Anthology of Twentieth-Century
BRITISH AND IRISH POETRY

EDITED BY
Keith Tuma
Miami University

New York   Oxford
OXFORD UNIVERSITY PRESS
2001

Oxford University Press

Oxford   New York
Athens   Auckland   Bangkok   Bogotá   Buenos Aires   Calcutta
Cape Town   Chennai   Dar es Salaam   Delhi   Florence   Hong Kong   Istanbul
Karachi   Kuala Lumpur   Madrid   Melbourne   Mexico City   Mumbai
Nairobi   Paris   São Paulo   Shanghai   Singapore   Taipei   Tokyo   Toronto   Warsaw

and associated companies in
Berlin   Ibadan

Copyright © 2001 by Oxford University Press, Inc.

Published by Oxford University Press, Inc.
198 Madison Avenue, New York, New York, 10016
http://www.oup-usa.org

Oxford is a registered trademark of Oxford University Press

Library of Congress Cataloging-in-Publication Data

Anthology of twentieth-century British and Irish poetry / edited by Keith Tuma.
    p. cm.
    Includes bibliographical references.
    ISBN 0-19-512893-1 (acid-free paper)—ISBN 0-19-512894-X (pbk.: acid-free paper)
    1. English poetry—20th century. 2. English poetry—Irish authors. I. Title: Oxford
anthology of 20th century British and Irish poetry. II. Tuma, Keith, 1957–

PR1225 .O86 2000
821'.9108—dc21   00-041648

Printing number: 9 8 7 6 5 4 3 2 1

Printed in the United States of America
on acid-free paper

To the memory of
Donald Davie, Edward Dorn, and Douglas Oliver,
agents of transatlantic dialogue in poetry

CONTENTS

12644389

Contents ix

Edward Lucie-Smith had it right when he wrote that "to publish an anthology is to turn oneself into a pheasant on the first day of August."[1] He might have added that some pheasants are fatter targets than others. Some anthologies are free to limit their selections to represent the shape of a group, movement, or tendency, or perhaps several of them. Others have boundaries drawn by form, genre, or subject matter—war poems or love poems, for instance—or something else. Most do not attempt to represent anything so large as a century. But in editing this one I had an entire century to think about, and Britain and Ireland both.[2] I know full well that reviewers will nod to the impossibility of the task at hand and proceed immediately to their list of omitted poets. That response is part of the risk of editing such a book and not to be regretted. Anticipating it, editors of anthologies often prepare introductory statements outlining principles of selection, inevitably simplifying what are thousands of decisions in a narrative or rationale probably most useful for those who would use it against them. There is something tempting about the brevity of a statement like Philip Larkin's in the preface to his *The Oxford Book of Twentieth-Century English Verse* (1973): "In the end I found that my material fell into three groups: poems representing aspects of the talents of poets judged either by the age or by myself to be worthy of inclusion, poems judged by me to be worthy of inclusion without reference to their authors, and poems judged by me to carry with them something of the century in which they were written. Needless to say, the three groups are not equal in size, nor are they mutually exclusive." One might well leave it at that, with a statement simple if also a little disingenuous—how, for example, does one imagine an "age" as having come to a judgment? Larkin's preface said little more except to note that he had opted for "wide rather than deep representation."[3] As it happens there are particulars of Larkin's anthology I find myself admiring—the inclusion of poets still too little read thirty years later, such as Charlotte Mew, Ivor Gurney, F. R. Higgins, Charles Madge, and Rosemary Tonks; or his generous selection from the poetry of Basil Bunting, despite his dismissals of modernism elsewhere. This anthology shares these poets with Larkin's, but in other ways it is a very different book. So I had better say just a little more about how it was made.

I have tried to include poems that seem worthy of continuing consideration as exemplary poems within the history of an artform. That seems straightforward enough, and moreover not too remote from Larkin's first category above. If we understand his reference to "the age" to mean influential opinion—which leaves us to quarrel about which critical opinion has been and should be influential—my remarks below about efforts to listen to criticism and scholarship can be read as squaring me with his statement there as well. But in the end I am much less confident in my ability to represent such opinion as if it were uniform, a settled matter. There would be no point in editing this book if I meant to accommodate all views. Larkin's book omitted a good deal of what this one takes to be some of the most interesting poetry of this century, the poetry associated with varieties of modernism. This is an English, Scottish, Welsh, and Irish poetry that, once it is better known, will find its place on global maps Larkin himself notoriously professed little interest in. I am confident of that much.

Larkin's preference for "wide rather than deep representation" does not seem to consider the possibility that a single poet's career might offer a diversity or range of poetic practice greater than twenty other poets from the same period. In any case such a strategy seems more necessary the closer one moves toward the present, and that is one reason I have given considerable space here to recent poetry, where one's judgment is also inevitably most willful. But there is something more to be said about intentions like Larkin's, something that pertains to the whole book and century. From one point of view, an anthology of modern British and Irish poetry would do well to sketch as full a picture of the variety of modern poetic practices as possible. Subordinating questions of aesthetic value to questions of representation, it might include in sampling the poetry of the early century in England, for instance, the work of Edward Shanks or J. C. Squire alongside that of T. S. Eliot, as Larkin's book does. An editor especially attuned to the cultural studies methodologies current among scholars in today's universities might well want music-hall lyrics included beside the poems of Edith Sitwell and Rudyard Kipling, or verse whose interest primarily derives from what it can tell us about cultural history. One might want equally to represent the poetry of particular groups or regions. But while all of these rationales in editing an anthology are more or less credible, they do not exactly explain the approach taken in this anthology. Indicating the outlines of something near the total cultural field of poetic production was not my chief consideration. Nothing has been excluded here because of *a priori* categories such as "popular poetry" or *a priori* judgments concerning "accessibility" or some other loaded term. These categories and judgments are always worth questioning anyway, and they have been particularly hard on varieties of modernist poetry in England, for complex reasons often having little to do with the poetry itself. Nor has the mode, visibility, or status of publication been a determining factor here. If anything the independent, small press book has been valued as typically representing a labor of love undertaken by those closest to and most knowledgeable about poetry and whose pursuit of the art often involves small hope of financial reward. Nevertheless, it will be easy for informed readers to see that this book has, for instance, found little room for "light verse" and for varieties of popular poetry and song, with a few exceptions, such as Rudyard Kipling's "Gunga Din." There is, after all, Larkin's book, among many others in which some of the poems a few readers will find missing here can easily enough be found, whether they are "light verse" or something else.

I have not thought, for the most part, to allow the selection process to be guided by consideration of the ways in which poetry can be used to survey events or issues that are part of the history of Britain and Ireland in the twentieth century, and that also puts me a little at odds with Larkin's third category. That is, this anthology is less interested in history than it is in the history of poetry, and moreover in the history of poetry as a living, serious, vital artform. One author of a critical survey of twentieth-century poetry describes his intention "to focus on poetry in the glare of the events of the century, rather than in the light of aesthetic judgment, formal changes, and biographies of individual poets."[4] There is nothing to prevent this anthology from being of use to related modes of reading, but I have chosen to privilege the history of artifice rather than history per se. I find Veronica Forrest-Thomson's polemic in *Poetic Artifice* (1978) still timely: "It is all too easy for poets as well as critics to give in to the kind of reading which criticism often proposes and to assume that the important features of a poem are those which can be shown to contribute to a thematic synthesis stated in terms of the external world. The meaning of the poem is extended into the world; this extended meaning is assumed to be dominant, and if formal features are to become noteworthy components of a poem they must be assimilated to this extended meaning."[5] One need not be the formalist Forrest-Thomson was to understand that reading or evaluating poems without reflecting on "the components of poetic language" and other aesthetic matters impoverishes our understanding of the possibilities of poetry as an artform. Whether or not we agree with Ezra Pound's modernist proposition that "technique" is "the test of [a poet's] sincerity," it is worth insisting upon consideration of poetic technique in the reading and evaluation of poetry, and the making of an anthology is about evaluation no matter how wide a net is cast, or what other values enter into the selection of poems.[6] The significance of poetry beyond its status as a set of symptomatic texts or practices retrieved by and for history or critique depends upon discourses prepared to argue for particular poems and modes of facture as exemplary or flawed, on judgments determining what is groundbreaking or perfected or worn and boring. Some poems seem alive as possible resources for those who seek to know something about or to write poetry; others seem best left to the antiquarians and the cultural historians. You will choose your own terms.

It is not necessary to say, with Lucie-Smith, that there is something "disingenuous" about any "pretense to total objectivity" in an anthologist, but I am closer to Lucie-Smith than to some editors in imagining that the selections for this anthology reflect a kind of pluralism. I want to call it "critical pluralism" to underline my point above about aesthetic judgment, but I am afraid that "critical pluralism" suggests something ponderous and systematic. All it means here is that I began reading for this anthology understanding that there are many modes of poetry that informed readers, critics, and poets have found more or less valuable, and intending to exercise whatever negative capability allowed me to take poems and their advocates on their own terms. It will not be difficult to determine which critical voices I have found most persuasive, as I have cited them in the introductions to individual authors, excerpting remarks there that might offer possible points of entry into the poetry reprinted. These remarks are selected from essays written over the course of the century, and their authors sometimes explicitly disagree in their judgments and values concerning poetry. They range from poet-critics such as Forrest-Thomson and Basil Bunting, who have poems in the book, to many of the critics and scholars now writing most convincingly on modern and contemporary British and Irish poetry. That this anthology is large enough to contain multitudes is my hope; that its very format risks reducing to sameness poems from different places and times, and sometimes attached to practices and values either remote from one another or explicitly opposed, is one of my fears.

This anthology will be of most use to informed readers willing to take it on its own terms insofar as it introduces poets previously unknown to or undervalued by many critics and literary historians. There are quite a few such poets here, even from earlier in the century: I would count John Rodker, Mina Loy, Clere Parsons, Joseph Macleod, Thomas MacGreevy, Lynette Roberts, and Nicholas Moore among them. One hopes the book will have an equal value to such readers for its sketch of post-1945 poetry moving into the present. Even though the anthology is most capacious there, intent on including even very recent poetry in sufficient quantities to show the extent to which poetry remains vital in Britain and Ireland, it is surely also most contentious in its representation of recent decades. For I have paid little attention to reputations that strike me as ephemeral, as produced by newspapers or official agencies. I have paid little attention to awards and titles and searched instead among the publications and opinions of those who have little at stake beyond their love of poetry and hope for its future—this so as not to give the twenty-first century the impression that a contemporary equivalent of J. C. Squire is as likely to be of continuing interest as a contemporary equivalent of T. S. Eliot, Charlotte Mew, or Ivor Gurney. As it happens, it is the contemporary poetry that is most obviously indebted to an international modernism that has fared worst in many of the anthologies of British and Irish poetry published over the last thirty years, especially by major publishers in England, which until recently have seemed interested in perpetuating the influence of the Movement's anti-modernism as it emerged in the 1950s.[7] I find the logic that declared a British (or Irish) poetry engaged with modernist traditions somehow "foreign" to traditions purportedly more native or indigenous altogether suspect. As a number of the poets included here from earlier in the century demonstrate, it is simply no longer possible to pretend that modernism never happened in English poetry, and with Hugh MacDiarmid as arguably its most important early-century poet, Scotland also obviously was home to a poetry conscious of international modernism. (It should also be added that MacDiarmid's poetry was sometimes posed against the sentimental versifying of the Scottish kailyard as well as English verse.) Ireland too had a modernist practice beyond the towering presence of William Butler Yeats, who strikes some readers as a transitional figure and others as a modernist, in poets such as Thomas MacGreevy, Denis Devlin, Samuel Beckett, and Brian Coffey. In Wales there was Lynette Roberts, whose importance is just now becoming known to scholars and poets.

If one of the driving forces and also consequences of anti-modernism in England, especially over the last forty years, has been cultural insularity or so-called "little-englandism," I want to admit that there is a way in which this anthology might inadvertently promote a way of reading and studying poetry that shores up boundaries in a shrinking and interconnected world. Some of the poets who might be said to be among the most crucial influences on particular poems and poets included here—the American Ezra Pound and the Barbidian Edward Kamau Brathwaite for instance, the first important to discussions of modernism and the second to discussions of modernist, "post-colonial," and Black British poetry—are not part of the book. Since their work is available elsewhere, my hope was that I could devote pages that might have been offered to their work to figures less well-known or widely available. The list might be extended, even to poets writing in other languages. Such are the choices and frustrations of the anthologist. Faced by the limits of page counts and budgets, one necessarily falls back on arbitrary criteria, which here primarily involve insisting that the poets to be included were born in Britain or Ireland, or became citizens or spent important parts of their literary careers there. There are exceptions even here, of course, as Pound's case also demonstrates, given his London years. Again, I can only hope that the reader will seek out his work, perhaps in Cary Nelson's anthology *Modern American Poetry* (Oxford, 2000), a companion volume to this one.

One regret about these and other exclusions has to do with knowing that informed readers are not necessarily the most important readers of an anthology like this one, for informed readers need this book less than readers new to modern British and Irish poetry. This anthology will achieve its loftiest goal if it makes newer, younger readers want to search out poetry as it lives beyond this book, in individual volumes by the authors included here and many others beside them. An anthology should never be mistaken for the territory; it is one map of that territory. Academics sometimes like to speak of the role of books like this one in creating or revising a canon. Thus it can sometimes seem as if a poem's place in an anthology is its final destination (or its rest home, depending on one's values). But there are few poets who would prefer their work to be read only in an anthology. This is the case whatever the value of the anthology, and of course I think that this anthology has considerable value in offering a picture of British and Irish poetry unlike any other picture available. Anthologists, like critics, do have a role to play in canon formation, but in the end their influence is no greater than that of contemporary and future poets who will have to decide what work is most valuable to them as they continue to imagine the possibilities of poetic practice. Extending the range of the work widely available thus becomes crucial, and challenging or innovative work especially merits a place beside work many readers agree demonstrates accomplishment in known or widely accepted poetic modes.

It might be argued that the very idea of a canon of "modern British and Irish poetry" will be received differently and mean different things in the United States, Canada, Ireland, and the United Kingdom. Lucie-Smith, searching for reasons why modernist poetry in Britain has not had the profile of comparable poetries in the United States, points to differences in the courses of study adopted by universities, differences that are themselves based on distinct national and cultural histories: "The American sense of the past, of what is established and historic, remains different from ours. On their side of the Atlantic, for example, the year 1800 seems considerably more distant. Most of American literary history has taken place since that date; the bulk of ours happened before it. . . . In the twentieth century the modernist element has been an integral part of this American literature, and has perhaps been especially conspicuous in poetry. The result is that the study of modernist approaches and attitudes is a necessary background to the study of classic American texts—texts which in British terms may seem too recent even to merit inclusion as part of a standard degree course. These differences in approach mean that the academic study of English in England maintains a distinction between the classic and the modern which no longer exists in the United States" (26). This argument is a little dated and thus cannot account for more recent developments on both sides of the Atlantic. Moreover, it neglects the impetus given to the study of modern literature by English academics such as I. A. Richards, William Empson, and F. R. Leavis in the years before and after World War II. It probably also overstates the influence of the academic study of literature on poetic practice. Nevertheless, there is some truth in it.

If this anthology will find most of its readers in the United States, it is also destined to have readers in Britain, Ireland, Canada, and elsewhere. Some of these readers, perhaps in Britain and Ireland especially, will be eager to point out that I am an American, and that my insistence that twentieth-century British and Irish poetry be recognized for its contributions to modernism reflects American values. Forms of this insidious representational logic, in which national identity is paramount and citizenship magically confers authentic expertise, have had a devastating effect on much of the poetry produced in this century. It is surely not only in England that poetry has been narrowly celebrated for its value to the nation, as if it were only a form of cultural capital a nation or even a region might bank on or exchange. I was struck on a recent trip to Ireland by the giant photographs of Ireland's Nobel Prize winners in literature outside one gate at Dublin's airport, and I found myself pondering the irony that at least one of these writers—Samuel Beckett—had lived most of his life in exile and, like James Joyce, was long in being taken up by academic syllabi in Ireland. There is nothing wrong with a nation celebrating its poets, and I am not so naive as to believe that a modernist poetry might not equally be taken up by heritage or tourist industries, but there is indeed a problem with the use of reified or shallow notions of tradition to exclude whole ranges of poetry. The distorted rhetorics that can result from an appeal to something like national tradition or "Englishness" have far-reaching consequences on both the reading and writing of poetry; I can only allude to these here by noting that they have had some bearing on the fate of the more neglected poetries included in this anthology. To those who will say that my picture of twentieth-century British and Irish poetry is "Americanized" or reflects an interloper's agenda, I can say that showing the extent to which certain British and Irish poetry has participated in varieties of modernist practice might also be read as criticism of those who have claimed that modern American poetry is uniquely vital among modern poetries—to the point where the study of American poetry in American universities risks becoming parochial. I say this as a passionate reader of American poetry. But it is sadly true that over the last decade or two, contemporary British poetry in the United States has hardly been a raging concern; it has instead been dominated by a very few figures who have come to represent that poetry almost as tokens. Such neglect has a history, of course, which I cannot explore here except by citing a few remarks such as Yvor Winters's polemical statement that "England has not given us much notable poetry in the last 250 years," which dates from 1967.[8] In the introduction to the anthology in which I first studied modern British poetry as an undergraduate, to offer another example, the editors write that "the one poet of great power to emerge in England since the

'thirties was Dylan Thomas. . . . But British poetry has not broken through the barri-
ers of basically conventional virtuosity since Thomas. . . ."[9]

Let me try to say this another way. This book's emphasis, to the extent that an
emphasis on modernism emerges within its pluralist contours, is meant partly to
counter such remarks. But it also occurs to me that if there is one thing that would be
worse than the near total neglect of British poetry now characterizing American aca-
demic life it would be a suggestion like that made by some influential critics in England
associated with the Movement and its progeny. This is the suggestion that there has
been something like a continuous tradition of "Englishness" in English poetry, a tradi-
tion in which the poetry of Thomas Hardy figures as monumental and definitive. One
can admire Hardy's poetry without putting it to such uses, which reflect a politicized
definition of tradition as unconflicted and monolithic. The same might be said of
efforts to sketch a history of Irish poetry in which the poetry of Yeats gives way to the
poetry of Patrick Kavanagh, which in turn makes possible the poetry of Seamus
Heaney.

A much more important concern related to the fact that the bulk of this anthol-
ogy's readers will be American involves my decision not to include poetry written in
Scots Gaelic, Irish, or Welsh. These languages are simply not read in the United States,
however influential they have been for particular British and Irish writers, whether,
like Sorley Maclean, they write in Gaelic or, like Austin Clarke, F. R. Higgins, and Mau-
rice Scully, they have been attentive to the structures of some of its poetry.

This anthology, then—to use some contemporary jargon—is "revisionist." Perhaps
I can further clarify what I mean by that with a few remarks turned especially to its
representation of British poetry since 1945, but also looking backwards a little from
that date. To do so I turn once again to Edward Lucie-Smith's anthology. In the sec-
ond, 1985 edition of his *British Poetry Since 1945*, Lucie-Smith quotes from the intro-
duction to his earlier, 1970 edition of his anthology of that title:

> Poets in Britain are still coming to terms, not only with Britain's changed posi-
> tion in the world and the sudden upsurge of American literature, but with the
> fact of modernism itself. The past quarter of a century, with its pattern of
> action and reaction, has seen a painful adjustment to the fact that the mod-
> ern sensibility is here to stay. (23)

The reason Lucie-Smith quotes his own words, he writes, is that he has changed his
mind; he is no longer sure in 1985 that modernism has been absorbed by British
poetry:

> I now wonder if that adjustment really took place, at least in the sense in
> which I described, and, if it did, whether it wasn't ephemeral. The additions I
> have made to this book, whatever their other characteristics, have the general
> effect of making the collection seem more conservative, and indeed more
> insular, than it was previously. (23)

It will not surprise the reader if I say that I prefer Lucie-Smith's first edition to his
second. I think that I can understand what led him to believe that insular pressures
had reasserted themselves with sufficient force to erase the engagement with mod-
ernist and international poetries that had characterized some of the poetry of the
1960s anthologized in his earlier edition. The influential *Penguin Book of Contempo-
rary British Poetry* (1982), for instance, was largely inattentive to ongoing writing that
might have given him more hope. The point here is not to deride that anthology but
rather to insist that there was much that it excluded. It is certain that readers of this
book exploring the poetry written after Lucie-Smith's second edition was published
will not be able to say that modernism and experimentalism have disappeared as
forces in British and Irish poetry.

In mentioning a "pattern of action and reaction" to modernism in British poetry
between 1945 and 1970, Lucie-Smith extends a history of the century's poetry offered

in the introduction to A. Alvarez's more influential and less eclectic anthology *The New Poetry* (1962), and that history is worth repeating here. It is a history that can only seem potted, with any real scrutiny of the bewildering diversity and complexity of a century's worth of poetry in Britain and Ireland. In his famous introduction to his anthology, Alvarez argued that "the experimental techniques of Eliot and the rest never really took on [in Britain] because they were a distinctly American concern." Alvarez then describes the history of British poetry between 1930 and 1960 as a "series of negative feed-backs," which seemed to make Thomas Hardy's famous statement that "vers libre could come to nothing in England" prophetic.[10] Modernism is thus identified with that always nebulous thing and inexact term, free verse; Hardy is made modernism's other; and warring traditions are established as nicely discrete, the one American, the other English. According to this influential if inadequate narrative, the 1930s saw a group of poets led by W. H. Auden reacting against the "difficult" and "experimental" poetry of the 1920s. This was followed by the reaction to the Auden group among a group of neo-romantic poets led by Dylan Thomas; Alvarez claims that this reaction "took the form of anti-intellectualism." Then there was the rejection of this poetry of "wild, loose emotion" among the Movement poets of the 1950s, who chose instead to write a poetry—as their own anthologist Robert Conquest described it—"empirical in attitude," a poetry refusing "to abandon a rational structure and comprehensible language." Against this "short, academic-administrative . . . polite, knowledgeable, efficient, polished, and, in its quiet way, even intelligent" poetry, Alvarez posed yet another reaction said to represent a synthesis of the "formal intelligence" of the modernist Eliot and the "psychological insight" of the modernist D. H. Lawrence, notorious alternatives thanks to the criticism of F. R. Leavis and some less well-known remarks by Eliot himself. The key figures of Alvarez's new synthesis were Ted Hughes and several Americans who have since often been called "confessional poets"—Robert Lowell and Sylvia Plath especially. One need not reject a category like "major poet" to reject such a history alert only to a few poets and tendencies, a history that also has contributed substantially, I think, to simplistic ideas about national traditions. At least in identifying Lawrence and Eliot as attached to different ideas of modernism, Alvarez offers a view of early-century modernism that begins to admit some of its complexity. There is no one modernist poetic practice, no unified or single "modernism." This is not just a matter of saying that the Catholic modernism of Brian Coffey, for instance, is quite different from the polytheistic modernism of Ezra Pound. It is also to acknowledge that local contexts and traditions must be considered—that the poetry of Hugh MacDiarmid, for instance, might be read simultaneously as engaged with international poetic practices and with local Scottish ones.

One recent anthologist in need of definitions of modernism finds himself citing this one from *The Penguin Dictionary of Literary Terms and Theory*:

> As far as literature is concerned modernism reveals a breaking away from established rules, traditions and conventions, fresh ways of looking at man's function in the universe and many (in some cases remarkable) experiments in form and style. It is particularly concerned with language and how to use it (representationally or otherwise) and with *writing itself*.[11]

But this is vague enough to be nearly useless. It does not account for the argument of Laura Riding and Robert Graves in *A Survey of Modernist Poetry* (1927), for example, which tried to distinguish an "authentic 'advanced' poetry" from the poetry associated with two roughly contemporaneous "movements" important to the early-century history of English poetry, Imagism and Georgianism. The first is associated with the American poet Ezra Pound and the English poets T. E. Hulme and F. S. Flint among others, the second with Edward Marsh's popular anthologies; these gathered a poetry, much of it about the English countryside, often attacked by modernists like T. S. Eliot and

Edith Sitwell and sometimes viewed since by literary historians as an "other" to modernism. Riding and Graves describe the "general recommendations" of Georgian poetry as having to do with "the discarding of archaistic diction . . . and poetical constructions" and "formally religious, philosophic or improving themes in reaction to Victorianism; and all sad, wicked café-table themes in reaction to the 'nineties.'" The Imagists, they argue, "had decided beforehand the kind of poetry that was wanted by the time: a poetry to match certain up-to-date movements in music and art." Their imperatives concerning the need "to render particulars exactly," or so Graves and Riding argue, show them too concerned with the manner of presentation, whereas the authentic advanced poet will be "concerned with a reorganization of the matter (not in the sense of subject-matter but of poetic thought as distinguished from other kinds of thought) rather then the manner of poetry." Imagism is read as involving only a stylistic shift, a change of fashion, against which Graves and Riding posit a poetry seeking a more thoroughgoing revaluation of the poem as "thought-activity."[12] The point is not only that there are many modernist poetic practices but also that they are often opposed in important ways. The term "modernist" can be seen to be elastic enough to gather poets as different as Hugh MacDiarmid, Mina Loy, T. S. Eliot, Edith Sitwell, David Jones, John Rodker, and Thomas MacGreevy, just to name a few poets from the early century and from Scotland, England, and Ireland. And if the differences among these poets are as important as their similarities, can we be all that much more confident in a label like "Georgian" poetry? The most interesting writers, then or now, defy categories, as would seem obvious in reading Ivor Gurney and Edward Thomas, two poets who might be discussed with reference to Georgian poetry. One of the "revisionist" agendas of this anthology is to complicate the categories while discarding the potted histories, or rather while encouraging you, the reader, to rewrite those histories.

I suppose that this takes us back to the question of pluralism, to my desire to find poetry that seems most successful given its assumptions. Again I will not deny that I find some assumptions more credible than others. But in reading through the century's poetry to assemble this book I found myself struck again and again by how much interesting poetry there was to consider. The experience has left me skeptical of polemical claims like this: "The problem for any putatively postmodern poetry in Britain is that Britain has yet to go through a modernist period and, thanks to the efforts of [Sir John] Betjeman and [Philip] Larkin and their current disciples never will. . . . The only poets to embrace modernism's discourse of fragmentation and terseness, mythopoeia and modernity, and in its philosophical investigation of the interface between self, language and world in England were Basil Bunting . . . and David Jones."[13] The author of these remarks is a fine critical advocate of modernist and experimental poetry. I might be expected to agree with him to the extent that he is right that modernist poetry has not had much of a hearing in Britain, or in Ireland for that matter. But one of the points of this anthology is to give some of that poetry a hearing among other poetries, and thereby to remedy that situation a little. If it is true that modernism has not exactly triumphed in Britain and Ireland, that does not mean that it has not existed, or that we can be comfortable in our definitions of it— or even in our evaluation of it. All of that must be ongoing. Critical narratives concerning British and Irish poetry of the century just past must be rewritten for the new century, and if this book can make that even a little apparent it will have achieved something.

A few words of thanks now. This book would not have been possible if the need for it had not been recognized in the first place by my editor at Oxford University Press in New York, Tony English. His support from first to last has been steady and patient, and I thank also his assistant Charmaine Lim, who helped with permissions, and the book's production editor, Benjamin Clark. The original table of contents for the book was anonymously reviewed by a number of scholars and poets who made good suggestions for poems to include. Some of them have since become known to me, and so I would like to thank Robert Archambeau, Robert Hampson, Romana Huk, Mark Morrisson,

John Matthias, Carol Muske, and Vincent Sherry for their detailed notes about my plans for the book. For other general support and assistance crucial to the completion of the book I would like to thank Clive Bush, Richard Cook, Tom and Marla Dorward, Jay Finnan, John Goodby, Steve McCaffery, Karen Mac Cormack, Peter Middleton, Kevin Nolan, Peter Quartermain, James Reiss, Dianne Sadoff, Michael Schmidt, Allison Tuma, Diane Tuma, and my parents William and Marilyn Tuma.

Several years ago at a conference in London, Peter Barry argued in a paper that an anthology of British and Irish poetry that risked including experimental work would require good annotations in order to be truly useful. I was eager, then, when I agreed to edit this book, to find an assistant who would be able to help me provide such notes, especially considering that many of the poems included here had not previously been annotated. I was extraordinarily fortunate to persuade the Canadian scholar and editor Nate Dorward to undertake this task. Dorward has annotated all of the poems in the book. He deserves the credit for what is a remarkable scholarly achievement. But this was not Dorward's only role in this book. He also responded to my ideas for inclusions, suggested poets and poems to consider, cast a sharp editorial eye on nearly every sentence in the book, and put the manuscript together for Oxford University Press. My email files to Dorward contain over 2,000 messages related to this anthology. Quite simply, this book would not exist without him.

Of course no scholarship is a solo pursuit, and just as I have relied on existing criticism in my introductions to specific authors Dorward and I have also had help with the notes. We would like to thank the numerous poets who responded to queries about their poems. Several poets helped with annotation for other poets' work as well. Some poets were understandably skeptical about the value of notes for poems that are sometimes polysemous or rebarbative enough to make the very idea of notes controversial. Our defense of annotation to these writers invariably was to argue that our notes are not meant to be interpretive or to limit the reading of the poems. We hope that this is the case, and that readers of this book will peruse them simply as one resource and with a skeptical eye, understanding that, as is the case with all such notes, there is the possibility that we have neglected something important or that here and there we are simply wrong. These seem like obvious points, but they relate to what I have said above about anthologies; notes too can change and even distort the experience of reading a poem if the reader lets them. But since we have included them here, thanks are due to the scholars, poets, and individuals who helped with them. Ian Patterson, one of our finest scholars of modern poetry and a poet himself, deserves special thanks for having looked over the notes at his home in Cambridge, England. Thanks also to the following people for help with particular notes and queries: Gerda Barlow, Joseph Black, Carolyn Burke, Steven Burns, Richard Caddel, Roger Conover, Kelvin Corcoran, Fred D'Aguiar, Wendy Dare, Alex Davis, Thomas Dilworth, Jane Dorward, Tom Dorward, Ben Friedlander, Harry Gilonis, Ruth Grogan, Nick Halmi, Elizabeth James, Lee Jenkins, Frank Jordan, Mara Kalnins, Tim Kendall, David Kennedy, Michael Kirkham, Rodrigo Lazo, Tim Longville, Lizzie MacGregor, Sante Matteo, Peter Manson, Vance Maverick, Billy Mills, Donal Moriarty, Susan Neylan, John Pikoulis, Richard Price, Robin Purves, Gareth Reeves, Lyn Richards, Randolph Runyon, Susan Schreibman, Pete Smith, John Temple, William Walsh, George Walter, Nigel Wheale, and the members of the British-Poets listserv.

A final word concerning the dating of poems. The dates provided are, as a general rule, those of first collected appearance (there are some exceptions, as when a poem remains uncollected). In a few cases two dates are included, if there is warrant for it (e.g. Mina Loy's "English Rose" first appeared in 1923, but the sequence of which it is a part first appeared as a whole in 1982). When the date of composition is known, it is also included, preceding the date of composition and separated from it by a slash. Poems are, with a few exceptions (notably some of W. H. Auden's poems), presented in the final text decided on by the author, and thus may incorporate revisions later than the original publication date.

NOTES

1. "Introduction to the Revised Edition," *British Poetry Since 1945*, ed. Edward Lucie-Smith, London 1985, p. 22.

2. "Britain" and "British" are used as shorthand in this preface, as the terms will be challenged by some Scottish and Welsh readers and poets especially. The use of these terms is not meant to suggest a position on questions of "devolution" or the political and cultural history and identity of parts of "Britain" or Ireland.

3. "Preface," *The Oxford Book of Twentieth-Century English Verse*, London, 1973, pp. v–vi.

4. Peter Childs, *The Twentieth Century in Poetry: A Critical Survey*, London and New York, 1999, p. 13.

5. *Poetic Artifice: A Theory of Twentieth-Century Poetry*, Manchester, 1978, p. x.

6. "A Retrospect" (1918), *Literary Essays of Ezra Pound*, ed. T. S. Eliot, New York, 1935, p. 9.

7. Among the recent anthologies one might consider exceptions are *A Various Art*, ed. Andrew Crozier and Tim Longville (1987); *The New British Poetry*, ed. Gillian Allnutt, Fred D'Aguiar, Ken Edwards, and Eric Mottram (1988); *Floating Capital: New Poets from London*, ed. Adrian Clarke and Robert Sheppard (1991); *The New Poetry*, ed. Michael Hulse, David Kennedy, and David Morley (1993); *Conductors of Chaos*, ed. Iain Sinclair (1996); *Out of Everywhere: Linguistically Innovative Poetry by Women in North America & the UK*, ed. Maggie O'Sullivan (1996); *A State of Independence*, ed. Tony Frazer (1998); and *Other: British and Irish Poetry Since 1970*, ed. Richard Caddel and Peter Quartermain (1999). Except for *Other*, *Out of Everywhere*, and *The New Poetry*, these anthologies are generally not available in the United States; the others are out-of-print in Britain. All of them are concerned only with poetry post-1945 or poetry still more recent, and most of them are limited to "modernist" or "experimental" work. Listing other anthologies might not seem a wise thing for an editor of an anthology to do, but poetry is not about competition, and there are poems in these books and not in mine which I admire, including the poems of J. H. Prynne, who declined to be represented in this book. The publisher of another poet wanted fees deemed excessive. Were it not for necessarily limited budgets and pages, this book would be twice its current size. Some of the poets who might have been included in that book, a number of them working outside of modernist traditions, can be found in the anthologies mentioned elsewhere in this preface and edited by Lucie-Smith, Motion and Morrison, and O'Brien. Some of the poets most deserving inclusion are mentioned in the headnotes to authors represented in this anthology.

8. Yvor Winters, *Forms of Discovery*, Chicago, 1967, p. 347.

9. "Introduction," *Chief Modern Poets of Britain and America*, 5th ed. Vol. 1, ed. Gerald DeWitt Sanders, John Herbert Nelson, and M. L. Rosenthal, London and New York, 1970, p. 8.

10. "The New Poetry, Or Beyond the Gentility Principle," *The New Poetry*, ed. A. Alvarez, London, 1962, p. 21–32. The only source for Hardy's famous phrase is Robert Graves; the scholar John Lucas has in the pages of *PN Review* recently questioned the attribution, documenting also Hardy's interest in the work of T. S. Eliot and Ezra Pound.

11. Quoted in Sean O'Brien's introduction to his anthology *The Firebox: Poetry in Britain and Ireland after 1945*, London, 1998.

12. Laura Riding and Robert Graves, *A Survey of Modernist Poetry*, London, 1927, pp. 116–19.

13. Andrew Lawson, "Life After Larkin: Postmodern British Poetry," *Textual Practice* 3.3 (1990), p. 413.

ACKNOWLEDGMENTS

Pages xxix–xxxiii constitute an extension of the copyright page.

Fleur Adcock: "Against Coupling," "Ex-Queen Among the Astronomers," and "Leaving the Tate." Reprinted by permission of the author.

Moniza Alvi: *Carrying My Wife* (Bloodaxe Books, 2000). Reprinted by permission of Oxford University Press.

W. H. Auden: "The Watershed," "'Consider this and in our time,'" "The Secret Agent," and "Bones wrenched, weak whimper, lids wrinkled..." from *Collected Poems* by W. H. Auden, edited by Edward Mendelson. Copyright (c) 1934 and renewed 1962 by W. H. Auden. Reprinted by permission of Random House, Inc. "In Memory of Sigmund Freud" from *Collected Poems* by W. H. Auden, edited by Edward Mendelson. Copyright (c) 1940 and renewed 1968 by W. H. Auden. Reprinted by permission of Random House, Inc. "No Time" and "At the Grave of Henry James" from *Collected Poems* by W. H. Auden, edited by Edward Mendelson. Copyright (c) 1941 and renewed 1969 by W. H. Auden. Reprinted by permission of Random House, Inc. "In Praise of Limestone" from *Collected Poems* by W. H. Auden, edited by Edward Mendelson. Copyright (c) 1951 by W. H. Auden. Reprinted by permission of Random House, Inc. "Ode to Terminus" from *Collected Poems* by W. H. Auden, edited by Edward Mendelson. Copyright (c) 1968 by W. H. Auden. Reprinted by permission of Random House, Inc. "A Bride in the 30's" from *Collected Poems* by W. H. Auden, edited by Edward Mendelson. Copyright (c) 1937 and renewed 1965 by W. H. Auden. Reprinted by permission of Random House, Inc. Faber and Faber Ltd. as publishers.

W. H. Auden: "Bones wrenched, weak whimper, lids wrinkled..." from *The English Auden* by W. H. Auden, edited by Edward Mendelson. "The Watershed" and "The Secret Agent" from *Collected Poems* by W. H. Auden, edited by Edward Mendelson. Copyright (c) 1934 and renewed 1962 by W. H. Auden. Reprinted by permission of Random House, Inc. "'Consider this and in our time'" from *Selected Poems* by W. H. Auden, edited by Edward Mendelson. Copyright (c) 1934 and renewed 1962 by W. H. Auden. Reprinted by permission of Random House, Inc. "A Bride in the 30's" from *Collected Poems* by W. H. Auden, edited by Edward Mendelson. Copyright (c) 1937 and renewed 1965 by W. H. Auden. Reprinted by permission of Random House, Inc. "Spain" from *Selected Poems* by W. H. Auden, edited by Edward Mendelson. Sections VI and VII from "Sonnets from China," "Musée des Beaux Arts," "In Memory of W. B. Yeats," "September 1, 1939," "In Memory of Sigmund Freud" from *Collected Poems* by W. H. Auden, edited by Edward Mendelson. Copyright (c) 1940 and renewed 1968 by W. H. Auden. Reprinted by permission of Random House, Inc. "No Time" and "At the Grave of Henry James" from *Collected Poems* by W. H. Auden, edited by Edward Mendelson. Copyright (c) 1941 and renewed 1969 by W. H. Auden. Reprinted by permission of Random House, Inc. "Nones" from *Collected Poems* by W. H. Auden, edited by Edward Mendelson. "In Praise of Limestone" from *Collected Poems* by W. H. Auden, edited by Edward Mendelson. Copyright (c) 1951 by W. H. Auden. Reprinted by permission of Random House, Inc. "Ode to Terminus" from *Collected Poems* by W. H. Auden, edited by Edward Mendelson. Copyright (c) 1968 by W. H. Auden. Reprinted by permission of Random House, Inc.

Samuel Beckett: "Enueg I," "Enueg II," and "Ooftish" from *Collected Poems in English and French* by Samuel Beckett. Reprinted by permission of Grove/Atlantic, Inc. "Enueg I" and "Enueg II" copyright (c) 1935 by Samuel Beckett; "Ooftish" copyright (c) 1938 by Samuel Beckett. Calder Publications Ltd. as the original copyright holder and publisher.

Caroline Bergvall: "Les jets de la Poupee" published by RemPress (Cambridge, England, 1999) as *Goan Atom: 1. jets-poupee*. Reprint permission granted by the author.

James Berry: "Letter to My Father from London" and "From Lucy: Englan a University," from *Hot Earth Cold Earth* (Bloodaxe Books, 1995).

Jean "Binta" Breeze: "Riddym Ravings" and "Cherry Tree Garden" from *Spring Cleaning* (Virago Press) by Jean "Binta" Breeze. Reprinted by permission of Little, Brown and Company (UK), a division of Time-Life Entertainment Group Limited.

Eavan Boland: "The Women Turns Herself into a Fish," "Listen. This is the Noise of Myth," and "In Exile," from *Outside History: Selected Poems 1980–1990* by Eavan Boland. Copyright (c) 1990 by Eavan Boland. Reprinted by permission of W.W. Norton & Company, Inc and by permission of Carcanet Press Limited.

Basil Bunting: All selections from *Complete Poems* (Bloodaxe Books, 2000).

Mary Butts: "Corfe." Reprinted by permission of the Estate of Mary Butts.

Brian Catling: "The Stumbling Block its Index." Reprinted by permission of the author.

Austin Clarke: "Forget Me Not." Reprinted by permission of R. Dardis Clarke, 21 Pleasants Street, Dublin 8.

Bob Cobbing: "wan do tree," "[LION LENIN LEONORA]," and "[ALEVIN BARS CAUSAPSCAL]," from *Bob Jubile,* published by New River (London, 1990). Reprinted by permission of the author.

Brian Coffey: "HEADROCK" and *Advent,* part I. Reprinted by permission of Dedalus Press.

Cris Cheek: *'stranger.'* Reprint permission granted by the author.

Andrew Crozier: "The Veil Poem." Reprinted by permission of the author.

Nancy Cunard: Extracts from *Parallax.* Reprinted by permission of the Estate of Nancy Cunard.

David Dabydeen: "Coolie Odyssey" and extracts from "Turner." Reprint permission granted by Jonathan Cape as publisher.

Elizabeth Daryush: "Still-life," "'Children of wealth in your warm nursery,'" and "News-reel," from *Collected Poems* by Elizabeth Daryush. Reprinted by permission of Carcanet Press Limited.

Donald Davie: "Hearing Russian Spoken," "Rejoinder to a Critic," "Rodez," "Out of East Anglia," "A Conditioned Air," and "Inditing A Good Matter," from *Collected Poems* by Donald Davie. Reprinted by permission of Carcanet Press Limited.

Walter de la Mare: "The Listeners," "Miss Loo," and "The Old Summerhouse," from *The Complete Poems of Walter de la Mare* (London: Faber, 1969; New York: Knopf, 1970). Reprinted by permission of The Literary Trustees of Walter de la Mare, and the Society of Authors as their representative.

Denis Devlin: "Lough Derg" and "Obstacle Basilisk" from *Collected Poems* with the permission of Wake Forest University Press and Dedalus Press.

Keith Douglas: "Simplify me when I'm dead," "These grasses, ancient enemies," "Mersa," "Dead Men," "Cairo Jag," "*Vergissmeinnicht*," "Aristocrats," and "How to Kill," from *The Complete Poems* by Keith Douglas. Reprinted by permission of Faber and Faber Limited and the Estate of Keith Douglas.

Carol Ann Duffy: "Standing Female Nude" from *Standing Female Nude* by Carol Ann Duffy (Anvil Press Poetry, 1985). "And How Are We Today?" and "Psychopath" from *Selling Manhattan* by Carol Ann Duffy (Anvil Press Poetry, 1987). "Translating the English, 1989" and "Poet for Our Times" from *The Other Country* by Carol Ann Duffy (Anvil Press Poetry, 1990).

T. S. Eliot: "The Love Song of J. Alfred Prufrock," "Gerontion," and "The Waste Land" from *Collected Poems 1909–1962* by T. S. Eliot. Reprinted by permission of Faber and Faber Ltd. as publishers. "Little Gidding," from *Four Quartets.* Copyright (c) 1942 by T. S. Eliot and renewed 1970 by Esme Valerie Eliot, reprinted by permission of Harcourt, Inc. and Faber and Faber Ltd.

William Empson: "Plenum and Vacuum," "Villanelle," "Reflections from Rochester," and "Sonnet," from *Collected Poems* by William Empson. Reproduced with permission of Curtis Brown Ltd., London, on behalf of the Estate of William Empson. Copyright (c) William Empson 1935, 1940, 1949, 1955.

Elaine Feinstein: "Marriage," "Exile," and "For Brighton, Old Bawd," from *Selected Poems* by Elaine Feinstein. Reprinted by permission of Carcanet Press Limited.

Ian Hamilton Finlay: "Orkney Lyrics," from *Dancers Inherit the Party.* Reprint permission granted by Polygon. "Sea-Poppy 1" and "Sea-Poppy 2." Reprint permission granted by author.

Allen Fisher: "African Mission," "defamiliarizing_____*: 38," and "Mummers' Strut" reprinted by permission of author.

Roy Fisher: *The Dow Low Drop* (Bloodaxe Books, 1996)

Ford Madox Ford: "The Starling" from *Collected Poems* (Manchester: Carcanet, 1997). Reprinted by permission of Carcanet Press Limited.

Veronica Forrest-Thomson: "Cordelia: or, 'A Poem Should Not Mean, But Be'" from *Collected Poems and Translations* (London, Lewes and Berkeley: Allardyce, Barnett Publishers, 1990) and *Selected Poems* (London: Invisible Books, 1999). Copyright (c) Veronica Forrest-Thomson 1976, 1990. Copyright (c) Allardyce, Barnett Publishers 1990. Reprinted by permission of Allardyce, Barnett Publishers.

David Gascoyne: "And the Seventh Dream is the Dream of Isis," "Baptism," "The Rites of Hysteria," and "The Cubical Domes," from David Gascoyne's *Selected Poems.* Reprinted by permission of Enitharmon Press, London, 1994.

W. S. Graham: "The Nightfishing," "A Note to the Difficult One," and "Language Ah Now You Have Me." Reprint permissions and copyright granted by the Estate of W. S. Graham.

Robert Graves: "Warning to Children," "The Legs," "To Juan at the Winter Solstice" and "The White Goddess," from *Complete Poems.* Reprinted by permission of Carcanet Press Limited.

Bill Griffiths: "Reekie." Reprinted by permission of author.

Thom Gunn: "The Unsettled Motorcyclist's Vision of His Death," "Confessions of the Life Artist," "Moly," "See-saw," "A Sketch of the Great Dejection," and "Lament," from *Collected Poems* by Thom Gunn. Copyright (c) 1994 by Thom Gunn. Reprinted by permission of Faber and Faber Ltd.

Ivor Gurney: "First Time In," "La Gorgue," "Laventie," "The Bare Line of the Hill," "The Bohemians," and "Sea-Marge." Reprinted from *The Collected Poems of Ivor Gurney,* edited by P. J. Kavanagh (1982), by permission of Oxford University Press.

Tony Harrison: *V.* by Tony Harrison. Copyright (c) 1990 by Tony Harrison. Reprinted by permission of Farrar, Straus and Giroux, LLC.

Alan Halsey: "Answering a New Year Letter, 1989" and "Self-Portrait in a '90s Bestiary" from *Reasonable Distance* (Cambridge: Equipage, 1992). "An Essay on Translation" from *Shadow Recension* (Southwick: Pages, 1996). "An Essay on Translation" and "Self Portrait in a '90s Bestiary" from *Wittgenstein's Devil: Selected Writing 1978–98* (Exeter: Stride Publications, 2000).

Lee Harwood: "When the geography was fixed," "The Blue Mosque," and "Salt Water." Reprinted by permission of author.

Randolph Healy: "Colonies of Belief." Reprint permission granted by The Beau Press. Part 1 of *Arbor Vitae.* Reprint permission granted by author.

Seamus Heaney: "Bogland," "North," "Singing School," "Oysters," "The Toome Road," "The Underground," parts VII and XII of "Station Island," and "The Mud Vision," from *Opened Ground: Selected Poems 1966–1996* by Seamus Heaney. Copyright (c) 1998 by Seamus Heaney. Reprinted by permission of Farrar, Straus and Giroux, LLC and Faber and Faber Ltd.

W. N. Herbert: "The Anxiety of Information" and "The Postcards of Scotland" from *Cabaret McGonagall* (Bloodaxe Books, 1996). Permission granted by author.

Geoffrey Hill: "Genesis" from *New Collected Poems 1952–1992.* Copyright (c) 1994 by Geoffrey Hill. Reprinted by permission of Houghton Mifflin Co. All rights reserved. Previously published in *For the Unfallen* (1959) and *Collected Poems* (Penguin Books, 1985). Copyright (c) Geoffrey Hill, 1959, 1985. "Ovid in the Third Reich," "September Song," and "History as Poetry" from *New Collected Poems 1952–1992.* Copyright (c) 1994 by Geoffrey Hill. Reprinted by permission of Houghton Mifflin Co. All rights reserved. Previously published in *King Log* (1968) and *Collected Poems* (Penguin Books, 1985). Copyright (c) Geoffrey Hill, 1968, 1985. Extracts from "Mercian Hymns," from *New Collected Poems 1952–1992.* Copyright (c) 1994 by Geoffrey Hill. Reprinted by permission of Houghton Mifflin Co. Previously published in *Mercian Hymns* (1971) and *Collected Poems* (Penguin Books, 1985). Copyright (c) Geoffrey Hill, 1971, 1985. Extracts from "The Mystery of the Charity of Charles Péguy" from *New Collected Poems 1952–1992.* Copyright (c) 1994 by Geoffrey Hill. Reprinted by permission of Houghton Mifflin Co. All rights reserved. Previously published as *The Mystery of the Charity of Charles Peguy* (1983) and *Collected Poems* (Penguin Books, 1985). Copyright (c) Geoffrey Hill, 1983, 1985. "Respublica" from *New Collected Poems 1952–1992.* Copyright (c) 1994 by Geoffrey Hill. Reprinted by permission of Houghton Mifflin Co. All rights reserved. Extracts from *The Triumph of Love* by Geoffrey Hill. Copyright (c) 1998 by Geoffrey Hill. Reprinted by permission of Houghton Mifflin Co. All rights reserved. Penguin Books, 1999. Copyright (c) Geoffrey Hill, 1998.

Ted Hughes: "View of a Pig," "Pike," "Out," "Pibroch," "Crow Hears Fate Knock on the Door," and "Wodwo," from *Selected Poems 1957–1967* by Ted Hughes. Copyright (c) 1972 by Ted Hughes. Reprinted by permission of Harper & Row, HarperCollins Publishers, Inc., and Faber and Faber Ltd. as publishers. Extracts from *Gaudete* from *New Selected Poems* by Ted Hughes. Copyright (c) 1982 by Ted Hughes. Reprinted by permission of HarperCollins Publishers, Inc., and Faber and Faber Ltd. as publishers. "Flounders" from *Birthday Letters.* Copyright (c) 1998 by Ted Hughes. Reprinted by permission of Farrar, Straus and Giroux, LLC and Faber and Faber Ltd. as publishers.

John James: "Good Old Harry" and "Inaugural Address." Reprinted by permission of the author.

Elizabeth Jennings: "Choices," "Fountain," and "On Its Own" from *Collected Poems.* Permissions granted by David Higham Associates and Carcanet Press Ltd.

David Jones: Extract from *In Parenthesis* by David Jones. Extract from "Rite and Fore-Time" and "Angle-Land" from *The Anathemata* by David Jones. "A, a, a, Domine Deus" from *The Sleeping Lord* by David Jones. Reprinted by permission of Faber and Faber Ltd.

Trevor Joyce: "The Turlough," "Cry Help," and "Tohu-bohu," Reprinted by permission of author.

Patrick Kavanagh: Parts I and IX of *The Great Hunger*, "Father Mat" and "Canal Bank Walk." Reprinted by permission of the Trustees of the Estates of Patrick Kavanagh, c/o Peter Fallon, Literary Agent, Loughcrew, Oldcastle Co., Meath, Ireland.

Jackie Kay: *The Adoption Papers* (Bloodaxe Books, 1991).

Thomas Kinsella: "Baggot Street Deserta" and "Ritual of Departure." Reprinted by permission of the author.

Rudyard Kipling: "Gunga Din," "Sestina of the Tramp-Royal," and two poems from "Epitaphs of the War." Reprinted by permission of A. P. Watt Ltd. on behalf of the National Trust for Places of Historic Interest or Natural Beauty.

Frank Kuppner: "Eclipsing Binaries" from *What? Again? Selected Poems* by Frank Kuppner. Reprinted by permission of Carcanet Press Limited.

R. F. Langley: "Saxon Landings" and "Man Jack" from *Collected Poems.* Reprinted by permission of Carcanet Press Limited.

Philip Larkin: "Church Going" and "Toads" from *The Less Deceived* by permission of The Marvell Press, England and Australia. "Water," "The Whitsun Weddings," "An Arundel Tomb," "High Windows," "Going, Going," "Homage to a Government," "This Be The Verse," and "The Explosion," from *Collected Poems* by Philip Larkin. Copyright (c) 1988, 1989 by the Estate of Philip Larkin. Reprinted by permission of Farrar, Straus and Giroux, LLC and Faber and Faber Ltd.

D. H. Lawrence: "Willy Wet-Leg," "Andraitx.-Pomegranate Flower," and "Bavarian Gentians" from *The Complete Poems of D. H. Lawrence*, edited by V. de Sola Pinto and F. W. Roberts. Copyright (c) 1964, 1971 by Angelo Ravagli and C. M. Weekly, Executors of the Estate of Frieda Lawrence Ravagli. Used by permission of Viking Penguin, a division of Penguin Putnam Inc. Permissions granted by Pollinger Limited and the Estate of Frieda Lawrence Ravagli.

Tom Leonard: "Six Glasgow Poems" and "A Priest Came on at Merkland Street." Reprinted by permission of author.

Liz Lochhead: "Mirror's Song" from *Dreaming Frankenstein.* Reprinted by permission of Polygon. "Bagpipe Muzak, Glasgow 1990" from *Bagpipe Muzak* by Liz Lochhead (Penguin Books, 1991). Copyright (c) Liz Lochhead, 1991.

Tony Lopez: "Brought Forward" from *False Memory.* Copyright (c) Tony Lopez, The Figures, Great Barrington, MA, 1998.

Mina Loy: "Der Blinde Junge" and "Italian Pictures" from *The Lost Lunar Baedeker.* Copyright (c) 1996 by the Estate of Mina Loy. Reprinted by permission of Farrar, Straus and Giroux, LLC and Carcanet Press Limited. "English Rose" from *Anglo-Mongrels and the Rose.* Reprint permissions granted by the Estate of Mina Loy.

Norman MacCaig: "High Street, Edinburgh," "Nude in a fountain," "Celtic cross," and "Intrusion." Reprinted by permission of Chatto & Windus.

Hugh MacDiarmid: Excerpts from *The Drunk Man Looks at the Thistle*, "On a Raised Beach" and an excerpt from *In Memoriam James Joyce*, from *Selected Poetry.* Copyright (c) 1992 by Michael Grieve. Reprinted by permission of New Directions Publishing Corp. and by permission of Carcanet Press Limited.

Helen Macdonald: "Taxonomy," "Blackbird/Jackdaw/*Turdus/corvus/merula/monedula*," "Section VIII," and "Poem." Reprint permission granted by author.

Thomas MacGreevy: "De Civitate Hominum," "The Six Who Were Hanged," and "Homage to Hieronymus Bosch," from *The Collected Poems of Thomas MacGreevy*, edited by Susan Schreibman. Reprinted by permission of The Catholic University of America Press.

Sorley MacLean: "The Island" and "Going Westward" from *From Wood to Ridge* by Sorley MacLean. Reprinted by permission of Carcanet Press Limited.

Joseph Gordon Macleod: "Cancer, or the Crab," from *The Ecliptic*. Reprinted by permission of the estate of the author.

Louis MacNeice: "An Eclogue for Christmas," "Valediction," "Snow," and "Carrickfergus," from *Collected Poems*. Reprinted by permission of David Higham Associates.

Barry MacSweeney: Extracts from *Hellhound Memos*. Permission granted by the author.

Charles Madge: "Obsessional," "Delusions I," "Delusions III," "Delusions V," "Delusions VII," and "Countries of the Dead II," from *Of Love, Time and Places* (Anvil Press Poetry, 1994).

Derek Mahon: "A Garage in Co. Cork" and "Courtyards in Delft" from *The Hunt By Night*, with the permission of Wake Forest University Press. "The Snow Party" "A Disused Shed in Co. Wexford," "Courtyards in Delft," and "A Garage in Co. Cork," from *Selected Poems* by Derek Mahon. Reprinted by permission of The Peters, Fraser and Dunlop Group Limited on behalf of Derek Mahon.

E. A. Markham: "The Sea" from *Human Rites* (Anvil Press Poetry, 1984). "Towards the End of a Century," "Grandmotherpoem," and "The Mother's Tale," from *Towards the End of a Century* (Anvil Press Poetry, 1989).

Medbh McGuckian: "Tulips," "The Seed-Picture" and "Slips," from *The Flower Master and Other Poems* (1993). Reprinted by kind permission of the author and The Gallery Press. "Aviary" from *Venus and the Rain* (1994). Reprinted by kind permission of the author and The Gallery Press. "The War Ending" from *Marconi's Cottage* (1991). Reprinted by kind permission of the author and The Gallery Press. "The Albert Chain" from *Captain Lavender* (1994). Reprinted by kind permission of the author and The Gallery Press.

Drew Milne: "A Garden of Tears." Reprint permission granted by Alfred David Editions.

Christopher Middleton: "Hearing Elgar Again" and "The Prose of Walking Back to China" from *111 Poems*. Reprinted by permission of Carcanet Press Limited.

Charlotte Mew: "The Farmer's Bride," "Fame," "On the Road to the Sea," "Arracombe Wood," and "Monsieur Qui Passe" from *Collected Poems and Selected Prose* by Charlotte Mew. Reprinted by permission of Carcanet Press Limited.

Geraldine Monk: *La Quinta del Sordo* (Writers Forum, 1980) and "Where?" Reprint permission granted by the author.

Harold Monro: "Bitter Sanctuary." Reprint permission granted by Monro Harold Estates.

John Montague: "The Trout," "A Bright Day," "The Cage," "This Neutral Realm," and "The Well Dreams," from *Collected Poems* (1995) with permission of Wake Forest University Press and by kind permission of the author and The Gallery Press.

Nicholas Moore: "Song," "Ideas of Disorder at Torquay," and "Portman Restaurant" from *Longings of the Acrobats* by Nicholas Moore. Reprinted by permission of Carcanet Press Limited. "Leap Year" reprinted by permission of Peter Riley.

Paul Muldoon: "Incantata" from *Annals of Chile* by Paul Muldoon. Copyright (c) 1994 by Paul Muldoon. Reprinted by permission of Farrar, Straus and Giroux, LLC and Faber and Faber Ltd.

Edwin Muir: "The Old Gods," "The Three Mirrors," and "The Horses" from *Collected Poems* by Edwin Muir. Copyright (c) 1960 by Willa Muir. Used by permission of Oxford University Press, Inc. and Faber and Faber Ltd.

Grace Nichols: "The Fat Black Woman Remembers," "The Fat Black Woman Versus Politics," and "Skanking Englishman Between Trains" from *The Fat Black Woman's Poems* by Grace Nichols. Reprinted by permission of Little, Brown and Company (UK), a Division of Time-Life Entertainment Group Limited. "Long-Man" from *Sunris*. Reproduced with permission of Curtis Brown Ltd, London, on behalf of Grace Nichols. Copyright (c) Grace Nichols 1996.

Maggie O'Sullivan: "Starlings," "Garb," and "Hill Figures," from *In the House of the Shaman*. Reprinted by permission of Reality Street Editions.

Clere Parsons: "Corybantic," "Photogravure," "Different," and "Interruption," from *The Air Between: Poems of Clere Parsons (1908–1931)*, introduction by T. W. Sutherland and with an afterword by Edouard Roditi (Cloudforms Series, Newcastle upon Tyne, 1989). Reprinted by permission of Cloud.

Tom Pickard: "A History Lesson from My Son on Hadrian's Wall," "Energy," and "The Double D Economy." Copyright (c) Tom Pickard, 1994. First published in 1994 in *Tiepin Eros* by Bloodaxe Books Ltd.

F. T. Prince: "Strafford." Reprinted by permission of Sheep Meadow Press.

Craig Raine: "An Inquiry into Two Inches of Ivory" and "A Martian Sends a Postcard Home." Reprinted by permission of David Godwin Associates.

Tom Raworth: "Wedding Day," "You've Ruined My Evening/You've Ruined My Life," "South America," extracts from *Logbook*, extracts from "Sentenced to Death," extracts from *Eternal Sections*, and "Out of the Picture." Reprinted by permission of the author.

Peter Reading: Extract from *Stet*, from *Collected Poems*, Volume 2 (Bloodaxe Books, 1996).

Peter Redgrove: "Against Death," "Young Women with the Hair of Witches and No Modesty," "The British Museum Smile," and "Mothers and Child," from *The Moon Disposes: Poems 1954–1987*. Reprinted by permission of Secker & Warburg and David Higham Associates.

Carlyle Reedy: "The Slave Ship," from the anthology *Out of Everywhere*, edited by Maggie O'Sullivan. Reprinted by permission of Reality Street Editions.

Denise Riley: "Affections must not" from *Dry Air* by Denise Riley (Virago Press). Reprinted by permission of Little, Brown and Company (UK), a Division of Time-Life Entertainment Group Limited and Reality Street Editions. "Affections must not" from *Dry Air* by Denise Riley (Virago Press). Reprinted by permission of Little, Brown and Company (UK), A Division of Time-Life Entertainment Group Limited. "Lure, 1963," "When it's time to go," "Pastoral," "Wherever you are, be somewhere else," and "Knowing in the real world," from *Selected Poems* by Denise Riley (Reality Street Editions). Reprinted by permission of Reality Street Editions.

John Riley: "Czargrad." Reprinted by permission of the Estate of John Riley.

Peter Riley: Extracts from *Lines on the Liver* (London: Ferry Press, 1981). Extracts from *Excavations, Part One*, books 1 and 2 from *Distant Points* (London: Reality Street Editions, 1995). Reprinted by permission of Reality Street Editions. Extracts from *Excavations, Part One*, book 3 from *Chicago Review* 43, no. 3 (1997). Reprinted by permission of the *Chicago Review*.

Lynette Roberts: Parts IV and V of *Gods with Stainless Ears*. Reprint permission granted by the Estate of Lynette Roberts.

John Rodker: "A Slice of Life," "The Music Hall," "Hymn to Love" and "I'd have loved you as you deserved had we been frogs," from *Poems & Adolphe 1920* by John Rodker. Reprinted by permission of Carcanet Press Limited.

Isaac Rosenberg: "The Jew," "Break of Day in the Trenches," "Louse Hunting," and "Dead Man's Dump." Reprint permission granted by Isaac Rosenberg's copyright-holder.

Siegfried Sassoon: "A Working Party," "The Rear-Guard," and "The General." Copyright (c) Siegfried Sassoon. Reprinted by permission of George Sassoon.

Tom Scott: "Johnie Raw Prays for His Lords and Maisters" from *The Collected Shorter Poems of Tom Scott*. Reprinted by permission of Chapman Agenda Publications, The Estate of Tom Scott.

Maurice Scully: "Fire," from *Steps*. Reprinted by permission of Reality Street Editions.

Jo Shapcott: "Phrase Book," "The Mad Cow in Love," and "Mad Cow Dance," from *Her Book: Poems 1988–1998* by Jo Shapcott. Reprinted by permission of Faber and Faber Ltd. as publishers.

Robert Sheppard: "The Materialization of Soap 1947" and "Internal Exile 1." Reprint permission granted by author.

Jon Silkin: "Death of a Son," "First it was Singing," "Dandelion," "A Daisy," and "A Word About Freedom." Reprinted by permission of author.

C. H. Sisson: "A Letter to John Donne," "The Desert," "Au Clair de la Lune," and "Place," from *Collected Poems* by C. H. Sisson. Reprinted by permission of Carcanet Press Limited.

Edith Sitwell: "Ass-Face," "The Bat," "Fox Trot," "Sir Beelzebub," and "The Canticle of the Rose," from *Collected Poems* by Edith Sitwell. Reprinted by permission of David Higham Associates and Sinclair Stevenson.

Stevie Smith: "Souvenir de Monsieur Poop," "Not Waving but Drowning," "My Hat," "The Celts," "Pretty" and "Black March," from *Collected Poems of Stevie Smith*. Copyright (c) 1972 by Stevie Smith. Reprinted by permission of New Directions Publishing Corp.

Dylan Thomas: "The force that through the green fuse drives the flower" and "To-day, this insect" from *The Poems of Dylan Thomas*. Copyright (c) 1939 by New Directions Publishing Corp. Reprinted by permission of New Directions Publishing Corp. "Our eunuch dreams" from *The Poems of Dylan Thomas*. Copyright (c) 1952, 1953 by Dylan Thomas. Reprinted by permission of New Directions Publishing Corp. "Over Sir John's hill," from *The Poems of Dylan Thomas*. Copyright (c) 1952 by Dylan Thomas. Reprinted by permission of New Directions Publishing Corp. Permission granted by David Higham Associates.

Charles Tomlinson: "Aesthetic," "Distinctions," "Saving the Appearances," "Swimming Chenango Lake," "Prometheus," "Annunciation," "The Plaza," and "The Garden." Reprinted by permission of the author.

Rosemary Tonks: "The Sofas, Fogs and Cinemas," "The Little Cardboard Suitcase," and "The Ice-cream Boom Towns." Reprinted by permission of Sheil Land Associates Ltd.

Gael Turnbull: "George Fox, from his Journals," extracts from "Twenty Words, Twenty Days," and "Thighs Gripping," from *While Breath Persist* (Erin, Ontario: The Porcupine's Quill, 1992). Permission granted by The Porcupine's Quill, Inc.

Catherine Walsh: Part Three of *Pitch*. Copyright (c) Catherine Walsh. Reprinted by permission of Pig Press as the original publisher.

Sylvia Townsend Warner: "Nelly Trim," "East London Cemetery," "King Duffus," and "Anne Donne," from *Selected Poems* by Sylvia Townsend Warner. Reprinted by permission of Carcanet Press Limited.

Anna Wickham: "Self Analysis," "Meditation at Kew," and "Divorce." Reprint permission granted by George Hepburn and Margaret Hepburn.

John Wilkinson: "bayonetted," "snap crackle & pop," and "You've got some lip," from *Sarn Helen*. Reprint permission granted by the author.

W. B. Yeats: "Sailing to Byzantium," "The Tower," and "Among School Children." Reprinted with the permission of Scribner, a Division of Simon & Schuster, from *The Collected Poems of W. B. Yeats*, Revised Second Edition edited by Richard J. Finneran. Copyright (c) 1928 by Macmillian Publishing Company; copyright renewed (c) 1956 by Georgie Yeats. "Byzantium" and "Crazy Jane Talks with the Bishop." Reprinted with the permission of Scribner, a Division of Simon & Schuster from *The Collected Poems of W. B. Yeats*, Revised Second Edition edited by Richard J. Finneran. Copyright (c) 1933 by Macmillian Publishing Company; copyright renewed (c) 1961 by Bertha Georgie Yeats. "Lapis Lazuli," "Under Ben Bulben," "The Circus Animals' Desertion," and "Politics." Reprinted with the permission of Scribner, a Division of Simon & Schuster, from *The Collected Poems of W. B. Yeats*, Revised Second Edition edited by Richard J. Finneran. Copyright (c) 1940 by Georgie Yeats; copyright renewed (c) 1968 by Bertha Georgie Yeats, Michael Butler Yeats, and Anne Yeats. Reprinted permission granted by A. P. Watt Ltd. "To the Rose Upon the Rood of Time," "The Lake Isle of Innisfree," "Who Goes with Fergus?," "The Valley of the Black Pig," "September 1913," "The Witch," "The Peacock," "The Dolls," "A Coat," "The Wild Swans at Coole," "Easter 1916," "The Second Coming," "A Prayer for my Daughter," and "Leda and the Swan." Reprinted by permission of A. P. Watt Ltd. on behalf of Michael B. Yeats.

Benjamin Zephaniah: *City Psalms* (Bloodaxe Books, 1992).

THOMAS HARDY (1840–1928)

H ARDY WAS BORN AT HIGHER BOCKHAMPTON, NEAR DORCHESTER IN DORSET, AND
educated at local schools. At 16 he was apprenticed to a church architect and later
he studied with the architect Arthur Bloomfield in London, continuing in this pro-
fession until the success of his novel *Far from the Madding Crowd* (1874) enabled him
to work full-time at writing. In 1874, he married Emma Gifford, the "voiceless ghost"
of "After a Journey" and other poems that also acknowledge that "Things were not
lastly as firstly well / With us." Between 1871 and 1896, Hardy published seventeen
novels and collections of short stories until the hostile public reaction to *Tess of the
D'Urbervilles* (1891) and *Jude the Obscure* (1896) prompted him to give up fiction. His
first poems date from the 1860s, but manuscripts for these poems have not survived,
and it is not known to what extent the poems in his first book, *Wessex Poems* (1898),
revise earlier poems. Six more volumes of poems were published in his lifetime,
including *Time's Laughingstocks* (1909), *Satires of Circumstance* (1914), and *Moments
of Vision* (1917); *Winter Words* (1928) appeared posthumously. His verse drama *The
Dynasts* was published in three volumes (1904–08). After his wife's death in 1912,
Hardy married Florence Dugdale in 1914; her biography of the poet and novelist was
largely ghosted by Hardy. Though *Jude the Obscure* was controversial for its purported
obscenity and his poetry for the most part unenthusiastically received, Hardy's repu-
tation grew to the point where, late in life, honors were heaped upon him, including
the Order of Merit, honorary degrees from Oxford and Cambridge, and the gold
medal of the Royal Society of Literature.

Irving Howe writes that "We can read [Hardy] as a philosopher spinning fables
of determinism, an elegist of rural simplicities, a poet of tenderness, a Christian
whose faith has been hollowed by skepticism, a country pagan whose mind is covered
over with Christian pieties, an imaginative historian of the revolutionary changes in
nineteenth-century moral consciousness, an autodidact who keeps stumbling into
sublimities of intuition."[1] Ideas in Hardy's poems that might have been derived from
Charles Darwin, Herbert Spencer, Thomas Henry Huxley, or the German "Higher
Criticism" become part of a drama of conflicting perspectives and values. David
Perkins argues that Hardy's complexity is such that "Hard-won convictions of reason
are maintained with fidelity and yet massively countered by allegiances of feeling—
and perhaps by a remembrance that reason, like everything else, evolves historically."[2]
If Hardy is an ironist, pity often gets the last word, as Donald Davie remarked.[3] While

---

[1] "Thomas Hardy," *Atlantic Brief Lives: A Biographical Companion to the Arts,* ed. Louis Kronenberger,
Boston, 1971, p. 348.
[2] *A History of Modern Poetry: From the 1890s to the High Modernist Mode,* Cambridge, MA, 1976, p. 145.
[3] *Thomas Hardy and British Poetry,* New York, 1972, p. 33.

his poetry is admired for its descriptive realism, there is an archetypal quality to some of its vignettes, such as the meeting of lovers on the bridge in "The Harbour Bridge," one of those poems with the remote and steely perspective that Auden spoke of as Hardy's "hawk's vision."[4]

Of the nearly 1,000 poems in Hardy's *Collected Poems*, only 141 duplicate stanzaic patterns. While there are formal continuities across the work, such as a fondness for lines mixing anapests and iambs and a preference for arranging stanzas in a quasi-architectural visual symmetry, much of the interest of Hardy's versification comes from its expressive idiosyncrasies. The ghosted autobiography links a "cunning irregularity" in "the character of his meters and stanzas, that of stress rather than syllable, poetic texture rather than poetic veneer," to the "Gothic art-principle" and "the principle of spontaneity . . . found in mouldings, tracery, and such like."[5] Hardy's diction, which can contain seemingly awkward words such as "powerfuller" and odd coinages such as "outskeleton" and "upfinger," was once described by F. R. Leavis as including "the romantic poetical, the prosaic banal, the archaistic, the erudite, the technical, the dialect word, the brand-new Hardy coinage."[6] As with the poetry of Gerard Manley Hopkins, it is precisely the unpredictable and exuberant inventiveness of Hardy's language and forms that most holds our attention today.

---

[4] Quoted in Perkins, p. 149.
[5] Florence Emily Hardy, *The Life of Thomas Hardy, 1840–1928*, London, 1962, p. 300.
[6] Quoted in Perkins, p. 146.

Hap

If but some vengeful god would call to me
From up the sky, and laugh: 'Thou suffering thing,
Know that thy sorrow is my ecstasy,
That thy love's loss is my hate's profiting!'

5   Then would I bear it, clench myself, and die,
Steeled by the sense of ire unmerited;
Half-eased in that a Powerfuller than I
Had willed and meted me the tears I shed.

But not so. How arrives it joy lies slain,
10   And why unblooms the best hope ever sown?
—Crass Casualty obstructs the sun and rain,
And dicing Time for gladness casts a moan. . . .
These purblind Doomsters had as readily strown
Blisses about my pilgrimage as pain.

1866 / 1898

Title: *Hap:* chance (arch.); fortune (whether good or bad)
11: *Casualty:* chance
12: *for:* instead of: "Time's throw of the dice turns up a moan instead of gladness"
13: *purblind Doomsters:* obtuse (literally "partly blind") Fates

Neutral Tones

We stood by a pond that winter day,
And the sun was white, as though chidden of God,
And a few leaves lay on the starving sod;
    —They had fallen from an ash, and were gray.

5   Your eyes on me were as eyes that rove
Over tedious riddles of years ago;
And some words played between us to and fro
    On which lost the more by our love.

The smile on your mouth was the deadest thing
10   Alive enough to have strength to die;
And a grin of bitterness swept thereby
    Like an ominous bird a-wing. . . .

Since then, keen lessons that love deceives,
And wrings with wrong, have shaped to me
15   Your face, and the God-curst sun, and a tree,
    And a pond edged with grayish leaves.

1867 / 1898

The Subalterns

I

'Poor wanderer,' said the leaden sky,
    'I fain would lighten thee,
But there are laws in force on high
    Which say it must not be.'

II

5   —'I would not freeze thee, shorn one,' cried
    The North, 'knew I but how
To warm my breath, to slack my stride;
    But I am ruled as thou.'

III

    —'To-morrow I attack thee, wight,'
10   Said Sickness. 'Yet I swear
I bear thy little ark no spite,
    But am bid enter there.'

2: *chidden of*: chided by
3: *starving*: frozen (dial.)

Title: *Subaltern:* a subordinate; in the British Army, an officer occupying the rank below captain.
2: *fain would:* would be glad to (arch.)
9: *wight:* person (arch.)
11: *ark:* body. See 2 Corinthians 5:1–4 for the body as "tabernacle."

IV

—'Come hither, Son,' I heard Death say;
        'I did not will a grave
15   Should end thy pilgrimage to-day,
        But I, too, am a slave!'

V

We smiled upon each other then,
        And life to me had less
Of that fell look it wore ere when
20   They owned their passiveness.

1901

The Darkling Thrush

I leant upon a coppice gate
        When Frost was spectre-gray,
And Winter's dregs made desolate
        The weakening eye of day.
5   The tangled bine-stems scored the sky
        Like strings of broken lyres,
And all mankind that haunted nigh
        Had sought their household fires.

The land's sharp features seemed to be
10   The Century's corpse outleant,
His crypt the cloudy canopy,
        The wind his death-lament.
The ancient pulse of germ and birth
        Was shrunken hard and dry,
15   And every spirit upon earth
        Seemed fervourless as I.

At once a voice arose among
        The bleak twigs overhead
In a full-hearted evensong
20   Of joy illimited;

19: *fell:* cruel, terrible

Title: *Darkling:* in darkness (arch.). The word suggests several earlier poets' use of it: e.g., "the wakeful
    bird / Sings darkling, and in shadiest covert hid / Tunes her nocturnal note" (Milton, *Paradise Lost*
    3:38–40); "Darkling I listen" (Keats, "Ode to a Nightingale"); "And we are here as on a darkling plain /
    Swept with confused alarms of struggle and flight, / Where ignorant armies clash by night." (Matthew
    Arnold, "Dover Beach").
1: *coppice:* a wood of small trees grown for the purposes of periodical cutting
4: *eye of day:* i.e., the sun
6: *broken lyres:* Hardy alludes to the Aeolian harp (wind-harp), for the Romantic poets a symbol of
    Nature's action on the mind. See, e.g., Coleridge's "The Eolian Harp," or Shelley's "Ode to the West
    Wind": "Make me thy lyre, even as the forest is: / What if my leaves are falling like its own!"
10: *outleant:* outstretched (Hardy's coinage)
13: *germ:* germination
19: *evensong:* church service held just before sunset

An aged thrush, frail, gaunt, and small,
    In blast-beruffled plume,
Had chosen thus to fling his soul
    Upon the growing gloom.

25   So little cause for carolings
    Of such ecstatic sound
Was written on terrestrial things
    Afar or nigh around,
That I could think there trembled through
30   His happy good-night air
Some blessed Hope, whereof he knew
    And I was unaware.

            31 December 1900 / 1901

The Man He Killed

    'Had he and I but met
    By some old ancient inn,
We should have sat us down to wet
    Right many a nipperkin!

5   'But ranged as infantry,
    And staring face to face,
I shot at him as he at me,
    And killed him in his place.

    'I shot him dead because—
10   Because he was my foe,
Just so: my foe of course he was;
    That's clear enough; although

    'He thought he'd 'list, perhaps,
    Off-hand like—just as I—
15   Was out of work—had sold his traps—
    No other reason why.

    'Yes; quaint and curious war is!
    You shoot a fellow down
You'd treat if met where any bar is,
20   Or help to half-a-crown.'

            1902 / 1909

Date: Despite Hardy's date this poem was first published as "By the Century's Deathbed" in the 29 Dec. 1900 issue of *Graphic*.

4: *nipperkin*: a small drinking vessel, containing less than half a pint
13: *'list*: enlist
15: *traps*: belongings
20: *half-a-crown*: a coin worth two shillings and sixpence in the old British monetary system—i.e., a small amount of money.

Channel Firing

That night your great guns, unawares,
Shook all our coffins as we lay,
And broke the chancel window-squares,
We thought it was the Judgment-day

5   And sat upright. While drearisome
Arose the howl of wakened hounds:
The mouse let fall the altar-crumb,
The worms drew back into the mounds,

The glebe cow drooled. Till God called, 'No;
10   It's gunnery practice out at sea
Just as before you went below;
The world is as it used to be:

'All nations striving strong to make
Red war yet redder. Mad as hatters
15   They do no more for Christés sake
Than you who are helpless in such matters.

'That this is not the judgment-hour
For some of them's a blessed thing,
For if it were they'd have to scour
20   Hell's floor for so much threatening. . . .

'Ha, ha. It will be warmer when
I blow the trumpet (if indeed
I ever do; for you are men,
And rest eternal sorely need).'

25   So down we lay again. 'I wonder,
Will the world ever saner be',
Said one, 'than when He sent us under
In our indifferent century!'

And many a skeleton shook his head.
30   'Instead of preaching forty year,'
My neighbour Parson Thirdly said,
'I wish I had stuck to pipes and beer.'

This poem was written four months before the outbreak of World War I on 4 August 1914; Hardy later
called it "prophetic."
Title: *Channel Firing:* gunnery practice on battleships in the English Channel
3: *chancel window-squares:* The chancel is the section of the church behind the altar-rails, which contains
the altar and is reserved for the clergymen and choir. The stained-glass window over the altar typically
contains numerous small diamond-shaped panes.
4: The dead have mistaken the gunfire for the last trumpet that will announce the Last Judgment.
7: *altar-crumb:* a fragment of consecrated wafer from the service; this indicates the minister's negligence,
since no remnants should be left over.
9: *glebe:* a portion of church land assigned to a clergyman as part of his benefice, to supplement his
income
28: *indifferent:* not differing (arch.)—i.e., equally warlike

Again the guns disturbed the hour,
Roaring their readiness to avenge,
35　　　As far inland as Stourton Tower,
And Camelot, and starlit Stonehenge.

April 1914 / 1914

'I Found Her Out There'

I found her out there
On a slope few see,
That falls westwardly
To the salt-edged air,
5　　　Where the ocean breaks
On the purple strand,
And the hurricane shakes
The solid land.

I brought her here,
10　　　And have laid her to rest
In a noiseless nest
No sea beats near.
She will never be stirred
In her loamy cell
15　　　By the waves long heard
And loved so well.

So she does not sleep
By those haunted heights
The Atlantic smites
20　　　And the blind gales sweep,
Whence she often would gaze
At Dundagel's famed head,

35: *Stourton Tower:* King Alfred's Tower, a monument near Stourton, Wiltshire, built in 1766 and commemorating the site where he repelled the invading Danes in 879; situated on a ridge, it is visible for miles around.

36: *Camelot:* the legendary castle said to be the seat of the King Arthur

Stonehenge: a large circle of standing stones located on Salisbury Plain. According to modern archeology it was built in several stages from c. 3100 BC to c. 1500 BC; in Hardy's time it was wrongly thought to be a Druidic temple.

"'I Found Her Out There'" and "After a Journey" come from *Poems of 1912–13,* a section of *Satires of Circumstance* whose reticent title indicates their source in Hardy's mourning the death of his first wife, Emma, in November 1912. Hardy's work as an architect's assistant had taken him to Cornwall in 1870 for a brief visit to sketch St. Juliot Church in preparation for its restoration. There he met Emma Gifford, the rector's sister-in-law; a few months later he returned to court her. They married in 1874, but the marriage was not a success: by the time of her death, Hardy and his wife lived in separate parts of their house at Max Gate and met only once a day at dinner; she had also become increasingly mentally unstable. Her unexpected death shocked Hardy into warmly recalling their early days of courtship, and he continued to mourn her for the rest of his life, much to the dismay of his second wife, Florence, whom he married in 1914.

9: Emma Hardy was buried in Stinsford, Dorset, next to other members of the Hardy family.

14: *Loam* is a fertile soil containing clay, sand, and decomposed vegetable matter.

22: *Dundagel's famed head:* Tintagel Head, the site of ruins traditionally held to be those of the castle where King Arthur was born.

While the dipping blaze
Dyed her face fire-red;

25   And would sigh at the tale
Of sunk Lyonnesse,
As a wind-tugged tress
Flapped her cheek like a flail;
Or listen at whiles
30   With a thought-bound brow
To the murmuring miles
She is far from now.

Yet her shade, maybe,
Will creep underground
35   Till it catch the sound
Of that western sea
As it swells and sobs
Where she once domiciled,
And joy in its throbs
40   With the heart of a child.

1912 / 1914

After a Journey

Hereto I come to view a voiceless ghost;
   Whither, O whither will its whim now draw me?
Up the cliff, down, till I'm lonely, lost,
   And the unseen waters' ejaculations awe me.
5   Where you will next be there's no knowing,
     Facing round about me everywhere,
       With your nut-coloured hair,
And gray eyes, and rose-flush coming and going.

Yes: I have re-entered your olden haunts at last;
10   Through the years, through the dead scenes I have tracked you;
What have you now found to say of our past—
    Scanned across the dark space wherein I have lacked you?
Summer gave us sweets, but autumn wrought division?
    Things were not lastly as firstly well
15   With us twain, you tell?
But all's closed now, despite Time's derision.

I see what you are doing: you are leading me on
    To the spots we knew when we haunted here together,
The waterfall, above which the mist-bow shone
20   At the then fair hour in the then fair weather,

26: *sunk Lyonnesse:* a mythic part of Cornwall associated with Arthurian legend, traditionally said to have
  sunk beneath the sea.
31: *murmuring miles:* i.e., the sea
38: *domiciled:* resided

After a Journey: The poem is set in Pentargan Bay, in Cornwall; Hardy visited Cornwall for the first time
  since the days of his courtship in March 1913.

And the cave just under, with a voice still so hollow
   That it seems to call out to me from forty years ago,
     When you were all aglow,
And not the thin ghost that I now fraily follow!

25   Ignorant of what there is flitting here to see,
   The waked birds preen and the seals flop lazily,
Soon you will have, Dear, to vanish from me,
   For the stars close their shutters and the dawn whitens hazily.
Trust me, I mind not, though Life lours,
30   The bringing me here; nay, bring me here again!
    I am just the same as when
Our days were a joy, and our paths through flowers.

1914

from Satires of Circumstance

II. In Church

'And now to God the Father,' he ends,
And his voice thrills up to the topmost tiles:
Each listener chokes as he bows and bends,
And emotion pervades the crowded aisles.
5   Then the preacher glides to the vestry-door,
And shuts it, and thinks he is seen no more.

The door swings softly ajar meanwhile,
And a pupil of his in the Bible class,
Who adores him as one without gloss or guile,
10 Sees her idol stand with a satisfied smile
And re-enact at the vestry-glass
Each pulpit gesture in deft dumb-show
That had moved the congregation so.

1910 / 1914

VI. In the Cemetery

'You see those mothers squabbling there?'
Remarks the man of the cemetery.
'One says in tears, "'*Tis mine lies here!*"
Another, "*Nay, mine, you Pharisee!*"

1: *And now to God the Father*: The phrase is from the formula used toward the end of the sermon, which
  announces the return to the written service.
5: *vestry*: a room in or attached to the church in which the vestments are kept and where they are put on.
12: *dumb-show*: mute reenactment

2: *man of the cemetery*: sexton
4: *Pharisee*: strictly, a self-righteous person or hypocrite (after the name of the strictly observant Jewish
  sect whose members opposed Jesus); here used more generally to mean "liar."

5   Another, "*How dare you move my flowers*
       And put your own on this grave of ours!"
       But all their children were laid therein
       At different times, like sprats in a tin.

10   'And then the main drain had to cross,
       And we moved the lot some nights ago,
       And packed them away in the general foss
       With hundreds more. But their folks don't know,
       And as well cry over a new-laid drain
       As anything else, to ease your pain!'

                                                  1910 / 1914

The Pity of It

       I walked in loamy Wessex lanes, afar
       From rail-track and from highway, and I heard
       In field and farmstead many an ancient word
       Of local lineage like 'Thu bist', 'Er war',

5   'Ich woll', 'Er sholl', and by-talk similar,
       Nigh as they speak who in this month's moon gird
       At England's very loins, thereunto spurred
       By gangs whose glory threats and slaughters are.

       Then seemed a Heart crying: 'Whosoever they be
10   At root and bottom of this, who flung this flame
       Between kin folk kin tongued even as are we,

       'Sinister, ugly, lurid, be their fame;
       May their familiars grow to shun their name,
       And their brood perish everlastingly.'

                                                  1915 / 1917

11: *foss:* grave (arch.)

The Pity of It: This poem and the next appear in a section of *Moments of Vision* (1917) entitled "Poems of
  War and Patriotism."
1: *Loam* is a fertile soil containing clay, sand, and decomposed vegetable matter.
  Wessex: the name Hardy gives in his fiction and poetry to the southwest of England.
4–5: The recognizable traces of German in these phrases—meaning "You are," "He was," "I will," and "He
  shall"—point to the English language's Anglo-Saxon roots. Dialects of English often preserve archaisms
  that have disappeared from standard English.
6–7: *gird / At England's very loins:* (1) "gird at": jeer at; (2) "gird one's loins": prepare for battle
13: *familiars:* friends or associates

In Time of 'the Breaking of Nations'

I

Only a man harrowing clods
 In a slow silent walk
With an old horse that stumbles and nods
 Half asleep as they stalk.

II

5 Only thin smoke without flame
 From the heaps of couch-grass;
Yet this will go onward the same
 Though Dynasties pass.

III

Yonder a maid and her wight
10 Come whispering by:
War's annals will cloud into night
 Ere their story die.

1915 / 1916, 1917

Snow in the Suburbs

Every branch big with it,
 Bent every twig with it;
Every fork like a white web-foot;
Every street and pavement mute:
5 Some flakes have lost their way, and grope back upward, when
Meeting those meandering down they turn and descend again.
 The palings are glued together like a wall,
 And there is no waft of wind with the fleecy fall.

A sparrow enters the tree,
10 Whereon immediately

Though "In Time of 'the Breaking of Nations'" was first published during World War I, its scene comes
 from a memory of 1870, during the Franco-Prussian War, when Hardy was courting Emma Gifford: as
 he later wrote, "On the day that the bloody battle of Gravelotte was fought they were reading Tennyson
 in the grounds of the rectory. It was at this time and spot that Hardy was struck by the incident of the
 old horse harrowing the arable field in the valley below, which, when in far later years it was recalled to
 him by a still bloodier war, he made into the little poem of three verses entitled "In Time of 'the Break-
 ing of Nations'"." (*The Life and Work of Thomas Hardy*, ed. Michael Millgate, London, 1984, pp. 81–82).
Title: See Jeremiah 51:20, where God pronounces the destruction of Babylon: "Thou [Israel] art my battle-
 ax and weapons of war: for with thee will I break in pieces the nations, and with thee will I destroy king-
 doms."
6: *couch-grass*: a common weed, troublesome to farmers
9: *wight*: man (arch.)
11: *cloud*: Hardy's second thought; earlier texts have "fade."

7: *palings*: fence-stakes

> A snow-lump thrice his own slight size
> Descends on him and showers his head and eyes,
> And overturns him,
> And near inurns him,
> 15 And lights on a nether twig, when its brush
> Starts off a volley of other lodging lumps with a rush.
>
> The steps are a blanched slope,
> Up which, with feeble hope,
> A black cat comes, wide-eyed and thin;
> 20 And we take him in.

1925

The Harbour Bridge

> From here, the quay, one looks above to mark
> The bridge across the harbour, hanging dark
> Against the day's-end sky, fair-green in glow
> Over and under the middle archway's bow:
> 5 It draws its skeleton where the sun has set,
> Yea, clear from cutwater to parapet;
> On which mild glow, too, lines of rope and spar
> Trace themselves black as char.
>
> Down here in shade we hear the painters shift
> 10 Against the bollards with a drowsy lift,
> As moved by the incoming stealthy tide.
> High up across the bridge the burghers glide
> As cut black-paper portraits hastening on
> In conversation none knows what upon:
> 15 Their sharp-edged lips move quickly word by word
> To speech that is not heard.
>
> There trails the dreamful girl, who leans and stops,
> There presses the practical woman to the shops,
> There is a sailor, meeting his wife with a start,
> 20 And we, drawn nearer, judge they are keeping apart.
> Both pause. She says: 'I've looked for you. I thought
> We'd make it up.' Then no words can be caught.
> At last: 'Won't you come home?' She moves still nigher:
> ''Tis comfortable, with a fire.'

6: *cutwater:* the wedge-shaped base of the bridge pier meant to divide the water and break up ice
 parapet: low wall at the side of a bridge
7: *rope and spar:* i.e., of ships.
9: A *painter* is a rope attached to the bow of a boat for tying it fast.
10: *bollards:* posts on the quay to which ropes are made fast
12: *burghers:* citizens
13: *cut black-paper portraits:* the literal meaning of "silhouettes"
20: *keeping:* living

25   'No,' he says gloomily. 'And, anyhow,
       I can't give up the other woman now:
       You should have talked like that in former days,
       When I was last home.' They go different ways.
       And the west dims, and yellow lamplights shine:
30   And soon above, like lamps more opaline,
       White stars ghost forth, that care not for men's wives,
            Or any other lives.

                                                        1925

He Never Expected Much
[or]
A Consideration

[A reflection] ON MY EIGHTY-SIXTH BIRTHDAY

          Well, World, you have kept faith with me,
               Kept faith with me;
          Upon the whole you have proved to be
               Much as you said you were.
5   Since as a child I used to lie
          Upon the leaze and watch the sky,
          Never, I own, expected I
               That life would all be fair.

          'Twas then you said, and since have said,
10   Times since have said,
          In that mysterious voice you shed
               From clouds and hills around:
          'Many have loved me desperately,
          Many with smooth serenity,
15   While some have shown contempt of me
               Till they dropped underground.

          'I do not promise overmuch,
               Child; overmuch;
          Just neutral-tinted haps and such,'
20   You said to minds like mine.
          Wise warning for your credit's sake!
          Which I for one failed not to take,
          And hence could stem such strain and ache
               As each year might assign.

                                                        1928

Title: The title and subtitles reproduce the alternatives Hardy was considering when his death interrupted
   his revision of the manuscript.
6: *leaze:* pasture (dial.)
19: *haps:* occurrences or accidents (arch.)

GERARD MANLEY HOPKINS (1844–1889)

W HEN HOPKINS'S POETRY WAS INTRODUCED TO THE WORLD BY ROBERT
Bridges in 1918, Bridges felt obliged to apologize for what he took for odd and
obscure moments in the poems. Less than two decades later F. R. Leavis was able to
proclaim the same poems "key to a decisive reordering of the traditions of English
poetry."[1] Less preoccupied with supposed rules of verse than Bridges, more recent
readers of Hopkins often delight in what cannot help but immediately strike them: the
sonic splendor, even excess, of his poetry's music. Hopkins will cluster words and
stresses, punctuating the line to emphasize or exaggerate a sound effect, forcing
attention on the density of words and phrases as they are sounded. The sheer wonder
and plenty of language seemed to him evidence that God "hath raised up a horn of
salvation for us."[2] Onomatopoeic effects are common, as in these lines from "Tom's
Garland":

> Low be it: lustily he his low lot (feel
> That ne'er need hunger, Tom; Tom seldom sick,
> Seldomer heartsore; that treads through, prickproof, thick
> Thousands of thorns, thoughts) swings through.[3]

Like working-class Tom treading through his trials, not least of which are his
thoughts, the movement from the first alliterative chain—*l*—to the last—*th*—slows
our reading, allowing us to linger with individual words and ponder words linked by
sound, until eventually we emerge triumphant on the far side of the parenthesis. Verse
like this, outside of traditional metrical patterns, was as unconventional in Hopkins's
day as in our own, requiring him to devise, for his correspondents and for himself, a
new set of prosodic terms and procedures. Many a student since has had initial enthu-
siasm unnecessarily squashed by scansion exercises requiring definitions of "sprung
rhythm," "counterpoint rhythm," and "outriding feet." While it is true that Hopkins
was an eclectic and learned reader capable of mining forms such as the Welsh cyng-
hanedd for sonic resources, his habit of "scanning by accents and stresses alone" also
has some of its roots in the popular and demotic, "in nursery rhymes and popular jin-
gles," as he noted in a letter.[4]

Hopkins was born at Stratford, Essex, the oldest of eight children in a middle-
class home. After Highgate School he attended Balliol College, Oxford, where Walter
Pater was his tutor and where he began his lifelong friendship with Bridges. Oxford

---

[1] *New Bearings in English Poetry*, London, 1932, p. 195.
[2] "An Early Diary" (September 24, 1863), *Poems and Prose*, ed. W. H. Gardner, London, 1953, p. 90.
[3] *Poems and Prose*, p. 64.
[4] Letter to R. W. Dixon, October 5, 1878, *Selected Poetry and Prose*, p. 187.

also introduced Hopkins to the influence of the Oxford Movement (begun in 1833) and its effort to establish the authority and catholicity of the English Church. In 1866, John Henry Cardinal Newman received Hopkins into the Roman Catholic Church. After two years teaching at Newman's Oratory School in Edgbaston, he entered the Novitiate of the Society of Jesus in 1868. Since the Jesuits viewed fame as, in Hopkins's words, "the most dangerous and dazzling of all attractions," he resolved to give up writing poetry. In 1876, when Franciscan nuns were among those lost in the shipwreck of the *Deutschland*, Hopkins, encouraged by his rector, began writing poetry again. "The Wreck of the Deutschland" was rejected by a Jesuit journal for being too difficult, and Hopkins's work would not appear in print until the Bridges edition. Nor was publication pursued. After 1876, he continued to write while working in Chesterfield, London, Oxford, and various industrial parishes. A brief tenure in Glasgow was followed by an appointment in Greek and Latin at University College, Dublin. At times feeling alien in this new location and uncertain of his chosen work, Hopkins wrote to a friend that "the melancholy I have all my life been subject to has become of late . . . more distributed, constant, and crippling."[5] His spiritual struggles in this period are evident in late poems such as "Carrion Comfort," written in the years preceding his early death from typhoid fever.

Hopkins once wrote in an entry in his journal that he had "noticed the smell of the big cedar, not just in passing it but always at a patch of sunlight a little way off."[6] The descriptive sensuousness of such writing, which owes something to John Ruskin's example, is everywhere present in Hopkins's nature poems, which celebrate the singularity of the natural object as visible sign of spiritual grace. Hopkins developed a personal spiritual vocabulary with terms such as "inscape" (the uniqueness or distinctiveness of a thing or object of sense) and "instress" (the energy that shapes this distinctiveness); these terms are often discussed with reference to the medieval theologian Duns Scotus and his ideas of haecceity or "thisness."

---

[5] Quoted in Norman White, *Hopkins: A Literary Biography*, Oxford, 1992, p. 392.
[6] *Selected Poems and Prose*, p. 131.

God's Grandeur

The world is charged with the grandeur of God.
    It will flame out, like shining from shook foil;
    It gathers to a greatness, like the ooze of oil
Crushed. Why do men then now not reck his rod?
5   Generations have trod, have trod, have trod;
    And all is seared with trade; bleared, smeared with toil;
    And wears man's smudge and shares man's smell: the soil
Is bare now, nor can foot feel, being shod.

We are indebted to the annotations of N.H. Mackenzie in *A Reader's Guide to the Poetry of Gerard Manley Hopkins* (London, 1981) and his Oxford English Texts edition of Hopkins, and Catherine Phillips's edition in the Oxford Authors series.

1: *charged*: as with electricity. "All things therefore are charged with love, are charged with God and if we know how to touch them give off sparks and take fire, yield drops and flow, ring and tell of him" (*Sermons and Devotional Writings*, 1959, p. 195)

2: *shook foil*: "I mean foil in its sense of leaf or tinsel. . . . Shaken goldfoil gives off broad glares like sheet lightning and also, and this is true of nothing else, owing to its zigzag dints and creasings and network of small many cornered facets, a sort of fork lightning too" (letter to Robert Bridges, 4 Jan 1883).

4: *Crushed*: i.e., from olives
    reck: pay heed to

And, for all this, nature is never spent;
10   There lives the dearest freshness deep down things;
And though the last lights off the black West went
        Oh, morning, at the brown brink eastwards, springs—
Because the Holy Ghost over the bent
        World broods with warm breast and with ah! bright wings.

1877 / 1918

"As kingfishers catch fire"

As kingfishers catch fire, dragonflies draw flame;
        As tumbled over rim in roundy wells
        Stones ring; like each tucked string tells, each hung bell's
Bow swung finds tongue to fling out broad its name;
5   Each mortal thing does one thing and the same:
        Deals out that being indoors each one dwells;
        Selves—goes its self; *myself* it speaks and spells,
Crying *What I do is me: for that I came.*

I say more: the just man justices;
10   Keeps grace: that keeps all his goings graces;
Acts in God's eye what in God's eye he is—
        Christ. For Christ plays in ten thousand places,
Lovely in limbs, and lovely in eyes not his
        To the Father through the features of men's faces.

c. 1877 / 1918

The Windhover

TO CHRIST OUR LORD

I caught this morning morning's minion, king-
        dom of daylight's dauphin, dapple-dáwn-drawn Falcon, in his riding
        Of the rólling level úndernéath him steady áir, and stríding
High there, how he rung upon the rein of a wimpling wing

13: *Holy Ghost:* the Holy Spirit, present at the Creation: see Genesis 1:2, and Milton: "thou from the first / Wast present, and with mighty wings outspread / Dove-like sat'st brooding on the vast abyss / And mad'st it pregnant" (*Paradise Lost* 1:19–22).
    bent: curved (like the earth's surface); but the word also suggests mankind's warping of the natural order.

2: *roundy:* round (dial.)
3: *tucked:* plucked (dial.)
7: *selves:* The verb (Hopkins's coinage) is explained by the rest of the line.
9: *justices:* i.e., acts justly

Title: *Windhover:* a kestrel, so named for its hovering in midair while searching the ground for prey
1: *minion:* the favorite of a sovereign
2: *dauphin:* the eldest son (and heir) of the King of France
    dapple-dawn-drawn: The words may be read in many ways, but the primary sense is perhaps "drawn forth by the dappled dawn."
4: "The wimpling wing . . . is a rein from the bird to the air it rides and controls, and the bird . . . is also a bell ringing and jingling upon that moving rein" (Geoffrey Grigson).
    wimpling: the meandering or rippling of a stream (Scots). The wimple is a part of a nun's headdress under the veil that covers the forehead, sides of the face and neck.

5　　　In his ecstacy! then off, off forth on swing,
　　　　　　As a skate's heel sweeps smooth on a bow-bend: the hurl and gliding
　　　　　　Rebuffed the big wind. My heart in hiding
　　　　Stirred for a bird,—the achieve of, the mastery of the thing!

　　　　Brute beauty and valour and act, oh, air, pride, plume, here
10　　　　　　Buckle! AND the fire that breaks from thee then, a billion
　　　　Times told lovelier, more dangerous, O my chevalier!

　　　　No wónder of it: shéer plód makes plóugh down síllion
　　　　Shine, and blue-bleak embers, ah my dear,
　　　　　　Fall, gáll themsélves, and gásh góld-vermílion.

　　　　　　　　　　　　　　　　　　　1877 / 1918

Pied Beauty

　　　　Glory be to God for dappled things—
　　　　　　For skies of couple-colour as a brinded cow;
　　　　　　　For rose-moles all in stipple upon trout that swim;
　　　　Fresh-firecoal chestnut-falls; finches' wings;
5　　　　　　Landscape plotted and pieced—fold, fallow, and plough;
　　　　　　And áll trades, their gear and tackle and trim.

　　　　All things counter, original, spáre, strange;
　　　　　　Whatever is fickle, frecklèd (who knows how?)
　　　　　　With swíft, slów; sweet, sóur; adázzle, dím;
10　　　He fathers-forth whose beauty is pást change:
　　　　　　　　　　　　Práise hím.

　　　　　　　　　　　　　　　　　　　1877 / 1918

6: The tension of the sharp turn made by a skater suggests the image of a bent *bow*.

10: *Buckle*: join (together); also possibly "give way, collapse" (i.e., fall). MacKenzie argues strongly for the first sense, which suggests that all the qualities given in line 9 fuse "here" in a moment of inscape. (In this reading, the hawk does not—as other critics hold—here dive to snatch its prey.)

11: *chevalier*: knight, horseman

12: *sillion*: furrow (from the French "sillon"). See Virgil, *Georgics* i.43–6: "in Spring . . . let the ploughshare begin to become brilliant from rubbing against the furrow."

14: *gall*: break the surface of; wound. The line's imagery of descent and wounds suggests the incarnation and crucifixion of Christ.

Title: *Pied*: having two or more colors

2: *brinded*: a variant of "brindled": streaked, tabby

4: *fresh-firecoal chestnut-falls*: "Chestnuts as bright as coals or spots of vermilion" (Hopkins, *Journals and Papers*, ed. Humphry House and Graham Storey, London, 1959, p.189)

　　Finches' wings have light-coloured bands.

5: A "piece" is a plot of land; to "piece" is to patch or join together (thus here suggesting the patchwork arrangement of fields).

　　fold, fallow, and plough: enclosed pasturage and land both uncultivated and ploughed

6: *trim*: equipment

7: *counter*: contrary

　　spare: plain; meager

10: *fathers-forth*: creates

　　past change: unchanging

Spring and Fall

<small>TO A YOUNG CHILD</small>

Margaret, are you grieving
Over Goldengrove unleaving?
Leaves, like the things of man, you
With your fresh thoughts care for, can you?
5   Ah! as the heart grows older
It will come to such sights colder
By and by, nor spare a sigh
Though worlds of wanwood leafmeal lie;
And yet you *will* weep and know why.
10   Now no matter, child, the name:
Sorrow's springs are the same.
Nor mouth had, no nor mind, expressed
What héart héard of, ghóst guéssed:
It is the blight man was born for,
15   It is Margaret you mourn for.

1880 / 1918

Inversnaid

This dárksome búrn, hórseback brówn,
His rollrock highroad roaring down,
In coop and in comb the fleece of his foam
Flutes and low to the lake falls home.

5   A wíndpuff-bónnet of fáwn-fróth
Turns and twindles over the broth
Of a póol so pítchblack, féll-frówning,
It rounds and rounds Despair to drowning.

Degged with dew, dappled with dew
10   Are the groins of the braes that the brook treads through,

---

8: *leafmeal lie:* lie piecemeal in leaves. Like "wanwood," a coinage; it also suggests the leaves' becoming "meal" (powder) as they decay on the forest floor.
9: *will:* insist on
13: *ghost:* spirit

Title: *Inversnaid:* a small hamlet on Loch Lomond in Scotland (famous in Hopkins's time as the setting of Wordsworth's "To a Highland Girl"); also the name of the waterfall made by the stream called Arklet Water as it courses to the Loch.
1: *burn:* small stream (Scots)
3: *coop:* perhaps "narrow channel"; *comb:* perhaps "ridge"
4: *flutes:* "has the appearance of fluting" (the ornamental ridges of a column)
6: *twindles:* possibly "gives birth to twins" (dial.); or perhaps coined from "dwindles" and "twists" or "twines"
7: *fell:* fiercely
8: *rounds:* "turns around," but also "whispers to" and "rebukes." The pool invites the despairing to drown themselves.
9: *Degged:* sprinkled (dial.)
10: *the groins of the braes:* the folds and declivities of the steep hillsides of the river valley

Wiry heathpacks, flitches of fern,
And the beadbonny ash that sits over the burn.

What would the world be, once bereft
Of wet and of wildness? Let them be left,
15   O let them be left, wildness and wet;
Long live the weeds and the wilderness yet.

1881 / 1918

"I wake and feel the fell of dark, not day"

I wake and feel the fell of dark, not day.
What hours, O what black hours we have spent
This night! what sights you, heart, saw; ways you went!
And more must, in yet longer light's delay.

5   With witness I speak this. But where I say
Hours I mean years, mean life. And my lament
Is cries countless, cries like dead letters sent
To dearest him that lives alas! away.

I am gall, I am heartburn. God's most deep decree
10   Bitter would have me taste: my taste was me;
Bones built in me, flesh filled, blood brimmed the curse.

Selfyeast of spirit a dull dough sours. I see
The lost are like this, and their scourge to be
As I am mine, their sweating selves; but worse.

c. 1885–1886 / 1918

11: *heathpacks:* heather; MacKenzie notes that the variety *Erica* "has stiff branches which tangle into packs."
  flitches: "flakes of bracken, stiff and russet-brown, like thin slices from a tree-trunk" (MacKenzie)
12: *beadbonny ash:* "the mountain ash (rowan) gay with scarlet berries in autumn." (MacKenzie)

1: *fell:* a blow, or the pelt of an animal; the adjective "fell" means "cruel, terrible."
7: *dead letters:* letters undeliverable due to, e.g., a wrong address
9: *gall . . . heartburn:* bitterness . . . embitterment; but "gall" is literally a secretion of the liver that aids digestion, "heartburn," indigestion.
10: *Bitter would have me taste:* would have me taste bitterness
12: *Yeast* that is too old will become sour and lose its ability to make *dough* rise.
13ff: See *Sermons*, pp. 241–4, where Hopkins says that the damned are punished in Hell according to their sins on Earth: "we are our own tormentors, for every sin we then shall have remorse and with remorse torment" (241–2)

"No worst, there is none."

No worst, there is none. Pitched past pitch of grief,
More pangs will, schooled at forepangs, wilder wring.
Comforter, where, where is your comforting?
Mary, mother of us, where is your relief?
5   My cries heave, herds-long; huddle in a main, a chief-
Woe, wórld-sorrow; on an áge-old ánvil wínce and síng—
Then lull, then leave off. Fury had shrieked 'No ling-
Ering! Let me be fell: force I must be brief.'
O the mind, mind has mountains; cliffs of fall
10   Frightful, sheer, no-man-fathomed. Hold them cheap
May who ne'er hung there. Nor does long our small
Durance deal with that steep or deep. Here! creep,
Wretch, under a comfort serves in a whirlwind: all
Life death does end and each day dies with sleep.

c. 1885–1886 / 1918

[Carrion Comfort]

Not, I'll not, carrion comfort, Despair, not feast on thee;
Not untwist—slack they may be—these last strands of man
In me ór, most weary, cry *I can no more.* I can;
Can something, hope, wish day come, not choose not to be.

5   But ah, but O thou terrible, why wouldst thou rude on me
Thy wring-earth right foot rock? lay a lionlimb against me? scan
With darksome devouring eyes my bruisèd bones? and fan,
O in turns of tempest, me heaped there; me frantic to avoid thee and flee?

Why? That my chaff might fly; my grain lie, sheer and clear.
10   Nay in all that toil, that coil, since (seems) I kissed the rod,
Hand rather, my heart lo! lapped strength, stole joy, would laugh, cheer.

Cheer whóm though? The héro whose héaven-handling flúng me, fóot tród
Me? or mé that fóught him? O whích one? is it eách one? That níght, that
    year
Of now done darkness I wretch lay wrestling with (my God!) my God.

c. 1885–1886 / 1918

1: *No worst, there is none:* i.e., there is no limit to the increase of the speaker's torment.
2: *schooled at forepangs:* taught by earlier pains
3: *Comforter:* the translation of "paraclete," a traditional epithet of the Holy Ghost
8: *fell:* cruel, terrible; *force:* perforce
12: *durance:* endurance
13: *a comfort serves:* i.e., a shelter that serves

1: In Christian tradition *Despair* is one of the greatest of sins: the abandonment of hope in one's salvation,
  and the denial of God's ability or willingness to assist in one's salvation. It is often associated with sui-
  cide, as in Spenser, *The Faerie Queene* 1.9.
5: *rude:* harshly
7: *fan:* not just "drive air upon" but "winnow" (grain). See Matthew 3:12 and Luke 3:17.
10: *coil:* turmoil
    kissed the rod: accepted chastisement; perhaps the meaning here is, as Phillips suggests, "accepted
depression and despair as tests set by God."
13–14: See Genesis 32:24–30, where Jacob wrestles with God for the space of a night.

Spelt from Sibyl's Leaves

Earnest, earthless, equal, attuneable, | vaulty, voluminous, . . . stupendous
Evening strains to be tíme's vást, | womb-of-all, home-of-all, hearse-of-all
    night.
Her fond yellow hornlight wound to the west, | her wild hollow hoarlight
    hung to the height
Waste; her earliest stars, earlstars, | stars principal, overbend us,
5   Fíre-féaturing héaven. For éarth | her béing has unbóund; her dápple is at
    énd, as-
Tray or aswarm, all throughther, in throngs; | self ín self stéepèd and
    páshed—qúite
Disremembering, dismembering | all now. Heart, you round me right
With: Óur évening is óver us; óur night | whélms, whélms, ánd will énd us.
Only the beakleaved boughs dragonish | damask the tool-smooth bleak
    light; black,
10   Ever so black on it. Óur tale, O óur oracle! | Lét life, wáned, ah lét life
    wínd
Off hér once skéined stained véined varíety | upon, áll on twó spools; párt,
    pen, páck
Now her áll in twó flocks, twó folds—bláck, white; | ríght, wrong; réckon
    but, réck but, mínd
But thése two; wáre of a wórld where bút these | twó tell, éach off the
    óther; of a ráck
Where, selfwrung, selfstrung, sheathe- and shelterless, | thoúghts agáinst
    thoughts ín groans grínd.

                                            c. 1886 / 1918

Title: *Sibyl's Leaves:* see the medieval Latin hymn "Dies Irae," which is used in the Catholic requiem mass: "Day of wrath, that day when the world is consumed to ash as David and the Sibyl testify." The Sibyl was the name given to various ancient oracles; her prophecies were inscribed on palm leaves. (She appears in the "Dies Irae" because of the *Sibylline Oracles,* a collection of supposedly authentic sibylline prophecies confirming Jewish and Christian doctrines, and actually the work of Jewish and Christian writers.)
1: *equal:* MacKenzie suggests a pun on "even" and "evening" (one 19th-century dictionary suggests an etymological connection); *attuneable:* a coinage, perhaps meaning "susceptible (and conducive) to harmony"; *vaulty:* i.e., arching over like the vaults of a church; *stupendous:* causing fear or amazement
2: "Evening . . . strains to become time's vast night, the final and universal darkness ('hearse-of-all') which would match the primal chaos out of which the cosmos was born ('womb-of-all')." (MacKenzie)
3: *fond:* perhaps "insipid; sickly-flavored" (dial.); *hornlight:* the light from a horn lantern (one with windows of thin pieces of horn); *hoarlight:* see *Journals* p. 199: "the burnished or embossed forehead of sky over the sundown; of beautiful 'clear' / Perhaps the zodiacal light."
4: *waste:* i.e., fade away
6: *throughther:* confused, disorderly (dial.); *pashed:* reduced to pulp (dial.)
7: *round:* rebuke
8: *whelms:* engulfs; overwhelms
9: *damask the tool-smooth bleak light:* ornament the light "like a black wavy pattern in damask steel" (MacKenzie)
12: *two flocks, two folds:* at the Last Judgment, Christ "shall separate [the nations] one from another, as a shepherd divideth his sheep from the goats" (Matt. 25:31–33)
    reck: pay heed to

That Nature is a Heraclitean Fire
and of the comfort of the Resurrection

Cloud-puffball, torn tufts, tossed pillows | flaunt forth, then chevy on an
   air-
Built thoroughfare: heaven-roysterers, in gay-gangs | they throng; they glit-
   ter in marches.
Down roughcast, down dazzling whitewash, | wherever an elm arches,
Shivelights and shadowtackle in long | lashes lace, lance, and pair.
5   Delightfully the bright wind boisterous | ropes, wrestles, beats earth bare
Of yestertempest's creases; in pool and rutpeel parches
Squandering ooze to squeezed | dough, crust, dust; stanches, starches
Squadroned masks and manmarks | treadmire toil there
Footfretted in it. Million-fuelèd, | nature's bonfire burns on.
10 But quench her bonniest, dearest | to her, her clearest-selvèd spark
Man, how fast his firedint, | his mark on mind, is gone!
Both are in an únfathomable, all is in an enormous dark
Drowned. O pity and indig | nation! Manshape, that shone
Sheer off, disseveral, a star, | death blots black out; nor mark
15   Is any of him at all so stark
But vastness blurs and time | beats level. Enough! the Resurrection,
A heart's-clarion! Away grief's gasping, | joyless days, dejection.
           Across my foundering deck shone
A beacon, an eternal beam. | Flesh fade, and mortal trash
20 Fall to the residuary worm; | world's wildfire, leave but ash:
           In a flash, at a trumpet crash,
I am all at once what Christ is, | since he was what I am, and

---

Title: The Greek philosopher Heraclitus (c. 540 BC–480 BC) believed that fire was the basic substance of
  the universe. This substance existed in its purest form as a hot wind outside the earth's atmosphere. For
  Heraclitus the amount of fire, water, and earth in the universe remained constant, but each substance
  was constantly changing into another—atmospheric "fire" becoming rain, the ocean producing land, etc.
1: *chevy:* race
2: *roysterers:* carousers; revellers
3–4: "Shafts of sunlight and shadow lace, lance, and form pairs *down* . . . roughcast or whitewashed walls,
  wherever a tree interposes." (MacKenzie)
3: *roughcast:* a mixture of lime and gravel used for plastering the outside of walls
4: *shive:* splinter (dial.)
  shadowtackle: i.e., the shadow resembles that cast by the ropes of a ship's tackle (rigging)
5: *ropes:* perhaps in the obsolete sense of "grabs hold of"
6: *rutpeel:* a coinage, suggesting either the puddles in the ruts left by wheels ("peel": pool [dial.]) or the
  ruts' drying (peeling) mud.
8–9: *treadmire toil there / Footfretted in it:* i.e., "(that) arduous toil marked there with footprints" ("tread-
  mire" is coined from "treadmill," "footfretted" from "footprinted")
11: *firedint:* coined from "dint" (a mark)
14: *disseveral:* from "dissever" (to separate, sever) and "several" (distinct)
15: *stark:* strong (arch.)
20: A *residuary* legatee is one to whom the residue of an estate is left.
21ff: cf 1 Cor. 15, where Christ's incarnation and resurrection guarantee the resurrection of his followers:
  "We shall not all sleep, but we shall all be changed, in a moment, in the twinkling of an eye, at the last
  trump: for the trumpet shall sound, and the dead shall be raised incorruptible, and we shall be changed.
  For this corruptible must put on incorruption, and this mortal must put on immortality" (1 Cor. 15:51–53).

This Jack, joke, poor potsherd, | patch, matchwood, immortal diamond,
　　　　Is immortal diamond.

1888 / 1918

Justus quidem tu es, Domine,

si disputem tecum; verumtamen justa loquar ad te: quare via
impiorum prosperatur? etc

JEREM. XII I.

　　Thou art indeed just, Lord, if I contend
　　With thee; but, sir, so what I plead is just.
　　Why do sinners' ways prosper? and why must
　　Disappointment all I endeavour end?

5　　Wert thou my enemy, O thou my friend,
　　How wouldst thou worse, I wonder, than thou dost
　　Defeat, thwart me? Oh, the sots and thralls of lust
　　Do in spare hours more thrive than I that spend,

　　Sir, life upon thy cause. See, banks and brakes
10　　Now, leavèd how thick! lacèd they are again
　　With fretty chervil, look, and fresh wind shakes

　　Them; birds build—but not I build; no, but strain,
　　Time's eunuch, and not breed one work that wakes.
　　Mine, O thou lord of life, send my roots rain.

1889 / 1918

23: *Jack:* an ordinary man or labourer
　patch: fool, clown; also, a bit or piece
　matchwood: tinder or matchstick

Lines 1–4 of this poem paraphrase Jer. 12:1; the poem's images of flourishing and sterility draw more
　loosely on the rest of Jer. 12.
7: *thralls:* slaves
9: *brakes:* thickets
11: *fretty chervil:* cow parsley, "whose flowers are delicate, white, and lacy" (Phillips); *fretty:* either "inter-
　laced" (like a trellis) or "serrated, with leaves finely divided in toothed segments" (MacKenzie).
13: *eunuch:* see Matt. 19:12, where the chaste are said to "have made themselves eunuchs for the kingdom
　of heaven's sake."

RUDYARD KIPLING (1865–1936)

"THERE MUST BE BORN A POET WHO SHALL GIVE THE ENGLISH *THE* SONG OF their own, own country—which is to say, of about half the world," Kipling wrote in *American Notes*. The "Saga of the Anglo-Saxon all round the earth," he continued, should be a paean combining the "swing of the *Battle Hymn of the Republic* with *Britannia needs no Bulwarks,* the skirl of the *British Grenadiers* with that perfect quickstep, *Marching Through Georgia,* and at the end the wail of the *Dead March.*"[1] This remark offers us a glimpse of the jingoistic ballad-maker whose "singleness of intention in attempting to convey no more . . . than can be taken in on one reading or hearing" T. S. Eliot thought needed defending.[2] Several of Kipling's many ballads, such as "Danny Deever" and "Gunga Din," and the hymn "Recessional," written for Jubilee Day 1897, were for many years as widely known as his children's stories still are. His many topical and occasional poems, his thumping rhythms, loud rhymes, and caricatured dialect led Eliot to write "We expect to have to defend a poet against the charge of obscurity; we have to defend Kipling against the charge of excessive lucidity. . . . We expect a poet to be ridiculed because his verse does not appear to scan; we must defend Kipling against the charge of writing jingles."[3] While few would contest the superiority of his prose, poems by Kipling, such as "Common Form" and "A Dead Statesman," written after his only son was killed in World War I, remain powerful whatever one makes of the dynamics of literary taste in the modernist period or the symptomatic status of Kipling's political and moral sentiments as a man of the Empire.

Kipling was born in Bombay, where he spent his first six years before being sent to live in England with his father's relatives, whose horrific treatment of the young boy is described in several stories. After attending a school founded by army and navy officers, he returned to India at 17 to work as a journalist, gaining experience of the Indian and Anglo-Indian life that would become the subject of some of his most famous novels and stories. After marrying an American, he lived in Vermont from 1892 to 1896; later he returned to England, residing in Sussex. In 1907, he became the first English writer to be awarded the Nobel Prize.

---

[1] *American Notes* (1889), London, 1930, p. 238.
[2] "Rudyard Kipling," *On Poetry and Poets,* New York, 1957, p. 270.
[3] Ibid., p. 266.

Gunga Din

You may talk o' gin and beer
When you're quartered safe out 'ere,
An' you're sent to penny-fights an' Aldershot it;
But when it comes to slaughter
5   You will do your work on water,
An' you'll lick the bloomin' boots of 'im that's got it.
Now in Injia's sunny clime,
Where I used to spend my time
A-servin' of 'Er Majesty the Queen,
10   Of all them blackfaced crew
The finest man I knew
Was our regimental bhisti, Gunga Din.
        He was 'Din! Din! Din!
   'You limpin' lump o' brick-dust, Gunga Din!
15   'Hi! Slippy *hitherao!*
     'Water, get it! *Panee lao,*
   'You squidgy-nosed old idol, Gunga Din.'

The uniform 'e wore
Was nothin' much before,
20   An' rather less than 'arf o' that be'ind,
For a piece o' twisty rag
An' a goatskin water-bag
Was all the field-equipment 'e could find.
When the sweatin' troop-train lay
25   In a sidin' through the day,
Where the 'eat would make your bloomin' eyebrows crawl,
We shouted 'Harry By!'
Till our throats were bricky-dry,
Then we wopped 'im 'cause 'e couldn't serve us all.
30   It was 'Din! Din! Din!
   'You 'eathen, where the mischief 'ave you been?
    'You put some *juldee* in it
   'Or I'll *marrow* you this minute
   'If you don't fill up my helmet, Gunga Din!'

35   'E would dot an' carry one
Till the longest day was done;

We are indebted for several of our notes to *Rudyard Kipling,* ed. Daniel Karlin (Oxford, 1999).

Gunga Din is based loosely on Juma, a water-carrier for the Frontier Force regiment of the Guides at the siege of Delhi in July 1857 during the Indian Mutiny. He was selected by his comrades as the bravest man in the regiment.

3: "'When you're called out to deal with minor disturbances and swagger around as you do in barracks'. Aldershot, near Guildford in Surrey, is still an important military base." (Karlin)

12: *bhisti:* water-carrier

15: *Slippy hitherao:* come here quickly

16: *Panee lao:* "Bring water swiftly" (Kipling's note)

27: *Harry By!:* "O brother" (Kipling)

32: *put some juldee in it:* "Be quick" (Kipling)

33: *marrow you:* "Hit you" (Kipling)

35: *dot an' carry one:* i.e., walk with a limping gait ("dot and carry one," a phrase from the teaching of basic arithmetic, was slang for a someone with a wooden leg)

An' 'e didn't seem to know the use o' fear.
If we charged or broke or cut,
You could bet your bloomin' nut,
40 'E'd be waitin' fifty paces right flank rear.
With 'is mussick on 'is back,
'E would skip with our attack,
An' watch us till the bugles made 'Retire,'
An' for all 'is dirty 'ide
45 'E was white, clear white, inside
When 'e went to tend the wounded under fire!
      It was 'Din! Din! Din!'
  With the bullets kickin' dust-spots on the green.
    When the cartridges ran out,
50   You could hear the front-ranks shout,
  'Hi! ammunition-mules an' Gunga Din!'

I shan't forgit the night
When I dropped be'ind the fight
With a bullet where my belt-plate should 'a' been.
55 I was chokin' mad with thirst,
An' the man that spied me first
Was our good old grinnin', gruntin' Gunga Din.
'E lifted up my 'ead,
An' he plugged me where I bled,
60 An' 'e guv me 'arf-a-pint o' water green.
It was crawlin' and it stunk,
But of all the drinks I've drunk,
I'm gratefullest to one from Gunga Din.
    It was 'Din! Din! Din!
65   ''Ere's a beggar with a bullet through 'is spleen;
    'E's chawin' up the ground,
    'An' 'e's kickin' all around:
  'For Gawd's sake git the water, Gunga Din!'

'E carried me away
70 To where a dooli lay,
An' a bullet come an' drilled the beggar clean.
'E put me safe inside,
An' just before 'e died,
'I 'ope you liked your drink,' sez Gunga Din.
75 So I'll meet 'im later on
At the place where 'e is gone—
Where it's always double drill and no canteen.
'E'll be squattin' on the coals
Givin' drink to poor damned souls,
80 An' I'll get a swig in hell from Gunga Din!
    Yes, Din! Din! Din!

38: *broke:* broke ranks; made a disorderly retreat
   cut: either "fled" or perhaps "advanced rapidly"
39: *nut:* head
41: *mussick:* "Water-skin" (Kipling)
54: *belt-plate:* buckle
70: *dooli:* stretcher

You Lazarushian-leather Gunga Din!
　　Though I've belted you and flayed you,
　　By the livin' Gawd that made you,
85　　You're a better man than I am, Gunga Din!

1892

Sestina of the Tramp-Royal

　　Speakin' in general, I 'ave tried 'em all—
　　The 'appy roads that take you o'er the world.
　　Speakin' in general, I 'ave found them good
　　For such as cannot use one bed too long,
5　　But must get 'ence, the same as I 'ave done,
　　An' go observin' matters till they die.

　　What do it matter where or 'ow we die,
　　So long as we've our 'ealth to watch it all—
　　The different ways that different things are done,
10　　An' men an' women lovin' in this world;
　　Takin' our chances as they come along,
　　An' when they ain't, pretendin' they are good?

　　In cash or credit—no, it aren't no good;
　　You 'ave to 'ave the 'abit or you'd die,
15　　Unless you lived your life but one day long,
　　Nor didn't prophesy nor fret at all,
　　But drew your tucker some'ow from the world,
　　An' never bothered what you might ha' done.

　　But, Gawd, what things are they I 'aven't done?
20　　I've turned my 'and to most, an' turned it good,
　　In various situations round the world—
　　For 'im that doth not work must surely die;
　　But that's no reason man should labour all
　　'Is life on one same shift—life's none so long.

25　　Therefore, from job to job I've moved along.
　　Pay couldn't 'old me when my time was done,
　　For something in my 'ead upset it all,
　　Till I 'ad dropped whatever 'twas for good,
　　An', out at sea, be'eld the dock-lights die,
30　　An' met my mate—the wind that tramps the world!

82: *Lazarushian-leather:* Russian leather is a durable leather used for bookbinding; the speaker presumably refers to Gunga Din's skin. However, the word also alludes to the parable of the rich man and the beggar Lazarus (Luke 16): the rich man in hell sees Lazarus in Abraham's bosom; "And he cried and said, Father Abraham, have mercy on me, and send Lazarus, that he may dip the tip of his finger in water, and cool my tongue; for I am tormented in this flame." But Abraham refuses, saying that between the blessed and the damned "a great gulf is fixed."

17: *tucker:* keep; daily bread

It's like a book, I think, this bloomin' world,
Which you can read and care for just so long,
But presently you feel that you will die
Unless you get the page you're readin' done,
35   An' turn another—likely not so good;
But what you're after is to turn 'em all.

Gawd bless this world! Whatever she 'ath done—
Excep' when awful long—I've found it good.
So write, before I die, ''E liked it all!'

                                                        1896

from Epitaphs of the War

COMMON FORM

If any question why we died,
Tell them, because our fathers lied.

A DEAD STATESMAN

I could not dig: I dared not rob:
Therefore I lied to please the mob.
Now all my lies are proved untrue
And I must face the men I slew.
5   What tale shall serve me here among
Mine angry and defrauded young?

                                                        1919

WILLIAM BUTLER YEATS (1865–1939)

I N THE LATE ESSAY "A GENERAL INTRODUCTION TO MY WORK" (1937), YEATS WRITES THAT "It was a long time before I had made a language to my liking; I began to make it when I discovered some twenty years ago that I must seek, not as Wordsworth thought, words in common use, but a powerful and passionate syntax, and a complete coincidence between period [sentence] and stanza."[1] Yeats's role in and view of modern Irish culture and politics, his eclectic use of materials taken from Irish myth, English poetic traditions, Noh drama, and a host of other sources including Plato, Plotinus, Emanuel Swedenborg, Madame Blavatsky, and the *Upanishads*—these are matters of great interest, but they do not explain Yeats's stature among modern poets. Writing in 1974, Basil Bunting argued that "if [Yeats's] philosophic, theosophic, magical quasi-religion was trivial and by origin insincere, politics and religion were not his business except in the sense that they are everyone's business. He was a poet." Bunting feared that Yeats's aristocratic love of order and ceremony would repulse contemporary readers; thus it was necessary to argue that it was first of all Yeats's attention to "rhythm and vowel sequence and what the Welsh have codified but the rest of us grope for to hold the sounds of our verse together" that he valued.[2] Bunting's remark is worth remembering even if we agree with T. S. Eliot that Yeats is one of the few poets "who are part of the consciousness of an age that cannot be understood without them."[3] Eliot thought that Yeats's political, cultural, and religious views would ultimately have to enter into judgment of his poetry. Even Bunting admits, "It is true that he loaded his conception of being a poet with all manner of lofty moral responsibilities, which seemed to claim authority in politics and religion."

Yeats began in the wake of the Pre-Raphaelites and, by the turn of the century, had already defined the poetic modes we associate with the Celtic Twilight and Symbolist poetry in English. This alone would have been sufficient to assure him our continuing attention, but Yeats is by most definitions a major poet because, mid-career, he forged a new poetic style. The incantatory rhythms of his early ballads and poems based on Irish myth, the trance-music of dream-like association and indefinite reference that Yeats developed among the poets of the Rhymers Club in the 1890s, gave way in the first decades of the century to a new concreteness in idiom and an idea of poetry as excited, passionate talk. Yeats indicated that he wanted the new style to seem effortless and improvisational, but, as Hugh Kenner reminds us, "a sentence cannot pretend to be improvised as it makes its elaborate way among rhyming markers toward

---

[1] *Essays and Introductions*, New York, 1968, p. 521.
[2] "Yeats Recollected," quoted in *Basil Bunting: Man and Poet*, ed. Carroll F. Terrell, Orono, ME, 1981, p. 252.
[3] "Yeats," *On Poetry and Poets*, London, 1957, p. 308.

an unforeseeable, necessarily foreseen close where rhyme and syntax and thought are resolved together." This "magisterial" style of "weighty deliberation," Kenner adds, presents a "poet-mage of resolute concatenated statement, modelled on a lyrical Augustanism that never was."[4] To travel from early to late Yeats is also to witness a poet who began by mixing aestheticism and wistful nationalism suddenly gain the ability to accommodate in his poetry a new, more urgently public commentary based in complex if idiosyncratic theories of historical cycles and archetypes of culture and human personality.

It is the later rather than the earlier poems that now seem to guarantee Yeats a position within the history of a "modernist" poetry. C. H. Sisson's description of Yeats as "a poet of the end of the nineteenth century rather than a beginner of the twentieth," and his preference for the "languid charm" of poems up through *The Green Helmet* (1910) offers a minority view.[5] (Sisson finds the later work excessively theatrical, too self-conscious about the poet's public role.) The more common view is the one Yeats's one-time secretary Ezra Pound expressed in his review of *Responsibilities* (1914): Yeats was already "immortal" for having "brought in the sound of keening and the skirl of the Irish ballads," had no need to reinvent himself but had managed to do just that in striking a "manifestly new note" of "prose directness," which made his poetry "gaunter, seeking a greater hardness of outline."[6] The volumes following *Responsibilities* contain the poems for which Yeats is most remembered, such as "Easter 1916," one of the century's most famous political poems, or "The Second Coming," with its apocalyptic tone and mention of "some revelation . . . at hand."

Yeats was born in Dublin. His father was John Butler Yeats, a cosmopolitan intellectual and a painter, a skeptical voice never altogether lost to Yeats; Yeats's need to counter the materialist and utilitarian values of modernity are sometimes traced to conversations with his father. Yeats's mother's family, the Pollexfens, came from rural Sligo. He was raised and educated in London, Sligo, and eventually Dublin as a Protestant, part of the Anglo-Irish Ascendency culture, which offered Yeats heroes such as Jonathan Swift and Edmund Burke. Under the influence of the Fenian leader John O'Leary and later Maud Gonne, Yeats was active in nationalist politics in the late 1880s and 1890s, and these were also the years he led the Celtic or Irish Literary Revival. The Revival's representations of Irish myth and folk tradition belong to a larger, late nineteenth-century revival of interest in "folk" cultures throughout Britain and Europe: the Royal Irish Academy began its study of ancient Irish culture in the decades prior to Yeats's birth. Yeats's own views of an Irish peasantry embodying a spirituality that mixed Druidism and Christianity might be described as romantic. The 1890s also saw Yeats extending his lifelong study of occult and theosophic writing, which together with the work of William Blake (which Yeats edited) offered him models for the esoteric symbolism presented in his poetry. Near the end of the century, Yeats began to turn his attention to drama, and in 1906 he was named with Lady Gregory and J. M. Synge to direct the recently established Abbey Theatre. Yeats's involvement with the Irish dramatic movement left him often caught in the crossfire between British authorities and Irish nationalists, and, as Douglas Archibald writes, between 1903 and 1916 he was "most typically disillusioned and estranged; he recognizes the points of tension between the two Irelands and he has to face the disparity between the ideal nation prophesied by The Revival and the state as it was actually emerging."[7] In 1916, the year of the Easter Rising in Dublin, Yeats bought the Norman tower at Ballylee that would become an important symbol in his late poems. In 1922, he was invited to become a member of the new Irish Free State's senate, where he served for

---

4 *A Colder Eye: The Modern Irish Writers,* New York, 1983, p. 186.
5 *English Poetry 1900–1950,* London, 1971, p. 179.
6 "The Later Yeats," *Literary Essays of Ezra Pound,* ed. T. S. Eliot, 1935, p. 378.
7 *Yeats,* Syracuse, NY, 1986, p. 81.

six years. The Nobel Prize for Literature was awarded him in 1923. He became a highly visible public figure in all spheres of Irish life, and remained so after leaving office. In his last years, he was given to conservative, even reactionary statements, which have led to speculation about his relationship to the Blueshirts in Ireland and to fascist ideas.

Among the numerous contemporaries with an important role in Yeats's writing are Lady Gregory and Maud Gonne, and something should be said about them here. Lady Gregory, Yeats's patron, a playwright and folklorist, owned an estate at Coole Park that came to symbolize for Yeats classical and aristocratic ideals interwoven with national pride, all that he most valued in Anglo-Irish culture. Yeats's relationship with Maud Gonne is more complex. She was not only the inspiration for his early nationalist activities but also his ideal love, someone, Hugh Kenner suggests, who could serve the poetry like the Immortal Lady incarnate rhapsodized by the English Pre-Raphaelites. Gonne repeatedly rebuffed Yeats's advances. In 1903, she married Major John MacBride, and that together with her political extremism distanced her from Yeats, but she remained important to his poetry until the end. In 1917, Yeats married the Englishwoman Georgie Hyde-Lees; they had two children.

Yeats's poetry, as David Perkins explains, often explores a series of oppositions "between nature and art, youth and age, body and soul, passion and wisdom, beast and man, creative violence and order, revelation and civilization, poetry and responsibility, and time and eternity." Such contrasts and "antithetical thinking" often led Yeats to posit as an ideal what he called "unity of being." Like many other modernists, Yeats searched historical civilizations for examples of cultures that seemed to have made possible a life meeting his ideal, and Byzantine culture became the chief example for its "artifice of eternity." The degree to which the oppositions named above are ever resolved by the poetry is open to debate; the body and desire, for instance, remain restless presences in Yeats's poetry right to the very end. If, in Yeats's view, the supernatural might be defined as whole and unified being, that still left him with the question, as David Perkins writes, of "whether even in a fleeting moment the human is capable of such completeness."[8]

---

[8] *A History of Modern Poetry: From the 1890s to the High Modernist Mode*, Cambridge, MA, 1976, p. 596.

To the Rose upon the Rood of Time

Red Rose, proud Rose, sad Rose of all my days!
Come near me, while I sing the ancient ways:
Cuchulain battling with the bitter tide;
The Druid, grey, wood-nurtured, quiet-eyed,
5   Who cast round Fergus dreams, and ruin untold;

Our glosses are indebted at several points to A. Norman Jeffares, *A New Commentary on the Poems of W.B. Yeats* (Stanford, 1984).

Title: *Rood:* cross. The image is of the Rose of Eternity on the Cross of Time; this was the symbol of the Rosicrucian order, an occult brotherhood with origins in the seventeenth century. It symbolized the union of woman (rose) and man (cross); the four classical elements with the fifth, quintessence; and the mystical union of time and eternity. In a note from 1925 Yeats says that "the quality symbolised as The Rose differs from the Intellectual Beauty of Shelley and of Spenser in that I have imagined it as suffering with man and not as something pursued and seen from afar." This poem introduces Yeats's volume *The Rose.*

3: The Irish hero Cuchulain unwittingly killed his own son, and went to his death fighting the waves of the sea; the story is told in Yeats's "Cuchulain's Fight with the Sea" in *The Rose.*

4–5: Yeats alludes to his "Fergus and the Druid," also in *The Rose*. The mythical king Fergus MacRoy, wishing for wisdom, begs the Druid for his "bag of dreams"; when it is opened, he has a vision in which he sees all his prior incarnations, but which leaves him drained and despairing.

And thine own sadness, whereof stars, grown old
In dancing silver-sandalled on the sea,
Sing in their high and lonely melody.
Come near, that no more blinded by man's fate,
10 I find under the boughs of love and hate,
In all poor foolish things that live a day,
Eternal beauty wandering on her way.

Come near, come near, come near—Ah, leave me still
A little space for the rose-breath to fill!
15 Lest I no more hear common things that crave;
The weak worm hiding down in its small cave,
The field-mouse running by me in the grass,
And heavy mortal hopes that toil and pass;
But seek alone to hear the strange things said
20 By God to the bright hearts of those long dead,
And learn to chaunt a tongue men do not know.
Come near; I would, before my time to go,
Sing of old Eire and the ancient ways:
Red Rose, proud Rose, sad Rose of all my days.

1892

The Lake Isle of Innisfree

I will arise and go now, and go to Innisfree,
And a small cabin build there, of clay and wattles made:
Nine bean-rows will I have there, a hive for the honey-bee,
And live alone in the bee-loud glade.

5   And I shall have some peace there, for peace comes dropping slow,
Dropping from the veils of the morning to where the cricket sings;
There midnight's all a glimmer, and noon a purple glow,
And evening full of the linnet's wings.

I will arise and go now, for always night and day
10 I hear lake water lapping with low sounds by the shore;
While I stand on the roadway, or on the pavements grey,
I hear it in the deep heart's core.

1888 / 1893

23: *Eire:* Ireland

Title: *Innisfree:* a small island in Lough Gill, County Sligo.
2: *wattles:* interlaced rods and twigs, which are spread with mud and used as a building material.
7: *purple glow:* Yeats explained in a radio broadcast that the glow is from the reflection of heather in the
  water. "Innisfree" means "heather island."

Who Goes with Fergus?

Who will go drive with Fergus now,
And pierce the deep wood's woven shade,
And dance upon the level shore?
Young man, lift up your russet brow,
5   And lift your tender eyelids, maid,
And brood on hopes and fears no more.

And no more turn aside and brood
Upon love's bitter mystery;
For Fergus rules the brazen cars,
10   And rules the shadows of the wood,
And the white breast of the dim sea
And all dishevelled wandering stars.

1893

The Valley of the Black Pig

The dews drop slowly and dreams gather: unknown spears
Suddenly hurtle before my dream-awakened eyes,
And then the clash of fallen horsemen and the cries
Of unknown perishing armies beat about my ears.
5   We who still labour by the cromlech on the shore,
The grey cairn on the hill, when day sinks drowned in dew,
Being weary of the world's empires, bow down to you,
Master of the still stars and of the flaming door.

1899

Title: *Fergus*: in Irish myth, Fergus MacRoy, king of Ulster, is tricked by his wife Ness into abdicating in favour of her son Conchubar. Yeats's version is indebted to "The Abdication of Fergus MacRoy," a nineteenth-century retelling by Sir Samuel Ferguson, where Fergus is also a poet; he tires of rule and abdicates in order to spend the rest of his life in peace, hunting in the woods.
9: *brazen cars*: chariots

Title: Yeats commented: "The Irish peasantry have for generations comforted themselves, in their misfortunes, with visions of a great battle, to be fought in a mysterious valley called, 'The Valley of the Black Pig', and to break at last the power of their enemies." In another note he wrote that the Black Pig was an archetype "of cold and of winter that awake in November, the old beginning of winter, to do battle with the summer, and with the fruit and leaves" and hence a symbol of "the darkness that will at last destroy the gods and the world."
5: *cromlech*: a prehistoric stone construction, in which a stone lintel lies atop upright stones
6: *cairn*: a prehistoric pile of stones marking a gravesite

September 1913

What need you, being come to sense,
But fumble in a greasy till
And add the halfpence to the pence
And prayer to shivering prayer, until
5   You have dried the marrow from the bone?
For men were born to pray and save:
Romantic Ireland's dead and gone,
It's with O'Leary in the grave.

Yet they were of a different kind,
10   The names that stilled your childish play,
They have gone about the world like wind,
But little time had they to pray
For whom the hangman's rope was spun,
And what, God help us, could they save?
15   Romantic Ireland's dead and gone,
It's with O'Leary in the grave.

Was it for this the wild geese spread
The grey wing upon every tide;
For this that all that blood was shed,
20   For this Edward Fitzgerald died,
And Robert Emmet and Wolfe Tone,
All that delirium of the brave?
Romantic Ireland's dead and gone,
It's with O'Leary in the grave.

12   Yet could we turn the years again,
And call those exiles as they were

Title: When first published in the *Irish Times* (8 Sept. 1913) the poem was titled "Romance in Ireland / (On reading much of the correspondence against the Art Gallery)." Sir Hugh Lane, nephew of Yeats's patron, Lady Gregory, had offered his collection of French Impressionist paintings to Dublin, on the condition that a gallery be built to house them. The Dublin Corporation rejected a design by Edwin Lutyens for a bridge gallery over the River Liffey; in response Lane bequeathed the collection to the National Gallery in London. (In 1915 Lane drowned when the *Lusitania* was sunk by a German submarine, a few months after adding an unwitnessed codicil to his will leaving the paintings to Dublin. Yeats tirelessly lobbied for Lane's last wish to be obeyed; only decades later was an agreement reached in which the collection was shared between London and Dublin.) The "correspondence" of Yeats's original title was that appearing in popular Catholic newspapers; Yeats was disgusted by the philistine views expressed there about modern art.
1: *you:* i.e., the Irish Catholic middle class
8: John *O'Leary* (1830–1907) was a leader of the Fenian nationalist movement. Arrested by the British in 1865, he was sentenced to 20 years, a sentence later commuted to 15 years' exile; he lived in Paris, returning to Dublin in 1885. O'Leary was a mentor of Yeats, and his political views and personality were a strong influence upon him; so too were the books by Irish authors he lent Yeats from his library.
17: *wild geese:* Irishmen who served in the armies of France, Spain, and Austria because of the Penal Laws of 1691, which prevented them from holding commissions in the British army.
20–21: In 1798 *Wolfe Tone* (1763–98) led French forces to Ireland to support an uprising against the British; captured and condemned to death, he committed suicide in prison. Lord *Edward Fitzgerald* (1763–98), Member of Parliament for Athy and Kildare, was part of Wolfe Tone's uprising; he died of wounds received when resisting arrest. *Robert Emmet* (1778–1803) led a revolt against the English in 1803 and was executed for high treason.

In all their loneliness and pain,
You'd cry, 'Some woman's yellow hair
Has maddened every mother's son':
30   They weighed so lightly what they gave.
But let them be, they're dead and gone,
They're with O'Leary in the grave.

1913 / 1914

I. The Witch

Toil and grow rich,
What's that but to lie
With a foul witch
And after, drained dry,
5   To be brought
To the chamber where
Lies one long sought
With despair?

1912 / 1914

II. The Peacock

What's riches to him
That has made a great peacock
With the pride of his eye?
The wind-beaten, stone-grey,
5   And desolate Three Rock
Would nourish his whim.
Live he or die
Amid wet rocks and heather,
His ghost will be gay
10   Adding feather to feather
For the pride of his eye.

1913–1914 / 1914

28–29: i.e., your prosaic minds could not conceive that Irish patriots acted out of sheer love of country.

The Peacock: Hugh Kenner notes that Yeats likely had in mind the Pennells' *Life of Whistler* (the artist James McNeill Whistler [1834–1903]): "on page 301 we find the master's tart appraisal of riches ('It is better to live on bread and cheese and paint beautiful things than to live like Dives and paint pot-boilers') and five pages later his proposal for 'a great peacock ten feet high.'" (Kenner, *A Colder Eye*, New York, 1983). The design, never executed, was intended for the Boston Library.
5: The *Three Rock* Mountain overlooks Dublin.

The Dolls

A doll in the doll-maker's house
Looks at the cradle and bawls:
'That is an insult to us.'
But the oldest of all the dolls,
5   Who had seen, being kept for show,
Generations of his sort,
Out-screams the whole shelf: 'Although
There's not a man can report
Evil of this place,
10   The man and the woman bring
Hither, to our disgrace,
A noisy and filthy thing.'
Hearing him groan and stretch
The doll-maker's wife is aware
15   Her husband has heard the wretch,
And crouched by the arm of his chair,
She murmurs into his ear,
Head upon shoulder leant:
'My dear, my dear, O dear,
20   It was an accident.'

1913 / 1914

A Coat

I made my song a coat
Covered with embroideries
Out of old mythologies
From heel to throat;
5   But the fools caught it,
Wore it in the world's eyes
As though they'd wrought it.
Song, let them take it,
For there's more enterprise
10   In walking naked.

1912 / 1914

The Dolls: "The fable for this poem came into my head while I was giving some lectures in Dublin. I had noticed once again how all thought among us is frozen into 'something other than human life.'" (Yeats's note)

A Coat: This poem signals Yeats's turning away from his earlier Celtic Twilight style, a style that had become imitated by other Irish poets.

The Wild Swans at Coole

The trees are in their autumn beauty,
The woodland paths are dry,
Under the October twilight the water
Mirrors a still sky;
5   Upon the brimming water among the stones
Are nine-and-fifty swans.

The nineteenth autumn has come upon me
Since I first made my count;
I saw, before I had well finished,
10   All suddenly mount
And scatter wheeling in great broken rings
Upon their clamorous wings.

I have looked upon those brilliant creatures,
And now my heart is sore.
15   All's changed since I, hearing at twilight,
The first time on this shore,
The bell-beat of their wings above my head,
Trod with a lighter tread.

Unwearied still, lover by lover,
20   They paddle in the cold
Companionable streams or climb the air;
Their hearts have not grown old;
Passion or conquest, wander where they will,
Attend upon them still.

25   But now they drift on the still water,
Mysterious, beautiful;
Among what rushes will they build,
By what lake's edge or pool
Delight men's eyes when I awake some day
30   To find they have flown away?

1916 / 1917

7: Yeats first visited Lady Gregory's estate, Coole Park, in 1896, but the visit he has in mind is that of 1897, when he was in a state of deep unhappiness from Maud Gonne's rejection of his love.

27: Later, on a 1928 visit, Yeats saw a pair of swans with three cygnets, and told Lady Gregory, "I have known your lake for thirty years, and that is the first time a swan has built here. That is a good omen."

Easter 1916

I have met them at close of day
Coming with vivid faces
From counter or desk among grey
Eighteenth-century houses.
5   I have passed with a nod of the head
Or polite meaningless words,
Or have lingered awhile and said
Polite meaningless words,
And thought before I had done
10   Of a mocking tale or a gibe
To please a companion
Around the fire at the club,
Being certain that they and I
But lived where motley is worn:
15   All changed, changed utterly:
A terrible beauty is born.

That woman's days were spent
In ignorant good-will,
Her nights in argument
20   Until her voice grew shrill.
What voice more sweet than hers
When, young and beautiful,
She rode to harriers?
This man had kept a school
25   And rode our wingèd horse;
This other his helper and friend
Was coming into his force;
He might have won fame in the end,
So sensitive his nature seemed,
30   So daring and sweet his thought.
This other man I had dreamed
A drunken, vainglorious lout.
He had done most bitter wrong
To some who are near my heart,
35   Yet I number him in the song;

On April 24, 1916, the Irish Volunteers, some 700 members of the Irish Republican Brotherhood, occupied
the center of Dublin and proclaimed an independent Irish Republic. British soldiers crushed the upris-
ing after five days of fighting. Yeats's poem was prompted by the court-martial and execution of fifteen
of the rebellion's leaders in May of that year.
14: *motley:* the multicoloured garb of a jester or fool
17: *That woman:* The Countess Constance (Con) Markiewicz, née Gore-Booth (1868–1927) took part in
the Rebellion; her death sentence was commuted. Yeats had met her in 1894.
23: *rode to harriers:* participated in hare hunting
24: *This man:* Patrick Pearse (1879–1916), leader of the rebellion; he was the founder of a boys' school, a
poet, and a participant in the Gaelic language movement.
25: *wingèd horse:* Pegasus, the symbol of poetry
26: *This other:* Thomas MacDonagh (1876–1916), poet and playwright, taught English at University Col-
lege, Dublin; his play *When the Dawn is Come* was staged at the Abbey Theatre in 1908.
31: *This other man:* Major John MacBride, husband of Maud Gonne; they married in 1903 and separated
two years after.
34: *some:* Maud Gonne and her daughter Iseult

He, too, has resigned his part
In the casual comedy;
He, too, has been changed in his turn,
Transformed utterly:
40 A terrible beauty is born.

Hearts with one purpose alone
Through summer and winter seem
Enchanted to a stone
To trouble the living stream.
45 The horse that comes from the road,
The rider, the birds that range
From cloud to tumbling cloud,
Minute by minute they change;
A shadow of cloud on the stream
50 Changes minute by minute;
A horse-hoof slides on the brim,
And a horse plashes within it;
The long-legged moor-hens dive,
And hens to moor-cocks call;
55 Minute by minute they live:
The stone's in the midst of all.

Too long a sacrifice
Can make a stone of the heart.
O when may it suffice?
60 That is Heaven's part, our part
To murmur name upon name,
As a mother names her child
When sleep at last has come
On limbs that had run wild.
65 What is it but nightfall?
No, no, not night but death;
Was it needless death after all?
For England may keep faith
For all that is done and said.
70 We know their dream; enough
To know they dreamed and are dead;
And what if excess of love
Bewildered them till they died?
I write it out in a verse—
75 MacDonagh and MacBride
And Connolly and Pearse
Now and in time to be,
Wherever green is worn,
Are changed, changed utterly:
80 A terrible beauty is born.

1916 / 1921

68: The British Parliament had passed the Home Rule Bill in 1913, granting Ireland a measure of independence, but had suspended it in 1914 with the outbreak of World War I, promising to enact it after the war's end.
76: The trade union leader James *Connolly* (1870–1916) was the rebels' military commander.
78: *Green* was the symbolic color of the Irish Nationalists; the traditional ballad "The Wearing of the Green" memorializes the failed 1803 uprising.

The Second Coming

Turning and turning in the widening gyre
The falcon cannot hear the falconer;
Things fall apart; the centre cannot hold;
Mere anarchy is loosed upon the world,
5 The blood-dimmed tide is loosed, and everywhere
The ceremony of innocence is drowned;
The best lack all conviction, while the worst
Are full of passionate intensity.

Surely some revelation is at hand;
10 Surely the Second Coming is at hand.
The Second Coming! Hardly are those words out
When a vast image out of *Spiritus Mundi*
Troubles my sight: somewhere in sands of the desert
A shape with lion body and the head of a man,
15 A gaze blank and pitiless as the sun,
Is moving its slow thighs, while all about it
Reel shadows of the indignant desert birds.
The darkness drops again; but now I know
That twenty centuries of stony sleep
20 Were vexed to nightmare by a rocking cradle,
And what rough beast, its hour come round at last,
Slouches towards Bethlehem to be born?

1919 / 1921

A Prayer for my Daughter

Once more the storm is howling, and half hid
Under this cradle-hood and coverlid
My child sleeps on. There is no obstacle
But Gregory's wood and one bare hill
5 Whereby the haystack- and roof-levelling wind,
Bred on the Atlantic, can be stayed;
And for an hour I have walked and prayed
Because of the great gloom that is in my mind.

I have walked and prayed for this young child an hour
10 And heard the sea-wind scream upon the tower,

Title: Yeats's title is drawn from the Christian belief in Christ's Second Coming, but its prophecy is instead of a figure resembling the Antichrist of 1 John 2:18 or the Beast of the book of Revelation.
1: *gyre:* Yeats represented the process of history as a pair of interlocking cones (gyres); he imagines the present age as traveling along the path of a gyre (that representing "objective life"—"All our scientific, democratic, fact-accumulating, heterogeneous civilisation," as Yeats put it in a note) as it expands, like the bird flying in wider and wider circles; when it reaches the end (the cone's base) a new era, of "subjective life," will violently come into being.
12: *Spiritus Mundi:* Yeats's term for a storehouse of archetypal images drawn on by the poet
19: *twenty centuries:* i.e., the two millennia of Christianity, which began in Christ's cradle

Title: Anne Yeats, the first child of Yeats and his wife George, was born on 26 February 1919. The poem is set at their home, Thoor Ballylee, a Norman tower near Coole Park, Lady Gregory's estate.

And under the arches of the bridge, and scream
In the elms above the flooded stream;
Imagining in excited reverie
That the future years had come,
15   Dancing to a frenzied drum,
Out of the murderous innocence of the sea.

May she be granted beauty and yet not
Beauty to make a stranger's eye distraught,
Or hers before a looking-glass, for such,
20   Being made beautiful overmuch,
Consider beauty a sufficient end,
Lose natural kindness and maybe
The heart-revealing intimacy
That chooses right, and never find a friend.

25   Helen being chosen found life flat and dull
And later had much trouble from a fool,
While that great Queen, that rose out of the spray,
Being fatherless could have her way
Yet chose a bandy-leggèd smith for man.
30   It's certain that fine women eat
A crazy salad with their meat
Whereby the Horn of Plenty is undone.

In courtesy I'd have her chiefly learned;
Hearts are not had as a gift but hearts are earned
35   By those that are not entirely beautiful;
Yet many, that have played the fool
For beauty's very self, has charm made wise,
And many a poor man that has roved,
Loved and thought himself beloved,
40   From a glad kindness cannot take his eyes.

May she become a flourishing hidden tree
That all her thoughts may like the linnet be,
And have no business but dispensing round
Their magnanimities of sound,
45   Nor but in merriment begin a chase,
Nor but in merriment a quarrel.
O may she live like some green laurel
Rooted in one dear perpetual place.

My mind, because the minds that I have loved,
50   The sort of beauty that I have approved,
Prosper but little, has dried up of late,
Yet knows that to be choked with hate
May well be of all evil chances chief.
If there's no hatred in a mind
55   Assault and battery of the wind
Can never tear the linnet from the leaf.

26: *a fool:* Menelaus, whose wife Helen deserted him for Paris; the "trouble" is the Trojan War.
27: Aphrodite, goddess of love, was born from sea-foam; she married the lame blacksmith-god Hephaestus.

An intellectual hatred is the worst,
So let her think opinions are accursed.
Have I not seen the loveliest woman born
60   Out of the mouth of Plenty's horn,
Because of her opinionated mind
Barter that horn and every good
By quiet natures understood
For an old bellows full of angry wind?

65   Considering that, all hatred driven hence,
The soul recovers radical innocence
And learns at last that it is self-delighting,
Self-appeasing, self-affrighting,
And that its own sweet will is Heaven's will;
70   She can, though every face should scowl
And every windy quarter howl
Or every bellows burst, be happy still.

And may her bridegroom bring her to a house
Where all's accustomed, ceremonious;
75   For arrogance and hatred are the wares
Peddled in the thoroughfares.
How but in custom and in ceremony
Are innocence and beauty born?
Ceremony's a name for the rich horn,
80   And custom for the spreading laurel tree.

1919 / 1921

Sailing to Byzantium

I

That is no country for old men. The young
In one another's arms, birds in the trees
—Those dying generations—at their song,
The salmon-falls, the mackerel-crowded seas,

59ff: Yeats had grown more and more out of sympathy with Maud Gonne's increasingly militant political views.

Title: *Byzantium:* ancient Constantinople. In *A Vision* Yeats wrote: "I think if I could be given a month of Antiquity and leave to spend it where I chose, I would spend it in Byzantium, a little before Justinian opened St. Sophia and closed the Academy of Plato. I think I could find in some little wine-shop some philosophical worker in mosaic who could answer all my questions, the supernatural descending nearer to him than to [the Neoplatonist philosopher] Plotinus even, for the pride of his delicate skill would make what was an instrument of power to princes and clerics, a murderous madness in the mob, show as a lovely flexible presence like that of a perfect human body. I think that in early Byzantium, maybe never before or since in recorded history, religious, aesthetic and practical life were one, that architect and artificers . . . spoke to the multitude and the few alike. The painter, the mosaic worker, the worker in gold and silver, the illuminator of sacred books, were almost impersonal, almost perhaps without the consciousness of individual design, absorbed in their subject-matter and that the vision of a whole peo-ple. They could copy out of old gospel books those pictures that seemed as sacred as the text, and yet weave all into a vast design, the work of many that seemed the work of one, that made building, picture, pattern, metal-work of rail and lamp, seem but a single image. . . ." (*A Vision,* 1937, pp. 279–80). For more on Byzantium, see the note to the title of John Riley's "Czargrad," below (p. 605).

1: The *country* of this stanza is both Ireland (as indicated by line 4's *salmon-falls*) and the mythical Celtic island paradise of Tir na nÓg ("The Land of Youth").

5   Fish, flesh, or fowl, commend all summer long
Whatever is begotten, born, and dies.
Caught in that sensual music all neglect
Monuments of unageing intellect.

II

An aged man is but a paltry thing,
10   A tattered coat upon a stick, unless
Soul clap its hands and sing, and louder sing
For every tatter in its mortal dress,
Nor is there singing school but studying
Monuments of its own magnificence;
15   And therefore I have sailed the seas and come
To the holy city of Byzantium.

III

O sages standing in God's holy fire
As in the gold mosaic of a wall,
Come from the holy fire, perne in a gyre,
20   And be the singing-masters of my soul.
Consume my heart away; sick with desire
And fastened to a dying animal
It knows not what it is; and gather me
Into the artifice of eternity.

IV

25   Once out of nature I shall never take
My bodily form from any natural thing,
But such a form as Grecian goldsmiths make
Of hammered gold and gold enamelling
To keep a drowsy Emperor awake;
30   Or set upon a golden bough to sing
To lords and ladies of Byzantium
Of what is past, or passing, or to come.

1926 / 1927

The Tower

I

What shall I do with this absurdity—
O heart, O troubled heart—this caricature,
Decrepit age that has been tied to me
As to a dog's tail?
           Never had I more

13: Medieval Irish bards learned their craft at bardic *singing schools*.
19: *perne in a gyre*: spin in a spiral. For "gyre" see note to line 1 of "The Second Coming," above: the speaker is asking the sages to reenter historical time long enough to carry him back with them to eternity.
27ff: "I have read somewhere that in the Emperor's palace at Byzantium was a tree made of gold and silver, and artificial birds that sang." (Yeats)

Title: *The Tower.* Thoor Ballylee; see note to the title of "A Prayer for my Daughter," p. 40.

5 Excited, passionate, fantastical
 Imagination, nor an ear and eye
 That more expected the impossible—
 No, not in boyhood when with rod and fly,
 Or the humbler worm, I climbed Ben Bulben's back
10 And had the livelong summer day to spend.
 It seems that I must bid the Muse go pack,
 Choose Plato and Plotinus for a friend
 Until imagination, ear and eye,
 Can be content with argument and deal
15 In abstract things; or be derided by
 A sort of battered kettle at the heel.

II

 I pace upon the battlements and stare
 On the foundations of a house, or where
 Tree, like a sooty finger, starts from the earth;
20 And send imagination forth
 Under the day's declining beam, and call
 Images and memories
 From ruin or from ancient trees,
 For I would ask a question of them all.

25 Beyond that ridge lived Mrs. French, and once
 When every silver candlestick or sconce
 Lit up the dark mahogany and the wine,
 A serving-man, that could divine
 That most respected lady's every wish,
30 Ran and with the garden shears
 Clipped an insolent farmer's ears
 And brought them in a little covered dish.

 Some few remembered still when I was young
 A peasant girl commended by a song,
35 Who'd lived somewhere upon that rocky place,
 And praised the colour of her face,
 And had the greater joy in praising her,
 Remembering that, if walked she there,
 Farmers jostled at the fair
40 So great a glory did the song confer.

9: *Ben Bulben:* a mountain north of Sligo

12: *Plato and Plotinus:* philosophers who serve here as symbols of a belief in transcendence. Yeats later noted that he had mischaracterized Plotinus, who believed that "soul is the author of all living things" (compare lines 148–52 below) and did not discount temporal existence.

25ff: "Mrs. French lived at Peterswell in the eighteenth century and was related to Sir Jonah Barrington who [in *Personal Sketches of his own Time*] described the incident of the ears and the trouble that came of it." (Yeats's note). Of this and the following stanzas he notes, "The persons mentioned are associated by legend, story and tradition with the neighbourhood of Thoor Ballylee or Ballylee Castle, where the poem was written."

33ff: "The peasant beauty and the blind poet are Mary Hynes and Raftery, and the incident of the man drowned in Cloone Bog is recorded in my *Celtic Twilight*." (Yeats). The blind Gaelic poet Anthony Raftery (1784–1834) celebrated Hynes in a song.

And certain men, being maddened by those rhymes,
Or else by toasting her a score of times,
Rose from the table and declared it right
To test their fancy by their sight;
45 But they mistook the brightness of the moon
For the prosaic light of day—
Music had driven their wits astray—
And one was drowned in the great bog of Cloone.

Strange, but the man who made the song was blind;
50 Yet, now I have considered it, I find
That nothing strange; the tragedy began
With Homer that was a blind man,
And Helen has all living hearts betrayed.
O may the moon and sunlight seem
55 One inextricable beam,
For if I triumph I must make men mad.

And I myself created Hanrahan
And drove him drunk or sober through the dawn
From somewhere in the neighbouring cottages.
60 Caught by an old man's juggleries
He stumbled, tumbled, fumbled to and fro
And had but broken knees for hire
And horrible splendour of desire;
I thought it all out twenty years ago:

65 Good fellows shuffled cards in an old bawn;
And when that ancient ruffian's turn was on
He so bewitched the cards under his thumb
That all but the one card became
A pack of hounds and not a pack of cards,
70 And that he changed into a hare.
Hanrahan rose in frenzy there
And followed up those baying creatures towards—

O towards I have forgotten what—enough!
I must recall a man that neither love
75 Nor music nor an enemy's clipped ear
Could, he was so harried, cheer;
A figure that has grown so fabulous
There's not a neighbour left to say
When he finished his dog's day:
80 An ancient bankrupt master of this house.

57ff: *Hanrahan:* "Hanrahan's pursuit of the phantom hare and hounds is from my *Stories of Red Hanrahan*" (Yeats). His pursuit ends at the house of the beautiful fairy queen Echtge. Too tongue-tied to ask her who she is, his sanity is taken away from him by her attendant crones; it is implied that Echtge was in fact waiting for Hanrahan's love. He becomes a wandering, half-mad poet.
65: *bawn:* The usual sense of the word is "fortified enlosure" or "cattlefold." In the original story the setting was in fact a barn.
74ff: "the old bankrupt man lived about a hundred years ago. According to one legend he could only leave the Castle upon a Sunday because of his creditors, and according to another he hid in the secret passage." (Yeats).

Before that ruin came, for centuries,
Rough men-at-arms, cross-gartered to the knees
Or shod in iron, climbed the narrow stairs,
And certain men-at-arms there were
85   Whose images, in the Great Memory stored,
Come with loud cry and panting breast
To break upon a sleeper's rest
While their great wooden dice beat on the board.

As I would question all, come all who can;
90   Come old, necessitous, half-mounted man;
And bring beauty's blind rambling celebrant;
The red man the juggler sent
Through God-forsaken meadows; Mrs. French,
Gifted with so fine an ear;
95   The man drowned in a bog's mire,
When mocking Muses chose the country wench.

Did all old men and women, rich and poor,
Who trod upon these rocks or passed this door,
Whether in public or in secret rage
100   As I do now against old age?
But I have found an answer in those eyes
That are impatient to be gone;
Go therefore; but leave Hanrahan,
For I need all his mighty memories.

105   Old lecher with a love on every wind,
Bring up out of that deep considering mind
All that you have discovered in the grave,
For it is certain that you have
Reckoned up every unforeknown, unseeing
110   Plunge, lured by a softening eye,
Or by a touch or a sigh,
Into the labyrinth of another's being;

Does the imagination dwell the most
Upon a woman won or woman lost?
115   If on the lost, admit you turned aside
From a great labyrinth out of pride,
Cowardice, some silly over-subtle thought
Or anything called conscience once;
And that if memory recur, the sun's
120   Under eclipse and the day blotted out.

85: *Great Memory:* see note to "Anima Mundi" in line 12 of "The Second Coming," p. 40.
88: "The ghosts have been seen at their game of dice in what is now my bedroom" (Yeats)
90: *half-mounted man:* the bankrupt owner; the phrase implies a person of questionable social status.
92: *red man:* i.e., Red Hanrahan

III

It is time that I wrote my will;
I choose upstanding men
That climb the streams until
The fountain leap, and at dawn
125 Drop their cast at the side
Of dripping stone; I declare
They shall inherit my pride,
The pride of people that were
Bound neither to Cause nor to State,
130 Neither to slaves that were spat on,
Nor to the tyrants that spat,
The people of Burke and of Grattan
That gave, though free to refuse—
Pride, like that of the morn,
135 When the headlong light is loose,
Or that of the fabulous horn,
Or that of the sudden shower
When all streams are dry,
Or that of the hour
140 When the swan must fix his eye
Upon a fading gleam,
Float out upon a long
Last reach of glittering stream
And there sing his last song.
145 And I declare my faith:
I mock Plotinus' thought
And cry in Plato's teeth,
Death and life were not
Till man made up the whole,
150 Made lock, stock and barrel
Out of his bitter soul,
Aye, sun and moon and star, all,
And further add to that
That, being dead, we rise,
155 Dream and so create
Translunar Paradise.
I have prepared my peace
With learned Italian things
And the proud stones of Greece,
160 Poet's imaginings
And memories of love,
Memories of the words of women,
All those things whereof
Man makes a superhuman
165 Mirror-resembling dream.

132: Yeats celebrates two representatives of a Protestant Irish patriotism: Edmund *Burke* (1729–1797), Irish-born politician, orator and political thinker; Henry *Grattan* (1746–1820), Protestant Irish leader, who campaigned unsuccessfully against the Act of Union and fought for Catholic emancipation.
136: *fabulous horn:* the Horn of Plenty
156: *translunar:* unchanging, because beyond the lunar phases of historical change set forth in Yeats's *A Vision,* or in his poem *"The Phases of the Moon."*

As at the loophole there
The daws chatter and scream,
And drop twigs layer upon layer.
When they have mounted up,
170   The mother bird will rest
On their hollow top,
And so warm her wild nest.

I leave both faith and pride
To young upstanding men
175   Climbing the mountain-side,
That under bursting dawn
They may drop a fly;
Being of that metal made
Till it was broken by
180   This sedentary trade.

Now shall I make my soul,
Compelling it to study
In a learned school
Till the wreck of body,
185   Slow decay of blood,
Testy delirium
Or dull decrepitude,
Or what worse evil come—
The death of friends, or death
190   Of every brilliant eye
That made a catch in the breath—
Seem but the clouds of the sky
When the horizon fades,
Or a bird's sleepy cry
195   Among the deepening shades.

                                    1925 / 1928

Leda and the Swan

A sudden blow: the great wings beating still
Above the staggering girl, her thighs caressed
By the dark webs, her nape caught in his bill,
He holds her helpless breast upon his breast.

181: *make my soul*: prepare for death

Leda and the Swan: The poem was commissioned by George Russell ("AE") for *The Irish Statesman*, but its first periodical appearance was instead in *The Dial*, June 1924. "I wrote Leda and the Swan because the editor of a political review asked me for a poem. I thought, 'After the individualist, demagogic movement, founded by Hobbes and popularized by the Encyclopaedists and the French Revolution, we have a soil so exhausted that it cannot grow that crop again for centuries'. Then I thought, 'Nothing is now possible but some movement from above preceded by some violent annunciation'. My fancy began to play with Leda and the Swan for metaphor, and I began this poem; but as I wrote, bird and lady took such possession of the scene that all politics went out of it, and my friend tells me that his 'conservative readers would misunderstand the poem'." (Yeats's note). The god Zeus took the form of a swan to rape the girl Leda, who afterwards laid eggs from which hatched Helen, Clytemnestra, and the twins Castor and Pollux. Helen became the wife of Menelaus; her abduction by Paris precipitated the Trojan War. Clytemnestra became the wife of Menelaus's brother Agamemnon, leader of the Greeks; upon his return

5   How can those terrified vague fingers push
             The feathered glory from her loosening thighs?
             And how can body, laid in that white rush,
             But feel the strange heart beating where it lies?

             A shudder in the loins engenders there
10   The broken wall, the burning roof and tower
             And Agamemnon dead.
                        Being so caught up,
             So mastered by the brute blood of the air,
             Did she put on his knowledge with his power
             Before the indifferent beak could let her drop?

1923 / 1928

Among School Children

I

             I walk through the long schoolroom questioning;
             A kind old nun in a white hood replies;
             The children learn to cipher and to sing,
             To study reading-books and history,
5   To cut and sew, be neat in everything
             In the best modern way—the children's eyes
             In momentary wonder stare upon
             A sixty-year-old smiling public man.

II

             I dream of a Ledaean body, bent
10   Above a sinking fire, a tale that she
             Told of a harsh reproof, or trivial event
             That changed some childish day to tragedy—
             Told, and it seemed that our two natures blent
             Into a sphere from youthful sympathy,
15   Or else, to alter Plato's parable,
             Into the yolk and white of the one shell.

III

             And thinking of that fit of grief or rage
             I look upon one child or t'other there
             And wonder if she stood so at that age—

from the war she murdered him. Early drafts of the poem were called "Annunciation": just as the angel's annunciation to the Virgin Mary marks the start of Christian history, the rape of Leda is the origin of a new historical epoch.

Among School Children: Yeats visited St. Otteran's School, run according to Montessori principles, in February 1926, and later praised it in the Senate in a report on the condition of Irish schools.

9: *Ledaean body*: Maud Gonne, identified here with Leda's daughter, Helen of Troy; for Leda see "Leda and the Swan," above. Leda laid three eggs, of which one did not hatch; "Castor and Clytaemnestra broke the one shell, Helen and Pollux the other" (Yeats, *A Vision*, 1937, p. 51).

15: In Plato's *Symposium*, Aristophanes argues that mankind was originally a hermaphroditic creature with four legs and four arms. Zeus divided it in two like a cooked egg, creating the male and female sexes; human love is an attempt to restore the original unity.

20　　For even daughters of the swan can share
　　　Something of every paddler's heritage—
　　　And had that colour upon cheek or hair,
　　　And thereupon my heart is driven wild:
　　　She stands before me as a living child.

IV

25　　Her present image floats into the mind—
　　　Did Quattrocento finger fashion it
　　　Hollow of cheek as though it drank the wind
　　　And took a mess of shadows for its meat?
　　　And I though never of Ledaean kind
30　　Had pretty plumage once—enough of that,
　　　Better to smile on all that smile, and show
　　　There is a comfortable kind of old scarecrow.

V

　　　What youthful mother, a shape upon her lap
　　　Honey of generation had betrayed,
35　　And that must sleep, shriek, struggle to escape
　　　As recollection or the drug decide,
　　　Would think her son, did she but see that shape
　　　With sixty or more winters on its head,
　　　A compensation for the pang of his birth,
40　　Or the uncertainty of his setting forth?

VI

　　　Plato thought nature but a spume that plays
　　　Upon a ghostly paradigm of things;
　　　Solider Aristotle played the taws
　　　Upon the bottom of a king of kings;
45　　World-famous golden-thighed Pythagoras
　　　Fingered upon a fiddle-stick or strings
　　　What a star sang and careless Muses heard:
　　　Old clothes upon old sticks to scare a bird.

25: *present image:* Gonne in old age was thin and skeletal in appearance.

26: *Quattrocento finger:* that of a fifteenth-century Italian painter. An earlier version had "Da Vinci finger."

28: cf. "Esau selleth his birthright for a mess of pottage," chapter heading to Genesis 25 in the Geneva Bible. Yeats intimates a judgment on Gonne's increasing political extremism; compare "A Prayer for my Daughter," lines 59–64 (p. 42).

34: "I have taken the 'honey of generation' from Porphyry's essay on 'The Cave of the Nymphs', but find no warrant in Porphyry for considering it the 'drug' that destroys the 'recollection' of prenatal freedom. He blamed a cup of oblivion given in the zodiacal sign of Cancer" (Yeats). *On the Cave of the Nymphs* by the Neoplatonist philosopher Porphyry (232/3 – c.305) is a commentary on the symbolism of the cave in book 13 of *The Odyssey.* According to Porphyry, unborn souls are lured toward generation by the parents' sexual pleasure (symbolized by the honey in the cave).

41–48: Yeats sent a draft of this stanza to Olivia Shakespear in a letter: "Here is a fragment of my last curse on old age. It means that even the greatest men are owls, scarecrows, by the time their fame has come."

41: *Plato* believed this world was only a copy of a world of ideal forms.

43: *Aristotle* was tutor to the future Alexander the Great; he is "solider" both because of his use of the *taws*—the birch—and because he believed that this world was the authentic one.

45: The philosopher *Pythagoras* was said to have had a golden thigh. In Pythagoreanism, "all is number"; Pythagoras is credited with discovering that musical intervals could be expressed as ratios of vibrating lengths of string; the Pythagoreans believed that the movement of the spheres produced a cosmic harmony.

VII

Both nuns and mothers worship images,
50   But those the candles light are not as those
That animate a mother's reveries,
But keep a marble or a bronze repose.
And yet they too break hearts—O Presences
That passion, piety or affection knows,
55   And that all heavenly glory symbolise—
O self-born mockers of man's enterprise;

VIII

Labour is blossoming or dancing where
The body is not bruised to pleasure soul,
Nor beauty born out of its own despair,
60   Nor blear-eyed wisdom out of midnight oil.
O chestnut tree, great rooted blossomer,
Are you the leaf, the blossom or the bole?
O body swayed to music, O brightening glance,
How can we know the dancer from the dance?

1926 / 1928

Byzantium

The unpurged images of day recede;
The Emperor's drunken soldiery are abed;
Night resonance recedes, night-walkers' song
After great cathedral gong;
5   A starlit or a moonlit dome disdains
All that man is,
All mere complexities,
The fury and the mire of human veins.

Before me floats an image, man or shade,
10   Shade more than man, more image than a shade;
For Hades' bobbin bound in mummy-cloth
May unwind the winding path;
A mouth that has no moisture and no breath
Breathless mouths may summon;
15   I hail the superhuman;
I call it death-in-life and life-in-death.

Byzantium: Yeats wrote in his 1930 diary: "Subject for a poem. . . . Describe Byzantium as it is in the system [i.e., that of *A Vision*] towards the end of the first Christian millennium. A walking mummy. Flames at the street corners where the soul is purified, birds of hammered gold singing in the golden trees, [dolphins] in the harbour, offering their backs to the wailing dead that they may carry them to Paradise." See "Sailing to Byzantium," p. 42.
5: *dome:* the dome of the sixth-century church of Hagia Sophia in Constantinople (Byzantium).
11: *Hades* is the realm of the underworld; thus the *bobbin* is probably the spirit around which the mummy's cloth is wound. The sense here is perhaps that the thread of "life" of a dead person does not have to be wound on to the bobbin in a constant direction, as with the living: the bobbin of the dead can go into reverse, freeing the spirits of the dead, in this case a mummy, to reenter the mortal world.
14: *Breathless:* perhaps "breathless from wonder"

Miracle, bird or golden handiwork,
More miracle than bird or handiwork,
Planted on the star-lit golden bough,
20   Can like the cocks of Hades crow,
Or, by the moon embittered, scorn aloud
In glory of changeless metal
Common bird or petal
And all complexities of mire or blood.

25   At midnight on the Emperor's pavement flit
Flames that no faggot feeds, nor steel has lit,
Nor storm disturbs, flames begotten of flame,
Where blood-begotten spirits come
And all complexities of fury leave,
30   Dying into a dance,
An agony of trance,
An agony of flame that cannot singe a sleeve.

Astraddle on the dolphin's mire and blood,
Spirit after spirit! The smithies break the flood,
35   The golden smithies of the Emperor!
Marbles of the dancing floor
Break bitter furies of complexity,
Those images that yet
Fresh images beget,
40   That dolphin-torn, that gong-tormented sea.

1930 / 1932

Crazy Jane Talks with the Bishop

I met the Bishop on the road
And much said he and I.
'Those breasts are flat and fallen now,
Those veins must soon be dry;
5   Live in a heavenly mansion,
Not in some foul sty.'

'Fair and foul are near of kin,
And fair needs foul,' I cried.
'My friends are gone, but that's a truth
10   Nor grave nor bed denied,
Learned in bodily lowliness
And in the heart's pride.

'A woman can be proud and stiff
When on love intent;
15   But Love has pitched his mansion in

28: *blood-begotten spirits:* presumably human spirits
34: *the flood:* i.e., both the sea and the flood of incoming spirits

The place of excrement;
For nothing can be sole or whole
That has not been rent.'

1931 / *1933*

Lapis Lazuli

FOR HARRY CLIFTON

I have heard that hysterical women say
They are sick of the palette and fiddle-bow,
Of poets that are always gay,
For everybody knows or else should know
5   That if nothing drastic is done
Aeroplane and Zeppelin will come out,
Pitch like King Billy bomb-balls in
Until the town lie beaten flat.

All perform their tragic play,
10   There struts Hamlet, there is Lear,
That's Ophelia, that Cordelia;
Yet they, should the last scene be there,
The great stage curtain about to drop,
If worthy their prominent part in the play,
15   Do not break up their lines to weep.
They know that Hamlet and Lear are gay;
Gaiety transfiguring all that dread.
All men have aimed at, found and lost;
Black out; Heaven blazing into the head:
20   Tragedy wrought to its uttermost.
Though Hamlet rambles and Lear rages,
And all the drop-scenes drop at once
Upon a hundred thousand stages,
It cannot grow by an inch or an ounce.

25   On their own feet they came, or on shipboard,
Camel-back, horse-back, ass-back, mule-back,
Old civilisations put to the sword.
Then they and their wisdom went to rack:

Clifton gave Yeats a lapis luzuli carving in 1935 for his 70th birthday. Yeats wrote Dorothy Wellesley: "some-one has sent me a present of a great piece carved by some Chinese sculptor into the semblance of a mountain with temple, trees, paths and an ascetic and pupil about to climb the mountain. Ascetic, pupil, hard stone, eternal theme of the sensual east. The heroic cry in the midst of despair. But no, I am wrong, the east has its solutions always and therefore knows nothing of tragedy. It is we, not the east, that must raise the heroic cry."

1: The *women* are *hysterical* because of contemporary political events: in 1936, when the poem was writ-ten, Hitler invaded the Rhineland.

6: German *Zeppelins* (dirigibles) bombed London during World War I.

7: Yeats rewrites lines from "The Ballad of the Boyne": "King William threw his bomb-balls in / And set them all on fire." William III defeated the former king, the Catholic James II, in 1690 on the banks of Ireland's River Boyne (an event whose ritual commemoration still lies at the heart of Northern Irish Protestant politics).

No handiwork of Callimachus,
30   Who handled marble as if it were bronze,
Made draperies that seemed to rise
When sea-wind swept the corner, stands;
His long lamp-chimney shaped like the stem
Of a slender palm, stood but a day;
35   All things fall and are built again,
And those that build them again are gay.

Two Chinamen, behind them a third,
Are carved in lapis lazuli,
Over them flies a long-legged bird,
40   A symbol of longevity;
The third, doubtless a serving-man,
Carries a musical instrument.

Every discoloration of the stone,
Every accidental crack or dent,
45   Seems a water-course or an avalanche,
Or lofty slope where it still snows
Though doubtless plum or cherry-branch
Sweetens the little half-way house
Those Chinamen climb towards, and I
50   Delight to imagine them seated there;
There, on the mountain and the sky,
On all the tragic scene they stare.
One asks for mournful melodies;
Accomplished fingers begin to play.
55   Their eyes mid many wrinkles, their eyes,
Their ancient, glittering eyes, are gay.

1936 / 1938

Under Ben Bulben

I

Swear by what the sages spoke
Round the Mareotic Lake
That the Witch of Atlas knew,
Spoke and set the cocks a-crow.

29: *Callimachus*: Greek sculptor of the fifth century BC, reputed inventor of the Corinthian column and the first to use the running borer on marble; he was famed for his work's elaborate, stylized drapery. He was said to have made the lamp that burned perpetually at the Erechtheum, a temple on the Acropolis in Athens.

Ben Bulben is a mountain near Sligo.
2: *Lake Mareotis* lies near Alexandria in Egypt, the center of learning of the classical world.
3: *Witch of Atlas*: Yeats wrote in an essay of the protagonist of Shelley's "The Witch of Atlas": "When the Witch has passed in her boat from the caverned river, that is doubtless her own destiny, she passes along the Nile 'by Moeris and the Mareotid lakes,' and sees all human life shadowed upon its waters in shadows that 'never are erased but tremble ever'; and in 'many a dark and subterranean street under the Nile'—new caverns—and along the bank of the Nile; and as she bends over the unhappy, she compares unhappiness to the strife that 'stirs the liquid surface of man's life'; and because she can see the reality of things she is described as journeying 'in the calm depths' of 'the wide lake' we journey over unpiloted." (*Essays and Introductions*, London, 1961, p. 85)

5　　　　　　　　Swear by those horsemen, by those women
　　　　　　　　Complexion and form prove superhuman,
　　　　　　　　That pale, long-visaged company
　　　　　　　　That airs an immortality
　　　　　　　　Completeness of their passions won;
10　　　　　　　Now they ride the wintry dawn
　　　　　　　　Where Ben Bulben sets the scene.

　　　　　　　　Here's the gist of what they mean.

II

　　　　　　　　Many times man lives and dies
　　　　　　　　Between his two eternities,
15　　　　　　　That of race and that of soul,
　　　　　　　　And ancient Ireland knew it all.
　　　　　　　　Whether man die in his bed
　　　　　　　　Or the rifle knocks him dead,
　　　　　　　　A brief parting from those dear
20　　　　　　　Is the worst man has to fear.

　　　　　　　　Though grave-diggers' toil is long,
　　　　　　　　Sharp their spades, their muscles strong,
　　　　　　　　They but thrust their buried men
　　　　　　　　Back in the human mind again.

III

25　　　　　　　You that Mitchel's prayer have heard,
　　　　　　　　'Send war in our time, O Lord!'
　　　　　　　　Know that when all words are said
　　　　　　　　And a man is fighting mad,
　　　　　　　　Something drops from eyes long blind,
30　　　　　　　He completes his partial mind,
　　　　　　　　For an instant stands at ease,
　　　　　　　　Laughs aloud, his heart at peace.
　　　　　　　　Even the wisest man grows tense
　　　　　　　　With some sort of violence
35　　　　　　　Before he can accomplish fate,
　　　　　　　　Know his work or choose his mate.

IV

　　　　　　　　Poet and sculptor, do the work,
　　　　　　　　Nor let the modish painter shirk
　　　　　　　　What his great forefathers did,
40　　　　　　　Bring the soul of man to God,
　　　　　　　　Make him fill the cradles right.

5: *horsemen:* i.e., supernatural riders
25: The Irish nationalist John *Mitchel* (1815–1875) founded the *United Irishman* newspaper in 1843; he was transported to Australia, escaped to the United States, and returned to Ireland in 1874, to become an MP. Yeats quotes Mitchel's prayer for war with England in *Jail Journal* (1854), a parody of "Give us peace in our time, O Lord," from the Church of Ireland evening service.

Measurement began our might:
Forms a stark Egyptian thought,
Forms that gentler Phidias wrought.

45 Michael Angelo left a proof
On the Sistine Chapel roof,
Where but half-awakened Adam
Can disturb globe-trotting Madam
Till her bowels are in heat,
50 Proof that there's a purpose set
Before the secret working mind:
Profane perfection of mankind.

Quattrocento put in paint
On backgrounds for a God or Saint
55 Gardens where a soul's at ease;
Where everything that meets the eye,
Flowers and grass and cloudless sky,
Resemble forms that are or seem
When sleepers wake and yet still dream,
60 And when it's vanished still declare,
With only bed and bedstead there,
That heavens had opened.
                                  Gyres run on;
When that greater dream had gone
Calvert and Wilson, Blake and Claude,
65 Prepared a rest for the people of God,
Palmer's phrase, but after that
Confusion fell upon our thought.

V

Irish poets, learn your trade,
Sing whatever is well made,
70 Scorn the sort now growing up
All out of shape from toe to top,
Their unremembering hearts and heads
Base-born products of base beds.
Sing the peasantry, and then
75 Hard-riding country gentlemen,
The holiness of monks, and after
Porter-drinkers' randy laughter;

44: *Phidias:* the Greek sculptor (c. 490–430 BC), best known now for his sculptures for the Parthenon.
45: *Michelangelo*'s fresco shows a reclining Adam stretching his hand out to God, whose hand is reciprocally outstretched.
52: Yeats's respect for the creative power of art is such that he proposes that it affects the generation of children.
53: *Quattrocento:* the fifteenth century
62: *Gyres:* see note to line 1 of "The Second Coming", p. 40.
64: Edward *Calvert* (1799–1883) was a disciple of the poet-painter William *Blake*; Richard *Wilson* (1714–1782) was an English landscape painter influenced by the work of *Claude* Lorrain (1600–1682).
66: Samuel *Palmer* (1805–1881), another disciple of Blake, wrote of Blake's illustrations to Virgil: "There is in all such a misty and dreamy glimmer as penetrates and kindles the inmost soul . . . the drawing aside of the fleshly curtain, and the glimpse which all the most holy, studious saints and sages have enjoyed, of the rest which remains to the people of God." The phrase itself alludes to Hebrews 4:9: "There remaineth therefore a rest to the people of God."

Sing the lords and ladies gay
That were beaten into the clay
80   Through seven heroic centuries;
Cast your mind on other days
That we in coming days may be
Still the indomitable Irishry.

VI

Under bare Ben Bulben's head
85   In Drumcliff churchyard Yeats is laid.
An ancestor was rector there
Long years ago, a church stands near,
By the road an ancient cross.
No marble, no conventional phrase;
90   On limestone quarried near the spot
By his command these words are cut:
      Cast a cold eye
      On life, on death.
      Horseman, pass by!

1938 / 1939

The Circus Animals' Desertion

I

I sought a theme and sought for it in vain,
I sought it daily for six weeks or so.
Maybe at last, being but a broken man,
I must be satisfied with my heart, although
5   Winter and summer till old age began
My circus animals were all on show,
Those stilted boys, that burnished chariot,
Lion and woman and the Lord knows what.

II

What can I but enumerate old themes?
10   First that sea-rider Oisin led by the nose
Through three enchanted islands, allegorical dreams,
Vain gaiety, vain battle, vain repose,
Themes of the embittered heart, or so it seems,
That might adorn old songs or courtly shows;
15   But what cared I that set him on to ride,
I, starved for the bosom of his faery bride?

80: *seven heroic centuries*: i.e., since the Anglo-Norman invasion of Ireland in the twelfth century.
85: *Drumcliff*: a village to the north of Sligo, lying under the slopes of Ben Bulben. The "ancestor" was
  Rev. John Yeats (1774–1846).
94: *Horseman*: presumably one of the supernatural horsemen of part I.

7: *Those stilted boys*: Yeats gestures towards the ancient Irish heroes of his early work.
10ff: Yeats is recalling his early narrative poem *The Wanderings of Oisin* (1889).

And then a counter-truth filled out its play,
The Countess Cathleen was the name I gave it;
She, pity-crazed, had given her soul away,
20 But masterful Heaven had intervened to save it.
I thought my dear must her own soul destroy,
So did fanaticism and hate enslave it,
And this brought forth a dream and soon enough
This dream itself had all my thought and love.

25 And when the Fool and Blind Man stole the bread
Cuchulain fought the ungovernable sea;
Heart-mysteries there, and yet when all is said
It was the dream itself enchanted me:
Character isolated by a deed
30 To engross the present and dominate memory.
Players and painted stage took all my love,
And not those things that they were emblems of.

III

Those masterful images because complete
Grew in pure mind, but out of what began?
35 A mound of refuse or the sweepings of a street,
Old kettles, old bottles, and a broken can,
Old iron, old bones, old rags, that raving slut
Who keeps the till. Now that my ladder's gone,
I must lie down where all the ladders start,
40 In the foul rag-and-bone shop of the heart.

                                    1937–1938 / 1939

Politics

*'In our time the destiny of man presents its meanings
in political terms.'*
                                    THOMAS MANN

How can I, that girl standing there,
My attention fix
On Roman or on Russian
Or on Spanish politics?
5 Yet here's a travelled man that knows
What he talks about,
And there's a politician
That has read and thought,
And maybe what they say is true
10 Of war and war's alarms,
But O that I were young again
And held her in my arms.

                                    1938 / 1939

18: Yeats wrote *The Countess Cathleen* for Maud Gonne, who played the title role in its first production in
1899. The countess sells her soul in order to rescue the peasants in time of famine, but is saved from
damnation.
25: The *Fool* and *Blind Man* are characters in Yeats's play *On Baile's Strand* (1903); the play tells of Cuchu-
lain's death, fighting the sea.

Politics: The poem was written on 23 May 1938; Stalin and Mussolini were in power, the Spanish Civil War
was still raging, and a slide into European or world war seemed inevitable.

CHARLOTTE MEW (1869–1928)

MEW WAS BORN INTO THE FAMILY OF A PROSPEROUS ARCHITECT AND LIVED MOST OF her life in Bloomsbury. She graduated from Lucy Harrison's School for Girls and attended lectures at University College, London. A brother and a sister having been institutionalized for insanity, Mew was fearful of hereditary insanity, and mental illness is a theme in some of her poems. Distressed at the death of her sister Anne in 1927, she entered a nursing home for treatment for neurasthenia (a term for what might no less inexactly be called a "nervous breakdown" today). In 1928 she committed suicide by ingesting a half-bottle of the disinfectant Lysol. Admirers of her poetry and prose included Thomas Hardy, who helped Mew obtain a Civil List pension, Harold Monro, whose Poetry Bookshop published her first volume, Robert Bridges, John Masefield, Virginia Woolf, and Marianne Moore. Her first published story appeared in the second issue of *The Yellow Book*. Her poems were collected in *The Farmer's Bride* (1916), an expanded edition of which appeared in 1921, and posthumously in *The Rambling Sailor* (1929). Early fame, especially for "The Farmer's Bride," was followed until recently by neglect. Her *Collected Poems and Prose* appeared in 1981.

The more prosaic moments in Mew's syntax and idiom have led readers to draw comparisons with Hardy. Her best poems, such as "Madeleine in Church" and "On the Road to the Sea," hover between dramatic and interior monologue. The latter poem offers us a view of consciousness divided between obsessional erotic attraction and the knowledge that such attraction has no basis beyond fantasy. As Val Warner writes, Mew had in her youth "an Anglo-Catholic phase" and was impressed by what she saw of the effects of Roman Catholicism in French life and culture; the religion offered her a drama of passionate self-sacrifice even if, in the end, it did not claim her adherence.[1] She took from the poets of the 1890s a romanticized and furtive interest in prostitutes' lives and explored the uses to which female sexuality is put. Celeste M. Schenck argues that "whereas Djuna Barnes's lesbian eroticism . . . no longer provokes surprise, Mew's lyric exploration of the same themes within the confines of meter and rhyme has been overlooked," praising Mew's "sexual frankness" while discussing poems that evoke "both delight in female sexuality and conflict over its homo-erotic expression."[2] Mew was an admirer of Emily Brontë, whose lines from "The Philosopher" might describe her own despair: "Had I but seen his glorious eye / Once light the clouds that wilder me; / I ne'er had raised this coward cry / To cease to think, and cease to be."

---

[1] Introduction to Charlotte Mew, *Collected Poems and Selected Prose,* ed. Val Warner, Manchester, England, 1997, p. xi.

[2] "Charlotte Mew," *The Gender of Modernism: A Critical Anthology,* ed. Bonnie Kime Scott, Bloomington, 1990, pp. 317–18.

The Farmer's Bride

Three Summers since I chose a maid,
Too young maybe—but more's to do
At harvest-time than bide and woo.
    When us was wed she turned afraid
Of love and me and all things human;
Like the shut of a winter's day
Her smile went out, and 'twasn't a woman—
    More like a little frightened fay.
        One night, in the Fall, she runned away.

"Out 'mong the sheep, her be," they said,
'Should properly have been abed;
But sure enough she wasn't there
Lying awake with her wide brown stare.
So over seven-acre field and up-along across the down
We chased her, flying like a hare
Before our lanterns. To Church-Town
    All in a shiver and a scare
We caught her, fetched her home at last
    And turned the key upon her, fast.

She does the work about the house
As well as most, but like a mouse:
    Happy enough to chat and play
    With birds and rabbits and such as they,
    So long as men-folk keep away.
"Not near, not near!" her eyes beseech
When one of us comes within reach.
    The women say that beasts in stall
    Look round like children at her call.
    I've hardly heard her speak at all.

Shy as a leveret, swift as he,
Straight and slight as a young larch tree,
Sweet as the first wild violets, she,
To her wild self. But what to me?

The short days shorten and the oaks are brown,
    The blue smoke rises to the low grey sky,
One leaf in the still air falls slowly down,
    A magpie's spotted feathers lie
On the black earth spread white with rime,
The berries redden up to Christmas-time.
    What's Christmas-time without there be
    Some other in the house than we!

She sleeps up in the attic there
Alone, poor maid. 'Tis but a stair

8: *fay:* fairy
30: *leveret:* young hare

Betwixt us. Oh! my God! the down,
45   The soft young down of her, the brown,
The brown of her—her eyes, her hair, her hair!

1916

Fame

Sometimes in the over-heated house, but not for long,
       Smirking and speaking rather loud,
       I see myself among the crowd,
Where no one fits the singer to his song,
5   Or sifts the unpainted from the painted faces
Of the people who are always on my stair;
They were not with me when I walked in heavenly places;
       But could I spare
In the blind Earth's great silences and spaces,
10   The din, the scuffle, the long stare
       If I went back and it was not there?
Back to the old known things that are the new,
The folded glory of the gorse, the sweet-briar air,
To the larks that cannot praise us, knowing nothing of what we do,
15   And the divine, wise trees that do not care.
Yet, to leave Fame, still with such eyes and that bright hair!
God! If I might! And before I go hence
       Take in her stead
       To our tossed bed,
20 One little dream, no matter how small, how wild.
Just now, I think I found it in a field, under a fence—
A frail, dead, new-born lamb, ghostly and pitiful and white,
       A blot upon the night,
       The moon's dropped child!

1916

Arracombe Wood

Some said, because he wud'n spaik
       Any words to women but Yes and No,
Nor put out his hand for Parson to shake
       He mun be bird-witted. But I do go
5   By the lie of the barley that he did sow,
And I wish no better thing than to hold a rake
       Like Dave, in his time, or to see him mow.

5: *painted:* made-up
13: *gorse:* the gorsebush, which has yellow flowers
    sweet-briar: eglantine, a type of wild rose
24: To *drop* is to give birth to a lamb.

4: *mun be bird-witted:* must be half-witted

Put up in churchyard a month ago,
"A bitter old soul," they said, but it wadn't so.
His heart were in Arracombe Wood where he'd used to go
To sit and talk wi' his shadder till sun went low,
Though what it was all about us'll never know.
     And there baint no mem'ry in the place
     Of th' old man's footmark, nor his face;
     Arracombe Wood do think more of a crow—
'Will be violets there in the Spring: in Summer time the spider's lace;
     And come the Fall, the whizzle and race
Of the dry, dead leaves when the wind gies chase;
     And on the Eve of Christmas, fallin' snow.

1916

On the Road to the Sea

We passed each other, turned and stopped for half an hour, then went our
    way,
    I who make other women smile did not make you—
But no man can move mountains in a day.
    So this hard thing is yet to do.

But first I want your life:—before I die I want to see
    The world that lies behind the strangeness of your eyes,
There is nothing gay or green there for my gathering, it may be,
      Yet on brown fields there lies
A haunting purple bloom: is there not something in grey skies
          And in grey sea?
    I want what world there is behind your eyes,
    I want your life and you will not give it me.

    Now, if I look, I see you walking down the years,
    Young, and through August fields—a face, a thought, a swinging dream
      perched on a stile—;
    I would have liked (so vile we are!) to have taught you tears
          But most to have made you smile.

    To-day is not enough or yesterday: God sees it all—
Your length on sunny lawns, the wakeful rainy nights—; tell me—(how
    vain to ask), but it is not a question—just a call—;
Show me then, only your notched inches climbing up the garden wall,
          I like you best when you were small.

      Is this a stupid thing to say
        Not having spent with you one day?
    No matter; I shall never touch your hair
    Or hear the little tick behind your breast,
        Still it is there,
        And as a flying bird

8: *Put up*: buried
11: *shadder*: shadow
18: *gies*: gives

Brushes the branches where it may not rest
          I have brushed your hand and heard
The child in you: I like that best.

30   So small, so dark, so sweet; and were you also then too grave and wise?
        Always I think. Then put your far off little hand in mine;—Oh! let it
          rest;
I will not stare into the early world beyond the opening eyes,
        Or vex or scare what I love best.

        But I want your life before mine bleeds away—
35   Here—not in heavenly hereafters—soon,—
        I want your smile this very afternoon,
    (The last of all my vices, pleasant people used to say,
        I wanted and I sometimes got—the Moon!)

        You know, at dusk, the last bird's cry,
40   And round the house the flap of the bat's low flight,
        Trees that go black against the sky
    And then—how soon the night!

No shadow of you on any bright road again,
And at the darkening end of this—what voice? whose kiss? As if you'd say!
45   It is not I who have walked with you, it will not be I who take away
        Peace, peace, my little handful of the gleaner's grain
    From your reaped fields at the shut of day.

        Peace! Would you not rather die
        Reeling,—with all the cannons at your ear?
50   So, at least, would I,
    And I may not be here
To-night, to-morrow morning or next year.
Still I will let you keep your life a little while,
          See dear?
55   *I have made you smile.*

                                     1921

Monsieur Qui Passe

Quai Voltaire

A purple blot against the dead white door
In my friend's rooms, bathed in their vile pink light,
I had not noticed her before
She snatched my eyes and threw them back at me:
5   She did not speak till we came out into the night,
Paused at this bench beside the kiosk on the quay.

Title: The French title might be rendered as "The Visitor" or "Ships in the Night."
Subtitle: The *Quay Voltaire* is on the Seine, in Paris.
1: The title indicates that the speaker is a man. The *purple blot* is the woman of line 3.

God knows precisely what she said—
I left to her the twisted skein,
Though here and there I caught a thread,—
10   Something, at first, about "the lamps along the Seine,
And Paris, with that witching card of Spring
Kept up her sleeve,—why you could see
The trick done on these freezing winter nights!
While half the kisses of the Quay—
15   Youth, hope,—the whole enchanted string
Of dreams hung on the Seine's long line of lights."

Then suddenly she stripped, the very skin
Came off her soul,—a mere girl clings
Longer to some last rag, however thin,
20   When she has shown you—well—all sorts of things:
"If it were daylight—oh! one keeps one's head—
But fourteen years!—No one has ever guessed—
The whole thing starts when one gets to bed—
Death?—If the dead would tell us they had rest!
25   But your eyes held it as I stood there by the door—
One speaks to Christ—one tries to catch His garment's hem—
One hardly says as much to Him—no more:
It was not you, it was your eyes—I spoke to them."

She stopped like a shot bird that flutters still,
30   And drops, and tries to run again, and swerves.
The tale should end in some walled house upon a hill.
My eyes, at least, won't play such havoc there,—
Or hers— But she had hair!—blood dipped in gold;
And here she left me throwing back the first odd stare.
35   Some sort of beauty once, but turning yellow, getting old.
Pouah! These women and their nerves!
God! but the night *is* cold!

                                                                        1929

18: *a mere girl*: i.e., as opposed to a sexually experienced woman
26: For the Christian imagery see Matt. 14:35–36 and especially 9:20–22: "a woman, which was diseased
with an issue of blood twelve years, came behind [Jesus], and touched the hem of his garment: For she
said within herself, If I may but touch his garment, I shall be whole. But Jesus turned him about; and
when he saw her, he said, Daughter, be of good comfort; thy faith hath made thee whole. And the woman
was made whole from that hour."

WALTER DE LA MARE (1873–1956)

Walter de la Mare was born in Charlton in Kent and attended St. Paul's Cathedral School in London. From 1890 to 1908 he worked for the Anglo-American (Standard) Oil Company as a clerk. A Civil List pension awarded him by the Asquith government combined with income from reviewing allowed him thereafter to support himself as a full-time writer. His reputation as a poet reached its height with the publication of *The Listeners and Other Poems* in 1912 and the inclusion of his poems in the first two Georgian anthologies a few years later, but it never altogether recovered from F. R. Leavis's dismissal of him as "the belated last poet of the Romantic tradition" in *New Bearings in English Poetry* (1932).[1] Late praise from W. H. Auden, T. S. Eliot, and I. A. Richards did little to rescue his poetry from neglect, though de la Mare's children's verse and his novel *Memoirs of a Midget* (1921) have sustained an audience for his work beyond readers of modernist poetry. Leavis had little use for the "fairy-tale atmosphere" he found in de la Mare's mellifluous verse: "he has formed habits that make impossible such a frank recognition of the human plight as he seems to offer. The apparent recognition is not the frankness it pretends to be but an insidious enhancement of the spell, which is the more potent to soothe and lull when it seems to be doing the opposite."[2] Other readers have found de la Mare's fascination with an uncanny experience tinged with the macabre too close to the poetry of the Rossettis. But Michael Kirkham has argued that de la Mare's dream-world has little of the "flight from an actuality felt to be alien" characteristic of the Pre-Raphaelites who influenced him; he defined dreams in the introduction to his *Behold, This Dreamer* (1939) as "meaningful communings between self and self, revelations of the spirit within."[3] Moreover, de la Mare's poetry is more various than it is typically given credit for being. That he was aware of developments in modern poetry, which he chose not to pursue, and possessed a considerable critical intelligence is evident in the essays collected in *Pleasures and Speculations* (1940).

---

[1] *New Bearings in English Poetry*, London, 1932, p. 56
[2] Ibid., p. 53.
[3] *Dictionary of Literary Biography*, vol. 19, ed. Donald E. Stanford, Detroit, 1983, p. 112; *Behold, This Dreamer* quoted in the same.

Miss Loo

When thin-strewn memory I look through,
I see most clearly poor Miss Loo;
Her tabby cat, her cage of birds,
Her nose, her hair, her muffled words,
5   And how she'd open her green eyes,
As if in some immense surprise,
Whenever as we sat at tea
She made some small remark to me.
It's always drowsy summer when
10   From out the past she comes again;
The westering sunshine in a pool
Floats in her parlour still and cool;
While the slim bird its lean wires shakes,
As into piercing song it breaks;

15   Till Peter's pale-green eyes ajar
Dream, wake; wake, dream, in one brief bar.
And I am sitting, dull and shy,
And she with gaze of vacancy,
And large hands folded on the tray,
20   Musing the afternoon away;
Her satin bosom heaving slow
With sighs that softly ebb and flow,
And her plain face in such dismay,
It seems unkind to look her way:
25   Until all cheerful back will come
Her gentle gleaming spirit home:
And one would think that poor Miss Loo
Asked nothing else, if she had you.

1912

The Listeners

'Is there anybody there?' said the Traveller,
   Knocking on the moonlit door;
And his horse in the silence champed the grasses
   Of the forest's ferny floor:
5   And a bird flew up out of the turret,
   Above the Traveller's head:
And he smote upon the door again a second time;
   'Is there anybody there?' he said.
But no one descended to the Traveller;
10   No head from the leaf-fringed sill
Leaned over and looked into his grey eyes,
   Where he stood perplexed and still.
But only a host of phantom listeners
   That dwelt in the lone house then
15   Stood listening in the quiet of the moonlight
   To that voice from the world of men:
Stood thronging the faint moonbeams on the dark stair,

That goes down to the empty hall,
Hearkening in an air stirred and shaken
20   By the lonely Traveller's call.
And he felt in his heart their strangeness,
    Their stillness answering his cry,
While his horse moved, cropping the dark turf,
    'Neath the starred and leafy sky;
25 For he suddenly smote on the door, even
    Louder, and lifted his head:—
'Tell them I came, and no one answered,
    That I kept my word,' he said.
Never the least stir made the listeners,
30   Though every word he spake
Fell echoing through the shadowiness of the still house
    From the one man left awake:
Ay, they heard his foot upon the stirrup,
    And the sound of iron on stone,
35 And how the silence surged softly backward,
    When the plunging hoofs were gone.

1912

The Old Summerhouse

This blue-washed, old, thatched summerhouse—
Paint scaling, and fading from its walls—
How often from its hingeless door
I have watched—dead leaf, like the ghost of a mouse,
5 Rasping the worn brick floor—
The snows of the weir descending below,
And their thunderous waterfall.

Fall—fall: dark, garrulous rumour,
Until I could listen no more.
10 Could listen no more—for beauty with sorrow
Is a burden hard to be borne:
The evening light on the foam, and the swans, there;
That music, remote, forlorn.

1938

1: *washed*: painted

FORD MADOX FORD (1873–1939)

FORD, WHO PUBLISHED OVER EIGHTY BOOKS, IS BEST KNOWN FOR HIS NOVELS, MOST notably *The Good Soldier* (1915) and the four books of *Parade's End: Some Do Not* (1924), *No More Parades* (1925), *A Man Could Stand Up* (1926), and *Last Post* (1928). His studies of Henry James and Joseph Conrad and remarks concerning matters such as literary "impressionism" still find an audience among students of literature. But, despite the efforts of poets as different as Basil Bunting, Robert Lowell, and Kenneth Rexroth to increase the audience for Ford's poetry, it remains little read. Perhaps this is because, as Bunting admits, Ford "published bad poems—perhaps more bad than good." Yet Bunting, in citing "The Starling" in a lecture, insists that "[Ezra] Pound is not being merely loyal to a friend when he insists on the part Ford played in changing English poetry in the early years of this century. Ford at his best uses language that is not merely current but conversational. Ford at his best names *things* and lets them evoke the emotion without mentioning it. He had not the gift of monumental brevity, but he uses repetition for a kind of hypnotic effect: uses it quite consciously, without trying to disguise it."[1] In naming Ford as a precursor to modernist poetry, Bunting is surely remembering Pound's having credited Ford with the statement that "poetry should be written at least as well as prose" in an essay on "the prose tradition in verse."[2] To the end, Ford remained for Pound the dedicated "stylist" he wrote of in his *Hugh Selwyn Mauberley* (1920). Pound's obituary for his friend later remembered that "[Ford] felt the errors of contemporary style to the point of rolling . . . on the floor of his temporary quarters in Gissen when my third volume displayed me trapped, fly-papered, gummed and strapped down in a jejune provincial effort to learn, *mehercule*, the stilted language that then passed for 'good English' in the arthritic milieu that held control of the respected British critical circles. . . ."[3] Pound's obituary also remembers the neglect Ford suffered in Britain. Lowell, noting that Ford's legendary generosity to younger writers extended to generations beyond Pound's, writes that "When I knew Ford in America [1937], he was out of cash, out of fashion, and half out of inspiration, a half-German, half-English exile in love with the French, and able to sell his books only in the United States." The former editor of two of the century's most important journals, the *English Review* (1908–1910) and *Transatlantic Review* (1924–1925), was then lecturing at American colleges, picking up "armloads of Loeb Classics" at every stop to work on his massive study *The March of Literature* (1938).[4]

---

[1] "Precursors," in *Basil Bunting on Poetry*, ed. Peter Makin, Baltimore, 1999, p. 111.
[2] "The Prose Tradition in Verse," *Literary Essays of Ezra Pound*, ed. T. S. Eliot, New York, 1935, p. 373.
[3] "Ford Madox (Hueffer) Ford; Obit," in Ezra Pound, *Selected Prose 1909–1965*, ed. William Cookson, New York, 1968, pp. 461–62.
[4] "Ford Madox Ford," in Robert Lowell, *Collected Prose*, New York, 1987, pp. 3–4.

Ford was born Ford Hermann Hueffer in Merton, Surrey. His father was a German music critic and his mother the daughter of the Pre-Raphaelite painter Ford Madox Brown. He was educated at Praetoria House, Folkestone and University College, London. He met Joseph Conrad in 1898, and their first collaborative work, *The Inheritors,* appeared in 1901, to be followed by *Romance* in 1903. A *Collected Poems* appeared in 1914, the year before Hueffer enlisted in the army; his experience in World War I informs not only some of his best fiction but also *On Heaven, and Poems Written in Active Service* (1918). After the war Hueffer moved to a farm in Sussex and changed his German name to Ford. He then moved in 1922 to France. His last years were divided between America and France. *New Poems* appeared in 1927 and *Collected Poems*—including "Buckshee," "Temps de Sécheresse," "Coda" and other poems praised by Lowell—in 1936. The most recent *Selected Poems,* edited by Max Saunders, was published in 1997.

The Starling

It's an odd thing how one changes! . . .
Walking along the upper ranges
Of this land of plains
In this month of rains,
5   On a drying road where the poplars march along,
Suddenly,
With a rush of wings flew down a company,
A multitude, throng upon throng,
Of starlings,
10   Successive orchestras of wind-blown song,
Whirled, like a babble of surf,
On to the roadside turf—

And so, for a mile, for a mile and a half . . . a long way
Flight followed flight,
15   Thro' the still, grey light
Of the steel-grey day,
Whirling beside the road in clamorous crowds,
Never near, never far, in the shade of the poplars and clouds!

It's an odd thing how one changes! . . .
20   And what strikes me now as most strange is,
After the starlings had flown
Over the plain and were gone,
There was one of them stayed on alone
On a twig; it chattered on high,
25   Lifting its bill to the sky,
Distending its throat,
Crooning harsh note after note,
In soliloquy,
Sitting alone.

30   And, after a hush,
It gurgled as gurgles a well,
Warbled as warbles a thrush,
Had a try at the sound of a bell

And mimicked a jay . . .
35   But I,
Whilst the starling mimicked on high,
Pulsing its throat and its wings,
I went on my way
Thinking of things
40   Onwards, and over the range
And that's what is strange.

I went down 'twixt tobacco and grain,
Descending the chequerboard plain
Where the apples and maize are,
45   Under the loop-holed gate
In the village wall
Where the goats clatter over the cobbles
And the intricate, straw-littered ways are . . .
The ancient watchman hobbles,
50   Cloaked, with his glasses of horn at the end of his nose,
With velvet short hose
And a three-cornered hat on his pate,
And his pike-staff and all;
And he carries a proclamation—
55   An invitation
To great and small,
Man and beast,
To a wedding feast;
And he carries a bell and rings . . .
60   From the steeple looks down a saint,
From a doorway a queenly peasant
Looks out, in her bride gown of lace,
And her sister, a quaint little darling
Who twitters and chirps like a starling.
65   And this little old place,
It's so quaint,
It's so pleasant,
And the watch bell rings and the church bell rings
And the wedding procession draws nigh,
70   Bullock carts, fiddlers and goods;
But I
Pass on my way to the woods
Thinking of things.

Years ago, I'd have stayed by the starling,
75   Marking the iridescence of his throat,
Marvelling at the change in his note;
I'd have said to the peasant child: 'Darling,
Here's a groschen and give me a kiss!' . . . I'd have stayed
To sit with the bridesmaids at table
80   And have taken my chance
Of a dance

78: *groschen:* a German 10-pfennig coin

With the bride in her laces
Or the maids with the blond, placid faces
And ribbons and crants in the stables. . . .

85   But the church bell still rings
And I'm far away out on the plain,
In the grey weather among the tobacco and grain,
And the village and gate and the wall
Are a long grey line with the church over all.
90   And miles and miles away in the sky
The starlings go wheeling round on high
Over the distant ranges.
The violin strings
Thrill away and the day grows more grey.
95   And I. . . . I stand thinking of things.
Yes, it's strange how one changes! . . .

1912

84: *crants:* garlands

EDWARD THOMAS (1878–1917)

THOMAS WAS BORN IN LONDON AND GREW UP IN LAMBETH, A LONDON SUBURB. HIS parents were Welsh, his father a civil servant. He was educated at Battersea Grammar School, St. Paul's School, and Lincoln College at Oxford University. While still at Oxford, he married Helen Noble, the daughter of the critic and editor James Ashcroft Noble. Following the birth of a son and Thomas's graduation, the family took up residence in Kent, often struggling with poverty. Having already published reviews and a first book, *The Woodland Life* (1897), Thomas continued his literary career by writing a series of biographical and topographical books, including a study of the Victorian naturalist Richard Jeffries. Thomas did not begin writing poetry until the last years of his life; Robert Frost is often credited with recognizing the poet in the prose writer, though Frost would later downplay his role. In 1915, Thomas enlisted in the Artists' Rifles and took up military life with great enthusiasm. He spent two years in England as a map-reading instructor and continued to write poems. In 1916, he was commissioned as a second lieutenant. A year later, he was sent to France. He was killed by a shell blast in the first hour of the Arras offensive on April 9, 1917.

Because many of his poems invoke rustic and natural settings and describe country encounters, Thomas is often grouped with the Georgian poets. But in writing to Frost he was openly critical of the "rhetorical" verse of Rupert Brooke, perhaps the most representative Georgian poet, and for all of their apparent conventionality in subject matter Thomas's poems often reject Georgian mannerisms of rhythm and diction. He shared with Frost an interest in the relationship of "speech and literature," admiring "simple words and unemphatic rhythms."[1] C. H. Sisson argues that "The irregularity and straggling rhythms of his verse, and the happy invention of his language, are far beyond what was achieved by more explicit innovators. And he understood as well as Ford Madox Ford or [Ezra] Pound that no poem could be good at all that contained definite purple patches."[2] In the end, Thomas is less descriptive "nature poet" than poet of melancholy introspection, especially in his shorter lyrics but also in longer narrative poems such as "The Other." Sisson observes that "The stimulus which occasions a poem does not overwhelm him; it rattles a chain of connections which take him back into the depths of his history."[3]

---

[1] Edward Thomas, *Selected Letters,* ed. R. George Thomas, Oxford, 1995, p. 112.
[2] *English Poetry 1900–1950,* London, 1971, p. 79.
[3] Ibid., p. 74.

The Other

The forest ended. Glad I was
To feel the light, and hear the hum
Of bees, and smell the drying grass
And the sweet mint, because I had come
5   To an end of forest, and because
Here was both road and inn, the sum
Of what's not forest. But 'twas here
They asked me if I did not pass
Yesterday this way. 'Not you? Queer.'
10   'Who then? and slept here?' I felt fear.

I learnt his road and, ere they were
Sure I was I, left the dark wood
Behind, kestrel and woodpecker,
The inn in the sun, the happy mood
15   When first I tasted sunlight there.
I travelled fast, in hopes I should
Outrun that other. What to do
When caught, I planned not. I pursued
To prove the likeness, and, if true,
20   To watch until myself I knew.

I tried the inns that evening
Of a long gabled high-street grey,
Of courts and outskirts, travelling
An eager but a weary way,
25   In vain. He was not there. Nothing
Told me that ever till that day
Had one like me entered those doors,
Save once. That time I dared: 'You may
Recall'—but never-foamless shores
30   Make better friends than those dull boors.

Many and many a day like this
Aimed at the unseen moving goal
And nothing found but remedies
For all desire. These made not whole;
35   They sowed a new desire, to kiss
Desire's self beyond control,
Desire of desire. And yet
Life stayed on within my soul.
One night in sheltering from the wet
40   I quite forgot I could forget.

A customer, then the landlady
Stared at me. With a kind of smile
They hesitated awkwardly:
Their silence gave me time for guile.
45   Had anyone called there like me,
I asked. It was quite plain the wile
Succeeded. For they poured out all.
And that was naught. Less than a mile
Beyond the inn, I could recall
50   He was like me in general.

He had pleased them, but I less.
I was more eager than before
To find him out and to confess,
To bore him and to let him bore.
55   I could not wait: children might guess
I had a purpose, something more
That made an answer indiscreet.
One girl's caution made me sore,
Too indignant even to greet
60   That other had we chanced to meet.

I sought then in solitude.
The wind had fallen with the night; as still
The roads lay as the ploughland rude,
Dark and naked, on the hill.
65   Had there been ever any feud
'Twixt earth and sky, a mighty will
Closed it: the crocketed dark trees,
A dark house, dark impossible
Cloud-towers, one star, one lamp, one peace
70   Held on an everlasting lease:

And all was earth's, or all was sky's;
No difference endured between
The two. A dog barked on a hidden rise;
A marshbird whistled high unseen;
75   The latest waking blackbird's cries
Perished upon the silence keen.
The last light filled a narrow firth
Among the clouds. I stood serene,
And with a solemn quiet mirth,
80   An old inhabitant of earth.

Once the name I gave to hours
Like this was melancholy, when
It was not happiness and powers
Coming like exiles home again,
85   And weaknesses quitting their bowers,
Smiled and enjoyed, far off from men,
Moments of everlastingness.
And fortunate my search was then
While what I sought, nevertheless,
90   That I was seeking, I did not guess.

That time was brief: once more at inn
And upon road I sought my man
Till once amid a tap-room's din
Loudly he asked for me, began
95   To speak, as if it had been a sin,
Of how I thought and dreamed and ran

67: *crocketed*: Crockets are small carved knobs in the shape of buds or curled-up leaves; in Gothic archi-
   tecture rows of crockets often decorate the edges of spires, pinnacles, etc.
77: *firth*: inlet

After him thus, day after day:
He lived as one under a ban
For this: what had I got to say?
100   I said nothing. I slipped away.

And now I dare not follow after
Too close. I try to keep in sight,
Dreading his frown and worse his laughter.
I steal out of the wood to light;
105   I see the swift shoot from the rafter
By the inn door: ere I alight
I wait and hear the starlings wheeze
And nibble like ducks: I wait his flight.
He goes: I follow: no release
110   Until he ceases. Then I also shall cease.

                                                                1914 / 1918

Adlestrop

Yes. I remember Adlestrop—
The name, because one afternoon
Of heat the express-train drew up there
Unwontedly. It was late June.

5   The steam hissed. Someone cleared his throat.
No one left and no one came
On the bare platform. What I saw
Was Adlestrop—only the name

And willows, willow-herb, and grass,
10   And meadowsweet, and haycocks dry,
No whit less still and lonely fair
Than the high cloudlets in the sky.

And for that minute a blackbird sang
Close by, and round him, mistier,
15   Farther and farther, all the birds
Of Oxfordshire and Gloucestershire.

                                                                1915 / 1917

The Wasp Trap

This moonlight makes
The lovely lovelier
Than ever before lakes
And meadows were.

5   And yet they are not,
Though this their hour is, more

98: *ban:* curse

Title: *Wasp Trap:* a jam jar, empty but still sticky, with water at the bottom to drown wasps.

Lovely than things that were not
Lovely before.

Nothing on earth,
And in the heavens no star,
For pure brightness is worth
More than that jar,

For wasps meant, now
A star—long may it swing
From the dead apple-bough,
So glistening.

1915 / 1918

A Cat

She had a name among the children;
But no one loved though someone owned
Her, locked her out of doors at bedtime
And had her kittens duly drowned.

In Spring, nevertheless, this cat
Ate blackbirds, thrushes, nightingales,
And birds of bright voice and plume and flight,
As well as scraps from neighbours' pails.

I loathed and hated her for this;
One speckle on a thrush's breast
Was worth a million such; and yet
She lived long, till God gave her rest.

1915 / 1918

Rain

Rain, midnight rain, nothing but the wild rain
On this bleak hut, and solitude, and me
Remembering again that I shall die
And neither hear the rain nor give it thanks
For washing me cleaner than I have been
Since I was born into this solitude.
Blessed are the dead that the rain rains upon:
But here I pray that none whom once I loved
Is dying to-night or lying still awake
Solitary, listening to the rain,
Either in pain or thus in sympathy
Helpless among the living and the dead,
Like a cold water among broken reeds,
Myriads of broken reeds all still and stiff,
Like me who have no love which this wild rain
Has not dissolved except the love of death,
If love it be for what is perfect and
Cannot, the tempest tells me, disappoint.

1916 / 1917

HAROLD MONRO (1879–1932)

A TIRELESS ADVOCATE OF MODERN POETRY IN MOST OF ITS FORMS, MONRO remains better known for having been for twenty years at the center of the poetry world in London than for his own poems. The son of an English engineer of Scottish ancestry, he was born in Belgium and attended public school at Radley and then Caius College at Cambridge. After work as a land agent in Ireland, he lived briefly in Haslemere, where he came into contact with a community of craftsmen dedicated to Fabian socialism and the ideals of William Morris. His famous Poetry Bookshop hosted its first public reading—or "poetry squash" as they were sometimes called—in January 1913. Devoted to the recitation or performance of poetry as a practice essential to the art and a means of securing an audience for new poetry, Monro was able to transcend the sometimes fractious divisions among poets of his era, hosting everyone from Futurists and Imagists to Georgians and, as editor and publisher, promoting their work. In his criticism he defended "experimenters breaking the old rules," while also arguing that "most of the best modern work is interesting as experiment rather than achievement."[1] The Poetry Bookshop published the five volumes of Edward Marsh's anthology *Georgian Poetry* (1912–22) and also Pound's *Des Imagistes* (1915). In 1912, Monro founded and edited the *Poetry Review* in association with the Poetry Society. *Poetry and Drama*, which he began in 1913, was brought to a premature end by World War I, in which Monro served with the Royal Artillery and Intelligence. From 1919 to 1929, he edited *Chapbook*. His volumes of poems include *Poems* (1906), *Judas* (1907), *Before Dawn* (1911), *Children of Love* (1916), *Strange Meetings* (1917), *Real Property* (1922), and *The Earth for Sale* (1928). A *Collected Poems* with introductions by F. S. Flint and T. S. Eliot appeared posthumously in 1933.

If Monro was eclectic in his tastes, leaning in the direction of the modernists, the trajectory of his poetry is also idiosyncratic. Eliot's introduction is at pains to distinguish the earlier poems from Georgian conventions, but poems such as "Week-End," about escaping to the countryside, or the once much-anthologized "Milk for the Cat" have little to do with the modernism of Pound, Eliot, and others. Conrad Aiken noted Monro's preoccupation with "daily, personal experience . . . observed almost religiously as it flows from moment to moment."[2] Eliot seems to be referring to the very late poem "Bitter Sanctuary," published in his journal *The Criterion* six months before Monro's death, when he writes that "the centre of his interest is never in the visible world at all, but in the spectres and the 'bad dreams' which live inside the skull, in the ceaseless

---

1 Quoted in Robert H. Ross, *The Georgian Revolt 1910–1922: Rise and Fall of a Poetic Ideal*, Carbondale, 1965, p. 64.
2 *Scepticisms: Notes on Contemporary Poetry*, New York, 1919, p. 212.

question and answer between two human beings. To get inside his world takes some trouble, and it is not a happy or sunny world to stay in. . . . The external world, as it appears in his poetry, is manifestly but the mirror of the darker world within."[3]

---

[3] "Critical Note," *The Collected Poems of Harold Monro*, ed. Alida Monro, London, 1933, pp. xv–xvi.

Bitter Sanctuary

I

She lives in the porter's room; the plush is nicotined.
Clients have left their photos there to perish.
She watches through green shutters those who press
To reach unconsciousness.
5   She licks her varnished thin magenta lips,
She picks her foretooth with a finger nail,
She pokes her head out to greet new clients, or
To leave them (to what torture) waiting at the door.

II

Heat has locked the heavy earth,
10   Given strength to every sound,
He, where his life still holds him to the ground,
In anæsthesia, groaning for re-birth,
Leans at the door.
From out the house there comes the dullest flutter;
15   A lackey; and thin giggling from behind that shutter.

III

His lost eyes lean to find and read the number.
Follows his knuckled rap, and hesitating curse.
He cannot wake himself; he may not slumber;
While on the long white wall across the road
20   Drives the thin outline of a dwindling hearse.

IV

Now the door opens wide.

He: "Is there room inside?"
She: "Are you past the bounds of pain?"
He: "May my body lie in vain
25   Among the dreams I cannot keep!"
She: "Let him drink the cup of sleep."

V

Thin arms and ghostly hands; faint sky-blue eyes;
Long drooping lashes, lids like full-blown moons,

Clinging to any brink of floating skies:
30   What hope is there? What fear?—Unless to wake and see
Lingering flesh, or cold eternity.

O yet some face, half living, brings
Far gaze to him and croons:
She: "You're white. You are alone.
35   Can you not approach my sphere?"
He: "I'm changing into stone."
She: "Would I were! Would *I* were!"
Then the white attendants fill the cup.

VI

In the morning through the world,
40   Watch the flunkeys bring the coffee;
Watch the shepherds on the downs,
Lords and ladies at their toilet,
Farmers, merchants, frothing towns.

But look how he, unfortunate, now fumbles
45   Through unknown chambers, unheedful stumbles.
Can he evade the overshadowing night?
Are there not somewhere chinks of braided light?

VII

How do they leave who once are in those rooms?
Some may be found, they say, deeply asleep
50   In ruined tombs.
Some in white beds, with faces round them. Some
Wander the world, and never find a home.

1933

MINA LOY (1882–1966)

L OY WAS BORN MINA GERTRUDE LOWY IN LONDON AND GREW UP IN BLOOMSBURY AND
West Hampstead. Her father emigrated from Hungary as a young man and became
a successful tailor's cutter in London and later a merchant; her mother came from a
lower middle-class family in suburban Bromley. Loy describes their courtship and
marriage in the section of the partly autobiographical long poem *Anglo-Mongrels and
the Rose* entitled "English Rose," in which her father is "Exodus" and her mother
"Alice" or the "English Rose." The conflict between her father's Jewish immigrant
identity and her mother's Evangelical background and high regard for English ances-
try and Victorian moral and cultural values helps account for much in Loy's work and
life. A kind of mysticism, for instance, seems to emerge in *Anglo-Mongrels and the
Rose* and is posed as an alternative to her mother's religious practice, which Loy found
to be based upon a denial of the profane world and the purportedly "impure" body.
Loy was educated in Hampstead and then at several art schools in London, Munich,
and Paris. She met her first husband, the painter Stephen Haweis, in Paris; most of
their unhappy marriage was spent in Florence among the English colony there. In
Florence she also met the Americans Carl Van Vechten, Mabel Dodge, and Gertrude
Stein, and the Italian Futurists F. T. Marinetti and Giovanni Papini. Loy's three "Ital-
ian Pictures" present vignettes of her life in Florence and surrounding areas; these are
perhaps the closest approximation to Futurist painting in English poetry. Loy's grow-
ing dissatisfaction with the militarism and misogyny of the Futurists is evident in sev-
eral early poems satirizing the movement, and also in her lyric sequence "Songs to
Joannes," portions of which were published by the American magazine *Others* prior to
Loy's arrival in New York in 1916 (the same journal would later publish the entire
sequence). In New York, Loy met the leading figures of the New York Dada art world
and the *Others* circle, including William Carlos Williams, Marcel Duchamp, and
Arthur Cravan, later to become Loy's second husband. Cravan's mysterious disap-
pearance or death in Mexico in 1918 would haunt Loy for the rest of her life and is
addressed in several of her poems. In New York, Loy was named by the *New York
Evening Sun* as the quintessential modern woman for her progressive stance vis-à-vis
art, poetry, fashion, and feminist politics. In 1923, Loy settled in Paris with her two
daughters. With the support of Peggy Guggenheim and Laurence Vail, she sustained
a business making and selling lamps, lampshades, and glass novelties, while continu-
ing to paint and to write poems and fiction; her novel *Insel,* based on her friendship
in the 1930s with the German surrealist painter Richard Oelze, was published posthu-
mously. After her business failed, Loy worked as the Paris agent for her son-in-law
Julien Levy's New York art gallery. In 1936, she returned to New York, where she lived
for many years in the Bowery, out of view of the literary and art worlds in which she
had briefly been a celebrity, though never forgotten by admirers including Duchamp,

Basil Bunting, Louis Zukofsky, Ezra Pound, Djuna Barnes, and Joseph Cornell. In 1953, Loy moved to Aspen to be near her daughters, and in 1958, Jonathan Williams and Jargon Books published a selection of her poems entitled *Lunar Baedeker and Time-Tables,* which began the nearly forty-year process of recovering her poetry for a wider public.

While Loy's poems, drawings, and paintings were published in some of the most famous avant-garde magazines of her day, the only book published in her lifetime prior to the Jargon edition was *Lunar Baedecker* (sic), which appeared in 1923. Across the decades of her critical neglect, including the years in the Bowery, when Loy seems to have been uninterested in publishing poems or exhibiting her assemblages based on observations of New York street life, Loy's reputation was sustained by just a few critical comments. Her polysyllabic poems, in which poeticisms are undermined and a seemingly non-poetic and arcane idiom is slowed by exaggerated alliteration and rhyme, had provoked Ezra Pound's discussion of *logopoeia,* that "dance of the intelligence among words and ideas," which Pound later glossed as poetry emphasizing "the context we *expect* to find with the word" for purposes of "ironical play."[1] Yvor Winters spoke of the movement of her poems "from deadly stasis to stasis" as it resulted in "an ominous grandeur, like that of a stone idol become animate and horribly aware," and of Loy's "strange feeling for the most subterranean of human reactions."[2] Loy had one exchange with John Rodker and knew British writers and artists such as Wyndham Lewis and Bunting, but her admiration for the United States and the support she received there during her career were such that she has often been thought of as an American poet; she was naturalized as an American citizen in 1946. But given her origins together with the influence of figures such as William Blake and Dante Gabriel Rossetti on her work, she deserves a place in British as well as American canons; indeed her work, like the work of much of the international avant-garde, shows the limits of such national categories. The critique of genteel customs in "English Rose" was almost entirely unknown in Britain during her lifetime, but it anticipates by forty years similar critiques offered by A. Alvarez and others in the 1960s and does so in a poetry altogether unlike any other written in the twentieth century.

---

[1] "Marianne Moore and Mina Loy" (1918), *Selected Prose 1909–1965,* ed. William Cookson, New York, 1973, p. 424; "How to Read" (1929), *Literary Essays of Ezra Pound,* ed. T. S. Eliot, New York, 1935, p. 25.
[2] "Mina Loy," *The Dial,* vol. 80, no. 6, 1926, p. 496.

Italian Pictures

JULY IN VALLOMBROSA

Old lady sitting still
Pine trees standing quite still
Sisters of mercy   whispering
Oust the Dryad

5   O consecration of forest
To the uneventful

We are indebted for some of our notes to Roger Conover's edition of Loy's selected poems, *The Lost Lunar Baedeker* (New York, 1996)

Loy "spent the summer of 1914 recovering from a nervous breakdown, psychological illness, or depression of some kind in the Apennine mountain village of Vallombrosa, province of Florence. . . . Only in the fall of 1914 would [she] return to 54, Costa San Giorgio, her hilltop residence in Florence (ca. 1907–16)." (Conover).

I cannot imagine anything
Less disputably respectable
Than prolonged invalidism in Italy
10   At the beck
Of a British practitioner

Of all permissible pastimes
Attendant upon chastity
The one with which you can most efficiently insult
15   Life
Is your hobby of collecting death-beds
Blue Nun

So wrap the body in flannel and wool
Of superior quality from the Anglo-American
20   Until that ineffable moment
When Rigor Mortis
Divests it of its innate impurity

While round the hotel
Wanton Italian matrons
25   Discuss the better business of bed-linen
To regular puncture of needles

The old lady has a daughter
Who has been spent
In chasing moments from one room to another
30   When the essence of an hour
Was in its passing
With the passionate breath
Of the bronchitis-kettle
And her last little lust
35   Lost itself in a saucer of gruel

But all this moribund stuff
Is not wasted
For there is always Nature
So its expensive upkeep
40   Goes to support
The loves
Of head-waiters

THE COSTA SAN GIORGIO

We English make a tepid blot
On the messiness
Of the passionate Italian life-traffic
Throbbing the street   up   steep
5   Up   up   to the porta

33: The inhalation of steam relieves the symptoms of *bronchitis*.

Title: The *Costa San Giorgio* is a steep street in Florence; Loy lived there amidst a community of English
 expatriates. At its top is the Porta San Giorgio gate (built 1324), decorated with a fresco by Bernardo
 Daddi which depicts the Virgin and Child with Saints Giorgio (George) and Sigismund.

Culminating
In the stained frescoe of the dragon-slayer

The hips of women sway
Among the crawling children they produce
10   And the church hits the barracks
Where
The greyness of marching men
Falls through the greyness of stone

Oranges half-rotten are sold at a reduction
15   Hoarsely advertised as broken heads
BROKEN HEADS   and the barber
Has an imitation mirror
And Mary preserve our mistresses from seeing us as we see ourselves
Shaving
20   ICE CREAM
Licking is larger than mouths
Boots than feet
Slip   Slap   and the string dragging
And the angle of the sun
25   Cuts the whole lot in half

And warms the folded hands
Of a consumptive
Left outside   her chair is broken
And she wonders how we feel
30   For we walk very quickly
The noonday cannon
Having scattered the neighbour's pigeons

The smell of small cooking
From luckier houses
35   Is cruel to the maimed cat
Hiding
Among the carpenter's shavings
From three boys
—One holding a bar—
40   Who nevertheless
Born of human parents
Cry when locked in the dark

Fluidic blots of sky
Shift among roofs
45   Between bandy legs
Jerk patches of street

Interrupted by clacking
Of all the green shutters
From which
50   Bits of bodies
Variously leaning
Mingle eyes with the commotion

For there is little to do
The false pillow-spreads

55   Hugely initialed
       Already adjusted
       On matrimonial beds
       And the glint on the china virgin
       Consummately dusted

60   Having been thrown
       Anything or something
       That might have contaminated intimacy
       OUT
       Onto the middle of the street

Costa Magic

                    Her father
       Indisposed to her marriage
       And a rabid man at that
       My most sympathetic daughter
5   Make yourself a conception
       As large as this one
       Here
       But with yellow hair

       From the house
10   Issuing   Sunday dressed
       Combed precisely
                    SPLOSH
       Pours something
       Viscous
15   Malefic
       Unfamiliar

       While listening up   I hear my husband
       Mumbling   Mumbling
       Mumbling   at the window
20   Malediction
            Incantation
       Under an hour
       Her hand to her side   pressing
            Suffering
25   Being bewitched
       Cesira fading
       Daily   daily   feeble   softer

       The doctor   Phthisis
       The wise woman   says to take her
30   So we   following her instruction
       I and the neighbour
       Take her—

       The glass rattling
       The rain slipping

15: *Malefic:* (of magic) causing harm or evil
28: *Phthisis:* consumption, tuberculosis

35 I and the neighbour and her aunt
Bunched together
And Cesira
Droops across the cab

Fields and houses
40 Pass   like the pulling out
Of sweetmeat ribbon
From a rascal's mouth
Till
A wheel in a rut
45 Jerks back my girl on the padding
And the hedges into the sky

Coming to the magic tree

Cesira becomes as a wild beast
          A tree of age

50 If Cesira should not become as a wild beast
It is merely Phthisis
This being the wise woman's instruction

Knowing she has to die
We drive home
55 To wait
She certainly does in time

It is unnatural in a Father
Bewitching a daughter
Whose hair   down   covers her thighs

1914 / 1923

from Anglo-Mongrels and the Rose

English Rose

Early English everlasting
      quadrate Rose
      paradox-Imperial
trimmed with some travestied flesh
5 tinted with bloodless duties   dewed
with Lipton's teas
and grimed with crack-packed
herd-housing
petalling

Loy's *Anglo-Mongrels and the Rose* is a long semi-autobiographical narrative poem; Exodus, introduced in the first section of the poem, is modeled on Loy's Jewish father; Alice (or sometimes "Ada") on her mother.
Title: The *rose* is the traditional symbol of England. Heraldic and symbolic representations are usually modeled on the dog-rose, whose flowers have somewhat squared-off ("quadrate") outer edges, and which bloom from late May or early June to early August.

10   the prim gilt
            penetralia
            of a luster-scioned
            core-crown

            Rose of arrested impulses
15   self-pruned
            of the primordial attributes
            a tepid heart   inhibiting
            with tactful terrorism
            the Blossom Populous
20   to mystic incest with its ancestry
            establishing
            by the divine right of self-assertion
            the post-conceptional
            virginity of Nature
25   wiping
            its pink paralysis
            across the dawn of reason
            A World-Blush
            glowing from
30   a never-setting-sun
            Conservative Rose
            storage
            of British Empire-made pot-pourri
            of dry dead men   making a sweetened smell
35   among a shrivelled collectivity

            Which august dust
            stirred by
            the trouser-striped prongs of statesmanship
            (whenever politic)
40   rises upon the puff of press alarum
            and whirling itself
            deliriously around the   unseen
            Bolshevik   subsides
            in ashy circularity
45   "a wreath" upon the   unknown
            soldier's grave

            And Jehovah   strikes—
            through the fetish
            of the island hedges—
50   Exodus
            who on his holiday
            (induced
            by the insidious pink
            of Albion's ideal)
55   is looking for a rose

            And the rose
            rises

11: *penetralia:* inner sanctum
54: *Albion:* traditional name for Britain

from the green
of a green lane
60   rosily-stubborn
and robustly round

Under a pink print
sunbonnet
the village maid
65   scowls at the heathen

        Albion
        in female form
        salutes the alien Exodus

staring so hard—
70   warms his nostalgia
on her belligerent innocence

The maidenhead
drooping her lid
and pouting her breast

75   forewarns
his amity

Amorphous meeting
in the month of May

This Hebrew
80   culled by Cupid on a thorn
            of the rose
lays siege
            to the thick hedgerows
            where she blows
85   on Christian Sundays

She
            simpering in her
            ideological pink
He
90   loaded with Mosaic
            passions that amass
            like money

            implores her to take pity upon him
            and come and be a "Lady in the City"

95   Maiden emotions
breed
on leaves of novels
where anatomical man
has no notion
100   of offering other than the bended knee
to femininity

84: *blows:* blossoms

and purity
passes in pleasant ways
as the cows graze

105   For in those days
when Exodus courted the rose
literature was supposed to elevate us

So the maid   with puffy
bosom   where Jerusalem
110   dreams to ease
his head of calculations
in the Zero of ecstasy
and a little huffy
bristles   with chastity

115   For this is the last Judgment
when Jehovah
roars   "Open your mouth!
and I will tell you what you have been reading"

Exodus had been reading
120   Proverbs
making sharp distinction
between the harlot
and the Hausfrau   arraying
her offspring in scarlet
125   approving
such as garner good advice like grain
and such as know enough
to come in from the rain

The would be
130   secessionist from Israel's etiquette
(shielding pliant Jewesses from shame
less glances
and the giving
of just percentages
135   to matrimonial intermediaries)
is spiritually   intrigued
by the Anglo-Saxon phenomenon
of Virginity
delightfully
140   on its own   defensive!

This pouting
pearl beyond price
flouts

120ff: cf. Prov. 7:6–27 (on the harlot) and 31:10–31 (on the virtuous woman: "all her household are clothed
with scarlet").
135: Traditional Jewish culture frowned on direct courtship; instead the services of professional match-
makers were employed.
142: *pearl beyond price*: cf. Matt. 13:45–46, where salvation is a "pearl of great price"; and Prov. 31:10: "Who
can find a virtuous woman? for her price is far above rubies."

the male pretentions
145   to its impervious surface

Alice the gentile
Exodus the Jew
after a few
feverish tiffs
150   and reparations
chiefly conveyed in exclamations—
a means of expression
modified by lack of experience—
unite their variance
155   in marriage

Exodus
Oriental
mad to melt
with something softer than himself
160   clasps with soothing pledges
his wild rose of the hedges

While she
expecting
the presented knee
165   of chivalry
repels
the sub-umbilical mystery
of his husbandry
hysterically

170   His passionate-anticipation
of warming in his arms
his rose   to a maturer coloration
which was all of aspiration
the grating upon civilization
175   of his sensitive organism
had left him

splinters upon an adamsite
opposition
of nerves like stalactites

180   This dying chastity
had rendered up no soul
yet they pursued their conjugal
dilemmas   as is usual
with people
185   who know   not what they do
but know   that what they do
is not illegal

177: *adamsite*: a greenish-black form of mica
185: cf. Christ's words of forgiveness on the cross: "Father, forgive them; for they know not what they do"
(Luke 23:34)

Deep in the névrosé
night   he
190   peruses his body
divested of its upholstery
        firmly insensitive
        in mimicry
of its hypothetical model—
195   a petal
of the English rose
an abstracted Ada
in myopic contemplation
of the incontemplatable
200   compound rosette
of peerless negations

That like other Gods
has never appeared
leaving itself to be inferred
205   Whereof
it is not seemly
that the one petal
shall apprehend
of the other petals
210   their conformity

For of this Rose
wherever it blows
it is certain
that an impenetrable pink curtain
215   hangs between it and itself
and in metaphysical vagrance
it passes beyond the ken
of men unless
possessed
220   of exorbitant incomes
And Then—
merely indicating its presence
by an exotic fragrance

A rose—
225   that like religions
before
becoming amateur—
enwraps itself
in esoteric
230   and exoteric
dimensions:
the official
and inofficial

188: *névrosé:* neurotic
197: *Ada:* another name for Alice
230: *Exoteric* knowledge is that permitted currency outside a circle of initiates or disciples (as opposed to
   esoteric knowledge).

        social   morale
235   The outer
        classes
        accepting the official
        of the inner
        as a plausible
240   gymnastic
        for disciplining the inofficial
        "flesh and devil"
        to the ap   parent impecca   bility
        of the English

245   And for Empire
        what form could be superior
        to the superimposed
        slivers
        of the rose?

250   The best
        is this compressed
        all round-and-about
        itself conformation
        never letting out
255   subliminal infection
        from hiatuses
        in its sub-roseal skeleton

        Its petals hung
        with tongues
        that under the supervision
260   of the Board of Education
        may never sing in concert—
        for some
        singing h
        flat and some
265   h sharp 'The Arch
        angels sing H'

        There reigns a disproportionate
        dis'armony
        in the English Hanthem
270 ·   And for further information
        re the Rose—
        and what it does to the nose
        while smelling it

        See *Punch*

1923, 1982

242: cf. the Litany in the Book of Common Prayer: "from all the deceits of the world, the flesh, and the devil, Good Lord, deliver us."

263: *h* in German music notation is (in English style) b-natural.

274: *Punch:* the noted English periodical, founded in 1841, and famous for its satirical humour and its caricatures and cartoons. The particular image Loy has in mind remains untraced.

Der Blinde Junge

The dam Bellona
littered
her eyeless offspring
Kriegsopfer
upon the pavements of Vienna

Sparkling precipitate
the spectral day
involves
the visionless obstacle

this slow blind face
pushing
its virginal nonentity
against the light

Pure purposeless eremite
of centripetal sentience

Upon the carnose horologe of the ego
the vibrant tendon index moves not

since the black lightning desecrated
the retinal altar

Void and extinct
this planet of the soul
strains from the craving throat
in static flight upslanting

A downy youth's snout
nozzling the sun
drowned in dumbfounded instinct

Listen!
illuminati of the coloured earth
How this expressionless "thing"
blows out damnation and concussive dark

Upon a mouth-organ

1923

Title: "The Blind Youth" (German)
1: *dam*: mother; *Bellona* was the Roman goddess of war.
4: *Kriegsopfer*: war victim
14: *eremite*: hermit
16: *carnose*: fleshy
    horologe: clock
17: *index*: hand of a clock
28: *illuminati*: people who claim arcane or special enlightenment

T. E. HULME (1883–1917)

"THE GREAT AIM IS ACCURATE, PRECISE AND DEFINITE DESCRIPTION," HULME wrote in his famous essay "Romanticism and Classicism." As polemicist, aesthetic theorist, and translator of the work of Continental thinkers such as Henri Bergson, Hulme's influence on the development of modernist poetry in English was considerable. Opposed to romanticism's "sentimental" view of man as "intrinsically good" and the emotionalism and "vagueness" of its poetry, he announced the dawn of a new "classical" era that would understand man as "intrinsically limited, but disciplined by order and tradition" and supplant "debauched" romantic conventions with "dry hardness" and exactitude.[1] In meetings and lectures at his Poets' Club in Soho, he promulgated the aesthetic ideas that would ultimately help shape Imagist poetry. From nineteenth-century French psychologists he took the concept of "l'image" and the theory that the immediate data of sensory experience are prior to language; from Bergson he took the idea that "intuition" offers a more holistic way of apprehending reality than reasoning or intellection. Such premises led to strictures against "abstract" language and "ornamental" imagery familiar to many students of modernist poetry and from Ezra Pound's early critical prose. One of Hulme's formulations was as follows: "Images in verse are not mere decoration, but the very essence of an intuitive language."[2] Hulme's poems try to juxtapose or simultaneously present images with a minimum of discursive apparatus; many of the comparatively few poems he wrote in his brief life were written to exemplify his core aesthetic principles.

Thomas Ernest Hulme was born in Endon in north Staffordshire. He attended Cambridge University until being dismissed, reportedly for a brawl with a policeman; he then studied science at University College, London. In 1906, he went to Canada, where he worked as a laborer on the western prairies. In 1907, he returned to England, and then lived in Belgium briefly before settling again in London. The proto-imagist poem "Autumn" was written and published in 1908; by 1909, Hulme's Poets' Club was attracting figures such as F. S. Flint and Ezra Pound. Wyndham Lewis, who called him "Hulme of Original Sin," was one of many visual artists and poets present at other meetings, held from 1911 until the start of the war, at Hulme's house in London. In 1914, Hulme enlisted in the Honourable Artillery Company. He was killed in France in 1917. His most famous poems first appeared as a group in *The New Age* and then as a postscript to Ezra Pound's *Ripostes* (1912). His essays were gathered and edited by Herbert Read as *Speculations* (1924). An edition of the collected poems and fragments together with selected essays appeared in 1998.

---

[1] *Selected Writings*, ed. Patrick McGuinness, Manchester, 1998, pp. 68–83.
[2] Ibid., p. 80.

Autumn

A touch of cold in the Autumn night—
I walked abroad,
And saw the ruddy moon lean over a hedge
Like a red-faced farmer.
5   I did not stop to speak, but nodded,
And round about were the wistful stars
With white faces like town children.

1912

The Embankment

(The fantasia of a fallen gentleman on a cold, bitter night.)

Once, in finesse of fiddles found I ecstasy,
In the flash of gold heels on the hard pavement.
Now see I
That warmth's the very stuff of poesy.
5   Oh, God, make small
The old star-eaten blanket of the sky,
That I may fold it round me and in comfort lie.

1912

Conversion

Lighthearted I walked into the valley wood
In the time of hyacinths,
Till beauty like a scented cloth
Cast over, stifled me. I was bound
5   Motionless and faint of breath
By loveliness that is her own eunuch.

Now pass I to the final river
Ignominiously, in a sack, without sound,
As any peeping Turk to the Bosphorus.

1912

These three poems first appeared in book form in an appendix to Ezra Pound's *Ripostes* (1912), "The Complete Poetical Works of T.E. Hulme."

Conversion: 7ff: It was the alleged practice of the Turks to dispose of unwanted wives or concubines by tying them in a sack and throwing them in the Bosphorus at night.

from Fragments

Old houses were scaffolding once
               and workmen whistling.

*

The lark crawls on the cloud
Like a flea on a white body.

*

The flounced edge of a skirt,
            recoiling like waves off a cliff.

*

When she speaks, almost her breasts touch me.
Backward leans her head.

1921

As a Fowl

As a fowl in the tall grass lies
Beneath the terror of the hawk,
The tressed white light crept
Whispering with hand on mouth mysterious
5   Hunting the leaping shadows in straight streets
By the white houses of old Flemish towns.

1960

Fragments: These fragments come from a selection posthumously published in *The New Age*.

ANNA WICKHAM (1884–1947)

Born in Wimbledon, Wickham spent her youth in Australia. She returned to London in 1905, attending Tree's Academy of Acting on a scholarship. After studying opera with De Reszke in Paris, she began a career as an opera singer, but later took up social welfare work with working-class mothers. Among the literary figures Wickham came to know while dividing her time between London and Paris was the American writer and patron Natalie Barney, with whom she corresponded between 1926 and 1937. Wickham was extraordinarily prolific as a poet, writing 1,400 poems in twenty years, many of them polemical satires of English middle-class life and all of them employing traditional and popular forms to emphasize a bluntly comic rhyming. Her criticism of the limits enforced on women's lives and sexuality by marriage is suggested by "Meditation at Kew," which Celeste Schenck views as "the poetic version" of her feminist manifesto *The League for the Protection of the Imagination of Women. Slogan: World's Management by Entertainment* (1938).[1] Widely anthologized in its day, Wickham's uneven writing has not fared well after its early fame but deserves to be known as an alternative to the feminist experimentalism of her contemporaries Mina Loy and Gertrude Stein. Her volumes of poetry include *The Man with a Hammer* (1916), *The Little Old House* (1921), and *Richards' Shilling Selections* (1936).

---

[1] *The Gender of Modernism: A Critical Anthology,* ed. Bonnie Kime Scott, Bloomington, 1990, p. 614.

Divorce

    A voice from the dark is calling me.
    In the close house I nurse a fire.
    Out in the dark cold winds rush free
    To the rock heights of my desire.
5   I smother in the house in the valley below,
    Let me out to the night, let me go, let me go.

    Spirits that ride the sweeping blast,
    Frozen in rigid tenderness,
    Wait! for I leave the fire at last
10   My little-love's warm loneliness.

I smother in the house in the valley below,
Let me out to the night, let me go, let me go.

High on the hills are beating drums.
Clear from a line of marching men
15   To the rock's edge the hero comes
He calls me and he calls again.
On the hill there is fighting, victory or quick death,
In the house is the fire, which I fan with sick breath.
I smother in the house in the valley below,
20   Let me out to the dark, let me go, let me go.

1916

Self Analysis

The tumult of my fretted mind
Gives me expression of a kind;
But it is faulty, harsh, not plain—
My work has the incompetence of pain.

5   I am consumed with slow fire,
For righteousness is my desire;
Towards that good goal I cannot whip my will,
I am a tired horse that jibs upon a hill.

I desire Virtue, though I love her not—
10   I have no faith in her when she is got:
I fear that she will bind and make me slave,
And send me songless to the sullen grave.

I am like a man who fears to take a wife,
And frets his soul with wantons all his life.
15   With rich unholy foods I stuff my maw;
When I am sick, then I believe in law.

I fear the whiteness of straight ways—
I think there is no colour in unsullied days.
My silly sins I take for my heart's ease,
20   And know my beauty in the end disease.

Of old there were great heroes, strong in fight,
Who, tense and sinless, kept a fire alight:
God of our hope, in their great name,
Give me the straight and ordered flame.

1921

8: *jibs*: refuses to proceed; balks

Meditation at Kew

Alas! for all the pretty women who marry dull men,
Go into the suburbs and never come out again,
Who lose their pretty faces and dim their pretty eyes,
Because no one has skill or courage to organize.

5   What do these pretty women suffer when they marry?
They bear a boy who is like Uncle Harry,
A girl who is like Aunt Eliza, and not new,
These old dull races must breed true.

I would enclose a common in the sun,
10   And let the young wives out to laugh and run;
I would steal their dull clothes and go away,
And leave the pretty naked things to play.

Then I would make a contract with hard Fate
That they see all the men in the world and choose a mate,
15   And I would summon all the pipers in the town
That they dance with Love at a feast, and dance him down.

From the gay unions of choice
We'd have a race of splendid beauty and of thrilling voice.
The World whips frank, gay love with rods,
20   But frankly, gaily shall we get the gods.

                                                              1921

D. H. LAWRENCE (1885–1930)

"HARDY WAS A MAJOR POET. LAWRENCE WAS A MINOR PROPHET," THE AMERICAN POET Kenneth Rexroth once wrote, adding that Lawrence belonged, like Blake and Yeats, to the "greater tradition."[1] While, unlike Rexroth, W. H. Auden believed that writers who are "both artists and apostles" risk neglect when their message is absorbed or repudiated, he admitted that in his own youth it was "Lawrence's message that seemed most powerful."[2] In novels such as *Women in Love* (1920) and prose books such as *Fantasia of the Unconscious* (1922), Lawrence proffered his views of the relationship of self and other, of love and sexuality, and human and non-human worlds. A few sentences from his essay on Edgar Allan Poe will suggest the fervor of his moral propositions: "The root of all evil is that we all want this spiritual gratification, this flow, this apparent heightening of life, this knowledge, this valley of many-coloured grass . . . giving ecstasy. We want all this without resistance. . . . We ought to pray to be resisted and resisted to the bitter end. We ought to decide to have done at last with craving."[3]

David Herbert Lawrence was born in Eastwood, Nottinghamshire, his father a miner, his mother an ex-schoolteacher. He attended Nottingham High School for three years and later Nottingham University College, studying for a teacher's certificate. In 1912, he met the German-born Frieda Weekley (neé von Richthofen), the wife of his professor at Nottingham, and eloped with her to Germany. Short of money, often in poor health and his marriage fraught, Lawrence nevertheless managed to write continuously while traveling to or living in Ceylon, Australia, the United States, and Mexico. His attraction to the cultures of the latter two nations is evident in many books and in his desire to found an ideal community in New Mexico.

Along with his novels and stories, literary criticism and travel books, Lawrence published ten books of poetry. Though some of his earliest poems appeared in the first of the famous Georgian anthologies, Lawrence's poems have generally found fewer supporters in England than in America, where his remarks on American life and literature have also won him admirers such as William Carlos Williams and Charles Olson. In the preface to the American edition of *New Poems* (1918), Lawrence criticized the "gem-like lyrics" of Shelley and Keats, arguing on behalf of a "poetry of the immediate present. In the immediate present there is no perfection, no consummation, nothing finished . . . Life, the ever-present, knows no finality . . . Give me noth-

---

[1] Introduction, D. H. Lawrence, *Selected Poems*, 1947, p. 4.
[2] "D. H. Lawrence," *The Dyer's Hand and Other Essays*, New York, 1962, p. 277.
[3] D. H. Lawrence, *Studies in Classic American Literature*, New York, 1923, p. 82.

ing fixed, set, static."[4] In poems such as "Pomegranate" and "Snake" from *Birds,
Beasts, and Flowers* (1923), Lawrence is able to mimic the buoyant informality of
speech in a manner that would lead the skeptical but admiring W. H. Auden to say
that "he wrote for publication in exactly the same way that he spoke in private."[5]

---

[4] Quoted in Auden, p. 297.
[5] Auden, p. 288.

Under the Oak

You, if you were sensible,
When I tell you the stars flash signals, each one dreadful,
You would not turn and answer me
'The night is wonderful.'

5   Even you, if you knew
How this darkness soaks me through and through, and infuses
Unholy fear in my vapour, you would pause to distinguish
What hurts, from what amuses.

For I tell you
10   Beneath this powerful tree, my whole soul's fluid
Oozes away from me as a sacrifice steam
At the knife of a Druid.

Again I tell you, I bleed, I am bound with withies,
My life runs out.
15   I tell you my blood runs out on the floor of this oak,
Gout upon gout.

Above me springs the blood-born mistletoe
In the shady smoke.
But who are you, twittering to and fro
20   Beneath the oak?

What thing better are you, what worse?
What have you to do with the mysteries
Of this ancient place, of my ancient curse?
What place have you in my histories?

1918

12: *Druids* were ancient Celtic priests; oak and mistletoe had important functions in Celtic religion, as did
  ritual human sacrifice.
13: *withies:* willow branches, used as cords

Pomegranate

You tell me I am wrong.
Who are you, who is anybody to tell me I am wrong?
I am not wrong.

In Syracuse, rock left bare by the viciousness of Greek women,
5   No doubt you have forgotten the pomegranate-trees in flower,
Oh so red, and such a lot of them.

Whereas at Venice,
Abhorrent, green, slippery city
Whose Doges were old, and had ancient eyes,
10   In the dense foliage of the inner garden
Pomegranates like bright green stone,
And barbed, barbed with a crown.
Oh, crown of spiked green metal
Actually growing!

15   Now in Tuscany,
Pomegranates to warm your hands at;
And crowns, kingly, generous, tilting crowns
Over the left eyebrow.

And, if you dare, the fissure!

20   Do you mean to tell me you will see no fissure?
Do you prefer to look on the plain side?

For all that, the setting suns are open.
The end cracks open with the beginning:
Rosy, tender, glittering within the fissure.

25   Do you mean to tell me there should be no fissure?
No glittering, compact drops of dawn?
Do you mean it is wrong, the gold-filmed skin, integument, shown
    ruptured?

For my part, I prefer my heart to be broken.
It is so lovely, dawn-kaleidoscopic within the crack.

1923

4: The reference is to "the stone quarries of ancient Greek Syracuse 'where the Athenian youths, prison-ers-of-war, died so horribly' (*Letters* iii.509)" (Lawrence, *Selected Poems*, ed. Mara Kalnins, London, 1992). *Syracuse* defeated the Athenian Sicilian Expedition during the Peloponnesian War.
   the viciousness of Greek women: "Presumably the triumph of the women over the Athenians imprisoned and dying in the latomy, the stone quarry, but there is no reference in [the contemporary historian] Thucydides to any 'viciousness'." (Kalnins)
9: The *Doge* was the highest official in Venetian government, until the office was abolished in the late eighteenth century.
27: *integument:* rind

Snake

A snake came to my water-trough
On a hot, hot day, and I in pyjamas for the heat,
To drink there.

In the deep, strange-scented shade of the great dark carob-tree
5   I came down the steps with my pitcher
And must wait, must stand and wait, for there he was at the trough before
  me.

He reached down from a fissure in the earth-wall in the gloom
And trailed his yellow-brown slackness soft-bellied down, over the edge of
  the stone trough
And rested his throat upon the stone bottom,
10   And where the water had dripped from the tap, in a small clearness,
He sipped with his straight mouth,
Softly drank through his straight gums, into his slack long body,
Silently.

Someone was before me at my water-trough,
15   And I, like a second comer, waiting.

He lifted his head from his drinking, as cattle do,
And looked at me vaguely, as drinking cattle do,
And flickered his two-forked tongue from his lips, and mused a moment,
And stooped and drank a little more,
20   Being earth-brown, earth-golden from the burning bowels of the earth
On the day of Sicilian July, with Etna smoking.

The voice of my education said to me
He must be killed,
For in Sicily the black, black snakes are innocent, the gold are venomous.

25   And voices in me said, If you were a man
You would take a stick and break him now, and finish him off.

But must I confess how I liked him,
How glad I was he had come like a guest in quiet, to drink at my water-
  trough
And depart peaceful, pacified, and thankless,
30   Into the burning bowels of this earth?

Was it cowardice, that I dared not kill him?
Was it perversity, that I longed to talk to him?
Was it humility, to feel so honoured?
I felt so honoured.

35   And yet those voices:
If you were not afraid, you would kill him!

21: Mount *Etna* is an active volcano on the east coast of Sicily.

And truly I was afraid, I was most afraid,
But even so, honoured still more
That he should seek my hospitality
40   From out the dark door of the secret earth.

He drank enough
And lifted his head, dreamily, as one who has drunken,
And flickered his tongue like a forked night on the air, so black,
Seeming to lick his lips,
45   And looked around like a god, unseeing, into the air,
And slowly turned his head,
And slowly, very slowly, as if thrice adream,
Proceeded to draw his slow length curving round
And climb again the broken bank of my wall-face.

50   And as he put his head into that dreadful hole,
And as he slowly drew up, snake-easing his shoulders, and entered farther,
A sort of horror, a sort of protest against his withdrawing into that horrid
      black hole,
Deliberately going into the blackness, and slowly drawing himself after,
Overcame me now his back was turned.

55   I looked round, I put down my pitcher,
I picked up a clumsy log
And threw it at the water-trough with a clatter.

I think it did not hit him,
But suddenly that part of him that was left behind convulsed in undigni-
      fied haste,
60   Writhed like lightning, and was gone
Into the black hole, the earth-lipped fissure in the wall-front,
At which, in the intense still noon, I stared with fascination.

And immediately I regretted it.
I thought how paltry, how vulgar, what a mean act!
65   I despised myself and the voices of my accursed human education.

And I thought of the albatross,
And I wished he would come back, my snake.

For he seemed to me again like a king,
Like a king in exile, uncrowned in the underworld,
70   Now due to be crowned again.

And so, I missed my chance with one of the lords
Of life.
And I have something to expiate;
A pettiness.

1923

66: Killing an *albatross* was bad luck, according to sailors; see Coleridge's *The Rime of the Ancient Mariner.*

Swan

Far-off
at the core of space
at the quick of time
beats
5   and goes still
the great swan upon the waters of all endings
the swan within vast chaos, within the electron.

For us
no longer he swims calmly
10   nor clacks across the forces furrowing a great gay trail
of happy energy,
nor is he nesting passive upon the atoms,
nor flying north desolative icewards
to the sleep of ice,
15   nor feeding in the marshes,
nor honking horn-like into the twilight.—

But he stoops, now
in the dark
upon us;
20   he is treading our women
and we men are put out
as the vast white bird
furrows our featherless women
with unknown shocks
25   and stamps his black marsh-feet on their white and marshy flesh.

1929

Willy Wet-Leg

I can't stand Willy wet-leg,
can't stand him at any price.
He's resigned, and when you hit him
he lets you hit him twice.

1929

6: See Gen. 1:2: "And the Spirit of God moved upon the face of the waters"; the Holy Spirit is tradition-
ally conceived of as a dove (as in, e.g., Milton, *Paradise Lost* 1.19–22).
20: *treading:* mating with

4: Willy obeys Christ's injunction to turn the other cheek (Matt. 5:39).

Andraitx.—Pomegranate Flowers

It is June, it is June
the pomegranates are in flower,
the peasants are bending cutting the bearded wheat.

The pomegranates are in flower
5   beside the high-road, past the deathly dust,
and even the sea is silent in the sun.

Short gasps of flame in the green of night, way off
the pomegranates are in flower,
small sharp red fires in the night of leaves.

10   And noon is suddenly dark, is lustrous, is silent and dark
men are unseen, beneath the shading hats;
only, from out the foliage of the secret loins
red flamelets here and there reveal
a man, a woman there.

1932

Bavarian Gentians

Not every man has gentians in his house
in soft September, at slow, sad Michaelmas.

Bavarian gentians, big and dark, only dark
darkening the day-time, torch-like, with the smoking blueness of Pluto's
    gloom,
5   ribbed and torch-like, with their blaze of darkness spread blue
down flattening into points, flattened under the sweep of white day
torch-flower of the blue-smoking darkness, Pluto's dark-blue daze,
black lamps from the halls of Dis, burning dark blue,
giving off darkness, blue darkness, as Demeter's pale lamps give off light,
10   lead me then, lead the way.

Reach me a gentian, give me a torch!
let me guide myself with the blue, forked torch of this flower
down the darker and darker stairs, where blue is darkened on blueness
even where Persephone goes, just now, from the frosted September
15   to the sightless realm where darkness is awake upon the dark
and Persephone herself is but a voice
or a darkness invisible enfolded in the deeper dark
of the arms Plutonic, and pierced with the passion of dense gloom,
among the splendour of torches of darkness, shedding darkness on the lost
    bride and her groom.

1929 / 1932

Title: *Andraitx:* a town and port area in the west of Majorca, one of Spain's Balearic Islands.

4: *Pluto:* ruler of Dis, the classical underworld. Persephone, the daughter of Demeter, goddess of agriculture, was abducted by Pluto when she was picking flowers. Demeter pleaded with Zeus for her daughter's return, but because Persephone had eaten some pomegranate seeds while below, she could only return to the world for half the year.

SIEGFRIED SASSOON (1886–1967)

S ASSOON IS BEST KNOWN FOR TWO BOOKS OF POETRY HE PUBLISHED DURING WORLD War I, *The Old Huntsman* (1917) and, especially, *Counter-Attack* (1918). He was raised at Weirleigh in western Kent, his father a descendant of Mesopotamian Jewish merchants, his mother, Theresa Georgiana Thornycraft, a gentile of the landed gentry. More sportsman than scholar, Sassoon was educated at New Beacon School and Marlborough College, and then briefly attended Clare College at Cambridge before enlisting in 1914. After a short stint with the cavalry, he was commissioned as an officer in the Royal Welch Fusiliers and saw his first combat in the Somme offensive, where 420,000 British soldiers were killed. In 1916, he was awarded the Military Cross for venturing unordered into no-man's-land to rescue wounded soldiers. Back in England, he met the pacifists in Lady Ottoline Morrell's circle and, in 1917, published "A Soldier's Declaration," protesting the "political errors and insincerities for which the fighting men are being sacrificed." He returned to combat in 1918 and was once more decorated for his bravery, before being shot in the head and evacuated to England. The years after the war saw other volumes, including the social satire of *Satirical Poems* (1926) and religious poems in advance of and following his conversion to Roman Catholicism in 1957, but the war remained Sassoon's subject in fictionalized memoir and autobiography.

The didacticism of Sassoon's famous war poems has not always fared well, especially among those readers who have assimilated the aesthetics of modernism. John Lucas writes that "What propels Sassoon into the most memorable of his war poems is that very English feeling of outraged decency. He loathed all the things it was proper to loathe: the callous incompetence of generals, the warmongering hysteria of those who did not have to fight, the hypocritical patriotism of the home front. In a clutch of poems he spoke out against these things, and he did so in ways that may be called verse journalism. His language is invariably reach-me-down, his rhythms slack or gruffly approximate. Just occasionally the journalism goes up a notch or two."[1] Others would insist that the direct colloquial speech and gruesome imagery of poems that document horrors like the encounter with a dead German soldier described in "The Rear-Guard" helped establish a newly "realistic" war poetry.

---

[1] *Modern English Poetry from Hardy to Hughes*, Totowa, NJ, 1986, p. 79.

A Working Party

Three hours ago he blundered up the trench,
Sliding and poising, groping with his boots;
Sometimes he tripped and lurched against the walls
With hands that pawed the sodden bags of chalk.
5   He couldn't see the man who walked in front;
Only he heard the drum and rattle of feet
Stepping along barred trench boards, often splashing
Wretchedly where the sludge was ankle-deep.

Voices would grunt 'Keep to your right—make way!'
10 When squeezing past some men from the front-line:
White faces peered, puffing a point of red;
Candles and braziers glinted through the chinks
And curtain-flaps of dug-outs; then the gloom
Swallowed his sense of sight; he stooped and swore
15 Because a sagging wire had caught his neck.

A flare went up; the shining whiteness spread
And flickered upward, showing nimble rats
And mounds of glimmering sand-bags, bleached with rain;
Then the slow silver moment died in dark.
20 The wind came posting by with chilly gusts
And buffeting at corners, piping thin.
And dreary through the crannies; rifle-shots
Would split and crack and sing along the night,
And shells came calmly through the drizzling air
25 To burst with hollow bang below the hill.
Three hours ago he stumbled up the trench;
Now he will never walk that road again:
He must be carried back, a jolting lump
Beyond all need of tenderness and care.

30 He was a young man with a meagre wife
And two small children in a Midland town;
He showed their photographs to all his mates,
And they considered him a decent chap
Who did his work and hadn't much to say,
35 And always laughed at other people's jokes
Because he hadn't any of his own.

That night when he was busy at his job
Of piling bags along the parapet,
He thought how slow time went, stamping his feet
40 And blowing on his fingers, pinched with cold.
He thought of getting back by half-past twelve,
And tot of rum to send him warm to sleep

Title: A *working party* is a small party of men, volunteered or under orders, got together to carry out some
  specific task (in this case sandbagging the trenches).
42: *tot*: a small (regulation) measure

In draughty dug-out frowsty with the fumes
Of coke, and full of snoring weary men.

45   He pushed another bag along the top,
Craning his body outward; then a flare
Gave one white glimpse of No Man's Land and wire;
And as he dropped his head the instant split
His startled life with lead, and all went out.

1916 / 1917

The Rear-Guard

(Hindenburg Line, April 1917)

Groping along the tunnel, step by step,
He winked his prying torch with patching glare
From side to side, and sniffed the unwholesome air.

Tins, boxes, bottles, shapes too vague to know;
5   A mirror smashed, the mattress from a bed;
And he, exploring fifty feet below
The rosy gloom of battle overhead.

Tripping, he grabbed the wall; saw some one lie
Humped at his feet, half-hidden by a rug,
10   And stooped to give the sleeper's arm a tug.
'I'm looking for headquarters.' No reply.
'God blast your neck!' (For days he'd had no sleep,)
'Get up and guide me through this stinking place.'
Savage, he kicked a soft, unanswering heap,
15   And flashed his beam across the livid face
Terribly glaring up, whose eyes yet wore
Agony dying hard ten days before;
And fists of fingers clutched a blackening wound.

Alone he staggered on until he found
20   Dawn's ghost that filtered down a shafted stair
To the dazed, muttering creatures underground
Who hear the boom of shells in muffled sound.
At last, with sweat of horror in his hair,
He climbed through darkness to the twilight air,
25   Unloading hell behind him step by step.

1917 / 1918

43: *frowsty:* stuffy, musty
44: *coke:* a type of fuel derived from coal

Subtitle: *Hindenburg Line:* a reserve system of trenches on the German Front; the British made an assault
  on it beginning on 9 April 1917—the Battle of Arras—but after a month of fighting had failed to break
  through it.
2: *winked:* flashed

The General

'Good-morning; good-morning!' the General said
When we met him last week on our way to the line.
Now the soldiers he smiled at are most of 'em dead,
And we're cursing his staff for incompetent swine.
5   'He's a cheery old card,' grunted Harry to Jack
As they slogged up to Arras with rifle and pack.

.   .   .   .

But he did for them both by his plan of attack.

1917 / 1918

2: *the line:* Troops on both sides on the Western Front in World War I occupied vast systems of trenches stretching through France and Belgium to the sea which served as shelter against attack; these were known as "the Line."
6: *Arras:* a town in northern France: the Arras sector of the Western Front was under British control.

EDITH SITWELL (1887–1964)

S ITWELL WAS BORN INTO AN ARISTOCRATIC FAMILY WITH AN AN ANCIENT NAME AND A reputation for eccentricity. Her father, Sir George Sitwell, is said once to have painted blue Chinese figures on his white cows to beautify the grounds at Renishaw Hall. Her younger brothers, Osbert and Sacheverell, also pursued literary careers. In her autobiography she writes of periods of unhappiness going back to a childhood in which "I was unpopular with my parents from the moment of my birth, and . . . in disgrace for being a female."[1] Gertrude Stein and the Russian painter Paul Tchelitchew are among the people she remembers with fondness. After self-publishing *The Mother and Other Poems* in 1915, Sitwell and her brothers edited the anti-Georgian publication *Wheels* (1916–1921). In 1923, she performed the poems from *Façade* first privately and then at London's Aeolian Hall to the accompaniment of music composed by William Walton. Noel Coward walked out on the performance, and others were outraged when Sitwell sat with her back to the audience speaking and chanting poems into a sengerphone (a bullhorn of sorts). What they took for a theatrical display of hostility Sitwell said was meant to force the audience to attend to the poetry's sonic qualities. Dismissed by F. R. Leavis as "belong[ing] to the history of publicity rather than of poetry," criticized by Geoffrey Grigson, Wyndham Lewis, and others, Sitwell fought back in the essays of *Aspects of Modern Poetry* (1934). After World War II, she enjoyed great success on lecture tours in the United States, but her reputation, always shadowed by controversy, began to fade in the late 1950s. In 1954, she was made Dame Commander of the Order of the British Empire. In 1955, she became a Roman Catholic. Other books include *Street Songs* (1942) and *Collected Poems* (1954).

Few today will accept at face value Sitwell's explanation of her experiments in *Façade*—she hoped, for instance, that using two rhymes placed together at the end of successive lines in "Fox Trot" would suggest "leaps in the air":[2] " 'Sally, Mary, Mattie, what's the matter, why cry?' / The huntsman and the reynard-coloured sun and I sigh." However, the reader will surely apprehend something of the rhythm of the dances particular poems seek to imitate or suggest, and the poems also deserve consideration for their social critique as it alternates with a lyricism sometimes approaching antic despair. Sitwell's poetry after *Façade* takes on different forms and tonalities; "The Canticle of the Rose" represents one of the first efforts to respond directly in poetry to the fact of nuclear weapons.

---

[1] Edith Sitwell, *Taken Care Of: The Autobiography of Edith Sitwell*, London, 1965, p. 15.
[2] Quoted in G. A. Cevasco, *The Sitwells: Edith, Osbert, and Sacheverell*, Boston, 1987, p. 28.

from Façade

4. Ass-Face

Ass-Face drank
The asses' milk of the stars . . .
The milky spirals as they sank
From heaven's saloons and golden bars,
5   Made a gown
For Columbine,
Spirting down
On sands divine
By the asses' hide of the sea
10   (With each tide braying free).
And the beavers building Babel
Beneath each tree's thin beard,
Said, 'Is it Cain and Abel
Fighting again we heard?'
15   It is Ass-Face, Ass-Face,
Drunk on the milk of the stars,
Who will spoil their houses of white lace—
Expelled from the golden bars!

1922

6. The Bat

Castellated, tall,
From battlements fall
Shades on heroic
Lonely grass,
5   Where the moonlight's echoes die and pass.
Near the rustic boorish,
Fustian Moorish
Castle wall of the ultimate Shade,
With his cloak castellated as that wall, afraid,
10   The mountebank doctor,
The old stage quack,
Where decoy-duck dust
Began to clack,
Watched Heliogabalusene the Bat
15   In his furred cloak hang head down from the flat
Wall, cling to what is convenient,
Lenient.
'If you hang upside down with squeaking shrill,
You will see dust, lust, and the will to kill,
20   And life is a matter of which way falls

The Bat: 1: *castellated:* having battlements, the gapped parapets at the top of castle walls.
7: *Fustian:* bombastic
14: *Heliogabalusene:* Heliogabalus, Roman emperor from AD 218–222, was infamous for his depravity and
  sensual excess.

Your tufted turreted Shade near these walls.
For muttering guttering shadow will plan
If you're ruined wall, or pygmy man,'
Said Heliogabalusene, 'or a pig,
25   Or the empty Caesar in tall periwig.'
And the mountebank doctor,
The old stage quack,
Spread out a black membraned wing of his cloak
And his shuffling footsteps seem to choke,
30   Near the Castle wall of the ultimate Shade
Where decoy-duck dust
Quacks, clacks, afraid.

                                                        1922

22. Fox Trot

                    Old
                        Sir
                            Faulk,
        Tall as a stork,
5   Before the honeyed fruits of dawn were ripe, would walk,
        And stalk with a gun
        The reynard-coloured sun,
        Among the pheasant-feathered corn the unicorn has torn, forlorn the
        Smock-faced sheep
10   Sit
            And
                Sleep;
        Periwigged as William and Mary, weep . . .
        'Sally, Mary, Mattie, what's the matter, why cry?'
15   The huntsman and the reynard-coloured sun and I sigh;
        'Oh, the nursery-maid Meg
        With a leg like a peg
        Chased the feathered dreams like hens, and when they laid an egg
        In the sheepskin
20   Meadows
        Where
        The serene King James would steer
        Horse and hounds, then he
        From the shade of a tree
25   Picked it up as spoil to boil for nursery tea,' said the mourners. In the
        Corn, towers strain,
        Feathered tall as a crane,
        And whistling down the feathered rain, old Noah goes again—
        An old dull mome

Title: *Fox Trot:* a popular dance (or its accompanying music)
7: *reynard:* fox
13: *William and Mary:* William of Orange, the Protestant son-in-law of Britain's Catholic King James II
    (1633–1701), invaded Britain in 1688 at the invitation of British rebels who opposed a Catholic monarchy.
    James fled the country; William and his wife Mary were then jointly offered the throne, becoming
    William III and Mary II.
29: *mome:* fool

30   With a head like a pome,
     Seeing the world as a bare egg,
     Laid by the feathered air; Meg
     Would beg three of these
     For the nursery teas
35   Of Japhet, Shem, and Ham; she gave it
     Underneath the trees,
     Where the boiling
     Water
       Hissed,
40   Like the goose-king's feathered daughter—kissed
     Pot and pan and copper kettle
     Put upon their proper mettle,
     Lest the Flood—the Flood—the Flood begin again through these!

1922

37. Sir Beelzebub

     When
     Sir
     Beelzebub called for his syllabub in the hotel in Hell
        Where Proserpine first fell,
5   Blue as the gendarmerie were the waves of the sea,

       (Rocking and shocking the barmaid).

     Nobody comes to give him his rum but the
     Rim of the sky hippopotamus-glum
     Enhances the chances to bless with a benison
10   Alfred Lord Tennyson crossing the bar laid
     With cold vegetation from pale deputations
     Of temperance workers (all signed In Memoriam)
     Hoping with glory to trip up the Laureate's feet,

       (Moving in classical meters) . . .

15   Like Balaclava, the lava came down from the
     Roof, and the sea's blue wooden gendarmerie
     Took them in charge while Beelzebub roared for his rum.

       . . . None of them come!

1922

30: *pome:* apple
35: *Japhet, Shem, and Ham:* the sons of Noah (and thus the ancestors of all mankind)

Title: *Beelzebub:* a Philistine god, in Christian interpretation god of the underworld and "prince of the
   devils" (Matt. 12:24). In Milton's *Paradise Lost* he is one of the chief devils under Satan.
3: *syllabub:* a drink made of milk, curdled with wine or cider and sweetened
4: *Proserpine:* daughter of the goddess Demeter; she was abducted by Hades, ruler of the underworld, who
   made her his queen.
5: *gendarmerie:* French police force
10ff: *Tennyson:* Sitwell alludes to Tennyson's "Crossing the Bar," *In Memoriam* and "The Charge of the
   Light Brigade" (which concerns the Crimean War's Battle of Balaclava).

The Canticle of the Rose

To Geoffrey Gorer

The Rose upon the wall
Cries—'I am the voice of Fire:
And in me grows
The pomegranate splendour of Death, the ruby, garnet, almandine
5   Dews: Christ's Wounds in me shine.

I rise upon my stem,
The Flower, the whole Plant-being, produced by Light
With all Plant-systems and formations. . . . As in Fire
All elements dissolve, so in one bright
10   Ineffable essence all Plant-being dissolves to make the Flower.

My stem rises bright:
Organic water polarised to the dark
Earth-centre, and to Light.'

Below that wall, in Famine Street
15   There is nothing left but the heart to eat

And the Shade of Man. . . . Buyers and sellers cry
'Speak not the name of Light—
Her name is Madness now. . . . Though we are black beneath her kiss
As if she were the Sun, her name is Night:
20   She has condemned us, and decreed that Man must die.'

There was a woman combing her long hair
To the rhythm of the river flowing. . . .
She sang 'All things will end—
Like the sound of Time in my veins growing:
25   The hump on the dwarf, the mountain on the plain,
The fixed red of the rose and the rainbow's red,
The fires of the heart, the wandering planet's pain—
All loss, all gain—
Yet will the world remain!'

30   The song died in the Ray. . . . Where is she now?
Dissolved, and gone—
And only her red shadow stains the unremembering stone.

Title: *Canticle:* a song or hymn ("The Canticles" are the Song of Solomon).
This poem is the last of "Three Poems of the Atomic Age" in Sitwell's *Collected Poems.* She wrote it "after
  reading that new vegetation was beginning to sprout at Hiroshima" (Victoria Glendinning, *Edith Sitwell:
  A Unicorn Among Lions,* London: 1981, p. 269).
4: *almandine:* a dark red garnet
6ff: "These verses contain references to Oken" (Sitwell). Lorenz Oken (1779–1851) was a German philoso-
  pher of natural science. "During 1947 and 1948 [Sitwell] had copied passages from Lorenz Oken's *Ele-
  ments of Physiophilosophy* into her working notebooks: 'An animal is a flower without a stem'; 'The plant
  is an animal retarded by the darkness, the animal is a plant blossoming directly through the light, and
  devoid of root.'" (Glendinning, p. 268).
30–32: "Transcript of an eye-witness' description of Nagasaki after the falling of the atomic bomb."
  (Sitwell)

And in Famine Street the sellers cry
'What will you buy?

35   A dress for the Bride?'
(But all the moulds of generation died
Beneath that Ray.)
                              'Or a winding-sheet?'
(Outworn. . . . The Dead have nothing left to hide.)

40   'Then buy' said the Fate arisen from Hell—
That thing of rags and patches—
'A box of matches!
For the machine that generated warmth
Beneath your breast is dead. . . . You need a fire
45   To warm what lies upon your bone. . . .
Not all the ashes of your brother Men
Will kindle that again—
Nor all the world's incendiaries!
Who buys—Who buys—?
50   Come, give me pence to lay upon my staring lidless eyes!'

But high upon the wall
The Rose where the Wounds of Christ are red
Cries to the Light
'See how I rise upon my stem, ineffable bright
55   Effluence of bright essence. . . . From my little span
I cry of Christ, Who is the ultimate Fire
Who will burn away the cold in the heart of Man. . . .
Springs come, springs go. . . .
'I was reddere on Rode than the Rose in the rayne.'
60   'This smel is Crist, clepid the plantynge of the Rose in Jerico.'

1948

50: Coins are traditionally placed on the eyes of the dead, supposedly to keep the lids from opening with
the onset of rigor mortis. Cf. also T.S. Eliot, *The Waste Land*: "Pressing lidless eyes and waiting for a
knock upon the door" (138). Other details here are similarly indebted to *The Waste Land*: compare line
21 with "A woman drew her long black hair out tight" (378); or the conclusion with Eliot's collage of quo-
tations (426–434).

59: "Anturs of Arthur, 1394" (Sitwell). Modern editions of *The Awntyrs off Arthure at the Terne Wathelyne*
give "I was radder of rode then rose in the ron" (161)—"I had a rosier complexion than the rose in the
thicket." (Sitwell instead takes "rode" to mean "rood"—the Cross.) The speaker is the ghost of Queen
Guinevere's mother, remembering her beauty when she was alive.

60: The source (slightly altered) is a sermon by the theologian John Wyclif (c.1320–1384) (*Selected Eng-
lish Works*, vol. I, Oxford, 1869, p. 108); "clepid": named. A note on the preceding page explains that "Jeri-
cho" means "place of fragrance."

ELIZABETH DARYUSH (1887–1977)

D ARYUSH WAS THE DAUGHTER OF POET LAUREATE ROBERT BRIDGES AND MARY Monica Waterhouse Bridges, whose father was the famous architect Alfred Waterhouse. Except for four years in Persia (Iran) with her husband Ali Akbar Daryush, she lived most of her life at Chilswell on Boar's Hill, overlooking Oxford. With some notable exceptions—appreciations by the American poet-critic Yvor Winters and, much later, the British poet-critics Roy Fuller and Donald Davie—her work has been little discussed. Winters, who thought that "England has not given us much notable poetry in the past two hundred and fifty years," wrote that she was the best English poet between T. Sturge Moore and Thom Gunn.[1] Daryush's use of syllabic meters, an alternative to the dominant modern English tradition of accentual-syllabic verse as well as to free verse, is one point of interest for Winters and others. The syllabic meter is present in "Still-Life," the last lines of which Winters found "unforgettable in the melancholy of their cadence."[2] "Children of wealth" is, by contrast, written in the more familiar accentual-syllabic meter. As Davie noted, both poems, like others Daryush began writing in the 1930s, show Daryush "registering and responding to the profound changes that have transformed the world of the English gentry"—the world she was born into—in the twentieth century.[3] She titled many of her collections simply *Verses,* the first in 1930. Six collections appeared in the 1930s, a *Selected Poems* edited by Winters in 1948, and *Verses: Seventh Book* in 1971. Her *Collected Poems* was published in 1976.

---

[1] *Forms of Discovery,* Chicago, 1967, p. 347.
[2] Quoted in Donald Davie, "The Poetry of Elizabeth Daryush," introduction to Elizabeth Daryush, *Collected Poems,* Manchester, U.K. 1976, p. 15.
[3] Davie, "The Poetry of Elizabeth Daryush," p. 15.

Still-life

Through the open French window the warm sun
lights up the polished breakfast-table, laid
round a bowl of crimson roses, for one—
a service of Worcester porcelain, arrayed
5   near it a melon, peaches, figs, small hot
rolls in a napkin, fairy rack of toast,

1: *French window:* a door-length, hinged window, which may be used as a door
4: *Worcester porcelain:* manufactured by the notable factory in Worcester (founded in 1751)

butter in ice, high silver coffee pot,
and, heaped on a salver, the morning's post.

10   She comes over the lawn, the young heiress,
from her early walk in her garden-wood
feeling that life's a table set to bless
her delicate desires with all that's good,

that even the unopened future lies
like a love-letter, full of sweet surprise.

                                            1936

"Children of wealth in your warm nursery"

Children of wealth in your warm nursery,
Set in the cushioned window-seat to watch
The volleying snow, guarded invisibly
By the clear double pane through which no touch
5   Untimely penetrates, you cannot tell
What winter means; its cruel truths to you
Are only sound and sight; your citadel
Is safe from feeling, and from knowledge too.

Go down, go out to elemental wrong,
10   Waste your too round limbs, tan your skin too white;
The glass of comfort, ignorance, seems strong
Today, and yet perhaps this very night

You'll wake to horror's wrecking fire—your home
Is wired within for this, in every room.

                                            1938

News-reel

A glare-lit wall-cliff; windows row on row
Glare-lit, too, from within; at each a face—
Three, four dazed faces—looking down, down . . . space
Is drawn out here; time pauses, crawls, slow, slow . . .
5   Those tiny too-short wisps of white, I know,
Are knotted sheets . . . Where is the reaching grace
Of fire-chute, ladder? . . . O delayed help, race
Rashlier . . . madly! . . . The picture passes . . . O

But how roused feeling follows it . . . first soars
10   To those high furnace-traps, with terror sees
The street's abyss . . . flies down then, stands afreeze
With powerless pity; then leaps hours, explores

In chill of dawn, rooms charred, sky-roofed, where mind
Stumbles, a stranger, fears what it may find.

                                            1971

"Children of wealth": 2: *window-seat*: an upholstered seat fixed inside a windowed recess or bay-window

EDWIN MUIR (1887–1959)

M UIR'S FAMILY WERE TENANT FARMERS IN THE ORKNEY ISLANDS TO THE NORTH OF Scotland's mainland. When he was fourteen, he and his family moved to Glasgow where, in just a few years, Muir's parents and two brothers died. Life in the Orkneys was agrarian and influenced by a strict Calvinism, which seems to have contributed to Muir's psychological distress and religious turmoil, but the Orkneys remained for him the site of an archetypal and idyllic order to contrast with the modern, industrialized life of Glasgow. His early poems and prose appeared in A. R. Orage's *New Age,* and Orage's advice to the entirely self-educated Muir to study one author closely helped generate aphorisms in the manner of the German philosopher Friedrich Nietzsche; these are collected in Muir's first book, *We Moderns* (1918). Muir married the classics scholar Willa Anderson in 1919, and they spent the years between 1919 and 1945 in various locations on the continent and in England and Scotland. For three years after World War II, he directed the British Institute in Prague until the consolidation of Communist control made life intolerable for him there. In 1950, he was named Warden of Newbattle Abbey College in Scotland. In 1955, he was the Charles Eliot Norton Professor of Poetry at Harvard.

Muir's criticism helped make him, with Hugh MacDiarmid, one of the two most influential Scottish writers of the first half of the century. Though he supported MacDiarmid's early poetry, Muir's relationship to the Scottish literary renaissance was always ambivalent, and after he wrote in *Scott and Scotland* (1936) that Scottish writers would best be served by adopting the English language and engaging English literary traditions, the two writers often criticized one another's work, MacDiarmid describing Muir's views of Scottish poetry and language as "deplorable" and "supercilious."[1] While the contrast with MacDiarmid has led some of Muir's critics to focus on the more normative idioms and textures of Muir's poems, it is worth remembering that the matter of Scotland—its cultural history as shaped by the two Unions and the deterministic philosophy and work ethic of Calvinism—was no less his concern than MacDiarmid's. Political and personal experience are typically refracted by his poems' abstract and mythopoeic mode, their address to the historical moment being, in the words of Seamus Heaney, "eschatological if somewhat somnambulistic."[2] Muir's poems often have as their first subject the relationship of time and the timeless or edenic; they draw on such diverse sources as Jung, Blake, the Old Testament, and Greek literature for myths and archetypes. The influence of the German poet Friedrich Hölderlin has been suggested by readers seeking to explain a language of "old gods and goddesses"; others point to Muir's description of his religious experi-

---

[1] *The Company I've Kept,* Berkeley, 1967, p. 143.
[2] "The Impact of Translation," *The Government of the Tongue,* London, 1988, p. 41.

ence in 1939 to suggest that, despite his never having become a churchgoing Christian, Muir's later work reflects a Christian Platonism. Other books include *The Labyrinth* (1949), *Collected Poems 1921–1951* (1952), and the critical survey *The Present Age* (1939). Muir also collaborated with his wife in translating the work of Franz Kafka.

The Old Gods

Old gods and goddesses who have lived so long
Through time and never found eternity,
Fettered by wasting wood and hollowing hill,

You should have fled our ever-dying song.
5   The mound, the well, and the green trysting tree,
They are forgotten, yet you linger still.

Goddess of caverned breast and channelled brow
And cheeks slow hollowed by millenial tears,
Forests of autumns fading in your eyes,

10   Eternity marvels at your counted years
And kingdoms lost in time, and wonders how
There could be thoughts so bountiful and wise

As yours beneath the ever-breaking bough,
And vast compassion curving like the skies.

                       1943

The Three Mirrors

I looked in the first glass
And saw the fenceless field
And like broken stones in grass
The sad towns glint and shine.
5   The slowly twisting vine
Scribbled with wrath the stone,
The mountain summits were sealed
In incomprehensible wrath.
The hunting roads ran on
10   To round the flying hill

The Three Mirrors: In a 1940 essay, "Yesterday's Mirror: Afterthoughts to an Autobiography," Muir wrote: "Art is the sum of the moments in which men have glanced into that yesterday which can never change . . . that mirror in which all the forms of life lie outspread." There are "three ways in which men may look into that mirror— . . . the glance of experience which discerns a world where wrong triumphs and right suffers; . . . the glance of the man who in maturity has kept a memory of his childhood" and "sees in the mirror an indefeasible rightness beneath the wrongness of things"; and the vision of the mystic, who sees "a world in which both good and evil have their place legitimately: in which the king on his throne and the rebel raising his flag in the market place, the tyrant and the slave, the assassin and the victim, each plays a part in a supertemporal drama which at every moment, in its totality, issues in glory and meaning and fulfilment."

And bring the quarry home.
But the obstinate roots ran wrong,
The lumbering fate fell wrong,
The walls were askew with ill,
Askew went every path,
The dead lay askew in the tomb.

I looked in the second glass
And saw through the twisted scroll
In virtue undefiled
And new in eternity
Father and mother and child,
The house with its single tree,
Bed and board and cross,
And the dead asleep in the knoll.
But the little blade and leaf
By an angry law were bent
To shapes of terror and grief,
By a law the field was rent,
The crack ran over the floor,
The child at peace in his play
Changed as he passed through a door,
Changed were the house and the tree,
Changed the dead in the knoll,
For locked in love and grief
Good with evil lay.

If I looked in the third glass
I should see evil and good
Standing side by side
In the ever standing wood,
The wise king safe on his throne,
The rebel raising the rout,
And each so deeply grown
Into his own place
He'd be past desire or doubt.
If I could look I should see
The world's house open wide,
The million million rooms
And the quick god everywhere
Glowing at work and at rest,
Tranquillity in the air,
Peace of the humming looms
Weaving from east to west,
And you and myself there.

                                              1946

The Horses

Barely a twelvemonth after
The seven days war that put the world to sleep,
Late in the evening the strange horses came.
By then we had made our covenant with silence,

5   But in the first few days it was so still
       We listened to our breathing and were afraid.
       On the second day
       The radios failed; we turned the knobs; no answer.
       On the third day a warship passed us, heading north,
10   Dead bodies piled on the deck. On the sixth day
       A plane plunged over us into the sea. Thereafter
       Nothing. The radios dumb;
       And still they stand in corners of our kitchens,
       And stand, perhaps, turned on, in a million rooms
15   All over the world. But now if they should speak,
       If on a sudden they should speak again,
       If on the stroke of noon a voice should speak,
       We would not listen, we would not let it bring
       That old bad world that swallowed its children quick
20   At one great gulp. We would not have it again.
       Sometimes we think of the nations lying asleep,
       Curled blindly in impenetrable sorrow,
       And then the thought confounds us with its strangeness.

       The tractors lie about our fields; at evening
25   They look like dank sea-monsters couched and waiting.
       We leave them where they are and let them rust:
       'They'll moulder away and be like other loam'.
       We make our oxen drag our rusty ploughs,
       Long laid aside. We have gone back
30   Far past our fathers' land.
                                    And then, that evening
       Late in the summer the strange horses came.
       We heard a distant tapping on the road,
       A deepening drumming; it stopped, went on again
35   And at the corner changed to hollow thunder.
       We saw the heads
       Like a wild wave charging and were afraid.
       We had sold our horses in our fathers' time
       To buy new tractors. Now they were strange to us
40   As fabulous steeds set on an ancient shield
       Or illustrations in a book of knights.
       We did not dare go near them. Yet they waited,
       Stubborn and shy, as if they had been sent
       By an old command to find our whereabouts
45   And that long-lost archaic companionship.
       In the first moment we had never a thought
       That they were creatures to be owned and used.
       Among them were some half-a-dozen colts
       Dropped in some wilderness of the broken world,
50   Yet new as if they had come from their own Eden.
       Since then they have pulled our ploughs and borne our loads,
       But that free servitude still can pierce our hearts.
       Our life is changed; their coming our beginning.

                                                    1956

T. S. ELIOT (1888–1965)

ELIOT'S *THE WASTE LAND* WAS FIRST PUBLISHED IN THE INAUGURAL ISSUE OF HIS journal *The Criterion* in October 1922 and appeared in the United States a few weeks later in the November issue of the *Dial*. American and British editions, with Eliot's notes added, followed in the next months. English reviewers met the poem with a mixture of respect and befuddlement, the critic J. C. Squire calling the poem incomprehensible, but it was not long until the poem was widely recognized as the "justification" of the "modern movement," to use the words of Eliot's associate Ezra Pound. Eliot's biographer Peter Ackroyd notes that much of the poem's early fame was due not to reviewers but to "undergraduates and young writers who saw it as a revelation of a modern sensibility."[1] The poem quickly became crucial to a criticism it helped shape—the work of I. A. Richards, William Empson, and F. R. Leavis in England, and of "New Critics" such as Robert Penn Warren and Cleanth Brooks in the United States. These critics in turn defined the study of modern literature in the decades ahead as modernism entered the university. Leavis's remarks in *New Bearings in English Poetry* (1932) about the "rich disorganization of the poem" are typical of early efforts to link the poem's form and methods to a post-war crisis: "The seeming disjointedness is intimately related to the erudition that has annoyed so many readers and to the wealth of literary borrowings and allusions. These characteristics reflect the present state of civilization. The traditions and cultures have mingled, and the historical imagination makes the past contemporary; no one tradition can digest so great a variety of materials, and the result is a break-down of forms and the irrevocable loss of that sense of absoluteness which seems necessary to a robust culture."[2] The idea that the poem's montage of voices and idioms and its juxtaposition of fragments from St. Augustine, Dante, Shakespeare, Baudelaire, Verlaine, music-hall jingles, and other sources was only a "seeming disjointedness" encouraged readings that restored unity to the poem beyond its fractured surface. Here Eliot's notes to the poems concerning Jessie Weston's and Sir James Frazer's studies of Grail romance and "primitive" fertility rituals seemed helpful in considering the thematic elements of the poem, as did remarks in Eliot's own criticism, such as his description of the "mythic method" of James Joyce's *Ulysses*: "In using the myth, in manipulating a continuous parallel between contemporaneity and antiquity, Mr. Joyce is pursuing a method which others must pursue after him. . . . It is simply a way of controlling, or ordering, of giving a shape to the immense panorama of futility and anarchy which is contemporary his-

---

[1] *T. S. Eliot: A Life,* New York, 1984, p. 128.
[2] *New Bearings in English Poetry,* London, 1932, p. 90.

tory."[3] *The Waste Land*'s networks of allusions and symbols were also often read for their expression of an alienated view of modern urban life and sexuality. This well-meaning and often useful criticism probably contributed to the poem's reputation for obscurity, which Pound disputed as early as 1924, describing the poem as "an emotional unit" and insisting that it did not matter to his enjoyment of the poem that he had not read Jessie Weston: "This demand for clarity in every particular of a work, whether essential or not, reminds me of the Pre-Raphaelite painter who was doing a twilight scene but rowed across the river in daytime to see the shape of the leaves on the further bank, which he then drew in with further detail."[4]

Hugh Kenner argued in a book written at the height of Eliot's international and academic reputation that Eliot "commands vast influence, partly through moral consistency, partly through inscrutability, partly because, in an academic context, his prose is so quotable. The details of his poetic effects, furthermore, belong to an extremely conventional category: the tradition of the turned aphorism and the weighty line. That they also subvert this tradition is a consideration that has vaguely troubled many readers, who accordingly suppose that the poet and the tradition-loving critic are two different men."[5] As Eliot's "vast influence" was due in part to his criticism, it is useful to cite a few of its most famous claims and definitions. In "Tradition and the Individual Talent," one of the essays collected in *The Sacred Wood* (1920), Eliot stated his "Impersonal theory of poetry": "the more perfect the artist, the more completely separate in him will be the man who suffers and the mind which creates; the more perfectly will the mind digest and transmute the passions which are its materials." In the same essay he argued for a mode of criticism "directed not upon the poet but upon the poetry," and he defined "tradition" as "a living whole of all the poetry that has ever been written," an "ideal order" of "monuments" that is "modified by the introduction of the new (the really new) work of art among them." In "Hamlet," an essay in the same volume, he argued for a mode of poetic expression that would seek out and use an "objective correlative": "The only way of expressing emotion in the form of art is by finding an 'objective correlative'; in other words, a set of objects, a situation, a chain of events which shall be the formula of that particular emotion; such that when the external facts, which must terminate in sensory experience, are given, the emotion is immediately evoked." These remarks together with Eliot's efforts on behalf of Dante, Metaphysical poetry, and Jacobean drama, his devaluation (at first) of Milton's poetry and chastising of Georgians for their "inbred" poetry were part of a campaign that helped to establish an Anglo-American critical consensus that obtained for nearly forty years. From the 1930s forward, Eliot's interest in "the mind of Europe" was expressed in a criticism increasingly conservative and neo-classical in its values. His subjects expanded to religion, culture, and education in books such as *For Lancelot Andrewes* (1928), *After Strange Gods* (1934), *The Idea of a Christian Society* (1940), and *Notes Towards the Definition of Culture* (1948). His description of Stuart England in the late sixteenth and early seventeenth century as an ideal society with an "autocratic civil Government" which "controlled and worked with a strongly national Church"; his outlining of a "dissociation of sensibility" in modernity; and his description of himself in 1928 as a "classicist in literature, royalist in politics, and Anglo-Catholic in religion" reflected views influenced by writers such as Charles Maurras and Julien Benda. Eliot's emphasis was increasingly on the value of order and hierarchy. *After Strange Gods*, "Gerontion," and a few other poems in his second volume contain anti-Semitic passages.

After the publication of *Four Quartets* (1935–1942), it became tempting to map a trajectory in Eliot's poetry moving from the "fragments . . . shored against my ruins" in *The Waste Land* to the "drawing of this Love and the voice of this Calling" in "Lit-

---

3 "Ulysses, Order, and Myth" (1923), *Poems and Prose*, New York, 1998, p. 218.
4 Quoted in Hugh Kenner, *The Invisible Poet: T. S. Eliot*, New York, 1959, p. 152.
5 Kenner, p. x.

tle Gidding" (1942) twenty years later, from post-World War I devastation to an affirmation of faith and England amid World War II. Stylistically, the poems of *Four Quartets* are very different from *The Waste Land*. Whereas, Kenner writes, the earlier poem worked "by accumulation" and did not "relax its mantic intensity," what distinguished the later work was "sinuous easy gravity," "meditative poise," and "pellucid certainty of cadence and diction."[6] David Perkins describes the *Four Quartets'* return to "the language of reflection and generation," adding that the poems are "the culmination of twentieth-century symbolism": "the title proposes that the poem resembles music. Specific lines and passages activate the semantic suggestions and emotional overtones of words while precluding determinate meaning. Eliot impedes denotation by verbal contradiction, vagueness, ambiguousness, failure of logical sequence, and paradox."[7] The poems' settings include both the United States and Britain, thereby following Eliot's family history and concluding with the poet in England. Their central subject is time—the relationship of the eternal and the temporal, which are seen to intersect in the Church. "Little Gidding's" resonant conclusion, in which "the fire and the rose are one," resolves the paradoxes explored throughout *Four Quartets*.

Eliot was born in St. Louis. His father was a successful businessman and his mother an amateur poet, active with charities and cultural events. His grandfather was a Unitarian minister from New England who went on to found Washington University in St. Louis. Eliot was educated at Harvard, where he studied subjects including Sanskrit and Indian literature and came under the influence of the humanist Irving Babbitt. It is during this period that he read Arthur Symons' *The Symbolist Movement in Literature* (1899), which introduced him to nineteenth-century French poets including Jules Laforgue, one of the sources of the version of modernist irony evident in "Prufrock" and other of Eliot's early poems. Eliot then studied at the Sorbonne in Paris and at Merton College, Oxford, where he finished a doctoral thesis on the idealist philosopher F. H. Bradley (he was never to return to Harvard to accept the degree). In 1914 he met Pound, who convinced him to settle permanently in England. In the same year, "The Love Song of J. Alfred Prufrock," one of a series of poems completed before Eliot met Pound, was published in *Poetry* magazine. The following year he married Vivien Haigh-Wood. The marriage was troubled, and the couple separated in 1932; Haigh-Wood died in an institution in 1947. Eliot taught briefly before beginning a career at Lloyds Bank in London in 1917, also the year his first book, *Prufrock and Other Observations*, was published. *Poems* followed in 1919. He became assistant editor of *The Egoist* and, in 1922, began his quarterly *The Criterion*. Elizabethan and Jacobean drama had been a significant influence on Eliot's poetry from the beginning, and after *The Waste Land* and "Ash-Wednesday" (1930), Eliot's attention turned increasingly to poetic drama. His plays *The Rock* (1934), *Murder in the Cathedral* (1935), *The Family Reunion* (1939), *The Cocktail Party* (1950), *The Confidential Clerk* (1954), and *The Elder Statesmen* (1959) met with varying success. In 1925, Eliot left Lloyds to work for the publishing house Faber and Faber, where the poets he was eventually to publish included W. H. Auden, Stephen Spender, Joseph Macleod, Lynette Roberts, Charles Madge, Edwin Muir, Dylan Thomas, David Jones, and George Barker. Eliot became a British subject and a member of the Anglican church in 1927. In 1948, he was awarded the Nobel Prize for Literature. He married his second wife, Valerie Fletcher, in 1957.

---

6 Ibid., p. 290.
7 *A History of Modern Poetry: Modernism and After*, Cambridge, MA, 1987, p. 27.

The Love Song of J. Alfred Prufrock

S'io credessi che mia risposta fosse
a persona che mai tornasse al mondo,
questa fiamma staria senza più scosse.
Ma per ciò che giammai di questo fondo
non tornò vivo alcun, s'i'odo il vero,
senza tema d'infamia ti rispondo.

Let us go then, you and I,
When the evening is spread out against the sky
Like a patient etherised upon a table;
Let us go, through certain half-deserted streets,
5   The muttering retreats
Of restless nights in one-night cheap hotels
And sawdust restaurants with oyster-shells:
Streets that follow like a tedious argument
Of insidious intent
10   To lead you to an overwhelming question . . .
Oh, do not ask, 'What is it?'
Let us go and make our visit.

In the room the women come and go
Talking of Michelangelo.

15   The yellow fog that rubs its back upon the window-panes,
The yellow smoke that rubs its muzzle on the window-panes,
Licked its tongue into the corners of the evening,
Lingered upon the pools that stand in drains,
Let fall upon its back the soot that falls from chimneys,
20   Slipped by the terrace, made a sudden leap,
And seeing that it was a soft October night,
Curled once about the house, and fell asleep.

And indeed there will be time
For the yellow smoke that slides along the street
25   Rubbing its back upon the window-panes;
There will be time, there will be time
To prepare a face to meet the faces that you meet;
There will be time to murder and create,
And time for all the works and days of hands
30   That lift and drop a question on your plate;
Time for you and time for me,
And time yet for a hundred indecisions,
And for a hundred visions and revisions,
Before the taking of a toast and tea.

Epigraph: These words are spoken by Guido de Montefeltro, whose soul is encountered by Dante in the eighth Circle of Hell in the *Inferno*. Enrobed in fire, he can only speak through a tongue of flame. "If I thought my answer were to one who would return to the world, this flame would shake no more. But since no-one has ever returned alive from this depth, if what I hear is true, I answer you without fear of infamy" (*Inferno* 27.61–66).
29: *Works and Days,* by the Greek poet Hesiod (fl. 700 BC), is a didactic poem celebrating agricultural labor.

35   In the room the women come and go
         Talking of Michelangelo.

         And indeed there will be time
         To wonder, 'Do I dare?' and, 'Do I dare?'
         Time to turn back and descend the stair,
40   With a bald spot in the middle of my hair—
         (They will say: 'How his hair is growing thin!')
         My morning coat, my collar mounting firmly to the chin,
         My necktie rich and modest, but asserted by a simple pin—
         (They will say: 'But how his arms and legs are thin!')
45   Do I dare
         Disturb the universe?
         In a minute there is time
         For decisions and revisions which a minute will reverse.

         For I have known them all already, known them all—
50   Have known the evenings, mornings, afternoons,
         I have measured out my life with coffee spoons;
         I know the voices dying with a dying fall
         Beneath the music from a farther room.
               So how should I presume?

55   And I have known the eyes already, known them all—
         The eyes that fix you in a formulated phrase,
         And when I am formulated, sprawling on a pin,
         When I am pinned and wriggling on the wall,
         Then how should I begin
60   To spit out all the butt-ends of my days and ways?
               And how should I presume?

         And I have known the arms already, known them all—
         Arms that are braceleted and white and bare
         (But in the lamplight, downed with light brown hair!)
65   Is it perfume from a dress
         That makes me so digress?
         Arms that lie along a table, or wrap about a shawl.
               And should I then presume?
               And how should I begin?

                     .   .   .   .   .

70   Shall I say, I have gone at dusk through narrow streets
         And watched the smoke that rises from the pipes
         Of lonely men in shirt-sleeves, leaning out of windows? . . .

         I should have been a pair of ragged claws
         Scuttling across the floors of silent seas.

                     .   .   .   .   .

75   And the afternoon, the evening, sleeps so peacefully!
         Smoothed by long fingers,
         Asleep . . . tired . . . or it malingers,

─────────────────────

52: See *Twelfth Night* (1.1.4): "That strain again, it had a dying fall."

Stretched on the floor, here beside you and me.
Should I, after tea and cakes and ices,
80   Have the strength to force the moment to its crisis?
But though I have wept and fasted, wept and prayed,
Though I have seen my head (grown slightly bald) brought in upon a platter,
I am no prophet—and here's no great matter;
I have seen the moment of my greatness flicker,
85   And I have seen the eternal Footman hold my coat, and snicker,
And in short, I was afraid.

    And would it have been worth it, after all,
After the cups, the marmalade, the tea,
Among the porcelain, among some talk of you and me,
90   Would it have been worth while,
To have bitten off the matter with a smile,
To have squeezed the universe into a ball
To roll it towards some overwhelming question,
To say: 'I am Lazarus, come from the dead,
95   Come back to tell you all, I shall tell you all'—
If one, settling a pillow by her head,
    Should say: 'That is not what I meant at all.
    That is not it, at all.'

    And would it have been worth it, after all,
100   Would it have been worth while,
After the sunsets and the dooryards and the sprinkled streets,
After the novels, after the teacups, after the skirts that trail along the
      floor—
And this, and so much more?—
It is impossible to say just what I mean!
105   But as if a magic lantern threw the nerves in patterns on a screen:
Would it have been worth while
If one, settling a pillow or throwing off a shawl,
And turning toward the window, should say:
    'That is not it at all,
110   That is not what I meant, at all.'

      .   .   .   .   .

    No! I am not Prince Hamlet, nor was meant to be;
Am an attendant lord, one that will do
To swell a progress, start a scene or two,
Advise the prince; no doubt, an easy tool,
115   Deferential, glad to be of use,
Politic, cautious, and meticulous;
Full of high sentence, but a bit obtuse;

82: John the Baptist was executed by Herod in order to please Salome, who had requested his head on a
   platter (Mark 6:14–29; Matt. 14:1–12).
92: cf. "To His Coy Mistress" by Andrew Marvell (1621–1678): "Let us roll all our strength, and all / Our
   sweetness, up into one ball: / And tear our pleasures with rough strife, / Thorough the iron gates of life."
94: *Lazarus:* the man raised by Christ from the dead (John 11:1–44); see also the different Lazarus of the
   parable of Dives and Lazarus (Luke 16:19–31).
113: *progress:* a royal journey, upon which the sovereign would be accompanied by his courtiers
117ff: The description here recalls Polonius in *Hamlet. high sentence:* lofty speeches; sententiousness

At times, indeed, almost ridiculous—
Almost, at times, the Fool.

120   I grow old . . . I grow old . . .
I shall wear the bottoms of my trousers rolled.

Shall I part my hair behind? Do I dare to eat a peach?
I shall wear white flannel trousers, and walk upon the beach.
I have heard the mermaids singing, each to each.

125   I do not think that they will sing to me.

I have seen them riding seaward on the waves
Combing the white hair of the waves blown back
When the wind blows the water white and black.

We have lingered in the chambers of the sea
130   By sea-girls wreathed with seaweed red and brown
Till human voices wake us, and we drown.

1910–1911 / 1917

Gerontion

*Thou hast nor youth nor age
But as it were an after dinner sleep
Dreaming of both.*

Here I am, an old man in a dry month,
Being read to by a boy, waiting for rain.
I was neither at the hot gates
Nor fought in the warm rain
5   Nor knee deep in the salt marsh, heaving a cutlass,
Bitten by flies, fought.
My house is a decayed house,
And the Jew squats on the window sill, the owner,
Spawned in some estaminet of Antwerp,
10   Blistered in Brussels, patched and peeled in London.
The goat coughs at night in the field overhead;
Rocks, moss, stonecrop, iron, merds.
The woman keeps the kitchen, makes tea,
Sneezes at evening, poking the peevish gutter.
15   I an old man,
A dull head among windy spaces.

Title: "little old man" (Greek)
Epigraph: *Measure for Measure* 3.1.32–34; the Duke, disguised as a friar, is consoling the condemned
   Claudio by telling him of the transience and futility of life.
3: Thermopylae (literally "hot gates"), a narrow pass on the east coast of central Greece, was the location
   of a battle between the Greeks and invading Persians in 480 BC.
9: *estaminet:* tavern
12: *stonecrop:* a type of plant that grows on rocks and walls
     merds: excrement
14: *gutter.*i.e., guttering fire

Signs are taken for wonders. 'We would see a sign!'
The word within a word, unable to speak a word,
Swaddled with darkness. In the juvescence of the year
20   Came Christ the tiger

In depraved May, dogwood and chestnut, flowering judas,
To be eaten, to be divided, to be drunk
Among whispers; by Mr. Silvero
With caressing hands, at Limoges
25   Who walked all night in the next room;
By Hakagawa, bowing among the Titians;
By Madame de Tornquist, in the dark room
Shifting the candles; Fräulein von Kulp
Who turned in the hall, one hand on the door. Vacant shuttles
30   Weave the wind. I have no ghosts,
An old man in a draughty house
Under a windy knob.

After such knowledge, what forgiveness? Think now
History has many cunning passages, contrived corridors
35   And issues, deceives with whispering ambitions,
Guides us by vanities. Think now
She gives when our attention is distracted
And what she gives, gives with such supple confusions
That the giving famishes the craving. Gives too late
40   What's not believed in, or if still believed,
In memory only, reconsidered passion. Gives too soon
Into weak hands, what's thought can be dispensed with
Till the refusal propagates a fear. Think
Neither fear nor courage saves us. Unnatural vices
45   Are fathered by our heroism. Virtues
Are forced upon us by our impudent crimes.
These tears are shaken from the wrath-bearing tree.

The tiger springs in the new year. Us he devours. Think at last
We have not reached conclusion, when I

17ff: The Pharisees demanded that Jesus prove his divinity by performing a miracle: "Master, we would see a sign from thee" (Matt. 12:38). Eliot quotes a 1618 Christmas sermon by Lancelot Andrewes (1555–1626). Andrewes is discussing the Angel's speech to the shepherds (Luke 2:12): "And this shall be a sign unto you; ye shall find the Child swaddled, and laid in a cratch [manger]." He says: "Signs are taken for wonders. 'Master, we would fain see a sign,' (Mat. xii. 38), that is a miracle. And in this sense [the biblical passage] is a sign to wonder at. Indeed, every word here is a wonder. . . . *Verbum infans* [both 'the infant Word' and 'the unspeaking Word'], the Word without a word; the eternal Word not able to speak a word; 1. a wonder sure. 2. And . . . swaddled; and that a wonder too. 'He,' that (as in the thirty-eighth of Job (v.9) He saith), 'taketh the vast body of the main sea, turns it to and fro, as a little child, and rolls it about with the swaddling bands of darkness;'—He to come thus into clouts, Himself!" See also John 1:1,14: "In the beginning was the Word, and the Word was with God, and the Word was God. . . . And the Word was made flesh, and dwelt among us."
19: *juvescence:* Eliot's contraction of "juvenescence," the state of youth
21: *flowering judas:* a flowering tree so named from the popular belief that Judas hanged himself from such a tree
22: *eaten . . . divided . . . drunk:* as are the bread and wine that symbolize Christ's body and blood in the communion service
26: *Titians:* paintings by the Venetian artist Titian (1488/90–1576)
32: *knob:* hill
47: *wrath-bearing tree:* presumably either the flowering judas or the Garden of Eden's tree of knowledge

50   Stiffen in a rented house. Think at last
        I have not made this show purposelessly
        And it is not by any concitation
        Of the backward devils.
        I would meet you upon this honestly.
55   I that was near your heart was removed therefrom
        To lose beauty in terror, terror in inquisition.
        I have lost my passion: why should I need to keep it
        Since what is kept must be adulterated?
        I have lost my sight, smell, hearing, taste and touch:
60   How should I use them for your closer contact?

        These with a thousand small deliberations
        Protract the profit of their chilled delirium,
        Excite the membrane, when the sense has cooled,
        With pungent sauces, multiply variety
65   In a wilderness of mirrors. What will the spider do,
        Suspend its operations, will the weevil
        Delay? De Bailhache, Fresca, Mrs. Cammel, whirled
        Beyond the circuit of the shuddering Bear
        In fractured atoms. Gull against the wind, in the windy straits
70   Of Belle Isle, or running on the Horn.
        White feathers in the snow, the Gulf claims,
        And an old man driven by the Trades
        To a sleepy corner.

                        Tenants of the house,
75   Thoughts of a dry brain in a dry season.

                                                1919 / 1920

52: *concitation:* stirring up
68: *Bear:* Ursa Major (also known as the Great Bear or Big Dipper), a constellation in the Northern Hemi-
    sphere
70: The Strait of *Belle Isle* lies between Newfoundland and Labrador on the east coast of Canada; it is the
    northern entrance from the Atlantic Ocean to the Gulf of St. Lawrence.
    Horn: the southernmost tip of South America
71: The *Gulf* current is part of a system of currents in the North Atlantic.
72: *Trades:* the trade winds, blowing westward towards the equator

The Waste Land

'Nam Sibyllam quidem Cumis ego ipse oculis meis vidi in
ampulla pendere, et cum illi pueri dicerent:
Σίβυλλα τί θέλεις; *respondebat illa:* ἀποθανεῖν θέλω.'

For Ezra Pound
IL MIGLIOR FABBRO.

I. The Burial of the Dead

    April is the cruellest month, breeding
Lilacs out of the dead land, mixing
Memory and desire, stirring
Dull roots with spring rain.
5   Winter kept us warm, covering
Earth in forgetful snow, feeding
A little life with dried tubers.
Summer surprised us, coming over the Starnbergersee
With a shower of rain; we stopped in the colonnade,
10   And went on in sunlight, into the Hofgarten,
And drank coffee, and talked for an hour.
Bin gar keine Russin, stamm' aus Litauen, echt deutsch.
And when we were children, staying at the arch-duke's,
My cousin's, he took me out on a sled,
15   And I was frightened. He said, Marie,

"Not only the title, but the plan and a good deal of the incidental symbolism of the poem were suggested by Miss Jessie L. Weston's book on the Grail legend: *From Ritual to Romance* (Cambridge). Indeed, so deeply am I indebted, Miss Weston's book will elucidate the difficulties of the poem much better than my notes can do; and I recommend it (apart from the great interest of the book itself) to any who think such elucidation of the poem worth the trouble. To another work of anthropology I am indebted in general, one which has influenced our generation profoundly; I mean [Sir James Frazer's] *The Golden Bough*; I have used especially the two volumes *Adonis, Attis, Osiris*. Anyone who is acquainted with these works will immediately recognise in the poem certain references to vegetation ceremonies." (Eliot's note).

Weston's book draws on Frazer's comparative study of ancient fertility myths to outline an archetypal myth that lies behind Christianity and behind the Arthurian legend of the quest for the Holy Grail (the lost cup in which Joseph of Arimathea caught the blood of Christ on the cross). In this myth, the Fisher King is impotent due to either maiming or illness; as a result his lands are laid under a curse and his people are likewise infertile. The curse is lifted only by the arrival of a stranger who puts or answers a series of ritual questions. Weston links this myth to the Grail quest, in which a knight comes to the Chapel Perilous, where he must put a series of questions about the Grail and the Lance (that pierced Christ's side); once he has done this the land and people are restored to fertility. The Fisher King is thus parallel to vegetation gods such as the Greek Adonis, the Phrygian Attis, and the Egyptian Osiris, whose deaths and rebirths are represented in rituals of sacrifice that are meant to ensure the rebirth of new vegetation out of winter's sterility. We have given Eliot's notes to individual lines in quote marks below.

Epigraph: "With my own eyes now, I myself saw the Sibyl at Cumae hanging in a bottle; and when the boys said to her, 'Sibyl, what do you want?', she would answer, 'I wish to die.'" (Petronius, *Satyricon*, ch. 48). The Sibyl was a prophetess whom Apollo offered anything she wished if she became his lover. She asked to live as long as the grains of sand in a pile, but neglected to ask for eternal youth; as she aged she shrank and eventually was suspended in a bottle from the ceiling of her cave in Cumae.

Dedication: *il miglior fabbro*: "the better craftsman"; Eliot quotes Dante's words on the Provençal poet Arnaut Daniel (*Purgatorio* 26.117). The final shape of *The Waste Land* owed much to the keen editorial eye of Eliot's friend, the American poet Ezra Pound (1885–1972).

Title: The funeral service in the Book of Common Prayer is called "The Order for the Burial of the Dead."

8: *Starnbergersee*: a lake near Munich

10: *Hofgarten*: a park in Munich

12: "I am not Russian at all; I come from Lithuania; I am a real German." (German)

15: The character *Marie* is based on the Countess Marie Larisch, the niece and confidante of the Austrian Empress Elizabeth; though the details in these lines appear in her book *My Past* (1913), Eliot's source was an actual conversation with the Countess herself.

Marie, hold on tight. And down we went.
In the mountains, there you feel free.
I read, much of the night, and go south in the winter.

What are the roots that clutch, what branches grow
20   Out of this stony rubbish? Son of man,
You cannot say, or guess, for you know only
A heap of broken images, where the sun beats,
And the dead tree gives no shelter, the cricket no relief,
And the dry stone no sound of water. Only
25   There is shadow under this red rock,
(Come in under the shadow of this red rock),
And I will show you something different from either
Your shadow at morning striding behind you
Or your shadow at evening rising to meet you;
30   I will show you fear in a handful of dust.

                    Frisch weht der Wind
                    Der Heimat zu
                    Mein Irisch Kind
                    Wo weilest du?

35   'You gave me hyacinths first a year ago;
'They called me the hyacinth girl.'
—Yet when we came back, late, from the hyacinth garden,
Your arms full, and your hair wet, I could not
Speak, and my eyes failed, I was neither
40   Living nor dead, and I knew nothing,
Looking into the heart of light, the silence.
Oed' und leer das Meer.

Madame Sosostris, famous clairvoyante,
Had a bad cold, nevertheless
45   Is known to be the wisest woman in Europe,
With a wicked pack of cards. Here, said she,

17: The line is a translation of a German cliché.

20: "Cf. Ezekiel II, i." God addresses Ezekiel: "Son of man, stand upon thy feet, and I will speak unto thee."

23: "Cf. Ecclesiastes XII, v." This speaks of coming "evil days" "when they shall be afraid of that which is high, and fears shall be in the way, and the almond tree shall flourish, and the grasshopper shall be a burden, and desire shall fail; because a man goeth to his long home; and the mourners go about the streets."

25: See Isaiah 32.2, which speaks of the coming of a savior who "shall be as an hiding place from the wind, and a covert from the tempest; as rivers of water in a dry place; as the shadow of a great rock in a weary land."

30: See John Donne's *Devotions upon Emergent Occasions* (1624), Meditation 4: "what's become of man's great extent and proportion, when himself shrinks himself, and consumes himself to a handful of dust."

31–34: "V. Tristan und Isolde, I, verses 5–8." ("V.": *vide*, "see".) The lines are sung by a sailor of his absent sweetheart: "The wind blows fresh to the homeland. My Irish darling, where do you linger?"

42: "Id. III, verse 24." ("Id.": *idem*, the same.) Tristan lies dying, waiting for his lover Isolde to come, but the shepherd on the lookout for her ship reports: "Desolate and empty the sea."

43: *clairvoyante:* fortuneteller

46: *pack of cards:* the Tarot; Weston's book discusses the symbolism of its four suits—the cup, lance, sword, and dish. "I am not familiar with the exact constitution of the Tarot pack of cards, from which I have obviously departed to suit my own convenience. The Hanged Man, a member of the traditional pack, fits my purpose in two ways: because he is associated in my mind with the Hanged God of Frazer, and because I associate him with the hooded figure in the passage of the disciples of Emmaus in Part V. The Phoenician Sailor and the Merchant appear later; also the 'crowds of people', and Death by Water is executed in Part IV. The Man with Three Staves (an authentic member of the Tarot pack) I associate, quite arbitrarily, with the Fisher King himself."

Is your card, the drowned Phoenician Sailor,
(Those are pearls that were his eyes. Look!)
Here is Belladonna, the Lady of the Rocks,
50   The lady of situations.
Here is the man with three staves, and here the Wheel,
And here is the one-eyed merchant, and this card,
Which is blank, is something he carries on his back,
Which I am forbidden to see. I do not find
55   The Hanged Man. Fear death by water.
I see crowds of people, walking round in a ring.
Thank you. If you see dear Mrs. Equitone,
Tell her I bring the horoscope myself:
One must be so careful these days.

60   Unreal City,
Under the brown fog of a winter dawn,
A crowd flowed over London Bridge, so many,
I had not thought death had undone so many.
Sighs, short and infrequent, were exhaled,
65   And each man fixed his eyes before his feet.
Flowed up the hill and down King William Street,
To where Saint Mary Woolnoth kept the hours
With a dead sound on the final stroke of nine.
There I saw one I knew, and stopped him, crying: 'Stetson!
70   'You who were with me in the ships at Mylae!
'That corpse you planted last year in your garden,
'Has it begun to sprout? Will it bloom this year?
'Or has the sudden frost disturbed its bed?
'O keep the Dog far hence, that's friend to men,
75   'Or with his nails he'll dig it up again!
'You! hypocrite lecteur!—mon semblable,—mon frère!'

47: *Phoenician Sailor*: the Phoenicians were notable sailors and merchants in the Mediterranean in the first millennium BC.

48: In *The Tempest*, the spirit Ariel sings to Ferdinand, telling him (falsely) of his father's death: "Full fathom five thy father lies; / Of his bones are coral made; / Those are pearls that were his eyes: / Nothing of him that doth fade, / But doth suffer a sea-change / Into something rich and strange" (1.2.399–404).

51: *Wheel*: i.e., the Wheel of Fortune (symbolizing life's unpredictable reverses of fortune)

60: "Cf. Baudelaire: 'Fourmillante cité, cité pleine de rêves, / Où le spectre en plein jour raccroche le passant.'" From Baudelaire's "Les Sept Vieillards" ("The Seven Old Men"): "Swarming city, city full of dreams, / Where the spectre accosts the passerby in broad daylight."

63: "Cf. Inferno III, 55–57: 'si lunga tratta / di gente, ch'io non averei creduto / che morte tanta n'avesse disfatta.'" ("such a huge stream of people, that I should never have believed death had undone so many.") This is Dante's reaction to seeing a crowd of souls just inside the gate of Hell, placed there because they did no good nor evil in life, and those angels who neither rebelled with Satan nor supported God.

64: "Cf. Inferno IV, 25–27: 'Quivi, secondo che per ascoltare, / non avea piante mai che di sospiri / che l'aura eterna facevan tremare.'" ("Here, so far as listening could tell me, the only lamentations were sighs, which made the eternal air tremble.") Dante is in Limbo, where reside the souls of virtuous heathens who lived before the time of Christ.

68: "A phenomenon which I have often noticed." The church of St. Mary Woolnoth, on the corner of Lombard Street and King William Street, is in London's City district—its financial and business area; the people in the crowd are on their way to work.

70: *Mylae*: The Battle of Mylae (260 BC), a naval conflict (part of the First Punic War) in which the Romans defeated a Carthaginian fleet.

74–75: "Cf. the Dirge in Webster's *The White Devil*." This runs: "But keep the wolf far thence, that's foe to men, / For with his nails he'll dig them up again." (John Webster, *The White Devil* (1612), 5.4.101–02)

76: "V. Baudelaire, Preface to *Fleurs du Mal*." In Baudelaire's poem it is Ennui that is the greatest of human vices: "you know him well, hypocrite reader—my double—my brother!"

II. A GAME OF CHESS

The Chair she sat in, like a burnished throne,
Glowed on the marble, where the glass
Held up by standards wrought with fruited vines
80 From which a golden Cupidon peeped out
(Another hid his eyes behind his wing)
Doubled the flames of sevenbranched candelabra
Reflecting light upon the table as
The glitter of her jewels rose to meet it,
85 From satin cases poured in rich profusion.
In vials of ivory and coloured glass
Unstoppered, lurked her strange synthetic perfumes,
Unguent, powdered, or liquid—troubled, confused
And drowned the sense in odours; stirred by the air
90 That freshened from the window, these ascended
In fattening the prolonged candle-flames,
Flung their smoke into the laquearia,
Stirring the pattern on the coffered ceiling.
Huge sea-wood fed with copper
95 Burned green and orange, framed by the coloured stone,
In which sad light a carvèd dolphin swam.
Above the antique mantel was displayed
As though a window gave upon the sylvan scene
The change of Philomel, by the barbarous king
100 So rudely forced; yet there the nightingale
Filled all the desert with inviolable voice
And still she cried, and still the world pursues,
'Jug Jug' to dirty ears.
And other withered stumps of time
105 Were told upon the walls; staring forms
Leaned out, leaning, hushing the room enclosed.
Footsteps shuffled on the stair.
Under the firelight, under the brush, her hair
Spread out in fiery points
110 Glowed into words, then would be savagely still.

'My nerves are bad to-night. Yes, bad. Stay with me.
Speak to me. Why do you never speak. Speak.
  What are you thinking of? What thinking? What?
I never know what you are thinking. Think.'

Title: Eliot glances at two plays by Thomas Middleton (1580–1627): the satirical *A Game at Chess* and, more significantly, the tragedy *Women Beware Women* (see note to line 137 below).

77: "Cf. *Antony and Cleopatra*, II, ii, l.190." Eliot parodically adapts Enobarbus's description of Cleopatra.

92: "Laquearia. V. *Aeneid*, I, 726: 'dependent lychni laquearibus aureis / incensi, et noctem flammis funalia vincunt.'" ("flaming torches hang from the gold-panelled ceiling, and the night is pierced by the flaring lights")

98: "Sylvan scene. V. Milton, *Paradise Lost*, IV, 140." The scene is the Garden of Eden, as first glimpsed by Satan.

99: "V. Ovid, *Metamorphoses*, VI, Philomela." Tereus raped his wife Procne's sister Philomela and cut out her tongue to prevent her telling of it. She conveyed her story to Procne by depicting it in a piece of needlework; they then killed Procne's son Itys and served his flesh in a meal to Tereus. Tereus attempted to kill them in revenge, but instead all three were turned into birds: Philomela became a nightingale, Procne a swallow, and Tereus a hoopoe.

100: "Cf. Part III, l. 204."

103: *Jug Jug*: conventional representation of the nightingale's song in Elizabethan poetry

115   I think we are in rats' alley
        Where the dead men lost their bones.

            'What is that noise?'
                        The wind under the door.
            'What is that noise now? What is the wind doing?'
120   Nothing again nothing.
                                                            'Do
            'You know nothing? Do you see nothing? Do you remember
            Nothing?'

            I remember
125   Those are pearls that were his eyes.
            'Are you alive, or not? Is there nothing in your head?'
                                                            But

        O O O O that Shakespeherian Rag—
        It's so elegant
130   So intelligent
            'What shall I do now? What shall I do?
        I shall rush out as I am, and walk the street
        With my hair down, so. What shall we do tomorrow?
        What shall we ever do?'
135   The hot water at ten.
        And if it rains, a closed car at four.
        And we shall play a game of chess,
        Pressing lidless eyes and waiting for a knock upon the door.

            When Lil's husband got demobbed, I said—
140   I didn't mince my words, I said to her myself,
        HURRY UP PLEASE ITS TIME
        Now Albert's coming back, make yourself a bit smart.
        He'll want to know what you done with that money he gave you
        To get yourself some teeth. He did, I was there.
145   You have them all out, Lil, and get a nice set,
        He said, I swear, I can't bear to look at you.
        And no more can't I, I said, and think of poor Albert,
        He's been in the army four years, he wants a good time,
        And if you don't give it him, there's others will, I said.
150   Oh is there, she said. Something o' that, I said.
        Then I'll know who to thank, she said, and give me a straight look.
        HURRY UP PLEASE ITS TIME
        If you don't like it you can get on with it, I said.
        Others can pick and choose if you can't.
155   But if Albert makes off, it won't be for lack of telling.
        You ought to be ashamed, I said, to look so antique.

115: "Cf. Part III, l. 195."
118: "Cf. Webster: 'Is the wind in that door still?'" (John Webster, *The Devil's Law Case*, 3.2). ("in that door": in that direction)
126: "Cf. Part I, l. 37, 48."
128–130: Eliot quotes from a popular song of 1912, "That Shakespeherian Rag."
137: "Cf. the game of chess in Middleton's *Women Beware Women*." In this play Bianca is seduced by the duke, while the procuress Livia plays a game of chess with Bianca's mother-in-law in order to distract her; the moves in the game of seduction are paralleled by the moves in the chessgame.
139: *demobbed:* demobilized (i.e., discharged from the army after the end of World War I).
141: The traditional English bartender's call at closing-time.

(And her only thirty-one.)
I can't help it, she said, pulling a long face,
It's them pills I took, to bring it off, she said.
160 (She's had five already, and nearly died of young George.)
The chemist said it would be all right, but I've never been the same.
You *are* a proper fool, I said.
Well, if Albert won't leave you alone, there it is, I said,
What you get married for if you don't want children?
165 HURRY UP PLEASE ITS TIME
Well, that Sunday Albert was home, they had a hot gammon,
And they asked me in to dinner, to get the beauty of it hot—
HURRY UP PLEASE ITS TIME
HURRY UP PLEASE ITS TIME
170 Goonight Bill. Goonight Lou. Goonight May. Goonight.
Ta ta. Goonight. Goonight.
Good night, ladies, good night, sweet ladies, good night, good night.

III. THE FIRE SERMON

  The river's tent is broken; the last fingers of leaf
Clutch and sink into the wet bank. The wind
175 Crosses the brown land, unheard. The nymphs are departed.
Sweet Thames, run softly, till I end my song.
The river bears no empty bottles, sandwich papers,
Silk handkerchiefs, cardboard boxes, cigarette ends
Or other testimony of summer nights. The nymphs are departed.
180 And their friends, the loitering heirs of City directors;
Departed, have left no addresses.
By the waters of Leman I sat down and wept . . .
Sweet Thames, run softly till I end my song,
Sweet Thames, run softly, for I speak not loud or long.
185 But at my back in a cold blast I hear
The rattle of the bones, and chuckle spread from ear to ear.

A rat crept softly through the vegetation
Dragging its slimy belly on the bank
While I was fishing in the dull canal
190 On a winter evening round behind the gashouse
Musing upon the king my brother's wreck
And on the king my father's death before him.

159: *it:* i.e., an abortion
161: *chemist:* druggist
166: *gammon:* ham
172: Ophelia's farewell (*Hamlet* 4.5.72–73), her last words in the play before she drowns herself.
Title: See Eliot's note to line 308.
176: "V. Spenser, *Prothalamion.*" Spenser's poem celebrates the 1596 double betrothal of the two eldest daughters of the Earl of Worcester; Eliot quotes the poem's refrain. The nymphs of the Thames strew flowers upon the daughters (as symbolized by swans), and sing a song in celebration.
182: Cf. Psalm 137: "By the rivers of Babylon, there we sat down; yea, we wept, when we remembered Zion." *Leman* is the French name for the Lake of Geneva in Switzerland; Eliot convalesced in 1921 in the nearby town of Lausanne during the composition of *The Waste Land.*
185–86: Cf. Andrew Marvell, "To His Coy Mistress": "But at my back I always hear / Time's wingèd chariot hurrying near."
191–92: "Cf. *The Tempest,* I, ii." Eliot alludes to Ferdinand's speech just before Ariel's song "Full fathom five": "Sitting on a bank, / Weeping again the King my father's wrack, / This music crept by me upon the waters."

White bodies naked on the low damp ground
And bones cast in a little low dry garret,
195 Rattled by the rat's foot only, year to year.
But at my back from time to time I hear
The sound of horns and motors, which shall bring
Sweeney to Mrs. Porter in the spring.
O the moon shone bright on Mrs. Porter
200 And on her daughter
They wash their feet in soda water
Et O ces voix d'enfants, chantant dans la coupole!

Twit twit twit
Jug jug jug jug jug jug
205 So rudely forc'd.
Tereu

      Unreal City
Under the brown fog of a winter noon
Mr. Eugenides, the Smyrna merchant
210 Unshaven, with a pocket full of currants
C.i.f. London: documents at sight,
Asked me in demotic French
To luncheon at the Cannon Street Hotel
Followed by a weekend at the Metropole.

215   At the violet hour, when the eyes and back
Turn upward from the desk, when the human engine waits
Like a taxi throbbing waiting,
I Tiresias, though blind, throbbing between two lives,

196: "Cf. Marvell, *To His Coy Mistress.*"

197: "Cf. Day, *Parliament of Bees*: 'When of the sudden, listening, you shall hear, / A noise of horns and hunting, which shall bring / Actaeon to Diana in the spring, / Where all shall see her naked skin . . . '" *The Parliament of Bees* is a pastoral play by John Day (1574–1640). The hunter Actaeon caught sight of Diana, goddess of hunting and of chastity, bathing on Mount Cithaeron; in revenge she turned him into a stag, and he was killed by his own hounds.

199–201: "I do not know the origin of the ballad from which these lines are taken: it was reported to me from Sydney, Australia."

202: "V. Verlaine, *Parsifal.*" ("And O those children's voices, singing in the dome!"). Verlaine's poem refers to Wagner's *Parsifal*, where Parsifal, after a ceremony of foot-washing, enters the Grail Castle. There he restores the wounded Fisher King, Amfortas, to health by touching him with his sacred spear, lifting the curse on the waste land, and announces that he is now king himself. The opera ends with the sound of children's voices singing Christ's praise from the dome of the castle.

206: The shortened form of Tereus's name comes from John Lyly's *Campaspe* (1584): "O 'tis the ravished nightingale. / Jug, jug, jug, jug, tereu! she cries."

211: "The currents were quoted at a price 'cost insurance and freight to London'; and the Bill of Lading, etc., were to be handed to the buyer upon payment of the sight draft."

213: *Cannon Street Hotel:* attached to Cannon Street Station in the City.

214: *Metropole:* a luxury hotel in the seaside resort of Brighton

218: "Tiresias, although a mere spectator and not indeed a 'character', is yet the most important personage in the poem, uniting all the rest. Just as the one-eyed merchant, seller of currants, melts into the Phoenician Sailor, and the latter is not wholly distinct from Ferdinand Prince of Naples, so all the women are one woman, and the two sexes meet in Tiresias. What Tiresias *sees*, in fact, is the substance of the poem. The whole passage from Ovid is of great anthropological interest." Eliot quotes *Metamorphoses* 3.320–38, which tells how Tiresias, born a man, was transformed into a woman after striking two copulating snakes with his stick; seven years later, encountering the same snakes again, he struck them and was again a man. Jupiter and Juno, disagreeing over whether women or men get greater pleasure from sex, asked Tiresias to adjudicate: he agreed with Jove that women receive more pleasure, and in anger Juno struck him blind; as recompense, Jupiter gave him the gift of prophecy.

Old man with wrinkled female breasts, can see
220   At the violet hour, the evening hour that strives
        Homeward, and brings the sailor home from sea,
        The typist home at teatime, clears her breakfast, lights
        Her stove, and lays out food in tins.
        Out of the window perilously spread
225   Her drying combinations touched by the sun's last rays,
        On the divan are piled (at night her bed)
        Stockings, slippers, camisoles, and stays.
        I Tiresias, old man with wrinkled dugs
        Perceived the scene, and foretold the rest—
230   I too awaited the expected guest.
        He, the young man carbuncular, arrives,
        A small house agent's clerk, with one bold stare,
        One of the low on whom assurance sits
        As a silk hat on a Bradford millionaire.
235   The time is now propitious, as he guesses,
        The meal is ended, she is bored and tired,
        Endeavours to engage her in caresses
        Which still are unreproved, if undesired.
        Flushed and decided, he assaults at once;
240   Exploring hands encounter no defence;
        His vanity requires no response,
        And makes a welcome of indifference.
        (And I Tiresias have foresuffered all
        Enacted on this same divan or bed;
245   I who have sat by Thebes below the wall
        And walked among the lowest of the dead.)
        Bestows one final patronising kiss,
        And gropes his way, finding the stairs unlit . . .

        She turns and looks a moment in the glass,
250   Hardly aware of her departed lover;
        Her brain allows one half-formed thought to pass:
        'Well now that's done: and I'm glad it's over.'
        When lovely woman stoops to folly and
        Paces about her room again, alone,
255   She smoothes her hair with automatic hand,
        And puts a record on the gramophone.

221: "This may not appear as exact as Sappho's lines, but I had in mind the 'longshore' or 'dory' fisherman, who returns at nightfall." Eliot has in mind Fragment 149: "Evening Star, that brings back all that the shining Dawn has sent far and wide, you bring back the sheep, the goat, and the child back to its mother."
231: *carbuncular*: pimply
234: *Bradford* is a manufacturing town in northern England, stereotypically the place of origin of millionaires who made their fortunes from sales of woollen goods during World War I.
245–46: In Sophocles' *Oedipus Rex* it is Tiresias who reveals that the curse under which Thebes is suffering has been called down by its king Oedipus's (unknowing) murder of his father and marrying of his mother. In the *Odyssey*, Odysseus consults Tiresias in the underworld.
253: "V. Goldsmith, the song in *The Vicar of Wakefield*." The seduced Olivia sings: "When lovely woman / stoops to folly and / finds too late that men betray / What charm can soothe her melancholy, / What art can wash her guilt away? / The only art her guilt to cover, / To hide her shame from every eye, / To give repentance to her lover / And wring his bosom—is to die."

    'This music crept by me upon the waters'
    And along the Strand, up Queen Victoria Street.
    O City city, I can sometimes hear
260 Beside a public bar in Lower Thames Street,
    The pleasant whining of a mandoline
    And a clatter and a chatter from within
    Where fishmen lounge at noon: where the walls
    Of Magnus Martyr hold
265 Inexplicable splendour of Ionian white and gold.

       The river sweats
       Oil and tar
       The barges drift
       With the turning tide
270   Red sails
       Wide
       To leeward, swing on the heavy spar.
       The barges wash
       Drifting logs
275   Down Greenwich reach
       Past the Isle of Dogs.
           Weialala leia
           Wallala leialala

       Elizabeth and Leicester
280   Beating oars
       The stern was formed
       A gilded shell
       Red and gold
       The brisk swell
285   Rippled both shores
       Southwest wind
       Carried down stream
       The peal of bells
       White towers
290   Weialala leia
           Wallala leialala

257: "V. *The Tempest,* as above." See lines 191–92 and note.

263: *fishmen:* fish-sellers

264: "The interior of St. Magnus Martyr is to my mind one of the finest among Wren's interiors. See *The Proposed Demolition of Nineteen City Churches:* (P.S. King & Son, Ltd.)." Built in 1676, it still stands, at the corner of Lower Thames and Fish Streets, between London Bridge and the London fishmarket.

266: "The Song of the (three) Thames-daughters begins here. From line 292 to 306 inclusive they speak in turn. V. *Götterdämmerung,* III, i: the Rhine-daughters." Eliot alludes to the Rhine-daughters' song in Wagner's *The Twilight of the Gods,* in which they lament their river's loss of its beauty with the loss of the gold of the Nibelungs; lines 277–78 are the refrain of their song.

275–76: *Greenwich* is a London borough on the south side of the Thames; opposite it is the *Isle of Dogs* (in fact a peninsula).

279: "V. [J.A.] Froude, *[The Reign of] Elizabeth,* Vol. I, ch. iv, letter of De Quadra [Spanish bishop and ambassador to England] to Philip of Spain: 'In the afternoon we were in a barge, watching the games on the river. (The Queen) was alone with Lord Robert [Earl of Leicester] and myself on the poop, when they began to talk nonsense, and went so far that Lord Robert at last said, as I was on the spot there was no reason why they should not be married if the queen pleased.'"

'Trams and dusty trees.
Highbury bore me. Richmond and Kew
Undid me. By Richmond I raised my knees
295   Supine on the floor of a narrow canoe.'

'My feet are at Moorgate, and my heart
Under my feet. After the event
He wept. He promised "a new start."
I made no comment. What should I resent?'

300   'On Margate Sands.
I can connect
Nothing with nothing.
The broken fingernails of dirty hands.
My people humble people who expect
305   Nothing.'
                    la la

To Carthage then I came

Burning burning burning burning
O Lord Thou pluckest me out
310   O Lord Thou pluckest

burning

IV.   DEATH BY WATER

Phlebas the Phoenician, a fortnight dead,
Forgot the cry of gulls, and the deep sea swell
And the profit and loss.
315   A current under sea
Picked his bones in whispers. As he rose and fell
He passed the stages of his age and youth
Entering the whirlpool.
                            Gentile or Jew
320   O you who turn the wheel and look to windward,
Consider Phlebas, who was once handsome and tall as you.

293–94: "Cf. *Purgatorio*, V. 133: 'Ricorditi di me, che son la Pia; / Siena mi fe', disfecemi Maremma.'"
("Remember me, who am La Pia; Siena made me, Maremma undid me.") La Pia, Lady of Siena, was
murdered at Maremma by her husband's orders. *Highbury* is a residential suburb in North London; *Rich-
mond* and *Kew* are riverside districts on the Thames west of London.

296: *Moorgate:* an area in the east of the City of London

300: *Margate Sands:* a seaside resort on the Thames estuary in Kent. Eliot began *The Waste Land* while
convalescing there in late 1921.

307: "V. St. Augustine's *Confessions* [3.1]: 'to Carthage then I came, where a cauldron of unholy loves sang
all about mine ears.'" Augustine is speaking of the sensual temptations that assailed him in his youth.

308: "The complete text of the Buddha's Fire Sermon (which corresponds in importance to the Sermon
on the Mount) from which these words are taken, will be found translated in the late Henry Clarke War-
ren's *Buddhism in Translation* (Harvard Oriental Series). Mr. Warren was one of the great pioneers of
Buddhist studies in the Occident." In the Fire Sermon Buddha preached that all existence is afire with
"the fire of passion . . . , with the fire of hatred, with the fire of infatuation."

309: "From St. Augustine's *Confessions* again. The collocation of these two representatives of eastern and
western asceticism, as the culmination of this part of the poem, is not an accident." Augustine wrote: "I
entangle my steps with these outward beauties, but Thou pluckest me out, O Lord, Thou pluckest me
out."

V. WHAT THE THUNDER SAID

After the torchlight red on sweaty faces
After the frosty silence in the gardens
After the agony in stony places
325   The shouting and the crying
Prison and palace and reverberation
Of thunder of spring over distant mountains
He who was living is now dead
We who were living are now dying
330   With a little patience

Here is no water but only rock
Rock and no water and the sandy road
The road winding above among the mountains
Which are mountains of rock without water
335   If there were water we should stop and drink
Amongst the rock one cannot stop or think
Sweat is dry and feet are in the sand
If there were only water amongst the rock
Dead mountain mouth of carious teeth that cannot spit
340   Here one can neither stand nor lie nor sit
There is not even silence in the mountains
But dry sterile thunder without rain
There is not even solitude in the mountains
But red sullen faces sneer and snarl
345   From doors of mudcracked houses
                        If there were water
And no rock
If there were rock
And also water
350   And water
A spring
A pool among the rock
If there were the sound of water only
Not the cicada
355   And dry grass singing
But sound of water over a rock
Where the hermit-thrush sings in the pine trees
Drip drop drip drop drop drop drop
But there is no water

Title: see note to line 401. "In the first part of Part V three themes are employed: the journey to Emmaus, the approach to the Chapel Perilous (see Miss Weston's book) and the present decay of eastern Europe." For the journey, see Luke 24:13ff: two disciples traveling to Emmaus (a village some distance from Jerusalem) on the day of the Resurrection are joined by Christ, but do not recognize him. When they reach Emmaus they invite him to eat with them; he blesses the bread, upon which they recognize him; he then vanishes.

322ff: These lines touch on Christ's agony in the Garden of Gethsemane, arrest, trial, and crucifixion.

339: *carious*: rotting

354: *cicada*: grasshopper: see line 23 and its note.

357: "This is *Turdus aonalaschkae pallasii*, the hermit-thrush which I have heard in Quebec Province. Chapman says (*Handbook of Birds of Eastern North America*) 'it is most at home in secluded woodland and thickety retreats. . . . Its notes are not remarkable for variety or volume, but in purity and sweetness of tone and exquisite modulation they are unequalled.' Its 'water-dripping song' is justly celebrated."

360   Who is the third who walks always beside you?
       When I count, there are only you and I together
       But when I look ahead up the white road
       There is always another one walking beside you
       Gliding wrapt in a brown mantle, hooded
365   I do not know whether a man or a woman
       —But who is that on the other side of you?

       What is that sound high in the air
       Murmur of maternal lamentation
       Who are those hooded hordes swarming
370   Over endless plains, stumbling in cracked earth
       Ringed by the flat horizon only
       What is the city over the mountains
       Cracks and reforms and bursts in the violet air
       Falling towers
375   Jerusalem Athens Alexandria
       Vienna London
       Unreal

       A woman drew her long black hair out tight
       And fiddled whisper music on those strings
380   And bats with baby faces in the violet light
       Whistled, and beat their wings
       And crawled head downward down a blackened wall
       And upside down in air were towers
       Tolling reminiscent bells, that kept the hours
385   And voices singing out of empty cisterns and exhausted wells.

       In this decayed hole among the mountains
       In the faint moonlight, the grass is singing
       Over the tumbled graves, about the chapel
       There is the empty chapel, only the wind's home.
390   It has no windows, and the door swings,
       Dry bones can harm no one.
       Only a cock stood on the rooftree
       Co co rico co co rico
       In a flash of lightning. Then a damp gust
395   Bringing rain

       Ganga was sunken, and the limp leaves
       Waited for rain, while the black clouds
       Gathered far distant, over Himavant.

360: "The following lines were stimulated by the account of one of the Antarctic expeditions (I forget which, but I think one of Shackleton's): it was related that the party of explorers, at the extremity of their strength, had the constant delusion that there was *one more member* than could actually be counted."
367–77: "Cf. Hermann Hesse, *Blick ins Chaos* [*A Glimpse into Chaos,* 1920]." Eliot quotes a passage that refers to the Russian Revolution and other events in Europe: "Already half of Europe, already at least half of Eastern Europe, on the way to Chaos, drives drunkenly in spiritual frenzy along the edge of the abyss, sings drunkenly, as though singing hymns, as Dmitri Karamazov sang [in Dostoevsky's *The Brothers Karamazov*]. The offended bourgeois laughs at the songs; the saint and the seer hear them with tears."
393: The cry of the cock supposedly dispels spirits with the coming of the dawn; it also marked Peter's third denial of Christ (Matthew 26).
396: *Ganga:* the sacred Indian river Ganges
398: *Himavant:* a holy mountain in the Himalaya range

The jungle crouched, humped in silence.
400   Then spoke the thunder
        DA
        Datta: what have we given?
        My friend, blood shaking my heart
        The awful daring of a moment's surrender
405   Which an age of prudence can never retract
        By this, and this only, we have existed
        Which is not to be found in our obituaries
        Or in memories draped by the beneficent spider
        Or under seals broken by the lean solicitor
410   In our empty rooms
        DA
        Dayadhvam: I have heard the key
        Turn in the door once and turn once only
        We think of the key, each in his prison
415   Thinking of the key, each confirms a prison
        Only at nightfall, aethereal rumours
        Revive for a moment a broken Coriolanus
        DA
        Damyata: The boat responded
420   Gaily, to the hand expert with sail and oar
        The sea was calm, your heart would have responded
        Gaily, when invited, beating obedient
        To controlling hands

                                              I sat upon the shore
425   Fishing, with the arid plain behind me
        Shall I at least set my lands in order?
        London Bridge is falling down falling down falling down
        Poi s'ascose nel foco che gli affina

401: *Da*: The sound of the thunder. "'Datta, dayadhvam, damyata' (Give, sympathize, control). The fable of the meaning of the Thunder is found in the *Brihadaranyaka—Upanishad*, 5, 1." To each of the world's three groups of beings—gods, demons and men—the Creator Deity Prajapati said "DA": each interpreted it differently—the gods were asked to "control" themselves, men to "give" alms, and demons to "be compassionate." "This is what the divine voice, the Thunder, repeats when he says DA, DA, DA: 'Control yourselves; give alms; be compassionate.'"
408: "Cf. Webster, *The White Devil*, V, vi: '. . . they'll remarry / Ere the worm pierce your winding-sheet, ere the spider / Make a thin curtain for your epitaphs.'"
412ff: "Cf. *Inferno*, XXXIII, 46: 'ed io senti chiavar l'uscio di sotto / all' orribile torre.' ['and below I heard the horrible tower being locked up'.]" This is spoken by the soul of Ugolino, who with his family was locked up in a tower; starving, he devoured his children. Eliot adds: "Also F. H. Bradley [(1846–1924), British idealist philosopher,] *Appearance and Reality*, p. 306. 'My external sensations are no less private to my self than are my thoughts or my feelings. In either case my experience falls within my own circle, a circle closed on the outside; and, with all its elements alike, every sphere is opaque to the others which surround it. . . . In brief, regarded as an existence which appears in a soul, the whole world for each is peculiar and private to that soul.'"
417: *Coriolanus*, in Shakespeare's play of that name, is a Roman war-hero; his pride and contempt for the Roman mob lead to his fall from favor and banishment. In revenge he joins the Volscians in an attack against Rome, but is persuaded to call it off by his mother; he dies, betrayed by the Volscian Aufidius.
425: "V. Weston: *From Ritual to Romance*; chapter on the Fisher King."
426: "Thus saith the Lord, Set thine house in order: for thou shalt die, and not live." (Isaiah 38:1)
428: "V. *Purgatorio*, XXVI, 148. '"Ara vos prec per aquella valor / que vos guida al som de l'escalina, / sovenha vos a temps de ma dolor." / Poi s'ascose nel foco che li affina.'" Dante is being addressed by the Provençal poet Arnaut Daniel: "'And I pray you, by the virtue that leads you to the top of this staircase, be mindful in due time of my pain.' Then he dove back into that fire which refines them."

Quando fiam uti chelidon—O swallow swallow
430   *Le Prince d'Aquitaine à la tour abolie*
These fragments I have shored against my ruins
Why then Ile fit you. Hieronymo's mad againe.
Datta. Dayadhvam. Damyata.
          Shantih shantih shantih

                                        1921–1922 / 1922

From Four Quartets

Little Gidding

I

Midwinter spring is its own season
Sempiternal though sodden towards sundown,
Suspended in time, between pole and tropic.
When the short day is brightest, with frost and fire,
5   The brief sun flames the ice, on pond and ditches,
In windless cold that is the heart's heat,
Reflecting in a watery mirror
A glare that is blindness in the early afternoon.
And glow more intense than blaze of branch, or brazier,
10   Stirs the dumb spirit: no wind, but pentecostal fire
In the dark time of the year. Between melting and freezing
The soul's sap quivers. There is no earth smell
Or smell of living thing. This is the spring time
But not in time's covenant. Now the hedgerow

429: "V. *Pervigilium Veneris*. Cf. Philomela in Parts II and III." The line is spoken by the narrator of the anonymous late Latin poem "The Vigil of Venus": "When shall I be like the swallow?" In this poem Procne is the nightingale, Philomela the swallow: "the maid of Tereus sings under the poplar shade, so that you would think musical trills of love came from her mouth, and not a sister's complaint of a barbarous husband. . . . She sings, we are mute. When will my spring come? When shall I be like the swallow, that I may cease to be silent? I have lost the Muse in silence, nor does Apollo regard me." Eliot also alludes to A.C. Swinburne's "Itylus": "Swallow, my sister, O sister swallow, / How can thy heart be full of spring?"

430: "V. Gerard de Nerval [1808–1855], Sonnet *El Desdichado* ['The Disinherited']." Nerval's speaker is like "The Prince of Aquitaine, of the ruined tower."

432: "V. Kyd's *Spanish Tragedy*." In *The Spanish Tragedy* by Thomas Kyd (1557?–1595), subtitled "Hieronymo is Mad Again," Hieronymo is driven mad by the murder of his son. Asked to provide a court entertainment, he replies: "Why, then, I'll fit you!" (i.e., accommodate you); he arranges for his son's murderers to take part in the play and be killed onstage.

434: "Shantih. Repeated as here, a formal ending to an Upanishad. 'The Peace which passeth understanding' [Phil. 4:7] is our equivalent to this word." The Upanishads are commentaries on the Vedas, the ancient Hindu scriptures.

Little Gidding: This poem is the last of the *Four Quartets*. In Eliot's scheme, each poem of the *Quartets* corresponds to one of the four elements: that of "Little Gidding" is fire.

Title: *Little Gidding* was an Anglican religious community in Huntingdonshire founded in 1625 by Nicholas Ferrar; Charles I, who held it in great esteem, visited it three times. The community was broken up by the Puritans in 1647. Its church was restored in 1714 and again in 1853.

2: *Sempiternal:* eternal

10: *pentecostal fire:* the feast of Pentecost celebrates the descent of the Holy Spirit on the heads of the apostles: "And suddenly there came a sound from heaven, as of a rushing mighty wind. . . . And there appeared unto them cloven tongues, like as of fire, and it sat upon each of them. And they were all filled with the Holy Ghost, and began to speak with other tongues, as the Spirit gave them utterance" (Acts 2:2–4).

15 Is blanched for an hour with transitory blossom
Of snow, a bloom more sudden
Than that of summer, neither budding nor fading,
Not in the scheme of generation.
Where is the summer, the unimaginable
20 Zero summer?

If you came this way,
Taking the route you would be likely to take
From the place you would be likely to come from,
If you came this way in may time, you would find the hedges
25 White again, in May, with voluptuary sweetness.
It would be the same at the end of the journey,
If you came at night like a broken king,
If you came by day not knowing what you came for,
It would be the same, when you leave the rough road
30 And turn behind the pig-sty to the dull façade
And the tombstone. And what you thought you came for
Is only a shell, a husk of meaning
From which the purpose breaks only when it is fulfilled
If at all. Either you had no purpose
35 Or the purpose is beyond the end you figured
And is altered in fulfilment. There are other places
Which also are the world's end, some at the sea jaws,
Or over a dark lake, in a desert or a city—
But this is the nearest, in place and time,
40 Now and in England.

If you came this way,
Taking any route, starting from anywhere,
At any time or at any season,
It would always be the same: you would have to put off
45 Sense and notion. You are not here to verify,
Instruct yourself, or inform curiosity
Or carry report. You are here to kneel
Where prayer has been valid. And prayer is more
Than an order of words, the conscious occupation
50 Of the praying mind, or the sound of the voice praying.
And what the dead had no speech for, when living,
They can tell you, being dead: the communication
Of the dead is tongued with fire beyond the language of the living.
Here, the intersection of the timeless moment
55 Is England and nowhere. Never and always.

II

Ash on an old man's sleeve
Is all the ash the burnt roses leave.
Dust in the air suspended

24: *may*: the (white) blossoms of hawthorn
27: *broken king*: Charles I, who last visited Little Gidding in secret after his defeat at the battle of Naseby
in the Civil War.

Marks the place where a story ended.
60   Dust inbreathed was a house—
The wall, the wainscot and the mouse.
The death of hope and despair,
        This is the death of air.

There are flood and drouth
65   Over the eyes and in the mouth,
Dead water and dead sand
Contending for the upper hand.
The parched eviscerate soil
Gapes at the vanity of toil,
70   Laughs without mirth.
        This is the death of earth.

Water and fire succeed
The town, the pasture and the weed.
Water and fire deride
75   The sacrifice that we denied.
Water and fire shall rot
The marred foundations we forgot,
Of sanctuary and choir.
        This is the death of water and fire.

80   In the uncertain hour before the morning
        Near the ending of interminable night
        At the recurrent end of the unending
After the dark dove with the flickering tongue
        Had passed below the horizon of his homing
85   While the dead leaves still rattled on like tin
Over the asphalt where no other sound was
        Between three districts whence the smoke arose
        I met one walking, loitering and hurried
As if blown towards me like the metal leaves
90   Before the urban dawn wind unresisting.
        And as I fixed upon the down-turned face
That pointed scrutiny with which we challenge
        The first-met stranger in the waning dusk
        I caught the sudden look of some dead master
95   Whom I had known, forgotten, half recalled
        Both one and many; in the brown baked features
        The eyes of a familiar compound ghost
Both intimate and unidentifiable.
        So I assumed a double part, and cried
100   And heard another's voice cry: 'What! are *you* here?'

78: *sanctuary and choir:* these are parts of a church: the sanctuary contains the altar, and is joined to the nave (the main body of the church) by the choir.
80ff: The indentation pattern in these lines imitates the terza rima structure of Dante's *Divine Comedy.* Eliot was a nighttime firewatcher in London during the German Blitz in World War II. The encounter described in this passage takes place during his patrol after an air raid.
83: *dark dove:* the German bomber
97: This encounter is modeled on Dante's encounter in Hell with the spirit of his teacher, Brunetto Latini (*Inferno* 15); the *ghost* is regarded by many commentators as a *compound* of W.B. Yeats, Jonathan Swift, and Latini.
99: The speaker assumes a *double part* bzecause his cry translates that of Dante to Latini (*Inferno* 15.29).

Although we were not. I was still the same,
   Knowing myself yet being someone other—
   And he a face still forming; yet the words sufficed
To compel the recognition they preceded.
105   And so, compliant to the common wind,
   Too strange to each other for misunderstanding,
In concord at this intersection time
   Of meeting nowhere, no before and after,
   We trod the pavement in a dead patrol.
110   I said: 'The wonder that I feel is easy,
   Yet ease is cause of wonder. Therefore speak:
   I may not comprehend, may not remember.'
And he: 'I am not eager to rehearse
   My thoughts and theory which you have forgotten.
115   These things have served their purpose: let them be.
So with your own, and pray they be forgiven
   By others, as I pray you to forgive
   Both bad and good. Last season's fruit is eaten
And the fullfed beast shall kick the empty pail.
120   For last year's words belong to last year's language
   And next year's words await another voice.
But, as the passage now presents no hindrance
   To the spirit unappeased and peregrine
   Between two worlds become much like each other,
125   So I find words I never thought to speak
   In streets I never thought I should revisit
   When I left my body on a distant shore.
Since our concern was speech, and speech impelled us
   To purify the dialect of the tribe
130   And urge the mind to aftersight and foresight,
Let me disclose the gifts reserved for age
   To set a crown upon your lifetime's effort.
   First, the cold friction of expiring sense
Without enchantment, offering no promise
135   But bitter tastelessness of shadow fruit
   As body and soul begin to fall asunder.
Second, the conscious impotence of rage
   At human folly, and the laceration
   Of laughter at what ceases to amuse.
140   And last, the rending pain of re-enactment
   Of all that you have done, and been; the shame
   Of motives late revealed, and the awareness
Of things ill done and done to others' harm
   Which once you took for exercise of virtue.
145   Then fools' approval stings, and honour stains.
   From wrong to wrong the exasperated spirit

123: *peregrine*: wandering
127: Yeats died on 28 January 1939 in France; only after the end of World War II could his remains return
   to Ireland.
129: Eliot quotes a line from Stéphane Mallarmé's "Le Tombeau d'Edgar Poe": "Donner un sense plus pur
   aux mots de la tribu."
138–39: cf. Yeats's "Swift's Epitaph," a translation of Swift's own Latin: "Savage indignation there / Can-
   not lacerate his breast."

Proceeds, unless restored by that refining fire
Where you must move in measure, like a dancer.'
The day was breaking. In the disfigured street
150   He left me, with a kind of valediction,
And faded on the blowing of the horn.

III

There are three conditions which often look alike
Yet differ completely, flourish in the same hedgerow:
Attachment to self and to things and to persons, detachment
155   From self and from things and from persons; and, growing between them,
                    indifference
Which resembles the others as death resembles life,
Being between two lives—unflowering, between
The live and the dead nettle. This is the use of memory:
For liberation—not less of love but expanding
160   Of love beyond desire, and so liberation
From the future as well as the past. Thus, love of a country
Begins as attachment to our own field of action
And comes to find that action of little importance
Though never indifferent. History may be servitude,
165   History may be freedom. See, now they vanish,
The faces and places, with the self which, as it could, loved them,
To become renewed, transfigured, in another pattern.
Sin is Behovely, but
All shall be well, and
170   All manner of thing shall be well.
If I think, again, of this place,
And of people, not wholly commendable,
Of no immediate kin or kindness,
But some of peculiar genius,
175   All touched by a common genius,
United in the strife which divided them;
If I think of a king at nightfall,
Of three men, and more, on the scaffold
And a few who died forgotten
180   In other places, here and abroad,
And of one who died blind and quiet,
Why should we celebrate
These dead men more than the dying?
It is not to ring the bell backward

147: *refining fire:* see note to line 428 of *The Waste Land*; also cf. the purifying flames in Yeats's poem
    "Byzantium," stanza 4 (p. 52).
151: Ghosts are said to be dispelled at dawn at the sound of cock-crow: cf. *Hamlet* 1.1.162: "It faded on the
    crowing of the cock." The "horn" is also the All Clear signal after the raid.
168ff: cf. Chapter 27 of the *Showings* of the fourteenth-century mystic Dame Julian of Norwich: "Sin is
    behovely, but all shall be well, and all shall be well, and all manner of thing shall be well." *Behovely*: "nec-
    essary" (to the divine plan).
178: Charles I was beheaded on 30 January 1649; his two principal advisers, Thomas Wentworth, Earl of
    Strafford, and William Laud, Archbishop of Canterbury, had been executed by Parliament in 1641 and
    1645, respectively.
181: The poet John Milton was a supporter of Cromwell; in his early 40s he went blind.
184: "the alarm called 'ringing the bell backward' is sounded by striking a peal of bells up the scale, begin-
    ning with the bass" (Grover Smith, *T.S. Eliot's Poetry and Plays: A Study in Sources and Meaning*,
    Chicago, 1974, p. 293).

185   Nor is it an incantation
        To summon the spectre of a Rose.
        We cannot revive old factions
        We cannot restore old policies
        Or follow an antique drum.
190   These men, and those who opposed them
        And those whom they opposed
        Accept the constitution of silence
        And are folded in a single party.
        Whatever we inherit from the fortunate
195   We have taken from the defeated
        What they had to leave us—a symbol:
        A symbol perfected in death.
        And all shall be well and
        All manner of thing shall be well
200   By the purification of the motive
        In the ground of our beseeching.

IV

        The dove descending breaks the air
        With flame of incandescent terror
        Of which the tongues declare
205   The one discharge from sin and error.
        The only hope, or else despair
            Lies in the choice of pyre or pyre—
            To be redeemed from fire by fire.

        Who then devised the torment? Love.
210   Love is the unfamiliar Name
        Behind the hands that wove
        The intolerable shirt of flame
        Which human power cannot remove.
            We only live, only suspire
215   Consumed by either fire or fire.

V

        What we call the beginning is often the end
        And to make an end is to make a beginning.
        The end is where we start from. And every phrase
        And sentence that is right (where every word is at home,
220   Taking its place to support the others,
        The word neither diffident nor ostentatious,
        An easy commerce of the old and the new,
        The common word exact without vulgarity,

186: *spectre of a Rose:* This is the title of a ballet performed by the Ballets Russes; but, more pertinently, the *Rose* is the symbol of the Tudor kings whose last representative was Elizabeth I.
201: Cf. Julian of Norwich, chapter 41, on prayer, where God says: "I am ground of thy beseeching."
202ff: The dove in this stanza is now both the bomber and the symbol of the Holy Ghost.
212: When Hercules deserted his wife Deineira for Iole, Deineira sent him the shirt of Nessus, which she was falsely told would win back his love; it was in fact poisoned, and it clung to Hercules' flesh, causing him such terrible suffering that he killed himself by immolation on a pyre.
214: *suspire:* breathe

The formal word precise but not pedantic,
225   The complete consort dancing together)
Every phrase and every sentence is an end and a beginning,
Every poem an epitaph. And any action
Is a step to the block, to the fire, down the sea's throat
Or to an illegible stone: and that is where we start.
230   We die with the dying:
See, they depart, and we go with them.
We are born with the dead:
See, they return, and bring us with them.
The moment of the rose and the moment of the yew-tree
235   Are of equal duration. A people without history
Is not redeemed from time, for history is a pattern
Of timeless moments. So, while the light fails
On a winter's afternoon, in a secluded chapel
History is now and England.

240   With the drawing of this Love and the voice of this Calling

We shall not cease from exploration
And the end of all our exploring
Will be to arrive where we started
And know the place for the first time.
245   Through the unknown, remembered gate
When the last of earth left to discover
Is that which was the beginning;
At the source of the longest river
The voice of the hidden waterfall
250   And the children in the apple-tree
Not known, because not looked for
But heard, half-heard, in the stillness
Between two waves of the sea.
Quick now, here, now, always—
255   A condition of complete simplicity
(Costing not less than everything)
And all shall be well and
All manner of thing shall be well
When the tongues of flame are in-folded
260   Into the crowned knot of fire
And the fire and the rose are one.

                                                           1942

240: A quotation from the anonymous fourteenth-century mystical text *The Cloud of Unknowing*.

Butts was raised at Salterns, her family's estate near Poole on the Dorset coast. Her father Frederick, a naval captain, was descended from Thomas Butts, a friend and patron of William Blake. When he died, death-duties forced the sale of his large collection of Blake's watercolors, portraits, engravings, and sketches. Reaction to the sale of family heirlooms and despair at the development of uncorrupted regions of Dorset color Butts's autobiography, *The Crystal Cabinet* (1937), which ends by detailing the visionary experience she associated with the ancient landscape of the Badbury Rings. For Butts as for Ezra Pound, H. D., Jane Harrison, and other modernist writers, the spirit of romance and felt presence of the divinities of polytheistic lore offered alternatives to Christian and secular worlds: "Some such knowledge was awakening in me, a 'divine property of first seeing' . . . perception of a hierarchized universe, awakened by every order in the external world. Tide-pull and upthrust of trunk and root, of bulb and seed."[1] The ruins of Corfe Castle are part of her mystical landscape. Nathalie Blondel notes that the poem "Corfe," "while ostensibly centering on the Dorset village of Corfe Castle . . . resonates with even older allusion."[2] Butts writes that "when I remember you Corfe, I remember Delphi / Because your history also is a mystery of God."

Butts was educated at St. Leonard's School for Girls in St Andrews and Westfield College, London. During World War I, she was part of a circle that included Pound, H. D., Richard Aldington, May Sinclair, and Ford Madox Ford. In 1918, she married the poet and publisher John Rodker but left him, shortly after the birth of their daughter, for Cecil Maitland, a Scottish painter and writer. She moved with Maitland to Paris, where her acquaintances included Mina Loy, Jean Cocteau, Djuna Barnes, and Sylvia Beach. In Paris she began experimenting with drugs and the black magic of Aleister Crowley. In 1930, she returned to England and married the painter and cartoonist Gabriel Aiken. Her books of prose include *Ashe of Rings* (1925), *Imaginary Letters* (1928, illustrated by Cocteau), *Armed with Madness* (1928), *The Death of Felicity Taverner* (1932), and the historical novels *The Macedonian* (1933) and *Scenes from the Life of Cleopatra* (1935). Her poems have yet to be collected in a book; "Corfe," which had the alternate title "A Song to Keep People Out of Dorset," was selected by the American poet Louis Zukofsky for *An 'Objectivists' Anthology* in 1932.

Like a number of women writers of her generation, Butts was long better known for her appearance in memoirs than for her own writing, but her work has always sus-

---

[1] *The Crystal Cabinet* (1937), expanded edition Manchester, UK, 1988, p. 276
[2] *Mary Butts: Scenes from the Life*, Kingston, NY, 1998, p. 293.

tained a small group of admirers. Robin Blaser, remembering the interest in it among writers of the San Francisco Renaissance, such as Robert Duncan and Jack Spicer, praises her "special intelligence" concerning the spiritual and sexual being of men and women, adding that, for Butts, magic "is not the practice of abracadabra, but a kind of awareness, a loosening of the connections defined by the banal and the ordinary."[3]

---

[3] Afterword to Mary Butts, *Imaginary Letters*, Vancouver, 1979, p. 69.

Corfe

Corfe, the hub of a wheel
Where the green down-spokes turning
Embrace an earth-cup of smoke and ghosts and stone.
The sea orchestrates
5   The still dance in the cup
Danced for ever, the same intricate sobriety
Equivocal, adored.

But when I remember you Corfe, I remember Delphi
Because your history also is a mystery of God.

10   'And God is no blind man and God is our father:'
But like lovers
Your cup is full of the courts of other princes
Disputing you.

Very sweet is the Sacred Wood
15   In the gold clearing, in the mustard patch;
But at night comes a change
Like a gold ball thrown out
And a black ball thrown in
(Not sunset behind Tyneham Cap
20   On a night without a moon.)
But a shift of potencies
Like a black ball thrown in
And a gold ball thrown out
And the players are princes
25   Of the turf and the weed
And the wind-moulded trees
And the hazel thicket
And the red blackberry thorn.

Never trust a hemlock
30   An inch above your mouth.
An ice-green hemlock

Title: *Corfe* Castle is a medieval castle in Dorset, now in ruins.
8: *Delphi*: the ancient Greek town, site of the Oracle of Apollo
9: *mystery*: religious rite
14: *Sacred Wood*: the phrase alludes to Sir James Frazer's work of comparative anthropology, *The Golden Bough*; it also thus touches on T.S. Eliot's use of Frazer in *The Waste Land* and elsewhere (Eliot's first book of criticism was called *The Sacred Wood*).
19: *Tyneham Cap* is a nearby ridge of chalk downland.

       Is a lover
       In the wood.
       Now every way the wind blows this sweetie goes
35   In the south
       Where goes the leaf of the rose
       And the evergreen tree.

II

       Inside the house, above the wood
       Look out of the tall windows squared
40   With wood-strips painted white.
       The wild grass runs up the wild hill
       The wild hill runs up the wild sky
       The wild sky runs over itself
       And goes nowhere.

45   A man crosses the rough grass
       Up the wild hill;
       Strong graceless kharki legs in silhouette
       Tired and tough, treading the hill down.

       He will not wear it down
50   Let him try!
       He is here only because this place is
       A button on the bodies of the green hills.

III

       God keep the Hollow Land from all wrong!
       God keep the Hollow Land going strong!
55   A song a boy made in a girl
       Brother and sister in a car
       Over the flints, upon the turf
       Beside the crook-backed angry thorn
       Under the gulls, above the dead
60   To where the light made the grass glass.

       Until they came to the world's end
       The sea below and under them
       The gulls above and over them
       And through the thunder and the wailing
65   Sun full of wings was over them
       In a glass world made out of grass.
       'God keep the Hollow Land from all wrong!
       God keep the Hollow Land going strong!
       Curl horns and fleeces, straighten trees,
70   Multiply lobsters, assemble bees.

       Give it to us for ever, take our hints
       Knot up its roads for us, sharpen its flints.

47: *kharki*: khaki
53: *The Hollow Land* is a romance by William Morris (1834–1896); Butts's invocation is modeled on the
   poem that ends Morris's book ("Christ keep the Hollow Land / All the summer-tide . . .").

Pour the wind into it, the thick sea rain,
Blot out the landscape and destroy the train.

75   Turn back our folk from it, we hate the lot
Turn the American and turn the Scot;
Take unpropitious the turf, the dust
If the sea doesn't get'em then the cattle must.

Make many slugs where the stranger goes
80   Better than barbed wire the briar rose;
Swarm on the down-tops the flint men's hosts
Taboo the barrows, encourage ghosts.

Arm the rabbits with tigers' teeth
Serpents shoot from the soil beneath
85   By pain in belly and foot and mouth
Keep them out of our sacred south.'

                                                        1932

81: *flint men:* i.e., men from the Stone Age

ISAAC ROSENBERG (1890–1918)

THE CHILD OF JEWISH ÉMIGRÉS FROM WESTERN RUSSIA, ROSENBERG WAS BORN IN Bristol. He moved with his family to London at the age of seven and was educated in the East End. At 14, he left school to be apprenticed to a firm of engravers. With the financial support of another Jewish family, he attended the Slade School of Art from 1911 to 1914, where he studied with David Bomberg and produced prize-winning portraits and drawings. Poor health forced him to leave England in 1914 for South Africa, where he attempted to support himself by writing and lecturing. A year later he was back in London. He enlisted in 1915 to secure a separation allowance for his mother and was sent in 1916 to the trenches in France as a private. In 1918, he was killed in action. His first collection of poems, *Night and Day*, was published at his own expense in 1912 and gained the attention of Ezra Pound and Gordon Bottomley. He began a correspondence with Edward Marsh, who published one of his poems in *Georgian Poetry 1916–1917*. Two other pamphlets appeared in his lifetime. In 1922, Bottomley edited a posthumous collection introduced by Laurence Binyon, but Rosenberg's work was not widely recognized until the appearance of his *Collected Works* in 1937. Geoffrey Hill has written of the "skilful juxtaposing of elevated and banal diction" in Rosenberg's poetry, and in this and other ways Rosenberg has closer affinities with modernist poetry than any other British poet of World War I, with the exception of David Jones.[1] The "sardonic rat" addressed in "Break of Day in the Trenches" bespeaks Rosenberg's sensibility as it identifies with this common and commonly detested animal whose "cosmopolitan sympathies" in moving between German and English lines the soldier cannot share. Rosenberg's consciousness of the social status of Jews in England becomes the explicit subject of his simple but forceful poem "The Jew."

---

[1] Quoted in Christopher Ricks, *The Force of Poetry*, Oxford, 1984, p. 364.

The Jew

Moses, from whose loins I sprung,
Lit by a lamp in his blood
Ten immutable rules, a moon
For mutable lampless men.

5   The blonde, the bronze, the ruddy,
       With the same heaving blood,
       Keep tide to the moon of Moses,
       Then why do they sneer at me?

                                        1916 / 1922

Break of Day in the Trenches

       The darkness crumbles away.
       It is the same old druid Time as ever,
       Only a live thing leaps my hand,
       A queer sardonic rat,
5   As I pull the parapet's poppy
       To stick behind my ear.
       Droll rat, they would shoot you if they knew
       Your cosmopolitan sympathies.
       Now you have touched this English hand
10   You will do the same to a German
       Soon, no doubt, if it be your pleasure
       To cross the sleeping green between.
       It seems you inwardly grin as you pass
       Strong eyes, fine limbs, haughty athletes,
15   Less chanced than you for life,
       Bonds to the whims of murder,
       Sprawled in the bowels of the earth,
       The torn fields of France.
       What do you see in our eyes
20   At the shrieking iron and flame
       Hurled through still heavens?
       What quaver—what heart aghast?
       Poppies whose roots are in man's veins
       Drop, and are ever dropping;
25   But mine in my ear is safe—
       Just a little white with the dust.

                                        1916 / 1922

Louse Hunting

       Nudes—stark and glistening,
       Yelling in lurid glee. Grinning faces
       And raging limbs
       Whirl over the floor one fire.

Title: *The trenches* were opposing systems of defensive excavations on the Western Front in World War I; often only a few meters apart, the trenches served as troops' living quarters and only means of shelter.
2: *druid*: an ancient Celtic priest
5: *parapet*: the mound along the front of the trench
  Red *poppies* bloomed in the fields of Belgium and France where the war was fought; the flowers have since become the symbol of World War I. For commentary on the flower and Rosenberg's poem, see chapter 7 of Paul Fussell, *The Great War and Modern Memory* (London, 1975).

5   For a shirt verminously busy
       Yon soldier tore from his throat, with oaths
       Godhead might shrink at, but not the lice.
       And soon the shirt was aflare
       Over the candle he'd lit while we lay.

10   Then we all sprang up and stript
       To hunt the verminous brood.
       Soon like a demons' pantomime
       The place was raging.
       See the silhouettes agape,
15   See the gibbering shadows
       Mixed with the battled arms on the wall.
       See gargantuan hooked fingers
       Pluck in supreme flesh
       To smutch supreme littleness.
20   See the merry limbs in hot Highland fling
       Because some wizard vermin
       Charmed from the quiet this revel
       When our ears were half lulled
       By the dark music
25   Blown from Sleep's trumpet.

1917 / 1922

Dead Man's Dump

       The plunging limbers over the shattered track
       Racketed with their rusty freight,
       Stuck out like many crowns of thorns,
       And the rusty stakes like sceptres old
5   To stay the flood of brutish men
       Upon our brothers dear.

       The wheels lurched over sprawled dead
       But pained them not, though their bones crunched,
       Their shut mouths made no moan,
10   They lie there huddled, friend and foeman,
       Man born of man, and born of woman,
       And shells go crying over them
       From night till night and now.

       Earth has waited for them
15   All the time of their growth
       Fretting for their decay:
       Now she has them at last!
       In the strength of their strength
       Suspended—stopped and held.

19: *smutch:* smudge
20: *Highland fling:* a vigorous Scottish dance

1: *limbers:* wagons (here carrying barbed wire)

20   What fierce imaginings their dark souls lit
Earth! have they gone into you?
Somewhere they must have gone,
And flung on your hard back
Is their souls' sack,
25   Emptied of God-ancestralled essences.
Who hurled them out? Who hurled?

None saw their spirits' shadow shake the grass,
Or stood aside for the half used life to pass
Out of those doomed nostrils and the doomed mouth,
30   When the swift iron burning bee
Drained the wild honey of their youth.

What of us, who flung on the shrieking pyre,
Walk, our usual thoughts untouched,
Our lucky limbs as on ichor fed,
35   Immortal seeming ever?
Perhaps when the flames beat loud on us,
A fear may choke in our veins
And the startled blood may stop.

The air is loud with death,
40   The dark air spurts with fire
The explosions ceaseless are.
Timelessly now, some minutes past,
These dead strode time with vigorous life,
Till the shrapnel called 'an end!'
45   But not to all. In bleeding pangs
Some borne on stretchers dreamed of home,
Dear things, war-blotted from their hearts.

A man's brains splattered on
A stretcher-bearer's face;
50   His shook shoulders slipped their load,
But when they bent to look again
The drowning soul was sunk too deep
For human tenderness.

They left this dead with the older dead,
55   Stretched at the cross roads.

Burnt black by strange decay,
Their sinister faces lie
The lid over each eye,
The grass and coloured clay
60   More motion have than they,
Joined to the great sunk silences.

Here is one not long dead;
His dark hearing caught our far wheels,
And the choked soul stretched weak hands

34: *ichor*: the ethereal liquid that flowed in the veins of the Greek gods

65   To reach the living word the far wheels said,
The blood-dazed intelligence beating for light,
Crying through the suspense of the far torturing wheels
Swift for the end to break,
Or the wheels to break,
70   Cried as the tide of the world broke over his sight.

Will they come? Will they ever come?
Even as the mixed hoofs of the mules,
The quivering-bellied mules,
And the rushing wheels all mixed
75   With his tortured upturned sight,
So we crashed round the bend,
We heard his weak scream,
We heard his very last sound,
And our wheels grazed his dead face.

1917 / 1922

71: *Will they come?*: see note on p. 206 to Wilfred Owen's "Disabled", lines 45–46.

IVOR GURNEY (1890–1937)

GURNEY WAS BOTH A POET AND A NOTABLE COMPOSER. THE SON OF A TAILOR, HE WAS born in Gloucester between the River Severn and the Cotswold Hills; this region, its Roman and Danish past still tangible presences in the landscape, is the touchstone of much of his poetry. He was educated at King's School and a member of the Gloucester Cathedral Choir between 1900 and 1906; from 1906 to 1911, he was a pupil of the Cathedral organist. In 1911, he won a scholarship to the Royal College of Music, London, where he remained until volunteering for service in World War I. An infantryman in northern France, he was wounded in the arm and then later gassed. In 1918, he was discharged with "deferred shell-shock." In 1919, he returned to the Royal College of Music and studied with Vaughan Williams. For a few years afterwards, he worked a series of jobs while beginning to manifest symptoms of a mental illness of which he had shown signs even before the war. Having threatened to commit suicide, he was committed to a Gloucester asylum in 1922 and then moved to another in Dartford, Kent, where he remained until his death.

Two books of poems were published in his lifetime: *Severn and Somme* (1917) and *War's Ember's* (1919). His first music publication, *Five Elizabethan Songs,* appeared in 1920. Public recognition of his music came soon after his death, but the extent and nature of the poetry written after the first two books was unknown for many years. Editions of the poems edited by Edmund Blunden in 1954, Leonard Clark in 1973, P. J. Kavanagh in 1982, and most recently R. K. R. Thornton and George Walter, have gradually brought more, though not all, of the poetry into print. Previously known as a minor war poet and a songwriter in the tradition of Renaissance courtier poets such as Thomas Campion, Gurney could now be seen to have drawn on a far wider range of experience than just his war years. Even as a war poet, moreover, he differs from Owen, Sassoon, and Graves; whereas these poets "reacted against the war rhetoric of their elders with indignation and tell us truths we ought to have guessed," Kavanagh writes, "Gurney gives us pictures we would not have imagined," the French woman serving bread and coffee to soldiers in "La Gorgue" for instance.[1] In later poems such as "Sea-Marge," Gurney is still more difficult to categorize. Geoffrey Grigson pointed to Gurney's position "in-between" Georgianism and Modernism, noting that description of landscape in his poetry transcends sentimental attachments to the countryside: "What distinguishes the type of Georgian utterance—if those novel raisers of the dead, Philip Larkin and Sir John Betjeman, will allow me to say so—is a time-serving timidity and thinness of diction of the kind Ivor Gurney was rejecting, the kind appropriate to an unexacting superficial view of nature and of individual and social man. . . . If to begin

---

[1] Introduction, *Selected Poems of Ivor Gurney,* ed. P. J. Kavanagh, Oxford, 1990, p. xi.

with Gurney's attachment to Cotswold and Severn might be construed as Georgian, he very soon raises description and presentation to exulting."[2]

[2] "A Modernist Incomplete: Ivor Gurney" (1973), *Blessings, Kicks and Curses,* London, 1982, p. 116.

First Time In

After the dread tales and red yarns of the Line
Anything might have come to us; but the divine
Afterglow brought us up to a Welsh colony
Hiding in sandbag ditches, whispering consolatory
5   Soft foreign things. Then we were taken in
To low huts candle-lit, shaded close by slitten
Oilsheets, and there the boys gave us kind welcome,
So that we looked out as from the edge of home.
Sang us Welsh things, and changed all former notions
10   To human hopeful things. And the next day's guns
Nor any line-pangs ever quite could blot out
That strangely beautiful entry to war's rout;
Candles they gave us, precious and shared over-rations—
Ulysses found little more in his wanderings without doubt.
15   'David of the White Rock', the 'Slumber Song' so soft, and that
Beautiful tune to which roguish words by Welsh pit boys
Are sung—but never more beautiful than there under the guns' noise.

1922–1924 / 1982

La Gorgue

The long night, the short sleep, and La Gorgue to wander,
So be the Fates were kind and our Commander;
With a mill, and still canal, and like-Stroudway bridges.
One looks back on these as Time's truest riches
5   Which were so short an escape, so perilous a joy
Since fatigues, weather, line trouble or any whimsical ploy
Division might hatch out would have finished peace.

There was a house there, (I tell the noted thing)
The kindest woman kept, and an unending string

1: *the Line:* Troops on both sides on the Western Front in World War I occupied vast systems of trenches stretching through France and Belgium to the sea which served as shelter against attack; these were known as "the Line."
7: *Oilsheets:* sheets of (waterproof) oilskin cloth
14: *Ulysses:* Odysseus, whose twenty years' wanderings on his return home to Ithaca after Troy's defeat are told in the *Odyssey*

Title: *La Gorgue:* in Northern France, a mile or so behind the front line: the site of Gurney's brigade's headquarters in 1916.
3: *Stroud* is a district of Gloucestershire, and also a town.
6: *fatigues:* various duties, such as repairing equipment, supplying rations, and stores for the front line, etc.
   line trouble: i.e., severe fighting

10   Of privates as wasps to sugar went in and out.
         Friendliness sanctified all there without doubt,
         As lovely as the mill above the still green
         Canal where the dark fishes went almost unseen.
         B Company had come down from Tilleloy
15   Lousy, thirsty, avid of any employ
         Of peace; and this woman in leanest times had plotted
         A miracle to amaze the army-witted.
         And this was café-au-lait as princes know it,
         And fasting, and poor-struck; dead but not to show it.
20   A drink of edicts, dooms, a height of tales.
         Heat, cream, coffee; the maker tries and fails,
         The poet too, where such thirst such mate had.
         A campaign thing that makes remembrance sad.

         There was light there, too, in the clear North French way.
25   It blessed the room, and bread, and the mistress giver,
         The husband for his wife's sake, and both for a day
         Were blessed by many soldiers tired however;
         A mark in Time, a Peace, a Making-delay.

                                1922–1924 / 1982

Laventie

         One would remember still
         Meadows and low hill
         Laventie was, as to the line and elm row
         Growing through green strength wounded, as home elms grow.
5   Shimmer of summer there and blue autumn mists
         Seen from trench-ditch winding in mazy twists.
         The Australian gunners in close flowery hiding
         Cunning found out at last, and smashed in the unspeakable lists.
         And the guns in the smashed wood thumping and grinding.
10   The letters written there, and received there,
         Books, cakes, cigarettes in a parish of famine,
         And leaks in rainy times with general all-damning.
         The crater, and carrying of gas cylinders on two sticks
         (Pain past comparison and far past right agony gone),
15   Strained hopelessly of heart and frame at first fix.

         Café-au-lait in dug-outs on Tommies' cookers,
         Cursed minniewerfs, thirst in eighteen-hour summer.
         The Australian miners clayed, and the being afraid

14: The company is returning from fighting: *Tilleloy* was a nearby town, on the front.

Title: *Laventie:* a French village, near La Gorgue and Tilleloy, a mile from the front line; Gurney's battalion was "in reserve" there in 1916. Its inhabitants remained there and continued farming in the surrounding area despite its promixity to the front line. Surrounding the village were British gun batteries.
16: *Tommies':* English soldiers'
17: *minniewerfs:* German trench-mortars
18: *miners:* Huge mines were dug under the lines and then filled with explosives, to be detonated later.

20 Before strafes, sultry August dusk time than death dumber—
And the cooler hush after the strafe, and the long night wait—
The relief of first dawn, the crawling out to look at it,
Wonder divine of dawn, man hesitating before Heaven's gate.
(Though not on Cooper's where music fire took at it.
Though not as at Framilode beauty where body did shake at it)
25 Yet the dawn with aeroplanes crawling high at Heaven gate
Lovely aerial beetles of wonderful scintillate
Strangest interest, and puffs of soft purest white—
Seeking light, dispersing colouring for fancy's delight.
Of Machonachie, Paxton, Tickler and Gloucester's Stephens;
30 Fray Bentos, Spiller and Baker, odds and evens
Of trench food, but the everlasting clean craving
For bread, the pure thing, blessèd beyond saving.
Canteen disappointments, and the keen boy braving
Bullets or such for grouse roused surprisingly through
35 (Halfway) Stand-to.
And the shell nearly blunted my razor at shaving;
Tilleloy, Fauquissart, Neuve Chapelle, and mud like glue.
But Laventie, most of all, I think is to soldiers
The town itself with plane trees, and small-spa air;
40 And vin, rouge-blanc, chocolat, citron, grenadine:
One might buy in small delectable cafés there.
The broken church, and vegetable fields bare;
Neat French market-town look so clean,
And the clarity, amiability of North French air.

45 Like water flowing beneath the dark plough and high Heaven,
Music's delight to please the poet pack-marching there.

1922–1924 / 1954

The Bare Line of the Hill

The bare line of the hill
Shows Roman and
A sense of Rome hangs still
Over the land.

5 So that one looks to see
Steel gleam, to hear

23–24: *Cooper's* Hill and the town of *Framilode* are in Gloucestershire.
29ff: These are tinned rations of various kinds; *Maconochie* was tinned stew; *Stephens*, a brand of jam made in Gloucester; *Fray Bentos*, corned beef.
35: Every day at dawn and dusk, all soldiers in the trench would be commanded to "Stand to"—stand in readiness for a possible attack.
37: *Tilleloy, Fauquissart, Neuve Chappelle*: towns situated on the front line
40: *vin, rouge-blanc, chocolat, citron, grenadine*: red and white wine, hot chocolate, lemon cordial, pomegranate juice

Voices outflung suddenly
Of the challenger.

10 Yet boom of the may-fly
The loudest thing
Is of all under the sky
Of the wide evening.

And the thing metal most
The pond's last sheen
15 Willow shadow crossed
But still keen.

How long, how long before
The ploughland lose
Sense of that old power?
20 The winds, the dews

Of twice ten hundred years
Have dimmed no jot
Of Roman thought there, fears,
Triumphs unforgot.

25 Has Caesar any thought
In his new place, of lands
Far west, where cohorts fought,
Watched at his commands?

Carausius, Maximus,
30 Is all let slip, then why
Does Rome inherit thus
Dominate memory

So royally that Here
And Now are nothing known?
35 The regal and austere
Mantle of Rome is thrown

As of old—about the walls
Of hills and the farm—the fields.
Scabious guards the steeps,
40 Trefoil the slopes yield.

1921–1922 / 1973

29: *Carausius:* a general from the Low Countries who seized the Roman provinces of Britain circa 287 and ruled them independently from the central government in Rome; he was later assassinated.
  Maximus: commander of the Roman army in Britain: in 383 he usurped the throne of the western empire from the emperor Gratian. He was defeated in 388.
36: *Mantle:* i.e., toga
39: *Scabious:* a flowering herb
40: *Trefoil:* a plant resembling clover

The Bohemians

Certain people would not clean their buttons,
Nor polish buckles after latest fashions,
Preferred their hair long, putties comfortable,
Barely escaping hanging, indeed hardly able;
5   In Bridge and smoking without army cautions
Spending hours that sped like evil for quickness,
(While others burnished brasses, earned promotions).
These were those ones who jested in the trench,
While others argued of army ways, and wrenched
10   What little soul they had still further from shape,
And died off one by one, or became officers.
Without the first of dream, the ghost of notions
Of ever becoming soldiers, or smart and neat,
Surprised as ever to find the army capable
15   Of sounding 'Lights out' to break a game of Bridge,
As to fear candles would set a barn alight:
In Artois or Picardy they lie—free of useless fashions.

1925–1926 / 1954

Sea-Marge

Pebbles are beneath, but we stand softly
On them, as on sand, and watch the lacy edge
Of the swift sea

Which patterns and with glorious music the
5   Sands and round stones. It talks ever
Of new patterns.

And by the cliff-edge, there, the oakwood throws
A shadow deeper to watch what new thing
Happens at the marge.

1926–1929 / 1954

3: *putties:* or puttees: strips of cloth wound round the leg between ankle and knee as a form of gaiter
17: The French regions of *Artois* and *Picardy* were scenes of some of the bloodiest fighting of World War I.

Title: *Marge:* margin

HUGH MACDIARMID (1892–1978)

"HUGH MACDIARMID" WAS THE *NOM DE PLUME* OF CHRISTOPHER MURRAY GRIEVE, the most influential and internationally respected Scottish poet of the century. "I'll hae nae haulf-way hoose, but aye be whaur / Extremes meet," MacDiarmid wrote in *A Drunk Man Looks at the Thistle* (1926), and his work considered over his career can seem a mass of contradictions. He was a Scottish nationalist and a Communist often at odds with the National Party of Scotland and the Communist Party of Great Britain. He was a materialist and atheist with a deep interest in mystical traditions and the *élan vital* of Henri Bergson. He believed in "genius" and an intellectual elite but also in the "common man"—whom he was nevertheless prone to chastising for ignorance and sentimentality. In his role as didact and vanguard polemicist, MacDiarmid helped to forge a Scottish Renaissance with what must have seemed at times a Nietzschean act of will. *A Drunk Man Looks at the Thistle* is partly about the possibility of writing a Scottish national epic with an international purchase, and begins by acknowledging the exhaustion of the poem's speaker and, more generally, Scottish culture itself. It proceeds to hold out hope that "A greater Christ, a greater Burns, may come," while fearing that "The maist they'll dae is to gi'e bigger pegs / To folly and conceit to hank their rubbish on." Later in the poem the thistle of Scotland becomes Ygdrasil, the cosmic tree. To imagine a Scotland that would move beyond its marginal position within the United Kingdom and its parochial "kailyard" tradition's sentimental, elegiac representation of Scotland, MacDiarmid allied himself with a range of international voices: the Russians Dostoevsky, Lenin, and Leo Shestov, and others including Nietzsche, Marx, and Charles Doughty. *A Drunk Man* also represents itself at one point as a response to T. S. Eliot's *The Waste Land*. Its ambition owes less to the poetry of Robert Burns (alluded to at the beginning of the poem) than to medieval Scottish makars such as Dunbar and Henryson. Rena Grant argues that its "trajectory" suggests "how desire, whether as sexual or as sublimated into imaginative or political enterprises, works against its own abjection" and asks "what strategies one might use to speak from a place that, on the one hand, has been written as the picturesque . . . and, on the other hand, has been claimed as laudably conformist."[1]

The chief strategy is revealed by the poem's own lexicon. For *A Drunk Man*, MacDiarmid mined dictionaries of archaic Scots words and mixed these with various regional idioms to extend vernacular Scots towards a "synthetic Scots," which he hoped would constitute a language capable of presenting the complexities and ambitions of Scottish culture. Other poems immediately following *A Drunk Man*, includ-

---

[1] "Synthetic Scots: Hugh MacDiarmid's Imagined Community," *Hugh MacDiarmid: Man and Poet*, ed. Nancy Gish, Orono, 1992, p. 194.

ing *To Circumjack Cencrastus* (1930), similarly employed an idiom that no particular Scottish speaker would use, but MacDiarmid then abandoned it for an English-language poetry many readers find every bit as "synthetic," if in different ways. The ontological meditation of "On A Raised Beach," a poem Roderick Watson calls "with T. S. Eliot's *Four Quartets* . . . one of the finest and most troubling philosophical poems of our century," begins in a dictionary-derived language nearly as other to everyday use as the perdurable reality of stone that prompts the poet's meditations.[2]

Many of MacDiarmid's later poems, including *In Memoriam James Joyce,* are taken from *Mature Art,* a vast poem that occupied MacDiarmid from 1933 until his death. Because it never appeared entire in an authorized form, and because MacDiarmid continued to revise it as he published sections of the poem in journals and books, its structure has generated controversy. W. N. Herbert argues that that bulk of the poem was written by the early 1940s, and that it might be reconstructed as a six-volume poem consisting of the *Cornish Heroic Song for Valda Trevlyn, The Red Lion, The Battle Continues, The Kind of Poetry I Want, In Memoriam James Joyce,* and *Impavidi Progrediamur.*[3] In total, despite many years of extreme poverty, MacDiarmid managed to write 1,500 pages of poetry, and beyond that thousands of pages of journalism and autobiography. From Christianity to Hinduism, from the discourses of contemporary science to the latest article in the *TLS,* his poetry increasingly pulled everything into its vortex, and his habit of transcribing passages from his reading into his poetry led, in the mid-1960s, to questions about plagiarism. While modernist poetry often incorporates texts via collage, MacDiarmid's late work seemed vulnerable to this charge, because of the extent of his borrowing and failure to acknowledge sources. MacDiarmid defended his practice by referring to other examples of poetic collaboration and by speaking of himself, in *The Kind of Poetry I Want,* as a "passionate lover / Of every creative effort the whole world over."[4]

MacDiarmid was born in Langholm, Dumfriesshire, near the English border, and educated at Langholm Academy. A more informal education resulted from spending part of his youth living in post-office buildings containing a substantial library. In 1908, he went to Edinburgh as a pupil-teacher at Broughton Junior Student Centre. He began his career as a journalist, writing for and editing a variety of publications until the start of World War I, during which he served in the Royal Army Medical Corps. After the war, he settled in Montrose and resumed his journalistic work. In 1922, he founded and edited *The Scottish Chapbook.* In the same year, he became Town Councillor, Parish Councillor, and Justice of the Peace for Montrose. In 1928, he became a founding member of the National Party of Scotland. The next year, he went to London to work for a radio journal, beginning what turned out to be several unhappy years in England. He moved in 1933 to the Shetland island Whalsay, where he and his second wife Valda Trevlyn lived for nine years in a cottage without plumbing or electricity. In 1934, he joined the Communist Party of Great Britain; he was expelled four years later for "nationalist deviation." During World War II, he was conscripted for National Service and then transferred to the Merchant Service. In 1950, he was awarded a Civil List pension, which eased his ongoing financial difficulties. He rejoined the Communist Party in 1956, just as intellectuals everywhere were leaving it in droves because the Soviet Union had squashed the threatened counter-revolution in Hungary. In 1957, he read his poems in Peking. A few years later, he debated

---

2 "Landscapes of Mind and Word: MacDiarmid's Journey to the Raised Beach and Beyond," *Hugh Mac-Diarmid: Man and Poet,* p. 231.
3 *To Circumjack MacDiarmid: The Poetry and Prose of Hugh MacDiarmid,* Oxford, 1992, pp. 157–225.
4 *The Complete Poems of Hugh MacDiarmid,* ed. Michael Grieve and W. R. Aitken, London, 1978, vol. 2, p. 1030.

on the same side with Malcolm X, defending extremism. Eliot Weinberger remembers that "The words he wanted on his tombstone were 'A disgrace to the community.'"[5]

---

[5] "Introduction," Hugh MacDiarmid, *Selected Poetry*, ed. Alan Riach and Michael Grieve, New York, 1992, p. xix.

from A Drunk Man Looks at the Thistle

> *Vast imbecile mentality of those*
> *Who cannot tell a thistle from a rose.*
> *This is for others. . . .*
>
> SACHEVERELL SITWELL

[Sic Transit Gloria Scotiae]

    I amna fou' sae muckle as tired—deid dune.
    It's gey and hard wark coupin' gless for gless
    Wi' Cruivie and Gilsanquhar and the like,
    And I'm no' juist as bauld as aince I wes.

5   The elbuck fankles in the coorse o' time,
    The sheckle's no' sae souple, and the thrapple
    Grows deef and dour: nae langer up and doun
    Gleg as a squirrel speils the Adam's apple.

    Forbye, the stuffie's no' the real Mackay.
10   The sun's sel' aince, as sune as ye began it,
    Riz in your vera saul: but what keeks in
    Noo is in truth the vilest "saxpenny planet."

Section titles were added at the publisher's request to MacDiarmid's 1962 *Collected Poems;* they were dropped in the final *Complete Poems,* but for reasons of convenience in referring to the poem we have supplied them in brackets. Our annotations make use of MacDiarmid's glossary in the *Complete Poems;* we are also indebted to Kenneth Buthlay's edition of *A Drunk Man* (Edinburgh, 1987).
Epigraph: *Sacheverell Sitwell* (1897–1988) was the younger brother of the poet Edith Sitwell.

Title: "Thus passes the glory of Scotland" (Latin). "Sic transit gloria mundi" ("Thus passes the glory of the world") is said, as flax is symbolically burned, during the ceremony for the coronation of a new Pope.
1: *fou':* drunk; *sae muckle:* so much; *deid dune:* dead beat
2: *gey and hard:* very hard; *coupin':* upending
3: *Cruivie and Gilsanquhar:* the speaker's drinking-companions, "called as was the custom not by their surnames but by the names of their farms" (MacDiarmid).
4: *bauld:* strong, healthy
5: *elbuck fankles:* elbow becomes clumsy
6: *sheckle:* wrist; *thrapple:* throat
7: *deef:* numb
8: *Gleg:* eager; *speils:* climbs
9: *Forbye:* besides; *the stuffie:* whisky
10: *aince:* once
11: *keeks:* peeps
12: *saxpenny planet:* Sir Walter Scott wrote in a letter of the Scottish novelist James Hogg: "There is an old saying of the seaman's, 'every man is not born to be a boatswain', and I think I have heard of men born under a sixpenny planet, and doomed never to be worth a groat [a coin worth fourpence]. I fear something of this vile sixpenny influence had gleamed in at the cottage window when poor Hogg first came squeaking into the world."

And as the worth's gane doun the cost has risen.
Yin canna thow the cockles o' yin's hert
15   Wi'oot ha'en' cauld feet noo, jalousin' what
The wife'll say (I dinna blame her fur't).

It's robbin' Peter to pey Paul at least. . . .
And a' that's Scotch aboot it is the name,
Like a' thing else ca'd Scottish nooadays
20   —A' destitute o' speerit juist the same.

(To prove my saul is Scots I maun begin
Wi' what's still deemed Scots and the folk expect,
And spire up syne by visible degrees
To heichts whereo' the fules ha'e never recked.

25   But aince I get them there I'll whummle them
And souse the craturs in the nether deeps,
—For it's nae choice, and ony man su'd wish
To dree the goat's weird tae as weel's the sheep's!)

Heifetz in tartan, and Sir Harry Lauder!
30   Whaur's Isadora Duncan dancin' noo?
Is Mary Garden in Chicago still
And Duncan Grant in Paris—and me fou'?

Sic transit gloria Scotiae—a' the floo'ers
O' the Forest are wede awa'. (A blin' bird's nest
35   Is aiblins biggin' in the thistle tho'? . . .
And better blin' if'ts brood is like the rest!)

You canna gang to a Burns supper even
Wi'oot some wizened scrunt o' a knock-knee

14: *Yin:* one; *thow:* warm
15: *ha'en':* having; *jalousin':* guessing
19: *a' thing:* everything
21: *maun:* must
23: *spire:* climb; *syne:* then
24: *heichts:* heights; *recked:* reckoned (with)
25: *whummle:* overturn
26: *craturs:* creatures
27: *nae:* no; *su'd:* should
28: "to suffer (or endure) the goat's fate too as well as the sheep's": at the Last Judgment Christ "shall separate [the nations] one from another, as a shepherd divideth his sheep from the goats" (Matt. 25:32).
29ff: A tartan-dressed Jascha *Heifetz* (the European classical violinist) and *Sir Harry Lauder* (Scottish music-hall comedian popular in England and overseas) represent the artistic bankruptcy of a Scotland inhospitable to the genuine artistry of the dancer *Duncan* (who was actually American, despite her Scottish-sounding surname), the soprano *Garden*, or *Grant*, the Bloomsbury painter.
34: *are wede awa':* have vanished. "The flowers of the forest are a' wede away" is the refrain of a number of Scottish songs that lament the catastrophic defeat of the Scottish army at Flodden in 1513.
35: *aiblins biggin':* perhaps building
37: *gang:* go
    Burns supper: celebrating the birthday of the Scottish poet Robert Burns (1759–1796); haggis (a pudding made from sheep's offal, cooked in its stomach) is the food traditionally served on the occasion.
38: *scrunt:* midget

Chinee turns roon to say, "Him Haggis—velly goot!"
40   And ten to wan the piper is a Cockney.

No' wan in fifty kens a wurd Burns wrote
But misapplied is a'body's property,
And gin there was his like alive the day
They'd be the last a kennin' haund to gi'e—

45   Croose London Scotties wi' their braw shirt fronts
And a' their fancy freen's, rejoicin'
That similah gatherings in Timbuctoo,
Bagdad—and Hell, nae doot—are voicin'

Burns' sentiments o' universal love,
50   In pidgin English or in wild-fowl Scots,
And toastin' ane wha's nocht to them but an
Excuse for faitherin' Genius wi' *their* thochts.

A' *they've* to say was aften said afore
A lad was born in Kyle to blaw aboot.
55   What unco fate mak's *him* the dumpin'-grun'
For a' the sloppy rubbish they jaw oot?

Mair nonsense has been uttered in his name
Than in ony's barrin' liberty and Christ.
If this keeps spreedin' as the drink declines,
60   Syne turns to tea, wae's me for the *Zeitgeist*!

Rabbie, wad'st thou wert here—the warld hath need,
And Scotland mair sae, o' the likes o' thee!
The whisky that aince moved your lyre's become
A laxative for a' loquacity.

65   O gin they'd stegh their guts and haud their wheesht
I'd thole it, for "a man's a man," I ken,
But though the feck ha'e plenty o' the "a' that,"
They're nocht but zoologically men.

41: *kens*: knows
42: *a'body*: everybody
43: *gin*: if; *the day*: today
44: *kennin'*: understanding; *gi'e*: give
45: *Croose*: self-important; *Scotties*: Scots; *braw*: grand
46: *freen's*: friends
48: *doot*: doubt
51: *nocht*: nothing
52: *thochts*: thoughts
54: *A lad*: Burns (who wrote the song "There was a lad was born in Kyle"); *blaw*: boast
55: *unco*: strange
60: *Zeitgeist*: the spirit of the age
61: See Wordsworth's "London, 1802": "Milton! Thou shouldst be living at this hour; / England hath need of thee"; the Romantics admired Milton as both a poet and champion of political liberty.
62: *mair*: more
65: *stegh*: stuff; *haud their wheesht*: shut up
66: *thole*: bear; *a man's a man*: see Burns' "For a' that and a' that": "What though on hamely fare we dine, / Wear hoddin grey, and a' that, / Gie fools their silks, and knaves their wine, / A Man's a Man for a' that."
67: *feck*: majority

I'm haverin', Rabbie, but ye understaun'
70   It gets my dander up to see your star
A bauble in Babel, banged like a saxpence
'Twixt Burbank's Baedeker and Bleistein's cigar.

There's nane sae ignorant but think they can
Expatiate on *you,* if on nae ither.
75   The sumphs ha'e ta'en you at your wurd, and, fegs!
The foziest o' them claims to be a—Brither!

Syne "Here's the cheenge"—the star o' Rabbie Burns.
Sma' cheenge, "Twinkle, Twinkle." The memory slips
As G. K. Chesterton heaves up to gi'e
80   "The Immortal Memory" in a huge eclipse,

Or somebody else as famous if less fat.
You left the like in Embro in a scunner
To booze wi' thieveless cronies sic as me.
I'se warrant you'd shy clear o' a' the hunner

85   Odd Burns Clubs tae, or ninety-nine o' them,
And haud your birthday in a different kip
Whaur your name isna ta'en in vain—as Christ
Gied a' Jerusalem's Pharisees the slip

—Christ wha'd ha'e been Chief Rabbi gin he'd lik't!—
90   Wi' publicans and sinners to forgether,
But, losh! the publicans noo are Pharisees,
And I'm no' shair o' maist the sinners either.

But that's aside the point! I've got fair waun'ert.
It's no' that I'm sae fou' as juist deid dune,
95   And dinna ken as muckle's whaur I am
Or hoo I've come to sprawl here 'neth the mune.

69: *haverin':* rambling
71: *banged like a saxpence:* " 'Bang went sixpence' is the pay-off line of a comic anecdote illustrating the
parsimony of the stereotyped Scotsman in London" (Buthlay).
72: cf. T.S. Eliot's "Burbank with a Baedeker: Bleistein with a Cigar." "MacD takes these two American
tourists to suggest the commercialisation of culture, of which the Burns Cult was a Scottish example"
(Buthlay).
74: *Expatiate:* speak at length
75: *sumphs:* blockheads; *fegs!:* faith!
76: *foziest:* softest (of rotten vegetables), stupidest
77: *cheenge:* i.e., the change from the sixpence of line 71. The song "The Star o' Robbie Burns" is sung at
Burns suppers.
79: The (portly) English author G.K. *Chesterton* spoke at a London Burns Club Supper in 1923.
82: *Embro:* Edinburgh; *in a scunner:* in disgust
83: *thieveless:* profligate; *sic:* such
84: *hunner:* hundred
86: *haud:* hold; *kip:* lodging or brothel
88: *Pharisees:* the strictly observant Jewish sect whose members opposed Jesus; self-righteous or hypo-
critical people.
90: *forgether:* meet. For Christ's parable of the *publican* (tax-gatherer) and the Pharisee see Luke 18:9–14.
MacDiarmid in the next line puns on *publicans* in the sense of "owners of public houses."
92: *shair o' maist:* sure of most of
93: *fair waun'ert:* quite confused
96: *hoo:* how; *'neth:* beneath

That's it! It isna me that's fou' at a',
But the fu' mune, the doited jade, that's led
Me fer agley, or 'mogrified the warld.
100   —For a' I ken I'm safe in my ain bed.

Jean! Jean! Gin *she's* no' here it's no' *oor* bed,
Or else I'm dreamin' deep and canna wauken,
But it's a fell queer dream if this is no'
A real hillside—and thae things thistles and bracken!

105   It's hard wark haud'n by a thocht worth ha'en'
And harder speakin't, and no' for ilka man;
Maist Thocht's like whisky—a thoosan' under proof,
And a sair price is pitten on't even than.

As Kirks wi' Christianity ha'e dune,
110   Burns Clubs wi' Burns—wi' a'thing it's the same,
The core o' ocht is only for the few,
Scorned by the mony, thrang wi'ts empty name.

And a' the names in History mean nocht
To maist folk but "ideas o' their ain,"
115   The vera opposite o' onything
The Deid 'ud awn gin they cam' back again.

A greater Christ, a greater Burns, may come.
The maist they'll dae is to gi'e bigger pegs
To folly and conceit to hank their rubbish on.
120   They'll cheenge folks' talk but no' their natures, fegs!

[The Barren Fig]

[707]   *O Scotland is*
           THE barren fig.
           Up, carles, up
710   *And roond it jig.*

98: *doited jade:* confused horse
99: *fer agley:* far astray
100: *ain:* own
102: *wauken:* wake
103: *fell:* very
104: *thae:* those
105: *haud'n by:* holding onto
106: *ilka:* every
107: *sair:* dear; *pitten:* put
109: *Kirks:* Churches
111: *ocht:* anything
112: *thrang:* busy
116: *awn:* own to, claim
119: *hank:* fasten

708: *barren fig:* "Now in the morning, as [Jesus] returned into the city, he hungered. And when he saw a fig tree in the way, he came to it, and found nothing thereon, but leaves only, and said unto it, Let no fruit grow on thee henceforward for ever. And presently the fig tree withered away." (Matt. 21:18–19)
709: *carles:* men

Auld Moses took
A dry stick and
Instantly it
Floo'ered in his hand.

715   *Pu' Scotland up,*
And wha can say
It winna bud
And blossom tae.

A miracle's
720   *Oor only chance.*
Up, carles, up
And let us dance!

[Yank Oot Your Orra Boughs]

[1004]   *Yank oot your orra boughs, my hert!*

1005   God gied man speech and speech created thocht,
He gied man speech but to the Scots gied nocht
Barrin' this clytach that they've never brocht
To onything but sic a Blottie O
As some bairn's copybook micht show,

1010   A spook o' soond that frae the unkent grave
In which oor nation lies loups up to wave
Sic leprous chuns as tatties have
That cellar-boond send spindles gropin'
Towards ony hole that's open,

1015   Like waesome fingers in the dark that think
They still may widen the ane and only chink
That e'er has gi'en mankind a blink

711ff: MacDiarmid conflates the flowering of Aaron's rod (Numbers 17:8) with Moses' turning his rod into
    a serpent (Exodus 4:2–3, 7:8–12).
715: *Pu'*: pull
717: *winna*: will not
718: *tae*: too

Title: *Orra*: useless; not up to much. Buthlay cites John 15:1–3: "I am the true vine, and my Father is the
    husbandman. Every branch in me that beareth not fruit he taketh away: and every branch that beareth
    fruit he purgeth it, that it may bring forth more fruit. Now ye are clean through the word which I have
    spoken unto you."
1004: *hert*: heart
1005: *gied*: gave
1007: *clytach*: meaningless chatter
1008: *Blottie O*: a children's pencil and paper game
1009: *bairn*: child
1010: *frae*: from; *unkent*: unknown
1011: *loups*: leaps
1012: "such leprous sprouts as potatoes have"
1013: *spindles*: shoots
1015: *waesome*: sorrowful

O' Hope—tho' ev'n in that puir licht
They s'ud ha'e seen their hopeless plicht.

1020   This puir relation o' my topplin' mood,
This country cousin, streak o' churl-bluid,
This hopeless airgh 'twixt a' we can and should,
This Past that like Astarte's sting I feel,
This arrow in Achilles' heel.

1025   *Yank oot your orra boughs, my hert!*

Mebbe we're in a vicious circle cast,
Mebbe there's limits we can ne'er get past,
Mebbe we're sentrices that at the last
Are flung aside, and no' the pillars and props
1030   O' Heaven foraye as in oor hopes.

Oor growth at least nae steady progress shows,
Genius in mankind like an antrin rose
Abune a jungly waste o' effort grows,
But to Man's purpose it mak's little odds,
1035   And seems irrelevant to God's. . . .

Eneuch? Then here you are. Here's the haill story.
Life's connached shapes too'er up in croons o' glory,
Perpetuatin', natheless, in their gory
Colour the endless sacrifice and pain
1040   That to their makin's gane.

The roses like the saints in Heaven treid
Triumphant owre the agonies o' their breed,
And wag fu' mony a celestial heid
Abune the thorter-ills o' leaf and prick
1045   In which they ken the feck maun stick.

Yank oot your orra boughs, my hert!

1020: *puir:* poor
1021: *churl-bluid:* vulgar blood
1022: *airgh:* lack
1023: *Astarte:* Phoenician goddess of sex and the moon
1028: *sentrices:* scaffolding
1030: *foraye:* forever
1032: *antrin:* rare
1033: *Abune:* above
1036: *Eneuch:* enough; *haill:* whole
1037: *connached:* abused, spoiled; *too'er:* tower; *croons:* crowns
1038: *natheless:* nonetheless
1040: *gane:* gone
1041: *treid:* tread
1043: *mony:* many
1044: *Abune:* above; *thorter-ills:* obstructions, difficulties
1045: *feck:* majority

A mongrel growth, jumble o' disproportions,
Whirlin' in its incredible contortions,
Or wad-be client that an auld whore shuns,
1050 Wardin' her wizened orange o' a bosom
Frae importunities sae gruesome,

Or new diversion o' the hormones
Mair fond o' procreation than the Mormons,
And fetchin' like a devastatin' storm on's
1055 A' the uncouth dilemmas o' oor natur'
Objectified in vegetable maitter.

Yank oot your orra boughs, my hert!

And heed nae mair the foolish cries that beg
You slice nae mair to aff or pu' to leg,
1060 You skitin' duffer that gars a'body fleg,
—What tho' you ding the haill warld oot o' joint
Wi' a skier to cover-point!

Yank oot your orra boughs, my hert!

There *was* a danger—and it's weel I see't—
1065 Had brocht ye like Mallarmé to defeat:—
"Mon doute, amas de nuit ancienne, s'achève
En maint rameau subtil, qui, demeuré les vrais
Bois mêmes, prouve, hélas! que bien seul je m'offrais
Pour triomphe la faute idéale de roses."

1070 *Yank oot your orra boughs, my hert! . . .*

1926

1049: *wad-be*: would-be
1054: *on's*: on us
1058–62: This stanza uses cricketing terms. "Off" and "leg" are terms for the left and right sides of the field, depending on whether the batsman is left- or right-handed: the "off side" is that facing the batsman as he stands to receive the ball; the "leg side" is that behind him.
1059: *pu'*: pull
1060: *skitin'*: wild-hitting; *gars a'body fleg*: frightens everyone
1061: *ding*: strike
1062: *skier*: a ball struck high in the air; here caught by the *cover-point* (one of the fielding positions), thus getting the batsman out.
1064: *weel*: well
1066–1069: "The line which precedes these in Mallarmé's poem is 'Aimai-je un rêve?' and Wilfred Thorley translates the passage thus:—'Loved I Love's counterfeit? / My doubts, begotten of the long night's heat, / Dislimn the woodland till my triumph shows / As the flawed shadow of a frustrate rose.'" (Mac-Diarmid). The passage is from "L'après-midi d'un faune" ("The Afternoon of a Faun," 1876).

On a Raised Beach

To James H. Whyte

All is lithogenesis—or lochia,
Carpolite fruit of the forbidden tree,
Stones blacker than any in the Caaba,
Cream-coloured caen-stone, chatoyant pieces,
5   Celadon and corbeau, bistre and beige,
Glaucous, hoar, enfouldered, cyathiform,
Making mere faculae of the sun and moon,
I study you glout and gloss, but have
No cadrans to adjust you with, and turn again
10   From optik to haptik and like a blind man run
My fingers over you, arris by arris, burr by burr,
Slickensides, truité, rugas, foveoles,
Bringing my aesthesis in vain to bear,
An angle-titch to all your corrugations and coigns,
15   Hatched foraminous cavo-rilievo of the world,
Deictic, fiducial stones. Chiliad by chiliad
What bricole piled you here, stupendous cairn?

We are indebted at several points to the glossary in MacDiarmid's *Selected Poetry,* ed. Alan Riach and Michael Grieve (Manchester, 1992). Those interested in MacDiarmid's use of sources here should consult W.N. Herbert's *To Circumjack Cencrastus: The Poetry and Prose of Hugh MacDiarmid* (Oxford, 1992), pp. 129–36, which details his use of Theodora Bosanquet's *Paul Valéry* (London, 1933).

Title: *Raised Beach*: a former beach, now above sea level. The poem was written during MacDiarmid's stay on Whalsay, one of Scotland's Shetland Islands; the raised beach is on the nearby island of Linga.

1: *lithogenesis*: the process of formation of stones
   lochia: watery discharge following childbirth; "the word is associated with metaphors of parturition (or 'the act of bringing forth') in Nietzsche and Soloview, and may refer to the evolution or 'second birth' of consciousness" (Riach and Grieve).

2: *carpolite fruit*: fossil fruit

3: *Caaba*: a shrine located in the centre of the Great Mosque of Mecca; it encloses a sacred black stone, which is kissed by pilgrims to Mecca.

4: *caen-stone*: a light-yellow stone used for building
 chatoyant: cat's-eye stone, which changes in appearance when viewed from different angles

5: *Celadon*: pale green; *corbeau*: dark green verging on black; *bistre*: a brown pigment made from soot

6: *Glaucous*: dull or pale green; *hoar*: white or greyish white; *enfouldered*: black as a thundercloud; charged with lightning; *cyathiform*: shaped like a drinking glass

7: *faculae*: bright spots on the sun

8: *glout*: a scowl or frown; weather that looks dark and threatening is said to "glout."

9: *cadrans*: an instrument that adjusts a gemstone while it is being cut

10: *from optik to haptik*: from the sense of sight to that of touch

11: *arris*: sharp edge; *burr*: rough edge

12: A *slickenside* is a polished mineral or rock surface in a mass of rock, caused by pressure and friction. *truité*: a delicately crackled surface (said of ceramics); *rugas*: wrinkles or ridges; *foveoles*: tiny pits

13: *aesthesis*: sensory perception

14: *angle-titch*: a worm used as fishing-bait; *coigns*: corners

15: *Hatched*: carved with parallel lines (e.g., to shade part of an engraving); *foraminous*: perforated; *cavo-rilievo*: a relief carving in which the highest portions are left at the same level as the original surface, which remains around its edges

16: *Deictic*: directly demonstrating (said of a logical argument); *fiducial*: serving as a basis of reckoning; trustworthy; *Chiliad*: thousand

17: *bricole*: a medieval engine for throwing stones; *cairn*: a pile of stones marking a site (e.g., a gravesite or boundary)

What artist poses the Earth écorché thus,
Pillar of creation engouled in me?
20   What eburnation augments you with men's bones,
Every energumen an Endymion yet?
All the other stones are in this haecceity it seems,
But where is the Christophanic rock that moved?
What Cabirian song from this catasta comes?

25   Deep conviction or preference can seldom
Find direct terms in which to express itself.
Today on this shingle shelf
I understand this pensive reluctance so well,
This not discommendable obstinacy,
30   These contrivances of an inexpressive critical feeling,
These stones with their resolve that Creation shall not be
Injured by iconoclasts and quacks. Nothing has stirred
Since I lay down this morning an eternity ago
But one bird. The widest open door is the least liable to intrusion,
35   Ubiquitous as the sunlight, unfrequented as the sun.
The inward gates of a bird are always open.
It does not know how to shut them.
That is the secret of its song,
But whether any man's are ajar is doubtful.
40   I look at these stones and know little about them,
But I know their gates are open too,
Always open, far longer open, than any bird's can be,
That every one of them has had its gates wide open far longer
Than all birds put together, let alone humanity,
45   Though through them no man can see,
No man nor anything more recently born than themselves
And that is everything else on the Earth.
I too lying here have dismissed all else.
Bread from stones is my sole and desperate dearth,
50   From stones, which are to the Earth as to the sunlight
Is the naked sun which is for no man's sight.
I would scorn to cry to any easier audience
Or, having cried, to lack patience to await the response.
I am no more indifferent or ill-disposed to life than death is;
55   I would fain accept it all completely as the soil does;
Already I feel all that can perish perishing in me
As so much has perished and all will yet perish in these stones.
I must begin with these stones as the world began.

18: *écorché*: flayed; an ecorché is an artistic representation of a figure without skin, in order to show the muscles for study.

19: *engouled*: held in an animal's mouth (a term from heraldry)

20: *eburnation*: a diseased condition of bone or cartilage, in which it becomes hard as ivory

21: *energumen*: a person possessed by a devil; *Endymion*: a youth loved by Selene, goddess of the moon; she made him sleep eternally in a cave, so that she could visit him unobserved.

22: *haecceity*: "thisness," individuality (a word coined by the medieval Scottish theologian Duns Scotus)

23: *Christophanic*: pertaining to the appearance of Christ after his death. The stone rolled away from the entrance to Christ's tomb after his resurrection.

24: *Cabirian song*: a song in worship of the ancient gods the Cabeiri, worshipped on the islands of the Greek archipelago
  catasta: a stage or bed used in torture; also, a block on which slaves were exposed for sale

Shall I come to a bird quicker than the world's course ran?
60   To a bird, and to myself, a man?
            And what if I do, and further?
I shall only have gone a little way to go back again
And be like a fleeting deceit of development,
Iconoclasts, quacks. So these stones have dismissed
65 All but all of evolution, unmoved by it,
(Is there anything to come they will not likewise dismiss?)
As the essential life of mankind in the mass
Is the same as their earliest ancestors yet.

Actual physical conflict or psychological warfare
70   Incidental to love or food
Brings out animal life's bolder and more brilliant patterns
            Concealed as a rule in habitude.
            There is a sudden revelation of colour,
            The protrusion of a crest,
75   The expansion of an ornament,
—But no general principle can be guessed
From these flashing fragments we are seeing,
These foam-bells on the hidden currents of being.
The bodies of animals are visible substances
80 And must therefore have colour and shape, in the first place
Depending on chemical composition, physical structure, mode of growth,
Physiological rhythms and other factors in the case,
But their purposive function is another question.
Brilliant-hued animals hide away in the ocean deeps;
85 The mole has a rich sexual colouring in due season
Under the ground; nearly every beast keeps
Brighter colours inside it than outside.
What the seen shows is never anything to what it's designed to hide,
The red blood which makes the beauty of a maiden's cheek
90 Is as red under a gorilla's pigmented and hairy face.
Varied forms and functions though life may seem to have shown
They all come back to the likeness of stone,
So to the intervening stages we can best find a clue
In what we all came from and return to.
95 There are no twirly bits in this ground bass.

We must be humble. We are so easily baffled by appearances
And do not realise that these stones are one with the stars.
It makes no difference to them whether they are high or low,
Mountain peak or ocean floor, palace, or pigsty.
100 There are plenty of ruined buildings in the world but no ruined stones.
No visitor comes from the stars
But is the same as they are.

95: *ground bass*: "a bass-passage of four or eight bars in length, constantly repeated with a varied melody
  and harmony" (OED)

—Nay, it is easy to find a spontaneity here,
An adjustment to life, an ability
105   To ride it easily, akin to 'the buoyant
Prelapsarian naturalness of a country girl
Laughing in the sun, not passion-rent,
But sensing in the bound of her breasts vigours to come
Powered to make her one with the stream of earthlife round her,'
110   But not yet as my Muse is, with this ampler scope,
This more divine rhythm, wholly at one
With the earth, riding the Heavens with it, as the stones do
And all soon must.
But it is wrong to indulge in these illustrations
115   Instead of just accepting the stones.
It is a paltry business to try to drag down
The arduous furor of the stones to the futile imaginings of men,
To all that fears to grow roots into the common earth,
As it soon must, lest it be chilled to the core,
120   As it will be—and none the worse for that.
Impatience is a poor qualification for immortality.
Hot blood is of no use in dealing with eternity.
It is seldom that promises or even realisations
Can sustain a clear and searching gaze.
125   But an emotion chilled is an emotion controlled;
This is the road leading to certainty,
Reasoned planning for the time when reason can no longer avail.
It is essential to know the chill of all the objections
That come creeping into the mind, the battle between opposing ideas
130   Which gives the victory to the strongest and most universal
Over all others, and to wage it to the end
With increasing freedom, precision, and detachment
A detachment that shocks our instincts and ridicules our desires.
All else in the world cancels out, equal, capable
135   Of being replaced by other things (even as all the ideas
That madden men now must lose their potency in a few years
And be replaced by others—even as all the religions,
All the material sacrifices and moral restraints,
That in twenty thousand years have brought us no nearer to God
140   Are irrelevant to the ordered adjustments
Out of reach of perceptive understanding
Forever taking place on the Earth and in the unthinkable regions around it;
This cat's cradle of life; this reality volatile yet determined;
This intense vibration in the stones
145   That makes them seem immobile to us)
But the world cannot dispense with the stones.
They alone are not redundant. Nothing can replace them
Except a new creation of God.

I must get into this stone world now.
150   Ratchel, striae, relationships of tesserae,

103–109: This passage derives from p. 209 of F.R. Leavis's *New Bearings in English Poetry* (London, 1932).
   The quote marks indicate Leavis's quotation of a poem by Ronald Bottrall.
150: *Ratchel*: loose pieces of stone lying atop firm rock
    striae: ridges
    tesserae: the cubes of a mosaic

          Innumerable shades of grey,
          Innumerable shapes,
      And beneath them all a stupendous unity,
      Infinite movement visibly defending itself
155   Against all the assaults of weather and water,
      Simultaneously mobilised at full strength
      At every point of the universal front,
          Always at the pitch of its powers,
          The foundation and end of all life.
160   I try them with the old Norn words—hraun
      Duss, rønis, queedaruns, kollyarun;
      They hvarf from me in all directions
      Over the hurdifell—klett, millya hellya, hellyina bretta,
      Hellyina wheeda, hellyina grø, bakka, ayre,—
165   And lay my world in kolgref.

      This is no heap of broken images.
      Let men find the faith that builds mountains
      Before they seek the faith that moves them. Men cannot hope
      To survive the fall of the mountains
170   Which they will no more see than they saw their rise
      Unless they are more concentrated and determined,
      Truer to themselves and with more to be true to,
      Than these stones, and as inerrable as they are.
      Their sole concern is that what can be shaken
175   Shall be shaken and disappear
      And only the unshakeable be left.
      What hardihood in any man has part or parcel in the latter?
      It is necessary to make a stand and maintain it forever.
      These stones go through Man, straight to God, if there is one.
180   What have they not gone through already?
      Empires, civilisations, aeons. Only in them
      If in anything, can His creation confront Him.

160: *Norn*: the Norse dialect formerly spoken on Scotland's Orkney and Shetland islands, which were
   Scandinavian possessions from the ninth century until 1472. In these lines MacDiarmid draws on "The
   Old Shetland Place-Names," from *The Dialect and Place Names of Shetland* (1897) by Jakob Jakobsen.
      hraun: a rough or rocky place
161: *Duss*: "*Duss*, O.N. *dys*, means a (thrown up) heap. . . . in Danish *'dysse'* is a cairn or stone-heap"
   (Jakobsen)
      rønis: "There are several heights by the name of *Røni* (*Røn*) in Shetland. It is O.N. *hraun*, which
   denotes originally a rough or rocky place, a wilderness. . . . In placenames the word denotes a rocky hill
   (knoll, brae) or plateau." Thus *queedaruns*: white hills; *kollyarun*: round-topped hill
162: *hvarf*: turn, disappear
163: *hurdifell*: "a steep rocky hill, full of downfallen boulders" (Jakobsen)
      klett: "*Klett* (O.N. *klett-r*) denotes a (piece of) rock and is also applied collectively to the shore rocks,
   a stretch of low rocky shore." (Jakobsen)
      millya hellya: between the smooth rocks
      hellyina bretta: the steep rock
164: *Hellyina wheeda*: the white rock
      hellyina grø: the grey rock
      bakka: "*Bakka*, O.N. *bakki*, is the old word for cliff or 'banks' (steep, rocky shore)." (Jakobsen)
      ayre: "*Ayre* means beach or a piece of sandy (gravelly) shore" (Jakobsen)
165: "There is an expression used in [the Shetland island of] Yell: 'to lay onything in *kolgref*': to do any-
   thing roughly, especially in delving: to leave the ground in a rough state (Icel. *kolgröf* denotes a pit for
   burning coals)." (Jakobsen)
166: *heap of broken images*: see T. S. Eliot, *The Waste Land*: "What are the roots that clutch, what branches
   grow / Out of this stony rubbish? Son of man, / You cannot say, or guess, for you know only / A heap of
   broken images" (19–22).

They came so far out of the water and halted forever.
That larking dallier, the sun, has only been able to play
185   With superficial by-products since;
The moon moves the waters backwards and forwards,
But the stones cannot be lured an inch farther
Either on this side of eternity or the other.
Who thinks God is easier to know than they are?
190   Trying to reach men any more, any otherwise, than they are?
These stones will reach us long before we reach them.
Cold, undistracted, eternal and sublime.
They will stem all the torrents of vicissitude forever
With a more than Roman peace.

195   Death is a physical horror to me no more.
I am prepared with everything else to share
Sunshine and darkness and wind and rain
And life and death bare as these rocks though it be
In whatever order nature may decree,
200   But, not indifferent to the struggle yet
Nor to the ataraxia I might get
By fatalism, a deeper issue see
Than these, or suicide, here confronting me.
It is reality that is at stake.
205   Being and non-being with equal weapons here
Confront each other for it, non-being unseen
But always on the point, it seems, of showing clear,
Though its reserved contagion may breed
This fancy too in my still susceptible head
210   And then by its own hidden movement lead
Me as by aesthetic vision to the supposed
Point where by death's logic everything is recomposed,
Object and image one, from their severance freed,
As I sometimes, still wrongly, feel 'twixt this storm beach and me.
215   What happens to us
Is irrelevant to the world's geology
But what happens to the world's geology
Is not irrelevant to us.
We must reconcile ourselves to the stones,
220   Not the stones to us.
Here a man must shed the encumbrances that muffle
Contact with elemental things, the subtleties
That seem inseparable from a humane life, and go apart
Into a simple and sterner, more beautiful and more oppressive world,
225   Austerely intoxicating; the first draught is overpowering;
Few survive it. It fills me with a sense of perfect form,
The end seen from the beginning, as in a song.
It is no song that conveys the feeling
That there is no reason why it should ever stop,
230   But the kindred form I am conscious of here

194: *Roman peace*: or *Pax Romana*, the state of relative peace throughout the Mediterranean world from
  the reign of Augustus (27 BC–AD 14) to that of Marcus Aurelius (161–180).
201: *ataraxia*: stoical indifference

Is the beginning and end of the world,
The unsearchable masterpiece, the music of the spheres,
Alpha and Omega, the Omnific Word.
These stones have the silence of supreme creative power,
235   The direct and undisturbed way of working
Which alone leads to greatness.
What experience has any man crystallised,
What weight of conviction accumulated,
What depth of life suddenly seen entire
240   In some nigh supernatural moment
And made a symbol and lived up to
With such resolution, such Spartan impassivity?
It is a frenzied and chaotic age,
Like a growth of weeds on the site of a demolished building.
245   How shall we set ourselves against it,
Imperturbable, inscrutable, in the world and yet not in it,
        Silent under the torments it inflicts upon us,
            With a constant centre,
With a single inspiration, foundations firm and invariable;
250   By what immense exercise of will,
Inconceivable discipline, courage, and endurance,
        Self-purification and anti-humanity,
            Be ourselves without interruption,
                Adamantine and inexorable?
255   It will be ever increasingly necessary to find
In the interests of all mankind
Men capable of rejecting all that all other men
        Think, as a stone remains
Essential to the world, inseparable from it,
260   And rejects all other life yet.
Great work cannot be combined with surrender to the crowd.
        —Nay, the truth we seek is as free
From all yet thought as a stone from humanity.
Here where there is neither haze nor hesitation
265   Something at least of the necessary power has entered into me.
I have still to see any manifestation of the human spirit
That is worthy of a moment's longer exemption than it gets
From petrifaction again—to get out if it can.
All is lithogenesis—or lochia;
270   And I can desire nothing better,
An immense familiarity with other men's imaginings
Convinces me that they cannot either
(If they could, it would instantly be granted
—The present order must continue till then)
275   Though, of course, I still keep an open mind,
A mind as open as the grave.
You may say that the truth cannot be crushed out,
That the weight of the whole world may be tumbled on it,

233: *Alpha and Omega*: "I am Alpha and Omega, the beginning and the ending, saith the Lord" (Rev. 1:8);
  Omnific: all-creating
242: *Spartan impassivity*: Ancient Sparta was a military oligarchy whose citizens were trained as warriors,
  cultivating the virtues of stoicism and toughness.
254: *Adamantine*: exceedingly hard ("adamant" being a mythical type of stone of unbreakable hardness)

And yet, in puny, distorted, phantasmal shapes albeit,
280   It will braird again; it will force its way up
Through unexpectable fissures? look over this beach.
What ruderal and rupestrine growth is here?
What crop confirming any credulities?
Conjure a fescue to teach me with from this
285   And I will listen to you, but until then
Listen to me—Truth is not crushed;
It crushes, gorgonises all else into itself.
The trouble is to know it when you see it?
You will have no trouble with it when you do.
290   Do not argue with me. Argue with these stones.
Truth has no trouble in knowing itself.
This is it. The hard fact. The inoppugnable reality,
Here is something for you to digest.
Eat this and we'll see what appetite you have left
295   For a world hereafter.
I pledge you in the first and last crusta,
The rocks rattling in the bead-proof seas.

O we of little faith,
As romanticists viewed the philistinism of their days
300   As final and were prone to set over against it
Infinite longing rather than manly will—
Nay, as all thinkers and writers find
The indifference of the masses of mankind,—
So are most men with any stone yet,
305   Even those who juggle with lapidary's, mason's, geologist's words
And all their knowledge of stones in vain,
Tho' these stones have far more differences in colour, shape and size
Than most men to my eyes—
Even those who develop precise conceptions to immense distances
310   Out of these bleak surfaces.
All human culture is a Goliath to fall
To the least of these pebbles withal.
A certain weight will be added yet
To the arguments of even the most foolish
315   And all who speak glibly may rest assured
That to better their oratory they will have the whole earth
For a Demosthenean pebble to roll in their mouths.

I am enamoured of the desert at last,
The abode of supreme serenity is necessarily a desert.

280: *braird*: sprout (Scot)
282: *ruderal*: growing on ruins or stone-rubbish
  rupestrine: growing on rocks
284: *fescue*: teacher's pointing-stick
287: *gorgonises*: turns to stone
292: *inoppugnable*: uncontrovertible
296: *crusta*: a hard coating; a layer of the earth; and a cocktail served in a glass with a sugar-encrusted rim
297: *bead-proof*: (said of alcohol) very strong; from the erroneous belief that strong alcohol will carry bubbles after shaking.
305: *lapidary*: someone who works with gemstones
317: The Greek orator *Demosthenes* cured his speech impediment by practicing speaking with pebbles in his mouth.

320   My disposition is towards spiritual issues
       Made inhumanly clear; I will have nothing interposed
       Between my sensitiveness and the barren but beautiful reality;
       The deadly clarity of this 'seeing of a hungry man'
       Only traces of a fever passing over my vision
325   Will vary, troubling it indeed, but troubling it only
       In such a way that it becomes for a moment
       Superhumanly, menacingly clear—the reflection
       Of a brightness through a burning crystal.
       A culture demands leisure and leisure presupposes
330   A self-determined rhythm of life; the capacity for solitude
       Is its test; by that the desert knows us.
       It is not a question of escaping from life
       But the reverse—a question of acquiring the power
       To exercise the loneliness, the independence, of stones,
335   And that only comes from knowing that our function remains
       However isolated we seem fundamental to life as theirs.
                We have lost the grounds of our being,
                We have not built on rock.
       Thinking of all the higher zones
340   Confronting the spirit of man I know they are bare
       Of all so-called culture as any stone here;
       Not so much of all literature survives
       As any wisp of scriota that thrives
       On a rock—(interesting though it may seem to be
345   As de Bary's and Schwendener's discovery
       Of the dual nature of lichens, the partnership,
       Symbiosis, of a particular fungus and particular alga).
       These bare stones bring me straight back to reality.
                I grasp one of them and I have in my grip
350   The beginning and the end of the world,
       My own self, and as before I never saw
       The empty hand of my brother man,
       The humanity no culture has reached, the mob.
       Intelligentsia, our impossible and imperative job!

355   'Ah!' you say, 'if only one of these stones would move
       —Were it only an inch—of its own accord.
                This is the resurrection we await,
       —The stone rolled away from the tomb of the Lord.
                I know there is no weight in infinite space,
360   No impermeability in infinite time,
       But it is as difficult to understand and have patience here
                As to know that the sublime
       Is theirs no less than ours, no less confined
       To men than men's to a few men, the stars of their kind.'
365   (The masses too have begged bread from stones,
                From human stones, including themselves,
                And only got it, not from their fellow-men,
                But from stones such as these here—if then.)

343: *scriota*: The word is untraced. Perhaps MacDiarmid meant the script lichen (*Graphis scripta*).
345: The nineteenth-century German botanists *de Bary* and *Schwendener* discovered that lichen was not
an individual plant but an alga and a fungus growing together symbiotically.

Detached intellectuals, not one stone will move,
370   Not the least of them, not a fraction of an inch. It is not
       The reality of life that is hard to know.
    It is nearest of all and easiest to grasp,
    But you must participate in it to proclaim it.
    —I lift a stone; it is the meaning of life I clasp
375   Which is death, for that is the meaning of death;
    How else does any man yet participate
       In the life of a stone,
    How else can any man yet become
    Sufficiently at one with creation, sufficiently alone,
380   Till as the stone that covers him he lies dumb
    And the stone at the mouth of his grave is not overthrown?
    —Each of these stones on this raised beach,
       Every stone in the world,
    Covers infinite death, beyond the reach
385   Of the dead it hides; and cannot be hurled
    Aside yet to let any of them come forth, as love
       Once made a stone move
     (Though I do not depend on that
       My case to prove).
390   So let us beware of death; the stones will have
    Their revenge; we have lost all approach to them,
    But soon we shall become as those we have betrayed,
    And they will seal us fast in our graves
    As our indifference and ignorance seals them;
395   But let us not be afraid to die.
    No heavier and colder and quieter then,
    No more motionless, do stones lie
       In death than in life to all men.
    It is not more difficult in death than here
400   —Though slow as the stones the powers develop
    To rise from the grave—to get a life worth having;
    And in death—unlike life—we lose nothing that is truly ours.

    Diallage of the world's debate, end of the long auxesis,
    Although no ébrillade of Pegasus can here avail,
405   I prefer your enchorial characters—the futhorc of the future—
    To the hieroglyphics of all the other forms of Nature.
    Song, your apprentice encrinite, seems to sweep
    The Heavens with a last entrochal movement;
    And, with the same word that began it, closes
410   Earth's vast epanadiplosis.

1933 / 1934

403: *Diallage*: (1) [pronounced *di-ál-a-jee*] in rhetoric, the bringing to bear of multiple arguments upon a single point; (2) [pronounced *dí-al-edge*] a type of green mineral
    auxesis: rhetorical digression
404: *ébrillade*: the check given a horse by its rider (by jerking one rein) when it refuses to turn
    Pegasus: the winged horse of Greek legend, symbol of poetic inspiration
405: *enchorial*: the demotic type of ancient Egyptian writing (as opposed to the hieroglyphic and hieratic forms)
    futhorc: the Runic alphabet
407: *encrinite*: a fossil crinoid (sea-lily)
408: *entrochal*: wheeling; "entrochi" are the wheel-like plates of which some crinoids are composed.
410: *epanadiplosis*: a rhetorical device in which a sentence begins and ends with the same word

from In Memoriam James Joyce

[629]   Let the only consistency
630   In the course of my poetry
            Be like that of the hawthorn tree
            Which in early Spring breaks
            Fresh emerald, then by nature's law
            Darkens and deepens and takes
635   Tints of purple-maroon, rose-madder and straw.

            Sometimes these hues are found
            Together, in pleasing harmony bound.
            Sometimes they succeed each other. But through
            All the changes in which the hawthorn is dight,
640   No matter in what order, one thing is sure
            —The haws shine ever the more ruddily bright!

            And when the leaves have passed
            Or only in a few tatters remain
            The tree to the winter condemned
645   Stands forth at last
                Not bare and drab and pitiful,
            But a candelabrum of oxidised silver gemmed
            By innumerable points of ruby
            Which dominate the whole and are visible
650   Even at considerable distance
            As flame-points of living fire.
            That so it may be
            With my poems too at last glance
            Is my only desire.

655   All else must be sacrificed to this great cause.
            I fear no hardships. I have counted the cost.
            I with my heart's blood as the hawthorn with its haws
            Which are sweetened and polished by the frost!
            See how these haws burn, there down the drive,
660   In this autumn air that feels like cotton wool,
            When the earth has the gelatinous limpness of a body dead as a whole
            While its tissues are still alive!

            Poetry is human existence come to life,
            The glorious energy that once employed
665   Turns all else in creation null and void,
            The flower and fruit, the meaning and goal,
            Which won all else is needs removed by the knife
            Even as a man who rises high
            Kicks away the ladder he has come up by.

635: *madder*: red
639: *dight*: dressed, arrayed
669: cf. the *Tractatus Logico-Philosophicus* of Ludwig Wittgenstein (1889–1951), proposition 6.54: "My propositions serve as elucidations in the following way: anyone who understands me eventually recognizes them as nonsensical, when he has used them—as steps—to climb up beyond them. (He must, so to speak, throw away the ladder after he has climbed up it.)"

670   This single-minded zeal, this fanatic devotion to art
           Is alien to the English poetic temperament no doubt,
           'This narrowing intensity' as the English say,
           But I have it even as you had it, Yeats, my friend,
           And would have it with me as with you at the end,
675   I who am infinitely more un-English than you
           And turn Scotland to poetry like those women who
           In their passion secrete and turn to
           Musk through and through!

           So I think of you, Joyce, and of Yeats and others who are dead
680   As I walk this Autumn and observe
           The birch tremulously pendulous in jewels of cairngorm,
           The sauch, the osier, and the crack-willow
           Of the beaten gold of Australia;
           The sycamore in rich straw-gold;
685   The elm bowered in saffron;
           The oak in flecks of salmon gold;
           The beeches huge torches of living orange.

           Billow upon billow of autumnal foliage
           From the sheer high bank glass themselves
690   Upon the ebon and silver current that floods freely
           Past the shingle shelves.
           I linger where a crack willow slants across the stream,
           Its olive leaves slashed with fine gold.
           Beyond the willow a young beech
695   Blazes almost blood-red,
           Vying in intensity with the glowing cloud of crimson
           That hangs about the purple bole of a gean
           Higher up the brae face.

           And yonder, the lithe green-grey bole of an ash, with its boughs
700   Draped in the cinnamon-brown lace of samara.
           (And I remember how in April upon its bare twigs
           The flowers came in ruffs like the unshorn ridges
           Upon a French poodle—like a dull mulberry at first,
           Before the first feathery fronds
705   Of the long-stalked, finely-poised, seven-fingered leaves)—
           Even the robin hushes his song
           In these gold pavilions.

681: *cairngorm*: a yellow or smoke-brown quartz found in Scotland
682: *sauch*: a type of low-growing willow
    osier: a willow whose tough branches are used in basket-work
    crack-willow: a type of willow with brittle branches
690: *ebon*: black
697: *gean*: the wild cherry tree (Scots)
698: *brae*: the steep bank of a river valley (Scots)
700: *samara*: the winged, one-seeded fruit of the ash

Other masters may conceivably write
Even yet in C major
710   But we—we take the perhaps 'primrose path'
To the dodecaphonic bonfire.

They are not endless these variations of form
Though it is perhaps impossible to see them all.
It is certainly impossible to conceive one that doesn't exist.
715   But I keep trying in our forest to do both of these,
And though it is a long time now since I saw a new one
I am by no means weary yet of my concentration
On phyllotaxis here in preference to all else,
All else—but my sense of sny!

720   The gold edging of a bough at sunset, its pantile way
Forming a double curve, tegula and imbrex in one,
Seems at times a movement on which I might be borne
Happily to infinity; but again I am glad
When it suddenly ceases and I find myself
725   Pursuing no longer a rhythm of duramen
But bouncing on the diploe in a clearing between earth and air
Or headlong in dewy dallops or a moon-spairged fernshaw
Or caught in a dark dumosity, or even
In open country again watching an aching spargosis of stars.

1937–1939 / *1955*

708ff: The avant-garde composer Arnold Schoenberg (1874–1951) invented the 12-tone (dodecaphonic)
system of composition, which treats all notes of the chromatic scale as of equal importance and dis-
penses with an audible key. Despite his innovations, he is reputed to have said, "There is still much good
music to be written in C major."

710: The quoted phrase is from *Hamlet* 1.3.50, but MacDiarmid has in mind *Macbeth* 2.3.19: "the primrose
way to th'everlasting bonfire."

718: *phyllotaxis*: the arrangement of leaves on a plantstem

719: *sny*: The sense of the word MacDiarmid had in mind remains untraced. The *OED* records only a noun
that means (in shipbuilding) "the upwards curve of a plank"; and a dialect verb meaning "to teem,
abound, be infested" (with something).

720: *pantile*: a roofing tile with an ogee (S-shaped) cross-section.

721: See *OED*, "tegula" sb 2, quotation from 1871: "The Roman tiles were of two kinds, flat tiles [tegulae]
and smaller curved tiles [imbrices]. The flat tiles had raised rims at the sides . . . The small curved tiles
were . . . laid over the joined edges . . . and formed a complete protection for the joint." Thus a combi-
nation of convex imbrex and concave tegula would produce an S-shaped curve like a pantile.

725: *duramen*: the hard central wood of a tree

726: *diploe*: the green cellular matter of which leaves are made

727: *dallops*: patches of grass or weeds
    spairged: besprinkled (Scots)
    fernshaw: fern-thicket

728: *dumosity*: bramble-thicket

729: *spargosis*: distention of the breasts from excess milk

Sylvia Townsend Warner (1893–1978)

WARNER WAS BORN IN HARROW, MIDDLESEX, AND EDUCATED PRIVATELY. INTENDing to pursue a career in music, she turned to musicology after World War I, and was the only female editor of the ten-volume *Tudor Church Music* (1925–1930). With the encouragement of T. F. Powys and David Garnett, she began a literary career that resulted in numerous novels and collections of short stories, together with translations, biographies, and poetry. Her first novel, *Lolly Willowes* (1926), became the first American Book of the Month selection, and throughout her lifetime her stories regularly appeared in the *New Yorker*. With her companion, the poet Valentine Ackland, she went to Spain, working for the Red Cross and attending the congress of anti-Fascist writers; in 1935, she joined the British Communist Party. Warner's novels include *Mr. Fortune's Maggot* (1927), *The Corner That Held Them* (1948), generally considered her masterpiece, and *The Flint Anchor* (1954). Her volumes of poetry include *Espalier* (1925), the novel in verse *Opus 7* (1931), *King Duffus and Other Poems* (1968), and *Collected Poems* (1983). For these and other accomplishments, she was made a fellow of the Royal Society of Literature and an honorary member of the American Academy of Arts and Letters.

Noting the "half-modern, half-archaic blend of naïveté and erudition" in her poems, Louis Untermeyer once described Warner as a "feminine Thomas Hardy," but her biographer and editor Claire Harman detects "an air of learned mischief . . . which is far from Hardyesque."[1] In a late interview, Warner said that she was "more at home with seventeenth-century poetry than with any other. I'm a very great admirer of Dryden, because Dryden can say anything."[2] While it is no more fair to Warner's poetry to call it "Drydenesque" than "Hardyesque," the two comparisons do indicate something of the technique of her best poems. "King Duffus" uses a form rarely employed—triplets—as its narrative extends motifs concerning witches and the supernatural also found in Warner's fiction. "Anne Donne" might be an example of the "learned mischief" Harman mentions; the poem's outrageously repeated pun is borrowed from John Donne but used here to hint at Warner's view of the child-bearing labors of Donne's wife Anne. The range of Warner's poetic modes, which include satire, burlesque, lyric, the verse novel, Tudor metrical conceits, and Communist ballads, can only be hinted at. "East London Cemetery," one of her finest poems, suggests the work of Emily Dickinson.

---

[1] *Modern British Poetry: A Critical Anthology*, 5th ed., New York, 1942, p. 408; Claire Harman quoted in Donald Davie, *Under Briggflatts: A History of Poetry in Great Britain 1960–1988*, Chicago, 1989, p. 231.
[2] *P. N. Review*, vol. 23, 1981, p. 36.

Nelly Trim

'Like men riding,
The mist from the sea
Drives down the valley
And baffles me.'
'Enter, traveller,
Whoever you be.'

By lamplight confronted
He staggered and peered;
Like a wet bramble
Was his beard.
'Sit down, stranger,
You look a-feared.'

Shudders rent him
To the bone,
The wet ran off him
And speckled the stone.
'Dost bide here alone, maid?'
'Yes, alone.'

As he sat down
In the chimney-nook
Over his shoulder
He cast a look,
As if the night
Were pursuing; she took

A handful of brash
To mend the fire,
He eyed her close
As the flame shot higher;
He spoke—and the cattle
Moved in the byre.

'Though you should heap
Your fire with wood,
'Twouldn't warm me,
Nor do no good,
Unless you first warm me
As a maiden should.'

With looks unwavering,
With breath unstirred,
She took off her clothes
Without a word;
And stood up naked
And white as a curd.

25: *brash*: branches, twigs
30: *byre*: cowshed

He breathed her to him
With famished sighs,
45   Against her bosom
He sheltered his eyes,
And warmed his hands
Between her thighs.

Strangely assembled
50   In the quiet room,
Alone alight
Amidst leagues of gloom,
So brave a bride,
So sad a groom;

55   And strange love-traffic
Between these two;
Nor mean, nor shamefaced—
As though they'd do
Something more solemn
60   Than they knew:

As though by this greeting
Which chance had willed
'Twixt him so silent
And her so stilled,
65   Some pledge or compact
Were fulfilled.

Made for all time
In times unknown,
'Twixt man and woman
70   Standing alone
In mirk night
By a tall stone.

His wayfaring terrors
All cast aside,
75   Brave now the bridegroom
Quitted the bride;
As he came, departing—
Undenied.

But once from darkness
80   Turned back his sight
To where in the doorway
She held a light:
'Goodbye to you, maiden,'
'Stranger, good night.'

85   Long time has this woman
Been bedded alone.
The house where she dwelt
Lies stone on stone:
She'd not know her ash-tree,
90   So warped has it grown.

But yet this story
Is told of her
As a memorial;
And some aver
95   She'd comfort thus any
Poor traveller.

A wanton, you say—
Yet where's the spouse,
However true
100   To her marriage-vows,
To whom the lot
Of the earth-born allows

More than this?—
To comfort the care
105   Of a stranger, bound
She knows not where,
And afraid of the dark,
As his fathers were.

                          1923–1924 / 1925

East London Cemetery

Death keeps—an indifferent host—
this house of call,
whose sign-board wears no boast
save Beds for All.

5   Narrow the bed, and bare,
and none too sweet.
No need, says Death, to air
the single sheet.

Comfort, says he, with shrug,
10   is but degree,
and London clay a rug
like luxury,

to him who wrapped his bones
in the threadbare hood
15   blood wove from weft of stones
under warp of foot.

                          1927 / 1982

King Duffus

When all the witches were haled to the stake and burned;
When their least ashes were swept up and drowned,
King Duffus opened his eyes and looked round.

For half a year they had trussed him in their spell:
5   Parching, scorching, roaring, he was blackened as a coal.
Now he wept like a freshet in April.

Tears ran like quicksilver through his rocky beard.
Why have you wakened me, he said, with a clattering sword?
Why have you snatched me back from the green yard?

10   There I sat feasting under the cool linden shade;
The beer in the silver cup was ever renewed,
I was at peace there, I was well-bestowed:

My crown lay lightly on my brow as a clot of foam,
My wide mantle was yellow as the flower of the broom,
15   Hale and holy I was in mind and in limb.

I sat among poets and among philosophers,
Carving fat bacon for the mother of Christ;
Sometimes we sang, sometimes we conversed.

Why did you summon me back from the midst of that meal
20   To a vexed kingdom and a smoky hall?
Could I not stay at least until dewfall?

1948 / 1968

Anne Donne

I lay in in London;
And round my bed my live children were crying,
And round my bed my dead children were singing.
As my blood left me it set the clappers swinging:

Title: *King Duffus* of Scotland (ruled 961–965) suffered from a mysterious illness brought on by witch-craft. The witches were discovered by the King's Guards in the act of melting a wax image of the king on the fire; they were put to death, and the King immediately recovered.
6: *freshet*: stream

Title: *Anne Donne:* The poet John Donne (1572–1631) was in the employ of Sir Thomas Egerton, Lord Keeper of the Great Seal, when in 1601 he surreptitiously married Anne More, Egerton's niece; the result was his dismissal from his job, a spell in prison at the instigation of her father, and the blighting of his career. According to the seventeenth-century biographer Izaak Walton, Donne ended his letter to Anne informing her of his dismissal with the phrase "John Donne, Anne Donne, Undone." Warner conflates this story with a second: Donne accompanied his patron Sir Robert Drury in 1612 to Paris, though he did so reluctantly because Anne was pregnant at the time. One day he saw an apparition, which he reported to Drury: "I have seen a dreadful vision since I saw you: I have seen my dear wife pass twice by me through this room, with her hair hanging about her shoulders, and a dead child in her arms." Twelve days later came the news that the baby was stillborn. Anne eventually died at the age of 33, having given birth to ten children (of whom seven survived her) and suffered two stillbirths.

5 Tolling, jarring, jowling, all the bells of London
   Were ringing as I lay dying—
   John Donne, Anne Donne, Undone!

   Ill-done, well-done, all done.
   All fearing done, all striving and all hoping,
10 All weanings, watchings, done; all reckonings whether
   Of debts, of moons, summed; all hither and thither
   Sucked in the one ebb. Then, on my bed in London,
   I heard him call me, reproaching:
   Undone, Anne Donne, Undone!

15 Not done, not yet done!
   Wearily I rose up at his bidding.
   The sweat still on my face, my hair dishevelled,
   Over the bells and the tolling seas I travelled,
   Carrying my dead child, so lost, so light a burden,
20 To Paris, where he sat reading
   And showed him my ill news. That done,
   Went back, lived on in London.

1948 / 1968

5: *jowling*: ringing (dial.)

THOMAS MACGREEVY (1893–1967)

MACGREEVY PUBLISHED ONLY ONE BOOK OF POETRY IN HIS LIFETIME, *POEMS* (1934), but he has emerged in recent decades as a foundational figure for an Irish poetry fully participating in the aesthetic initiatives of international modernism. Beyond the poems he published, there is the fact that MacGreevy knew many writers among the London and Parisian avant-gardes and corresponded with the American modernist poet Wallace Stevens. Some scholars have speculated that his failure to win wider recognition for his work in Ireland eventually limited his poetic output; except for a few poems written late in life MacGreevy appears largely to have abandoned poetry after *Poems* was published. Nevertheless, as J. C. C. Mays writes, since the 1960s Mac-Greevy has been "the man . . . around whom a largely ignored tradition of international modernism . . . happened." A devout Catholic, committed republican and cultural nationalist, MacGreevy differs from some Irish nationalists, Mays adds, "in the selflessness and range of his extra-national sympathies": "His idea of national identity took other national identities into account and welcomed their fructifying influence."[1] MacGreevy's *Collected Poems* (1991) includes poems on World War I, the Easter Uprising and the Irish Civil War, satirical sketches of Anglo-Irish and Dublin culture, and a series of epiphanic and religious poems. Like T. S. Eliot's *The Waste Land,* his poems can be allusive and citational, collagist and dialogic in their use of many "voices" and even, in one case, a fragment of musical notation. Other poems, as Tim Armstrong suggests, show "no sign of abandoning lyric; it is the poet's voice—the 'I'—which bears the burden of witnessing to his times, taking the burden of petition and at its best finding a confluence of personal and collective feeling, as at the end of 'The Six Who Were Hanged,' with its insistent time and place."[2]

MacGreevy was born in Tarbert, County Kerry; his father was a policeman, his mother a primary school teacher. He attended national school until the age of sixteen and then studied privately for the civil service, beginning work for the British civil service in Dublin in 1910. In 1917, he joined the British Army, eventually to become a second lieutenant in the Royal Field Artillery. He saw action at Ypres Salient and the Somme and was wounded twice. After the war, he attended Trinity College, Dublin. In 1924, he moved to London and began writing criticism for *The Criterion, The Times Literary Supplement,* and other journals while working as deputy lecturer at the National Gallery. While based in Paris between 1927 and 1933, he wrote monographs on Eliot and Richard Aldington and an essay on "The Catholic Element in [James Joyce's] *Work in Progress [Finnegans Wake].*" With his friend Samuel Beckett and others, he signed

---

[1] "How is MacGreevy a Modernist?", *Modernism and Ireland: The Poetry of the 1930s,* ed. Patricia Coughlan and Alex Davis, Cork, 1995, pp. 107, 111.
[2] "Muting the Klaxon: Poetry, History, and Irish Modernism," *Modernism and Ireland,* p. 56.

the "Verticalist manifesto" published in Eugene and Maria Jolas' avant-garde magazine *transition*. In 1933, he returned to London and began work on a study of the Irish painter Jack B. Yeats; it was eventually published in 1945. In 1948, he was made Chevalier de l'ordre de la Legion d'honneur by the French government for services to the arts. In 1950, he was appointed Director of the National Gallery of Ireland.

De Civitate Hominum

To A.S.F.R.

The morning sky glitters
Winter blue.
The earth is snow-white,
With the gleam snow-white answers to sunlight,
5   Save where shell-holes are new,
Black spots in the whiteness—

A Matisse ensemble.

The shadows of whitened tree stumps
Are another white.

10   And there are white bones.

Zillebeke Lake and Hooge,
Ice gray, gleam differently,

Like the silver shoes of the model.

The model is our world,
15   Our bitch of a world.
Those who live between wars may not know
But we who die between peaces
Whether we die or not.

It is very cold
20   And, what with my sensations
And my spick and span subaltern's uniform,
I might be the famous brass monkey,
The *nature morte* accessory.

We are indebted for several of our notes to Susan Schreibman's edition of MacGreevy's *Collected Poems* (Dublin and London, 1991).

MacGreevy joined the British Army in March 1917 and later that year was sent to the Ypres Salient in Belgium, location of some of the fiercest fighting of World War I (and also of "Zillebeke Lake and Hooge" [11] and the town of "Gheluvelt" [30]).

Title: "Of the City of Men." *The City of God,* by St. Augustine (354–430), contrasts worldly, sinful society with the City of God.

Dedication: Alexander Stewart Frere Reeves (1892–1984) was managing director for Heinemann, publisher of MacGreevy's *Poems.* He was a close friend of the poet's, and had served in the Royal Flying Corps during World War I.

7: Henri *Matisse* (1869–1954), the French painter known for his vivid explorations of color

22: "'It is cold enough to freeze the balls off a brass monkey'. The phrase, originally a naval expression, refers to a metal fixture on ships (the brass monkey) used to carry cannon balls. In very cold weather the metal would contract, thus causing the balls to slide off." (Schreibman)

23: *nature morte:* a still-life (though punning on the sense of "dead nature"); "an accessory is any object or figure not belonging to the principal subject of the picture, but added solely to furnish background." (Schreibman)

Morte . . . !
25 'Tis still life that lives,
Not quick life—

There are fleece-white flowers of death
That unfold themselves prettily
About an airman
30 Who, high over Gheluvelt,
Is taking a morning look round,
All silk and silver
Up in the blue.

I hear the drone of an engine
35 And soft pounding puffs in the air
As the fleece-white flowers unfold.

I cannot tell which flower he has accepted
But suddenly there is a tremor,
A zigzag of lines against the blue
40 And he streams down
Into the white,
A delicate flame,
A stroke of orange in the morning's dress.

My sergeant says, very low, 'Holy God!
45 'Tis a fearful death.'

Holy God makes no reply
Yet.

1927 / 1934

The Six Who Were Hanged

The sky turns limpid green.
The stars go silver white.
They must be stirring in their cells now—

Unspeaking likely!

5 Waiting for an attack
With death uncertain
One said little.

For these there is no uncertainty.

The sun will come soon,
10 All gold.

26: *quick*: a pun: both "rapid" and "full of life"

The Six Who Were Hanged: On 14 March 1921, six Republican prisoners were hanged by the British at Mountjoy Jail in Dublin. MacGreevy witnessed the crowd that assembled, chanting and praying, outside the prison that morning.

1–10: "MacGreevy . . . evokes the flag of Ireland in the first lines by interweaving green, white and gold into the imagery of the poem. He chooses gold, rather than the conventional orange, in deference to popular nationalist custom alluding to the papal flag of gold and white." (Schreibman)

'Tis you shall have the golden throne—

It will come ere its time.
It will not be time,
Oh, it will not be time,
15   Not for silver and gold,
Not with green,
Till they all have dropped home,
Till gaol bells all have clanged,
Till all six have been hanged.

20   And after?
Will it be time?

There are two to be hanged at six o'clock,
Two others at seven,
And the others,
25   The epilogue two,
At eight.
The sun will have risen
And two will be hanging
In green, white and gold,
30   In a premature Easter.

The white-faced stars are silent,
Silent the pale sky;
Up on his iron car
The small conqueror's robot
35   Sits quiet.
But *Hail Mary! Hail Mary!*
They say it and say it,
These hundreds of lamenting women and girls
Holding Crucified Christs.

40   *Daughters of Jerusalem . . .*

Perhaps women have Easters.

There are very few men.
Why am I here?

At the hour of our death
45   At this hour of youth's death,
Hail Mary! Hail Mary!
Now young bodies swing up

11: quoted from "Dark Rosaleen," a patriotic poem by James Clarence Mangan (1803–1849). The "you" addressed in the poem is Rosaleen, a personification of Ireland.
30: In 1921 Easter fell on 27 March.
33: *iron car:* an armored car; the *robot* is a British soldier.
40: "And there followed him a great multitude of people, and of women, who bewailed and lamented him. But Jesus turning to them, said: Daughters of Jerusalem, weep not over me; but weep for yourselves, and for your children" (Luke 23:27–28, Douay translation)
44: The women are reciting consecutive Hail Marys; "at the hour of our death" comes from the end of the Hail Mary, "Hail Mary!" (46) from the beginning.

Then
Young souls
50   Slip after the stars.
Hail Mary! Hail Mary!

Alas! I am not their Saint John—

Tired of sorrow,
My sorrow, their sorrow, all sorrow,
55   I go from the hanged,
From the women,
I go from the hanging;
Scarcely moved by the thought of the two to be hanged,
I go from the epilogue.

60   *Morning Star, Pray for us!*

What, these seven hundred years,
Has Ireland had to do
With the morning star?

And still, I too say,
65   *Pray for us.*

                                        1927–1929 / 1934

Homage to Hieronymus Bosch

A woman with no face walked into the light;
A boy, in a brown-tree norfolk suit,
Holding on
Without hands
5   To her seeming skirt.

She stopped,
And he stopped,
And I, in terror, stopped, staring.

52: *Saint John*: "Traditionally the only male follower of Jesus present at the Crucifixion. He was given the
responsibility of caring for the Virgin Mary after the death of Jesus (John 19:26–7)." (Schreibman)
60: *Morning star*: an epithet for the Virgin Mary in the litany (which follows the rosary)
61: *seven hundred years*: i.e., since the occupation of Ireland by the Anglo-Normans in the twelfth century.

Homage to Hieronymus Bosch: This poem is based on an incident from MacGreevy's days at Trinity Col-
lege. "When I was a student a number of us, 17 in all I think, who were ex-British officers asked the
Provost of Trinity College to send an appeal on our behalf for the reprieve of a student of the National
University who was captured in an ambush and condemned to be hanged. It was believed he had been
tortured by the Black and Tans and our appeal was that he should be reprieved only long enough for it
to be verified that he had British justice and not torture. Only two or three of the signatories were nation-
alists. But the Provost refused to have anything to do with the appeal and Kevin Barry was hanged. We
were the inhabitants of the nursery in the poem. John Bernard the nursery governor, etc., etc. The well
of St Patrick is in the grounds of Trinity College which used before the Reformation to be the abbey of
All Hallows. That is the kernel of the poem but the spirit of Ireland, powerful and powerless, shabby and
inspiring and a dozen other things is knocking about the whole time." (MacGreevy, cited by Schreib-
man)
Title: *Hieronymus Bosch* (c.1450–1516), the Flemish painter, known for the grotesquerie of his images.
2: A *norfolk suit* consists of a belted brown-tweed jacket and knee breeches.

Then I saw a group of shadowy figures behind her.

10   It was a wild wet morning
        But the little world was spinning on.

        Liplessly, somehow, she addressed it:
        The book must be opened
        And the park too.

15   I might have tittered
        But my teeth chattered
        And I saw that the words, as they fell,
        Lay, wriggling, on the ground.

        There was a stir of wet wind
20   And the shadowy figures began to stir
        When one I had thought dead
        Filmed slowly out of his great effigy on a tomb near by
        And they all shuddered
        He bent as if to speak to the woman
25   But the nursery governor flew up out of the well of Saint Patrick,
        Confiscated by his mistress,
        And, his head bent,
        Staring out over his spectacles,
        And scratching the gravel furiously,
30   Hissed—
                The words went *pingg!* like bullets,
                Upwards past his spectacles—
        Say nothing, I say, say nothing, say nothing!
        And he who had seemed to be coming to life
35   Gasped,
        Began hysterically, to laugh and cry,
        And, with a gesture of impotent and half-petulant despair,
        Filmed back into his effigy again.

        High above the Bank of Ireland
40   Unearthly music sounded,
        Passing westwards.

13: *The book must be opened:* see Apocalypse (Revelation) 5:2–5.

14: "The park here has to do symbolically with the four green fields of Irish tradition and more particu-
larly with the Dublin squares that are still closed except to residents." (MacGreevy) The "four green
fields" are the four provinces of Ireland (Ulster, Connaught, Munster, and Leinster). The "squares" are
the private gardens of upper-class residents (and here symbolic of privilege and oppression).

22: *great effigy:* "The best-known tomb with an effigy near by is that of Strongbow (Richard fitz Gilbert de
Clare) in Christ Church Cathedral." Strongbow invaded Ireland in 1170, and gained control of Waterford
and Dublin; his holding Dublin against the siege of Roderic, King of Ireland, was instrumental in the
1171 Norman conquest of Ireland.

26: "Queen Elizabeth I founded Trinity College, Dublin on lands confiscated from the Priory of All Hal-
lows." (Schreibman)

39: The Irish Parliament House on College Green, built in 1729, was, after the 1800 Act of Union abol-
ished the Irish Parliament, converted to a bank. "It was the dream of all Nineteenth Century National-
ists to see an independent Irish Parliament established there again." (MacGreevy)

40–41: "In Ireland we tend as a result of a poem written by Thomas Davis about 1840 ['The West's Asleep']
to regard the west of Ireland as the spirit of the nation. When the west is awake, that spirit is awake.
When the west is asleep, that spirit is asleep." (MacGreevy). Also see the unearthly music in *Antony and
Cleopatra* 4.3, signifying Antony's desertion by the god Hercules; and T.S. Eliot's parody of this in "Bur-
bank with a Baedeker: Bleistein with a Cigar."

Then, from the drains,
Small sewage rats slid out.
They numbered hundreds of hundreds, tens, thousands.
45 Each bowed obsequiously to the shadowy figures
Then turned and joined in a stomach dance with his brothers and sisters.
Being a multitude, they danced irregularly.
There was rat laughter,
Deeper here and there,
50 And occasionally she-rat cries grew hysterical.
The shadowy figures looked on, agonized.
The woman with no face gave a cry and collapsed.
The rats danced on her
And on the wriggling words
55 Smirking.
The nursery governor flew back into the well
With the little figure without hands in the brown-tree clothes.

1934

WILFRED OWEN (1893–1918)

O WEN WAS BORN IN OSWESTRY, SHROPSHIRE. HIS FATHER WAS A MINOR RAILWAY
official; his mother is said to have been puritanical but devoted to her children,
especially Wilfred. He was educated at Birkenhead and Shrewsbury Technical Col-
lege, worked for a period in a country parish, taught English in Bordeaux, then in 1915
joined the army. In June 1916, he was commissioned as a second lieutenant in the
Manchester regiment. A first tour of duty ended when Owen was sent back from the
lines after seeing a fellow officer blown to bits beside him in the trenches; recovering
in a hospital, he met Siegfried Sassoon and Robert Graves. In his second tour of duty,
he won the Military Cross. A month later he was killed on the Sambre canal, only a
week before the Armistice.

Owen's preface to his poems notes that "This book is not about heroes. English
poetry is not yet fit to speak of them." His subject, he added, is "the pity of War": "All
a poet can do today is warn."[1] While only five of his poems were published in his life-
time, Owen's reputation quickly grew after Sassoon published an edition of the poems
in 1920; his poetry presented an antidote to the sentimental patriotism of the poems
famous during the war itself, such as Rupert Brooke's "The Soldier": "If I should die,
think only this of me: / That there's some corner of a foreign field / That is for ever
England. There shall be / In that rich earth a richer dust concealed." C. Day Lewis
held Owen above all other war poets as the one who "came home deepest to my gen-
eration, so that we could never again think of war as anything but a vile, if necessary,
evil."[2]

Paul Fussell has demonstrated that Owen's "sentimental homoerotic theme" was
shaped by Victorian literary conventions and already established in his pre-war poetry;
the war provided him with the extreme circumstances wherein male companionship
could be celebrated and contrasted with violence and barbarism, as in "Arms and the
Boy." Noting the prevalence of erotic detail in many of the poems, Fussell writes that
it is the presence of "the palpable body" that distinguishes Owen's poetry from that of
other war poets: "To speak of 'sufferings' is not enough; one must see and feel the
bloody head cradled dead on one's own shoulder."[3] In details such as the bleeding
thigh of "Disabled" a culture linking war and sport comes under bitterly ironic
scrutiny.

---

[1] Preface, *The Collected Poems of Wilfred Owen*, ed. C. Day Lewis, London, 1964, p. 31.
[2] Introduction, *The Collected Poems of Wilfred Owen*, 1964, p. 12
[3] *The Great War and Modern Memory*, London, 1975, pp. 286–96.

Dulce et Decorum Est

Bent double, like old beggars under sacks,
Knock-kneed, coughing like hags, we cursed through sludge,
Till on the haunting flares we turned our backs
And towards our distant rest began to trudge.
5   Men marched asleep. Many had lost their boots
But limped on, blood-shod. All went lame; all blind;
Drunk with fatigue; deaf even to the hoots
Of tired, outstripped Five-Nines that dropped behind.

Gas! GAS! Quick, boys!—An ecstasy of fumbling,
10   Fitting the clumsy helmets just in time;
But someone still was yelling out and stumbling,
And flound'ring like a man in fire or lime . . .
Dim, through the misty panes and thick green light,
As under a green sea, I saw him drowning.

15   In all my dreams, before my helpless sight,
He plunges at me, guttering, choking, drowning.

If in some smothering dreams you too could pace
Behind the wagon that we flung him in,
And watch the white eyes writhing in his face,
20   His hanging face, like a devil's sick of sin;
If you could hear, at every jolt, the blood
Come gargling from the froth-corrupted lungs,
Obscene as cancer, bitter as the cud
Of vile, incurable sores on innocent tongues,—
25   My friend, you would not tell with such high zest
To children ardent for some desperate glory,
The old Lie: Dulce et decorum est
Pro patria mori.

1917–1918 / 1920

Strange Meeting

It seemed that out of battle I escaped
Down some profound dull tunnel, long since scooped
Through granites which titanic wars had groined.

Yet also there encumbered sleepers groaned,
5   Too fast in thought or death to be bestirred.

Dulce et Decorum Est: This poem was originally dedicated to Jessie Pope, author of children's books and
of books such as *Jessie Pope's War Poems* and *Simple Rhymes for Stirring Times.*
Title: Horace, *Odes* 3.2.13. "The famous Latin tag means of course *It is sweet and meet to die for one's coun-
try. Sweet!* and *decorous!*" (letter from Owen to his mother)
8: *Five-Nines:* 5.9-inch-caliber shells
12: *lime:* calcium oxide, a caustic substance
13: *panes:* the windows of the gas mask

Strange Meeting: The manuscript of this poem suggests that Owen may not have considered it finished.
The last draft is in ink; the final line is a later addition in pencil (subsequently inked in), and a penciled
arrow moves the current line 39 to the poem's last or second-to-last line.

Then, as I probed them, one sprang up, and stared
With piteous recognition in fixed eyes,
Lifting distressful hands, as if to bless.
And by his smile, I knew that sullen hall,—

10   By his dead smile I knew we stood in Hell.

With a thousand pains that vision's face was grained;
Yet no blood reached there from the upper ground,
And no guns thumped, or down the flues made moan.
'Strange friend,' I said, 'here is no cause to mourn.'

15   'None,' said that other, 'save the undone years,
The hopelessness. Whatever hope is yours,
Was my life also; I went hunting wild
After the wildest beauty in the world,
Which lies not calm in eyes, or braided hair,

20   But mocks the steady running of the hour,
And if it grieves, grieves richlier than here.
For by my glee might many men have laughed,
And of my weeping something had been left,
Which must die now. I mean the truth untold,

25   The pity of war, the pity war distilled.
Now men will go content with what we spoiled,
Or, discontent, boil bloody, and be spilled.
They will be swift with swiftness of the tigress.
None will break ranks, though nations trek from progress.

30   Courage was mine, and I had mastery,
Wisdom was mine, and I had mastery:
To miss the march of this retreating world
Into vain citadels that are not walled.
Then, when much blood had clogged their chariot-wheels,

35   I would go up and wash them from sweet wells,
Even with truths that lie too deep for taint.
I would have poured my spirit without stint
But not through wounds; not on the cess of war.
Foreheads of men have bled where no wounds were.

40   'I am the enemy you killed, my friend.
I knew you in this dark: for so you frowned
Yesterday through me as you jabbed and killed.
I parried; but my hands were loath and cold.
Let us sleep now. . . .'

                                     1918 / 1920

25: In a draft preface to a planned collection of his poems, Owen wrote: "My subject is War, and the pity of War. The Poetry is in the pity."
38: *cess:* Perhaps the word is coined from "cesspool" (thus meaning "excrement") or is short for "abscess."

Arms and the Boy

Let the boy try along this bayonet-blade
How cold steel is, and keen with hunger of blood;
Blue with all malice, like a madman's flash;
And thinly drawn with famishing for flesh.

5   Lend him to stroke these blind, blunt bullet-leads,
Which long to nuzzle in the hearts of lads,
Or give him cartridges whose fine zinc teeth
Are sharp with sharpness of grief and death.

For his teeth seem for laughing round an apple.
10   There lurk no claws behind his fingers supple;
And God will grow no talons at his heels,
Nor antlers through the thickness of his curls.

1918 / 1920

Disabled

He sat in a wheeled chair, waiting for dark,
And shivered in his ghastly suit of grey,
Legless, sewn short at elbow. Through the park
Voices of boys rang saddening like a hymn,
5   Voices of play and pleasure after day,
Till gathering sleep had mothered them from him.

*   *   *

About this time Town used to swing so gay
When glow-lamps budded in the light blue trees,
And girls glanced lovelier as the air grew dim,—
10   In the old times, before he threw away his knees.
Now he will never feel again how slim
Girls' waists are, or how warm their subtle hands.
All of them touch him like some queer disease.

*   *   *

There was an artist silly for his face,
15   For it was younger than his youth, last year.
Now, he is old; his back will never brace;
He's lost his colour very far from here,
Poured it down shell-holes till the veins ran dry,
And half his lifetime lapsed in the hot race
20   And leap of purple spurted from his thigh.

*   *   *

Arms and the Boy: cf. Dryden's translation of the opening of Vergil's *Aeneid*: "Arms and the man I sing."
4: *drawn*: elongated and flattened by hammering

One time he liked a blood-smear down his leg,
After the matches, carried shoulder-high.
It was after football, when he'd drunk a peg,
He thought he'd better join.—He wonders why.
25   Someone had said he'd look a god in kilts,
That's why; and maybe, too, to please his Meg,
Aye, that was it, to please the giddy jilts
He asked to join. He didn't have to beg;
Smiling they wrote his lie: aged nineteen years.
30   Germans he scarcely thought of; all their guilt,
And Austria's, did not move him. And no fears
Of Fear came yet. He thought of jewelled hilts
For daggers in plaid socks; of smart salutes;
And care of arms; and leave; and pay arrears;
35   Esprit de corps; and hints for young recruits.
And soon, he was drafted out with drums and cheers.

*   *   *

Some cheered him home, but not as crowds cheer Goal.
Only a solemn man who brought him fruits
Thanked him; and then enquired about his soul.

*   *   *

40   Now, he will spend a few sick years in institutes,
And do what things the rules consider wise,
And take whatever pity they may dole.
Tonight he noticed how the women's eyes
Passed from him to the strong men that were whole.
45   How cold and late it is! Why don't they come
And put him into bed? Why don't they come?

1917–1918 / 1920

21–22: Owen parodies A.E. Housman's "To an Athlete Dying Young": "The time you won your town the race / We chaired you through the market-place; / Man and boy stood cheering by, / And home we brought you shoulder-high."

23: *peg*: brandy and soda-water

27: *jilts*: fickle women

33: *daggers in plaid socks*: The protagonist here is serving in a Scottish regiment; its dress uniform would include the traditional small ornamental dagger called a "skene-dhu," carried in the stocking.

34: *pay arrears*: back pay

45–46: *Why don't they come* . . . : "Dominic Hibberd calls attention to 'a mocking echo of the slogan on a recruiting poster, probably put out in 1914, which shows soldiers in action and in need of reinforcements. The slogan reads, "Will they never come?". . . . The parallel in this poem between playing football and serving in the Army reflects the recruiting drives that had been made at football matches earlier in the war.'" (Jon Stallworthy's note)

JOHN RODKER (1894–1955)

RODKER WAS BORN IN MANCHESTER AND MOVED WITH HIS FAMILY SIX YEARS
later to the East End in London, where he was educated at the Board School and
the Jews Free School. He was a conscientious objector during World War I and twice
arrested. In 1917, after a hunger strike led to his hospitalization, he was courtmartialed
and sentenced to six months in Wandsworth Prison before being transferred to a work
settlement. By this point, Rodker had begun a literary career, which saw early poems
and prose published in *The New Age, Poetry and Drama,* and *The Egoist.* He had also
met Ezra Pound and Wyndham Lewis, and his interest in the theater had led him to
become associated with the "Choric School" based in Chelsea; this group was exper-
imenting with the performance of poetry as dance. In 1919, Rodker succeeded Pound
as the editor of *The Little Review* and, with his wife Mary Butts, established the Ovid
Press, which was to publish Pound's *Hugh Selwyn Mauberley* and collections of draw-
ings by Edward Wadsworth, Wyndham Lewis, and Henri Gaudier-Brzeska, among
other books. Based in Paris during much of the 1920s, Rodker continued his lifelong
work as a publisher, bringing out work by Pound, Le Corbusier, Paul Valéry, and oth-
ers. He published three volumes of poetry during his lifetime; other books include
Memoirs of Other Fronts (1932) and the experimental novella *Adolphe 1920* (1929),
which Pound thought an advance on the methods of James Joyce's *Ulysses.*

In Rodker's poetic development, an early fascination with the macabre probably
deriving from French Symbolist poetry eventually leads to investigations of lyric sub-
jectivity informed by reading in Sigmund Freud, the Italian Futurists, and Rodker's
other modernist peers. His poetry's idiosyncratic spacings, punctuation, and rhythms
derive partly from the theater experiments of the Choric School. Andrew Crozier
argues that "in Rodker we find neither the erasure of the writing subject, nor the
ironic objectification of the dramatic subject in its imputed language: both of them
modes which constituted the modernity of Pound and Eliot. Furthermore, we find
quite the reverse of [Wyndham] Lewis's theoretical dissociation of mind and body.
Somatic effect is continuous with psychic affect, in a way that removes the new sen-
sations of the mechanical environment from simple astonishment and intellectual
fascination."[1] Rodker's representations of sexuality and desire deserve comparison
with the work of other, more celebrated modernists such as Mina Loy and D. H.
Lawrence; "I'd have loved you as you deserved had we been frogs" offers a view of
alienated male sexuality worth reading beside more famous lines from T. S. Eliot's *The
Waste Land.*

---

[1] Introduction, *Poems & Adolphe 1920,* ed. Andrew Crozier, Manchester, 1996, p. xvii.

A Slice of Life

The sky broods over the river—
The waves tumble and flee.
And down go the dead things ever
Down to the sea.

5   A dog, an empty keg,
An outworn hat.
And with a broken leg
A pregnant cat.

1914

The Music Hall

The group soul anguished drives up to the vane;
Shivers over the clamant band,
And tremulously sinks upon its padded seat, . . .
With such a pleasant shiver of the bowels.
5   (The first faint peristalt . . .)
And a thin hunger somewhere.
Beauty or woman; something not over-rare
That will absorb the thrill, the gushing energic thrill. . . .
We watch and smoke . . . our trembling hands
10   That flutter for a space an arc of light
With acrid trailing fume. . . .
But oh . . . the hunger. . . .

1914

Hymn to Love

Ave Maria, Stella Maris
Ah Paris
Yet even in London,
Brantôme, Whitman,
5   Vatsyayana.

Even so
can it be merely

The Music Hall: 1: *vane*: "weathervane," thus, metonymically, the roof of the theater
2: *clamant*: clamorous
5: *peristalt*: contraction of the intestine (as part of the process of elimination)
8: *energic*: full of energy

Hymn to Love: 1: "Hail Mary, Star of the Sea" (cf. the medieval Latin hymn "Ave Maris Stella")
3: Pierre de Bourdeille, Seigneur de *Brantôme* (c.1540–1614), was the French author of *The Lives of Gal-
lant Ladies,* a memoir of the sexual exploits of the nobility of his times.
5: The *Kāma Sūtra* is attributed to the fifth-century sage *Vatsyayana.*

a matter of
(quoting De Gourmont)
10   mucous surfaces?

O impossible virginity
of ductless glands!
The agony!

Yet maybe they too are happy.

15   For I have heard
there *is* an odour of sanctity
and it is real—
like musty clothes—
but the odour of venery,
20   goats and laurels—
is flung
six feet through a room,
and remaining,
fires lovers to perpetuate it.

25   Restraints!
coyness—blushes,
trembling knees,
fluttering eyelids,
working throttle-
30   mad hands—
how terrible your impotence!
how pitiful!

A bull in a slaughter-house,
his knees in curdled blood—
35   weeps.

First loves.
Tragedies of incompetence—
misunderstandings—
tragedies of haste and fear.

40   Second loves.
Tragedies of satiety;
clever and wanton aimlessness.

Third loves.
Bah!

45   When the moon's full
yellow, sordid, wrinkled—

9: The Symbolist author Rémy *de Gourmont* (1858–1915) wrote *Physique de l'amour: essai sur l'instinct sexuel*; Ezra Pound's translation, *The Natural Philosophy of Love,* was published by Rodker in 1922.
16: Saints were said to give forth a divinely fragrant odor.
19: *venery*: lust
20: *Goats* are a traditional symbol of lust.

we rise to the surface of our
velleities—Ascidians—
to play at passion
50   yellow and wrinkled.

Ave Maria Stella Maris.
White Ewe of the Canting Crew

1920

I'd have loved you as you deserved had we been frogs

Where did I hear of two smooth frogs
clasped among rushes
in love and death:
rigid and with spread fingers.

5   And we   men
all brain, all heart, hot blood;
turn lightly, then
'Ah, weren't we once friends?'

1920

48: *velleities*: desires
    Ascidians: sea squirts

DAVID JONES (1895–1974)

INTRODUCING THE 1961 EDITION OF DAVID JONES'S *IN PARENTHESIS* (1937), T. S. ELIOT wrote: "as for the writer himself, he is a Londoner of Welsh and English descent. He is decidedly a Briton. He is also a Roman Catholic, and he is a painter who has painted some beautiful pictures and designed some beautiful lettering. All these facts about him are important." Eliot then names Jones, James Joyce, Ezra Pound, and himself as four writers profoundly affected by World War I. Among the four, he adds, it is only Jones who fought in the war, only Jones who is "decidedly a Briton."[1] Jones was also "tardiest" to publish, as Eliot writes, and his work has since been the least read and studied, especially in North America, where the Welsh words that appear throughout *The Anathemata* (1952) require glosses for pronunciation as well as meaning. Jones was aware of the difficulties presented by such words, which will be no less "foreign" to many British readers; this is one reason for his own notes to the poem. They are words that are partly meant as "material deposits" evoking "exact historic over-tones and under-tones," ways of keeping "past transactions" from being "trodden under foot"—that is, of acknowledging cultural traditions at risk or already obliterated.[2]

The Anathemata shows us the "matter of Britain" in a text mixing poetry and poetic prose in a "heap of all that I could find . . . blessed things that have taken on what is cursed and the profane things that somehow are redeemed: the delights and also the 'ornaments,' both in the primary sense of gear and paraphernalia and in the sense of what simply adorns; the donated and votive things, the things dedicated after whatever fashion, the things in some sense made separate, being laid up from other things; things, or some aspect of them, that partake of the extra-utile and of the gratuitous; things that are the signs of something other; together with those signs that not only have the nature of a sign, but are themselves, under some mode, what they signify."[3] The poem's title means, Jones wrote, "Things set up, lifted up, or in whatever manner made over to the gods." Taking its structure from the Roman Catholic Mass, it consists of a montage of scenes beginning in prehistory and presenting the birth of Aphrodite, the founding of Rome and London and the Celtic culture of Wales and Britain following the Roman conquest; the longer excerpt included here concerns the arrival of the Angles. Fragments from the poet's own past are mixed among Britain's composite cultural tradition.

The earlier book *In Parenthesis* represents the experience of common soldiers in World War I while also alluding to Arthurian myth, Aneirin's *Y Gododdin* and Shake-

---

[1] "A Note of Introduction," *In Parenthesis* (1937), London, 1963, p. vii.
[2] David Jones, *Epoch and Artist*, London, 1959, p. 107.
[3] The same, p. 124.

speare's histories. The shape of the book suggests comparisons with Joyce's *Ulysses*: description and narrative are presented beside or against the evident patterns of a literary and mythic past. Noting in his preface that he had not intended a "War Book," Jones wrote that "I have only tried to make a shape in words, using as data the complex of sights, sounds, fears, hopes, apprehensions, smells, things exterior and interior, the landscape and paraphernalia of that singular time and of those particular men."[4] The narrative follows its protagonist, John Ball, among soldiers in the trenches and in an engagement in which he is wounded. John Matthias finds "at the center of its fire-swept mazes an extraordinary and otherworldly calm," adding that "*In Parenthesis* produces an effect more characteristic . . . of Benjamin Britten's settings of Wilfred Owen's poems in his *War Requiem* than of Owen's poems themselves. Its catharsis is shattering and lasting, but it does not induce the catharsis of tragedy. . . . Still less does it generate the kinetic emotions which some of its readers would like to find in it (which doesn't mean that we fail to count the dead: we do), nor yet does it dramatize the merely passive suffering that Yeats objected to in war poems. It redeems the time."[5] Such "redemption" or healing finds one embodiment in the figure of the Queen of the Woods, who appears in the passage excerpted below from the poem's end. Jones writes that "The tutelary spirit of the wood . . . bestows her gifts 'according to precedence'—that is, according to the hidden degrees of 'valour' of these men now dead, which obviously no living man could assess. For though there is a truth in what is meant by 'Death the Leveller' there is, I think, a far more important truth in seeing it the opposite way round. This I tried to express in the words: 'Life the leveller hugs her impudent equality—she may proceed at once to less discriminating zones.' "[6]

Joyce and Eliot, Eric Gill and the French Catholic theologian Jacques Maritain each might be spoken of as influences on Jones's work and aesthetic principles as both poet and painter. But perhaps it is the German historian of culture Oswald Spengler's *The Decline of the West* that is best read beside Jones's poetry. In his essay "The Myth of Arthur" Jones writes that "Spengler had very special insight into the cyclic character of the periods of decline, and certainly the trend, as far as we can see, of the contemporary world, verifies a number of his conclusions."[7] That Jones had differences with Spengler is evident in his last phrase here, but Spengler surely contributed to Jones's sense of living at the end of a cycle of culture, or after what he referred to as the "Break" brought about by World War I. The Queen of the Woods, Kathleen Henderson Staudt writes, points to Spengler's "use of female figures to reflect the natural order and the cycles of birth and death." Staudt adds that Jones's use of "female figures to celebrate the fundamental creatureliness of all human life" reverses "a traditionally misogynistic strain in Christianity that sees woman as the temptress . . . Jones reinterprets this tradition by celebrating the life of the flesh as a divine gift."[8]

Cultural conservatism is not uncommon among the first generation of modernist poets, especially from the 1930s forward, and Jones's dedication to preserving a tradition gives us again Eliot's "Briton." Relevant here is the passage in his preface to *In Parenthesis* in which he cites and agrees with a critic who finds that it is the "loyalty to lost causes of western Britain that has given our national tradition its distinctive character," arguing that the middle ages "were not far wrong in choosing Arthur, rather than Alfred or Edmund or Harold, as the central figure of the national heroic legend."[9] The methods of Jones's poetry are modernist in insisting on "the many strata" of cultural deposits and interpretation between the poet and Arthur, as the Vic-

---

[4] David Jones, Preface, *In Parenthesis*, p. x.
[5] *Introducing David Jones: A Selection of His Writings*, ed. John Matthias, London, 1980, p. 18.
[6] David Jones quoted in Matthias, ibid., p. 23.
[7] *Epoch and Artist*, p. 242.
[8] *At the Turn of a Civilization: David Jones and Modern Poetics*, Ann Arbor, 1994, p. 140.
[9] Christopher Dawson quoted in *In Parenthesis*, p. xiii.

torian poet Alfred Lord Tennyson, in his *Idylls of the King* (1859), could not. But if the textual palimpsests of myth and culture are not easily read, Jones will ultimately settle on an Arthur who is "conveyor of order, even to the confines of chaos; he is redeemer in the strict sense of the word."[10] As Jones wrote in the late poem "A, a, a, Domine Deus," his poems feel "for His Wounds/in nozzles and containers."

Jones was born in Brockley, Kent. He grew up in suburban London and was raised in the English and Anglican culture of his mother, though his father's Welsh background prompted an early interest in Welsh culture. (Except for a few childhood visits and some more extended visits in the 1920s and 1930s, Jones never lived in Wales.) He trained as a visual artist at the Camberwell Art Academy before serving in the trenches in World War I. After the war he studied at the Westminster School of Art, joining Eric Gill's community of craftsmen in Ditchling afterwards. He converted to Roman Catholicism in 1921. A trip to Jerusalem undertaken in 1934, after a doctor had recommended travel as therapy for recurring bouts of neurasthenia, became crucial to his later work, which deals in part with similarities between Roman and British military occupations of Palestine. After the war, having suffered another attack of neurasthenia, Jones spent a year in a nursing home at Harrow-on-the-Hill, where psychotherapy enabled him to complete *The Anathemata*, which he had begun in the early 1940s. He spent the last decades of his life in Harrow. Poems beyond the two book-length works are collected in *The Sleeping Lord and Other Fragments* (1974) and *The Roman Quarry* (1981), Jones's essays in *Epoch and Artist* (1959) and *The Dying Gaul* (1978).

---

10 "The Myth of Arthur," *Epoch and Artist,* p. 237.

from In Parenthesis

from Part 7: The five unmistakable marks

[946]   And to Private Ball it came as if a rigid beam of great weight
flailed about his calves, caught from behind by ballista-baulk
let fly or aft-beam slewed to clout gunnel-walker
below below below.
950   When golden vanities make about,
                    you've got no legs to stand on.
He thought it disproportionate in its violence considering
the fragility of us.
The warm fluid percolates between his toes and his left boot
955   fills, as when you tread in a puddle—he crawled away in the
opposite direction.

Title: *The five unmistakable marks:* Cf. Lewis Carroll's "The Hunting of the Snark" II.58; Carroll's Snark can be identified by its taste ("meagre and hollow, but crisp"), its "habit of getting up late," its lack of a sense of humor, its "fondness for bathing-machines," and its ambition. Carroll's poem ends with the Baker, one of the hunting party's members, finding a Snark; but it turns out to be a fearsome Boojum, and by the time the others arrive at the scene the Baker has vanished without trace.

946: *Private Ball* is the protagonist of *In Parenthesis;* in this final section of the poem his company is assaulting German positions in a wood at the Battle of the Somme. Ball has just been shot in the legs by a machine gun.

947: A *ballista* is a catapult, which here has fired a *baulk,* a beam of wood.

948: *gunnel-walker:* a sailor walking the gunwales, who is caught from behind by the sail's boom.

949: Cf. the chorus of the song "'Twas a Friday night when we set sail": "Oh the stormy seas do swell / And the stormy winds do blow, / And we jolly sailors are up are up aloft / And the land-lubbers lying down below below below / And the landlubbers lying down below."

950: "Cf. song, *The Golden Vanity.*" (Jones)

It's difficult with the weight of the rifle.
Leave it—under the oak.
Leave it for a salvage-bloke
960   let it lie bruised for a monument
dispense the authenticated fragments to the faithful.
It's the thunder-besom for us
it's the bright bough borne
it's the tensioned yew for a Genoese jammed arbalest and a
965   scarlet square for a mounted *mareschal,* it's that county-mob
back to back. Majuba mountain and Mons Cherubim and
spreaded mats for Sydney Street East, and come to Bisley
for a Silver Dish. It's R.S.M. O'Grady says, it's the soldier's
best friend if you care for the working parts and let us be 'av-
970   ing those springs released smartly in Company billets on wet
forenoons and clickerty-click and one up the spout and you
men must really cultivate the habit of treating this weapon with
the very greatest care and there should be a healthy rivalry
among you—it should be a matter of very proper pride and
975   Marry it man! Marry it!
Cherish her, she's your very own.
        Coax it man coax it—it's delicately and ingeniously made
—it's an instrument of precision—it costs us tax-payers,
money—I want you men to remember that.
980   Fondle it like a granny—talk to it—consider it as you would
        a friend—and when you ground these arms she's not a rooky's
        gas-pipe for greenhorns to tarnish.
    You've known her hot and cold.
You would choose her from among many.

962: *besom*: broom; Jones is imagining it as a lightning bolt, such as were wielded by the Norse thunder-god Thor.

963: In Virgil's *Aeneid* Aeneas bears the Golden *Bough* in order to descend into the underworld. According to Sir James Frazer, in *The Golden Bough* (abridged ed., London, 1922, p. 163), it was an oak bough; the oak was sacred to the Roman thunder-god Jupiter.

964: *tensioned yew*: English longbow
    arbalest: crossbow; presumably its rewinding mechanism is jammed. Crossbows were no match for the longbow, being slower and more cumbersome to reload.

965: *scarlet square*: a block of redcoats waiting to fire
    mareschal: the general of a foreign army

966: *back to back*: "The Gloucestershire Regiment, during an action near Alexandria, in 1801, about-turned their rear rank and engaged the enemy back to back." (Jones)
    The Boers defeated the British at the Battle of *Majuba* Hill in 1881 during the Boer War.
    Mons Cherubim: Soldiers reported seeing huge angels in the sky at the 1914 Battle of Mons, the first major engagement of British troops in World War I.

967: *Sydney Street East*: "It is said that in 'The Battle of Sydney Street' under Mr. Churchill's Home Secretaryship mats were spread on the pavement for troops firing from the prone position." (Jones). Jones alludes to the most notorious incident of Winston Churchill's home secretaryship: in January 1911, members of a gang of Latvian anarchists were discovered hiding out in a house in East London's Sidney Street. Police surrounded the house; Churchill sent troops, and came to the scene himself to witness the siege. The house caught fire, and Churchill directed that the fire brigade not intervene; two bodies were found in the rubble.
    Bisley: the location of the annual British shooting championships, at which the army teams, as well as amateurs, would compete.

968: *R.S.M. O'Grady says*: "Refers to mythological personage figuring in Army exercises, the precise describing of which would be tedious. Anyway these exercises were supposed to foster alertness in dull minds—and were a curious blend of the parlour game and military drill." (Jones). R.S.M.: Regimental Sergeant-Major.

968ff: *soldier's best friend . . .* : "I have employed here only such ideas as were common to the form of speech affected by Instructors in Musketry." (Jones)

981: *ground these arms*: rest the rifle on the ground while holding it upright before oneself

985   You know her by her bias, and by her exact error at 300, and
        by the deep scar at the small, by the fair flaw in the grain,
        above the lower sling-swivel—
        but leave it under the oak.

        Slung so, it swings its full weight. With you going blindly on
990   all paws, it slews its whole length, to hang at your bowed neck
        like the Mariner's white oblation.
            You drag past the four bright stones at the turn of Wood
        Support.

        It is not to be broken on the brown stone under the gracious
995   tree.
            It is not to be hidden under your failing body.
            Slung so, it troubles your painful crawling like a fugitive's
        irons.

        The trees are very high in the wan signal-beam, for whose slow
1000   gyration their wounded boughs seem as malignant limbs,
        manœuvring for advantage.
            The trees of the wood beware each other
                            and under each a man sitting;
        their seemly faces as carved in a sardonyx stone; as undiademed
1005   princes turn their gracious profiles in a hidden seal, so did
        these appear, under the changing light.

        For that waning you would believe this flaxen head had for its
        broken pedestal these bent Silurian shoulders.
            For the pale flares extinction you don't know if under his
1010   close lids, his eye-balls watch you. You would say by the turn
        of steel at his wide brow he is not of our men where he leans
        with his open fist in Dai's bosom against the White Stone.

        Hung so about, you make between these your close escape.

        The secret princes between the leaning trees have diadems
1015   given them.
            Life the leveller hugs her impudent equality—she may pro-
        ceed at once to less discriminating zones.

        The Queen of the Woods has cut bright boughs of various
        flowering.

986: *small*: the place where the stick narrows

991: The protagonist of Coleridge's "The Rime of the Ancient Mariner" shoots an albatross; his fellow
sailors, deeming this bad luck, hang the body about his neck.
    oblation: a victim offered in sacrifice

992ff: *You drag past* . . . : "Cf. *Chanson de Roland,* lines 2259–2396, which relate how Roland, knowing that
death is near for him, would break his sword on the brown stone, but it will not break, and how among
the heaps of dead an enemy watches him, and how he lies by the white stone & the stone of sardonyx,
and hides his sword *Durendal* under his body and dies." (Jones) The *Chanson de Roland* is a medieval
French epic poem detailing the heroic death in battle of Roland at the Battle of Roncesvalles.
    Wood Support: Wood Support Trench, at the edge of the wood: Ball is crawling back to the British
line.

1008: *Silurian*: Welsh (the *Silures* were an ancient tribe inhabiting southeast Wales). In this paragraph
Jones juxtaposes two decapitations: it looks as though a German head is on Welsh shoulders; in the next
Ball wonders whether the German is alive and dangerous.

1012: *Dai*: a Welsh soldier

1018: *Queen of the Woods*: This figure is a fertility goddess drawn from Frazer's *Golden Bough*; he identi-
fies her with the goddess Diana (see 1922 edition, p. 163).

1020   These knew her influential eyes. Her awarding hands can pluck for each their fragile prize.

She speaks to them according to precedence. She knows what's due to this elect society. She can choose twelve gentle-men. She knows who is most lord between the high 1025   trees and on the open down.

Some she gives white berries
                some she gives brown
Emil has a curious crown it's
                made of golden saxifrage.
1030   Fatty wears sweet-briar,
he will reign with her for a thousand years.
For Balder she reaches high to fetch his.
Ulrich smiles for his myrtle wand.
That swine Lillywhite has daisies to his chain—you'd hard-
1035   ly credit it.
She plaits torques of equal splendour for Mr. Jenkins and Billy Crower.
Hansel with Gronwy share dog-violets for a palm, where they lie in serious embrace beneath the twisted tripod.
1040   Siôn gets St. John's Wort—that's fair enough.
Dai Great-coat, she can't find him anywhere—she calls both high and low, she had a very special one for him.
Among this July noblesse she is mindful of December wood —when the trees of the forest beat against each other because 1045   of him.
She carries to Aneirin-in-the-nullah a rowan sprig, for the glory of Guenedota. You couldn't hear what she said to him, because she was careful for the Disciplines of the Wars.

At the gate of the wood you try a last adjustment, but slung 1050   so, it's an impediment, it's of detriment to your hopes, you had best be rid of it—the sagging webbing and all and what's left of your two fifty—but it were wise to hold on to your mask.

You're clumsy in your feebleness, you implicate your tin-hat 1055   rim with the slack sling of it.

1032: *Balder*: a dead German soldier, like Emil, Ulrich and Hansel, mentioned in the following lines along with the dead British soldiers. The name is taken from the Norse god Balder, for whom mistletoe was the only substance that could cause him harm. He was killed by a shaft of mistletoe hurled at him by the blind god Höd at the instigation of the evil Loki.

1033: *Myrtle* boughs were worn by initiates at the Eleusinian mysteries of ancient Greece.

1036: A *torque* is a metal collar consisting of twisted precious metal shaped into a loop; it was a characteristic neck ornament of the ancient Britons.

1038: The leaf of a *palm* tree was in classical times worn as a symbol of victory.

1039: *tripod*: of a machine gun

1040: *St. John's Wort*: said to offer protection against the fairies

1041: The character *Dai Greatcoat* had earlier been blown to pieces.

1043: *noblesse*: group of noblemen

1046: *Aneirin*: the sixth-century Welsh poet: his *Y Gododdin* memorializes the fallen members of an ill-fated expedition sent from Gododdin to take Catraeth from the invading Saxons. *nullah*: river

1047: *Guenadota*: "The north-west parts of Wales" (Jones)

1048: *Disciplines of the Wars*: the phrase is spoken by the Welsh Captain Fluellen, in *Henry V* 3.2.

1051: *webbing*: harness, cloth strap

1052: *two fifty*: .250 ammunition

1053: *mask*: i.e., gas mask

Let it lie for the dews to rust it, or ought you to decently
cover the working parts.
　　Its dark barrel, where you leave it under the oak, reflects
the solemn star that rises urgently from Cliff Trench.
1060　　It's a beautiful doll for us
it's the Last Reputable Arm.
　　But leave it—under the oak,
leave it for a Cook's tourist to the Devastated Areas and crawl
as far as you can and wait for the bearers.

1065　Mrs. Willy Hartington has learned to draw sheets and so has
Miss Melpomené; and on the south lawns,
men walk in red white and blue
under the cedars
and by every green tree
1070　and beside comfortable waters.

But why dont the bastards come—
Bearers!—stret-cher bear-errs!
or do they divide the spoils at the Aid-Post.
　　But how many men do you suppose could bear away a third
1075　of us:
drag just a little further—he yet may counter-attack.

Lie still under the oak
next to the Jerry
and Sergeant Jerry Coke.
1080　　The feet of the reserves going up tread level with your fore-
　　　head; and no word for you; they whisper one with another;
　　　　pass on, inward;
these latest succours:
green Kimmerii to bear up the war.

1085　Oeth and Annoeth's hosts they were
who in that night grew

1056: cf. *Othello* 1.2.59: "Keep up your bright swords, for the dew will rust 'em"

1059: *solemn star*: a signaling flare

1061: *Last Reputable Arm*: "Jones and the other soldiers had a sense of their rifles being the last humane weapon, already being superseded by machine guns and artillery, instruments of mechanical mass destruction." (Thomas Dilworth, in correspondence)

1063: Thomas *Cook* is a travel agency. "This may appear to be an anachronism, but I remember in 1917 discussing with a friend the possibilities of tourist activity if peace ever came. I remember we went into details and wondered if the unexploded projectile lying near us would go up under a holiday-maker, and how people would stand to be photographed on our parapets. I recall feeling very angry about this, as you do if you think of strangers ever occupying a house you live in, and which has, for you, particular associations." (Jones)

1066: *Melpomené* was the Greek Muse of tragedy.

1067: *red white and blue*: the colors of the Union Jack, the British flag

1068ff: The phrasing is from the Old Testament but the source is Frazer: "among the green woods and beside the still waters of the lonely hills" (p. 167).

1073: "The R.A.M.C. [Royal Army Medical Corps] was suspected by disgruntled men of the fighting units of purloining articles from the kit of the wounded and the dead. Their regimental initials were commonly interpreted: 'Rob All My Comrades'." (Jones)

1076: *he*: i.e., the Germans: Jones noted in an earlier part of the poem: "He, him, his—used by us of the enemy at all times."

1078: *Jerry*: German

1084: *Kimmerii*: inhabitants of Cimmeria, a land where according to legend the sun never shone.

1085–88: "Cf. Englyn 30 of the *Englynion y Beddeu*, 'The Stanzas of the Graves'. See Rhys, *Origin of the Englyn, Y Cymmrodor*, vol. xviii. Oeth and Annoeth's hosts occur in Welsh tradition as a mysterious body

younger men
younger striplings.

1090 The geste says this and the man who was on the field . . . and
who wrote the book . . . the man who does not know this
has not understood anything.

1937

from The Anathemata

from I: Rite and Fore-Time

[162] At this unabiding Omphalos
    this other laughless rock
at the stone of division
165   above the middle water-deeps
at the turn of time
    not at any time, but
at this acceptable time.
From the year of
170   the lord-out-of-Ur
about two millennia.
Two thousand lents again
    since the first barley mow.
Twenty millennia (and what millennia more?)
175 Since he became
        man master-of-plastic.

Who were his *gens*-men or had he no *Hausname* yet
no *nomen* for his *fecit*-mark
    the Master of the Venus?
180 whose man-hands god-handled the Willendorf stone
    before they unbound the last glaciation

---

of troops that seem to have some affinity with the Legions. They were said to 'fight as well in the covert as in the open'. Cf. *The Iolo MSS.*" (Jones) (*Legions:* Jones refers to legends of lost Roman Legions on the Welsh borders.)

1089: *geste:* tale. "Cf. *Chanson de Roland,* lines 2095–8. . . . I have used Mr. René Hague's translation." (Jones)

The Anathemata: Besides Jones's own annotations, we have also made use of René Hague's *A Commentary on The Anathemata of David Jones* (Toronto and Buffalo, 1977) and Henry Summerfield's *An Introductory Guide to* The Anathemata *and the* Sleeping Lord *Sequence of David Jones* (Victoria, BC, 1979).

Rite and Fore-Time: 162ff: The *laughless rock* is Agelastos Petra at ancient Eleusis, site of the Eleusinian Mysteries in honor of the goddess Demeter. But the setting of this passage is Jerusalem: "The great rock over which the temple of Jerusalem was built was regarded not only as the navel [*omphalos*] of the world but as separating the waters of the abyss under the earth from the celestial waters." (Jones)

170: "It is usually supposed that Abraham moved north-west up the Euphrates valley from 'Ur of the Chaldees' about 2,000 BC. The cultivation of grain had begun in Mesopotamia at least by 4,000 BC." (Jones)

176: *plastic:* the visual arts. "The first examples of visual art so far (1940) discovered date from about 20,000 BC. There is evidence of artefacture, of a sort, twenty thousand and more years earlier still, e.g. flints and marked stones, but these are hardly 'visual art' in the accepted sense." (Jones)

177: *gens:* clan (Latin); *Hausname:* clan-name (German)

178: *nomen:* one's middle name (in Latin), signifying one's *gens*
    fecit-mark: maker's signature (*fecit:* "he made")

180: The *Willendorf Venus* is a prehistoric fertility symbol, a carved image of a woman with exaggeratedly large breasts and hips; see Jones's note to line 198 below.

for the Uhland Father to be-ribbon *die blaue Donau*
      with his Vanabride blue.
O long before they lateen'd her Ister

185   or Romanitas manned her gender'd stream.

O Europa!

                how long and long and long and
very long again, before you'll maze the waltz-forms in gay
Vindobona in the ramshackle last phases; or god-shape the

190   modal rhythms for nocturns in Melk in the young-time; or
plot the Rhaetian limits in the Years of the City.
          But already he's at it
the form-making proto-maker
busy at the fecund image of her.

195   Chthonic? why yes
but mother of us.
      Then it is these abundant *ubera,* here, under the species
of worked lime-rock, that gave suck to the lord? She that
they already venerate (what other could they?)

200   her we declare?
Who else?
      And see how they run, the juxtaposed forms,
brighting the vaults of Lascaux; how the linear is wedded
to volume, how they do, within, in an unbloody manner,

205   under the forms of brown haematite and black manganese on
the graved lime-face, what is done, without,
          far on the windy tundra
at the kill

182: "In Northern myth, Uhland is the abode of the gods of the atmosphere, the *Luftraum*. Vanabride is
Freyja, a kind of Teutonic Venus. White cats draw her car across the blue sky and her myth seems in part
confused with that of Frigg the wife of Odin. She is the most beautiful of the Vanir and half the departed
(who die bravely) are hers." (Jones).
    die blaue Donau: the blue Danube
184: *lateen'd her Ister*: (1) gave the Latin name "Ister" to the lower Danube; (2) sailed it with lateens, a type
of Mediterranean sailing ship.
185: *Romanitas*: Romanness. The grammatical gender of "Ister" is masculine in Latin, but that of the Ger-
man "Donau" is feminine.
189: *Vindobona*: Latin name of Vienna
190: *modal*: using one of the modes of church music
    nocturns: one of the divisions of matins (church office performed either at midnight or daybreak)
    Melk: "The reference is to the Benedictine abbey of Melk, in Austria, which I am told was one of the
great centres of church music." (Jones)
191: "Cf. the *Limes Raetiae*, which marked the limits of the civilized world in the Danube district." (Jones)
    the Years of the City: i.e., of the Roman Empire.
195: *Chthonic*: of the underworld; literally, in or under the earth
197: *ubera*: breasts (Latin)
    species: outward appearance (as said of the bread and wine of the mass, whose appearance conceals
Christ's flesh and blood)
198–199: *She that they already venerate*: "The reference is to the first work of plastic art in-the-round
known to us, the little limestone sculpture just over four inches high, of very ample proportions, known
as 'the Venus of Willendorf'. It is dated, I believe, as contemporary with some of the recently discovered
Lascaux cave-paintings, and is of the same Aurignacian culture of 20–25,000 BC. If it is a 'Venus' it is very
much a Venus Genetrix, for it emphasizes in a very emphatic manner the nutritive and generative phys-
iognomy. It is rather the earliest example of a long sequence of mother-figures, earth-mothers and
mother goddesses, that fuse in the Great-Mother of settled civilizations—not yet, by a long, long way,
the Queen of Heaven, yet, nevertheless, with some of her attributes; in that it images the generative and
the fruitful and the sustaining, at however primitive and elementary, or, if you will, 'animal' a level;
though it is slovenly to use the word 'animal' of any art-form, for the making of such forms belongs only
to man." (Jones).
203: The images of animals on the cave-walls at *Lascaux* formed part of magical hunting rituals.

that the kindred may have life.
210   O God!
O the Academies!

What ages since
his other marvel-day
                    when times turned?
215   and *how* turned!
When
          (How?
          from early knocking stick or stane?)
the first New Fire wormed
220   at the Easter of Technics.
What a holy Saturn's day!
O vere beata nox!

                    A hundred thousand equinoxes
(less or more)
225   since they cupped the ritual stones
for the faithful departed.

III: Angle-Land

Did he strike soundings off Vecta Insula?
          or was it already the gavelkind *ígland?*
Did he lie by
          in the East Road?

211: *Academies:* i.e., of classical and post-classical art.

218: *stane:* stone (Scots)

219: *wormed:* referring to "the first little creeping glow of red, followed by the curl of flame and wisp of smoke in the charcoal" (Hague)

222: "*O vere beata nox,* 'O truly blessed night'. See the *Exsultet* chanted by the deacon at the blessing of the Paschal Candle which is lighted from a fire of charcoal newly kindled by striking flint. This occurs once in the annual cycle, in the spring, on Easter Saturday. From the new fire so kindled the lamps and candles used during the ensuing twelve months are subsequently lit." (Jones).

225: "Although Neanderthal man of 40 to 60,000 BC appears not to be regarded by the anthropologists as a direct ancestor of ourselves, nevertheless it would seem to me that he must have been 'man', for his burial-sites show a religious care for the dead. At his places of interment the covering stones have revealed ritual markings; moreover food-offerings, weapons and possibly a life-symbol (a horn) have been found buried with him. Further, the hollow markings ('cup-marks') are similar to those which characterize the sacred stones of tens of thousands of years afterwards, in the New Stone Age culture which began, as far as Western Europe is concerned, as recently as *c.* 5,000 BC, or later, to continue among some primitive peoples to this day, in some parts of the world." (Jones)

Title: The preceding sections of *The Anathemata* contain the figure of a sea captain, whose ship moves both over seas and in time; as this section opens the poem has reached the beginnings of Anglo-Saxon England, sometime between the fifth and eighth centuries.

1: *Vecta Insula:* Roman name for the Isle of Wight, off the south coast of England

2: *ígland:* island (Old English). In the system of *gavelkind* a tenant's land was at his death divided equally among his sons. "When I wrote this I was associating the system of gavelkind with the Isle of Wight solely on account of its being occupied by Jutes, who also occupied Kent, which country is particularly associated with that system and there is evidence of a sort of succession by gavelkind in the Jutish area in Hampshire opposite Wight." (Jones)

4: *East Road:* a sheltered area on the south coast of Kent where ships can anchor. A ship heading from the North Sea down the coast of England to the Isle of Wight would pass through it.

5   was it a kindly *numen* of the Sleeve that headed him clear of
                South Sand Head?
                Did he shelter in the Small Downs?
                Keeping close in, did he feel his way
                between the Flats and the Brake?
10   But, what was her draught, and, what was the ocean doing?
                    Did he stand on toward the Gull?
                did his second mate sound
                    with more than care?
                was it perforce or Fortuna's rudder, circumstance or superb
15   pilotage or clean oblation
                  that sheered him from smother
                (the unseen necropolis banking to starboard of her).
                Or was it she
                    Sea-born and Sea-star
20   whose own, easy and free
                    the pious matlos are
                or, was it a whim of Poseidon's
                (master o' the cinque masters o' lodemanage)
                whose own the Island's approaches are
25   that kept her?
                Was the Foreland?
                    was the Elbow?
                under fog.
                  He might have been deeped in the Oaze!
30   Or
                  by the brumous numen drawn on

5: *numen*: spirit (Latin)

   Sleeve: the English Channel

6: *South Sand Head*: the southwestern tip of Goodwin Sands, a treacherous series of shoals off the east coast of Kent

7: *Small Downs*: a sheltered area of the sea off the east coast of Kent, north of Deal

9: *the Flats*: the Sandwich Flats, alongside part of the east coast of Kent

   The *Gull* Stream is a channel between Goodwin Sands and *the Brake*, a shallow area nearer the shore.

11: *stand on*: continue his course

14: *Fortuna*: Roman goddess of fortune; she is often depicted carrying a rudder

15: *oblation*: religious offering

16: *sheered*: to sheer is "to direct a vessel obliquely" (Hague).

   smother: "(1) thick fog; (2) water in confused motion" (Summerfield)

17: *necropolis*: graveyard. "It so happens that it was at Deal, c.1903, that 'I first beheld the ocean' and I particularly remember that sometimes, in certain conditions of weather and tide, a number of hulks were visible on the Goodwins which then seemed like a graveyard of ships." (Jones)

19: Aphrodite, Greek goddess of love, was born from sea-foam; the Virgin Mary is traditionally called "Stella Maris" (star of the sea).

21: *matlos*: matelots (sailors). "Cf. Archbishop David Mathew, *British Seamen*, p. 48, 'Easy and gallant they defend the freedom of the seas and the shores of England'. And cf. song, *All the Nice Girls Love a Sailor*, line 5, 'Bright and breezy, free and easy.' " (Jones)

22: *Poseidon*: Greek god of the sea

23: "'Cinque' and 'lodemanage' to be said as in English, indeed as in Cockney English. (Each of the Cinque Ports had a pilot called the Master of Lodemanage.)" (Jones). The Cinque Ports were five ports along the Kent and Sussex coast that in medieval times supplied men and ships to the Royal Navy.

   lodemanage: pilotage

26–27: The *Elbow* is a dangerous shoal off the North *Foreland,* a point of land that projects from the northeast coast of Kent.

29: "Cf. Oaze Deep, an area of water so named in the mouth of the Thames." (Jones)

31: *brumous numen*: spirit of mist

or
in preclear visibility
by the invisible wind laboured
35   it might have been Dogger or Well
to bank her a mound
without a sheet to wrap her
without a shroud to her broken back.
Past where they placed their *ingas*-names
40   where they speed the coulter deep
in the open Engel fields
to this day.
How many poles
of their broad Angle hidage
45   to the small scattered plots, to the lightly furrowed *erwau*,
that once did quilt Boudícca's róyal *gwely?*

Past where they urn'd their calcined dead from Schleswig
over the foam.

(Close the south-west wall of the chester, without the orbit,
50   if but a stone's throw: you don't want to raise an Icenian
Venta's Brettisc ghost.
He'll latin-runes tellan in his horror-coat standing:
IAM REDIT ROMA
his lifted palm his VERBVM is.)

55   Past where the ancra-man, deeping his holy rule
in the fiendish marsh

33: *preclear*: very clear
35: *Dogger* Bank is a dangerous shallow area off the northeast coast of England; *Well* Bank is a sandbank
off the coast of Lincolnshire
39: *ingas*: Anglo-Saxon placenames ending in "-ingas"
40: *coulter*: a vertical blade attached to a ploughshare; see Jones's note to line 45.
41: *Engel*: cf. St. Gregory the Great's epigram upon seeing some Anglo-Saxon children: "Non Angli sed
Angeli" (Not Angles but angels); "engel" is German for "angel."
43: A *pole* was 30.25 square yards; a *hide* was an indeterminate measure: the amount of land needed to
support a man and his family.
45: "*Erwau*, plural of *erw*, acre; érr-wye (err as in the Latin *errare*), accent on first syllable. Not in fact an
acre or any fixed unit, but land equally divided among the members of a plough-team under the Celtic
system of co-aration." (Jones)
46: "*gwely*, gwel-ly, bed, but also used of the collective lands of a group. Typical Celtic ploughing was less
deep than that of subsequent invaders." (Jones). The British queen *Boudícca* led her tribe, the Icenians,
in a failed revolt against the Romans in 60 AD.
47: *calcined*: burnt to powder
    Schleswig: The Angles are thought to have come from the northern part of Germany, which is in mod-
ern times the province of Schleswig-Holstein. They practiced cremation of the dead.
49: *chester*: Roman walled town
51: *Venta*: After their defeat at the hands of the Romans the Icenians became a small tribal community
whose capital was Venta Icenorum (in modern-day Norfolk)
    Brettisc: British. "Pronounce bret-tish." (Jones)
52: "He [one of the newcomers] will puzzle out the Latin letters"
    horror-coat: armor
53: "NOW ROME RETURNS"
54: *VERBVM*: word. The raised palm salute was used in the Roman army—and also by the Italian Fas-
cists, who liked to stress Italy's ancient Roman heritage.
55: "The Mercian saint, Guthlac, when an anchorite on Crowland island in the Fens [of East Anglia], hear-
ing the speech of surviving Britons thought it the language of devils." (Jones)

            at the *Geisterstunde*
            on *Calangaeaf* night
        heard the bogle-*baragouinage*.
60   Crowland-*diawliaidd*
        Wealisc-man lingo speaking?
            or Britto-Romani gone *diaboli*?
        or Romanity gone *Wealisc*?
        Is Marianus wild Meirion?
65   is Sylvánus
                Urbigéna's son?
        has toga'd Rhufon
                (gone Actaeon)
        come away to the Wake
70   in the bittern's low aery?
        along with his towny
                Patricius gone the *wilde Jäger*?

        From the *fora*
                to the forests.
75   Out from *gens Romulûm*
            into the *Weal*-kin
        dinas-man gone *aethwlad*
        cives gone wold-men
                        . . . from Lindum to London
80   bridges broken down.

        What was his *Hausname*?
            he whose North Holstein urn
        they sealed against the seep of the Yare?

57: *Geisterstunde:* witching-hour, midnight
58: "*Calangaeaf,* Winter Calands, November 1, cal-lan-gei-av, accent on ei pronounced as in height." (Jones)
59: *baragouinage:* gibberish (French)
60: "*diawliaidd,* devils, deeowl-yithe, accent on first syllable." (Jones)
61: *Wealisc:* Welsh. "Pronounce wye-lish." (Jones)
62: *diaboli:* devils (Latin)
64: "The Roman name Marianus gave Meirion in Welsh; hence 'Merioneth' [Meirionnydd, a region of Wales]." (Jones)
65–66: These Latin names mean, respectively, "woodsman" and "city-born." "Urbigena; cf. Urbgen in Nennius, Urien in the Romances. The late Gilbert Sheldon wrote: 'The Latin name *Urbigena,* city-born, is disguised as Urien'. Pronounce as urr-bee-gain-ah, accent on gain." (Jones)
67: "Rhufon, rhiv-von, Romanus"
68: *Actaeon:* the mythical hunter, who was turned into a stag by the goddess Diana and killed by his own hounds.
69: *Wake:* vigil; but Jones also alludes to the Anglo-Saxon hero Hereward the Wake, who held out in 1070–1071 in the Fens against the Normans.
72: *wilde Jäger:* wild huntsman (German)
73: *fora:* Roman forums
75: *gens Romulûm:* race of the Romuleans (descended from Romulus, founder of Rome)
76: *Weal-kin:* "Cf. *Wealcyn* used by the Teutonic invaders of any group of kindred within those lands which had been part of Roman Britain. Pronounce, wa-ahl." (Jones)
77: "*dinas,* city, din-ass, accent on first syllable. *aethwlad,* outlaw, aeth-oolahd, ae as ah+eh, accent on first syllable." (Jones)
78: *cives:* citizens (Latin); *wold-men:* forest-men
79: *Lindum:* Roman name for Lincoln
81: *Hausname:* clan-name (German)
83: *Yare:* a river in Norfolk

If there are *Wealas* yet
85   in the Waltons
    what's the cephalic index of the *môrforynion*, who knell
    the bell, who thread the pearls that were Ned Mizzen's eyes,
    at the five fathom line off the Naze?
                    On past the low low lands of the Holland that
90 Welland winds to the Deepings north of the Soke
    past where Woden's gang *is gens Julia* for Wuffingas new to
    old Nene and up with the Lark
    past the south hams and the north tons
    past the weathered thorps and
95   the Thorpe
    that bore, that bred
                            him whom Nike did bear
    her tears at flood
    and over the scatter of the forebrace bitts
100   down to the orlop
    at twenty five minutes after one of the clock
    in the afternoon, on a Monday
    twelve days before the Calends of November
    outside the Pillars
105   where they closed like a forest
                        . . . in 13 fathoms' water
    unanchored in the worsening weather.

84: "*Wealas*, wa-ahl-ass, plural of *Wealh*, a Welshman." (Jones)
85: Several Norfolk towns, such as Walton-on-the-Naze, have names that include the word *Walton* (a contraction of "walled town").
86: *cephalic index*: the ratio of the breadth to the length of the skull, a measurement supposedly indicative of racial characteristics
    "*môrforynion*, water-maidens, mōrr-vorr-un-yon, accent on third syllable." (Jones)
86ff: cf. Ariel's song in *The Tempest*: "Full fathom five thy father lies; / Of his bones are coral made; / Those are pearls that were his eyes. . . . / Sea nymphs hourly ring his knell." *Ned Mizzen* is a sailor who appears elsewhere in *The Anathemata*.
88: *the Naze*: a headland on the coast of Essex
89: *Holland*: a district of southern Lincolnshire; the Welland runs through it and empties into the Wash. "The Low Low Lands of Holland" is an English folksong.
90: *Deepings*: the town of Market Deeping and the neighboring villages of West Deeping, Deeping Gate and Deeping St. James lie on the Welland.
Soke: the Soke of Peterborough, an area of Northamptonshire adjacent to Holland.
91–92: "The Wuffingas, that during the fifth-century invasions made settlements in the Fen country, through which flow the Nene and the Lark, seem later on to have claimed descent from both Odin and Caesar." (Jones)
91: *Woden*: or Odin, ruler of the Germanic pantheon
    gens Julia: clan of Julius Caesar
93–94: *ham* ("home"), *ton* ("town") and *thorp* ("village") are Old English words which are still present in English placenames.
97: *him*: Lord Nelson, the English admiral, who was born in Burnham Thorpe, Norfolk, in 1758. At the battle of Trafalgar he sailed on the *Victory* (*Nike* was the Greek goddess of victory).
99: *forebrace bitts*: deck posts to which forebraces (ropes for handling the foresail) are attached.
100: *orlop*: a ship's lowest deck. Nelson was wounded during the battle by a sniper; he was carried below decks, where he died. The battle was, however, won by the British.
103: *Calends*: first day of the month
104: *Pillars*: the Pillars of Hercules, usually identified as the Rock of Gibraltar and Mount Hacho on the African coast; Cape Trafalgar, Spain, is at the western extreme of the Strait of Gibraltar.
105–107: "See Collingwood's dispatch to the Admiralty Lords as reported in *The Times* of Nov. 7th, 1805, giving particulars of the action on Monday, October 21, 1805, and also James, *Naval History*, Vol. IV, 1837 edtn. 'Seeing by the direction of her course that the Victory was about to follow the example of the Royal-Sovereign, the French and Spanish ships ahead of the British weather column closed like a forest.' p. 38.

Far drawn on away

from the island's field-floor, upwards of a hundred fathoms
110   over where, beyond where, in the fifties, toward the sixties,
north latitude

all our easting waters

are confluent with the fathering river and tributary to him:
where Tamesis, Great Ouse, Tyne from the Wall's end, de-
115   marking Tweed, Forth that winds the middle march, Tummel
and wide looping Tay (that laps the wading files when Birnam
boughs deploy toward Dunsinane—out toward the Goat
Flats),
Spey of the Symbol stones and Ness from the serpentine mere
120   all mingle Rhenus-flow

and are oned with him

in Cronos-*meer*.
I speak of before the whale-roads or the keel-paths were from
Orcades to the fiord-havens, or the greyed green wastes that
125   they strictly grid
quadrate and number on the sea-green *Quadratkarte*

one eight six one G
for the fratricides

of the latter-day, from east-shore of Iceland
130   *bis Norwegen*

'To add to the perilous condition of the British fleet and prizes, the ships were then in 13 fathoms' water, with the shoals of Trafalgar but a few miles to leeward.' p. 87." (Jones)

108ff: The narrative returns to the British Isles, moving northwards (the English Channel is at the 50th parallel; the 60th is in Scotland); the "field-floor" is the comparatively shallow part of the North Sea from the Strait of Dover to the coast of southern Yorkshire. The rivers listed are progressively more northerly.

114: *Tamesis*: the Thames (Latin)

    Great Ouse: a river flowing into the Wash

    The river *Tyne* reaches the sea near Wallsend, at the eastern end of Hadrian's Wall, a Roman wall stretching from coast to coast in northern Britain.

115: Part of the river *Tweed* lies on the Anglo-Scottish border.

    The (circuitous) river *Forth* runs from the Scottish Highlands into the Lowlands; *march*: border.

    The *Tummel* flows into the *Tay*, which empties into the North Sea. In *Macbeth* Macduff's army camouflages itself with boughs from *Birnam* Wood; they would have had to cross the Tay to get to Macbeth's castle at *Dunsinane*.

117–18: *Goat flats*: "the probable literal meaning of 'Carse of Gowrie,' the Gaelic-based name of a level area on the north side of the Tay estuary." (Summerfield)

119: *Spey*: a river flowing into the North Sea; the "Symbol stones" are either "stones carved and inscribed by the Picts in northern and eastern Scotland in the first millennium A.D." (Summerfield) or "the fantastic glacial deposits of the Spey river and valley" (Hague).

    Ness: a river flowing from Loch Ness–"serpentine" for its supposed monster.

120: *Rhenus*: the Rhine; "Before Britain became an island, the Rhine and Thames were parts of a single vast river system which drained into a basin in what is now part of the North Sea." (Summerfield)

122: *Chronos-meer*: the Sea of Chronos, "the name used by the Classical writers for the unexplored northern waters." (Jones)

123–25: Jones is bringing the narrative up to the moment of writing, during World War II. "Whale-road" and "keel-path" are Old-English-style poeticisms for the sea. Scotland's Orkney Islands (the *Orcades*, in Latin) were the base for the British Navy; during the war the German Navy (over- and underwater) operated in the Atlantic and the North Sea.

126: *Quadratkarte*: a map marked with a square grid (German)

130: *bis Norwegen*: to Norway (German). "I had in mind a squared chart issued for special service requirements by the German Naval Command, described as *Europäisches Nordmeer. Ostküste von Island bis Norwegen, 1861 G.*, on which the grid, numerals and other markings are imposed in green on a large-scale map of that area. Date *c.* 1940." (Jones)

(O Balin O Balan!
          how blood you both
the *Brudersee*
          toward the last pháse
135   of our dear West.)

                                               1952

A, a, a, Domine Deus

I said, Ah! what shall I write?
I enquired up and down.
          (He's tricked me before
with his manifold lurking-places.)
5   I looked for His symbol at the door.
I have looked for a long while
          at the textures and contours.
I have run a hand over the trivial intersections.
I have journeyed among the dead forms
10   causation projects from pillar to pylon.
I have tired the eyes of the mind
          regarding the colours and lights.
I have felt for His Wounds
          in nozzles and containers.
15   I have wondered for the automatic devices.
I have tested the inane patterns
          without prejudice.
I have been on my guard
          not to condemn the unfamiliar.
20   For it is easy to miss Him
          at the turn of a civilisation.
    I have watched the wheels go round in case I might see the
living creatures like the appearance of lamps, in case I might see
the Living God projected from the Machine. I have said to the
25   perfected steel, be my sister and for the glassy towers I thought I
felt some beginnings of His creature, but *A, a, a, Domine Deus,*
my hands found the glazed work unrefined and the terrible
crystal a stage-paste . . . *Eia, Domine Deus.*

                              1938, 1966 / 1974

131: "Cf. Malory Bk. II, Cp. 18. How Balin met with his brother Balan and how each slew each other
unknown [i.e., not knowing they were brothers]." (Jones)

133: *Brudersee:* brother-sea (German)

135: Jones has in mind the historical theories of Oswald Spengler, who in *The Decline of the West*
(1918–1922) argued that modern Western civilization had peaked in the Middle Ages and had ever since
been on the decline.

Title: The title is from the Latin version of Jer. 1:6: "Ah, Lord God! behold, I cannot speak; for I am a
child."

27–28: "And the likeness of the firmament upon the heads of the living creature was as the colour of the
terrible crystal, stretched forth over their heads above." (Ezek. 1:22)

ROBERT GRAVES (1895–1985)

G RAVES GREW UP IN A HIGH VICTORIAN HOUSEHOLD VISITED BY LUMINARIES SUCH AS Algernon Swinburne and spent his last years as something of a cult figure, entertaining writers and movie stars at his home in Majorca. The celebrity of his last decades owed a good deal to his prose, especially his historical novels *I, Claudius* and *Claudius the God* (both 1934) and *The White Goddess: A Historical Grammar of Poetic Myth* (1948). In *The White Goddess,* Graves writes that "My thesis is that the language of poetic myth anciently current in the Mediterranean and Northern Europe was a magical language bound up with popular religious ceremonies in honour of the Moon-goddess, or Muse, some of them dating from the Old Stone Age, and that this remains the language of true poetry."[1] Though its scholarship has not been well received by professional scholars of myth, *The White Goddess*'s plea for the "return of the goddess" and a "female sense of orderliness" found receptive audiences in the United States and England in the 1950s and the 1960s. Graves's poetry has realist and classicist elements and often takes up the traditional subjects of lyric, love especially. In the 1950s, a few of the poets of the Movement found Graves's independence from modernism exemplary, admiring his use of traditional forms and plain diction if not his celebration of the White Goddess.

Graves was born in Wimbledon and educated at Charterhouse. He said that the family's pedigree was "good as far as the reign of Henry VII."[2] His first poetry appeared while he served as an infantry officer in World War I, though C. H. Sisson argues that "The war, in which Graves performed so notably and from which he suffered prolonged nervous consequences, did not concentrate his mind," adding that Graves's more impressive war poetry was written "when war haunted him from a distance."[3] After the war he married Nancy Nicholson, the daughter of the painter Sir William Nicholson, and attended St. John's College, Oxford. In 1925, the couple went with their acquaintance the American poet Laura Riding to Egypt; the relationship with Riding was crucial to Graves's work but disastrous for his marriage. With Riding, Graves wrote *A Survey of Modernist Poetry* (1927), which was to influence the New Critics in the United States and William Empson's critical writing in England. In 1929, Graves published *Goodbye to All That,* a memoir detailing his war experience, the breakup of his marriage, and his general disillusionment with postwar England. That same year, he moved with Riding to Majorca, where they remained until the Spanish Civil War forced their evacuation in 1936. For several years afterwards, Graves and

---

[1] *The White Goddess: A Historical Grammar of Poetic Myth,* New York, 1948, p. vi.
[2] Quoted in C. H. Sisson, *English Poetry 1900–1950,* London, 1971, p. 188.
[3] Ibid., p. 190.

Riding lived in various locations in Europe and the United States; by 1939, their relationship had ended and Graves was back in England, where he remained throughout World War II. With his second wife, Beryl Hodge, he settled in Majorca permanently in 1946. Graves was professor of poetry at Oxford from 1961 to 1966. Among his many books are editions of his *Collected Poems* published in 1955 and 1975.

Warning to Children

Children, if you dare to think
Of the greatness, rareness, muchness,
Fewness of this precious only
Endless world in which you say
5   You live, you think of things like this:
Blocks of slate enclosing dappled
Red and green, enclosing tawny
Yellow nets, enclosing white
And black acres of dominoes,
10   Where a neat brown paper parcel
Tempts you to untie the string.
In the parcel a small island,
On the island a large tree,
On the tree a husky fruit.
15   Strip the husk and pare the rind off:
In the kernel you will see
Blocks of slate enclosed by dappled
Red and green, enclosed by tawny
Yellow nets, enclosed by white
20   And black acres of dominoes,
Where the same brown paper parcel—
Children, leave the string alone!
For who dares undo the parcel
Finds himself at once inside it,
25   On the island, in the fruit,
Blocks of slate about his head,
Finds himself enclosed by dappled
Green and red, enclosed by yellow
Tawny nets, enclosed by black
30   And white acres of dominoes,
With the same brown paper parcel
Still unopened on his knee.
And, if he then should dare to think
Of the fewness, muchness, rareness,
35   Greatness of this endless only
Precious world in which he says
He lives—he then unties the string.

1929

The Legs

There was this road,
And it led up-hill,
And it led down-hill,
And round and in and out.

5   And the traffic was legs,
Legs from the knees down,
Coming and going,
Never pausing.

And the gutters gurgled
10   With the rain's overflow,
And the sticks on the pavement
Blindly tapped and tapped.

What drew the legs along
Was the never-stopping,
15   And the senseless, frightening
Fate of being legs.

Legs for the road,
The road for legs,
Resolutely nowhere
20   In both directions.

My legs at least
Were not in that rout:
On grass by the roadside
Entire I stood,

25   Watching the unstoppable
Legs go by
With never a stumble
Between step and step.

Though my smile was broad
30   The legs could not see,
Though my laugh was loud
The legs could not hear.

My head dizzied, then:
I wondered suddenly,
35   Might I too be a walker
From the knees down?

Gently I touched my shins.
The doubt unchained them:
They had run in twenty puddles
40   Before I regained them.

1931

To Juan at the Winter Solstice

There is one story and one story only
That will prove worth your telling,
Whether as learned bard or gifted child;
To it all lines or lesser gauds belong

5   That startle with their shining
Such common stories as they stray into.

Is it of trees you tell, their months and virtues,
Or strange beasts that beset you,
Of birds that croak at you the Triple will?

10 Or of the Zodiac and how slow it turns
Below the Boreal Crown,
Prison of all true kings that ever reigned?

Water to water, ark again to ark,
From woman back to woman:

15 So each new victim treads unfalteringly
The never altered circuit of his fate,
Bringing twelve peers as witness
Both to his starry rise and starry fall.

Or is it of the Virgin's silver beauty,

20 All fish below the thighs?
She in her left hand bears a leafy quince;
When with her right she crooks a finger, smiling,
How may the King hold back?
Royally then he barters life for love.

25 Or of the undying snake from chaos hatched,
Whose coils contain the ocean,

Title: "This was begun just before, and completed just after, the birth of my seventh child on December
21, 1945. The *winter solstice* is the traditional birthday of all the 'Solar Heroes' or 'Demons of the Year' of
antiquity, such as the Greek gods Apollo, Dionysus, Zeus, Hermes, Syrian Tammuz, Hercules, the Irish
demi-gods Lugh and Cuchulain, the Egyptian Horus, and the Welsh Merlin and Llew Llaw. In Celtic
popular mythology they are sometimes represented as poetically gifted infants who confound the bards
or magicians of the court where they first appear. Their fate is bound up with that of the Moon Goddess
who appears to them in her different characters at different seasons of the year, that is to say at differ-
ent years of their life, as successively mother, lover, and layer-out. This poem epitomizes the theme of
the Solar Hero's invariable fate, with circumstances deduced from all the relevant mythologies. That this
one story and one story only is the central infinitely variable theme of all poetry is the true, firm con-
tention of my *The White Goddess: A Historical Grammar of Poetic Myth. . . .*" (Graves, qtd. in *Complete
Poems*, vol 2, Manchester, 1997, pp. 329–30)
9: *Triple will:* Another name for Graves's White Goddess is the "Threefold Goddess" (in her roles as
mother, bride, and layer-out).
11: "*Boreal Crown* is [the constellation] Corona Borealis, alias the Cretan Crown, which in Thracean-
Libyan mythology, carried to Bronze Age Britain, was the purgatory where Solar Heroes went after death:
in Welsh it was called 'Caer Arianrhod' (the castle of the goddess Arianrhod—mother of the hero Llew
Llaw)." (Graves, ibid.)
19ff: In *The White Goddess* (1961 ed.), Graves links as versions of a Muse figure the Virgin Mary, the
medieval St. Bridget ("Mary of the Gael"), "the ancient pagan Sea-goddess Marian" and the mermaid;
"Marian always held [the quince] in her hand as a love-gift" (p. 395).
25: *snake:* cf. Graves's *The Greek Myths* 1 (describing the creation of the universe from the union of
Eurynome, Goddess of All Things, and the serpent Ophion); 103.2 (describing the Babylonian sea-
monster Tiamat) and 137.d, 2 (describing Heracles' jumping down a sea-monster's throat and emerging
victorious after three days' battle inside).

Into whose chops with naked sword he springs,
Then in black water, tangled by the reeds,
Battles three days and nights,
30   To be spewed up beside her scalloped shore?

Much snow is falling, winds roar hollowly,
The owl hoots from the elder,
Fear in your heart cries to the loving-cup:
Sorrow to sorrow as the sparks fly upward.
35   The log groans and confesses:
There is one story and one story only.

Dwell on her graciousness, dwell on her smiling,
Do not forget what flowers
The great boar trampled down in ivy time.
40   Her brow was creamy as the crested wave,
Her sea-grey eyes were wild
But nothing promised that is not performed.

1945 / 1946

The White Goddess

All saints revile her, and all sober men
Ruled by the God Apollo's golden mean—
In scorn of which we sailed to find her
In distant regions likeliest to hold her
5   Whom we desired above all things to know,
Sister of the mirage and echo.

It was a virtue not to stay,
To go our headstrong and heroic way
Seeking her out at the volcano's head,
10   Among pack ice, or where the track had faded
Beyond the cavern of the seven sleepers:
Whose broad high brow was white as any leper's,
Whose eyes were blue, with rowan-berry lips,
With hair curled honey-coloured to white hips.

33: *loving-cup*: a tankard or goblet, often two-handled, passed from hand to hand at feasts (such as Christ-mas) as the guests pledge friendship to one another.
35: "The *log* is the Yule log, burned at the year's end." (Graves, *Collected Poems* vol 2, p. 330)
39: "The *great boar* kills practically all the heroes (even Zeus, according to one account) at the fall of the year." (Graves, ibid.). Cf. the Greek myth of the goddess Aphrodite's mortal lover Adonis, who was killed by a boar; *The White Goddess*, p. 210, gives a list of mythic parallels.

Title: The *White Goddess* is the "Muse, the Mother of All Living," who according to Graves lies behind all religions and all true poetry (Graves, *The White Goddess*, 1961 ed, p. 24).
2: *Apollo* was the Greek god of youth, music, and the sun, represented as a beautiful young man. *Golden mean*: temperance and moderation; the avoidance of excess (see Horace, *Odes* 2.10)
10: *pack ice*: in polar seas, large pieces of ice floating in the water pack together, making a near-solid mass that is impassable to ships.
11: According to legend, seven Christian youths of Ephesus took shelter from the emperor Decius's per-secution of Christians by hiding in a cave; they fell into a slumber, awaking two centuries later.

15   Green sap of Spring in the young wood a-stir
Will celebrate the Mountain Mother,
And every song-bird shout awhile for her;
But we are gifted, even in November
Rawest of seasons, with so huge a sense
20   Of her nakedly worn magnificence
We forget cruelty and past betrayal,
Heedless of where the next bright bolt may fall.

1948

NANCY CUNARD (1896–1965)

Born into one of England's shipping fortunes, Cunard spent most of her adult life in France, where she enjoyed considerable celebrity for her wealth, glamor, and lifestyle. Mina Loy wrote that she possessed the "lone fragility / of mythological queens,"[1] and Harold Acton remembered that she "inspired half the poets and novelists of the twenties. They saw her as the Gioconda of the Age."[2] From 1928 to 1931, she ran the Hours Press, which published Ezra Pound's *A Draft of XXX Cantos* and Samuel Beckett's *Whoroscope*. In 1928, she met the African-American jazz pianist Henry Crowder; her controversial 855-page anthology *Negro* (1935), containing contributions by Langston Hughes, Countee Cullen, René Crevel, Pound, and many others, was dedicated to him. Her relationship with Crowder and progressive stance on race relations set her at odds with her family.

Cunard was active as a journalist, translator, publisher, and African art collector; she was also an anti-Fascist political activist during the Spanish Civil War and World War II. Her early poetry appeared in the volumes *Outlaws* (1921) and *Sublunary* (1923). The impact of her association with modernists like Pound begins to appear in poems such as "Simultaneous" (1924) and "In Provins" (1925), which employ characteristic Poundian rhythms and collage and share Pound's interest in the culture and history of Provence. The book-length poem *Parallax*, published in 1925 by Leonard and Virginia Woolf's Hogarth Press, follows T. S. Eliot's *The Waste Land* in some of the particulars of its cadences, imagery, diction, and figure ("Sunday creeps in silence / under suspended smoke, / And curdles defiant in unreal sleep").[3] "Parallax" is the apparent displacement of an object caused by a change in the position from which the object is viewed; the poem self-consciously explores a postwar crisis of value and perspective ("One for another / I have changed my prisons; / held fast, as the flame stands, locked in the prism").

---

[1] "Nancy Cunard," *The Lost Lunar Baedeker*, ed. Roger L. Conover, New York, 1996, p. 103.
[2] "Nancy Cunard: Romantic Rebel," *Nancy Cunard: Brave Poet, Indomitable Rebel*, ed. Hugh Ford, New York, 1968, p. 73.
[3] *Parallax*, London, 1925, p. 10.

from Parallax

*"Many things are known as some are seen, that is by Paralaxis,
or at some distance from their true and proper being."*
SIR THOMAS BROWNE

. . . .

165   London—
                youth and heart-break
       Growing from ashes.
       The war's dirges
       Burning, reverberate—burning
170   Now far away, sea-echoed, now in the sense,
       Taste, mind, uneasy quest of what I am—
       London, the hideous wall, the jail of what I am,
             With fear nudging and pinching
       Keeping each side of me
175   Down one street and another, lost—
       Returned to search through adolescent years
       For key, for mark of what was done and said.
       Do ghosts alone possess the outworn decade?
       Souls fled, bones scattered—
180   And still the vigilant past
       Crowds, climbs, insinuates its whispering vampire-song:
       (No more, oh never, never . . .)
       Are the living ghosts to the dead, or do the dead disclaim
       This clutch of hands, the tears cast out to them?
185   Must one be courteous, halve defunct regrets,
       Present oneself as host to 'Yester-year'?

       By the Embankment I counted the grey gulls
       Nailed to the wind above a distorted tide.
       On discreet waters
190   In Battersea I drifted, acquiescent.
       And on the frosted paths of suburbs
       At Wimbledon, where the wind veers from the new ice,
       Solitary.
       In Gravesend rusty funnels rise on the winter noon
195   From the iron-crane forests, with the tide away from the rank mud.
       Kew in chestnut-time, September in Oxford Street
       Through the stale hot dust—
       And up across the murk to Fitzroy Square
       With a lemon blind at one end, and the halfway spire
200   Attesting God on the right hand of the street—
       London—
             Old.
       Dry bones turfed over by reiterant seasons,

Epigraph: Cunard quotes the *Christian Morals* (II.3) of *Sir Thomas Browne* (1605–1682), doctor, antiquarian, and noted writer of prose.

190ff: *Battersea* is on the Thames' south bank; *Wimbledon* is eight miles southwest of the City of London; *Gravesend* is a port on the Thames downstream of London.

196: *Kew* is a London area south of the Thames, where the Royal Botanic Gardens are located—cf. "Go down to Kew in lilac-time," from "The Barrel Organ," by Alfred Noyes (1880–1958). *Oxford Street* is a London shopping area.

Dry graves filled in, stifled, built upon with new customs.

205 Well, instead—
The south, and its enormous days;
Light consuming the sea, and sun-dust on the mountain,
Churn of the harbour, the toiling and loading, unloading
By tideless seas
210 In a classic land, timeless and hot.
Trees
Bowed to the immemorial Mistral
The evergreens, the pines,
Open their fans—
215   Red-barked forest,
        O vast, brown, terrible,
        Silent and calcinated.
        Moonstruck, dewless . . .
     Or further
220 I know a land . . . red earth, ripe vines and plane-trees,
A gulf of mournful islands, best from afar.
The sunset's huge surrender
Ripens the dead-sea fruit in decaying saltmarsh.
Then brain sings out to the night in muffled thirds,
225 Resumes the uneasy counting and the planning—

      What wings beat in my ears
The old tattoo of journeys?
Why dreamer, *this* is the dream,
The question's answer. And yet, and yet,
230   The foot's impatient (. . . where?)
                  the eye is not convinced,
Compares, decides what's gone was better,
Murmurs about 'lost days' . . .
Sit then, look in the deep wells of the sky,
235 Compose the past—
     Dry moss, grey stone,
     Hill ruins, grass in ruins
     Without water, and multitudinous
     Tintinnabulation in poplar leaves;
240   A spendrift dust from desiccated pools,
     Spider in draughty husks, snail on the leaf—
        Provence, the solstice.
     And the days after,
By the showman's travelling houses, the land caravels
245 Under the poplar—the proud grapes and the burst grape-skins.
Arles in the plain, Miramas after sunset-time

212: *Mistral*: a cold, strong wind of southern France that blows down the Rhône River valley towards the Mediterranean Sea

217: *calcinated*: literally "burnt; reduced to powder": perhaps the reference is to dry, chalky earth beneath the pines.

223: *dead-sea fruit*: alluding to the legendary trees on the shore of the Dead Sea, whose fruit looked attractive to the eye but tasted of ashes

239: *Tintinnabulation*: ringing like bells

240: *spendrift*: spray

244: *caravels*: small ships

246ff: *Arles* and *Miramas* are cities in Provence (a region in the southeast of France), *Les Baux* a small village. Arles is situated on the *Camargue* plain.

In a ring of lights,
And a pale sky with a sickle-moon.
Thin winds undress the branch, it is October.
250   And in Les Baux
An old life slips out, patriarch of eleven inhabitants—
'Fatigué' she said, a terse beldam by the latch,
'Il est fatigué, depuis douze ans toujours dans le même coin.'

. . . .

. . . Then I was walking in the mountains,
And drunk in Cortona, furiously,
505   With the black wine rough and sour
from a Tuscan hill;
Drunk and silent between the dwarfs and the cripples
And the military in their intricate capes
Signed with the Italian star.
510   Eleven shuddered in a fly-blown clock.
O frustrations, discrepancies,
I had you to myself then!
To count and examine,
Carve, trim, pare—and skewer you with words.
515   Words . . . like the stony rivers
Anguished and dry.
Words clouding, spoiling, getting between one and the mark,
Falsely perpetuating—'Why he was thus,
Self-painted, a very personal testimony
520   Of half-expression'—and oh the hypocrisy
Of the surrender in the written word . . .
(Yet taken from this
The discerning estimate of 'what you've been'—)
What now can be remembered that was seen
525   Long ago? (always long ago.)
The empty seas, the unpeopled landscape,
and the sullen acre
Trodden out in revolt—
Associations
530   Called in unmerited resurrection
Of what's accomplished, dead—
These, and the chasing of the immortal Question,
The hunted absolute.
In the shade of the bitter vine
535   I sit, instructed fool and phœnix-growth,
Ash-from-my-ash that made me, that I made
Myself in the folded curve of Origin—
Heredities disclaim, will not explain
All prior mischiefs in the bone, the brain—
540   Only a ponderous mirror holds
The eyes that look deep and see but the eyes again.

One for another
I have changed my prisons;

252: *beldam*: old woman
253: "He's tired, after twelve years still in the same corner."
504: *Cortona* is a town in Tuscany, in western Italy; Tuscany is known for its red Chianti wine.
535: The *phoenix* is a mythical bird that never died, but instead would immolate itself on a pyre and be reborn in the ashes.

Held fast, as the flame stands, locked in the prism—
545   And at one end I see
Beauty of other times, mirage of old beauty
Down a long road, clear of the strands and patches of associations,
Keen, resurrected, very clear—
—And at one side
550   The symbol of the vacant crossroads,
Then the veiled figure waiting at the crossroads
Leaning against the wind,
              urging, delaying . . .
(I have come for you, Peer!)
555   —And behind me
The candles of thoughtful nights,
And the green months, solitary,
Across dividing seas—
And again behind me, the cities
560   Rising on the inexpressible meaning of their streets,
Unaltering—and the eyes lifting over a wine-glass,
Holding the inexpressible,
              playing terror against acceptance—
Eyes, and siren voices lost at dawn . . .
565   Only the empty dawn
Comes, over the harbour; with the getting-back to day,
The resumed love-songs and the rhythms of illusion.
—And around me
Legend of other times on dry gold background,
570   Pitted with slow insinuations
Probings of now defunct animalculæ. . .
Worm, mighty and dead, established in the paint and the tapestries,
Having ended your statements.
Only the statement, the unalterable deed only
575   Stands, and is no more than a halt on the track—
—And at last, before me
In fierce rise and fall of impetuous seasons,
The articulate skeleton
In clothes grown one with the frame,
580   At the finger-post waiting, aureoled with lamentations.
'Hail partner, that went as I
In towns, in wastes—I, shadow,
Meet with you—I that have walked with recording eyes
Through a rich bitter world, and seen
585   The heart close with the brain, the brain crossed by the heart—
        I that have made, seeing all,
          Nothing, and nothing kept, nor understood
          Of the empty hands, the hands impotent through time that lift
            and fall
          Along a question—
590   Nor of passing and re-passing
By the twin affirmations of never and for-ever,
        In doubt, in shame, in silence.'"

1925

571: *animalculae*: microscopic animals
581: An *aureole* is the gold disc of light surrounding the head of holy figures in medieval art.

Austin Clarke (1896–1974)

CLARKE WAS BORN IN DUBLIN AND EDUCATED AT BELVEDERE COLLEGE, THE SCHOOL immortalized by James Joyce's *A Portrait of the Artist as a Young Man* (1916), and University College, Dublin. There he studied with Thomas MacDonagh, who was later executed by the British for his part in the Easter Uprising. After the success of the first of several early books based on the mythological stories of the Ulster and Fenian cycles, a series of events including the death of his father led to a nervous breakdown. In 1921, after a brief marriage and the loss of a university appointment, he moved to England, where he lived for fifteen years, supporting himself by book reviewing. He continued to publish poetry, together with plays and novels—several of which were unavailable in Ireland due to the strict censorship policies of the Irish Free State. His poems gradually shifted their attention from the ancient cycles to the medieval period of Celtic-Romanesque Ireland. In 1933, he was asked to serve as judge at the Oxford Festival of Spoken Poetry, an experience that led Clarke to found a verse-speaking society upon his eventual return to Ireland in 1937. With the death of Yeats in 1939, he became Ireland's most celebrated poet: elected to the presidency of the Irish chapter of P. E. N., broadcasting regularly on Radio Eireann, staging his drama at the Abbey Theatre. Amid this success there was also the less flattering recognition of Samuel Beckett's sneering portrait of Clarke as "Austin Ticklepenny" in *Murphy* (1938). In the 1940s, Clarke was primarily occupied with the theatre, but he would reemerge as a poet with books including *Ancient Lights* (1955), *The Horse-Eaters* (1960), and the justly celebrated *Mnemosyne Lay in Dust* (1966), a long poem describing his mental breakdown of many years earlier.

Though his work is occasionally in a comic vein, Clarke is best known, as Maurice Harmon writes, for his "poetry of guilt, sexual repression and social satire," for topical and aggressively secular poems reflecting his struggle with the fervent Catholicism of Irish society in the early years of political autonomy.[1] Like his friend F. R. Higgins, Clarke deployed the assonantal patterns characteristic of Irish verse in his English poetry. He glossed this element of his technique as follows: "Assonance is more elaborate in Gaelic than in Spanish poetry. In the simplest forms the tonic word at the end of the line is supported by an assonance in the middle of the next line. The use of internal pattern of assonance in English, though more limited in its possible range, changes the pivotal movement of the lyric stanza."[2] Thematically, "Forget Me Not" offers a memorable exposition of the humanistic values Clarke thought were threatened by a modern and materialistic culture. Here the rhythms of the horses his ances-

---

[1] Maurice Harmon, *Austin Clarke: A Critical Introduction*, Dublin, 1989, p. 38.
[2] Austin Clarke, quoted in Harmon, p. 22.

tors knew are linked to the vitality of poetry; Clarke names the rhythms of his open-
ing lines in the prosodic terms immediately following them.

Forget Me Not

Up the hill,
Hurry me not;
Down the hill,
Worry me not;
5   *On the level,*
Spare me not,
In the stable,
Forget me not.

Trochaic dimeter, amphimacer
10   And choriamb, with hyper catalexis,
Grammatical inversion, springing of double
Rhyme. So we learned to scan all, analyse
Lyric and ode, elegy, anonymous patter,
For what is song itself but substitution?
15   Let classical terms unroll, with a flourish, the scroll
Of baccalaureate.   Coleridge had picked
That phrase for us—*vergiss-mein-nicht,* emblem
Of love and friendship, delicate sentiments.
Forget-me-nots, forget-me-nots:
20   Blue, sunny-eyed young hopefuls! He left a nosegay,
A keepsake for Kate Greenaway.

                    Child climbed
Into the trap; the pony started quick
As fly to a flick and Uncle John began
Our work-a-day, holiday jingle.
                        Up the hill,
25   *Hurry me not.*
                  Down the hill,
Worry me not.
                  Verse came like that, simple
As join-hands, yet ambiguous, lesson
Implied, a flower-puzzle in final verb
And negative. All was personification

9ff: Clarke describes the versification of the children's rhyme just quoted. *Trochaic:* with falling stress pat-
terns (a trochee is a foot consisting of a stressed followed by an unstressed syllable); *dimeter:* a line with
two feet per line; *amphimacer:* a foot of three syllables, stressed-unstressed-stressed; *choriamb:* a foot of
four syllables, stressed-unstressed-unstressed-stressed; *hyper catalexis:* extra syllables after the last foot
in a line; *double rhyme:* rhyming on the last two feet of a line, as in lines 2 and 4.
17: *vergiss-mein-nicht:* "forget-me-not" (German). The forget-me-not appears in Coleridge's poem "The
Keepsake," with a footnote: "One of the names (and meriting to be the only one) of the *Myosotis Scor-
pioides Palustris.* . . . It has the same name over the whole Empire of Germany (*Vergissmeinnicht*) and,
we believe, in Denmark and Sweden."
21: *Kate Greenaway:* nineteenth-century children's author and illustrator
22: *trap:* a small one-horse carriage

30   As we drove on: invisibility
        Becoming audible. A kindness spoke,
        Assumed the god; consensus everywhere
        In County Dublin. Place-names, full of Sunday,
        Stepaside, Pass-if-you-can Lane, Hole in the Wall.
35   Such foliage in the Dargle hid Lovers Leap,
        We scarcely heard the waters fall-at-all.
        Often the open road to Celbridge: we came back
        By Lucan Looks Lovely, pulled in at the Strawberry Beds,
        Walked up the steep of Knockmaroon. Only
40   The darkness could complete our rounds. The pony
        Helped, took the bit. Coat-buttoned up, well-rugg'd
        I drowsed till the clatter of city sets, warning
        Of echoes around St. Mary's Place, woke me;
        But I was guarded by medal, scapular
45   And the *Agnus Dei* next my skin, passing
        That Protestant Church. Night shirt, warm manger, confusion
        Of premise, creed; I sank through mysteries
        To our oblivion.
                    Ora pro nobis
     Ora pro me.
                'Gee up,' 'whoa,' 'steady,' 'hike,'
50   'Hike ow'a that.' Rough street-words, cheerful, impatient:
        The hearers knew their own names as well. Horses,
        Men, going together to daily work; dairy
        Cart, baker's van, slow dray, quick grocery
        Deliveries. Street-words, the chaff in them.
55   Suddenly in Mountjoy Street, at five o'clock
        Yes, five in the evening, work rhymed for a minute with sport.
        Church-echoing wheel-rim, roof-beat, tattle of harness
        Around the corner of St. Mary's Place:
        Cabs, outside cars, the drivers unranked in race
60   For tips; their horses eager to compete,
        With spark and hubbub, greet with their own heat
        Galway Express that puffed to Broadstone Station.
        They held that Iron Horse in great esteem
        Yet dared the metamorphosis of steam.
65   Soon they were back again. I ran to watch
        As Uncle John in elegant light tweeds
        Drove smartly by on his outside car, talking

41: *rugg'd*: wrapped in a coverlet
42: *sets*: granite paving stones
44: *scapular*: a wide band of cloth with a hole for the head, worn front-to-back over the shoulders by priests (i.e., the rug worn by the child)
45: *Agnus Dei*: "Lamb of God" (hence the image of a lamb)
48–49: "Pray for us / Pray for me" (Latin): alluding to the Hail Mary, a principal prayer of the Catholic Church: "Holy Mary, Mother of God, pray for us sinners, now and at the hour of our death."
49: *hike*: stop
50: *Hike ow'a that*: "Stop out of that": i.e., "stop doing that"
53: *dray*: a brewers' low cart without sides, used to carry barrels
54: *chaff*: banter
59: *outside cars*: carriages that carry four riders, seated two on each side, back to back (as opposed to "inside cars," which face each other)

Over his shoulder to a straight-up fare
Or two, coaxing by name his favourite mare;
70   The best of jarvies, his sarcastic wit
Checked by a bridle rein; and he enlarged
My mind with two Victorian words. Grown-ups
Addressed him as Town Councillor, Cab
And Car Proprietor!

Horse-heads above me,
75   Below me. Happy on tram top, I looked down
On plaited manes, alighted safely, caught
Sidelong near kerb, perhaps, affectionate glance
As I passed a blinker. Much to offend the pure:
Let-down or drench, the sparrows pecking at fume,
80   The scavengers with shovel, broom. But, O
When horse fell down, pity was there: we saw
Such helplessness, girth buckled, no knack in knee,
Half-upturned legs—big hands that couldn't unclench.
A parable, pride or the like, rough-shod,
85   Or goodness put in irons, then, soul uplifted
Bodily; traffic no longer interrupted.
Strength broadened in narrow ways. Champions went by,
Guinness's horses from St. James's Gate:
Their brasses clinked, yoke, collar shone at us:
90   Light music while they worked. Side-streets, alleys
Beyond St. Patrick's, floats unloading, country
Colt, town hack, hay-cart, coal-bell. Often the whip-crack,
The lash of rein. Hand-stitch in the numb of pain
At school. Religious orders plied the strap
95   On us, but never on themselves. Each day, too,
Justice tore off her bandage in Mountjoy Street.
The Black Maria passed, van o' the poor.
Weeks, months clung to those bars, cursed, or stared, mute.
Children in rags ran after that absenting,
100   Did double time to fetlocks. Solemnity
For all; the mournful two or four with plumes,
Hooves blackened to please your crape. The funerals
Go faster now. Our Christianity
Still catching up with All is Vanity.

105   Nevertheless,
Nature had learned to share our worldliness,
Well-pleased to keep with man the colours in hide,
Dappling much, glossing the chestnut, sunshading the bays,

70: *jarvies*: coachmen
75: *tram top*: the top deck of an open-topped tram
78: *Blinkers* are leather screens on horses' headgear, which prevent them from looking sideways.
88: *St. James's Gate*: Guiness's Brewery, in James Street
91: *St. Patrick's*: St. Patrick's Cathedral
97: *Black Maria*: a van for conveying prisoners to jail
100: *A fetlock* is a tuft of hair on the back of a horse's leg.
104: *All is Vanity*: cf. Eccles. 1:2

To grace those carriage wheels, that *vis-à-vis*
110   In the Park. Let joy cast off a trace, for once,
High-stepping beyond the Phoenix Monument
In the long ago of British Rule, I saw
With my own eyes a white horse that unfabled
The Unicorn.

Mechanised vehicles:
115   Horse-power by handle-turn. My Uncle John
Lost stable companions, drivers, all. Though poor,
He kept his last mare out on grass. They aged
Together. At twenty-one, I thought it right
And proper.

How could I know that greed
120   Spreads quicker than political hate? No need
Of propaganda. Good company, up and down
The ages, gone: the trick of knife left, horse cut
To serve man. All the gentling, custom of mind
And instinct, close affection, done with. The unemployed
125   Must go. Dead or ghosted by froths, we ship them
Abroad. Foal, filly, farm pony, bred for slaughter:
What are they now but hundredweights of meat?
A double trade. Greed with a new gag of mercy
Grants happy release in our whited abbatoirs.
130   'Gentlemen, businessmen, kill on the spot! O
That,' exclaim the good, 'should be your motto.
Combine in a single trade all profits, save
Sensitive animals from channelling wave,
Continental docking, knackering down.
135   We dread bad weather, zig-zag, tap of Morse.'
Well-meaning fools, who only pat the horse
That looks so grand on our Irish half-crown.

I've more to say—

Men of Great Britain
Openly share with us the ploughtail, the field-spoil,

109: *vis-à-vis*: a carriage seating two people facing each other
111: *Phoenix Monument*: This monument, built in 1745 by Lord Chesterfield, is on the main road through Phoenix Park.
125ff: Clarke dealt with the export of Irish horses to the Continent for slaughter in several poems. In a note to "Knacker Rhymes" he wrote: "Traffic in these sensitive creatures had been quietly and discreetly increasing for some time, but on Dec. 17th. 1959, the loss of forty-eight horses at sea during a storm drew public attention to what had been going on. Protection Societies, both here and in Great Britain, have chosen the lesser of two evils, thereby showing short-sightedness and remarkable stupidity. Instead of advocating total abolition of this new slave trade and appealing to decent citizens, they ask for an export trade in horse meat and are even raising subscriptions to start this new industry. Cars now carry the brutal slogan: 'Stop exporting horses. Start meat factories here.' "
133: *channelling wave*: i.e., that of the English Channel
137: *half-crown*: a coin worth an eighth of a pound.

140   Trucking in Europe what we dare not broil
     At home.
                      Herodotus condemned
     Hippophagy.
                            And Pliny, also.
                                 Besieged towns
     Denied it.
                      Stare now at Pegasus. The blood
     Of the Medusa weakens in him.
                           Yet all the world
145   Was hackneyed once—those horses o' the sun,
     Apollo's car, centaurs in Thessaly.
     Too many staves have splintered the toy
     That captured Troy. The Hippocrene is stale.
     Dark ages; Latin rotted, came up from night-soil,
150   New rush of words; thought mounted them. Trappings
     Of palfrey, sword-kiss of chivalry, high song
     Of grammar. Men pick the ribs of Rosinante
     In restaurants now. Horse-shoe weighs in with saddle
     Of meat.
               Horseman, the pass-word, courage shared
155   With lace, steel, buff.
                       Wars regimented
     Haunches together. Cities move by in motor
     Cars, charging the will. I hear in the lateness of Empires,
     A neighing, man's cry in engines. No peace, yet,
     Poor draggers of artillery.
                   The moon
160   Eclipsed: I stood on the Rock of Cashel, saw dimly
     Carved on the royal arch of Cormac's Chapel
     Sign of the Sagittary, turned my back
     On all that Celtic Romanesque; thinking

141ff: The fourth-century Greek historian *Herodotus* and the natural historian *Pliny* the Elder (23–79) both condemned *hippophagy*, the eating of horses.

143: The winged horse *Pegasus*, symbol of poetic inspiration, sprang from the blood of the slain monster Medusa; the fountain Hippocrene, on Mount Helicon, was created by a blow of his hoof.

145: A *hackney* is a horse suitable for riding or driving.

146: *Apollo*, the Greek god of light, music and poetry, was sometimes identified with the sun-god Helios, who drove his chariot east to west in the sky every day. *Thessaly*, in northeastern Greece, was the legendary home of the Centaurs.

147: *toy*: the Trojan Horse, a giant wooden horse built by the Greeks, inside which was concealed the Greek army; the Trojans were deceived into taking it inside the walls of Troy, permitting the Greeks to sack the city.

149ff: Clarke has in mind the decay of classical learning in the Middle Ages and its revival in the Renaissance. "*Palfrey*" is a medieval word for a light saddle-horse; the medieval ethos of *chivalry* was parodied in the Renaissance author Cervantes' *Don Quixote* (*Rosinante* was Don Quixote's horse).

153: *saddle*: punning on the sense of "joint [of meat]"

154: Horsemanship was an essential accomplishment of the Renaissance gentleman or gentlewoman. *Buff* leather was used in military outfits.

159: Cavalry proved useless in World War I against modern *artillery*; horses were instead used for dragging the weaponry that had made them useless in battle.

160: *Rock of Cashel*: in Co. Tipperary, a ruined medieval religious site. It is the location of *Cormac's Chapel*, which contains the zodiacal relief mentioned (a *sagittary* is a centaur wielding a bow and arrow).

163: The *Celtic Romanesque* period of Medieval Ireland was from the fifth-century arrival of St. Patrick (bringing Christianity to the island) to the Anglo-Norman invasion in 1171.

Of older story and legend, how Cuchullain,
165   Half man, half god-son, tamed the elemental
Coursers: dear comrades: how at his death
The Gray of Macha laid her mane upon his breast
And wept.
                                I struggled down
From paleness of limestone.
                                Too much historied
170   Land, wrong in policies, armings, hope in prelates
At courts abroad! Rags were your retribution,
Hedge schools, a visionary knowledge in verse
That hid itself. The rain-drip cabin'd the dream
Of foreign aid . . . Democracy at last.
175   White horses running through the European mind
Of the First Consul. Our heads were cropped like his.
New brow; old imagery. A Gaelic poet,
Pitch-capped in the Rebellion of '98.
Called this Republic in an allegory
180   The Slight Red Steed.
                                Word-loss is now our gain:
Put mare to stud. Is Ireland any worse
Than countries that fly-blow the map, rattle the sky,
Drop down from it? Tipsters respect our grand sires,
Thorough-breds, jumpers o' the best.
185   Our grass still makes a noble show, and the roar
Of money cheers us at the winning post.
So pack tradition in the meat-sack, Boys,
Write off the epitaph of Yeats.

164ff: In Celtic legend the two horses the *Grey of Macha* and the Black of Saingliu rose out of a lake; they were tamed by the hero *Cuchullain* and became his chariot horses. The Grey of Macha had great love for his master, refusing to be saddled and weeping tears of blood before Cuchullain's last, fatal battle.

170–71: *hope in prelates / At courts abroad*: alluding to the longstanding hope for military assistance from Catholic countries abroad against English rule.

172: *Hedge schools*, open-air schools for children, provided education for the rural Catholic population during the eighteenth and nineteenth centuries (during the period of the Penal Laws, under which Catholics were forbidden to teach in schools). Gaelic poets often earned a living teaching in hedge schools.

   visionary knowledge in verse: i.e., the Gaelic bardic tradition; it "hid itself" because the old bardic order died out after the mid-seventeenth century; thereafter Gaelic poetry went into serious decline, dying out as a literary language in the nineteenth century until the revival of the twentieth century. "Visionary" alludes to the Gaelic form of the *aisling* (vision or dream poem). By the time of the Penal Laws the *aisling* had become a heavily politicized form, in which the poet meets a female embodiment of Ireland, who prophesies its release from bondage by the intervention of a Catholic power from overseas.

173–74: The Irish revolutionary leader Wolfe Tone attempted to lead a French invasion of Ireland in 1796, but the ships were dispersed by a storm after they reached the coast of west Cork and Kerry.

175: *White horses*: crested waves

176: *First Consul*: Napoleon; he was known as "the little crop-head," after his favored hairstyle. The Irish rebels of the 1798 rebellion were known as "croppies" because they cut their hair short to show their sympathy with the French Revolution.

178: *Pitch-capped*: The rebels of 1798 were tortured by putting a cap lined with pitch on their head and setting fire to it. The *Gaelic poet* remains unidentified.

188: see the last lines of Yeats's "Under Ben Bulben": "Cast a cold eye / On life, on death. / Horseman, pass by!"

I'll turn

To jogtrot, pony bell, say my first lesson:

190
      Up the hill,
      Hurry me not;
      Down the hill,
      Worry me not;
      On the level,
195   *Spare me not,*
      In the stable,
      Forget me not.

      Forget me not.

1963

F. R. HIGGINS (1896–1941)

FREDERICK ROBERT HIGGINS WAS BORN IN FOXFORD, COUNTY MAYO, INTO A UNIONist Protestant family, his father an engineer. He grew up in County Meath. At 14, he began clerking for a building firm but was eventually fired for attempting to organize a branch of the Clerical Worker's Union, which then employed him. He edited trade-union journals and Ireland's first magazine for women, which produced only two issues, *Welfare* and *Farewell*. In 1915, Higgins met Austin Clarke, who shared his interests in folklore and Gaelic literature; in the 1930s, Higgins was a close associate of W. B. Yeats.

In his notes to *The Dark Breed* (1927), Higgins wrote that "The racial strength of a Gaelic aristocratic mind—with its vigorous colouring and hard emotion—is easily recognised in Irish poetry, by those acquainted with the literature of our own people." He went on to observe that "The younger poets generally express themselves through idioms taken from Gaelic speech; they impose on English verse the rhythm of a gapped music, and through their music we still hear echoes of secret harmonies and the sweet twists still turning today through many a quaint Connacht song . . . the memories of an ancient and rigorous technique."[1] In this effort to imitate some of the formal properties of Irish poetry in English-language poetry, Higgins resembles his friend Austin Clarke. Gregory Shirmer argues that Higgins "probably owed more than a little to J. M. Synge's influence" in taking the west of Ireland "as the center of authentic Irish culture," which also represented "a personal rebellion for him," given his father's Unionist sympathies.[2] Praised by Hugh MacDiarmid and—with less fervor—Samuel Beckett in his day, Higgins's poetry is not often read of late but remains of interest for its place in an Irish folk-poetic tradition, which includes the works of figures such as Padraic Colum and Joseph Campbell. His other books include *Island Blood* (1925), *Arable Holdings* (1933), and *The Gap of Brightness* (1940).

---

[1] *The Dark Breed*, London, 1927, p. 66.
[2] *Out of What Began: A History of Irish Poetry in English*, Ithaca and London, 1998, p. 297.

A Plea

Come, poets, hear the flails; bright grain is leaping
In your stone homes where old men slept in flowers;
Although the harps are still and wine is out,
I have a lip of wine to heal all drought
5   Beneath the glitter of this laughing goblet,
That Patric netted from the salmon's mouth.

For I'm more youthful than the youth of Fintan,
More beautiful than any grace in Deirdre,
And even Aoife never rivalled me
10   With tides of riches, gathered after she
Became the crane, that hid within her crane skin
The winking jewels of a morning sea.

Then rise and taste this red wine; strings are chirping!
And from my wild lip take each tidal treasure—
15   That tides, too full below the crane's grey skin,
Have washed with music through the harp of Finn,
Whose tunes, too seldom heard where bells are noisy,
Are hidden in me till the strings begin!

Look up! the hounds are out and swift black horses
20   Have stript new glens and hoofed the mountain grasses,
Chasing slow daylight over Muckish Mor;
Until quick stars seem javelins to the boar
And distant lakes are stepping-stones of moonlight
Across the darkness to the first grey shore.

25   These are no goblet dreams, sung by three voices—
That laughing string, these strings of tears and slumber;
Then, poets, sing, before my wine is gone;
O poets, you in whom my beauty shone,

"Some allusions in this retrospective poem are derived from Ossianic sources and from incidents in the Fenian saga. One of these incidents concerns the loss of Caoilte's goblet: according to an old bard, that brilliant jewel fell from the hero's fingers into a pool of great depth, and its recovery was only possible with the coming of Christianity, when eventually it was recovered by Saint Patrick through the aid of a salmon. Further use is made of an old poem regarding the magical transformation of Aoife into the form of a crane, condemned to spend a bitter life upon sea water; after its death, Mananaun of the Sea took the skin of that crane for a treasure bag, and with him its glittering contents were increased by each heaping of the tide." (Higgins's note). The Ossianic ballads are a collection of Gaelic poems composed between the eleventh and eighteenth centuries; they are resolutely pagan and anticlerical, elegizing the pre-Christian past and painting a hostile portrait of St. Patrick as a bigoted cleric.

7: "Fintan was a very remote figure in Irish mythology, who, having passed through many incarnations, is recorded to have made his appearance again in Ireland centuries after the Christian era, when he was accepted as an authority on matters of prehistoric accuracy." (Higgins)

8: *Deirdre:* heroine of *The Fate of the Sons of Usnech* in the Ulster Cycle of Irish legends

16: "The harp of Finn held three strings capable of producing on all hearers sorrow, smiles, or slumber at its player's will." (Higgins)

20: *stript:* sped over

22: Boars and boar hunting were celebrated in Celtic myth. Boars have been extinct in Ireland since the twelfth century.

Come flush me with new praise, for I am Ireland,
30   Grown old and ashen with a touch of dawn!

1927

Auction!

To Lynn Doyle

Listen, you graziers, men of stealth,
Gentlemen jobbers, heavy in dung;
I've under this hammer: miles of green wealth,
An eel-run slipped from the river's tongue,
5   A house of ghosts and that among
Gardens where even the Spring is old;
So gather around, the sale is on
And nods and winks spell out in gold
Going, going, gone.

10   Who bids for that stone wall and gate?
Come, gentlemen, their worth is known
To you who stared against their weight
And stared so long that O you've grown,
With eyes of hunger, hard as stone;
15   Now they'll no more hang out the sun
Nor gaol the best of grass that's grown;
These walls are yours, their day is done,
Going, going, gone.

And there's the timber you have cashed,
20   Weighed and measured in a squint:
Fatherly trees that from a past
Of windy traffic made a mint
Of golden rings for their heart's content—
They'll make the teeth of sawmills water;
25   So better your bids; and here's hint,
The Boyne will be your gentle carter,
Going, going, gone.

Well, boys alive, and who'd desire
Keener bidding, neater fight;
30   Even the skin-flint kindles fire,
Even the tight-lipped purses bite
At fields, that seemed one green delight
To slyly dream upon in pubs—
When the last drinks were out of sight;
35   So easy on, men, spare my lugs,
Going, going, gone.

Now, I'll knock down to this fine throng
The spacious park—once great and grand—

2: *jobbers:* traders
26: *Boyne:* a river in Co. Meath
28: *boys alive:* an interjection
35: *lugs:* ears
37: *knock down:* sell

That Higgins mortgaged for a song;
40   For even had old Euclid planned
Its blue prints with his gilded hand,
See there before you: grace gone wild
And beauty run to earth, a land
Of gentleness that's all shop-soiled,
45   *Going, going, gone.*

But that's the best soil cropped for coin;
Good money there like mushrooms creep
Out of pastures where the Boyne
Drains the heavy fields of sleep;
50   Why, even look, the frail winds heap
Fierce silver on the sally hedge
And sods are fortunes going cheap—
Enough to put your teeth on edge:
Going, going, gone.

55   So the last field falls to a nod,
Falls from a red indentured deed
To you whose hearts throb on the sod,
Beef-belted, pea-eyed men of Meath;
You've got the lot by nothing said,
60   Indeed, you speak that common tongue
Of silence spoken by the dead—
For in close darkness all is one,
Going, going, gone.

Jobbers in land! And so you pass
65   The graces by and only yawn;
Ah, what to you this genteel grass,
This willowed, bronzed, umbrellaed lawn
As calm as when Palm Sunday shone
Through aisles of elm where Stella drove
70   With Doctor Swift to Evensong,
While crows in each black chapter strove;
Going, going, gone.

These things are now not worth a curse—
Faint patterns from a willow plate;
75   Look at the house! What could be worse
Than that old peacock roost of late?

40: *Euclid:* the ancient Greek geometrician
51: *sally:* or sallow: a low-growing willow
65: *the graces:* i.e., a statue of the Graces, Greek goddesses of fertility
68: *Palm Sunday:* the Sunday before Easter
70: Jonathan *Swift* (1667–1745), noted satirist and Dean of St. Patrick's in Dublin, maintained an endur-
    ing but apparently Platonic friendship with Esther Johnson (whom he called "Stella") until her death in
    1728.
    Evensong: the Evening Prayer service of the Anglican Chuch
71: *chapter:* "The body of canons of a collegiate or cathedral church, presided over by the dean" (*OED*)
74: *willow plate:* a plate decorated with the popular imitation-Chinese "willow pattern," a stylized land-
    scape including a bridge (see lines 96–97).

Its rooky stair sways at your weight
To rooms of yellow, blue and pink
Where feather-brainlings titivate
80   And then cold shoulder those they think
Going, going, gone.

Well, God be with the days of power—
Those ending with the crinoline,
When strength shone like an oak in flower
85   From minds that tied their time between
Old books, old wine and ladies seen
All musical in candlelight;
What then seemed bright by now seems mean
With things of wisdom, grace and might
90   *Going, going, gone.*

So the old home goes to the wall,
As goes its garden—so select—
With Time's green fingers slipping all;
The plum-trees keep the walls erect,
95   While ivies hold the stones intact;
And what seemed cribbed from Chinese schools,
That bridge-design! it, too, is wrecked
On a mosaic of midnight pools
Going, going, gone.

100 Then take for nothing that moss-house,
Once hedge-school to a gentle breed;
You'll see it, if the light allows,
Beyond the bee-hives hid beneath
Nettle-stock and chicken-weed;
105 So fare you well, well may you keep
These lands—my people's, yes, indeed—
For I've their dreams, in me they sleep,
Going, going, gone.

1940

77: *rooky:* creaky, unsteady
79: *titivate:* doll themselves up
100: *moss-house:* a garden shelter covered in moss
101: *Hedge schools,* open-air schools for children, provided education for the rural Catholic population
   during the eighteenth and nineteenth centuries (when Catholics were forbidden to teach in schools).

BASIL BUNTING (1900–1985)

Bunting was born in Scotswood-on-Tyne, the son of a doctor who became general practitioner to the miners of Montague Pit, and a mother who was the daughter of a local mine manager. He was educated at Quaker schools in West Riding of Yorkshire and Leighton Park in Berkshire. During World War I, he was a conscientious objector and served 18 months at Wormwood Scrubs and other prisons. After the war, he attended the London School of Economics until, bored with economics, he quit to look for work, eventually becoming secretary to Harry Barnes, MP. Taking temporary work as an artists' model, barman, and ditch digger in Paris in the early 1920s, he met Ezra Pound. In Paris he also had a stint as sub-editor for Ford Madox Ford's *Transatlantic Review*. After a brief period on the Tuscany coast working on sand boats, Bunting returned to London, where he took up writing music reviews for the *Outlook*. He then lived in Germany and, after marrying Marian Gray Culver, an American he met in Venice, he lived briefly in the United States, where in New York he met Louis Zukofsky and William Carlos Williams. In the early 1930s, Bunting lived with his family in Rapallo, Italy, where Pound and Yeats were living, the latter for half of each year. Both older poets were admirers of Bunting's poems.

After *Redimiculum Matellarum* (Necklace of Chamber Pots) was privately published in Milan in 1930, Bunting had some of its poems published in *Poetry* (Chicago), one poem appearing in the 1931 "Objectivist" issue edited by Zukofsky. He contributed to *Poetry*'s less well-known "English Number" a year later. In 1933, a group of his poems appeared in Ezra Pound's *Active Anthology*, published by Faber and Faber; the anthology was attacked by F. R. Leavis and other critics, but largely ignored. Reviews and a translation of part of Firdosi's *Shanameh* would appear in T. S. Eliot's *The Criterion* during the same decade, but Pound's anthology was the only substantial collection of Bunting's poems to appear in England until the 1960s. (An American edition of his earlier poems appeared in 1950.) In the late 1930s, Bunting and family lived in the Canary Islands; these were years when work was difficult to find, and shortly after leaving the Canaries for England his marriage ended, his wife moving back to the United States with the children. When World War II broke out Bunting was in Los Angeles, hoping for work as a movie extra, but he came back to England to enlist. He began service based in Scotland, escorting North Sea convoys to Murmansk. Later, partly because of his knowledge of classical Persian, he was sent to Persia, where he was put in charge of a unit of Bakhtiari and Luri tribesmen and eventually took a commission as Squadron Leader. Bunting's activities in the war are the stuff of legend or the movies: he traveled from Baghdad to Tripoli and the battle of Wadi Akarat, helped organize Eisenhower's warroom for the Sicilian campaign, and did much else: some of this experience helps shape his World War II poem, *The Spoils* (1951). After the war, he was Vice Consul at Isfahan and then head of political intelligence for Persia, Iraq, and Saudi Arabia. His knowledge of the region's nomadic tribes apparently proved useful as the Soviets, British, and Americans sought to influence developments in the region, but the full extent of Bunting's activities during this period are still unknown. After marrying the Armenian Silla Alladallien, Bunting resigned from his Foreign Office post in Iran and worked as a correspondent for *The Times* until, in 1952, Mossadeq expelled him from the country, suspecting that he was a British agent. Finding employment hard to come by in England, Bunting supported his second family with tiresome jobs such as proofreading train schedules and stock exchange reports for the *Newcastle Evening Chronicle*. He wrote little or nothing for a decade until, in 1963, the young Newcastle poet Tom Pickard sought him out. Encouraged by interest among younger British and American poets and the emerging culture of poetry readings and small-press modernist poetry, Bunting began writing poems again. After Pickard and Gael Turnbull published *The Spoils* in 1965, Fulcrum in the same year brought out *Loquitur, First Book of Odes*, and the poem for which Bunting remains best known, *Briggflatts*. With the publication of *Briggflatts*, his reputation grew quickly, and in the late 1960s and early 1970s, he held several visiting appointments at Canadian and American universities. In 1972, he was president of the Poetry Society and in 1974, president of Northern Arts. A *Collected Poems* appeared in 1968, his edition of Ford Madox Ford's *Selected Poems* in 1971, and in 1976 an edition of the poems of the late-nineteenth-century northern miner-poet Joseph Skipsey.

For some readers, Bunting is the foremost English modernist poet of the century, a poet who began with aesthetic values similar to those defended by Pound and Eliot and who went on to write his own distinctive modernist poetry. Others would stress his place in a northern tradition, including the Gawain poet and Wordsworth. Bunting translated classical Persian and Roman poetry and, extending Pound's example in *Homage to Sextus Properties*, adapted and versified Kamo-no-Chomei's twelfth-century Japanese prose in his "Chomei at Toyama." His lyrics or "odes" rarely repeat their forms, and they include several efforts to write in English versions of quantitative measures. Add to this Bunting's emphasis on "condensare" or condensation in writing and his collage of passages from Villon and Dante in several early longer poems, and one has the beginnings of a modernism that emphasizes craftsmanship and the music of poetry above all else. Much of what Bunting valued in writing he came later in life to see as being properties of classical Persian and Northumbrian art: "It's not easy, first to simplify detail til only the barest essentials of the detail are left; second to weave an enormous amount of such details into an intricate pattern which yet keeps perfect balance and proportion."[1]

Bunting referred to his long poems as "sonatas," suggesting that in their "musical form" they have affinities with the sonatas of Domenico Scarlatti. The five sections plus coda of *Briggflatts* employ such a "musical" organization, modulating between different prosodies. Bunting called the poem "an autobiography," but it is also a meditation on time and ambition and a celebration of Northumbrian craft and tradition. Insisting in characteristic fashion that "*Briggflatts* is a poem: it needs no explanation" and that "The sound of the words spoken aloud is itself the meaning," Bunting described this poem thick in Northumbrian rhythms, idiom, and references as follows: "Commonplaces provide the poem's structure: spring, summer, autumn, winter of the year and of man's life, interrupted in the middle and balanced around Alexander [the Great]'s trip to the limits of the world and its futility, and sealed and signed at the end by a confession of our ignorance. Love and betrayal are spring's adventures, the wisdom of elders and the remoteness of death, hardly more than a gravestone. In summer there is no rest from ambition and lust of experience, never final. Those fail who try to force their destiny, like Eric [Bloodaxe]; but those who are resolute to submit, like my version of Pasiphae, may bring something new to birth, be it only a monster." Elsewhere in the same note

---

[1] "The Art of Poetry" (1970), quoted in *Basil Bunting: Man and Poet*, ed. Carroll F. Terrell, Orono, 1980, p. 234.

Bunting is at pains to distinguish his views from those of his early mentors and friends Pound, Eliot, and Yeats. He poses a combination of stoic resignation and anarchistic individualism against the "hierarchy and order" valued in different ways by the older modernists. In philosophy, Bunting adds, "I have most sympathy with Lucretius and his masters, content to explain the world one atom at a time; with Spinoza who saw all things as God, though not with his wish to demonstrate that logically; and with David Hume, the doubter."[2] *Briggflatts'* title refers to a Quaker meeting house in the north of England, and in late interviews Bunting often acknowledged his interest in the "silence" of the Quaker meeting, adding that "I have no use for religion conceived as church forms or as believing as historical fact what are ancient parables, but I do believe that there is a possibility of a kind of reverence for the whole creation which I feel we ought to have in our bones if we don't, a kind of pantheism I suppose."[3]

---

[2] *A Note on Briggflatts*, Durham, 1989.
[3] Quoted in *Basil Bunting: Man and Poet*, p. 271.

from First Book of Odes

3.

To Peggy Mullett

I am agog for foam. Tumultuous come
with teeming sweetness to the bitter shore
tidelong unrinsed and midday parched and numb
with expectation. If the bright sky bore
5   with endless utterance of a single blue
unphrased, its restless immobility
infects the soul, which must decline into
an anguished and exact sterility
and waste away: then how much more the sea
10   trembling with alteration must perfect
our loneliness by its hostility.
The dear companionship of its elect
deepens our envy. Its indifference
haunts us to suicide. Strong memories
15   of sprayblown days exasperate impatience
to brief rebellion and emphasise
the casual impotence we sicken of.
But when mad waves spring, braceletted with foam,
towards us in the angriness of love
20   crying a strange name, tossing as they come
repeated invitations in the gay
exuberance of unexplained desire,
we can forget the sad splendour and play
at wilfulness until the gods require
25   renewed inevitable hopeless calm
and the foam dies and we again subside
into our catalepsy, dreaming foam,
while the dry shore awaits another tide.

1926 / 1930

27: *catalepsy:* a state of trance or seizure

8.

Each fettered ghost slips to his several grave.

Loud intolerant bells (the shrinking nightflower closes
tenderly round its stars to baulk their hectoring)
orate to deaf hills where the olive stirs and dozes
in easeless age, dim to farce of man's fashioning.

5   Shepherds away! They toll throngs to your solitude
and their inquisitive harangue will disembody
shames and delights, all private features of your mood,
flay out your latencies, sieve your hopes, fray your shoddy.

The distant gods enorbed in bright indifference
10 whom we confess creatures or abstracts of our spirit,
unadored, absorbed into the incoherence,
leave desiccated names: rabbits sucked by a ferret.

                                              1928 / 1930

15.

Nothing
substance utters or time
stills and restrains
joins design and

5   supple measure deftly
as thought's intricate polyphonic
score dovetails with the tread
sensuous things
keep in our consciousness.

10 Celebrate man's craft
and the word spoken in shapeless night, the
sharp tool paring away
waste and the forms
cut out of mystery!

15 When taut string's note
passes ears' reach or red rays or violet
fade, strong over unseen
forces the word
ranks and enumerates . . .

Epigraph: Milton, "On the Morning of Christ's Nativity," line 234: in Milton's poem the coming of Christ
  dispels the false gods of other religions just as the coming of dawn dispels ghosts.
8: *shoddy*: a type of cloth made from yarn obtained from torn-up wool rags; clothing made from this cloth

17: *fade*: i.e., pass the limits of the humanly visible spectrum, either toward infrared or ultraviolet

20   mimes clouds condensed
    and hewn hills and bristling forests,
    steadfast corn in its season
    and the seasons
    in their due array,

25   life of man's own body
    and death . . .
         The sound thins into melody,
    discourse narrowing, craft
    failing, design
30   petering out.

    Ears heavy to breeze of speech and
    thud of the ictus.

                  1930 / 1931

17.

To Mina Loy

Now that sea's over that island
so that barely on a calm day sun sleeks
a patchwork hatching of combed weed
over stubble and fallow alike
5 I resent drowned blackthorn hedge, choked ditch,
gates breaking from rusty hinges,
the submerged copse,
Trespassers will be prosecuted.

Sea's over that island,
10 weed over furrow and dungheap:
but how I should recognise the place
under the weeds and sand
who was never in it on land I dont know:
some trick of refraction,
15 a film of light in the water crumpled and spread
like a luminous frock on a woman walking
alone in her garden.

Oval face, thin eyebrows wide of the eyes,
a premonition in the gait
20 of this subaqueous persistence
of a particular year—
for you had prepared it for preservation
not vindictively, urged
by the economy of passions.

32: *ictus:* metrical stress (in a foot of verse); literally, a blow

Dedication: *Mina Loy:* see p. 80.
3: *hatching:* a fine pattern of lines (as in, e.g., cross-hatching)

25   Nobody said: She is organising
        these knicknacks her dislike collects
        into a pattern nature will adopt and perpetuate.

        Weed over meadowgrass, sea over weed,
        no step on the gravel.
30   Very likely I shall never meet her again
        or if I do, fear the latch as before.

                                        1930 / 1950

28.

        You leave
        nobody else
        without a bed

        you make
5   everybody else
        thoroughly at home

        I'm
        the only one
        hanged
10   in your
        halter

        you've driven
        nobody else mad
        but me.

                                        1935 / 1941

30. The Orotava Road

        Four white heifers with sprawling hooves
                    trundle the waggon.
                Its ill-roped crates heavy with fruit sway.
        The chisel point of the goad, blue and white,
5   glitters ahead,
                a flame to follow lance-high in a man's hand
        who does not shave. His linen trousers
                    like him want washing.
                You can see his baked skin through his shirt.
10   He has no shoes and his hat has a hole in it.
                        'Hu! vaca! Hu! vaca!'
                he says staccato without raising his voice;

Title: *Orotava*: a town on Tenerife, one of the Canary Islands. The islands, which belong to Spain, lie in
  the Atlantic off the coast of Africa.

'Adios caballero' legato but
in the same tone.
15   Camelmen high on muzzled mounts
boots rattling against the panels
of an empty
packsaddle do not answer strangers.
Each with his train of seven or eight tied
20   head to tail they
pass silent but for the heavy bells
and plip of slobber dripping from
muzzle to dust;
save that on sand their soles squeak slightly.
25 Milkmaids, friendly girls between
fourteen and twenty
or younger, bolt upright on small
trotting donkeys that bray (they arch their
tails a few inches
30   from the root, stretch neck and jaw forward
to make the windpipe a trumpet)
chatter. Jolted
cans clatter. The girls' smiles repeat
the black silk curve of the wimple
35   under the chin.
Their hats are absurd doll's hats
or flat-crowned to take a load.
All have fine eyes.
You can guess their balanced nakedness
40 under the cotton gown and thin shift.
They sing and laugh.
They say 'Adios!' shyly but look back
more than once, knowing our thoughts
and sharing our
45 desires and lack of faith in desire.

1935 / 1950

11: *Hu! vaca!:* "Hey! cow!" (Spanish)
12: *staccato:* sharply (as opposed, in music, to *legato:* smoothly)
13: *Adios caballero:* "Goodbye, sir"

from Briggflatts

An Autobiography

For Peggy

Son los pasariellos del mal pelo exidos

The spuggies are fledged

I.

    Brag, sweet tenor bull,
    descant on Rawthey's madrigal,
    each pebble its part
    for the fells' late spring.
5   Dance tiptoe, bull,
    black against may.
    Ridiculous and lovely
    chase hurdling shadows
    morning into noon.
10   May on the bull's hide
    and through the dale
    furrows fill with may,
    paving the slowworm's way.

    A mason times his mallet
15   to a lark's twitter,
    listening while the marble rests,
    lays his rule
    at a letter's edge,
    fingertips checking,
20   till the stone spells a name
    naming none,
    a man abolished.
    Painful lark, labouring to rise!
    The solemn mallet says:
25   In the grave's slot
    he lies. We rot.

"The Northumbrian tongue travel has not taken from me sometimes sounds strange to men used to the koine or to Americans who may not know how much Northumberland differs from the Saxon south of England. Southrons would maul the music of many lines in Briggflatts.

"*An autobiography,* but not a record of fact. . . . The truth of the poem is of another kind." (Bunting)

Title: The title is the "name of a small hamlet in the Pennine mountains in a very beautiful situation in what [Americans] call a valley but which [Northerners] call a dale" (Bunting, quoted in Victoria Forde, *The Poetry of Basil Bunting,* Newcastle upon Tyne, 1991, p. 213). As a teenager Bunting was educated at a Quaker school in Ackworth in West Yorkshire; he stayed at Brigflatts (as it is usually spelled) during the school holidays upon the invitation of a school friend.

Epigraph: The second sentence is Bunting's translation of the first (from the *Libro de Alexandre,* a medieval Spanish poem recounting the life of Alexander the Great).

 spuggies: "little sparrows" (Bunting)

2: The River *Rawthey* runs past Brigflatts.

4: *fells:* stretches of moorland hills

6: *may:* "the flower, as haw is the fruit, of the thorn." (Bunting)

13: *slowworm:* a legless lizard

Decay thrusts the blade,
wheat stands in excrement
trembling. Rawthey trembles.
30   Tongue stumbles, ears err
for fear of spring.
Rub the stone with sand,
wet sandstone rending
roughness away. Fingers
35   ache on the rubbing stone.
The mason says: Rocks
happen by chance.
No one here bolts the door,
love is so sore.

40   Stone smooth as skin,
cold as the dead they load
on a low lorry by night.
The moon sits on the fell
but it will rain.
45   Under sacks on the stone
two children lie,
hear the horse stale,
the mason whistle,
harness mutter to shaft,
50   felloe to axle squeak,
rut thud the rim,
crushed grit.

Stocking to stocking, jersey to jersey,
head to a hard arm,
55   they kiss under the rain,
bruised by their marble bed.
In Garsdale, dawn;
at Hawes, tea from the can.
Rain stops, sacks
60   steam in the sun, they sit up.
Copper-wire moustache,
sea-reflecting eyes
and Baltic plainsong speech
declare: By such rocks
65   men killed Bloodaxe.

42: *lorry:* a flat, low-sided wagon
47: *stale:* urinate
50: *felloe:* the outer circumference of a wheel
57: *Garsdale* is a dale above Brigflatts.
58: *Hawes* is a town in Wensleydale.
    can: a metal container with handle and cover
63ff: "Northumbrians should know Eric *Bloodaxe* but seldom do, because all the school histories are writ-
ten by or for southrons. Piece his story together from the Anglo-Saxon Chronicle, the Orkneyinga Saga,
and Heimskringla, as you fancy." (Bunting). The tenth-century Viking king Eric *Bloodaxe* lost the throne
of Norway bequeathed him by his father King Harald; he sailed with his followers westwards (over the
Baltic Sea) to the British Isles. There he became ruler of the Orkney Islands (off Scotland) and York,
which he gained and lost twice. After his second expulsion from York he was betrayed and murdered at
Stainmore.
63: *plainsong:* a rhythmically free liturgical chant sung in unison

Fierce blood throbs in his tongue,
lean words.
Skulls cropped for steel caps
huddle round Stainmore.
70   Their becks ring on limestone,
whisper to peat.
The clogged cart pushes the horse downhill.
In such soft air
they trudge and sing,
75   laying the tune frankly on the air.
All sounds fall still,
fellside bleat,
hide-and-seek peewit.

Her pulse their pace,
80   palm countering palm,
till a trench is filled,
stone white as cheese
jeers at the dale.
Knotty wood, hard to rive,
85   smoulders to ash;
smell of October apples.
The road again,
at a trot.
Wetter, warmed, they watch
90   the mason meditate
on name and date.

Rain rinses the road,
the bull streams and laments.
Sour rye porridge from the hob
95   with cream and black tea,
meat, crust and crumb.
Her parents in bed
the children dry their clothes.
He has untied the tape
100   of her striped flannel drawers
before the range. Naked
on the pricked rag mat
his fingers comb
thatch of his manhood's home.

105   Gentle generous voices weave
over bare night
words to confirm and delight
till bird dawn.

69: *Stainmore:* a stretch of high pennines near Brigflatts
70: *becks:* streams. "We have burns in the east, *becks* in the west, but no brooks or creeks." (Bunting)
78: *peewit:* lapwing
82: "local Wensleydale cheese (made in Hawes) . . . is as white as the limestone of the Wensleydale fells"
  (Ric Caddel, in correspondence)
94: *hob:* a projection at the back or side of a fireplace on which the kettle may be kept warm

Rainwater from the butt
110   she fetches and flannel
to wash him inch by inch,
kissing the pebbles.
Shining slowworm part of the marvel.
The mason stirs:
115   Words!
Pens are too light.
Take a chisel to write.

Every birth a crime,
every sentence life.
120   Wiped of mould and mites
would the ball run true?
No hope of going back.
Hounds falter and stray,
shame deflects the pen.
125   Love murdered neither bleeds nor stifles
but jogs the draftsman's elbow.
What can he, changed, tell
her, changed, perhaps dead?
Delight dwindles. Blame
130   stays the same.

Brief words are hard to find,
shapes to carve and discard:
Bloodaxe, king of York,
king of Dublin, king of Orkney.
135   Take no notice of tears;
letter the stone to stand
over love laid aside lest
insufferable happiness impede
flight to Stainmore,
140   to trace
lark, mallet,
becks, flocks
and axe knocks.

Dung will not soil the slowworm's
145   mosaic. Breathless lark
drops to nest in sodden trash;
Rawthey truculent, dingy.
Drudge at the mallet, the may is down,
fog on fells. Guilty of spring
150   and spring's ending
amputated years ache after
the bull is beef, love a convenience.
It is easier to die than to remember.
Name and date
155   split in soft slate
a few months obliterate.

112: *pebbles:* i.e., testicles

CODA

A strong song tows
us, long earsick.
Blind, we follow
rain slant, spray flick
5   to fields we do not know.

Night, float us.
Offshore wind, shout,
ask the sea
what's lost, what's left,
10   what horn sunk,
what crown adrift.

Where we are who knows
of kings who sup
while day fails? Who,
15   swinging his axe
to fell kings, guesses
where we go?

1965

from Second Book of Odes

II.

At Briggflatts meetinghouse

Boasts time mocks cumber Rome. Wren
set up his own monument.
Others watch fells dwindle, think
the sun's fires sink.

5   Stones indeed sift to sand, oak
blends with saints' bones.
Yet for a little longer here
stone and oak shelter

silence while we ask nothing
10   but silence. Look how clouds dance
under the wind's wing, and leaves
delight in transience.

1975 / 1977

Ode *11:* Sir Christopher *Wren* (1632–1723) designed St Paul's Cathedral in London. He is buried there
under a simple marble slab; on the wall is inscribed: "Lector, si monumentum requiris, circumspice"
(Reader, if it is a monument you seek, look around you).
3: *fells:* moorland hills

12.

Perche no spero

Now we've no hope of going back,
cutter, to that grey quay
where we moored twice and twice unwillingly
cast off our cables to put out at the slack
5   when the sea's laugh was choked to a mutter
and the leach lifted hesitantly with a stutter
and sulky clack,

how desolate the swatchways look,
cutter, and the chart's stained,
10   stiff, old, wrinkled and uncertain,
seeming to contradict the pilot book.
On naked banks a few birds strut
to watch the ebb sluice through a narrowing gut
loud as a brook.

15   Soon, while that northwest squall wrings out its cloud,
cutter, we'll heave to
free of the sands and let the half moon do
as it pleases, hanging there in the port shrouds
like a riding light. We have no course to set,
20   only to drift too long, watch too glumly, and wait,
wait.

1980 / 1985

Epigraph: *Perche no spero*: an abbreviated quotation of "Because I do not hope to return," the first line of
  "Ballata, written in exile at Saranza" by Guido Cavalcanti (c.1255–1300); Bunting's poem is a kind of
  translation of the Cavalcanti.
2: *cutter*: a small one-masted ship
6: *leach*: or leech: "Either vertical edge of a square sail; the aft edge of a fore-and-aft sail" (*OED*)
8: *swatchways*: narrow channels between shoals or across sandbanks
19: *riding light*: a light displayed by a ship when it is riding at anchor

STEVIE SMITH (1902–1971)

FLORENCE MARGARET ("STEVIE") SMITH WAS BORN IN HULL, YORKSHIRE. HER FATHER joined the North Sea Patrol when she was three and Smith rarely saw him. A year later, her mother moved the family to Palmers Green, a London suburb. The home in Palmers Green, described as "a house of female habitation" in one autobiographical poem, was to be Smith's for the rest of her life.[1] After her mother's early death, Smith was cared for by her aunt Margaret Annie Spear, the "Lion of Hull" in Smith's novels. She was educated at Palmers Green High School and London Collegiate School for Girls and then took a secretarial position with the magazine publishers George Newnes, where she worked in various capacities for thirty years. Her first book, *Novel on Yellow Paper,* appeared in 1936 and was widely praised. She continued to publish novels and poetry but without much critical attention until the 1960s, when Smith's poetry was acclaimed by Philip Larkin, Sylvia Plath, Muriel Rukeyser, and the American poet-publisher James Laughlin, whose New Directions Press published the American edition of Smith's *Selected Poems* (1964). In the same decade, Smith also became known as a performer of her poems, reading once in 1966 to an audience of 8,000 at the Royal Albert Hall. In 1969, she was awarded the Queen's Gold Medal for Poetry. Her life has been the subject of a stage play and film featuring Glenda Jackson.

The first-time reader of Smith will notice her use of the rhythms of popular verse and nursery rhymes, and of figures and devices from fairy tales. These borrowings serve to suggest tonal and emotional registers that the poems allude to ironically or deflect into melancholy lyricism. Certainly the apparent simplicity of form can be belied by the complex relationship of multiple voices in a poem such as "Not Waving but Drowning." Philip Larkin wrote that "For all the freaks and sports of her fancy, for all her short pieces that are like rejected *Pansies* and her long pieces that are like William Blake rewritten by Ogden Nash, Miss Smith's poems speak with the authority of sadness."[2] A number of Smith's poems explore the Anglican faith in which she was raised; others identify and satirize middle-class expectations for women. Smith's poems were often accompanied by her own sketches, which serve not so much to illustrate the poems as to comment on them. As Romana Huk writes, the figure drawn for "Not Waving but Drowning" is not the "he" of the poem but a woman "waist-deep or emergent" and "outlined by fragments of the text's 'male' carapace at her shoulder and head."[3]

---

[1] "A House of Mercy," *Collected Poems,* New York, 1983, p. 410.
[2] "Frivolous and Vulnerable," *Required Writing: Miscellaneous Pieces 1955–1982,* London, 1983, p. 158.
[3] "Eccentric Concentrism: Traditional Poetic Forms and Refracted Discourse in Stevie Smith's Poetry," *Contemporary Literature,* vol. 34, no. 2, 1993, p. 249.

Souvenir de Monsieur Poop

I am the self-appointed guardian of English literature,
I believe tremendously in the significance of age;
I believe that a writer is wise at 50,
Ten years wiser at 60, at 70 a sage.
5   I believe that juniors are lively, to be encouraged with discretion and
        snubbed,
I believe also that they are bouncing, communistic, ill mannered and, of
        course, young.
But I never define what I mean by youth
Because the word undefined is more useful for general purposes of abuse.
I believe that literature is a school where only those who apply themselves
        diligently to their tasks acquire merit.
10   And only they after the passage of a good many years (see above).
But then I am an old fogey.
I always write more in sorrow than in anger.
I am, after all, devoted to Shakespeare, Milton,
And, coming to our own times,
15   Of course
Housman.
I have never been known to say a word against the established classics,
I am in fact devoted to the established classics.
In the service of literature I believe absolutely in the principle of division;
20   I divide into age groups and also into schools.
This is in keeping with my scholastic mind, and enables me to trounce
Not only youth
(Which might be thought intellectually frivolous by pedants) but also peri-
        odical tendencies,
To ventilate, in a word, my own political and moral philosophy.
25   (When I say that I am an old fogey, I am, of course, joking.)
English literature, as I see it, requires to be defended
By a person of integrity and essential good humour
Against the forces of fanaticism, idiosyncrasy and anarchy.
I perfectly apprehend the perilous nature of my convictions
30   And I am prepared to go to the stake
For Shakespeare, Milton,
And, coming to our own times,
Of course
Housman.
35   I cannot say more than that, can I?
And I do not deem it advisable, in the interests of the editor to whom I am
        spatially contracted,
To say less.

1938

12: Horatio says that the ghost of Hamlet's father had "A countenance more in sorrow than in anger" (*Hamlet* 1.2.231).
16: The classical scholar and poet A.E. *Housman* (1859–1936) wrote *A Shropshire Lad* (1896), one of the most popular books of poetry of the time.
24: *ventilate*: make public; express

Not Waving but Drowning

Nobody heard him, the dead man,
But still he lay moaning:
I was much further out than you thought
And not waving but drowning.

5   Poor chap, he always loved larking
And now he's dead
It must have been too cold for him his heart gave way,
They said.

10   Oh, no no no, it was too cold always
(Still the dead one lay moaning)
I was much too far out all my life
And not waving but drowning.

1957

My Hat

Mother said if I wore this hat
I should be certain to get off with the right sort of chap
Well look where I am now, on a desert island
With so far as I can see no one at all on hand
5   I know what has happened though I suppose Mother wouldn't see
This hat being so strong has completely run away with me
I had the feeling it was beginning to happen the moment I put it on
What a moment that was as I rose up, I rose up like a flying swan
As strong as a swan too, why see how far my hat has flown me away
10   It took us a night to come and then a night and a day
And all the time the swan wing in my hat waved beautifully
Ah, I thought, How this hat becomes me.
First the sea was dark but then it was pale blue
And still the wing beat and we flew and we flew
15   A night and a day and a night, and by the old right way
Between the sun and the moon we flew until morning day.
It is always early morning here on this peculiar island
The green grass grows into the sea on the dipping land
Am I glad I am here? Yes, well, I am,
20   It's nice to be rid of Father, Mother and the young man
There's just one thing causes me a twinge of pain,
If I take my hat off, shall I find myself home again?
So in this early morning land I always wear my hat
Go home, you see, well I wouldn't run a risk like that.

1957

The Celts

I think of the Celts as rather a whining lady
Who was beautiful once but is not so much so now
She is not very loving, but there is one thing she loves
It is her grievance which she hugs and takes out walking.

5   The Celtic lady likes fighting very much for freedom
But when she has got it she is a proper tyrant
Nobody likes her much when she is governing.

The Celtic lady is not very widely popular
But the English love her oh they love her very much
10   Especially when the Celtic lady is Irish they love her
Which is odd as she hates them then more than anyone else.
When she's Welsh the English stupidly associate her chiefly
With national hats, eisteddfods and Old Age Pensions.
(They don't think of her at all when she is Scotch, it is rather a problem.)

The Celts. 13: The pointed hat is part of the Welsh women's national costume, and is worn by school-children annually on St David's Day. *Eisteddfods* are formal assemblies of Welsh bards gathered for competition, a tradition going back to medieval times; in modern times the tradition has been revived as the Royal National Eisteddfod, a more general annual celebration of the arts. The Welsh Liberal politician (later Prime Minister) Lloyd George was responsible for the introduction of national social insurance with the 1911 National Insurance Act.

15   Oh the Celtic lady when she's Irish is the one for me
          Oh she is so witty and wild, my word witty,
          And flashing and spiteful this Celtic lady we love
          All the same she is not so beautiful as she was.

                                          1957

Pretty

Why is the word pretty so underrated?
In November the leaf is pretty when it falls
The stream grows deep in the woods after rain
And in the pretty pool the pike stalks

5   He stalks his prey, and this is pretty too,
The prey escapes with an underwater flash
But not for long, the great fish has him now
The pike is a fish who always has his prey

And this is pretty. The water rat is pretty
10   His paws are not webbed, he cannot shut his nostrils
As the otter can and the beaver, he is torn between
The land and water. Not 'torn', he does not mind.

The owl hunts in the evening and it is pretty
The lake water below him rustles with ice
15   There is frost coming from the ground, in the air mist
All this is pretty, it could not be prettier.

Yes, it could always be prettier, the eye abashes
It is becoming an eye that cannot see enough,
Out of the wood the eye climbs. This is prettier
20   A field in the evening, tilting up.

The field tilts to the sky. Though it is late
The sky is lighter than the hill field
All this looks easy but really it is extraordinary
Well, it is extraordinary to be so pretty.

25   And it is careless, and that is always pretty
This field, this owl, this pike, this pool are careless,
As Nature is always careless and indifferent
Who sees, who steps, means nothing, and this is pretty.

So a person can come along like a thief—pretty!—
30   Stealing a look, pinching the sound and feel,
Lick the icicle broken from the bank
And still say nothing at all, only cry pretty.

Cry pretty, pretty, pretty and you'll be able
Very soon not even to cry pretty
35   And so be delivered entirely from humanity
This is prettiest of all, it is very pretty.

                                          1966

Black March

I have a friend
At the end
Of the world.
His name is a breath

5   Of fresh air.
He is dressed in
Grey chiffon. At least
I think it is chiffon.
It has a
10   Peculiar look, like smoke.

It wraps him round
It blows out of place
It conceals him
I have not seen his face.

15   But I have seen his eyes, they are
As pretty and bright
As raindrops on black twigs
In March, and heard him say:

I am a breath
20   Of fresh air for you, a change
By and by.

Black March I call him
Because of his eyes
Being like March raindrops
25   On black twigs.

(Such a pretty time when the sky
Behind black twigs can be seen
Stretched out in one
Uninterrupted
30   Cambridge blue as cold as snow.)

But this friend
Whatever new names I give him
Is an old friend. He says:

Whatever names you give me
35   I am
A breath of fresh air,
A change for you.

1971

30: *Cambridge blue:* light blue (the Cambridge university color in athletic contests with Oxford; Oxford's color being dark blue)

JOSEPH GORDON MACLEOD (1903–1984)

MACLEOD'S CAREER AS A POET BEGAN WITH GREAT PROMISE AND ENDED IN near total obscurity. His first book, *The Ecliptic* (1930), was published by Faber and Faber, and its appearance led the American editor Morton Dauwen Zabel to proclaim in *Poetry* magazine a new "dawn" in British poetry heralded by the work of Macleod, Basil Bunting, and W. H. Auden. In the same magazine, Bunting praised the "skill and impetus" of the poem's versification and added that "*The Ecliptic* interested me more than any new thing since [Eliot's] *The Waste Land*."[1] Probably through Bunting, Macleod began a correspondence with Ezra Pound, who praised *The Ecliptic* in letters to friends and remembered Macleod in Canto CXIV. But Macleod's early success was limited and temporary; he had difficulty finding a publisher for his second collection, *Foray of Centaurs* (1931), and gradually came to believe that there was no audience for the kind of modernist poetry he was writing. That belief and his commitment to leftist politics led him to abandon the poetic mode of *The Ecliptic*. He then began writing social realist poetry indebted to folk traditions and documenting life in the Hebrides and the Highlands of Scotland; these poems were published under the pseudonym "Adam Drinan." The most notable of the Drinan books is *The Men of the Rocks* (1942); several of the Drinan poems have been included in anthologies of Scottish literature. A final book containing poems set in Florence, *An Old Olive Tree*, appeared under his own name in 1971.

Joseph Todd Gordon Macleod was born in Ealing, Middlesex and educated at Rugby School and Balliol College, Oxford. As he wrote in a note on his career, most of his adult life was "spent in the performing arts (theatre, politics, broadcasting)."[2] From 1933 to 1936, he was lessee and director of the Festival Theatre in Cambridge. In 1937, he was secretary for the Huntingtonshire Divisional Labour Party and a parliamentary candidate. From 1938 to 1945, he was a newsreader and commentator for the BBC in London and then from 1946 to 1947, managing director of the Scottish National Film Studios. In 1946, he toured Holland as a guest of the Dutch government, and the next year he toured the U.S.S.R. as a guest of the Soviet government. Besides poetry, he published several plays, the novel *Overture to Cambridge: A Satirical Story* (1934), several books on Soviet and British theater, a memoir of his life at the BBC, and the biography *The Sisters d'Aranyi* (1969). His last years were spent in Florence.

The Ecliptic is a poem in twelve sections based on the signs of the zodiac; they employ a wide range of poetic modes, from free verse to rhymed couplets. Macleod wrote in the book's preface that "Each sign . . . contributes to a single consciousness" as the

---

[1] "English Poetry Today," *Poetry*, vol. 39, no. 5, 1932, p. 268.
[2] Quoted in George Bruce, "Joseph Gordon Macleod," *Contemporary Poets*, 3rd ed., New York, 1980, p. 961.

poem traces the development and conflicts of a representative self. "Cancer," the poem's fourth section, is glossed by the poet as follows: "There is a phase in the twenties when . . . disintegration becomes almost complete. The will fails. The whole world seems to be a chaos of contradictory meaning without faith or effort."[3] The poem's allusions to classical myth and culture and occasional use of collage suggest the influence of Pound and Eliot. William Blake is also a presiding spirit in this long poem attempting a synthesis of first-generation modernist poetry and English traditions.

---

[3] *The Ecliptic*, p. 8.

from The Ecliptic

Cancer, or, The Crab

Moonpoison, mullock of sacrifice,
Suffuses the veins of the eyes
Till the retina, mooncoloured,
Sees the sideways motion of the cretin crab
5   Hued thus like a tortoise askew in the glaucous moonscape
A flat hot boulder it
Lividly in the midst of the Doldrums
Sidles
The lunatic unable to bear the silent course of constellations
10   Mad and stark naked
Sidles
The obol on an eyeball of a man dead from elephantiasis
Sidles
All three across heaven with a rocking motion.
15   The Doldrums: 'region of calms and light baffling winds near Equator.'

But the calms are rare
The winds baffling but not light
And the drunken boats belonging to the Crab Club
Rock hot and naked to the dunning of the moon
20   All in the pallescent Sargasso weed
And windbound, seeking distraction by the light of deliverance
For
What are we but the excrement of non-existent noon?
      (Truth like starlight crookedly)

The *ecliptic* is the path taken in the course of a year by the sun through the constellations of the zodiac; each section of MacLeod's poem, titled after a sign of the zodiac, deals with successive stages in the mental and emotional growth of modern man. According to MacLeod's synopsis in the preface, in his youth man "revolt[s] against all control and authority," leading him to "destandardize himself at the cost of disintegrating himself." He summarizes "Cancer": "There is a phase in the twenties when this disintegration becomes almost complete. The will fails. The whole world seems to be a chaos of contradictory meaning without faith or effort."
1: *mullock*: rubbish
5: *glaucous*: bluish-white
12: *obol*: an ancient Greek silver coin; coins were traditionally placed on the eyes of the dead.
elephantiasis: a condition associated with the disease filariasis, involving the grotesque enlargement of limbs or the scrotum
18: *drunken boats*: alludes to the visionary poem "Le Bateau Ivre" ("The Drunken Boat") by Arthur Rimbaud (1854–1891).
20: *pallescent*: becoming pale (i.e., from moonlight)

25   What are we all but 'burial grounds abhorred by the moon'?
     And did the Maoris die of measles? So do we.

     But there is no snow here, nor lilies.
     The night is glutinous
     In a broad hearth crisscross thorn clumps
30   Smoulder: distant fireback of copse
     Throws back silence: glassen ashes gleam in pond
     The constellations which have stopped working (?)
     Shimmer. No dead leaf jumps.
     On edge of lawn a glowworm
35   Hangs out its state-recognized torchlamp
     Blocks of flowers gape dumb as windows with blinds drawn
     And in the centre the rugate trees
     Though seeming as if they go up in smoke
     Are held like cardboard where they are.
40   Bluehot it is queer fuel to make the moon move.

     Agesias said: 'Nero was an artist because he murdered his mother
     Sensibility (subliminal) is of more importance than moral obligation (pran-
          dial).'
        But Agesias paints cottages in watercolours and fears his own mother
     Barbarieus said: 'I am passionately in love with Gito who spurns me for
          Praxinoê'
45   But until he saw them together he was merely disturbed by Gito's eye-
          lashes
     Galônus said: 'The subsequent shrivelling of an orchid doesn't alter the
          value of its beauty.'
     Decanus said: 'Joy in nothing. Either dies joy or what produced it.'
        But Galônus is attractive to women, Decanus obese, poor, obtuse.
     Epinondas said: 'I have been a liar, now no longer so.'
50   Zeuxias said: 'What I have always been, I shall remain, a fool.'
        Is it better to be self-deceived or lazy?
     Epator was drunk for two days: Theodorus traced his disease to college,
          Iphogenês saw God and died,
     And so down the Alphabet, aye, and the Persian,
     With variegated gutturals and sibilants, the Gaelic with diphthongs and
          triphthongs,
55   Choctaw with three different clicks
     Each letter is somebody
     But the Crab is nobody
     Nobody
     Nobody
60   A ganglion of neurotic imitations
     Composed of each letter in turn
     Jointed by conflicts he does not want
     A word that never existed with a sense nobody can understand.
     Suffering for the sins his father refused to commit

25: Macleod quotes "Spleen," poem 76 of Baudelaire's *The Flowers of Evil* (1857): "I am a cemetery abhorred by the moon."
26: The native *Maori* population of New Zealand was devastated by European diseases after explorers began visiting it in the seventeenth century.
30: *fireback:* the back wall of a fireplace
37: *rugate:* wrinkled
41: The Roman emperor *Nero* had his mother, the ruthless Agrippina, put to death in 59 AD.
60: *ganglion:* cluster of nerve cells

65 He sits and thinks about the twiddling toes of Gunerita
    A boy-girl or girl-boy of an average pulchritude
    Haunted by phantoms of his female self
    Whom he has never seen but composed himself, thus:
        Breasts of Augustina brains of Beatrice
70   Arms of Capucine on the motherliness of Dorothea
        Eyes of Evelyn in the brow of Francesca
        Fragrance of Gretchen with the understanding of Helen
    This he desires, but despises:
    Bhah!
75 Always sideways, crabs walk.

    Either he is not fit for this world
    Or this world not fit for him. But which?
    After all this pain of development is there neither interval nor reward?
    They lured him with promises,
80 Now it has all slipped sideways
    What is the good, I ask you, of going into a melting-pot
    If fated to melt again after getting out of it?
    The answers are: He is not out of it
    Determined to budge not from yon slippery rock
85 Not a yard, no, nor an inch, no, nor a barleycorn's breadth
    For Chance is not blind but unimpedable
    And we call it blind because
    Since we frustrate it only by chance
    We prefer to shut our own eyes.

90 The crab however crawls on.

    He must therefore be a crab subnormal.
    One day, one of his foreclaws, assembled as usual by many men,
    Being longer than the other, turns and pinches his tentacles
    With the other he pinches the persons that assembled the long one
95 Next day the short one, equally alien, is the longer
    And the process is reversed.
    In mass production one hand never knows
    The evil the other is inspiring it to do
    This is a heretic even to the faiths he fails to believe
100 So worthless, awkward, unintelligible,
    The crab crawls on.

    He has suffered because he was ugly
    Let him be cruel now that he is attractive
    Caring not whether he fructifies cruelty or is merely hard on self.
105 We trap our goldfinch trapping our souls therewinged
    Sacrifice our mad gods to the madder gods:
    We hymn the two sons of Leda and Zeus Aegis-bearer
    We don't. We drink and drivel. My
        poor Catullus, do stop being such a

105ff: MacLeod is touching on earlier sections of the poem: in "Taurus" the *goldfinch* is, in the words of
the preface, "an unintelligible voice whose authority the child recognizes with a romantic misunder-
standing, but is made to reject"; the "two sons of Leda and Zeus" are the twins Castor and Pollux, who
were transformed into the constellation Gemini. *Aegis* is the name of Zeus's shield.
109–28: A rendition of poem 8 of the Latin poet Catullus (c.84 BC–c.54 BC)

110   Fool. Admit that lost which as you watch is
      gone. O, once the days shone very bright for
      you, when where that girl you loved so (as no
      other will be) called, you came and came. And
      then and there were odd things done and many
115   which you wanted and she didn't not want.
      Yes indeed the days shone very bright for
      you. But now she doesn't want it.
                              Don't you either,
      booby. Don't keep chasing her. Don't live in
120   misery, carry on, be firm, be hardened.
      Goodbye, girl: Catullus is quite hardened,
      doesn't want you, doesn't ask, if you're not
      keen—though sorry you'll be to be not asked.
      Yes, poor sinner . . . what is left in life for
125   you? Who'll now go with you? Who'll be attracted?
      Whom'll you love now? Whom say you belong to?
      Whom'll you now kiss? Whose lips'll you nibble?
      —Now you, Catullus! you've decided to be hardened.

      How can I be hardened when the whole world is fluid?
130   O Aphroditê Pandêmos, your badgers rolling in the moonlit
      Corn blue-bloom-covered carpeting the wind
      Wind humming like distant rooks
      Distant rooks busy like factory whirring metal
      Whirring metallic starlings bizarre like cogwheels missing teeth
135   These last grinning like the backs of old motor cars
      Old motor cars smelling of tragomaschality
      Tragomaschality denoting the triumph of self over civilization
      Civilization being relative ours to Greek
                    Greek to Persian
140   Persian to Chinese
      Chinese politely making borborygms to show satisfaction
      Satisfaction a matter of capacity
      Capacity not significance: otherwise with an epigram
      Epigrams—poems with a strabismus
145   Strabismus being as common spiritually as optically the moon
      The moon tramping regular steps like a policeman past the houses of the
            Zodiac
      And the Zodiac itself, whirling and flaming sideways
      Circling from no point returning through no point
      Endlessly skidding as long as man skids, though never moving,
150   Wavers, topples, dissolves like a sandcastle into acidity.

      Is there nothing more soluble, more gaseous, more imperceptible?
      Nothing.

                                                      1930

130: *Aphroditê,* goddess of love, was traditionally given the epithet *Pandêmos,* "of all the people."
136: *tragomaschality:* pungent armpit sweat
141: *borborygms:* rumblings in the intestines; Macleod presumably means "burps," the customary Chinese
  way of showing satisfaction with a meal.
144: *strabismus:* inability to align both eyes on an object; a squint

PATRICK KAVANAGH (1904–1967)

"I HAVE NEVER BEEN MUCH CONSIDERED BY THE ENGLISH CRITICS. . . . BUT FOR MANY years I have learned not to care, and I have learned that the basis of literary criticism is usually the ephemeral." This remark, prefacing Kavanagh's *Collected Poems* (1964), gives us something of the Irish poet who has become powerfully identified with "an Irish note that is not dependent on backwards looks towards the Irish tradition, not an artful retrieval of poetic strategies from another tongue but a ritualistic drawing out of patterns of run and stress in the English language as it is spoken in Ireland" (Seamus Heaney).[1] Less concerned to note Kavanagh's rejection of the formal strategies and interest in myth characteristic of the Irish Revival, Robert Creeley similarly describes a "tone, a prosody intimate with a voice speaking" which "engage[s] a whole people's communal language" to make of "common, human experience" a "profoundly simple, wondrous music."[2] But Kavanagh's poetry is not only a poetry of country or peasant idioms: "Somehow or other I have a belief in poetry as a mystical thing, and a dangerous thing," he said in his preface. "Canal Bank Walk" is the most famous expression of his mysticism. "The woes of the poor" are the subject of the long poem *The Great Hunger*, which begins with an ironic allusion to the Gospel of John ("Clay is the word and clay is the flesh") and shows how empty the consolations of Catholicism could seem to Kavanagh as they met the realities of the peasant farmer's life.

Kavanagh knew these realities well: "Looking back, I see that the big tragedy for the poet is poverty. I had no money and no profession except that of small farmer. And I had the misfortune to live the worst years of my life through a period when there were no Arts Councils . . . for the benefit of young poets."[3] Kavanagh was born in Inniskeen, County Monaghan, and left school at an early age to work as a hired hand and farmer. He moved permanently to Dublin in 1939, where he made his living by writing reviews for the *Irish Times* and other papers. With his brother Peter, he edited the short-lived *Kavanagh's Weekly*, a journal devoted to literature and politics. In 1952, after he was attacked in an unsigned article in the magazine *The Leader*, he initiated a libel suit, one of the most famous literary lawsuits of the century. By this point, "Paddy" was a famous personality in Dublin, but he was also desperately poor. Kavanagh lost the jury trial. The decision was appealed and a new trial ordered, but Kavanagh was ill with lung cancer, and the case had to be settled out of court—a "pyrrhic victory," his brother wrote.[4] After leaving the hospital where he had a lung removed, Kavanagh had the epiphany that is recorded in "Canal Bank Walk." In 1955,

---

1 *Preoccupations: Selected Prose 1968–1978,* London, 1980, p. 123.
2 "A True Poet," *Patrick Kavanagh: Man and Poet,* ed. Peter Kavanagh, Orono, 1986, p. 312.
3 "Author's Note," *The Great Hunger,* New York, 1964, pp. xiii–xiv
4 "The Kavanagh Case," *Patrick Kavanagh: Man and Poet,* p. 142.

he was appointed extra-mural lecturer at University College, Dublin and at last found a meager financial stability. The last years of his life were troubled by alcoholism and regular controversy in the *Irish Times,* but Kavanagh's international reputation also grew with readings and lectures in England and the United States.

from The Great Hunger

I

Clay is the word and clay is the flesh
Where the potato-gatherers like mechanized scare-crows move
Along the side-fall of the hill—Maguire and his men.
If we watch them an hour is there anything we can prove
5   Of life as it is broken-backed over the Book
Of Death? Here crows gabble over worms and frogs
And the gulls like old newspapers are blown clear of the hedges, luckily.
Is there some light of imagination in these wet clods?
Or why do we stand here shivering?
10   Which of these men
Loved the light and the queen
Too long virgin? Yesterday was summer. Who was it promised marriage to
    himself
Before apples were hung from the ceilings for Hallowe'en?
We will wait and watch the tragedy to the last curtain
15   Till the last soul passively like a bag of wet clay
Rolls down the side of the hill, diverted by the angles
Where the plough missed or a spade stands, straitening the way.

A dog lying on a torn jacket under a heeled-up cart,
A horse nosing along the posied headland, trailing
20   A rusty plough. Three heads hanging between wide-apart
Legs. October playing a symphony on a slack wire paling.
Maguire watches the drills flattened out
And the flints that lit a candle for him on a June altar
Flameless. The drills slipped by and the days slipped by
25   And he trembled his head away and ran free from the world's halter,
And thought himself wiser than any man in the townland
When he laughed over pints of porter
Of how he came free from every net spread
In the gaps of experience. He shook a knowing head
30   And pretended to his soul

Some of our annotations are indebted to Antoinette Quinn's edition of Kavanagh's *Selected Poems* (London: Penguin, 1996).

Title: The poem is named after the Irish Potato Famine of 1845–1849; but the poem deals instead with the spiritual and sexual hunger of its protagonist, whose devotion to his mother and sense of sin keeps him from ever marrying.

I: 1: Cf. John 1:14: "And the Word was made flesh, and dwelt among us"

11–12: *the queen / Too long virgin:* probably the Virgin Mary

13: *apples were hung . . . :* a variant on bobbing for apples

17: *straitening the way:* a parody of John the Baptist's cry: "Make straight the way of the Lord" (John 1:23)

21: *paling:* fence

22: *drills:* the rows where the plants had been growing

26: *townland:* township

That children are tedious in hurrying fields of April
Where men are spanging across wide furrows.
Lost in the passion that never needs a wife—
The pricks that pricked were the pointed pins of harrows.
35   Children scream so loud that the crows could bring
The seed of an acre away with crow-rude jeers.
Patrick Maguire, he called his dog and he flung a stone in the air
And hallooed the birds away that were the birds of the years.

Turn over the weedy clods and tease out the tangled skeins.
40   What is he looking for there?
He thinks it is a potato, but we know better
Than his mud-gloved fingers probe in this insensitive hair.

'Move forward the basket and balance it steady
In this hollow. Pull down the shafts of that cart, Joe,
45   And straddle the horse,' Maguire calls.
'The wind's over Brannagan's, now that means rain.
Graip up some withered stalks and see that no potato falls
Over the tail-board going down the ruckety pass—
And *that's* a job we'll have to do in December,
50   Gravel it and build a kerb on the bog-side. Is that Cassidy's ass
Out in my clover? Curse o' God—
Where is that dog?
Never where he's wanted.' Maguire grunts and spits
Through a clay-wattled moustache and stares about him from the height.
55   His dream changes again like the cloud-swung wind
And he is not so sure now if his mother was right
When she praised the man who made a field his bride.

Watch him, watch him, that man on a hill whose spirit
Is a wet sack flapping about the knees of time.
60   He lives that his little fields may stay fertile when his own body
Is spread in the bottom of a ditch under two coulters crossed in Christ's
      Name.

He was suspicious in his youth as a rat near strange bread
When girls laughed; when they screamed he knew that meant
The cry of fillies in season. He could not walk
65   The easy road to his destiny. He dreamt
The innocence of young brambles to hooked treachery.
O the grip, O the grip of irregular fields! No man escapes.
It could not be that back of the hills love was free
And ditches straight.
70   No monster hand lifted up children and put down apes
As here.
                         'O God if I had been wiser!'
That was his sigh like the brown breeze in the thistles.
He looks towards his house and haggard. 'O God if I had been wiser!'

32: spanging: leaping
47: *Graip*: dig; a graip is a pronged instrument used for digging.
48: *ruckety*: uneven, not level
59: *wet sack*: Workers wore sacks like aprons over their trousers when working in wet fields.
61: A *coulter* is an iron blade fixed in front of a ploughshare.
74: *haggard*: that part of the farmyard where straw and hay are stored

75   But now a crumpled leaf from the whitethorn bushes
        Darts like a frightened robin, and the fence
        Shows the green of after-grass through a little window,
        And he knows that his own heart is calling his mother a liar.
        God's truth is life—even the grotesque shapes of its foulest fire.

80   The horse lifts its head and crashes
        Through the whins and stones
        To lip late passion in the crawling clover.
        In the gap there's a bush weighted with boulders like morality,
        The fools of life bleed if they climb over.

85   The wind leans from Brady's, and the coltsfoot leaves are holed with rust,
        Rain fills the cart-tracks and the sole-plate grooves;
        A yellow sun reflects in Donaghmoyne
        The poignant light in puddles shaped by hooves.

        Come with me, Imagination, into this iron house
90   And we will watch from the doorway the years run back,
        And we will know what a peasant's left hand wrote on the page.
        Be easy, October. No cackle hen, horse neigh, tree sough, duck quack.

IX

355   He gave himself another year,
        Something was bound to happen before then—
        The circle would break down
        And he would curve the new one to his own will.
        A new rhythm is a new life
360   And in it marriage is hung and money.
        He would be a new man walking through unbroken meadows
        Of dawn in the year of One.

        The poor peasant talking to himself in a stable door—
        An ignorant peasant deep in dung.
365   What can the passers-by think otherwise?
        Where is his silver bowl of knowledge hung?
        Why should men be asked to believe in a soul
        That is only the mark of a hoof in guttery gaps?
        A man is what is written on the label.
370   And the passing world stares but no one stops
        To look closer. So back to the growing crops
        And the ridges he never loved.
        Nobody will ever know how much tortured poetry the pulled weeds on the
            ridge wrote
        Before they withered in the July sun,
375   Nobody will ever read the wild, sprawling, scrawling mad woman's signa-
            ture,

81: *whins:* gorsebushes
82: *passion:* a rhubarb-like plant
85: *coltsfoot:* a type of weed; *rust:* a plant disease caused by fungi
86: *sole-plate:* horseshoe
87: *Donaghmoyne:* a parish adjacent to Inniskeen (and once part of Inniskeen parish)

The hysteria and the boredom of the enclosed nun of his thought.
Like the afterbirth of a cow stretched on a branch in the wind
Life dried in the veins of these women and men:
The grey and grief and unlove,
380   The bones in the backs of their hands,
And the chapel pressing its low ceiling over them.

Sometimes they did laugh and see the sunlight,
A narrow slice of divine instruction.
Going along the river at the bend of Sunday
385   The trout played in the pools encouragement
To jump in love though death bait the hook.
And there would be girls sitting on the grass banks of lanes
Stretch-legged and lingering staring—
A man might take one of them if he had the courage.
390   But 'No' was in every sentence of their story
Except when the public-house came in and shouted its piece.

The yellow buttercups and the bluebells among the whin bushes
On rocks in the middle of ploughing
Was a bright spoke in the wheel
395   Of the peasant's mill.
The goldfinches on the railway paling were worth looking at—
A man might imagine then
Himself in Brazil and these birds the Birds of Paradise
And the Amazon and the romance traced on the school map lived again.

400   Talk in evening corners and under trees
Was like an old book found in a king's tomb.
The children gathered round like students and listened
And some of the saga defied the draught in the open tomb
And was not blown.

1942

Father Mat

I

In a meadow
Beside the chapel three boys were playing football.
At the forge door an old man was leaning
Viewing a hunter-hoe. A man could hear
5   If he listened to the breeze the fall of wings—
How wistfully the sin-birds come home!

It was Confession Saturday, the first
Saturday in May; the May Devotions
Were spread like leaves to quieten

4: *hunter-hoe:* horse-drawn implement for loosening soil or scraping up weeds
8: *May Devotions:* an evening service held throughout May in honor of the Virgin Mary

10   The excited armies of conscience.
          The knife of penance fell so like a blade
          Of grass that no one was afraid.

          Father Mat came slowly walking, stopping to
          Stare through gaps at ancient Ireland sweeping
15   In again with all its unbaptized beauty:
          The calm evening,
          The whitethorn blossoms,
          The smell from ditches that were not Christian.
          The dancer that dances in the hearts of men cried:
20   Look! I have shown this to you before—
          The rags of living surprised
          The joy in things you cannot forget.

          His heavy hat was square upon his head,
          Like a Christian Brother's;
25   His eyes were an old man's watery eyes,
          Out of his flat nose grew spiky hairs.
          He was a part of the place,
          Natural as a round stone in a grass field;
          He could walk through a cattle fair
30   And the people would only notice his odd spirit there.

          His curate passed on a bicycle—
          He had the haughty intellectual look
          Of the man who never reads in brook or book;
          A man designed
35   To wear a mitre,
          To sit on committees—
          For will grows strongest in the emptiest mind.

          The old priest saw him pass
          And, seeing, saw
40   Himself a medieval ghost.
          Ahead of him went Power,
          One who was not afraid when the sun opened a flower,
          Who was never astonished
          At a stick carried down a stream
45   Or at the undying difference in the corner of a field.

                              II

          The Holy Ghost descends
          At random like the muse
          On wise man and fool,
          And why should poet in the twilight choose?

24: *Christian Brother*: member of a lay Christian congregation founded in 1802 to provide education to
poor Catholic children
46: *Holy Ghost*: the feast of Pentecost commemorates the descent of the Holy Spirit on the heads of the
apostles, giving them the gifts of tongues (Acts 2).

50   Within the dim chapel was the grey
        Mumble of prayer
        To the Queen of May—
        The Virgin Mary with the schoolgirl air.

        Two guttering candles on a brass shrine
55   Raised upon the wall
        Monsters of despair
        To terrify deep into the soul.

        Through the open door the hum of rosaries
        Came out and blended with the homing bees.
60   The trees
        Heard nothing stranger than the rain or the wind
        Or the birds—
        But deep in their roots they knew a seed had sinned.

        In the graveyard a goat was nibbling at a yew,
65   The cobbler's chickens with anxious looks
        Were straggling home through nettles, over graves.
        A young girl down a hill was driving cows
        To a corner at the gable-end of a roofless house.

        Cows were milked earlier,
70   The supper hurried,
        Hens shut in,
        Horses unyoked,
        And three men shaving before the same mirror.

III

        The trip of iron tips on tile
75   Hesitated up the middle aisle,
        Heads that were bowed glanced up to see
        Who could this last arrival be.

        Murmur of women's voices from the porch,
        Memories of relations in the graveyard.
80   On the stem
        Of memory imaginations blossom.

              In the dim
        Corners in the side seats faces gather,
        Lit up now and then by a guttering candle
85   And the ghost of day at the window.
        A secret lover is saying
        Three Hail Marys that she who knows
        The ways of women will bring
        Cathleen O'Hara (he names her) home to him.
90   Ironic fate! Cathleen herself is saying
        Three Hail Marys to her who knows

52: *Queen of May*: the Virgin Mary; but Kavanagh alludes ironically to the secular folk festival of May Day, involving dances around a "maypole" and the election of a Queen for the day.

The ways of men to bring
Somebody else home to her—
'O may he love me.'
95   What is the Virgin Mary now to do?

IV

From a confessional
The voice of Father Mat's absolving
Rises and falls like a briar in the breeze.
As the sins pour in the old priest is thinking
100   His fields of fresh grass, his horses, his cows,
His earth into the fires of Purgatory.
It cools his mind.
'They confess to the fields,' he mused,
'They confess to the fields and the air and the sky,'
105   And forgiveness was the soft grass of his meadow by the river;
His thoughts were walking through it now.

His human lips talked on:
'My son,
Only the poor in spirit shall wear the crown;
110   Those down
Can creep in the low door
On to Heaven's floor.'

The Tempter had another answer ready:
'Ah lad, upon the road of life
115   'Tis best to dance with Chance's wife
And let the rains that come in time
Erase the footprints of the crime.'

The dancer that dances in the hearts of men
Tempted him again:
120   'Look! I have shown you this before;
From this mountain-top I have tempted Christ
With what you see now
Of beauty—all that's music, poetry, art
In things you can touch every day.
125   I broke away
And rule all dominions that are rare;
I took with me all the answers to every prayer
That young men and girls pray for: love, happiness, riches—'
O Tempter! O Tempter!

V

130   As Father Mat walked home
Venus was in the western sky

120ff: Cf. Satan's temptation of Christ (Matt. 4:1–11)
131: The planet Venus, named after the Greek goddess of love, is called "the evening star" because it is vis-
ible in the west with the setting of the sun.

And there were voices in the hedges:
'God the Gay is not the Wise.'

'Take your choice, take your choice,'
135   Called the breeze through the bridge's eye.
'The domestic Virgin and Her Child
Or Venus with her ecstasy.'

1947

Canal Bank Walk

Leafy-with-love banks and the green waters of the canal
Pouring redemption for me, that I do
The will of God, wallow in the habitual, the banal,
Grow with nature again as before I grew.
5   The bright stick trapped, the breeze adding a third
Party to the couple kissing on an old seat,
And a bird gathering materials for the nest for the Word
Eloquently new and abandoned to its delirious beat.
O unworn world enrapture me, encapture me in a web
10   Of fabulous grass and eternal voices by a beech,
Feed the gaping need of my senses, give me ad lib
To pray unselfconsciously with overflowing speech
For this soul needs to be honoured with a new dress woven
From green and blue things and arguments that cannot be proven.

1960

Title: This poem records a revelatory experience of Kavanagh's, which he considered his rebirth as a poet through his losing his "messianic compulsion": it occurred during his convalescence after an operation to treat his lung cancer. "I sat on the bank of the Grand Canal [in Dublin] in the summer of 1955 and let the water lap idly on the shores of my mind. My purpose in life was to have no purpose." (Preface to *Collected Poems*).
1–2: Antoinette Quinn points out that the imagery in these lines is that of baptism.

BRIAN COFFEY (1905–1995)

COFFEY WAS BORN IN DÚN LAOGHAIRE NEAR DUBLIN AND ATTENDED CLONGOWES Wood College and University College, Dublin, where he studied mathematics, physics, and chemistry. Living in Paris during the 1930s, he pursued a doctorate in scholastic philosophy at the Institute Catholique, studying with the neo-Thomist philosopher and aesthetician Jacques Maritain. He then spent the war years in London. After submitting his doctoral thesis in 1947, he became an assistant professor of Philosophy at St. Louis University in Missouri. In 1952, he returned to London, where he taught mathematics until 1972. His first book, *Poems* (1930), included poems by Denis Devlin. Other early books include *Three Poems* (1933) and *Third Person* (1938). Coffey's activities in this first phase of his literary career also included reviewing for T. S. Eliot's journal *The Criterion*. After taking his position at St. Louis University, Coffey did not publish another book until *Missouri Sequence* (1962), which was followed by *Selected Poems* (1971), *Advent* (1975, 1986), and *Death of Hektor* (1982). *Leo*, with drawings by Geoffrey Prowse, was published in a special Brian Coffey issue of the *Irish University Review* in 1975. He also published a translation of Stéphane Mallarmé's *Un Coup de Dés* in 1965 and of Pablo Neruda's love poems in 1973.

In 1934, Samuel Beckett declared Coffey, with Denis Devlin, "without question the most interesting of the youngest generation of Irish poets."[1] With Thomas Mac-Greevy, Devlin, and Beckett himself, Coffey has often been identified with international modernism. *Advent*'s syntactically compressed, meditative mode introduces propositions and questions concerning ontology and religion, such as "Who opposes world world crucifies" and "Why is this hanging wreck forsaken the remedy for world."[2] The poem contests orthodoxies of popular belief in its pursuit of a Christ immanent in the world, recording the struggle to wake to hopefulness from a "place dice dead," its reference to "dice" suggesting Stéphane Mallarmé's famous poem, which Coffey was translating while writing *Advent*. Coffey's Catholic modernism, as Alex Davis argues, must be distinguished from forms of modernism reflecting what Coffey's mentor, Jacques Maritain, called "angelism": "the striving of human intelligence to attain the spiritual autonomy reserved, in Thomism, for creatures unbound by material individuation." For Maritain and Coffey any such idealism risked producing an escapist poetry; Wallace Stevens and Rainer Maria Rilke, for instance, are two poets whose work might be said to reveal the human propensity to "forget matter" and suppress our "utter dependency upon the earth." In Mallarmé's poetics of chance and contingency this "angelism" implodes as "the imposition of order reaches its negative

---

1 "Recent Irish Poetry" (1934), *Disjecta: Miscellaneous Writings and a Dramatic Fragment*, ed. Ruby Cohn, New York, 1984, p. 75.
2 *Advent*, London, 1986, p. 40.

apotheosis in the randomly thrown dice of the poetic act."[3] *Advent,* by contrast, demands a poetry inseparable from the particulars of person and circumstance:

> We are always in human circumstances
> no angels and prone to forget
> we can work only from point to point[4]

---

[3] "'Poetry is Ontology': Brian Coffey's Poetics," *Modernism and Ireland: The Poetry of the 1930s,* ed. Patricia Coughlan and Alex Davis, Cork, 1995, pp. 162–64.

[4] *Advent,* p. 41.

H E A D R O C K

```
     I p s o f a c t o p a p e r A n s w e r a l l q u e s t i
     o n s t a k i n g a l l y o u r t i m e O N E W h a t h a
     v e y o u f o r g o t t e n A r e y o u b e y o n d d o u
     b t i n g y o u r m o t i v e s ' h o n e s t y W h o m d
  5  i d y o u s u p p o s e i n w h o s e s k i n l a s t t i
     m e y o u m a d e i t T W O I s y o u r m o t h e r a t h
     o m e d e a r e o r d o y o u m e n t a l l y r e s e r
     v e / p r u d e n t l y d i s s i m u l a t e W h o ' s l
     y i n g n o w T H R E E C a n d a m n a t i o n b e a m a
 10  t t e r o f r o u t i n e a d m i n C o u l d y o u o r g
     a n i s e a n d m a i n t a i n i n a n i n q u i s i t i o n
     w o u l d y o u A r e y o u t h a t s t r o n g r e a l l
     y F O U R A r e y o u p u s h e d f o r t i m e y e t D i
     d y o u t a k e y o u r p i l l A n d h a v e y o u f o u
 15  n d a p l a c e t o h i d e i n t o h i d e f r o m F I V
     E W h a t a b o u t y o u r m o t h e r D o y o u d r i n
     k u n u s u a l l y m u c h w a t e r t h e s e d a y s S
     I X W h e n y o u w e r e b e a t i n g y o u r w i f e d
     i d s h e s m i l e a n d i f s o w h y S E V E N W h o a
 20  r e y o u W h e r e a r e y o u W h e n a r e y o u W h a
     t d i d t h e n t h G a d a r e n e s w i n e s a y t o t
     h e ( n + 1 ) t h o n t h e w a y d o w n E I G H T W a s
     y o u r M a a g o o d c h a p y o u r f a t h e r w o r s
     h i p p e d w h e n h e c h a s e d y o u r l i t t l e s
 25  i s t e r t o t h e t o o l s h e d N I N E A c t u a l l
     y A k c h e l l i F r a n k l y s p e a k i n g M a n t o
     m a n / W o m a n t o w o m a n d i d y o u e v e r l o v
     e a n y o n e d e a d E v e r o w n e d a b o d T E N D o
     y o u a g r e e t h a t i t i s f a i r c o m m e n t o n
 30  F U Z Z ' S v i e w o f t h e e v i l t h a t i s a b r o
     a d i n o u r l a n d t h a t M a n t h e r e i s M a n t
     h e r e i s a b s o l u t e l y M a n M a n t h e r e i s
```

N O E S C A P E

1971

10: *admin:* administration (colloq.)

21: *the nth Gadarene swine:* see Mark 5:1–14: Jesus exorcises a madman possessed by a legion of devils, sending them into a herd of swine, which throw themselves into the sea off a cliff. In mathematics "n" is often used to denote any arbitrary number.

from Advent

I

Who wakes now being here if not one alone

where where lifts no sail no dew cools
far stars of their purity presage none
voiceless unfeatured unrapturing deep
5   own the place dice dead naught to please

But waking not like from sleep to sleep

Does eye but open on mere daily wont
hard habit plain the deadhand forest lichen
habit hostile to hope foiling wish in rifled heart
10   continue one does one will pliant desperate

Let but at shadow gate sound sudden garden bell
no change   sign signal far flame whatever   none

Count hours waiting as so many sleepers
or at nightfall decide to seek light in vain
15   one day yes the barque will glide out of long night seas
slide into yellow sand at break of day

Now neither one nor th'other   This   A heartbeat dropped
and on the piazza busy men no longer   thin statue-shades

Unquiet house it is   darkness solid
20   like what wake-light once showed   shadows pressing
From tumbled citadel one stared at air
shaped by walls   rigid like speech frozen

Unsafe unhappy chance   promised no joy no egress
it is constraint to narrowness it's patience
25   with need with sentence   no angel calls here

Title: *Advent:* in the Church calendar, a period of preparation for the coming of Christ at Christmas; it is
a penitential season that includes the four preceding Sundays. "Advent" is also the term given to the
anticipated second coming of Christ.

2–5: This stanza's images come from *Un coup de dés jamais n'abolira le hasard* (*A Throw of the Dice Never
Will Abolish Chance*) by Stéphane Mallarmé (1842–1898); Coffey was translating this famously enigmatic
poem during the composition of *Advent.* For Mallarmé the universe is one from which God has disap-
peared, and is thus an "Abyss" without meaning, contingent; our condition is one of "shipwreck." The
poem's hero-figure is a "master" or mariner who launches a sail into "the tempest," just as the poet makes
a "throw of the dice" in the act of creation. Mallarmé's conclusion is ambiguous, both suggesting that
such struggles cannot abolish contingency and found meaning, and hinting at the possibility of a (quasi-
religious) transcendence: "NOTHING / WILL TAKE PLACE / BUT PLACE / EXCEPTED /
PERHAPS / A CONSTELLATION." Mallarmé's poem is an expression of the "crisis" of modernity,
which Coffey both draws on in *Advent* and (as a Christian) separates himself from.

15: *barque:* boat; in an interview Coffey said that the image of a boat sliding onto the sand came from a
dream he had in 1930 ("Brian Coffey: An Interview," by Parkman Howe, *Éire-Ireland* 13:1 [Spring 1978]).

20: *wake-light:* the light from candles around the body at a wake

21: *tumbled citadel:* perhaps alluding to the sonnet "El Desdichado" ("The Disinherited"), by Gerard de
Nerval (1808–1855): "I am the widower—dim, disconsolate—/ The Aquitainian prince in the ruined tower.
/ My star is dead, my constellated lute / Emblazoned with the black sun of despair." (trans. Derek Mahon).

If one stared through a wall
one would stare at a staring eye

Watch iris poppy lily flower expectant turn
unabashed welcoming wind or bee
30   Whose is this waiting for interminable waiting to end
who feeds back whom to whom   sells self short

So shaped solids men-like appeared to peer
Wind moved dust at heel   Wind's voices
Dust rose   Dust fell   Ever the same anew

35   When wind moved bell to ring night rushed in
made dark solid   bound power   and aimless

one waited   no reason to wait

Come from far to planet-fall   where no man lies

Like a view in a frame a peak in clear sky

40   Thence over paradisal sea over heavenly plain
gaze gaze   the sea the sea   Eden unbounded
ten-thousand-welcoming sea
and view yes view plain   Eden just come to be
fruitful the openarmed

45   Early victories on the upward path after
ranges chasms dawn-grey crests beginnings

There's mellow sun immeasurable horn of plenty and green
saurian ease it seemed limitless age after age

a world of its own   fulfilled   utterly fulfilled

50   Do memories suffuse flesh from that far back
the behind all archetypes   that silent world
Thence did height and length and breadth and depth
pre-stress primal slime   Do our dreams roam
that ever-recurring sea that pathless plain fading into pale sky
55   What absent heart might there have soared to the stars

41: *the sea the sea*: quoted from the *Anabasis* (4.7.24) of Xenophon (c.428–c.354 BC), an account of a military expedition led by Cyrus the Younger against his elder brother Artaxerxes II, king of Persia. His force, which included 10,000 Greek mercenaries, was defeated at Cunaxa, and Cyrus was killed; but the Greeks refused to surrender. Their retreat took them over the mountains of Armenia and through heavy fighting; when they climbed Mount Theches and saw the safe haven of the Black Sea, they shouted "*thalassa, thalassa!*" (the sea, the sea!).
48: *saurian*: pertaining to lizards (or, here, dinosaurs)
53: *pre-stress*: alluding to prestressed concrete, used in construction: while it is setting tensioned steel rods or wires are introduced into the concrete, so that after setting it is under compression and thus strengthened.

Tyrannic roaring   wrenched roots   gulped screams
millions of days and nights and unrecorded

Pollen-haze   trees spreading above feeding swarms
weather so constant dreaming it smooths one's brow
60   It was there the first of autumns laid leaf-carpet down
on a whole planet re-echoing thunder-tread
and not a single word broke the silence

Other oceans   and pain dreams   sighs soar
hateful the cold-blue sky the water-cold
65   Long it is since sail-man half-saw Blessed Isles
shift and waver on apple-sky at sea-rim
Those loners   circumvagrant wave after wave
of ocean   douse in heart faint fires
only grief alive in weather-beaten slaves

70   Other plains   and who now rises to toil-face
from mound tell barrow villa manor town
city glass and concrete walls like no hands and groping
The lonely people and not a seat to rest on
Move on Move on   No instant still   Broken
75   though sun reflect a Tir-na-n'og from factory roof
grief alone alive in ashen cheek

Straightened   no hill no valley   a working world
custom-built for no saviour Brother Big

Peace and security   barrel-bottom pittance
80   peace absence of choice
security presence of chains

Women alone men alone   barefaced the walls
constraint and blind eyes to play the guide

In the darkhouse They ask   "Who are you"
85   *Who are They* and you say perhaps so to please
"I am Flea Ghost" and They say   *Who are They*

56: *Tyrannic:* alluding to the large carnivorous dinosaur *Tyrannosaurus rex*

61: *thunder-tread:* alluding to the *Brontosaurus* ("thunder-lizard"), a huge plant-eating dinosaur.

65: *Blessed Isles:* in classical myth, these were somewhere in the west; the favorites of the Gods were taken there after their death to dwell in eternal joy.

71: Coffey names these traces of human building in historical order of their construction. A *tell* is an artificial mound formed by the accumulated ruins of earlier settlements. A *barrow* is an ancient gravemound. The *villa* is a classical Roman villa (country residence).

74: *Move on Move on:* the traditional policeman's words in telling a vagrant to get going

75: *Tir-na-n'og:* the supernatural land of eternal youth in Irish myth (akin to the Blessed Isles)

84: *darkhouse:* a darkened room in which a madman is housed

86: The poet-painter William Blake met the watercolorist and astrologer John Varley (1779–1842) in 1818; thereafter Blake frequently visited Varley's quarters for late-night sessions where he would draw spirits that came to him in visions. Blake once drew the ghost of a flea (half-flea, half-human, with a forked tongue); the subsequent oil painting he made of the image is one of his most frightening and visionary pictures.

          "Not ghostly but wit"   and you answer
          Are They Who   "You're funny today" and you turn
          to file-bank flick tabs enquire
90   "Do you like me" and They say "Call again
          when you trust"   "We" They say "care"

          Take care you ponder   Care not to touch
          care not to touch   care not to touch
          What's avoided three times ain't there

95   Under the hill I found the foiled people
          under the hill witted with witless endure
          under the hill give not take not

          Observe power-seeker court his frog people
          treacly-tempting voice promise to fetch them in
100   words to soothe he gives them words like *gold*
          silver comfort ease verb sap for the would-be-wise

          Who could he avoid it would slave his time in mines
          grub in rubble for gold in darkness chase silver vein
          or who but a fool would twitch in comfort ease
105   half-sleep in passing cloud by-passing peaks awake

          We and you and they greet us and you and them

          Such is one   us all some of you none of them

          How different from doll or angel in one's style
          action outside the doll's inane action still under dread angel gaze
110   but to surpass self's choosing at whose touch does self
          sacrifice self in freedom no selfwards motion shares

          Helpless crowd proceeds in fear that earns no wisdom
          How to turn off helplessness and waking face
          like eagle soaring the hopelessness that sours clay

115   Grey wisps of pain curl in wings and clueless we crawl
          when curtain falls on tired troupers from emptied hall
          We had seen in them ourselves plain

89: *file-bank:* i.e., a card-index

94: *What's avoided three times ain't there:* see Lewis Carroll, *The Hunting of the Snark* (1.8): "What I tell you three times is true."

101: *verb sap:* from the Latin tag, "verbum sapienti est" ("a word to the wise is enough")

108ff: Coffey draws on the Fourth *Duino Elegy,* by Rainer Maria Rilke (1875–1926), in which Rilke expresses disgust with "half-filled human masks" and prefers the puppet show, saying he will gaze "so hard at it that, finally, / To balance my gaze a performing angel has to come / And jerk the puppets into life" (trans. Ian Patterson). Rilke is drawing here on Heinrich von Kleist's essay "On the Marionette Theatre" (1810), which claims that "Grace appears most purely in that human form in which conscious-ness is either nonexistent or infinite, i.e., in the marionette or in the god." See also Rilke's essay "Some Reflections on Dolls" (1914).

109: *dread angel:* "Every angel is terrifying" (First *Duino Elegy*).

like valley opened by sun-shaft splitting swagging cloud
and out there stand forever the petrified trees

120   Oh might we walk again in fancy that wood by stream
note flash of spotted shaft bark of silk-white stem
skill that dams water it will bridge no fall
see us as simple selves on well-worn trail

Not that way with us not that way with human kind
125   we modify what we find and our markings yield no shore

Did Blake who gave a voice to dew ask
what hand what touch then or then a once event
induced in clay or stone metal or jade
the not yet heard of the not yet seen

130   And time and time so we see unglad unprofiting by death
souls stripped of honour gone to no return
the while blood dripped house burned new slave screaming ran
and so we see rubble where hand and touch did raise
Venus in bone laurel in flint marble cycladic head
135   maternal sorrow to writhe out of stone and instant sheer
bird in space bronze flight

Earthly vanishment   person and handiwork gone
We breathe in absence the negative abolished deeds

We say "We've had it" "Who can win" "Lost on both sides"
140   We soothe sour selves with "What recks it"
grab scraps of laugh-it-off pleasure now
at last to retch up scraps of knotted script
in hospice ward unreadied no great deed done

To dine on stone golden mountain arctic flower
145   the small advantage what's not

118: *swagging:* hanging heavily; cf. "The Argument" from Blake's *The Marriage of Heaven and Hell:* "Hungry clouds swag on the deep."

126: In Blake's *The Book of Thel* its protagonist lives in a dewy paradise; her questions about life's transience are answered by a lily of the valley, a cloud, a clod of clay and a worm (though not a dewdrop).

127: See Blake's poem "The Tyger": "Tyger, Tyger, burning bright, / In the forests of the night: / What immortal hand or eye, / Could frame thy fearful symmetry?"

134: Coffey compresses a history of ancient art into the line. *Venus* figures—small sculptured female figures with pronounced breasts and hips—were characteristic of Paleolithic art, and evidently functioned as fertility symbols. The *laurel in flint* is a Stone-Age flint arrowhead in the shape of a laurel leaf. The Bronze Age civilization of the *Cyclades* (a group of islands in the Aegean Sea) is famed for its white marble figurines.

135: *maternal sorrow:* Coffey likely has in mind Michelangelo's *Pietà.*

136: *bird in space:* the title of a number of bronze sculptures by Constantin Brancusi (1876–1957). Modernist artists often turned to ancient art for inspiration.

140: *What recks it:* What does it matter

144: *To dine on stone:* cf. "Hunger," a poem in *Une Saison en Enfer (A Season in Hell)* by Arthur Rimbaud (1854–1891): "If I have any appetite it is for rocks and stones"; the *arctic flower* is from Rimbaud's "Barbare" ("Barbarian," *Illuminations*): "The banner of raw meat against the silk of seas and arctic flowers; (they do not exist)." The *golden mountain* perhaps comes from the Grimms' fairy tale "The King of the Golden Mountain." For Coffey these poetical impossibilities are of questionable value: "the small advantage what's not."

Try the runner palm trees tell his dream
he cannot lengthen limbs cuts no knots

Let climber who heals no proud wounds
re-echoing "Because it was there"
150   from the top stare benevolent at lesser fry
self-commended go down to swallow unreflecting cheers
No dice there   Here today tomorrow wan

And rulers we call them eyes clamouring love-me-love-me-do
those magic men from water bowls display white hands
155   unsoiled that ease no pain inverted alchemists

The great deed no child's play
of ten-foot Texans sprinkling sunsets across their squatting broads
nor funny game of fancy men for Isthar Queen
Real exit scrubbed by real return
160   can you do that for us you miracle men

Think world with you
think total voiding all whatever naughted and you too
if once all with us were naught
could aught ever be

165   Yet we are here   Is it ourselves alone and unfulfilled

Want   Want   Want   Want   Want

So we moan and cry and rage and beg and beg an answer

Has no one he she or it called today

1975

147: *cuts no knots:* in Greek legend, whoever undid the Gordian knot was prophesied to rule all Asia. It defeated all attempts until Alexander the Great cut it with his sword.

148: *proud:* punning on "proud flesh," overgrown flesh around a healing wound

149: Asked why he wanted to climb Mount Everest, the mountaineer George Leigh Mallory (1886–1924) replied "Because it's there."

153: *love-me-love-me-do:* a sardonic reference to the Beatles' song "Love Me Do"

154: *display white hands:* as did Pontius Pilate (Matt. 27:24)

158: *fancy men:* paramours, lovers
    Isthar: the Mesopotamian goddess of love and war, sometimes called "Queen of the Universe."

159: *Real exit . . . real return:* Christ's death and resurrection

161: Coffey summarizes the third proof of the existence of God in the medieval theologian Thomas Aquinas's *Summa Theologica* (Part 1, Question 2, Third Article): all things in nature "are possible to be and not to be." "Therefore, if everything can not-be, then at one time there was nothing in existence"; and if there was nothing in the past, then even now there would still be nothing in existence. Thus, says Aquinas, there must be something whose existence is *necessary,* that cannot not-be; and since "every necessary thing either has its necessity caused by another, or not," and "it is impossible to go on to infinity in necessary things which have their necessity caused by another," there must be some necessarily existing being whose necessity comes of itself—i.e., God.

165: *ourselves alone:* Sinn Fein (Gaelic: "Ourselves") is an Irish nationalist party founded in 1907, its name alluding to Thomas Davis's ballad "Ourselves Alone." At the end of the war of independence the name was retained by those republicans who rejected the 1921 Anglo-Irish Treaty, but the movement went into decline after the Civil War, and was electorally demolished by de Valera's Fianna Fail. (This section of the poem was probably written before the creation, in the context of the renewed troubles in Northern Ireland, of the modern Sinn Fein party.)

WILLIAM EMPSON (1906–1984)

E MPSON'S *COLLECTED POEMS* (1955) IS A SLIM VOLUME, CONTAINING ONLY 56 POEMS. Syntactically dense, paradoxical and punning, Empson's "metaphysical" poems— the term refers to the poetic mode of John Donne rather than to philosophy—have the appeal of well-honed arguments. Learned references, Latinate words, a tone of intellection can make his poems bristle with confident proposition, until we note the unexpected usage or comparison in pursuit of comic effect: "Lucretius could not credit centaurs; / Such bicycle he deemed asynchronous" ("Invitation to Juno").[1] Similarly, while Empson will allude to abstruse concepts from science not always standard fare for poetry, he is not above using a colloquial idiom: "For all the loony hooters can be bought / On the small ball" ("Sonnet").[2] The typical effect is a kind of resonance one might well call wit, an exactitude one recognizes after the fact. If their dominant tenor is sardonic, the poems can also suggest strong emotion—anger at the vapid political discourse of the day, despair at life's complexities unraveling into meaning- lessness and forgetfulness: "It is this deep blankness is the real thing strange. / The more things happen to you the more you can't / Tell or remember even what they were" ("Let it go").[3] Many of the poems can be usefully glossed by Empson's own crit- icism, among the most influential of his era—the study of poetic ambiguity in his first book, *Seven Types of Ambiguity* (1930), the argument with Christianity in the last book published in his lifetime, *Milton's God* (1961). Empson's poems were praised by F. R. Leavis and influenced a host of poets from Richard Eberhart and John Wain to Richard Wilbur and Veronica Forrest-Thomson. Forrest-Thomson writes that "As poet, theorist, and critic Empson illustrates the most fruitful tensions in the poetic culture of the century and provides many suggestive points of departure."[4]

Empson was descended from landed gentry and grew up on a 4,000-acre estate beside the river Ouse in Yorkshire. He was educated at Winchester College and Mag- dalene College at Cambridge University, where his tutor was I. A. Richards. At Cam- bridge, he edited the magazine *Experiment* with Jacob Bronowski and Hugh Sykes Davies. He taught at universities in Japan and China and subsequently became pro- fessor of English at Sheffield University. In 1979, he was knighted for his services to arts and letters in England.

---

[1] *Collected Poems,* London, 1955, p. 5.
[2] Ibid., p. 83.
[3] Ibid., p. 81.
[4] *Poetic Artifice: A Theory of Twentieth-Century Poetry,* Manchester, UK, 1978, p. xiv.

Plenum and Vacuum

Delicate goose-step of penned scorpions
Patrols its weal under glass-cautered bubble;
Postpones, fire-cinct, their suicide defiance,
Pierced carapace stung in mid vault of bell.

5   From infant screams the eyes' blood-gorged veins
Called ringed orbiculars to guard their balls;
These stays squeeze yet eyes no relief ensanguines,
These frowns, sphincter, void-centred, burst wrinkled hold-alls.

Matter includes what must matter enclose,
10   Its consequent space, the glass firmament's air-holes.
Heaven's but an attribute of her seven rainbows.
It is Styx coerces and not Hell controls.

1935

Villanelle

It is the pain, it is the pain, endures.
Your chemic beauty burned my muscles through.
Poise of my hands reminded me of yours.

What later purge from this deep toxin cures?
5   What kindness now could the old salve renew?
It is the pain, it is the pain, endures.

We are indebted to Philip and Averil Gardner's *The God Approached: A Commentary on the Poems of William Empson* (London: Chatto & Windus, 1978) for some of our glosses.

Plenum and Vacuum: "The thought supposed to be common to the examples is that the object has become empty so that one is left with an unescapable system of things each nothing in itself." (Empson's note)
Title: *Plenum:* a space completely filled with matter
1: Scorpions are said to "kill themselves when put under glass and frightened with fire; Darwin tried this, but I forget whether it was true or not." (Empson's note)
2: *weal:* commonweal, nation; but also "the scar of a burn, made as the glass was"; and "the gain [weal] of death" (Empson)
   cautered: cauterized
3: *cinct:* encircled
5–8: "'The veins produced eye muscles to guard the eyeballs from screams.' The screaming-fit is supposed to be abandoned by civilised people, so that the machinery of facial expression depends on a central reality no longer present." (Empson)
7: *stays:* supports; corsets
   ensanguines: "makes bloody or hopeful" (Empson)
9: Matter includes space, which in turn includes matter. "Matter *includes* space on relativity theory, in a logical not spatial sense, because from a given distribution of matter you might calculate the space-time in which it seems to move freely. The line is not meant to be read as anapaests [i.e., the stress is on 'what']." (Empson). Matter includes space because atoms are composed of smaller particles with space between them.
10: "the space not in our space-time, which we cannot enter, is thought of as glass with the universe as a bubble in it." (Empson)
11: *seven:* from the seven colors of the spectrum
12: The *Styx* is one of the rivers surrounding Hades, the underworld of classical mythology; its waters were lethal, and Milton called it "the flood of deadly hate" (*Paradise Lost* 2.577). "'Noviens Styx interfusa coercet' ['Styx imprisons with his ninefold circles': Virgil, *Aeneid* 6.439]; not Hell but its surrounding hatred is real and a cause of action." (Empson)

The infection slept (custom or change inures)
And when pain's secondary phase was due
Poise of my hands reminded me of yours.

10   How safe I felt, whom memory assures,
Rich that your grace safely by heart I knew.
It is the pain, it is the pain, endures.

My stare drank deep beauty that still allures.
My heart pumps yet the poison draught of you.
15   Poise of my hands reminded me of yours.

You are still kind whom the same shape immures.
Kind and beyond adieu. We miss our cue.
It is the pain, it is the pain, endures.
Poise of my hands reminded me of yours.

                                                          1935

Reflection from Rochester

"But wretched Man is still in arms for Fear."

"From fear to fear, successively betrayed"—
By making risks to give a cause for fear
(Feeling safe with causes, and from birth afraid),

By climbing higher not to look down, by mere
5   Destruction of the accustomed because strange
(Too complex a loved system, or too clear),

By needing change but not too great a change
And therefore a new fear—man has achieved
All the advantage of a wider range,

10   Successfully has the first fear deceived,
Thought the wheels run on sleepers. This is not
The law of nature it has been believed.

Increasing power (it has increased a lot)
Embarrasses "attempted suicides,"
15   Narrows their margin. Policies that got

Epigraph: see "A Satire against Mankind", by John Wilmot, Earl of Rochester (1647–1680): "For hunger or for love they [animals] fight or tear, / Whilst wretched Man is still [i.e., always] in arms for fear; / For fear he arms, and is of arms afraid, / By fear, to fear, successively betrayed." (139–42). In this passage Rochester argues, as Empson's poem puts it, that such perpetual fear is "not / The law of nature."

11: *sleepers:* the timbers that hold up railway tracks, though Empson also puns on "sleeping people" (perhaps "sleeping fears")

13–15: "The idea is that nationalist war is getting to a crisis because the machines make it too dangerous and expensive to be serviceable even in the queer marginal ways it used to be." (Empson). This idea is expressed by the metaphor of someone who makes a suicide attempt without actually intending to kill himself; the increasing power of gas stoves has shrunk the margin for error and increased the chance of actual death.

"Virility from war" get much besides;
The mind, as well in mining as in gas
War's parallel, now less easily decides

On a good root-confusion to amass
20   Much safety from irrelevant despair.
Mere change in numbers made the process crass.

We now turn blank eyes for a pattern there
Where first the race of armament was made;
Where a less involute compulsion played.
25   "For hunger or for love they bite and tear."

                                                        1940

Sonnet

Not wrongly moved by this dismaying scene
    The thinkers like the nations getting caught
    Joined in the organising that they fought
To scorch all earth of all but one machine.

5   It can be swung, is what these hopers mean,
        For all the loony hooters can be bought
        On the small ball. It can then all be taught
And reconverted to be kind and clean.

A more heartening fact about the cultures of man
10   Is their appalling stubbornness. The sea
Is always calm ten fathoms down. The gigan-

-tic anthropological circus riotously
Holds open all its booths. The pygmy plan
    Is one note each and the tune goes out free.

                                                        1945

17–21: "The mind uses unconscious processes (mining underground) and an outpouring of loose words, sometimes poisonous (gas); the reasons that make the thought of a country succeed can be as queer as the reasons that sometimes make war good for it, and a mere change of proportion might make either fail to work any longer." (Empson)

22–25: We now look for models in the behavior of animals, whose "compulsion" is at least less "involute" (curved in on itself; complex) than ours.

13–14: The "pygmy plan" is that of lines 1–8. "This *free* I am afraid only sounds an offensively false use of the great emotive term, implying merely that the pygmies and the rest of us had better be 'left alone.' This may be true of pygmies, but I was trying to give the word the impact of a contradiction. . . . The pygmy method of singing (on the sound-track of an excellent travel film) sounded spontaneous though it was a grotesque and extreme example of collectivism." (Empson)

SAMUEL BECKETT (1906–1989)

THE MAJORITY OF THE POEMS BECKETT CHOSE TO INCLUDE IN HIS *COLLECTED POEMS in English and French* (1977) were written in the 1930s. Partly because he published few poems, and partly because he is widely regarded as among the most important novelists and dramatists of the century, Beckett's poems have received little attention. This is surprising given the way that his prose, in books such as *Watt* (1953) and *Pour finir encore et autres foirades* ([1976]; in English *Fizzles* [1976]), often points to the arbitrariness of generic distinctions between prose fiction and poetry. A good deal of what one finds in Beckett's prose can be found in miniature in his poems—the choleric personality obsessed with the absurdity and complexity of the most mundane events, the crisis of the subject in a world torn free of its moorings in Christianity, the low comedy of the body and of daily life. The poems are not as fully realized as the prose, but they have a small but significant place within modernist and Irish poetry. Beckett's observations concerning Irish poetry in his essay "Recent Irish Poetry" (1934) link him with a group of poets including his friends Thomas MacGreevy, Denis Devlin, and Brian Coffey. "Oisin, Cuchulain, Maeve, Tir-nanog, the Táin Bo Cuailgne, Yoga, the Crone of Beare"—these Irish characters and myths were only sentimental décor, he wrote, used by "antiquarians" and "thermolators."[1] While Beckett cared little for the parochial interests of the Irish Literary Revival, his poems are equally skeptical of another tendency in a more international modernism—the "mythical method" T. S. Eliot located in James Joyce's *Ulysses*. In the narrative fragments of "Eneug I" the speaker wanders an Eliotic wasteland on "ruined feet" in "a wrecked wind" but remains curiously ambivalent about "the mind annulled"; unlike Eliot, Beckett is never nostalgic for a culturally rich past, refusing "the arctic flowers / that do not exist." As Patricia Coughlan writes, Beckett "is quite outside the kinship of Eliot and Yeats in shoring fragments against their ruins or seeking Unity of Being, just as he cannot share his Irish contemporaries' enthusiasm for the nation."[2]

Beckett was born near Dublin in Foxrock, and raised as a Protestant by a deeply religious mother. He was educated at Portora Royal School, Enniskillen, and Trinity College, Dublin. After lecturing in Belfast and Paris (where he first met Joyce and MacGreevy) and then in Dublin at Trinity College, he abandoned an academic career. He spent five years living in Germany, France, Ireland, and London before settling permanently in Paris. During World War II, he was part of the French Resistance and had to leave Paris in 1942 to avoid arrest by the Gestapo. Among his plays, collections

---

[1] Reprinted in *Disjecta: Miscellaneous Writings and a Dramatic Fragment by Samuel Beckett*, ed. Ruby Cohn, New York, 1984, p. 71.
[2] "'The Poetry is Another Pair of Sleeves,'" in *Modernism and Ireland: The Poetry of the 1930s*, ed. Patricia Coughlan and Alex Davis, Cork, 1995, p. 179.

of stories, and novels are *More Pricks than Kicks* (1934), *Murphy* (1938), *Molloy* (1951), *Malone Muert* ([1951]; in English *Malone Dies* [1958]), *En attendant Godot* ([1952]; in English *Waiting for Godot* [1955]), *L'Innommable* ([1953]; in English *The Unnamable* [1960]), and *Krapp's Last Tape* (1958). His poems in English were first published in *Whoroscope* (1930) and *Echo's Bones* (1934). Beckett was awarded the Nobel Prize for Literature in 1969.

Enueg I

        Exeo in a spasm
        tired of my darling's red sputum
        from the Portobello Private Nursing Home
        its secret things
5   and toil to the crest of the surge of the steep perilous bridge
        and lapse down blankly under the scream of the hoarding
        round the bright stiff banner of the hoarding
        into a black west
        throttled with clouds.

10   Above the mansions the algum-trees
        the mountains
        my skull sullenly
        clot of anger
        skewered aloft strangled in the cang of the wind
15   bites like a dog against its chastisement.

        I trundle along rapidly now on my ruined feet
        flush with the livid canal;
        at Parnell Bridge a dying barge
        carrying a cargo of nails and timber
20   rocks itself softly in the foaming cloister of the lock;
        on the far bank a gang of down and outs would seem to be mending a
            beam.

        Then for miles only wind
        and the weals creeping alongside on the water
        and the world opening up to the south

We are indebted for some of our notes to Lawrence Harvey's *Samuel Beckett: Poet and Critic* (Princeton, 1970).

Title: Beckett's note to this and the next poem: "Written in the form of a Provençal dirge or lament. The poet at the time was a lecturer at Trinity College." Beckett is actually fusing two poetic genres, the *planh* (a lament) and the *enueg* ("vexation"), a discontinuous list of things that annoy the poet.

1: *Exeo:* "I depart" (Latin)

3: "The Portobello House is a very real building that still exists, facing the Grand Canal in south Dublin." (Harvey)

4: *its secret things:* quoted from Dante, *Inferno* 3.21: the "secret things" are those of Hell, whose gate Dante has just entered with his guide Virgil.

6: *hoarding:* a fence made of boards put up around a construction site (usually covered with advertise-ments)

10: *algum-trees:* mentioned in the Bible (2 Chron. 2:8, 9:10–11; 1 Kings 10:11): a name for sandalwood. "Used because of the similarity to the Greek *algos* ('pain')" (Harvey).

14: *cang:* a wooden frame worn round the neck, used in China as a kind of portable pillory

18: *Parnell Bridge:* named after the Irish nationalist leader Charles Stuart Parnell (1846–1891)

25   across a travesty of champaign to the mountains
        and the stillborn evening turning a filthy green
        manuring the night fungus
        and the mind annulled
        wrecked in wind.

30   I splashed past a little wearish old man,
        Democritus,
        scuttling along between a crutch and a stick,
        his stump caught up horribly, like a claw, under his breech, smoking.
        Then because a field on the left went up in a sudden blaze
35   of shouting and urgent whistling and scarlet and blue ganzies
        I stopped and climbed the bank to see the game.
        A child fidgeting at the gate called up:
        "Would we be let in Mister?"
        "Certainly" I said "you would."
40   But, afraid, he set off down the road.
        "Well" I called after him "why wouldn't you go on in?"
        "Oh" he said, knowingly,
        "I was in that field before and I got put out."
        So on,
45   derelict,
        as from a bush of gorse on fire in the mountain after dark,
        or in Sumatra the jungle hymen,
        the still flagrant rafflesia.

        Next:
50   a lamentable family of grey verminous hens,
        perishing out in the sunk field,
        trembling, half asleep, against the closed door of a shed,
        with no means of roosting.
        The great mushy toadstool,
55   green-black,
        oozing up after me,
        soaking up the tattered sky like an ink of pestilence,
        in my skull the wind going fetid,
        the water . . .

60   Next:
        on the hill down from the Fox and Geese into Chapelizod
        a small malevolent goat, exiled on the road,
        remotely pucking the gate of his field;
        the Isolde Stores a great perturbation of sweaty heroes,
65   in their Sunday best,

25: *champaign:* open country
30: *wearish:* wizened
31: The Greek philosopher *Democritus* (460 BC–c.370 BC), often called "the laughing philosopher," presented an early atomic theory of matter.
35: *ganzies:* jerseys. The players are playing hurling, an Irish sport similar to field hockey, promoted by the Gaelic Athletic Association as part of the cultural nationalism of the 1890s on.
48: *rafflesia:* a parasitic Sumatran plant, noted for its gigantic flowers and foul smell
61: *Fox and Geese:* a small suburb; *Chapelizod* is a town outside Dublin, where a bridge crosses the River Liffey.
63: *pucking:* butting; but the Gaelic word for a male goat is *pocán.*
64: The *Isolde Stores* are no longer in existence; the name alludes to the Celtic legend of the doomed lovers Tristan and Isolde (as does Chapelizod, "Chapel of Isolde").

come hastening down for a pint of nepenthe or moly or half and half
from watching the hurlers above in Kilmainham.

Blotches of doomed yellow in the pit of the Liffey;
the fingers of the ladders hooked over the parapet,
70   soliciting;
a slush of vigilant gulls in the grey spew of the sewer.

Ah the banner
the banner of meat bleeding
on the silk of the seas and the arctic flowers
75   that do not exist.

1935

Enueg II

world world world world
and the face grave
cloud against the evening

de morituris nihil nisi

5   and the face crumbling shyly
too late to darken the sky
blushing away into the evening
shuddering away like a gaffe

veronica mundi
10   veronica munda
gives us a wipe for the love of Jesus

sweating like Judas
tired of dying
tired of policemen
15   feet in marmalade

66: *nepenthe*: a drug said to induce forgetfulness of trouble or sorrow

    moly: a magical herb, like nepenthe mentioned in the *Odyssey*. Odysseus's shipmates are turned into swine by the sorceress Circe; Odysseus, protected by moly given him by the god Hermes, compels Circe to restore his shipmates to human shape.

    half and half: a mixture of ale and porter

67: *Kilmainham*: a Dublin suburb; Parnell was imprisoned in Kilmainham Gaol in 1881, and in more recent memory it had housed members of the IRA.

72ff: This stanza translates a sentence from Rimbaud's prose-poem "Barbare" ("Barbarian") in *Illumina-tions*. The passage runs: "Long after the days and the seasons, and people and countries. / The banner of raw meat against the silk of seas and arctic flowers; (they do not exist). / Recovered from the old fanfares of heroism,—which still attack the heart and head,—far from the old assassins."

4: The Latin tag "De mortuis nil nisi bonum" ("Of the dead say nothing but good") is altered to "Of those about to die say nothing but. . . ."; Beckett may also echo the traditional salute of gladiators to the Roman Emperor: "Ave Caesar, morituri te salutant" ("Hail Caesar, those who about to die salute you").

8: *gaffe*: faux pas; but Beckett may have the image of a ship's sail in mind (a "gaff" is a spar on which the top of a fore-and-aft sail is extended).

9–10: "veronica of the world / pure veronica." Veronica is a legendary woman said to have wiped Christ's brow with her kerchief as he carried the cross to Golgotha; the kerchief is said to have been imprinted with the image of his face.

perspiring profusely
heart in marmalade
smoke more fruit
the old heart the old heart
20   breaking outside congress
doch I assure thee
lying on O'Connell Bridge
goggling at the tulips of the evening
the green tulips
25   shining round the corner like an anthrax
shining on Guinness's barges

the overtone the face
too late to brighten the sky
doch doch I assure thee

1935

Ooftish

offer it up plank it down
Golgotha was only the potegg
cancer angina it is all one to us
cough up your T.B. don't be stingy
5   no trifle is too trifling not even a thrombus
anything venereal is especially welcome
that old toga in the mothballs
don't be sentimental you won't be wanting it again
send it along we'll put it in the pot with the rest
10   with your love requited and unrequited
the things taken too late the things taken too soon
the spirit aching bullock's scrotum
you won't cure it you won't endure it
it is you it equals you any fool has to pity you
15   so parcel up the whole issue and send it along
the whole misery diagnosed undiagnosed misdiagnosed
get your friends to do the same we'll make use of it
we'll make sense of it we'll put it in the pot with the rest
it all boils down to blood of lamb

1938

18: cf. the 1930s advertising slogan, "Eat more fruit."
21: Harvey notes Beckett's use of "the German *doch* for lack of an English equivalent of the strong con-
    tradictory positive"; the line could be rendered: "but, yes, truly I assure thee."
22: *O'Connell Bridge:* Dublin's main bridge over the Liffey
26: Barges are floating barrels of *Guinness* (a dark stout) down the river.

Title: *Ooftish:* "The title is a Yiddish expression meaning 'put your money down on the table.'" (Beckett).
    "The starting point for the poem was a sermon [Beckett] had once heard in Ireland. The preacher, in
    describing his visits to the sick, confessed, 'What gets me down is pain. The only thing I can tell them is
    that the crucifixion was only the beginning. You must contribute to the kitty.'" (Harvey)
2: *Golgotha* ("skull") was the hill on which Christ was crucified. A *potegg* is "a dummy nest egg for a fowl"
    (Harvey).
5: *thrombus:* blood-clot
7: *toga:* a reference to the *toga virilis*, worn by Roman boys to indicate having reached puberty, and used
    metonymically to refer to potency
19: *blood of lamb:* i.e., the blood of Christ (Rev 7:14)

W. H. AUDEN (1907–1973)

REVIEWING AUDEN'S WORK IN 1932, GEOFFREY GRIGSON WROTE OF AN "ANGRY POET" and a verse "distinguished by the most extraordinary vigour."[1] Two years later, Auden's international reputation was sufficiently established for the American poet-critic Robert Penn Warren to describe him as "the satirist of the English 'poetic renascence,'" words echoing *Poetry* magazine's earlier proclamation of a "new dawn" in British poetry.[2] The reception of Auden's early work was not uniform—Stephen Spender wrote defending the poetry against charges of "obscurity"—but Auden's early success was such that few in the 1930s would have contested his status as the leading poet of his generation. To the end of his life Auden remained one of the most influential poets writing in English, though there is much less critical consensus about the value of his later poetry.

It is something of a convention now to divide Auden's poetry into early and late, with several roughly contemporary key events serving as a dividing line: his departure for the United States shortly before the outbreak of World War II, his return to the Anglican church of his youth, the death of his mother in 1941. For the most part, it is the "English Auden" of the 1930s whose reputation has fared better, though the influence of the later Auden on a generation of American poets including James Merrill, Anthony Hecht, and Richard Wilbur cannot be overestimated. We can see the tendency to judge the early work against the late in the remarks of Philip Larkin, who in 1960 stated what he took to be the consensus view: Auden was "a tremendously exciting English social poet full of energetic unliterary knock-about and unique lucidity of phrase" who became "an engaging, bookish, American talent, too verbose to be memorable and too intellectual to be moving."[3] Similarly, C. H. Sisson praises the precocious facility with verse forms evident in early poems but goes on to say that this same facility "vitiates most of Auden's later work": "The trouble about Auden's verse in discursive vein is that he is not, as he writes, in the process of discovering something for himself; he is the pedagogue or doctor advising others what truth is."[4] Thinking of Auden's influence in the United States, the American poet Karl Shapiro complained that Auden "brought to perfection what everyone nowadays [1960] calls the Academic Poem."[5] For Shapiro's epithet "academic" others would substitute words such as urbane and cosmopolitan. About the only matter critics in various camps will agree

---

1 "The Poet and the Enemy," rpt. in *W. H. Auden: The Critical Heritage,* ed. John Haffenden, London, 1983, p. 106.
2 Rpt. in Haffenden, p. 129.
3 "What's Become of Wystan?" in *Required Writing: Miscellaneous Pieces 1955–1982,* London, 1983, p. 123.
4 *English Poetry 1900–1950,* London, 1971, p. 211.
5 *In Defense of Ignorance,* New York, 1960, p. 126.

on is that a poetry and poetics identified with the center of a post-World War II consensus culture in Britain and the United States is unimaginable without Auden's later work.

The early Auden is credited by the same readers as "the first 'modern' poet, in that he could employ modern properties unselfconsciously" (Larkin) and as the source of a "revolution in diction," which could exploit the possibilities for poetry of "all the jargons, from social science to advertising, accepting them as current languages of communication, allowing for just enough irony of tone to save himself from being identified with these jargons" (Shapiro). The early Auden assimilated Anglo-Saxon syntax and the stark idioms of Icelandic sagas along with imagery and techniques derived from sources as diverse as John Skelton, Thomas Hardy, T. S. Eliot, Laura Riding, and Bertolt Brecht. "The stress of Anglo-Saxon metre and the gnomic clunk of Anglo-Saxon phrasing were pulled like a harrow against the natural slope of social speech and iambic lyric," Seamus Heaney writes, celebrating Auden's openings, wherein a reader is "set down in the middle of a cold landscape, blindfolded, turned rapidly around, unblindfolded, ordered to march and to make sense of every ominous thing encountered from there on."[6] The early Auden was at the center of a group of associated poets—Stephen Spender, C. Day Lewis, Louis MacNeice, Bernard Spencer—who became spokesmen for a generation, voicing a leftist critique of England's rigid social structure and contemporary decadence, as expressed by Auden in his psychologized landscapes and images of closed factories and abandoned machines. This was the modernist Auden of *Poems* and also the *The Orators* (1932), perhaps his most experimental book, the Auden who was assimilating in prose and poetry the views of Freud, Marx, and D. H. Lawrence.

The concentrated manner of Auden's early verse had already been replaced by a more relaxed and colloquial style by the time of "Letter to Lord Byron" (1936), with its pastiche of Byron's *Don Juan,* but it is the more explicitly Horatian style of the verse essays and epistles of the 1940s that has seemed to many to reflect his move away from liberal humanism and an explicitly politicized stance toward a Christian existentialism influenced by Kierkegaard and Reinhold Niebuhr. Debate on the value of early and late poems has often crystallized around Auden's practice of revision; numerous essays and books have responded to his decision to omit poems from his canon or to cut or revise lines that he later came to feel were dishonest. This debate is inevitable, given the career trajectory sketched above, the changing circumstances of the world he lived in, and Auden's remarkable productivity, positively Victorian in its dimensions and reflecting a similar work ethic.

In her memoir of Auden, Hannah Arendt stresses the importance to him of years spent in Germany at the end of the Weimar republic, when "Carpe diem was practiced daily" in a culture of "animal *tristesse.*" This is one context, she argues, for Auden's later Christian moralism and political quietism: "There was nothing more admirable in him than his complete sanity and his firm belief in the sanity of the mind; all kinds of madness were in his eyes lack of discipline—'naughty, naughty', as he used to say. The main thing was to have no illusions and to accept no thoughts, no theoretical systems that would blind you against reality."[7] Among Auden's greatest work reflecting his Christianity is the sequence of Horatian odes entitled "Horae Canonicae," his meditation on the Crucifixion as its meaning is reenacted in everyday lives.

Auden was raised in Birmingham and educated at Gresham's School, Holt and Christ Church, Oxford. His first book, *Poems,* was privately printed by Stephen Spender in 1928 and then accepted by Eliot for publication by Faber and Faber in 1930. The years between found him in Germany and teaching school in England. *The Orators* appeared in 1932; it was later nearly renounced by Auden. During the mid-1930s, Auden was also associated with Rupert Doone's Group Theatre, which produced his

---

6 "Sounding Auden," *The Government of the Tongue,* London, 1988, p. 117.
7 "Remembering Wystan H. Auden," *W. H. Auden: A Tribute,* ed. Stephen Spender, London, 1975, p. 184.

play *The Dance of Death* (1933) and several others written with Christopher Isherwood, including *The Dog Beneath the Skin* (1935). Working with the GPO Film Unit in 1935, he met Benjamin Britten, who later set some of Auden's poems to music. In 1935, he married Erika Mann, the daughter of the novelist Thomas Mann, so that she could obtain a British passport to leave Nazi Germany. A trip to Iceland with Louis MacNeice produced their jointly written *Letters from Iceland* (1937). In 1937, Auden spent several months in Spain in support of the Loyalist, anti-fascist cause; he had meant to drive an ambulance but was put to work writing propaganda for broadcasts that reached only the local English-speaking audience. In 1938, he went with Isherwood to China to witness the hostilities between China and Japan; the co-authored *Journey to a War* (1939) followed. *Another Time* appeared in 1940; it contains some of Auden's most famous poems, including "September 1, 1939" and "Museé des Beaux Arts" and the first poems he wrote in America. After Auden emigrated to the United States in January 1939 (he was to become a U.S. citizen in 1946), he was based primarily in Brooklyn, where he assisted with a boarding-house for artists, while also teaching at various colleges, including Swarthmore and Bryn Mawr. At the end of World War II, he was briefly in Europe with the U.S. Army as a civilian researcher with an honorary rank, but New York remained his home until, in later years, he began dividing his time between New York and a house near Vienna, with periodic stays on a Mediterranean island near Naples. In New York, Auden met his lifelong companion Chester Kallman, who collaborated with him for several of the opera librettos Auden wrote in the United States, including one for Igor Stravinsky's *The Rake's Progress*, which opened in 1951. The 1940s saw a series of longer works: "New Year Letter" in *The Double Man* (1941); "For the Time Being" (subtitled "A Christmas Oratorio") and "The Sea and the Mirror" (subtitled "A Commentary on Shakespeare's *The Tempest*") in *For the Time Being* (1944); and *The Age of Anxiety: A Baroque Eclogue* (1947), which won a Pulitzer Prize. Auden's reputation in the United States was confirmed by Random House's publication in 1945 of *The Collected Poetry*, which was to be reprinted numerous times and sell upwards of 50,000 copies. For this volume Auden reordered, revised, and omitted older poems, provided titles for poems previously untitled, and included twenty-one new poems written after *Another Time*, including versions of some of his most famous verse letters. The major books of the 1950s were *Nones* (1951) and *The Shield of Achilles* (1955), the latter containing "In Praise of Limestone," "Bucolics," and the entire sequence of "Horae Canonicae." In 1956, Auden was professor of poetry at Oxford. He was judge and editor of the Yale Younger Poets Series from 1947 to 1959, selecting first books by writers including John Ashbery and Adrienne Rich. *Homage to Clio* was published in 1960, to be followed over the next decade by a host of publications, the most important of them editions of his earlier poems and collections of his essays, including *The Dyer's Hand and Other Essays*, which appeared in 1962, the year Auden also became a fellow of Christ Church, Oxford. In the last few years before his death in Vienna, Auden produced two collections, *City without Walls* (1969) and *Epistle to a Godson* (1972). *Thank You, Fog* appeared posthumously in 1974. Most of Auden's poetry is now collected in two volumes edited by his executor Edward Mendelson, *Collected Poems* (1976) and *The English Auden* (1978). He also edited many collections, including the *Oxford Book of Light Verse* (1938); Auden's defense of that genre bears continuing consideration.

"Bones wrenched, weak whimper, lids wrinkled . . ."

Bones wrenched, weak whimper, lids wrinkled, first dazzle known,
World-wonder hardened as bigness, years, brought knowledge, you:
Presence a rich mould augured for roots urged—but gone,
The soul is tetanus; gun-barrel burnishing
5   In summer grass, mind lies to tarnish, untouched, undoing,
Though body stir to sweat, or, squat as idol, brood,
Infuriate the fire with bellows, blank till sleep
And two-faced dream—'I want', voiced treble as once
Crudely through flowers till dunghill cockcrow, crack at East.
10   Eyes, unwashed jewels, the glass floor slipping, feel, know Day,
Life stripped to girders, monochrome. Deceit of instinct,
Features, figure, form irrelevant, dismissed
Ought passes through points fair plotted and you conform,
Seen yes or no, too just for weeping argument.

1927 / 1928

The Secret Agent

Control of the passes was, he saw, the key
To this new district, but who would get it?
He, the trained spy, had walked into the trap
For a bogus guide, seduced by the old tricks.

5   At Greenhearth was a fine site for a dam
And easy power, had they pushed the rail
Some stations nearer. They ignored his wires:
The bridges were unbuilt and trouble coming.

The street music seemed gracious now to one
10   For weeks up in the desert. Woken by water
Running away in the dark, he often had
Reproached the night for a companion
Dreamed of already. They would shoot, of course,
Parting easily two that were never joined.

1928 / 1928

We are indebted at several points to John Fuller's *W.H. Auden: A Commentary* (London, 1998). We have generally followed Auden's final (1966) versions of texts; when we have not done so this is indicated in the notes.

Auden dropped "Bones wrenched, weak whimper, lids wrinkled . . ." from his canon from 1933 onwards.
3: *mould:* soil
4: *tetanous:* infected with tetanus (lockjaw)

14: This line is from the Old English poem "Wulf and Eadwacer": "þaet mon eaþe tosliteð þaette naefre gesomnad waes" ("They can easily part that which was never joined together"). The poem is spoken by a woman separated from her lover by the enmity of their clans.

The Watershed

Who stands, the crux left of the watershed,
On the wet road between the chafing grass
Below him sees dismantled washing-floors,
Snatches of tramline running to a wood,
5   An industry already comatose,
Yet sparsely living. A ramshackle engine
At Cashwell raises water; for ten years
It lay in flooded workings until this,
Its latter office, grudgingly performed.
10   And, further, here and there, though many dead
Lie under the poor soil, some acts are chosen,
Taken from recent winters; two there were
Cleaned out a damaged shaft by hand, clutching
The winch a gale would tear them from; one died
15   During a storm, the fells impassable,
Not at his village, but in wooden shape
Through long abandoned levels nosed his way
And in his final valley went to ground.

Go home, now, stranger, proud of your young stock,
20   Stranger, turn back again, frustrate and vexed:
This land, cut off, will not communicate,
Be no accessory content to one
Aimless for faces rather there than here.
Beams from your car may cross a bedroom wall,
25   They wake no sleeper; you may hear the wind
Arriving driven from the ignorant sea
To hurt itself on pane, on bark of elm
Where sap unbaffled rises, being spring;
But seldom this. Near you, taller than grass,
30   Ears poise before decision, scenting danger.

1927 / 1928

"Consider this and in our time"

Consider this and in our time
As the hawk sees it or the helmeted airman:
The clouds rift suddenly—look there
At cigarette-end smouldering on a border
5   At the first garden party of the year.
Pass on, admire the view of the massif
Through plate-glass windows of the Sport Hotel;
Join there the insufficient units

3ff: The observer sees the remnants of the nineteenth-century lead-mining industry. The *washing-floors* were where crushed ore was sieved to extract galena (lead sulfide).

"Consider this and in our time": Text: 1930; later texts, beginning in 1945, are titled "Consider," with lines 42–49 omitted.
6: *massif*: mountain

Dangerous, easy, in furs, in uniform
10   And constellated at reserved tables
Supplied with feelings by an efficient band
Relayed elsewhere to farmers and their dogs
Sitting in kitchens in the stormy fens.

Long ago, supreme Antagonist,
15   More powerful than the great northern whale
Ancient and sorry at life's limiting defect,
In Cornwall, Mendip, or the Pennine moor
Your comments on the highborn mining-captains,
Found they no answer, made them wish to die
20   —Lie since in barrows out of harm.
You talk to your admirers every day
By silted harbours, derelict works,
In strangled orchards, and the silent comb
Where dogs have worried or a bird was shot.
25   Order the ill that they attack at once:
Visit the ports and, interrupting
The leisurely conversation in the bar
Within a stone's throw of the sunlit water,
Beckon your chosen out. Summon
30   Those handsome and diseased youngsters, those women
Your solitary agents in the country parishes;
And mobilise the powerful forces latent
In soils that make the farmer brutal
In the infected sinus, and the eyes of stoats.
35   Then, ready, start your rumour, soft
But horrifying in its capacity to disgust
Which, spreading magnified, shall come to be
A polar peril, a prodigious alarm,
Scattering the people, as torn-up paper
40   Rags and utensils in a sudden gust,
Seized with immeasurable neurotic dread.

Financier, leaving your little room
Where the money is made but not spent,
You'll need your typist and your boy no more;
45   The game is up for you and for the others,
Who, thinking, pace in slippers on the lawns
Of College Quad or Cathedral Close,
Who are born nurses, who live in shorts
Sleeping with people and playing fives.
50   Seekers after happiness, all who follow
The convolutions of your simple wish,
It is later than you think; nearer that day
Far other than that distant afternoon

14: *Antagonist:* The name "Satan" means "adversary" in Hebrew. Both the Old English *Bestiary* and Milton's *Paradise Lost* (1.200) compare Satan and the whale.
17: *Cornwall* and *Mendip* (a district in Somerset) are in southern England; the *Pennines* are a system of mountains and hills in northern England.
20: *barrows:* gravemounds
23: *comb:* or coomb, a hollow or valley on the side of a hill
49: *fives:* a ballgame played in English public schools

Amid rustle of frocks and stamping feet
55   They gave the prizes to the ruined boys.
You cannot be away, then, no
Not though you pack to leave within an hour,
Escaping humming down arterial roads:
The date was yours; the prey to fugues,
60   Irregular breathing and alternate ascendancies
After some haunted migratory years
To disintegrate on an instant in the explosion of mania
Or lapse for ever into a classic fatigue.

1930 / 1930

A Bride in the 30's

Easily you move, easily your head,
And easily, as through leaves of an album, I'm led
Through the night's delights and the day's impressions,
Past tenement, river, upland, wood,
5   Though sombre the sixteen skies of Europe
            And the Danube flood.

Looking and loving, our behaviours pass
Things of stone, of steel and of polished glass;
Lucky to Love the strategic railway,
10   The run-down farms where his looks are fed,
And in each policed unlucky city
            Lucky his bed.

He from these lands of terrifying mottoes
Makes worlds as innocent as Beatrix Potter's;
15   Through bankrupt countries where they mend the roads,
Along unending plains his will is,
Intent as a collector, to pursue
            His greens and lilies.

Easy for him to find in your face
20   A pool of silence or a tower of grace,
To conjure a camera into a wishing-rose,
Simple to excite in the air from a glance

59ff: John Fuller notes that the illnesses here "can all be found expounded in William McDougall's *An Outline of Abnormal Psychology* (1926). 'Fugues' . . . are a form of amnesia involving compulsive travel; 'irregular breathing' is a symbolic symptom in abnormal psychology . . . ; '*alternate ascendancies*' . . . are cases of alternating personalities with reciprocal amnesia like fugues; while for the 'explosion of mania' the reader may refer to McDougall's explanation . . . of anger as a secondary feature of mania."

Title: The earlier version of "A Bride in the 30's" was dedicated to Olive Mangeot, a friend and employer of Auden's friend Christopher Isherwood; the dedication and title are somewhat obfuscatory, as the "bride" was a male lover of Auden's (see Edward Mendelson, *Early Auden*, 1983, pp. 222ff).

5–6: The *sixteen skies* "probably represent Portugal, Spain, France, Switzerland, Italy, Belgium, Luxemburg, Netherlands, Germany, Austria, Czechoslovakia, Poland, Hungary, Yugoslavia, Albania and Greece (omitting Britain, of course, and also Bulgaria and Romania, the countries of 'the Danube flood')." (Fuller)

Horses, fountains, a side-drum, a trombone,
    The cosmic dance.

25   Summoned by such a music from our time,
Such images to sight and audience come
As Vanity cannot dispel or bless,
Hunger and fear in their variations,
Grouped invalids watching movements of birds,
30   And single assassins,

Ten desperate million marching by,
Five feet, six feet, seven feet high,
Hitler and Mussolini in their wooing poses,
Churchill acknowledging the voters' greeting,
35   Roosevelt at the microphone, van der Lubbe laughing,
        And our first meeting.

But Love except at our proposal
Will do no trick at his disposal,
Without opinions of his own performs
40   The programme that we think of merit,
And through our private stuff must work
        His public spirit.

Certain it became, while still incomplete,
There were prizes for which we would never compete:
A choice was killed by each childish illness,
45   The boiling tears amid the hot-house plants,
The rigid promise fractured in the garden,
        And the long aunts.

While every day there bolted from the field
Desires to which we could not yield,
50   Fewer and clearer grew our plans,
Schemes for a life-time, sketches for a hatred,
And early among my interesting scrawls
        Appeared your portrait.

55   You stand now before me, flesh and bone
That ghosts would like to make their own:
Beware them, look away, be deaf,
When rage would proffer her immediate pleasure
Or glory swap her fascinating rubbish
60   For your one treasure.

Be deaf, too, standing uncertain now,
A pine-tree shadow across your brow,

31: *Ten desperate million:* i.e., from the economic depression of the 1930s that affected America and
Europe
35: The Dutch Communist Marius *van der Lubbe* was convicted of arson for the 27 Feb 1933 burning of
Berlin's Reichstag (parliament) building. The fire gave Hitler the opportunity to consolidate the Nazi dic-
tatorship by assuming emergency powers. It was widely supposed that the fire was actually the work of
the Nazis themselves.

To what I hear and wish I did not,
The voice of Love saying lightly, brightly,
65   "Be Lubbe, be Hitler, but be my good,
        Daily, nightly."

Trees are shaken, mountains darken,
But the heart repeats, though we would not hearken:
"Yours the choice to whom the gods awarded
70   The language of learning, the language of love,
Crooked to move as a money-bug, as a cancer,
        Or straight as a dove".

1934 / 1936

Spain

Yesterday all the past. The language of size
Spreading to China along the trade-routes; the diffusion
    Of the counting-frame and the cromlech;
Yesterday the shadow-reckoning in the sunny climates.

5   Yesterday the assessment of insurance by cards,
The divination of water; yesterday the invention
    Of cartwheels and clocks, the taming of
Horses. Yesterday the bustling world of the navigators.

Yesterday the abolition of fairies and giants,
10   The fortress like a motionless eagle eyeing the valley,
        The chapel built in the forest;
Yesterday the carving of angels and alarming gargoyles;

The trial of heretics among the columns of stone;
Yesterday the theological feuds in the taverns
15   And the miraculous cure at the fountain;
Yesterday the Sabbath of witches; but to-day the struggle.

Yesterday the installation of dynamos and turbines,
The construction of railways in the colonial desert;
        Yesterday the classic lecture
20   On the origin of Mankind. But to-day the struggle.

"Spain" was printed in 1937 as a pamphlet (royalties from which went to Medical Aid for Spain); it was then published in 1940 as "Spain 1937"; Auden excluded it from his 1966 *Collected Shorter Poems*. We print here the 1937 text; the 1940 revisions include the deletion of lines 69–76 and 85–88 and the rewriting of lines 93–94 (see note below).

Title: In 1936 the right-wing Nationalist rebels led by General Franco launched a military challenge to the legitimate left-wing Republican government of Spain, pitching the country into civil war. The Spanish Civil War (1936–1939) had much wider reverberations outside Spain, being seen as part of the wider struggle between Communism and Fascism; the Comintern (Communist International) organized International Brigades of volunteers from all over the world to fight on the Republican side. Auden was in Spain between January and March 1937 as part of a medical unit organized by the Spanish Medical Aid Committee.

3: *cromlech*: a prehistoric stone construction, in which a stone lintel lies atop upright stones

13: Auden has in mind the Spanish Inquisition, instituted in 1478 to persecute Jews, Muslims, and heretics.

Yesterday the belief in the absolute value of Greek,
The fall of the curtain upon the death of a hero;
    Yesterday the prayer to the sunset
And the adoration of madmen. But to-day the struggle.

25   As the poet whispers, startled among the pines,
Or where the loose waterfall sings compact, or upright
    On the crag by the leaning tower:
"O my vision. O send me the luck of the sailor."

And the investigator peers through his instruments
30   At the inhuman provinces, the virile bacillus
    Or enormous Jupiter finished:
"But the lives of my friends. I inquire. I inquire."

And the poor in their fireless lodgings, dropping the sheets
Of the evening paper: "Our day is our loss, O show us
35   History the operator, the
Organiser, Time the refreshing river."

And the nations combine each cry, invoking the life
That shapes the individual belly and orders
    The private nocturnal terror:
40   "Did you not found the city state of the sponge,

"Raise the vast military empires of the shark
And the tiger, establish the robin's plucky canton?
    Intervene. O descend as a dove or
A furious papa or a mild engineer, but descend."

45   And the life, if it answers at all, replies from the heart
And the eyes and the lungs, from the shops and squares of the city
    "O no, I am not the mover;
Not to-day; not to you. To you, I'm the

"Yes-man, the bar-companion, the easily-duped;
50   I am whatever you do. I am your vow to be
    Good, your humorous story.
I am your business voice. I am your marriage.

"What's your proposal? To build the just city? I will.
I agree. Or is it the suicide pact, the romantic
55   Death? Very well, I accept, for
I am your choice, your decision. Yes, I am Spain."

Many have heard it on remote peninsulas,
On sleepy plains, in the aberrant fishermen's islands
    Or the corrupt heart of the city,
60   Have heard and migrated like gulls or the seeds of a flower.

42: *canton:* a small territorial division of a country
47: *the mover:* i.e., the Prime Mover, God.

They clung like burrs to the long expresses that lurch
Through the unjust lands, through the night, through the alpine tunnel;
    They floated over the oceans;
They walked the passes. All presented their lives.

65   On that arid square, that fragment nipped off from hot
Africa, soldered so crudely to inventive Europe;
    On that tableland scored by rivers,
Our thoughts have bodies; the menacing shapes of our fever

Are precise and alive. For the fears which made us respond
70   To the medicine ad. and the brochure of winter cruises
    Have become invading battalions;
And our faces, the institute-face, the chain-store, the ruin

Are projecting their greed as the firing squad and the bomb.
Madrid is the heart. Our moments of tenderness blossom
75   As the ambulance and the sandbag;
Our hours of friendship into a people's army.

To-morrow, perhaps the future. The research on fatigue
And the movements of packers; the gradual exploring of all the
    Octaves of radiation;
80   To-morrow the enlarging of consciousness by diet and breathing.

To-morrow the rediscovery of romantic love,
The photographing of ravens; all the fun under
    Liberty's masterful shadow;
To-morrow the hour of the pageant-master and the musician,

85   The beautiful roar of the chorus under the dome;
To-morrow the exchanging of tips on the breeding of terriers,
    The eager election of chairmen
By the sudden forest of hands. But to-day the struggle.

To-morrow for the young the poets exploding like bombs,
90   The walks by the lake, the weeks of perfect communion;
    To-morrow the bicycle races
Through the suburbs on summer evenings. But to-day the struggle.

To-day the deliberate increase in the chances of death,
The conscious acceptance of guilt in the necessary murder;

93–94: The 1940 text changes this to "To-day the inevitable increase in the chances of death; / The conscious acceptance of guilt in the fact of murder." The change likely responds to George Orwell's attack on them in "Political Reflections on the Crisis" (*The Adelphi*, Dec. 1938) as an example of an "utterly irresponsible intelligentsia"'s obscuring the difference between murder as a word and as an act. Orwell attacked the lines again in "Inside the Whale," this time reading them as a defence of Stalinist purges; though it did not influence Auden's revisions, having appeared some months after the publication of the 1940 text, the latter essay has remained influential upon the poem's reception. Auden later defended the original lines: "I was *not* excusing totalitarian crimes but only trying to say what, surely, every decent person thinks if he finds himself unable to adopt the absolute pacifist position. (1) To kill another human being is always murder and should never be called anything else. (2) In a war, the members of two rival groups try to murder their opponents. (3) *If* there is such a thing as a just war, then murder can be necessary for the sake of justice." (qtd. in Monroe K. Spears, *The Poetry of W.H. Auden*, New York, 1963, p.157).

95   To-day the expending of powers
        On the flat ephemeral pamphlet and the boring meeting.

        To-day the makeshift consolations: the shared cigarette,
        The cards in the candlelit barn, and the scraping concert,
            The masculine jokes; to-day the
100   Fumbled and unsatisfactory embrace before hurting.

        The stars are dead. The animals will not look.
        We are left alone with our day, and the time is short, and
            History to the defeated
        May say Alas but cannot help nor pardon.

                                                1937 / *1937, 1940*

from Sonnets from China

VI

        He watched the stars and noted birds in flight;
        A river flooded or a fortress fell:
        He made predictions that were sometimes right;
        His lucky guesses were rewarded well.

5   Falling in love with Truth before he knew Her,
        He rode into imaginary lands,
        By solitude and fasting hoped to woo Her,
        And mocked at those who served Her with their hands.

        Drawn as he was to magic and obliqueness,
10   In Her he honestly believed, and when
        At last She beckoned to him he obeyed,

        Looked in Her eyes: awe-struck but unafraid,
        Saw there reflected every human weakness,
        And knew himself as one of many men.

VII

        He was their servant (some say he was blind),
        Who moved among their faces and their things:
        Their feeling gathered in him like a wind
        And sang. They cried "It is a God that sings",

5   And honoured him, a person set apart,
        Till he grew vain, mistook for personal song
        The petty tremors of his mind or heart
        At each domestic wrong.

Sonnets From China: These sonnets first appeared under the title "In Time of War" as part of *Journey to a War* (1939), a collaborative account by Auden and Christopher Isherwood of their trip to China in 1938 during the Sino-Japanese War.

10   Lines came to him no more; he had to make them
    (With what precision was each strophe planned):
    Hugging his gloom as peasants hug their land,

    He stalked like an assassin through the town,
    And glared at men because he did not like them,
    But trembled if one passed him with a frown.

1938 / 1939

Musée des Beaux Arts

    About suffering they were never wrong,
    The Old Masters: how well they understood
    Its human position; how it takes place
    While someone else is eating or opening a window or just walking dully
        along;
5   How, when the aged are reverently, passionately waiting
    For the miraculous birth, there always must be
    Children who did not specially want it to happen, skating
    On a pond at the edge of the wood:
    They never forgot
10   That even the dreadful martyrdom must run its course
    Anyhow in a corner, some untidy spot
    Where the dogs go on with their doggy life and the torturer's horse
    Scratches its innocent behind on a tree.

    In Brueghel's *Icarus*, for instance: how everything turns away
15   Quite leisurely from the disaster; the ploughman may
    Have heard the splash, the forsaken cry,
    But for him it was not an important failure; the sun shone
    As it had to on the white legs disappearing into the green
    Water; and the expensive delicate ship that must have seen
20   Something amazing, a boy falling out of the sky,
    Had somewhere to get to and sailed calmly on.

1938 / 1939, 1940

In Memory of W. B. Yeats

(*d. Jan. 1939*)

I

    He disappeared in the dead of winter:
    The brooks were frozen, the airports almost deserted,
    And snow disfigured the public statues;
    The mercury sank in the mouth of the dying day.

Title: Auden visited the Musées Royaux des Beaux-Arts in Brussels in 1938. Besides describing *Landscape with the Fall of Icarus* by Pieter Bruegel the Elder (c.1525–69), Auden borrows details from other of his paintings: the horse scratching its behind is from *The Massacre of the Innocents,* and lines 5–8 draw on *The Numbering at Bethlehem* and *Winter Landscape with Skaters and a Bird Trap.*

In Memory of W. B. Yeats: Text: 1966. We have noted some of Auden's revisions from the 1940 text below.

5   What instruments we have agree
           The day of his death was a dark cold day.

           Far from his illness
           The wolves ran on through the evergreen forests,
           The peasant river was untempted by the fashionable quays;
10   By mourning tongues
           The death of the poet was kept from his poems.

           But for him it was his last afternoon as himself,
           An afternoon of nurses and rumours;
           The provinces of his body revolted,
15   The squares of his mind were empty,
           Silence invaded the suburbs,
           The current of his feeling failed; he became his admirers.

           Now he is scattered among a hundred cities
           And wholly given over to unfamiliar affections,
20   To find his happiness in another kind of wood
           And be punished under a foreign code of conscience.
           The words of a dead man
           Are modified in the guts of the living.

           But in the importance and noise of to-morrow
25   When the brokers are roaring like beasts on the floor of the Bourse,
           And the poor have the sufferings to which they are fairly accustomed,
           And each in the cell of himself is almost convinced of his freedom,
           A few thousand will think of this day
           As one thinks of a day when one did something slightly unusual.

30   What instruments we have agree
           The day of his death was a dark cold day.

II

           You were silly like us; your gift survived it all:
           The parish of rich women, physical decay,
           Yourself. Mad Ireland hurt you into poetry.
35   Now Ireland has her madness and her weather still,
           For poetry makes nothing happen: it survives
           In the valley of its making where executives
           Would never want to tamper, flows on south
           From ranches of isolation and the busy griefs,
40   Raw towns that we believe and die in; it survives,
           A way of happening, a mouth.

5–6: The original version of these lines (and lines 30–31) read: "O all the instruments agree / The day of his death was a dark cold day."

25: *Bourse:* stock exchange

32: *You were silly like us:* Auden likely has particularly in mind Yeats's occultism.

33: *the parish of rich women:* Auden has in mind Yeats's patron Lady Gregory, and his later friendships with aristocratic women such as Dorothy Wellesley.

III

Earth, receive an honoured guest:
William Yeats is laid to rest.
Let the Irish vessel lie
45   Emptied of its poetry.

In the nightmare of the dark
All the dogs of Europe bark,
And the living nations wait,
Each sequestered in its hate;

50   Intellectual disgrace
Stares from every human face,
And the seas of pity lie
Locked and frozen in each eye.

Follow, poet, follow right
55   To the bottom of the night,
With your unconstraining voice
Still persuade us to rejoice;

With the farming of a verse
Make a vineyard of the curse,
60   Sing of human unsuccess
In a rapture of distress;

In the deserts of the heart
Let the healing fountain start,
In the prison of his days
65   Teach the free man how to praise.

1939 / *1939, 1940*

42ff: This section's tetrameter couplets echo those of Yeats's late poem "Under Ben Bulben," first published shortly after his 28 January 1939 death. They also suggest the style of William Blake: compare lines 50ff with his poem "London."

45: The earlier text has three more stanzas following this line:

Time that is intolerant
Of the brave and innocent,
And indifferent in a week
To a beautiful physique,

Worships language and forgives
Everyone by whom it lives;
Pardons cowardice, conceit,
Lays its honours at their feet.

Time that with this strange excuse
Pardoned Kipling and his views,
And will pardon Paul Claudel,
Pardons him for writing well.

Rudyard Kipling held strongly imperialist views; those of poet-playwright Paul Claudel (1868–1955) were strongly right-wing and Catholic. Yeats's own politics became increasingly right-wing and anti-democratic in his old age.

46–47: Europe was heading toward the outbreak of World War II in September of that year.

59: *the curse*: i.e., God's curse upon Adam for eating from the Tree of Knowledge, that he would have to gain sustenance through agricultural labor.

September 1, 1939

I sit in one of the dives
On Fifty-Second Street
Uncertain and afraid
As the clever hopes expire
5   Of a low dishonest decade:
Waves of anger and fear
Circulate over the bright
And darkened lands of the earth,
Obsessing our private lives;
10   The unmentionable odour of death
Offends the September night.

Accurate scholarship can
Unearth the whole offence
From Luther until now
15   That has driven a culture mad,
Find what occurred at Linz,
What huge imago made
A psychopathic god:
I and the public know
20   What all schoolchildren learn,
Those to whom evil is done
Do evil in return.

Exiled Thucydides knew
All that a speech can say
25   About Democracy,
And what dictators do,
The elderly rubbish they talk
To an apathetic grave;
Analysed all in his book,
30   The enlightenment driven away,
The habit-forming pain,
Mismanagement and grief:
We must suffer them all again.

Into this neutral air
35   Where blind skyscrapers use
Their full height to proclaim

Text: 1939; this poem was excluded from the 1966 *Collected Shorter Poems*: see note to line 88.

Title: The date is that of Hitler's invasion of Poland; the *clever hopes* of line 4 are those of the 1938 Munich Agreement, the failed attempt at appeasing Germany's ambitions by permitting its annexation of the Sudetenland.

2: *Fifty-Second Street*: in New York

14: Auden sees the history of German nationalism, and more generally of Western culture, as beginning with Martin *Luther's* instigation of the Protestant Reformation.

16: *Linz*: capital of Upper Austria, the place of Hitler's childhood

17: *imago*: "Unconscious prototypical or stereotypical figure which orientates the subject's way of appre- hending other people; it derives from real and phantasied relationships in infancy" (Laplanche and Pon- talis, *The Language of Psycho-Analysis*).

23: *Thucydides*: the Greek historian and military commander (c.460 BC–c.404 BC), author of the *History of the Peloponnesian War*; his failure to prevent the Spartans from seizing the Athenian colony of Amphipolis led to his being exiled from Athens.

The strength of Collective Man,
Each language pours its vain
Competitive excuse:
40   But who can live for long
In an euphoric dream;
Out of the mirror they stare,
Imperialism's face
And the international wrong.

45   Faces along the bar
Cling to their average day:
The lights must never go out,
The music must always play,
All the conventions conspire
50   To make this fort assume
The furniture of home;
Lest we should see where we are,
Lost in a haunted wood,
Children afraid of the night
55   Who have never been happy or good.

The windiest militant trash
Important Persons shout
Is not so crude as our wish:
What mad Nijinsky wrote
60   About Diaghilev
Is true of the normal heart;
For the error bred in the bone
Of each woman and each man
Craves what it cannot have,
65   Not universal love
But to be loved alone.

From the conservative dark
Into the ethical life
The dense commuters come,
70   Repeating their morning vow,
"I will be true to the wife,
I'll concentrate more on my work,"
And helpless governors wake
To resume their compulsory game:
75   Who can release them now,
Who can reach the deaf,
Who can speak for the dumb?

All I have is a voice
To undo the folded lie,

59: *Nijinsky*: Vaslav Nijinsky (1890–1950), the great Russian ballet dancer, who danced in Sergey Diaghilev's Ballets Russes; he succumbed to schizophrenia in 1919 and was institutionalized for the rest of his life. The diary he wrote as he descended into madness was published in 1936: the passage Auden quotes runs: "Some politicians are hypocrites like Diaghilev, who does not want universal love, but to be loved alone. I want universal love."
77: *Who can speak for the dumb?*: cf. Prov. 21.8

80   The romantic lie in the brain
   Of the sensual man-in-the-street
   And the lie of Authority
   Whose buildings grope the sky:
   There is no such thing as the State
85   And no one exists alone;
   Hunger allows no choice
   To the citizen or the police;
   We must love one another or die.

   Defenceless under the night
90   Our world in stupor lies;
   Yet, dotted everywhere,
   Ironic points of light
   Flash out wherever the Just
   Exchange their messages:
95   May I, composed like them
   Of Eros and of dust,
   Beleaguered by the same
   Negation and despair,
   Show an affirming flame.

           1939 / 1939, 1940

In Memory of Sigmund Freud

(d. Sept. 1939)

When there are so many we shall have to mourn,
when grief has been made so public, and exposed
  to the critique of a whole epoch
  the frailty of our conscience and anguish,

5 of whom shall we speak? For every day they die
among us, those who were doing us some good,
  who knew it was never enough but
  hoped to improve a little by living.

  Such was this doctor: still at eighty he wished
10 to think of our life from whose unruliness

88: Auden omitted this poem from the 1966 *Collected Shorter Poems* because of this line. "Rereading a poem of mine, *1st September, 1939,* after it had been published, I came to the line 'We must love one another or die' and said to myself: 'That's a damned lie! We must die anyway.' So, in the next edition, I altered it to 'We must love one another and die'. This didn't seem to do either, so I cut the stanza. Still no good. The whole poem, I realized, was infected with an incurable dishonesty—and must be scrapped." (qtd. in Fuller). (The sequence of revision was actually somewhat different: the 1945 *Collected Poetry* omits the stanza; it reappeared in 1955 with "and die" in Oscar Williams' *New Pocket Anthology of American Verse*.) One reason for Auden's suppression of the poem, however, was the (mis)quotation of this line in a 1964 television ad from Lyndon B. Johnson's presidential campaign (Edward Mendelson, *Later Auden,* New York, 1999, p. 478).

1: *so many we shall have to mourn:* i.e., so many people whom we shall have to mourn: Auden has the recent outbreak of World War II in mind.

> so many plausible young futures
> with threats or flattery ask obedience,

> but his wish was denied him: he closed his eyes
> upon that last picture, common to us all,
15   of problems like relatives gathered
> puzzled and jealous about our dying.

> For about him till the very end were still
> those he had studied, the fauna of the night,
>   and shades that still waited to enter
20   the bright circle of his recognition

> turned elsewhere with their disappointment as he
> was taken away from his life interest
>   to go back to the earth in London,
> an important Jew who died in exile.

25 Only Hate was happy, hoping to augment
> his practice now, and his dingy clientele
>   who think they can be cured by killing
> and covering the gardens with ashes.

> They are still alive, but in a world he changed
30 simply by looking back with no false regrets;
>   all he did was to remember
> like the old and be honest like children.

> He wasn't clever at all: he merely told
> the unhappy Present to recite the Past
35   like a poetry lesson till sooner
> or later it faltered at the line where

> long ago the accusations had begun,
> and suddenly knew by whom it had been judged,
>   how rich life had been and how silly,
40   and was life-forgiven and more humble,

> able to approach the Future as a friend
> without a wardrobe of excuses, without
>   a set mask of rectitude or an
> embarrassing over-familiar gesture.

45 No wonder the ancient cultures of conceit
> in his technique of unsettlement foresaw
>   the fall of princes, the collapse of
> their lucrative patterns of frustration:

> if he succeeded, why, the Generalised Life
50 would become impossible, the monolith
>   of State be broken and prevented
> the co-operation of avengers.

23: Freud escaped to England after Hitler's 1938 annexation of Austria.

Of course they called on God, but he went his way
down among the lost people like Dante, down
55   to the stinking fosse where the injured
lead the ugly life of the rejected,

and showed us what evil is, not, as we thought,
deeds that must be punished, but our lack of faith,
         our dishonest mood of denial,
60   the concupiscence of the oppressor.

If some traces of the autocratic pose,
the paternal strictness he distrusted, still
         clung to his utterance and features,
         it was a protective coloration

65   for one who'd lived among enemies so long:
if often he was wrong and, at times, absurd,
         to us he is no more a person
         now but a whole climate of opinion

under whom we conduct our different lives:
70   Like weather he can only hinder or help,
         the proud can still be proud but find it
         a little harder, the tyrant tries to

make do with him but doesn't care for him much:
he quietly surrounds all our habits of growth
75   and extends, till the tired in even
         the remotest miserable duchy

have felt the change in their bones and are cheered,
till the child, unlucky in his little State,
         some hearth where freedom is excluded,
80   a hive whose honey is fear and worry,

feels calmer now and somehow assured of escape,
while, as they lie in the grass of our neglect,
         so many long-forgotten objects
         revealed by his undiscouraged shining

85   are returned to us and made precious again;
games we had thought we must drop as we grew up,
         little noises we dared not laugh at,
         faces we made when no one was looking.

But he wishes us more than this. To be free
90   is often to be lonely. He would unite
         the unequal moieties fractured
         by our own well-meaning sense of justice,

54: *like Dante:* i.e., in his descent to Hell as described in the *Inferno.*
55: *fosse:* ditch
91: *moieties:* halves, portions

95

would restore to the larger the wit and will
the smaller possesses but can only use
　　　for arid disputes, would give back to
the son the mother's richness of feeling:

but he would have us remember most of all
to be enthusiastic over the night,
　　　not only for the sense of wonder

100

it alone has to offer, but also

because it needs our love. With large sad eyes
its delectable creatures look up and beg
　　　us dumbly to ask them to follow:
they are exiles who long for the future

105

that lies in our power, they too would rejoice
if allowed to serve enlightenment like him,
　　　even to bear our cry of "Judas",
as he did and all must bear who serve it.

110

One rational voice is dumb. Over his grave
the household of Impulse mourns one dearly loved:
　　　sad is Eros, builder of cities,
and weeping anarchic Aphrodite.

1939 / 1940

No Time

Clocks cannot tell our time of day
For what event to pray,
Because we have no time, because
We have no time until

5

We know what time we fill,
Why time is other than time was.

Nor can our question satisfy
The answer in the statue's eye.
Only the living ask whose brow

10

May wear the Roman laurel now:
The dead say only how.

What happens to the living when they die?
Death is not understood by death: nor you, nor I.

1940 / 1941

111ff: *Aphrodite,* Greek goddess of love, was mother of *Eros* (Cupid).

"No Time" was originally a verse footnote to line 13 of *New Year Letter* (1941).

At the Grave of Henry James

The snow, less intransigeant than their marble,
Has left the defence of whiteness to these tombs,
        And all the pools at my feet
Accommodate blue now, echo such clouds as occur
5   To the sky, and whatever bird or mourner the passing
        Moment remarks they repeat.

While rocks, named after singular spaces
Within which images wandered once that caused
        All to tremble and offend,
10   Stand here in an innocent stillness, each marking the spot
Where one more series of errors lost its uniqueness
        And novelty came to an end.

To whose real advantage were such transactions,
When worlds of reflection were exchanged for trees?
15   What living occasion can
Be just to the absent? Noon but reflects on itself,
And the small taciturn stone, that is the only witness
        To a great and talkative man,

Has no more judgement than my ignorant shadow
20   Of odious comparisons or distant clocks
        Which challenge and interfere
With the heart's instantaneous reading of time, time that is
A warm enigma no longer to you for whom I
        Surrender my private cheer,

25   As I stand awake on our solar fabric,
That primary machine, the earth, which gendarmes, banks
        And aspirin pre-suppose,
On which the clumsy and sad may all sit down, and any who will
Say their a-ha to the beautiful, the common locus
30   Of the Master and the rose,

Shall I not especially bless you as, vexed with
My little inferior questions, I stand
        Above the bed where you rest,
Who opened such passionate arms to your *Bon* when It ran
35   Towards you with Its overwhelming reasons pleading
        All beautifully in Its breast?

With what an innocence your hand submitted
To those formal rules that help a child to play,
        While your heart, fastidious as
40   A delicate nun, remained true to the rare noblesse

Text: 1966. This text is a third the length of the 1941 version.
34: *Bon:* James's term in his notebooks for the guardian angel of his inspiration
35–36: *overwhelming reasons . . . breast:* "a direct quotation from a [James] notebook entry about *The Ivory
    Tower,* 4 January 1910. . . . The phrase was also used of Mrs Brookenham's ingratiations in *The Awkward
    Age,* chapter 14." (Fuller)

Of your lucid gift and, for its love, ignored the
    Resentful muttering Mass,

Whose ruminant hatred of all that cannot
Be simplified or stolen is yet at large:
45   No death can assuage its lust
To vilify the landscape of Distinction and see
The heart of the Personal brought to a systolic standstill,
    The Tall to diminished dust.

Preserve me, Master, from its vague incitement;
50   Yours be the disciplinary image that holds
    Me back from agreeable wrong
And the clutch of eddying Muddle, lest Proportion shed
The alpine chill of her shrugging editorial shoulder
    On my loose impromptu song.

55   All will be judged. Master of nuance and scruple,
Pray for me and for all writers, living or dead:
    Because there are many whose works
Are in better taste than their lives, because there is no end
To the vanity of our calling, make intercession
60   For the treason of all clerks.

1941 / 1941, 1945

In Praise of Limestone

If it form the one landscape that we, the inconstant ones,
    Are consistently homesick for, this is chiefly
Because it dissolves in water. Mark these rounded slopes
    With their surface fragrance of thyme and, beneath,
5   A secret system of caves and conduits; hear the springs
    That spurt out everywhere with a chuckle,
Each filling a private pool for its fish and carving
    Its own little ravine whose cliffs entertain
The butterfly and the lizard; examine this region
10   Of short distances and definite places:
What could be more like Mother or a fitter background
    For her son, the flirtatious male who lounges
Against a rock in the sunlight, never doubting
    That for all his faults he is loved; whose works are but
15   Extensions of his power to charm? From weathered outcrop
    To hill-top temple, from appearing waters to
Conspicuous fountains, from a wild to a formal vineyard,
    Are ingenious but short steps that a child's wish

47: *systolic*: contracted; the heart beats through a rhythmic alternation of systole and diastole (dilation).
60: Julien Benda's *La Trahison des clercs* (1927; *The Treason of the Intellectuals*) was an attack on the politicization of intellectual culture.

In Praise of Limestone: The poem's landscape is the Island of Ischia, located in the northwest entrance to the Bay of Naples, in southern Italy; it is a popular health and vacation resort. Auden spent his summers there from 1948 to 1957. Its landscape recalls for Auden his childhood in the Pennines, a limestone area of central England.

To receive more attention than his brothers, whether
20   By pleasing or teasing, can easily take.

Watch, then, the band of rivals as they climb up and down
        Their steep stone gennels in twos and threes, at times
Arm in arm, but never, thank God, in step; or engaged
        On the shady side of a square at midday in
25 Voluble discourse, knowing each other too well to think
        There are any important secrets, unable
To conceive a god whose temper-tantrums are moral
        And not to be pacified by a clever line
Or a good lay: for, accustomed to a stone that responds,
30   They have never had to veil their faces in awe
Of a crater whose blazing fury could not be fixed;
        Adjusted to the local needs of valleys
Where everything can be touched or reached by walking,
        Their eyes have never looked into infinite space
35 Through the lattice-work of a nomad's comb; born lucky,
        Their legs have never encountered the fungi
And insects of the jungle, the monstrous forms and lives
        With which we have nothing, we like to hope, in common.
So, when one of them goes to the bad, the way his mind works
40   Remains comprehensible: to become a pimp
Or deal in fake jewellery or ruin a fine tenor voice
        For effects that bring down the house, could happen to all
But the best and the worst of us . . .
                         That is why, I suppose,
45 The best and worst never stayed here long but sought
        Immoderate soils where the beauty was not so external,
        The light less public and the meaning of life
Something more than a mad camp. "Come!" cried the granite wastes,
        "How evasive is your humor, how accidental
50 Your kindest kiss, how permanent is death." (Saints-to-be
        Slipped away sighing.) "Come!" purred the clays and gravels,
"On our plains there is room for armies to drill; rivers
        Wait to be tamed and slaves to construct you a tomb
In the grand manner: soft as the earth is mankind and both
55   Need to be altered." (Intendant Caesars rose and
Left, slamming the door.) But the really reckless were fetched
        By an older colder voice, the oceanic whisper:
"I am the solitude that asks and promises nothing;
        That is how I shall set you free. There is no love;
60 There is only the various envies, all of them sad."

They were right, my dear, all those voices were right
And still are; this land is not the sweet home that it looks,
        Nor its peace the historical calm of a site
Where something was settled once and for all: A backward
65   And dilapidated province, connected

22: *gennels:* narrow passages between houses (or, here, rocks)
35: "The MS draft . . . helps to explain the odd 'nomad's comb' at line 35, since it contrasts the 'male nude at rest, the temple on the promontory' with 'the portable objects of migrants, bracelets, seals, combs / infinity through a lattice'." (Fuller)

To the big busy world by a tunnel, with a certain
    Seedy appeal, is that all it is now? Not quite:
It has a worldly duty which in spite of itself
    It does not neglect, but calls into question
70   All the Great Powers assume; it disturbs our rights. The poet,
    Admired for his earnest habit of calling
The sun the sun, his mind Puzzle, is made uneasy
    By these marble statues which so obviously doubt
His antimythological myth; and these gamins,
75   Pursuing the scientist down the tiled colonnade
With such lively offers, rebuke his concern for Nature's
    Remotest aspects: I, too, am reproached, for what
And how much you know. Not to lose time, not to get caught,
    Not to be left behind, not, please! to resemble
80   The beasts who repeat themselves, or a thing like water
    Or stone whose conduct can be predicted, these
Are our Common Prayer, whose greatest comfort is music
    Which can be made anywhere, is invisible,
And does not smell. In so far as we have to look forward
85   To death as a fact, no doubt we are right: But if
Sins can be forgiven, if bodies rise from the dead,
    These modifications of matter into
Innocent athletes and gesticulating fountains,
    Made solely for pleasure, make a further point:
90   The blessed will not care what angle they are regarded from,
    Having nothing to hide. Dear, I know nothing of
Either, but when I try to imagine a faultless love
    Or the life to come, what I hear is the murmur
Of underground streams, what I see is a limestone landscape.

1948 / 1948, 1951

from Horae Canonicae

4. Nones

What we know to be not possible,
    Though time after time foretold
By wild hermits, by shaman and sybil
    Gibbering in their trances,
5   Or revealed to a child in some chance rhyme
    Like *will* and *kill,* comes to pass
Before we realize it. We are surprised
    At the ease and speed of our deed
And uneasy: It is barely three,
10   Mid-afternoon, yet the blood

74: *gamins*: street urchins
82: The Book of *Common Prayer* is the liturgical book of the Anglican Church.
88: The *athletes* are statues, carved from marble (which is itself limestone recrystallized by metamorphic geological processes).

The *Horae Canonicae*—Canonical Hours—are regular church services, based upon the events of the Crucifixion, and are held at set times during the day; *Nones* is the service held at 3 p.m., the time of Christ's death on the cross.
3: *sybil*: prophetess

Of our sacrifice is already
    Dry on the grass; we are not prepared
For silence so sudden and so soon;
    The day is too hot, too bright, too still,
15   Too ever, the dead remains too nothing.
    What shall we do till nightfall?

The wind has dropped and we have lost our public.
    The faceless many who always
Collect when any world is to be wrecked,
20   Blown up, burnt down, cracked open,
Felled, sawn in two, hacked through, torn apart,
    Have all melted away. Not one
Of these who in the shade of walls and trees
    Lie sprawled now, calmly sleeping,
25   Harmless as sheep, can remember why
    He shouted or what about
So loudly in the sunshine this morning;
    All if challenged would reply
—"It was a monster with one red eye,
30   A crowd that saw him die, not I."—
The hangman has gone to wash, the soldiers to eat:
    We are left alone with our feat.

The Madonna with the green woodpecker,
    The Madonna of the fig-tree,
35   The Madonna beside the yellow dam,
    Turn their kind faces from us
And our projects under construction,
    Look only in one direction,
Fix their gaze on our completed work:
40   Pile-driver, concrete-mixer,
Crane and pick-axe wait to be used again,
    But how can we repeat this?
Outliving our act, we stand where we are,
    As disregarded as some
45   Discarded artifact of our own,
    Like torn gloves, rusted kettles,
Abandoned branch-lines, worn lop-sided
    Grindstones buried in nettles.

This mutilated flesh, our victim,
50   Explains too nakedly, too well,
The spell of the asparagus garden,
    The aim of our chalk-pit game; stamps,
Birds' eggs are not the same, behind the wonder
    Of tow-paths and sunken lanes,
55   Behind the rapture on the spiral stair,
    We shall always now be aware
Of the deed into which they lead, under
    The mock chase and mock capture,
The racing and tussling and splashing,
60   The panting and the laughter,
Be listening for the cry and stillness
    To follow after: wherever

The sun shines, brooks run, books are written,
 There will also be this death.

65 Soon cool tramontana will stir the leaves,
 The shops will re-open at four,
The empty blue bus in the empty pink square
 Fill up and depart: we have time
To misrepresent, excuse, deny,
70 Mythify, use this event
While, under a hotel bed, in prison,
 Down wrong turnings, its meaning
Waits for our lives. Sooner than we would choose
 Bread will melt, water will burn,
75 And the great quell begin, Abaddon
 Set up his triple gallows
At our seven gates, fat Belial make
 Our wives waltz naked; meanwhile
It would be best to go home, if we have a home,
80 In any case good to rest.

That our dreaming wills may seem to escape
 This dead calm, wander instead
On knife edges, on black and white squares,
 Across moss, baize, velvet, boards,
85 Over cracks and hillocks, in mazes
 Of string and penitent cones,
Down granite ramps and damp passages,
 Through gates that will not relatch
And doors marked *Private*, pursued by Moors
90 And watched by latent robbers,
To hostile villages at the heads of fjords,
 To dark chateaux where wind sobs
In the pine-trees and telephones ring,
 Inviting trouble, to a room,
95 Lit by one weak bulb, where our Double sits
 Writing and does not look up.

That, while we are thus away, our own wronged flesh
 May work undisturbed, restoring
The order we try to destroy, the rhythm
100 We spoil out of spite: valves close
And open exactly, glands secrete,
 Vessels contract and expand
At the right moment, essential fluids
 Flow to renew exhausted cells,
105 Not knowing quite what has happened, but awed
 By death like all the creatures

65: *tramontana:* a cool Mediterranean north wind
75: *quell:* destruction, slaughter
 Abaddon: the angel of the bottomless pit in Revelation 9:11
77: *Belial:* a devil; in Milton's *Paradise Lost* he is a devil representing profligacy and lewdness.
86: *penitent cones: nieves penitentes,* upright blades of ice up to several meters tall that form on the surface of glaciers

Now watching this spot, like the hawk looking down
    Without blinking, the smug hens
Passing close by in their pecking order,
110   The bug whose view is balked by grass,
Or the deer who shyly from afar
    Peer through chinks in the forest.

1950 / 1951, 1955

Ode to Terminus

The High Priests of telescopes and cyclotrons
keep making pronouncements about happenings
    on scales too gigantic or dwarfish
    to be noticed by our native senses,

5   discoveries which, couched in the elegant
euphemisms of algebra, look innocent,
    harmless enough but, when translated
    into the vulgar anthropomorphic

tongue, will give no cause for hilarity
10   to gardeners or house-wives: if galaxies
    bolt like panicking mobs, if mesons
    riot like fish in a feeding-frenzy,

it sounds too like Political History
to boost civil morale, too symbolic of
15   the crimes and strikes and demonstrations
    we are supposed to gloat on at breakfast.

How trite, though, our fears beside the miracle
that we're here to shiver, that a Thingummy
    so addicted to lethal violence
20   should have somehow secreted a placid

tump with exactly the right ingredients
to start and to cocker Life, that heavenly
    freak for whose manage we shall have to
    give account at the Judgement, our Middle-

25   -Earth, where Sun-Father to all appearances
moves by day from orient to occident,
    and his light is felt as a friendly
    presence not a photonic bombardment,

Title: *Terminus:* the Roman god of limits and boundary stones
1: *cyclotrons:* particle accelerators
11: *Mesons* are a class of sub-atomic particles.
21: *tump:* mound, small hill
22: *cocker:* bring up a child affectionately
23: *manage:* control, care; but also the obsolete sense of "age of maturity; manhood"
24–25: *Middle-Earth:* translation of "Midgard," the Norse word for this world (as opposed to Asgard, the
    world of the gods)

where all visibles do have a definite
30   outline they stick to, and are undoubtedly
            at rest or in motion, where lovers
            recognize each other by their surface,

where to all species except the talkative
have been allotted the niche and diet that
35   become them. This, whatever micro-
            -biology may think, is the world we

really live in and that saves our sanity,
who know all too well how the most erudite
            mind behaves in the dark without a
40   surround it is called on to interpret,

how, discarding rhythm, punctuation, metaphor,
it sinks into a drivelling monologue,
            too literal to see a joke or
            distinguish a penis from a pencil.

45   Venus and Mars are powers too natural
to temper our outlandish extravagance:
            You alone, Terminus the Mentor,
            can teach us how to alter our gestures.

God of walls, doors and reticence, nemesis
50   overtakes the sacrilegious technocrat,
            but blessed is the City that thanks you
            for giving us games and grammar and metres.

By whose grace, also, every gathering
of two or three in confident amity
55   repeats the pentecostal marvel,
            as each in each finds his right translator.

In this world our colossal immodesty
has plundered and poisoned, it is possible
            You still might save us, who by now have
60   learned this: that scientists, to be truthful,

must remind us to take all they say as a
tall story, that abhorred in the Heav'ns are all
            self-proclaimed poets who, to wow an
            audience, utter some resonant lie.

                                    May 1968 / 1968, 1969

40: *surround*: environment; frame
44: *Penis* and *pencil* both derive from the Latin word for "tail."
45: *Venus and Mars*: goddess of love and god of war, respectively
49: *nemesis*: divine vengeance
55: The Christian feast of *Pentecost* commemorates the Holy Spirit's gift of tongues to Christ's disciples.

LOUIS MACNEICE (1907–1963)

"THIS BOOK IS A PLEA FOR IMPURE POETRY, THAT IS, FOR POETRY CONDITIONED BY THE poet's life and the world around him," MacNeice wrote in the preface to his *Modern Poetry* (1938), a book critical of the "bookishness, obscurity, [and] intellectual superiority" of T. S. Eliot, Ezra Pound, and other modernists. Much of Eliot's work he called "defeatist." Observing that "The poet seems no longer organic to the community," MacNeice argued for "communication" with a more general readership, for the poet as "Man at his most self-conscious, but this means consciousness of himself as man, not consciousness of himself as poet."[1] In practice this meant a tone of familiarity, a conversational idiom, a self-consciously topical range of concerns, the poet as "a blend of the entertainer and the critic or informer."[2] There is also something of the poet-as-journalist evident in the commentary of his *Autumn Journal,* as for example in a passage in which the fears of cultural decline MacNeice shared with many poets and intellectuals of his generation give way to this well-schooled advice: "It is so hard to imagine / A world where the many would have a chance without / A fall in the standard of intellectual living / And nothing be left that the highbrow cared about. / Which fears must be suppressed."[3] Like other members of the "Auden group," MacNeice's basic sympathies were leftist, but he never joined the Communist party, and, despite his support for causes such as the Valencia government in Spain, his political and cultural views suggest liberal probity more than radical enthusiasm. Recently, MacNeice has garnered attention from Irish poets and critics—here, too, the expatriate Northerner can seem "impure," resistant to "racial blood-music," insisting that the mixing of English and Irish culture in Ireland be admitted, writing to a friend that he wished "one could either live in Ireland or feel oneself in England."[4] Edna Longley writes that "MacNeice's affiliations with Britain gave him a fresh vantage-point from which to criticise both Nationalism and Unionism."[5] The satirical "Valediction," which addresses MacNeice's sense of the endemic ills of Irish culture, includes his recognition that he "cannot deny my past to which my soul is wed."

Born in Belfast, MacNeice moved with his family soon afterwards to Carrickfergus. His father was a clergyman and eventually a bishop in the Church of Ireland, who identified himself with the West of Ireland and held heterodox opinions on Home Rule. His mother, beset by mental illness, died when MacNeice was seven. At ten, he

---

[1] *Modern Poetry,* Oxford, 1938, pp. 1–30.
[2] Ibid., p. 197.
[3] *The Collected Poems of Louis MacNeice,* London, 1966.
[4] Quoted in Edna Longley, *The Living Stream: Literature and Revisionism in Ireland,* Newcastle upon Tyne, 1994, p. 201, p. 142.
[5] Longley, p. 139.

was sent to a preparatory school in Dorset, continuing his education at Marlborough College and Merton College, Oxford; he would not return to Ireland to live. After taking his B. A., he lectured on classics at Birmingham University, the University of London, and as a visitor at Cornell. After being barred from active service in World War II because of bad eyesight, he went to work for the BBC in London, where he created more than 150 scripts. He had early success as a poet with *Poems* (1935), following that collection with *Letter from Iceland* (1937, co-authored with W. H. Auden), *Autumn Journal* (1939), *Autumn Sequel* (1943), and *Solstices* (1961), among other volumes.

An Eclogue for Christmas

    A. I meet you in an evil time.

    B.   The evil bells

      Put out of our heads, I think, the thought of everything else.

    A. The jaded calendar revolves,

      Its nuts need oil, carbon chokes the valves,

5   The excess sugar of a diabetic culture

      Rotting the nerve of life and literature;

      Therefore when we bring out the old tinsel and frills

      To announce that Christ is born among the barbarous hills

      I turn to you whom a morose routine

10   Saves from the mad vertigo of being what has been.

    B. Analogue of me, you are wrong to turn to me,

      My country will not yield you any sanctuary,

      There is no pinpoint in any of the ordnance maps

      To save you when your towns and town-bred thoughts collapse,

15   It is better to die *in situ* as I shall,

      One place is as bad as another. Go back where your instincts call

      And listen to the crying of the town-cats and the taxis again,

      Or wind your gramophone and eavesdrop on great men.

    A. Jazz-weary of years of drums and Hawaiian guitar,

20   Pivoting on the parquet I seem to have moved far

      From bombs and mud and gas, have stuttered on my feet

      Clinched to the streamlined and butter-smooth trulls of the elite,

      The lights irritating and gyrating and rotating in gauze—

      Pomade-dazzle, a slick beauty of gewgaws—

25   I who was Harlequin in the childhood of the century,

      Posed by Picasso beside an endless opaque sea,

      Have seen myself sifted and splintered in broken facets,

      Tentative pencillings, endless liabilities, no assets,

      Abstractions scalpelled with a palette-knife

30   Without reference to this particular life.

      And so it has gone on; I have not been allowed to be

      Myself in flesh or face, but abstracting and dissecting me

      They have made of me pure form, a symbol or a pastiche,

      Stylized profile, anything but soul and flesh:

35   And that is why I turn this jaded music on

      To forswear thought and become an automaton.

    B. There are in the country also of whom I am afraid—

13: *ordnance maps:* official government maps
15: *in situ:* in my (original) place
22: *trulls:* prostitutes

Men who put beer into a belly that is dead,
Women in the forties with terrier and setter who whistle and swank
40   Over down and plough and Roman road and daisied bank,
Half-conscious that these barriers over which they stride
Are nothing to the barbed wire that has grown round their pride.

A. And two there are, as I drive in the city, who suddenly perturb—
The one sirening me to draw up by the kerb
45   The other, as I lean back, my right leg stretched creating speed,
Making me catch and stamp, the brakes shrieking, pull up dead:
She wears silk stockings taunting the winter wind,
He carries a white stick to mark that he is blind.

B. In the country they are still hunting, in the heavy shires
50   Greyness is on the fields and sunset like a line of pyres
Of barbarous heroes smoulders through the ancient air
Hazed with factory dust and, orange opposite, the moon's glare,
Goggling, yokel-stubborn through the iron trees,
Jeers at the end of us, our bland ancestral ease;
55   We shall go down like palaeolithic man
Before some new Ice Age or Genghiz Khan.

A. It is time for some new coinage, people have got so old,
Hacked and handled and shiny from pocketing they have made bold
To think that each is himself through these accidents, being blind
60   To the fact that they are merely the counters of an unknown Mind.

B. A Mind that does not think, if such a thing can be,
Mechanical Reason, capricious Identity.
That I could be able to face this domination nor flinch—

A. The tin toys of the hawker move on the pavement inch by inch
65   Not knowing that they are wound up; it is better to be so
Than to be, like us, wound up and while running down to know—

B. But everywhere the pretence of individuality recurs—

A. Old faces frosted with powder and choked in furs.

B. The jutlipped farmer gazing over the humpbacked wall.
70   A. The commercial traveller joking in the urinal.

B. I think things draw to an end, the soil is stale.

A. And over-elaboration will nothing now avail,
The street is up again, gas, electricity or drains,
Ever-changing conveniences, nothing comfortable remains
75   Un-improved, as flagging Rome improved villa and sewer
(A sound-proof library and a stable temperature).
Our street is up, red lights sullenly mark
The long trench of pipes, iron guts in the dark,
And not till the Goths again come swarming down the hill
80   Will cease the clangour of the pneumatic drill.
But yet there is beauty narcotic and deciduous
In this vast organism grown out of us:
On all the traffic-islands stand white globes like moons,
The city's haze is clouded amber that purrs and croons,
85   And tilting by the noble curve bus after tall bus comes
With an osculation of yellow light, with a glory like chrysanthemums.

50: Cremation of the bodies of the heroic and noble on *pyres* was characteristic of many pre-Christian societies.
79: From the third century on, the Roman Empire suffered from the assaults of the *Goths*.
81: *deciduous:* transitory
86: *osculation:* kiss
    glory: surrounding circle of light

B. The country gentry cannot change, they will die in their shoes
From angry circumstance and moral self-abuse,
Dying with a paltry fizzle they will prove their lives to be
90 An ever-diluted drug, a spiritual tautology.
They cannot live once their idols are turned out,
None of them can endure, for how could they, possibly, without
The flotsam of private property, pekinese and polyanthus,
The good things which in the end turn to poison and pus,
95 Without the bandy chairs and the sugar in the silver tongs
And the inter-ripple and resonance of years of dinner-gongs?
Or if they could find no more that cumulative proof
In the rain dripping off the conservatory roof?
What will happen when the only sanction the country-dweller has—
100 A. What will happen to us, planked and panelled with jazz?
Who go to the theatre where a black man dances like an eel,
Where pink thighs flash like the spokes of a wheel, where we feel
That we know in advance all the jogtrot and the cake-walk jokes,
All the bumfun and the gags of the comedians in boaters and toques,
105 All the tricks of the virtuosos who invert the usual—
B. What will happen to us when the State takes down the manor wall,
When there is no more private shooting or fishing, when the trees are all
cut down,
When faces are all dials and cannot smile or frown—
A. What will happen when the sniggering machine-guns in the hands of the
young men
110 Are trained on every flat and club and beauty parlour and Father's den?
What will happen when our civilization like a long-pent balloon—
B. What will happen will happen; the whore and the buffoon
Will come off best; no dreamers, they cannot lose their dream
And are at least likely to be reinstated in the new regime.
115 But one thing is not likely—
A.   Do not gloat over yourself,
Do not be your own vulture; high on some mountain shelf
Huddle the pitiless abstractions bald about the neck
Who will descend when you crumple in the plains a wreck.
Over the randy of the theatre and cinema I hear songs
120 Unlike anything—
B.   The lady of the house poises the silver tongs
And picks a lump of sugar, 'ne plus ultra' she says
'I cannot do otherwise, even to prolong my days'—
A. I cannot do otherwise either, tonight I will book my seat—
B. I will walk about the farm-yard which is replete
125 As with the smell of dung so with memories—
A. I will gorge myself to satiety with the oddities
Of every artiste, official or amateur,
Who has pleased me in my role of hero-worshipper
Who has pleased me in my role of individual man—

93: *polyanthus:* a garden primrose
104: *boaters:* straw hats
    toques: brimless hats
119: *randy:* noisy reveling
121: *ne plus ultra:* I can do no more (Latin)

130   B. Let us lie once more, say, 'What we think, we can'
       The old idealist lie—
    A.   And for me before I die
       Let me go the round of the garish glare—
    B.   And on the bare and high
       Places of England, the Wiltshire Downs and the Long Mynd
       Let the balls of my feet bounce on the turf, my face burn in the wind
135   My eyelashes stinging in the wind, and the sheep like grey stones
       Humble my human pretensions—
    A.   Let the saxophones and the xylophones
       And the cult of every technical excellence, the miles of canvas in the gal-
          leries
       And the canvas of the rich man's yacht snapping and tacking on the seas
       And the perfection of a grilled steak—
    B.   Let all these so ephemeral things
140   Be somehow permanent like the swallow's tangent wings:
       Goodbye to you, this day remember is Christmas, this morn
       They say, interpret it your own way, Christ is born.

                                                           1933 / 1935

Valediction

       Their verdure dare not show . . . their verdure dare not show . . .
       Cant and randy—the seals' heads bobbing in the tide-flow
       Between the islands, sleek and black and irrelevant
       They cannot depose logically what they want:
5   Died by gunshot under borrowed pennons,
       Sniped from the wet gorse and taken by the limp fins
       And slung like a dead seal in a boghole, beaten up
       By peasants with long lips and the whisky-drinker's cough.
       Park your car in the city of Dublin, see Sackville Street
10   Without the sandbags in the old photos, meet
       The statues of the patriots, history never dies,
       At any rate in Ireland, arson and murder are legacies
       Like old rings hollow-eyed without their stones
       Dumb talismans.
15   See Belfast, devout and profane and hard,
       Built on reclaimed mud, hammers playing in the shipyard,
       Time punched with holes like a steel sheet, time
       Hardening the faces, veneering with a grey and speckled rime
       The faces under the shawls and caps:
20   This was my mother-city, these my paps.
       Country of callous lava cooled to stone,
       Of minute sodden haycocks, of ship-sirens' moan,
       Of falling intonations—I would call you to book

133: *Wiltshire Downs:* the Marlborough Downs in Wiltshire, a steep grass-covered chalk escarpment
    the Long Mynd: part of the Shropshire Hills; unlike the rest of the Hills, its summit is covered not by
forest but by bare heather.

2: *randy:* noisy revelry
9: *Sackville Street:* location of Dublin's General Post Office; it was the locus of fighting in both the Easter
1916 rebellion and the 1922–1923 Civil War. It is now named O'Connell Street.

I would say to you, Look;
25   I would say, This is what you have given me
Indifference and sentimentality
A metallic giggle, a fumbling hand,
A heart that leaps to a fife band:
Set these against your water-shafted air
30   Of amethyst and moonstone, the horses' feet like bells of hair
Shambling beneath the orange cart, the beer-brown spring
Guzzling between the heather, the green gush of Irish spring.
Cursèd be he that curses his mother. I cannot be
Anyone else than what this land engendered me:
35   In the back of my mind are snips of white, the sails
Of the Lough's fishing-boats, the bellropes lash their tails
When I would peal my thoughts, the bells pull free—
Memory in apostasy.
I would tot up my factors
40   But who can stand in the way of his soul's steam-tractors?
I can say Ireland is hooey, Ireland is
A gallery of fake tapestries,
But I cannot deny my past to which my self is wed,
The woven figure cannot undo its thread.
45   On a cardboard lid I saw when I was four
Was the trade-mark of a hound and a round tower,
And that was Irish glamour, and in the cemetery
Sham Celtic crosses claimed our individuality,
And my father talked about the West where years back
50   He played hurley on the sands with a stick of wrack.
Park your car in Killarney, buy a souvenir
Of green marble or black bog-oak, run up to Clare,
Climb the cliff in the postcard, visit Galway city,
Romanticize on our Spanish blood, leave ten per cent of pity
55   Under your plate for the emigrant,
Take credit for our sanctity, our heroism and our sterile want
Columba Kevin and briny Brandan the accepted names,
Wolfe Tone and Grattan and Michael Collins the accepted names,
Admire the suavity with which the architect

46: *a hound and a round tower:* national symbols: an Irish wolfhound and one of the round towers char-
acteristic of early Irish monastic settlements. Cf. MacNeice's autobiography *The Strings are False* (Lon-
don, 1965), pp. 50–51: "My father had a brand of writing-paper which came in boxes decorated with a
round tower and an ancient Irish wolfhound; whenever I looked at this trademark I felt a nostalgia, sweet
and melting, for the world where that wolfhound belonged. All these things were old and being old were
good."
48: *Celtic crosses* are tall, free-standing, ornately carved stone crosses found on medieval Irish monastic
sites. Their most distinctive feature is a ring about the cross's center.
49: *The West* of Ireland is its most rural and poorest area; the places listed in lines 51–53 are all in the west.
50: *hurley:* a form of field-hockey
52: Connemara, in Co. Galway, is known for its green-streaked *marble.*
    bog-oak: ancient oak preserved in a peat bog
54: In popular belief Spanish blood was introduced into the Irish population after ships from the Spanish
Armada foundered off the Irish coast in 1588.
55: *emigrant:* i.e., to the U.S.A. (an exodus that had its beginnings in the Irish Potato Famine of the 1840s
and still continued into the twentieth century)
57: *Columba Kevin and briny Brandan:* medieval Irish saints; St. Brandan (or Brendan) was a noted trav-
eler, the subject of the tenth-century *Navigatio Brendani* ("Voyage of Brendan").
58: *Wolfe Tone and Grattan and Michael Collins* are heroes of Irish nationalist history, the first two eigh-
teenth-century figures, the latter twentieth-century.

60   Is rebuilding the burnt mansion, recollect
         The palmy days of the Horse Show, swank your fill,
         But take the Holyhead boat before you pay the bill;
         Before you face the consequence
         Of inbred soul and climatic maleficence
65   And pay for the trick beauty of a prism
         In drug-dull fatalism.
         I will exorcize my blood
         And not to have my baby-clothes my shroud
         I will acquire an attitude not yours
70   And become as one of your holiday visitors,
         And however often I may come
         Farewell, my country, and in perpetuum;
         Whatever desire I catch when your wind scours my face
         I will take home and put in a glass case
75   And merely look on
         At each new fantasy of badge and gun.
         Frost will not touch the hedge of fuchsias,
         The land will remain as it was,
         But no abiding content can grow out of these minds
80   Fuddled with blood, always caught by blinds;
         The eels go up the Shannon over the great dam;
         You cannot change a response by giving it a new name.
         Fountain of green and blue curling in the wind
         I must go east and stay, not looking behind,
85   Not knowing on which day the mist is blanket-thick
         Nor when sun quilts the valley and quick
         Winging shadows of white clouds pass
         Over the long hills like a fiddle's phrase.
         If I were a dog of sunlight I would bound
90   From Phoenix Park to Achill Sound,
         Picking up the scent of a hundred fugitives
         That have broken the mesh of ordinary lives,
         But being ordinary too I must in course discuss
         What we mean to Ireland or Ireland to us;
95   I have to observe milestone and curio
         The beaten buried gold of an old king's bravado,
         Falsetto antiquities, I have to gesture,
         Take part in, or renounce, each imposture;
         Therefore I resign, goodbye the chequered and the quiet hills
100   The gaudily-striped Atlantic, the linen-mills
         That swallow the shawled file, the black moor where half
         A turf-stack stands like a ruined cenotaph;
         Goodbye your hens running in and out of the white house

---

60: *mansion:* a mansion of the Anglo-Irish Ascendancy, burnt down in the political turmoil of the nineteenth and early twentieth century.
61: *Horse Show:* the annual show held by the Royal Dublin Society beginning in 1864.
62: *Holyhead boat:* the ferry from Dun Laoghire (near Dublin) to Holyhead, a port and resort on Anglesey, Wales.
72: *in perpetuum:* forever
81: The River *Shannon* is the longest in Ireland; where it reaches Lough Derg there is a fish ladder that permits them to pass upriver to spawn.
90: From one end of Ireland to the other: *Phoenix Park* is in Dublin; *Achill Sound* is the bridge that connects the island of Achill, on the west coast, to the mainland.

Your absent-minded goats along the road, your black cows
105   Your greyhounds and your hunters beautifully bred
Your drums and your dolled-up Virgins and your ignorant dead.

1934 / *1935*

Snow

The room was suddenly rich and the great bay-window was
Spawning snow and pink roses against it
Soundlessly collateral and incompatible:
World is suddener than we fancy it.

5   World is crazier and more of it than we think,
Incorrigibly plural. I peel and portion
A tangerine and spit the pips and feel
The drunkenness of things being various.

And the fire flames with a bubbling sound for world
10   Is more spiteful and gay than one supposes—
On the tongue on the eyes on the ears in the palms of one's hands—
There is more than glass between the snow and the huge roses.

1935 / *1935*

Carrickfergus

I was born in Belfast between the mountain and the gantries
    To the hooting of lost sirens and the clang of trams:
Thence to Smoky Carrick in County Antrim
    Where the bottle-neck harbour collects the mud which jams

5   The little boats beneath the Norman castle,
    The pier shining with lumps of crystal salt;
The Scotch Quarter was a line of residential houses
    But the Irish Quarter was a slum for the blind and halt.

The brook ran yellow from the factory stinking of chlorine,
10   The yarn-mill called its funeral cry at noon;
Our lights looked over the lough to the lights of Bangor
    Under the peacock aura of a drowning moon.

The Norman walled this town against the country
    To stop his ears to the yelping of his slave

Title: *Carrickfergus:* a town in Northern Ireland, on the north shore of Belfast Lough. Carrickfergus Castle lies on a rocky spur above the harbor. MacNeice's account of his childhood here may be usefully compared with that in *The Strings are False,* chapters 4–9, especially chapter 8.
11: *Bangor:* town on the opposite shore of Belfast Lough

15   And built a church in the form of a cross but denoting
             The list of Christ on the cross in the angle of the nave.

         I was the rector's son, born to the anglican order,
             Banned for ever from the candles of the Irish poor;
         The Chichesters knelt in marble at the end of a transept
20   With ruffs about their necks, their portion sure.

         The war came and a huge camp of soldiers
             Grew from the ground in sight of our house with long
         Dummies hanging from gibbets for bayonet practice
             And the sentry's challenge echoing all day long;

25   A Yorkshire terrier ran in and out by the gate-lodge
             Barred to civilians, yapping as if taking affront:
         Marching at ease and singing 'Who Killed Cock Robin?'
             The troops went out by the lodge and off to the Front.

         The steamer was camouflaged that took me to England—
30   Sweat and khaki in the Carlisle train;
         I thought that the war would last for ever and sugar
             Be always rationed and that never again

         Would the weekly papers not have photos of sandbags
             And my governess not make bandages from moss
35   And people not have maps above the fireplace
             With flags on pins moving across and across—

         Across the hawthorn hedge the noise of bugles,
             Flares across the night,
         Somewhere on the lough was a prison ship for Germans,
40   A cage across their sight.

         I went to school in Dorset, the world of parents
             Contracted into a puppet world of sons
         Far from the mill girls, the smell of porter, the salt-mines
             And the soldiers with their guns.

                                                    1937 / 1938

15: *church:* the medieval Church of St. Nicholas; it is renowned for its 1625 monument to Lord Chicester,
Lord Deputy of Ireland from 1604 to 1614.
16: *list:* tilt
       nave: the main section of a church, in the form of a long narrow hall; the *transepts* (line 19) are the
two sections at right angles to the nave in a cross-shaped church.
18: In the Catholic church votive *candles* are lit and placed in front of a religious image as a symbol of
prayer.
30: *Carlisle:* in Northern England, on the Scottish border
41: *Dorset:* a county in southwest England

CLERE PARSONS (1908–1931)

PARSONS WAS BORN IN INDIA AND EDUCATED AT ST. PAUL'S SCHOOL AND CHRIST Church, Oxford. He was active in undergraduate poetry circles at Oxford that included Louis MacNeice, Edouard Roditi, Bernard Spencer, and Stephen Spender, editing and contributing poems and essays to *Oxford Poetry* and *The Oxford Outlook*. He suffered from a severe case of diabetes and died at twenty-three. T. S. Eliot paid tribute to him in *The Criterion* in 1931, and Parsons's thirty-page volume, entitled *Poems*, was assembled by Herbert Read and published by Faber in 1932. More recently, these poems and others published in magazines have been gathered in *The Air Between: Poems of Clere Parsons* (1989). In his introduction to this volume, T. W. Sutherland cites an obituary indicating that Parsons was "ready to sacrifice the prospect of a literary career to social service" and lines from a poem by Geoffrey Grigson describing him as one "who revered the mind's integrity / Whose hand was against strife / Whose love for the lowly."[1] Parsons's poems, however, show little of his interest in politics. In the afterword to the same volume, Roditi remembers that, among Oxford undergraduate poets, it was Parsons and Spencer who shared his interest in the modernist poetry published in France and the United States. Having met the editors of the Cambridge avant-garde magazine *Experiment*, Parsons started a magazine that reflected its influence, *Sir Galahad*. An interest in a "pure poetry" (derided by MacNeice a few years later) is announced in the second strophe of Parsons's "Introduction": "Mallarmé for a favour / teach me to achieve / the rigid gesture won only with labour / and comparable to the ease / balance and strength with which the ballet-dancer / sustains her still mercurial pose in air."[2] C. H. Sisson has praised "the work— and not merely the sentiment—of a poet who is setting out to learn his trade as Pound and Eliot set out," noting "a quality at once airy and metallic" in the music of Parsons's verse line.[3]

---

[1] *The Air Between: Poems of Clere Parsons,* Newcastle upon Tyne, 1989, p. 12.
[2] Ibid., p. 15.
[3] *English Poetry 1900–1950,* London, 1971, p. 217.

Corybantic

Closing our books we walked into the air
It was the touch of life the genuine sense
Of the old part played as a new adventure
Future and past merged in the present tense

5   Blow when you will according to your nature
Eager March wind promise of vernal scent
Pagan in youth not unnaturally her
Demonic limbs this close constraint resent

1932

Photogravure

Io   Io   Io
    Sing the white birds
    Io   Io

Enter these tarnished woods
5   Where tensely
The summer broods.

Flystung in pools kneedeep to cool their hooves
Indolent and immobile the cows brood
Or lazily raise listlessly swish
10   And droop
            their tails

Climb gravely upon slow wings
Slower than Time utter your cries
La la you are holy birds
15   Dead sailors look through your eyes

Pol-
perro   Io   Io
                China clouds

Irresolute against heaven's Wedgewood blue.

1932

Title: The *Corybantes* were (male) priests of the goddess Cybele, whom they celebrated with orgiastic rites involving wild dancing and music.

Title: *Photogravure:* a print produced from an engraved plate made from a photograph
1: *Io:* a Latin or Greek interjection (expressing joy, pain, etc.)
15: According to an old sailors' superstition, storm petrels (a type of seabird) are the incarnations of the souls of dead seamen.
16–17: *Polperro* is a fishing village in Cornwall.
19: *Wedgewood blue:* a light shade of blue, a specialty of the Wedgwood porcelain firm.

Different

Not to say what everyone else was saying
not to believe what everyone else believed
not to do what everybody did,
then to refute what everyone else was saying
5   then to disprove what everyone else believed
then to deprecate what everybody did,

was his way to come by understanding

how everyone else was saying the same as he was saying
believing what he believed
10   and did what doing

1932

Interruption

The deep sun leisurely with mottled gray-
plumed wings closefurls the stippled day
in which they tentatively their souls paraded
in bodies attached by surest threads of silk
5   like monocles they dangled for effect;
each in ornate deliberate words bedecked
dancing attendance in slow modes of speech
in pauses rich to encourage confidence . . .
No hurry at all no hurry let the words fall
10   plumb, and roll gravely each like a cannon-ball
dislodged from proud pedestal or monument
gathering pace down dusky slopes of sense.
Time to gesture with hands, time to exhibit
how subtle and fine is thought it will not fit
15   (sometimes) into those labelled grooves of sound
we docket Latin, French, German, English . . .
Memory obfuscates and fancy obscures
also these sentences which slacken and pause;
causeless intrude the Quarter Boys of Rye
20   and early golfers walking on Camber dunes.

1932

19: *Rye* is a town in Sussex, near the coast; the *Quarter Boys* (jacks in the form of boys that strike the quarter-hours) are those of its church, St Mary's. Camber Sands, nearby, is the location of a noted golf course.

DENIS DEVLIN (1908–1959)

D EVLIN WAS BORN IN GREENOCK, SCOTLAND TO IRISH PARENTS. THE FAMILY returned to Ireland in 1920, and Devlin attended first Belvedere College, then the diocesan seminary at All Hallow's College, Clonliffe, and finally University College, Dublin, where he took first-class honors in both English and French. In 1931, he was awarded an M.A. for his thesis on Montaigne and moved to Paris to continue his studies at the Sorbonne. After a brief stint in the English Department at University College, Dublin, Devlin entered the Department of Foreign Affairs to begin a successful career as an overseas diplomat. He held a series of diplomatic posts in Washington D. C., London, Turkey, and Italy. In 1958, he was named ambassador to Italy. Devlin translated modern French poets, including St. John-Perse, Paul Valéry, and René Char. His books of poetry include the self-published *Poems* (with Brian Coffey, 1930), *Lough Derg and Other Poems* (1946), and, posthumously, *Selected Poems* (1963), edited by the American poets Allen Tate and Robert Penn Warren, and *The Heavenly Foreigner* (1967), edited by Brian Coffey.

Devlin is often grouped with Thomas MacGreevy, Brian Coffey, and Samuel Beckett—four international modernists among modern Irish poets. But as a group these poets do not share much beyond a rejection of the Irish Literary Revival's parochialism and the empiricism of the Irish traditions associated with Patrick Kavanagh and Austin Clarke. Devlin in particular seems more simply outside than consciously opposed to prevailing Irish modes. Randall Jarrell once compared Devlin's poetry unfavorably to Louis MacNeice's, calling it "distracting," "rhetorical," and "unevenly assertive": "the reader realizes he is being taken on an expensive, cultivated, expected series of digressions, a Grand Tour."[1] Noting some of the same qualities, Beckett praised the "abstruse self-consciousness" of Devlin's syntactically dense and "overimaged" poems, arguing that "art has nothing to do with clarity, does not dabble in the clear and does not make clear."[2] J. C. C. Mays writes of Devlin's poetry's "self-checking" manner; "the poems turn over in their length, take off suddenly in unanticipated directions, double-back."[3] The stylistic tendencies that all of these remarks point to might be explained by what Stan Smith describes as the "central paradox for Devlin: if language is a tract on which the soul constructs itself from moment to moment, it is also an impermanent and treacherous ground."[4] Brian Coffey thought that the

---

[1] Randall Jarrell, *Poetry and the Age*, New York, 1953, p. 204.
[2] "Denis Devlin" (1938), *Disjecta: Miscellaneous Writings and a Dramatic Fragment*, ed. Ruby Cohn, New York, 1984, p. 94.
[3] Introduction, *Collected Poems of Denis Devlin*, ed. J.C.C. Mays, Dublin, 1989, p. 34.
[4] "'Precarious Guest': The Poetry of Denis Devlin," *Modernism and Ireland: The Poetry of the 1930s*, ed. Patricia Coughlan and Alex Davis, Cork, 1995, p. 233.

reserve and quietism of Devlin's poetry owed something to his seminary education. The philosophy and theology of Blaise Pascal is a pervasive influence. "Lough Derg," first published during World War II, meditates upon the value of the ancient religious pilgrimage to Lough Derg in Donegal.

Lough Derg

The poor in spirit on their rosary rounds,
The jobbers with their whiskey-angered eyes,
The pink bank clerks, the tip-hat papal counts,
And drab, kind women their tonsured mockery tries,
5   Glad invalids on penitential feet
Walk the Lord's majesty like their village street.

With mullioned Europe shattered, this Northwest,
Rude-sainted isle would pray it whole again:
(Peasant Apollo! Troy is worn to rest.)
10   Europe that humanized the sacred bane
Of God's chance who yet laughed in his mind
And balanced thief and saint: were they this kind?

Low rocks, a few weasels, lake
Like a field of burnt gorse; the rooks caw;
15   Ours, passive, for man's gradual wisdom take
Firefly instinct dreamed out into law;
The prophets' jewelled kingdom down at heel
Fires no Augustine here. Inert, they kneel;

All is simple and symbol in their world,
20   The incomprehended rendered fabulous.
Sin teases life whose natural fruits withheld
Sour the deprived nor bloom for timely loss:

Title: Station Island, in *Lough Derg,* a lake in County Donegal, has been a site of religious pilgrimage since early Christian times, bringing pilgrims from Ireland and all over Europe. St. Patrick is said to have descended a cave there to Purgatory. The three-day pilgrimage involves a routine of prayer, fasting, and walking barefoot around stone circles ("beds"), thought to be the remains of ancient monastic cells.

1: *poor in spirit:* "Blessed are the poor in spirit, for theirs is the kingdom of heaven." (Matt. 5:3)
   rosary: in the Catholic church, a string of beads used to number a series of formulaic prayers recited while contemplating Christ's life, divided into three groups of five scenes, known as the Joyful, Sorrowful, and Glorious Mysteries.

2: *jobbers:* traders

3: The honorific title of *papal count* is bestowed by the Pope.

7: *mullioned Europe shattered:* This poem first appeared in periodical form in 1942, during World War II. A *mullion* is a vertical division in a window (characteristic of Gothic church architecture).

8: *Rude:* uneducated; St. Patrick, Ireland's national saint, greatly regretted his lack of higher education.

9: *Apollo* supported *Troy* in the Trojan War.

10ff: The stark mystery of God's grace, as exemplified by the story in Luke 23:39–43 of the thieves crucified alongside Christ (of whom one was saved, the other damned), was later tempered in Europe by secular humanism.

12: *were they this kind?:* An earlier version runs "but not this kind"; Devlin is comparing the thief and saint of legend with the people of stanza 1.

14: *gorse:* gorsebush; an undesirable plant, it would be often cleared by burning.

17ff: Devlin ironically identifies the Irish Free State with the New Jerusalem (Rev. 21); where cumulative knowledge ("gradual wisdom") is ignored in favor of "instinct dreamed out into law," there is no place for a modern St. Augustine (354–430), the great Christian theologian and author of *The City of God.*

Clan Jansen! less what magnanimity leavens
Man's wept-out, fitful, magniloquent heavens

25　　Where prayer was praise, O Lord! the Temple trumpets
Cascaded down Thy sunny pavilions of air,
The scroll-tongued priests, the galvanic strumpets,
All clash and stridency gloomed upon Thy stair;
The pharisees, the exalted boy their power
30　　Sensually psalmed in Thee, their coming hour!

And to the sun, earth turned her flower of sex,
Acanthus in the architects' limpid angles;
Close priests allegorized the Orphic egg's
Brood, and from the Academy, tolerant wranglers
35　　Could hear the contemplatives of the Tragic Choir
Drain off man's sanguine, pastoral death-desire.

It was said stone dreams and animal sleeps and man
Is awake; but sleep with its drama on us bred
Animal articulate, only somnambulist can
40　　Conscience like Cawdor give the blood its head
For the dim moors to reign through druids again.
O first geometer! tangent-feelered brain

Clearing by inches the encircled eyes,
Bolder than the peasant tiger whose autumn beauty
45　　Sags in the expletive kill, or the sacrifice
Of dearth puffed positive in the stance of duty
With which these pilgrims would propitiate
Their fears; no leafy, medieval state

23: *Jansenism* was a harshly moralistic form of Catholicism subscribing to the doctrines of Cornelius Jansen (1585–1638), in particular his deterministic conception of God's grace.

25ff: See Christ's warning: "when thou doest thine alms, do not sound a trumpet before thee, as the hypocrites do in the synagogues and in the streets, that they may have glory of men. . . . And when thou prayest, thou shalt not be as the hypocrites are: for they love to pray standing in the synagogues and in the corners of the streets, that they may be seen of men. . . . But thou, when thou prayest, enter into thy closet, and when thou hast shut thy door, pray to thy Father which is in secret" (Matthew 6:2–6). Despite its hypocrisy, Devlin suggests, such behavior at least showed a *magnanimity* that modern Irish Catholicism lacks.

29: *pharisees*: a strictly observant Jewish sect who were opponents of Christ; their name is now synonymous with hypocrisy and self-righteousness. They *sensually psalmed* the coming of Christ (the *exalted boy*) in that they failed to fully understand the biblical texts they spoke aloud, which prophesied the Messiah's coming.

32: Stylized representations of *acanthus* leaves adorned the capitals of Corinthian columns in classical Greek architecture.

33: In the legends of the ancient Greek *Orphic* cult, the god of Life was born from an *egg* laid by Chronos (Time), in turn creating a world containing gods and men.

34: *Academy*: the school of philosophy founded in Athens by Plato

35: *Tragic Choir*: the Chorus of Greek tragedy; according to Aristotle's *Poetics*, the purpose of tragedy is *catharsis*, the purging of the spectator's emotions of pity and fear.

37ff: Devlin seems to have in mind the philosopher Gottfried Leibniz (1646–1716), for whom the universe was composed of "monads," which all possess the faculty of consciousness to varying degrees.

39ff: "only when sleepwalking can Conscience, like Cawdor, permit violent actions." Macbeth, Thane of Cawdor, became King of Scotland through murdering King Duncan as he slept.

41: The rites performed by the *druids*, ancient Celtic priests, included human sacrifice.

42: *O first geometer*: i.e., the brain

45: *expletive*: literally, "filling"

Of paschal cathedrals backed on earthy hooves
50   Against the craftsmen's primary-coloured skies
Whose gold was Gabriel on the patient roofs,
The parabled windows taught the dead to rise,
And Christ the Centaur, in two natures whole,
With fable and proverb joinered body and soul.

55   Water withers from the oars. The pilgrims blacken
Out of the boats to masticate their sin
Where Dante smelled among the stones and bracken
The door to Hell (O harder Hell where pain
Is earthed, a casuist sanctuary of guilt!).
60   Spirit bureaucracy on a bet built

Part by this race when monks in convents of coracles
For the Merovingian centuries left their land,
Belled, fragrant; and honest in their oracles
Bespoke the grace to give without demand,
65   Martyrs Heaven winged nor tempted with reward.
And not ours, doughed in dogma, who never have dared

Will with surrogate palm distribute hope:
No better nor worse than I who, in my books,
Have angered at the stake with Bruno and, by the rope
70   Watt Tyler swung from, leagued with shifty looks
To fuse the next rebellion with the desperate
Serfs in the sane need to eat and get;

Have praised, on its thunderous canvas, the Florentine smile
As man took to wearing his death, his own,
75   Sapped crisis through cathedral branches (while
Flesh groped loud round dissenting skeleton)
In soul, reborn as body's appetite:
Now languisht back in body's amber light,

49: *paschal*: Easter

50: The *craftsmen* are the illuminators of medieval manuscripts, which often contained paintings executed in bright colors and gold leaf.

51: *Gabriel*: the archangel Gabriel

54: *joinered*: joined together, like pieces of wood in carpentry; Christ was a carpenter (Mark 6:3).

57: The poet *Dante* according to legend conceived the idea for his *Divine Comedy* from visiting the cave at Lough Derg.

61ff: The early Irish church is celebrated for its learning and for its missionary activities in Scotland, northern England, and western Europe. Until 751 it was independent from Rome.

61: *coracles*: small, wicker-framed boats, covered with hide or fabric

62: The Frankish *Merovingian* dynasty (476–750) is traditionally considered the "first race" of the kings of France.

69: The doctrines of the Italian Renaissance philosopher Giordano *Bruno* (1548–1600) were censured by the Church; he was captured by the Inquisition and burned at the stake.

70: *Watt Tyler* was leader of the Kentish rebels in the Peasants' Revolt of 1381 in England. Protests against the unpopular poll-tax culminated in a march on London by rebels from Kent and Essex; during negotiations with Richard II, Tyler was stabbed to death (not hanged) by the Mayor of London.

73: *Florentine smile*: i.e. that of the *Mona Lisa*, painted by the Florentine painter Leonardo Da Vinci (1452–1519).

74ff: The passage is obscure, but the sense seems to be: man's sense of himself as an individual—of personal mortality and bodily appetites—grew because of humanism, which was also responsible for the Protestant schism from the Roman Catholic Church; ultimately it was responsible for modern secularism.

78: *Now languisht*: now (the soul) is reduced to languor.

Now is consumed. O earthly paradise!
80   Hell is to know our natural empire used
Wrong, by mind's moulting, brute divinities.
The vanishing tiger's saved, his blood transfused.
Kent is for Jutes again and Glasgow town
Burns high enough to screen the stars and moon.

85   Well may they cry who have been robbed, their wasting
Shares in justice legally lowered until
Man his own actor, matrix, mould and casting,
Or man, God's image, sees his idol spill.
Say it was pride that did it, or virtue's brief:
90   To them that suffer it is no relief.

All indiscriminate, man, stone, animal
Are woken up in nightmare. What John the Blind
From Patmos saw works and we speak it. Not all
The men of God nor the priests of mankind
95   Can mend or explain the good and broke, not one
Generous with love prove communion;

Behind the eyes the winged ascension flags,
For want of spirit by the market blurbed,
And if hands touch, such fraternity sags
100   Frightened this side the dykes of death disturbed
Like Aran Islands' bibulous, unclean seas:
Pietà: but the limbs ache; it is not peace.

Then to see less, look little, let hearts' hunger
Feed on water and berries. The pilgrims sing:
105   Life will fare well from elder to younger,
Though courage fail in a world-end, rosary ring.
Courage kills its practitioners and we live,
Nothing forgotten, nothing to forgive,

We pray to ourself. The metal moon, unspent
110   Virgin eternity sleeping in the mind,
Excites the form of prayer without content;
Whitethorn lightens, delicate and blind,
The negro mountain, and so, knelt on her sod,
This woman beside me murmuring *My God! My God!*

1946

83: The *Jutes* were a Germanic people who invaded England in the fifth century and settled in Kent; *Glasgow* was hit by German bombing raids during World War II.

88: *spill:* both "topple" and "kill"

92: What *John* of *Patmos* saw was the Apocalypse, which he set down in the Book of Revelation.

100: *the dykes of death:* In Greek Mythology, the afterlife realm of Hades could only be reached by crossing the river Styx.

101: The *Aran Islands,* in the mouth of Galway Bay, are 30 miles from the mainland; the waters around them are treacherous.

102: *Pietà:* an artistic representation—notably the sculpture by Michelangelo—of the Virgin Mary's holding the dead body of Christ in her lap

106: At the end of the contemplation of each Mystery in the rosary, one says, "Glory be to the Father, and to the Son, and to the Holy Spirit. As it was in the beginning, is now, and ever shall be, world without end. Amen."

113ff: *and so . . . This woman:* "and in the same way does this woman lighten the (metaphorical) dark mountain"

Obstacle Basilisk

Down the path through treacherous years blood-dried
My cold-sweat horse, with his incredulous ears,
Ticks off each bandit landmark as we ride,
With friendly snuffling shows he shares my fears.
5   Those damp rhinoceroses, the mountains, shamble
Past; and hasty clouds tear like bramble
Into its spectral seven the dying light;
The stirrup foot, the reins, renege their lordships,
A mile below is a breastful of warships
10   In a heroic harbour, menacing, tight.

An old priest's nag pulls up, cries askance
At our disarticulated style:
"Halleluia! halleluia!" In fractious dance
His legs curve like a weak smile.

15   Then sundown at the city gates
Defended by a groom and three sick colts
My horse backs away and defecates,
Transformed into a whippet, off he bolts:
I have lived with nobility of emotion,
20   Thought out my honour, justified my rise:
Is this mean groom my measure? he, my harm?
Shall thus his fear degrade me, slow my arm?
The basilisk, my mercy in his eyes,
Unmans us both; we fade in slow motion
25   By invisible spider-camera webbed; our cue,
Predestined, robs us of the will to do.

Or could I ever break the servile charm
And gain one step, in scrupulous alarm?

1946

Title: The *Basilisk* was a mythical reptile whose gaze was fatal to the observer.
7: *spectral seven:* the seven colors of the spectrum

LYNETTE ROBERTS (1909–1995)

"THERE IS A GOOD CASE FOR SAYING THAT [ROBERTS] IS THE ONE AND ONLY LATINO-Welsh modernist," Nigel Wheale writes.[1] Roberts was born in Buenos Aires to parents of Welsh descent and educated in Argentina and at the Central School for Arts and Crafts in London. She spent World War I in England while her father fought on the Western Front and, following the post-war death of her mother in Argentina, moved to London. After marrying the Welsh poet and editor Keidrych Rhys, she moved to Llanybri, South Carmarthshire, a village in Wales where she spent the 1940s, her most productive period as a writer. Roberts was known to and her work as poet and painter respected by several of the major literary figures of the decade: Wyndham Lewis and Edith Sitwell, among others. She corresponded with David Jones and Robert Graves, submitting materials for Graves's *The White Goddess*, though ultimately writing him that "Parts of your theory [are] totally wrong."[2] Dylan Thomas attended her wedding, and Roberts knew other Welsh writers such as Alun Lewis and Vernon Watkins. Faber and Faber published her first book of poetry, *Poems*, in 1944; a pamphlet entitled *An Introduction to Village Dialect with Seven Stories* was published by the Druid Press in the same year. *Gods with Stainless Ears*, subtitled "a heroic poem," was written between 1941 and 1943, though not published until 1951. During the period of its composition Roberts's husband was on active duty with coastal batteries as Swansea was attacked by Nazi bombers. These and other specific historical events, such as the downing of a pilot off the coast, are part of the background to the poem's visionary narrative. After Roberts and Rhys were divorced in 1949, she moved to London but published little beyond *The Endeavor: Captain Cook's First Voyage to Australia* (1954). In recent decades interest in her work has been slowly building.

"Essentially an elliptical narrative presenting different aspects of the war's impact on the village and coastal area near Llanybri," Wheale writes, *Gods with Stainless Ears* bears comparison with T. S. Eliot's *Four Quartets* and H. D.'s *Trilogy* as modernist sequences responding to the blitz. In her preface, Roberts says the poem's subject is "universal, and the tragedy one of too many"; her further comment that "my own [tragedy], though part may be expressed, is outside the page," perhaps glances at the miscarriage she suffered during the war. The poem's fourth section, "Cri Madonna," is a dramatic monologue in which an unnamed speaker elegizes a child lost among the other casualties of war; Roberts's note states that "The struggle for birth under these conditions suggests a comparison with the Madonna, which becomes the nucleus and theme of the whole poem." The narrative concludes in a fifth section, which gives us, as Roberts's prefatory "argument" says, "the gunner returned, and faithful to his girl;

---

[1] "Lynette Roberts: legend and form in the 1940s," *Critical Quarterly*, vol. 36, no. 3, 1994, p. 5.
[2] Quoted in Wheale, p. 7.

they rise through the strata of the sky to seek peace and solace from the sun" and "love in harmony on cloud in fourth dimensional state." The lovers are ultimately forced to return to Earth where the gunner-poet, resolved "to free the [Welsh] dragon, and take fate in his own hands," and "walks meekly" into the "Mental Home for Poets," leaving the girl to look upon a "hard and new chemical dawn breaking up the traditional sky-line." The poem's dense and semantically rich line has some affinities with New Romantic and New Apocalypse poetry, in which, in Wheale's words, "a version of musi-cality is privileged over sense," here meeting "a counter-tendency, which is a vigorous interest in etymology and in uncommon meanings of specific words."[3] In her preface Roberts writes that "congested words, images, and certain hard metallic lines are intro-duced with deliberate emphasis to represent a period of muddled and intense thought which arose out of the first years of conflict."[4]

---

[3] Wheale, p. 9.
[4] *Gods with Stainless Ears*, p. 11.

from Gods with Stainless Ears

Part IV: Cri Madonna

Un eich amynedd un ddi-feth,
Un yn eich croes a'ch cri,
Mair, mam Iesu o Nasareth
A' Mari o Llanybri.

DYFNALLT

ARGUMENT

Of birth. Of uneventful birth. Owing to lack of money and to emotional strain death cuts in, double death, loss of lover and child. The struggle for birth under these conditions suggests a comparison with the Madonna, which becomes the nucleus and theme of the whole poem. *That the birth of flesh and blood is every-where a noble event and that lives of all nationalities must be considered sacred— not to be callously destroyed.* Of the girl's distraction. Humiliation at her dou-ble loss. Stanzas of discordant fifths prevail. Cherubs weep, and a desolation and deadness of spirit is felt as after raids. The uselessness of the soldiers' jobs is intensified as they empty latrine buckets in the rain. Making them, since to rebel at this particular time would bring about the country's defeat, *our heroes. The heroes unknown who braved and bore, each a private crucifix.*

 I, rimmeled, awake before the dressing sun:
 Alone I, pent up incinerator, serf of satellite gloom

We would like to gratefully acknowledge the assistance of John Pikoulis and Nigel Wheale in the assem-bly of these glosses.

Title: "The Cry of the Madonna"

Epigraph: "The same your patience unfailing, / The same your cross and your cry, / Mary, mother of Nazareth / And Mary of Llanybri." "The above translation is from one of Dyfnallt's poems 'Cri Madonna'. He is one of our poets and a leading Nonconformist minister. I should like to point out here, that I have intentionally used Welsh quotations as this helps to give the conscious compact and culture of another nation. The village of Llanybri, around which this poem is set, is Welsh speaking." (Roberts)

1: *Rimmel* was the name of a cosmetics manufacturer: presumably, from weeping the speaker's eyes look like they are ringed with black make-up.

Cower around my cradled self; find crape-plume
In a work-basket cast into swaddling clothes
5   Forcipated from my mind after the foetal fall:

Rising ashly, challenge blood to curb—compose—
Martial mortal, face a red mourning alone.
To the star of the third magnitude O my God,
Shriek, sear my swollen breasts, send succour
10   To sift and settle me.—This the labour of it . . .

But reality worse than the pain intrudes,
And no near doctor for six days. This
Also is added truth. Razed for lack of
Incomputable finance. For womb was
15   Fresh as the day and solid as your hand.

BLOOD OF ALL MEN. DRENCHED ANCESTORS OF WAR
WHETHER GERMAN. BRITISH. RUSSIAN. OR HIDE
FROM SOME OTHER FOREIGN FIELD: REMEMBER AGAIN
BLOOD IS HUMAN. BORN AT COST. REMEMBER THIS
20   ESPECIALLY YOU TAWDRY LAIRDS AND JUGGLERS OF MINT.

So double hurt was hard to console. Heart hatched
Shrived nerves each day in valley clove. Stretched
Mind tight into scarlet umbrella. Slatched
Nowhere the deflated ropes of blood. Wrenched
25   Harbouring heartbreak that is a crack grailed.

O where was my consoler. Where O where
You double beast down. Callous Cymru.
O love beaten. By loss humiliated.
Stretched out in muslin distress. Bound
30   By an iron wreath scattered with coloured beads.

O my people immeasurably alone.
No ringfinger: with the tips of my nails glazed
With sorrow with solemn gravity. Crown tipped sideways;
Ears blown back like lilac; with set face
35   And dry lids, waiting for Love's Arcade.

O LOVE was there no barddoniaeth?
No billing birds to be—coinheritor?

The night sky is braille in a rock of frost.

5: *Forcipated:* extracted with forceps
8: *star of the third magnitude:* i.e. a distant star ("magnitude" is the astronomical measure of a star's
   brightness). If Roberts had a particular star in mind it remains unidentified.
14: *Incomputable finance:* "During this war the Government allowed apes at the Zoo thirty shillings per
   week for their food, while soldiers' wives received seventeen shillings and sixpence per week to cover
   food, rent, clothing, and the security and protection of a child." (Roberts)
20: *LAIRDS:* landed proprietors (Scots)
23: *Slatched:* slackened
27: *Cymru:* Wales
36: *barddoniaeth:* poetry, verse (Welsh)

Why wail ribbon head. Crystallized cherubic
40   Cluster of stars. Why weep spilling splints to
Steelgraze the sky. Why shrillcold cerulean
Flesh with identity tacked hot on your wing.
Why dribble prick-ears, scintillating in an up

And down nailmourn. Tumbling to earth an icy precision
45   Of pins, distilling flies and peacock fins,
Tears in flames on fire, scorching air as they
Splash into heavier spills of quavering
Silver, drops, seels resinate woe, chills hedge and

Chilblain glades. Grisaille freezes the sense; crines
50   The gills into a drill motion; stills-shrills
The singing birds to kill; drips rills
From envelopes, pustule eyes and hat. With
Urinal taint instils mind with a perilled dampness;

Fells skilled discipline to halls of humidity
55   Engraving clothes to trail balustrades without
Flesh; to a wilderness of pavements blue crayoned
With telegrams, where by a trick of air, owners
And cats remain, trying in mid-air to force riseup

Their own smashed brick. These men have brothers,
60   Are wived. And in dredging buckets of steam
Through stable-showers, men sway with the slush,
Dreamwhile teeming out cables and rope
Stretch barb wire tight across the crimped moon.

Wringing out moisture from mind and mouth,
65   Pulverizing a haze to gauze their contorted feature,
Inebriate mouths cratered: others with lime fresh
On briared cheeks cut Easter Island shadows, elongating
Into weathered struts that strain all clouds for height.

On the lowering of the Dandelion Sun brail umbrage
70   For their pall: for those hovering above us tall as a
Siren's wail . . . pocked and pale as pumice stone . . .

41: *splints:* splinters
48: *seels:* closes up: in falconry, hawks' eyes are temporarily "seeled" (sewn shut) as part of the taming
process.
49: *Grisaille:* literally "grey": a method of painting which creates a three-dimensional appearance through
using only layered shades of grey
    crines: shrinks
56: *blue crayoned:* "A line of knotted string covered with miscellaneous notes: 'For Higgs & Porters try oo
Downing Street.'—'I won't be more than five minutes John Evans'—'Still carrying on Riggs and Rogues
Ltd.' These, and tragic words interspersed, clipped on with safety-pins, wire, hairpins: or emergency
signs chalked up with blue crayons on cracked and broken pavements; and behind this rain-washed line
of dripping notes—a cloud of dust—SPACE—and wideways stretch of sheltered rubble." (Roberts)
67: *Easter Island shadows:* "Huge mathematical heads and shoulders which grate against the fierce storms
of the tropics; and puzzle us still, whether they stand outside the British Museum or on the bleak plains
of Easter Island. *A Prismatic Art,* each feature cut, alters in expression with the movement of the sun, so
that he is grinning under the evening light, may sneer before the rising of the sharp dawn." (Roberts)
69: *brail:* haul up (a sail) by the brails, small ropes at the edges
    umbrage: both "offense, anger" and "shadow, shade" (such as that of a canopy of leaves)

Mother-shrivelled with tansy tears: and those from
Accumulators, with eyes vacant as motor horns

Who shutter out the bleakness and blink in their
75 Own way. In quiet corners men yawn out death.
Commiserately sodden. Here rain contravariant:
Here in discord and disobedience:
Probable mutiny and desertion: night splashes up

Mullions in heavy hayloads: lights up shiny
80 Pailettes on rawset faces: spits up frogs
And tins to fidget their bowels. Dodging
Pillars of rain; pails overbrimming swishswashing;
Drenching rifty suits, their steel shoulders subscribing

Thin laminations of grief. O my people here
85 With labour illused and minds deranged. . . .
Through rivets of light; *Here are your Heroes.*
While high up, swallowsoft. . . .
Marine butterflies flood out the whole estuary.

72: *tansy:* an herb with a bitter taste
76: *contravariant:* perhaps "unvarying" or "hostile to change"
79: *Mullions:* vertical pane-separators of windows
80: *Pailettes:* spangles

Part V

. . . mi a glywais lais y pedwerydd anifail yn dywedyd, Tyred, a gwêl.
Ac mi a edrychais; ac wele farch gwelw-las: ac enw'r hwn oedd yn
eistedd arno oedd Marwolaeth: ac yr oedd Uffern yn canlyn gydâg ef.
A rhoddwyd iddynt awdurdod ar y bedwaredd ran o'r ddaear, i ladd â
chleddyf, ac â newyn, ac â marwolaeth, ac â bwystfilod y ddaear.

A phan agorodd efe y bumed sîl, mi a welais dan yr allor eneidiau'r
rhai a laddesid am air Duw, ac am y dystiolaeth oedd ganddynt.

A hwy a lefasant â llef uchel, gan ddywedyd, Pa hyd, Arglwydd,
sanctaidd a chywir, nad ydwyt yn barnu ac yn dial ein gwaed ni ar y
rhai sydd yn trigo ar y ddaear?

A gynau gwynion a roed i bob un ohonynt;

Datguddiad, Pennod VI

ARGUMENT

The same bay plated with ice. Industrial war progressing and the anxiety for after-war commerce and competitive air-lines. The soldiers recognizing this futility, but also, not without some faith in social and economic changes. The gunner returned, and faithful to his girl, they rise through the strata of the sky to seek peace and solace from the sun. Their love in harmony on cloud in fourth dimensional state. But memory bringing with it a consciousness of war—responsibility—they work towards this end. Fail. For the world demands their return, and down through the lower strata of the earth they travel, to the wounded bay where no human contact is found, only pylons, telegraph wires, and a monstrous placard which reads: 'Mental Home for Poets'. The gunner interned under pressure, resolves to free the dragon, and take fate in his own hands. The symbol having been already introduced in Part I of this poem when the woodpecker seen as a 'dragon of wings' introduced the gunner's identity. He walks meekly into the Mental Home. The girl turns away: towards a hard and new chemical dawn breaking up the traditional skyline.

> Air white with cold. Cycloid wind prevails.
> On ichnolithic plain where no step stirs
> And winter hardens into plate of ice:
> Shoots an anthracite glitter of death
5 > From their eyes,—these men shine darkly.

> With stiff betrayal; dark suns on pillows
> Of snow. But not eclipsed, for out of cauterized
> Craters, a conclave of architects with
> Ichnographic plans, shall bridge stronger
10 > Ventricles of faith. They know also

Epigraph: "I heard the voice of the fourth beast say, Come and see. And I looked, and behold a pale horse: and his name that sat on him was Death, and Hell followed with him. And power was given unto them over the fourth part of the earth, to kill with sword, and with hunger, and with death, and with the beasts of the earth. And when he had opened the fifth seal, I saw under the altar the souls of them that were slain for the word of God, and for the testimony which they held: And they cried with a loud voice, say-ing, How long, O Lord, holy and true, dost thou not judge and avenge our blood on them that dwell on the earth? And white robes were given unto every one of them." (Rev. 6:7–11)
1: A *cycloid* is the curve traced by a point on the circumference of a circle as it rolls along a straight line.
2: *ichnolithic:* An "ichnolite" is a fossilized footprint.
4: *anthracite:* a hard natural coal
9: *Ichnographic plans:* ground-plans
10: A *ventricle* is a cavity in a bodily organ—as in, e.g., the ventricles of the heart or of the brain.

Etonic vows: the abstractions which may arise:
That magnates out of prefabricated
Glass, may build Chromium Cenotaphs—
Work and pay for all! Contract aerodromes
15   To lift planes where ships once crawled, over

Baleful continents to the Caribbean Crane,
Down, to the Southern Christ of Palms.
Back on red competitive lines: chasing
Chinese blocks of uranium: above pack-ice
20   Snapping like wolves on Siberian shores.

Over wails of boracic and tundra torn wounds,
Darkening 'peaked' Fuji-yama, clearing
Cambrian caves where xylophone reeds hide
Menhir glaciers and appointed feet.
25   Out of this hard. Out of this sheet of zinc.

We by centrifugal force . . . rose softly. . . .
Faded from bloodsight. We, he and I ran
On to a steel escalator, the white
Electric sun drilling down on the cubed ice;
30   Our cyanite flesh chilled on aluminium

Rail. Growing taller, our demon diminishing
With steep incline. Climbed at gradient
'42; on to a trauma stratus
Where a multitude of birds, each wing
35   A sunset against sheet of ice, dipped

And flew throughout our cloth piercing folds
Of pain and fear. Higher through moist
And luminous dust: up breathless to a jungle of
Winedamp, out of gravity and territorial
40   Sight on to a far outer belt muscling-in

The Earth's curve. In such spirals of air
Sailed ketch and kestrel, fighting propeller,
Swastika wings and grey rubber rafts: this strange

11: *Eton* is a prestigious boys' school to which the sons of the elite are sent. (The usual adjective is "Eton-ian.")

14: *aerodromes*: airfields

16: *Caribbean Crane*: "The poet Hart Crane 'who made a perfect dive' off the S.S. *Orizaba*, and was drowned in the Caribbean on 26th April 1932 [actually the 27th]." (Roberts' note).

18: *red competitive lines*: presumably the red lines on a map marking air or sea routes

19: A *Chinese block* is a slotted wooden block used by a percussionist.
    pack-ice: in polar seas, large pieces of ice floating in the water will "pack" together, making a near-solid mass which is impassable to ships. The "snapping" sounds are from pieces of ice rubbing together.

22: *Fuji-yama*: Mount Fuji, in Japan

23: *Cambrian*: the Cambrian Period (dating from about 540 to 505 million years ago) is the earliest period of the Paleozoic Era. The name literally means "Welsh."

24: *Menhir*: a prehistoric monument in the form of an upright monolith

30: *cyanite*: a blue-colored mineral, sometimes used as a gemstone

33: *stratus*: a broad sheet of low cloud

42: *ketch*: a type of sailing boat

45

Evidence reconciliating as
Tide and shape floated by on swift moving layer.

Out of it. Out of it. To a ceiling and clarity
Of *Peace*. Sweet white air varied as syllables.
Spray of air fresh, fragrant as beehive glossed
Over with beech. So quiet a terrace to tune-in-to

50

With Catena shine round each cell of light

To laze carelessly in the Crown of the Sky;
But timeless minds held us victims
To the sour truth. *War and responsibility.*
He, of Bethlehem treading a campaign

55

Of clouds the fleecy cade purring at his side:

Sun, serene sense, tinting page of his face roan.
Bent over wooden table and glazed chart
And with compass and astronomical calculations
He, again at my side, pricked lines and projected

60

Latitudes so that we stood we cared not

How, upside down over South American canes.
Boots proved cumbersome at the height. Bleak battledress
Irritating as old salvaged reed collar;
Black and gravel wings pinned to his heart,

65

A grief already told. In such radium

Activity—white starlings—suspended
On string like Calder 'stills'—shivered
Like morning stars in fresh open sky
I contented in this fourth dimensional state

70

Past through, him and the table, pursued

50: *Catena:* "Born Biagio, *c.* 1470–1531. A Venetian pupil from Bellini's Bottega [studio-shop]. His paint-ing in the National Gallery, 'Saint Jerome in his Study', resembles my own convent upbringing, so that I connect him with the fragrance of beeswax—peace—serene pervading warmth of the southern air." (Roberts)

54: Roberts' husband Keidrych Rhys was born in the Welsh village of *Bethlehem*.
   campaign: field

55: *cade:* a young animal (such as a lamb or colt) reared by hand as a pet

63: *reed collar:* "Used in this village on an occasional horse. The collar is made of woven reeds and has no outer leather cover: the shade is olive-green: neatness and firmness of craftsmanship something which we have carelessly lost. I have also seen one plaited in straw." (Roberts)

64: *wings:* Roberts has in mind the R.A.F. wings worn on service uniforms.

66: *white starlings:* "January 1943, there was a column in the *Western Mail* by an ornithologist saying that a white starling had been seen flying over Carmarthen. The starling has appeared in Welsh mythology more than once: and was 'dispatch rider' for Branwen when it flew and took her message from Ireland to Wales, so that she might be delivered of her unhappiness and *hiraeth* [homesickness] for Wales." (Roberts). Branwen, the Welsh wife of the King of Ireland, was consigned to work in the kitchen of the Irish court after war broke out between Wales and Ireland. After three years, she managed to send a mes-sage back to Wales by means of a pet starling.

67: *Calder 'stills':* the American sculptor Alexander Calder (1898–1976) was known for his "mobiles," kinetic sculptures that often involved the suspension of their delicately balanced parts in the air, their shape constantly changing in the currents of the air. (Calder called his conventional sculptures "stabiles," perhaps the source of Roberts' word "stills.")

My own work slightly *below* him. In
Sandals and sunsuit lungs naked to the light,
Sitting on chair of glass with no fixed frame
Leaned to the swift machine threading over twill;
75   'Singer's' perfect model scrolled with gold,

Chromium wheel and black structure, firm on
Mahogany plinth. Nails varnished with
Chanel shocking! Ears jewelled: light hand
Tipped with dorcas' silver thimble tracing thin
80   Aertex edge: trimmings, and metal buttons

Stitched by hand. Slim needle and strong sharp
Thread. Coats' cotton-twist No. 48. Excelling always as
Soldier shirt finished floated down to earth.
But cold at night. We wrapt our own mystery
85   Around us; trailed in cerulean mosquito nets

As kale canopy lifted from cooler zones below.
Pack of stars in full cry icing the heavens
As we were compelled to descend. *Disendowed,*
By the State. By will of those hankering
90   After pig standards of gold. The fall was heavy,

Too sudden for our laughter so that we
Took it with us; dragged it slowly down through
Waled skylanes. Shocked Capricorn and Cancer who
Winked to control us like Belisha beacons.
95   Tacked out of our course into opaline dusk.

A huge silence ashiver. Huge Witness dwells.
In Celestial Study to right and left lucid
Eyes pay tribute, angel secretaries with
Paper wings—and paper so scarce—dyed mauve-scarlet
100   With chemical rings; speech blue behind aniline minds.

Away from this. Flattery. God-Hypocrisy.
Not even a whisper escaped our lips as we
Continued in sharp descent, like old minesweepers
Creaking through boisterous storms, *our own God*
105   *Within us.* Down into xerophilous air clarion snow

75: The speaker is using a *Singer* sewing machine.
78: One of the colors created by Chanel was "shocking" pink.
79: *dorcas:* a Dorcas Society—the name comes from Acts 9:36—is a ladies' church association for making
    clothes for the poor.
80: *Aertex:* a modern cotton cellular fabric used for blouses
82: The thread is manufactured by a company named *Coats;* the number 48 designates a color.
86: *kale:* a type of cabbage
93: *Waled:* ribbed, striped
94: *Belisha beacons:* pedestrian-crossing lights, consisting of a flashing orange globe on a post
99: The *paper* was *scarce* due to rationing.
100: The chemical *aniline* is used to manufacture dye.
105: *xerophilous:* (of a plant or animal) adapted to a dry climate; dry

Percolating, oölite flakes warm as
Owl tufts or deciduous leaves. Falling on
Flesh with the lightness of moths. Without breath
Or bell of joy lurched slipped-slid into icy
110   Vacuums. Fell out of frozen cylinders. Flew

Earthwards like arctic terns the spangled
Mirrors still on our wings. Colder. Continuous as *newsreel,*
Quadrillion cells spotting the air, stinging
The face like a swarm of bees. Lower. A vitreous green
115   Paperweight—the sky is greenglaze with snow flying

Upwards zionwards. Such iconic sky bears promise.
Dredging slowly down, veiling shield of sky hard.
Cold. Austere. Tumbled over each other lurched
Into the dark penumbra: then, through a
120   Rift as suddenly, the solid stone of earth

Rushed up; hit us hotly as household iron.
Over this maimed cadaverous globe, the wind
Had streaked each ridge with piercing prongs
Of a curry comb, leaving here and there
125   A thin sheet of aluminium which shone from out

Of the Earth's crust. Over set currents
Of ice, emerald streams and blue electric lakes
Worked simultaneously to purify the
World . . . down driving down . . . following the thin
130   Strokes of mapping pens stretching page of

Music over vast terrain. This, and stronger
Network of rails: pylons and steel installations
The only landmarks of our territory . . .
Down, to this bleak telegraphic planet and its solid
135   Pyramids of canvas. Down, gunner and black

Madonna with heart of tin; surrounded
By fluttering greed of ravens, their
Beaks of bone breaking up the wounds of winter;
Croak; a mad voice sunk down a sink. The attendant
140   Curlews at the forage edge wearing moth-eaten

Shawls; shagreen legs brittle as ember twigs.
Pipe plaintive descants that sharpen the shale.

106: *oölite:* a limestone composed of small egg-shaped granules formed around grains of sand
111–12: *spangled / Mirrors:* i.e., snowflakes
119: They are passing from the light of the celestial realm to the realm of *penumbra* (partial shadow), and
then to the (spiritually and physically) darkened earth itself.
124: *curry comb:* a metal comb used to groom horses
135: *Pyramids of canvas:* i.e., military tents
135–36: *gunner and black / Madonna with heart of tin:* i.e., Rhys and Roberts (a "black" Madonna because
of her miscarriage in Part IV)
141: *shagreen:* an untanned leather with a granulated surface, dyed green

From ascending stirrups steps to the sun, down,
Dragged-down we descended the slimerot ladders,
145   Rats withdrawing each foot: rust worn where other

Boots had rung. To the Bay known before,
The warm and stagnant air raising wellshafts
Of putrid flesh sunk deep in desert sands. Stepped out onto
Blue blaze of snow. Barbed wire. No man of bone.
150   A placard to the right which concerned us:

Mental Home For Poets. He alone on this
Isotonic plain: against a jingle of Generals
And Cabinet Directors determined
A stand. Declared a Faith. Entered 'Foreign
155   Field' like a Plantagenet King: his spirit

Gorsefierce: hands like perfect quatrains.
Green spindle tears seep out of closed lids . . .
Mourn murmuring . . . remembering my brother.
His Cathedral mind in Bedlam. Sign and
160   Lettering-black grail of quavering curves.

Distrained . . . mallowfrail . . . turned to where.
But *to-day which is to-morrow.*

Salt spring from frosted sea filters palea light
Raising tangerine and hard line of rind on the
165   Astringent sky. Catoptric on waterice he of deep love
Frees dragon from the glacier glade
Sights death fading into chilblain ears.

                                        1941–1943 / 1951

151: *He alone* is Rhys, but in the *Mental Home* Roberts alludes to the fate of her brother Dymock. He had
     wanted to join the war but was not allowed to.
152: *Isotonic:* literally "equally stretched, of equal tension or tone": thus perhaps "flat, level" and "tensed."
155: *Plantagenet King:* "Lordship of Commote Penrhyn, owned by Edward I, Prince of Wales, during the
     Hundred Years' War and which consisted of a pasture and grange surrounding the present villages of
     Llanybri and Llanstephan: Edward, the Prince of Wales, at the same time also owned a larger portion of
     the Duchy of Cornwall." (Roberts)
156: *Gorsefierce:* "Leguminosae: Ulex [a type of bush] and Genista [broom] both words of Celtic origin.
     The gorse is to be found in early Triads and Welsh literature of the sixth century: a favourite flower with
     King Alfred and the Anglo-Saxons: and worn later as a cognizance by the Plantagenet kings. In the lan-
     guage of flowers gorse symbolizes anger. A resisting spirit throughout the severest weather, when a sheet
     of piercing yellow covers the hills blossoming in this valley: November, December, January, and Febru-
     ary." (Roberts)
160: *Lettering-black grail of quavering curves:* i.e., the sign is in a Gothic ("black-letter") typeface.
161: *Distrained:* incarcerated
163: *palea:* the bract enclosing the flower of grasses. But this may be a misprint for "pale," "paler," or
     "pale a."
165: *Catoptric:* reflecting (as in a mirror)

NORMAN MacCAIG (1910–1996)

MacCaig was born in Edinburgh and educated at the University of Edinburgh. His career as a primary school teacher was interrupted by World War II, during which MacCaig was a conscientious objector and served a term of imprisonment. In 1970, he became Lecturer in Poetry at the University of Stirling. MacCaig is, Alan Bold writes, "generally regarded as the finest English-writing Scottish poet since [Edwin] Muir."[1]

MacCaig's early poems led him to be identified with the New Apocalypse movement of Henry Treece, J. F. Hendry, Nicholas Moore, and others. His poems appeared in the movement's anthologies *The New Apocalypse* (1939) and *The White Horsemen* (1940), and his first two books, *Far Cry* (1943) and *The Inward Eye* (1946), consist primarily of love poetry fusing surrealist and romantic poetic conventions. MacCaig came to dislike the poems in what he thought of as an obscurantist mode and moved away from the style in *Riding Lights* (1956), the first book represented in his *Collected Poems* (1985; 1990). His mature poems employ a more ironic and conversational mode and accessible subject matter, his favorite subjects being, in Bold's words, "landscape, animals, people."[2] Douglas Dunn writes that "Ordinariness as the human condition forms something like an intellectual foundation in MacCaig's poetry," while wondering also if MacCaig's affection for metaphor and simile, "and his intellectual concern with seeming, with appearances" stems from his earliest work; at any rate there is, in the later work, "an uncommon anxiety for meaning, as well as for the lucidity of whatever can be seen clearly."[3] MacCaig's sense of the limits of perception and the "disturbing" otherness of the world are evident in the last lines of "Intrusion," which speak of the "No Man's Land that lies / between me and everything." Unlike his friend Hugh MacDiarmid, MacCaig cultivated an "apolitical astringency . . . which can seem to embody an interesting *evasion* of history and politics, or a mischievous superiority that refuses to take seriously the aspirations, sometimes opposed, with which large numbers of citizens are besotted."[4] There is a grim, ironic reference to "useless battle[s] lost" in his poem "High Street, Edinburgh." Dunn remembers that MacCaig called himself a "Zen Calvinist. . . . In spite of its flippancy I take the description to indicate a secular understanding of what he takes to be sacred, as well as the ethical, rational tug of his poetry while surrounded by detailed, natural epiphanies."[5]

1 *Modern Scottish Literature*, Harlow, 1983, p. 66.
2 Ibid., p. 68.
3 "'As a Man Sees': On Norman MacCaig's Poetry," *Verse*, vol. 7, no. 2, 1990, pp. 62–63.
4 Ibid., pp. 56–57.
5 Ibid., p. 67.

High Street, Edinburgh

Here's where to make a winter fire of stories
And burn dead heroes to keep your shinbones warm,
Bracing the door against the jackboot storm
With an old king or two, stuffing the glories
5   Of rancid martyrs with their flesh on fire
Into the broken pane that looks beyond Fife
Where Alexander died and a vain desire,
Hatched in Macbeth, sat whittling at his life.

Across this gulf where skeins of duck once clattered
10   Round the black Rock and now a tall ghost wails
Over a shuddering train, how many tales
Have come from the hungry North of armies shattered,
An ill cause won, a useless battle lost,
A head rolled like an apple on the ground;
15   And Spanish warships staggering west and tossed
On frothing skerries; and a king come to be crowned.

Look out into this brown November night
That smells of herrings from the Forth and frost;
The voices humming in the air have crossed
20   More than the Grampians; East and West unite,
In dragonish swirlings over the city park,
Their tales of deaths and treacheries, and where
A tall dissolving ghost shrieks in the dark
Old history greets you with a Bedlam stare.

25   He talks more tongues than English now. He fetches
The unimagined corners of the world
To ride this smoky sky, and in the curled

Title: *High Street* is a section of the Royal Mile, a street running through Edinburgh's historic Old Town section.

7: The Scottish king *Alexander* III (ruled 1249–1286) was one of the most successful of medieval Scottish kings; he died in Fife, killed when his horse fell over a cliff.

8: *Macbeth* was awarded the title of Thane of Cawdor after defeating the Norwegians at Fife (*Macbeth* 1.2).

10: *Rock:* Castle Rock in Edinburgh's Old Town, a black basalt crag 443 feet above sea level and surmounted by a castle. The main rail link between Glasgow and Edinburgh runs past the Rock; the *ghost* is the white steam from the train's steam whistle.

12ff: MacCaig is touching on the strife-filled history of relations between England and Scotland. The *ill cause won* perhaps alludes to the 1314 Battle of Bannockburn, at which the Scots decisively defeated the English. The Scottish army, with King James IV and the cream of the Scottish nobility, were in 1513 annihilated by the English at the Battle of Flodden. Mary, Queen of Scots was in 1579 forced to flee Scotland for England, where she was kept captive by Queen Elizabeth's government; having been convicted of involvement in a plot against Elizabeth, she was beheaded in 1587. After the Spanish Armada's defeat by the English in 1588, the fleet's remnants were forced to return to Spain by sailing around the north tip of Scotland, and suffered further losses in their passage through the harsh North Atlantic gales. Mary's son, King James VI, in 1603 succeeded to the throne of England and became James I (and, with the union of the crowns, the last king of Scotland to have actually resided on Scottish soil).

16: *skerries:* an Orkney word for rocks or islets in the sea, often covered at high tide; the Orkneys are a group of islands off the north coast of Scotland.

18: Edinburgh is located near the Firth of *Forth*.

20: The *Grampian* Mountains make up the central part of Scotland's northern Highlands region.

Autumnal fog his phantoms move. He stretches
His frozen arm across three continents
30   To blur this window. Look out from it. Look out
From your November. Tombs and monuments
Pile in the air and invisible armies shout.

c. 1955–1957 / 1985

Nude in a fountain

Clip-clop go water-drops and bridles ring—
Or, visually, a gauze of water, blown
About and falling and blown about, discloses
Pudicity herself in shameless stone,
5   In an unlikely world of shells and roses.

On shaven grass a summer's litter lies
Of paper bags and people. One o'clock
Booms on the leaves with which the trees are quilted
And wades away through air, making it rock
10   On flowerbeds that have blazed and dazed and wilted.

Light perches, preening, on the handle of a pram
And gasps on paths and runs along a rail
And whitely, brightly in a soft diffusion
Veils and unveils the naked figure, pale
15   As marble in her stone and stilled confusion.

And nothing moves except one dog that runs,
A red rag in a black rag, round and round
And that long helmet-plume of water waving,
In which the four elements, hoisted from the ground,
20   Become this grace, the form of their enslaving.

Meeting and marrying in the midmost air
Is mineral assurance of them all;
White doldrum on blue sky; a pose of meaning
Whose pose is what is explicit; a miracle
25   Made, and made bearable, by the water's screening.

The drops sigh, singing, and, still sighing, sing
Gently a leaning song. She makes no sound.
They veil her, not with shadows, but with brightness;
Till, gleam within a glitter, they expound
30   What a tall shadow is when it is whiteness.

A perpetual modification of itself
Going on around her is her; her hand is curled
Round more than a stone breast; and she discloses

4: *Pudicity:* modesty
7: A piece of artillery on the ramparts of Edinburgh Castle fires a blank shell every day at 1:00 pm.

The more than likely in an unlikely world
35   Of dogs and people and stone shells and roses.

1960

Celtic cross

The implicated generations made
This symbol of their lives, a stone made light
By what is carved on it.
                                        The plaiting masks,
5   But not with involutions of a shade,
What a stone says and what a stone cross asks.

Something that is not mirrored by nor trapped
In webs of water or bag-nets of cloud;
The tangled mesh of weed
10   lets it go by.
Only men's minds could ever have unmapped
Into abstraction such a territory.

No green bay going yellow over sand
Is written on by winds to tell a tale
15   Of death-dishevelled gull
                                        or heron, stiff
As a cruel clerk with gaunt writs in his hand
—Or even of light, that makes its depths a cliff.

Singing responses order otherwise.
20   The tangled generations ravelled out
In links of song whose sweet
                                        strong choruses
Are these stone involutions to the eyes
Given to the ear in abstract vocables.

25   The stone remains, and the cross, to let us know
Their unjust, hard demands, as symbols do.
But on them twine and grow
                                        beneath the dove
Serpents of wisdom whose cool statements show
30   Such understanding that it seems like love.

1960

Title: A *Celtic cross* is one the center of which is surrounded by a circle; medieval stone crosses were
   carved with ornately interweaving tracery.
1: *implicated*: literally, "tangled, intertwined"
19: *responses*: or responsories: anthems sung by a soloist and choir alternately. In this stanza MacCaig has
   in mind the polyphony of medieval church music.
29: Cf. Matt. 10:16: "be ye therefore wise as serpents, and harmless as doves."

Intrusion

We sat by a Scottish stream
in Massachusetts.
A groundhog observed us,
its whiskered face peering
from a hole in the ground
like a cartoon from World War I
and through the still, bright air
flew birds whose names
I did not know.

Suddenly, in front of us,
thirty yards away,
a twenty foot limb
crashed from an elm tree.

Now, three weeks later,
in a Scottish house in Scotland,
I tell myself
it was one of a million
dramatic acts
in the world of nature's
perpetually symbolic play
that, if we had not been there,
would have taken place anyway.

But it disturbs me. I try
to see it as no other than
the Scottish water crimpling away
through America and
the watchful face peering
from its dugout across
the No Man's Land that lies
between me and everything.

1968

2: MacCaig is presumably sitting by Dunbar Brook, in Franklin County, Massachusetts.
25: *crimpling:* wrinkling, crinkling

SORLEY MACLEAN /
SOMHAIRLE MACGILL-EAIN (1911–1996)

MACLEAN HAS BEEN CALLED THE POET RESPONSIBLE FOR BRINGING SCOTS GAELIC poetry into the present and praised for his mastery of that poetry's complex internal, end, and cross-rhyming; his own translations of his Gaelic poems bear consideration also. Whereas Gaelic poetry had long been regarded as the province of sentiment and nostalgia, MacLean's work, Alan Bold writes, is "international, his passions . . . both sensual and political, and his greatest poems . . . both heroic and elegiac."[1] The use of Gaelic suggests a commitment to Scottish autonomy, but in "I do not see. . . . ," written during the Spanish Civil War, MacLean despairs of the limits of poetry in times of political crisis: "I do not see the sense of my toil / putting thoughts in a dying tongue / now when the whoredom of Europe / is murder erect and agony." In MacLean's *Dain do Eimhir* (*Songs to Eimhir,* 1943), the Spanish Civil War is the background to poems about a love affair. In other books MacLean's poems move between traditional lyric subject matter and his commentary and meditation on class struggle, cold war politics, the legacy of the nineteenth-century clearances, and other political subjects. "The Island," with its lyric celebration of place, indicates one tendency in MacLean's work, even as such celebration is complicated by an elegiac recognition that the world the poet knows is passing away. Another, more documentarian tendency is suggested by the World War II poem, "Going Westwards." Juxtaposing this poem with the war poems of Keith Douglas, Donald Davie writes that "Here [in Maclean's poem] the poetic tradition that is called on to try to do justice to the desert battles is not the English, but another at least as ancient: the Gaelic tradition in which the celebration of martial valour—some may think it bloodthirsty, others will call it heroic—bulks larger than in the English tradition. . . . It is interesting to ask whether the Gaelic poet . . . finds his inherited tradition encumbering or enabling. And the answer is surely: both."[2]

MacLean was born Somhairle MacGhill-Eain in Osgaig on Raasay Island in Scotland. He was educated at Portree High School on the Isle of Skye and at the University of Edinburgh. He served in the Signal Corps in North Africa, where he was wounded in combat. He taught in schools in Skye and Edinburgh and was headmaster at the Plockton Secondary School in Wester Ross from 1956 to 1972. His books include *Spring tide and Neap tide: Selected Poems 1932–72* (1977) and *From*

---

[1] *Modern Scottish Literature,* Harlow, 1983, p. 93.
[2] *Under Briggflatts: A History of Poetry in Great Britain 1960–1988,* Chicago, 1989, p. 27.

Wood to Ridge: Collected Poems in Gaelic and English (1989), both with English translations by the author.

The Island

You gave me the valuable enough
and some mettlesome talent,
struggle, danger and pleasant high spirits
on the rugged tops of the Cuillin,
5   and under me a jewel-like island,
love of my people, delight of their eyes;
the Seven and the rest in Portree,
exercise of brain and spirit, strife
of Skye camans on the river bught,
10   battle-joy, joyous company
and the nights of Edinbane,
beauty, drink and poets' novelties,
wit, satire, delight in full,
the Skye spirit at its height;
15   and nights on the slope of Lyndale,
the great Island with its many hills
lying in peace in the twilight,
grey-faced till the breaking of the sky.

O great Island, Island of my love,
20   many a night of them I fancied
the great ocean itself restless
agitated with love of you
as you lay on the sea,
great beautiful bird of Scotland,
25   your supremely beautiful wings bent
about many-nooked Loch Bracadale,
your beautiful wings prostrate on the sea
from the Wild Stallion to the Aird of Sleat,
your joyous wings spread
30   about Loch Snizort and the world.

O great Island, my Island, my love
many a night I lay stretched
by your side in that slumber

The translations are the poet's own.

Title: The Isle of Skye is one of Scotland's Hebrides islands; it is known in Gaelic as An t-Eilean Sgitheanach ("The Winged Island") or just An t-Eilean, "The Island." MacLean was born on the nearby island of Raasay and went to school in Portree in Skye; the placenames in the poem are all locations on Skye.
4: *the Cuillin:* the Cuillin Hills, in southern Skye
7: *the Seven:* the seven liberal arts of the traditional curriculum
9: *camans:* sticks used in shinty, a game similar to field hockey
   bught: the flat ground enclosed by a river bend
28: Neist Point, "The Wild Stallion," is the westernmost tip of Skye; the *Aird of Sleat* is the southernmost tip.

when the mist of twilight swathed you.
35 My love every leaflet of heather on you
from Rudha Hunish to Loch Slapin,
and every leaflet of bog-myrtle
from Stron Bhiornaill to the Garsven,
every tarn, stream and burn a joy
40 from Romisdale to Brae Eynort,
and even if I came in sight of Paradise,
what price its moon without Blaven?

Great Island, Island of my desire,
Island of my heart and wound,
45 it is not likely that the strife
and suffering of Braes will be seen requited
and it is not certain that the debts
of the Glendale Martyr will be seen made good;
there is no hope of your townships
50 rising high with gladness and laughter,
and your men are not expected
when America and France take them.

Pity the eye that sees on the ocean
the great dead bird of Scotland.

1940

Going Westwards

I go westwards in the Desert
with my shame on my shoulders,
that I was made a laughing-stock
since I was as my people were.

5 Love and the greater error,
deceiving honour spoiled me,

36: *Rudha Hunish* is the northernmost tip of Skye, *Loch Slapin* a sea-loch in the south.
38: *Stron Bhiornaill* is the northernmost end of the great ridge of Tròndairnis, the northernmost "wing" of Skye; *Garsven* is a peak in the south of the Cuillins.
39: *tarn*: small mountain lake
40: *Romisdale* is in Tròndairnis; *Brae Eynort* is the uplands on the north side of Loch Eynort, in the south of Skye.
42: *Blaven*: a mountain to the east of the Cuillins
46: The *Braes* is a region of Skye. It was in 1882 the scene of a violent confrontation between policemen and crofters (tenant-farmers); the crofters in order to protest their living conditions and high rent had been withholding rent, and when police from the mainland were sent in to enforce evictions the "Battle of the Braes" took place.
48: *Glendale* is a valley in Skye; it was the home of John MacPherson, who led the crofters in their protests; he was with four other men sentenced to short jail sentences in Edinburgh for his activities.
52: Beginning in the mid-nineteenth century, many crofters emigrated overseas—some voluntarily, others because forced to by the landlords.

with a film of weakness on my vision,
squinting at mankind's extremity.

Far from me the Island
10   when the moon rises on Quattara,
far from me the Pine Headland
when the morning ruddiness is on the Desert.

Camus Alba is far from me
and so is the bondage of Europe,
15   far from me in the North-West
the most beautiful grey-blue eyes.

Far from me the Island
and every loved image in Scotland,
there is a foreign sand in History
20   spoiling the machines of the mind.

Far from me Belsen and Dachau,
Rotterdam, the Clyde and Prague,
and Dimitrov before a court
hitting fear with the thump of his laugh.

25   Guernica itself is very far
from the innocent corpses of the Nazis,
who are lying in the gravel
and in the khaki sand of the Desert.

There is no rancour in my heart
30   against the hardy soldiers of the Enemy,
but the kinship that there is among
men in prison on a tidal rock

waiting for the sea flowing
and making cold the warm stone;
35   and the coldness of life (is)
in the hot sun of the Desert.

But this is the struggle not to be avoided,
the sore extreme of human-kind,

9: *the Island:* Skye; see note to the title of the preceding poem.
10: The *Qattara* Depression is an arid basin in northwestern Egypt. It formed the southern terminus to the British defense lines at El-Alamein during World War II.
11: An Aird Ghiuthais ("The Promontory of the Pine") is a peninsula of the island of Raasay.
13: *Camus Alba:* a small bay in Raasay with white shingle and sand
21: *Belsen and Dachau:* German concentration camps
22: *Rotterdam:* major European port in The Netherlands; it had fallen to the Germans in 1940.
    The river *Clyde* flows through Glasgow, and is the location of its important shipbuilding industry (and thus was a target for German attack).
    Prague had fallen to the Germans when they invaded Czechoslovakia.
23: The Bulgarian Communist leader Georgi *Dimitrov* (1882–1949) was tried by the Nazis in connection with the 27 Feb 1933 burning of the Reichstag (parliament) building in Berlin; he conducted his own defense and was acquitted.
25: *Guernica:* in Spain; in 1937, during the Spanish Civil War, it was heavily bombed by German planes assisting Franco's right-wing Nationalists.

and though I do not hate Rommel's army
40   the brain's eye is not squinting.

And be what was as it was,
I am of the big men of Braes,
of the heroic Raasay MacLeods,
of the sharp-sword Mathesons of Lochalsh;
45   and the men of my name—who were braver
when their ruinous pride was kindled?

1942–1943 / 1977

39: Erwin *Rommel* (1891–1944) was commander of the German troops in North Africa.
42: *Braes* is a distrinct of Skye (see lines 46ff of the preceding poem).

F. T. PRINCE (b. 1912)

IN A RECENT POEM, PRINCE, PONDERING WHAT IT MEANS TO WRITE "WHAT NOBODY peruses," decides that he can at least "Think, how in databanks one snoozes / Safe in the bosom of the Muses / With Larkins, Harrisons, and Hugheses."[1] Prince has long been a poet's poet, praised by those who would seem to agree on little else, such as Donald Davie and John Ashbery, his work too little known beyond such informed readers. The one exception is the much-anthologized "Soldiers Bathing," a remarkable poem in which Prince contemplates "war's sorrow and disgrace" as he has experienced it in life and art and ultimately offers a Christian vision of "Strange gratitude, as if evil itself were beautiful, / And [I] kiss the wound in thought, while in the west / I watch a streak of red that might have issued from Christ's breast."[2] Perhaps, as Prince speculates in "Not a Paris Review Interview," his reputation has suffered from his preference for longer poems that encroach upon the territory of the novelist and historian. His imaginary interlocutor in that poem asks him "But could one, not unfairly, / Argue that you have suppressed your / Identity, or tried— / See the persons and occasions / In long pieces as evasions?"[3] "Strafford" is an example of a poem taking up an historical person, Thomas Wentworth, the advisor to Charles I, dubbed "Black Tom Tyrant" for his activities on behalf of the king in Ireland and England; he was eventually executed for treason. But Prince's interests are not limited to "Old histories, pale, stained, yet beautiful": Strafford's story is partly about duty and character and the challenges and conflicts of public life, Strafford "being of the kind / That are by nature never satisfied." Other poems about Michelangelo and Rupert Brooke suggest Prince's ability to write meditative poems beginning with historical persons. He is skilled not only in so-called traditional forms but in rarely used ones as well, including the *strambotto,* an Italian precursor to the sonnet, which, as Prince notes, had not been employed in English since Sir Thomas Wyatt.

Frank Templeton Prince was born to English parents in Kimberley, South Africa. He left South Africa in 1931 to study at Balliol College, Oxford. In the 1930s, he met T. S. Eliot, who published one of Prince's poems in *The Criterion,* and W. B. Yeats. In 1937, he converted to Roman Catholicism. After graduate study at Princeton University he worked at the Institute of International Affairs in London. During World War II, he served in the Intelligence Corps of the British Army. After the war, he began teaching at the University of Southampton. He has also held visiting positions at universities in Canada, the United States, and Jamaica, as well as at Oxford and Cam-

---

1 "Finis Coronat Opus," *Collected Poems: 1935–1992,* Riverdale-on-Hudson, 1993, p. 301.
2 *Collected Poems,* p. 57.
3 *Collected Poems,* p. 248.

bridge. His books include critical studies and editions of Milton and Shakespeare, as well as *Poems* (1938), *Soldiers Bathing and Other Poems* (1954), *Drypoints of the Hasidim* (1975), and *Collected Poems: 1935–1992* (1993).

Strafford

Fi à faute de courage, je n'en aye que trop.

I

Dark steel, the muffled flash
On iron sleeve and cuff; black storm of armour,
Half-moons and wedges, scaly wings and hinges,
Ovals and quadrilaterals and cylinders
5   Moulded in nightshade metal.
                  So he stands
With rod and sword of office, living fingers
Poised lightly on the sword-hilt, pale and still,

Wentworth, the black-browed Yorkshire magnate, with a rent-roll
10   Matched only by his pedigree, the long list
Of Norman-English quarters and alliances—
His patent granting D'Arcys and Despensers,
Latimers, Talboys, Ogles; Maud of Cambridge,
Quincy of Winchester; Grantmesnil of Hinckley,
15   Peveril of Nottingham, Ferrers Earl of Digby;
And crowned by John of Gaunt, Plantagenet.

And still the dark eyes gloom beneath the bent brows
As if impatient of himself, his greatness

Title: Thomas Wentworth (1593–1641; created Earl of *Strafford* in 1640) was one of Charles I's most trusted and feared advisors. The eldest son of a Yorkshire landowner, he became MP for Yorkshire and then Pontefract; he was initially an opponent to the Crown because of his opposition to Charles's war policies against Spain and France, but in 1628, was elevated to the peerage, and in quick succession became lord president of the North and a member of the Privy Council. In 1633, he became lord deputy of Ireland. These were the years of Charles's "Personal Rule" (1629–1640), when the king dispensed with summoning Parliament; this style of government was suited to Wentworth, who was dedicated to Charles and possessed a deep-seated sense of order and authority. His administration of the North and later Ireland was authoritarian and highly effective; he rigidly enforced the royal prerogative (often enriching himself in the process), and made himself many enemies. Wentworth was recalled by Charles in 1639 to help quell a Scottish rebellion; he and his friend Archbishop Laud advised Charles to recall Parliament to vote money for the war. But a recalcitrant Parliament and a pair of military failures proved disastrous; in 1640 a second recalled Parliament made it its first order of business to impeach Strafford, and in 1641 he was beheaded.
Epigraph: "Never mind lack of courage [or spirit], I've got too much of it." (French); the source is a letter of Strafford's from 1640, written as he was departing for Ireland to deal with the task of getting a newly convened Irish Parliament to vote subsidies to Charles I (see line 91 below and note); the passage may be found on p. 275 of *Thomas Wentworth: First Earl of Strafford, 1593–1641*, by C.V. Wedgwood (London, 1961). Passages in quotation marks in the poem are drawn, with some reworking, from Strafford's own words.
1ff: Prince has in mind here the 1633 Van Dyck portrait of Strafford, now in the collection of the National Portrait Gallery.
12ff: Wentworth's ancestral record includes grants of lands and title to much of the medieval aristocracy, culminating in the English prince *John of Gaunt* (1340–1399). The letters *patent* granting lands to his family forebears would have come from the king.

Rooted in limitation, strength and weakness
20   Of fiery piercing mind, that wears the waning body;
And still resentful to be so resented
Pleads for his power and purpose, 'chaste ambition',
For 'power as much as may be, that may be power to do more good';
Yet as we read it further, pleads for pity:

25   'Pity me for the power that drives me onward,
Far from content and quiet, yet farther, wider, climbing higher,
Haunted by thirst and shadow, to slip the bar of shadow
Lurking within, but finding greater darkness—
Envy attending me, black clouds above the world's abyss,
30   Black streams that crawl below,
Envy, death's rivers.'

II

Old histories, pale, stained, yet beautiful,
Unfold from yellowing papers, tarnished print,
Their tales of times of trouble, fear and war,
35   Dry death and living love.
                  And still unsatisfied
Strafford lives on, he being of the kind
That are by nature never satisfied.

'Ever desiring best things, never satisfied
40   That I had done enough, but did desire
Always, I might do better . . .'
So he in sadness at the trial,
And long before, in letter after letter
We see the difficulty draw him on—
45   Not for the greatness only, but the difficulty,
And will to do what others will not do,
Well knowing what he does:
                       'I know, I know
And see the pinnacles I go upon,
50   Danger at every step, left solitary,
Left lonely in the heat of the day,
To bear it out alone . . .
                  'And so have reason
To carry my eyes along, and know that all my actions
55   Are cast into the balance, weighed and fingered,
And rubbed and tested whether gross or light';
And so defies them, flashing in despite,
'Content a' God's name!
So let them take me up and cast me down.
60   If I do not prove paragon, fall square
In every coign of duty to my master,
Let me perish, and may no man pity me!'

51: cf. Matt. 20:12, in the parable of the vineyard: "These last have wrought but one hour, and thou hast
  made them equal to us, which have borne the burden and heat of the day."
58: *a'*: in
61: *coign*: cornerstone

III

So to his master's work. And what a master!
Stubborn and yet irresolute, immovable
65 Always in wrong positions, only wavering in the right;
Thinking himself most gracious, but cold-hearted;
Cross-grained and peevish, far too fond of money;
Pleased as a woman with his easy cunning;
Anxious and yet self-righteous, self-justified
70 Yet sensitive to every rub or rumour.
—With that small elegance, that sad shut face,
Sullenly delicate, that wan mean dignity! . . .

Wentworth would have him King, uphold him King;
And for that narrow nature toiled and wrestled,
75 And had indeed upheld him for ten years
Caught in the closing circle of his rule:
Governing like a king away in Ireland—
Faithfully drawing odium on himself, the distant servant,
From sharking lords and lawyers—dealing justice,
80 Planted and dug and watered, pruned and fostered
Till the poor cried 'Never so good a Lord Deputy!'
And the King's purse was filled—to fatten courtiers.

IV

But to subdue two Kingdoms, distempered by their bungling King?
Come to his aid alone and patch his blunders,
85 Tied to the hot Archbishop and cold Church?
Enter the crumbling warrens of the Court,
Phosphorescent in decay, and tainted Council,
With Arundel and Holland, Henry Vane
And all 'the Queen's men' itching for his ruin?

90 Yet never had he done so much, so quickly:
Ireland and back again, his mind on fire
To force his failing body—there and back,
Armed with four subsidies and public vows.
And ill already, to the captain's terror
95 Puts out from Howth, beats out the storm to Chester
Through twenty hours of torment, where he touches

77: Cf. the judgment of Wentworth's contemporary Sir Thomas Roe: "He rules Ireland like a King" (quoted in Wedgwood, p. 169).

83: Charles had created widespread resentment in England through the levying of "ship money," a non-parliamentary tax imposed on coastal cities and counties, which he revived from medieval times in order to secure funding without calling Parliament. Charles's attempt to impose a version of the Anglican Prayer Book on a mostly presbyterian Scotland, conducted with the advice of William Laud, Archbishop of Canterbury, and the Scottish bishops, resulted in riots in Edinburgh in 1637 and precipitated the "Prayer Book Rebellion" that led to war with Scotland in 1639.

88: These figures were enemies of Strafford's at court: Thomas Howard, Earl of *Arundel* (who as Lord High Steward eventually presided over Strafford's trial); Henry Rich, Earl of *Holland;* and the Secretary of State Sir *Henry Vane* (who was to testify against Strafford at his trial). The Queen's faction—which included Holland and Vane—was hostile to Strafford and Laud.

91: In March 1640, a month before the assembling of the English Parliament, Wentworth managed to secure from the Irish Parliament four subsidies for Charles and a resolution that further grants would be made if needed.

Half-dead with pain but, carried on to London,
Hurries to Charles and grips the wavering Council:

Bears down his enemies—the Queen his convert—
100 Levies, advises and devises, puts to shame,
And counsels a new Parliament; it meets,
But dashed and snatched away by Vane,
Leaves him alone again.
                                    And so at length
105 Comes a new General and unprovided,
To that 'lost business' in the North, and there
They have him in their noose, their traitors' truce—
The league with Scotland.

V

Yet in the 'strange mistaking of these times'
110 (He will not say, their taste for blood and lies)
Something breaks out of him, astonishing
Old friends and enemies alike, so new
It seemed in him, a gentleness, a sweetness,
Born of the wreck of fortune, 'this my night.'

115 Was it a confidence in innocence—
For anyone can see his innocence?
'God's hand is with us, and to my best judgement
We rather win than lose . . .'
                                    And as it lingered,
120 'All will be well, and every hour
Brings us more hope than other.'

Or was it faith in that poor Stuart's word
That he should never die while Charles was King?

Or was it over and above,
125 That 'Strafford would not die a fool'?
And when that fettered angel
Of his burning, winged intelligence
Had seen the blood and malice that men love,

101: Wentworth played a crucial role in Charles's decision to reconvene Parliament in order to fund a second war against the Scots (though this decision in fact took place before the Irish Parliament). It convened in April 1640, but refused to vote the king the subsidies necessary to fund his war on the Scots and instead concentrated on airing grievances. Vane presented Parliament with the king's offer to waive collection of the much-hated ship money on condition it vote him 12 subsidies, but his refusal to settle for a smaller number led to a deadlock that forced Charles to dissolve Parliament.

105: Strafford was given the command of the English troops; but, outnumbered and poorly paid and disciplined, they panicked under Scottish cannonfire at Newburn that August and were routed; the Scots seized the whole of Northumberland and Durham.

108: After the dissolution of the first ("Short") Parliament, the Scots acted in league with its leading MPs, pressing Charles to call a new Parliament where their grievances might be dealt with.

122: Charles was forced to call a Parliament in November of 1640. Strafford, hated by the populace and the chief target of both Parliament and the Scots, contemplated fleeing the country but was assured by Charles of his protection. He attempted to reach Westminster to impeach the king's Parliamentary enemies for treasonable correspondence with the Scots; but before he could do so he was himself impeached by the leader of the Commons, John Pym.

For all their godly rage and godly lies;
130   Still looking back on faith and right
He found his reasons bathed in light,
And 'being upon his life and children',
Learning patience after strife,
Wrote the absolving letter
135   To the King, and in all sadness
Placed in his hands the 'things most loved, most dreaded,
Death or Life.'

'Sir, my consent herein shall more acquit you
To God, than all the world can do beside';
140   'There is no injury done to a willing man.'
'To say, Sir, that there hath not been a strife
Within me, were to make me less than man,
God knows . . .'
                        And thinking still of Will and Nan,
145   'My poor son and his sisters',
He will beg for them the King's regard
'No more or less hereafter, than hereafter
Their father may seem worthy of this death.'

VI

So ends the letter. Two days later Charles
150   Had signed the warrant weeping, while the mob
Cumbered the yard at Whitehall.
Judges and Bishops barrenly opined:
'As it was put to us, the case was treason';
'Kings have two consciences, the public cloaks you here.'
155   Juxon alone said 'Follow your own conscience.'
So this earl ended.

                        And the lasting moral?
Something on geese and mice, or rats and lions?
An eagle torn by jackals?
160   'Strafford's innocent blood
Taught Charles to die'?
                        For after seven years,
He reckoned it the purchase of his death:
'An unjust sentence
165   That I suffered once to pass me by,
Brings me an unjust sentence.'

132: "being concerned with the conduct of his life and the welfare of his children"
134: As the trial against Strafford proceeded, it became clear that the evidence against him was weak; Strafford defended himself so skilfully that it was feared he would be acquitted. Pym therefore introduced a bill of attainder that simply declared him guilty; this, unlike the trial, required the king's signature. Strafford wrote a letter to the king releasing him from his vow.
155: William *Juxon* was Bishop of London and Charles's Lord High Treasurer.
161: Charles had hoped that the execution of Strafford would placate his opponents, but England instead slipped into civil war, from which the Parliamentary side emerged victorious. In 1649, Charles was tried and executed. Like Strafford, his dignified behavior at the execution impressed all who were present, even his enemies.

VII

But turning to the great man from the small,
Should we not think of Strafford after all
As of the kind
170   Who 'pilgrim it out here'
Some years, and 'tug and tow',
But labour, drudge unconsciously, to find
Their way to self-destruction?
And further, in the way assigned,
175   As one who tasted justice by injustice, murdered here,
His thirst for justice quenched when all is clear,
And he is right and they are wrong and he can say
'They have my body, but my soul is God's',
Remembering the words of Jacques Molay.

180   —The silver river ruffled in the breeze,
Running by grey mud-banks; the glimmering hill-circle
Closes, and opens wider . . .
                        And at dawn,
And coming from the Tower he sees
185   The sun lift up his head, and lifting up his head,
He goes forth 'like a general breathing victory,
That leads a loving army',
But with no army to be led,
And walks between the people thick as trees.
190   Mounting the scaffold, granted time for speech—
Delivered standing on the hollow wood,
And turning words and gestures to the multitude;
Unheard by most and yet, it may be, not misunderstood:
As first, he thinks it strange a people should
195   'Choose to begin their happiness in blood';
Submits to death as voted for their good, the common good,
But not as just: 'Here we misjudge each other;
Righteous judgement, that shall come hereafter.'
And so he ends 'forgiving all the world
200   From my dislodging soul.'
                      Then kisses Ussher and his brother,
Unbuttons at the neck, puts up his hair,
Forgives the axe his coming stroke,
And having knelt awhile in prayer
205   —The head falls from the block,
Caught up and held, the people shout approof
And shake the air.
One touch of azure breaks the cloudy crumbling roof
Hung far above the tumult,
210   And the piece of paper whence he read

179: *Jacques de Molay* (1243–1314) was the last great master of the Knights Templars, a religious military
  order; the Templars were suppressed by Philip IV of France and Pope Clement V, and Molay was burned
  at the stake.
201: James *Ussher*, Archbishop of Armagh and Primate of Ireland, had counselled Charles against assent-
  ing to Strafford's execution.

Flutters and drops, unheeded
For the trophy of the bleeding head;
But gathered up by Rushworth,
Creased, and speckled with a faded red
215   Comes to be published after fifty years
—When most who could remember would be dead,

Or only wished that Strafford were forgotten.

                                                             1963

213: John *Rushworth* (1612–1690) was the author of *Historical Collections of Private Passages of State* (8 vols, 1659–1721), which contains his eyewitness account of Strafford's trial.

CHARLES MADGE (1912–1996)

MADGE WAS BORN IN JOHANNESBURG, SOUTH AFRICA, AND EDUCATED AT WIN-chester College and Magdalene College, Oxford, where he studied with I. A. Richards. He left Cambridge in 1935 to work as a correspondent for the *Daily Mirror*. In 1937, Madge and Tom Harrisson founded Mass-Observation, a project of collaborative anthropology and sociology, which was active throughout the late 1930s and the 1940s. Mass-Observation's intention was to document the persistence of myth and superstition in the mass psychology of Britain; Madge recruited volunteer correspondents to keep diaries of everyday life in locations such as Blackpool and for occasions such as the coronation of George VI. "Mass-Observation wants to find out why human beings are suggestible and how they can protect themselves against suggestions which do not help them to survive,"[1] an early bulletin for the organization proclaimed, echoing Madge's sentiments about the role of the novel in a contemporaneous critical essay: "If the novelist has any function in our age, it is to delineate the relationship of an individual to his class, on the basis of scientific materialism."[2] Mass-Observation's publications were attacked for the amateurism of their analytical methods, but the project remains of interest for its effort to give the ordinary citizen a voice while circumventing more official media, as well as for insights resulting from the observation of behavior then too little analyzed—from music-hall jokes to holiday sex. In 1940, Madge and Harrisson undertook for the Ministry of Information a study of the effect of the blitz on civilian morale; the next year, Madge broke from Harrisson and joined John Maynard Keynes in studying consumption and saving patterns. In 1950, Madge became professor of sociology at Birmingham University, where he worked until 1970.

Madge had early success as a poet. His poems had already appeared in several influential anthologies by the time his first book, *The Disappearing Castle,* was published in 1937. His poetry reflects the influence of W. H. Auden, but it often departs from Auden in its harshly embittered ironies and idiosyncratic mixture of surrealist and documentarian elements. Many of the poems in *The Disappearing Castle* suggest a poetic equivalent for the Marxist and sociological analysis Madge published in his work with Mass-Observation. The sequence "Delusions," for instance, examines subjects such as "bourgeois" fantasies concerning leisure and science and the dream of revolution among "the great unruly crowd." Madge followed his first book with *The Father Found* in 1941, but did not publish another volume until *Of Love, Time and Places,* his selected poems, appeared in 1993.

---

[1] Quoted in James Buzard, "Mass Observation, Modernism, and Auto-ethnography," *Modernism/Modernity,* vol. 4, no. 3, 1997, p. 108.
[2] Quoted in David Margolies, *"Left Review* and Left Literary Theory," *Culture and Crisis in Britain in the Thirties,* ed. Jon Clark, Margot Heinemann, et al., London, 1979, p. 70.

Obsessional

No justice can be done
To the sunlost tribes
Where they sit musing
In their stony arbours

5   Whose brains are yolks
The ages have matured
Into their existence
As selfish primaries

Communications for them
10   Link up their eyes
Those stones that gaze
In unrestricted emptiness

The rule of myriads
The counting of souls
15   The range of classes
Absorption of being

On their forked brows
Hunger and lightning
Reveal the mountain
20   Of the supersensible.

                                          1935 / 1937

Delusions I

Where are the dancing girls? They are not here.
Not here? Then back into the night again,
The night of images that disappear
And reappear to mock the tired brain.

5   We have no home. Our bourgeois home is wrecked.
We seek instead the shadowy consolation
Of glimmering alcohol, and still expect
The unexpected of our own creation.

For we create—proud tyrants of a moment—
10   Bright visions, born between despair and fear,
And, in possessing them, survive our torment.
Where are the dancing girls? They are not here.

They are not here. They are not in the street.
No corner holds them, and no glass swing door

Obsessional: 20: *supersensible:* not apprehensible to the senses; spiritual

15   Admits us to the presence. Still we meet
The blank appearance that we met before:

Glittering spectacle of the lonely bar
And the society which there forgets
Itself, while the routine of things that are
20   In fantasies that are not, dissipates.

Behind the glasses and the polished board,
Behind the faces as they change and smile,
Promises of delusion seem assured
And homeless wanderers soothe their long exile.

25   Beyond the printed words that catch their eyes,
And the chance gleam of some suspended sign,
May fall the blissful moment of surprise
When the dull bourgeois can become divine.

1937

Delusions III

Pillage the great unruly crowd invites
To take the bourgeois palaces by storm.
The sheets of glass, the softly shaded lights
Attract, induce the ugly murmuring swarm.

5   Fingers that grab, and hands that overturn
Obey their prompted nostrils over-wrought
With female scent diffused, and rebels burn
What in their slavery they would once have bought.

Into charred ash high priced silks disappear,
10   Up blazes all the furniture of class
And frightened lift-girls fill the shafts with fear
Wounded by splinters of the shivering glass.

Basement and mezzanine with turmoil swell,
But look! Some little Lenin of the mob
15   Breaks with harsh reprimand the lustful spell
Raising his voice: 'Our task is not to rob

'Since not to us but to the workers' state
These folded silks, this glittering trash belong.
For us meanwhile more pregnant works await
20   Than useless vengeance adding wrong to wrong.

'No doubt in time you too such silks shall wear
When luxury shall crown the common toil
And jewels glitter in the shop girl's hair
And gold and silver round her wrists shall coil

11: *lift-girls:* elevator attendants

25   'Symbols of love, relating then no more
       To the exploited, suffering, human mass,
       Incentive to no vast imperial war
       But innocent and valueless as glass.

       'Then bide your time. That time has not come yet.
30   Meantime replace the spoil, put out the flames.
       At every entrance let a guard be set.'
       Thus in his generous anger he exclaims.

       The guilty crowd recoils; passion subsides,
       Passion that long had known the secret goad
35   Of property that on men's shoulders rides:
       They glimpsed her, bowed beneath the insulting load.

       The moment came. She fell into their power.
       Her, disinvested, helpless now they saw,
       But felt, as they rushed forward to deflower,
40   The bayonet of proletarian law.

       See, as they stumble out upon the kerb,
       The brain still glowing with desire undone,
       They turn their backs upon the pile superb
       And return home, the last illusion gone.

                                                           1937

Delusions V

       The lion evening is untamed because
       Some broken relics from the past of man
       Exert their splendid force against the laws,
       Being liberated and American.

5   'Evil, be thou my good.' Declining sun
       Shaking his head in the disastered west
       Completes the moral pilgrimage, begun
       With secret tremblings of an exile's breast.

       Domestic Adam, father of the race,
10   Haunts the recess of every homely tree
       And his injunctions mark the human face
       With darkening wrinkles of malignity.

       Flinging away his broken crusts and pans,
       A panting savage hurries to the woods,

38: *disinvested:* unclothed

5: *Evil, be thou my good:* Said by Satan in Milton's *Paradise Lost*, 4.110.

15   And in ecstatic ruin dumbly stands
    Glad to behold the murder of his goods.

    The light recedes and the grey chimneys rise
    Against the noisy havoc, tall and grim.
    Reflections of the fire catch human eyes,
20   And each man waits the fate that waits for him.

1937

Delusions VII

    Interior castle of the feudal soul
    And architecture of theology,
    Monad of self and particular whole,
    Your doors are open now invitingly.

5   What space there is within these hoary walls,
    What freedom for the psychic autocrat!
    From sky to tower here the swallow falls;
    This is the midnight trysting of the bat.

    Each book a cell that holds an ancient monk,
10   Each brick a meditation fed with time,
    Foundation into rock-unconscious sunk,
    And minarets that like Spinoza climb.

    Such is that temple where the holy queen
    Blesses the torture chamber and the rack:
15   In image always, never person, seen,
    Long draperies falling behind her back.

    She dominates, whether as Abstract Will,
    Brennpunkt, inverted Sex, or racial dream,
    The old collective phantom lingering still
20   To fascinate, to murder and to seem.

1937

3: *Monad:* an ultimate unit of being; in the philosophy of G. W. Leibniz (1646–1716), the universe consists entirely of self-contained monads, which possess the power of perception to varying degrees. Those monads with the highest powers of perception are souls; the objects of the material world are the appearances of collections of monads. Monads are said to be "windowless" because not open to influence from the outside: their perceptions are not caused by external objects but are determined from within, conveying truth about objects only because of the pre-established harmony between all monads that is arranged by God.

12: The *Ethics* of the philosopher Baruch *Spinoza* (1632–77) climbs from elementary, supposedly self-evident propositions to the highest of metaphysical principles in the manner of a geometrical proof.

17–18: Madge is speaking of Nazi ideology and its origins in nineteenth-century theories. *Abstract Will* perhaps alludes to the philosopher Arthur Schopenhauer's *The World as Will and Representation. Brennpunkt* means "focal point" (but Madge's reference remains unidentified). *Inversion* was the late nineteenth-century scientific term for homosexuality; *racial dream* refers to eugenics and social Darwinist theories.

Countries of the Dead II

There is a passage   from the vault
into an adjacent   invisible bedroom of
        those where flies   crawl boring or
spaces filled with bodies, universal catacombs
5   sleep   the woods   of sleep instead
so letters can be introduced   keyholes
or under the door   a bride, led by hand
        into water   or crumble into dust
a pageant of representational figures   mutes
10   inspiration   a valley of bones
some were forks   spoons
drawers full of intimate remembrances
        a labyrinth of prose   bookworms
gilding the wooden blocks   names of demigods
15   an inscription   difficult
no scholar can decipher   forces   unknown
        or negatively   groping
on to the end   of tactile sensation
        restoring   a dead man
20   life   in that
        underworld   overgrown
        a little crevice   centipedes find
a way through   solitude.

1937

DYLAN THOMAS (1914–1953)

THOMAS WAS BORN AT SWANSEA IN SOUTH WALES AND EDUCATED AT SWANSEA Grammar School, where his father was the English master. He left school at sixteen to work for the *South Wales Daily Post* and continued to write freelance pieces for the paper after leaving it in 1932. Thereafter, like many others at the height of the depression, Thomas was essentially unemployed. Much of his poetry, even the later work, has its origins in notebooks kept between 1930 and 1934. In 1933, Thomas began publishing poems in many of the most respected London periodicals, and the next year his first book, *18 Poems,* appeared. In 1936, the second, *Twenty-five Poems,* was published and enthusiastically praised by Edith Sitwell. The next year, Thomas married Caitlin Macnamara and moved to Laugharne in Wales; for several years they lived in the lodgings of friends and relatives. In the early 1940s, Thomas was back in London, working sporadically for the BBC and as a scriptwriter for Strand Films; he settled permanently in Laugharne with his wife and children in 1949. *Portrait of the Artist as a Young Dog,* a book of quasi-autobiographical stories, appeared in 1940, *New Poems* in 1943, and *Selected Writings* in 1946. With these publications and the success of his theatrical and sonorous reading of poetry on the BBC's Third Programme in the years immediately following World War II, Thomas became one of the two or three most famous poets in England. His celebrity increased with several extensive American reading tours in the early fifties; his activities on these tours have been amply documented. Thomas was an alcoholic for most of his adult life, and in 1953, while staying in New York for rehearsals and public readings of his radio play *Under Milk Wood* (1954), he began to show signs of various physical and psychological ailments. One night he told a friend that he had drunk eighteen straight whiskies; a day later he lapsed into a coma. Four days later he was dead.

From the middle of his brief career until roughly 1980, Thomas's poetry attracted a vast amount of critical attention, and he was praised by many fellow poets, including Hugh MacDiarmid and Vernon Watkins. His poetry was quickly recognized as a neoromantic alternative to the urbane ironies of the Auden group and as a precursor of the New Apocalypse movement. Critics responding to a poetry that seemed to privilege sound over sense while employing archetypal imagery argued about the influence of Sigmund Freud and Surrealism on the poems, but Thomas was careful to state the limits of his interest in both. While he had been present for the Surrealist Exhibition in London in 1936, he rejected what the Surrealists called "automatic writing" and insisted that his poems were the product of intentional, labored construction. Similarly, early critics speculated about Thomas's indebtedness to Welsh poetry, but Thomas knew no Welsh and owed his density of sound to writers such as Gerard Manley Hopkins and his interest in myth and the bardic voice to William Blake and the Bible. George Barker wrote that Thomas "married the art of poetry not in a registry office or a library or a lecture room, but in church."[1] While Thomas can be read as a religious poet, his images and propositions addressing the simultaneously creative and destructive energies of nature and sexuality have more in common with mystical traditions than Christian doctrine. Since roughly 1980, Thomas's reputation has been in decline, while the reputation of other neo-romantic poets such as W. S. Graham has been on the rise, but, as Neil Corcoran argues, "the way the world is read through, or dreamed across, the human body in this poetry makes Thomas overdue for a contemporary . . . reassessment."[2]

---

[1] "On the Death of Dylan Thomas," *Essays,* London, 1970, p. 58.
[2] *English Poetry Since 1940,* Harlow, 1993, p. 43.

The force that through the green fuse drives the flower

The force that through the green fuse drives the flower
Drives my green age; that blasts the roots of trees
Is my destroyer.
And I am dumb to tell the crooked rose
5   My youth is bent by the same wintry fever.

The force that drives the water through the rocks
Drives my red blood; that dries the mouthing streams
Turns mine to wax.
And I am dumb to mouth unto my veins
10   How at the mountain spring the same mouth sucks.

The hand that whirls the water in the pool
Stirs the quicksand; that ropes the blowing wind
Hauls my shroud sail.
And I am dumb to tell the hanging man
15   How of my clay is made the hangman's lime.

The lips of time leech to the fountain head;
Love drips and gathers, but the fallen blood
Shall calm her sores.
And I am dumb to tell a weather's wind
20   How time has ticked a heaven round the stars.

And I am dumb to tell the lover's tomb
How at my sheet goes the same crooked worm.

1934

15: The bodies of the hanged were placed in quicklime (calcium oxide) so that they might be the more completely expunged.

Our eunuch dreams

I

Our eunuch dreams, all seedless in the light,
Of light and love, the tempers of the heart,
Whack their boys' limbs,
And, winding-footed in their shawl and sheet,
5   Groom the dark brides, the widows of the night
Fold in their arms.

The shades of girls, all flavoured from their shrouds,
When sunlight goes are sundered from the worm,
The bones of men, the broken in their beds,
10   By midnight pulleys that unhouse the tomb.

II

In this our age the gunman and his moll,
Two one-dimensioned ghosts, love on a reel,
Strange to our solid eye,
And speak their midnight nothings as they swell;
15   When cameras shut they hurry to their hole
Down in the yard of day.

They dance between their arclamps and our skull,
Impose their shots, throwing the nights away;
We watch the show of shadows kiss or kill,
20   Flavoured of celluloid give love the lie.

III

Which is the world? Of our two sleepings, which
Shall fall awake when cures and their itch
Raise up this red-eyed earth?
Pack off the shapes of daylight and their starch,
25   The sunny gentlemen, the Welshing rich,
Or drive the night-geared forth.

The photograph is married to the eye,
Grafts on its bride one-sided skins of truth;
The dream has sucked the sleeper of his faith
30   That shrouded men might marrow as they fly.

IV

This is the world: the lying likeness of
Our strips of stuff that tatter as we move
Loving and being loth;

4: *winding-footed:* coined from "winding-sheet," a burial sheet
25: *Welshing:* to "welsh" (with a lowercase "w") is to fail to repay a gambling debt; the word contains an
ironic pun in its capitalization, as Dylan Thomas was Welsh.

The dream that kicks the buried from their sack
35   And lets their trash be honoured as the quick.
This is the world. Have faith.

For we shall be a shouter like the cock,
Blowing the old dead back; our shots shall smack
The image from the plates;
40   And we shall be fit fellows for a life,
And who remain shall flower as they love,
Praise to our faring hearts.

1934

To-day, this insect

To-day, this insect, and the world I breathe,
Now that my symbols have outelbowed space,
Time at the city spectacles, and half
The dear, daft time I take to nudge the sentence,
5   In trust and tale have I divided sense,
Slapped down the guillotine, the blood-red double
Of head and tail made witnesses to this
Murder of Eden and green genesis.

The insect certain is the plague of fables.

10   This story's monster has a serpent caul,
Blind in the coil scrams round the blazing outline,
Measures his own length on the garden wall
And breaks his shell in the last shocked beginning;
A crocodile before the chrysalis,
15   Before the fall from love the flying heartbone,
Winged like a sabbath ass this children's piece
Uncredited blows Jericho on Eden.

The insect fable is the certain promise.

Death: death of Hamlet and the nightmare madmen,
20   An air-drawn windmill on a wooden horse,
John's beast, Job's patience, and the fibs of vision,
Greek in the Irish sea the ageless voice:

10: *caul:* a membrane enclosing the foetus inside the womb; it was traditionally a good omen for a baby
to be born with a portion of the caul still covering its head.
16: *sabbath ass:* The holiday of Palm Sunday celebrates Jesus' entry into Jerusalem riding an ass (Matt. 21;
John 12:14).
17: *Jericho:* The Israelites laid siege to this city, destroying its walls with a blast of sound from their priests'
trumpets (Joshua 6).
20: *air-drawn windmill:* Don Quixote mistook windmills for giants; also cf. Macbeth's hallucination: "the
air-drawn dagger" (*Macbeth* 3.4.61).
    wooden horse: the Greek army won the siege of Troy by constructing and hiding inside a giant wooden
horse; the Trojans foolishly took the horse inside the city gates.
21: *John's beast:* of the Apocalypse (Rev. 13)
22: *Greek in the Irish sea:* alluding to Odysseus, whose travels as told in Homer's *Odyssey* are paralleled by
those of Leopold Bloom around Dublin in James Joyce's novel *Ulysses*.

'Adam I love, my madmen's love is endless,
No tell-tale lover has an end more certain,
25   All legends' sweethearts on a tree of stories,
My cross of tales behind the fabulous curtain.'

1936

Over Sir John's hill

Over Sir John's hill,
The hawk on fire hangs still;
In a hoisted cloud, at drop of dusk, he pulls to his claws
And gallows, up the rays of his eyes the small birds of the bay
5   And the shrill child's play
Wars
Of the sparrows and such who swansing, dusk, in wrangling hedges.
And blithely they squawk
To fiery tyburn over the wrestle of elms until
10   The flash the noosed hawk
Crashes, and slowly the fishing holy stalking heron
In the river Towy below bows his tilted headstone.

Flash, and the plumes crack,
And a black cap of jack-
15   Daws Sir John's just hill dons, and again the gulled birds hare
To the hawk on fire, the halter height, over Towy's fins,
In a whack of wind.
There
Where the elegiac fisherbird stabs and paddles
20   In the pebbly dab filled
Shallow and sedge, and 'dilly dilly,' calls the loft hawk,
'Come and be killed,'
I open the leaves of the water at a passage
Of psalms and shadows among the pincered sandcrabs prancing

25   And read, in a shell,
Death clear as a buoy's bell:
All praise of the hawk on fire in hawk-eyed dusk be sung,
When his viperish fuse hangs looped with flames under the brand
Wing, and blest shall
30   Young
Green chickens of the bay and bushes cluck, 'dilly dilly,
Come let us die.'

25: *tree:* i.e., the Cross
26: *fabulous:* i.e., depicting fables (such as a medieval tapestry)

7: *swansing:* According to legend the swan sang a ravishingly beautiful song as it died.
9: *Tyburn,* in London, was where public hangings were held until the end of the eighteenth century.
12: *Towy:* one of two rivers that run into the estuary at Laugharne, Wales, the location of Sir John's Hill
(and of Thomas's cottage).
15: *gulled:* fooled, tricked
20: *dab:* a type of small flatfish
21: *dilly dilly:* see the nursery rhyme "Mrs Bond": "John Ostler, go fetch me a duckling or two; / Cry Dilly,
dilly, dilly, dilly, come and be killed."

We grieve as the blithe birds, never again, leave shingle and elm,
The heron and I,
35   I young Aesop fabling to the near night by the dingle
Of eels, saint heron hymning in the shell-hung distant

Crystal harbour vale
Where the sea cobbles sail,
And wharves of water where the walls dance and the white cranes stilt.
40   It is the heron and I, under judging Sir John's elmed
Hill, tell-tale the knelled
Guilt
Of the led-astray birds whom God, for their breast of whistles,
Have mercy on,
45   God in his whirlwind silence save, who marks the sparrows hail,
For their souls' song.
Now the heron grieves in the weeded verge. Through windows
Of dusk and water I see the tilting whispering

Heron, mirrored, go,
50   As the snapt feathers snow,
Fishing in the tear of the Towy. Only a hoot owl
Hollows, a grassblade blown in cupped hands, in the looted elms,
And no green cocks or hens
Shout
55   Now on Sir John's hill. The heron, ankling the scaly
Lowlands of the waves,
Makes all the music; and I who hear the tune of the slow,
Wear-willow river, grave,
Before the lunge of the night, the notes on this time-shaken
60   Stone for the sake of the souls of the slain birds sailing.

1952

35: *dingle:* wooded valley
45: For *God in his whirlwind silence,* see Job 38:1, 40:6. God is traditionally said to take note even of the
   fall of a sparrow (Matthew 10:29).
52: *Hollows:* calls out
58: *grave:* engrave

C. H. SISSON (b. 1914)

CHARLES HUBERT SISSON WAS BORN IN BRISTOL AND EDUCATED AT THE UNIVERSITY OF Bristol and afterwards in Germany and France. In 1936, he began a career in the Civil Service, which would eventually make him under secretary in the Ministry of Labour. During World War II, he served in India. Sisson's professional life in political administration helped generate an extensive body of prose, including *The Spirit of British Administration* (1959), *The Case of Walter Bagehot* (1972), and some of the essays collected in *The Avoidance of Literature* (1978), which addresses issues such as the relationship of Church and State and the role of the Crown in the perpetuation of sovereignty. In *The Case of Walter Bagehot,* for instance, Sisson writes that "The final point in the State must rest on a certain incomprehension, and incomprehension is the beginning of theology. Few people now would imagine that they knew what was meant by the Divine Right of Kings, but any one might reach the point of mystification as to the coherence and persistence of national entities, which the hereditary monarchy so well expresses."[1] Sisson remembers that his political and cultural views were greatly affected by reading the works of Charles Maurras and T. E. Hulme in his post-graduate years, and the literary criticism in *The Avoidance of Literature* as well as *English Poetry 1900–1950* (1971) reflects the influence of T. S. Eliot and Ezra Pound. Sisson has translated Catullus, Virgil, Horace, Ovid, Lucretius, and Dante, and his books of poetry include *The London Zoo* (1961), *Numbers* (1965), *In The Trojan Ditch: Collected Poems and Selected Translations* (1974), and *Exactions* (1980). Between 1977 and 1984, Sisson and Donald Davie joined Michael Schmidt in editing the *PN Review,* often contributing editorials.

While Sisson's poetry occasionally reflects the influence of modernists such as Pound and Eliot, a Drydenesque plain style is perhaps its most distinctive characteristic. An interest in nursery rhymes can manifest itself as well, as in this glum passage from "Au Claire de la Lune": "This is the end of everything, of everything, of everything / This is the end of everything / On Christmas Day in the morning." "The less / we mean / The more / we say" Sisson writes in beginning the same poem; that proposition seems to shape much of his poetry. Ironic, deeply sceptical, Sisson's poetry confronts the instabilities of identity and perception and tests a Christian faith with the limits of reason and the possibility of meaninglessness. Donald Davie writes that "The drama of *Exactions* is precisely in the spectacle of Sisson hauling himself out of the scepticism which is, in the poems printed first [such as "The Desert" and "Place"]

---

[1] Quoted in Donald Davie, *Under Briggflatts: A History of Poetry in Great Britain 1960–1988,* Chicago, 1989, p. 107.

more abysmal and terrifying than most people have experienced or can contemplate without extreme discomfort."[2]

---

[2] Ibid., p. 190.

A Letter to John Donne

*On 27 July 1617, Donne preached at the parish church
at Sevenoaks, of which he was rector, and was
entertained at Knole, then the country residence of Richard
Sackville, third Earl of Dorset.*

    I understand you well enough, John Donne
    First, that you were a man of ability
    Eaten by lust and by the love of God
    Then, that you crossed the Sevenoaks High Street
5   As rector of Saint Nicholas:
    I am of that parish.

    To be a man of ability is not much
    You may see them on the Sevenoaks platform any day
    Eager men with despatch cases
10   Whom ambition drives as they drive the machine
    Whom the certainty of meticulous operation
    Pleasures as a morbid sex a heart of stone.

    That you should have spent your time in the corruption of courts
    As these in that of cities, gives you no place among us:
15   Ability is not even the game of a fool
    But the click of a computer operating in a waste
    Your cleverness is dismissed from the suit
    Bring out your genitals and your theology.

    What makes you familiar is this dual obsession;
20   Lust is not what the rutting stag knows
    It is to take Eve's apple and to lose
    The stag's paradisal look:
    The love of God comes readily
    To those who have most need.

25   You brought body and soul to this church
    Walking there through the park alive with deer
    But now what animal has climbed into your pulpit?
    One whose pretension is that the fear
    Of God has heated him into a spirit
30   An evaporated man no physical ill can hurt.

Title: The poet *John Donne* (1572–1631) attempted to pursue a career at court, but lost his position as sec-
retary to Sir Thomas Egerton, Keeper of the Seal, after eloping with Egerton's niece Anne More. There-
after he lived in poverty, all his efforts to secure employment failing; he reluctantly took orders in the
Anglican Church after King James I made it clear he would only appoint Donne to a church position.
Donne—who was born a Catholic and when a younger man had composed the love poetry for which he
is now celebrated—rose to become Dean of St. Paul's in 1621.

Well might you hesitate at the Latin gate
Seeing such apes denying the church of God:
I am grateful particularly that you were not a saint
But extravagant whether in bed or in your shroud.
35   You would understand that in the presence of folly
I am not sanctified but angry.

Come down and speak to the men of ability
On the Sevenoaks platform and tell them
That at your Saint Nicholas the faith
40   Is not exclusive in the fools it chooses
That the vain, the ambitious and the highly sexed
Are the natural prey of the incarnate Christ.

1965

The Desert

I

This is the only place that I inhabit:
The desert.
No drop of water: no palm trees: nothing.
No gourd, no cactus: sand
5   Heaped on all sides like mountainous seas
To drown in.
Luckily I cannot see myself, I am alone
No mirror, glass, plastic left by an Arab
Nothing
10   I cannot say it too often
Nothing.
The sand itself would diminish if I said yes.
No rascally Bedouin,
Praying mantis, or nice people
15   —A mirage of them, occasionally.
But they are not there, any more than I,
For all my vocables, eyes, 'I's,
Other impedimenta of the desert
—Khaki shirt, shorts, chapli,
20   Mess-tin, for nothing to eat;
Water-bottle, nothing in it.
It is an amusing end, because desired.

2

Alone
But to say 'alone' would be to give validity
25   To a set of perceptions which are nothing at all
—A set as these words are

17: *vocables:* words (considered with reference to their shape rather than meaning)
18: *impedimenta:* equipment
19: *chapli:* sandals (Urdu)

Set down
Meaninglessly on paper, by nobody.
There were friends, they have faded into the distance;
30   With my disintegration the vision becomes blurred,
Rather, disintegrated, each bit
For all I know
Tied to a separate nothing, not I.
Enough of laughter, which echoes like a tin eccentric
35   Round the edge of the desert:
Tears would be ridiculous
If I could shed them,
Eyes shed them, one
Then another again, weeping
40   For different things, not joined.

Shatter the retina so that the eyes are many
—Hailstones, now, it can be sand for all I care.
The damned unrepairable, I sit
Like a vehicle sanded up, the desert
45   Is frequent with images.
Could night come, that would effect a change,
But the sun blazes:
'I am all you have to fear, extreme, hot, searing
But the end is dust, and soon.'

1980

Au Clair de la Lune

The less
        we mean
The more
        we say

5   The less we mean the more we say:
Put together like that, marvellous.

I see no point in meaning,
Nor any;
Reason is deluded, old hag.
10   No need to talk of the affective, Love:
The machine itself is enough.

There is no entry into any city
There is nothing but fornication,
Parties picked, packed and
15   Repeated.

34: *eccentric:* a mechanism that uses a turning shaft fixed off-center to a disk in order to generate a back-and-forth motion

Title: "In Moonlight" (French)

No bloody nonsense about the king of hosts:
No arsing around with the dialectical process.
There is nothing up against the wall
But the prick stopped in the plaster

20   This is the end of everything, of everything, of everything
This is the end of everything
On Christmas Day in the morning.

So I came through that territory
With camels, at least I had the hump,
25   Down several deserts where there were wind-breaks
—Sliding on the dunes patched with light:
They fell under my feet like truculent reality,
Would not be still, offer foot-hold to foot-fall, feet
Sank, ankles sank, the knees
30   Found the sand flowing about them.

Motion stopped, except the hands waving
Hip hip hooray.
They are gone at last,
Under

35   Starting from nothing, returning
To the same place or no-place;
Passing *outre* only to pass beyond nothing
Into nothing
—A spacious place, I expect
40   Too big for you:
Where salvation was expected, hardly by me
But arranged in order for those who expected it:
A pile of rocks heaped, gigantic pebbles,
Weathered at least by some trick of the centuries.

45   A great bowl of sand. I alone am the moon-figure
Walking there.
Is there no hovel for fornication?
The palace of luxury which is alone worth finding?
An old hermit, sitting at the door—it is myself—
50   And inside,
Her limbs stretched on a bed, rationality
—Smooth as lard.

1980

16: *king of hosts*: cf. Psalm 24:10: "The Lord of hosts, he is the King of glory."
20–22: cf. the Christmas carol "I Saw Three Ships": "I saw three ships come sailing in, / On Christmas Day, on Christmas Day, / I saw three ships come sailing in, / On Christmas Day in the morning." Also cf. T.S. Eliot's parody of the children's rhyme "Here we go round the mulberry bush" in 'The Hollow Men": "Here we go round the prickly pear / Prickly pear prickly pear / Here we go round the prickly pear / At five o'clock in the morning."
37: *outre*: "beyond" (French)
48: *luxury*: lechery

Place

We have only to live and see what happens
—Nothing perhaps; for it may be that history,
As Mairet remarked, is coming to an end
And we shall wander around without meaning.

5   That is what most of us would like, and it is death
However it puts on the masks and opinions of life.
If we live here, it is indeed here that we live.
We cannot afford to scoff at the *pays natal*,
Unless our minds are to be born without content;

10   Nor at the acres in which we spend our childhood,
Unless the things we see are of no account,
Do not fill our minds, are nothing but generalities.
What do we see? Faces on a television screen
Which are more vivid than those we pass in the street.

15   So we live no-where, but somewhere there is a *place*
Where life is lived, a kingdom of the blest,
Perhaps, in which the programmes are prepared.

1980

3: Philip *Mairet* (1886–1975) was editor of the Social Credit journal the *New English Weekly* after the death
of its founder A. R. Orage.
8: *pays natal:* native country

DAVID GASCOYNE (b. 1916)

GASCOYNE'S SURREALIST POEMS, PUBLISHED AS A COLLECTION WHEN HE WAS ONLY twenty, together with his translations of French Surrealist poets, make him one of the most important of a small group of English Surrealists, including Hugh Sykes Davies and Roger Roughton. In the introduction to his *Collected Poems*, Gascoyne tells the story of how he came to title his surrealist book *Man's Life is This Meat* (1936). The poet-critic Geoffrey Grigson, whose magazine *New Verse* published Gascoyne's poems, randomly opened a sample book of printer's typefaces for Gascoyne's examination. On the bottom of one page were the words "man's life is," and on the top of the next "this meat"—and so Gascoyne had his title.[1] "And the Seventh Dream is the Dream of Isis" was the first of Gascoyne's surrealist poems; like others it deploys hallucinatory imagery to show the body in a state of dissolution, its boundaries transgressed.

Gascoyne's *Short Survey of Surrealism* (1935) identifies two areas of Surrealist research. One interest was "automatism, spontaneous and 'pure' poetry, and the idea of the synonymity of poetry and dream. Parallel with these features, in the realm of art, may be placed collage and frottage, and the development of the idea of the element of anonymity and chance in artistic creation." More recently, Gascoyne continued, surrealism explored the artist's ability to impose "the image of his desires and obsessions upon the concrete, daylight world of objective reality; he actively takes part in 'accidents.' "[2] Gascoyne's account of his title would seem to locate his early work as part of his second, more conscious surrealist practice.

Gascoyne was born in Harrow outside London and spent his youth in England and Scotland. He attended the Choir School at Salisbury and Regent Street Polytechnic in Central London. In 1933, he first visited France, and for part of the 1930s and again after the war he lived in Paris. Friends made in the 1930s included Kathleen Raine, Humphrey Jennings, and Charles Madge, through whom he became involved, in 1936, with "Mass-Observation," a project initiated by social anthropologists to study everyday behavior. He joined the Communist party in 1936, and broadcast in English for the propaganda ministry in Barcelona but became "disillusioned by Communist hostility to the anarchists and the Trotskyite P.O.U.M."[3] From 1954 to 1964, he lived in Paris and Aix-en-Provence. He moved to the Isle of Wight to live with his parents in 1964, after experiencing a mental breakdown; by 1979, Gascoyne was able to write

---

1 "Introductory Notes," *Collected Poems 1988,* Oxford, 1988, p. xv.
2 Quoted in Rob Jackaman, *The Course of English Surrealist Poetry Since the 1930s*, Lewiston, New York, 1989, p. 40.
3 Philip Gardner, "David Gascoyne," *Dictionary of Literary Biography,* vol. 20, ed. Donald E. Stanford, Detroit, 1983, p. 143.

that he had recovered from ongoing problems with depression and paranoia. Following the surrealist poetry, Gascoyne's work increasingly explores metaphysical and religious themes. Discussing the "quiet music" of the later poems and contrasting their "searching of his own and others' wounds" with the more "clinical" approach of W. H. Auden, C. H. Sisson argues that "Gascoyne values psychology as a possible route to the truth not as a technique which enables you to put somebody right."[4] *Hölderlin's Madness* appeared in 1938, followed by the well-received *Poems, 1937–1942* (1943). Since *A Vagrant, and Other Poems* (1950) and his radiophonic poem *Night Thoughts*, produced by the BBC in 1955 and published a year later, Gascoyne has written little poetry, though the 1988 edition of *Collected Poems* includes a few more recent poems. Sisson adds that "One has to go back to the most inventive period of the century, the years preceding the First World War, to find anything like . . . the degree of disjunction from his immediate predecessors which Gascoyne showed."[5]

---

[4] *English Poetry 1900–1950*, London, 1971, p. 258.
[5] Ibid., p. 256.

And the Seventh Dream is the Dream of Isis

1

    white curtains of infinite fatigue
    dominating the starborn heritage of the colonies of St Francis
    white curtains of tortured destinies
    inheriting the calamities of the plagues of the desert
5   encourage the waistlines of women to expand
    and the eyes of men to enlarge like pocket-cameras
    teach children to sin at the age of five
    to cut out the eyes of their sisters with nail-scissors
    to run into the streets and offer themselves to unfrocked priests
10   teach insects to invade the deathbeds of rich spinsters
    and to engrave the foreheads of their footmen with purple signs
    for the year is open the year is complete
    the year is full of unforeseen happenings
    and the time of earthquakes is at hand

15   today is the day when the streets are full of hearses
    and when women cover their ring fingers with pieces of silk
    when the doors fall off their hinges in ruined cathedrals
    when hosts of white birds fly across the ocean from america
    and make their nests in the trees of public gardens
20   the pavements of cities are covered with needles
    the reservoirs are full of human hair
    fumes of sulphur envelop the houses of ill-fame
    out of which bloodred lilies appear.

    across the square where crowds are dying in thousands
25   a man is walking a tightrope covered with moths

2

    there is an explosion of geraniums in the ballroom of the hotel
    there is an extremely unpleasant odour of decaying meat

arising from the depetalled flower growing out of her ear
her arms are like pieces of sandpaper
30   or wings of leprous birds in taxis
and when she sings her hair stands on end
and lights itself with a million little lamps like glow-worms
you must always write the last two letters of her christian name
upside down with a blue pencil
35   she was standing at the window clothed only in a ribbon
she was burning the eyes of snails in a candle
she was eating the excrement of dogs and horses
she was writing a letter to the president of france

3

the edges of leaves must be examined through microscopes
40   in order to see the stains made by dying flies
at the other end of the tube is a woman bathing her husband
and a box of newspapers covered with handwriting
when an angel writes the word TOBACCO across the sky
the sea becomes covered with patches of dandruff
45   the trunks of trees bust open to release streams of milk
little girls stick photographs of genitals to the windows of their homes
prayerbooks in churches open themselves at the death service
and virgins cover their parents' beds with tealeaves
there is an extraordinary epidemic of tuberculosis in yorkshire
50   where medical dictionaries are banned from the public libraries
and salt turns a pale violet colour every day at seven o'clock
when the hearts of troubadours unfold like soaked mattresses
when the leaven of the gruesome slum-visitors
and the wings of private airplanes look like shoeleather
55   shoeleather on which pentagrams have been drawn
shoeleather covered with vomitings of hedgehogs
shoeleather used for decorating wedding-cakes
and the gums of queens like glass marbles
queens whose wrists are chained to the walls of houses
60   and whose fingernails are covered with little drawings of flowers
we rejoice to receive the blessing of criminals
and we illuminate the roofs of convents when they are hung
we look through a telescope on which the lord's prayer has been written
and we see an old woman making a scarecrow
65   on a mountain near a village in the middle of spain
we see an elephant killing a stag-beetle
by letting hot tears fall onto the small of its back
we see a large cocoa-tin full of shapeless lumps of wax
there is a horrible dentist walking out of a ship's funnel
70   and leaving behind him footsteps which make noises
on account of his accent he was discharged from the sanatorium
and sent to examine the methods of cannibals
so that wreaths of passion-flowers were floating in the darkness
giving terrible illnesses to the possessors of pistols
75   so that large quantities of rats disguised as pigeons
were sold to various customers from neighbouring towns
who were adepts at painting gothic letters on screens
and at tying up parcels with pieces of grass
we told them to cut off the buttons on their trousers

80   but they swore in our faces and took off their shoes
       whereupon the whole place was stifled with vast clouds of smoke
       and with theatres and eggshells and droppings of eagles
       and the drums of the hospitals were broken like glass
       and glass were the faces in the last looking-glass.

1936

Baptism

Have had enough barbarity
But enough too of illusion
Dreams of peace

Walking in the water
5   Or upon it
With wet fingers on the brow
And sombre eyes turned upwards
No longer expectant but prepared
Have had enough of was . . .

10   Statement:
If you are with us you are red.

1935, 1988

The Rites of Hysteria

In the midst of the flickering sonorous islands
The islands with liquid gullets full of mistletoe-suffering
Where untold truths are hidden in fibrous baskets
And the cold mist of decayed psychologies stifles the sun
5   An arrow hastening through the zone of basaltic honey
An arrow choked by suppressed fidgetings and smokey spasms
An arrow with lips of cheese was caught by a floating hair

The perfumed lenses whose tongues were tied up with wire
The boxes of tears and the bicycles coated with stains
10   Swam out of their false-bottomed nests into clouds of dismay
Where the gleams and the moth-bitten monsters the puddles of soot
And a half-strangled gibbet all cut off an archangel's wings
The flatfooted heart of a memory opened its solitary eye
Till the freak in the showcase was smothered in mucus and sweat

15   A cluster of insane massacres turns green upon the highroad
Green as the nadir of a mystery in the closet of a dream
And a wild growth of lascivious pamphlets became a beehive
The afternoon scrambles like an asylum out of its hovel
The afternoon swallows a bucketful of chemical sorrows
20   And the owners of rubber pitchforks bake all their illusions
In an oven of dirty globes and weedgrown stupors

Now the beckoning nudity of diseases putrifies the saloon
The severed limbs of the galaxy wriggle like chambermaids
The sewing-machine on the pillar condenses the windmill's halo
25   Which poisoned the last infanta by placing a tooth in her ear
When the creeping groans of the cellar's anemone vanished
The nightmare spun on the roof a chain-armour of handcuffs
And the ashtray balanced a ribbon upon a syringe

An opaque whisper flies across the forest
30   Shaking its trailing sleeves like a steaming spook
Till the icicle stabs at the breast with the bleeding nipple
And bristling pot-hooks slit open the garden's fan
In the midst of the flickering sonorous hemlocks
A screen of hysteria blots out the folded hemlocks
35   And feathery eyelids conceal the volcano's mouth.

                                                                                    1936

The Cubical Domes

Indeed indeed it is growing very sultry
The Indian feather pots are scrambling out of the room
The slow voice of the tobacconist is like a circle
Drawn on the floor in chalk and containing ants
5   And indeed there is a shoe upon the table
And indeed it is as regular as clockwork
Demonstrating the variability of the weather
Or denying the existence of manu altogether
For after all why should love resemble a cushion
10   Why should the stumbling-block float up towards the ceiling
And in our attic it is always said
That this is a sombre country the wettest place on earth
And then there is the problem of living to be considered
With its vast pink parachutes full of underdone mutton
15   Its tableaux of the archbishops dressed in their underwear
Have you ever paused to consider why grass is green
Yes greener at least it is said than the man in the moon
Which is why
The linen of flat countries basks in the tropical sun
20   And the light of the stars is attracted by transparent flowers
And at last is forgotten by both man and beast
By helmet and capstan and mermerised nun
For the bounds of my kingdom are truly unknown
And its factories work all night long
25   Producing the strongest canonical wastepaper-baskets
And ant-eaters' skiing-shoes
Which follow the glistening murders as far as the pond
And then light a magnificent bonfire of old rusty nails

25: *infanta*: daughter of a Spanish or Portuguese monarch

8: In Indian myth *Manu* is the first man and the author of the *Manu-smṛti*, an important Sanskrit code of law.

And indeed they are paid by the state for their crimes
30 There is room for them all in the conjuror's musical-box
There is still enough room for even the hardest of faces
For faces are needed to stick on the emperor's walls
To roll down the stairs like a party of seafaring christians
Whose hearts are on fire in the snow.

1936, 1965

NICHOLAS MOORE (1918–1986)

Nicholas Moore, the son of philosopher G. E. Moore and nephew of poet T. Sturge Moore, was born in Cambridge and educated at The Dragon School, Oxford, Dartington Hall, and Cambridge. In 1938, he began *Seven,* a journal that helped give birth to the Apocalyptic movement; his poems then appeared in the two most important anthologies of that movement, *The New Apocalypse* (1939) and *The White Horseman* (1941), and his reputation as a leading poet of the generation following W. H. Auden's was established. Except for a brief period during World War II when as a conscientious objector Moore worked on farms in East Anglia, he spent the 1940s in Cambridge, commuting to London and working in the offices of J. Meary Tambimuttu, the influential editor of *Poetry* (London). His poems continued to appear in journals associated with Apocalyptic and neo-romantic poetry and in collections including *A Book for Priscilla: Poems* (1941), *The Glass Tower* (1944), and *Recollections of the Gala: Selected Poems, 1943–1948* (1949). His reputation extended to the United States; Wallace Stevens was a correspondent. Then, in the 1950s, after his wife left him and Moore was diagnosed with diabetes, he stopped writing and disappeared from public view when tastes shifted under the influence of the Movement. He moved to suburban Kent and worked as a horticulturalist until his diabetes made this impossible. In the early 1960s, he began writing poetry again but without regaining his former reputation: only three small books were published in the remainder of his lifetime. One of them, *Spleen* (1973), contains thirty-one translations of one poem by Charles Baudelaire, an unprecedented gesture that bears more examination than it has received to date. Some of the work from Moore's later period is collected in *Lacrimae Rerum* (1986) and *Longings of the Acrobats,* a selected poems published in 1990.

For the most part literary historians, when they remember Moore at all, remember him for early poems such as "The Ruin and the Sun," a poem about the Spanish Civil War. "Ideas of Disorder at Torquay," which dates from the early 1940s, alludes in its title to Stevens's "The Idea of Order at Key West" but addresses the question of order in explicitly social and political terms, imagining the voices of old women in Torquay fearful of the "Russian fantasy" and the changes World War II seemed to promise. Of Moore's later poems, such as "Leap Year," Peter Riley notes that "Since nobody was listening, the poetry could be 'anything'. Long meditations, short epigrams, rhymed and unrhymed, measured and unmeasured, sonnets, songs, ballads, blues, straight philosophical statements, symbolic landscapes, surrealist figurations, imagist traces, jokes and nonsense, poems in gobbledegook, outrageous travesty and satire, calm description, detective poems, jazz poems, cricket poems, haiku, doggerel, pure 1940s lyrics and persona narratives."[1] This stylistic eclecticism forged against the orthodoxies of the moment indicates not only the freedom afforded by neglect but an integrity, independence, and craftsmanship much admired by poets such as Riley, who seek to challenge a literary history too comfortable in its categories to account for a poet like Moore.

---

[1] "Nicholas Moore in the 1960s and 1970s," *Conductors of Chaos*, ed. Iain Sinclair, London, 1996, p. 415.

Song

A little onion lay by the fireplace,
It had a burning mansion painted on one side,
On the other it had a rat and a pair of whiskers.
I said, My love, this reminds me of you,
5   But she put out the candle and said, Go to bed.
I cannot remember, said the madman.

The mouse on the floor and the bat on the ceiling
Batten on my memory, O make my bed soon,
Before I see her again, or before the doctor shoots me,
10   Or the white nurse straps me to my bed like mother.
The midnight lady has lost her echo.
I only remember the onion, the egg, and the boy.
O that was me, said the madman.

1940 / 1941

Ideas of Disorder at Torquay

I

The trams still run in some kind of array,
Along the seafront with its curled white foam
And reminiscent gardens on the rocks,
Goldenrod, saxifrage, imperious lupins
5   Waving a kind of welcome to the sea:
The trams still run against the times' dismay,
Leaving an old-world order in Torquay.

II

And there the aunts sit with their gorgeous knitting,
Watching the children's kites high in the bay:
10   The needles go click-click against the sky,
The cloud and sunshine, and the rocking sea,
The flowers and the nurses. In the bay

Ideas of Disorder At Torquay: See Wallace Stevens, "The Idea of Order at Key West." *Torquay* (pronounced *tor-key*) is a popular sea resort in Devon, in the southwest of England.
1: *trams*: streetcars

The little steamers puff their purple smoke
As if to say order in everything.

III

15 And the hotels on the majestic front
Fill up with visitors, old, ancient ladies,
And proud magnates from factory and bank.
In the ballrooms they hum God-save-the-King,
Among the flowery asters and the dark . . .
20 Dun dowagers with breasts of precious pearl,
Lords and ladies out of a distant world.

IV

Meanwhile the vulgar in their hordes disdain
The imperial order, and the rabble ride
Upon what trains they can to Blackpool Pier,
25 To look for lights they used to know. Click-click.
The Torquay needles clack to help the troops,
While what wild engineers grab Blackpool buns,
Hoping to find an old-world holiday.

V

Such reading sends a shudder of disgust . . .
30 As who would not, among lupins and roses,
Watching the quiet foam of Devon water,
And doing duty with wound reams of wool,
Contemplating disorder . . . Who would not
Protest that such order might be destroyed?
35 The same thrilling distaste runs through the roses,
As cold disaster in detective stories.

VI

And murmurs heave the quiet, contented ladies,
Whose withered bosoms hold bright emerald jewels,
As if to say the young are so, so strange,
40 As if to say the world was in its ruins,
With such experiments, with such wild fancies,
The Russian fantasy. And edibles
Run out because of war, and chew on grief
Becomes the order of the day, old ladies.

VII

45 The trams still run. In the white-ribbed café,
It is still possible to take coffee,

24: *Blackpool* is a resort town in Lancashire, popular with the Lancashire working classes.
27: *buns:* cakes or sweet buns
42: *Russian fantasy:* i.e., the Communist social experiment
42–43: *edibles / Run out:* due to shortages and rationing during World War II

Or in the gorgeous flower-perfect lounge
Sip gentle teas. Order is possible.
The lupins and the saxifrage have it.
50   So does the welcoming and battling sea,
The gentle rocks. But something holds dismay
Like a round moon upon faded Torquay.
Something, the essence of a change that seems
A breaking up of order, something grave
55   Troubles the waters of contentment, moves
The old, cold ladies to a troubled love.

1941–1942 / 1942

Portman Restaurant

(FOR JOSÉ WILSON)

Be true to what? The image,
Right for its eminence, traces
On the table-cloth a pattern, true
No doubt to many places,

5   Zero, the ubiquitous
Everywhere-to-be-found answer.
Here, where the image dives
And twists like a drunken dancer,

I lift the coffee to my lips,
10   Running over the page with rhythms
Everywhere-to-be-noted. That
Does nothing to the people with whom—

Just as casually as they—I
Operate: for the food is tender,
15   Satisfactorily cooked and the eye,
Everywhere-to-be-looking, will wander

Invincibly from image to image.
So this is poetry? The bland-eyed, obtrusive
Airforce officer calmly
20   Breathes the air, illusive,

Everywhere-questioning, noticeable in
Anger. It is as though these faces,
Until now the still familiar human,
Turned to stone or broke to pieces

25   In his calm hands like bread. And questions
Fall automatically from the position,
Until then certain, of his lady's
Light shoulders. Is this the condition,

Capable in poetry, of all
30   Rare beauties? O the blazing,

Everywhere-to-be-met-with image is
After all the point. To be choosing

This, to be knowing it. That,
Until we learn a better grace of faces,
35   Remains our task not to be broken. For,
Everywhere-turning, the image falls to pieces.

1944 / 1950

Leap Year

You can't jump out of the window for poetry
Or leave yourself lying broken in the courtyard.
The goddess is there, even if you aren't,
Saying, 'You cannot do this. You must inhabit the body,'
5   And you have this uncomfortable habitancy
To keep up against all odds, against

The pricking needles of fate, the man in the bowler,
The journalist under the stairs, the most uncorpselike
Body of love on the bed, the red eggs
10   Crawling between the grey scrolls of your brain.
'Resist, you must resist,' she tells you, and quietly places
Forget-me-nots in your eyes, black gentians at your ears.

1960s or 1970s / 1996

W. S. GRAHAM (1918–1986)

WILLIAM SYDNEY GRAHAM WAS BORN IN GREENOCK, SCOTLAND AND EDUCATED AT Greenock High School. At fourteen, he was apprenticed as a draughtsman to an engineering firm and then attended Stow College, Glasgow, taking classes in structural engineering. In 1938, he was awarded a bursary to Newbattle Abbey College, where he studied literature for a year. During the war years Graham worked various jobs in Galway, Dublin, and Clydeside, and taught briefly in an experimental school in southwest Scotland. In 1944, Graham and his companion Nessie Dunsmuir moved to Cornwall; after they separated in 1947, Graham spent a year teaching at New York University. Returning to Britain in 1948, he lived in London and briefly in Paris before marrying Dunsmuir in 1954 and settling in Cornwall, near the artists' community of St. Ives, where Graham came to befriend several of the painters resident there, including Bryan Wynter and Roger Hilton. The poverty that Graham experienced throughout much of his life eased a little with the patronage of the Canadian poet-professor Robin Skelton in the 1970s and a Civil List pension awarded in 1974.

Graham's earlier poems, as collected in *Cage Without Grievance* (1942), *2nd Poems* (1945), and *The White Threshold* (1949), were often compared to the work of Dylan Thomas, though what similarities are evident result less from the influence of Thomas on Graham than shared reading in poets such as Hopkins, Arthur Rimbaud, and Hart Crane. With the publication of *The Nightfishing* in 1955, Graham emerged from Thomas's shadow, but the success of the Movement's attack on neo-romanticism in the 1950s prevented his poetry from receiving the acclaim it deserved, despite influential advocates such as T. S. Eliot and Hugh MacDiarmid. As Tony Lopez suggests in his study of Graham, it was not until after *Malcolm Mooney's Land* (1970), *Implements in their Places* (1977), and especially *Collected Poems 1942–1977* (1979) that Graham began to be recognized as "a major British poet whose work is quite different from anything else we have—quite independent, that is, from the dominant trend in British poetry since the 1950s."[1]

G. S. Fraser described Graham shortly after the publication of "The Nightfishing" as "a man struggling concretely with the problem of identity-in-change." Using the poem's own metaphors, he noted that "Language is the boat with which we ride the flux, a flux which, like the sea, is in some sense our source and at once threatens us and feeds us."[2] At one important and "concrete" level the poem's seven sections of varying meters describe a night's voyage fishing for herring, but the poem's ultimate concerns are philosophical—the nature of being-in-the-world, the possibility of self-

---

[1] *The Poetry of W. S. Graham*, Edinburgh, 1989, p. 9.
[2] Review of *The Nightfishing*, *London Magazine*, vol. 2, no. 9, 1955, pp. 67–9.

knowledge within the flux of experience and language, where "Each word is but a longing / Set out to break from a difficult home. Yet in / Its meaning I am." What makes "The Nightfishing" remarkable, James Dickey argued along slightly different lines, is not only a setting where "only essentials have their being ... a kind of inhuman mystery against which the human 'I' is better defined than on land" but also "the impacted, constantly-changing-about-a-center imagery, and the broken, rocky-mouthed, irresistible surge of [its] rhythms."[3]

Graham's later poems, such as "Language Ah Now You Have Me," are dense with puns and substitutions. They create what Lopez calls an "in-between realm that lies, in [Martin] Heidegger's words, 'between men and gods'. ... Through his monsters, beasts, and gods, Graham characterized language as a given, living, and animate being."[4]

---

[3] *Babel to Byzantium: Poets & Poetry Now,* New York, 1968, p. 45.
[4] Lopez, p. 129.

The Nightfishing

I

Very gently struck
The quay night bell.

Now within the dead
Of night and the dead
5   Of my life I hear
My name called from far out.
I'm come to this place
(Come to this place)
Which I'll not pass
10   Though one shall pass
Wearing seemingly
This look I move as.
This staring second
Breaks my home away
15   Through always every
Night through every whisper
From the first that once
Named me to the bone.
Yet this place finds me
20   And forms itself again.
This present place found me.
Owls from on the land.
Gulls cry from the water.
And that wind honing
25   The roof-ridge is out of
Nine hours west on the main
Ground with likely a full
Gale unwinding it.

We are indebted at several points to Tony Lopez's *The Poetry of W.S. Graham* (Edinburgh, 1989).

2: *bell:* of a buoy, which clangs as the sea moves it, serving as a position marker in fog or on a dark night
26–27: *the main / Ground:* the main commercial fishing ground west of Cornwall, known as the Irish Box.

30
Gently the quay bell
Strikes the held air.

Strikes the held air like
Opening a door
So that all the dead
Brought to harmony
35
Speak out on silence.

I bent to the lamp. I cupped
My hand to the glass chimney.
Yet it was a stranger's breath
From out of my mouth that
40
Shed the light. I turned out
Into the salt dark
And turned my collar up.

And now again almost
Blindfold with the bright
45
Hemisphere unprised
Ancient overhead,
I am befriended by
This sea which utters me.

The hull slewed out through
50
The lucky turn and trembled
Under way then. The twin
Screws spun sweetly alive
Spinning position away.

Far out faintly calls
55
The continual sea.

Now within the dead
Of night and the dead
Of all my life I go.
I'm one ahead of them
60
Turned in below.
I'm borne, in their eyes,
Through the staring world.

The present opens its arms.

2

To work at waking. Yet who wakes?
65
Dream gives awake its look. My death
Already has me clad anew.

37: *glass chimney*: i.e., of the lamp
45: *unprised*: opened; the stars become visible as the ship moves away from onshore lights.
49–50: "I think that 'slew' here means pushing through water and 'lucky turn' is a turn from the pilot chan-
nel close to harbour out into the sea." (Lopez, in correspondence)
52: *Screws*: screw propellers

We'll move off in this changing grace.
The moon keels and the harbour oil
Looks at the sky through seven colours.

70   When I fell down into this place
My father drew his whole day's pay,
My mother lay in a set-in bed,
The midwife threw my bundle away.

Here we dress up in a new grave,
75   The fish-boots with their herring scales
Inlaid as silver of a good week,
The jersey knitted close as nerves
Of the ground under the high bracken.
My eyes let light in on this dark.

80   When I fell from the hot to the cold
My father drew his whole day's pay,
My mother lay in a set-in bed,
The midwife threw my bundle away.

3

I, in Time's grace, the grace of change, sail surely
85   Moved off the land and the skilled keel sails
The darkness burning under where I go.
Landvoices and the lights ebb away
Raising the night round us. Unwinding whitely,
My changing motive pays me slowly out.
90   The sea sails in. The quay opens wide its arms
And waves us loose.

So I would have it, waved from home to out
After that, the continual other offer,
Intellect sung in a garment of innocence.
95   Here, formal and struck into a dead stillness,
The voyage sails you no more than your own.
And on its wrought epitaph fathers itself
The sea as metaphor of the sea. The boat
Rides in its fires.

100   And nursed now out on movement as we go,
Running white from the bow, the long keel sheathed
In departure leaving the sucked and slackening water
As mingled in memory; night rises stooped high over
Us as our boat keeps its nets and men and
105   Engraves its wake. Our bow heaves hung on a likely
Bearing for fish. The Mor Light flashes astern
Dead on its second.

68: *keels:* presumably "enters or pushes through the water like a ship's keel"
72: *set-in bed:* a bed built in an alcove. "The phrase 'a set-in bed' means a bed set into the thickness of the wall, a kind of square cave." (Graham, quoted in Lopez, p. 67)
89: To *pay out* a rope is to slacken it and permit it to run out.
106: *Mor Light:* lighthouse. "Mor" is Cornish for the sea.

Across our moving local of light the gulls
Go in a wailing slant. I watch, merged
110 In this and in a like event, as the boat
Takes the mild swell, and each event speaks through.
They speak me thoroughly to my faintest breath.
And for what sake? Each word is but a longing
Set out to break from a difficult home. Yet in
115 Its meaning I am.

The weather's come round. For us it's better broken.
Changed and shifted above us, the sky is broken
Now into a few light patches brightly ground
With its rough smithers and those swells lengthening
120 Easy on us, outride us in a slow follow
From stern to stem. The keel in its amorous furrow
Goes through each word. He drowns, who but ill
Resembled me.

In those words through which I move, leaving a cry
125 Formed in exact degree and set dead at
The mingling flood, I am put forward on to
Live water, clad in oil, burnt by salt
To life. Here, braced, announced on to the slow
Heaving seaboards, almost I am now too
130 Lulled. And my watch is blear. The early grey
Air is blowing.

It is that first pallor there, broken, running
Back on the sheared water. Now the chill wind
Comes off the shore sharp to find its old mark
135 Between the shoulderblades. My eyes read in
The fixed and flying signs wound in the light
Which all shall soon lie wound in as it slowly
Approaches rising to break wide up over the
Brow of the sea.

140 My need reads in light more specially gendered and
Ambitioned by all eyes that wide have been
Me once. The cross-tree light, yellowing now,
Swings clean across Orion. And waned and very
Gently the old signs tilt and somersault
145 Towards their home. The undertow, come hard round,
Now leans the tiller strongly jammed over
On my hip-bone.

It is us at last sailed into the chance
Of a good take. For there is the water gone
150 Lit black and wrought like iron into the look
That's right for herring. We dropped to the single motor.

119: *smithers*: fragments; here, fragments of lit cloud
130: The speaker's *watch* (his turn as look-out) is *blear* (dim—i.e., difficult in the predawn light).
136: *fixed and flying signs*: respectively, the moon and stars, and fish-eating birds.
142: *cross-tree light*: A light hanging from a cross-member on the mast that here seems (from the viewer's position) to move over the constellation Orion.

The uneasy and roused gulls slid across us with
Swelled throats screeching. Our eyes sharpened what
Place we made through them. Now almost the light
155   To shoot the nets,

And keep a slow headway. One last check
To the gear. Our mended newtanned nets, all ropes
Loose and unkinked, tethers and springropes fast,
The tethers generous with floats to ride high,
160   And the big white bladder floats at hand to heave.
The bow wakes hardly a spark at the black hull.
The night and day both change their flesh about
In merging levels.

No more than merely leaning on the sea
165   We move. We move on this near-stillness enough
To keep the rudder live and gripped in the keel-wash.
We're well hinted herring plenty for the taking,
About as certain as all those signs falling
Through their appearance. Gulls settle lightly forward
170   Then scare off wailing as the sea-dusk lessens
Over our stern.

Yes, we're right set, see, see them go down, the best
Fishmarks, the gannets. They wheel high for a moment
Then heel, slip off the bearing air to plummet
175   Into the schooling sea. It's right for shooting,
Fish breaking the oiled water, the sea still
Holding its fires. Right, easy ahead, we'll run
Them straight out lined to the west. Now they go over,
White float and rope

180   And the net fed out in arm-lengths over the side.
So we shoot out the slowly diving nets
Like sowing grain. There they drag back their drifting
Weight out astern, a good half-mile of corks
And bladders. The last net's gone and we make fast
185   And cut the motor. The corks in a gentle wake,
Over curtains of water, tether us stopped, lapped
At far last still.

It is us no more moving, only the mere
Maintaining levels as they mingle together.
190   Now round the boat, drifting its drowning curtains
A grey of light begins. These words take place.
The petrel dips at the water-fats. And quietly
The stillness makes its way to its ultimate home.

157: Tanner's ooze is used to preserve fishnets.
158: *springropes:* ropes put out from the end or side of a boat at anchor and made fast to the anchor's cable
173: *Gannets* are fish-eating seabirds; they dive headfirst into the sea to capture fish.
175: *shooting:* release of the nets
192: *petrel:* a small nocturnal seabird
    water-fats: oil or grease left floating on the water by nets or boats

The bilges slap. Gulls wail and settle.
195   It is us still.

At last it's all so still. We hull to the nets,
And rest back with our shoulders slacked pleasantly.
And I am illusioned out of this flood as
Separate and stopped to trace all grace arriving.
200   This grace, this movement bled into this place,
Locks the boat still in the grey of the seized sea.
The illuminations of innocence embrace.
What measures gently

Cross in the air to us to fix us so still
205   In this still brightness by knowledge of
The quick proportions of our intricacies?
What sudden perfection is this the measurement of?
And speaks us thoroughly to the bone and has
The iron sea engraved to our faintest breath,
210   The spray fretted and fixed at a high temper,
A script of light.

So I have been called by my name and
It was not sound. It is me named upon
The space which I continually move across
215   Bearing between my courage and my lack
The constant I bleed on. And, put to stillness,
Fixed in this metal and its cutting salts,
It is this instant to exact degree,
And for whose sake?

220   It is this instant written dead. This instant,
Bounded by its own grace and all Time's grace,
Masters me into its measurement so that
My ghostly constant is articulated.
Then suddenly like struck rock all points unfix.
225   The whole east breaks and leans at last to us,
Ancient overhead. Yet not a break of light
But mingles into

The whole memory of light, and will not cease
Contributing its exiled quality.
230   The great morning moves from its equivalent
Still where it lies struck in expressed proportion.
The streaming morning in its tensile light
Leans to us and looks over on the sea.
It's time to haul. The air stirs its faint pressures,
235   A slat of wind.

194: The *bilges* are the lowest part of the interior of a boat; wastes collect there (the water which is heard
   to "slap"), to be later pumped out.
196: *hull:* drift
210: *fretted:* patterned
232: *tensile light:* the phrase is from Ezra Pound's 1947 translation of Confucius's *The Unwobbling Pivot*,
   ch. 26, sect. 10. Other versions of the phrase appear in Pound's Cantos 74 and 90.
235: *slat:* sudden gust

We are at the hauling then hoping for it
The hard slow haul of a net white with herring
Meshed hard. I haul, using the boat's cross-heave
We've started, holding fast as we rock back,
240   Taking slack as we go to. The day rises brighter
Over us and the gulls rise in a wailing scare
From the nearest net-floats. And the unfolding water
Mingles its dead.

Now better white I can say what's better sighted,
245   The white net flashing under the watched water,
The near net dragging back with the full belly
Of a good take certain, so drifted easy
Slow down on us or us hauled up upon it
Curved in a garment down to thicker fathoms.
250   The hauling nets come in sawing the gunwale
With herring scales.

The air bunches to a wind and roused sea-cries.
The weather moves and stoops high over us and
There the forked tern, where my look's whetted on distance,
255   Quarters its hunting sea. I haul slowly
Inboard the drowning flood as into memory,
Braced at the breathside in my net of nerves.
We haul and drift them home. The winds slowly
Turn round on us and

260   Gather towards us with dragging weights of water
Sleekly swelling across the humming sea
And gather heavier. We haul and hold and haul
Well the bright chirpers home, so drifted whitely
All a blinding garment out of the grey water.
265   And, hauling hard in the drag, the nets come in,
The headrope a sore pull and feeding its brine
Into our hacked hands.

Over the gunwale over into our deep lap
The herring come in, staring from their scales,
270   Fruitful as our deserts would have it out of
The deep and shifting seams of water. We haul
Against time fallen ill over the gathering
Rush of the sea together. The calms dive down.
The strident kingforked airs roar in their shell.
275   We haul the last

238ff: The boat is rocking back behind the waves as they haul the nets in over the gunwale (the upper edge
  of the boat's side), then rocking as it were forward (going to), enabling them to take up the slack that was
  pulled taut on the backward rock.
254: tern: a small diving seabird with a forked tail
255: Quarters: traverses ground in search of game
263: chirpers: "On certain parts of the coast, herring are sometimes called 'chirpers' because they emit a
  slight chirp as their airsac collapses when they come in on the net." (Graham, quoted in Lopez, p. 72)
274: strident kingforked airs: alluding to the trident of Neptune, Greek god of the sea

Net home and the last tether off the gathering
Run of the started sea. And then was the first
Hand at last lifted getting us swung against
Into the homing quarter, running that white grace
280   That sails me surely ever away from home.
And we hold into it as it moves down on
Us running white on the hull heeled to light.
Our bow heads home

Into the running blackbacks soaring us loud
285   High up in open arms of the towering sea.
The steep bow heaves, hung on these words, towards
What words your lonely breath blows out to meet it.
It is the skilled keel itself knowing its own
Fathoms it further moves through, with us there
290   Kept in its common timbers, yet each of us
Unwound upon

By a lonely behaviour of the all common ocean.
I cried headlong from my dead. The long rollers,
Quick on the crests and shirred with fine foam,
295   Surge down then sledge their green tons weighing dead
Down on the shuddered deck-boards. And shook off
All that white arrival upon us back to falter
Into the waking spoil and to be lost in
The mingling world.

300   So we were started back over that sea we
Had worked widely all fish-seasons and over
Its shifting grounds, yet now risen up into
Such humours, I felt like a farmer tricked to sea.
For it sailed sore against us. It grew up
305   To black banks that crossed us. It stooped, beaked.
Its brine burnt us. I was chosen and given.
It rose as risen

Treachery becomes myself, to clip me amorously
Off from all common breath. Those fires burned
310   Sprigs of the foam and branching tines of water.
It rose so white, soaring slowly, up
On us, then broke, down on us. It became a mull
Against our going and unfastened under us and
Curdled from the stern. It shipped us at each blow.
315   The brute weight

282: *heeled:* leaning
284: *blackbacks:* waves dark from thunderclouds overhead (though "soaring" also suggests a pun on
"blackbacked gulls")
294: *Quick:* rapid; but also in the older senses "alive," "lively," or "pregnant"; in the Bible, for instance,
Christ is judge of "the quick and the dead" (Acts 10:42 etc.).
     shirred: ruffled (like fabric decorated with ornamental "shirring")
308: *clip:* embrace
312: *mull:* promontory or headland (Scots)
314: *shipped us:* flooded us with water from the waves' breaking over the ship's side

Of the living sea wrought us, yet the boat sleeked lean
Into it, upheld by the whole sea-brunt heaved,
And hung on the swivelling tops. The tiller raised
The siding tide to wrench us and took a good
320 Ready hand to hold it. Yet we made a seaway
And minded all the gear was fast, and took
Our spell at steering. And we went keeled over
The streaming sea.

See how, like an early self, it's loath to leave
325 And stares from the scuppers as it swirls away
To be clenched up. What a great width stretches
Farsighted away fighting in its white straits
On either bow, but bears up our boat on all
Its plaiting strands. This wedge driven in
330 To the twisting water, we rode. The bow shores
The long rollers.

The keel climbs and, with screws spinning out of their bite,
We drive down into the roar of the great doorways,
Each time almost to overstay, but start
335 Up into again the yelling gale and hailing
Shot of the spray. Yet we should have land
Soon marking us out of this thick distance and
How far we're in. Who is that poor sea-scholar,
Braced in his hero,

340 Lost in his book of storms there? It is myself.
So he who died is announced. This mingling element
Gives up myself. Words travel from what they once
Passed silence with. Here, in this intricate death,
He goes as fixed on silence as ever he'll be.
345 Leave him, nor cup a hand to shout him out
Of that, his home. Or, if you would, O surely
There is no word,

There is not any to go over that.
It is now as always this difficult air
350 We look towards each other through. And is there
Some singing look or word or gesture of grace
Or naked wide regard from the encountered face,
Goes ever true through the difficult air?
Each word speaks its own speaker to his death.
355 And we saw land

At last marked on the tenting mist and we could
Just make out the ridge running from the north
To the Black Rosses, and even mark the dark hint

316: *sleeked:* glided
325: *scuppers:* openings in the ship's side that permit water to run out
332: "The 'bite' is the water when the propellors are in it (it is what the screws bite on); here the uneven
  progress of the ship moving through heavy seas has the keel and propellors briefly sticking out in the air."
  (Lopez, in correspondence)
358: *Black Rosses:* or Black Head—"ros" in Cornish is a promontory or headland.

Of Skeer well starboard. Now inside the bight
360   The sea was loosening and the screws spun steadier
Beneath us. We still shipped the blown water but
It broke white, not green weight caved in on us.
In out of all

That forming and breaking sea we came on the long
365   Swell close at last inshore with the day grey
With mewing distances and mist. The rocks rose
Waving their lazy friendly weed. We came in
Moving now by the world's side. And O the land lay
Just as we knew it well all along that shore
370   Akin to us with each of its dear seamarks. And lay
Like a mother.

We came in, riding steady in the bay water,
A sailing pillar of gulls, past the cockle strand.
And springing teal came out off the long sand. We
375   Moved under the soaring land sheathed in fair water
In that time's morning grace. I uttered that place
And left each word I was. The quay-heads lift up
To pass us in. These sea-worked measures end now.
And this element

380   Ends as we move off from its formal instant.
Now he who takes my place continually anew
Speaks me thoroughly perished into another.
And the quay opened its arms. I heard the sea
Close on him gently swinging on oiled hinges.
385   Moored here, we cut the motor quiet. He that
I'm not lies down. Men shout. Words break. I am
My fruitful share.

4

Only leaned at rest
Where my home is cast
390   Cannonwise on silence
And the serving distance.

O my love, keep the day
Leaned at rest, leaned at rest.

Only breathed at ease
395   In that loneliness
Bragged into a voyage
On the maintaining image.

359: *Skeer:* a rock about two miles offshore
     bight: bay
366: *mewing:* from mews (seagulls)
373: *cockle strand:* a stretch of sea shore where one may gather cockles (small edible molluscs)
374: A *teal* is a type of duck.

O my love, there we lay
Loved alone, loved alone.

400   Only graced in my
Changing madman who
Sings but has no time
To divine my room.

O my love, keep the day
405   Leaned at rest, leaned at rest.

What one place remains
Home as darkness quickens?

5

So this is the place. This
Is the place fastened still with movement,
410   Movement as calligraphic and formal as
A music burned on copper.

At this place
The eye reads forward as the memory reads back.
At this last word all words change.
415   All words change in acknowledgement of the last.
Here is their mingling element.
This is myself (who but ill resembles me).
He befriended so many
Disguises to wander in on as many roads
420   As cross on a ball of wool.
What a stranger he's brought to pass
Who sits here in his place.
What a man arrived breathless
With a look or word to a few
425   Before he's off again.

Here is this place no more
Certain though the steep streets
And High Street form again and the sea
Swing shut on hinges and the doors all open wide.

6

430   As leaned at rest in lamplight with
The offered moth and heard breath
By grace of change serving my birth,

And as at hushed called by the owl,
With my chair up to my salt-scrubbed table,
435   While my endured walls kept me still,

411: Musical scores were printed from copperplate etchings.

I leaned and with a kind word gently
Struck the held air like a doorway
Bled open to meet another's eye.

Lie down, my recent madman, hardly
440   Drawn into breath than shed to memory,
For there you'll labour less lonely.

Lie down and serve. Your death is past.
There the fishing ground is richest.
There contribute your sleight of cast.

445   The rigged ship in its walls of glass
Still further forms its perfect seas
Locked in its past transparences.

You're come among somewhere the early
Children at play who govern my way
450   And shed each tear which burns my eye.

Thus, shed into the industrious grave
Ever of my life, you serve the love
Whose motive we are energies of.

So quietly my words upon the air
455   Awoke their harmonies for ever
Contending within the ear they alter.

And as the lamp burned back the silence
And the walls caved to a clear lens,
The room again became my distance.

460   I sat rested at the grave's table
Saying his epitaph who shall
Be after me to shout farewell.

7

Far out, faintly rocked,
Struck the sea bell.

465   Home becomes this place,
A bitter night, ill
To labour at dead of.
Within all the dead of
All my life I hear
470   My name spoken out
On the break of the surf.
I, in Time's grace,
The grace of change, am

445: *rigged ship:* i.e., a miniature ship in a bottle

Cast into memory.
475 What a restless grace
To trace stillness on.

Now this place about me
Wakes the night's twin shafts
And sheds the quay slowly.
480 Very gently the keel
Walks its waters again.
The sea awakes its fires.
White water stares in
From the harbour-mouth.
485 And we run through well
Held off the black land
Out into the waving
Nerves of the open sea.

My dead in the crew
490 Have mixed all qualities
That I have been and,
Though ghosted behind
My sides spurred by the spray,
Endure by a further gaze
495 Pearled behind my eyes.
Far out faintly calls
The mingling sea.

Now again blindfold
With the hemisphere
500 Unprised and bright
Ancient overhead,

This present place is
Become made into
A breathless still place
505 Unrolled on a scroll
And turned to face this light.

So I spoke and died.
So within the dead
Of night and the dead
510 Of all my life those
Words died and awoke.

1955

478: *shafts*: the driveshafts that turn the screws
495: Cf. Shakespeare's "Those are pearls that were his eyes" (*The Tempest* 1.2.401), and also T. S. Eliot's
quotation of this line in *The Waste Land*, lines 48 and 125.

A Note to the Difficult One

This morning I am ready if you are,
To hear you speaking in your new language.
I think I am beginning to have nearly
A way of writing down what it is I think
5   You say. You enunciate very clearly
Terrible words always just beyond me.

I stand in my vocabulary looking out
Through my window of fine water ready
To translate natural occurrences
10   Into something beyond any idea
Of pleasure. The wisps of April fly
With light messages to the lonely.

This morning I am ready if you are
To speak. The early quick rains
15   Of Spring are drenching the window-glass.
Here in my words looking out
I see your face speaking flying
In a cloud wanting to say something.

1977

Language Ah Now You Have Me

I

Language ah now you have me. Night-time tongue,
Please speak for me between the social beasts
Which quick assail me. Here I am hiding in
The jungle of mistakes of communication.

5   I know about jungles. I know about unkempt places
Flying toward me when I am getting ready
To pull myself together and plot the place
To speak from. I am at the jungle face
Which is not easily yours. It is my home
10   Where pigmies hamstring Jumbo and the pleasure
Monkey is plucked from the tree. How pleased I am
To meet you reading and writing on damp paper
In the rain forest beside the Madron River.

11: *wisps of April:* "little bits of cloud blown off at the edge by wind" (Tony Lopez, in correspondence)
14: *quick:* full of life

10: "pigmies hunt elephants by hobbling them with ropes and following them until they fall over exhausted" (Lopez, in correspondence).
13: *Madron* is the tiny village in west Cornwall where Graham lived for the latter half of his life. West Cornwall is the wettest part of Southern Britain.

2

Which is my home. The great and small breathers,
15   Experts of speaking, hang and slowly move
To say something or spring in the steaming air
Down to do the great white hunter for ever.

3

Do not disturb me now. I have to extract
A creature with its eggs between the words.   .
20   I have to seize it now, otherwise not only
My vanity will be appalled but my good cat
Will not look at me in the same way.

4

Is not to look. We are the ones hanging
On here and there, the dear word's edge wondering
25   If we are speaking clearly enough or if
The jungle's acoustics are at fault. Baboon,
My soul, is always ready to relinquish
The safe hold and leap on to nothing at all.
At least I hope so. Language now you have me
30   Trying to be myself but changed into
The wildebeest pursued or the leo pard
Running at stretch beside the Madron River.

5

Too much. I died. I forgot who I was and sent
My heart back with my bearers. How pleased I am
35   To find you here beside the Madron River
Wanting to be spoken to. It is my home
Where pigmies hamstring Jumbo and the pleasure
Monkey is plucked from the tree.

1977

TOM SCOTT (1918–1995)

A COMMENT TOM SCOTT MADE IN AN INTERVIEW OFFERS A WAY OF READING THE genre of his "Johnie Raw Prays for His Lords and Maisters," the mock-petition: "here I would use the word, not 'satire', but another vein of the Scottish tradition, 'flyting', which can be utterly scurrilous. . . ."[1] Like much of the poetry of this life-long socialist and Scottish nationalist, "Johnie Raw" is a frontal assault on the dominant political, educational, and cultural institutions of modern—and in this case English—society. Kathleen Raine situates Scott's poems within a Scottish tradition in which "poetry comes from, and addresses itself to, the poor and proud people of croft and bothie."[2] The mode of address in his poems is typically bardic, public, even didactic, the idiom used a heightened vernacular Scots extending back to the "Inglis" used by William Dunbar in the fifteenth century. The forms of Scott's poetry as well as his sense of poetic vocation owe much not only to Scottish makars like Dunbar but also to the late medieval French poet François Villon, whose poetry Scott translated brilliantly enough to earn the praise of Ezra Pound and T. S. Eliot. To hear Scott talk about Villon, whose "gallusness" or audacity he shares, is to hear provocative statements on the history of language and speech in the British Isles: "20th century Scots has more in common with medieval French than it does with 20th century English, which is one of the reasons I got on so well with Villon. Scots was killed by the reformation. One of the Catholics accused the reformers of 'knappin Soudron' [kidnapping southern forms of English], in contempt of oor mither language. And that was true. And we got the English Bible thereafter, and the whole English tradition began there, so really Scots was arrested at the medieval level. When you come back to it and want to use the full canon of Scots, not content just to write wee lyrics, you've got to go back to medieval Scots."[3]

Scott was born in Glasgow, the son of a laborer much like the one celebrated in his most famous book, *Brand the Builder* (1975). He was educated at Hyndland Secondary School in Glasgow and at Madras College in St. Andrews and, years later, received his M. A. and Ph.D. from the University of Edinburgh. He worked as a laborer-apprentice in his grandfather's building firm. Scott began writing poems in English but "I was seeking my tradition, and somehow I found it via Europe [in Sicily] when I got out of the shadow of England."[4] His books include *The Ship and Ither Poems* (1963), whose title-poem deals with the sinking of the Titanic and the political strife of the century following it, *At the Shrine o the Unkent Sodger: A Poem for Recita-*

---

[1] Tom Scott, "Interview with Joy Hendry," *Agenda*, vol. 30, no. 4, p. 65.
[2] "Tom Scott and the Bardic Lineage," *Agenda*, vol. 30, no. 4, p. 86.
[3] "Interview with Joy Hendry," p. 62.
[4] Ibid., p. 60.

422

tion (1968), and *The Tree: An Animal Fable* (1977), in which the poem's zoological material required the poet to write in English: "when you come to try to take on board science . . . you find that the Scots vocabulary just isn't there."[5] Scott also wrote about Dunbar's poetry, and edited several collections of Scottish verse.

---

[5] Ibid., p. 69.

Johnie Raw Prays for His Lords and Maisters

For England, God, we gie our thanks.
Lang may she protect us Scots
Frae reid-clawed Rooshans and saft-pawed Yanks
And aa thae ither barbarous lots.
5   Gin we'd a government o wir ain
Whit dangers micht frae them assail us
There's nae sayin, we dinna ken.
Sae be thankit, Lord, for Westminster Palace.

Be thankit, tae, for the MPs in it,
10   Puir humble dogs wha for our saik
Are flypit wi whups their ilka minute
Like sauls in hell, till their droddums ache.
Tho I've heard ill-farrant tykes declare
They're nocht but a wheen uisless blethers,
15   A safety-valve to let aff het air,
Yet bless them, Lord, whaur their like foregaithers.

And bless their lords and maisters tae,
Thae cabinet chiels, aa government linkin,
That selflessly baith nicht and day
20   Relieve thir dogs o the trauchle o thinkin.
They rin the hoose like an Old Boys' club,
And, daily torkit by the Inquisition,
Help mak Decisions, their depairtments' nub,
For gey wee pey and recognition.

1: *gie:* give
4: *aa:* all
   thae: those
5: *Gin:* if
   wir ain: our own
7: *dinna ken:* do not know
9: *MPs:* Members of Parliament
11: *flypit wi whups:* flayed with whips. A party whip is an MP in charge of insuring party members' attendance during important votes.
   ilka: every
12: *droddums:* backsides
13: *ill-farrant tykes:* ill-natured people with axes to grind
14: "They're nothing but a bunch of useless drivellers."
16: *foregaithers:* assembles
18: *chiels:* men
20: *trauchle:* trouble
22: *torkit:* tortured
24: *gey wee:* very little

25   And, Lord—I scarce can bring mysel
        To mention sic an awesome name—
        The Prime Meenister Himsel,
        Wha duis aa the wark, gets aa the blame,
        Wha wields the lash, brings the pack to heel,
30   Toots the horn, cries Tally-ho,
        Taxes the tod his brush as weel,
        Maun be like You, God, here below.

        Hou can a man o mortal mak
        Bear sic a load, endure sic pain,
35   Cairry haill empires on his back,
        Flee round the warld and hame again?
        Ay, and wi great Presses on his skull.
        Whit saint achieved sic self-negation?
        This blend o Mithra and the buhll,
40   O bless him, Lord, for the British nation.

        And bless our blessed Tories, Lord,
        Designed by You for ayebydan rule
        By hook or by crook, bribe or sword,
        Tho their younger set maun play the fool.
45   For while land and money rule the free
        Few, our bonds will be wider set,
        Privilege and birth in harmonie,
        O mak thae mighty mightier yet!

        But juist as guid (in their ain sichts
50   And faur be't frae me, Lord, to decry them)
        Are our apprentice Labour lichts;
        Puir fags, gey sair their seniors try them.
        They'll learn in time to forget aboot classes
        And obey the financiers, like wyce bairns:
55   But lord, meantime it's hard on the masses
        Tinan red meat for redder herrins.

30: *Tally-ho:* the cry announcing the sighting of the fox in a fox-hunt
31: *tod:* fox
    brush: tail
33: *mak:* form; constitution
34: *sic:* such
35: *haill:* whole
36: *Flee:* fly
39: *Mithra,* the ancient Iranian god of light, friendship, and contracts and oaths, is said to have slain the cosmic bull whose blood makes the earth fertile.
42: *ayebydan:* eternal
44: *maun:* must
49: *guid:* good
    sichts: sights
50: *faur be't frae me:* far be it from me
52: *fags:* drudges; in English public schools, a *fag* is a junior student who has to perform tasks for a senior.
    gey sair: very sorely
54: *wyce bairns:* sensible children
56: *Tinan:* losing
    herrins: herrings

But the masses tae will hae to learn
To forget their wicked socialism
And be content to work and earn
60   In a state o bolshidemocfascism
Run for them by the muddle class leaders
Trained the Eton and Oxbridge way.
They'll dam weel hae to gie owre, the bleeders,
The dream that producers should be owners tae.

65   But, Lord, remember abune them aa,
Oor liberal idealist boys,
The darlins o TV, stage and haa,
And circus, and ither popular joys.
Gie them the pouer, and suin ye'll find
70   There are nae problems left to see:
Aa will dissolve in the liberal mind
Like saccharine in NAAFI tea.

But faur abuin aa, I speir your blessin
On the London Clubs, for as aabody kens,
75   It's in their premises and messin
Decisions are made, no in lesser dens
Like the Hooses o Commons or the Lords.
I've even heard that You yoursel
Hae been seen foregaitheran at their boards
80   Wi Your opposite number, the Leader o Hell.

But talk o duty minds me o the cream,
The very curds and whey o Britain:
The Diplomats are whit ithers seem,
And serve on their feet as ithers dae sittin,
85   Except for lunches, dinners, even
Breakfasts I hear, nou that weemen are in.
The Foreign Office is next door to Hevin
For public schoolboys free frae sin.

But bless abuin aa the Treasurie
90   As it soars abuin its Whitehall peers
Like Pegasus, in harmonie
Wi aa the faur-aff music o the spheres,

63: *gie owre:* abandon
65: *abune:* above
67: *haa:* hall
72: *NAAFI:* the Navy, Army and Airforce Institutes; the reference is to army canteen food.
73: *speir:* ask
74: *aabody:* everybody
75: *messin:* dinners
83: *seem:* i.e., only seem
90: *Whitehall:* an area near the Houses of Parliament that contains numerous government offices, including the Treasury; often shorthand for "government bureaucracy."
91: *Pegasus:* the winged horse of Greek myth, symbol of poetic inspiration
92: *music o the spheres:* According to classical lore, each planet was inhabited by an angel who sang in harmony with all the others.

Transmutin their ayebydan law
In an even mair ayebydan nay.
95   Penny-wise, pound-foolish, aa
Ithers hing in ilk word they say.

And ilka word is genius-pickit
To protect us frae cauld winds o truth
And in white (washed) papers oot is trickit
100   In prose wad baffle even You, forsooth!
At ilka Easter they celebrate
The rise o Our Budget frae the grave,
And His Very Body demonstrate
For the fowk wha dout He's come to save.

105   And baith the legal beagle packs
Are dogs, I hear, that've had their day,
For accoontants are better at income tax,
And cheaper by faur in every way.
They dinna rook puir saints and sinners
110   Wi double fees for advisers and pleaders,
Nor eat their clients at cannibal dinners
In archaic temples, like the legal bleeders.

But talkin o temples, there's the kirk,
God's and Mammon's mairriage bed,
115   Ministered by eloquent, lowan stirks,
Their treisures in land established,
Like their ideas in feudalism.
But, Lord, it's better, as You weel ken,
To keep them taen up wi the world and schism
120   Than leein aboot you to gullible men.

Their bishops come and their bishops go,
But the Sees gang on for ever,
And Ceylon can mell wi the Arctic snow
On Lambeth lawn by London's river.
125   But bless them aa, for whiteer they be,
They'll spoil nae sport in Vanity fair,

96: *hing:* hang
99: A "white paper" is a government publication presented to Parliament, such as a statement of policy or proposal for legislation.
    oot is trickit: is tricked out
100: *wad:* that would
109: *dinna rook:* do not cheat
113: *kirk:* church
114: *Mammon:* "Ye cannot serve God and mammon [wealth]" (Matt. 6:24)
115: *lowan stirks:* lowing bulls
118: *weel ken:* know well
119: *taen up:* busy
122: *Sees:* bishops' seats of office
123–24: *mell:* mingle. "Bishops from all over the world can rub shoulders at tea parties on the Lambeth Palace lawn"; *Lambeth* Palace is the London residence of the Archbishop of Canterbury.
125: *whiteer:* whatever
126: *Vanity fair:* symbol of the world's vanities in John Bunyan's *Pilgrim's Progress* (1678).

For papist or Protestant, established or free,
It's the Tory-Lib-Lab party at prayer.

And at the heid o aa is the Faerie Queen,
130 Yokin a Knox wi a Canterbury ram,
A gracious star on the movin screen.
Nae ruler she, but the English Mam,
Wife and mither, lovin and fecunt,
Lookin on the bright side, tholan the worst,
135 Pretendan she's only a modest Secont
And her a Constitutional First.

Bless her, and bless her cuisins tae,
The deuks and rooks and airls and coonts
And aa their honorable progenie.
140 Whaur wad we be athoot them and their hunts?
Atween them aa they hae mair land
Nor even the Forestry Commission's
Or the Kirk's—and I understand
Their lochs and rivers are their ain pishins.

145 But, Lord, the skies that roar abuin the land
Are brichter faur wi universal clouds,
Thir universities that aye command
Admiration frae the Hevin-aspirin crowds.
And Oxbridge sails serene abuin them aa
150 But little changed since Geoffrey Chaucer's day,
Never touchin the grimy earth ava,
As they float on high in their metaphysic way.

Whaur, O Lord, wad our class-system be
But for thae stalwart maisters o the class?
155 Gone, as in France, in dull equalitie,
Nae fowr degrees rankit abuin the mass.
Our theories in practice wad hae foundert,

127: The "established church" is the official one (the Church of England or, in Scotland, the Presbyterian Church); all other Protestant denominations are thus "free churches."
129: *Faerie Queen*: i.e., Elizabeth II; the title character of Edmund Spenser's *The Faerie Queene* (1590–1609) represents Queen Elizabeth I.
130: "linking Scottish and English churches" (John *Knox* was a sixteenth-century Scottish divine).
133: *fecunt*: fecund
134: *tholan*: enduring
135–36: Constitutional power resides with the Queen but actual power is wielded by Parliament. (Scott may also have in mind her being Elizabeth the *Second*.)
138: *rooks*: noblemen (literally, castles in the game of chess); Scott perhaps also glances at the meaning "cheats, swindlers."
140: *athoot*: without
141: *Atween*: between
     hae: have
142: *Nor*: than
144: *pishins*: pissings
151: *ava*: at all
156: *fowr degrees*: presumably a reference to the medieval Three Estates—clergy, nobles, townsmen—augmented by the later addition of the press.

The makar owre the talker been upraised:
Conformitie by genius had been soundert,
160   Mere originalitie ower-praised.

Waterloo wes focht ablow Big Tom,
Trafalgar won and lost upon the Cam.
Wioot Halls there'd been nae atom bomb,
And clockwise port made possible Vietnam.
165   Whaurever's Love destroyed by Intellect,
Or lesser breeds for notions are napalmed,
The Oxbridge claim to credit can be staked,
And the dead in academic robes embalmed.

Preserve them, lord, and wi them Privilege,
170   Lest education should be thocht a right,
Or production o persons, no juist minds, engage
The dons in a soul-o-learnin's black night.
'Fewer is better', as Hitler micht hae said,
'And only the few Aryans better still'.
175   So preserve our Oxbridge, Lord, as it wes made
As the Tory-Lib-Lab party's charm-schuil.

But dinna forget the 'varsities o the masses,
Thir educational slums for low degrees,
Tho little better nor glorifeed evenin classes,
180   They're fine for brain-washin rebels and geniuses,
And peyin dons frae Oxbridge graduatit,
Critics as guid as ever slew a bard,
Praised mediocritie, got a Pound hatit—
Front-line fighters for the arrière-garde.

185   Thae puir provincial academics pine,
Entombed alive in heaps o mouldy bricks,
For the higher life maist o them kent langsyne,
Lodged in the Isis-Cam's alma matrix.
Gin it wesnae, Lord, for yon hungry lust for pouer

158: *makar*: poet
159: *soundert*: sundered, split open
161: *ablow*: below
    Napoleon's army received its final defeat in 1815 at the hands of British and Prussian forces at the
Battle of *Waterloo*. The Duke of Wellington, who led the British forces, is reputed to have later said, "The
battle of Waterloo was won on the playing fields of Eton [Britain's most elite public school]." *Big Tom* is
the bell of Christ Church College, in Oxford.
162: Napoleon's navy lost the Battle of *Trafalgar* to the British in 1805. The River *Cam* flows through Cam-
bridge; punting on the Cam is a popular student pastime.
163: *Wioot*: without
    Halls: i.e., the colleges and their dining halls.
164: A decanter of *port* is traditionally passed around the table clockwise.
183: The American modernist poet Ezra *Pound* (1885–1972) spent the years 1908–1919 in London.
187: *kent langsyne*: know long ago
188: The *Isis* is the part of the Thames flowing by Oxford University.
    alma matrix: punning on "alma mater"; a "matrix" is a womb.
189: *wesnae*: was not
    yon: that

190   Maist o them hide ablow an ootward grace,
        Few o them wad byde—for be sure
        Arrogance lurks ahent their humble face.

        It shows itsel in scholarship, ye ken,
        The ramstam, slapdash wey they gang at things
195   Wad fill a lifetime for proper Oxbridge men:
        Dependan on whitna pairts a man brings.
        There's Dr. Quibble nou been fifteen year
        By MacGonagallian problems sairly vexed:
        But some o thae new lads believe, I hear,
200   That a poem is mair important nor the text.

        Sic heresies as thir will never dae,
        Worship o poems abuin the sacred Text,
        Sae I'd ask ye, Lord, to visit dule and wae
        On aa put the Muses first, and scholarship next.
205   Blast them, Lord, wi brimstane and hellfire,
        Destroy them, hurl them doun to Hell!
        Curse their talents and ill-faured desire!
        Mak suir their heretic books will never sell!

        Remember, tae, the Fourth Estate,
210   (No, I dinnae mean the wage-slaves)
        The chiels that really educate
        The fowk, frae their cradles til their graves—
        The Press, God Bless them (and God, You ken
        Hou muckle they aa need Your blessin)
215   And see they learn to lee like honest men,
        And no behave like some Muse's messan.

        Journalists shouldnae be sae shy
        And mimosa-like, ahent their words,
        But learn frae their maisters to hae a guid 'I'—
220   Prent their ain money, mak theirsels lords.
        Gin Shakespeare'd been alive the-day,
        The Fleet wad hae claimed him, no the Globe,

190: *ablow:* below
191: *byde:* remain
194: *ramstam:* headstrong
        gang: go
196: *whitna pairts:* whatever ability
198: The Scottish poet William *McGonagall* (1825 or 1830–1902) is famed for "The Tay Bridge Disaster,"
   by general consensus the worst poem in the English language.
203: *dule:* sorrow
207: *ill-faured:* wrongful
209: *Fourth Estate:* the press
212: *til:* to
214: *Hou muckle:* how much
215: *lee:* lie
216: *messan:* cur
218: *ahent:* behind; the *mimosa* plant, or "sensitive-plant," will shrink to the touch.
221: *the-day:* today
222: *Fleet:* Fleet Street, traditional home of newspaper publishers

And owre the Impress he'd held his sway
As the greatest ever xenophobe.

225   But, Lord, abuin aa bless London city,
Whaur the native London fog is made
To hide frae us sic scenes o pitie
As wad put Dickens in the shade:
For there the gangs o Old School slaves
230   Toil at the oars o the British galley
And ken nae rest till they reach their graves,
Or faa unduin in some luckless sally.

And Holy God, hae mercy there
On thae puir baests in the Stock Exchange,
235   The torkit buhll and baitit bear,
The jobber-tykes, fiky wi the mange.
I dinnae ken, but God, I'm suir
Hell itsel hes nae waur to show,
And I wonder You can be sae sair
240   On sic dumb brutes here below.

For bankers, Lord, as weill I pray:
Puir things, for aa the miracles they enact
Lendin fowk millions they dinnae hae,
Credit by nocht but Confidence backt,
245   Tho at real eneuch an Interest rate,
Syne gettin peyed whit they didnae lend
Plus Interest—as wealth they create
Ex nihil, money for nothing, in the end.

And yet I've heard it said
250   That the Bank is England's in nocht but name.
That nae maitter whit decision's made,
Zurich can scupper it juist the same.
'Britons never shall be slaves'
Except til Europe and the IMF.

223: *Impress:* either a club named The Empress or perhaps just the long form of "Press."
225: *London city:* the financial and commercial section of London
229: *Old School:* a reference to the giving of jobs on an old-school-tie basis
232: *faa unduin:* fall undone
235: *Bear-baiting*—the setting of dogs on a captive bear—was a popular entertainment in earlier centuries.
236: *jobber-tykes:* working dogs
        fiky: itchy
238: *waur:* worse
239: *sair:* hard
245: *eneuch:* enough
246: *syne:* then; thus
248: *Ex nihil:* out of nothing
252: *Zurich:* i.e., Swiss banks
253: Cf. "Rule Britannia," by the eighteenth-century Scottish poet James Thomson: "Rule, Britannia, rule
  the waves; / Britons never will be slaves."
254: *IMF:* International Monetary Fund

255   Britannia aiblins rules the waves,
         But her kitchen's ruled by a foreign Chef.

         And in ony case, the Lady Pru
         And her sisters, promise ti ensure
         That even the Bank's mechanical crew
260   Hae less and less toil til endure.
         To keep their auld usurious sway
         The banks tak less o stock than bearins
         And gang in for Insurance tae,
         On pain o lossin half their fairins.

265   And whit, dear God, wad the heicher proles
         Wioot their Buildin Societies dae?
         Whaur else wad they get sic generous doles?
         At 100%, near gien away!
         And yet it's queer sic institutions
270   Are sae unco laith to show their books:
         A body micht think, frae their convolutions,
         They were nocht but a pack o spivs and crooks.

         But oor financiers mair nor aa
         I pray for, Lord, for they maist need it.
275   They aye risk the farthest faa
         And are aye the easiest misleadit.
         No juist oor British anes I mean,
         But furriners, like wee Aristotle—
         A lad o pairts, but fair owregien
280   I'm telt, til actresses, gamblin and the bottle.

         And syne there are oor Corporations,
         The Levers, ICI and Shell,
         And ither siclike fabrications
         Made for the man that buys and sells.
285   Bless them, Lord, for God they need it
         Sae sair they're temptit by the Deil
         Whase infernal pouers til them he cedit,
         Wi hauf the kingriks o the earth as weill.

255: *aiblins:* perhaps
257: *the Lady Pru:* the Prudential Insurance Company
262: *bearins:* The reference is presumably both to bearer bonds and to Barings Bank.
264: *fairins:* profits
265: *heicher:* higher
266: *Building Societies:* mutual (i.e. not-for-profit) societies that accept deposits and then use their funds to lend on mortgage to people who wish to buy their own houses
270: *unco laith:* strangely loath
271: *A body:* one
272: *spivs:* petty crooks
273: *mair nor aa:* more than all the rest
278: *Aristotle:* Aristotle Onassis (1906–1975), the Greek shipping magnate
279: *lad o pairts:* talented boy
282: *The Levers:* Unilever, twin companies based in London and Rotterdam, which own companies all over the world that produce household items.
     ICI: Imperial Chemical Industries, a London-based corporation
286: *Deil:* Devil
288: *hauf the kingriks:* half the kingdoms

And bless the lords o income tax
290   Wha keep us aa frae gettin fat,
Like bloodsuckers on craiturs' backs,
Lampreys, or vampires, and things like that.
We've had nae need since echteen hunder
To pey a leech to bleed us white:
295   The tax-boys dae't wi faur less blunder,
And wi faur less sting for their bigger bite.

And Lord, bless aa directors tae,
Whether o companie, screen or stage,
Their jaguars, wives and muckle pay,
300   Thir Round Table knights o the usurie age,
Their country hooses, their public schuil weans,
Their super-tax and heavy drinkin,
Their attackit herts and attackin brains:
For wioot them we'd be lost, I'm thinkin.

305   Thir Lords and Maisters I declare
Are aa entitlit for to be
Mentioned in a puir man's prayer,
Singly and collectivelie.
Confirm them in their pouer, Lord,
310   Owre us puir sinners in this tearfu glen,
To rule for aye, by sceptre and sword,
Til your ain glorie, God—Aimen!

1974, 1993

293: *echteen hunder:* 1800
294: *leech:* doctor; in past centuries they used leeches to bleed patients, then considered an effective form
  of medical treatment.
300: *Thir:* these
301: *weans:* children. A British "public school" would in North America be called a "private school."

KEITH DOUGLAS (1920–1944)

DOUGLAS WAS BORN IN TUNBRIDGE WELLS, THE ONLY CHILD OF A MOTHER WHO SUF-fered recurring attacks of encephalitis and a father who deserted the family when Douglas was eight. He was educated at Christ's Hospital and Merton College, Oxford, where his tutor was Edmund Blunden. In his two years at Oxford, Douglas edited the magazine *The Cherwell* and published poems in several journals. In 1940, he enlisted and trained to be a cavalry officer, and then was sent in 1941 to Egypt where he was retrained for a tank regiment and became a camouflage expert at divisional headquarters. In 1942, he drove himself to the battlefield at El Alamein to join the combat; his adventures as a tank commander are recounted in his narrative *Alamein to Zem Zem,* published posthumously in 1946. After being wounded by a land mine in 1943, he was sent to a hospital in Palestine. The only volume of poetry published in his lifetime, *Selected Poems,* appeared in 1943, thanks to the interest of J. M. Tambimuttu, the influential editor of *Poetry* (London) and Editions Poetry London. By late 1943, Douglas was back in Britain, training for the invasion of Europe and working on his poetry manuscripts and desert narrative. He was killed in action on June 9, 1944, three days after the Normandy invasion began. The first edition of his *Collected Poems* was published in 1951. A selection introduced by Ted Hughes appeared in 1964 and the *Complete Poems* in 1979.

The British soldier poets of World War II, including Sidney Keyes, Alun Lewis, Hamish Henderson, and Douglas, had the example of Wilfred Owen and other poets of the First World War to contend with; Douglas noted as much in a famous letter. The fame of these same predecessors might in part account for the comparative obscurity of the later generation. Thanks to the efforts of G. S. Fraser, Douglas's editor and biographer Desmond Graham, and Ted Hughes, Douglas slowly emerged to become the most celebrated poet of the group. Finally, Douglas's poems are as different from Owen's or Sassoon's as the two wars were different. Writing from Palestine to his friend J. C. Hall about his new poems that abandoned an earlier lyricism, Douglas tells him that "My rhythms, which you find enervated, are carefully chosen to enable the poems to be read as significant speech: I see no reason to be either musical or sonorous about things at present. . . . I suppose I reflect the cynicism and the careful absence of expectation (it is not quite the same as apathy) with which I view the world. As many others to whom I have spoken, not only civilians and British soldiers, but German[s] and Italians, are in the same state of mind, it is a true reflection."[1] In his 1987 introduction to *The Complete Poems,* Ted Hughes remarks on the

---

[1] Keith Douglas, *The Complete Poems,* 3rd ed., ed. Desmond Graham, New York, 1998, pp. 134–35.

remote, dispassionate, professional soldier's voice of some of Douglas's most famous poems: "The incisive nimble glance, the uniquely tempered music, the simple, point-blank, bull's-eye statement, the tensile delicacy, are all part of Douglas' effort to confront reality undeluded, and as it were on its own terms, and yet maintain detachment and self-control."[2]

---

[2] Ibid., p. xix.

Simplify me when I'm dead

Remember me when I am dead
and simplify me when I'm dead.

As the processes of earth
strip off the colour and the skin
take the brown hair and blue eye

and leave me simpler than at birth
when hairless I came howling in
as the moon came in the cold sky.

Of my skeleton perhaps
so stripped, a learned man will say
'He was of such a type and intelligence,' no more.

Thus when in a year collapse
particular memories, you may
deduce, from the long pain I bore

the opinions I held, who was my foe
and what I left, even my appearance
but incidents will be no guide.

Time's wrong-way telescope will show
a minute man ten years hence
and by distance simplified.

Through that lens see if I seem
substance or nothing: of the world
deserving mention or charitable oblivion

not by momentary spleen
or love into decision hurled
leisurely arrive at an opinion.

Remember me when I am dead
and simplify me when I'm dead.

?1941 / 1951

These grasses, ancient enemies

These grasses, ancient enemies
waiting at the edge of towns,
conceal a movement of live stones,
the lizards with hooded eyes
5   of hostile miraculous age.

It is not snow on the green spurs
of hilltops, only towns of white
whose trees are populous with fruit;
with girls whose velvet beauty is
10   handed down to them, gentle ornaments.

Somewhere in the hard land
and vicious scrub, or fertile place
of women and productive trees
you think you see a devil stand
15   fronting a creature of good intention

or fair apples where the snake plays—
don't you? Sweet leaves but poisonous,
or a mantrap in a gay house
a murderer with a lover's face
20   seem to you the signs of this country?

But devil and angel do not fight,
they are the classic Gemini
for whom it's vital to agree
whose interdependent state
25   this two-faced country reflects. Curiously

though foreigners we surely shall
prove this background's complement
the kindly visitors who meant
so well all winter but at last fell
30   unaccountably to killing in the spring.

1941 / 1951

Mersa

This blue halfcircle of sea
moving transparently
on sand as pale as salt
was Cleopatra's hotel:

22: *Gemini:* Castor and Pollux, twin sons of Leda; Castor was mortal, Pollux immortal. When Castor was killed, Pollux refused his own immortality as it would separate them, so Zeus permitted them to live together half the year in the underworld, half with the gods on Mount Olympus.

Mersa: Marsa Matruh, a town on Egypt's Mediterranean coast. The site was once the location of the Ptolemaic city of Paraetonium, where Cleopatra and Mark Antony took refuge after their defeat at the Battle of Actium.

5   here is a guesthouse built
         and broken utterly, since.
         An amorous modern prince
         lived in this scoured shell.

         Now from the skeletal town
10   the cherry skinned soldiers stroll down
         to undress to idle on the white beach.
         Up there, the immensely long road goes by

         to Tripoli: the wind and dust reach
         the secrets of the whole
15   poor town whose masks would still
         deceive a passer-by;

         faces with sightless doors
         for eyes, with cracks like tears
         oozing at corners. A dead tank alone
20   leans where the gossips stood.

         I see my feet like stones
         underwater. The logical little fish
         converge and nip the flesh
         imagining I am one of the dead.

                                        1942–1944 / 1946

Dead Men

         Tonight the moon inveigles them
         to love: they infer from her gaze
         her tacit encouragement.
         Tonight the white dresses and the jasmin scent
5   in the streets. I in another place
         see the white dresses glimmer like moths. Come

         to the west, out of that trance, my heart—
         here the same hours have illumined
         sleepers who are condemned or reprieved
10   and those whom their ambitions have deceived;
         the dead men, whom the wind
         powders till they are like dolls: they tonight

         rest in the sanitary earth perhaps
         or where they died, no one has found them
15   or in their shallow graves the wild dog
         discovered and exhumed a face or a leg
         for food: the human virtue round them
         is a vapour tasteless to a dog's chops.

         All that is good of them, the dog consumes.
20   You would not know, now the mind's flame is gone,
         more than the dog knows: you would forget

but that you see your own mind burning yet
and till you stifle in the ground will go on
burning the economical coal of your dreams.

25   Then leave the dead in the earth, an organism
not capable of resurrection, like mines,
less durable than the metal of a gun,
a casual meal for a dog, nothing but the bone
so soon. But tonight no lovers see the lines
30   of the moon's face as the lines of cynicism.

And the wise man is the lover
who in his planetary love revolves
without the traction of reason or time's control
and the wild dog finding meat in a hole
35   is a philosopher. The prudent mind resolves
on the lover's or the dog's attitude for ever.

                                        1946

Cairo Jag

Shall I get drunk or cut myself a piece of cake,
a pasty Syrian with a few words of English
or the Turk who says she is a princess—she dances
apparently by levitation? Or Marcelle, Parisienne
5   always preoccupied with her dull dead lover:
she has all the photographs and his letters
tied in a bundle and stamped *Décedé* in mauve ink.
All this takes place in a stink of jasmin.

But there are the streets dedicated to sleep
10   stenches and the sour smells, the sour cries
do not disturb their application to slumber
all day, scattered on the pavement like rags
afflicted with fatalism and hashish. The women
offering their children brown-paper breasts
15   dry and twisted, elongated like the skull,
Holbein's signature. But this stained white town
is something in accordance with mundane conventions—
Marcelle drops her Gallic airs and tragedy
suddenly shrieks in Arabic about the fare
20   with the cabman, links herself so
with the somnambulists and legless beggars:
it is all one, all as you have heard.

35: The etymological root of "cynicism" is the Greek word for "dog." The Cynics were ancient philosophers who advocated asceticism and disregard for social convention and the sense of shame. The most famous Cynic, Diogenes, led the life of a vagabond: his nickname, "The Dog," was bestowed on the group as a whole.

7: *Décedé*: deceased

16: *The Ambassadors,* a 1533 painting by Hans Holbein the Younger, contains a distorted object in the foreground that when viewed in a curved mirror is revealed to be a skull.

But by a day's travelling you reach a new world
the vegetation is of iron
25   dead tanks, gun barrels split like celery
the metal brambles have no flowers or berries
and there are all sorts of manure, you can imagine
the dead themselves, their boots, clothes and possessions
clinging to the ground, a man with no head
30   has a packet of chocolate and a souvenir of Tripoli.

1943 / 1946

Aristocrats

The noble horse with courage in his eye,
clean in the bone, looks up at a shellburst:
away fly the images of the shires
but he puts the pipe back in his mouth.

5   Peter was unfortunately killed by an 88;
it took his leg away, he died in the ambulance.
I saw him crawling on the sand, he said
It's most unfair, they've shot my foot off.

How can I live among this gentle
10   obsolescent breed of heroes, and not weep?
Unicorns, almost,
for they are fading into two legends
in which their stupidity and chivalry
are celebrated. Each, fool and hero, will be an immortal.

15   These plains were their cricket pitch
and in the mountains the tremendous drop fences
brought down some of the runners. Here then
under the stones and earth they dispose themselves,
I think with their famous unconcern.
20   It is not gunfire I hear, but a hunting horn.

1943 / 1946

Aristwocrats: Earlier versions of Douglas's *Complete Poems* print a variant text entitled "Sportsmen." "Lt.
  Col. J. D. Player, killed in Tunisia, Enfidaville, Feb. 1943, left £3000 to the Beaufort hunt, and directed
  that the incumbent of the living in his gift should be 'a man who approves of hunting, shooting, and all
  manly spots, which are the backbone of the nation.'" (Douglas). Player actually died 24 April 1943.
5: *88:* German tank armed with an 88-millimeter gun
15: *pitch:* playing field
16: *drop fences:* fences in a steeplechase horserace

Vergissmeinnicht

Three weeks gone and the combatants gone
returning over the nightmare ground
we found the place again, and found
the soldier sprawling in the sun.

5   The frowning barrel of his gun
overshadowing. As we came on
that day, he hit my tank with one
like the entry of a demon.

Look. Here in the gunpit spoil
10   the dishonoured picture of his girl
who has put: *Steffi. Vergissmeinnicht*
in a copybook gothic script.

We see him almost with content,
abased, and seeming to have paid
15   and mocked at by his own equipment
that's hard and good when he's decayed.

But she would weep to see today
how on his skin the swart flies move;
the dust upon the paper eye
20   and the burst stomach like a cave.

For here the lover and killer are mingled
who had one body and one heart.
And death who had the soldier singled
has done the lover mortal hurt.

1943 / 1946

How to Kill

Under the parabola of a ball,
a child turning into a man,
I looked into the air too long.
The ball fell in my hand, it sang
5   in the closed fist: *Open Open*
Behold a gift designed to kill.

Now in my dial of glass appears
the soldier who is going to die.
He smiles, and moves about in ways
10   his mother knows, habits of his.
The wires touch his face: I cry
NOW. Death, like a familiar, hears

Title: "Forget me not" (German)

12: *familiar*: an evil spirit under the control of a sorceror

and look, has made a man of dust
of a man of flesh. This sorcery
15   I do. Being damned, I am amused
to see the centre of love diffused
and the waves of love travel into vacancy.
How easy it is to make a ghost.

The weightless mosquito touches
20   her tiny shadow on the stone,
and with how like, how infinite
a lightness, man and shadow meet.
They fuse. A shadow is a man
when the mosquito death approaches.

c. 1943 / 1946

BOB COBBING (b. 1920)

COBBING WAS BORN IN ENFIELD, MIDDLESEX AND EDUCATED AT ENFIELD GRAMMAR School and Bognor Training College. He has worked as a civil servant, farmer, teacher, and manager of a bookshop; since 1967, he has been a freelance writer and performer. In 1952, Cobbing began the Writers Forum Workshop, as it has been called for many years now, a workshop devoted to experimental poetry that has had among its participants numerous poets resident in England, including Lee Harwood, Anselm Hollo, and Lawrence Upton, and visiting writers from Europe and North America. The workshop began publishing books—often small, mimeographed editions—in 1963, including work by Allen Ginsberg, the Austrian Ernst Jandl, the Canadian bpNichol, and the Czech Jiri Valoch. Among the hundreds of Writers Forum publications are numerous works by Cobbing himself, including *Kurrirrurriri* (1967), *Sonic Icons* (1970), *Alphapitasuite* (1973), and *Hydrangea* (1975). Among Cobbing's books published by other imprints are *Bill Jubobe: Selected Texts, 1942–1975* (Coach House, 1976) and *Bob Jubile: Selected Work, 1944–1990* (New River Project, 1991). Cobbing's output extends to LP and cassette recordings of his sound poetry, often performed with musicians or other sound poets or with his longstanding group Birdyak.

Performance has long been central to Cobbing's activities and aesthetic choices; he understands some of his texts as scores for single or multi-voiced reading. His work belongs in a tradition of experimental poetry that extends back through the tape-recorder productions of Henri Chopin in the 1950s to the Dada performances of Hugo Ball, Raouel Hausmann, Kurt Schwitters, and others in the 1920s, and back beyond Dada to Lewis Carroll and others. This tradition seeks to extend the possibilities of poetry by staying alert to the extra-semantic and paralinguistic dimensions of communication. While his work in intermedia and the painterly values evident in some texts leave the critic in search of labels, Cobbing has discussed some of his work within the context of "concrete sound poetry," identifying "two lines of development." One line attempts "to come to terms with scientific and technological development" by humanizing the machine, asserting artistic control over machines designed for non-artistic uses.[1] At a practical level this has meant, for instance, making texts and images in which an "original" in a photocopier is moved to distort the image of the original and produce something else. Another tradition perhaps closer to Cobbing's heart seeks a "return to the primitive, to incantation and ritual, to the coming together again of music and poetry, the amalgamation with movement and dance, the growth

---

[1] "Concrete Sound Poetry 1950–1970," *The Avant-Garde Tradition in Literature*, ed. Richard Kostelanetz, Buffalo, 1982, p. 390.

of the voice to its full physical powers again as part of the body."[2] The samples reproduced here offer a glimpse of the visual and auditory imagination of Cobbing's work as it explores the conventions of the page.

---

[2] Ibid., p. 391.

[wan do tree]

**wan
do
tree
fear
fife
seeks
siphon
eat
neighing
den
elephan'
twirl**

1977

[LION LENIN LEONORA]

```
LION   LENIN   LEONORA   LAMB
HEARTLESS   RESTIVE   RESOLUTE
BEAT   HABIT   RABBLE   APPLE   PIZZA
ROOT   TOOTLE   FLUORESCENT   CRESCENT
CAUSE   BECAUSE   BETRAYED   MOON
WAY   WRY   WRIGGLE   RENDER   LIGHT
OUT   NECK   CHEW      TUDOR   HOUSE
LAW   SUIT   SUET      STUART   ROOM
LESS LIKELY   RAW      MEAT   MATE
ON    UP    OVER   OTHERWISE   WISDOM
GOING   FOREARMED   TOOTHLESS   TOOTH
FORWARD   FORSOOTH   FEATHERWEIGHT   FEVER
LOOKING   SEEKING   SUMMARY    SO   FEW
                         DEW   DROP
GLASS   GLASTONBURY    BURIAL   BRUTAL
GLAZED   CRAZED   DEFIANT   DEVIANT
LAZER   RAZOR   DEFINITIVE   DELETE
     TEACHER
TREAT   TREACHERY   TREACLE   TRUNCATE
TREND   TRESTLE   NESTING   STUNG
FLUNG   FLING   DONG   LUMINOUS   LEERING
LECHEROUS   LUNCHEON   LUCIFER   LINK
CUFF   ROUGH   VOUCHER
            WROUGHT   IRON   GATE
CRATE   GRATER   GRATEFUL   DEAD
DEADENING   DUNDERHEAD   HEAD   DRESS
HUSTLE   CRUST   CRIMPING   CRUMB
CRUMBLE
```

1982

21: *DONG LUMINOUS:* cf. the nonsense poem "The Dong with the Luminous Nose" by Edward Lear (1812–1888).

[ALEVIN BARS CAUSAPSCAL]

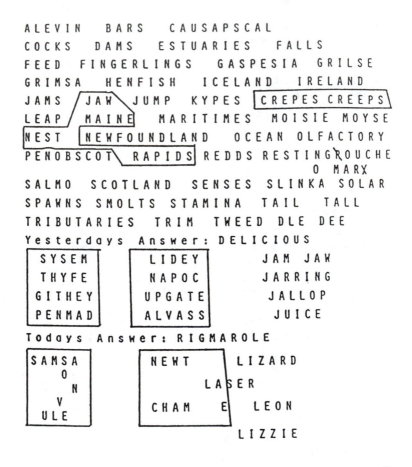

```
ALEVIN    BARS    CAUSAPSCAL
COCKS    DAMS   ESTUARIES    FALLS
FEED   FINGERLINGS    GASPESIA   GRILSE
GRIMSA    HENFISH    ICELAND    IRELAND
JAMS    JAW    JUMP   KYPES   CREPES CREEPS
LEAP    MAINE    MARITIMES    MOISIE   MOYSE
NEST    NEWFOUNDLAND    OCEAN   OLFACTORY
PENOBSCOT    RAPIDS   REDDS   RESTIGOUCHE
                                O MARX
SALMO   SCOTLAND   SENSES   SLINKA   SOLAR
SPAWNS   SMOLTS   STAMINA   TAIL    TALL
TRIBUTARIES   TRIM   TWEED  DLE  DEE
Yesterdays   Answer:  DELICIOUS
   SYSEM        LIDEY        JAM JAW
   THYFE        NAPOC        JARRING
   GITHEY       UPGATE       JALLOP
   PENMAD       ALVASS       JUICE

Todays   Answer:  RIGMAROLE
SAMSA          NEWT        LIZARD
   O
      N               LASER
   V
ULE            CHAM    E   LEON

                            LIZZIE
```

1982

The words in the first half of the poem concern the Atlantic salmon (*Salmo salar*); they mostly refer to stages in its life (*alevin, fingerlings, grilse, henfish, smolt*) and to rivers where it is found (Quebec's *Causapscal* and *Moisie* rivers and *Gaspesia* peninsula; Iceland's *Grimsa*, Maine's *Penobscot*). The hooked jaw of a male salmon is called a *kype*; a *redd* is a nest built by the fish to spawn in. *Slinka*: "to hatch" (Swedish).

PHILIP LARKIN (1922–1985)

L ARKIN IS THE MOST WIDELY CELEBRATED AND ARGUABLY THE FINEST POET OF THE
  Movement, a group of English poets that emerged in the 1950s and set the terms
for much of the poetry of the next several decades. As Robert Conquest noted in his
introduction to *New Lines* (1956), an anthology that helped to establish the Movement
poets as a group, these poets rejected modernist and neo-romantic poetic modes for
a poetry "empirical in its attitude" and characterized by "rational structure and com-
prehensible language."[1] While recent critics have been at some pains to show that
Larkin's poetry sustains an engagement with the proto-modernism of W. B. Yeats and
the French Symbolists, Larkin's own account of his poetic development had it that his
early Yeats influence was abandoned after his first book *The North Ship* (1945), to be
replaced by a lasting allegiance to the poetry of Thomas Hardy. Thus it is not surpris-
ing that much has been made of Larkin's relationship to Hardy as it extends what the
poet Andrew Motion argues is a "specifically English line" of poetry including Words-
worth, Tennyson, Edward Thomas, and W. H. Auden, poets intent on using the lan-
guage of everyday speech and addressing "the relationship between themselves and
their towns or landscapes."[2] Larkin's contemporary Donald Davie similarly argued in
Thomas Hardy and British Poetry (1972) that Larkin is a "Hardyesque poet" in whom
"we recognize . . . the seasons of present-day England."[3] Both remarks point to the
self-consciously plain idiom of the poems as they pursue a public utterance stripped
of bardic afflatus. Some have understood Larkin's subject matter—post-Christian
English society and the post-pastoral English landscape—and his often ironic tone as
indicating an anti-cosmopolitan, "little-englander" sensibility; Larkin's dismissals of
modern jazz, painting, literature, and academic life contributed to a public persona
A. Alvarez once characterized as "the image of the post-war Welfare State Englishman
. . . gauche but full of agnostic piety . . . just like the man next door."[4] But Larkin's
poetry is more various than its reputation for dour pessimism and anecdotes of a dis-
appointed middle class suggests. The famous persona turns out to be theatrical and
impish as often as it is grim and debunking; and irony and realism often co-exist with
sentiments bordering on Georgian nostalgia. As Motion indicates, the "typical struc-
ture of his poems" involves "a debate between hope and hopelessness, between ful-
fillment and disappointment."[5]

---

[1] Introduction, *New Lines,* London, 1956, p. xii.
[2] Andrew Motion, *Philip Larkin,* London, 1982, p. 19.
[3] *Thomas Hardy and British Poetry,* New York, 1972, p. 64.
[4] "Introduction: The New Poetry, or, Beyond the Gentility Principle," *The New Poetry,* ed. A. Alvarez, Har-
 mondsworth, 1962, p. 24.
[5] Motion, p. 72.

Larkin was born at Coventry, Warwickshire and educated at King Henry VIII School in Coventry and St. John's College, Oxford, where he was a contemporary of fellow Movement poet Kingsley Amis. In 1943, he began a career as a librarian at a public library in Wellington, Shropshire; subsequently he worked as a librarian at University College, Leicester and Queen's University, Belfast before taking a position at the Brynmor Jones Library in Hull. After the death of Poet Laureate Sir John Betjeman in 1984, Larkin was offered the Laureateship, which he refused.

Larkin's novel *Jill* was published in 1946, a second novel, *A Girl in Winter,* in 1947. His second collection of poems, *The Less Deceived,* appeared in 1955, *The Whitsun Weddings* in 1964, and *High Windows* in 1974. His critical prose is collected in *Required Writing: Miscellaneous Pieces 1955–1982* (1983).

Church Going

Once I am sure there's nothing going on
I step inside, letting the door thud shut.
Another church: matting, seats, and stone,
And little books; sprawlings of flowers, cut
5   For Sunday, brownish now; some brass and stuff
Up at the holy end; the small neat organ;
And a tense, musty, unignorable silence,
Brewed God knows how long. Hatless, I take off
My cycle-clips in awkward reverence,

10   Move forward, run my hand around the font.
From where I stand, the roof looks almost new—
Cleaned, or restored? Someone would know: I don't.
Mounting the lectern, I peruse a few
Hectoring large-scale verses, and pronounce
15   'Here endeth' much more loudly than I'd meant.
The echoes snigger briefly. Back at the door
I sign the book, donate an Irish sixpence,
Reflect the place was not worth stopping for.

Yet stop I did: in fact I often do,
20   And always end much at a loss like this,
Wondering what to look for; wondering, too,
When churches fall completely out of use
What we shall turn them into, if we shall keep
A few cathedrals chronically on show,
25   Their parchment, plate and pyx in locked cases,
And let the rest rent-free to rain and sheep.
Shall we avoid them as unlucky places?

Or, after dark, will dubious women come
To make their children touch a particular stone;

9: The speaker removes, rather than his hat, his *cycle-clips,* metal clips used to confine a cyclist's pants at the ankle, to avoid their becoming tangled in the bicycle chain.
14: *large-scale:* i.e., printed in large type for reading aloud
17: *Irish sixpence:* of no value in England
25: *pyx:* the box containing the communion wafers, usually made of precious metal

30   Pick simples for a cancer; or on some
       Advised night see walking a dead one?
       Power of some sort or other will go on
       In games, in riddles, seemingly at random;
       But superstition, like belief, must die,
35   And what remains when disbelief has gone?
       Grass, weedy pavement, brambles, buttress, sky,

       A shape less recognisable each week,
       A purpose more obscure. I wonder who
       Will be the last, the very last, to seek
40   This place for what it was; one of the crew
       That tap and jot and know what rood-lofts were?
       Some ruin-bibber, randy for antique,
       Or Christmas-addict, counting on a whiff
       Of gown-and-bands and organ-pipes and myrrh?
45   Or will he be my representative,

       Bored, uninformed, knowing the ghostly silt
       Dispersed, yet tending to this cross of ground
       Through suburb scrub because it held unspilt
       So long and equably what since is found
50   Only in separation—marriage, and birth,
       And death, and thoughts of these—for which was built
       This special shell? For, though I've no idea
       What this accoutred frowsty barn is worth,
       It pleases me to stand in silence here;

55   A serious house on serious earth it is,
       In whose blent air all our compulsions meet,
       Are recognised, and robed as destinies.
       And that much never can be obsolete,
       Since someone will forever be surprising
60   A hunger in himself to be more serious,
       And gravitating with it to this ground,
       Which, he once heard, was proper to grow wise in,
       If only that so many dead lie round.

                                                              1954 / 1955

Toads

       Why should I let the toad *work*
              Squat on my life?
       Can't I use my wit as a pitchfork
              And drive the brute off?

30: *simples:* medicinal herbs
41: The nave and chancel are separated by a rood screen, surmounted by a *rood-loft*, a gallery containing
   a crucifix.
44: *gown-and-bands:* clergymen's clothes; *bands:* a collar with two hanging strips
       myrrh: a gum resin that is an ingredient in incense
46: *ghostly:* both "supernatural" and "spiritual"
53: *frowsty:* stale, stuffy

5   Six days of the week it soils
                With its sickening poison—
           Just for paying a few bills!
                That's out of proportion.

           Lots of folk live on their wits:
10   Lecturers, lispers,
           Losels, loblolly-men, louts—
                They don't end as paupers;

           Lots of folk live up lanes
                With fires in a bucket,
15   Eat windfalls and tinned sardines—
                They seem to like it.

           Their nippers have got bare feet,
                Their unspeakable wives
           Are skinny as whippets—and yet
20   No one actually *starves*.

           Ah, were I courageous enough
                To shout *Stuff your pension!*
           But I know, all too well, that's the stuff
                That dreams are made on:

25   For something sufficiently toad-like
                Squats in me, too;
           Its hunkers are heavy as hard luck,
                And cold as snow,

           And will never allow me to blarney
30   My way to getting
           The fame and the girl and the money
                All at one sitting.

           I don't say, one bodies the other
                One's spiritual truth;
35   But I do say it's hard to lose either,
                When you have both.

                                        1954 / 1955

Nothing To Be Said

           For nations vague as weed,
           For nomads among stones,
           Small-statured cross-faced tribes
           And cobble-close families

11: *Losels, loblolly-men:* good-for-nothings and scoundrels
23–24: cf. *The Tempest,* 4.1.156–58: "We are such stuff / As dreams are made on; and our little life / Is
   rounded with a sleep."

5   In mill-towns on dark mornings
Life is slow dying.

So are their separate ways
Of building, benediction,
Measuring love and money
10   Ways of slow dying.
The day spent hunting pig
Or holding a garden-party,

Hours giving evidence
Or birth, advance
15   On death equally slowly.
And saying so to some
Means nothing; others it leaves
Nothing to be said.

1961 / 1964

Water

If I were called in
To construct a religion
I should make use of water.

Going to a church
5   Would entail a fording
To dry, different clothes;

My liturgy would employ
Images of sousing,
A furious devout drench,

10   And I should raise in the east
A glass of water
Where any-angled light
Would congregate endlessly.

1954 / 1964

The Whitsun Weddings

That Whitsun, I was late getting away:
    Not till about
One-twenty on the sunlit Saturday
Did my three-quarters-empty train pull out,
5   All windows down, all cushions hot, all sense
Of being in a hurry gone. We ran

The Whitsun Weddings: Whitsun: Whit Sunday, the Anglican term for the holiday of Pentecost, celebrated the seventh Sunday after Easter. The following Monday was a statutory bank holiday, thus making it a long weekend.

Behind the backs of houses, crossed a street
Of blinding windscreens, smelt the fish-dock; thence
The river's level drifting breadth began,
10   Where sky and Lincolnshire and water meet.

All afternoon, through the tall heat that slept
    For miles inland,
A slow and stopping curve southwards we kept.
Wide farms went by, short-shadowed cattle, and
15   Canals with floatings of industrial froth;
A hothouse flashed uniquely: hedges dipped
And rose: and now and then a smell of grass
Displaced the reek of buttoned carriage-cloth
Until the next town, new and nondescript,
20   Approached with acres of dismantled cars.

At first, I didn't notice what a noise
    The weddings made
Each station that we stopped at: sun destroys
The interest of what's happening in the shade,
25   And down the long cool platforms whoops and skirls
I took for porters larking with the mails,
And went on reading. Once we started, though,
We passed them, grinning and pomaded, girls
In parodies of fashion, heels and veils,
30   All posed irresolutely, watching us go,

As if out on the end of an event
    Waving goodbye
To something that survived it. Struck, I leant
More promptly out next time, more curiously,
35   And saw it all again in different terms:
The fathers with broad belts under their suits
And seamy foreheads; mothers loud and fat;
An uncle shouting smut; and then the perms,
The nylon gloves and jewellery-substitutes,
40   The lemons, mauves, and olive-ochres that

Marked off the girls unreally from the rest.
    Yes, from cafés
And banquet-halls up yards, and bunting-dressed
Coach-party annexes, the wedding-days
45   Were coming to an end. All down the line
Fresh couples climbed aboard: the rest stood round;
The last confetti and advice were thrown,
And, as we moved, each face seemed to define
Just what it saw departing: children frowned
50   At something dull; fathers had never known

25: *skirls*: shrieks
43: *bunting-dressed*: bunting is a fabric used to make flags or, as here, festive decorations.
44: *Annexes* were sometimes built on to pubs and hotels to accommodate the *coach-parties* that stopped
   there for refreshment; they were intended to stop the traditional bars from becoming suddenly jammed
   up with customers.

Success so huge and wholly farcical;
   The women shared
The secret like a happy funeral;
While girls, gripping their handbags tighter, stared
55   At a religious wounding. Free at last,
And loaded with the sum of all they saw,
We hurried towards London, shuffling gouts of steam.
Now fields were building-plots, and poplars cast
Long shadows over major roads, and for
60   Some fifty minutes, that in time would seem

Just long enough to settle hats and say
   I nearly died,
A dozen marriages got under way.
They watched the landscape, sitting side by side
65   —An Odeon went past, a cooling tower,
And someone running up to bowl—and none
Thought of the others they would never meet
Or how their lives would all contain this hour.
I thought of London spread out in the sun,
70   Its postal districts packed like squares of wheat:

There we were aimed. And as we raced across
   Bright knots of rail
Past standing Pullmans, walls of blackened moss
Came close, and it was nearly done, this frail
75   Travelling coincidence; and what it held
Stood ready to be loosed with all the power
That being changed can give. We slowed again,
And as the tightened brakes took hold, there swelled
A sense of falling, like an arrow-shower
80   Sent out of sight, somewhere becoming rain.

1958 / 1964

An Arundel Tomb

Side by side, their faces blurred,
The earl and countess lie in stone,
Their proper habits vaguely shown
As jointed armour, stiffened pleat,
5   And that faint hint of the absurd—
The little dogs under their feet.

Such plainness of the pre-baroque
Hardly involves the eye, until
It meets his left-hand gauntlet, still

65: *Odeon:* name of a chain of cinemas
66: *bowl:* in cricket, to pitch the ball to the batsman

Title: The tomb of the Earl of *Arundel* and his wife is in Chichester Cathedral, West Sussex. After the
   poem's composition Larkin discovered that the joined hands were the result of a nineteenth-century
   restoration.
3: *habits:* apparel, garments

10   Clasped empty in the other; and
       One sees, with a sharp tender shock,
       His hand withdrawn, holding her hand.

       They would not think to lie so long.
       Such faithfulness in effigy
15   Was just a detail friends would see:
       A sculptor's sweet commissioned grace
       Thrown off in helping to prolong
       The Latin names around the base.

       They would not guess how early in
20   Their supine stationary voyage
       The air would change to soundless damage,
       Turn the old tenantry away;
       How soon succeeding eyes begin
       To look, not read. Rigidly they

25   Persisted, linked, through lengths and breadths
       Of time. Snow fell, undated. Light
       Each summer thronged the glass. A bright
       Litter of birdcalls strewed the same
       Bone-riddled ground. And up the paths
30   The endless altered people came,

       Washing at their identity.
       Now, helpless in the hollow of
       An unarmorial age, a trough
       Of smoke in slow suspended skeins
35   Above their scrap of history,
       Only an attitude remains:

       Time has transfigured them into
       Untruth. The stone fidelity
       They hardly meant has come to be
40   Their final blazon, and to prove
       Our almost-instinct almost true:
       What will survive of us is love.

                    1956 / 1964

High Windows

       When I see a couple of kids
       And guess he's fucking her and she's
       Taking pills or wearing a diaphragm,
       I know this is paradise

5   Everyone old has dreamed of all their lives—
       Bonds and gestures pushed to one side

33: *an unarmorial age:* one indifferent to heraldic arms

Like an outdated combine harvester,
And everyone young going down the long slide

To happiness, endlessly. I wonder if
10 Anyone looked at me, forty years back,
And thought, *That'll be the life;*
No God any more, or sweating in the dark

About hell and that, or having to hide
What you think of the priest. He
15 *And his lot will all go down the long slide*
Like free bloody birds. And immediately

Rather than words comes the thought of high windows:
The sun-comprehending glass,
And beyond it, the deep blue air, that shows
20 Nothing, and is nowhere, and is endless.

1967 / 1974

Going, Going

I thought it would last my time—
The sense that, beyond the town,
There would always be fields and farms,
Where the village louts could climb
5 Such trees as were not cut down;
I knew there'd be false alarms

In the papers about old streets
And split-level shopping, but some
Have always been left so far;
10 And when the old part retreats
As the bleak high-risers come
We can always escape in the car.

Things are tougher than we are, just
As earth will always respond
15 However we mess it about;
Chuck filth in the sea, if you must:
The tides will be clean beyond.
—But what do I feel now? Doubt?

Or age, simply? The crowd
20 Is young in the M1 café;
Their kids are screaming for more—
More houses, more parking allowed,
More caravan sites, more pay.
On the Business Page, a score

Going, Going: 20: The *M1* was the U.K.'s first motorway; it runs north from London as far as Leeds (in west Yorkshire).
23: *caravan sites:* trailer parks (for holidaying at seaside locations)

25   Of spectacled grins approve
                    Some takeover bid that entails
                    Five per cent profit (and ten
                    Per cent more in the estuaries): move
                    Your works to the unspoilt dales
30   (Grey area grants)! And when

                    You try to get near the sea
                    In summer . . .
                                It seems, just now,
                    To be happening so very fast;
                    Despite all the land left free
35   For the first time I feel somehow
                    That it isn't going to last,

                    That before I snuff it, the whole
                    Boiling will be bricked in
                    Except for the tourist parts—
40   First slum of Europe: a role
                    It won't be so hard to win,
                    With a cast of crooks and tarts.

                    And that will be England gone,
                    The shadows, the meadows, the lanes,
45   The guildhalls, the carved choirs.
                    There'll be books; it will linger on
                    In galleries; but all that remains
                    For us will be concrete and tyres.

                    Most things are never meant.
50   This won't be, most likely: but greeds
                    And garbage are too thick-strewn
                    To be swept up now, or invent
                    Excuses that make them all needs.
                    I just think it will happen, soon.

                                            1972 / 1974

Homage to a Government

Next year we are to bring the soldiers home
For lack of money, and it is all right.
Places they guarded, or kept orderly,
Must guard themselves, and keep themselves orderly.

30: *Grey area grants:* grants given to encourage development in *grey areas,* those in poor economic health
37–38: *the whole / Boiling:* the whole lot
45: *guildhalls:* the surviving medieval guildhalls in small shire towns; no longer having any administrative
   function, they are used for local functions, Womens' Institute markets, etc.

Homage to a Government: Larkin began this poem in January 1968, in response to the government's deci-
   sion to close the British base in Aden (now part of Yemen). The British had maintained a presence there
   since the beginning of the nineteenth century.

5   We want the money for ourselves at home
Instead of working. And this is all right.

It's hard to say who wanted it to happen,
But now it's been decided nobody minds.
The places are a long way off, not here,
10   Which is all right, and from what we hear
The soldiers there only made trouble happen.
Next year we shall be easier in our minds.

Next year we shall be living in a country
That brought its soldiers home for lack of money.
15   The statues will be standing in the same
Tree-muffled squares, and look nearly the same.
Our children will not know it's a different country.
All we can hope to leave them now is money.

                                       1969 / 1974

This Be The Verse

They fuck you up, your mum and dad.
   They may not mean to, but they do.
They fill you with the faults they had
   And add some extra, just for you.

5   But they were fucked up in their turn
   By fools in old-style hats and coats,
Who half the time were soppy-stern
   And half at one another's throats.

Man hands on misery to man.
10   It deepens like a coastal shelf.
Get out as early as you can,
   And don't have any kids yourself.

                                         1971 / 1974

The Explosion

On the day of the explosion
Shadows pointed towards the pithead:
In the sun the slagheap slept.

Down the lane came men in pitboots
5   Coughing oath-edged talk and pipe-smoke,
Shouldering off the freshened silence.

This Be The Verse: Title: Cf. Robert Louis Stevenson's "Requiem": "This be the verse you grave for me."

The Explosion: Larkin is evoking the mining communities of the past (rather than of the 1970s).
2: *pithead:* the entrance to the mineshaft

One chased after rabbits; lost them;
Came back with a nest of lark's eggs;
Showed them; lodged them in the grasses.

10   So they passed in beards and moleskins,
Fathers, brothers, nicknames, laughter,
Through the tall gates standing open.

At noon, there came a tremor; cows
Stopped chewing for a second; sun,
15   Scarfed as in a heat-haze, dimmed.

The dead go on before us, they
Are sitting in God's house in comfort,
We shall see them face to face—

Plain as lettering in the chapels
20   It was said, and for a second
Wives saw men of the explosion

Larger than in life they managed—
Gold as on a coin, or walking
Somehow from the sun towards them,

25   One showing the eggs unbroken.

                                        1970 / 1974

10: *moleskins:* clothes made of moleskin (a heavy cotton fabric), such as trousers
18: see 1 Cor. 13:12.

DONALD DAVIE (1922–1995)

IN BOOKS OF LITERARY CRITICISM AND LITERARY HISTORY, INCLUDING *PURITY OF DICTION in English Verse* (1952), *Articulate Energy: An Inquiry into the Syntax of English Poetry* (1955), *Ezra Pound: Poet as Sculptor* (1964), *Thomas Hardy and British Poetry* (1972), and *Under Briggflatts: A History of Poetry in Great Britain 1960–1988* (1989), Davie established himself, in Britain and the United States, as the most influential critical among the Movement writers of the 1950s. Davie often criticized the insularity of British poetry in referring to the writing of Ezra Pound and Charles Olson, but he also defended "an English or British difference" and the tradition he associated with the poetry of Thomas Hardy. He was an advocate of conventions of English syntax that he felt sustained the "tacit compact or contract between writer and reader."[1] Critical of the bardic posture or egoism of many neo-romantic poets, equally suspicious of the "self-sufficient" symbolist poem and modernist form, Davie sought to link neo-Augustan poetic values with civic virtues and democratic politics. In a polemical passage in *Purity of Diction,* he wrote: "the development from imagism in poetry to fascism in politics is clear and unbroken. . . . One could almost say . . . that to dislocate syntax in poetry is to threaten the rule of law in the civilized community."[2] In later years, Davie's criticism reflected his respect for the poetry of Basil Bunting, of interest to him equally for its debt to modernism and for Bunting's Quakerism, and his own developing commitment to Christianity. Davie's poetry, from the Movement verse of *Brides of Reason* (1955) through the exploration of North American history and tradition in *A Sequence for Francis Parkman* (1961) to the late religious poems of *To Scorch or Freeze* (1988) sustains his preference for the conversational and urbane rather than the romantic or ecstatic, but all of the poems are typically more self-questioning than his sometimes dogmatic prose. Poems such as "Rodez" suggest the influence of the modernist poetry he often wrote ambivalently about.

Davie was born in Barnsley, Yorkshire and educated at the local grammar school. After serving in the Royal Navy during World War II, he attended Cambridge University, where he earned a Ph.D. He lectured in Dublin and Cambridge before becoming Professor of English at Essex in 1964. In 1968, he emigrated to the United States, where he was Professor of English at Stanford and then Vanderbilt University before retiring and returning to England. Davie was a translator of Boris Pasternak's poetry and published essays on Polish and Russian literature. He also edited collections of Augustan and Christian verse. Some of his other books of poems are *The Forests of Lithuania* (1959), *Essex Poems* (1969), *Six Epistles to Eva Hesse* (1970), *The Shires* (1974), and *The Battered Wife and Other Poems* (1982). Other prose includes *The Poet in the Imaginary*

---

[1] "Postscript 1975," *Articulate Energy,* rev. ed., London, 1975, p. xii.
[2] *Purity of Diction in English Verse,* p. 99.

Museum: Essays of Two Decades (1977), *These the Companions* (1982), and *A Gathered Church: The Literature of the English Dissenting Interest 1700–1930* (1978).

Hearing Russian Spoken

Unsettled again and hearing Russian spoken
I think of brokenness perversely planned
By Dostoievsky's debauchees; recall
The 'visible brokenness' that is the token
5   Of the true believer; and connect it all
With speaking a language I cannot command.

If broken means unmusical I speak
Even in English brokenly, a man
Wretched enough, yet one who cannot borrow
10   Their hunger for indignity nor, weak,
Abet my weakness, drink to drown a sorrow
Or write in metres that I cannot scan.

Unsettled again at hearing Russian spoken,
'Abjure politic brokenness for good',
15   I tell myself. 'Recall what menaces,
What self-loathings must be re-awoken:
This girl and that, and all your promises
Your pidgin that they too well understood.'

Not just in Russian but in any tongue
20   Abandonment, morality's soubrette
Of lyrical surrender and excess,
Knows the weak endings equal to the strong;
She trades on broken English with success
And, disenchanted, I'm enamoured yet.

1957

Rejoinder to a Critic

You may be right: 'How can I dare to feel?'
May be the only question I can pose,
'And haply by abstruse research to steal
From my own nature all the natural man'

3: Davie might have in mind a number of characters in the works of the Russian novelist Fyodor *Dostoievsky* (1821–1881); see, e.g., the dialogue concerning "debauchery" between Raskolnikov and Svidrigaylov in Part 6, Chapter 3 of *Crime and Punishment* (1867).
20: *soubrette:* the role of coquettish maid-servant in French comedy
22. *endings:* i.e., grammatical endings: "knows that grammatical niceties are unimportant"

Title: "The poem was written as a reply to Martin Seymour-Smith, who had criticized Davie in the Oxford magazine *Departure* for 'constantly seeking a critico-academic excuse for postponing an attempt to write poetry of a wider range'." (Blake Morrison, *The Movement: English Poetry and Fiction of the 1950s*, Oxford, 1980, p. 106)
3–4: Quoted from Coleridge's "Dejection: An Ode", 89–90

5   *My* sole resource. And I do not suppose
     That others may not have a better plan.

     And yet I'll quote again, and gloss it too
     (You know by now my liking for collage):
     Donne could be daring, but he never knew,
10   When he inquired, 'Who's injured by my love?'
     Love's radio-active fall-out on a large
     Expanse around the point it bursts above.

     'Alas, alas, who's injured by my love?'
     And recent history answers: Half Japan!
15   Not love, but hate? Well, both are versions of
     The 'feeling' that you dare me to . . . Be dumb!
     Appear concerned only to make it scan!
     How dare we now be anything but numb?

                                                              1957

Rodez

     Northward I came, and knocked in the coated wall
     At the door of a low inn scaled like a urinal
     With greenish tiles. The door gave, and I came

     Home to the stone north, every wynd and snicket
5   Known to me wherever the flattened cat
     Squirmed home to a hole between housewall and paving.

     Known! And in the turns of it, no welcome,
     No flattery of the beckoned lighted eye
     From a Rose of the rose-brick alleys of Toulouse.

10   Those more than tinsel garlands, more than masks,
     Unfading wreaths of ancient summers, I
     Sternly cast off. A stern eye is the graceless

     Bulk and bruise that at the steep uphill
     Confronts me with its drained-of-colour sandstone
15   Implacably. The Church. It is Good Friday.

     Goodbye to the Middle Ages! Although some
     Think that I enter them, those centuries
     Of monkish superstition, here I leave them

     With their true garlands, and their honest masks,
20   Every fresh flower cast on the porch and trodden,
     Raked by the wind at the Church door on this Friday.

10: Quoted from John Donne's "The Canonization."

Title: *Rodez:* a town in the south of France
4: *wynd and snicket:* narrow street and alleyway
9: *Toulouse:* a city in southern France; its architecture is characterized by the use of rose-red brick.

Goodbye to all the centuries. There is
No home in them, much as the dip and turn
Of an honest alley charmingly deceive us.

25   And yet not quite goodbye. Instead almost
Welcome, I said. Bleak equal centuries
Crowded the porch to be deflowered, crowned.

                                                    1969

Out of East Anglia

Pacific: in Russian as
In our language
Peaceful is the word
For that last sea at the edge;
5   And nearer than the Americas'
Awesome, vertical falls
Into the Western Ocean
The imperceptible, tempting
Declivity, inanition!

10   Sometimes when all this side
Of England seems to hang
Suspenseful on that slide,
How peace might be is near.

                                                    1969

A Conditioned Air

A wind I know blows dirt
In and out of the town that I was born in,
The same wind blowing the same dirt in and out,
Coal-dirt, grit. No odorous cloud-cleaving
5   Typhoon of Crusoe grew upon the West
To satisfy your hunger for afflatus,
Masters of the last
Century, attending
A plaint in the mouth of the hearth, a night of
10   Wind. The wind

Title: *East Anglia:* an eastern region of England; physically, it is low and undulating, with its east coast on
the North Sea. It is also the location of U.S. Air Force bases; the poem was written during the Cold War.
4: The Pacific Ocean is ringed by a chain of volcanoes and mountain ranges that includes those in North-
eastern Siberia and on the west coast of the United States.
9: *Declivity:* downwards slope
    inanition: exhausted indifference; emptying-out
12: *Suspenseful:* both "suspended" and "full of suspense"

5: *Typhoon:* the typhoon that led to the shipwreck of Robinson *Crusoe* in Defoe's novel
6: *afflatus:* inspiration (lit. "breath")
7ff: Davie has in mind the Romantic poets, perhaps especially Coleridge for his "Frost at Midnight" and
    "Dejection," and Shelley for his "Ode to the West Wind."

Was a draught in the flue of England. I attend
How the electric motor
Gulps and recovers and
The image on the television screen
15   Contracts and distends like a reptilian eye,
As somewhere the high wind slaps at a power-line
Out in the country. In the howling quick
Of the bud the branches suffer
Retardations much as you did. I,
20   Before an empty hearth
In an unfocused house,
Behind me the quietly blasting
Hot-air grille, attend
The delicate movements of
25   Conditioned airs
I learn to love, as small
As that is, and as prompt
In its dispersed and shaking service. My
Storm-window's foggy polythene claps and billows.

1969

Inditing A Good Matter

I find nothing to say,
I am heavy as lead.
I take small satisfaction
in anything I have said.

5   Evangelists want your assent,
be it cringing, or idle, or eager.
God shrugs. We taste dismay,
as sharp as vinegar.

He shrugs. How can He care
10   what *billets-doux* we send Him,
how much we applaud? Such coxcombs
inclined to commend Him!

My heart had been inditing
a good matter. My tongue
15   was the pen of a ready writer
who had been writing too long.

17–18: *the howling quick / Of the bud*: cf. "the howling storm" in Blake's "The Sick Rose"
19: *Retardations*: Davie likely has in mind the early deaths of Shelley, Keats, and Byron.
21: *unfocused*: "Focus" means "fireplace, hearth" in Latin.

Title: *Inditing*: writing down. "My heart is inditing a good matter: I speak of the things which I have made touching the King; my tongue is the pen of a ready writer." (Ps. 45:1).
10: *billets-doux*: love-letters

Whoever supposes his business
is to commend and bless
is due for this comeuppance:
20   feeling it less and less.

But I find something to say.
I pump it out, heavy as lead:
'Buoy me up out of the shadow
of your ramparts overhead.'

25   Like one of those vanished performers
on an afternoon-matinée console,
I arise:
   'Admit to your rock
this ready, this shriven, soul.'

           1988

25ff: Davie has in mind old-fashioned live accompaniments to silent films: a cinema organist would rise, complete with *organ,* from the depths of the building, playing as he came.

JAMES BERRY (b. 1924)

BERRY WAS BORN IN BOSTON, JAMAICA, AND BROUGHT UP IN THE COASTAL VILLAGE OF Fair Prospect. He lived in the United States prior to moving to London in 1948. He is the editor of two ground-breaking anthologies of Caribbean and Black British poetry, *Bluefoot Traveller* (1976; 1981) and *News for Babylon* (1984), and is well-known for performances of his poetry and for poetry programs presented on British television and radio. He has toured Sweden, Germany, and Poland for the British Council and been active in multicultural education. His books of poetry include *Fractured Circles* (1979), *Lucy's Letter and Loving* (1982), *Chain of Days* (1985), and *Hot Earth Cold Earth* (1995). He has also published stories and books for children, including the poetry collection *When I Dance* (1988). He lives in Brighton, England.

In Berry's poems, Fred D'Aguiar writes, "we see a wide-ranging creole emerging, at once closely affiliated to the English spoken here [in Britain] and to the more radical forms of creole associated with the Jamaican countryside. . . . As we move from one poem to the next linguistic continents are crossed."[1] Berry is fond of incorporating folk proverbs in his poems, as in "From Lucy: Englan a University." In other poems, such as "Folk Proverbs Found Poems" these proverbs are offered in a series of epigrams that delight in creole rhythms Berry has "found": "Is a blessing me come me see you / eye-to-eye joy is a love."[2] Berry's best-known poems are the persona poems wherein "Lucy" writes from London to her friend Leela in Jamaica; some continuities as well as differences in Berry's work might be contemplated by comparing the Lucy poem included here with another epistolary poem written in a more standard idiom, "Letter to My Father from London." Some of the poems in *In Chain of Days* and elsewhere are concerned with Berry's ancestral roots in Africa; he has explained that "I needed to go back to my African roots with my hurt, anger and a complaining voice."[3] Other poems such as the two represented here explore the differences between Caribbean and British life. Berry's poems can reflect as well as explore nostalgia for life beyond Britain, but they are also concerned with the radical otherness of the two cultures, and the difficulties of understanding one culture from the perspective of the other. He writes in "Letter to My Father from London" that "You cannot measure the twig-man / image you launched before me / with bloated belly / with bulged eyes of famine / insistent from hoardings and walls / here on world highstreets / holding a bowl to every passerby." Nor is Berry content to settle in a sentimental politics of victimization: "You still don't understand / how a victim is guilty as accomplice."

---

1 "Have you been here long? Black Poetry in Britain," in *New British Poetries: The Scope of the Possible*, ed. Robert Hampson and Peter Barry, Manchester, 1993, p. 60.
2 *Hot Earth Cold Earth*, Newcastle upon Tyne, 1995, p. 30.
3 Preface, *Hot Earth Cold Earth*, p. 9.

Letter to My Father from London

Over the horizon here
you say I told you
animals are groomed like babies
and shops hang wares
5   like a world of flame trees in bloom

Lambs and calves and pigs hang empty
and ships crowd the port

You say no one arrives back
for the breath once mixed becomes
10   an eternal entanglement

You say unreason eats up the youth
and rage defeats him

Elders cannot be heroes
when the young wakes up centrally
15   ragged or inflated on the world
and the ideal of leisure does
not mean a bushman's pocketless time

An enchanter has the face of cash
without sweat
20   and does not appear barefooted
bursting at elbows and bottom

He has the connections and craft
to claim the sun in gold
and the moon in diamond

25   You cannot measure the twig-man
image you launched before me
with bloated belly
with bulged eyes of famine
insistent from hoardings and walls
30   here on world highstreets
holding a bowl to every passerby

You still don't understand
how a victim is guilty as accomplice

1985

From Lucy: Englan a University

Darlin, you did ask a good question.
You know, and I know, how white folks
can go on, bout they need a holiday,
and manage get it cross
5   they 'adventurous', they 'curious',

and land up in Africa
and India and China, etcetera, etcetera.

Well, darlin, Westindians come
get known as travellers for food
10   and clothes: not folks who did long
to feel somewhere else,
long to touch snow with eyeball,
and all curious too to see
horseback lords at home, at fireside
15   maybe thinkin how they did long
for company of bushman, and did long
to take in sounds
and feelin's of jungle places.

And all in all, sweetheart, though
20   our move was blind date to Mother
Country, it look now it did carry
far-sightedness. And I swear
heavn did know something bout it.

Darlin, when real person get seen
25   in black figure, like when real
human get known in white figure,
is celebration, is teatime all roun,
or rum and blackcurrant. And still
I get surprise, when I see
30   somebody posh behavin like
a hungrybelly in we distric there.

And real news this, me dear!
From distric there, another
barefoot boy is makin mark.
35   Fool-Fool Boy-Joe son come get degree,
education degree here in London:
and Bareback-Buddy is teacher now.
Bareback teachin. He teachin
black and white children mix together.
40   Leela, you see how what
you don know is older than you?

Sweetheart, we mus remember you know
how ol people did say, 'Man is more
than a flock of birds.'

1985

IAN HAMILTON FINLAY (B. 1925)

"MY VERSE IS NOT A *SINGLE* THING SINCE IT HAS CHANGED OVER THE YEARS. ON THE other hand, I have usually tried for the same ends—lucidity, clarity, a resolved complexity. . . . In the context of this time, it is not the job of poetry to 'expand consciousness' but to offer a modest example of a decent set of order."[1] So Finlay writes in a note for *Contemporary Poets,* outlining a continuity in his art as it has progressed from the early lyrics collected in *The Dancers Inherit the Party* (1960) and *Glasgow Beasts, an a Burd* (1961). A neo-classical "resolved complexity" also characterizes his concrete poetry—the typewriter poems of *Telegrams from my Windmill* (1964), the poster poems such as *Star/Steer* (1966), and poem-prints such as *homage to gomringer* (1972). Because Finlay's work spans and mixes media, including photos, sculpture, allegorical gardens, and the printed page, it belongs to an avant-garde tradition challenging generic categories, but in his case avant-gardism exists comfortably with traditionalism. His work often alludes to classicist moments of the past, the stone aircraft carriers in his garden at Stonypath remembering war-galleys represented in Roman gardens, the installation *A View of the Temple* (1987) acknowledging the French Revolution by framing the viewer's sight of a distant temple with guillotines inscribed with mottoes from Saint-Just's prose. The poems from *The Dancers Inherit the Party,* dating from the period prior to his emergence as one of Britain's most celebrated concrete poets, resemble the work of the American poet Lorine Niedecker in the way they mix folk materials—then a little out of fashion in Scotland following MacDiarmid's assault on kailyard sentimentality—with the austere formalism of Objectivist poetry such as Louis Zukofsky's. Each development in Finlay's career has been influential. His next book, *Glasgow Beasts,* prepared the ground for poets such as Tom Leonard by employing a Glaswegian demotic idiom; Hugh MacDiarmid, perhaps the only Scottish poet of the century with greater influence, described it as "written in the language of the gutter."[2]

Finlay was born in Nassau, Bahamas but returned with his parents to Scotland as a child. He lived in Perthshire and on the Orkney island of Rousay before settling in a shepherd's cottage on four acres of land at Stonypath, where he began creating his garden, later named Little Sparta. Through Gael Turnbull and his magazine and press *Migrant,* which published *The Dancers* in 1960, he made contact with American poets including Niedecker, Zukofsky, and Robert Creeley. Between 1961 and 1968, he edited *Poor. Old. Tired. Horse,* which together with his friend Edwin Morgan's translations

---

[1] *Contemporary Poets,* 6th ed., New York, 1996, p. 342.
[2] Quoted in Alec Finlay, Afterword to *The Dancers Inherit the Party and Glasgow Beasts,* Edinburgh, 1996, p. 109.

introduced a range of international avant-garde poetry to Scotland. By the early 1960s, Finlay was in contact with poets and artists such as Ad Reinhart, Ernst Jandl, and the Noigandres group of concrete poets in Brazil. Throughout the sixties, his publications defined the possibilities of concrete poetry (even more than most poetry, this work is best viewed in its original contexts). In the 1980s, Finlay became entangled in two widely publicized controversies, the first involving the Strathclyde Regional Council's effort to designate his "Garden Temple" ("a non-profit building with a spiritual purpose" for Finlay) as a commercial gallery, the second resulting from French critics absurdly accusing him of Nazi sympathies after they misread a series of inscribed marble blocks, one of which had the letters "SS" (as part of "Osso," the Italian word for "bone"). Given his prolific production across and among artforms, one can understand the contemporary Scottish critic Robert Crawford's statement that "Finlay is our [Scottish] avant-garde."[3]

---

[3]Quoted in Alec Finlay, p. 97.

Orkney Lyrics

1 PEEDIE MARY CONSIDERS THE SUN

The peedie sun is not so tall
He walks on golden stilts
Across, across, across the water
But I have darker hair.

2 THE ENGLISH COLONEL EXPLAINS AN ORKNEY BOAT

The boat swims full of air.
You see, it has a point at both
Ends, sir, somewhat
As lemons. I'm explaining

5   The hollowness is amazing. That's
The way a boat
Floats.

3 MANSIE CONSIDERS PEEDIE MARY

Peedie Alice Mary is
My cousin, so we cannot kiss.
And yet I love my cousin fair:
She wears her seaboots with such an air.

Title: The *Orkney* Islands lie 20 miles north of the Scottish mainland.
Peedie Mary Considers the Sun: Title: "'Peedie' is the Orkney word for 'wee'." (Finlay)
Mansie Considers Peedie Mary: "Many Orkney girls have two Christian names, and many Orkney men are called 'Mansie', which is the diminutive of 'Magnus'." (Finlay)

4 MANSIE CONSIDERS THE SEA IN THE MANNER OF HUGH MACDIARMID

The sea, I think, is lazy,
It just obeys the moon
—All the same I remember what Engels said:
'Freedom is the consciousness of necessity'.

5 FOLK SONG FOR POOR PEEDIE MARY

Peedie Mary
Bought a posh
Big machine
To do her wash.

5   Peedie Mary
Stands and greets,
Where dost thoo
Put in the peats?

Silly Peedie
10   Mary thoo
Puts the peats
Below, baloo.

Peedie Mary
Greets the more,
15   What did the posh paint
Come off for?

6 JOHN SHARKEY IS PLEASED TO BE IN SOURIN AT EVENING

How beautiful, how beautiful, the mill
—Wheel is not turning though the waters spill
Their single tress. The whole old mill
Leans to the West, the breast.

1960

Mansie Considers the Sea . . . : Title: For MacDiarmid, see p. 166.
Folk Song for Poor Peedie Mary: 6: *greets*: weeps
John Sharkey: . . . : Title: *Sourin* is a place on Rousay, one of the Orkney Islands.

Sea-Poppy 1

1968

Sea-Poppy 2

1968

ASA BENVENISTE (1925–1990)

WHEN BENVENISTE PUBLISHED *THROW OUT THE LIFE LINE LAY OUT THE Corse* in 1983, the book's subtitle was *Poems 1965–1985*. The joke was on the pretensions and conventions of such volumes; Benveniste gathered not just the past but two years of a silent future. This playful humility is evident in his poems. A "Valediction" to his selected work explains that "Most of the poems here have a basis in domestic experience, though it may be hard to believe, and this may explain my treatment of that subject with an irresistible and concerned silliness; domestic life lends itself easily to a complex comedy of language."[1] Benveniste's wit is more oblique than boisterous; many of his poems are miniatures, as if mixing and distilling techniques taken from a variety of sources: Mallarmé, William Carlos Williams, Dada and Surrealism, a first generation New York School poetry, Erik Satie's music, Chinese and Japanese traditions. One section of the book, "The Alchemical Cupboard," contains a sequence of poems reflecting ten years of study "into the sources of Kabbalistic congruities." Its epigraph from David Meltzer suggests that reading the Kabbalah, like reading poetry, involves "the study of and submission to the mysteries of the word."[2] Another, "Tabellae Linnaei," is a sequence about "naming," responding to the "genera tables" and "runic / approximations" of the Swedish botanist Carolus Linnaeus: "Paged oblique against English light / oily black letterpress and I know / enough to read perhaps 2 words: / acknowledge, subjective. . . ."[3] For all of his affiliations with a cosmopolitan avant-garde, Benveniste is in many ways a traditional lyric poet, as is especially evident in *Pommes Poems* (1988), which contains a sequence of love poems for the artist Agneta Falk (including "Blue Crêpe") and a sonnet sequence. "Oh happiness, you're like a green face / lighting up a giant cigarette / that never goes out but falls from the window" Benveniste writes in one poem.[4] But the last few lines from "An End to It" suggest the book's dominant tone, which has more to do with vulnerability and woundedness and the Psalms: "But the grass loves me now. / It lays itself on my body / and ties my hands mercifully together / so that they lift not any element / outside their own tenderness. / And the sun is on me too / and the outline of its kiss / and the delirious wounds on my cheek / and the cold surface of their chimes."[5]

A Sephardic Jew, Benveniste was born in the Bronx. He was in Europe during World War II and, after returning to the United States for a few years, moved to Paris

---

[1] *Throw Out the Life Line Lay Out the Corse*, London, 1983, p. 7.
[2] Quoted in the same, p. 50.
[3] Ibid., p. 122.
[4] "Short Scene Sonnets," *Pommes Poems*, Todmorden, 1988, p. 51.
[5] *Pommes Poems*, p. 32.

in 1948. There he studied at the Sorbonne and, with George Solomos, started the magazine *Zero,* which ran through 1956 as Benveniste moved first to Tangier and then, in 1950, to Britain. Writers published by *Zero* include William Carlos Williams, Christopher Isherwood, and James Baldwin. Detesting life in the United States, Benveniste settled permanently in Britain and was a crucial part of its small press publishing culture, starting Trigram Press in 1965: its over fifty books and broadsides presented work by poets as different as George Barker, Anselm Hollo, Gavin Ewart, J. H. Prynne, and Tom Raworth, and by artists including Jim Dine, Andy Warhol, and Glen Baxter. In the late 1970s, Benveniste moved from London to open a bookshop in West Yorkshire. His books of poetry also include *Poems of the Mouth* (1966), *The Atoz Formula* (1969), *Count Three* (1969), *Edge* (1975), *Loose Use* (1977), and *Invisible Ink* (1989).

First Words

    I don't remember writing the word christendom before
    and except for 'tribe' won't trouble you
    with O E D definitions
                          other words come to mind: however
5   is one of them: cocktail: temperature falling:
    cunnilingus: power failure—
                      but 'armoire'
    is closer to the truth! ah! the efficacy
    of transformation: the ability to transcend
10   ethnic differences: *la lune* for example belongs to
    Houston Texas and the tricks some poets play
    on their wives—
                I love you Maud
    I hope we meet sometime quickly
15   on the way to Wimbledon

                                              1972

Georgic

    They ascend from still wheat
    off the horizon
    biblical radius the sky darkens
    I don't feel much these days anyway
5   flies popping from my eyebrows
    which is about all that can be said
    for history

    and one other fact:
    the transplantation of yarrow

3: O E D: The *Oxford English Dictionary*
10: *la lune:* "the moon" (French). Houston's Lyndon B. Johnson Space Center is the command post for flights by U.S. astronauts.
15: *Wimbledon:* part of the Merton borough of Greater London

Title: A *georgic* is a didactic poem that gives instruction on farming.

10   from China to English verges
on deliberate botanical

poem

1972

Bird Appeal

We are one with nature O!
don't go away rizla never
leave me
        for a start the golden
5   gouge comes wrapped in ampoules
of mild pain killer for mild
pain
        not as precise as some
social poems perhaps
10   or miscellaneous objects

In another description
the sea rages against specific
bananas
        a form of lockjaw
15   keeps the peanut boats from ever
coming into harbour
                'craw craw'
the gentle gulls remark
'when will it end?
20   say when'
          NEVER
says the intuitive arrow
NEVER

1983

Blue Crêpe

The sky lowers itself to my book
and your reading of it as blue,
Materia prima, are, as if the touch
was perfectly defined, the terminal
5   occurrence when ceiling plaster floated
along the surface of crêpes normandes
steeped in biting calvados. I thought of you

10: *verges*: both verb and noun (meaning a grass edging to a road or flowerbed)

2: *rizla*: a brand of rolling paper for tobacco
5: *ampoules*: sealed glass flasks or capsules containing medicine ready for hypodermic injection

3: *Materia prima*: "first matter" (Latin), the original matter from which the material world was formed.
7: *calvados*: alcohol distilled from cider; named after Calvados, a department of Normandy, France

on the channel boat, speculating on your arrival
in Honfleur to research the Boudin mysteries.
10   Such light, the blue wind bleaching shingle
to an almost undefinable white.

There will always be you in my mind mingling
with the discomforts such as tremble and decisions
about range, colour and definitions of space,
15   what I have to do each time I persuade
response, the gesture of feinting at
a tender but acrimonious embrace, like a pug.

And the reactive move you make of it each time
(I want to underline its dangers)
20   my pitch which never gets finished within
the perfection I know of, to which I return
with new ambitions and patrician idiocies,
excising, curtaining against the adjectival
and shadowed bird as I reach out for my black songs,
25   that music, and make flowers of them, moving towards
your marvellous doctrines, taking no one
with me except always you
or simply your own translucent symmetry.

1988

9: The French landscape painter Eugène *Boudin* (1824–98) was born in *Honfleur,* a seaport in Calvados.

ELIZABETH JENNINGS (b. 1926)

JENNINGS IS THE ONLY ROMAN CATHOLIC AMONG MOVEMENT POETS, AND THERE IS MUCH about her poems that suggests that her relationship with that group of poets was largely circumstantial. With the exception of a few prose poems, she does, like most of the Movement poets, prefer traditional verse forms, but, as Michael Schmidt has written, her poetry does not employ the "reductive irony" of Movement poets and is more given to "trust and faith" than "wariness."[1] Poems such as "On Its Own" and "Choices" offer readers an intimacy and directness shaped and intensified by the restraints of form. "Fountain," Jennings's own favorite among her poems, is much more than an example of the tourist poems popular in the 1950s. Beginning in the world of the senses and urging us beyond them toward contemplation of the "deepest wonder," it might be thought of as Jennings's *ars poetica*, perhaps as a Christian reworking of the Roman poet Horace's ode "O fons Bandusiae" (*Odes*, Book 3, Poem 13).

Jennings was born in Boston, Lincolnshire. She moved to Oxford as a child and was educated at Oxford High School and St. Anne's College, Oxford, where she received her Master's degree in English Language and Literature. At Oxford she met Philip Larkin, John Wain, and Kingsley Amis, three poets she would later be grouped with as part of the Movement. After graduation Jennings worked as an advertising copywriter and then as librarian at the Oxford City Library. Her first book, *Poems*, appeared in 1953. A second book, *A Way of Looking* (1955), won the Somerset Maugham prize in 1956. Money accompanying the prize allowed her to spend three months in Italy, where many of the poems in her third book, *A Sense of the World* (1958), were written, including "Fountain." After returning to England, she worked as a reader for the publishers Chatto and Windus. In the early 1960s, she suffered a mental breakdown. *Every Changing Shape* (1961), a critical study of poetry and mysticism, was written during her recovery, together with two books of poems detailing her struggle with depression, *Recoveries* (1964) and *The Mind Has Mountains* (1966). *Collected Poems* was published in 1987.

---

[1] *Eleven British Poets*, London, 1989, p. 114.

Choices

Inside the room I see the table laid,
Four chairs, a patch of light the lamp has made

And people there so deep in tenderness
They could not speak a word of happiness.

5   Outside I stand and see my shadow drawn
Lengthening the clipped grass of the cared-for lawn.

Above, their roof holds half the sky behind.
A dog barks bringing distances to mind.

Comfort, I think, or safety then, or both?
10   I warm the cold air with my steady breath.

They have designed a way to live and I,
Clothed in confusion, set their choices by:

Though sometimes one looks up and sees me there,
Alerts his shadow, pushes back his chair

15   And, opening windows wide, looks out at me
And close past words we stare. It seems that he

Urges my darkness, dares it to be freed
Into that room. We need each other's need.

1958

Fountain

Let it disturb no more at first
Than the hint of a pool predicted far in a forest,
Or a sea so far away that you have to open
Your window to hear it.
5   Think of it then as elemental, as being
Necessity,
Not for a cup to be taken to it and not
For lips to linger or eye to receive itself
Back in reflection, simply
10   As water the patient moon persuades and stirs.

And then step closer,
Imagine rivers you might indeed embark on,
Waterfalls where you could
Silence an afternoon by staring but never
15   See the same tumult twice.
Yes come out of the narrow street and enter
The full piazza. Come where the noise compels.
Statues are bowing down to the breaking air.

20
Observe it there—the fountain, too fast for shadows,
Too wild for the lights which illuminate it to hold,
Even a moment, an ounce of water back;
Stare at such prodigality and consider
It is the elegance here, it is the taming,
The keeping fast in a thousand flowering sprays,

25
That builds this energy up but lets the watchers
See in that stress an image of utter calm,
A stillness there. It is how we must have felt
Once at the edge of some perpetual stream,
Fearful of touching, bringing no thirst at all,

30
Panicked by no perception of ourselves
But drawing the water down to the deepest wonder.

1958

On Its Own

Never the same and all again.
Well, no same loss will tear me through
Or the same pain grip me if you
Go on your way. I yet shall gain

5
Knowledge and never wish unknown
The arguments that reach the bone,

The feelings which lay waste the heart.
No tidy place, no, I will have
All the destructiveness of love

10
If I can know, beyond the hurt,
Happiness waits or partly so
But not like once and long ago.

My world shall be dramatic then,
No repetitions, many acts,

15
A few hard treaties, broken tracts,
And peace made stronger yet by pain
Accepted but not chosen when
Love is its own and not again.

1980

CHRISTOPHER MIDDLETON (b. 1926)

MIDDLETON WAS BORN IN TRURO, CORNWALL AND EDUCATED AT FELSTED SCHOOL IN Essex and, after service in the Royal Air Force, at Merton College, Oxford, where he completed work for his PhD in 1954. He taught at the University of Zürich for two years and then for eleven years at King's College, University of London. In 1966, he became Chair of the Department of Germanic Languages and Literatures at the University of Texas, Austin, where he taught until his retirement. Middleton has published translations of Swiss and German writers, including Robert Walser, Gottfried Benn, Hugo von Hoffmansthal, Friedrich Hölderlin, Christa Wolf, and, with Michael Hamburger, Paul Celan and Günter Grass. His books of poetry and criticism include *Torse 3: Poems 1949–1961* (1962), *Our Flowers and Nice Bones* (1969), *The Lonely Suppers of W. V. Balloon* (1975), *Pataxanadu and other prose* (1977), *Bolshevism in Art, and other expository writings* (1978), *Carminalenia* (1980), *Selected Writings* (1989), *Intimate Chronicles* (1996), and *Jackdaw Jiving: selected essays on poetry and translation* (1998).

The elliptical movement of Middleton's poem for his mother, "Hearing Elgar Again," in which he writes that "life is all / A wandering," might be considered beside the following remark from one of his essays: "If I prefer the archipelagic zigzag to to the sturdy continuous 'prose tradition' of English, it is because the latter has been made, somehow, inaccessible to me by experiences of my own, which are not American experiences."[1] As his last phrase indicates, Middleton has sometimes felt as estranged from the poetry prevailing in his adopted country as from the post-Movement verse of his native England. "Reflections on a Viking Prow" (1983), for instance, is critical of "confessional poetry," celebrating a history of the artifact as icon and promoting a view of artifice that has nothing to do with "foregrounding . . . subjective compulsions [and] cataloguing impressions" or "hanging an edict from an anecdote."[2] In the same essay, Middleton argues that "To recapture poetic reality in a tottering world, we may have to revise, once more, the idea of a poem as an expression of the 'contents' of a subjectivity. Some poems, at least, and some types of poetic language, constitute structures of a singularly radiant kind, where 'self-expression' has undergone a profound change of function. We experience these structures, if not as revelations of being, then as apertures upon being."[3] Middleton's reference to "apertures upon being" reflects the influence of Martin Heidegger's philosophy, which together with the poetry of Hölderlin and Rilke and traditions of shamanic song underwrite his

---

[1] "For Marton, Erwin, and Miklos," *The Pursuit of the Kingfisher*, Manchester, 1883, p. 48.
[2] *Selected Writings*, Manchester, 1989, p. 284.
[3] Ibid., p. 283.

post-Cartesian view of the relationship of self and world, in which one seeks to "retrieve matter into the rumorous life of reflection."[4] Ian Gregson argues that "The Prose of Walking Back to China" refers to Middleton's "ideal poetic project, in which the act of poetic composition—through its restructuring and defamiliarising strategies—can reconstitute experience by restoring its origins."[5] The poem glosses its own movement in the phrase "But you only find the place to stand / By moving as you may."

---

[4] Ibid., p. 300.
[5] *Contemporary Poetry and Postmodernism,* New York, 1996, p. 162.

Hearing Elgar Again

FOR D.M.M. AT 75

Not crocked exactly, but in a doze,
There I was, before supper time: Elgar,
Stop your meteoric noise, the glory
Leaves me cold; then it was
5   I woke to the melody—

Back, a place, 1939, and people
Singing, little me among them,
Fresh from a holiday
Summer, beside the Cornish sea, I sang
10   In chorus with a hundred English people.

You choose to live, as far as possible,
Spontaneously. So life is all
A wandering—curious orchestra, the whole
Sound of it accords with such
15   Invention of melody, song half-buried

By tympani, trombones, the glorious hot
Imperium. A life proceeds,
It is all, all of it, found in the instant:
Look, flowing, a friend shone, but wizards,
20   Drunken, forgot what I have to say

And underneath, in her garlic subway,
Busbied Persephone stands and waves
Her tambourine, a rabbit
Drums little feet on a village green, the snare
25   A moon halo strangling him.

Mother—we have gone on while others,
We remember, flew as ash into the sky.

1: *crocked:* dead-beat, exhausted
3: The piece of music is "Land of Hope and Glory," the first of the *Pomp and Circumstance* marches by Sir Edward Elgar (1857–1934) and a traditional expression of musical patriotism.
17: *Imperium:* empire
22: A *busby* is a tall fur hat worn by guardsmen. *Persephone* was carried off from the world above by Hades, king of the underworld in Greek myth, to become his queen.
26–27: The *others* who *flew as ash into the sky* are death-camp victims, their bodies having been incinerated.

To what? We have gone
On, dense trees, birdsong in cool petals
30   Never the ignored sustenance;

Rolling music is what deceives us, only
An appetite springs from the core,—
Melody, in a flash,
A harsh frog croaks in the creek now,
35   A bit of rain has touched my hand. Why?

1980

The Prose of Walking Back to China

The poem began when I walked out,
Early, discovering forty minutes to go
Before the traffic would raise its roar.
It was nothing at all but the motion
5   Of walking, nothing at all
But the sight of a fish head in a heap
Of trash in a pail, a flower, an egg shell,
Until I began to compose it in my head.
And until
10   An amazed man with a beard scooped
Colour photos out of a cardboard box
Close to a wall, and a couple of doors away
A dog discovered a bone in a bin,
My skin thickened. A mouldy lemon
15   Took the first heat of day in the Rue Madame
As I turned to the left
And an old lady
Hosing the pavement said: 'Il faut
Arroser, hein?' with a laugh, and I
20   Actually found the words to say: 'La rosée même,
Madame, c'est vous.'
Was this the poem? Up Rue Vavin it went,
With shirts in a window, was
It this, the stacks of little magnetic cakes
25   In the patisserie where schoolgirls go,
And this, in La Rotonde, the waiter of
Two years ago not recognizing me?
The trash truck whines as it grinds
Rot to powder; the poem
30   Attacked by fleets of random objects
Had no purity or perspective whatever.
Ninety tomorrow Marc Chagall declares
You are nothing if you have
Materialist ideas. A capless man
35   Sponges down the glass walls of the bus shelter.

18ff: "You have to water it, don't you?" . . . "You're the morning dew yourself."
32: *Marc Chagall* (1887–1985), the (Belorussian-born) French painter

Again I scan the print, see: Nuclear reactors,
Negociations, a charge of treason,
Crucial support, failed to progress,
Emigrate to Israel, why do the words
40 Come in the plodding rhythm of the poem
If the poem isn't? Now the sun's heat
Goes up another notch, I gulp
The last of the coffee and trundle on,
Along the Boulevard Montparnasse,
45 Crisscrossing it
For a line of books, a cluster of lamps,
A Syrian store with distinctive
Waistcoats, coral and silver on display,
Suddenly arrive, walking the poem,
50 There where the chestnut trees in full leaf
Frame lawns punctuated by statues.
The sprinkler's long horizontal bar
Rotating flung the water up in a fan,
So that it fell
55 Far across the grass and over the wavering
Fronds (at least I thought
These were 'fronds'), it dripped from the beards
Of bronze lions topping the pedestal
Of an old lamp, this might be
60 A thing to watch, like the poem
You can't write, ever, this
Machine dispensed
Freshness, beginning
Everywhere it touched, for sparrows
65 And the grass at least. I
Sat in the sun which had risen
Above the long green wave
Of Indistinguishable Trees, in the dust
My boots were settling among
70 Delicate prints of the feet of birds,
A broken egg shell, also a naked
Razor blade. The blackbird
Is listening for a Worm, he
Can place it by a slight
75 Shift of his head, and I was listening
For the poem, but heard, placeable nowhere,
Pure low Bach notes on a flute,
The flute
Undulates, the dove's flight
80 Undulates, descending spray
Fans out like nervous wings from shoulder blades
And floats to earth as the flute again
Soars upward. A dog trotted across
The sunlit opposite street. A gnat
85 Glittered for an instant in mid-air.
From where I am the flute is clear,
I cross the grass to be closer, it has gone,
Almost, into the traffic's roar.
A woman in an open window says
90 'Yes, I hear it, sometimes, yes,

But I don't know, I live here, yes,
But really I don't know,' and on she went
With the ironing. Could she be
A scalded grandchild of one of those women
95   The musician took through a secret door
In Saint-Merry? Not for bewitching as
Her grandma had been? The flute
Plays on and on and I thought
Not the moon is seen but fingers pointing,
100   How could she ever tell me
What can't be matched by dharma?
Perspective makes a space intelligible,
But you only find the place to stand
By moving as you may, for luck, so nothing,
105   Nothing in the voice
Guides the poem but a wave
Continually broken,
And restored in a time to be perceived,
As the flute is perceived, at origin,
110   Before creation.

                                        1980

94ff: In "Le Musicien de Saint-Merry," a poem by Guillaume Apollinaire (1880–1918), a mysterious strol-
ling musician attracts, Pied-Piper-like, all the women who hear his flute. Musician and women enter a
house and vanish forever.
101: *dharma:* in Buddhism, the universal truth or moral law common to all individuals, as proclaimed by
the Buddha.

CHARLES TOMLINSON (b. 1927)

Discussing his early poem "The Art of Poetry" in an interview, Tomlinson says that "In arguing for words to earn their keep, I was arguing for a kind of exactness in face of the object, which meant an exactness of feeling in the writer. I meant that you must enter into a relationship with things, that you must use your eyes and see what they were offering you—what, at first, you might not notice. I suppose I learned this lesson from Ruskin's *Modern Painters*."[1] Tomlinson's phenomenological poems make relationship their dominant theme—the relationship of perceiver and perceived in the space-time continuum, of poem and reader. His poems are thick with descriptive detail, but they are never merely descriptive, offering instead wary contemplation of what Tomlinson speaks of as "openings through place into mystery. Place—this place—speaks to me more than the dogmas of any religion, and it speaks to me of very fundamental things: time, death, what we have in common with the animals, what things are like when you stop talking and look, what Eden is like, what a center is."[2] His remark here might be considered beside the "angel of appearances" mentioned in "Annunciations," the "domestic miracle" of an endlessly renewed light spilling from "a grail of origin."

Tomlinson has written about his friendship with and debt to American poets such as Marianne Moore and George Oppen in *Some Americans* (1981), and his poetry was at first better received in the United States than in his native England. His first mature book, *The Necklace* (1955), was helped to publication by an introduction written by his mentor and friend Donald Davie, and his second, *Seeing Is Believing* (1958; 1960), was first published in the United States thanks to the critic Hugh Kenner. Tomlinson's work draws substantially on American modernism, but critics have also noted a neo-Augustan diction and moral sensibility reflecting his engagement with English traditions. As translator, Tomlinson has produced versions of César Vallejo, Octavio Paz, Antonio Machado, and Giuseppe Ungaretti, and he has collaborated with Paz and other poets.

Born in Stoke-on-Trent, Staffordshire, and educated locally and at Queen's College, Cambridge and the Royal Holloway and Bedford Colleges of the University of London, Tomlinson taught for many years at the University of Bristol. Among his many books are the volumes of poetry *American Scenes and Other Poems* (1966), *The Way of a World* (1969), *Written on Water* (1972), *The Way In and Other Poems* (1974), *The Shaft* (1978), *The Flood* (1981), *The Return* (1987), *Annunciations* (1989), *The Door*

---

[1] Charles Tomlinson and Alan Ross, "Words on Water: An Interview," *Charles Tomlinson: Man and Artist,* ed. Kathleen O'Gorman, Columbia, Missouri, 1988, p. 25

[2] Ibid., p. 35.

in the Wall (1992), and *Jubilation* (1995). He has edited *The Oxford Book of Verse in English Translation* (1980) and *William Carlos Williams: Selected Poems* (1985). Tomlinson is also a respected visual artist, noted especially for his use of collage and the surrealist technique called decalcomania, in which paint or ink is spread out on a sheet of paper and a second sheet is pressed onto the first and quickly drawn off, creating forms used as the basis of a new picture.

Aesthetic

Reality is to be sought, not in concrete,
But in space made articulate:
The shore, for instance,
Spreading between wall and wall;
5   The sea-voice
Tearing the silence from the silence.

1955

Distinctions

The seascape shifts.

Between the minutest interstices of time
Blue is blue.

A pine-branch
5   Tugs at the eye: the eye
Returns to grey-blue, blue-black or indigo
Or it returns, simply,
To blue-after-the-pine-branch.

Here, there is no question of aberrations
10   Into pinks, golds or mauves:
This is the variation Pater indicated
But failed to prove.

Art exists at a remove.
Evocation, at two,
15   Discusses a blue that someone
Heard someone talking about.

1958

11: *Pater:* Walter Pater (1839–94), novelist and art critic.

Saving the Appearances

The horse is white. Or it
appears to be under this
November light that could
well be October. It goes
5   as nimbly as a spider does
but it is gainly: the great
field makes it small
so that it seems
to crawl out of the distance
10   and to grow not larger
but less slow. Stains
on its sides show where
the mud is and the power
now overmasters the fragility
15   of its earlier bearing. Tall
it shudders over one and bends
a full neck, cropping
the foreground, blotting
the whole space back.
20   behind those pounding feet.
Mounted, one feels the sky
as much the measure of the event
as the field had been, and all
the divisions of the indivisible
25   unite again, or seem
to do as when the approaching
horse was white, on this
November unsombre day
where what appears, is.

1966

Swimming Chenango Lake

Winter will bar the swimmer soon.
    He reads the water's autumnal hesitations
A wealth of ways: it is jarred,
    It is astir already despite its steadiness,
5   Where the first leaves at the first
    Tremor of the morning air have dropped
Anticipating him, launching their imprints
    Outwards in eccentric, overlapping circles.
There is a geometry of water, for this
10   Squares off the clouds' redundances
And sets them floating in a nether atmosphere

Title: To *save the appearances* is to reconcile the observed facts of celestial motion with one's astronomi-
cal theories, when these appear in contradiction, as, e.g., adherents of the Ptolemaic account of the cos-
mos were forced to do.

Title: *Chenango Lake* is in New York State. Tomlinson has commented usefully on this poem in *The Poem
as Initiation* (Hamilton, NY, 1968).

All angles and elongations: every tree
Appears a cypress as it stretches there
And every bush that shows the season,
15 A shaft of fire. It is a geometry and not
A fantasia of distorting forms, but each
Liquid variation answerable to the theme
It makes away from, plays before:
It is a consistency, the grain of the pulsating flow.
20   But he has looked long enough, and now
Body must recall the eye to its dependence
As he scissors the waterscape apart
And sways it to tatters. Its coldness
Holding him to itself, he grants the grasp,
25 For to swim is also to take hold
On water's meaning, to move in its embrace
And to be, between grasp and grasping, free.
He reaches in-and-through to that space
The body is heir to, making a where
30   In water, a possession to be relinquished
Willingly at each stroke. The image he has torn
Flows-to behind him, healing itself,
Lifting and lengthening, splayed like the feathers
Down an immense wing whose darkening spread
35 Shadows his solitariness: alone, he is unnamed
By this baptism, where only Chenango bears a name
In a lost language he begins to construe—
A speech of densities and derisions, of half-
Replies to the questions his body must frame
40   Frogwise across the all but penetrable element.
Human, he fronts it and, human, he draws back
From the interior cold, the mercilessness
That yet shows a kind of mercy sustaining him.
The last sun of the year is drying his skin
45 Above a surface a mere mosaic of tiny shatterings,
Where a wind is unscaping all images in the flowing obsidian,
The going-elsewhere of ripples incessantly shaping.

                                        1969

Prometheus

Summer thunder darkens, and its climbing
Cumulae, disowning our scale in the zenith,
Electrify this music: the evening is falling apart.
Castles-in-air; on earth: green, livid fire.

Title: *Prometheus* was the Titan who, in Greek legend, brought fire down from the heavens for the use of mankind. "'Prometheus' refers to the tone-poem by Scriabin and to his hope of transforming the world by music and rite." (Tomlinson's note). Aleksandr Nikolayevitch Scriabin (1872–1915) intended his *Prometheus: The Poem of Fire* (1911) to be performed accompanied by changing colors projected by a special color keyboard.
2: *Cumulae:* cumulus clouds (rounded in shape, with a flat base)

5   The radio simmers with static to the strains
           Of this mock last-day of nature and of art.

       We have lived through apocalypse too long:
           Scriabin's dinosaurs! Trombones for the transformation
       That arrived by train at the Finland Station,
10   To bury its hatchet after thirty years in the brain
       Of Trotsky. Alexander Nikolayevitch, the events
           Were less merciful than your mob of instruments.

       Too many drowning voices cram this waveband.
           I set Lenin's face by yours—
15   Yours, the fanatic ego of eccentricity against
           The systematic son of a schools inspector
       Tyutchev on desk—for the strong man reads
           Poets as the antisemite pleads: 'A Jew was my friend.'

       Cymballed firesweeps. Prometheus came down
20   In more than orchestral flame and Kérensky fled
       Before it. The babel of continents gnaws now
           And tears at the silk of those harmonies that seemed
       So dangerous once. You dreamed an end
           Where the rose of the world would go out like a close in music.

25   Population drags the partitions down
           And we are a single town of warring suburbs:
       I cannot hear such music for its consequence:
           Each sense was to have been reborn
       Out of a storm of perfumes and light
30   To a white world, an in-the-beginning.

       In the beginning, the strong man reigns:
           Trotsky, was it not then you brought yourself
       To judgement and to execution, when you forgot
           Where terror rules, justice turns arbitrary?
35   Chromatic Prometheus, myth of fire,
           It is history topples you in the zenith.

       Blok too, wrote The Scythians
           Who should have known: he who howls
       With the whirlwind, with the whirlwind goes down.
40   In this, was Lenin guiltier than you
       When, out of a merciless patience grew
           The daily prose such poetry prepares for?

9–11: Lenin returned to Russia from his refuge in *Finland* to instigate the Bolshevik coup of October 1917 against the provisional government of Kerensky. Leon *Trotsky* (1879–1940) was the military leader of the Bolsheviks; he lost the political struggle with Stalin after Lenin's death, and was exiled. He was assassinated in his Mexican home by a Stalinist agent.

17: *Tyutchev:* the Russian poet Fyodor Ivanovich Tyutchev (1803–1873), a favorite author of Lenin's.

20: After the abdication of the Tsar in February 1917 Aleksandr Fyodorovich *Kerensky*, a moderate socialist revolutionary, became the leader of the Russian provisional government.

37: *Blok:* Aleksandr Aleksandrovich Blok (1880–1921), the Russian Symbolist poet; his ode "The Scythians" is addressed to Europe, speaking of Russia's messianic role in the new world order and warning the West not to interfere or be consumed.

Scriabin, Blok, men of extremes,
    History treads out the music of your dreams
45 Through blood, and cannot close like this
    In the perfection of anabasis. It stops. The trees
Continue raining though the rain has ceased
    In a cooled world of incessant codas:

Hard edges of the houses press
50   On the after-music senses, and refuse to burn,
Where an ice cream van circulates the estate
    Playing Greensleeves, and at the city's
Stale new frontier even ugliness
    Rules with the cruel mercy of solidities.

1969

Annunciation

The cat took fright
at the flashing wing of sunlight
as the thing
entered the kitchen, angel of appearances,
5 and lingered there.

What was it the sun
had sent to say
by his messenger, this solvent ray,
that charged and changed
10 all it looked at, narrowing even the eye of a cat?

Utensils caught a shine
that could not be used, utility
unsaid by this invasion
from outer space, this gratuitous occasion
15 of unchaptered gospel.

'I shall return,' the appearance promised,
'I shall not wait for the last
day—every day
is fortunate even when you catch
20 my ray only as a gliding ghost.

What I foretell
is the unaccountable birth each time
my lord the light, a cat and you
share this domestic miracle:
25 it asks the name anew

46: *anabasis*: marching

Title: The poem responds to the painting *Annunciation* (c. 1527), by Lorenzo Lotto (reproduced on the
cover of Tomlinson's *Annunciations*); it depicts an angel hailing the Virgin Mary as she prays in one cor-
ner of a domestic scene. A cat—a traditional symbol of evil—leaps in fright away from the angel; above,
God leans out of a cloud, pointing at Mary.

of each thing named
when an earlier, shining dispensation
reached down into mist
and found the solidity
30   these windows and these walls surround,

and where each cup,
dish, hook and nail
now gathers and guards the sheen
drop by drop
35   still spilling-over
out of the grail of origin.'

1989

The Plaza

People are the plot
and what they do here—
which is mostly sit
or walk through. The afternoon sun
5   brings out the hornets:
they dispute with no one, they too
are enjoying their ease
along the wet brink of the fountain,
imbibing peace and water
10   until a child arrives,
takes off his shoe
and proceeds methodically
to slaughter them. He has the face
and the ferocious concentration
15   of one of those Aztec gods
who must be fed on blood.
His mother drags him away, half-shod,
and then puts back the shoe
over a dusty sock.
20   Some feet go bare, some sandalled,
like these Indians who march through
—four of them—carrying a bed
as if they intended to sleep here.
Their progress is more brisk
25   than that of the ants at our feet
who are removing—some
by its feelers, some
supporting it on their backs—
a dead moth
30   as large as a bird.
As the shadows densen
in the gazebo-shaped bandstand
the band are beginning to congregate.

Annunciation: 27: dispensation: In Christian theology, there have historically been three dispensations
(divinely ordained religious systems): the Patriarchal, Mosaic, and Christian.

The air would be tropical
35   but for the breath of the sierra:
it grows opulent on the odour
of jacaranda and the turpentine
of the shoeshine boys
busy at ground-level,
40   the squeak of their rags on leather
like an angry, repeated bird-sound.
The conductor rises,
flicks his score with his baton—
moths are circling the bandstand light—
45   and sits down after each item.
The light falls onto the pancakes
of the flat military hats
that tilt and nod
as the musicians under them
50   converse with one another—then,
the tap of the baton. It must be
the presence of so many flowers enriches the brass:
tangos take on a tragic air,
but the opaque scent
55   makes the modulation into waltz-time seem
an invitation—not to the waltz merely—
but to the thought that there may be
the choice (at least for the hour)
of dying like Carmen
60   then rising like a flower.
A man goes by, carrying a fish
that is half his length
wrapped in a sheet of plastic
but nobody sees him. And nobody hears
65   the child in a torn dress
selling artificial flowers,
mouthing softly in English, 'Flowerrs'.
High heels, bare feet
around the tin cupola of the bandstand
70   patrol to the beat of the band:
this is the democracy
of the tierra templada—a contradiction
in a people who have inherited
so much punctilio, and yet
75   in all the to-and-fro
there is no frontier set:
the shopkeepers, the governor's sons,
the man who is selling balloons
in the shape of octopuses, bandannaed heads
80   above shawled and suckled children
keep common space
with a trio of deaf mutes
talking together in signs,
all drawn to the stir

59: *Carmen:* i.e., in Bizet's opera *Carmen*
72: *tierra templada:* "temperate country" (Spanish)
74: *punctilio:* adherence to custom and formal manners

85   of this rhythmic pulse
     they cannot hear. The musicians
     are packing away their instruments:
     the strollers have not said out their say
     and continue to process
90   under the centennial trees.
     A moon has worked itself free
     of the excluding boughs
     above the square, and stands
     unmistily mid-sky, a precisionist.
95   The ants must have devoured their prey by this.
     As for the fish . . . three surly Oaxaqueños
     are cutting and cooking it
     to feed a party of French-speaking Swiss
     at the Hotel Calesa Real.
100   The hornets that failed to return
     stain the fountain's edge,
     the waters washing and washing away at them,
     continuing throughout the night
     their whisperings of ablution
105   where no one stirs,
     to the shut flowerheads and the profuse stars.

                 1989

The Garden

FOR PAULA AND FRED

              And now they say
     Gardens are merely the expression of a class
Masterful enough to enamel away
     All signs of the labour that produced them.
5   This crass reading forgets that imagination
         Outgoes itself, outgrows aim
And origin; forgets that art
     Does not offer the sweat of parturition
As proof of its sincerity. The guide-book, too,
10   Dislikes this garden we are descending through
On a wet day in Gloucestershire. It speaks
     Accurately enough of windings and of water,
Half-lost pavilion, mossy cascade,
     But is afraid 'the style is thin.' One must smile
15   At the irritability of critics, who
         Impotent to produce, secrete over what they see
Their dislike or semi-assent, then blame
     The thing they have tamed for being tame.
But today, see only how
20   Laden in leaves, the branchwork canopy—

96: *Oaxaqueños:* inhabitants of Oaxaca, in Mexico, the setting of the poem
104: *ablution:* washing

The Garden: The setting is Stancombe Park, near Dursley, in Gloucestershire.
8: *parturition:* giving birth

Bough on bough, rearing a dense
   Mobile architecture—shudders beneath its finery
In cool July. Heat, no doubt,
   Would flesh out the secret of this garden where
25   (Or so it's said) the man who imagined it
   Could wind down to find
His gypsy inamorata waiting there
   By the hidden lake.
                     There are three lakes here
30   And a fluttering curtain of rain that falls
   Differently in each. The first
Lies open to the farmland and it takes
   The full gust and disordering of the weather
Across its surface. The second—
35   We have descended further now
Bending our way in under each low bough—
   Shelters between the hills' high shoulders,
And so the green, smooth plain of water
   Lies taut under the nail-points of the rain.
40   We must enter next a key-hole door
   Into darkness: through a rough window-slit
We catch a runnel wrinkling over stone,
   And the pool that stretches to receive it
So fills the aperture we can not take in
45   Its true extent: we are all eye—
Which is not eye enough to outdo
   The dark we are trying to gaze out through.
A twist in the tunnel: light! We are delivered
   And now we can freely move
50   Beneath a pergola 'in the precise arch'
   (I quote to show the disapproval I disapprove)
'Of a railway terminus.' This is no end
   However, but the start of the final lake.
You can see the rain withdraw across
55   This widest of the waters, the transparent scrim
Suddenly towed aside, and calm
   Flowing up to its receding hem:
Fish in the cloudy depths might well be swimming
   Through sky such as threatens us still.
60   We have the hill to re-ascend, and do,
   Up to the formal garden at its summit:
The statuary, the espaliered avenue
   Ignore the twisting path. The descent
To the hidden lake now hoards from sight
65   The walks and walls, the subterranean door
Into an imaginary place that time
   Turned real. The imagination hovers here
Half rebuked, with its Doric and Chinese;

27: *inamorata*: lover
42: *runnel*: small stream
50: *pergola*: a covered walk, formed from arched trellis-work overgrown with plants
55: *scrim*: a scrim (semi-transparent) curtain
62: *espaliered*: with fruit trees or shrubs trained to grow flat on trellises or against walls
68: *Doric*: a style of ancient Greek architecture

Nor can a planned secretiveness outdo
70   The cool green of that chamber
      Shut from view beneath the gloom
Of the copper beech. Its tent conceals
      Not darkness, but an inner room,
An emerald cell of leaves whose light
75   Seems self-sustaining, and its floor
A ground for the reconciling of our dreams
      With what is there.
                 So here we stand,
We two, and two from another land,
80   To meditate the gift we did not ask—
The work of seasons and of hands unseen
      Tempering time. What has not disappeared
Is a design that grew—ultimately to include
      (Beside plants of oriental and American species)
85 Us four, in its playful image of infinity,
      The whole of it assembled with a view
To generations beyond the planter's: there is nothing here
      We shall ever own, nothing that he owns now,
In those reflections of summer trees on water,
90   This composure awaiting the rain and snow.

1989

THOMAS KINSELLA (b. 1928)

K INSELLA WAS BORN IN DUBLIN AND EDUCATED AT O'CONNELLS SCHOOL AND UNI-
versity College, Dublin. From 1946 to 1965, he worked in the Irish Civil Service.
He then taught in the United States, first at Southern Illinois University and for many
years at Temple University, where he was professor of English and founder and direc-
tor of the Temple-in-Dublin Irish tradition program. He has been the director of the
Dolmen Press and Cuala Press in Dublin. In 1972, he founded the Peppercanister
Press, which has issued much of his later work, beginning with *Butcher's Dozen*
(1972), Kinsella's response to the Widgery Tribunal's report on the violence in Derry
on January 30, 1972 ("Bloody Sunday"). Among his dozens of books and pamphlets are
The Starlit Eye (1952), *Another September* (1958), *Downstream* (1962), *Nightwalker and
Other Poems* (1968), *Notes from the Land of the Dead and Other Poems* (1972), *Pepper-
canister Poems 1972–1978* (1979), *Blood and Family* (1988), and *Poems 1956–1994*
(1996). He is the translator of the ancient Irish epic *The Táin* (1969) and other Irish-
language poetry. He has edited *The New Oxford Book of Irish Verse* (1986) and pub-
lished criticism including *The Dual Tradition: An Essay on Poetry and Politics in Ire-
land* (1995).

Much of Kinsella's work as translator, editor, and critic can be contextualized by
a reading of his influential essay "The Divided Mind" (1973), which outlines the dilem-
mas of the modern Anglo-Irish writer who necessarily cannot be fully at home in tra-
ditions of English poetry. The essay describes the "gapped, discontinuous, polyglot
tradition" the Anglo-Irish poet assumes as a simultaneously disabling and enabling
fact of Irishness and modernity, and proclaims Joyce rather than Yeats as Kinsella's
most significant model.[1] Kinsella's familiarity with the work of William Carlos
Williams and Ezra Pound has also shaped some of his later poems. Arguing that Kin-
sella's work as a translator is evident in his poems' "dream-like or nightmare states in
which Irish historical experience and mythological motifs are interwoven with images
from the creative and psychological life," Neil Corcoran notes that the claims of "The
Divided Mind" are put more "optimistically" in the introduction to Kinsella's Oxford
anthology, which speaks of "two linguistic entities in dynamic interaction."[2]

Like Austin Clarke's work, which he has edited, Kinsella's poems are often set in
Dublin, and exude an urban ennui and disappointment with the failure of modern
Irish culture and politics to live up to the hopes of a revolutionary past. "Baggot Street
Deserta," one of his most anthologized early poems, presents the late-night medita-
tions of a speaker who is "alien" to himself as well as to his past, and has nothing but

---

[1] *Poetry and Ireland Since 1800: A Source Book,* ed. Mark Storey, London, 1988, pp. 207–16.
[2] *After Yeats and Joyce: Reading Modern Irish Literature,* Oxford, 1997, p. 12.

scorn for romantic images of rural Ireland. His wisdom resembles that of Albert Camus' Sisyphus; he has no choice but to *"Endure and let the present punish."* Like many of his poems, "Rituals of Departure" sets Kinsella's family history beside the history of Dublin after the Act of Union, making the torn "roots" of the potato famine of the 1840s representative of the direction of recent Irish history and articulating the poet's anxieties about traditions and origins now irrecoverable.

Baggot Street Deserta

Lulled, at silence, the spent attack.
The will to work is laid aside.
The breaking-cry, the strain of the rack,
Yield, are at peace. The window is wide
5   On a crawling arch of stars, and the night
Reacts faintly to the mathematic
Passion of a cello suite
Plotting the quiet of my attic.
A mile away the river toils
10   Its buttressed fathoms out to sea;
Tucked in the mountains, many miles
Away from its roaring outcome, a shy
Gasp of waters in the gorse
Is sonneting origins. Dreamers' heads
15   Lie mesmerised in Dublin's beds
Flashing with images, Adam's morse.

A cigarette, the moon, a sigh
Of educated boredom, greet
A curlew's lingering threadbare cry
20   Of common loss. Compassionate,
I add my call of exile, half-
Buried longing, half-serious
Anger and the rueful laugh.
We fly into our risk, the spurious.

25   Versing, like an exile, makes
A virtuoso of the heart,
Interpreting the old mistakes
And discords in a work of Art
For the One, a private masterpiece
30   Of doctored recollections. Truth
Concedes, before the dew, its place
In the spray of dried forgettings Youth
Collected when they were a single
Furious undissected bloom.
35   A voice clarifies when the tingle
Dies out of the nerves of time:

Title: *Baggot Street* is a street in Dublin, noted as a locus of bohemian activity and night-life. *Deserta:* deserted
9: *river:* Dublin's River Liffey
25–26: Cf. W.B. Yeats, "Easter 1916": "Too long a sacrifice / Can make a stone of the heart."

Endure and let the present punish.
Looking backward, all is lost;
The Past becomes a fairy bog
40   Alive with fancies, double crossed
By pad of owl and hoot of dog,
Where shaven, serious-minded men
Appear with lucid theses, after
Which they don the mists again
45   With trackless, cotton-silly laughter;
Secretly a swollen Burke
Assists a decomposing Hare
To cart a body of good work
With midnight mutterings off somewhere;
50   The goddess who had light for thighs
Grows feet of dung and takes to bed,
Affronting horror-stricken eyes,
The marsh bird that children dread.

I nonetheless inflict, endure,
55   Tedium, intracordal hurt,
The sting of memory's quick, the drear
Uprooting, burying, prising apart
Of loves a strident adolescent
Spent in doubt and vanity.
60   All feed a single stream, impassioned
Now with obsessed honesty,
A tugging scruple that can keep
Clear eyes staring down the mile,
The thousand fathoms, into sleep.

65   Fingers cold against the sill
Feel, below the stress of flight,
The slow implosion of my pulse
In a wrist with poet's cramp, a tight
Beat tapping out endless calls
70   Into the dark, as the alien
Garrison in my own blood
Keeps constant contact with the main
Mystery, not to be understood.
Out where imagination arches
75   Chilly points of light transact
The business of the border-marches
Of the Real, and I—a fact
That may be countered or may not—
Find their privacy complete.

80   My quarter-inch of cigarette
Goes flaring down to Baggot Street.

1958

46–47: The nineteenth-century murderers William *Burke* and William *Hare* were Irish-born; they operated in Edinburgh, murdering victims in order to sell their corpses to a medical school for dissection. Here they become figures of academic literary dissection, enemies of the goddess of poetry.
55: *intracordal:* inside the heart
76: *border-marches:* frontiers

Ritual of Departure

I

Open the soft string that clasps in series
A dozen silver spoons, and spread them out,
Matched perfectly, one maker and to the year,
Brilliant in use from the first inheritor.

5   A stag crest stares from the soft solid silver
With fat cud lips and jaws that could crack bones.
The stag heart stumbles, rearing at bay,
Rattling a trophied head, slavering silver.

*

A portico, beggars moving on the steps.
10   A horserider locked in soundless greeting,
Bowed among dogs and dung. A panelled vista
Closing on pleasant smoke-blue far-off hills.

The same city distinct in the same air,
More open in an earlier evening light,
15   In sweet-breathing death-ease after forced Union.
Domes, pillared, in the afterglow.

2

The ground opens. Pale wet potatoes
Fall into light. The black soil falls from their flesh,
From the hands that tear them up and spread them out,
20   Perishable roots to eat.

Fields dying away
Among white rock and red bog—saturated
High places traversed by spring sleet,
Thrust up through the thin wind into pounding silence.

Farther South: landscape with ancestral figures.
25   Names settling and intermixing on the earth.

The poem is a meditation on Kinsella's departure for the United States in 1965, moving into more general
reflections on past dispossessions in Irish history and their impact on his ancestors.
13: *the same city*: Dublin, here after the 1801 Act of Union, which joined Great Britain and Ireland under
the name of the United Kingdom, abolishing the Irish Parliament.
20: The Irish Potato Famine of 1845–1849 had catastrophic consequences for the island's population: over
a million people died from starvation and disease; about 1.5 million emigrated to the United States and
Britain.

The seed in slow retreat into bestial silence.
Faces sharpen and grow blank, with eyes for nothing.

*

And their children's children vanished in the city lanes.

I saw the light enter from the laneway
30   Through the scullery, and creep to the foot of the stairs
Over grey floorboards, and sink in plush
In the staleness of an inner room.

I scoop at the earth and sense famine,
A sourness in the clay. The roots tear softly.

3

35   A man at the moment of departure, turning
To leave, treasures some stick of furniture
With slowly blazing eyes, or the very door
Broodingly with his hand as it falls shut.

1968

GAEL TURNBULL (b. 1928)

Turnbull was born in Edinburgh to a Scottish father and a Swedish-American mother. Part of his youth was spent in Winnipeg, Canada, where his father, a Presbyterian minister, had charge of a church during World War II. After studying natural science at Cambridge University, Turnbull took a degree in medicine at the University of Pennsylvania. His first medical practice was in Ontario, where he also began his literary career by publishing poems in Canadian magazines. Introduced by a friend to Cid Corman's influential magazine *Origin,* Turnbull began publishing there among poets such as Robert Creeley, Charles Olson, and William Bronk. In 1956, he returned to England and started Migrant Books, which published English editions of Black Mountain poets first published by Origin Press and Jargon Books in the United States. In England he found a few English poets, such as the older Basil Bunting and his contemporary Roy Fisher, who shared his interest in the modernist traditions deriving from the work of Ezra Pound and William Carlos Williams. Jobs for doctors being scarce in England, Turnbull lived in California from 1958 and 1964, where *Migrant* began its run as a magazine and the renamed Migrant Press began publishing books by poets including Ian Hamilton Finlay, Edward Dorn, and Edwin Morgan. After 1964, Turnbull worked as a general practitioner and anaesthetist in England, then retired to Edinburgh in 1989.

Turnbull's books include *A Trampoline: Poems 1952–1964* (1968), *Scantlings: Poems 1964–1969* (1970), *Residues* (1976), and *While Breath Persist* (1992). His long poem, *Twenty Words, Twenty Days,* first published in *Poetry* (Chicago), consists of twenty sections, each generated by the random choice of a word from a dictionary. In a syntax moving across fragments of narrative and descriptive detail in probing, qualifying phrases—"coiling, uncoiling, recoiling / returning, turning"—Turnbull mediates on the possible uses of each of his key words as they allow him to evaluate his experience and the experience of others. David Miller has remarked on the poem's "largely conversational tone, the non-rhetorical and anti-decorative, spare and economical (although not highly compressed) language, and the quietly stated, or understated, impress of emotion," adding that it is "a close kin of that 'poetry-in-prose' which is so notable in contemporary writing."[1]

---

[1] "Heart of Saying: The Poetry of Gael Turnbull," *New British Poetries: The Scope of the Possible,* ed. Robert Hampson and Peter Barry, Manchester, UK, 1993, p. 191.

George Fox, from his Journals

Who had openings within
as he walked in the fields.

(and saw a great crack through the earth)

5   who went by eye across hedge and ditch toward the
       spires of the steeple-houses, until he came to
       Lichfield, and then barefoot in the market place,
       unable to contain, crying out,

       and among friends
       of much tenderness of conscience,
10   of a spirit by which all things might be judged
       by waiting
       for openings within, which would answer each other

(and after that crack, a great smoke)

       and in a lousy stinking place, low in the ground,
15   without even a bed, among thirty convicts, where
       he was kept almost half a year, the excrement over
       the top of his shoes,

       as he gathered his mind inward,
       a living hope arose

20   (and after that smoke, a great shaking)

       but when he heard the bell toll to call people to
       the steeple-house, it struck at his life; for it
       was like a market-bell, to call them that the
       priest might sell his wares,
25   such as fed upon
       words, and fed one another with words until they
       had spoken themselves dry, and who raged when they
       were told, 'The man in leather breeches is here. . . .'

       a tender man
30   with some experience
       of what had been opened to him.

                                                c. 1962, 1968

Title: *George Fox* (1624–1691) was the founder of the Society of Friends (or Quakers). He stressed the
importance of the inward light of inspiration rather than the mere "words" of scriptural revelation, and
in his *Journal* (an account of his life dictated in his old age) he recounted his direct religious experiences,
which he called "openings." He traveled by foot as an itinerant preacher throughout the Midlands and
north of England; later he visited Ireland and parts of Europe and the American colonies. Because of
their refusal to honor the authority of the government or the established church, pay tithes or take oaths,
Fox and his associates were frequently persecuted and imprisoned.
5: Fox refused to accept that a church was any better as a place to worship God than an ordinary house,
and so distinguished a church as no different except for its having a *steeple*.
28: *leather breeches:* Fox's favored garb; "he found them very durable and practical. It was considered quite
eccentric at the time." (Turnbull, in correspondence)

from Twenty Words, Twenty Days

XVII

to prevent abrasion—
        DEMULCENT—

an agent and an action—
           and I, up half the night working,
5   so today my eyesockets burn, my lips tingle—

my attention drifting in lapses, despite effort, despite all
resolve—
       with flushes, then chills—
                clarity through a haze—

10   nausea upon euphoria—
           and I cling to one strand . . .
the next instant . . . and the one after . . . and . . .

and pause, to breathe deeply, and hear within my ears,
a sound—
15   as if all carried by wheels on rails—
                  chuck,
chuck . . . chock, chock . . . a pulse—
            the universe
unfurled, sliding yonder where I was, where I may be—

20   to an end-point, to a fixity—
         with sleep as a pit—
                  and
fatigue: a mercy, an opiate—
         and as reported in the paper:
25   the Wankel engine, for the first time in a commercial car,
at the Motor Show—
        essentially a single rotary piston
without reciprocating parts, attractive for its simplicity
and excellent torque—
30   with an almost complete lack of
frictional surfaces at which wear could occur—

XVIII

as against: '. . . the first genius of our age. . . .'

Turner, according to a contemporary—
        this afternoon,
reading a magazine, a collection of poems by living

XVII: 2: *DEMULCENT*: any substance that soothes or protects an abraded mucous membrane.
XVIII: 2: *Turner*: J. M. W. Turner (1771–1851), the English landscape painter. His later work moved into
  explorations of light and abstraction that anticipated Impressionism by several decades.

5   authors, all their writing, the mass of it—
                                                so prolix an
           effort—
                     and gloom, not that it can't be read, but can, so
           much of it, so apt, with such singleness, such a pain to be
10   urgent—
                     and I, busy as with a Meccano set, a language
           of nuts, bolts and tin struts, contriving phrases as one
           might improvise toys—
                                for ingenuity, and as a pastime—
15   'Turn the handle. A string runs on a pulley. A hook lifts
           a matchstick. It works!'—
                                a LATTICE—
                                          of bits, lacking
           better, a patchwork—
20   as against: watercolour, the
           'English medium'—
                                where the texture of the pigment
           is determined not merely by the brush but by what is
           given up as the strokes dry, by what is lost from the
25   paper—
                     a purity; but in that, without body, without
           protection against air, against light—
                                          so that what we have
           now in the galleries, mostly but hints—
30   even Ruskin,
           in *his* old age, saying, '. . . have lost something of their
           radiance, my Turners . . . though the best, in that sort,
           are but shadows. . . .
                                'of the day rising up, of the sun
35   shining through vapour . . . through interstices of
           cloud . . . in crannies, the light precipitate as dew . . .
           the colours flared. . . .'
                                '. . . with blue and yellow
           close together in some places, instead of green,' one critic
40   grumbled, 'as if *that* could fool anyone. . . .'

XIX

           Weyland Smith, worker in iron, shoer of horses, linker of
           chain-mail, himself perhaps chained—
                                          a captive, a refugee,
           and said to be lame, perhaps hamstrung when taken, who
5   toils for a master—
                                by the Ridgeway on the Berkshire

---

11: *Meccano set*: a toy construction set
30: The art critic John *Ruskin* (1819–1900) was prompted to write *Modern Painters* by the critical incom-
   prehension that greeted Turner's late works.
XIX: 1: Weyland the Smith, a smith of outstanding skill, is a figure in Scandinavian, German, and Anglo-
   Saxon legend. He was captured by the Swedish King Nídud, lamed to prevent his escape, and forced to
   work in the king's smithy. In revenge he killed Nídud's two sons and raped his daughter, then escaped by
   magically flying through the air. An ancient stone burial chamber (barrow) in Berkshire is known as Wey-
   land's Smithy; it is said that Weyland will shoe a traveler's horse if payment is left on a stone and the trav-
   eler absents himself while the work is done.

Downs, a ruined Long Barrow, ringed with elm, once
used as a forge and given his name, where the turf is alive
under foot and the granular stones, dark as rain clouds
10   on the horizon, lie half submerged where they have
tumbled—
                    and I remember it today, Pay Day, collecting
my cheque, my ration, to be used and hoarded—
                                                    I sign
15   for it, a slave's mark—
                        yet bread in my mouth, and a roof—
a FAMILIARITY—
                    of disgust and of necessity—
                                                    and in
20   that, a sort of reassurance, a persistence—
                                    even a pride, if
not always of craft, then at least of a certain minimal
agility—
                    as if also at the anvil, squeezing the bellows to
25   heat the charcoal to incandescence, the iron thrust deep
until softened, to be hammered and rehammered—
                                                    day
upon day—
                    sweat dripping onto the metal, sizzling
30   in beads, engraving the surface with whorls, with a
lace-tracery pattern—
                        myself imaged and marked—
                                                    as
bondsman—
35   and contriver—

XX

last night, crying out in my sleep (so that Jonnie had to
prod me until I stopped), '. . . but it's murder. . . .'
not in fear, but amazement where I was—
                                    a valley between
5   mountains, with boulders, bracken, straggled clouds down
to tree top, tents, canopies, dripping guy-ropes, banners—

and men: hulking, spare of words, their eyes bloodshot
from urgent travel and the smoke of charcoal braziers,
with rich brocade under their jerkins—
10   inhaling each other's
thought as one might scent—
                            their inmost being finding
sustenance far down, as plants with long tap-roots
growing out of a shale slope—
15   a world imagined, become

XX: 5: *straggled:* dispersed, spread out in untidy strands, like hair
6: *guy-ropes:* the ropes that steady a tent or canopy and prevent it from being blown away

imminent—
        but not mine and blundered into as I slept—

Powys (John Cowper) and his novel *Porius*—
                read so long
20   ago and so ill-remembered, yet unmistakable—
                    never
POOR—
      but a plethora, a gallimaufry—
              and this evening
25   the baby, as she fell asleep after happy struggle in a corner
of her crib, almost upside down, so abruptly, she was
so tired, with one last wail as if tumbled into a chasm—

puir wee thing—
          and I remember an Edinburgh room
30   and one saying, when I asked what he'd done that day,
how much—
       'I tore it up . . . I wisnae pure enough
when I wrote . . . I wisnae pure enough. . . .'
                          1963 / 1966

Thighs Gripping

Thighs gripping, hips
moving in pace—her face
suffused—each breath
short and quick
5   through spread lips,
she is possessed
and lost in the act

trotting
her horse down the lane.
                          1970

18: *Porius: A Romance of the Dark Ages* (1951) is a (very long) novel by the Welsh novelist John Cowper
  Powys (1872–1963).
28: *puir:* poor (Scots)
32: *wisnae:* was not (Scots)

JOHN MONTAGUE (b. 1929)

MONTAGUE WAS BORN IN BROOKLYN, NEW YORK, HIS FATHER HAVING BEEN FORCED to leave Ulster in 1925 because of his republican activities. At the age of four, Montague was sent to live with his father's sister in Garvaghey in County Tyrone. He attended the Catholic school of St. Patrick's College in Armagh and University College, Dublin. After traveling in Europe he returned to the United States in 1953, eventually teaching part-time at the Iowa Writers' Workshop, where he earned an M.F.A. in 1955. Among the poets Montague met in the United States were Robert Penn Warren, W. H. Auden, Robert Lowell, and William Carlos Williams. While living in the Bay Area he heard Allen Ginsberg read his recently published poem "Howl." In 1959, he returned to Dublin, working for Ireland's tourist board. In the early 1960s, Montague was Paris correspondent for the *Irish Times*. Later in the decade, he taught at the University of California, Berkeley and University College, Dublin. In 1972, Montague took a position at University College, Cork, making his home in Cork while also occasionally teaching at universities in North America and France. His many books include *Forms of Exile* (1958), *Poisoned Lands* (1961), *A Chosen Light* (1967), *Tides* (1970), *The Rough Field* (1972), *A Slow Dance* (1975), *The Great Cloak* (1978), *The Dead Kingdom* (1983), and *New Selected Poems* (1990). He is the editor of *The Faber Book of Irish Verse* (1974).

Montague's development as a poet has reflected, in Robert F. Garrett's words, "a gradual movement from a Joycean sense of exile and isolation toward what resembles a Yeatsian dramatization of history and family."[1] Much of his work is autobiographical, though in his use of the details of family and regional history he is, in modernist fashion, often in search of recurrent patterns and archetypes, or what he calls in one early poem "that dark permanence of ancient forms."[2] Montague's most famous and stylistically experimental book is *The Rough Field*, a sequence of poems meditating on Ulster history and the political "troubles" of the late 1960s; the book might be thought of as his effort to reconcile a romantic attachment to his personal and cultural origins with a cosmopolitan critique of contemporary events. Like *The Rough Field*, *The Dead Kingdom* is a sequence of interrelated poems and thus difficult to excerpt; the title refers to Munster, a province associated with female deities and the dead. As the poet sets out from Cork to attend his mother's funeral in Ulster, the "dead kingdom" becomes all of Ireland, the poet traveling back and forth across it through meditation on personal, historical, and mythic material in search of what the penultimate poem names as "The impulse in love / to name the place as / protection and solace; / an exact tenderness."

---

[1] *Modern Irish Poetry: Tradition and Continuity from Yeats to Heaney,* Berkeley, 1986, p. 201.
[2] "Like Dolmens Round My Childhood, The Old People," *Selected Poems,* Winston-Salem, 1982, p. 27.

The Trout

FOR BARRIE COOKE

Flat on the bank I parted
Rushes to ease my hands
In the water without a ripple
And tilt them slowly downstream
5   To where he lay, tendril-light,
In his fluid sensual dream.

Bodiless lord of creation,
I hung briefly above him
Savouring my own absence,
10   Senses expanding in the slow
Motion, the photographic calm
That grows before action.

As the curve of my hands
Swung under his body
15   He surged, with visible pleasure.
I was so preternaturally close
I could count every stipple
But still cast no shadow, until

The two palms crossed in a cage
20   Under the lightly pulsing gills.
Then (entering my own enlarged
Shape, which rode on the water)
I gripped. To this day I can
Taste his terror on my hands.

1967

A Bright Day

FOR JOHN MCGAHERN

At times I see it, present
   As a bright day, or a hill,
The only way of saying something
   Luminously as possible.

5   Not the accumulated richness
   Of an old historical language—
That musk-deep odour!
   But a slow exactness

Dedication: The Irish artist *Barrie Cooke* (b. 1931) is known for his depictions of the natural world, includ-
ing marine life.

Dedication: *John McGahern:* the contemporary Irish novelist and short story writer.

Which recreates experience
    By ritualizing its details—
10 Pale web of curtain, width
    Of deal table, till all

Takes on a witch-bright glow
    And even the clock on the mantel
15 Moves its hands in a fierce delight
    Of so, and so, and so.

1967

The Cage

My father, the least happy
man I have known. His face
retained the pallor
of those who work underground:
5 the lost years in Brooklyn
listening to a subway
shudder the earth.

But a traditional Irishman
who (released from his grille
10 in the Clark Street I.R.T.)
drank neat whiskey until
he reached the only element
he felt at home in
any longer: brute oblivion.

15 And yet picked himself
up, most mornings,
to march down the street
extending his smile
to all sides of the good,
20 (all-white) neighbourhood
belled by St Teresa's church.

When he came back
we walked together
across fields of Garvaghey
25 to see hawthorn on the summer
hedges, as though
he had never left;
a bend of the road

which still sheltered
30 primroses. But we
did not smile in
the shared complicity

The Cage: For the family background of this poem see the headnote above.
10: *I.R.T.:* Interborough Rapid Transit

of a dream, for when
weary Odysseus returns
35   Telemachus should leave.

Often as I descend
into subway or underground
I see his bald head behind
the bars of the small booth;
40   the mark of an old car
accident beating on his
ghostly forehead.

1972

This Neutral Realm

The great achievement of the South of Ireland was to stand aside.
                                        LOUIS MACNEICE

Here, too, they defied Adolf.
A platoon of the L.D.F.
drilled in the parochial hall,
shouldering Lee Enfields.
5   A war intimate as a game,
miles better than Indians,
like the splendid manoeuvres
when the regular army came.

We defended Abbeylara
10   watching the Northern road—
signposts all gone—
from a girdered haybarn,
rifles at the ready,
with dummy cartridges,
15   until Southern Command
came behind our backs:
took over the town.

So I and my cousin
were captured, condemned
20   to spend a warm afternoon
incubating in an armoured car,
peering through slits,

35: The wanderings of *Odysseus* back to Ithaca from the Trojan war took 20 years; his return was awaited
    faithfully by his wife Penelope and son *Telemachus.*

Title: The Republic of Ireland was officially neutral during World War II, while Northern Ireland was an
    important part of the Allied war effort.
Epigraph: for *Louis MacNeice* see p. 330.
2: *L.D.F.*: Local Defence Force
4: *Lee Enfields*: Lee-Enfield rifles
9: *Abbeylara*: a village in Co. Longford, in central Ireland
11: *signposts all gone*: i.e., to confuse any invaders
15: *Southern Command*: the regular Irish army

fingering the intricacy
of a mounted Bren gun.

25 So we learnt to defend
this neutral realm,
each holiday summer,
against all comers,
including the Allies
30 if they dared to cross over
(Hitler being frightened).
Eire's most somnolent time
while, at home, invasion
forces risked chilling seas
35 to assemble in Ulster.

Already seen through
the stereoscopic lens
of a solitary childhood,
our divided allegiances;
40 a mock and a real war:
Spitfire and Messerschmitt
twinned in fire, Shermans
lumbering through our hedges,
ungainly as dinosaurs, while
45 the South marched its toy
soldiers along the sideline.

1984

The Well Dreams

I

The well dreams;
liquid bubbles.

Or it stirs
as a water spider skitters across;
5 a skinny legged dancer.

Sometimes, a gross interruption;
a stone plumps in.
That takes a while to absorb,
to digest, much groaning
10 and commotion in the well's stomach
before it can proffer again
an almost sleek surface.

24: *Bren gun:* a machine gun
33ff: The British in 1938 relinquished occupation of three British naval bases in the Republic, and the
 Republic's neutrality meant that American and British troops and ships instead were forced to assemble
 in Ulster.
41: *Spitfire and Messerschmitt:* respectively, British and German World War II fighter planes
42: *Shermans:* (American-made) Sherman tanks

Even a pebble disturbs
that tremor laden meniscus,
that implicit shivering.
They sink towards the floor,
the basement of quiet,
settle into a small mosaic.

And the single eye
of the well dreams on,
a silent cyclops.

II

People are different.
They live outside, insist
in their world of agitation.
A man comes by himself,
singing or in silence,
and hauls up his bucket slowly—
an act of meditation—
or jerks it up angrily,
like lifting a skin,
sweeping a circle
right through his own reflection.

III

And the well recomposes itself.

Crowds arrive annually, on pilgrimage.
Votive offerings adorn the bushes;
a child's rattle, hanging silent
(except when the wind shifts it)
a rag fluttering like a pennant.

Or a tarnished coin is thrown in,
sinking soundlessly to the bottom.
Water's slow alchemy washes it clean:
a queen of the realm, made virgin again.

IV

Birds chatter above it.
They are the well's principal distraction,
swaying at the end of branches,
singing and swaying, darting excitement
of courting and nesting,
fending for the next brood,
who still seem the same robin,
thrush, blackbird or wren.

14: *meniscus*: the surface of a body of liquid, curved at its edges due to surface tension

The trees stay silent.
The storms speak through them.
Then the leaves come sailing down,
sharp green or yellow,
55   betraying the seasons,
till a flashing shield of ice
forms over the well's single eye:
the year's final gift,
a static transparence.

V

60   But a well has its secret.
Under drifting leaves,
dormant stones around
the whitewashed wall,
the unpredictable ballet
65   of waterbugs, insects,

There the wellhead pulses,
little more than a tremor,
a flickering quiver,
spasms of silence;
70   small intensities of mirth,
the hidden laughter of earth.

1984

THOM GUNN (b. 1929)

G UNN WAS BORN IN GRAVESEND, KENT, AND SPENT MUCH OF HIS YOUTH IN HAMP-
stead in London. He was educated at University College School, London, and
then, after two years of national service in the army, at Trinity College, Cambridge,
where he attended the lectures of F. R. Leavis. At Stanford University he studied with
Yvor Winters. With the exception of several brief residences in Berlin, London, and
New York, Gunn has remained in the Bay Area since settling in San Francisco in 1960.
From 1958 to 1966, he taught at the University of California, Berkeley full-time; from
1975 until his retirement in 1999, he was a visiting professor, teaching for one quarter
a year.

Very early in his poetic career, Gunn was identified as a Movement poet, though
as he has written in an autobiographical essay it was a surprise to him to learn that he
was part of this group: "The whole business now looks like a lot of categorizing fool-
ishness." Like some of his contemporaries, Gunn, in his earlier books especially,
"deliberately [eschewed] Modernism" in favor of a "turning back . . . to traditional
resources in structure and method." From an early age, Gunn was an avid reader of
English Renaissance lyric, and its influence persists in his poetry. Winters encouraged
his distrust for poems "used as a gymnasium for the ego."[1] Clive Wilmer describes
Gunn's approach to poetry as "at root impersonal: his first person, like Ralegh's or Jon-
son's or Hardy's, is unquestionably that of a particular man, but a man who expects
his individuality to be of interest in so far as it is a quality the reader shares with him."[2]
Wilmer's characterization of Gunn as a "philosophical hedonist" is also useful, but
Gunn's hedonism is rarely exuberant. "Moly" describes "a nightmare of beasthood,"
and the child-like rhythms and diction of "Seesaw" do not conceal the poem's quietly
despairing view of intimate relationships.

Gunn's years in the United States have made him a receptive reader of American
poets such as William Carlos Williams and Robert Duncan; Gunn credits Duncan
with making it possible for poets to "deal with overtly homosexual material . . . as a
matter of course," and some of Gunn's poems beginning with *Jack Straw's Castle*
(1976) reflect the influence of Duncan's work in their free verse and their more direct
treatment of sexuality.[3] The earliest Gunn poem included here, "An Unsettled Motor-
cyclist's Vision of His Death," shows some of the impact of American myth on his
poetry; he has described that myth as "the wild man part free spirit and part hood-

---

[1] "My Life Up to Now," *The Occasions of Poetry: Essays in Criticism and Autobiography*, expanded ed., San
Francisco, 1985, pp. 179–98.
[2] Introduction to *The Occasions of Poetry*, 1985, p. 11.
[3] "Homosexuality in Robert Duncan's Poetry," *The Occasions of Poetry*, 1985, p. 134.

lum," noting also that his poem anglicizes the myth.[4] The poem was first published in his second book, *The Sense of Movement* (1957), which followed *Fighting Terms* (1954). Other books of poetry include *My Sad Captains* (1961), *Moly* (1971), *The Passages of Joy* (1982), and *The Man With Night Sweats* (1992), which contains a remarkable series of poems about the AIDS crisis, including "Lament." Gunn's prose is collected in *The Occasions of Poetry: Essays in Criticism and Autobiography* (1982) and *Shelf Life: Essays, Memoirs, and an Interview* (1993).

---

[4] "My Life Up to Now," p. 187.

The Unsettled Motorcyclist's Vision of his Death

Across the open countryside,
Into the walls of rain I ride.
It beats my cheek, drenches my knees,
But I am being what I please.

5   The firm heath stops, and marsh begins.
Now we're at war: whichever wins
My human will cannot submit
To nature, though brought out of it.
The wheels sink deep; the clear sound blurs:
10   Still, bent on the handle-bars,
I urge my chosen instrument
Against the mere embodiment.
The front wheel wedges fast between
Two shrubs of glazed insensate green
15   —Gigantic order in the rim
Of each flat leaf. Black eddies brim
Around my heel which, pressing deep,
Accelerates the waiting sleep.

I used to live in sound, and lacked
20   Knowledge of still or creeping fact,
But now the stagnant strips my breath,
Leant on my cheek in weight of death.
Though so oppressed I find I may
Through substance move. I pick my way,
25   Where death and life in one combine,
Through the dark earth that is not mine,
Crowded with fragments, blunt, unformed;
While past my ear where noises swarmed
The marsh plant's white extremities,
30   Slow without patience, spread at ease
Invulnerable and soft, extend
With a quiet grasping toward their end.

And though the tubers, once I rot,
Reflesh my bones with pallid knot,
35   Till swelling out my clothes they feign
This dummy is a man again,
It is as servants they insist,

Without volition that they twist;
And habit does not leave them tired,
40   By men laboriously acquired.
Cell after cell the plants convert
My special richness in the dirt:
All that they get, they get by chance.

And multiply in ignorance.

1957

Confessions of the Life Artist

I

Whatever is here, it is
material for my art.

On the extreme shore of land,
and facing the disordered
5   rhythms of the sea, I taste
a summoning on the air.

I derive from these rocks, which
inhibit the sea's impulse.
But it is a condition,
10   once accepted, like air: air
haunted by the taste of salt.

II

I think, therefore I cannot
avoid thought of the morrow.
Outside the window, the birds
15   of the air and the lily
have lost themselves in action.
I think of the birds that sleep
in flight, of the lily's pale
waxy gleaming, of myself,
20   and of the morrow pending.
The one thing clear is that I
must not lose myself in thought.

III

You control what you can, and
use what you cannot.
                        Heady,
25   to hover above the winds,

12: Cf. "I think, therefore I am," said by the philosopher René Descartes in his *Discourse on Method* (1637).
14–15: *birds / of the air:* the phrase is biblical (2 Sam. 21:10; Eccles. 10:20); thus the *lily* might suggest Matt.
  6:28: "Consider the lilies of the field, how they grow: they toil not, neither do they spin."

buoyant with a sense of choice.
Circling over a city,
to reject the thousand, and
to select the one. To watch

30 the goodly people there, to
know that their blood circulates,
that it races as yours does,
live between extremities.

IV

But what of the unchosen?

35 They are as if dead. Their deaths,
now, validate the chosen.

Of course, being left as dead
may lead to the thing itself.
I read about them: and what

40 could be more fortifying
to one's own identity
than another's suicide?

If there are forbidden arts,
mine must indeed be of them.

V

45 She is immersed in despair,
but I am here, luckily.
She, become indefinite,
leans on me who am starkly
redefined at each moment,

50 aware of her need, and trained
to have few needs of my own.

As I support her, so, with
my magnificent control,
I suddenly ask: 'What if

55 she has the edge over me?'

VI

To give way to all passions,
I know, is merely whoring.
Yes, but to give way to none
is to be a whore-master.

60 I stride through the whore-house
when my girls are off duty,
I load them with chocolates,
but cannot for one moment

possess red hair like hers, fresh
cheeks or bee-stung lips like hers,
or a wasteful heart like hers.

VII

I elevate not what I
have, but what I wish to have,
and see myself in others.

There is a girl in the train
who emulates the bee-hive
of the magazine stars of
four years ago.
                    I blush at
the jibes that grow inside me,
lest someone should utter them.

Why was something evolved so
tender, so open to pain?

VIII

Here is a famous picture.

It is of a little Jew
in Warsaw, some years ago,
being hustled somewhere. His
mother dressed him that morning
warmly in cap and cloth coat.
He stares at the camera
as he passes. Whatever
those big shining dark eyes have
just looked on, they can see now
no appeal in the wide world.

IX

I grow old in the design.

Prophecies become fulfilled,
though never as expected,
almost accidentally,
in fact, as if to conform
to some alien order.

But I am concerned with my
own knowledge that the design
is everywhere ethical
and harmonious: circles
start to close, lines to balance.

X

100   The art of designing life
          is no excuse for that life.

          People will forget Shakespeare.
          He will lie with George Formby
          and me, here where the swine root.
105   Later, the solar system
          will flare up and fall into
          space, irretrievably lost.

          For the loss, as for the life,
          there will be no excuse, there
110   is no justification.

                                                            1967

Moly

          Nightmare of beasthood, snorting, how to wake.
          I woke. What beasthood skin she made me take?

          Leathery toad that ruts for days on end,
          Or cringing dribbling dog, man's servile friend,

5   Or cat that prettily pounces on its meat,
          Tortures it hours, then does not care to eat:

          Parrot, moth, shark, wolf, crocodile, ass, flea.
          What germs, what jostling mobs there were in me.

          These seem like bristles, and the hide is tough.
10   No claw or web here: each foot ends in hoof.

          Into what bulk has method disappeared?
          Like ham, streaked. I am gross—grey, gross, flap-eared.

          The pale-lashed eyes my only human feature.
          My teeth tear, tear. I am the snouted creature

15   That bites through anything, root, wire, or can.
          If I was not afraid I'd eat a man.

103: *George Formby* (1904–1961) was a British music-hall entertainer and virtuoso on the banjulele (a hybrid banjo-ukulele).

Title: *Moly*: a magical herb in Greek myth. In Homer's *Odyssey*, Odysseus's shipmates are turned into swine by the sorceress Circe; Odysseus, protected by moly given him by the god Hermes, compels Circe to restore his shipmates to human shape. Gunn has written: "It is no longer fashionable to praise LSD, but I have no doubt at all that it has been of the utmost importance to me, both as a man and as a poet. I learned from it, for example, a lot of information about myself that I had somehow blocked from my own view. And almost all of the poems that were to be in my next book, *Moly*, written between 1965 and 1970, have in some way however indirect to do with it" ("My Life Up to Now," *The Occasions of Poetry*, London, 1982, p. 192).

Oh a man's flesh already is in mine.
Hand and foot poised for risk. Buried in swine.

     I root and root, you think that it is greed,
20   It is, but I seek out a plant I need.

Direct me gods, whose changes are all holy,
To where it flickers deep in grass, the moly:

Cool flesh of magic in each leaf and shoot,
From milky flower to the black forked root.

25   From this fat dungeon I could rise to skin
And human title, putting pig within.

I push my big grey wet snout through the green,
Dreaming the flower I have never seen.

1971

Seesaw

song

Days are bright,
Nights are dark.
We play seesaw
In the park.

5   Look at me
And my friend
Freckleface
The other end.

Shiny board
10   Between my legs.
Feet crunch down
On the twigs.

I crouch close
To the ground
15   Till it's time:
Up I bound.

Legs go loose,
Legs go tight.
I drop down
20   Like the night.

Like a scales.
Give and take,
Take and give
My legs ache.

25   So it ends
      As it begins.
      Off we climb
      And no one wins.

1992

A Sketch of the Great Dejection

     Having read the promise of the hedgerow
     the body set out anew on its adventures.
     At length it came to a place of poverty,
     of inner and outer famine,
5   where all movement had stopped
     except for that of the wind, which was continual
     and came from elsewhere, from the sea,
     moving across unplanted fields and between headstones
     in the little churchyard clogged with nettles
10   where no one came between Sundays, and few then.
     The wind was like a punishment to the face and hands.
     These were marshes of privation:
     the mud of the ditches oozed scummy water,
     the grey reeds were arrested in growth,
15   the sun did not show, even as a blur,
     and the uneven lands were without definition
     as I was without potent words,
     inert.
          I sat upon a disintegrating gravestone.
20   How can I continue, I asked?
     I longed to whet my senses, but upon what?
     On mud? It was a desert of raw mud.
     I was tempted by fantasies of the past,
     but my body rejected them, for only in the present
25   could it pursue the promise,
         keeping open to its fulfilment.
     I would not, either, sink into the mud,
     warming it with the warmth I brought to it,
         as in a sty of sloth.
30   My body insisted on restlessness
         having been promised love,
     as my mind insisted on words
         having been promised the imagination.
     So I remained alert, confused and uncomforted.
35   I fared on and, though the landscape did not change,
     it came to seem after a while like a place of recuperation.

1992

Lament

Your dying was a difficult enterprise.
First, petty things took up your energies,
The small but clustering duties of the sick,
Irritant as the cough's dry rhetoric.
5   Those hours of waiting for pills, shot, X-ray
Or test (while you read novels two a day)
Already with a kind of clumsy stealth
Distanced you from the habits of your health.
    In hope still, courteous still, but tired and thin,
10 You tried to stay the man that you had been,
Treating each symptom as a mere mishap
Without import. But then the spinal tap.
It brought a hard headache, and when night came
I heard you wake up from the same bad dream
15 Every half-hour with the same short cry
Of mild outrage, before immediately
Slipping into the nightmare once again
Empty of content but the drip of pain.
No respite followed: though the nightmare ceased,
20 Your cough grew thick and rich, its strength increased.
Four nights, and on the fifth we drove you down
To the Emergency Room. That frown, that frown:
I'd never seen such rage in you before
As when they wheeled you through the swinging door.
25 For you knew, rightly, they conveyed you from
Those normal pleasures of the sun's kingdom
The hedonistic body basks within
And takes for granted—summer on the skin,
Sleep without break, the moderate taste of tea
30 In a dry mouth. You had gone on from me
As if your body sought out martyrdom
In the far Canada of a hospital room.
Once there, you entered fully the distress
And long pale rigours of the wilderness.
35 A gust of morphine hid you. Back in sight
You breathed through a segmented tube, fat, white,
Jammed down your throat so that you could not speak.
    How thin the distance made you. In your cheek
One day, appeared the true shape of your bone
40 No longer padded. Still your mind, alone,
Explored this emptying intermediate
State for what holds and rests were hidden in it.
    You wrote us messages on a pad, amused
At one time that you had your nurse confused
45 Who, seeing you reconciled after four years
With your grey father, both of you in tears,
Asked if this was at last your 'special friend'
(The one you waited for until the end).
'She sings,' you wrote, 'a Philippine folk song

"Lament" memorializes Gunn's friend, Allan Noseworthy.

50　To wake me in the morning . . . It is long
　　And very pretty.' Grabbing at detail
　　To furnish this bare ledge toured by the gale,
　　On which you lay, bed restful as a knife,
　　You tried, tried hard, to make of it a life
55　Thick with the complicating circumstance
　　Your thoughts might fasten on. It had been chance
　　Always till now that had filled up the moment
　　With live specifics your hilarious comment
　　Discovered as it went along; and fed,
60　Laconic, quick, wherever it was led.
　　You improvised upon your own delight.
　　I think back to the scented summer night
　　We talked between our sleeping bags, below
　　A molten field of stars five years ago:
65　I was so tickled by your mind's light touch
　　I couldn't sleep, you made me laugh too much,
　　Though I was tired and begged you to leave off.

　　Now you were tired, and yet not tired enough
　　—Still hungry for the great world you were losing
70　Steadily in no season of your choosing—
　　And when at last the whole death was assured,
　　Drugs having failed, and when you had endured
　　Two weeks of an abominable constraint,
　　You faced it equably, without complaint,
75　Unwhimpering, but not at peace with it.
　　You'd lived as if your time was infinite:
　　You were not ready and not reconciled,
　　Feeling as uncompleted as a child
　　Till you had shown the world what you could do
80　In some ambitious role to be worked through,
　　A role your need for it had half-defined,
　　But never wholly, even in your mind.
　　You lacked the necessary ruthlessness,
　　The soaring meanness that pinpoints success.
85　We loved that lack of self-love, and your smile,
　　Rueful, at your own silliness.
　　　　　　　　　　　　　　　　　Meanwhile,
　　Your lungs collapsed, and the machine, unstrained,
　　Did all your breathing now. Nothing remained
　　But death by drowning on an inland sea
90　Of your own fluids, which it seemed could be
　　Kindly forestalled by drugs. Both could and would:
　　Nothing was said, everything understood,
　　At least by us. Your own concerns were not
　　Long-term, precisely, when they gave the shot
95　—You made local arrangements to the bed
　　And pulled a pillow round beside your head.
　　　　And so you slept, and died, your skin gone grey,
　　Achieving your completeness, in a way.

　　Outdoors next day, I was dizzy from a sense
100　Of being ejected with some violence
　　From vigil in a white and distant spot

Where I was numb, into this garden plot
Too warm, too close, and not enough like pain.
I was delivered into time again
105   —The variations that I live among
Where your long body too used to belong
And where the still bush is minutely active.
You never thought your body was attractive,
Though others did, and yet you trusted it
110   And must have loved its fickleness a bit
Since it was yours and gave you what it could,
Till near the end it let you down for good,
Its blood hospitable to those guests who
Took over by betraying it into
115   The greatest of its inconsistencies
This difficult, tedious, painful enterprise.

1992

ELAINE FEINSTEIN (b. 1930)

R EADERS OF MODERN POETRY WILL FIND ELAINE FEINSTEIN'S NAME IN CHARLES
Olson's *Selected Writings* (1966), in which Olson's letter to Feinstein answering
queries about poetic form and speech rhythms is printed adjacent to his manifesto
"Projective Verse." The influence of Olson and his Black Mountain peers is far from
overwhelming but surely perceptible in Feinstein's early poems. The opening stanza of
"Marriage," for instance, pushes its prosaic syntax energetically forward, using a
comma where others would use a period in its second line, extending phrases across
line breaks to redirect or expand their reference. The effect is utterance accelerated,
made urgent; the poet is a woman on her feet talking (to modify a famous phrase), the
poem an act of coming-into-knowledge. Feinstein was one of the first English poets to
take up the challenge to the traditional verse forms of the 1950s represented by Olson
and his peers, and she has acknowledged that her reading in American poets ranging
from Emily Dickinson to Charles Reznikoff helped shape her work. But she has said
that she never shared the "passion for geography and local history nor the insistence
on uncorrected spontaneity" of her Black Mountain mentors, and has never felt part
of a group or movement of poets.[1] Perhaps even more than by American modernists
her work has been shaped by her experience in translating the Russian poet Marina
Tsvetayeva, whose biography Feinstein has also authored. Donald Davie writes that
"the affinity between the Russian poet and her Anglo-Jewish translator was not in the
first place any matter of idiom or style. Tsvetayeva seems to be . . . the undeniable
instance in our century of a woman poet who embraced the lyrical abandon, aban-
donment in life as well as writing." Discussing the place of Feinstein's collection *The
Magic Apple Trees* (1971) within the women's movement of the late 1960s and early
1970s, Davie adds that "her theme was and had to be the barely reconcilable tension
between herself as wife and mother, and herself as independent person."[2]

Feinstein was born in Boole, Lancashire and educated at Wyggeston Grammar
School, Leicester and Newnham College, Cambridge. She has lectured at Bishop
Stortford Training College and the University of Essex and is the author of numerous
novels and radio plays. Her books of poetry include *The Celebrants and Other Poems*,
(1973) in which the long title poem seeks to exorcise the cultural spells and "supersti-
tion" that have "bewitched . . . into a myth . . . anyone's cracked daughter," *The Feast
of Euridice* (1980), *Badlands* (1986), and *City Music* (1990).

---

[1] *Contemporary Poets*, 6th ed., ed. Thomas Riggs, New York, 1996, p. 329.
[2] *Under Briggflatts: A History of Poetry in Great Britain 1960–1988*, Chicago, 1989, pp. 91–2.

Marriage

Is there ever a new beginning when every
word has its ten years weight, can there be
what you call conversation between us?
Relentless you are as you push me
5   to dance and I lurch away from you
weeping, and yet can we bear to lie
silent under the ice together like
fish in a long winter?

A letter now from York is a reminder of
10   windless Rievaulx, the hillside moving through
limestone arches, in the ear's liquid the
whirr of dove notes: we were a fellowship of three
strangers walking in northern brightness, our
searches peaceful, in our silence the
15   resonance of stones only, any celibate
could look for such retreat, for me
it was a luxury to be insisted on
in the sight of those grass overgrown dormitories.

We have taken our shape from the
20   damage we do one another, gently as
bodies moving together at night, we amend
our gestures, softly we hold our places:
in the alien school morning in the
small stones of your eyes I know how
25   you want to be rid of us, you were
never a family man, your virtue is
lost, even alikeness deceived us
love, our spirits sprawl together
and both at last are distorted

30   and yet we go toward birthdays and other
marks   not wryly   not thriftily
waiting, for where shall we find it, a
joyous, a various world? in fury
we share, which keeps us, without
35   resignation: tender whenever we touch   what
else we share   this flesh   we
bring together   it hurts to
think of dying as we lie close

1969

10: *Rievaulx* is a ruined twelfth-century Cistercian abbey situated in a valley in North Yorkshire.

Exile

Estonian ghosts of
river birds within the
temples of his skull, ashes
of poets, girders of school houses:
5 these are the tired politics
that vein his eyes

scoop a pouch under his lower
lip. In our system
his vigour has aged into
10 rumours of miraculous
sexual prowess, yet
the gesture of his
pasty fist is continuous with
the sag of his cardigan

15 and his enemies are
quiet middle-aged men, who
move in the mist of invisible
English power. He is
unhunted and unforested in the fen:
20 like the rest of us.

1971

For Brighton, Old Bawd

Streets smelling of vinegar, fronted with junk
and monstrous sweet shops, here the sea slopes up as
bland as a green hill. And the air is a wash of

salt and brightness. This town has so transfigured
5 the silt of what lay in our mouths that
now we can lie happily awake together as

the first milk bottles go down on the
steps and the early lorries change gear
at the lights beneath us.

10 Though what is good in this city is frivolous
as the green tits on Mrs Fitzherbert's
pleasure palace, it retains the force

which is the magic of all bawdy, fit
forgiveness that true measure for every
15 shape of body and each mistaken piece of behaviour

1971

Title: *Brighton* is a seaside resort in East Sussex, popularized by George IV when he was Prince Regent.
11: Maria *Fitzherbert* (1756–1837) was George IV's secret wife.

TED HUGHES (1930–1998)

FROM HIS FIRST BOOK, *THE HAWK IN THE RAIN* (1957), TO HIS LAST, *BIRTHDAY Letters* (1998), Hughes sustained a readership matched by few English poets. His neo-primitivist, post-Lawrentian poems about the instinctual and often rapacious behavior of animals seemed, from one perspective, an unblinking revision of traditions of nature poetry. Against sentimental views of man's relationship to the non-human universe Hughes posits a radical otherness. The possibility of reading the same poems allegorically, however, which is encouraged by Hughes's occasional use of anthropomorphisms, has led critics to ask whether his view of a hostile and pitiless nature also indicates an atavistic celebration of the violent and animalistic as a superior mode of being. There is little doubt that the poems represent an assault on Christian pieties and the civic virtues promoted by varieties of liberal humanism. The shamanistic and visionary tone of some of Hughes's poetry was to critics such as A. Alvarez a welcome relief from the ironic urbanity and middle-class anomie of the Movement, but Anthony Thwaite has called the work "dogmatically pessimistic."[1] Similarly, Hughes's diction is for some Shakespearean and for others bombastic. His poems, which include those written in more traditional forms as well as those in varieties of free verse and longer sequences mixing free verse and prose, make him for some readers one of England's most experimental writers. For Veronica Forrest-Thompson, however, Hughes's poetry represents the triumph of a "sincerity" and purported "naturalness" that too often substitutes for technique; his versification can be as brutal as his sense of the poet's "predatory visionary role."[2] Such passionate responses are one testament to the stature and independence of Hughes's poetry.

The poems represented here sketch some of the formal and thematic concerns of what was an exceptionally prolific career. "View of a Pig" and "Pike," from his first two books *The Hawk in the Rain* and *Lupercal* (1960), sample Hughes's bestiary. "Wodwo," from the 1967 book of that title is the monologue of a wildman who imagines himself at "the exact centre" of creation. "Out," from the same volume, alludes to Hughes's father's experience in World War I, a subject often returned to by the poet, who also did much to promote the work of World War II poet Keith Douglas. The selections from *Gaudete* (1977), a book-length poem narrating the story of a changeling who assumes the body of an Anglican vicar (the fictional Reverend Nicholas Lumb) to have orgiastic sex with the women of the parish, are presented in that book's epilogue as the poems of Lumb found upon his return from the spirit-world. "Flounders" first

---

[1] A. Alvarez, "Introduction: The New Poetry, or Beyond the Gentility Principle," *The New Poetry*, ed. A. Alvariez, Harmondsworth, 1962, p. 31. Anthony Thwaite, *Poetry Today: A Critical Guide to British Poetry 1960–1984*, Harlow, 1985, p. 59.
[2] *Poetic Artifice: A Theory of Twentieth-Century Poetry*, Manchester, 1978, pp. 146–58.

appeared in *Birthday Letters* (1998), Hughes's poems about his relationship with his first wife, the American poet Sylvia Plath; Hughes's work as her editor has been criticized, especially his selections for and ordering of her book *Ariel* (1965) and his destruction of part of her journal written in the month before her suicide.[3]

Hughes was born in Mytholmroyd, Yorkshire, in a landscape he often meditated on in his poetry. He was educated at Mexborough Grammar School and Pembroke College, Cambridge. Aside from those mentioned above, his many books include *Crow* (1970), *Cave Birds* (1975), *Moortown* (1979), *River* (1983), *Wolf-Watching* (1989), and *New Selected Poems* (1995). He also wrote many books for children and two principal prose works, *Shakespeare and the Goddess of Being* (1992) and *Winter Pollen* (1995). Hughes was appointed Poet Laureate in 1984.

---

[3] Marjorie Perloff, "The Two Ariels: The (Re)making of the Sylvia Plath Canon," *Poetic Artifice: Essays on Modernist and Postmodernist Lyric*, Evanston, 1990, pp. 175–97.

View of a Pig

The pig lay on a barrow dead.
It weighed, they said, as much as three men.
Its eyes closed, pink white eyelashes.
Its trotters stuck straight out.

5   Such weight and thick pink bulk
Set in death seemed not just dead.
It was less than lifeless, further off.
It was like a sack of wheat.

I thumped it without feeling remorse.
10   One feels guilty insulting the dead,
Walking on graves. But this pig
Did not seem able to accuse.

It was too dead. Just so much
A poundage of lard and pork.
15   Its last dignity had entirely gone.
It was not a figure of fun.

Too dead now to pity.
To remember its life, din, stronghold
Of earthly pleasure as it had been,
20   Seemed a false effort, and off the point.

Too deadly factual. Its weight
Oppressed me—how could it be moved?
And the trouble of cutting it up!
The gash in its throat was shocking, but not pathetic.

25   Once I ran at a fair in the noise
To catch a greased piglet
That was faster and nimbler than a cat,
Its squeal was the rending of metal.

Pigs must have hot blood, they feel like ovens.
30   Their bite is worse than a horse's—
They chop a half-moon clean out.
They eat cinders, dead cats.

Distinctions and admirations such
As this one was long finished with.
35   I stared at it a long time. They were going to scald it,
Scald it and scour it like a doorstep.

1960

Pike

Pike, three inches long, perfect
Pike in all parts, green tigering the gold.
Killers from the egg: the malevolent aged grin.
They dance on the surface among the flies.

5   Or move, stunned by their own grandeur
Over a bed of emerald, silhouette
Of submarine delicacy and horror.
A hundred feet long in their world.

In ponds, under the heat-struck lily pads—
10   Gloom of their stillness:
Logged on last year's black leaves, watching upwards.
Or hung in an amber cavern of weeds

The jaws' hooked clamp and fangs
Not to be changed at this date;
15   A life subdued to its instrument;
The gills kneading quietly, and the pectorals.

Three we kept behind glass,
Jungled in weed: three inches, four,
And four and a half: fed fry to them—
20   Suddenly there were two. Finally one.

With a sag belly and the grin it was born with.
And indeed they spare nobody.
Two, six pounds each, over two feet long,
High and dry and dead in the willow-herb—

25   One jammed past its gills down the other's gullet:
The outside eye stared: as a vice locks—
The same iron in this eye
Though its film shrank in death.

A pond I fished, fifty yards across,
30   Whose lilies and muscular tench

11: *Logged:* heavy; sluggish

Had outlasted every visible stone
Of the monastery that planted them—

Stilled legendary depth:
It was as deep as England. It held
35   Pike too immense to stir, so immense and old
That past nightfall I dared not cast

But silently cast and fished
With the hair frozen on my head
For what might move, for what eye might move.
40   The still splashes on the dark pond,

Owls hushing the floating woods
Frail on my ear against the dream
Darkness beneath night's darkness had freed,
That rose slowly towards me, watching.

1960

Out

I THE DREAM TIME

My father sat in his chair recovering
From the four-year mastication by gunfire and mud,
Body buffeted wordless, estranged by long soaking
In the colours of mutilation.
5   His outer perforations
Were valiantly healed, but he and the hearth-fire, its blood-flicker
On biscuit-bowl and piano and table leg,
Moved into strong and stronger possession
Of minute after minute, as the clock's tiny cog
10   Laboured and on the thread of his listening
Dragged him bodily from under
The mortised four-year strata of dead Englishmen
He belonged with. He felt his limbs clearing
With every slight, gingerish movement. While I, small and four,
15   Lay on the carpet as his luckless double,
His memory's buried, immovable anchor,
Among jawbones and blown-off boots, tree-stumps, shellcases and craters,
Under rain that goes on drumming its rods and thickening
Its kingdom, which the sun has abandoned, and where nobody
20   Can ever again move from shelter.

II

The dead man in his cave beginning to sweat;
The melting bronze visor of flesh
Of the mother in the baby-furnace—
Nobody believes, it
25   Could be nothing, all
Undergo smiling at
The lulling of blood in

Their ears, their ears, their ears, their eyes
Are only drops of water and even the dead man suddenly
30   Sits up and sneezes—Atishoo!
Then the nurse wraps him up, smiling,
And, though faintly, the mother is smiling,
And it's just another baby.

As after being blasted to bits
35   The reassembled infantryman
Tentatively totters out, gazing around with the eyes
Of an exhausted clerk.

III   REMEMBRANCE DAY

The poppy is a wound, the poppy is the mouth
Of the grave, maybe of the womb searching—

40   A canvas-beauty puppet on a wire
Today whoring everywhere. It is years since I wore one.

It is more years
The shrapnel that shattered my father's paybook

Gripped me, and all his dead
45   Gripped him to a time

He no more than they could outgrow, but, cast into one, like iron,
Hung deeper than refreshing of ploughs

In the woe-dark under my mother's eye—
One anchor

50   Holding my juvenile neck bowed to the dunkings of the Atlantic.

So goodbye to that bloody-minded flower.

You dead bury your dead.
Goodbye to the cenotaphs on my mother's breasts.

Goodbye to all the remaindered charms of my father's survival

55   Let England close. Let the green sea-anemone close.

                                                        1967

53: *cenotaphs*: war memorials

Pibroch

The sea cries with its meaningless voice
Treating alike its dead and its living,
Probably bored with the appearance of heaven
After so many millions of nights without sleep,
5   Without purpose, without self-deception.

Stone likewise. A pebble is imprisoned
Like nothing in the Universe.
Created for black sleep. Or growing
Conscious of the sun's red spot occasionally,
10   Then dreaming it is the foetus of God.

Over the stone rushes the wind
Able to mingle with nothing,
Like the hearing of the blind stone itself.
Or turns, as if the stone's mind came feeling
15   A fantasy of directions.

Drinking the sea and eating the rock
A tree struggles to make leaves—
An old woman fallen from space
Unprepared for these conditions.
20   She hangs on, because her mind's gone completely.

Minute after minute, aeon after aeon,
Nothing lets up or develops.
And this is neither a bad variant nor a tryout.
This is where the staring angels go through.
25   This is where all the stars bow down.

1967

Wodwo

What am I? Nosing here, turning leaves over
Following a faint stain on the air to the river's edge
I enter water. What am I to split
The glassy grain of water looking upward I see the bed
5   Of the river above me upside down very clear
What am I doing here in mid-air? Why do I find
this frog so interesting as I inspect its most secret
interior and make it my own? Do these weeds
know me and name me to each other have they
10   seen me before, do I fit in their world? I seem
separate from the ground and not rooted but dropped
out of nothing casually I've no threads

Title: *Pibroch:* a set of mournful variations played on the bagpipes; a dirge

Title: *Wodwo:* The word comes from Middle English: Hughes commented, "A Wodwo is a sort of half-man half-animal spirit of forests" (*Poetry in the Making,* London, 1967, p. 62).

fastening me to anything I can go anywhere
I seem to have been given the freedom
15   of this place what am I then? And picking
bits of bark off this rotten stump gives me
no pleasure and it's no use so why do I do it
me and doing that have coincided very queerly
But what shall I be called am I the first
20   have I an owner what shape am I what
shape am I am I huge if I go
to the end on this way past these trees and past these trees
till I get tired that's touching one wall of me
for the moment if I sit still how everything
25   stops to watch me I suppose I am the exact centre
but there's all this what is it roots
roots roots roots and here's the water
again very queer but I'll go on looking

1967

Crow Hears Fate Knock on the Door

Crow looked at the world, mountainously heaped.
He looked at the heavens, littering away
Beyond every limit.
He looked in front of his feet at the little stream
5   Chugging on like an auxiliary motor
Fastened to this infinite engine.

He imagined the whole engineering
Of its assembly, repairs and maintenance—
And felt helpless.

10   He plucked grass-heads and gazed into them
Waiting for first instructions.
He studied a stone from the stream.
He found a dead mole and slowly he took it apart
Then stared at the gobbets, feeling helpless.
15   He walked, he walked
Letting the translucent starry spaces
Blow in his ear cluelessly.

Yet the prophecy inside him, like a grimace,
Was I will measure it all and own it all
20   and I will be inside it
as inside my own laughter
and not staring out at it through walls

Crow Hears Fate Knock on the Door: "Crow is a sequence of poems relating the birth, upbringing and
adventures of a protagonist of that name—a creature whose transformations tend from the primal and
elemental toward the human." (Hughes, foreword to *New Selected Poems*, New York, 1982). The
sequence contains multiple parodies of creation myths, its anti-hero Crow acting as a version of the
mythic Trickster figure.

OF MY EYE'S COLD QUARANTINE
FROM A BURIED CELL OF BLOODY BLACKNESS—

25   This prophecy was inside him, like a steel spring

Slowly rending the vital fibres.

1970

from Gaudete

"Collision with the earth has finally come"

Collision with the earth has finally come—
How far can I fall?

A kelp, adrift
In my feeding substance

5   A mountain
Rooted in stone of heaven

A sea
Full of moon-ghost, with mangling waters

Dust on my head
10   Helpless to fit the pieces of water
A needle of many Norths

Ark of blood
Which is the magic baggage old men open
And find useless, at the great moment of need

15   Error on error
Perfumed
With a ribbon of fury

"I see the oak's bride"

I see the oak's bride in the oak's grasp.

Nuptials among prehistoric insects
The tremulous convulsion
The inching hydra strength

Gaudete: These poems are part of the selection from the book *Gaudete* in Hughes's *Selected Poems:* his note there reads: "This is a long story in verse which outlines the last day of a changeling—a creature substituted for an Anglican clergyman, as an all but perfect duplicate, by powers of the other world, while the real clergyman remains in the other world as their prisoner (like Thomas the Rhymer in the Scots ballad). At the destruction of the changeling, the man of flesh and blood reappears, and the poems here are taken from his notebook—his diary of coming to his senses, or of trying to come to his senses."

1: *the oak's bride:* i.e., mistletoe

5   Among frilled lizards

Dropping twigs, and acorns, and leaves.

The oak is in bliss
Its roots
Lift arms that are a supplication
10   Crippled with stigmata
Like the sea-carved cliffs earth lifts
Loaded with dumb, uttering effigies
The oak seems to die and to be dead
In its love-act.

15   As I lie under it

In a brown leaf nostalgia

An acorn stupor.

"The grass-blade is not without"

The grass-blade is not without
The loyalty that never was beheld.

And the blackbird
Sleeking from common anything and worm-dirt
5   Balances a precarious banner
Gold on black, terror and exultation.

The grim badger with armorial mask
Biting spade-steel, teeth and jaw-strake shattered,
Draws that final shuddering battle cry
10   Out of its backbone.

Me too,
Let me be one of your warriors.

Let your home
Be my home. Your people
15   My people.

"Your tree—your oak"

Your tree—your oak
A glare

Of black upward lightning, a wriggling grab
Momentary
5   Under the crumbling of stars.

"I see the oak's bride": 5: *frilled lizards* are found in Australia and New Guinea; they have a neck frill which
can be erected to make the lizard appear suddenly larger, frightening off predators.

"The grass-blade is not without": 8: *strake*: a curved metal plate that forms part of the rim of a wooden
wheel

A guard, a dancer
At the pure well of leaf.

Agony in the garden. Annunciation
Of clay, water and the sunlight.
10   They thunder under its roof.
Its agony is its temple.

Waist-deep, the black oak is dancing
And my eyes pause
On the centuries of its instant
15   As gnats
Try to winter in its wrinkles.

The seas are thirsting
Towards the oak.

The oak is flying
20   Astride the earth.

1977

Flounders

Was that a happy day? From Chatham
Down at the South end of the Cape, our map
Somebody's optimistic assurance,
We set out to row. We got ourselves
5   Into mid-channel. The tide was flowing. We hung
Anchored. Northward-pulling, our baited leads
Bounced and bounced the bottom. For three hours—
Two or three sea-robins. Cruisers
Folded us under their bow-waves, we bobbed up,
10   Happy enough. But the wind
Smartened against us, and the tide turned, roughening,
Dragged seaward. We rowed. We rowed. We
Saw we weren't going to make it. We turned,
Cutting downwind for the sand-bar, beached
15   And wondered what next. It was there
I found a horse-shoe crab's carapace, perfect,
No bigger than a bee, in honey-pale cellophane.
No way back. But big, good America found us.
A power-boat and a pilot of no problems.
20   He roped our boat to his stern and with all his family
Slammed back across the channel into the wind,
The spray scything upwards, our boat behind
Twisting across the wake-boil—a hectic

8: *Agony in the garden:* Christ's night of prayer in Gethsemane before his arrest (Matt. 26:36ff).

1: *Chatham* is in Cape Cod, Massachusetts.
8: The *sea-robin,* or gurnard, is a type of bottom-dwelling fish.

Four or five minutes and he cast us off
In the lee of the land, but a mile or more
From our dock. We toiled along inshore. We came
To a back-channel, under beach-house gardens—marsh grass,
Wild, original greenery of America,
Mud-slicks and fiddler-crab warrens, as we groped
Towards the harbour. Gloom-rich water. Something
Suggested easy plenty. We lowered baits,
And out of about six feet of water
Six or seven feet from land, we pulled up flounders
Big as big plates, till all our bait had gone.
After our wind-burned, head-glitter day of emptiness,
And the slogging row for our lives, and the rescue,
Suddenly out of water easy as oil
The sea piled our boat with its surplus. And the day
Curled out of brilliant, arduous morning,
Through wind-hammered perilous afternoon,
Salt-scoured, to a storm-gold evening, a luxury
Of rowing among the dream-yachts of the rich
Lolling at anchor off the play-world pier.

How tiny an adventure
To stay so monumental in our marriage,
A slight ordeal of all that might be,
And a small thrill-breath of what many live by,
And a small prize, a toy miniature
Of the life that might have bonded us
Into a single animal, a single soul—

It was a visit from the goddess, the beauty
Who was poetry's sister—she had come
To tell poetry she was spoiling us.
Poetry listened, maybe, but we heard nothing
And poetry did not tell us. And we
Only did what poetry told us to do.

                                        1998

Fisher was born in Handsworth, Birmingham and has lived in the industrial Midlands his entire life, though in recent decades he has lived out of the city proper in a more rural area of northern Staffordshire. He attended Handsworth Grammar School and Birmingham University. He has worked as a lecturer at the Dudley College of Education, as the head of the Department of English and Drama at the Bordesley College of Education, and between 1972 and 1982, as a senior lecturer in American Studies at the University of Keele. Since 1946, he has also been a pianist in various jazz groups. His books include *City* (1961), *Ten Interiors with Various Figures* (1966), *The Ship's Orchestra* (1966), *The Cut Pages* (1971), *Matrix* (1971), *The Thing about Joe Sullivan* (1978), *A Furnace* (1986), *Birmingham River* (1994), and *The Dow Low Drop: New and Selected Poems* (1996).

In a note for *Contemporary Poets,* Fisher writes that "My work is grounded in the assumption that the human imagination creates and transacts the world, and must, in view of its record, be treated with the utmost vigilance so that its operations may be intimately understood and its malfunctions predicted."[1] Description in Fisher's poetry is "cognitive rather than perceptual," as Andrew Crozier has written, interrogating its own processes.[2] Fisher has been read as a descriptive realist and empiricist in the tradition of Hardy and Larkin and, because of his interest in the industrial landscapes and urban renewal of Birmingham, also as a poet of place in the line of Charles Olson and Edward Dorn. But he has been skeptical of both identifications, answering the latter by insisting that poems such as *City* make no effort "to invoke the historical meaning of the behavior of the people on the ground in anything like the way Olson does" and adding that "place in there is a way of exploring inner space."[3] Crozier argues that the "sustaining mode" of *City* is "alienation, the alienation of the observer from his world, of that world from its past, of life from death. . . ."[4] In the metonymic and deictic technique of much of his poetry, Fisher is clearly indebted to Ezra Pound's proposition that the natural object is the "adequate symbol" and William Carlos Williams's insistence on "no ideas but in things," but Fisher's work is equally marked by English Romanticism and a range of European avant-garde writing, including Surrealism. The prose poetry in *City* has few precedents in English writing, and Fisher has spoken of the influence of Rilke, Kafka, and Cocteau, as well as the "assemblage"

---

[1] *Contemporary Poets,* 6th edition, ed. Thomas Riggs, New York, 1996, p. 345.
[2] "Sign of Identity: Roy Fisher's A Furnace," *PN Review,* vol. 18, no. 3, 1992, p. 28.
[3] Jed Rasula and Mike Erwin, "An Interview with Roy Fisher," in Roy Fisher, *Nineteen Poems and an Interview,* 1975, p. 18.
[4] Crozier, p. 26.

of Russian constructivism. "Introit," the first section of the book-length sequence *A Furnace,* returns to the matter of *City,* but the sequence later moves beyond Birmingham to consider the metamorphosis of a number of European cities. As Peter Barry writes, "the major concern of *A Furnace* is energy, change, transformation, superimposition and process as such, viewed as transcendent entities."[5] Pondering the poem's reference to "timeless identities / riding in the flux," the "materialization" of which is present to "the guesswork of the senses," Crozier asks if the poem finally posits a "heterodox mysticism," concluding that it does not: "[The poem's] stress on human agency . . . is major: the signs that encode identity and culture originate in the same human desire, and by that desire we are attached to the world."[6]

---

[5] "'Fugitive from All Exegesis': Reading Roy Fisher's *A Furnace,*" *Dutch Quarterly Review of Anglo-American Letters,* vol. 18, no. 1, 1988, p. 4.
[6] Crozier, p. 32.

from City

The Entertainment of War

I saw the garden where my aunt had died
And her two children and a woman from next door;
It was like a burst pod filled with clay.

A mile away in the night I had heard the bombs
5   Sing and then burst themselves between cramped houses
With bright soft flashes and sounds like banging doors;

The last of them crushed the four bodies into the ground,
Scattered the shelter, and blasted my uncle's corpse
Over the housetop and into the street beyond.

10   Now the garden lay stripped and stale; the iron shelter
Spread out its separate petals around a smooth clay saucer,
Small, and so tidy it seemed nobody had ever been there.

When I saw it, the house was blown clean by blast and care:
Relations had already torn out the new fireplaces;
15   My cousin's pencils lasted me several years.

And in his office notepad that was given me
I found solemn drawings in crayon of blondes without dresses.
In his lifetime I had not known him well.

Those were the things I noticed at ten years of age:
20   Those, and the four hearses outside our house,
The chocolate cakes, and my classmates' half-shocked envy.

But my grandfather went home from the mortuary
And for five years tried to share the noises in his skull,
Then he walked out and lay under a furze-bush to die.

25   When my father came back from identifying the daughter
      He asked us to remind him of her mouth.
      We tried. He said 'I think it was the one'.

      These were marginal people I had met only rarely
      And the end of the whole household meant that no grief was seen;
30   Never have people seemed so absent from their own deaths.

      This bloody episode of four whom I could understand better dead
      Gave me something I needed to keep a long story moving;
      I had no pain of it; can find no scar even now.

      But had my belief in the fiction not been thus buoyed up
35   I might, in the sigh and strike of the next night's bombs
      Have realized a little what they meant, and for the first time been afraid.

The Poplars

      Where the road divides
      Just out of town
      By the wall beyond the filling-station
      Four Lombardy poplars
5   Brush stiff against the moorland wind.

      Clarity is in their tops
      That no one can touch
      Till they are felled,
      Brushwood to cart away:

10   To know these tall pointers
      I need to withdraw
      From what is called my life
      And from my net
      Of achievable desires.

15   Why should their rude and permanent virginity
      So capture me? Why should studying
      These lacunae of possibility
      Relax the iron templates of obligation
      Leaving me simply Man?

20   All I have done, or can do
      Is prisoned in its act:
      I think I am afraid of becoming
      A cemetery of performance.

4: *Lombardy poplars:* a thin, tall variety of poplar
17: *lacunae:* gaps (in a fragmentary text)

"Walking through the suburb at night"

Walking through the suburb at night, as I pass the dentist's house I
hear a clock chime a quarter, a desolate brassy sound. I know where it
stands, on the mantelpiece in the still surgery. The chime falls back
into the house, and beyond it, without end. Peace.

5   I sense the simple nakedness of these tiers of sleeping men and women
beneath whose windows I pass. I imagine it in its own setting, a mean
bathroom in a house no longer new, a bathroom with plank panelling,
painted a peculiar shade of green by an amateur, and badly preserved.
It is full of steam, so much as to obscure the yellow light and hide the
10 high, patched ceiling. In this dream, standing quiet, the private image
of the householder or his wife, damp and clean.

I see this as it might be floating in the dark, as if the twinkling point
of a distant street-lamp had blown in closer, swelling and softening to
a foggy oval. I can call up a series of such glimpses that need have no
15 end, for they are all the bodies of strangers. Some are deformed or dis-
eased, some are ashamed, but the peace of humility and weakness is
there in them all.

I have often felt myself to be vicious, in living so much by the eye, yet
among so many people. I can be afraid that the egg of light through
20 which I see these bodies might present itself as a keyhole. Yet I can
find no sadism in the way I see them now. They are warm-fleshed,
yet their shapes have the minuscule, remote morality of some mediaeval
woodcut of the Expulsion: an eternally startled Adam, a permanently
bemused Eve. I see them as homunculi, moving privately each in a
25 softly lit fruit in a nocturnal tree. I can consider without scorn or envy
the well-found bedrooms I pass, walnut and rose-pink, altars of tidy,
dark-haired women, bare-backed, wifely. Even in these I can see order.

I come quite often now upon a sort of ecstasy, a rag of light blowing
among the things I know, making me feel I am not the one for whom
30 it was intended, that I have inadvertently been looking through
another's eyes and have seen what I cannot receive.

I want to believe I live in a single world. That is why I am keeping my
eyes at home while I can. The light keeps on separating the world like
a table knife: it sweeps across what I see and suggests what I do not.
35 The imaginary comes to me with as much force as the real, the remem-
bered with as much force as the immediate. The countries on the map
divide and pile up like ice-floes: what is strange is that I feel no stress,
no grating discomfort among the confusion, no loss; only a belief that
I should not be here. I see the iron fences and the shallow ditches of
40 the countryside the mild wind has travelled over. I cannot enter that
countryside; nor can I escape it. I cannot join together the mild wind
and the shallow ditches, I cannot lay the light across the world and
then watch it slide away. Each thought is at once translucent and icily
capricious. A polytheism without gods.

1957–1961 / 1961

24: *homunculi:* tiny people

From an English Sensibility

There's enough wind
to rock the flower-heads
enough sun
to print their shadows
5   on the creosoted rail.

Already
this light shaking-up
rouses the traffic noise
out of a slurred riverbed
10   and lifts voices
as of battered aluminium cowls
toppling up;
black
drive chains racking the hot tiles.

15   Out in the cokehouse
cobweb
a dark mat
draped on the rubble in a corner
muffled
20   with a fog of glittering dust
that shakes
captive
in the sunlight
over pitted silver-grey
25   ghost shapes that shine through.

1965 / 1968

from A Furnace

To the memory of John Cowper Powys (1872–1963)

Introit

12 November 1958

November light low and strong
crossing from the left
finds this archaic
trolleybus, touches the side of it up
5   into solid yellow and green.

14: *tiles:* i.e., roof tiles
15: *cokehouse:* a building for storage of coke, a fuel derived from coal

Dedication: The novelist *John Cowper Powys's* works include *Wolf Solent* (1929) and *A Glastonbury Romance* (1932). "The poem is . . . an homage, from a temperament very different from his, to the profound, heterodox and consistent vision of John Cowper Powys, to whom I owe thanks for some words of exhortation he gave me in my youth and in his old age. More importantly, I am indebted to his writings for such understanding as I have of the idea that the making of all kinds of identities is a primary impulse which the cosmos itself has; and that those identities and that impulse can be acknowledged only by some form or other of poetic imagination." (Fisher, Preface to *A Furnace*).
Title: *Introit:* an introduction; the name of the introductory section of the Mass

This light is without
rarity, it is an oil,
amber and clear that binds in
this alone and suggests
10   no other. It is a pressing
medium, steady to a purpose.

And in the sun's ray through the glass
lifting towards low noon, I
am bound;
15   boots on the alloy
fenders that edge the deck,
lost out of the day
between two working calls
and planted alone
20   above the driver's head.
High over the roadway
I'm being swung out
into an unknown crosswise
route to a connection
25   at the Fighting Cocks
by way of Ettingshall;

old industrial road,
buildings to my left along the flat
wastes between townships
30   wrapped in the luminous
haze underneath the sun,
their forms cut clear and combined
into the mysteries, their surfaces
soft beyond recognition;

35   and as if I was made
to be the knifeblade, the light-divider,
to my right the brilliance strikes out perpetually
into the brick house-fields towards Wolverhampton,
their calculable distances
40   shallow with detail.

                    •

What is it, this
sensation as of freedom? Tang of
town gas, sulphur, tar,
settled among the heavy
45   separate houses behind
roadside planes, pale, patch-barked
and almost bare,
the last wide stiffened leaves
in tremor across their shadows
50   with trolley-standards of green cast iron

25–26: *Fighting Cocks* is a crossroads area near Wolverhampton, named after its pub; *Ettingshall* is a district on the Bilston-Wolverhampton road. Wolverhampton is a metropolitan district in the West Midlands, on the perimeter of the industrial "Black Country."
50: *trolley-standards:* trolley-cable posts. A trolley bus was a double-decker bus with road wheels, powered from overhead cables like a tramcar (trolley).

reared among them, the catenaries
stretching a net just over my guided head,
its roof of yellow metal.

A deserted, sun-battered theatre
55   under a tearing sky
is energy, its date 19□02
spread across its face, mark of
anomaly. And the road
from Bilston to Ettingshall begins
60   beating in. Whatever
approaches my passive taking-in,
then surrounds me and goes by
will have itself understood only
phase upon phase
65   by separate involuntary
strokes of my mind, dark
swings of a fan-blade
that keeps a time of its own,
made up from the long
70   discrete moments
of the stages of the street,
each bred off the last as if by
causality.
                    Because
75   of the brick theatre struck to the roadside
the shops in the next
street run in a curve, and
because of that there is raised up
with red lead on its girders
80   a gasworks
close beyond the roofs,

and because of the fold of the
folding in of these three to me
there comes a frame tower with gaps
85   in its corrugated cladding
and punched out of the sheets high
under its gable
a message in dark empty holes, USE GAS.

●

Something's decided
90   to narrate
in more dimensions than I can know
the gathering in
and giving out of the world on a slow
pulse, on a metered contraction
95   that the senses enquire towards

51: *catenaries*: i.e., trolley cables: a catenary is the curve formed by a string suspended from its two end-
     points.
59: *Bilston*: a small urban area near Wolverhampton
85: *cladding*: a covering (composed, e.g., of flakes of wood, sheet metal, slate, or tile), applied to the sur-
     face of a building—here, a steel-frame tower

but may not themselves
intercept. All I can tell it by
is the passing trace of it
in a patterned agitation of
100   a surface that shows only
metaphors. Riddles. Resemblances
that have me in the chute
as it meshes in closer, many modes
funnelling fast through one event,
105   the flow-through so
dense with association
that its colour comes up, dark
brownish green, soaked and
decomposing leaves
110   in a liquor.

•

And the biggest of all the apparitions,
the great iron
thing, the ironworks,
reared up on end into the bright
115   haze, makes quiet burning
if anything at all.

When the pulse-beat for it comes
it is revealed, set
back a little way, arrested,
120   inward, grotesque, prepared for.

Then gone by,
with the shallowing of the road
and the pulse's falling away
cleanly through a few more
125   frames of buildings, noise,
a works gate with cyclists;
the passing of it quite final, not a tremor
of the prospect at the crossroads;
open light, green paint on a sign,
130   the trolley wires
chattering and humming from somewhere else.

II. The Return

Whatever breaks
from stasis, radiance or dark
impending, and slides
directly and fast on its way, twisting

Title: cf. Ezra Pound's poem "The Return," a vision of the "tentative" return of the gods: "See, they return, one, and by one, / With fear, as half-awakened."

5 aspect in the torsions of the flow
 this way and that,
      then suddenly
 over,
   through a single
10 glance of another force touching it or
 bursting out of it sidelong,

 doing so
 fetches the timeless flux
 that cannot help but practise
15 materialization,
 the coming into sense,
 to the guesswork of the senses,
 the way in cold air
 ice-crystals, guessed at, come densely
20 falling from where they were not;

 and it fetches
 timeless identities
 riding in the flux with no
 determined form, cast out of the bodies
25 that once they were, or out of
 the brains that bore them;

 but trapped into water-drops,
 windows they glanced through
 or had their images
30 detained by and reflected
 or into whose molten glass the coloured oxides
 burned their qualities;

 like dark-finned fish embedded in ice
 they have life in them that can be revived.

   ●

35 There is ancient
 and there is seeming ancient;
 new, and seeming new—
 venerable cancer, old as the race,
 but so made as to bear
40 nothing but urgencies—

 there is persuading the world's
 layers apart with means
 that perpetually alter and annex,
 and show by the day what they can;

45 but still, with hardly a change to it,
 the other dream or intention: of encoding

31: *coloured oxides:* added to make stained glass
33–34: "Quoted from J. C. Powys, *Maiden Castle* (Macdonald, 1937)." (Fisher).

something perennial
and entering Nature thereby.

The masque for that
50   comes in its own best time
but in my place.

Bladelike and eternal, clear,
the entry into Nature
is depicted by
55   the vanishing of a gentleman
in black, and in portraiture,
being maybe a Doctor John
Dee, or Donne, or Hofmannsthal's
Lord Chandos,
60   he having lately walked
through a door in the air
among the tall
buildings of the Northern Aluminium Company
and become inseparable
65   from all other things, no longer
capable of being imagined
apart from them, nor yet of being
forgotten in his identity.

All of that is enacted
70   at the far top
of the field I was born in,

long slope of scrub, then pasture,
still blank on the map three hundred years
after the walkings of all such gentlemen
75   out of the air

then suddenly printed across with
this century, new, a single
passage of the roller
dealing out streets of terraces
80   that map like ratchet-strips, their gables
gazing in ranks above the gardens
at a factory sportsground,
a water-tower for steam-cranes, more
worksheds, and,
85   hulking along a bank
for a sunset peristyle, the long dark
tunnel-top roof of a football stadium.

49: *masque:* a form of entertainment popular among the sixteenth- and seventeenth-century English aris-
tocracy: it combined drama, spectacle, dance, and music, with members of the court themselves taking
many of the roles. The form's master was Ben Jonson, whose masques are characteristically celebrations
of a harmonious cosmic and social order.

57–58: *Doctor John Dee* (1527–1608), Elizabethan alchemist, astrologist, and mathematician.

58–59: *Lord Chandos* was a real Renaissance nobleman; but the "Lord Chandos Letter" is a fictional let-
ter by the Austrian poet and playwright Hugo von Hofmannsthal (1874–1929), in the form of a letter from
Lord Chandos to his friend Sir Francis Bacon. In it he speaks of how his youthful promise as a writer
withered when he mysteriously lost his faith in language.

86: *peristyle:* a colonnade surrounding a building

All so mild, so late
in that particular change;
90   still seeming new.
                    Some of it,
my streets—Kentish Road,
Belmont, Paddington, Malvern—
just now caught up and lacquered
95   as Urban Renewal, halted
in the act of tilting to break up
and follow the foundries out
and the stamping mills,
the heavy stuff; short lives, all of them.

100   But still through that place
to enter Nature; it was possible,
it was imperative.

Something always
coming out, back against the flow,
105   against the drive to be in,
                     close to the radio,
the school, the government's wars;

the sunlight, old and still,
heavy on dry garden soil,

110   and nameless mouths,
events without histories, voices,
animist, polytheist, metaphoric,
coming through;

the sense of another world
115   not past, but primordial,
everything in it
simultaneous, and moving
every way but forward.

Massive in the sunlight, the old woman
120   dressed almost all in black, sitting out
on a low backyard wall,
rough hands splayed on her sacking apron
with a purseful of change in the pocket,
black headscarf tight across the brow, black
125   cardigan and rough skirt, thick stockings,
black shoes worn down;
                   this peasant
is English, city born; it's the last
quarter of the twentieth century
130   up an entryway
in Perry Barr, Birmingham, and there's

98: *stamping mills:* "I was thinking of any machinery that renders waste unrecognisable" (Fisher, in correspondence).
122: *sacking:* a coarse fabric such as burlap
131: *Perry Barr:* a district of Birmingham, adjacent to Handsworth (Fisher's birthplace)

mint sprouting in an old
chimneypot. No imaginable
beginning to her epoch, and she's
135   ignored its end.

•

Timeless identities,
seeming long
like the one they called Achilles,
or short, like William Fisher,
140   age ten years, occupation, jeweller,
living in 1861 down Great King Street
in a household
headed by his grandmother, my ancestress
Ann Mason, fifty-seven, widow,
145   occupation, mangler; come in
from Hornton, back of Edge Hill,
where the masons were quarrying for Christminster.

•

These identities, recorded by authority
to be miniaturized; to be traceable
150   however small; to be material;
to have status in the record;
to have the rest,
the unwritten,
even more easily scrapped.

•

155   Mind
and language
and mind out of language again, and
language again and for ever

fall slack and pat
160   by defect of nature
into antinomies. Unless

thrown. And again
and repeatedly thrown
to break down the devil
165   his spirit; to pull down
the devil his grammar school,
wherein the brain

138: *Achilles:* the greatest of the Greek warriors in the *Iliad*
145: *mangler:* i.e., a laundry worker, operating a mangle (wringer) to press water out of clothes and linen before it was hung to dry
146: *Hornton:* a small village in North Oxfordshire; nearby is *Edge Hill,* a ridge that overlooks the site of, and gives its name to, a famous Civil War battle.
147: *Christminster:* the name used for Oxford in the novels of Thomas Hardy; Jude Fawley, protagonist of *Jude the Obscure,* dreams of studying at Christminster, but, coming from a humble background, can only work there as a mason.
164–65: *the devil / his spirit:* i.e., the devil's spirit: this form of the possessive was standard until the eighteenth century.

submits to be
cloven, up,
170   sideways and down
in all of its pathways;

where to convert
one term to its antithesis
requires that there be devised
175   an agent with authority—

and they're in. That's it. Who
shall own death? Spoken for,
and Lazarus the test case. Only Almighty
God could work that trick. Accept
180   that the dead have gone away to God through
portals sculpted in brass to deter,
horrific. The signs of it, passably
offensive in a cat or a herring,
in a man are made out
185   unthinkably appalling: *vide*
M. Valdemar's selfless
demonstration; drawn back and forth,
triumphantly racked in a passage without
extent, province of the agent,
190   between antithesis and thesis.

Sale and Lease-back. Perennial
wheeze. In the body's exuberance
steal it, whatever it is, sell it back again,
buy it in, cheap,
195   put it out to rent. If it's freedom, graciously
grant it,
            asking in return no more than
war service, wage-labour, taxes,
custodial schooling, a stitched-up
200   franchise. Trade
town futures for fields,
railroad food in, sell it on the streets.

And as if it were a military installation
specialize and classify and hide
205   the life of the dead.

178: *Lazarus*: the man raised from the dead by Jesus (see John 11).

185: *vide*: see

186: *M. Valdemar*: in Edgar Allan Poe's story "The Facts in the Case of M. Valdemar," he is put under hypnosis while he is dying; to the hypnotist's question "M. Valdemar, do you still sleep?" he replies "Yes;—no;—I *have been* sleeping—and now—now—*I am dead*." He continues in this state for seven months until he is roused from his hypnotized state, upon which he instantly decomposes to nothing.

190: *antithesis and thesis*: Fisher alludes to the philosophy of Hegel, in whose dialectical scheme of history and ideas thesis and antithesis lead eventually to a higher synthesis. The images of antithetical movement in this passage touch on the poem's core structural image, "the ancient figure of the double spiral, whose line turns back on itself at the centre and leads out again, against its own incoming curve" (Fisher's Preface).

192: *wheeze*: trick

•

Under that thunderous
humbug they've been persistently
coming and going, by way of
the pass-and-return valve between the worlds,
210   not strenuous; ghosts
innocent of time, none the worse
for their adventure, nor any better;

that you are dead
turns in the dark of your spiral,
215   comes close in the first hours after birth,
recedes and recurs often. Nobody
need sell you a death.

•

The ghosts' grown children
mill all day in the Public Search Office
220   burrowing out names for their own bodies, finding
characters with certificates but no
stories. Genetic behaviour,
scrabbling, feeling back across the spade-cut
for something; the back-flow of the genes'
225   forward compulsion suddenly
showing broken, leaking out, distressed.

•

They come anyway
to the trench,
the dead in their surprise,
230   taking whatever form they can
to push across. They've no news.
They infest the brickwork. Kentish Road
almost as soon as it's run up
out in the field, gets propelled
235   to the trench, the soot still fresh on it,
and the first few dozen faces
take the impress, promiscuously
with door and window arches;
Birmingham voices in the entryways
240   lay the law down. My surprise
stares into the walls.

1983–1985 / 1986

219: *Public Search Office:* part of the public records system; in particular the central office in London,
  where old registers of births, deaths, and marriages are available for consultation
232: *Kentish Road:* the street where Fisher was born and lived until the age of 23.

JON SILKIN (1930–1998)

S ILKIN WROTE THAT "IF IMAGISM IS IMPACTED WITH NARRATIVE . . . IMAGISTIC PROFILE is given substance and value."[1] His poems often fold sensuous description into a narrative or discursive structure; they can be candidly didactic in their treatment of moral and political questions. His longer political poems explore the meaning and impact of historical events: the collective suicide in 1190 of Jews in York to avoid forcible conversion to Christianity ("Astringencies") or miners' strikes in County Durham in the nineteenth century ("Killhope Wheel"). The two "Flower Poems" together with "A Word About Freedom and Dignity in Tel Aviv," "Death of a Son," and "First it was Singing" indicate something of Silkin's range as a lyric poet and show the extent to which "harm / Made me sing," as Silkin writes in "First it was Singing." Whether it is the common daisy or dandelion or Jewish devotion in modern-day Tel Aviv that is his subject, Silkin's lyric poems often wonder at the ability of forms of life to persist and even flourish in a world too often characterized by cruelty and will to power. He once wrote that the question dominating his work is "How does the Peaceable Kingdom make room for those creatures who do not want to belong to it, and would destroy it if it tried to bring them into its condition of love?"[2]

Silkin was born in London and educated at Wycliffe and Dulwich colleges and the University of Leeds. His first jobs were as a journalist, laborer, and teacher of English to foreign students; later he taught at the universities of Leeds and Newcastle and at universities in the United States, Australia, and Israel. In 1952, he founded the journal *Stand* in Newcastle upon Tyne, and except for a brief hiatus in the mid-fifties, he continued to edit or co-edit it until his death. His collections of poetry include *The Peaceable Kingdom* (1954), *The Two Freedoms* (1958), *Flower Poems* (1964), *Nature with Man* (1965), *Killhope Wheel* (1971), *Amana Grass* (1971), *The Principle of Water* (1974), and *The Ship's Pasture* (1986). He wrote on World War I poetry in *Out of Battle: The Poetry of the Great War* (1972; 1987) and edited the poems of Wilfred Owen. His anthology of "socially oriented" poems, *Poetry of the Committed Individual*, was published in 1973.

---

[1] *Contemporary Poets*, 6th ed., ed. Thomas Riggs, New York, 1996, p. 894.
[2] Ibid., p. 894.

Death of a Son

(who died in a mental hospital aged one)

Something has ceased to come along with me.
Something like a person: something very like one.
And there was no nobility in it
Or anything like that.

5 Something was there like a one year
Old house, dumb as stone. While the near buildings
Sang like birds and laughed
Understanding the pact

They were to have with silence. But he
10 Neither sang nor laughed. He did not bless silence
Like bread, with words.
He did not forsake silence.

But rather, like a house in mourning
Kept the eye turned in to watch the silence while
15 The other houses like birds
Sang around him.

And the breathing silence neither
Moved nor was still.

I have seen stones: I have seen brick
20 But this house was made up of neither bricks nor stone
But a house of flesh and blood
With flesh of stone

And bricks for blood. A house
Of stones and blood in breathing silence with the other
25 Birds singing crazy on its chimneys.
But this was silence,

This was something else, this was
Hearing and speaking though he was a house drawn
Into silence, this was
30 Something religious in his silence,

Something shining in his quiet,
This was different this was altogether something else:
Though he never spoke, this
Was something to do with death.

35 And then slowly the eye stopped looking
Inward. The silence rose and became still.
The look turned to the outer place and stopped,
With the birds still shrilling around him.
And as if he could speak

40 He turned over on his side with his one year
Red as a wound
He turned over as if he could be sorry for this
And out of his eyes two great tears rolled, like stones, and he died.

1954

First it was Singing

From the first cry
I was given music with which to speak,
Tramping the agape streets
The amazed faces

5   Turning, with their
Voices to laugh at the singer in the common
Street. From the first I was
Given a voice

To cry out with.
10   It was a peaceable music tuned in fear.
Later, it was death
But it was singing

First.
And from that it was I loved the hopping birds,
15   The limping fly
And the mad

Bee, stung to anger
In worship of summer. It was their speech, and my speech,
The Jewish stone and the
20   Animal rock

Rolling together that made me sing
Of our common lash, the white raised weal across
Our black back, I and
The hunted fox, the

25   Huge fly, his
Dangerous wings torn from his body
The seal tusking the sea,
As the dog bawls air.

It was our harm
30   Made me sing. Afterwards it was death,
Death of the stone
By stoning

The animal
By animals, but, first, singing.
35   Jew and animal singing first;
And afterwards, death.

1954

Dandelion

Slugs nestle where the stem
Broken, bleeds milk.
The flower is eyeless: the sight is compelled
By small, coarse, sharp petals,

5   Like metal shreds. Formed,
They puncture, irregularly perforate
Their yellow, brutal glare.
And certainly want to
Devour the earth. With an ample movement
10   They are a foot high, as you look.
And coming back, they take hold
On pert domestic strains.
Others' lives are theirs. Between them
And domesticity,
15   Grass. They infest its weak land;
Fatten, hide slugs, infestate.
They look like plates; more closely
Like the first tryings, the machines, of nature
Riveted into her, successful.

1965

A Daisy

Look unoriginal
Being numerous. They ask for attention
With that gradated yellow swelling
Of oily stamens. Petals focus them:
5   The eye-lashes grow wide.
Why should not one bring these to a funeral?
And at night, like children,
Without anxiety, their consciousness
Shut with white petals;

10   Blithe, individual.

The unwearying, small sunflower
Fills the grass
With versions of one eye.
A strength in the full look
15   Candid, solid, glad.
Domestic as milk.

In multitudes, wait,
Each, to be looked at, spoken to.
They do not wither;
20   Their going, a pressure
Of elate sympathy
Released from you.
Rich up to the last interval
With minute tubes of oil, pollen;
25   Utterly without scent, for the eye,
For the eye, simply. For the mind
And its invisible organ,
That feeling thing.

1965

A Word about Freedom and Identity in Tel-Aviv

Through a square sealed-off with
a grey & ornate house,
its length bent, for one corner of that,
a road leads off, got to down steps:
5   wide, terraced, ample.
The road's quiet, too; but nudges as
the square did not. Walking
some, below the city I heard
a pared, harsh cry, sustained
10 and hovering, between outrage
and despair; scraped by itself
into a wedge-shape opening on
inaccessibly demented hurt
it can't quite come at;
15 imitative, harsh, genuine.
A pet-shop four feet below
pavement level; in its front yard
a blue parrot, its open beak
hooked and black, the folded wings
20 irregularly lifting a little;
under which, dull yellow soft plumage,
the insides of itself, heaved, slightly.
Its tail was long, stiff. Long in stiffness
that at once bends entirely
25 if bent too much. And as it
turned in its cage, bending the tail
against the wires, it spoke
into the claw it raised
at its hooked face, the word
30 'torah, torah' in the hoarse, devotional
grief religious men speak with
rendering on God the law
their love binds them with. Done,
it cried its own cry, its claws tightening
35 onto its beak, shaking slowly
the whole face with the cry
from side to side. This cry was placed
by one Jew inside another. Not belonging though;
an animal of no distinct race,
40 its cry also human, slightly;
wired in, waiting; fed on
good seed a bit casually
planted. Granulated, sifted,
dry. The torah is:
45 suffering begets suffering, that is.

1971

30: "The Torah consists of the body of Jewish religious knowledge." (Silkin)

ROSEMARY TONKS (b. 1932)

TONKS QUIT PUBLISHING IN THE EARLY 1970S, REPORTEDLY AFTER BECOMING AN EVAN-gelical Christian. Her poetry has never entirely faded from view, and there have been recent indications of new interest, such as the inclusion of one of her poems in Sean O'Brien's anthology *The Firebox: Poetry in Britain and Ireland after 1945* (1998). She was born in London and educated at Wentworth School, from which she was expelled at the age of 16. Her career as a writer began in the same year with the publication of a children's story. After marrying at 19, she went with her husband to Karachi, Pakistan, where she began seriously to write poetry. Illnesses—typhoid and then polio—forced her to return to England, and later she spent a brief period in Paris. She wrote stories for the BBC, reviewed poetry for the BBC's European Service, and published a series of poetic novels including *Opium Fogs* (1963), *The Bloater* (1968), *Businessmen as Lovers* (1969), and *The Halt During the Chase* (1972). Her poems were published in the *Observer*, the *New Statesman, Encounter,* and *Poetry Review*; she read them on the BBC's Third Programme and recorded one of them for Argo. Her two books of poems are *Notes on Cafés and Bedrooms* (1963) and *Iliad of Broken Sentences* (1967).

Tonks's poems offer a stylized view of a late 1950s and early 1960s urban literary sub-culture afloat in hedonism and decadence, their speaker's persona shifting between Baudelairean ennui and exuberant disbelief at her "nervous, luxury civilization." Scenes of illicit love affairs in seedy hotels and café life in cities throughout Europe and the Middle East mingle with savvy reflection on the behavior of "men timid with women."[1] The pathetic pretensions of intellectuals and writers are a regular target. But Tonks's poems are often chatty and buoyant, more bemused than critical, sometimes self-deprecating. "The Sash Window" begins "Outside that house, I stood like a dog,"[2] and in the course of mocking the high-society xenophobia of those who blame "those damn foreign women" for "the whole trouble," the speaker of "The Little Cardboard Suitcase" tells us that "As a thinker" she is "a professional water-cabbage."[3] Elsewhere Tonks writes of students "pour[ing] politics into the brown walls" of a restaurant: "each man stuffs himself with ideas, he eats his pork newspaper."[4] The poems suggest a witty precociousness that resists earnestness, as if the poet finds life "irresistibly amusing"; they refuse to submit to those who would predict her likely "disreputable future."[5] Their diction and fondness for inventive exclamations can sometimes suggest French surrealist poetry: "The blind rubbers of the mouth of love!"[6]

---

[1] "Love Territory," *Notes on Cafés and Bedrooms*, p. 7.
[2] *Iliad of Broken Sentences*, p. 11.
[3] Ibid., p. 12.
[4] "Students In Bertorelli's," *Iliad of Broken Sentences*, p. 14.
[5] "The Little Cardboard Suitcase," p. 12.
[6] "Ace of Hooligans," *Notes on Cafés and Bedrooms*, p. 21.

The Sofas, Fogs, and Cinemas

I have lived it, and lived it,
My nervous, luxury civilization,
My sugar-loving nerves have battered me to pieces.

. . . Their idea of literature is hopeless.
5   Make them drink their own poetry!
Let them eat their gross novel, full of mud.

It's quiet; just the fresh, chilly weather . . . and he
Gets up from his dead bedroom, and comes in here
And digs himself into the sofa.
10   He stays there up to two hours in the hole—and talks
—Straight into the large subjects, he faces up to *everything*
It's . . . . . . damnably depressing.
(That great lavatory coat . . . the cigarillo burning
In the little dish . . . And when he calls out: "Ha!"
15   Madness!—you no longer possess your own furniture.)

On my bad days (and I'm being broken
At this very moment) I speak of my ambitions . . . and he
Becomes intensely gloomy, with the look of something jugged,
Morose, sour, mouldering away, with lockjaw. . . .

20   I grow coarser; and more modern (*I*, who am driven mad
By my ideas; who go nowhere;
Who dare not leave my frontdoor, lest an idea . . .)
All right. I admit everything, everything!

Oh yes, the opera (Ah, but the cinema)
25   He particularly enjoys it, enjoys it *horribly,* when someone's ill
At the last minute; and they specially fly in
A new, gigantic, Dutch soprano. He wants to help her
With her arias.   Old goat! Blasphemer!
He wants to help her with her arias!

30   No, I . . . go to the cinema,
I particularly like it when the fog is thick, the street
Is like a hole in an old coat, and the light is brown as laudanum.
. . . the fogs! the fogs! The cinemas
Where the criminal shadow-literature flickers over our faces,
35   The screen is spread out like a thundercloud—that bangs
And splashes you with acid . . . or lies derelict, with lighted waters in it,
And in the silence, drips and crackles—taciturn, luxurious.
. . . The drugged and battered Philistines
Are all around you in the auditorium . . .

40   And he . . . is somewhere else, in his dead bedroom clothes,
He wants to make me think his thoughts

18: *jugged:* confined

And they will be *enormous,* dull—(just the sort
To keep away from).
   . . . when I see that cigarillo, when I see it . . . smoking
45   And he wants to face the international situation . . .
Lunatic rages! Blackness! Suffocation!

—All this sitting about in cafés to calm down
Simply wears me out. And their idea of literature!
The idiotic cut of the stanzas; the novels, full up, gross.

50   I have lived it, and I know too much.
My café-nerves are breaking me
With black, exhausting information.

1967

The Little Cardboard Suitcase

Events pushed me into this corner;
I live in a fixed routine,
With my cardboard attaché case full of rotting books.
. . . If only I could trust my blood! Those damn foreign women
5   Have a lot to answer for, marrying into the family—

—The mistakes, the wrong people, the half-baked ideas,
And their beastly comments on everything. Foul.
But irresistibly amusing, that is the whole trouble.

With my cardboard suitcase full of occidental literature
10   I reached this corner, to educate myself
Against the sort of future they flung into my blood—
The events, the people, the ideas—the *ideas!*
And I alone know how disreputable and foreign.

But as a thinker, as a professional water-cabbage,
15   From my desk, of course, I shall dissolve events
As if they were of no importance . . . none whatever.

. . . And those women are to blame!
I was already half-way into my disreputable future,
When I found that they had thrown into my blood
20   With the mistakes, the people, the ideas (ideas indeed!)
This little cardboard suitcase . . . damned
Beloved women . . . and these books, opium, beef, God.

At my desk (lit by its intellectual cabbage-light)
I found them—and they are irresistibly amusing—
25   These thoughts that have been thrown into my blood.

1967

The Ice-cream Boom Towns

Hurry: we must go south to escape
The bubonic yellow-drink of our old manuscripts,
You, with your career, toad-winner, I with my intolerance.
The English seacoast is more oafish than a ham.

5 We can parade together softly, aloof
Like envoys in coloured clothes—on the promenades,
The stone sleeping-tables where the bourgeois bog down,
And the brilliant sea swims vigorously in and out.

There will be hot-house winds to blunt themselves
10 Against the wooden bathing-huts, and fall down senseless;
Lilos that swivel in the shallow, iced waves, half-submerged;
Skiffs—trying to bite into a sea that's watertight!

One whiff of it—careerist—and we fall down senseless,
Bivouacked! Your respirating, steep, electric head,
15 Filled by its nervous breakdown, will slumber narcotized
By the clear gas that trembles in the sandpit.

Under the pier will be an overdose of shadows—the Atlantic
Irrigates the girders with enormous, disembodied cantos,
Unless you're quick—they pull the clothes off your soul
20 To make it moan some watery, half-rotten stanzas.

Night! The plasterboard hotels that rattle shanty bedrooms
On the front, are waiting! Without gods, books, sex or family,
We'll sink to a vast depth, and lie there, musing, interlocked
Like deportees who undulate to phosphorescent booming.

1967

2: *bubonic:* i.e., poisonous: Tonks has in mind the bubonic plague.
11: A *Lilo* is a plastic, inflatable air-bed.
14: *Bivouacked:* encamped outside for the night
18: *cantos:* sections of a long poem (literally "songs")

PETER REDGROVE (b. 1932)

IN HIS ESSAY "RIMBAUD MY VIRGIL," REDGROVE WRITES OF HIS PURSUIT OF A "daily sacramental vision." Citing Rimbaud's insistence that the poet disorder or de-school his senses to arrive at a vision of the previously unknown, Redgrove claims that "It is not so much that we must 'make strange' as to be prepared to find life as strange as it is."[1] Redgrove has drawn on a broad set of influences—the psychology of Jung and John Layard, shamanism, alchemy, magic ("by magic we should mean 'unwounded perception'"), the natural sciences, feminist theory. His poems work to imagine what Neil Corcoran describes as an "internally coherent symbolic system or symbology, explicitly anti-Christian and pagan-organicist-pantheistic, and implicitly Gravesian and Jungian, a private imaginative system intruded upon and interrupted dissonantly and intermittently by 'official', public symbols and myths."[2] "We should become technicians of the sacred," Redgrove writes, "and study not the abstract ram-ifications of physics, but the actuality of psychological and biological sciences, remembering of course that any psychology which neglects the inner experience— and they all do this—is suspect and almost derelict unless we can give our own per-sonal and poetic testimony from actual experience."[3] A recurrent concern, as in the early poem "Against Death," is to locate the human within the larger non-human world, and the effort of the human to come to terms with the rhythms of a "natural world" as they involve cycles of birth and death. Corcoran remarks that "Insects . . . are perhaps his most exceptional symbol, with a resonance by turns (or even all at once) Blakean, Franciscan, and Christopher Smartian."[4]

Redgrove was born in Kingston, Surrey and educated at Taunton School, Somer-set, and Queen's College, Cambridge. He has worked in advertising and scientific journalism and, since 1966, as the resident author at Falmouth School of Art in Corn-wall. He was a member of the London incarnation of The Group and had poems in Phillip Hobsbaum and Edward Lucie Smith's *A Group Anthology* (1963). Redgrove's many books include *The Collector and Other Poems* (1960), *Dr. Faust's Sea-Spiral Spirit* (1972), *The Man Named East* (1985), and *My Father's Trapdoor* (1994). *The Wise Wound: Menstruation and Everywoman* (1986), a study of the taboos that have sur-rounded menstruation and menstrual sex, co-written with Penelope Shuttle, is a key text in understanding Redgrove's revisionist mythography.

---

[1] *Sulfur*, vol. 30, 1992, p. 176.
[2] *English Poetry since 1940*, Harlow, 1993, p. 143.
[3] *Sulfur*, p. 177.
[4] Corcoran, p. 144.

Against Death

We are glad to have birds in our roof
Sealed off from rooms by white ceiling,
And glad to glimpse them homing straight
Blinking across the upstairs windows,
5   And to listen to them scratching on the laths
As we bed and whisper staring at the ceiling.
We're glad to be hospitable to birds.
In our rooms, in general only humans come,
We keep no cats and dislike wet-mouthed dogs,
10   And wind comes up the floorboards in a gale,
So then we keep to bed: no more productive place
To spend a blustery winter evening and keep warm.
Occasionally a spider capsizes in the bath,
Blot streaming with legs among the soap,
15   Cool and scab-bodied, soot-and-suet,
So we have to suffocate it down the pipe
For none of us'd have dealings with it,
Like kissing a corpse's lips, even
Through the fingers, so I flood it out.
20   In our high-headed rooms we're going to breed
Many human beings for their home
To fill the house with children and with life,
Running in service of the shrill white bodies,
With human life but for sparrows in the roof,
25   Wiping noses and cleaning up behind,
Slapping and sympathising, and catching glimpses
Of each other and ourselves as we were then,
And let out in the world a homing of adults.

And if there ever should be a corpse in the house
30   Hard on its bedsprings in a room upstairs,
Smelling of brass-polish, with sucked-in cheeks,
Staring through eyelids at a scratching ceiling,
Some firm'd hurry it outdoors and burn it quick—
We'd expect no more to happen to ourselves
35   Our children gradually foregoing grief of us
As the hot bodies of the sparrows increase each summer.

1959

Young Women with the Hair of Witches
and no Modesty

'I loved Ophelia!'

I have always loved water, and praised it.
I have often wished water would hold still.
Changes and glints bemuse a man terribly:
There is champagne and glimmer of mists;

Epigraph: *Hamlet* 5.1.264

5   Torrents, the distaffs of themselves, exalted, confused;
     And snow splintering silently, skilfully, indifferently.
     I have often wished water would hold still.
     Now it does so, or ripples so, skilfully
     In cross and doublecross, surcross and countercross.
10   A person lives in the darkness of it, watching gravely;

     I used to see her straight and cool, considering the pond,
     And as I approached she would turn gracefully
     In her hair, its waves betraying her origin.
     I told her that her thoughts issued in hair like consideration of water,
15   And if she laughed, that they would rain like spasms of weeping,

     Or if she wept, then solemnly they held still,
     And in the rain, the perfumes of it, and the blowing of it,
     Confused, like hosts of people all shouting.
     In such a world the bride walks through dressed as a waterfall,
20   And ripe grapes fall and splash smooth snow with jagged purple,
     Young girls grow brown as acorns in their rainy climb towards oakhood,
     And brown moths settle low down among ivories wet with love.
     But she loosened her hair in a sudden tangle of contradictions,
     In cross and doublecross, surcross and countercross,
25   And I was a shadow in the twilight of her late displeasure.
     I asked water to stand still, now nothing else holds.

                                                          1972

The British Museum Smile

     None of the visitors from teeming London streets
     Smiles. The deeply-lined downtrodden faces
     Elbow the galleries. The sphinxes inside smile
     And the colossal faces.
5   The face of a king with shattered legs
     Smiles. And the guards smile. Their solitude
     Forms into a smile and the patience
     Of all the seated faces in navy uniforms
     On the little chairs with the deeply-marked cushions
10   Smiles. They have caught it from the sphinxes
     And the colossal kings and the powerful scribes
     With the stone incense-bowls who smile sweetly
     Over the smoky crowds. Some of the smiles
     Are printed on the air from the faces of the guards,
15   And the stone faces have dissolved a little in the air;
     Passing through and through the smiling galleries
     Rubs inch by inch the face into a smile,
     The smile of the king you pass (whose legs are sand),
     The imagined absent smiles of the drenched nereids
20   Whose headless robes blow back against their flesh

5: *distaffs*: staffs holding wool or flax for purposes of spinning

19: *nereids*: sea-nymphs

In many folded smiles, whose smiling heads
Are museum air; the mummies
With their gasping toothy grins
Under the polite smile-paintings of their coffin-shells
25   Lumbered here by ship and block and tackle
Scattering a trail of smiles; elsewhere
The nereid heads are pebbles or sand,
And who picks up the pebble smiles at its smoothness;
(And the sleek sand is made of microscopic nereid heads
30   Turning and kissing in the water of the tide
The smiles rubbing from quartz lip to lip,
Dissolving in the sea and flying on spume;
The mariners inhale, and smile.)

Such smiles have flittered down
35   Like pipistrelles of Egypt on to the faces of the guards
And the smiling guards know something unknown to their crowds,
Something fallen from the sphinx that patters down
To fit you as you sit still on a stool
Polishing with your back those polished stones
40   For twenty years, or among those polished volumes
Not reading, but learning that smile. It took
Four thousand years to teach that smile
That flutters in these galleries among the guards
Who exchange mirrored smiles across glass cases; how
45   Did stone first catch it, that virus smile?

1981

Mothers and Child

I

The soft modelling for hours,
The soft handling.
Undressing, she forgets to say her prayers.

The town of wives, promenading,
5   Staring among the lighted beauty-shops
Which are shadows of the beauty that is above,

That is too bright to look at
Except in the shadowing of lipstick and powder,
Painting with colour, camera obscura,

35: *pipistrelles:* bats

Title: "Mother and Child" is the title of countless paintings of the Virgin Mary with the baby Jesus.
9: *camera obscura:* predecessor of the modern camera, a darkened box with a small aperture in one wall; the light through this hole casts an inverted external image on the opposite wall. This device was used in past centuries to indirectly view solar eclipses in order to avoid damaging the eyes.

10   This in the town of the two electricities,
       The powerhouse, lighting the shops,
       The wives, stiff in their orgasms

       With fingers stretched like starfish
       And eyes going like electric bulbs,
15   Witch-hair cracking the taut white pillow;

       And the stiff filamentous reach of the powerstation
       Incandescent also in its circuits
       Like some miraculous gestating glow-worm

       Or silk-spinner of tungsten
20   That shines with that power,
       The elastic of magnetism,

       For whirl wheel within wheel
       It comes spitting
       Into the lamps, over the sheets

25   Of the great metropolis of rooms
       And the lighted villages of wives
       With the lover wanting the skin off

       Wanting the electricity in essence,
       The stripped wires,
30   Electricity with its rubber off,

       Electricity more naked than last time;
       He strokes for hours
       Mowing the magnetism,

       The sheets crackling,
35   The soft handling over and over,
       And gradually the first skins loosen;

       And the wives observe this recreation
       As the mother her rounding belly
       And wishes her child to be naked of it

40   Herself now willing her own birth
       As the fish skips out of the wave
       To be nude of the water

       Water that peels off water as it marches
       Nakedness off salt nakedness,
45   So that, undressing, she forgets to say her prayers,

       As water forgets, and reflects
       The beauty above her.

II

Or does she beam beauty up
To be bounced off the ceiling
50   Or off the man above her,

Transforming her beauty
Into his (and he needs it);
Her fighting-gear

A silk shirt,
55   Excellent accumulator of electricities,
Admirable rubbing battery of orgasms,

Or, as they say, Static,
For time stands still.
Such heroes as there might be

60   Awake when they touch her skin,
With a silent shout of recognition,
Skin which flutters unbearably

When they touch it sufficiently,
Like a moth beating in the light of the sheets,
65   The moth whose wings are flaming

Without being consumed;
And the wellspring where the more it is drawn
The more it flows;

While the wife as mother of herself opens
70   And draws herself off
That which steps out

Over the sill, the berth, the landing-place.

1985

GEOFFREY HILL (b. 1932)

HILL'S POEMS LIKE HIS ESSAYS CAN SEEM DRIVEN BY QUESTIONS INVOLVING THE MORAL-ity of poetry and the responsibilities of the poet confronting the limits of language and the hazards of interpretation. In his essay "Poetry as 'Menace' and 'Atonement,'" he writes that

> However much and however rightly we protest against the vanity of supposing [poetry] to be merely the 'spontaneous overflow of powerful feelings,' poetic utterance is nonetheless an utterance of the self, the self demanding to be loved, demanding love in the form of recognition and 'absolution.' The poet is perhaps the first to be dismayed by such a discovery and to seek the conversion of his 'daemon' to a belief in altruistic responsibility. But this dismay is as noth-ing compared to the shocking encounter with 'empirical guilt,' not as a man-ageable hypothesis, but as irredeemable error in the very substance and texture of his craft and pride. It is here that he knows the affliction of 'being fallen into the "they"' and yet it is here that his selfhood may be made at-one with itself. He may learn to live in his affliction, not with the cynical indifference of the reprobate but with the renewed sense of the vocation: that of necessarily bear-ing his peculiar unnecessary shame in a world growing ever more shameless.[1]

If rejecting the Romantic ego and self-expression hardly liberates the poet from the burden of the self, the utmost precision of craft likewise is inadequate in a world that is, as the theological idiom here suggests, not only fallen but "irredeemable." It might be that the poet's guilt or shame—at the failure of words or the failure of acts—is finally "unnecessary," but nevertheless such guilt will "necessarily" be borne: here the prose performs much as the poems often do. In the end, an integrity of craft that is itself "moral" is the poet's one consolation as he recognizes that enduring affliction is, after all, not his fate alone but a common condition. Beginning with his early poems about the Holocaust, Hill has often pondered the proposition that gives him the title for another essay: "Our word is our bond." "Modern poetry," he writes in that essay, "yearns for this sense of identity between doing and saying," but the very phrase "our word is our bond" is run aground on ambiguity, "bond" suggesting not only "covenant" or "fidu-ciary symbol" but also "shackle" or "arbitrary constraint."[2] It is perhaps not often enough noted that verbal play and structural ambiguity in Hill's poetry can be ludic and antic as well as despairing and agonized, as for example at times in the sequence *Mer-cian Hymns* (1971), a poem that mixes lines about the legendary eighth-century King of Mercia, Offa, with autobiographical and contemporary material identifying Offa as

---

[1] *The Lords of Limit: Essays on Literature and Ideas*, New York, 1984, p. 17.
[2] Ibid. p. 153.

"the presiding genius of the West Midlands," as Hill's note explains. Donald Hall writes of Hill that "if in the end he has contradicted everything that he has said, including his own contradictions, he has made an articulated structure, or representation, of the modern mind unable to find rest or resolution, defeated and beautiful in stillness."[3]

Hill was born in Bromsgrove, Worcestershire and educated at local schools and Keble College, Oxford. He taught for many years at the University of Leeds and has since been a fellow of Emmanuel College, Cambridge and a visiting professor at several other universities. He moved to the United States in 1988 and currently teaches at Boston University. His other books include *For the Unfallen: Poems 1952–1958* (1959), *King Log* (1968), *Tenebrae* (1978), *New and Collected Poems 1952–1992* (1994), *Canaan* (1996), and *The Triumph of Love* (1998). Some of his essays are collected in *The Lords of Limit* (1984) and *The Enemy's Country: Words, Contexture, and Other Circumstances of Language* (1991).

---

[3] Quoted in Vincent Sherry, *The Uncommon Tongue: The Poetry and Criticism of Geoffrey Hill*, Ann Arbor, 1987, p. 35.

Genesis

I

Against the burly air I strode
Crying the miracles of God.

And first I brought the sea to bear
Upon the dead weight of the land;
5   And the waves flourished at my prayer,
The rivers spawned their sand.

And where the streams were salt and full
The tough pig-headed salmon strove,
Ramming the ebb, in the tide's pull,
10   To reach the steady hills above.

II

The second day I stood and saw
The osprey plunge with triggered claw,
Feathering blood along the shore,
To lay the living sinew bare.

15   And the third day I cried: 'Beware
The soft-voiced owl, the ferret's smile,
The hawk's deliberate stoop in air,
Cold eyes, and bodies hooped in steel,
Forever bent upon the kill.'

III

20   And I renounced, on the fourth day,
This fierce and unregenerate clay,

Building as a huge myth for man
The watery Leviathan,

25 And made the long-winged albatross
Scour the ashes of the sea
Where Capricorn and Zero cross,
A brooding immortality—
Such as the charmed phoenix has
In the unwithering tree.

IV

30 The phoenix burns as cold as frost;
And, like a legendary ghost,
The phantom-bird goes wild and lost,
Upon a pointless ocean tossed.

So, the fifth day, I turned again
35 To flesh and blood and the blood's pain.

V

On the sixth day, as I rode
In haste about the works of God,
With spurs I plucked the horse's blood.

By blood we live, the hot, the cold,
40 To ravage and redeem the world:
There is no bloodless myth will hold.

And by Christ's blood are men made free
Though in close shrouds their bodies lie
Under the rough pelt of the sea;

45 Though Earth has rolled beneath her weight
The bones that cannot bear the light.

1952

Ovid in the Third Reich

non peccat, quaecumque potest peccasse negare,
solaque famosam culpa professa facit.
(AMORES, III, XIV)

I love my work and my children. God
Is distant, difficult. Things happen.
Too near the ancient troughs of blood
Innocence is no earthly weapon.

23: *Leviathan:* a Biblical sea monster (Job 41:1; Psalm 74:14)

26: The Tropic of *Capricorn* and the Prime Meridian cross in an empty stretch of the South Atlantic Ocean, some distance off the west coast of Africa.

28: *phoenix:* a mythical bird that lived in a tree in Arabia; it never died, but instead would immolate itself on a pyre and be reborn in the ashes.

Title: The Roman poet *Ovid* (43 BC–17 AD) was banished by the emperor Augustus to Tomis, on the Black Sea, for reasons that are unclear but in part involve his poem *Ars Amatoria* (*The Art of Love*). The speaker of the epigraph asks his unfaithful lover to hide her unfaithfulness from him: "Any woman is innocent who can deny having sinned, and only a confession of guilt makes her guilty."

5   I have learned one thing: not to look down
       So much upon the damned. They, in their sphere,
       Harmonize strangely with the divine
       Love. I, in mine, celebrate the love-choir.

1968

September Song

born 19.6.32—deported 24.9.42

Undesirable you may have been, untouchable
you were not. Not forgotten
or passed over at the proper time.

As estimated, you died. Things marched,
5   sufficient, to that end.
Just so much Zyklon and leather, patented
terror, so many routine cries.

(I have made
an elegy for myself it
10   is true)

September fattens on vines. Roses
flake from the wall. The smoke
of harmless fires drifts to my eyes.

This is plenty. This is more than enough.

1968

History as Poetry

Poetry as salutation; taste
Of Pentecost's ashen feast. Blue wounds.
The tongue's atrocities. Poetry
Unearths from among the speechless dead

5   Lazarus mystified, common man
Of death. The lily rears its gouged face

Title: Hill's title alludes to "September Song," a popular song by the German composer Kurt Weill (1900–1950), with lyrics by Maxwell Anderson. Weill, of Jewish birth, left Germany for the United States in the 1930s after the Nazis' rise to power.
Subtitle: *deported:* i.e., to a Nazi death camp. Christopher Ricks points out that Hill's birthdate is 18 June 1932 (18.6.32).
6: *Zyklon:* Zyklon-B, a cyanide gas used in the gas chambers; it was first employed in August 1942.

1: *salutation:* perhaps alluding to the angel's salutation of Mary at the Annunciation (Luke 1:28)
2: *Pentecost:* in the Christian church, the festival ("feast") celebrating the descent of the Holy Spirit on the heads of the apostles ("And there appeared unto them cloven tongues, like as of fire, and it sat upon each of them"), giving them the gift of tongues, and marking the origin of the Christian mission (Acts 2).
5: *Lazarus:* the dead man restored to life by Jesus (John 11)

From the provided loam. Fortunate
Auguries; whirrings; tarred golden dung:

10   'A resurgence' as they say. The old
Laurels wagging with the new: Selah!
Thus laudable the trodden bone thus
Unanswerable the knack of tongues.

1968

from Mercian Hymns

I

King of the perennial holly-groves, the riven sand-
stone: overlord of the M5: architect of the his-
toric rampart and ditch, the citadel at Tamworth,
the summer hermitage in Holy Cross: guardian of
5   the Welsh Bridge and the Iron Bridge: contractor
to the desirable new estates: saltmaster: money-
changer: commissioner for oaths: martyrologist:
the friend of Charlemagne.

'I liked that,' said Offa, 'sing it again.'

II

A pet-name, a common name. Best-selling brand, curt
graffito. A laugh; a cough. A syndicate. A specious
gift. Scoffed-at horned phonograph.

The starting-cry of a race. A name to conjure with.

10: *Selah!*: a word of uncertain meaning (possibly a musical direction) that appears frequently at the end
of verses in the Psalms.

Mercia was one of the principal kingdoms of Anglo-Saxon England. "The historical King Offa reigned over
Mercia (and the greater part of England south of the Humber) in the years AD 757–96. During early
medieval times he was already becoming a creature of legend. The Offa who figures in this sequence might
perhaps most usefully be regarded as the presiding genius of the West Midlands, his dominion enduring
from the middle of the eighth century until the middle of the twentieth (and possibly beyond). The indi-
cation of such a timespan will, I trust, explain and to some extent justify a number of anachronisms." (Hill)
Title: "The title of the sequence is a suggestion taken from *Sweet's Anglo-Saxon Reader* (1950 edn), pp.
170–80. A less immediate precedent is provided by the Latin prose-hymns or canticles of the early Chris-
tian Church. See Frederick Brittain, ed., *The Penguin Book of Latin Verse* (1962), pp. xvii, lv." (Hill)
I: 2: The *M5* motorway runs through what was Offa's Mercia.
3: The *rampart and ditch* are Offa's Dyke, constructed along his kingdom's border with Wales to mark its
boundaries; many sections of it are still visible.
    Tamworth: in Staffordshire; Offa built his palace there.
4: *summer hermitage*: summer retreat; *Holy Cross* is a town a few miles away from Hill's birthplace, Broms-
grove.
5: The *Iron Bridge*, spanning the River Severn in Shropshire, was the first cast-iron bridge; it was erected
in 1777–1779. The town of Ironbridge which grew up around it was one of the earliest centers of the
Industrial Revolution.
6: *saltmaster*: a collector of duties on imports of salt (once a valuable commodity)
7: *commissioner for oaths*: solicitor (in his function of witnessing sworn documents)
    martyrologist: a chronicler of the lives of Christian martyrs
8: *Charlemagne* (742–814) was king of the Franks and, from 800, Emperor of the West.
II: 1: *common name*: "cf. W. F. Bolton, *A History of Anglo-Latin Literature 597–1066* (1967), Vol. I, p. 191:
'But Offa is a common name'." (Hill)

III

On the morning of the crowning we chorused our re-
mission from school. It was like Easter: hankies
and gift-mugs approved by his foreign gaze, the
village-lintels curlered with paper flags.

5 We gaped at the car-park of 'The Stag's Head' where a
bonfire of beer-crates and holly-boughs whistled
above the tar. And the chef stood there, a king in
his new-risen hat, sealing his brisk largesse with
'any mustard?'

IV

I was invested in mother-earth, the crypt of roots
and endings. Child's-play. I abode there, bided my
time: where the mole

shouldered the clogged wheel, his gold solidus; where
5 dry-dust badgers thronged the Roman flues, the
long-unlooked-for mansions of our tribe.

V

So much for the elves' wergild, the true governance
of England, the gaunt warrior-gospel armoured in
engraved stone. I wormed my way heavenward for
ages amid barbaric ivy, scrollwork of fern.

5 Exile or pilgrim set me once more upon that ground:
my rich and desolate childhood. Dreamy, smug-faced,
sick on outings—I who was taken to be a king of
some kind, a prodigy, a maimed one.

VI

The princes of Mercia were badger and raven. Thrall
to their freedom, I dug and hoarded. Orchards
fruited above clefts. I drank from honeycombs of
chill sandstone.

5 'A boy at odds in the house, lonely among brothers.'
But I, who hadnone, fostered a strangeness; gave
myself to unattainable toys.

III: 1: Hill puns on "remission of sins," the priest's absolution of a sinner following confession.
IV: 1: "To the best of my recollection, the expression 'to invest in mother-earth' was the felicitous (and cor-
rect) definition of 'yird' given by Mr (now Sir) Michael Hordern in the programme *Call My Bluff* tele-
vised on BBC 2 on Thursday 29 January 1970." (Hill)
4: *solidus*: a Roman gold coin
V: 1: *wergild*: " 'the price set upon a man according to his rank' (OED) cf. D. Whitelock, *The Beginnings
of English Society* (1965 edn), ch. 5." (Hill). The price was paid to the man (or in the case of murder, to
his family) by whomever committed a crime against him.
VI: 1: *Thrall*: slave
5: The quotation is paraphrased from the noncanonical Psalm 151, a version of which is the first of the
Mercian Hymns included in *Sweet's Anglo-Saxon Reader*.

Candles of gnarled resin, apple-branches, the tacky
mistletoe. 'Look' they said and again 'look.' But
10   I ran slowly; the landscape flowed away, back to
its source.

In the schoolyard, in the cloakrooms, the children
boasted their scars of dried snot; wrists and
knees garnished with impetigo.

VII

Gasholders, russet among fields. Milldams, marlpools
that lay unstirring. Eel-swarms. Coagulations of
frogs: once, with branches and half-bricks, he
battered a ditchful; then sidled away from the
5   stillness and silence.

Ceolred was his friend and remained so, even after
the day of the lost fighter: a biplane, already
obsolete and irreplaceable, two inches of heavy
snub silver. Ceolred let it spin through a hole
10   in the classroom-floorboards, softly, into the
rat-droppings and coins.

After school he lured Ceolred, who was sniggering
with fright, down to the old quarries, and flayed
him. Then, leaving Ceolred, he journeyed for hours,
15   calm and alone, in his private derelict sandlorry
named *Albion*.

VIII

The mad are predators. Too often lately they harbour
against us. A novel heresy exculpates all maimed
souls. Abjure it! I am the King of Mercia, and
I know.

5   Threatened by phone-calls at midnight, venomous let-
ters, forewarned I have thwarted their imminent
devices.

Today I name them; tomorrow I shall express the new law.
I dedicate my awakening to this matter.

IX

The strange church smelled a bit 'high', of censers
and polish. The strange curate was just as ap-
propriate: he took off into the marriage-service.
No-one cared to challenge that gambit.

14: *impetigo*: an infectious skin disease, which used to be particularly common among schoolchildren
VII: 1: *Gasholders*: large tanks for holding gas; *marlpools*: pools in marl, a soil made of clay and chalk.
6: Hill takes the name *Ceolred* from that of a ninth-century bishop of Leicester.
15: *sandlorry*: sand truck
16: *Albion* is the ancient and traditional name for the island of Britain.
IX: 1: *high*: emphasizing the Catholic elements in the ritual of the Anglican Church

5 Then he dismissed you, and the rest of us followed,
   sheepish next-of-kin, to the place without the
   walls: spoil-heaps of chrysanths dead in their
   plastic macs, eldorado of washstand-marble.

10 Embarrassed, we dismissed ourselves: the three mute
   great-aunts borne away down St Chad's Garth
   in a stiff-backed Edwardian Rolls.

   I unburden the saga of your burial, my dear. You had
   lived long enough to see things 'nicely settled'.

X

   He adored the desk, its brown-oak inlaid with ebony,
   assorted prize pens, the seals of gold and base
   metal into which he had sunk his name.

5 It was there that he drew upon grievances from the
   people; attended to signatures and retributions;
   forgave the death-howls of his rival. And there
   he exchanged gifts with the Muse of History.

10 What should a man make of remorse, that it might
   profit his soul? Tell me. Tell everything to
   Mother, darling, and God bless.

   He swayed in sunlight, in mild dreams. He tested the
   little pears. He smeared catmint on his palm for
   his cat Smut to lick. He wept, attempting to mas-
   ter *ancilla* and *servus*.

XI

   Coins handsome as Nero's; of good substance and
   weight. *Offa Rex* resonant in silver, and the
   names of his moneyers. They struck with account-
   able tact. They could alter the king's face.

5 Exactness of design was to deter imitation; muti-
   lation if that failed. Exemplary metal, ripe for
   commerce. Value from a sparse people, scrapers of
   salt-pans and byres.

6: In ancient times burial sites were located outside city walls, which was considered an "unclean" place.

8: *macs:* mackintoshes

  eldorado of washstand-marble: i.e., a quantity of inexpensive (bathroom standard) marble headstones.

10: The church is named after *St Chad* (d. 672), the first bishop of Lichfield, who is credited with the Christianization of Mercia. *Garth* is presumably the streetname.

X: 7: Clio was the Greek *Muse of History.*

14: *ancilla and servus:* female and male servant (or slave) (Latin); these nouns are often used in examples in introductory Latin instruction.

XI: 1: *Nero* (37–68), Roman emperor notorious for his extravagance and for his persecution of Christians. *Offa Rex:* "King Offa" (Latin): "an inscription on his coins. See J. J. North, *English Hammered Coinage* (1963), Vol. I, pp. 52–60 and Plate III." (Hill)

8: *salt-pans:* shallow ponds near the sea, used to produce salt through the evaporation of seawater *byres:* cowsheds

10   Swathed bodies in the long ditch; one eye upstaring.
It is safe to presume, here, the king's anger. He
reigned forty years. Seasons touched and retouched
the soil.

Heathland, new-made watermeadow. Charlock, marsh-
marigold. Crepitant oak forest where the boar
15   furrowed black mould, his snout intimate with
worms and leaves.

XII

Their spades grafted through the variably-resistant
soil. They clove to the hoard. They ransacked
epiphanies, vertebrae of the chimera, armour of
wild bees' larvae. They struck the fire-dragon's
5   faceted skin.

The men were paid to caulk water-pipes. They brewed
and pissed amid splendour; their latrine seethed
its estuary through nettles. They are scattered
to your collations, moldywarp.

10   It is autumn. Chestnut-boughs clash their inflamed
leaves. The garden festers for attention: telluric
cultures enriched with shards, corms, nodules, the
sunk solids of gravity. I have raked up a golden
and stinking blaze.

XXVII

'Now when King Offa was alive and dead', they were
all there, the funereal gleemen: papal legate
and rural dean; Merovingian car-dealers, Welsh mercen-
aries; a shuffle of house-carls.

5   He was defunct. They were perfunctory. The ceremony
stood acclaimed. The mob received memorial vouch-
ers and signs.

13: *Charlock:* wild mustard
14: *Crepitant:* making a crackling sound
15: *mould:* earth
XII: 3: *epiphanies:* discoveries, revelations
9: *collations:* acts of bringing together (i.e., the molehills)
    moldywarp: mole
11: *telluric:* pertaining to the earth
12: *Corms,* also known as "solid bulbs," are the underground stems of certain plants, serving as reproduc-
tive structures.
XXVII: 1: "'Now when King Offa was alive and dead' is based on a ritual phrase used of various kings [i.e.,
upon their death], though not, as far as I am aware, of Offa himself. See Christopher Brooke, [*The Saxon
and Norman Kings* (1967 edn)], p. 39; R. H. M. Dolley, ed., *Anglo-Saxon Coins: Studies Presented to F. M.
Stenton* (1961), p. 220." (Hill)
3: The *Merovingians* were France's first dynasty of kings (476–750); by Offa's time the dynasty had come
to an end, supplanted by the Carolingian kings.
4: *house-carls:* the king's bodyguard

After that shadowy, thrashing midsummer hail-storm,
Earth lay for a while, the ghost-bride of livid
10   Thor, butcher of strawberries, and the shire-tree
dripped red in the arena of its uprooting.

XXVIII

Processes of generation; deeds of settlement. The
urge to marry well; wit to invest in the proper-
ties of healing-springs. Our children and our
children's children, o my masters.

5   Tracks of ancient occupation. Frail ironworks rust-
ing in the thorn-thicket. Hearthstones; charred
lullabies. A solitary axe-blow that is the echo
of a lost sound.

Tumult recedes as though into the long rain. Groves
10   of legendary holly; silverdark the ridged gleam.

XXIX

'Not strangeness, but strange likeness. Obstinate,
outclassed forefathers, I too concede, I am your
staggeringly-gifted child.'

So, murmurous, he withdrew from them. Gran lit the
5   gas, his dice whirred in the ludo-cup, he entered
into the last dream of Offa the King.

XXX

And it seemed, while we waited, he began to walk to-
wards us   he vanished

he left behind coins, for his lodging, and traces of
red mud.

1971

10: *Thor:* the god of thunder in Germanic myth
XXIX: 4: *Gran:* short for "grandmother"
5: *ludo:* a boardgame (also known as parcheesi)

from The Mystery of the Charity of Charles Péguy

4

[109]   This world is different, belongs to them—
110   the lords of limit and of contumely.
         It matters little whether you go tamely
         or with rage and defiance to your doom.

         This is your enemies' country which they took
         in the small hours an age before you woke,
115   went to the window, saw the mist-hewn
         statues of the lean kine emerge at dawn.

         Outflanked again, too bad! You still have pride,
         haggard obliquities: those that take remorse
         and the contempt of others for a muse,
120   bound to the alexandrine as to the *Code*

         Napoléon. Thus the bereaved soul returns
         upon itself, grows resolute at chess,
         in war-games hurling dice of immense loss
         into the breach; thus punitively mourns.

"Charles Péguy was born in 1873 into a family of barely literate peasants, to whom he subsequently devoted much eloquent homage, and died, an ageing infantry lieutenant of the Reserve, on the first day of the first Battle of the Marne in September 1914. He was a son of the people, of 'l'ancienne France', one of the last of that race as he conceived of it. His reputation, such as it was during his lifetime, was confined to a small intellectual élite: the few hundred readers of *Les Cahiers de la Quinzaine*, which he founded in 1900, and the dozen or so who attended the Thursday meetings in his little bookshop, the 'Boutique des Cahiers', in the shadow of the Sorbonne. A man of the most exact and exacting probity, accurate practicality, in personal and business relations, a meticulous reader of proof, he was at the same time moved by violent emotions and violently afflicted by mischance. Like others similarly wounded, he was perhaps smitten by the desirability of suffering." (from Hill's companion essay to the poem). Hill notes that Péguy was a "staunchly-committed Dreyfusard." (In 1894, the Jewish captain Alfred Dreyfus was convicted of selling military secrets to the Germans. Evidence mounted that the real culprit was another officer, Maj. Ferdinand Walsin Esterhazy, but the military refused to reopen the case; by 1898 the case had become a violently divisive political issue, with right-wing and clericalist factions supporting the army and the socialists split between the pro-Dreyfus faction of Jean Jaurès and those following the Marxist socialist Jules Guesde, who dismissed the affair as a bourgeois squabble. The most incriminating documents against Dreyfus were at this point discovered to be a forgery. Esterhazy fled the country; Dreyfus was found guilty by a second military trial but pardoned by the president of the republic; he was finally cleared in a 1906 civilian trial.) "Péguy was an admirer of the great socialist deputy Jean Jaurès throughout the period of the 'Affair'. By 1914 he was calling for his blood: figuratively, it must be said; though a young madman, who may or may not have been over-susceptible to metaphor, almost immediately shot Jaurès through the head." (Hill). Hill's title evokes Péguy's poem *Le Mystère de la charité de Jeanne d'Arc* (*The Mystery of the Charity of Joan of Arc*, 1910).

110: *the lords of limit:* "The phrase is Auden's, from an early poem 'Now from my window-sill I watch the night'. See Edward Mendelson, ed., *The English Auden* (1977), pp. 115–16." (Hill)
    contumely: insolence; contemptuous or humiliating abuse
116: *kine:* cattle. The allusion is to Pharaoh's dream in Gen. 41 of seven fat kine emerging from the Nile, followed by seven lean kine which eat up them up; it is correctly interpreted by Joseph correctly as a prophecy of seven bountiful years followed by seven years of famine. In Hill's poem Joseph/Péguy has awakened from a prophetic dream too late to do anything about it.
120: The *alexandrine* (twelve-syllable line) is the staple metrical form of French verse from the sixteenth century to the present.
120–21: The Napoleonic Code was established in 1804 with the aim of replacing the legal patchwork that existed in France prior to the revolutionary period with a civil code with a purely rational basis. With modifications it is still in force today.

125   This is no old Beauce manoir that you keep
       but the rue de la Sorbonne, the cramped shop,
       its unsold *Cahiers* built like barricades,
       its fierce disciples, disciplines and feuds,

       the camelot-cry of 'sticks!' As Tharaud says,
130   'all through your life the sound of broken glass.'
       So much for Jaurès murdered in cold pique
       by some vexed shadow of the belle époque,

       some guignol strutting at the window-frame.
       But what of you, Péguy, who came to 'exult',
135   to be called 'wolfish' by your friends? The guilt
       belongs to time; and you must leave on time.

       Jaurès was killed blindly, yet with reason:
       'let us have drums to beat down his great voice.'
       So you spoke to the blood. So, you have risen
140   above all that and fallen flat on your face

5

       among the beetroots, where we are constrained
       to leave you sleeping and to step aside
       from the fleshed bayonets, the fusillade
       of red-rimmed smoke like stubble being burned;

145   to turn away and contemplate the working
       of the radical soul—instinct, intelligence,
       memory, call it what you will—waking
       into the foreboding of its inheritance,

       its landscape and inner domain; images
150   of earth and grace. Across Artois the rois-mages
       march on Bethlehem; sun-showers fall
       slantwise over the kalefield, the canal.

       Hedgers and ditchers, quarrymen, thick-shod
       curés de campagne, each with his load,

125: *Beauce:* a region in northwest France; a flat, featureless plain, it is an important agricultural area, its main crops formerly wheat and sugar beets.

129: "*Les camelots du roi* was a right-wing, anti-Dreyfusard organization, prominent in the street-battles of the period." (Hill)

130: "Daniel Halévy, *Péguy and 'Les Cahiers de la Quinzaine',* translated from the French by Ruth Bethell (1946), p. 171: 'Always, all through his life, this sound of broken glass, to use Tharaud's expression'." (Hill)

131: The French socialist leader Jean *Jaurès* was assassinated during the war fever that followed the June 1914 assassination of Archduke Ferdinand; he had been attempting to secure a French-German rapprochement (and thus avert the onset of World War I), a position that had earned him the enmity of French nationalists such as Péguy.

132: *belle époque:* "the good old days"—the conventional phrase for the decade preceding World War I, as seen in retrospect

133: *guignol:* melodramatic puppet

138: Hill quotes from Péguy's 1914 denunciation of Jaurès.

150: *Artois:* a region of northern France; the scene of some of World War I's fiercest fighting, it was devastated by the war's end.

rois-mages: three Wise Men. The timeframe of the poem has moved back to 1873, the year of Péguy's birth.

154: *curés de campagne:* country priests

155   shake off those cares and burdens; they become,
       in a bleak visionary instant, seraphim

       looking towards Chartres, the spired sheaves,
       stone-thronged annunciations, winged ogives
       uplifted and uplifting from the winter-gleaned
160   furrows of that criss-cross-trodden ground.

       Or say it is Pentecost: the hawthorn-tree,
       set with coagulate magnified flowers of may,
       blooms in a haze of light; old chalk-pits brim
       with seminal verdure from the roots of time.

165   Landscape is like revelation; it is both
       singular crystal and the remotest things.
       Cloud-shadows of seasons revisit the earth,
       odourless myrrh borne by the wandering kings.

       Happy are they who, under the gaze of God,
170   die for the 'terre charnelle', marry her blood
       to theirs, and, in strange Christian hope, go down
       into the darkness of resurrection,

       into sap, ragwort, melancholy thistle,
       almondy meadowsweet, the freshet-brook
175   rising and running through small wilds of oak,
       past the elder-tump that is the child's castle.

       Inevitable high summer, richly scarred
       with furze and grief; winds drumming the fame
       of the tin legions lost in haystack and stream.
180   Here the lost are blest, the scarred most sacred:

       odd village workshops grimed and peppercorned
       in a dust of dead spiders, paper-crowned
       sunflowers with the bleached heads of rag dolls,
       brushes in aspic, clay pots, twisted nails;

185   the clinking anvil and clear sheepbell-sound,
       at noon and evening, of the angelus;
       coifed girls like geese, labourers cap in hand,
       and walled gardens espaliered with angels;

157: The great medieval cathedral at *Chartres* is a landmark on the Beauce plains.
158: An *ogive* is a diagonal rib or groin of a vault: two ogives cross each other at the vault's center; the word can also simply mean a pointed arch.
161: *Pentecost:* the church festival on the Sunday 50 days after Easter that commemorates the descent of the Holy Spirit on the heads of the apostles.
162: *may:* may-blossom
170: *terre charnelle:* "Charles Péguy, *Eve* (1913): '—Heureux ceux qui sont morts pour la terre charnelle, / Mais pourvu que se fût dans une juste guerre.'" (Hill) "Blessed are those who die for the flesh-and-blood earth, as long as it is in a just war." The passage in Péguy's poem from which this comes is modeled on the Beatitudes of the Sermon on the Mount (Matt. 5).
176: *tump:* a clump of trees
180: *blest:* punning on the French *blesser,* "to wound"
186: *angelus:* in the Catholic church, a bell that rings at morning, noon, and evening to call people to recite the angelus, a short prayer that commemorates the Incarnation.
188: *angels:* The reference is perhaps to the resemblance of espaliered branches to an angel's wings.

solitary bookish ecstasies, proud tears,
190   proud tears, for the forlorn hope, the guerdon
        of Sedan, 'oh les braves gens!', English Gordon
        stepping down sedately into the spears.

        Patience hardens to a pittance, courage
        unflinchingly declines into sour rage,
195   the cobweb-banners, the shrill bugle-bands
        and the bronze warriors resting on their wounds.

        These fatal decencies, they make us lords
        over ourselves: familial debts and dreads,
        keepers of old scores, the kindly ones
200   telling their beady sous, the child-eyed crones

        who guard the votive candles and the faint
        invalid's night-light of the sacrament,
        a host of lilies and the table laid
        for early mass from which you stood aside

205   to find salvation, your novena cleaving
        brusquely against the grain of its own myth,
        its truth and justice, to a kind of truth,
        a justice hard to justify. 'Having

        spoken his mind he'd a mind to be silent.'
210   But who would credit that, that one talent

190: *forlorn hope:* an Englishing of the Dutch *verloren hoop* ("lost troop"): a storming party; "reckless bravos" (*OED*)

    guerdon: reward

191: *Sedan:* a town in northeastern France which was the scene of a decisive 1870 defeat of the French troops in the Franco-German War.

    oh les braves gens: "ah, those brave fellows"

    The English general Charles George *Gordon* (1833–1885) became a popular hero for his heroic and doomed defense of Khartoum against Sudanese rebels. The classic image of his death comes from G. W. Joy's painting *Death of Gordon,* showing him coolly facing down spear-wielding attackers from the palace steps.

199: Hill alludes to the Furies of Greek legend, underworld deities who pursued those guilty of crimes against blood relatives; because people were loath to utter their name they were referred to euphemistically as the Eumenides ("the kindly ones").

200: Hill puns on "telling their beads"—saying prayers with the assistance of a rosary.

202: *invalid's night-light:* refers to the practice of bringing communion to a person in danger of death, with a lit candle signifying the presence of the consecrated host

204: See Hill's accompanying essay: "No one knows for certain whether he did, or did not, receive the sacrament on the Feast of the Assumption, shortly before he was killed. Estranged from the Church for a number of years, first by his militant socialist principles, then by the consequences of a civil marriage, he had, in 1908, rediscovered the solitary ardours of faith but not the consolations of religious practice. He remained self-excommunicate but adoring; his devotion most doggedly expressed in those two pilgrimages undertaken on foot, in June 1912 and July 1913, from Paris to the Cathedral of Notre Dame de Chartres. The purpose of his first journey, as a tablet in the Cathedral duly records, was to entrust his children to Our Lady's care."

205: *novena:* a period of nine days' public or private devotion, by which one hopes to obtain some special grace; they may be said in circumstances of special peril or need.

210: See Matt. 25: 14–30, the parable of the talents (an ancient unit of money): "the kingdom of heaven is as a man travelling into a far country, who called his own servants, and delivered unto them his goods. And unto one he gave five talents, to another two, and to another one." On his return, he asks to the servants what they have done; the first has by trade increased his five talents to ten, the second his two talents to four; but the third, afraid of losing the money, has buried it. The master praises the first two servants, and reproves the third as "wicked and slothful": "Thou oughtest . . . to have put my money to the exchangers, and then at my coming I should have received mine own with usury." Here Péguy is imagined as having earned "fruit" (interest) on the talent before reburying it.

dug from the claggy Beauce and returned to it
with love, honour, suchlike bitter fruit?

1983

Respublica

The strident high
civic trumpeting
of misrule. It is
what we stand for.

5   Wild insolence,
aggregates without
distinction. Courage
of common men:

spent in the ruck
10   their remnant witness
after centuries
is granted them

like a pardon.
And other fealties
15   other fortitudes
broken as named—

Respublica
brokenly recalled,
its archaic laws
20   and hymnody;

and destroyed hope
that so many times
is brought with triumph
back from the dead.

1994

211: *claggy:* heavy and sticky like wet clay

Title: *Respublica:* republic; state; commonwealth (Latin)

from The Triumph of Love

AND I SENT MESSENGERS VNTO THEM, SAYING, I AM
DOING A GREAT WORKE, SO THAT I CAN NOT COME
DOWN: WHY SHOULD THE WORKE CEASE, WHILEST I
LEAVE IT, AND COME DOWNE TO YOU?
NEHEMIAH 6:3

XXIII

What remains? You may well ask. Construction
or deconstruction? There is some poor
mimicry of choice, whether you build or destroy.
But the Psalms—they remain; and certain exultant
5   canzoni of repentance, secular oppugnancy. *Laus*
et vituperatio, the worst
remembered, least understood, of the modes.
Add political satire. Add the irrefutable
grammar of Abdiel's defiance.
10   And if not wisdom, then something
that approaches it nearly. And if not faith,
then something through which it is made possible
to give credence—if only to Isaiah's prophetically
suffering servant; if only by evidence
15   of the faithful women, Ruth and Naomi,
as they were, and as Rembrandt sees them,
the widowed generations, the irrevocable
covenant with Abraham which you
scarcely recall.

XXV

The hierarchies are here to be questioned. Lead on
Angelus Novus; show onetime experts presenting

The Triumph of Love: Hill's poem is in 150 sections, echoing the Bible's 150 Psalms.

Title: *The Triumph of Love* is the first of the *Trionfi,* a series of allegorical poems by the Italian poet Petrarch (1304–1374). It describes Petrarch's vision of the triumphal parade of Cupid.

Epigraph: The Book of *Nehemiah* tells how he supervised the rebuilding of the walls of Jerusalem. Hill quotes Nehemiah's reply to his enemies, who are attempting to lure him down from the walls in order to do him mischief.

XXIII: 5: A *canzone* is a poetic form used in medieval Italian or Provencal poetry; in section LV below Hill quotes from a famous canzone by Petrarch.

5–6: *Laus / et vituperatio:* praise and blame (Latin). The phrase comes from the beginning of the Latin translation of the medieval Islamic philosopher Averroes' paraphrase of Aristotle's *Poetics:* "Every poem and all poetic discourse is blame or praise . . . [of] the honourable or the base."

9: *Abdiel's defiance:* At Satan's initial meeting with his angels to plot their revolt against God, Abdiel is the only one to defy Satan, "in a flame of zeal severe" (Milton, *Paradise Lost* 5.803ff).

13: The Book of *Isaiah* prophesies the coming of a "servant" of the Lord—in Christian interpretation, Christ; see Isaiah 53:3.

15: The Book of *Ruth* tells how the Bethlehemite Elimelech, with his wife Naomi and his two sons, settled in the land of Moab; after his death, his sons took Moabite wives, Orpah and Ruth. After the sons' death, Naomi returned to Bethlehem; Orpah stayed behind, but Ruth came with her, saying, "whither thou goest, I will go; and where thou lodgest, I will lodge: thy people shall be my people, and thy God my God" (1:16).

18: *covenant with Abraham:* God's promise to bestow the land of Canaan—Palestine—on Abraham's descendants (Gen. 12ff)

XXV: 2: *Angelus Novus:* The Angel of History (Latin); the title of a painting by Paul Klee (1879–1940). The German thinker Walter Benjamin (1892–1940) wrote in *Theses on the Philosophy of History* IX: "A Klee painting named 'Angelus Novus' shows an angel looking as though he is about to move away from some-

aniline dyes as the intensest expressions
of coal-tar; let others develop 'man's
5   determinate action', for so Peirce dubbed it
in the wake of Chickamauga. Failing these,
bring others well-tried in the practical
worlds of illusion, builders of fabled masks,
their dancing clients
10   vanishing into the work
made up as lords and spiky blackamoors:
Unveil the dust-wrapped, post-war architects'
immediate prize-designs in balsa wood,
excelling fantasies, sparsely inhabited
15   by spaced-out, pinhead model citizens:
Florentine piazzas for Antarctica.
The augurs, finally: strangely possessed by doubt
whether to address the saturnine magistrates
concerning the asteroid, or the asteroid
20   on the nature of destiny and calculation.

XXXV

Even now, I tell myself, there is a language
to which I might speak and which
would rightly hear me;
responding with eloquence; in its turn,
5   negotiating sense without insult
given or injury taken.
Familiar to those who already know it
elsewhere as justice,
it is met also in the form of silence.

XXXIX

Rancorous, narcissistic old sod—what
makes him go on? We thought, hoped rather,
he might be dead. Too bad. So how
much more does he have of injury time?

thing he is fully contemplating. His eyes are staring, his mouth is open, his wings are spread. This is how one pictures the angel of history. His face is turned toward the past. Where we perceive a chain of events, he sees one single catastrophe which keeps piling wreckage upon wreckage and hurls it in front of his feet. The angel would like to stay, awaken the dead, and make whole what has been smashed. But a storm is blowing from Paradise; it has got caught in his wings with such violence that the angel can no longer close them. This storm irresistibly propels him into the future to which his back is turned, while the pile of debris before him grows skyward. This storm is what we call progress."

3: *aniline:* a chemical base used to make dyes; it is obtainable from coal-tar

5: Charles Sanders *Peirce* (1839–1914), the American scientist and philosopher

6: *Chickamauga:* the Battle of Chickamauga (1863) in the American Civil War

8: *masks:* i.e., masques, aristocratic entertainments popular in the sixteenth and seventeenth centuries: they involved acting, dance, and music, in which lords and ladies would take many of the roles.

17: *augurs:* soothsayers

18: *saturnine:* gloomy; surly

XXXIX: 4: *Injury time,* in soccer, is time added on at the end of a game (or a half) to make up for time lost while the game was temporarily stopped on account of a player's injury.

XL

For wordly, read worldly; for in equity, inequity;
for religious read religiose; for distinction
detestation. Take accessible to mean
acceptable, accommodating, openly servile.
Is that right, Missis, or is that right? I don't
care what I say, do I?

XLI

For iconic priesthood, read worldly pique and ambition.
Change insightfully caring to pruriently intrusive.
Delete chastened and humbled. Insert humiliated.
Interpret slain in the spirit as browbeaten to exhaustion.
For hardness of heart read costly dislike of cant.

XLII

Excuse me—excuse me—I did not
say the pain is lifting. I said the pain is in
the lifting. No—please—forget it.

XLIII

This is quite dreadful—he's become obsessed.
There you go, there you go—narrow it down to *obsession!*

XLIV

Cry pax. Not that anything is forgiven;
not that there seems anything new to forgive
in this assemblance. Not that the assemblance
might be tempted into the fertile
wilderness of unspirituality. Not that I
know the way out, or in. So be it;
let us continue to abuse one another
with the kiss of peace.

LV

Vergine bella—it is here that I require
a canzone of some substance. There are sound
precedents for this, of a plain eloquence
which would be perfect. But—
ought one to say, I am required; or, it is
required of me; or, it is requisite that I should
make such an offering, bring in such a tribute?
And is this real obligation or actual

XLIV: 1: *pax*: peace (Latin); in the schoolyard, it is spoken with crossed fingers by a child as a truce word.
3: *assemblance*: both "assembly" and "assemblage" (and perhaps glancing at "semblance")
LV: 1: *Vergine bella*: "beautiful Virgin": the words begin the last canzone of Petrarch's *Rime,* a supplication to the Virgin Mary.

pressure of expectancy? One cannot purchase
10   the goodwill of your arduously simple faith
as one would acquire a tobacconist's cum paper shop
or a small convenience store
established by aloof, hardworking Muslims.
Nor is language, now, what it once was
15   even in—wait a tick—nineteen hundred and forty-
five of the common era, when your blast-scarred face
appeared staring, seemingly in disbelief,
shocked beyond recollection, unable to recognize
the mighty and the tender salutations
20   that slowly, with innumerable false starts, the ages
had put together for your glory
in words and in the harmonies of stone.
But you have long known and endured all things
since you first suffered the Incarnation:
25   endless the extortions, endless the dragging
in of your name. *Vergine bella,* as you
are well aware, I here follow
Petrarch, who was your follower,
a sinner devoted to your service.
30   I ask that you acknowledge the work
as being contributive to your high praise,
even if no-one else shall be reconciled
to a final understanding of it in that light.

LX

Return of *Angelus Novus.* How that
must have shaken you—the anima
touched like a snare-drum
or the middle ear.
5   New conjugations, fine as hair-springs,
the seconds-hand twitching it-
self into shock.
Try it again—again you leap
aside and are riven.

LXI

A se stesso.
Not unworded. Enworded.
But in the extremity
of coherence. You will be taken up.
5   *A se stesso.*

23: cf. 1 Cor. 13:7: Charity "endureth all things."
LX: 2: *anima:* spirit; soul
5: A *hair-spring* is a delicate spring that regulates the balance wheel of a watch mechanism.
LXI: 1: *A se stesso:* "to himself" (Italian): this is the title of a poem by Giacomo Leopardi (1798–1837), in
  which he says, "Now be for ever still / Weary my heart. . . . Now you may despise / Yourself, nature, the
  brute / Power which, hidden, ordains the common doom, / And all the immeasurable emptiness of
  things." (trans. Heath-Stubbs).

LXII

A happy investment, Lord Trimalchio:
forasmuch as Blake laboured
in Hercules Buildings, and as 'up Dryden's
alley' is where he was set upon
5   to the unstinting plaudits of the trade;
as 'mob' and 'fun' came in at the same time:
forasmuch as the world stands,
in a small part, exposed for what it is—
tyrant-entertainment, master of the crowds.

LXIII

Those obscenities which—as you say—you fancy
perverting the consecration; you hear them all right
even if they are unspoken, as most are. It is
difficult always to catch the tacit
5   echoes of self-resonance. Is prayer
residual in imprecation? Only
as we equivocate. When I examine
my soul's heart's blood I find it the blood
of bulls and goats.
10   Things unspoken as spoken give us away.
What else can I now sell myself, filched
from Lenten *Hebrews*?

LXIV

Delete: sell myself; filched from. Inert:
tell myself; fetched from. For inert read insect.

CXLVII

To go so far with the elaborately-
vested Angel of Naked Truth:
and where are we, finally? Don't
say that—we are nowhere
5   finally. And nowhere are you—
nowhere are you—any more—more
cryptic than a schoolyard truce. Cry
Kings, Cross, or Crosses, cry Pax,

LXII: 1: *Trimalchio*: the vulgar, nouveau-riche patron of the lavish banquet recounted in the *Satyricon* of
Petronius (d. 66).
3: From 1790 to 1800 William *Blake* lived in 13 *Hercules Buildings*, Lambeth, in London; while living there
he was (in the words of his friend Captain J. G. Stedman) "mobb'd and robb'd." *Dryden* was attacked by
hired thugs in an alleyway near his home in 1679.
5: *the trade*: publishers and booksellers
6: The earliest *OED* citations of these words are from the early eighteenth century.
LXIII: 12: *Lenten Hebrews*: the epistle read for the fifth Sunday of Lent in the Anglican Church is Hebrews
9:11–15, on the supersession of the Old Covenant by the New. "If the blood of bulls and of goats, and the
ashes of an heifer sprinkling the unclean, sanctifieth to the purifying of the flesh; how much more shall
the blood of Christ, who through the eternal Spirit offered himself without spot to God, purge your con-
science from dead works to serve the living God!" (Heb. 9:13–14)
CXLVII: 7: Like *pax* these are all schoolboys' truce-words.

cry Pax, but to be healed. But to be
10   healed, and die!

CXLVIII

Obnoxious means, far back within itself,
easily wounded. But vulnerable, proud
anger is, I find, a related self
of covetousness. I came late
5   to seeing that. Actually, I had to be
shown it. What I saw was rough, and still
pains me. Perhaps it should pain me more.
Pride is our crux: be angry, but not proud
where that means vainglorious. Take Leopardi's
10   words or—to be accurate—BV's English
cast of them: when he found Tasso's poor
scratch of a memorial barely showing
among the cold slabs of defunct pomp. It
seemed *a sad and angry consolation.*
15   So—Croker, MacSikker, O'Shem—I ask you:
what are poems for? They are to console us
with their own gift, which is like perfect pitch.
Let us commit that to our dust. What
ought a poem to be? Answer, *a sad*
20   *and angry consolation.* What is
the poem? What figures? Say,
a sad and angry consolation. That's
beautiful. Once more? *A sad and angry*
consolation.

CXLIX

Obstinate old man—*senex*
sapiens, it is not. Is he still
writing? What is he writing now? He
has just written: I find it hard
5   to forgive myself. We are immortal. Where
was I?—

CL

Sun-blazed, over Romsley, the livid rain-scarp.

                                                     1998

CXLVIII: 1–2: The earlier meaning of "obnoxious" was "vulnerable."
10: *BV* was the pseudonym of the poet James Thomson (1834–1882), whose translations of Leopardi's prose
   are collected in *Essays, Dialogues, and Thoughts* (1905).
11: Torquato *Tasso* (1544–1595), the Italian poet, author of the epic *Gerusalemme Liberata* ("Jerusalem Lib-
   erated")
15: *Croker, MacSikker, O'Shem:* names given elsewhere in *The Triumph of Love* to Hill's niggling and cen-
   sorious critics.
CXLIX: 1–2: *senex / sapiens:* wise old man (Latin)
CL: 1: *Romsley* is a village, now swallowed up by the city of Birmingham, which is the site of a church
   sacred to St. Kenelm; it is a few miles away from Bromsgrove, Hill's birthplace. This final section is near-
   identical to the poem's first: "Sun-blazed, over Romsley, a livid rain-scarp."

FLEUR ADCOCK (b. 1934)

IN HER ANTHOLOGY OF WOMEN'S POETRY, ADCOCK WRITES THAT "IF I HAVE A THEORY about the tradition informing [women's] poetry it is that there is no particular tradition: there have been poets, and they have been individuals, and a few of them have influenced a few others."[1] Clair Buck, pointing to Adcock's criticism of "primal scream" writing, suggests that her work shows "a desire to advocate a humanism in which sexual difference would be transcended" and "an allegiance to a poetry espousing a moderate rationality, similar perhaps to the temperate reasonableness demanded by such Movement poets as Donald Davie and Philip Larkin. It is this allegiance that lies behind . . . Adcock's mobilization of an ideal of good poetry and the structuring value of art in opposition to unmediated experience."[2] Adcock's poetic styles range from the formally and syntactically balanced "The Ex-Queen Among the Astronomers" to the more conversational "Leaving the Tate."

Adcock was born in Papakura, New Zealand, and educated at Victoria University of Wellington. She emigrated to England in 1963. She has worked as a librarian and a freelance writer. Her books include *The Eye of the Hurricane* (1964), *High Tide in the Garden* (1971), *The Inner Harbour* (1979), *The Incident Book* (1986), *Time-Zones* (1991), and *Looking Back* (1997). She has edited the *Oxford Book of Contemporary New Zealand Poetry* (1983), *The Faber Book of Twentieth Century Women's Poetry* (1987), and, with Jacqueline Simms, *The Oxford Book of Creatures* (1995).

---

[1] *The Faber Book of Twentieth Century Women's Poetry,* London, 1987, p. 1.
[2] "Poetry and the Women's Movement in Postwar Britain," *Contemporary British Poetry: Essays in Theory and Criticism,* Albany, 1996, p. 92.

Against Coupling

I write in praise of the solitary act:
of not feeling a trespassing tongue
forced into one's mouth, one's breath
smothered, nipples crushed against the
5   ribcage, and that metallic tingling
in the chin set off by a certain odd nerve:

unpleasure. Just to avoid those eyes would help—
such eyes as a young girl draws life from,
listening to the vegetal
10   rustle within her, as his gaze
stirs polypal fronds in the obscure
sea-bed of her body, and her own eyes blur.

There is much to be said for abandoning
this no longer novel exercise—
15   for not 'participating in
a total experience'—when
one feels like the lady in Leeds who
had seen *The Sound of Music* eighty-six times;

or more, perhaps, like the school drama mistress
20   producing *A Midsummer Night's Dream*
for the seventh year running, with
yet another cast from 5B.
Pyramus and Thisbe are dead, but
the hole in the wall can still be troublesome.

25   I advise you, then, to embrace it without
encumbrance. No need to set the scene,
dress up (or undress), make speeches.
Five minutes of solitude are
enough—in the bath, or to fill
30   that gap between the Sunday papers and lunch.

1971

The Ex-Queen Among the Astronomers

They serve revolving saucer eyes,
dishes of stars; they wait upon
huge lenses hung aloft to frame
the slow procession of the skies.

5   They calculate, adjust, record,
watch transits, measure distances.
They carry pocket telescopes
to spy through when they walk abroad.

Spectra possess their eyes; they face
10   upwards, alert for meteorites,
cherishing little glassy worlds:
receptacles for outer space.

But she, exile, expelled, ex-queen,
swishes among the men of science

11: *polypal fronds:* the tentacles of a polyp (e.g., a sea anemone or coral)
23–24: *Pyramus and Thisbe:* the doomed lovers of the mock play-within-a-play of Shakespeare's *A Midsummer Night's Dream* 5.1; they conversed by night through a crack in a wall.
6: *transits:* passages of celestial bodies through the field of a telescope

15   waiting for cloudy skies, for nights
        when constellations can't be seen.

        She wears the rings he let her keep;
        she walks as she was taught to walk
        for his approval, years ago.
20   His bitter features taunt her sleep.

        And so when these have laid aside
        their telescopes, when lids are closed
        between machine and sky, she seeks
        terrestrial bodies to bestride.

25   She plucks this one or that among
        the astronomers, and is become
        his canopy, his occultation;
        she sucks at earlobe, penis, tongue

        mouthing the tubes of flesh; her hair
30   crackles, her eyes are comet-sparks.
        She brings the distant briefly close
        above his dreamy abstract stare.

                                                                    1979

Leaving the Tate

        Coming out with your clutch of postcards
        in a Tate Gallery bag and another clutch
        of images packed into your head you pause
        on the steps to look across the river

5   and there's a new one: light bright buildings,
        a streak of brown water, and such a sky
        you wonder who painted it—Constable? No:
        too brilliant. Crome? No: too ecstatic—

        a madly pure Pre-Raphaelite sky,
10   perhaps, sheer blue apart from the white plumes
        rushing up it (today, that is,
        April. Another day would be different

        but it wouldn't matter. All skies work.)
        Cut to the lower right for a detail:
15   seagulls pecking on mud, below
        two office blocks and a Georgian terrace.

27: *occultation*: the obscuring of a heavenly body by another in front of it

Title: London's *Tate* Gallery is located on the Thames bankside.

7: The landscape painter John *Constable* (1776–1837) was noted for his depiction of cloud forms.

8: John *Crome* (1768–1821), English landscape painter

9: The *Pre-Raphaelites* (a group of nineteenth-century artists including Dante Gabriel Rossetti, John Everett Millais, and Holman Hunt) were noted for the stylized vividness of their depiction of nature.

Now swing to the left, and take in plane-trees
bobbled with seeds, and that brick building,
and a red bus . . . Cut it off just there,
20   by the lamp-post. Leave the scaffolding in.

That's your next one. Curious how
these outdoor pictures didn't exist
before you'd looked at the indoor pictures,
the ones on the walls. But here they are now,

25   marching out of their panorama
and queuing up for the viewfinder
your eye's become. You can isolate them
by holding your optic muscles still.

You can zoom in on figure studies
30   (that boy with the rucksack), or still lives,
abstracts, townscapes. No one made them.
The light painted them. You're in charge

of the hanging committee. Put what space
you like around the ones you fix on,
35   and gloat. Art multiplies itself.
Art's whatever you choose to frame.

1986

33: *hanging committee:* the committee that decides inclusions in an exhibition

TONY HARRISON (b. 1937)

H ARRISON WAS BORN IN LEEDS AND ATTENDED LEEDS GRAMMAR SCHOOL AND LEEDS University, where he read Classics. He has lectured at Ahmadu Bello University in Nigeria and Charles University in Prague and held creative writing fellowships at several universities in the north of England. He was the resident dramatist for the National Theatre from 1977 to 1979. For many years now, Harrison has made his living as a freelance writer, producing poems, translations of poetry and drama by Molière, Racine, and Aeschylus, opera libretti, and poems for television and film. Harrison's use of so-called "obscenities" in *v.* generated controversy in Parliament and throughout Britain's press when Richard Eyre's film version of the poem was aired on Channel 4. His books of poetry include *The Loiners* (1970), *From the School of Eloquence and Other Poems* (1978), *Continuous: Fifty Sonnets from the School of Eloquence* (1981), *v.* (1985; second edition with press clippings 1987), *The Blasphemer's Banquet* (1989), *A Cold Coming: Gulf War Poems* (1991), and *The Gaze of the Gorgon* (1992). He is married to the opera singer Teresa Stratas and divides his time between Florida and Newcastle.

Harrison's poems often explore his working-class northern origins and the difficulty of affirming these in poetry. A classical education affords him a purportedly "cultured" idiom less familiar to those whose demotic, regional speech is often introduced within the poems. The conflicts Harrison maps are not only personal but representative; whatever hope for their resolution the poems present typically involves an appeal to the nation. We see this clearly in *v.*, where the point is not only to present the skinhead who insults the poet and defaces the Leeds graveyard as the poet's *alter ego* but as an alienated citizen whose obscenities and graffiti "art" might be redeemed by an act of vision. The "v" of versus (and via a pun "verses") is read as indicating oppositions between north and south, black and white, poor and rich, but the poem also links the "v" with Winston Churchill's World War II sign for victory, thereby remembering the national unity of a moment in the past as a means of stating hope for the future—this dream of reconciliation is part of the "humanism" critics sometimes find in Harrison's poems. Like Thomas Gray, whose "Elegy Written in a Country Churchyard" *v.* updates, Harrison includes his own epitaph in the poem; his use of it to ask readers to turn their backs on Leeds does not suggest a naive faith in the possibility of vision becoming reality. Blake Morrison has pointed out that in his use of traditional forms and syntax Harrison is studiously awkward as part of an endeavor to show that writing poems is labor, an activity opposed to the values of the leisured classes who have often been poetry's patrons: "his poems let us know they have come up the hard way; they are written with labour, and out of the labouring classes, and on behalf of Labour Party aspirations."[1] In recent work taking up the fatwa visited upon Salman Rushdie's *Satanic Verses* or the Gulf War, Harrison's work is self-consciously rhetorical, even while anxieties about the poet's ability to speak for the silent persist.

---

[1] "The Filial Art," *Tony Harrison,* ed. Neil Astley, Newcastle upon Tyne, 1991, p. 57.

V.

*"My father still reads the dictionary every day. He says your life
depends on your power to master words."*
ARTHUR SCARGILL
SUNDAY TIMES, 10 JANUARY 1982

Next millennium you'll have to search quite hard
to find my slab behind the family dead,
butcher, publican, and baker, now me, bard
adding poetry to their beef, beer and bread.

5   With Byron three graves on I'll not go short
of company, and Wordsworth's opposite.
That's two peers already, of a sort,
and we'll all be thrown together if the pit,

whose galleries once ran beneath this plot,
10   causes the distinguished dead to drop
into the rabblement of bone and rot,
shored slack, crushed shale, smashed prop.

Wordsworth built church organs, Byron tanned
luggage cowhide in the age of steam,
15   and knew their place of rest before the land
caves in on the lowest worked-out seam.

This graveyard on the brink of Beeston Hill's
the place I may well rest if there's a spot
under the rose roots and the daffodils
20   by which dad dignified the family plot.

If buried ashes saw then I'd survey
the places I learned Latin, and learned Greek,
and left, the ground where Leeds United play
but disappoint their fans week after week,

25   which makes them lose their sense of self-esteem
and taking a short cut home through these graves here
they reassert the glory of their team
by spraying words on tombstones, pissed on beer.

Epigraph: As head of the National Union of Mineworkers, *Arthur Scargill* called a strike in 1983 in response to pit closures instigated by the Conservative government of Margaret Thatcher. However, the National Coal Board had stockpiled coal ahead of time in anticipation of the strike; Thatcher's government defeated the union in 1984 with a combination of legislation and brute force.
9: *galleries:* underground horizontal passageways in a mine
12: *slack:* small fragments of coal; refuse
28: *pissed:* drunk

This graveyard stands above a worked-out pit.
30 Subsidence makes the obelisks all list.
One leaning left's marked FUCK, one right's marked SHIT
sprayed by some peeved supporter who was pissed.

Far-sighted for his family's future dead,
but for his wife, this banker's still alone
35 on his long obelisk, and doomed to head
a blackened dynasty of unclaimed stone,

now graffitied with a crude four-letter word.
His children and grandchildren went away
and never came back home to be interred,
40 so left a lot of space for skins to spray.

The language of this graveyard ranges from
a bit of Latin for a former Mayor
or those who laid their lives down at the Somme,
the hymnal fragments and the gilded prayer,

45 how people 'fell asleep in the Good Lord',
brief chisellable bits from the good book
and rhymes whatever length they could afford,
to CUNT, PISS, SHIT and (mostly) FUCK!

Or, more expansively, there's LEEDS v.
50 the opponent of last week, this week, or next,
and a repertoire of blunt four-letter curses
on the team or race that makes the sprayer vexed.

Then, pushed for time, or fleeing some observer,
dodging between tall family vaults and trees
55 like his team's best ever winger, dribbler, swerver,
fills every space he finds with versus Vs.

Vs sprayed on the run at such a lick,
the sprayer master of his flourished tool,
get short-armed on the left like that red tick
60 they never marked his work much with at school.

Half this skinhead's age but with approval
I helped whitewash a V on a brick wall.
No one clamoured in the press for its removal
or thought the sign, in wartime, rude at all.

65 These Vs are all the versuses of life
from LEEDS v. DERBY, Black/White
and (as I've known to my cost) man v. wife,
Communist v. Fascist, Left v. Right,

40: *skins:* skinheads
43: *Somme:* World War I's Battle of the Somme
64: i.e., during World War II it stood for "victory."

class v. class as bitter as before,
70   the unending violence of US and THEM,
personified in 1984
by Coal Board MacGregor and the NUM,

Hindu/Sikh, soul/body, heart v. mind,
East/West, male/female, and the ground
75   these fixtures are fought out on's Man, resigned
to hope from his future what his past never found.

The prospects for the present aren't too grand
when a swastika with NF (National Front)'s
sprayed on a grave, to which another hand
80   has added, in a reddish colour, CUNTS.

Which is, I grant, the word that springs to mind,
when going to clear the weeds and rubbish thrown
on the family plot by football fans, I find
UNITED graffitied on my parents' stone.

85   How many British graveyards now this May
are strewn with rubbish and choked up with weeds
since families and friends have gone away
for work or fuller lives, like me from Leeds?

When I first came here 40 years ago
90   with my dad to 'see my grandma' I was 7.
I helped dad with the flowers. He let me know
she'd gone to join my grandad up in Heaven.

My dad who came each week to bring fresh flowers
came home with clay stains on his trouser knees.
95   Since my parents' deaths I've spent 2 hours
made up of odd 10 minutes such as these.

Flying visits once or twice a year,
and though I'm horrified just who's to blame
that I find instead of flowers cans of beer
100   and more than one grave sprayed with some skin's name?

Where there were flower urns and troughs of water
and mesh receptacles for withered flowers
are the HARP tins of some skinhead Leeds supporter.
It isn't all his fault though. Much is ours.

105   5 kids, with one in goal, play 2-a-side.
When the ball bangs on the hawthorn that's one post
and petals fall they hum *Here Comes the Bride*
though not so loud they'd want to rouse a ghost.

72: *NUM*: National Union of Mineworkers. Sir Ian *MacGregor* (1912–1998), as head of the National Coal
  Board under Thatcher, played a key role in breaking the miners' strike.
78: *National Front*: an extreme right-wing group, characterized by aggressive racism and thuggery
103: *HARP*: a cheap brand of lager

They boot the ball on purpose at the trunk
110 and make the tree shed showers of shrivelled may.
I look at this word graffitied by some drunk
and I'm in half a mind to let it stay.

(Though honesty demands that I say *if*
I'd wanted to take the necessary pains
115 to scrub the skin's inscription off
I only had an hour between trains.

So the feelings that I had as I stood gazing
and the significance I saw could be a sham,
mere excuses for not patiently erasing
120 the word sprayed on the grave of dad and mam.)

This pen's all I have of magic wand.
I know this world's so torn but want no other
except for dad who'd hoped from 'the beyond'
a better life than this one, *with* my mother.

125 Though I don't believe in afterlife at all
and know it's cheating it's hard *not* to make
a sort of furtive prayer from this skin's scrawl,
his UNITED mean 'in Heaven' for their sake,

an accident of meaning to redeem
130 an act intended as mere desecration
and make the thoughtless spraying of his team
apply to higher things, and to the nation.

Some, where kids use aerosols, use giant signs
to let the people know who's forged their fetters
135 like PRI CE O WALES above West Yorkshire mines
(no prizes for who nicked the missing letters!).

The big blue star for booze, tobacco ads,
the magnet's monogram, the royal crest,
insignia in neon dwarf the lads
140 who spray a few odd FUCKS when they're depressed.

Letters of transparent tubes and gas
in Düsseldorf are blue and flash out KRUPP.
Arms are hoisted for the British ruling class
and clandestine, genteel aggro keeps them up.

145 And there's HARRISON on some Leeds building sites
I've taken in fun as blazoning my name,
which I've also seen on books, in Broadway lights,
so why can't skins with spraycans do the same?

110: *may:* hawthorn blossoms
142: *KRUPP:* a German manufacturer of steel and industrial machinery; until the end of World War II it
was also one of the world's biggest arms manufacturers.
144: *aggro:* aggressive or violent behaviour

But why inscribe these *graves* with CUNT and SHIT?
150   Why choose neglected tombstones to disfigure?
This pitman's of last century daubed PAKI GIT,
this grocer Broadbent's aerosolled with NIGGER?

They're there to shock the living, not arouse
the dead from their deep peace to lend support
155   for the causes skinhead spraycans could espouse.
The dead would want their desecrators caught!

Jobless though they are how can these kids,
even though their team's lost one more game,
believe that the 'Pakis', 'Niggers', even 'Yids'
160   sprayed on the tombstones here should bear the blame?

What is it that these crude words are revealing?
What is it that this aggro act implies?
Giving the dead their xenophobic feeling
or just a *cri-de-coeur* because man dies?

165   *So what's a* cri-de-coeur, *cunt? Can't you speak*
the language that yer mam spoke. Think of 'er!
Can yer only get yer tongue round fucking Greek?
Go and fuck yerself with cri-de-coeur!

'She didn't talk like you do for a start!'
170   I shouted, turning where I thought the voice had been.
She didn't understand yer fucking 'art'!
She thought yer fucking poetry obscene!

I wish on this skin's word deep aspirations,
first the prayer for my parents I can't make,
175   then a call to Britain and to all the nations
made in the name of love for peace's sake.

Aspirations, cunt! Folk on t'fucking dole
'ave got about as much scope to aspire
above the shit they're dumped in, cunt, as coal
180   *aspires to be chucked on t'fucking fire.*

'OK, forget the aspirations. Look, I know
United's losing gets you fans incensed
and how far the HARP inside you makes you go
but *all* these Vs: against! against! against!'

185   *Ah'll tell yer then what really riles a bloke.*
It's reading on their graves the jobs they did—
butcher, publican and baker. Me, I'll croak
doing t'same nowt ah do now as a kid.

151: *PAKI GIT:* racist slang: "Pakistani idiot"
164: *cri-de-coeur:* passionate protest
177: *dole:* unemployment insurance
188: *nowt:* nothing

'*ard birth ah wor, mi mam says, almost killed 'er.*
190   *Death after life on t'dole won't seem as 'ard!*
Look at this cunt, Wordsworth, organ builder,
this fucking 'aberdasher Appleyard!

If mi mam's up there, don't want to meet 'er
listening to me list mi dirty deeds,
195   *and 'ave to pipe up to St fucking Peter*
ah've been on t'dole all mi life in fucking Leeds!

Then t'Alleluias stick in t'angels' gobs.
When dole-wallahs fuck off to the void
what'll t'mason carve up for their jobs?
200   *The cunts who lieth 'ere wor unemployed?*

This lot worked at one job all life through.
Byron, 'Tanner', 'Lieth 'ere interred'.
They'll chisel fucking poet when they do you
and that, yer cunt, 's a crude four-letter word.

205   'Listen, cunt!' I said, 'before you start your jeering
the reason why I want this in a book
's to give ungrateful cunts like you a hearing!'
A book, yer stupid cunt, 's not worth a fuck!

'The only reason why I write this poem at all
210   on yobs like you who do the dirt on death
's to give some higher meaning to your scrawl.'
Don't fucking bother, cunt! Don't waste your breath!

'You piss-artist skinhead cunt, you wouldn't know
and it doesn't fucking matter if you do,
215   the skin and poet united fucking Rimbaud
but the *autre* that *je est* is fucking you.'

Ah've told yer, no more Greek . . . That's yer last warning!
Ah'll boot yer fucking balls to Kingdom Come.
They'll find yer cold on t'grave tomorrer morning.
220   *So don't speak Greek. Don't treat me like I'm dumb.*

'I've done my bits of mindless aggro too
not half a mile from where we're standing now.'
Yeah, ah bet yer wrote a poem, yer wanker you!
'No, shut yer gob a while. Ah'll tell yer 'ow . . .'

197: *gobs:* mouths
198: *dole-wallahs:* the long-term unemployed
210: *yobs:* hooligans
213: *piss-artist:* a general term of abuse; a person who when drunk (i.e., usually) has an exaggerated sense
of their own value, wit, or importance.
215: In a famous letter the French poet *Rimbaud* (1854–1891) announced his visionary vocation,
aiming to allow his consciousness to become a medium to the spiritual unknown; he encapsulated the
idea in the cryptic phrase, "Je est un autre": "I is another." Rimbaud's poetic career was remarkably
brief—after his teenage years he completely abandoned literature—and his vagabond, often sordid life
indeed combined the aspects of "skin and poet."

225   'Herman Darewski's band played operetta
       with a wobbly soprano warbling. Just why
       I made my mind up that I'd got to get her
       with the fire hose I can't say, but I'll try.

       It wasn't just the singing angered me.
230   At the same time half a crowd was jeering
       as the smooth Hugh Gaitskell, our MP,
       made promises the other half were cheering.

       What I hated in those high soprano ranges
       was uplift beyond all reason and control
235   and in a world where you say nothing changes
       it seemed a sort of prick-tease of the soul.

       I tell you when I heard high notes that rose
       above Hugh Gaitskell's cool electioneering
       straight from the warbling throat right up my nose
240   I had all your aggro in *my* jeering.

       And I hit the fire extinguisher ON knob
       and covered orchestra and audience with spray.
       I could run as fast you then. A good job!
       They yelled 'damned vandal' after me that day . . .'

245   *And then yer saw the light and gave up 'eavy!*
       And knew a man's not how much he can sup . . .
       Yer reward for growing up's this super-bevvy,
       a meths and champagne punch in t'FA Cup.

       Ah've 'eard all that from old farts past their prime.
250   *'ow now yer live wi' all yer once detested . . .*
       Old farts with not much left 'll give me time.
       Fuckers like that get folk like me arrested.

       Covet not thy neighbour's wife, thy neighbour's riches.
       Vicar and cop who say, to save our souls,
255   *Get thee beHind me, Satan, drop their breeches*
       and get the Devil's dick right up their 'oles!

       It was more a *working* marriage that I'd meant,
       a blend of masculine and feminine.
       Ignoring me, he started looking, bent
260   on some more aerosolling, for his tin.

225: *Herman Darewski* (1883–1947), British big-band leader, and composer of "Oh! What a Lovely War."
231: *Hugh Gaitskell* (1906–1963), one of the Leeds MPs, and leader of the Labour Party from 1955 until his
    death in 1963.
245: *'eavy:* bitter (beer)
246: *sup:* drink
247: *bevvy:* drink
248: *meths:* methylated spirits
    FA Cup: the cup presented to the winner of the annual Challenge Cup series held by the Football
Association

'It was more a *working* marriage that I mean!'
Fuck, and save mi soul, eh? That suits me.
Then as if I'd egged him on to be obscene
he added a middle slit to one daubed V.

265   *Don't talk to me of fucking representing*
the class yer were born into any more.
Yer going to get 'urt and start resenting
it's not poetry we need in this class war.

Yer've given yerself toffee, cunt. Who needs
270   *yer fucking poufy words. Ah write mi own.*
Ah've got mi work on show all ovver Leeds
like this UNITED 'ere on some sod's stone.

'OK!' (thinking I had him trapped) 'OK!'
'If you're so proud of it, then sign your name
275   when next you're full of HARP and armed with spray,
next time you take this short cut from the game.'

He took the can, contemptuous, unhurried
and cleared the nozzle and prepared to sign
the UNITED sprayed where mam and dad were buried.
280   He aerosolled his name. And it was mine.

The boy footballers bawl *Here Comes the Bride*
and drifting blossoms fall onto my head.
One half of me's alive but one half died
when the skin half sprayed my name among the dead.

285   Half versus half, the enemies within
the heart that can't be whole till they unite.
As I stoop to grab the crushed HARP lager tin
the day's already dusk, half dark, half light.

That UNITED that I'd wished onto the nation
290   or as reunion for dead parents soon recedes.
The word's once more a mindless desecration
by some HARPoholic yob supporting Leeds.

Almost the time for ghosts I'd better scram.
Though not given much to fears of spooky scaring
295   I don't fancy an encounter with mi mam
playing Hamlet with me for this swearing.

Though I've a train to catch my step is slow.
I walk on the grass and graves with wary tread
over these subsidences, these shifts below
300   the life of Leeds supported by the dead.

Further underneath's that cavernous hollow
that makes the gravestones lean towards the town.

264: *added a middle slit:* i.e., turning it into a stylized image of a woman's genitals

A matter of mere time and it will swallow
this place of rest and all the resters down.

305   I tell myself I've got, say, 30 years.
At 75 this place will suit me fine.
I've never feared the grave but what I fear's
that great worked-out black hollow under mine.

Not train departure time, and not Town Hall
310   with the great white clock face I can see,
coal, that began, with no man here at all,
as 300 million-year-old plant debris.

5 kids still play at making blossoms fall
and humming as they do *Here Comes the Bride.*
315   They never seem to tire of their ball
though I hear a woman's voice call one inside.

2 larking boys play bawdy bride and groom.
3 boys in Leeds strip la-la *Lohengrin.*
I hear them as I go through growing gloom
320   still years away from being skald or skin.

The ground's carpeted with petals as I throw
the aerosol, the HARP can, the cleared weeds
on top of dad's dead daffodils, then go,
with not one glance behind, away from Leeds.

325   The bus to the station's still the No. 1
but goes by routes that I don't recognise.
I look out for known landmarks as the sun
reddens the swabs of cloud in darkening skies.

Home, home, home, to my woman as the red
330   darkens from a fresh blood to a dried.
Home, home to my woman, home to bed
where opposites seem sometimes unified.

A pensioner in turban taps his stick
along the pavement past the corner shop,
335   that sells samosas now, not beer on tick,
to the Kashmir Muslim Club that was the Co-op.

House after house FOR SALE where we'd played cricket
with white roses cut from flour-sacks on our caps,
with stumps chalked on the coal-grate for our wicket,
340   and every one bought now by 'coloured chaps',

318: The "Bridal Song" from Wagner's *Lohengrin* is the source for "Here Comes the Bride."
320: *skald:* bard
335: *tick:* credit
338: The *white rose* is the emblem of Yorkshire, and thus of Yorkshire County Cricket Club.
339: In cricket the *wicket* defended by the batsman consists of three *stumps* (stakes).

dad's most liberal label as he felt
squeezed by the unfamiliar, and fear
of foreign food and faces, when he smelt
curry in the shop where he'd bought beer.

345 And growing frailer, 'wobbly on his pins',
the shops he felt familiar with withdrew
which meant much longer tiring treks for tins
that had a label on them that he knew.

And as the shops that stocked his favourites receded
350 whereas he'd fancied beans and popped next door,
he found that four long treks a week were needed
till he wondered what he bothered eating for.

The supermarket made him feel embarrassed.
Where people bought whole lambs for family freezers
355 he bought baked beans from check-out girls too harassed
to smile or swap a joke with sad old geezers.

But when he bought his cigs he'd have a chat,
his week's one conversation, truth to tell,
but time also came and put a stop to that
360 when old Wattsy got bought out by M. Patel.

And there, 'Time like an ever rolling stream' 's
what I once trilled behind that boarded front.
A 1000 ages made coal-bearing seams
and even more the hand that sprayed this CUNT

365 on both Methodist and C of E billboards
once divided in their fight for local souls.
Whichever house more truly was the Lord's
both's pews are filled with cut-price toilet rolls.

Home, home to my woman, never to return
370 till sexton or survivor has to cram
the bits of clinker scooped out of my urn
down through the rose-roots to my dad and mam.

Home, home to my woman, where the fire's lit
these still chilly mid-May evenings, home to you,
375 and perished vegetation from the pit
escaping insubstantial up the flue.

Listening to *Lulu*, in our hearth we burn,
as we hear the high Cs rise in stereo,

345: *pins:* legs
361: *Time like an ever rolling stream:* from the Methodist hymn "O God, our help in ages past" (Psalm 90, trans. Isaac Watts)
365: *C of E:* Church of England
371: *clinker:* solid remnants left after combustion
377: *Lulu:* an opera by the Viennese avantgarde composer Alban Berg (1885–1935); Harrison's wife, the soprano Teresa Stratas, sang the title role in the version recorded by Pierre Boulez for Deutsche Grammophon.

what was lush swamp club-moss and tree-fern
380   at least 300 million years ago.

Shilbottle cobbles, Alban Berg high D
lifted from a source that bears your name,
the one we hear decay, the one we see,
the fern from the foetid forest, as brief flame.

385   This world, with far too many people in,
starts on the TV logo as a taw,
then ping-pong, tennis, football; then one spin
to show us all, then shots of the Gulf War.

As the coal with reddish dust cools in the grate
390   on the late-night national news we see
police v. pickets at a coke-plant gate,
old violence and old disunity.

The map that's colour-coded Ulster/Eire's
flashed on again as almost every night.
395   Behind a tiny coffin with two bearers
men in masks with arms show off their might.

The day's last images recede to first a glow
and then a ball that shrinks back to blank screen.
Turning to love, and sleep's oblivion, I know
400   what the UNITED that the skin sprayed *has* to mean.

Hanging my clothes up, from my parka hood
may and apple petals, browned and creased,
fall onto the carpet and bring back the flood
of feelings their first falling had released.

405   I hear like ghosts from all Leeds matches humming
with one concerted voice the bride, the bride
I feel united to, *my* bride is coming
into the bedroom, naked, to my side.

The ones we choose to love become our anchor
410   when the hawser of the blood-tie's hacked, or frays.
But a voice that scorns chorales is yelling: *Wanker!*
It's the aerosolling skin I met today's.

My *alter ego* wouldn't want to know it,
his aerosol vocab would baulk at LOVE,
415   the skin's UNITED underwrites the poet,
the measures carved below the ones above.

381: *cobbles:* coal
386: *taw:* a marble used as a shooter
388: *Gulf War:* the Iran-Iraq war of the 1980s
391: *coke:* a fuel made from coal
393: *Ulster/Eire:* Northern Ireland and the Republic of Ireland

I doubt if 30 years of bleak Leeds weather
and 30 falls of apple and of may
will erode the UNITED binding us together.
420   And now it's your decision: does it stay?

Next millennium you'll have to search quite hard
to find out where I'm buried but I'm near
the grave of haberdasher Appleyard,
the pile of HARPs, or some new neonned beer.

425   Find Byron, Wordsworth, or turn left between
one grave marked Broadbent, one marked Richardson.
Bring some solution with you that can clean
whatever new crude words have been sprayed on.

If love of art, or love, gives you affront
430   that the grave I'm in's graffitied then, maybe,
erase the more offensive FUCK and CUNT
but leave, with the worn UNITED, one small v.

Victory? For vast, slow, coal-creating forces
that hew the body's seams to get the soul.
435   Will Earth run out of her 'diurnal courses'
before repeating her creation of black coal?

But choose a day like I chose in mid-May
or earlier when apple and hawthorn tree,
no matter if boys boot their ball all day,
440   cling to their blossoms and won't shake them free.

If, having come this far, somebody reads
these verses, and he/she wants to understand,
face this grave on Beeston Hill, your back to Leeds,
and read the chiselled epitaph I've planned:

445   *Beneath your feet's a poet, then a pit.*
Poetry supporter, if you're here to find
how poems can grow from (beat you to it!) *SHIT*
find the beef, the beer, the bread, then look behind.

                                                          1985

435: *diurnal courses*: cf. Wordsworth, "A Slumber Did My Spirit Seal"

JOHN RILEY (1937–1978)

R ILEY WAS BORN IN LEEDS AND EDUCATED AT LOCAL SCHOOLS AND, AFTER NATIONAL
service in the air force, at Pembroke College, Cambridge. After graduation he
taught in schools in and around Cambridge and Bicester (near Oxford). After giving
up teaching in the late 1960s, Riley lived briefly in Cornwall before returning to Leeds.
In 1973, he visited Istanbul, the former Constantinople and Byzantium, and, for Rus-
sians, Czargrad. In 1977, Riley was received into the Russian Orthodox Church. His
first book, *Ancient and Modern,* appeared in 1967. *What Reason Was: Poems 1967–1969*
(1970) takes its title from a phrase by the Russian writer Vladimir Solovyov: "So far,
love is for man what reason was for the animal world: it exists in its rudiments or
tokens, but not as yet in fact."[1] *Ways of Approaching* was published in 1973; *Prose
Pieces* in 1974. *The Collected Works* (1980) and *Selected Poems* (1995) appeared
posthumously. Riley also translated German and Russian poets, including Friedrich
Hölderlin and Osip Mandelstam. He was the business manager for Tim Longville's
Grosseteste Review, a journal that did much to further knowledge in Britain of the
work of American poets such as Charles Olson, George Oppen, William Bronk,
Robert Creeley, and Louis Zukofsky, and, as Grosseteste Press, published Riley, J. H.
Prynne, John James, Douglas Oliver, and other British poets. In 1978, Riley was mur-
dered by muggers in Leeds.

Tim Longville writes that "One of the sustaining maneuvers throughout Riley's
poetry is the way in which a superficially magisterial voice, announcing what is
known, is encroached on and called into question as the poem develops, to end, char-
acteristically, in a state of still-unsettled though subdued doubt."[2] The non-linear
movement of Riley's poems establishes them as sites for approaching and testing
knowledge, for weighing sensory data against idea, desire against the felt limits of lan-
guage. Andrew Duncan notes that "Riley avoids argument, and other rational proce-
dures, as part of the programme of love and contemplation, which reason could only
interrupt."[3] Insofar as Riley's poems are of interest for their theology, it is helpful to
know that Orthodox dogma stresses the mystery of divinity, balancing the nearness
and otherness of the Eternal; divinity is both transcendent *and* immanent. But
Andrew Crozier argues that Riley's poems must be read as "secular," if "not in the nar-
row sense of contradistinction from the sacred," since "The dominion of human
nature, the disjunction between it and the rest of creation, yet their permanent co-

---

1 Quoted in John Riley, *The Collected Works,* Wirksworth and Leeds, 1980, p. 68.
2 "John Riley," *Dictionary of Literary Biography* 40, ed. Vincent Sherry, Detroit, 1985, p. 492.
3 Andrew Duncan, "The Worm and the Coin: John Riley, *Selected Poems,*" *Angel Exhaust,* vol. 14, 1996,
  p. 82.

presence, nature plus man, constitute what is for John Riley's writing the world, and entail its existence both as immediate spiritual revelation and as instance of sacred history, uniting past and future. But the implicit concept of the sacral unity hovers over rather than informs the world as it is known by experience."[4] Riley's Byzantium or Czargrad has nothing to do with a Yeatsian "artifice of eternity" altogether "out of nature" and inhuman; the poem instead celebrates a state of spiritual desire in which "wisdom hovers / tangible, almost, between sense and idea" and the poet is prepared with "cupped hands / to get to know. . . ." "Czargrad," as these lines indicate, is more Rilkean than Yeatsian.

---

[4] "The World, The World: A Reading of John Riley's Poetry," *For John Riley,* Wirksworth, 1979, p. 97.

Czargrad

I

to get to know the flight of birds, blossoming
of lilac-bush tipped with white flame
see the movement of the wind and try
to reassemble quietness from the creakings of the house at night, night
5   when the blood-red sun leaves the room I'd have written a lot
having lots of thoughts and memories of lots of people
in a book of hours, meaning, hierarchies
an Easter greeting always, uncertainties
of private death dispelled, carried closely, nourished
10   and protected till the time for it and the Poet
subsumed in the poet
             blue
flowers yellow flowers a garden a dog a stick
and courage
15   but God decided differently
strangely unrecognisable almost beyond

Title: "Czargrad" is the Russian name for modern Istanbul (previously Constantinople), in Turkey. The site is strategically situated on a peninsula at the entrance to the Black Sea; the city lies on either side of the Bosporus Strait and thus is located in both Europe and Asia. The colony of Byzantium was founded by the Greeks at the site in the eighth century BC; in subsequent centuries it passed to the Persian Empire, then Alexander the Great, then the Roman Empire. The emperor Constantine I established a new imperial residence there in 324; in 330 it was refounded as the seat of the Roman Empire and renamed Constantinople. Under Constantine, Constantinople was declared a Christian city; its patriarch remains the official head of the Orthodox church. Constantinople remained as the capital of the eastern half of the Roman Empire—the Byzantine Empire—after the fall of Rome in the late fifth century. The Byzantine Empire lasted until Constantinople was overrun by the Ottomans in 1453; it then became the capital of the Ottoman Empire, until the Empire's fall in 1922.

The architecture of the city preserves many reminders of its past; many of the ancient Christian churches remain in use, some as mosques; the spectacular sixth-century domed church Hagia Sophia was converted to a mosque in 1453 and is now a museum. Christianity was introduced into Russia by Byzantine missionaries in the ninth century, and became the state religion in 988; the Russian church was a metropolitanate of the Byzantine patriarchate until becoming independent in 1448.

1: Riley adapts a line from "Helian" by the Austrian poet Georg Trakl (1887–1914), one more closely rendered by Riley in his poem "The World Itself, the Long Poem Foundered": "To trace, round-eyed, the flight of birds."

7: *book of hours:* a medieval book containing the prayers to be said at the "hours," the seven times of day appointed by the Church for prayer. Tim Longville has noted the influence of the poet Rainer Maria Rilke (1875–1926) on this passage; Rilke's first book of poems was called *The Book of Hours,* and "hierarchies" perhaps glances at the first *Duino Elegy:* "Who, if I cried out, would hear me among the angelic hierarchies?"

where we've been the ferns, far plants, anachronisms
rampant, uncoil, sticky and rain hours on end
this garden, prehistoric landscape
20   dirty public wandering to know
all cities to have heard and distinguished the cries
that women make and men in pleasure, in pain
the future stretched out as the past in faces
the god of grace floats high up over the cloud formation
25   hymns raised and lowered, seemingly not
getting any place, the common god
                                        what the sea
has to say, what we : after the blizzard they
jumped on sailors to get them in their coffins the schoolmaster
30   "consulted the elements" both flags we wave
in view, in view of, somewhat gaily : enough greenery
to get lost in temporarily
                                        reaching out, driven
from pillar to post of millennia blood
35   thickens, thins
                        to get to know
the flight of angels "I have not loved
my contemporaries, I've loved their beauty"
"and pitied myself improperly" *cette pourriture*
40   I think I hear there the whine of receding light
more than in most
                              not much
jasmine scent from the islands
the stink of colossal crime
45   still on West Europe

                                        2

delicate the wind through silken corn
a life without compromise
hills over hills unseen the sighing of the wind
weighty in the palm
50   wisdom hovers, unheld
tangible, almost, between sense and idea
the cupped hands
                        to get to know

and I could not help thinking of the wonders of the brain
55   that hears music
the soft moths the soft hills the soft nights the soft breezes
of Asia   .
and the music? gone, gone, but here and the form :
except, save (save) in the music of the line it is not, that's
60   the trick, mind

17: *anachronisms*: the earliest ferns are found in the fossil record as far back as the Carboniferous period
(360–286 million years ago).
28ff: This passage draws on nineteenth-century stories of Cornish coastal village life; Riley lived for a time
in the Cornish village of Fowey.
39: *cette pourriture*: "this rottenness" (French)
46: *corn*: i.e., wheat

stumbles at that, not imitating
nature but man's art we heard
a priest chant vespers to an empty church (save
for us, spectators) God
65 in the City . the brain sticks . proposes
formulations :

           a city
           of squatters, drum
           of the dancing bear at morning, past noon
70   both man and bear asleep in ruins, the bear's paw
           delicate . easy
                  a formulation

dome after dome and dome within dome
was . is . the caves within made
75 no space made all space having
rhythm and line and necessity
and duty perhaps in the poem one recites by heart
even to no auditors but beauty
a paradox in the very soft breezes
80 not apparent   for all
that one lives
              and is grateful
for all that without which
              and in spite of
85 in such plenitude the music
              comes of itself, were we
able .
       how make you hear is to say
how shall I hear . how shall I hear ? say it or how
90 hear exactly what was heard
                in the ruins
till the time
        or this :

there is a flower
95 whose colour I cannot see
of pervasive scent
           the name
of the end of all things, in all things .
                  the poem . the City .

100   a flight .

II

there are those who are prepared for the ruin
of empire and therefore empire endures
after ruin, a fish gliding to deeper water
there are those who are prepared for ruin
105 the wind a straight line from horizon to horizon
when the candle extinguished in its pool of water

63: *vespers*: the evening service in the hours of the church

releases the floodgate of moonlight silver
on shelf on bed on books on faces the measure
of our fall upward into night
110   iconostasis of our common misery
those who increased the measure of our love and left us
stillness : for memory is a contemplation
that rebirth is possible, that the song be established

where are they now, the people?
115   dispersed   .   the face of the earth   .   why not join with the exile's
recreation of what's gone, or lost, or never was?
                                             this
keeping house, a few precious objects,
clarities, the form of gratitude,
120   a gathered circle of light, strangeness
or the lifetime of a mind—hard fate

in retentive air legends persist :
songs made dearer when gone than ever they were,
sung by heroes, animal spirits
125   in what the storm disturbs and in what the storm
can not disturb, sense quickens
a painful building up of joy and love
gathers childhood's customs and the steady fields
sleek or gleaming, sounds border on ventriloquy,
130   an alien metallic power in this land,
gulls circle, silent, engrossed in the wind,
the composer returning to his people,
earth's face vanishing around him, *poeta
caecus*, this dream blindly dreamed
135   down to, back to, the face of it
the measure of it

a tiny world, self-reflected into infinity
the wind all the same about the house and words
hissed out in avoidance of error : what we're seeking
140   has little to do with belief
shadows violently on the window, thrown a hundred feet or more
and behind that between the turning pages a
shadowed space and (even) on the still white page
                              a concentration of attention such
145   deep well of love
                              bright cloud is
fixed
              that love
                              is never fulfilled

110: *iconostasis*: in the Eastern Orthodox Church, a wooden screen painted with religious iconography,
    positioned between the sanctuary (which holds the altar) and the rest of the church, and containing a
    door in the center. The priests consecrate the Eucharist hidden behind the screen and enter through the
    door to give communion to the congregation.
133–34: *poeta / caecus*: "the blind poet" (Latin)

150   but the ways
                        of approaching
                                        endless

                            III

                    Morning breeze morning breeze murmurs
                    on water trembles leaves
155   young trees above green branches
        birds cascade
                    sing sweetly the east
                    is bright.
                    See, already light's white
160   the sea a mirror
                    to clear sky
                    light frost pearled
                    the high hills golden.
                    Beauty of moving dawn.
165   The wind's your messenger you the wind's
                    the thirsting heart fulfilled

        and that the stars them
        selves on clear night the black
        birds' nests and budding trees un-
170   fold
                    morning breeze morning breeze murmurs
        sparrows rise so much together
        motionless with intense vibration of wing
                                    murmurs the breeze
175   on river flow
                        brown, green gradations
                                                silent
                    white-flecked
                                        sound, outward
180   curve
                    of time, each leaf a kingdom, the wind's
        your messenger, you the wind's
        ideal audience ideal auditor the song
                                    accomplishes the singer

                            †

185   shouts from across the valley
        raindrops pendant from the trees
        the one manner of knowing : to reach out
        as a leaf swivels in sunlight
        angel's wings to the limits of sky
190   and still the roar in his mind
        towered cloud domes, air cas-
        cades, swirls as water
        falls, from rock to rock the reverence
        due to an icon :

153: This stanza is a free translation of "Ecco mormorar l'onde . . . ," a madrigal by Claudio Monteverdi
    (1567–1643) setting words by the poet Torquato Tasso (1544–1595).

195   green of spring in the Carystian stones
                     crocus blooming in light of gold
                     blue cornflowers in white of snow

        and I apologise to the blackbird
        that there is higher in nature than him
200   to sound true note

                                    †

        till the stream overflows its banks
        overflows its banks and there is a face of waters
        and there is a face of waters
        and there is a face of waters
205   and so mirrored back to the known beyond which is
        nothing   imagination   levelled
        and beauty is residue after the bluebells
        lilac   and the stream
                                name your realities
210   in silence in secrecy or as much
        as the Word permits
        relate them to earthswing, stars, a very distant
        music through the plenitude of what is
        to what must be in plenitude of grasses
215   shooting overnight two feet high obliterating
        distance making the immediate vast
        submarine rooms in summer foliage trailing
        down rippled by currents a hunter
        hovers over parkland, wind soft feathers
220   this day
                    tendrils of passion flower vine round the morning star
        counterpoints of rigour
        clarity of the far white
        walls picked out
225   vapour
        trails, a routine with variations sun disc
        silent   warm enough
        for you? all windows
        alive with reflections air
230   cool still though in breeze, in shade so
        singing of first rain and
        the rain drop by drop makes holes in my song
        la pluie, goutte à goutte, the rain the rain drop by drop
        the power to be humble and clear forsook me
235   this world of moods and voices around silence

195: *Carystian stones:* Káristos, on the Greek island of Euboea, is renowned for its green and white
  cipollino marble.
221: *morning star:* the planet Venus. (There is a plant of this name, Star-of-Bethlehem, but Tim Longville
  has suggested that Riley is looking out of the window of his room, the inside of which is wreathed in the
  foliage, flowers, and tendrils of a potted passion flower, and through them seeing the actual morning
  star.)
233: *la pluie . . .* (French): translated in the next words

IV

weak in the light or a weakness in the light
                    and so the caravan approaches
greedy now for Spring, the minutest details
the pageant flight of love's victims;
240   caught between sun and moon there is disquiet
the age   almost through mouths of dead poets
the angelic song burns with its own bitterness
that the hand turns inward to the light too often
and darkness grows useless, unused the trees
245   flame higher, proclaim what is, caught
in desire   stillness in the house, delight still
ascent and descent still possible, labour of precision
the crows' thick wings pass overhead; life in-
tensified, held now
250   as albatross wings are a part of the wind

                              †

that the City exists
                    tints
of autumn brown and yellow, red
scarlets of autumns I shall never see but could not
255   in imagination better   and love
a willed deficiency of senses
how else could we bear, why else die   denied

no season is tranquil
recession of galaxies in a falling leaf
260   life blood   but shrinking the day
to insignificant concerns, deserted
leaves like rain

that the past the present and the future have no motion
no wearisome motion, steady thud of acorns
265   to the earth, information not opinion and
if we have learnt it is
that the hubbub is also texture of song,
the breath of exiles, survivors,
thought of home

                              †

270   birds off across November fields   mist
startling confidence tricks   a heron   slim wrists
the people one meets   what's to be done
with love
spread wider   identity   you
275   are invited we never
knew each other   hardly
for the years and circumstances begin life
naked   phenomena   dark, evenings, mornings
                    and
280   the

palaces the colonnades the prospects, domes, winter
dreams, rhythms of the world's desire
slanted sun circles to eye's limit
though the City is partly corruption, decay
285   a world of greys and greens and white under cloud
no nearer no further than fifty thousand years ago
by stems each of which is stable in itself
the City, jewelled in time
                                    I hear the sky go by
290   constellations, star seams in a darkening world

                                    †

faithful mirror in a lake and then
wind ruffles the waters and we raise our eyes
and the image   language of transparent love
meditation   formed of exactitude
295   the City's walls   fail

slight stir of air through grasses
curtains sucked in, out, to the breathing of the wind
the body being anxious, seedlings attentive
Ararat   the smooth-tongued rain

300   mouths of hills shrouded
bare rock triumphs where water flowed
yellow death   heavy, nothing
keep to the shady the deep paths
rhododendron-flanked, gross rose from clay
305   out of sun

arc of hand poised before the other
                                    precious
red rose on the pillow, a sea of perfume
its roots intact
310   and that the sun sets
blood-red sated with its own weight
below the bleached fields
that all that is done
all day the drone of a harvester
315   next field

                                                    1973, 1980

299: Mount *Ararat* is in eastern Turkey, near its borders with Armenia and Iran; it is the traditional rest-
ing place of Noah's Ark.

TOM RAWORTH (b. 1938)

Raworth was born in southeast London, the only child of an Irish-born mother and English father. He quit school at sixteen and worked a series of jobs. While working as an international phone operator in the early 1960s, he started the magazine *Outburst*, which published Ed Dorn, LeRoi Jones, Anselm Hollo, Larry Eigner, and Christopher Logue, among others, and founded Matrix Press, which brought out books by Dorn, Piero Heliczer, David Ball, and other poets. In 1965, with Barry Hall, he began the Goliard Press, which published Charles Olson's first British book, *West* (1966), and books by Ron Padgett and Tom Clark. These publishing ventures contributed substantially to the interest in the "New American" poetry in Britain. After Raworth's first collection of poems, *The Relation Ship,* appeared in 1966, Donald Davie, who admired it, encouraged him to resume his official education at Essex University. Raworth signed on for a B.A. in Spanish, spent time in Spain as part of his studies, and then completed translations of poetry and fiction by Vincente Huidobro and others to receive his M.A. He then left with his family for an extended stay in the United States (where he taught at several universities) and Mexico, returning to England in 1977 to take a position as visiting poet-in-residence at King's College, Cambridge. In the mid-1980s, he produced *Infolio,* a four-page magazine, the first forty issues of which were brought out daily, the last sixty weekly; some 200 writers and graphic artists from all over the world appeared in it. In 1991, Raworth taught at the University of Cape Town, the first European writer to be invited there in thirty years. He lives in Cambridge with his wife Val and grandson Cato.

Since *The Relation Ship,* Raworth has published over forty books and pamphlets of poetry, including *The Big Green Day* (1968), *Lion Lion* (1970), *Moving* (1971), *Act* (1973), *Logbook* (1977), *Writing* (1982), *Tottering State: New and Selected Poems 1963–1984* (1984; 2nd ed. 1988; 3rd ed. 2000), *Visible Shivers* (1987), *Eternal Sections* (1993), *Clean & Well Lit* (1996), and *Meadow* (1999). These books reflect artisanly and aesthetic values in their own right; several of them have been produced in collaboration with artists such as Joe Brainard, Frances Butler, and Jim Dine. Occasionally, as in *Catacoustics* (1991), Raworth has contributed his own doodles and drawings to the books; his collages and other work in the graphic arts have been exhibited in France and Italy. As a performer, Raworth is known for the speed of his delivery, which is tailored to the modular shape and mercurial movement of his poems. He has read throughout Europe, Britain, and North America, sometimes performing with musicians such as Steve Lacy and Joëlle Léandre.

Asked about the work of Charles Olson in 1972, Raworth told Barry Alpert that "I really have no sense of questing for knowledge. . . . My idea is to go the other way, you

know. And to be completely empty and then see what sounds."[1] Kit Robinson writes
that Raworth's earlier poems (such as "Wedding Day") "are condensed instants in the
language of daily life, marking quick shifts of attention. They register specific, isolated
points of view extended, or distended, in time, recording momentary distractions,
sound interference, sudden memory, views through glass, mirrors, funny and awkward
social complications, frustration at failure to push past immediate conditions, and
refusal to pretend more."[2] Affinities with Black Mountain and New York School poetry
are evident in the way these poems follow the poet in the process of discovering where
experience and the poem itself will lead him. Other early poems such as "You've Ruined
My Evening / You've Ruined My Life" suggest another understanding of the poem in
which the poem is an artifact constructed of theoretically movable parts rather than a
record of consciousness in time. These two tendencies in the work come together in
Raworth's poetry beginning with *Ace* (1974), in which syntactic disjunctions compli-
cate the reader's movement between short lines offering fragments of quotidian obser-
vation and statement. In moving from line to line in the poem, the reader is forced to
suspend or adjust understanding of what has just been read to consider new possibil-
ities for reference and meaning. This process rarely stops in Raworth's recent poems;
the desire for closure and completion is emphasized as closure's comforts are rejected.
The movement of Raworth's poetry should not prevent the reader from noting its clar-
ity of detail and the diversity of its tonal registers. The condensed analysis and sarcasm
of a phrase such as "europe, freud laughed" in *Catacoustics* gives way elsewhere to
anger and despair, and the poetry has moments of unaffected wonder as well, as is evi-
dent in one of the poems from *Eternal Sections* included here, in which we glimpse the
"brilliance of the orange lily / down the gangways, silent / in its broad bosom."

---

[1] "An Interview Conducted by Barry Alpert" (1972), reprinted in *Tom Raworth: An Exhibition*, Cambridge
Conference on Contemporary Poetry 8, 1998, n.p.
[2] "Tom Raworth," *Dictionary of Literary Biography* 40, ed. Vincent Sherry, Detroit, 1965, p. 467.

Wedding Day

      noise of a ring sliding onto a finger

      supposing he *did* say that?
      we came by the front
      sea fog twisting light above the pebbles
5   towards the cliffs towards the sea

      i made this pact, intelligence
      shall not replace intuition, sitting here
      my hand cold on the typewriter
      flicking the corner of the paper. he

10   came from the toilet wearing
      a suit, people
      didn't recognise him, down the length
      of corridor. the room
      was wooden, sunlight   we stood in a half circle

15   noise of two cine-cameras

      i wonder what's wrong with her
      face, she said, because

there's nothing wrong with it really   i
inhabit a place just to the left of that phrase. from

20   a bath the father took champagne later
whiskey. through the window we watched the frigate's
orange raft drifting to shore

i mean if you're taking *that*
attitude
25   we rode in a train watching the dog move

noise of a bicycle freewheeling downhill

1966

You've Ruined My Evening/You've Ruined My Life

i would be eight people and then the difficulties vanish
only as one i contain the complications
in a warm house roofed with the rib-cage of an elephant
i pass my grey mornings re-running the reels
5   and the images are the same but the emphasis shifts
the actors bow gently to me and i envy them
their repeated parts, their constant presence in that world

i would be eight people each inhabiting the others' dreams
walking through corridors of glass framed pages
10   telling each other the final lines of letters
picking fruit in one dream and storing it in another
only as one i contain the complications
and the images are the same, their constant presence in that world
the actors bow gently to each other and envy my grey mornings

15   i would be eight people with the rib-cage of an elephant
picking fruit in a warm house above actors bowing
re-running the reels of my presence in this world
the difficulties vanish and the images are the same
eight people, glass corridors, page lines repeated
20   inhabiting grey mornings roofed with my complications
only as one walking gently storing my dream

1968

South America

he is trying to write down a book he wrote years ago in his head
an empty candlestick on the windowsill   each day
of his life he wakes in paris to the sound of vivaldi in summer
and finds the space programme fascinating since he still doesn't know

---

South America: 3: *vivaldi in summer.* i.e., "Summer" from *The Four Seasons* by the composer Antonio
Vivaldi (c.1675–1741)

5   how radio works   as in the progress of art the aim is finally
       to make rules the next generation can break more cleverly   this
       morning he has a letter from his father saying "i have set my face
       as a flint against a washbasin in the lavatory. it seems to me
       almost too absurd and sybaritic"   how they still don't know
10   where power lies or how to effect change
       he clings to a child's book called 'all my things' which says:
       ball (a picture of a ball) drum (a picture of a drum) book (a picture of a
            book)

       all one evening he draws on his left arm with felt-tipped pens
       an intricate pattern   feels how the pain does give protection
15   and in the morning finds faint repetitions on the sheets, the inside
       of his thigh, his forehead   reaching this point
       he sees that he has written pain for paint   and it works better

                                                                    1970

from Logbook

page 106

       would have explained it. But asymptosy seems destined to
       leave it to Vespucci. The two styles fight even for my hand-
       writing. Their chemicals, even, produce nothing more than
       wax in the ears and an amazing thirst. That seems to 'even'
5   things, for those who regard it as a *balance,* or think the
       wind blows *one way.* The third day of our voyage was peri-
       lous. Multitudinous seas incarnadine. But the small craft that
       came out to meet us contained us and went sailing into the
       sunset, carrying only ten pages of my logbook (106, 291, 298,
10   301, 345, 356, 372, 399, 444 and 453), slightly charred by the
       slow still silent instant. And it was in that same instant (as
       everything is) that we recognised that in addition to our
       normal crew we had a stowaway—the author of *The Incredi-*
       ble Max who, alone and unaided, had, on a long string,
15   hauled the dinghy *Automatic Writing* (out from Deus ex
       Machinette)—or how else could he be explained? The elo-
       quence of his moustache (you will understand) bulged neatly
       over and under his belt. He spoke of himself as ceaselessly
       sweeping up the leaves that fall from the trees. We tried to
20   tell him about the other seasons—"Fall DOWN: Spring UP!"
       we made him repeat. "Fall DOWN: Sweep UP!" he added a

1: *asymptosy:* the quality of being asymptotic; an asymptote is a straight line, associated with a curve that
   continually approaches it without meeting it within a finite distance.
2: America was named after Amerigo *Vespucci* (1451–1512), the Florentine explorer of the New World.
7: *Multitudinous seas incarnadine: Macbeth* 2.2.61
15: Automatic writing is that produced rapidly in a trance; the procedure was used by spiritualists to take
   dictation from spirits, and by the Surrealists to produce texts supposedly exemplifying the unfettered
   operation of the unconscious.
15–16: *Deus ex Machinette:* from "deus ex machina" (god from the machinery): originally, a god descend-
   ing by means of a crane onto the stage of a Greek or Roman play; thus, any last-minute, contrived turn
   of events that resolves a difficulty.
20: cf. the mnemonic for Daylight Savings Time: "Spring forward; fall back."

page 453

I'm not going to make it to the lift in time, nor change my
name, and the dialogue echoes off the walls of the set. It's
the front room, and the queen's picture flickers into a limp
book called Jimi Hendrix because all books are dead and we
5   live where the edges overlap. The material is transparent,
but the seam is already ripping down from Orion. And I am
busily sweeping up the last few words in a country without
an ear, whose artists are busy filling in the colours they've
been allocated in the giant painting-by-numbers picture of
10   themselves, because they think an interview with the man
(now a physicist in Moscow) who was the boy on the Odessa
Steps *makes a connection.* Full moon. High tide. Because it's
all gesture, and nobody ever talked in words.

c. 1970 / 1977

from Sentenced to Death

"sentenced he gives a shape"

sentenced he gives a shape
by no means enthusiastic
to what he saw
this new empire had begun
5   slave trade
they were killed
his rabble
divined in one instant
coups d'état
10   regarded missionaries
as an elaborate plot
no journey can be quite
anything any more
pretensions would have been absurd

"curiously the whole thing had begun"

curiously the whole thing had begun
in a fit of shame
trying to get a housing programme
long before there was a tunisia
5   dancing, dancing where everyone had to
have very successful sex lives

---

page 453: 6: *Orion:* a constellation, representing the hunter of Greek legend
11: Raworth has in mind the famous Odessa Steps sequence from Eisenstein's film *The Battleship*
Potemkin (1925), where the revolting citizens are trapped on a series of stone steps between the Tsarist
militia above and the Cossacks below; a massacre ensues. Its most famous image is of a baby-carriage
plunging down the steps to its doom.

and should be designed to cope
with regard to fatty foods
presently replaced every two years
10   the rest of us we have no clothes
most stories reflected
within the geographical territory known as england
or is it the gentrified refuge?
or the unsupported carer?

"reversals of performance levels"

reversals of performance levels
an exaggeration of the lyric
cannot say anything worth reading
and thus form overlapping
5   interpretive procedures directed towards
certain plans of action
by which metaphors come to be made
many mournful images
repeated to dizziness or exhaustion
10   in a corresponding reduction
shift boundaries
bringing attention to form
within itself a multiple
continually traced

                        1986–1987 / 1988

from Eternal Sections

"in black tunics, middle-aged"

in black tunics, middle-aged
in the stationery store
every gesture, even
food: to it
5   thought which breaks
stereotypes which constitute
extenuated to the point
none of the action's promoters
the user experiences
10   no need of acting
dedicated to commerce
the history of our own
stiffness of manner
no longer aligned

"brilliance of the orange lily"

brilliance of the orange lily
down the gangways, silent

in its broad bosom
indifferent to the new
5   more delicate ways
never used now
watered silk subdued by time
within earshot
extinguished the lamp
10   hushed for a few moments
down they climbed
daring to look at it
before midnight
could be fashioned into words

"thoughts are in real time"

thoughts are in real time
after you've gone
they keep your body alive
sending bills
5   bankrupting
your children
reserving the right
to legally define
alive
10   perhaps
that technological blip
records decay
evening sunlight
first sense of spring

1988–1990 / 1993

Out of the Picture

the obsolete ammunition depot
unmissed and unreported
put it in categories
still glistened with dampness
5   suits seemed to be identical
through the window behind him
a battered cardboard box
won somewhere gambling
dim bell in his memory
10   was making a duplicate
to see if that needed explanation
sharply, and then, more gently
the door opened
three thousand miles east of home

"brilliance of the orange lily": 7: *watered silk:* a lustrous silk with a wavy pattern

15   we avoid old bones
        conscious that their territory
        enlarges the room
        by removing a partition
        in the mirror
20   disharmony seeped out
        surrounded by a strange culture
        message and hung up
        its heavy coating of dust
        whispering just loud enough
25   to create a disturbance
        finding words for sorrow
        still locked in combat
        in the expanding silence
        ties with wild designs
30   printed on them suited me
        to be places, camouflaged
        against the cult of personality
        panning over rough walls
        overshadowed modifications
35   into missing construction
        the remote camera
        revealed a huge space
        a kind of coma
        the last gasp of civil protest
40   he could not sleep, above
        starless and dark
        the cloudy sky
        was relieved only
        by electric blue traces
45   shivering with more than cold
        a tumbled slope of stones
        flexed and straightened
        warping space
        into a dozen planes
50   two total strangers
        retreated in panic
        without letting it appear
        the instrument of a secret
        attached to this procedure
55   by a sudden doubt
        pretending he was a robot
        respectable looking
        legs hot and itchy
        faces indistinct behind windows
60   look from all angles
        scornfully as
        wandering among dogs
        he is politely relieved of his wallet
        the corner of his mouth
65   under a white moustache
        pried off
        with an effective tool
        giving her the illusion
        of a small, dimly lit
70   parking lot

set well back from the road
looking at a calendar
he realised the image of a falling body
came from film
75. a slightly altered version
connected to these bombings
the smell of wood burning
should be in a museum
thought probably was
80 displayed on costumed models
back in the car then
slumped down in the seat
accompanied only by printed legends
his thoughts elsewhere
85 with the thousands of dead
each wrapped in newspaper
he wasn't intending to dig up more
someone high on the power ladder
meant nothing else would matter
90 before the call came
rain streaked the glass
preventing identification
between drizzle and mist
through a labyrinth of corridors
95 good feeling left
closing the door
fires that lined both sides
collapsed in sparks
riffled in the gusty breeze
100 remembered from previous days
nothing unusual on the street
not a word in the papers
nobody was interested
it didn't happen
105 in the taxi heading back
to avoid hysterical screaming
there was not one question
felt through thin black leather
after stretching his muscles
110 towards that cone of white light
with little jerky movements
spreading a cool odour of soap
suddenly he was flesh, meat
making tracking easy
115 she sobbed
behind her veil
fascinated by this ceremony
keeping emotion out of his voice
he glanced at the watch
120 its face stared back
cold air
whispered and fell silent
a slender stiff shank

123: *shank*: prison slang for a homemade knife

above the first vertebra
125 glancing around all the time
when the guard was killed
into a wilderness of lines
keeping things even
his inclination was to ignore
130 dislocation from reality
notice how it smells
slightly sympathetic
to the uncommitted
a bitterness he usually kept
135 to shield his face
during the autopsy
marks left by rodents
sure of security
sign and type the corpse
140 into something invisible
with pitiless neutrality
grunting and wheezing
a train makes an unscheduled stop
he's never heard before
145 suppressing an urge to look back
for something to read
partly in your mind
plastic, once transparent
can again be reunited
150 with old age wandering
in a public display
beside the mailbox
people with political connections
seemed neutral here
155 in that harmony
which conditions humans
in the crawlspace above the ceiling
their serious talking
rang some changes
160 under close surveillance
a voice that sounded like a cop
was hardly audible
buying bad information
only the molded plastic head
165 making a quick reflex move
struck him a terrible blow
skittering down the hall
eyes closed, singing
not words in any human language
170 he remembered the scene
parked under some cottonwoods
slightly out of focus
why not let the wound heal?
early in this assignment
175 he warned
a mixture of standard tourists
clustered around
the elegant camera bag

each holding a briefcase
180 that planting
a tape-recorded message
rated personal attention
music wasn't music any more
he shaved in three minutes
185 following her eyes
poured himself three shots
she wasn't worried
pressed harder on the gas
nothing out there except snow
190 on jet-velvet rocks
not the slightest clue
as her arm moved
in the cramped space
slowly towards his ribs
195 came away moist
making a polite movement
across the pillow
seeming to dance from darkness
shaking with rage
200 now that he was aware of it

1996

R. F. LANGLEY (b. 1938)

ROGER LANGLEY WAS BORN IN STAFFORDSHIRE, WHERE HE STILL RESIDES, AND educated at Jesus College, Cambridge. Until his retirement in 1999, he taught English and art history in secondary schools. His publications include *Hem* (1978), *Sidelong* (1981), *Twelve Poems* (1994), *Jack* (1998), and *Collected Poems* (2000). This does not constitute prolific production; Langley has said that his poems are often years in the making. Peter Riley, while noting that it is difficult to generalize about Langley's procedures, writes that "The textuality [of the poems] is strikingly difficult: we are not fully let in to the scene of action; phrases follow each other as if engendered from an inner site to which we cannot expect access; entities are referred to as if known . . . but remain unidentified. . . . The units of the poem, the word-groups it is made of, are of many kinds (images, remarks, descriptions, ideas, exclamations, narratives, dialogues, absurdities, references, slogans . . .) which are usually short and succeed each other with or without, usually without, the following-on procedures of addressed language. Quite often like a series of answers to questions which remain silent. A framework of 'scene' may emerge tentatively, but some detail suddenly transgresses it."[1] Autobiographical events can enter into the poems, as for instance in the phone call mentioned in "Man Jack," but the poem incorporates such detail while making autobiography neither more nor less than the other particulars of the poem; the poem is "referential" without ordering a hierarchy of referents or isolating an occasion.

In the journal *Angel Exhaust,* Langley tells an interviewer that "one inspiration [for "Man Jack"] is simply the dozens of columns in the *Oxford Dictionary* on the word 'jack'. And everything you can do with Jack, a sort of commonality of humanity that Jack might represent. And all of the different combinations he's been in: the names of flowers, Jacks and Jills, and Jack in the Beanstalks, and jack in the boxes and how Jack turns into Tom [in card games] and all the rest of it. . . . He's that little figure you see running along beside the train jumping over the hedges and swinging from the telegraph poles."[2] "Saxon Landings," as Langley indicates in the same interview, is about the Mildenhall Treasure, a trove of Roman artifacts discovered in the 1940s, especially the Great Dish, which depicts the triumph of Bacchus over Hercules and, on its central medallion, the head of the sea-god Oceanus. Langley also names as a source "a play about the Romans having to pull out of England under Saxon pressure, *The Long Sunset* by (R. C.) Sherriff. I think it was just having listened to that play on the radio that made me suddenly feel the trauma of throwing away a structured existence, bonfires going off at the bottom of the garden, and pagan shadows playing against them,

---

[1] *A Poetry in Favour of the World,* Cambridge, 1997, p. 1.
[2] "R. F. Langley interviewed by Bobby Walker," *Angel Exhaust,* vol. 13, 1996, p. 125.

and the likelihood of being massacred at any moment. And that's what got that going."[3] Despite having published comparatively few poems, Langley has a small but dedicated following, in part because his poems present such a variety of formal accomplishment, from the densely rhyming decasyllabics and circling sentences of "Man Jack" to the compressed and elided, monosyllable-dominated sentences that give the opening strophe of "Saxon Landing" its rhythms of fearful urgency.

---

3 "Propos Recuellis par R. F. Walker: Interview with Roger Langley," *Angel Exhaust*, vol. 14, 1997, p. 110.

Saxon Landings

1

Here is of all the very this
is at last to keep the signals
lit or soon, they might, who knows
for sure the shore to either
5   hand so quickly in the haze. And
this could, once, so it has been
solid and level, hold on, then
here is inside your head laid out
in zones of shells and leaves like
10   you always hoped, not real, but
cool, it throws white light in
your face would you step out
under trees under tumbling trees
hold it still in both hands.

2

15   Through by the door, in the fright
of it's done, it's shot in a
click, though it's not light yet
the smells are sharp the bricks
don't blink, you blind as you
20   tell it this is action action
action and the treasure, heavy
silver, warm lids, mother table,
olives and cheese and bread and
possessiveness of a simple love
25   the whole zoned, beaded and scrolled
just gloats, it just gloats and
push it somewhere away into soft
loam and leave it afloat there.

Title: For the details of the poem's composition see the headnote above. The Mildenhall Dish has three divisions: in the center is the head of the sea-god Oceanus, out of whose seaweed-like hair and beard leap dolphins; the circle surrounding this contains revelling nereids and sea-creatures; the outer circle shows the victory of Bacchus, god of wine, over Hercules in a drinking contest. Hercules is being carried off, dead drunk, by two satyrs; the rest of the frieze contains dancing maenads, satyrs, and the god Pan.

28: *loam:* a type of soil made up of clay, sand, and decomposed vegetable matter

3

Once they believed it but since it
30   is diction, the pipes in the wood
or limber vine and the bland
country where Bacchus and Pan
defeat Hercules. They lift him.
The drunk. Hush. Lay him down in
35   the sound of his name on the ground
of our home these are loan words we
never except as ledges of leaves of
shells this is keepsake and darling
and silver in moonlight is cold
40   twice cold, it throws white light
on your face you look blood
less in the porch's daze.

4

Your calm, my lady, has been
to have it your own, and known
45   hot to your ankles your knee
on the seat and talking windows
looking windows into arcady,
delectable, putting out white
poplar forming with your berry
50   mouth leaves or winter acorns
where your mood took listening
to there shall it suffice your
poet to have sung but this is
a very it cannot, slung on my
55   hips out my corner eye, rake
hell, orgies, waters, unlimited fury.

5

Save yourself stop this reflective you
can't think it sling it and run my
voice is quite shrill because while
60   you've been ships have beached, some
bird yelped, the face of a god looks
straight at you were eating off his
sacrilegious like a picnic his eyes
pop fish squeeze out his hair he really
65   rages lady! your chair spins his flashes
darken the windows his mane his mouth
is an open road under tormented forest
trees you walk gasping down his roaring
maw carrying your silver dish still
70   carrying you've been given a silver dish.

1978

36: A *loan word* is one borrowed from another language.
47: *arcady*: an idealized pastoral or rural scene
55–56: *rakehell*: an eighteenth-century term for a man of wild or promiscuous habits; a young blade

Man Jack

FOR JANE WILLIAMS AND BOB WALKER

So Jack's your man, Jack is your man in things.
And he must come along, and he must stay
close, be quick and right, your little cousin
Jack, a step ahead, deep in the hedge, on
5   edge, a kiss a rim, at pinch, in place, turn
face and tip a brim, each inch of him, the
folded leaf, the important straw. What for.
He's slippery and hot. He slides in blood.
Those lies he tells you, running alongside.
10   To and fro he ducks, and miserably
clicks and puckers up, and in his rage he
won't speak out, or only half. He's short. He's
dim. He'll clench his jaw. He's more than you can
take. He'll drop it all across the road and
15   spit and go. Over the years you'll have to
learn to pull him in and let him know. You'll
say, 'Today we'll have that, now, those other
apples. So. Oh but you'll fetch them like I
seem to think I dreamed you did, and they'll be
20   like they always should have been, in action,
apples in the apples, apples' apples,
through and through.' And then you'll see what he can
do. He'll fetch them in and put them roughly
in a row. The scent will almost be a presence
25   in the room. 'Oh, but it hurt,' he'll say, 'to
pick across the stones, the different stones.
So many different pains.' Oh Jack. You
hick. You grig. You hob. You Tom, and what not,
with your moans! Your bones are rubber. Get back
30   out and do it all again. For all the
world an ape! For all the world Tom poke, Tom
tickle and Tom joke! Go back and carry
logs into the hall. And wait with lifted
finger till the eave drops fall. Your task. The
35   jewel discovered by the monkey in
the shine. Fetch that, and make it much, and mine.
Sometimes it's best if I forget to ask.
An errand boy with nothing up his sleeve,
who stops to listen to the rigmarole
40   to find he cannot leave without he's bought
the dog. Time out of mind. Just bring
what you can find. Apples. Twigs. Icicles.
Pigs. The owl that watches as we try a
phonecall from the isolated box. Jane's
45   disembodied voice. The owl that hears her
words. The moon that thinks about her baby.

28: A *grig* can be a dwarf, a hen, or a small eel; a "merry grig" is a lively and high-spirited person. A *hob* is
a rustic, and also a sprite or hobgoblin.

Jack in the moon. Jane in Jill. The baby
coming sure and soon and bright and staring
at the apples which keep still. The owl had
50   no idea. More knew Tom fool. The apples
shine in everybody's eyes. Tom speaks
inside his cheeks. The moon talks from inside
his belly. The isolation sighs to think
of motherhood. We hear Jane's tiny words,
55   as does the owl, astonished, listening
in the roadside wood. Jack gleeks inside
his only box of tricks for what has come.
All thumbs, he Tibs his Tom. It's apples and
it's owls. He bobs and chops and nips until
60   it's Jill engaged in paradise, with the
enchanted pips. Just in the nick with
only magic left. No use at all to
look at him as if he were a jug. As
if he were. A twig is evidently
65   a love bouquet. The apples are a gift.
The spellbound owl sits round as such
upon a shelf. Its silence cries out loud
as if you touched it on a wound. It is
embarrassed and delighted with what Jack
70   has found. And that it had, itself, the wit
required to secretly decipher it.
Until there is a sudden dip into
a silence in the silence, and the owl
has turned his head away and, frightened, stepped
75   off on his long legs into air, into
an emptiness, left by Jack who is not
there. He's gone too far. Though nothing drops, there's
nothing caught. The twig is two. The gleek is
three. There'd be a mournival in the four
80   but no one's counting any more. It stops.
The apple is not fire. And yellow is
not sweet. Jane's voice from miles away is just
a speck and almost lost, but yet it is
distinctly Jane, uninfluenced by the moon
85   she has not seen, the roadside where she has
not been, the owl who thought to pick a peck,
the apples she will never eat. The Jane
who cannot tell us yet the baby's name.
And, undeclared like that, it wins the game.

                                                                        1993

56: *gleeks:* tricks; mocks; looks askew at. Gleek was also a three-person card game of the Renaissance, and
  Langley draws on its terminology: *Tib:* the ace of trumps; *Tom:* the jack (or "knave") of trumps; *gleek:*
  three-of-a-kind; *mournival:* four-of-a-kind.

CARLYLE REEDY (b. 1938)

Born in the United States, educated in the United States and France, Reedy has been resident in the United Kingdom since 1964. She became an important presence in the "pop" poetry scene vibrant in the 1960s and was one of half a dozen women to have poems in Michael Horovitz's counterculture anthology *Children of Albion* (1969). Her interest in performance extended from poetry cabaret to performance art and multimedia, and in the 1970s and 1980s she was active making and showing work at venues including the Royal Court Theatre, while also collaborating on projects such as Monkey Theatre and O Productions One. cris cheek describes the "Taoist patience, great humour, feminist insight, and . . . engaging touch with everyday objects" characteristic of her cross-artform practice: "Her work projected multiple characters and often alluded to compositional processes as philosophical states of attention. Much of it made use of materials directly associated with both writing and calligraphy. Further to this she makes elaborate and obsessively detailed collages. The work is often in continual states of arrival and departure as it progresses, becoming torn, erased, reinscribed, overwritten and discarded—all with great care and due respect paid to the precarious valences between immanent products and demotic flux."[1]

In her essay "Working Processes of a Woman Poet," Reedy discusses several modes employed in her poetry, beginning with "a poetry of image . . . based in the contemplation of things seen, in the material of the world and in the mind that looked upon them." Other work is designed with attention to "visual cinematic experience, written rather like a play, noted down with existential implication perceived as in a film."[2] Reedy's poems make full use of the typographical and visual resources of the book; some poems are arranged as if they were dispersed clusters of notes—single words and short phrases in cubes and columns. Conventions of reading and readerly attention are challenged as words are left to be joined in multiple combinations; one might also speak of a "mutuality," "spontaneity," and " 'egoless' attitude towards 'what comes up,' " values Reedy ascribes to her more explicitly collaborative work. The two fonts of "The Slave Ship" suggest two voices, or personal narrative and a more impersonal commentary, but the relationship between the two is more fluid and complex than that, partly because of the poem's spatial and syntactic gaps and sudden juxtapositions. Reedy's books of poetry include *Sculpted in This World* (1979), *The Orange Notebook* (1984), *Obituaries and Celebrations* (1995), and *Etruscan Reader 4* (1999), in which two of her sequences are gathered with work by Bob Cobbing and Maurice Scully.

---

[1] cris cheek, from an e-mail to the author, January 30, 2000.
[2] *Poets on Writing*, ed. Denise Riley, London, 1992, pp. 261–71.

The Slave Ship

chain beat me to death 3 am the 2nd
clattering against a door tonight I
    not slept I   all *its ring links, only clank*
smoke   lost return   *on the bone of my body*
5   head,   temple, *all over*   *to neck*   breast
in   pagan blue, plunging, *I so naked*
intake to belly   buttocks, the *charms*
they put you under, *it is not good,* what is used
with chains they put you in, in the hold of the ship
10   on in   the human in
    the white *voices sometime some one amongst us sing*
    change   in the mortal   *save*   the body
next to you would rot, hot all the time in the hold
    it does not heal,   *do not hear*
15   I want to hear, *I*   believe   *I be*
the story of   *blue black work of god*
    their voices come down through a hole
    words   fail, is it possible
    one he die and black blood rumble out his throat
20   put like   if this death   then
he twist up stiff going on   redemption,
    next on   *side of him she did not move for fear*
    self   *deathless*   *him go all stiff*
    she stare into nowhere like to live on the truth
25   live without any other food but truth *after*
she never right in her head after   and *die*
many   *die* and some will not *over*
Port-au-Prince she thin all the time
she walk roun because the test   *hard* on
30   their poor bodies,   *she don't know where she be*   *If only* care
she   *not die yet for awhile.* Only an old
self *I went down*   *the hole with my sister*
    make living awhile   if it does not,
in her pile of rug she had   *I had a pile of rag*

35   *did I smell bad, It don't smell alright*   the love
all there, *god's love,*   *Love all,* not
the reason being nobody but one   *mother*
is all, *put a chain on her she leg*   *she so thin*
    small possession   doled, each sip parched
40   *out it fall away from her*   *away*   *her skin*
it tore by where the chain slap the back
all around   in us,   the same
if you could die, you would like that
peace   if you could
45   you could sleep   get up off the chain

she told me because she young and pretty
those men June 2nd 8 a.m.
she without that   *dark*   you could see
50   *like a rose, she bruise up* for absolution
    in the route, no help, no harbour

you hope maybe that ship put into
to be saved.   important and big
in white lace, she all time set by that captain
55   *things which happen in this humanity,* in
      landscape of the roses with   leaves

the cook pot she banged on it with the silver
thorns.
         as a guide in   terrain,
60   what is happening *I got to tell my story*
again the chain beat me onto the death,
      losing individuality in some greater
clattering on the iron ring   the ring
      they stood up to say we have
65   caught *on the bone of the   woman*
by years of study   discovered
come here over to me but I came over
knowing this is not   being at the crux
       for that bone, you could hear
70   fast on the idea of   indivisible
it crunch and crack and saw the sea
over her body but then the man. . . . turned on to me.
i   hoped to get out in the sea over the side
      that moment much   unseen, being
75   removed, *pleading for about 3 days*
to throw myself quick over to be lightened
on   contrary   *even to forget my poor sister*
I   ready and strong   *then the man in stow*
he come up, with it all slow
80   living without for *I in awful pain, crackling*
      body temple crumbling down in an illusion
      sea so flat and black I could walk
sense disempower   soul   victim
     my leg all held   that was a very great/weight heavy
85   *only a babe* on a link *was left*
to whom *that he held back my arms so I could not* reach *the babe*
now in   time   soul infuse   each cell
reach across there, *in very slowdown time, she dyin' I saw that baby* die.
in the value of adversity rise conditions
90   lead the echo   soul back to its original
sound   like she bag of sighing dust all the breathe
came out that woman and she die right there.
divine   action   taking place
he pushed and beat on me til I back down
95   I fell . . .   it is safe to be alive   to be love
      peaceful with   trust in the lord
     I got myself awake my sister she say I sleep
one day   one other   purity   she
fusing with purity of non-matter come to try
100   *she can bittersweet fall on   the sharp plank*
      cut herself in the dark, the deep earth,   the body . . .
I wanted to change overnight find that woke up without bein' there
feeling   some dream   affliction
      solitude *after she die in the hole*
105   *I cry for so long I don't know*

tremblings and fears   screen-out   sorrow
        the creaking of that ship
in all my life, I have carried as a weight this
smell   death   to the healing
110   can such to look neither to the left nor right
nor make any concord   *not to make no move*
to call attention   *with rats which ruination on*
the skins of   feet, defeat   one devil
as god's child,   comfort   mother
115   heartbroken   her story   hear

once time all told about the slave galley
in the ship's hold.

                                    1996

E. A. MARKHAM (b. 1939)

EDWARD MARKHAM WAS BORN IN MONTSERRAT AND MOVED TO BRITAIN IN 1956. HE studied English and philosophy at the University of Wales (Lampeter) and has taught at Kilburn Polytechnic in London, Hull College of Higher Education, the University of Ulster, and recently at Lampeter. He directed the Caribbean Theatre Workshop in the West Indies and has worked as a media coordinator in Papua New Guinea. From 1985 to 1987, he edited the journal *Artrage*. Under the pseudonym Paul St Vincent, Markham published a number of books about his character Lambchops, a recent immigrant from the Caribbean; these often comic poems explore the poetic alter ego's Caribbean origins and love interests and also his confrontation with British society and prejudice: "Lambchops has potential / for violence. He's faking / says Pig in the wig / make him an example / of our collective self-defence."[1] Books published under Markham's own name include *Crossfire* (1972), *Family Matters* (1984), *Human Rites* (1984), *Living in Disguise* (1986), *Towards the End of a Century* (1989), and a collection of stories, *Something Unusual* (1986). He edited *Hinterland: Caribbean Poetry from the West Indies and Britain* (1989).

Markham's poetry does not limit itself to the idiomatic and colloquial forms of English that Barbidian poet Kamau Brathwaite has dubbed "nation-language." Writing about questions of identity and non-standard language use in poetry, Markham notes that he thinks of "nation-language and Standard English as the two languages in which my life must be lived; sometimes I think of Melanesian pidgin and French as two languages in which my life might be lived." He distrusts "the exclusivity of the British *versus* Caribbean cultural debate. Britain for me is part only—though an important part—of a European experience (I've worked in Sweden, Germany, France—the last in which I sometimes live): at times it's useful to identify this Europe as the old colonising power or as the new rich 'North'; more often just as the 'other' to the majority of black and blackish people in the world."[2] Markham's poems are various in tone and subject matter but often explore questions of ecological and gender politics as well as race relations. The partly self-critical "Grandmotherpoem" takes up his Caribbean past, in search of a voice "from the wreck" of the past, while understanding that the poet "at risk" must assume that voice "in a foreign garden." Acknowledging the demands for and the difficulty of determining what might count for "urgent" speech, "Towards the End of a Century" explores the morality of poetry late in the century, weighing the pressure to find a speech that might redeem the past

---

[1] "A Mugger's Game," *Hinterland: Caribbean Poetry from the West Indies & Britain,* ed. E. A. Markham, Newcastle upon Tyne, 1989, p. 200
[2] "Many Voices, Many Lives," *Hinterland,* p. 195.

against the need to live and write "differently" so as to be able "To start afresh, to deny the weight / Of my experience."

The Sea

It used to be at the bottom of the hill
and brought white ships and news
of a far land where half my life
was scheduled to be lived.

5   That was at least half a life ago
of managing without maps, plans, permanence
of a dozen or more addresses
of riding the trains like a vagrant.

Today, I have visitors. They come
10   long distances overland. They will be uneasy
and console me for loss of the sea.
I will discourage them.

1982

Towards the End of a Century

I

My hand is steady:
This, my friends, is no mannerism
From an adopted land. A mother's mother
Instructed us: *Do not grow old*
5   *In a place unkind to you.* This brought
Me back. The hand
Is no reek of manliness,
More the hint of some little way to go
Before words serve their sentence
10   To a final full-stop. Look, madam; look, sir:
Bless all who are gathered together in this
Non-holy place. My hand is steady.

Some who are confused
shift and turn away thinking this trick unworthy
15   of folk who declined a life abroad:
a hand not for shaking, free of gifts, unmagical.
A trick, like the boxer early in the century, taut,
plucking a fly out of air.
But not this, not here. You turn away,
20   right, perhaps, to be insulted. Some buy time
(for the hand is steady) till it be urgent.
Who will tell us when it is urgent?

Towards the End of a Century: Title: A *century* is 100 runs by a batsman in the game of cricket.

II A

She wants to know his colour
the blind one, black or white:
25   what is he wearing today?

And we say to her:
think of things nearer your age,
think of not seeing as your blessing.

She has outlived, out-thought us,
30   she will not play:
priest's coat or surgeon's:
what is the butcher's colour today?

Because she is blind,
because she's now the daughter
35   of her daughter, punishing, punished

we listen. Through her
they have deprived us of sanity,
they have aborted our line

of argument. And we, near death
40   are patient, huddled
with those who wear our blood,

white coats
black coats:
how can we embrace them like family?
45   How can we make them clean?

II B

Here is another part of the wood.
On a morning before we were born,
or later in the day, the year,
the thing we strive to recall
50   broke the tranquillity of this place.
None can remember when it ceased
being sacred. Some still worship here:
the barber cutting hair, the dentist
pulling teeth; others in from the sun.
55   (The musician and the dancer try to remind us
of what is lost—but they are outside.)
The travelling merchant gains audience
of sorts. Some sit, a few kneel. And over there
bodies are being bared as if for healing.

60   And in he strides without guns or bombs,
without words that hurt, that kill:
how is it done? He's ridiculous—
a blind man approaching sex with a stranger,
alert both to charity and to ridicule:
65   he is not ridiculous.

The musician and the dancer enter
to restore with memory time before pain.
We do not know how to dance to this music.

70   If we fail some will come
        and hold a conference here
        next year, each year
        for years.

III

We bring you news, of course,
From a far country. Bearers of gossip,
75   We have been moved on because
        This late in the century, all
        Have heard it. Safety in numbers, we come
        With no more hope than a messenger bringing bad news
        To Cleopatra. Some who have perished
80   Have been unlucky in their audience.

        I bring you news
        Not from obscure military men who force you
        To mispronounce their names;
        Not of mountains of skulls stored
85   By the last government, displayed by this one, used
        To confirm theories, to discredit us all.
        I bring no more news of slow, painful death
        Of a people . . . we have had this
        And have not used the knowledge.
90   So I bring you something manageable: this
        From a far country not at war. Yes,
        Fires have been lit in the house of your family.
        Bullets in the backs of children have stimulated
        Debate. For us, at the end of a century,
95   Who wish to influence debate, the price is high.
        Let us sing.

IV: A PROTEST

Even though it is this year, this century
and more of us are barren
and some who murder walk the streets
100   and are happy:
        and friends grow shifty and turn away
        from children (who have so long, so little
        time to live):
        and each of us can match a bad experience
105   told over dinner:
        and glasses, dentures and other aids
        now live with us:

78: See *Antony and Cleopatra* 2.5, where Cleopatra maltreats the messenger who brings news of Antony's
marriage.

Some resist,
like a casualty of this group
110   draining away poison piped into the head,
or get through the day without ache;
some who might preach a sermon from this text
and think better of it.

v: On Another Field, An Ally: A West Indian Batsman Talks us Towards the Century

for Malcolm Marshall and Michael Holding, resting . . .

Into the nineties, into the nineties
115   Ten to go, ten runs, don't panic . . .
Think Bradman . . . never got out when into the nineties

Nerves of steel, drive them through legs
Beginning to buckle *think* the three W's *think* Clive Lloyd
Think Richards and all those ruling heads

120   On the coin of cricket. And relax. Now where am I?
Lost in the arms of voluptuous Anna. *Fin
de siècle*, recalling the days of immortal Kanhai

Hooking to the boundary from a prone position.
Cravats & decadence. Good ball. *Christ!*
125   Man in white coat weighing the decision

To point the finger, legalized gun
With power to run the 'Man of the Match'
Out of town. Not guilty. Not guilty, my old son

If I say it myself. A lapse
130   In concentration quickly repaired by nailing
The Will against any further collapse

This side of the century. Here behind the barricades
Stretching from 'Clifton' and Gordon 'Le Corbusier' Greenidge
Through 'homelier' architects of our days

112: *text*: the biblical passage of which the sermon is an exposition

Dedication: *Malcolm Marshall* (1958–2000) and *Michael Holding* (b.1959), West Indian cricketers noted as fast bowlers; they were important in West Indies winning sides in the 1980s.

116: "[Don]Bradman [b.1908, Australian cricketer,] was never out in the nineties in a Test Match. His Test batting average was 99.94; of major batsmen, Sid Barnes came next with 63.05." (Markham)

118: *the three W's*: "Weekes, Worrell, Walcott—three of the greatest and most devastating stroke-makers ever to appear in the same team. They played for West Indies from 1947 for over a decade." (Markham) *Clive Lloyd*: the great Guyanese cricketer; he became in the 1980s the most successful captain in West Indies cricketing history.

119: Vivian *Richards* (b.1952) was one of the greatest and most explosive of batsmen.

122: "Kanhai was famous for ending up on his seat after he had swept a four to leg." (Markham)

125: *Man in the white coat*: umpire

127: *Man of the Match*: the player judged the most valuable player of the match

133: " 'Clifton' is Roy Fredericks' middle name. He was a fine, aggressive opening batsman." (Markham) *Gordon Greenidge* was a skilled and aggressive opening batsman.

"Le Corbusier and Frank Lloyd Wright: contrasting architects; the Swiss aggressive, explosive and arrogant in concrete, while Wright's mainly wooden buildings were seen as an unobtrusive extension of the American domestic landscape." (Markham)

135　　Of glory—the team's Frank Lloyd Wrights—
　　　　Up against pollution, thinning ozone, treeless forests
　　　　In the tropics etc., each run lifts you to the heights

　　　　Of vertigo. And for you down there, Miss X, Mrs Patel
　　　　At the corner-shop, this wicket guarantees
140　　Orgasms, guarantees that this last exile suits you well.

　　　　And damn it, I'm out. *Out?* There's no morality to this game.
　　　　Protesting genocide and burying your head
　　　　In sweet Anna's thighs, it's all the same.

　　　　The butcher of dreams, man in white coat
145　　Offers no reprieve, his butchershop in Hounslow in need
　　　　Of more meat. Yet again I've missed the boat

　　　　Of the century. Breach in the wall.
　　　　Bowled through the gate. Marooned from the grand
　　　　Ocean liners: SS Sobers & Headley; not by formidable Wes Hall

150　　Line of destroyers; no *chinaman* or finger-lickin' spin
　　　　To obscurity—just a *gift* with your name on it
　　　　Lacking spite, Physics or Philosophy, innocuous as sin.

　　　　Like I say, there's no morality in this game.
　　　　Protesting genocide or burying your head
155　　In sweet Anna's thighs, it's all the same.

VI: Face to Face

　　　　1

　　　　my house shifts
　　　　like the loose tooth
　　　　of an ailing
　　　　monster.
160　　I extract it
　　　　and we trespass
　　　　among the clouds
　　　　in unpolluted seas
　　　　through a road-map
165　　of foreign languages.

145: *Hounslow:* a London suburb
148: *gate:* the gap sometimes displayed between bat and pad when the batsman plays a loose stroke
149: *SS Sobers & Headley:* "The style and authority of Sobers and Headley at the batting crease recall the majestic Lady Boats—ocean liners that used to ply the Caribbean region between the wars." (Markham, in correspondence)
　　Wes Hall (b.1937), born in Barbados, one of the fastest bowlers produced by the West Indies
150: *chinaman:* "a disguised off-break with leg-break action bowled by a left-handed bowler to a right-handed batsman. This, to a left-hander, is the 'googly'." (Markham). "Off" and "leg" are terms for the left and right sides of the field, depending on whether the batter is left- or right-handed: the "off side" is that facing the batsman as he stands to receive the ball; the "leg side" is that behind him. The chinaman and googly aim to deceive the batsman: the bowler's hand seems to be spinning the ball so that it will break in one direction when it hits the ground when in fact he is spinning it to break in the opposite direction.
Title: *Face to Face:* 1 Cor. 13:12: "For now we see through a glass, darkly; but then face to face"

Occasionally I return
to the monster
who greets me
with a sharp grin,
170   its rows of houses hurting
like new teeth.
What does it say
after years of learning
to speak?
175   'I am not yours,'
a grin? a grimace?
'I am not yours.'

    2

he pauses to think
of his name carved
180   in a foreign wood.
It recurs this time
with a sigh on stern
lips of a too-late
wife. The after-dinner
185   joke under Provençal
olive spills wine
in its memory. And now
in the country of his birth,
the accusing, exhausted soil
190   the accusing, self-ripened tree
confront each other.
Branches wilt
as they must. Friends
help opponents to cut
195   them away and disagree
about what will grow.

    3

the man peered at me across
his life and apologized
in a voice I have sometimes used
200   in private. 'Man, you leave it late . . .
to come back. The place gone down now.
Used to work your people's land
in the old days.' The disappearing patch
of garden, the orphaned fruit-
205   trees, the 'ruin' from a past
decade tugged my memory back
to childhood—so many buying the lottery
of escape. Here, what was shelved
gathered more than dust; the memory
210   put in deep-freeze on our exit, melted:
the power-cut a controlled accident.
Now the body of your time lies
ill-preserved, unaesthetic. Recognition rinsed
my mind and his face
215   like spray from a hose: he stood guilty,

the bright lad in the class giving
the wrong answer, prickling us with hope
and unease. Now his face, furrowed
unlike the land, is an error no one
220   meant. I owe him tribute, like the land.
I bring him comfort in my news.

'*I have been reading the endings of novels.*
I have celebrated with strangers
"Solidarity" in their struggle.
225   *I have been consoled by friends*
In their paid-for homes,
And have observed the final shape
Of their families: I am whittled
By their need. These are the old films.
230   *You have seen it all, they say;*
How it works, what to avoid: you
Are the envy of us all starting out behind.'

And I vow to do things differently,
To start afresh, to deny the weight
235   Of my experience. Of our experience.

                                                        1989

Grandmotherpoem

(FOR GRANDMOTHER MARGARET, 'MISS DOVIE', 1867–1953)

thinking many things, grandmother
I can't trap the memory, itself like a kite
to blanket us without coarsening our pact:
it is not cold climate, not famine relief that triggers this need.
5   Though more than the annual hat of fashion must clothe us in words.
So I put it off, more and more play the errant;
with dissecting verbs occupy this or that high table where the world lies
        bloated.

You must be asking when this apprenticeship will end?
Running & jumping, ball-games, preaching and Latin were early fantasies.
10   Now, wandering in a garden far from us, I step
on the wrong end of a rake
and crack my skull: the yellow scream of grandmother burns the head.
Surprise, a hint of things malordained, skids me past *us*
till embarrassment makes it safe: this is an accident.
15   A third time I step on the rake: *this is god!* 'Boy, wha happenin?'
I am at risk in the world. This is no accident.
Something leaking through my head has value.
It wines, it lusts, it fills empties fills my space.
Its logic meanders like a stone too heavy for the stream.

6: *errant:* knight-errant; messenger; wanderer; prodigal child

20   It heaves sense against sense cascading down the boneface
        while the wet of mothermother drips into thimble: my bucket, my ocean.
        And the kite is a cloud of badness dribbling, drizzling a parable.
        From somewhere maleness spits defiance to hold soft matter in its rock of
            stubbornness

        from the wreck, debris of grandmotherpoem
25   and a thing not recognized as fear of rakes.
        Bits of me, long abandoned, floating past
        jostle one another like strangers on a march.
        The voice which breaks from its full set of teeth
        comes like a uniform, polished: we are at risk.
30   Grandmother, grandmother, her bath over, smelling of bay rum & bible
        knows how bad habits, like long years abroad, and the profession of male-
            ness,
        lead to ugly bumps on the head. So men must cover theirs.
        In my hat, in a foreign garden, when the leaf is about to fall from its tree,
        grandmother appears to speak to me:

                                                                    1989

The Mother's Tale

So many terrible people are people still
GAVIN EWART

        Goodness, she said:
        Unless you eat this,
        Unless you get to bed

        The black man
5   Will get you
        And that's worse than

        Being dead.
        You're all at sea now
        In above your head:

10   The grasping hand
        Reaching out to you
        From land

        Is folly. Just realize
        I didn't make you try that one
15   For size.

        He's everything
        I promised
        Though he won't sing

30: *bay rum:* an aromatic substance (used to perfume the bath)

Epigraph: *Gavin Ewart* (1916–95), British poet specializing in light verse

And dance.
And if he doesn't beat you, well
That's by chance.

I'm truly sorry for being right
Though we must take
Delight

In the buff-
Coloured darlings. Yes,
It's been rough

For all of us,
Determined to meet this setback
Without fuss.

We've been here before
With the Wars and bullies:
It's just a bore

In a home like this
To have brought on
With the bedtime kiss

When this game began
Something rather worse
Than the stock policeman.

1989

JOHN JAMES (b. 1939)

J AMES WAS BORN IN CARDIFF AND, SINCE LEAVING WALES IN 1957, HAS LIVED IN Bristol, London, and Cambridge. Educated at Bristol and Keele Universities, he teaches at Anglia Polytechnic University in Cambridge. From 1963 to 1969, he edited *R* magazine, as well as its associated press. James has curated shows by painters including Tom Phillips and Bruce McLean, and collaborated with Phillips and Andrew Crozier in *In One Side & Out the Other* (1970) and with McLean and Dirk Buwalda in *Bruce McLean: Berlin/London* (1983). His pamphlets and books include *mmm . . . ah yes* (1967), *The Welsh Poems* (1967), *The Small Henderson Room* (1969), *Letters from Sarah* (1973), *Striking the Pavilion of Zero* (1975), *A Theory of Poetry* (1977), *War* (1978), *Berlin Return* (1983), *Dreaming Flesh* (1991), and *Schlegel Eats a Bagel* (1996).

Several of James's readers have noted that, among the poets affiliated with small press publications in Britain, particularly those whose work appears in the anthology *A Various Art* (1987), James seems most deserving of a popular audience. Often topical, occasionally using lines from rock lyrics and mixing references to high and popular culture, James's poetry "speaks of public places and should be heard in them," Peter Riley has said.[1] The regular use of the present tense and paratactic organization offers the poems their sense of immediacy and improvisation; with their buoyant and confident persona moving through a rush of heterogeneous detail, observation, and statement, they unfold like a euphoric pedestrian's walk across town. Models include the poems of Vladimir Mayakofsky and Frank O'Hara, though there is more anger in James than in O'Hara: the theatricalized self in many of his early poems is more manic, the wit more aggressive than bemused, the irony more Punk than cosmopolitan. John Wilkinson notes that O'Hara is "an unlikely model for a communist Welsh heterosexual poet. James's poetry is simply more phallic than O'Hara's, being line-driven rather than fluently stanzaic, and while O'Hara is *of* his milieu (which is infinitely extensive) James is located *in* or *against* it."[2] "Inaugural Address," which suggests the "toasting" of reggae DJs, catalogs the "Babylon" of twentieth-century culture, repeating the names of its political monsters; the poem also attacks so-called "rational" urban planning and bureaucrat-approved modernist architecture. A "miniaturization of the Social Body" produced by media spectacle remains within the poem's critical sights, as James concludes in the voice of "Sky Junction," casting his alienation and counter-cultural romanticism in an appropriately banal image. "James's

---

[1] Peter Riley interviewed by Kelvin Corcoran, *Reality Studios*, vol. 8, nos. 1–4, 1986, p. 13.
[2] "Mexican Standoff in Practical Bondage Gear: An Appreciation of the Seventies Poetry of John James," *Angel Exhaust*, no. 13, 1996, p. 89.

poetry teaches," Wilkinson notes, that "the contradiction between attitudinising and seriousness and consistency of critical engagement is a productive one."[3]

---

[3] Ibid., pp. 86–7.

Good Old Harry

we go to sleep like anybody else
though some awake like bullets
like Romans
munch munch

5   we aren't Romans
we aren't Americans either
we drink a lot of beer
every nation has its own greatness

we are the English
10   easy-going & lazy
we sleep pretty well
& when we wake

we are usually pretty thirsty
but not for anything too drastic
15   you can trust us to be
wooden & quietly proud

of our laver bread
our dumplings
a tomato or two
20   does no one any harm

& if there did happen to be a bullet amongst us
it would never find anywhere to go
it would just keep travelling through the air
without hitting anything

25   we have thirty-eight rulers
which is very economical
& they are well protected from
tomatoes on the whole

we call them the cabinet
30   & cupboard is the name of the land

The poem was written in the wake of the unexpected victory of Edward Heath's Conservatives over Harold Wilson's Labour Party in the 1970 election. It is modeled on the poem "Zur Beruhigung" ["To Set Your Mind At Rest"] by the German poet Heinrich Heine (1797–1856), whose name was originally "Harry." Peter Branscombe translates several lines of the Heine poem as follows: "We are Germans, easy-going and worthy, we sleep a sound, vegetable sleep, and when we awake, we are usually thirsty, but not for the blood of our princes."
17: *laver bread:* a south Welsh delicacy made with seaweed; it is turned in oatmeal and fried with bacon for breakfast.

where everything is in its place again
the natural rulers

behaving like proper gentlemen again
eating a bit of cabbage
35 & sausage now & then
like the rest of us no doubt

when Edward goes for a walk
we take off our caps & wave them in the air
England is a mature nation
40 & is not a bit like America

1970, 1975

Inaugural Address

Good Day/you're in tune to If You're Going To Do It
Do It Alla Prima Time/

it's a Radio Babylon interference calling
a largesse of Delirius
5 more fundamental than America
ruddier than Silbury & more abused
greener than Mekonta &
mightier than the Wig in Wigan with a yellow in between/

Dreamier than the Kill in City
10 shinier than Krypton & more clear
more on top of it than Atlantis a
Blow Out on the Bauhaus
A Roll Over Old New Veau
A Knock Out on a Nico off the DD & D Co
15 A Granite Against Gropius/Toasting with The Hosting
No Touting for Bruno but
pouting & more tantalising than
Island Three the desiccated orifice of

Inaugural Address: This poem was commissioned by the artist Bruce McLean to open *The Masterwork /
Award Winning Fish-Knife,* a performance sculpture for the theatre in four parts created by Paul
Richards and Bruce McLean and first performed at The Riverside Studios, London, on 6 November 1979.
4: *Delirius:* the planet devoted to the gratification of pleasure in the work of the French sci-fi comic-book
artist Philippe Druillet.
6: *Silbury* Hill in Wiltshire is the largest prehistoric mound in Europe.
7–8: *Mekonta:* a city on Venus in the sci-fi comic-strip *Dan Dare*; Dan Dare's batman Digby was from
Wigan (a town near Manchester).
12: *Bauhaus:* the German school of design (1919–1933), founded by Walter Gropius
14: The German-born pop singer-composer *Nico* performed with the 1960s band The Velvet Underground
and went on to a solo career.
     DD & D Co: a distortion of DAAD (Deutscher Akademischer Austauschdienst: "German Academic
Exchange Service").
15: *Toasting:* in reggae, a D.J.'s singing or shouting of improvised lyrics over a record
16: *Bruno:* Bruno Taut (1880–1938), the innovative Berlin architect
18: *Island Three:* a space colony proposed by Gerard K. O'Neill in his book *The High Frontier: Human
Colonies in Space,* and later taken up by NASA.

The Woman with The Three of Everything she say
20   What on EARTH are Maltesers/what in THE WORLD
is a Power Tower/

A Cruising in a
3rd Century of The Decline
of Industrial Investment I & I for short The
25   Fantasia of The Plan Voisin Begat The Beaubourg
Glossier than La Ville Radieuse
& Sharper than Arcosanti The Architect
is The Invention of The Masterwork &
couldn't live without it/

30   Wrecking his Neck-Angle on the EuroStandard
we drift & mooch in the marinade of his metered Overspace
down on the Bogside Jesus & The Redevelopment Corporation
snicker into sight a fault in the beam-out from GPO Tower
back in Finance Capital/
35   neglected scabs of Venice Florence Rome Glasgow
flake under foot
on the black marble stairs of Milan Station

•

Inside The Riverside
Articulate Trace as Non-material form of Capital
40   blisters each side of your face with a blush
an intense blush blisters each side of your many faces
in the flux dance slab stance ba
lance of glittering felspar
the straitened moment speeding
45   in the ruinous curve of vinyl & circular dwelling
a cutting of deliberate gesture
in the passage of indelible act

•

20: *Maltesers:* a brand of candy ("the sweet with the less fattening centre")
21: *Power Tower:* a mobile truck with a hydraulic lift platform. One was used in the performance.
24: *I & I:* Rastafarian idiom for "we"
25ff: *Plan Voisin:* a visionary 1925 plan of the architect Le Corbusier (1887–1965) for the redevelopment of
the center of Paris, involving its demolition and rebuilding as an array of skyscrapers. The plan was never
implemented; nor was that for *La Ville Radieuse* ("The Radiant City"), his 1930 plan for the rebuilding of
Moscow. The Centre Pompidou (opened 1977), in Paris's Rue *Beaubourg,* a landmark of modernist archi-
tecture, is an enormous cultural centre which includes a museum of 20th-century art.
27: *Arcosanti* is a futurist Arizona city built in the 1970s by the Italian-born architect Paolo Soleri.
32: *Bogside:* the Catholic area of Derry, in Northern Ireland, and a focus of intense sectarian rioting in the
1960s and 1970s.
33: The *GPO Tower* is a landmark tower in central London (now renamed the BT Tower).
37: The Futurist architect Antonio Sant'Elia (1888–1916), spurred by a design competition for a new rail-
way in *Milan,* made a visionary series of drawings for a city of the future.
38: *The Riverside:* see the headnote to this poem

Good-bye Savonarola Brunelleschi Alberti Bramante
Good-bye Dublin The Centre Pompidou The Guggenheim
50 Ghiberti's doors are the doors to the biggest bank
The Los Angeles County Museum of Modern Art The Hayward
The National Gallery "West" Berlin & Hello Tokyo
Good-bye the Monumental Fault & the Faulty Monumental
Great Fish-Knives of the Future Hello/Good-bye
55 Good-bye you fully automated cities that keep operating after we have all
left
Good-bye computers transistors space-probes automation miniaturization
acid & San Francisco
Good-bye the Marlborough Good-bye Sir Humphrey Gilbert/
not a room to be had in all of Broadacre
though you may get there
60 on The Old Straight Track
By the Rights of Orthogonal Planning/

Good-bye Auschwitz Hello Angkor Vat Pol
Pot Napoleon III Pinochet Pinocchio of Chairman Hua
Haussmann Mussolini Sant'Elia The God
65 Father of High Tech & he with no lustre on his
bite in the echo chain of Sardis the thatcher the carter
Teheran the Arc of the Shah

48: These are figures from fifteenth-century Italy: the fiery preacher and reformer Girolamo *Savonarola;* and the architects Filippo *Brunelleschi* (noted for his dome to Florence's cathedral), Leon Battista *Alberti* and Donato *Bramante.*

49: New York's *Guggenheim* Museum, built in the 1950s, was designed by Frank Lloyd Wright.

50: Lorenzo *Ghiberti* (1378–1455), the Italian sculptor; his doors for the Baptistery of Florence's cathedral are one of the peaks of fifteenth-century Italian art.

51ff: James refers to the *Los Angeles County Museum of Modern Art,* noted for collections of Asian, Islamic, medieval, European, and modern art; the *Hayward* Gallery, on London's South Bank; and London's *National Gallery.*

57: *the Marlborough:* a commercial art gallery in London
The soldier and navigator *Sir Humphrey Gilbert* (1539–1583) was in Ireland from 1567–1570 and ruthlessly suppressed an uprising. He also planned a colonization of Munster and proposed similar schemes in North America; he claimed Newfoundland on behalf of Elizabeth I in 1583 but drowned at sea soon after.

58: *Broadacre* City was a community designed by Frank Lloyd Wright but never built.

60: In the 1920s Alfred Watkins' book *The Old Straight Track* popularized the (now discredited) idea of prehistoric "ley lines"—tracks in a straight line from hilltop to hilltop, with their routes marked by ponds, mounds, etc.

62: The focus of the poem shifts here to contemporary U.S. foreign policy. *Angkor Vat:* a twelfth-century temple complex in Cambodia; Angkor was the capital of the Khmer Empire from the ninth to the fifteenth century. *Pol Pot* was military leader of the Khmer Rouge, a Marxist guerilla organization that overthrew Cambodia's right-wing government in 1975. He was president of Cambodia from 1975 to 1979; his regime is estimated to have caused the deaths of at least a million Cambodians.

63ff: *Napoleon III* gave Baron *Haussmann* (1809–1891) virtually dictatorial powers in his role as Municipal Prefect of Paris; Haussmann created Paris's new straight boulevards by means of massive demolition and rebuilding.
General Augusto *Pinochet* was part of the (U.S.-supported) military coup that overthrew Salvador Allende's Marxist government in Chile, and assumed power in 1974. His regime was marked by brutal suppression of political dissent.
Hua Guofeng was premier of China from 1976 to 1980.

66: *Sardis:* ancient capitol of Lydia (in modern-day Turkey); it was destroyed by Tamerlane in 1402. The last king of Lydia, Croesus (reigned 560–546 BC), famed for his enormous wealth, ruled from this city.
James names the Conservative politician Margaret *Thatcher,* who became Britain's Prime Minister in 1979; and Jimmy *Carter,* President of the United States (1977–1981).

67: The rule of the *Shah* of Iran was brought down in 1979; he fled the country in January of that year, and its government was taken over by the Ayatollah Khomeini. The Shah came to the U.S. later that year for cancer treatment; on 4 Nov. 1979 Iranian students stormed the U.S. embassy in *Teheran* and took its diplomatic staff hostage, demanding that the Shah be extradited to Iran. Carter's failure to solve the hostage crisis was to lead to his failure to win a second term in office.

The Biggest McDonald's Advertisement In The World
Whose Cancer spreads easier than butter Kissinger
70   Rockefeller The Woman With The Three of Everything
Everything Terminates The Wedding
With Frozen InterContinental Rice/
Miniaturization of the Social Body
Into Occasional Table Arrangement
75   Micro-Explosion of the Thousands Transformer of Millions
peripheralized to the slotted sides of the votive Gold Heap
Market of Commodity Futures Miniaturized orgasm
of little yellow men spray from the planet edges
one by one
80   we drink & eat the sweat
& muscular steaks of Africa straight from the freezer
on Microwave Alert for The Republic
Sparta Miletus Periclean Athens:
The Acropolis Metropolis Necropolis Death Star Voiding
85   Hearthstones into 3D Vision Gelatine/

C'mon EveryBody/let me take your little pinkie
point your knees overhear
see me in the Arkle light of me anti-perspective altar back
shift your gear over here
90   get your fore-quarters into tune
& put them on this here blue plinth
Before your very stereoscopic vision
sky-junction Sky Junction
flux in sky junction Masterwork the flux of/
95   This is Sky Junction

                                                        1979 / 1987

69: Henry *Kissinger* was Secretary of State under Nixon and Ford.
70: Nelson A. *Rockefeller* was vice president under Ford; he was also a noted art collector.
83: The Peloponnesian War (431–404 BC) was fought between the Greek city-states of *Sparta* and *Athens;*
   the latter was ruled at the war's start by *Pericles* (495–429 BC), who was responsible for the development
   of both Athenian democracy and the Athenian empire.
   Miletus: an ancient Greek city, whose ruins are in modern Turkey; it was rebuilt in the fifth century
   BC according to a grid plan designed by Hippodamus.
84: Pericles was responsible for the rebuilding of the *Acropolis,* which had been devastated during Persian
   occupation.
   Necropolis: an ancient burial site
86: *C'mon Everybody* was an Eddie Cochran hit of 1958.
88: *Arkle light:* punning on "arc light" and on the name of the champion racehorse *Arkle*

LEE HARWOOD (b. 1939)

Harwood was born in Leicester and grew up in Chertsey (Surrey) and East London. He was educated at St. George's College, Weymouth and Queen Mary College, London. He has worked as a monumental mason's mate, librarian, bookseller, bus conductor, lecturer, and post office clerk. In the 1960s, he edited a series of little magazines including *Night Train*. In 1971 and 1972, he was writer-in-residence at the Aegean School of Fine Arts in Paros, Greece. In 1976, he was chairman of the Poetry Society. He has lived in London, Boston, San Francisco, Chicago, and, for part of the 1970s and since 1985, in Brighton. In 1977, he was an unsuccessful Labour candidate in county council elections in Sussex. Harwood has published several books, translating the poems of the French Dadaist Tristan Tzara and numerous collections of his own poems, including *The White Room* (1968), *Landscapes* (1969), *The Sinking Colony* (1970), *H. M. S. Little Fox* (1975), *Boston—Brighton* (1977), *Rope Boy to the Rescue* (1988), *Crossing the Frozen River: Selected Poems* (1988), and *In the Mists: Mountain Poems* (1993).

Harwood's extensive use of collage, his painterly details and intimate subject matter suggest affinities with the New York School poetry of John Ashbery and Frank O'Hara, as well as with that poetry's French models, affinities perhaps most apparent in Harwood's earlier and most influential volumes. But in remarking upon the "soft pearly focus" of Harwood's poems, Ashbery points us toward a significant difference between Harwood's work and that of his more ironic and urban American contemporaries.[1] A. Kingsley Weatherhead argues that "Harwood's details are often derived from uncertain sources, often rural scenes, small town or littoral, shards from memory, or fragments of melodrama. James Schuyler says the New York poets 'are affected most by the floods of paint in whose crashing surf we all scramble'; he would hardly have spoken thus about Harwood in the early poems, in which we are more conscious of mood spilling over than of mere pigment or its equivalent."[2] Harwood's lyricism also has a little more room for sentiment and for neo-romantic celebration of nature, even if such moments have more recently been increasingly juxtaposed with mention of social realities horrific enough to set his poetry's dreamy moments in poignant relief. Many poems from Harwood's *The White Room*, like "The Blue Mosque," set narrative elements within an open-ended reflection on poetic process and artifice. The poetry's sometimes prosaic rhythms and perspectives contrast the everyday with narrative details tending toward the exotic. Fragments as if cited from romance are

---

[1] Quoted in A. Kingsley Weatherhead, *The British Dissonance: Essays on Ten Contemporary Poets,* Columbia, Missouri, 1983, p. 174.
[2] Ibid., p. 174.

introduced and examined, then left as if abandoned rather than followed to their pos-
sible conclusions. Robert Sheppard has described the poetry's ability thereby to estab-
lish a "tension between . . . fictive elegance and a more 'straight-talking' discourse," a
technique that Harwood himself has called his "puritan-cavalier routine."[3]

---

[3] "Lee Harwood and the Poetics of the Open Work," *New British Poetries: The Scope of the Possible*, ed.
Robert Hampson and Peter Barry, Manchester, 1993, p. 219.

When the geography was fixed

FOR MARIAN

The distant hills are seen from the windows.
It is a quiet room, and the house is in a town
far from the capital.
The south-west province even now in spring
5   is warmer than the summer of the north.
The hills are set in their distance
from the town and that is where they'll stay.
At this time the colours are hard to name
since a whiteness infiltrates everything.
10   It could be dusk.
The memory and sound of chantings
is not so far away—it is only a matter
of the degree of veneer at that moment.
This is not always obvious and for many
15   undiscovered while their rhythm remains static.
It's all quite simple,
once past the door—and that's only a figure
of speech that's as clumsy as most symbols.
This formality is just a cover.

20   The hills and the room are both in
the white. The colours are here
inside us, I suppose. There's still a tower
on the skyline and it's getting more obscure.
When I say "I love you"—that means
25   something. And what's in the past
I don't know anymore—it was all ice-skating.
In the water a thick red cloud
unfurls upwards; at times it's almost orange.
A thin thread links something and there are
30   fingers and objects of superstition
seriously involved in this.

The canvas is so bare
that it hardly exists—though the painting
is quite ready for the gallery opening.
35   The clear droplets of water sparkle
and the orange-red cloud hangs quite seductively.

There is only one woman in the gallery now
who knows what's really happening on the canvas—

40 but she knew that already, and she
also instinctively avoided all explanations.
She liked the picture and somehow the delicate
hues of her complexion were reflected in it.
She was very beautiful and it soon became
obvious to everyone that the whole show
45 was only put on to praise her beauty.
Each painting would catch one of the colours
to be found in her skin and then play with it.
Though some critics found this delicacy
too precious a conceit, the landscape
50 was undeniable in its firmness
and the power that vibrated from the
colours chosen and used so carefully.

During the whole gallery-opening a record of primitive red
indian chants was played—and this music
55 seemed to come from the very distant hills
seen in every painting—their distance was
no longer fixed and they came nearer.
But recognitions only came when all
the veneer was stripped off
60 and the inexplicable accepted in the whiteness.

1968

The Blue Mosque

1

The blue mosque had one tower higher than all the others
and it was from this that the muezzin called the faithful
to prayer and thoughts of God:
"There is no god but the God."

5 The city which contained the mosque
is unnamed, as it is unmarked on the map.
The school atlas was equally useless, and history was more
of an amusement than most would admit.

If you will accept this story for what it is,
10 then you may well be amused or even pleased;
the actual reality is of no importance.

The facts and words—even whole lines—
could so easily be seen as matters of pure style.
Even the cheapest trinkets can mean more,
15 in the end, than any heavy act of conscious gratitude.

Title: The Sultan Ahmed Cami, built in the early seventeenth century in Constantinople (modern Istanbul, in Turkey), is known as the Blue Mosque, from the color of its tile work.
2: The *muezzin* calls the faithful to prayer five times daily from atop the minaret; his call begins "Allah is great" and ends "There is no god but Allah."

The towers, I believe, are called "minarets"—but this
accuracy is completely lost as it progresses.
All there really is is a deep concern for "charm"
and the "pleasant surprise".

2

20 Despite appearances and the first reflex reaction to this—
there could be more love in this acceptance
of the ludicrous and obvious
than in the many books with titles like
"Morals" or "Morality" or "Truth" or "Logic" or . . . .
25 and so on down the book shelves.

3

And now that the expedition was safe—
surely it was time for all the merchants
to thank their saviour and God?
—quarrels broke out almost immediately
30 over this order and precedence.
With the wilderness safe behind the city walls
it was not really unusual to see how quickly
memories and resolutions burst like soap bubbles,
and already few of them could even remember
35 the blackness of the storm clouds and,
least of all, their own helplessness and terror.

It was only a matter of days ago—
there was no question of it all being part of
some ancient riddle or alchemist's anagram.
40 It was all *too* simple, and that was why . . . .
books of authority and accepted formulas
were so violently seized.
The obvious and simple were like two men who
stood open-handed at the doors of the mosque.
45 It became essential for the merchants
to ignore them, if they were ever to continue as they were.

No one wanted the blood stains
on their own saddle cloth—yet . . . . .
The expedient had to be insisted on in private.
50 And the tanned hands' very openness—
that revealed pale tender palms
capable of so much love and gentleness
—was an unbearable threat.

4

The dull red neon in the bar windows and the "other things"
55 were left behind as they walked up Avenue B
to the brighter lights—there was no real malice
in this, nor in most actions in that city,

or any other town nearer or farther from home—
though "home" unfortunately is meaningless.

60   Is so much repetition always necessary?

When put bluntly again the question was
finally answered by "the man".
He said: "When faced with basic but *deep* emotions,
like (obvious, and so "extreme") love or fear, the common reaction
65   among this social and age group is to—
ONE: regard the experienc*ers* with hostility;
and TWO: urgently seek explanations (i.e. refuge)
for (i.e. from) the experience in the "copious realms"
of established reactions and common prejudice or
70   ignorance."
This was all pretty obvious. . . .

5

The muezzin, I'm sure, knew this,
and did not he proclaim the greatness of God
over the rooftops and the whole city every day
75   from his minaret in the blue mosque?
And, surely, when in the quiet of his study,
he knew that "the greatness of God" embraced
far more than the power of one individual?
Rather couldn't it be the power of this very openness,
80   whether in hands or love? The doors of the mosque.

There were so many books and already his head
began to ache. "Such is the life of a muezzin,"
he said, and laughed.

The sound of a fountain splashing in the courtyard
85   soothed him. This whole scene though
is only taken from another book—but
do the circumstances and scenery matter?
The mosque, the muezzin, even the expedition
that was claimed to be safe—
90   there can be no difference to their final reality
whether they exist only in the imagination
or in the physical world. It's only a matter
of the story holding people with its style
and lists of events, either curious or tender.

6

95   This preoccupation with words can only be boring
for the onlooker—painters arguing over the different
brands of paint—useless parallels.
What have any of these words to do with
praising a good man or a love?
100   No matter how exotic the decorations
and materials—the words always fail.
It's all been said before—and this

very questioning now heard only too often.
Even the clichés seem to contain less conceit
105 than the poem, and now the poem about the poem,
and the poem about the poem about the. . . .
and so on and on deeper into the cheap gaming house.

What has this to do or say with any weight
of the two men with open hands at the mosque
110 who will be murdered by the merchants' assassins?
or the good man that still knows how to love?
or the loved one whose kiss alone is beyond words?

The whole poem book must be left behind
(while I go to help the two men
115 and thank the good man), and then let it
be forgotten now we've become men and women.
And surely it's obvious to the simplest of men,
as it is for the muezzin to cry "There is no god but the God",
that I should now leave writing this poem
120 when it is so late at night,
and go lie with my love.
It is late, but such blindness
could not go on forever, thank God.

1968

Salt Water

IN MEMORY OF JOEY PEIRCE/HARWOOD, 11–14 MARCH 1997

The complexity of a coral reef
the creatures sunlight
shafting down through crystal sea
water the flicker of shadows
5 light wavering and fading
into the depths

Near the silver mirrored surface
bright yellow fish
flutter through the reef
10 crowded with the swaying tendrils
of coral and anemones,
smudges of algae, drifts of seaweed,
starfish and shellfish flowing,
through the canyons

15 The sun rises three times
The sun sets three times

over sea over land

on land
her blue grey eyes gaze at the world
20 in silence blink at the world

the world goes about
its usual business

"A fine view along the coast"
to be seen from a high building's
25   window one of many windows

"Polyps" the books say coral
a tube with a mouth at the end
surrounded by tendrils to catch
small creatures
30   A world of soft tissue
And the colours
white red orange
yellow green blue
purple   "natural pigments"
35   and those too changeable
when algae "lives within the tissue"

Many species Many depths
and the light filtered down
reducing reducing
40   And bright yellow fish
banded with peacock blue
flutter through the reef
Red fish Black fish
with lemon ringed eyes
45   flutter through the reef

How delighted she'd be
Her blue grey eyes gazing at this world
while cradled in her mother's
her father's arms
50   the world going about its usual business

A ship's bows cut the salt water
a phosphorescent trail in the tropic night

The phosphorus glitter of the sea
From the Greek
55   phos (light) -phoros (bringing)

Like her
as she came and went

Morning star

1998

SEAMUS HEANEY (b. 1939)

HEANEY WAS BORN AND RAISED IN COUNTY DERRY, NORTHERN IRELAND, AT HIS family's farm "Mossbawn." He was educated at Anahorish School, St. Columb's College, and Queen's University, Belfast, and then attended St. Joseph's College of Education in Belfast for his Teacher's Diploma. He lectured at St. Joseph's and then Queen's University until 1970, when he was offered a year-long visiting appointment at the University of California, Berkeley. Following the Bloody Sunday violence in 1972, he left Northern Ireland for a cottage in County Wicklow. From 1975 to 1981, he taught at Carysfort, a teacher's college in Dublin. In 1981, he accepted a position at Harvard University, where he taught one semester each year until 1996, spending the rest of the year at his home in Sandymount, Dublin. In 1988, he was appointed to a five-year term to lecture as Professor of Poetry at Oxford University. Heaney was awarded the Nobel Prize for Literature in 1995.

As his vita indicates, Heaney has been an international figure in poetry for many years now; he is the most celebrated Irish poet since Yeats. He has written of his admiration for Yeats's poems and Yeats's ability to make of his life and work a "continuum," but among Heaney's early models Patrick Kavanagh is more important.[1] The influence of English poetry, including Wordsworth, Hopkins, Ted Hughes, and the Movement is also evident in his early poems, but it was Kavanagh's work that authenticated Heaney's efforts to write about his rural Irish Catholic background. In his essay "The Sense of Place" (1977), Heaney writes that "Kavanagh's place names are there to stake out a personal landscape" and of the importance of a "feeling, assenting, equable marriage between the geographical country and the country of the mind."[2] In the same essay Heaney remembers that his experience of place in childhood was shaped by a "vestigial" sense of the sacred; many of his poems trace this vestigial sense from a perspective revealing the critical detachment he admired in Kavanagh, drawing analogies between cutting turf and writing, for instance, showing the poet in search of "living roots" but fearful that "he [has] no spade" up to the task. Heaney's second book, *Door into the Dark* (1969) concluded with "Bogland," signaling his interest in Irish bogs as sites and symbols of the preservation of life and culture. *Wintering Out* (1972), written after Heaney had read P. V. Glob's *The Bog People*, together with the next several volumes up through and including especially *North* (1975), extended his use of the bogs as a symbol, relating the violence in Northern Ireland to the ritual sacrifices of an Iron Age Jutland. With *Field Work* (1979), Heaney's work took a new direction

---

[1] "Yeats as an Example?" *Preoccupations: Selected Prose 1968–1978*, London, 1980, p. 100.
[2] *Preoccupations*, pp. 140, 132.

partly influenced by his reading in poets such as Robert Lowell, W. H. Auden, and the Eastern Europeans Czeslaw Milosz and Zbigniew Herbert. As Neil Corcoran writes, *Field Work* "contemplates the North from a position of withdrawal, composing a kind of luxuriant but anxious pastoral and a series of personal and national elegies in which the constant preoccupation with the kind of action a poem might represent is moved into another register: not the curt, clipped, lyrically disruptive and deliberate shapes" of the earlier books "but a more capacious, extended and socialised address."[3]

As Heaney's poetry has developed from that point, it has become clear that his *oeuvre* is, in Corcoran's words, "densely recessive," returning again and again to its major symbols and motifs, often to view them from a new and newly critical perspective. As autobiographical reflection has been fit into new molds such as the Dantesque structure of the title sequence in *Station Island* (1984), in which Heaney presents dialogues with dead friends, mentors, and James Joyce, Heaney's poetry has been obliged to confront his responsibilities as a public figure in Irish life. There has always been the sense that this fundamentally lyric poet wants to resist the bardic posturing that characterized some of the later Yeats, even while he has had to acknowledge that "as Kavanagh said, we have lived / In important places"—to quote from "Singing School." Heaney has made his commitments clear in public statements, as for instance when he insisted that his passport was "green" after Andrew Motion and Blake Morrison included him in *The Penguin Anthology of British Poetry* (1982). If critics have sometimes questioned his commitment to political causes, Heaney has not only addressed some of the questions they have raised in the essays collected in *Preoccupations* (1980), *The Government of the Tongue* (1988), and *The Redress of Poetry* (1995), but has also made meditation upon the social function of poetry one of his most important poetic motifs.

---

[3] *English Poetry since 1940,* Harlow, 1993, p. 182.

Bogland

FOR T. P. FLANAGAN

We have no prairies
To slice a big sun at evening—
Everywhere the eye concedes to
Encroaching horizon,

5   Is wooed into the cyclops' eye
Of a tarn. Our unfenced country
Is bog that keeps crusting
Between the sights of the sun.

They've taken the skeleton
10   Of the Great Irish Elk
Out of the peat, set it up,
An astounding crate full of air.

Dedication: *T.P. Flanagan* (b.1929), Irish artist; his painting *Boglands (for Seamus Heaney)* (1967) was the inspiration for this poem. See S.B. Kennedy, *T.P. Flanagan* (Blackrock / Portland, 1995), p. 83.
6: *tarn:* a small mountain lake
10: *Great Irish Elk:* an extinct Pleistocene species of elk noted for its gigantic antlers

Butter sunk under
More than a hundred years
15   Was recovered salty and white.
The ground itself is kind, black butter

Melting and opening underfoot,
Missing its last definition
By millions of years.
20   They'll never dig coal here,

Only the waterlogged trunks
Of great firs, soft as pulp.
Our pioneers keep striking
Inwards and downwards,

25   Every layer they strip
Seems camped on before.
The bogholes might be Atlantic seepage.
The wet centre is bottomless.

1969

North

I returned to a long strand,
the hammered curve of a bay,
and found only the secular
powers of the Atlantic thundering.

5   I faced the unmagical
invitations of Iceland,
the pathetic colonies
of Greenland, and suddenly

those fabulous raiders,
10   those lying in Orkney and Dublin
measured against
their long swords rusting,

those in the solid
belly of stone ships,
15   those hacked and glinting
in the gravel of thawed streams

9: *raiders:* Vikings. These Scandinavian pirate-explorers began settling in Iceland in the ninth century, and from there established colonies in Greenland. They first came to Scotland's Orkney Islands in the eighth century. The Vikings' first recorded appearance on the coast of Ireland was in 795, and thereafter they engaged in frequent plundering raids (seizing Dublin in 838). Gradually they established colonies and became traders in cooperation with the Irish; their power declined in the tenth century and was finally broken by their defeat by the Irish High King Brian Boru at the Battle of Clontarf in 1014.

were ocean-deafened voices
warning me, lifted again
in violence and epiphany.
20   The longship's swimming tongue

was buoyant with hindsight—
it said Thor's hammer swung
to geography and trade,
thick-witted couplings and revenges,

25   the hatreds and behind-backs
of the althing, lies and women,
exhaustions nominated peace,
memory incubating the spilled blood.

It said, 'Lie down
30   in the word-hoard, burrow
the coil and gleam
of your furrowed brain.

Compose in darkness.
Expect aurora borealis
35   in the long foray
but no cascade of light.

Keep your eye clear
as the bleb of the icicle,
trust the feel of what nubbed treasure
40   your hands have known.'

                                                                    1975

20: *longship*: a Viking ship, its length accommodating its many oarsmen
22: The *hammer*—representing the thunderbolt—was the principal attribute of the Scandinavian thun-
    der-god *Thor*.
26: *althing*: the Icelandic parliament
38: *bleb*: air-bubble

Singing School

Fair seedtime had my soul, and I grew up
Fostered alike by beauty and by fear;
Much favoured in my birthplace, and no less
In that beloved Vale to which, erelong,
I was transplanted . . .
WILLIAM WORDSWORTH, *THE PRELUDE*

He [the stable-boy] had a book of Orange rhymes, and the days
when we read them together in the hay-loft gave me the pleasure of
rhyme for the first time. Later on I can remember being told, when
there was a rumour of a Fenian rising, that rifles were being handed
out to the Orangemen; and presently, when I began to dream of my
future life, I thought I would like to die fighting the Fenians.
W. B. YEATS, *AUTOBIOGRAPHIES*

I   THE MINISTRY OF FEAR

FOR SEAMUS DEANE

Well, as Kavanagh said, we have lived
In important places. The lonely scarp
Of St Columb's College, where I billeted
For six years, overlooked your Bogside.
5   I gazed into new worlds: the inflamed throat
Of Brandywell, its floodlit dogtrack,
The throttle of the hare. In the first week
I was so homesick I couldn't even eat
The biscuits left to sweeten my exile.
10   I threw them over the fence one night
In September 1951
When the lights of houses in the Lecky Road
Were amber in the fog. It was an act
Of stealth.
              Then Belfast, and then Berkeley.

Title: Gaelic bards formed a special hereditary caste in medieval Ireland, with each bardic family establishing *schools* where their art was taught. Yeats had alluded to these schools in "Sailing to Byzantium" (see p. 42).
Second Epigraph: The *Orange* Order, founded in 1795 to uphold Protestant privilege in Ireland, remains a bastion of Protestant Unionist militancy in Northern Ireland, and is responsible for the annual July 12th Orange Parades. The *Fenians* were a secret Nationalist society of the mid-nineteenth century.
Title: *The Ministry of Fear*: The phrase is a paraphrase from Wordsworth (see the second line of the epigraph); it became the title of a Grahame Greene novel and the 1944 Fritz Lang movie based on it, about a man mistaken for a Nazi spy in wartime England.
Dedication: *Seamus Deane*: Irish critic, poet, and novelist, born in Derry's Bogside (its Catholic ghetto); he was a schoolmate of Heaney's at St Columb's College (secondary school) in Derry and a fellow student at Queen's University, Belfast.
1: For Patrick *Kavanagh*, see p. 275. Heaney quotes from "Epic": "I have lived in important places."
2: *scarp*: the steep face of a hill
14: Heaney taught at Queen's and then for a year at the University of California at *Berkeley*.

15   Here's two on's are sophisticated,
        Dabbling in verses till they have become
        A life: from bulky envelopes arriving
        In vacation time to slim volumes
        Despatched 'with the author's compliments'.
20   Those poems in longhand, ripped from the wire spine
        Of your exercise book, bewildered me—
        Vowels and ideas bandied free
        As the seed-pods blowing off our sycamores.
        I tried to write about the sycamores
25   And innovated a South Derry rhyme
        With *hushed* and *lulled* full chimes for *pushed* and *pulled*.
        Those hobnailed boots from beyond the mountain
        Were walking, by God, all over the fine
        Lawns of elocution.
                                    Have our accents
30   Changed? 'Catholics, in general, don't speak
        As well as students from the Protestant schools.'
        Remember that stuff? Inferiority
        Complexes, stuff that dreams were made on.
        'What's your name, Heaney?'
                                    'Heaney, Father.'
                                            'Fair
35   Enough.'
                    On my first day, the leather strap
        Went epileptic in the Big Study,
        Its echoes plashing over our bowed heads,
        But I still wrote home that a boarder's life
        Was not so bad, shying as usual.

40   On long vacations, then, I came to life
        In the kissing seat of an Austin 16
        Parked at a gable, the engine running,
        My fingers tight as ivy on her shoulders,
        A light left burning for her in the kitchen.
45   And heading back for home, the summer's
        Freedom dwindling night by night, the air
        All moonlight and a scent of hay, policemen
        Swung their crimson flashlamps, crowding round
        The car like black cattle, snuffing and pointing
50   The muzzle of a Sten gun in my eye:
        'What's your name, driver?'
                                    'Seamus . . .'
                                        Seamus?

        They once read my letters at a roadblock
        And shone their torches on your hieroglyphics,
        'Svelte dictions' in a very florid hand.

15: *on's*: of us
33: *on*: of. Cf. *The Tempest*, 4.1.156.
50: *Sten gun*: a submachine gun

55   Ulster was British, but with no rights on
        The English lyric: all around us, though
        We hadn't named it, the ministry of fear.

2 A Constable Calls

        His bicycle stood at the window-sill,
        The rubber cowl of a mud-splasher
        Skirting the front mudguard,
        Its fat black handlegrips

5   Heating in sunlight, the 'spud'
        Of the dynamo gleaming and cocked back,
        The pedal treads hanging relieved
        Of the boot of the law.

        His cap was upside down
10   On the floor, next his chair.
        The line of its pressure ran like a bevel
        In his slightly sweating hair.

        He had unstrapped
        The heavy ledger, and my father
15   Was making tillage returns
        In acres, roods, and perches.

        Arithmetic and fear.
        I sat staring at the polished holster
        With its buttoned flap, the braid cord
20   Looped into the revolver butt.

        'Any other root crops?
        Mangolds? Marrowstems? Anything like that?'
        'No.' But was there not a line
        Of turnips where the seed ran out

25   In the potato field? I assumed
        Small guilts and sat
        Imagining the black hole in the barracks.
        He stood up, shifted the baton-case

        Further round on his belt,
30   Closed the domesday book,
        Fitted his cap back with two hands,
        And looked at me as he said goodbye.

16: A perch is an area 16½ feet square; a rood contains 40 perches.
22: *Mangolds* (a type of beet) and *marrowstems* (a type of cabbage) are grown as food for livestock.
30: The *Domesday Book* records the survey of all landholdings in England carried out in 1086 under
   William the Conqueror.

A shadow bobbed in the window.
He was snapping the carrier spring
35   Over the ledger. His boot pushed off
And the bicycle ticked, ticked, ticked.

3 ORANGE DRUMS, TYRONE, 1966

The lambeg balloons at his belly, weighs
Him back on his haunches, lodging thunder
Grossly there between his chin and his knees.
He is raised up by what he buckles under.

5   Each arm extended by a seasoned rod,
He parades behind it. And though the drummers
Are granted passage through the nodding crowd,
It is the drums preside, like giant tumours.

To every cocked ear, expert in its greed,
10   His battered signature subscribes 'No Pope'.
The goatskin's sometimes plastered with his blood.
The air is pounding like a stethoscope.

4 SUMMER 1969

While the Constabulary covered the mob
Firing into the Falls, I was suffering
Only the bullying sun of Madrid.
Each afternoon, in the casserole heat
5   Of the flat, as I sweated my way through
The life of Joyce, stinks from the fishmarket
Rose like the reek off a flax-dam.
At night on the balcony, gules of wine,
A sense of children in their dark corners,
10   Old women in black shawls near open windows,
The air a canyon rivering in Spanish.

Title: The months of July and August are the "marching season," centered on the annual July 12th Orange Parade celebrating William III's 1689 victory over the forces of the Catholic James II at the Battle of the Boyne; it is an occasion of display of militant Protestant and Loyalist sympathies, its ritual involving the display of banner and flags and the beating of large drums called "lambegs." Parades are often deliberately routed past or through Catholic ghettos, often provoking sectarian rioting. *Tyrone* is a former county of Northern Ireland (no longer in existence after administrative reorganization in 1973).

Title: The Northern Irish government permitted a Protestant parade to go ahead in Derry on 12 August 1969, commemorating the lifting of James II's siege of the town in 1689; it led to violent clashes between Catholics and Protestants that escalated into the "Battle of the Bogside," with the police laying siege to the ghetto while its residents barricaded themselves in and lobbed stones and petrol bombs. After two days' battle British troops were sent in to quell the rioting, a measure that led to the permanent presence of the British Army in Northern Ireland and, in 1972, to the suspension of the Northern Irish parliament and the imposition of direct rule from Westminster.

2: *the Falls:* The Falls Road, a main road through Catholic west Belfast

3: The setting of this section is *Spain* under the right-wing authoritarian regime of Francisco Franco (1892–1975).

7: *flax-dam:* sheaves of flax after harvesting are steeped in a flax-dam (or "lint hole") filled with soft peaty water; they are left to rot for about a week, producing a foul stench and releasing poison into the water.

8: *gules:* red

We talked our way home over starlit plains
Where patent leather of the Guardia Civil
Gleamed like fish-bellies in flax-poisoned waters.

15 'Go back,' one said, 'try to touch the people.'
Another conjured Lorca from his hill.
We sat through death-counts and bullfight reports
On the television, celebrities
Arrived from where the real thing still happened.

20 I retreated to the cool of the Prado.
Goya's 'Shootings of the Third of May'
Covered a wall—the thrown-up arms
And spasm of the rebel, the helmeted
And knapsacked military, the efficient
25 Rake of the fusillade. In the next room,
His nightmares, grafted to the palace wall—
Dark cyclones, hosting, breaking; Saturn
Jewelled in the blood of his own children,
Gigantic Chaos turning his brute hips
30 Over the world. Also, that holmgang
Where two berserks club each other to death
For honour's sake, greaved in a bog, and sinking.

He painted with his fists and elbows, flourished
The stained cape of his heart as history charged.

5 FOSTERAGE

FOR MICHAEL MCLAVERTY

'Description is revelation!' Royal
Avenue, Belfast, 1962,
A Saturday afternoon, glad to meet
Me, newly cubbed in language, he gripped
5 My elbow. 'Listen. Go your own way.
Do your own work. Remember
Katherine Mansfield—*I will tell
How the laundry basket squeaked* . . . that note of exile.'

13: *Guardia Civil:* Spain's paramilitary national police force
16: The great Spanish poet Federico García *Lorca* (1898–1936) was murdered by Franco's Nationalists at the beginning of the Spanish Civil War (1936–1939). Lorca was shot to death at Víznar, a small hamlet on the slopes of the Sierra de Alfacar, northeast of Granada (in Andulusia).
20ff: Madrid's *Prado* houses the Goya paintings Heaney sees: *Third of May 1808,* showing the executions of Madrid insurgents at the hands of Napoleon's troops; the dark and horrific group of paintings known as the "black paintings," originally painted on the walls of Goya's house and later transferred to canvas, which includes *Saturn,* showing the god devouring one of his children; *The Colossus;* and *Duel with Clubs.*
30: *holmgang:* duel to the death

Title: It was a custom among the ancient Celtic nobility to send a son to live with another family for the entire course of his childhood, the aim being to give him a sense of the family and its closeness on a larger scale.
Dedication: As part of his postgraduate education course, early in 1962, Heaney was sent for his teaching practice to St Thomas Intermediate School, Ballymurphy, where the novelist and short-story writer *Michael McLaverty* was headmaster. He became a key literary guide and mentor.

But to hell with overstating it:
10   'Don't have the veins bulging in your Biro.'
And then, 'Poor Hopkins!' I have the *Journals*
He gave me, underlined, his buckled self
Obeisant to their pain. He discerned
The lineaments of patience everywhere
15   And fostered me and sent me out, with words
Imposing on my tongue like obols.

6 EXPOSURE

It is December in Wicklow:
Alders dripping, birches
Inheriting the last light,
The ash tree cold to look at.

5   A comet that was lost
Should be visible at sunset,
Those million tons of light
Like a glimmer of haws and rose-hips,

And I sometimes see a falling star.
10   If I could come on meteorite!
Instead I walk through damp leaves,
Husks, the spent flukes of autumn,

Imagining a hero
On some muddy compound,
15   His gift like a slingstone
Whirled for the desperate.

How did I end up like this?
I often think of my friends'
Beautiful prismatic counselling
20   And the anvil brains of some who hate me

As I sit weighing and weighing
My responsible *tristia*.
For what? For the ear? For the people?
For what is said behind-backs?

10: *Biro:* ballpoint pen

16: An *obol* is an ancient Greek coin; one was placed in the mouth of the dead so that they could pay the boatsman Charon for passage across the river Styx into the underworld.

1: Heaney moved to County *Wicklow* in the Republic of Ireland following the 1972 Bloody Sunday massacre in Derry (when British troops fired into a rioting crowd at a demonstration, killing thirteen people).

8: *haws:* fruit of the hawthorn

13ff: Heaney is thinking of David and Goliath.

22: *tristia:* "sorrows" (Latin). But the word refers more specifically to the *Tristia*, a book of poems written by the Roman poet Ovid after his banishment to Tomis, on the Black Sea. They are in the form of letters addressed to his wife and friends in Rome, which also indirectly plead with the Emperor Augustus to rescind his banishment. Heaney also perhaps has in mind the *Tristia* (1922) of the Russian poet Osip Mandelstam (1891–1938), written while he spent the years of the Russian Revolution and Civil War in the Crimea (on the Black Sea) and in Georgia.

25   Rain comes down through the alders,
        Its low conducive voices
        Mutter about let-downs and erosions
        And yet each drop recalls

        The diamond absolutes.
30   I am neither internee nor informer;
        An inner émigré, grown long-haired
        And thoughtful; a wood-kerne

        Escaped from the massacre,
        Taking protective colouring
35   From bole and bark, feeling
        Every wind that blows;

        Who, blowing up these sparks
        For their meagre heat, have missed
        The once-in-a-lifetime portent,
40   The comet's pulsing rose.

                                    1975

Oysters

        Our shells clacked on the plates.
        My tongue was a filling estuary,
        My palate hung with starlight:
        As I tasted the salty Pleiades
5   Orion dipped his foot into the water.

        Alive and violated
        They lay on their beds of ice:
        Bivalves: the split bulb
        And philandering sigh of ocean.
10   Millions of them ripped and shucked and scattered.

        We had driven to that coast
        Through flowers and limestone
        And there we were, toasting friendship,
        Laying down a perfect memory
15   In the cool of thatch and crockery.

30: *internee:* the reference is to the mass internment without trial of suspected members of the Provisional IRA in August 1971. 342 people were rounded up; the harsh and abusive treatment of internees was to become the subject of several governmental inquiries.

31: *inner émigré:* a term used in the former USSR of those sentenced to "internal exile" (often in Siberia's forced-labour camps). Mandelstam was condemned to internal exile in 1934 after writing a satire on Stalin; he died in a transit camp in far-eastern Siberia in 1938.

32: *Woodkerne* were seventeenth-century bands of Irishmen dispossessed of their land by English and Scottish settlers; they became outlaws, attacking planter settlements.

4: *Pleiades:* seven sisters who in Greek myth were pursued by the giant hunter Orion. They were turned into a constellation, as was Orion, who continues to pursue them across the sky.

Over the Alps, packed deep in hay and snow,
The Romans hauled their oysters south to Rome:
I saw damp panniers disgorge
The frond-lipped, brine-stung
20   Glut of privilege

And was angry that my trust could not repose
In the clear light, like poetry or freedom
Leaning in from sea. I ate the day
Deliberately, that its tang
25   Might quicken me all into verb, pure verb.

1979

The Toome Road

One morning early I met armoured cars
In convoy, warbling along on powerful tyres,
All camouflaged with broken alder branches,
And headphoned soldiers standing up in turrets.
5   How long were they approaching down my roads
As if they owned them? The whole country was sleeping.
I had rights-of-way, fields, cattle in my keeping,
Tractors hitched to buckrakes in open sheds,
Silos, chill gates, wet slates, the greens and reds
10   Of outhouse roofs. Whom should I run to tell
Among all of those with their back doors on the latch
For the bringer of bad news, that small-hours visitant
Who, by being expected, might be kept distant?
Sowers of seed, erectors of headstones . . .
15   O charioteers, above your dormant guns,
It stands here still, stands vibrant as you pass,
The invisible, untoppled omphalos.

1979

The Underground

There we were in the vaulted tunnel running,
You in your going-away coat speeding ahead
And me, me then like a fleet god gaining
Upon you before you turned to a reed
5   Or some new white flower japped with crimson
As the coat flapped wild and button after button

Title: The location (two miles from Heaney's birthplace) is strongly associated with the 1798 United Irishmen rebellion: the rebel Rody McCorley was hanged at Toomebridge.
8: A *buckrake* is a wide horse-drawn or tractor-drawn long-toothed rake for gathering hay.
11: *on the latch*: unlatched
17: Delphi was the location of the oracle of Apollo; the *omphalos* ("navel-stone") there supposedly marked the center of the world.

Title: *The Underground*: the London subway system
3–5: The nymph Syrinx, fleeing from the god Pan, was turned into a reed. The youth Hyacinthus was accidentally killed by a discus thrown by his admirer, the god Apollo; from his blood sprung the hyacinth.
5: *japped*: japanned (i.e., varnished)

Sprang off and fell in a trail
Between the Underground and the Albert Hall.

Honeymooning, mooning around, late for the Proms,
10   Our echoes die in that corridor and now
I come as Hansel came on the moonlit stones
Retracing the path back, lifting the buttons

To end up in a draughty lamplit station
After the trains have gone, the wet track
15   Bared and tensed as I am, all attention
For your step following and damned if I look back.

1984

from Station Island

VII

[377]   I had come to the edge of the water,
soothed by just looking, idling over it
as if it were a clear barometer

380   or a mirror, when his reflection
did not appear but I sensed a presence
entering into my concentration

on not being concentrated as he spoke
my name. And though I was reluctant
385   I turned to meet his face and the shock

is still in me at what I saw. His brow
was blown open above the eye and blood
had dried on his neck and cheek. 'Easy now,'

he said, 'it's only me. You've seen men as raw
390   after a football match . . . What time it was
when I was wakened up I still don't know

but I heard this knocking, knocking, and it
scared me, like the phone in the small hours,
so I had the sense not to put on the light

8: The Royal *Albert Hall* is one of London's principal concert halls: it holds the annual music festival known as the Proms (the Sir Henry Wood Promenade Concerts).

"*Station Island* is a sequence of dream encounters with familiar ghosts, set on Station Island on Lough Derg in Co. Donegal. The island is also known as St Patrick's Purgatory because of a tradition that Patrick was the first to establish the penitential vigil of fasting and praying which still constitutes the basis of the three-day pilgrimage. Each unit of the contemporary pilgrim's exercises is called a 'station,' and a large part of each station involves walking barefoot and praying round the 'beds,' stone circles which are said to be the remains of early medieval monastic cells." (Heaney). Heaney's poem follows a tradition of poetic meditations set at the location: see Patrick Kavanagh's "Lough Derg" (1942) and Denis Devlin's "Lough Derg" (reprinted in this volume).

395   but looked out from behind the curtain.
I saw two customers on the doorstep
and an old Land Rover with the doors open

parked on the street, so I let the curtain drop;
but they must have been waiting for it to move
400   for they shouted to come down into the shop.

She started to cry then and roll round the bed,
lamenting and lamenting to herself,
not even asking who it was. "Is your head

astray, or what's come over you?" I roared, more
405   to bring myself to my senses
than out of any real anger at her

for the knocking shook me, the way they kept it up,
and her whingeing and half-screeching made it worse.
All the time they were shouting, "Shop!

410   Shop!" so I pulled on my shoes and a sportscoat
and went back to the window and called out,
"What do you want? Could you quieten the racket

or I'll not come down at all." "There's a child not well.
Open up and see what you have got—pills
415   or a powder or something in a bottle,"

one of them said. He stepped back off the footpath
so I could see his face in the streetlamp
and when the other moved I knew them both.

But bad and all as the knocking was, the quiet
420   hit me worse. She was quiet herself now,
lying dead still, whispering to watch out.

At the bedroom door I switched on the light.
"It's odd they didn't look for a chemist.
Who are they anyway at this hour of the night?"

425   she asked me, with the eyes standing in her head.
"I know them to see," I said, but something
made me reach and squeeze her hand across the bed

before I went downstairs into the aisle
of the shop. I stood there, going weak
430   in the legs. I remember the stale smell

of cooked meat or something coming through
as I went to open up. From then on
you know as much about it as I do.'

'Did they say nothing?' 'Nothing. What would they say?'
435   'Were they in uniform? Not masked in any way?'
'They were barefaced as they would be in the day,

shites thinking they were the be-all and the end-all.'
'Not that it is any consolation
but they were caught,' I told him, 'and got jail.'

440   Big-limbed, decent, open-faced, he stood
forgetful of everything now except
whatever was welling up in his spoiled head,

beginning to smile. 'You've put on a bit of weight
since you did your courting in that big Austin
445   you got the loan of on a Sunday night.'

Through life and death he had hardly aged.
There always was an athlete's cleanliness
shining off him, and except for the ravaged

forehead and the blood, he was still that same
450   rangy midfielder in a blue jersey
and starched pants, the one stylist on the team,

the perfect, clean, unthinkable victim.
'Forgive the way I have lived indifferent—
forgive my timid circumspect involvement,'

455   I surprised myself by saying. 'Forgive
my eye,' he said, 'all that's above my head.'
And then a stun of pain seemed to go through him

and he trembled like a heatwave and faded.

XII

[682]   Like a convalescent, I took the hand
stretched down from the jetty, sensed again
an alien comfort as I stepped on ground

685   to find the helping hand still gripping mine,
fish-cold and bony, but whether to guide
or to be guided I could not be certain

for the tall man in step at my side
seemed blind, though he walked straight as a rush
690   upon his ashplant, his eyes fixed straight ahead.

Then I knew him in the flesh
out there on the tarmac among the cars,
wintered hard and sharp as a blackthorn bush.

688: The *tall man* is the novelist James Joyce (1882–1941), who by the end of his life was virtually blind;
the *ashplant* (ash walking-stick) is that of Stephen Dedalus in Joyce's novel *Ulysses*.

His voice eddying with the vowels of all rivers
695   came back to me, though he did not speak yet,
a voice like a prosecutor's or a singer's,

cunning, narcotic, mimic, definite
as a steel nib's downstroke, quick and clean,
and suddenly he hit a litter basket

700   with his stick, saying, 'Your obligation
is not discharged by any common rite.
What you do you must do on your own.

The main thing is to write
for the joy of it. Cultivate a work-lust
705   that imagines its haven like your hands at night

dreaming the sun in the sunspot of a breast.
You are fasted now, light-headed, dangerous.
Take off from here. And don't be so earnest,

so ready for the sackcloth and the ashes.
710   Let go, let fly, forget.
You've listened long enough. Now strike your note.'

It was as if I had stepped free into space
alone with nothing that I had not known
already. Raindrops blew in my face

715   as I came to and heard the harangue and jeers
going on and on. 'The English language
belongs to us. You are raking at dead fires,

rehearsing the old whinges at your age.
That subject people stuff is a cod's game,
720   infantile, like this peasant pilgrimage.

You lose more of yourself than you redeem
doing the decent thing. Keep at a tangent.
When they make the circle wide, it's time to swim

out on your own and fill the element
725   with signatures on your own frequency,
echo-soundings, searches, probes, allurements,

694: Joyce's novel *Finnegans Wake* works the names of rivers from all over the world into the prose, notably
in the "Anna Livia Plurabelle" section.
697: *cunning:* See Stephen Dedalus's final resolve in *A Portrait of the Artist as a Young Man:* "I will not
serve that in which I no longer believe whether it call itself my home, my fatherland or my church: and
I will try to express myself in some mode of life or art as freely as I can and as wholly as I can, using for
my defence the only arms I allow myself to use, silence, exile, and cunning."

elver-gleams in the dark of the whole sea.'
The shower broke in a cloudburst, the tarmac
fumed and sizzled. As he moved off quickly

730   the downpour loosed its screens round his straight walk.

                                                    1984

The Mud Vision

Statues with exposed hearts and barbed-wire crowns
Still stood in alcoves, hares flitted beneath
The dozing bellies of jets, our menu-writers
And punks with aerosol sprays held their own
5   With the best of them. Satellite link-ups
Wafted over us the blessings of popes, heliports
Maintained a charmed circle for idols on tour
And casualties on their stretchers. We sleepwalked
The line between panic and formulae, screentested
10   Our first native models and the last of the mummers,
Watching ourselves at a distance, advantaged
And airy as a man on a springboard
Who keeps limbering up because the man cannot dive.

And then in the foggy midlands it appeared,
15   Our mud vision, as if a rose window of mud
Had invented itself out of the glittery damp,
A gossamer wheel, concentric with its own hub
Of nebulous dirt, sullied yet lucent.
We had heard of the sun standing still and the sun
20   That changed colour, but we were vouchsafed
Original clay, transfigured and spinning.
And then the sunsets ran murky, the wiper
Could never entirely clean off the windscreen,
Reservoirs tasted of silt, a light fuzz
25   Accrued in the hair and the eyebrows, and some
Took to wearing a smudge on their foreheads
To be prepared for whatever. Vigils
Began to be kept around puddled gaps,
On altars bulrushes ousted the lilies
30   And a rota of invalids came and went
On beds they could lease placed in range of the shower.

A generation who had seen a sign!
Those nights when we stood in an umber dew and smelled

727: *elver:* a young eel

18: *lucent:* glowing
26: *wearing a smudge on their foreheads:* i.e., as is done in the Christian church on the penitential holiday
  of Ash Wednesday.

Mould in the verbena, or woke to a light
35   Furrow-breath on the pillow, when the talk
Was all about who had seen it and our fear
Was touched with a secret pride, only ourselves
Could be adequate then to our lives. When the rainbow
Curved flood-brown and ran like a water-rat's back
40   So that drivers on the hard shoulder switched off to watch,
We wished it away, and yet we presumed it a test
That would prove us beyond expectation.

We lived, of course, to learn the folly of that.
One day it was gone and the east gable
45   Where its trembling corolla had balanced
Was starkly a ruin again, with dandelions
Blowing high up on the ledges, and moss
That slumbered on through its increase. As cameras raked
The site from every angle, experts
50   Began their *post factum* jabber and all of us
Crowded in tight for the big explanations.
Just like that, we forgot that the vision was ours,
Our one chance to know the incomparable
And dive to a future. What might have been origin
55   We dissipated in news. The clarified place
Had retrieved neither us nor itself—except
You could say we survived. So say that, and watch us
Who had our chance to be mud-men, convinced and estranged,
Figure in our own eyes for the eyes of the world.

1987

45: *corolla:* flower
50: *post factum:* after-the-fact

PETER RILEY (b. 1940)

T OWARD THE END OF TRACKS AND MINESHAFTS (1983), RILEY WRITES: "DEEPER INTO stone than any technology can reach / is the stone in the heart."[1] Riley's appre-hension of the "Deep clarity of pure dread" has encouraged critics such as John Hall to link his meditative sequence with an "earlier (Christian) tradition of spiritual exer-cises and battles with meaning" while acknowledging that Riley's poems inhabit and address a post-Christian moment.[2] In writing of "uncertain belonging" Riley also seeks a civic address responsive to social conditions too often indicating "vast unwritable acts of mass brutality / always intended, by the errors of substitution, / to do good."[3] Clar-ity of purpose is one goal as it might emerge from a self more activity than essence:

> And the saint on his tiny island in the bay,
> like a doctor in his surgery, islanded off
> from the unhealing world and blasted out
> of self regard by pressure of work—love
> like this meets constantly the resistance of
> matter directly as the gardener where every shrub
> is won from nothing into the ancestral shield,
> and the stones rise to the hand.[4]

This is a poetry of moral urgency competing with despair before the opacity of the world: "Surely the fire is getting low; if we don't signal our love there will be no rea-son for dying."[5] The modernist collage of the first book in Riley's *Excavations* sequence, *Distant Points,* juxtaposes his own soliloquy or meditation with fragments "mined" from the archives of Tudor music and English lyric, setting both against the base line established by fragments from J. R. Mortimer's and Canon William Green-well's nineteenth-century accounts of the excavation of neolithic burial sites. Riley is equally at home in the more continuous and discursive stanzas of *Snow Has Settled [. . . .] Bury Me Here* (1997) or in the syllabic-based sonnets of *Ospita* (1987). His non-linear sequences include *Lines on the Liver* (1981) and *Tracks and Mineshafts.*

Riley was born near Manchester. He attended Pembroke College, Cambridge. Poets including Andrew Crozier, John Riley, Tim Longville, and J. H. Prynne, later iden-tified with a "Cambridge School," were his contemporaries at Cambridge, though Riley did not meet them until 1965. Interest in the "New American Poetry" as collected in

---

[1] *Tracks and Mineshafts,* Derbyshire, 1983, p. 68.
[2] "On *Lines on the Liver* and *Tracks and Mineshafts.*" *The Gig* 4/5, Nov. 1999–March 2000, p. 40.
[3] *Tracks and Mineshafts,* p. 68.
[4] Ibid., p. 74.
[5] Ibid., p. 16.

Donald Allen's famous anthology of that title is apparent in early Riley publications such as *Love/Strife Machine* (1969) and *The Linear Journal* (1973). For a brief period in the 1960s, Riley edited *The English Intelligencer,* a journal that housed the Cambridge School's first efforts to reimagine English poetry in the wake of Charles Olson, Jack Spicer, Frank O'Hara, and others. Riley lived in Hastings and then Hove, starting a thesis on T. F. Powys at the University of Sussex, and then took a teaching job at the University of Odense, Denmark. He returned to North Staffordshire and the University of Keele and wrote a thesis on Jack Spicer's poetry. In a variety of locations and holding a variety of jobs, he continued publishing poems while also taking part in the improvised music scene in London as a reviewer, interviewer, and occasional impresario. In recent years, he has lived in Cambridge, where he runs a catalog business for small-press poetry and publishes Poetical Histories. Other books and pamphlets include *Preparations* (1979), *Sea Watches* (1991), *Reader* (1992), *Lecture* (1993), *Alstonefield* (1995), *Author* (1998), and *Passing Measures: A Collection of Poems* (2000).

from Lines on the Liver

1.

Moving eastwards under symmetry towards no,
not yet home, not till I get there the west
pales the sky behind me a crimson slush a
dream of statement, slowly falling into bond.

5   But crammed with people and brokenness my solo
is concerted, I feel the tab on my collar, the
spine touch, and radial, you're always there.

I stick an ex libris
over a library stamp,
10   I walk the dark room.

2.

All that happened
and where's the poem of it?
—there in your surface speaking
your body writing your soul

5   tall
and never still
like the autumn grass

In the introductory prose section of *Lines on the Liver,* Riley speaks of the book's origins in "the process of moving house" from near Hartington to a house just outside Wirksworth, Derbyshire: this move was "not far, some 12 miles," but took him eastwards over the Peak District, a limestone dome that forms the southern termination of the Pennines, a range of mountains and hills that extends south from Northumberland. Riley's house was "well up an eastern valley-side, just off the limestone, facing west," overlooking the town of Wirksworth in the valley below. In the nineteenth century, the area's economy centered on lead mining; since the mines' closure it has shifted to limestone quarries.
Section 1: 8: ex libris: i.e., a bookplate: the phrase "ex libris" ("from the library of . . .") is often used on bookplates.

we could happen to
a Lycian double music
10   conjugates my throat weft

10. window piece

One of the little squares is out—a previous occupant
stretched polythene over the gap and sometimes at night
a moth flies straight into it, sudden thud.

cf. I think I'm "getting somewhere"
5   sudden thud
your back to me

The membrane holds. Ktd4Xe6!? black
moves. And now there's a dead moth
under the cover of ten years' diggings,
10   a streak of grease, and money dust

II.

Here out of my writing
your fingertips glow in the darkness
you climb into the valley

and I know my life can never be translated
5   out of this miserable little hole
full of novels and possibilities—
the very sides of it cut my hands

On the hard rocks of the heart vale
our sight ends. The magpie moth
10   lays her eggs in the wound.

17.

It's awful—there are owls and townships in the night
and I'm trembling because some Sales Manager
said "Now Look Here" on the 'phone.

No resolution is anticipated.
5   The owl, swooping over, looks ahead;

Section 2: 9: Lycian: an epithet of Apollo, Greek god of music
10: *conjugates:* conjoins; but with puns on "conjugal" and on the grammatical conjugation of a verb.
Section 10: 7: Ktd4Xe6!?: chess notation for "knight on square d4 captures a piece on e6." Exclamation
  points mark brilliant moves, question marks bad ones; the combination of the two means an unusual and
  interesting move, but one whose outcome is unclear.
Section 11: 9: magpie moth: a white moth with black (and some yellow) spots; it lays its eggs in wounds in
  plant stems.

the town sucks vision down its lamps
I quarry into night, a day's end.

Perhaps it's just that after so much
rooting in humanity
10   we need something to dry our hands on.

1981

from Excavations, Part One

FROM BOOK ONE: DISTANT POINTS

"the body in its final commerce"

1.   [1
the body in its final commerce: love and despair for a completed
memory or spoken heart *enclosed in a small inner dome of grey/drab-
coloured* [river-bed] *clay, brought from some distance* (from the valley
bottoms) and folded in, **So my journey ended** moulded in the
5   substance of arrival **I depart** *and a fire over the dome and a final
tumulus of local topsoil* /benign memorial where the heart is brought
to the exchange: death for life, relict for pain/ double-sealed, signed
and delivered—under all that press released to articulate its long
silence, long descended • tensed wing / spread fan / drumming over
10   the hill.

"folded in river clay"

2.   [C39
folded in river clay, the boat on the hilltop *lying East-West facing
upwards Right hand on Right shoulder Left arm across the body*
gradients of sleep, to die, to dream, or mean/ *Beyond his feet to the
East a row of three small circular pits or stake-holes* dawn trap as the
5   compass arc closes southwards and the heart is secured by azimuth,
all terrors past: **She only drave me to dispaire** /dead child, cancelled

---

Excavations: "These poems or meditations are concerned with the human burial deposits of the so-called
Neolithic/Bronze Age culture of what is now the Yorkshire Wolds, as documented in two books of late
19th Century tumulus excavation accounts: by JR Mortimer (1905) and Canon William Greenwell (1877)"
(Riley's note). In Book 1, Parts One and Two draw on Mortimer's *Forty Years' Researches in British and
Saxon Burial Mounds in East Yorkshire*, while Part Three draws on Greenwell's *British Barrows*. Numbers
in the righthand margin are those given the tumuli by their excavators ("C" is Mortimer's idiosyncratic
notation for "100": thus "C39" is tumulus 139). In the poems, italics mostly indicate where Riley is directly
reworking passages from these sources; boldface usually—though not always—indicates his working
from other source texts.
"the body in its final commerce": 6: *tumulus*: grave-mound
"folded in river clay": 5: In astronomy, the position of an object in the sky as seen by an observer on the
ground is measured by altitude and *azimuth;* the azimuth is the direction of the object in degrees clock-
wise from due south.
6: *She only drave me* . . . : from the anonymous poem "Awake, sweet love, thou art return'd," as set by the
composer John Dowland (1563–1626)

future in a satellite cloak hovering to SE. Yet the loss, folded into
history, sails adroit in the clay ship over commerce and habit, bound
for (to) this frozen screen where [cursive] we don't live, but do (love)
10 say, and cannot fail.

"carefully dismembered"

33.   [28: Life Hill

carefully dismembered [They are chucked into holocaust graves as
complete as they reached the end at; if you don't care who they are or
how they die you certainly don't care how they lie] for a purpose, a
scenario or buried score where the limbs gestate in the vocal and
5 brain cavities where the past becomes the future in chains of blood . . .
where a fallen god / *a shallow grave holding a dismembered human
body, mostly skull and leg bones . . . widely separated: one skull fragment
from the South top of the infill matched pieces from the bottom North*
Los smitten with astonishment: Frightend at the hurtling bones :
10 *two feet exactly in position at the south end of the grave,* a cremation
unit exactly above them /Where a fallen God stands on the earth
asking "What is this?" **The Eternals said: What is this? Death.
Urizen is a clod of clay.** on which the dancing continues, world-loss
survey, naming separate states **With numerous fete weell part and**
15 **mete** or touch casually in the night, seeking warmth with honour.

                                                          1995

FROM BOOK TWO: THIS CAROL THEY BEGAN THAT HOUR

"Sing to me"

81.   [65, 66

Sing to me, that half of you that's left. The upper half, containing the
air chambers and the arms and hands to work the bellows and the
fingers to stop. And I'll lie *crouched, on back, knees turned over to
right, head to West-South-West* listening to the singing **Sleepe fleshly
5 birth** of right and wrong stilled, of heart relay, of hope's gimlet in the
neck turning to that music **of the spheres** or very sound of death, the
snap | not quite south, as if pulled back slightly, my upper half faces
the sky and listens. The rest was burnt.

"*carefully dismembered*": 9: *Los smitten . . .* : This and the next boldface quotation are from Blake's *The Book of Urizen*, plates 8 and 6. Blake's narrative conflates the Biblical Creation and the Fall: Urizen, "primeval priest" and representative of false rationality, is responsible for the act of Creation, which divides Eternity, bringing on the wrath of the Eternals and leading to the Fall; Los, his counterpart (the "Eternal Prophet") attempts to heal the divisions in Eternity Urizen has caused but only ends up furthering them.
14: *numerous*: rhythmic and harmonious (as in a dance)
15: British prime minister Neville Chamberlain claimed to have secured "peace with honour" after negotiations with Germany in 1938.
Book Two: Title: see Shakespeare's song "It was a lover and his lass" (*As You Like It* 5.3.14–37): "This carol they began that hour, . . . / How that a life was but a flower."
"*Sing to me*": 6: In classical lore, each planet was inhabited by an angel singing in harmony with all the others, creating the *music of the spheres*.

10 Sing to me, what's left of me, half a person, the upper half, that
breathes and hearkens and learns to lie still. *hands to face* no pelvis, no
legs, no clay. / of left and right sundered, of gravity consigned to
healing *remains of a child to South-South-East* of the head not quite
vertical, as if drawn forward, over, to listen, to something that might
answer the pierced star soprano and restore to good all the time I've
15 known in the notation of that snap.

"Meaning spills"

88.   [57-55-58
Meaning spills, over the edge. The vortex has stabilisers, contingent
but discontinuous *two small mounds exactly to East and West of 55*
housing nothing much: a minimal human unit (E) / one jet button
(W) / the star-fighter has friends and relatives, whose irrelevance (cut
5 off from) forms a belt of subsequent purpose and even comfort across
wheat fields and factory estates in the path of the sun's decline where
wounds are dried. The clenched night has a sort of day as a sort of
canopy a sort of gravity or moment hinged on void points. Fa-la as
they say at the end of some songs, like a speeding ambulance.

"Leaving a simple state"

103.   [190
Leaving a simple state *a cremation placed in a trough in the floor of an*
oval pit five and a half feet long and aligned East-West unpersoned by
the dawning light in the narrow entrance *the deposit of ashes, also*
aligned East-West, was two and a half feet long, nearly the length of a
5 *tightly crouched inhumation* /unlimbed, unsexed, stuck in the crack
between days/ but something performed, or learnt, leaves a sign,—
Sign of what, sign which way? I don't know, it led to a bone on the
shore in blazing noon. And here, (you/she/it) who doesn't exist at all,
beside me, beckoning or tilting to affirm, again and again, the head
10 bowed over me, the long hair falling to the sides of my face. Willing to
give the self entire into succession as a unit, through a particular, for
a glimpse of renewal. And lightly graze the cheek in gratitude. The
bone glows on the edge of a life.

* * *

And look, the money runs shining into the ground.

                                                                     1995

"Meaning spills": 4: *star-fighter*: the phrase is borrowed from "The Ideal Star-Fighter," by the English poet
  J. H. Prynne (b. 1936).

"Ganesa dances"

112. (*Rothko: works on paper 1944–1969*)   [x

Ganesa dances, bearing the head, the head that wobbles and sways
and impedes the thought (of the dance) and the sense (of the world)
the gross lost head. Dances parameters of science and night. The
chalk swirls on the dance floor and spreads to the edge like a script
5   of urgent repair.

There in the page held out from the page, and the distance that clads
proximity, for it is time to go home. Quietly under the hospital walls
to the top of the town. To see the layered music twining into the far
fields, and the icing on the multitudes.

"'I arrived at a place mute of light'"

143. (*Installations by Gary Hill*)   [lxxxiv

"I arrived at a place mute of light." In the darkness the violet rods
tune up: pages on the floor, slowly becoming visible, open books
and documents /**these were once** (hopes, farewells) illegible, moving
surfaces slowly stirring dim forms of lip fingered, forearm stroked,
5   skin horizons stirring back and forth, cold burning/fleshly ghosts pale
grey in the seething paper ruled with horizontal lines, silent forms
meeting and separating in small cells scattered on the ground, dim
quires turning |slowly, repeatedly| touched lip, fluttered eye, turned
back. Some seven or eight (of them) each "much less than an entire
10   body, and burnt on the spot" the white wine of homing suspensions,
when any elsewhere cancels itself to complete fall. And the echo, the
ghosts in the corridor, the lives that were and shall be, totalling them-
selves in the margin. May we keep a charm or right of passage, a
unit, a piece of cheese, a pen in the hand, a yellow seal **The smalle**
15   **rayne** a voice recalled, awaited, a message understood, these things
that mean, these things agreed. After so long in darkness the star
sputters on the breast pocket and love is not fair. But love is not the
end.

1997

"*Ganesa dances*": Mark Rothko (1903–1970), the American abstract expressionist painter
1: *Ganesa:* Hindu god of wisdom and prudence, and of the home and hearth; he is represented with an
  elephant's head and a man's body.
"'*I arrived at a place mute of light*'": Gary Hill (b.1951), is an American artist working in video and instal-
  lation media; Riley attended an exhibition of his in 1993 at the Stedelijk Museum, Amsterdam.
1: *I arrived at a place mute of light:* from Dante's *Inferno* 5.28: Dante has just entered the second circle of
  Hell, which holds the lustful.
rods: rod-shaped receptors in the retina, responsible for black and white (hence night) vision.
14: Cf. the anonymous medieval lyric: "Western wind, when will thou blow, / The small rain down can
  rain? / Christ, if my love were in my arms / And I in my bed again!" ("can": does)

DEREK MAHON (b. 1941)

MAHON WAS BORN IN BELFAST AND EDUCATED AT THE ROYAL BELFAST ACADEMICAL Institution and Trinity College, Dublin. He has taught in England, France, Canada, Ireland, and the United States and been the writer-in-residence at institutions including the University of East Anglia and the New University of Ulster. For many years he worked in London as a journalist and as a screenwriter, adapting Irish novels for television. He has also been theater critic for the *Listener,* poetry editor of the *New Stateman,* features editor of *Vogue,* and a regular contributor to the *Irish Times.* His books of poetry include *Night-Crossing* (1968), *Lives* (1972), *The Snow Party* (1975), *The Hunt by Night* (1982), *Antarctica* (1985), *Selected Poems* (1991), and, most recently, *The Hudson Letter* (1995) and *The Yellow Book* (1997). He has translated Horace, Ovid, Rimbaud, Nerval, and Philippe Jaccottet.

Mahon rose to prominence as part of a group of Northern Irish poets (including Michael Longley, James Simmons, and Seamus Heaney) who came together in the mid-1960s at a writer's workshop led by Philip Hobsbaum, then teaching at Queen's University, Belfast. As a Protestant poet who has lived most of his writing life outside of Belfast and Ireland, Mahon has taken the poetry of Louis MacNeice as one important model, though his terser formalism typically avoids the chattier moments of MacNeice's poetry. Like MacNeice, Mahon often explores the complex emotions surrounding his distance from and attraction to Gaelic Ireland, and his poems combine a self-conscious and sometimes agonized touristic gaze on Ireland with the cosmopolitan perspective afforded by his knowledge of Continental, British, and American culture. Mahon's "The Snow Party" juxtaposes stanzas imitating Basho's poetry and describing the refined Japanese civilization of Basho's day with mention of political violence occurring simultaneously in Europe. Other poems confront more directly the question of poetry's responsibilities and efficacy, their irony sometimes turned inward, as when Mahon self-deprecatingly describes himself in "Dawn at St. Patrick's" as "a make-believe existentialist." The need for an art that lifts obscured human experience into the light of photographic, even redemptive representation, and the anxieties created by that need, are the focus of Mahon's most famous poem, "A Disused Shed in Co. Wexford."

The Snow Party

FOR LOUIS ASEKOFF

Bashō, coming
To the city of Nagoya,
Is asked to a snow party.

There is a tinkling of china
5   And tea into china;
There are introductions.

Then everyone
Crowds to the window
To watch the falling snow.

10   Snow is falling on Nagoya
And farther south
On the tiles of Kyōto.

Eastward, beyond Irago,
It is falling
15   Like leaves on the cold sea.

Elsewhere they are burning
Witches and heretics
In the boiling squares,

Thousands have died since dawn
20   In the service
Of barbarous kings;

But there is silence
In the houses of Nagoya
And the hills of Ise.

1975

Dedication: *Louis Asekoff* (b.1939), American poet
1: The poem describes a snow-watching party, a traditional social gathering in seventeenth-century Japan;
   its source is a brief mention in *The Records of a Weather-Exposed Skeleton*, a travel account mixing haiku
   and prose by the great Japanese poet *Basho* (1644–1694).

A Disused Shed in Co. Wexford

Let them not forget us, the weak souls among the asphodels.
SEFERIS, *MYTHISTOREMA*, TR. KEELEY AND SHERRARD

FOR J. G. FARRELL

Even now there are places where a thought might grow—
Peruvian mines, worked out and abandoned
To a slow clock of condensation,
An echo trapped for ever, and a flutter
5   Of wild-flowers in the lift-shaft,
Indian compounds where the wind dances
And a door bangs with diminished confidence,
Lime crevices behind rippling rain-barrels,
Dog corners for bone burials;
10 And in a disused shed in Co. Wexford,

Deep in the grounds of a burnt-out hotel,
Among the bathtubs and the washbasins
A thousand mushrooms crowd to a keyhole.
This is the one star in their firmament
15 Or frames a star within a star.
What should they do there but desire?
So many days beyond the rhododendrons
With the world waltzing in its bowl of cloud,
They have learnt patience and silence
20 Listening to the rooks querulous in the high wood.

They have been waiting for us in a foetor
Of vegetable sweat since civil war days,
Since the gravel-crunching, interminable departure
Of the expropriated mycologist.
25 He never came back, and light since then
Is a keyhole rusting gently after rain.
Spiders have spun, flies dusted to mildew
And once a day, perhaps, they have heard something—
A trickle of masonry, a shout from the blue
30 Or a lorry changing gear at the end of the lane.

There have been deaths, the pale flesh flaking
Into the earth that nourished it;
And nightmares, born of these and the grim
Dominion of stale air and rank moisture.
35 Those nearest the door grow strong—
'Elbow room! Elbow room!'

Epigraph: George *Seferis* (1900–1971), the Greek poet; the flower *asphodel* is said to cover the fields of Elysium.

Dedication: *J.G. Farrell* (1935–1979), the English novelist; his novel *Troubles* (1970) is set in Ireland in 1919, its setting a crumbling Anglo-Irish mansion, which has become a slightly run-down hotel.

21: *foetor:* stench

22: The passage of the Anglo-Irish Treaty in 1922 (creating the Irish Free State but excluding Northern Ireland and imposing an oath of allegiance to the British crown) led to civil war between the government and the Treaty's republican opponents.

24: *mycologist:* a specialist in mushrooms

The rest, dim in a twilight of crumbling
Utensils and broken pitchers, groaning
For their deliverance, have been so long
40   Expectant that there is left only the posture.

A half century, without visitors, in the dark—
Poor preparation for the cracking lock
And creak of hinges. Magi, moonmen,
Powdery prisoners of the old regime,
45   Web-throated, stalked like triffids, racked by drought
And insomnia, only the ghost of a scream
At the flash-bulb firing-squad we wake them with
Shows there is life yet in their feverish forms.
Grown beyond nature now, soft food for worms,
50   They lift frail heads in gravity and good faith.

They are begging us, you see, in their wordless way,
To do something, to speak on their behalf
Or at least not to close the door again.
Lost people of Treblinka and Pompeii!
55   'Save us, save us,' they seem to say,
'Let the god not abandon us
Who have come so far in darkness and in pain.
We too had our lives to live.
You with your light meter and relaxed itinerary,
60   Let not our naive labours have been in vain!'

                                           1975

Courtyards in Delft

Pieter de Hooch, 1659

FOR GORDON WOODS

Oblique light on the trite, on brick and tile—
Immaculate masonry, and everywhere that
Water tap, that broom and wooden pail
To keep it so. House-proud, the wives
5   Of artisans pursue their thrifty lives
Among scrubbed yards, modest but adequate.
Foliage is sparse, and clings. No breeze
Ruffles the trim composure of those trees.

No spinet-playing emblematic of
10   The harmonies and disharmonies of love;

45: *triffids*: the mobile, deadly plants of John Wyndham's 1951 science-fiction novel *The Day of the Triffids*
drouth: drought
54: Mahon joins *Treblinka*, a Nazi death camp in Poland, with the Italian city of *Pompeii*, destroyed in 79
  by the eruption of Mt. Vesuvius; the city with many of its inhabitants was perfectly preserved beneath
  volcanic ash, and excavated centuries later.

Some texts of "Courtyards in Delft" contain a fifth stanza.
Subtitle: *Pieter de Hooch* (1629–?1684), Dutch genre painter; he painted a number of domestic courtyard
  scenes; the scene of this poem comes from *Courtyard in Delft with Woman and Child* (1658).
9: De Hooch's great contemporary Jan Vermeer (1632–75) often painted women seated at the keyboard.

No lewd fish, no fruit, no wide-eyed bird
About to fly its cage while a virgin
Listens to her seducer, mars the chaste
Perfection of the thing and the thing made.
15   Nothing is random, nothing goes to waste.
We miss the dirty dog, the fiery gin.

That girl with her back to us who waits
For her man to come home for his tea
Will wait till the paint disintegrates
20   And ruined dikes admit the esurient sea;
Yet this is life too, and the cracked
Out-house door a verifiable fact
As vividly mnemonic as the sunlit
Railings that front the houses opposite.

25   I lived there as a boy and know the coal
Glittering in its shed, late-afternoon
Lambency informing the deal table,
The ceiling cradled in a radiant spoon.
I must be lying low in a room there,
30   A strange child with a taste for verse,
While my hard-nosed companions dream of fire
And sword upon parched veldt and fields of rain-swept gorse.

1981

A Garage in Co. Cork

Surely you paused at this roadside oasis
In your nomadic youth, and saw the mound
Of never-used cement, the curious faces,
The soft-drink ads and the uneven ground
5   Rainbowed with oily puddles, where a snail
Had scrawled its slimy, phosphorescent trail.

Like a frontier store-front in an old western
It might have nothing behind it but thin air,
Building materials, fruit boxes, scrap iron,
10   Dust-laden shrubs and coils of rusty wire,
A cabbage white fluttering in the sodden
Silence of an untended kitchen garden—

Nirvana! But the cracked panes reveal a dark
Interior echoing with the cries of children.
15   Here in this quiet corner of Co. Cork
A family ate, slept, and watched the rain

16: Mahon likely has in mind the work of Jan Steen (1626–1679), known for his lively and realistic depictions of everyday life, as in his painting *The World Upside-Down* (1663).
20: *esurient*: hungry

11: *cabbage white*: a type of butterfly whose caterpillars eat cabbage leaves

Dance clean and cobalt the exhausted grit
So that the mind shrank from the glare of it.

Where did they go? South Boston? Cricklewood?
20 Somebody somewhere thinks of this as home,
Remembering the old pumps where they stood,
Antique now, squirting juice into a chrome
Lagonda or a dung-caked tractor while
A cloud swam on a cloud-reflecting tile.

25 Surely a whitewashed sun-trap at the back
Gave way to hens, wild thyme, and the first few
Shadowy yards of an overgrown cart track,
Tyres in the branches such as Noah knew—
Beyond, a swoop of mountain where you heard,
30 Disconsolate in the haze, a single blackbird.

Left to itself, the functional will cast
A death-bed glow of picturesque abandon.
The intact antiquities of the recent past,
Dropped from the retail catalogues, return
35 To the materials that gave rise to them
And shine with a late sacramental gleam.

A god who spent the night here once rewarded
Natural courtesy with eternal life—
Changing to petrol pumps, that they be spared
40 For ever there, an old man and his wife.
The virgin who escaped his dark design
Sanctions the townland from her prickly shrine.

We might be anywhere but are in one place only,
One of the milestones of earth-residence
45 Unique in each particular, the thinly
Peopled hinterland serenely tense—
Not in the hope of a resplendent future
But with a sure sense of its intrinsic nature.

             1982

19: Both *Boston* and *Cricklewood* (an area of the London borough of Brent) have large populations of Irish origin.

23: *Lagonda:* an older British make of luxury saloon car

37ff: Ovid's *Metamorphoses* includes the story of Philemon and Baucis, a poor Phrygian couple who unknowingly entertained the disguised gods Zeus and Hermes, after the gods had been turned away by their rich neighbours. As a reward, they were saved from a flood that drowned the rest of the country, and their dwelling turned into a temple of which they became priest and priestess. They were granted their request that they die at the same time, being transformed into intertwining trees.

41: These lines perhaps allude loosely to the tale, also told in Ovid, of the virgin nymph Daphne; pursued by the god Apollo, she prayed to the river-god Peneus for deliverance and was transformed into a laurel tree.

ANDREW CROZIER (b. 1943)

CROZIER'S POETRY HAS BEEN INFLUENCED BY AN ENGLISH ROMANTIC TRADITION beginning with Wordsworth and Coleridge and moving up to writers of the 1940s, such as W. S. Graham and J. F. Hendry. It has equally been influenced by the American modernist poetry of William Carlos Williams, George Oppen, and Charles Olson. In its rejection of a neo-Platonic understanding of "forms" and a discourse of "ecology," which reveals our remoteness from the non-human world as it tries to remedy it, "The Veil Poem" seems partly informed by Olson's manifesto "Against Wisdom As Such." There Olson argues against an abstracted or reified understanding of wisdom "as such" and for a more "proper use of wisdom" as a "way of being or acting."[1] From the lines below the title where Crozier declares the poem's first section unfinished, to the poem's last lines, where "The dust beneath my / fingernails is all the wisdom I have / to take with me upstairs to my wife," Crozier's emphasis is on process and discovery. The domestic interiors of the poem and its sense of the world as simultaneously resistant to human understanding and available to be seen anew are typical of his work. Crozier's is a poetry repulsed by egotistical views of the self and language, profoundly democratic in its implications, as the last lines of "The Life Class" indicate: "Nothing is to be the sign / of a separate history. What is read out is the quality / of everyone's personal knowledge."[2] Edward Larissey notes how life "conceived as a process not to be arrogantly segmented by the ego" has a "stylistic correlative in Crozier's fondness for unpunctuated flows, in which one is constantly discovering new qualifications of preceding statements and is frequently uncertain of the precise interrelationship of the array of clauses."[3] It is as if the meditative syntax of Wordsworth's *The Prelude* had been accelerated and made nearly seamless.

Educated at Cambridge, Essex, and SUNY-Buffalo, Crozier teaches at the University of Sussex. In the 1960s, he founded the small but influential journal *The English Intelligencer*. He is also the founder of Ferry Press and, with Tim Longville, co-editor of *A Various Art* (1987), an anthology collecting thirteen English poets, including Anthony Barnett, Roy Fisher, J. H. Prynne, and John Riley. Among Crozier's volumes of poetry are *Loved Litter of Time Spent* (1967), *Walking on Grass* (1969), *Pleats* (1975), *High Zero* (1978), and a collected poems, *All Where Each Is* (1985). Crozier has published essays on George Oppen, Carl Rakosi, Roy Fisher, Donald

---

[1] "Against Wisdom as Such"(1954), Charles Olson, *Collected Prose,* ed. Donald Allen and Benjamin Friedlander, Berkeley, 1997, p. 262.
[2] *All Where Each Is,* London, 1985, p. 139.
[3] "Poets of *A Various Art:* J. H. Prynne, Veronica Forrest-Thomson, Andrew Crozier," *Contemporary British Poetry: Essays in Theory and Criticism,* ed. James Acheson and Romana Huk, Albany, 1996, p. 77.

Davie, the New Apocalypse, and recent British poetry. He edited a collection of
Rakosi's early poems and John Rodker's *Poems and Adolphe 1920* (1996).

The Veil Poem

FOR JEFFREY MORSMAN

0   (LEFT UNFINISHED

The garden clenched like a root, bare branches
evergreens, dry leaves, winter grass
quiet and still apart from the activity of birdlife
blackbird on the crazy paving, thrushes under the
5   hedge, two pigeons taken up in space
sparrows on every bush and twig

　　　　　　The light these days lasts
for a few hours, though here is no
yellow candle-light, and the storm I hear wind and rain
10   raging is an effect of bathwater
emptying into the drain outside or an electric motor
turning in the railway cutting down the road
the train that will take you into the city
through morning twilight and damp mists

1

15   In the dark there is a fretwork
that reveals a lightness beside it, gradually
a tree stands out from the hedge and
the rest of the garden, the sky lightens
and bleeds off at the edges, quite sharp
20   but not definite, the blueness has the frequency
of space and there is nothing else but whatever
has brought this tree here, quite taut
but flowing smoothly through its changes
I know it again and again and see how
25   set in one place as it is and small and
fragile I cannot dominate it, in the dark
or with my eyelids closed it will score
my face. Along a bright corridor the way
turns or is transected and is lost
30   in shadow, framed by a black latticed screen
its light foreshortened, lacking
depth. There is no radiant source within
these walls, they hold the sunlight to
define their intricate arcing.

2

35   What hides in darkness and what truths
it veils. Which side of these doors am I?

This arch might be the sky that bends over us
beneath which is our home, it is a wall
and outer skin beyond which we expire
40   like the breeze at evening. Let the wall be outside
for a change, my mind strangely free
amid this darkness. It has placed me
within these doors, they can have no secrets
from me any more. Though my judgement may falter
45   my feet are firmly placed and I can
walk with certainty, the cuts on my forehead will
heal easily, leaving no scars.

3

In nature everything, we suppose, connects up
with everything else, yet this garden
50   is no natural symbol but one of a series
a complex system displaying a process
which is its own symbol when the people
off the train come out their back doors
to potter about. They do this
55   at weekends or in the evening when it begins
to draw out, the struggle of what is light and
what dark seen thus to advantage in a
domestic, backyard setting. How nature
disguises herself, how like a woman, she has
60   turned from her solitary way, withholding
a unique gift of truth. For the hermetic
correspondence of forms hidden beneath appearance
we substitute the ideal market of ecology
gross and substantial. Though we would rob nature
65   of her profusion this arch the roof of the world
echoes prodigally down the corridor, its facings rendered
an exactly repeated tracery of magic in
cardinal numbers, at each diurnal arc
a hanging lamp mimics our sun.

4

70   Bend back the edges and pull what you see
into a circle. The ground you stand on
becomes an arc, the horizon another
each straight line swells out
leaving no single point at rest except

61ff: The *Hermetica* are a set of occult and alchemical writings attributed to the Egyptian god Thoth (Hermes Trismegistos ["Thrice-Greatest"]); they in fact date from the first to third centuries AD. "In a hermetic / magical view, the whole soul of the universe is expressed in each particle of it. . . . In hermetic doctrine—that shared by Henry and Thomas Vaughan, for example—earthly forms are drawn by magnetic sympathy towards their like, that is, to similar energic forces in the cosmos, as the morning cockerel is drawn to greet the sun because the sun's fire is in its spirit and its colouring in its feathers." (Douglas Oliver, "Andrew Crozier's Perceptions", *fragmente* 8 [Summer 1998]: 107–17, pp. 108–109)
67: *tracery*: ornamental openwork on walls or the arches of vaults, as in Gothic or Moorish architecture
68: *cardinal numbers*: numbers indicating quantity (1, 2, 3 . . .), rather than sequential order (1st, 2nd, 3rd . . .)

75　　where the pitch of your very uprightness
　　　bisects the projection of your focal plane.
　　　Here at the centre of every intersecting circle
　　　each infinite yet wholly itself
　　　whichever way you turn a way is offered
80　　for you to carry yourself, its knowledge
　　　will inundate you unless it is held
　　　along every inch of your skin, shaped as
　　　the grace you make for yourself. The starlings
　　　are all in place on the lawn, scattering
85　　up and down for little things, they rise
　　　in flight or plant their beaks into the earth.

5

　　　The coals in the stove glow red
　　　and heat the room. They settle slowly
　　　into themselves and something slips . . .
90　　You should never stop. The fire
　　　needs making up and I look round
　　　for a way out of the impasse.
　　　Colonnaded in a game of blind man's buff
　　　archways jostle on every side. I am
95　　here. Where are they? Which way
　　　am I beckoned, must I turn to find
　　　sanctuary, the arch which my eyes hide
　　　beyond another arch until I seek it out
　　　at the side or from a distance. I see it now
100　　barred by a line of small red triangles.

6

　　　I stand before the last arch, which makes
　　　a small enclosure with a rug and
　　　hangings and windows glazed with
　　　crumbling sunlight. The colours are black
105　　and gold and red, evening and dawn
　　　and when I close my eyes against them
　　　I see their pale capillary tracings.
　　　I am there, shaky, overwhelmed by
　　　the sense of it, piece mating to
110　　piece: blood, shit, and pus.

7

　　　The wind blows around the house
　　　and down the chimney, at night
　　　we are safe from it indoors yet it is

76: *focal plane:* "Where the straight lines connecting focal points are all on the same plane, i.e., a photo-
　　graphic film or plate; but more likely derived from reading on perspectival optics at this date than pho-
　　tography. . . . Here projected as field of vision when one is standing upright, and disregarding rapid eye
　　movement, hence 'no single point at rest'. If you want to visualise this imagine the cross-sights in a gun-
　　sight, & the gunner's concentration." (Crozier, in correspondence).
107: *capillary:* of the fine capillary veins of the eyelids

the same wind that briskly blew
115   the hair into our eyes this afternoon.
Yet it is not the same and never ends
Wisdom and Spirit of the Universe!
Thou Soul that art the Eternity of thought!
And giv'st to forms and images a breath
120   And everlasting motion! There is never
a last thing while we hold others
to us, this page, this carpet, this
green. You may walk in it until
you know each braided inch or let your eye
125   dwell on it till it reads itself, it is
as the green still springs up under
foot that you realise how the
illusions and transformations of magic
are different from birth and death.
130   There is always a page or carpet beyond
the arch, not hidden, green to the touch.

8

The electric light over the gateway
will show where you are. You
announce yourself on the bell-pull.
135   No special favour can be revealed here
beneath an arch which breaks off
against the edge of the sky. This is
the ordinary world, naturally incomplete and
in no wise to be verbally separated
140   from your picture of it. For words
are the wise men's counters, they do but
reckon with them, but they are the money
of fools. What you have come to say
no one can tell, you are wise
145   after your own knowledge and
the judgements you make. What wisdom there is
in the way you set it down, what else but
grace taken with you can carry you
back from the desert.

9

150   What I know has day by day
been drawn to me, and in my
sleep are drawn the images
which carry me forward to another day.
Vessel and vehicle, around one common model
155   we take and are taken, green all our
life long. Where we live would be
white in the sunlight, but is hemmed round
by our proper colour, and pressing in on

117ff: *Wisdom and Spirit* . . . : Wordsworth, *The Prelude* (1850) 1.401–4
140ff: *For words* . . . : from Thomas Hobbes' *Leviathan* (1651), I.iv ("Of Speech").

it too are the sea and the sky.
160 How can I know anything so grand
but from a postcard, not the tasteful
transcript of some old artifact but
the thing seen for the first time, banal and
awful as any literal image. The fire must
165 be banked down round a smouldering core
to keep in till morning. The dust beneath my
fingernails is all the wisdom I have
to take with me upstairs to my wife.

1972 / 1974

TOM LEONARD (b. 1944)

In "The Locust Tree in Flower, and why it had Difficulty Flowering in Britain" (1976), Leonard says that for many in Britain "If a piece of writing can't comfortably be read aloud in a 'correct' (Received Pronunciation) voice, then there must be something wrong with it. . . . And this might not merely apply to the grammar of the writing, but the semantic content as well: since the standard pronunciation, having to be bought, is the property of the propertied classes, then only such content as these classes do not find disagreeable can be 'correct.' "[1] As models for his own poetry, famous for its use of an orthography suggesting the speech of Glasgow's working class, Leonard has looked to William Carlos Williams, whom he honors in "Jist ti Let Yi No," written after Williams's. "This Is Just to Say." Beyond Williams, Leonard mentions as influences the early vernacular poems and concrete poetry of Ian Hamilton Finlay and the sound poetry of Bob Cobbing. These models indicate something of Leonard's range; there is much beyond the vernacular in his poems, including an emphasis on visual presentation and punning. "The Good Thief" is an early example of Leonard's orthography functioning at levels other than the mimetic: the phrase "ma right insane" is an idiomatic way of saying "Am I right in saying [. . . .]?" but the presence of the word "insane" impacts our sense of the poem. The poem sets the crucifixion in Glasgow at 3 P.M., the hour when football matches between the Catholic-supported Glasgow Celtic club and the Protestant-supported Glasgow Rangers typically take place, at a field nicknamed "Paradise." "A Priest Came on at Merkland Street" uses a more conventional orthography but shows some of the other tendencies the Scottish poet-critic Edwin Morgan has discussed in noting Leonard's interest in "the dramatic monologue, applied particularly to political subjects" and an "element of humor, sometimes fantastic and sometimes moderately black . . . and a recurring deadpan strangeness."[2]

Leonard was born in Glasgow and educated at Lourdes Secondary School and Glasgow University. He has worked a variety of mainly clerical jobs and been writer-in-residence at Glasgow and Strathclyde universities and Bell College of Technology. Many of the poems and essays from his early pamphlets and books are gathered in *Intimate Voices: Selected Work 1965–1983* (1984). More recent work can be found in *Reports from the Present: Selected Poetry and Prose 1982–1994* (1995) and in *Etruscan Reader V* (with Bill Griffiths and Tom Raworth, 1997). He has also published a biography of James ("B. V.") Thomson, *Places of the Mind* (1993). He lives in Glasgow.

---

[1] *Intimate Voices 1965–1983,* 1984 p. 96.
[2] *Contemporary Poets,* 6th ed., ed. Thomas Riggs, New York, 1996, p. 629.

Six Glasgow Poems

(1) THE GOOD THIEF

heh jimmy
yawright ih
stull wayiz urryi
ih

5   heh jimmy
ma right insane yirra pape
ma right insane yirwanny us jimmy
see it nyir eyes
wanny uz

10   heh

heh jimmy
lookslik wirgonny miss thi gemm
gonny miss thi GEMM jimmy
nearly three a cloke thinoo

15   dork init
good jobe theyve gote thi lights

(2) SIMPLE SIMON

thirteen bluddy years wi thim ih
no even a day aff
jiss gee im thi fuckin heave
weeks noatiss nur nuthin
5   gee im thi heave
thats aw

ahll tellyi sun
see if ah wiz Scot Symon
ahd tell thim wherrty stuff thir team

Title: *The Good Thief:* "The author was brought up to believe that Christ died on the cross promptly at three p.m. on Good Friday. Three p.m. is also usually the time at which football matches start. In Glasgow, Catholics generally support Glasgow Celtic, while Protestants generally support Glasgow Rangers. The Good Thief is therefore assumed to be a Celtic supporter, who addresses Christ shortly before 3 o'clock, as darkness descends on the earth. The reason for assuming that the Good Thief was a Celtic supporter is because Christ said to him, 'This night thou shalt be with me in Paradise'—and 'Paradise' is the nickname for Celtic's football ground." (Leonard's note from *Poems* [1973])

3: "still wi[th] us are you?"

6: "am I right in saying you're a Pape [Catholic]?"

12: *gemm:* game

14: *thinoo:* now

16: *lights:* i.e., floodlights. Darkness fell over the land when Christ was crucified.

3: *jiss gee:* just give

8: *Scot Symon:* manager of Glasgow Rangers from 1954 to 1967: he was sacked without warning.

10   thi hole fuckin lota thim
thats right

a bluddy skandal thats whit it iz
a bluddy skandal

sicken yi

(3) COLD, ISN'T IT

wirraw init thigithir missyz
geezyir kross

(4) A SCREAM

yi mist yirsell so yi did
we aw skiptwirr ferz njumptaffit thi lights
YIZIR AW PINE THEY FERZ THIMORRA
o it wizza scream
5   thaht big shite wiz dayniz nut

tellnyi jean
we wirraw shoutn backit im
rrose shoutit shi widny puhllit furra penshin
o yi shooda seeniz face
10   hi didny no wherrty look

thing iz tay
thirz nay skool thimorra
thi daft kunt wullny even getiz bluddy ferz

(5) THE MIRACLE OF THE BURD AND THE FISHES

ach sun
jiss keepyir chin up
dizny day gonabootlika hawf shut knife
inaw jiss cozzy a burd

5   luvur day yi
ach well

2: "gi[ve] us your cross"

1: *ye missed yirsell:* you missed some fun
2: "we all skipped our fares and jumped off at the lights"
3: "YOU[SE] ARE ALL PAYING THO[SE] FARES TOMORROW"
5: *dayiz nut:* "doing his nut" (going nuts)
8: *shi widny puhllit furra penshin:* "she wouldn't pull it for a pension"
11: *thing iz tay:* "[the] thing is, too"
13: *kunt:* a "cunt" in Glasgow idiom may be a person of either sex.

3: "going about like a half-shut knife": mooning about, going about disconsolately
4: "and all just 'cause of a bird [a woman]"
5: "love her, do you?"

gee it a wee while sun
thirz a loat merr fish in thi sea

(6) GOOD STYLE

helluva hard tay read theez init
stull
if yi canny unnirston thim jiss clear aff then
gawn
5   get tay fuck ootma road

ahmaz goodiz thi lota yiz so ah um
ah no whit ahm dayn
tellnyi
jiss try enny a yir fly patir wi me
10   stick thi bootnyi good style
so ah wull

1969

A Priest Came on at Merkland Street

A very thoughtful poem, being a canonical penance for sufferers of
psychosomatic asthma.

oh no
holy buttons
sad but dignified
and sitting straight across from me
5   a troubled soul
my son
christ
a bit of Mahler's Seventh might drown him
dah dum, da dum dah dee,
10   dah dah dah DAH da dah
da DAH, dah DEE da da da
DUM DUM dah dee
hello there
when I'm dead
15   when I think I'm dead
and I'm in my box
and it's all dark
and I'm wondering where the air's coming from
I'll see this curtain
20   and it will move to the side
and your great horrible leering face
how many times my son
and how long ago was this

Good Style: 4: *gawn:* go on
9: *fly:* clever, sly

bless me father for I am tinned
25 christ
maybe he's saying hail mary's
maybe he's praying for all the souls in purgatory
and really sincere
the nicest man in the world
30 he really loves people
hello father
I'm going to give you a smile
I'm going to give you the nicest smile in the world
it will be real love
35 there will be absolutely no sex
we will both be five years old
and we'll go to school together
play at weekends together
and you'll climb inside my box
40 laughing
lying together in the dark
innocent as hell
like after lights out in a school dormitory
cosy but exciting
45 and maybe God will look round the curtain
hello there
softly as God would say it
and we'll all go away together
away through his door
50 for ever
amen
I always spoil it
but maybe you'd spoil it yourself
maybe you wouldn't be five years old at all
55 and you'd climb inside my box
a troubled soul
my son
with a keyhole in your back
wind me up in the morning
60 and a button under your right arm
how many times my son
and a button under your left arm
how long ago was this
and a button in the back of your head
65 press to bless
and a tape recorder between your ears
from henceforth ye shall catch men
from henceforth ye shall catch men
from henceforth ye shall catch men
70 dah dum, da dum dah dee,
oh no
you won't catch me
maybe I'll be really dead
as dead as everyone else who has died
75 just lying in a box

67: *from henceforth ye shall catch men*: Christ's words to the apostles (Luke 5:10)

a box that somebody's made
a box for dead people
and I won't even know
christ
80   my name is Ozymandias
king of Leithland Road
Pollok
Glasgow SW3
and all the worrying
85   all the wanting to be five years old
imagine
the lone and level
far away
amen
90   only it's not the lone and level at all
for there's the Lansdowne Clinic for Functional Nervous Disorders
and the Southern General Hospital Department of Psychological Medicine
and Leverndale formerly known as Hawkhead Mental Asylum
I could write to a psychiatrist
95   a cry from the heart
dear sir
my name is Ozymandias
king of Leithland Road
and then there's the box
100   yours sincerely
maybe faithfully would be better
you know who
ps
I always spoil it
105   pps
I am awful lonely
ppps
I don't know what people are for
oh no
110   maybe I think about the box too much
maybe nobody else thinks about the box at all
at least not for long
not more than five minutes a day
or maybe ten minutes at the weekend
115   and that's all they need
they usually think about something else
they think about something else for hours on end
maybe I should do the same
I could draw up a plan
120   I could draw up a list of things to think about
everything but the box
and I'd think about them all day
I wouldn't think about the box at all
and then I'd go away home at night
125   and I'd have my tea
oxtail soup
a plate of potatoes and mince

80: *my name is Ozymandias*: cf. Shelley's sonnet "Ozymandias"

<pre>
            two slices of toasted cheese
            and a cup of tea
130   that would be fine
            that would be very nice indeed
            and then I'd go upstairs to my room
            and I'd sit down at the table
            and I'd write it out twenty times
135   I am going to die
            imagine
            maybe I'd get up in the morning
            with a big smile
            and I'd throw open the bedroom windows
140   hello there
            I have accepted the box
            I have accepted that I am going to die
            oh no
            maybe it wouldn't work at all
145   maybe I would just stay the same way for years
            just thinking about something else all day
            not thinking about the box at all
            and then just going away home at night
            just having my tea
150   just a cup of tea
            maybe a bun
            sad as hell
            wanting to be five years old
            christ
155   maybe I would tear up my plan
            maybe I would tear up my list of things to think about
            and I'd just go upstairs to my room
            away through my door
            for ever
160   with no button under my right arm
            I am going to die
            and no button under my left arm
            I am going to die
            and no button in the back of my head
165   I am going to die
            but a tape recorder between my ears
            I am going to die
            I am going to die
            I am going to die
170   dear Ozymandias
            there is nothing wrong with you at all
            my name is Ozymandias two
            correction
            my name is Ozymandias too
175   we are all in the box toogether
            correction
            we are all in the box twogether
            correction
            we are all in the box together
180   only indifferent ones
            sorry
            only in different ones
</pre>

yours sincerely
you know whoo
185   correction
you know whwo
correction
you know who
correction
190   "You Know Who"
imagine
maybe there's nothing wrong with me at all
maybe I'm just the same as everyone else who has lived
and I'll just put on a smile at the box
195   I'll just put on the nicest smile in the world
and a bit of Mahler's Seventh might drown it
dah dum, da dum dah dee,
dah dah dah DAH da dee
correction
200   da da da DAH da da
correction
dah dah dah DAH da dah
tick tock
tick
205   oh no
tick tock
tick
hello there
tick tock
210   tick
hello there everybody
tick tock
tick

tick tock
215   tick

tick tock
tick

     brackets watch him he has a stoop and funny eyes

                                                                 1970

CRAIG RAINE (b. 1944)

Raine's first two books of poetry, *The Onion, Memory* (1978) and *A Martian Sends a Postcard Home* (1979), made him one of the most celebrated poets of his generation. The title of his second book led reviewers, beginning with James Fenton, to identify Raine and Christopher Reid as members of a "Martian school" of poetry. The term points to their use of metaphor as a defamiliarizing device; the description of a vacuum cleaner as a grazing cow at the beginning of "An Enquiry into Two Inches of Ivory" is one example of the technique that spawned the label. "A Martian Sends a Postcard Home" might be read as extending the ancient genre of the riddle, and it also suggests one rationale for Raine's style; to imagine how a telephone would be viewed from the perspective of a "Martian" is to suggest the strangeness of the ordinary. Admiring critics have also linked Raine's techniques to those of predecessors such as John Donne, but the quirky premise of "A Martian Sends a Postcard Home" partakes as much of the ethos of television as of metaphysical poetry. Ian Gregson argues that Raine's "playfulness and wit—even in the face of solemn subject-matter, is most accurately defined by reference to the carnivalesque," remembering Raine's admiration for James Joyce's *Ulysses* and noting that his poems bring the sacred and the profane into close proximity.[1] Discussing the book-length poem *History: The Home Movie* (1994), Gregson argues that Raine is "in the company of satirists who have subverted human pretensions . . . [and is] in the broadest sense, a comic writer—he calls human values into question in order to reveal which are worth affirming."[2] Other books include *A Free Translation* (1981), *Rich* (1984), and *Clay. Whereabouts Unknown* (1996), which explores Raine's spiritual education. He has also written a libretto, *The Electrification of the Soviet Union* (1986) and a play, *"1953"* (1990).

Raine was born in Shildon, County Durham, and educated at Barnard Castle and Exeter College, Oxford. In the 1970s, he held several appointments as a lecturer at different colleges at Oxford and also worked as a freelance journalist. He co-edited *Quarto* in 1980 and was the poetry editor of the *New Statesman* in 1981. From 1981 to 1991, he was the poetry editor at Faber and Faber, returning to Oxford to teach in October 1991.

[1] *Contemporary Poetry and Postmodernism*, New York, 1996, p. 34.
[2] Ibid., p. 34.

An Enquiry into Two Inches of Ivory

We live in the great indoors:
the vacuum cleaner grazes
over the carpet, lowing,
its udder a swollen wobble . . .

5   At night, the switches stare
from every wall like flat-faced
barn-owls, and light ripens
the electric pear.

Esse is percipi—Berkeley knew
10   the gentle irony of objects, how
they told amusing lies and drew laughter,
if only we believed our eyes.

Daily things. Objects
in the museum of ordinary art.
15   Two armless Lilliputian queens
preside, watching a giant bathe.
He catches the slippery cubist fish
with perfumed eggs. Another
is a yogi on the scrubbing brush.
20   Water painlessly breaks his bent
Picasso legs.

Clothes queue up in the wardrobe,
an echo to the eye, or a jangle of Euclid.
The wall-phone wears a pince-nez
25   even in the dark—the flex
is Jewish orthodox.

Day begins.
The milkman delivers
penguins with their chinking atonal fuss.
30   Cups commemorate the War
of Jenkins' Ear.
Without thinking, the giant
puts a kettle on the octopus.

1978

Title: See Jane Austen's letter of 16 Dec. 1816 to her nephew Edward: "What should I do with your strong, manly, spirited sketches, full of variety and glow? How could I possibly join them on to the little bit (two inches wide) of ivory on which I work with so fine a brush, as produces little effect after much labour?"

9: *Esse is percipi:* "to be is to be perceived"; the philosopher George *Berkeley* (1685–1753) held that everything (save the spiritual) exists only insofar as it is perceived.

23: *a jangle of Euclid:* i.e., like a complicated diagram from a geometrical proof from Euclid's *Elements*.

25–26: The garments of Orthodox Jews are ornamented with tassels known as *tzitzit*.

30–31: *the War / of Jenkins' Ear:* a war between Britain and Spain that began in 1739, having been precipitated by an incident involving one Captain Robert Jenkins: his ear was cut off by Spanish coast guards when they boarded and pillaged his ship in the West Indies.

A Martian Sends a Postcard Home

Caxtons are mechanical birds with many wings
and some are treasured for their markings—

they cause the eyes to melt
or the body to shriek without pain.

5   I have never seen one fly, but
sometimes they perch on the hand.

Mist is when the sky is tired of flight
and rests its soft machine on ground:

then the world is dim and bookish
10   like engravings under tissue paper.

Rain is when the earth is television.
It has the property of making colours darker.

Model T is a room with the lock inside—
a key is turned to free the world

15   for movement, so quick there is a film
to watch for anything missed.

But time is tied to the wrist
or kept in a box, ticking with impatience.

In homes, a haunted apparatus sleeps,
20   that snores when you pick it up.

If the ghost cries, they carry it
to their lips and soothe it to sleep

with sounds. And yet, they wake it up
deliberately, by tickling with a finger.

25   Only the young are allowed to suffer
openly. Adults go to a punishment room

with water but nothing to eat.
They lock the door and suffer the noises

alone. No one is exempt
30   and everyone's pain has a different smell.

At night, when all the colours die,
they hide in pairs

and read about themselves—
in colour, with their eyelids shut.

                                                                          1979

1: *Caxtons:* i.e., books: William Caxton (1422–1491) was the first English printer.
13: The *Model T* was Ford's most popular model in the early part of the twentieth century.

EAVAN BOLAND (b. 1944)

BOLAND'S FATHER WAS A DIPLOMAT, AND AFTER BEING BORN IN DUBLIN SHE SPENT PART of her childhood in London and New York. She received a degree in English literature from Trinity College, Dublin, where she has also been writer-in-residence. She has taught at University College-Dublin and several universities in the United States, most recently at Stanford, where she teaches one quarter a year while continuing to maintain a permanent residence in suburban Dublin. Among Irish women poets, Boland is the most widely known in North America, both for her poems and for essays criticizing the masculinist traditions of Irish poetry, in which, as she has written, women have been represented as "figments of national expression": "The idea of the defeated nation being reborn as a triumphant woman was central to a certain kind of Irish poem. Dark Rosaleen. Cathleen ni Houlihan. The nation as woman; the woman as national muse."[1] Before Boland and women contemporaries such as the Irish-language poet Nuala Ní Dhomhnaill started publishing, Irish poetry was largely dominated by men, though there were women poets earlier in the century writing in Revival and post-Revival modes, including Mary Devenport O'Neill, Blanaid Salkeld, and Rhoda Coghill: "As far as I was concerned, it was the absence of women in the poetic tradition which allowed women in the poems to be simplified. The voice of a woman poet would, I was sure, have precluded such distortion. It did not exist."[2] Boland turned to American poets such as Adrienne Rich and Sylvia Plath for models; the latter's influence is evident here in "The Woman Turns Herself into a Fish," in which heightened sound effects underscore the speaker's self-denying objectification of her body. Many of Boland's poems explore women's domestic experience and desires; others, like "Listen. This is the Noise of Myth," directly address the distortions perpetuated by the poetry of the past. The title of Boland's sequence "Outside History," from which "In Exile" is taken, might be read as referring to the absence of women from the historical record or as naming a poetry that presents narratives "outside" or beyond those typical of historiographical writing. In the last poem of this elegiac and partly autobiographical sequence, Boland writes that "out of myth into history I move to be / part of that ordeal / whose darkness is / only now reaching me from those fields, those rivers, those roads clotted as / firmaments with the dead."[3] Among Boland's many books of poetry are *New Territory* (1967), *The War Horse* (1975), *In Her Own Image* (1980), *Night Feed* (1982), *The Journey* (1987), *Outside History* (1990), and *Collected Poems* (1995).

---

[1] Quoted in Patricia Boyle Haberstroh, *Women Creating Women: Contemporary Irish Women Poets,* Syracuse, 1996, p. 79.
[2] Ibid., p. 80.
[3] *Outside History,* Manchester, 1990, p. 50.

The Woman Turns Herself into a Fish

Unpod
the bag,
the seed.

Slap
5   the flanks back.
Flatten

paps.
Make finny
scaled

10   and chill
the slack
and dimple

of the rump.
Pout
15   the mouth,

brow the eyes
and now
and now

eclipse
20   in these hips,
these loins

the moon,
the blood
flux.

25   It's done.
I turn,
I flab upward

blub-lipped,
hipless
30   and I am

sexless,
shed
of ecstasy,

a pale
35   swimmer,
sequin-skinned,

pearling eggs
screamlessly
in seaweed.

40   It's what
        I set my heart on.
        Yet

        ruddering
        and muscling
45   in the sunless tons

        of new freedoms,
        still
        I feel

        a chill pull,
50   a brightening,
        a light, a light,

        and how
        in my loomy cold,
        my greens,

55   still
        she moons
        in me.

                                        1982

Listen. This is the Noise of Myth

        This is the story of a man and woman
        under a willow and beside a weir
        near a river in a wooded clearing.
        They are fugitives. Intimates of myth.

5   Fictions of my purpose. I suppose
        I shouldn't say that yet or at least
        before I break their hearts or save their lives
        I ought to tell their story and I will.

        When they went first it was winter; cold,
10   cold through the Midlands and as far West
        as they could go. They knew they had to go—
        through Meath, Westmeath, Longford,

        their lives unravelling like the hours of light—
        and then there were lambs under the snow
15   and it was January, aconite and jasmine
        and the hazel yellowing and puce berries on the ivy.

10: The *West* of Ireland is its most rural and poorest area. The progress in line 12 is in a westerly direction
starting from *Meath* in the northeast.
15: *aconite:* winter aconite, a variety of buttercup

They could not eat where they had cooked,
nor sleep where they had eaten
nor at dawn rest where they had slept.
20   They shunned the densities

of trees with one trunk and of caves
with one dark and the dangerous embrace
of islands with a single landing place.
And all the time it was cold, cold:

25   the fields still gardened by their ice,
the trees stitched with snow overnight,
the ditches full; frost toughening lichen,
darning lace into rock crevices.

And then the woods flooded and buds
30   blunted from the chestnut and the foxglove
put its big leaves out and chaffinches
chinked and flirted in the branches of the ash.

And here we are where we started from—
under a willow and beside a weir
35   near a river in a wooded clearing.
The woman and the man have come to rest.

Look how light is coming through the ash.
The weir sluices kingfisher blues.
The woman and the willow tree lean forward, forward.
40   Something is near; something is about to happen;

something more than Spring
and less than history. Will we see
hungers eased after months of hiding?
Is there a touch of heat in that light?

45   If they stay here soon it will be summer; things
returning, sunlight fingering minnowy deeps,
seedy greens, reeds, electing lights
and edges from the river. Consider

legend, self-deception, sin, the sum
50   of human purposes and its end; remember
how our poetry depends on distance,
aspect: gravity will bend starlight.

Forgive me if I set the truth to rights.
Bear with me if I put an end to this:
55   She never turned to him; she never leaned
under the sallow-willow over to him.

They never made love; not there; not here;
not anywhere; there was no winter journey;

56: *sallow-willow:* a type of low-growing willow

no aconite, no birdsong and no jasmine,
60   no woodland and no river and no weir.

Listen. This is the noise of myth. It makes
the same sound as shadow. Can you hear it?
Daylight greys in the preceptories.
Her head begins to shine

65   pivoting the planets of a harsh nativity.
They were never mine. This is mine.
This sequence of evicted possibilities.
Displaced facts. Tricks of light. Reflections.

Invention. Legend. Myth. What you will.
70   The shifts and fluencies are infinite.
The moving parts are marvellous. Consider
how the bereavements of the definite

are easily lifted from our heroine.
She may or she may not. She was or wasn't
75   by the water at his side as dark
waited above the Western countryside.

O consolations of the craft.
How we put
the old poultices on the old sores,
80   the same mirrors to the old magic. Look.

The scene returns. The willow sees itself
drowning in the weir and the woman
gives the kiss of myth her human heat.
Reflections. Reflections. He becomes her lover.

85   The old romances make no bones about it.
The long and short of it. The end and the beginning.
The glories and the ornaments are muted.
And when the story ends the song is over.

1986

63: A *preceptory* is a building housing a community of the Knights Templars, a medieval religious military
order of knighthood.

from Outside History

9: In Exile

The German girls who came to us that winter and
the winter after and who helped my mother fuel
the iron stove and arranged our clothes in wet
thicknesses on the wooden rail after tea was over,

5   spoke no English, understood no French. They were
sisters from a ruined city and they spoke rapidly
in their own tongue: syllables in which pain was
radical, integral; and with what sense of injury

the language angled for an unhurt kingdom—for
10   the rise, curve, kill and swift return to the wrist,
to the hood—I never knew. To me they were the sounds
of evening only, of the cold, of the Irish dark and

continuous with all such recurrences: the drizzle in
the lilac, the dusk always at the back door, like
15   the tinkers I was threatened with, the cat inching
closer to the fire with its screen of clothes, where

I am standing in the stone-flagged kitchen; there are
bleached rags, perhaps, and a pot of tea on the stove.
And I see myself, four years of age and looking up,
20   storing such music—guttural, hurt to the quick—

as I hear now, forty years on and far from where
I heard it first. Among these salt-boxes, marshes and
the glove-tanned colours of the sugar-maples, in
this New England town at the start of winter, I am

25   so much South of it: the soft wet, the light and
those early darks which strengthen the assassin's
hand; and hide the wound. Here, in this scalding air,
my speech will not heal. I do not want it to heal.

1990

10ff: Boland's image is drawn from hawking: the hawk returns to its owner's *wrist* with the kill, after which
   a *hood* is placed over its head.
15: *Tinkers,* like gypsies, were conventional bogeymen with which to threaten misbehaving children.
17: *stone-flagged:* paved with flagstones
22: A *salt-box* is a style of house characteristic of New England, with two stories in front and one in back,
   its roof steeply sloping towards the back.

ALLEN FISHER (b. 1944)

FISHER WAS BORN IN SOUTH LONDON AND EDUCATED AT BATTERSEA GRAMMAR SCHOOL. He worked for eleven years in a lead factory and later as a traveling salesman for a plastics company before beginning formal higher education at the age of 39 at Goldsmiths College in London. He then did graduate work in art history at Essex University. By 1988, when he took a position teaching art at the Hereford School of Art, Fisher had been publishing poems for over two decades. He was part of the Fluxus movement with the groups Fluxshoe and Fluxus England West in the early seventies, and he has been active in years since in painting, performance, and poetry. In 1974, he started his ongoing journal and press Spanner, publishing writers including Dick Higgins and John Cage. William Blake is one model for an integrated artistic activity across artforms, and Blake together with others such as Charles Olson, Joseph Beuys, Jackson Mac Low, Hugh MacDiarmid, Muriel Rukeyser, Ludwig Wittgenstein, and the Situationist theorist Raoul Vaneigem are among the most significant influences on Fisher's poetry. Fisher's eighty-plus pamphlets and books of poetry include those belonging to two sequences or "projects": *Place*, written between 1971 and 1979, and *Gravity as a consequence of shape*, begun in 1982. The *Place* project draws on reading in subjects as diverse as Taoism, catastrophe theory, and the history of London's rivers, but its dominant concerns are ecology, locality, and history, its particular focus London. Charles Olson's open-ended, process-based poetics and use of documentary sources are clearly a resource, but, as Clive Bush has argued, Fisher "rejects the epic hero of Olson's Maximus poems as a trans-cultural and trans-historical figure," substituting for Maximus the citizen of Lambeth, a poor London neighborhood.[1] Individual books are various in their prosodic and generic shapes, *Hooks* (1980) presenting meditation on process and complexity in an "open-field" format, *Unpolished Mirrors* (1985) including the dramatic monologues of fictional and historical characters. *Place Book One* (1974), *Stane: Place Book III* (1977), and *Becoming* (1978) are among the other books that make up *Place*. *Gravity as a consequence of shape* largely abandons the earlier "open-field" prosodies, opting often for narrative and using Blakean, quasi-archetypal figures such as the Engineer, Technician, and Burglar to embody the multiple and overlapping discourses with which meaning and experience are framed. Andrew Lawson describes these often carnivalesque poems as "dense, postmodernist allegories [operating] in a kind of continuous present where sensuous bodily experience merges with an eclectic, theoretical space whose values are polyphony, mobility, dissonance, alternative topologies, ways not so much of seeing ... but of *experiencing* space," adding that "Fisher does not believe in 'a single world',

---

[1] *Out of Dissent: A Study of Five Contemporary British Poets*, London, 1997, p. 103.

reality is composed of multiple paradigms."[2] Among the books of *Gravity* released to date are *Brixton Fractals* (1985), *Civic Crime* (1994), *Dispossession and Cure* (1994), and *Breadboard* (1995). *Scram* (1994) and the anthology *Future Exiles: Three London Poets* (with Bill Griffiths and Brian Catling, 1992) contain a wider sampling of work, including poems not a part of either project.

The range of Fisher's poetic facture is suggested by the distance between the post-objectivist word presentation and conceptual speed of "defamiliarizing _____*: 38" and the idiomatic narrative line and hardboiled persona of "African Mission," from Fisher's sequence "four novels." Fisher has written of "Mummers' Strut" in a lengthy note accompanying its publication in *West Coast Line* 29.2, detailing its "poetic strategy of slow discomposition, disruption of autobiographical voice through the use of many voices, aspiration to multiple and collage form through the pasting of many sources, many spacetimes, and a subversion of collage form through the use of re-narration, a simulation device evident elsewhere in this poet's work." Most of Fisher's aesthetic concerns—an interest in "incompleteness" and in meaning as use—are evident in the poem, which sets political realities and the anxiety produced by information overload against the desire for transcendent knowledge suggested by the "attempt / to see the stars."

---

2 "Life After Larkin: Postmodern British Poetry," *Textual Practice*, vol. 3, no. 3, p. 418.

from four novels

1. African Mission.

Johnny at the end of the table managed to choke back a great
snort of laughter. Perhaps this visit wont last long.
I say to myself, Bull's only Bull. It's an awful like, dear
father. I'm going to get me a real old bag, a squeezed orange
5   everyone's had a bash at.

Duckfoot Johnny made me till I got the tune with enough vigour
and emotion to satisfy him. Let's embroider this produced
little fiction. The chance to get in, wander round a little.
In my opinion what we should do is dance—
10   the only way to create the proper atmosphere for such an occasion.

Certainly I was still asleep. The whole atmosphere was soporific.
I simply stretched and grunted. I told myself I wasn't really
as tired as all that, fundamentally.
Duckfoot Johnny on his stool. Of course you love, how could
15   it be otherwise. A triumph of nature.

Slim, small, high, plump, firm, fragile, healthy
I felt a twinge of shame. It rose so sharply
that it would have knocked my head off
if I hadn't ducked
20   like a flash.

1974

defamiliarising _____*: 38

paint
happens

bar

norm

5   window   glass air

1983

Mummers' Strut

1

A technician turns the radio to
drown screams from neighbours

When the hungry come for food
the dog barks until they go

5   The connection fraught
with stray wires

Before this begins and now
it is bleeding and now the barking

drowns the screams and the
10   hungry have gone.

2

This is out of our range
This is out of our range

This is out of our range
.....

15   This is getting to be
This is getting to be

---

defamiliarising _____*: 38: According to the Russian Formalist literary theorist Viktor Shklovsky (1893–1984), the work of art attempts to lead to fresh perception of the world by disturbing habitual perception via the technique of *ostranenie* ('defamiliarization" or "making strange"). This poem is from a sequence based, Fisher notes, on "the note structure of Brian Ferneyhough's *Time and Motion Study for Bass Clarinet."*

Mummer's Strut: Title: This poem is part of Fisher's *Gravity as a consequence of shape* project, each of whose parts is named after a variety of dance. All numbered endnotes are Fisher's own, integral to the text; the matching notes may be found on p. 719. Fisher's commentary on the making of this poem may be found in *West Coast Line* 17 (Fall 1995).

This is getting to be
.....

I'm a Negative Creep
20   I'm a Negative Creep

I'm a Negative Creep
and I'm stoned[1]

Sometimes it works
and sometimes it doesn't

25   rock
it

begin another grasp
from the inside

rocket

3

30   So much so difficult to take in
Mule driver holds to

a raised path
in case of submersion.

Even as dew drops through
35   a window space the driver

can be seen holding the ropes' natural lubrication.
What was once cracking has become squeak

and then whistle
before the buckles rust.

40   Sodium ions are represented by two children
in the skins of nylon bears

dyed fluorescent blue
or ultramarine cut with steel and oil

Naturalists exchange informations on the relation
45   between bog bush crickets and the sound of dried grass

4

Openness, immediacy, eruptivity

Lability and suddenness

Answer to a boundary situation[2]

47: *Lability*: changeableness; "a further innuendo was laughter, as in 'labial'" (Fisher, in correspondence).

5

50   We marvel at the chemistry of minute flies and butterworts
as plants take up insects and in so doing feed

the insects' offspring in a flower display
stemmed away from the digestion.

6

Outline.
There's no outline

55   There's no such thing
All is Chiaro Scuro Poco Pend and Colouring[3]

7

A dog went over
the water without a wherry

A bone which he had stolen
60   he had in his mouth

As he swam
he saw the reflection

This is getting to me
This is getting to me

65   This is getting to me
.....

I just wanna take off
I just wanna take off

I just wanna take off
70   .....

8

In terms of local conditions

we need people to run it

who are not the enemy

9

The surface tension around
75   a glob of apple juice

49: *butterworts* are carnivorous plants, which trap insects with their sticky leaves.
56: *Poco Pend*: "poco" means "little"; "pend" perhaps suggests "penned."
58: *wherry*: boat

The banquet of smiles
dewy mead and sequester'd shed

Panted, prized, sacrificed
beneath the label from Safeways

80   *English Discovery* and
        For paction[4]

10

Climate no longer an obstacle
In civilised societies technicians are rich

A long story of robbery[5]
85   Wisdom taken from eloquence

Wisdom without eloquence
Without exception

perfection and finish
are unnatural[6]

90   Three lines on a panel
        an exchange between two Technicians

competes sequester'd derision
completes aesthetic decision[7]

The Burglar's postcard reads:
95   *taxis, diathesis, economia*

It is read as combining form into order
with a comprehension of flavours

in the best place
understand sub-atomic and cosmic time-space

100   For the Technician this will provide
        strength, utility and grace[8]

11

Where house is the first idea in building
a first matter of importance becomes load-bearing

this means wall, which leads to column
105   and a grace known as functional beauty[9]

79: *Safeways*: a chain store
80–81: The label indicates the apple's type—"English Discovery"—and that it is "For paction" (a paction
  is an agreement or contract; perhaps the sense is "for trade").
95: *taxis, diathesis, economia*: translated in line 101.

In every poem of truth
The Technician demands fiction

In every resemblance to the real
technique demands some incompleteness

110   Fiction and incompletion constitute the art
that she imitates[10]

Between a vertical face and shadow
there is transition that accentuates reflection

This increases in brightness
115   as it approaches the cosmic torus

It constitutes a reflex, cut by shades and bright lines
it fills up curvature and gives it value[11]

A competing technician projects a cosmos
expressed by a knot

120   characterised by friction
then the invention of nets[12]

                              12

This second Technician weighs empty ornament
against a high voltage cable

balancing between invention and hunger
125   as part of a search for concise form[13]

His eye, trained by what open, seen
tastes by acquaintance with obstinate rigour

He learns what enters through the window
untiringly toward the real

130   To draw from this
a subtle speculation

Fear and desire
to see some miraculous thing[14]

                              13

Introspection refuses to explain
135   the indescribable creation of meaning

The first Technician measures its trembles outside the world
in isolation from its use[15]

115: *cosmic torus*: Fisher notes in the entry for "torus (toroid.)" in *Ideas on the culture dreamed of* (1982)
    that "Andromeda viewed by radiotelescope" is in the shape of "a distorted doughnut."

14

<blockquote>
I buy a handgun at JSL
and next door get some lemon yellow
</blockquote>

140   before I'm banned from using it.
              It's so dull in Marks that a

<blockquote>
walk over the bridge is shot with
brilliance from a gap in the hills
</blockquote>

<blockquote>
edge of the Black Mountains lit
</blockquote>
145   from behind by a reflecting chrome.

15

<blockquote>
Started a new pen
trimming it then
</blockquote>

<blockquote>
a corner of page to try it
"Tell me
</blockquote>

150   "Tell me whether
              "Tell me how things are

<blockquote>
"Tell me if there was
</blockquote>

16

<blockquote>
The Technician stands down from our platform
to propose her limits on intervention
</blockquote>

155   They are characterised by the row—
              organise, assemble and mechanise

<blockquote>
You can achieve with a single machine
the work of several[16]
</blockquote>

17

<blockquote>
Understanding in a flash
</blockquote>
160   the grasp of rules

<blockquote>
her relations between consciousness
and complexity are clear[17]
</blockquote>

18

<blockquote>
She watches yellow brimstones fall from the sky
and turn purple on reaching the lawn
</blockquote>

138: *JSL:* "a gunshop in Church Street, Hereford, next door to the art materials shop. It recently closed and/or moved elsewhere." (Fisher, in correspondence)

141: *Marks:* Marks and Spencer, a clothing and food store chain

144: Part of Wales's *Black Mountains* is visible from Hereford.

165   when the bear trips
        on the sun dial base and

        discovers a silver watch where
        pear thuds tock the ear.

19

        Both technicians have modern literature
170   and several stabilities against

        this civil tradition
        against disease[18]

20

        Their self-consciousness
        of the very notion of a self

175   backflips a misconstrued
        pronoun

21

        Even as dew drops through
        a window space

        With a shudder I feel the stars
180   and name them differently once a day

22

        The line between sense and non-sense
        wider than both the areas it divides

23

        Chains grow in my head
        that pull the universe apart

24

185   The Technician and Burglar met at eleven
        or at least my sleep has been taken and

        I feel wiped out of the spacetime that fits
        a margin just before and after I awoke

in a passage, as the French call it, following
190   *The History of Sexuality,* a silence in which

the cupboard unfolds and the Burglar
who drops the Technician's ruler

leaves by the cat flap door
clutching a jar of birds

25

195   Technician turns the radio to
drown screams from neighbours

when the hungry come for food

26

The Burglar turns back
and becomes critical

200   asks what thought can achieve
under what conditions[19]

27

Shapeless stains

Light trembles

Tomorrow the Technician will
205   make the strap and the attempt[20]

to see the stars.[21]

NOTES

1. Kurt Cobain, fragments from his lyric sung for the Nirvana *Bleach* collection, 1989.
2. Helmuth Plessner. *Laughing and Crying: A Study of the Limits of Human Behavior,* trans. Jane Spencer Churchill and Marjorie Grene (Evanston: Northwestern UP. 1970).
3. William Blake. *Notebooks,* N61.
4. William Cowper. "Ode to Peace."
5. Peter Kropotkin. *The Conquest of Bread,* 1913.
6. Cicero. *De Optimo Genere Oratorum, Topica,* trans. H.M. Hubbell, Loeb Classical Library (London and Cambridge, MA: Heinemann and Harvard UP, 1976).
7. Pliny. *Natural History.* Vol. 9, book 35, trans. H. Rackham. Loeb Classical Library (London and Cambridge, MA: Heinemann and Harvard UP, 1968).

189: "*passage* is the French art historians use to describe Paul Cézanne's colour system. The system is unique to Cézanne (as far as I know). It relates to his method of arriving at a colour that mixes the related pigments, thus a green passage would derive from its proximity to a particular blue and a particular yellow. The word *passage* is useful because Cézanne's method lends itself to leading the eye through the canvas as if following a path through a landscape." (Fisher, in correspondence)

190: *The History of Sexuality* is a multivolume project by the French philosopher and historian Michel Foucault (1926–1984).

8. Vitruvius. *On Architecture*, Vol. 1, book 1, trans. Frank Granger (London and Cambridge, MA: Heinemann and Harvard UP, 1983).
9. G.W.F. Hegel. *Aesthetics: Lectures on Fine Art*, Vol. 2, trans. T.M. Knox (Oxford: Clarendon, 1975).
10. A.C. Quatremère de Quincy. *An Essay on the Nature, the End, and the Means of Imitation in the Fine Arts*, trans. J.C. Kent (1837): facsimile reprint London: 1979.
11. Eugene-Emmanuel Viollet-Le-Duc. *Lectures on Architecture*, vols 2 and 3, trans. Benjamin Bucknall (New York: 1987).
12. Gottfried Semper. *The Four Elements of Architecture and Other Writings*, trans. H.F. Mallgrave and W. Herrmann (Cambridge and New York: Cambridge UP, 1989).
13. Heinrich Tessenow. *House-Building and Such Things*, trans. Wilfred Wang (London: 1989).
14. *The Notebooks of Leonardo Da Vinci.* trans. by Serge Bramly; *Leonardo, The Artist and the Man*, 1988, trans. London 1992.p
15. Anthony Kenny quoting Wittgenstein in *The Legacy of Wittgenstein*, (Oxford: Blackwell, 1984).
16. Leonardo. op. cit. 14.
17. Wittgenstein, op. cit. 15.
18. Hugo von Hofmannsthal. *Buch der Freunde, Tagebuch-Aufzeikhnungen* (1929).
19. Ibid. 15.
20. Leonardo, op. cit. 14.
21. Dante Alighieri. *The Divine Comedy,* Temple Classics (London: Dent, 1909).

1995

TOM PICKARD (b. 1946)

Pickard was born in Newcastle upon Tyne and grew up in Tyneside. He left school at fourteen (though he later spent a year at Ruskin College, Oxford) and worked with a seed merchant, a construction company, and a wine merchant. From 1963 to 1972, he managed the Morden Tower Book Room in Newcastle, a vital regional venue for readings by British, American, and other modernist poets; from 1969 to 1973, he also ran the Ultima Thule Bookshop. Early in his literary career, Pickard served a literary apprenticeship with Basil Bunting, whom he encouraged to begin writing poetry again and who in turn introduced him to the work of American poets such as Louis Zukofsky and Lorine Niedecker. In the late 1960s, Pickard traveled to the United States, solidifying his friendship with poets including Edward Dorn, Allen Ginsberg, and Robert Creeley. In 1973, he moved to London and began writing scripts for radio programs and documentary films, including *The Jarrow March* (1976), which is about the march of the unemployed in London in 1936, *We Make Ships* (1988), *Birmingham Is What I Think With* (1991), and *The Shadow and the Substance* (1994); Pickard also directed the last three of these films. In 1976, he traveled to Warsaw, where he met Joanna Voit, a Polish artist whom he later married; thereafter he divided his time between London and Warsaw before returning to the north of England. He currently lives in Alston, Cumbria. Pickard's books of poems include *High on the Walls* (1968), *The Order of Chance* (1971), *Hero Dust: New and Selected Poems* (1979), *Tiepin Eros: New & Selected Poems* (1994), and *Fuckwind* (1999), the title of which is a sixteenth-century word for kestrel. He has collaborated with musicians including Peter Kirtley and Liane Carroll in recording songs from his most recent book.

Pickard's poems often employ an economical and deft lyricism, their idiom and content drawing on his origins in a working-class community in Northern England. A long poem, "Dancing Under Fire" (1971), owes something to Jungian theories of myth, making use of folk and popular materials and including fragments of songs. Pickard writes that "explanation / obscures the object" and, accordingly, most of his poems depend upon the precise presentation and arrangement of descriptive and expressive detail.[1] Never too far removed from popular forms and idioms, Pickard's love poems suggest an unabashedly direct, erotic speech that belies the precise music of their artifice. A pervasive political and cultural alienation is evident in other poems, such as "Energy" and "The Double D Economy," but the poems depend upon local observation and anecdote rather than rhetoric.

---

[1] Quoted in *Contemporary Poets*, ed. Thomas Riggs, 6th ed., New York, 1996, p. 862.

A History Lesson from My Son on Hadrian's Wall

On the edge of empire
running vallums along their arteries
keeps the generals off the streets.

A snake on the blade
5   said the man from the military museum.

What does a snake say?
He does several side steps
then strikes. A perfect symbol
to engrave on a sword.
10   *And a dangerous weapon*
in the hands of a Roman soldier.

The camp legionnaires wore enamelled armour
made by smithies sniffing mercurial fumes
from boiling quicksilver.

15   Everything is thinned and silenced suddenly
save for tree-topping Tornadoes
flying under radar.

Can we go to the pickets museum?
When were the Romans born?
20   *Who were their mothers?*
How does life begin?
Is my grandad dead?

The dig at Birdoswald fort,
sponsored by British Nuclear Fuels Ltd
25   is searching out the grain store.

Overlooking the Irthing
a stag in the gorge scatters
at the noise of our race
to the edge of the precipice.

30   As I ran out in front he said
the first one there loses.

1994

Title: *Hadrian's Wall:* a wall extending from coast to coast in the north of Britain, built at the command
  of the Emperor Hadrian in the second century AD.
2: *vallums:* the earthworks built behind the wall
16: *Tornadoes:* Tornado jet fighters
18: *pickets museum:* Pickard's son has "Picts" in mind; "having heard about the Picts in the Roman
  museum and no doubt from me about Thatcher's reactionary attack on organised labour [he] confused
  the two" (Pickard, in correspondence).
23: *Birdoswald:* a Roman fort on Hadrian's Wall, in the Irthing Valley section (in Cumbria)

Energy

The swallows on the TV aerial
face west and watch
the fellsides undulate
like dunes in the dusk.

5   They gather on the telephone wire.
Yesterday, fifty.
Today more than double that.

Quick clouds skim purple
off the fells.
10   These are the facts
I'm faxing down my line.

Slow flying jets under
a low lying sky.

They fly south
15   over armies assembled in the dust,
appear on radar screens
in the shape of cities,
disperse, with grains of sand
in a storm.

1994

The Double D Economy

Depravity and Deprivation

Back of the pub a rottweiler
ripped a kid's throat out.
Nanny broke baby skulls.
5 a.m. phone calls.
5   *Hello?*

There is no response.
The internal phone in the DSS
isn't working.
They only listen when you think
10   they aren't.

If there was a riot
I would have joined it.

This poem was written during the buildup to the 1990–1991 Gulf War.
3: *fellsides:* sides of moorland ridges

Title: *Double D:* the DD bra size; but also parodying social-work parlance of the 1980s—"depression and
  deprivation."
7: *DSS:* Department of Social Security

If I had a machine gun
I would have shot it.

15   Fuck Kung-fu all at once.
        Can't come against it hard on,
        you'll just leak all over
        the shatter-proof glass.
        Got to pour your outrage in a bottle,
20   light the fuse and throw it at the

        right moment,
        in congenial company.

        Or join the guerillas
        for a pair of boots.

25   Meanwhile who's for dinner?
        Eat leather.
        Lick hockle off the trough.

        Come joins us.

                                                    1994

27: *hockle*: phlegm
28: cf. the socialist marching song "Come and Join Us."

PETER READING (b. 1946)

R EADING WAS BORN IN LIVERPOOL AND EDUCATED AT ALSOP HIGH SCHOOL AND THE Liverpool College of Art, where he trained as a painter. After college he taught in a comprehensive school, lectured in art history at his former college, and for ten years worked menial jobs in agriculture. After a stint as writer-in-residence at Sunderland Polytechnic, he was a weighbridge operator at an agricultural feedmill in Shropshire, until he was fired in 1992 for refusing to wear the correct uniform. His many books include *For the Municipality's Elderly* (1974), *Tom O'Bedlam's Beauties* (1981), *C* (1984), *Ukulele Music* (1985), *Stet* (1986), *Perduta Gente* (1989), *Last Poems* (1994), the two-volume *Collected Poems* (1995–1996), and *Work In Regress* (1997).

Reading's earliest work reflects the influence of W. H. Auden and Gavin Ewart, but his most famous and controversial work is known primarily for two characteristics: a subject matter that has made him, in Tom Paulin's words, the poet of "the insane ugliness of British life" and "Junk Britain";[1] and the use or approximation of classical meters. Imitation of Alcaic and Alcmanic stanzas, classical hexameters, and other meters from Greek and Latin poetry is rare in English because, unlike Latin and Greek, English has no system for measuring the duration of vowel sounds, emphasizing stresses instead. While the critic Neil Roberts has wondered whether Reading's use of classical meters sacrifices the historical associations available to poets using English meters for a practice thereby "self-consciously gratuitous and ludic," one suspects that the non-Englishness of the meters is partly the point.[2] Many of Reading's books, such as *Stet* and *Ukulele Music,* are nearly impossible to excerpt because they consist of fragments cross-referenced and revisited throughout the whole of the book. *Stet* includes such seemingly disparate material as an interview with a physicist speaking about double quasars and "reasonless causal physics," doggerel poems that might have come straight from the obituaries or a greeting card, and idiomatic transcriptions of xenophobic political complaint. *Ukulele Music* includes notes from the maid "Viv," and *Perduta Gente* incorporates newspaper cuttings and other found materials such as textbook definitions of nausea and vomiting. Reading's angry, satirical, and rebarbative poems exclude little; they do not so much reflect on as embody the pervasive squalor of modern society. For some, this record of British cruelty and ignorance has made Reading the unofficial laureate of Thatcherite Britain, while others suspect that the intent to document contemporary chaos indicates a lapsed romantic. Reading seems to refer to his own screeds in the following lines from *Stet*: "Who do you think you are whining to? No reader wants / shares your bereavement."

---

[1] *Minotaur: Poetry and the Nation State,* Cambridge, MA, 1992, pp. 285–94.
[2] "Poetic Subjects: Tony Harrison and Peter Reading," *British Poetry from the 1950s to the 1990s,* ed. Gary Day and Brian Docherty, London, 1997, p. 56.

from Stet

465   Mixed mild and bitter—I thank you sir, kindly!
     Haven't I been proper rotten with flu like?
     Rotten with flu I been, all this week, I have.
     Been in bed all the week, missed the old voting—
     you know, the polling like, having the flu like.
470   Not as a vote off me'd make any change like.
     Fixed they am, all the same, all the same them lot.
     Once they gets Parlerment, hear no more of em.
     This is it, this is it—speak as I find, me.
     Speak as I find I does, all the same them lot.
475   Him as is standing's just same as them others.
     End up no better off. Bitter and mild please.
     I thank you kindly sir! You take old Churchill.
     That was the feller as showed em all, Churchill.
     That was the boy for the job was old Churchill.
480   That's what the country could do with now mister.
     Industry, you know like, that's what we need like.
     Soon be as dead as a yo-yo this country.
     Ask me like, and I'd say dead as a yo-yo.
     Soon be as dead as a yo-yo like, I'd say.
485   Still, that's the way as they wants it and that's the way as they'll get it.

     The tramp's scalp's indigo pus-oozing boil;
     sulphur dioxide piss-hued cumulus;
     a mac daubed with puked Chinese take-away—
     drooled noodly detail of a Jackson Pollock;
490   furred upside-down tench in a mauve canal . . .
     I sing the Grotty [no alternative].

     ' . . . terribly sad news . . . instantly . . . Motorway . . . '
     After your mother's letter I turn to a
        diary, through whose Wetmore Order
495   ornithological recollections

     stir, of a friendship early-established and
     special surviving global vicissitudes.
        Marvellous, those first close-shared eras
          mist-netting rarities, early migrants.

500   [Batty/unhealthy—verse at the best of times
     chunters to insubstantial minorities,

Title: *Stet:* "let it stand" (Latin): an editor's annotation, indicating that a previously marked change or
   deletion should be ignored.
465: *Mixed mild and bitter:* a drink of mixed mild and bitter ales
477: The speaker looks back nostalgically to England under Prime Minister Winston *Churchill.*
487: *cumulus:* a type of cloud
488: *mac:* mackintosh (raincoat); *take-away:* take-out food
488: *Jackson Pollock* (1912–1956), the American Abstract Expressionist painter
494: The *Wetmore Order* is the standard classification system for birds.
499: A *mist-net* is one with very fine threads, used for capturing birds for ringing or examination and release.
501: *chunters:* mutters

as for addressing lines to *dead men!*,
arrogant therapy/piffle, claptrap.]

505 East and west coast observatories fêted us
(icterine and melodious warblers,
thrill of *Phylloscopus bonelli,*
magnified instants of bright crisp focus)

even as that sad realm in the middle was gently expiring
devenustated but yet, even though feculent, *ours.*

510 [Therapy, whining, anxious to demonstrate
how the nice bard is awfully sad about
having his old pal flenched by crunched car—
others' bereavements don't marvel readers.]

25 years ago, we, at a spring's brink, tasted a chilled draught;
515 [Hippocrene hogwash] tonight, mawkish, I, solo, glut hock . . .

those days we charted our years by the dark swift coming and
going . . .

wants
[Who do you think you are whining to? No reader shares } your
bereavement
and it's pathetic and mad to address yourself to the dead.]

Similar, thank you squire, bitter and mild mixed.
520 I thank you kindly sir! Same with them Irish
and them Iramians—that Ayertolly,
him with the whiskers like, look out for him mate.
Lunatic, he is mate, L-O-O—listen,
all the same, them lot are, mad on religion.
525 All them religerous lot is fernatics.
Stick all them bleeders together and let em
blow bloody buggery out of each other—
Prodestant, Catherlic, Jews Isleramics.
Whisky's no good to you mister I tell you,
530 Not when you're lying down, any road mister.
I been in bed for two days with the flu like,
any road, thought as I'd just have a whisky—
get me back on to me feet as they say like—
any road, straight to me kidneys it went like.
535 Straight to the kidneys—that's lying down, that is.
Standing's the thing like if you drinks the whisky,
by-pass the kidneys the whisky will then like.
Don't touch the kidneys at all then like, standing.
Never lie down if you're drinking the whisky.

505: *icterine:* belonging to the songbird family
506: *Phylloscopus bonelli:* the taxonomic name for Bonelli's warbler
509: *devenustated:* disfigured
  feculent: filthy, befouled
512: *flenched:* cut up
515: *Hippocrene:* the fountain created by a blow of the hoof of Pegasus on Mount Helicon—an emblem
  of poetic inspiration. In Keats' "Ode to a Nightingale" it is wine—"the blushful Hippocrene"—that sym-
  bolizes poetic creativity.

540   All people got their own different religions.
               Obvious, that is like. Obvious, that is.
               No need to kill all them others what aren't yours.
               Them Sheeks with turbans on, thems just the same like.
               Also them terrorists—see in the *Sun* where
545   that lot let off a bomb? Lunatics them mate—
               L-U-N. Not to the kidneys, the *livers*—
               straight to the livers and buggers em up mate.
               Just half in there please squire. I thank you kindly!
      All got the diffrent idees like, so we got to accept it.

                                              1986

Thucydidean

      Continents then were affected by violent
          earthquakes, eclipses,
      withering droughts and subsequent famines,
          pestilent outbreaks . . .
5   Faced with the Plague, the ignorant Faculty
          shewed itself impotent;
      equally useless were all of our sciences,
          oracles, arts, prayers . . .
      Burning sensations occurred in our heads, our
10   eyes became bloodshot,
      inside our mouths there was bleeding from throat and
          tongue, we grew breathless,
      coughing and retching ensued, producing
          bile of all species,
15   genitals, fingers and toes became festered,
          diarrhoea burgeoned . . .

      Terrible was the despair into which all
          fell when they realized
      fully the weight and the magnitude of their
20   diresome affliction . . .
      Not enough living to bury the dead or
          cover the corpses . . .
      Seeing how swift and abrupt were the changes
          Fortune allotted
25   (money and life alike being transient
          under the Pestilence),
      profligate wretched citizens turned to
          lawless dishonour,
      heedless of gods and of law for they thought themselves
30   already sentenced—
      then was there bloody and slaughterous civil
          mass insurrection.

                                                1994

Title: The Greek historian *Thucydides* (c.460 BC–c.404 BC) wrote the *History of the Peloponnesian War;*
Reading is drawing on its eyewitness account (2.47–54) of the plague that afflicted Athens in 430–429 BC.

VERONICA FORREST-THOMSON (1947–1975)

IN HER INFLUENTIAL, POSTHUMOUSLY PUBLISHED CRITICAL STUDY *POETIC ARTIFICE: A Theory of Twentieth-Century Poetry* (1978), Forrest-Thomson argues that "Contemporary poetry has suffered from critics' disposition to make poetry above all a statement about the external world, and therefore it is now especially important somewhat to redress the balance, to stress the importance of artifice."[1] Influenced by the criticism of William Empson but taking issue with it, the book discusses the "most distinctive yet elusive features of poetry: all the rhythmic, phonetic, verbal, and logical devices which make poetry different from prose" and contains a fair amount of neoformalist polemic directed at modes of critical reading too quick to "reduce the strangeness of poetic language" to statements about the "non-verbal external world."[2] Its most pointed barbs are aimed at celebrated poems by Philip Larkin and Ted Hughes, its praise reserved for a range of poets including John Donne, Algernon Swinburne, T. S. Eliot, Ezra Pound, Sylvia Plath, John Ashbery, and J. H. Prynne. In the name of this and other poetry, she argues the need for "a theory of the devices of artifice, such as apparently non-sensical imagery, logical discontinuity, referential opacity, and unusual metrical and spatial organization."[3] Prynne writes in his memoir of Forrest-Thomson about her last poems' working "through this formal notion of artifice to allow into realisation forces she had tacitly been preparing to meet; a new invasion of subject. With great brilliance and courage she set fear against the formal irony of its literary anticipations."[4] The reader of "Cordelia: or, 'A Poem Should Not Mean, But Be'" is perhaps first struck by its bravura pastiche of famous lines of poetry. A flattened irony is what such pastiche has come to mean for many poets more recently, but the "larking up nightingales" evident in "Cordelia" seems part of a more anxious and painful writing; the speaker is intimate with but also outside literary traditions bespeaking masculinity and violence. The poem's partly aggressive, partly defensive chattiness is tinged with desperation, prepared to take on "bullying men" in the name of "the possibles of joy."

Forrest-Thomson was born in Malaya and grew up in Glasgow. She was educated at Liverpool and Cambridge University and taught at universities in Leicester and Birmingham. From 1971 to 1974, she was married to the critic Jonathan Culler. The collections of poetry published in her lifetime were *Identikit* (1967), *Twelve Academic Questions* (1970), *Language-Games* (1971)—its title reflecting her interest in the philosophy of Ludwig Wittgenstein—and *Cordelia: or, 'A Poem Should Not Mean, But Be'*

---

[1] *Poetic Artifice: A Theory of Twentieth-Century Poetry*, Manchester, UK, 1978, p. xi.
[2] Ibid., p. ix.
[3] Ibid., p. x.
[4] "Veronica Forrest-Thomson: A Personal Memoir," *On the Periphery*, 1976, n.p.

(1974). *On the Periphery* (1976), with the memoir by Prynne, and *Collected Poems and Translations* (1990), edited by Anthony Barnett, appeared posthumously. Forrest-Thomson died of an accidental overdose of sleeping pills the night before she was to read her poems in London.

Cordelia: or, 'A Poem Should Not Mean, But Be'

> To those who kiss in fear that they shall never kiss again
>
> To those that love with fear that they shall never love again
>
> To such I dedicate this rhyme and what it may contain.
>
> None of us will ever take the transiberian train
>
> 5   Which makes a very satisfactory refrain
>
> Especially as I can repeat it over and over again
>
> Which is the main use of the refrain.
>
> I with no middle flight intend the truth to speak out plain
> Of honour truth and love gone by that has come back again
> 10   The fact is one grows weary of the love that comes again.
> I may not know much about gods but I know that
> Eros is a strong purple god.
> And that there is a point where incest becomes
> Tradition. I don't mean that literally;
> 15   I don't love my brother or he me.
> We have been mutually avoiding each other
> For years and will continue to do so.
> Even I know about cross words—
> Something. The word you want is Dante.
> 20   He said he loved Beatrice. Whatever he did
> He didn't love Beatrice. At least the
> Beatrice Portinari whom history gives.
> He knew her and the point about all these
> Florentines is that they all were
> 25   Killing each other or dying of rapid
> Consumption. Beatrice died; Rossetti painted her

Title: *Cordelia:* the virtuous and faithful youngest daughter in *King Lear*. Forrest-Thomson's alternative title is quoted from "Ars Poetica" by the American poet Archibald MacLeish (1892–1982).

4: The Trans-Siberian Railroad runs from Moscow east to Vladivostok. Forrest-Thomson alludes to the poem *La Prose du Transsibérien et de la petite Jehanne de France* ("The Prose of the Trans-Siberian and of Little Jehanne of France," 1913), by Blaise Cendrars (1887–1961). It is a travelogue of his youthful trip on the line in the company of a young prostitute; they begin in Moscow and head east, but at the end of the trip the train mysteriously arrives in Paris.

8: cf. Milton, *Paradise Lost* 1.13–16: " . . . my advent'rous song, / That with no middle flight intends to soar / Above th'Aonian Mount, while it pursues / Things unattempted yet in prose or rhyme."

11–12: cf. T.S. Eliot's "The Dry Salvages", part I: "I do not know much about gods; but I think that the river / Is a strong brown god."

20: *Beatrice:* the object of Dante's love; her full name is not given in his poetry, but she has usually been identified with the historical Beatrice Portinari, the daughter of a noble Florentine family, who married Simone de' Bardi and died at the age of 24.

26: Dante Gabriel *Rossetti* (1828–1882), the English poet and painter, painted this scene from Dante's *Vita Nuova*, a collection of poems linked by prose commentary that tells the story of his love for Beatrice.

Cutting Dante in the street. Botticelli
Painted the rest: Simonetta Vespucci
Died of a rapid consumption (age 23)
30   Guliano dei Medici murdered by the altar rail (age 19)
Guido Cavalcanti died in exile (age 35)
Dante dei Aligeri died in exile (age 90)
Lorenzo dei Medici who lives for ever
Since he stayed there and commissioned
35   The paintings, and poems and statues
And if he also commissioned the deaths
I don't blame him. He didn't feel
Very magnificent when his brother
Was murdered in sanctuary.
40   Do you realise whoever did that
Would be excommunicated if, that is, if
He hadn't also murdered the papal legate,
His best friend.
I have lived long enough having seen one thing;
45   That term has an end.
It was getting dark on the platform of nowhere
When I who was anxious and sad came to you
Out of the rain. Out of the sound of the cold
Wind that blows time before and time after
50   Even Provence knows.
And as for this line I stole it from T. S. Eliot
And Ezra Pound and A. C. Swinburne. All very good
Poets to steal from since they are all three dead.
The love that is must always just contain
55   The glory of the love that was whatever be the pain.
We played at mates and mating and stopped up the drain.
Hear me. O Mister Poster I know
You have burnt me too brown you must boil me again
You simply have no notion how delightful it will
60   Be when they pick us up and throw us with the lobsters out to sea.
It is the lark, my love, and not the nightingale.
None of us will ever take the trans-siberian train.
She wanted to and was collecting people who did
I thought I did but now I know I don't.
65   It is the lark, my love, and not the nightingale.

27: The painter Sandro *Botticelli* (1445–1510) enjoyed the patronage of the Medici family. In the first half of this sentence Forrest-Thomson reworks a passage from Hugh Kenner's *The Pound Era* (Berkeley, 1971), p. 31.

33: The Florentine ruler *Lorenzo de' Medici* (1449–1492) was celebrated in Ezra Pound's *Cantos* for his lavish patronage of the arts.

44–45: cf. A. C. Swinburne, "Hymn to Proserpine": "I have lived long enough, having seen one thing, that love hath an end."

49: *time before and time after*: T.S. Eliot, "Burnt Norton", part III

50: cf. Pound's "The Flame": "Provence knew."

57: cf. the music-hall song "Oh Mister Porter (Whatever Shall I Do)."

58ff: These lines parody two poems from Lewis Carroll's *Alice's Adventures in Wonderland*, ch. 10: " 'Tis the voice of the Lobster: I heard him declare / 'You have baked me too brown, I must sugar my hair.' "; "You can really have no notion how delightful it will be / When they take us up and throw us, with the lobsters, out to sea!"

61: Cf. *Romeo and Juliet* 3.5.2–7: "*Juliet*: It was the nightingale and not the lark / That pierc'd the fearful hollow of thine ear. . . . *Romeo*: It was the lark, the herald of the morn, / No nightingale."

In fact I've never heard either bird
But people say they sound very similar.
And what the devil were Romeo and Juliet
About wasting their last moments
70   Listening to birds. Hah.
I like kicking up larks or
Larking up kicks. So do most poets
Including J. H. Prynne, the memorable poet
Who is happy to say that the U.L.
75   Has got his middle name wrong.
He claims it stands for Hah
But there is a limit. I know it all.
Riddle me riddle randy ree
Round and round in the snotgreen sea
80   When they pick us up and throw us
With the Joyces out to sea.
Tell us tale of Troy's downfall
We all would have liked to have been there.
The infernal Odyssos. He it was whose bile
85   Stirred up by envy and revenge destroyed
The mother of womankind. And Swinburne
Got a kick out of pain but I don't
I just get kicked.
I wish I didn't keep sounding like Richard the Third
90   Except that if I don't I tend to sound
Like Richard the Second. And who wants that.
I suppose I must sound like Richard the First.
What did he do?
Nothing I take it
95   I get a kick out of larking up nightingales.
Prynne says that if I don't come back
Safe from Sicily by the thirtieth April
They will send a posse.
March is the cruellest station
100   Taking on bullying men
And were you really afraid they would rape you?
No. I thought there would be grave difficulties.

73: *J. H.* (Jeremy Halward) *Prynne* (b. 1936), noted British modernist poet and fellow of Gonville and Caius
College, Cambridge.

74: *U.L.*: Cambridge University Library

79: *snotgreen sea*: quoted from James Joyce's *Ulysses* (1922), ch. 1

82: The line is a pastiche of medieval alliterative verse.

84: *Odyssos*: Odysseus, King of Ithaca, whose battle skills and wiles helped the Greeks win the Trojan war.
Homer's *Odyssey* tells of his many years' wanderings in his return to Ithaca from Troy, wanderings which
in Joyce's *Ulysses* are paralleled by the travels of his protagonist, Leopold Bloom, in Dublin during the
course of a single day.

84–86: cf. *Paradise Lost* 1.34–36, on Satan: "Th'infernal serpent; he it was, whose guile / Stirr'd up with
envy and revenge, deceiv'd / The mother of mankind"

87: Swinburne was a devotee of flagellation. Cf. the Cole Porter tune "I Get a Kick Out of You": "I get no
kick from champagne."

89ff: Shakespeare's *Richard III* portrays that king as a deformed villain; *Richard II*'s protagonist, weak and
vacillating, is eventually deposed. Richard I (Richard Lionheart) is traditionally one of the most popular
of English kings.

99: cf. the opening lines of *The Waste Land*. March is a particularly bleak railway station in Cam-
bridgeshire.

Not just that I was actively opposed
And so was every other man, woman and child
105   On that there train.
I was afraid they would kill me.
I may look stupid but I'm not
So simple as to think your name
Is Elizabeth Brown. Well. All right
110   My name is Veronica Forrest-Thomson.
Agammemnon was King of the Achaians at the time,
Priam, of the Trojans, Theseus, of the Athenians.
And like all Good Kings, they are dead.
In my day it was the done thing to side
115   With the Trojans for no better reason
Than that they lost. But me I back
Winners every time.
Mary Shelley may go to hell
As she thought she was going to anyway
120   And take Frankinsense with her.
I want her husband, alive and well.
Who, of course, also got killed.
Hardly surprising if he made a habit
Of reading Aiscylos while sailing.
125   He wasn't reading Aiscylos when he drowned.
Got cremated like a pagan king.
Not Agammemnon who, as I said, was king at the time
And lost, murderer of his daughter
Killed by his wife and (other) daughter.
130   Killed by his death killing his life.
Stabbed in the back in his bath.
I think of it every time I have a bath.
Though I have no sympathy at all
For that daughter and son.
135   I think it is unfair that Helen
Had everything, immortal beauty,
Lovers, cities destroyed and battles
Fought about her. And she just came home
And calmly went around being Menelaus' wife
140   While her twin sister, Clytemnestra
Was murdered by her son and daughter.

111ff: Agamemnon and Priam were the leaders, respectively, of the Greek and Trojan sides of the Trojan War; they both, like Theseus (who was driven from Athens by a rebellion and was murdered on the island of Scyros), came to violent ends.

113: *Good Kings:* The capitalization is a feature of the comic style of *1066 and All That* (1930), a mock British history guide by W. C. Sellar and R. J. Yeatman.

122: The poet Percy Bysshe Shelley (1792–1822) drowned while sailing in the Bay of Spezia.

127ff: The Greek fleet, sailing to assault Troy, was held by contrary winds at Aulis; the seer Calchas declared that Iphigenia, the daughter of Agamemnon, would have to be sacrificed to the goddess Artemis before the fleet could proceed. Aeschylus's tragedy *Agamemnon*, the first part of his *Oresteia* trilogy, tells of Agamemnon's return home, upon which he is murdered in his bath by his wife Clytemnestra and her lover Aegisthus. They in turn were murdered by Orestes with the assistance of Electra (the "daughter and son" of Agamemnon and Clytemnestra). (Having Electra—the "(other) daughter"—participate in the killing of Agamemnon is Forrest-Thomson's alteration to the story.)

135: The Trojan war was instigated by the Trojan Paris's abduction of Helen from her husband Menelaus. She and Clytemnestra were daughters of Leda.

And the Athenians acquitted them.
They would do, a nation of sophists.
Always betraying their allies and torturing
145 Women and children and enslaving people.
They even killed Socrates, their one good man,
Then Plato tried to be a philosopher king.
And got enslaved for his pains.
I wish they had kept him enslaved.
150 He escaped, of course, and wrote books
About how he would do it better
If he was in charge. All poets do that.
They are just as incompetent as the rest
If they try to organise things.
155 As witness my own efforts in that direction
Or those of my avatar, Agammemnon,
Who, as I say came home and was killed in his bath
Killing his wife and his daughter.
And if you don't know about this you ought to.
160 Read it in the *Iliad,* read it in the *Odyssey,*
Do not read it in Freud who is always wrong
Although even Freud didn't deserve a son like Lacan.
But first and last read me, the beloved
Who was killed in the general slaughter.
165 But rise again like John Donne
(read him too) I, Helen, I Iseult, I Guenevere,
I Clytemnestra and many more to come.
I did it, I myself, killing the King my father
Killing the King my mother, joining the King my brother.
170 It is the kick, my love, and not the nightingale
I like larking up kicks myself
But not kicking.
They that have power to hurt and do so
Should not be blamed by Shakespeare or anyone else
175 For hurting though such is the race of poets
That they will blame them anyway.
However it is a pretty productive process
Especially if one may be plumber as well as poet
And thus unstop the drain as well as writing
180 *Poetic Artifice* "Pain stopped play" and

142: In the third play of the *Oresteia, The Eumenides,* Orestes is acquitted of the murders he has committed by a tribunal of Athenian citizens presided over by the goddess Athena.

146: The Athenian philosopher *Socrates* was condemned to death for impiety.

147: In *The Republic Plato* sets forth an ideal republic whose rulers are "philosopher-kings." He did not, however, try to become a philosopher king himself nor was enslaved.

162: The French psychoanalyst Jacques *Lacan* (1901–1981) reinterpreted Freud in the light of structuralist linguistics; his work has had a strong influence on academic literary theory.

166: *Iseult* was the lover of Tristan in medieval romance. Queen *Guinevere* was the wife of King Arthur; her adultery with Sir Lancelot was a cause of the dissolution of the knightly fellowship of the Round Table.

168–69: cf *The Tempest,* 1.2.393: "Weeping again the King my father's wrack"; and Eliot, *The Waste Land,* 191–92.

173: cf. Shakespeare's sonnet 94: "They that have power to hurt, and will do none . . . "; this poem is discussed at length in Forrest-Thomson's *Poetic Artifice.*

180: One draft title of this poem was "Pain Stopped Play or 'The Twilight of the Gods' / for the Star." ("Rain stopped play" is the term used when a day of a cricket match is abandoned because of poor weather.) Another title was "Tradition and the Individual Talent," alluding to Eliot's essay of that title.

Several other books and poems including
1974 and All That (seriously though)
I, Veronica did it, truth-finding, truth-seeking
Muck-raking, bringing victory.

185 It was a horse, of course, in which the warriors hid
Pretending to bring peace
And they wouldn't speak to me, crouching in the dark
Like a lot of fools, hearing the voice of the goddess
In an alien city, I speak your tongue in my own city:

190 Cambridge or Camelot and you won't listen to me
Advised, of course, by Odyssos, solicitor, betrayer.
And when they had killed all the men, raped all the women etc.
Agammemnon came home and, as I said, was stabbed by his wife
In his bath. Anyway it is the lark, my love,

195 And not the nightingale. I follow the sacred footsteps of
Hippolyta, the blest, the best
That has been said or spoken well in any tongue
Read John Donne—the memorable dun.
Don't read Matthew Arnold; he's a fool

200 I am not Prince Thomas Aquinas F. H. Eliot
I am not an attendant lord either.
I am the king who lives.
Spring surprised us, running through the market square
And we stopped in Prynne's rooms in a shower of pain

205 And went on in sunlight into the University Library
And ate yogurt and talked for an hour.
You, You, grab the reins.
Drink as much as you can and love as much as you can
And work as much as you can

210 For you can't do anything when you are dead.

The motto of this poem heed
And do you it employ:
Waste not and want not while you're here
The possibles of joy.

1974

183: cf. Eliot, *The Waste Land*, 218
185: The Greeks won the Trojan war by an act of deception devised by Odysseus: he had them construct
a giant wooden horse, which he and a band of Greek warriors hid inside. Pretending to give up the war,
the Greek army sailed out of sight. They left behind Sinon, who, pretending to be a deserter, convinced
the Trojans to take the horse into the city, claiming it would make it impregnable. After nightfall the
Greeks emerged and sacked the city.
188ff: When the Trojan Horse was inside the walls of Troy, Helen, suspicious, walked round it calling out
the names of Greek warriors; Odysseus prevented them from answering.
196: The Amazon Hippolyta was the wife of Theseus, the legendary king of Athens.
196ff: In "The Function of Criticism at the Present Time," Matthew Arnold defined criticism as "a disin-
terested endeavour to learn and propagate the best that is known and thought in the world." Also see
Donne, "The First Anniversary" 443–45: "blessed maid, / Of whom is meant whatever hath been said, /
Or shall be spoken well by any tongue."
199ff: cf. Eliot's "Love Song of J. Alfred Prufrock," 111–19.
200: Eliot's Ph.D. dissertation was entitled *Knowledge and Experience in the Philosophy of F.H. Bradley*.
203ff: cf. Eliot, *The Waste Land*, 8ff

LIZ LOCHHEAD (b. 1947)

L OCHHEAD WAS BORN IN LANARKSHIRE, SCOTLAND, AND EDUCATED AT THE GLASGOW School of Art. She has taught art and been poet-in-residence at institutions in Britain and Canada, and is well known in Scotland for her stage and television plays. In the early 1970s, she was part of a class in creative writing led by Philip Hobsbaum at Glasgow University, also attended by Tom Leonard, Alasdair Gray, and James Kelman. Her earlier poetry was collected in *Memo for Spring* (1972), *The Grimm Sisters* (1981), and *Dreaming Frankenstein and Collected Poems* (1984), the latter two reflecting her interest in folktales and popular stories as sites for contesting and rewriting patriarchal values. Many of Lochhead's poems, like "Mirror's Song," dedicated to filmmaker Sally Potter, are about the difficulties of "woman giving birth to herself" amid the images, languages, and rituals of Scottish culture. Cairns Craig has argued that, in her poems, "the negation of a female identity becomes the index of a lost national identity."[1] *True Confessions and New Clichés* (1985) collects her songs, monologues, and other work written for performance and cabaret revue; the influence of populist and oral forms on texts that Lochhead prefers to call "recitations" is also apparent in *Bagpipe Muzak* (1991). Lochhead's "Bagpipe Muzak, Glasgow 1990," a pastiche of a famous poem by Louis MacNeice, responds to a moment when Scottish "devolution" was becoming a real possibility. The poem is less interested in mocking MacNeice's poem than in ridiculing the debased rhetoric of those for whom politics is little more than middle-class fashion, in a cosmopolitan Scotland where heroin and "pasta and pesto" are more part of the everyday landscape than Robert Burns's Tam O'Shanter.

---

[1] "From the Lost Ground: Liz Lochhead, Douglas Dunn, and Contemporary Scottish Poetry," *Contemporary British Poetry: Essays in Theory and Criticism,* Albany, 1996, p. 355.

Mirror's Song

FOR SALLY POTTER

Smash me looking-glass glass
coffin, the one
that keeps your best black self on ice.
Smash me, she'll smash back—
5   without you she can't lift a finger.

Dedication: *Sally Potter* (b. 1949), English filmmaker

Smash me, she'll whirl out like Kali,
trashing the alligator mantrap handbags
with her righteous karate.
The ashcan for the stubbed lipsticks
10   and the lipsticked butts,
the wet lettuce of fivers.
She'll spill the Kleenex blossoms,
the tissues of lies, the matted
nests of hair from the brushes'
15   hedgehog spikes, she'll junk
the dead mice and the tampons
the twinkling single eyes
of winkled out diamanté, the hatpins,
the whalebone and lycra,
20   the appleblossom and the underwires,
the chafing iron that kept them maiden,
the Valium and initialled hankies,
the lovepulps and the Librium,
the permanents and panstick and
25   Coty and Tangee Indelible,
Thalidomide and junk jewellery.

Smash me for your daughters and dead
mothers, for the widowed
spinsters of the first and every war—
30   let her
rip up the appointment cards for the
terrible clinics,
the Greenham summonses, that date
they've handed us. Let her rip.
35   She'll crumple all the
tracts and the adverts, shred
all the wedding dresses, snap
all the spike-heel icicles
in the cave she will claw out of—
40   a woman giving birth to herself.

1982

6: *Kali:* Indian goddess of destruction
11: *fivers:* five-pound notes
18: *diamanté:* a fabric covered in sparkling sequins
23: *Librium:* an antianxiety drug
24: *panstick:* a matt cosmetic in stick form
33: *Greenham summonses:* court summons for women arrested for protesting at the U.S. Trident airbase
at Greenham Common in England.

Bagpipe Muzak, Glasgow 1990

When A. and R. men hit the street
To sign up every second band they meet
Then marketing men will spill out spiel
About how us Glesca folk are really *real*
5   (Where once they used to fear and pity
These days they glamorise and patronise our city—
Accentwise once they could hear bugger all
That was not low, glottal or guttural,
Now we've 'kudos' incident'ly
10   And the Patter's street-smart, strictly state-of-the-art,
And our oaths are user-friendly).

It's all go the sandblaster, it's all go Tutti Frutti,
All we want is a wally close with Rennie Mackintosh putti.

Malkie Machismo invented a gismo for making whisky oot o'girders
15   He tasted it, came back for mair, and soon he was on to his thirders.
Rabbie Burns turned in his grave and dunted Hugh MacDiarmid,
Said: It's oor National Thorn, John Barleycorn, but I doot we'll ever learn
       it . . .

It's all go the Rotary Club, its all go 'The Toast Tae The Lassies',
It's all go Holy Willie's Prayer and plunging your dirk in the haggis.

20   Robbie Coltrane flew Caledonian MacBrayne
To Lewis . . . on a Sunday!
Protesting Wee Frees fed him antifreeze
(Why God knows) till he was comatose
And didnae wake up till the Monday.

Title: In 1990, Glasgow was declared European City of Culture, earning the ridicule of Glasgow writers
  such as Alaisdair Gray, James Kelman, Tom Leonard, and Lochhead. This poem is modeled on Louis
  MacNeice's "Bagpipe Music," which begins: "It's no go the merrygoround, it's no go the rickshaw, / All
  we want is a limousine and a ticket for the peepshow."
1: *A and R men:* artists and repertoire men, responsible for searching out new talent for record companies
4: *Glesca:* Glasgow
10: *the Patter:* Glasgow vernacular
12: *Tutti Frutti:* a television comedy-drama, shown on BBC Scotland in 1987, starring Robbie Coltrane and
  Emma Thompson, and concerning a Glasgow rock-and-roll band named The Majestics.
13: *wally close:* a tiled entryway to a tenement (supposedly a mark of higher social status); the stairwells
  of modern gentrified flats and lofts are often decorated with tiles stripped from original wally closes.
  Charles *Rennie Mackintosh* (1868–1928), Glasgow-born Art Nouveau architect and designer
  putti: cherubs
14: Irn-Bru, a popular Scottish soft-drink ("Scotland's Other National Drink"), is said in its slogan to be
  "Made in Scotland. From girders."—thus harking back to Glasgow's days of heavy labor and shipbuild-
  ing.
16: *dunted:* struck
18ff: The reference here is to the tradition of Burns Suppers, in celebration of the birthday of the Scot-
  tish national poet Robert Burns (1759–1796), at which the traditional meal is *haggis,* a pudding made
  from sheep's offal and cooked in its stomach. Traditionally the supper includes a sarcastic thanking of
  the women present (who have done the cooking and will do the cleaning-up.)
19: "Holy Willie's Prayer" is a poem by Burns.
  dirk: ceremonial knife
20: *Caledonian MacBrayne* is a ferry service (not an airline); Sunday ferry service is a fairly recent inno-
  vation, due to strong religious pressure against them.
22: *Wee Frees:* members of the Free Kirk (Church)

25   Aye it's Retro Time for Northern Soul and the whoop and the skirl o' the
          saxes.
     All they'll score's more groundglass heroin and venison filofaxes.
     The rent-boys preen on Buchanan Street, their boas are made of vulture,
     It's all go the January sales in the Metropolis of Culture.

     It's all go the PR campaign and a radical change of image—
30   Write Saatchi and Saatchi a blank cheque to pay them for the damage.

     Tam o'Shanter fell asleep
     To the sound of fairy laughter
     Woke up on the cold-heather hillside
     To find it was ten years after
35   And it's all go (again) the Devolution Debate and pro . . . pro . . . propor-
          tional representation.
     Over pasta and pesto in a Byres Road bistro, Scotland declares hersel' a
          nation.

     Margo McDonald spruced up her spouse for thon Govan By-Election
     The voters they selectit him in a sideyways *left* defection,
     The Labour man was awfy hurt, he'd dependit on the X-fillers
40   And the so-and-sos had betrayed him for thirty pieces of Sillars!

     Once it was no go the SNP, they were sneered at as 'Tory' and tartan
     And thought to be very little to do with the price of Spam in Dumbarton.
     Now it's all go the Nationalists, the toast of the folk and the famous
     —Of Billy Connolly, Muriel Gray and the Auchtermuchty Proclaimers.

45   It's all go L.A. lager, it's all go the Campaign for an Assembly,
     It's all go Suas Alba and winning ten-nil at Wembley.

25: *Northern Soul:* refers to the 1970s vogue in northern England for dancing to old funk and soul music.
A *skirl* is a shrill sound; the phrase *the whoop and the skirl* is a cliché for the sound of bagpipes.

26: *groundglass heroin:* i.e., heroin cut with ground glass
filofaxes: personal organizers

28: *January sales:* a UK tradition: the 1st of January sees stores slash their prices, creating hectic post-
Christmas bargain-hunting.

30: *Saatchi and Saatchi:* the public-relations firm; its posters with the slogan "Labour Isn't Working" and
a picture of a snaking dole queue helped Margaret Thatcher win her first term as Prime Minister in 1979.

31: *Tam o'Shanter* is the hero of Robert Burns's poem of that name; returning home, a little drunk, he
encounters a dancing group of witches and warlocks and narrowly escapes their clutches. (Lochhead
seems also to have the ballad "Thomas the Rymer" in mind, in which Thomas becomes the lover of a
fairy queen and disappears from the Earth for seven years).

35: A referendum on Scottish *devolution* (which would have granted Scotland limited legislative and exec-
utive powers within the UK) was held in 1979; more than half the voters voted for devolution, but the
vote was annulled because it was required that more than 40% of the electorate vote for devolution.

37: *Margo MacDonald* and her husband Jim *Sillars* are SNP (Scottish National Party) politicians; Sillars
won an important by-election in *Govan* (a constituency in Glasgow) from the Labour candidate in the
early 1980s.

44: *Billy Connolly:* a notable Scottish stand-up comedian
Muriel Gray: former presenter of a Channel Four music program called *The Tube* (and now a media
personality and horror novelist)
The *Proclaimers* (actually from Leith) were twin brothers who sang songs, accompanying themselves
on guitar; they had a number of hits, notably "Letter from America."

45: *L.A. lager:* a brand whose name stands for "Low Alcohol"
Assembly: i.e., a Scottish Assembly, as part of devolution

46: *Suas Alba:* a Gaelic-speaking, Highland-based pressure group
A victory for Scotland in the (now discontinued) annual Scotland v. England football match was all
the sweeter if it occurred at *Wembley* (the English national stadium).

Are there separatist dreams in the glens and the schemes?
Well . . . it doesny take Taggart to detect it!
Or to jalouse we hate the Government
50   And we patently didnae elect it.
So—watch out Margaret Thatcher, and tak' tent Neil Kinnock
Or we'll tak' the United Kingdom and brekk it like a bannock.

                                                              1991

47: *schemes:* i.e., housing schemes
48: *Taggart:* hero of a Glasgow TV detective series of the same name
49: *jalouse:* suspect
51: *Thatcher* was (Conservative) Prime Minister from 1979 to 1990; *Kinnock* was the leader of the opposing Labour Party from 1983 to 1992.
   tent: care
52: *bannock:* an unleavened cake made of oatmeal, barley, etc.

TREVOR JOYCE (b. 1947)

JOYCE WAS BORN IN DUBLIN AND SPENT HIS EARLY YEARS IN A CENTRAL DUBLIN TENE-
ment. He was educated at University College Dublin, where he read English and
philosophy, and University College, Cork, where he studied mathematical sciences.
In 1967, he and Michael Smith began the New Writers' Press in Dublin and two years
later produced the first issue of a poetry magazine, *The Lace Curtain,* which was ded-
icated to international modernism, highlighting neglected Irish modernists such as
Brian Coffey. Among the books published by New Writers' Press are an early transla-
tion of the poems of Jorge Luis Borges and collections by Coffey, Anthony Cronin, and
Desmond O'Grady. In 1984, Joyce moved to Cork, where he worked for over ten years
as a business analyst for Apple Computer. His early poems are collected in *Sole Glum
Trek* (1967), *Watches* (1969), and *Pentahedron* (1972). Unwilling to repeat himself,
Joyce quit writing in the early 1970s except to complete work on *The Poems of Sweeny
Peregrine* (1976), a translation of the Late Middle Irish poem *Buile Suibhne Geilt,*
which provided the base text also for Seamus Heaney's *Sweeney Astray* (1983). He
began writing again in 1990, and has since published *stone floods* (1995), *Syzygy* (1998),
Without Asylum (1998), and *with the first dream of fire they hunt the cold* (2000), his
collected poems.

John Goodby writes that Joyce's early poems as collected in *Pentahedron* reflect
"an eclectic, lyric experimentalism which owes much to [Georg] Trakl, the Eliot of
'Preludes,' [Arthur] Rimbaud and [Miroslav] Holub."[1] The vision of an exotic flower
in one poem leads the speaker to remember that "I have seen / the same textures in a
bed of leaves / where an anonymous carrion / was swathed in its own drowsy stench /
putrefying into unity / with the gold, beautiful leaves," and other poems also suggest
an aestheticism preoccupied with decay.[2] Joyce's extensive reading in Chinese and
Japanese poetry begins to manifest itself in *stone floods*—for instance in the adapta-
tions of renga form in "The Turlough." The theme of decay survives in poems such as
"The Course of Nature," which seems to pity "Poor angels" who weep "to witness /
such quick and irreversible decay" until we see that these same angels who would
gather the world into eternity are mauled by cats because their "high regard" distracts
them, leaving them oblivious to events in the world. It is as if the romanticism of Rilke
required as its appropriate antidote the stoic irony of Samuel Beckett. "Cry Help" and
"Tohu-bohu" reveal a similar refusal to rest content in visions of transcendence, and
if decay is a motif in his earlier, more expressive poems, Joyce's recent work turns a
less inward and more political eye on the destruction of "our civilized precincts /

---

1 Introduction to "Colonies of Belief: Ireland's Modernists," *Angel Exhaust,* vol. 17, 1999, p. 57.
2 "To an Exotic Flower," *Pentahedron,* Dublin, 1972, p. 15.

hocked for a pittance by wasters." In "Tohu-bohu" idioms borrowed from the worlds
of science and computer technologies mix with quotidian narrative and excerpts from
the Gnostic text "Thunder Perfect Mind." More recent work has absorbed influences
such as John Cage's procedural methods (*Syzygy*) while exploring the "sustained
bewilderment" resulting from globalized economies and information systems (*Without Asylum*).

The Turlough

FOR CELESTINE

It is raining elsewhere

Vertical rivers reverse
stone floods
the karst domain
5   each sink turns source

Rock brings forth fruit elsewhere

The action of the clock
runs down
through fissured hours
10   wells up lost time

All is not lost elsewhere

The emigrant returns
old loves
reach out their arms
15   gold leaves fly up

Time heals all wounds elsewhere

Bullet returns fire from flesh
to gun
the dried stain weeps
20   bone knits again

No mark gets the cold deck elsewhere

Boxed by his court of spades
Jack wakes
from his stone watch
25   that springs each arch

Title: "The turloughs [pronounced *tur-locks*] or winter lakes of western Ireland occur in areas of karstic
limestone. Rain falling on this land drains away through swallow-holes or sinks, but precipitation any-
where within the watershed may cause the water-table to rise again above the valley floor, whereupon
streams issue through the crevices by which they had previously drained away." (Joyce's note)
22: *Boxed*: Galway dialect for "shuffled"
23ff: "The rhyme London Bridge is Falling Down is taken to refer to the ancient practice of burying alive
a watchman beneath a newly-built bridge to prevent the stones being washed away." (Joyce)

London Bridge is falling down elsewhere

Circuits and gates collapse
in sand
the face the glass
30   composed breaks down

Raw head finds bloody bones elsewhere

Vast hands stop at the stretch
knuckle
of blazing gas
35   and wrist of stars

The gods explode this turn elsewhere

Red giant and white dwarf
come in
in a blue shift
40   Venus meets Mars

There is thunder now elsewhere

Under an incandescent sky
flash floods
spread out this lake
45   is on no map

1995

Cry Help

FOR BRIAN COFFEY

Cry help? You'll find me fast in my grave first
Who now could come if I did call
since our stronghold our hope our legitimate lord
has himself suffered seizure and failed?

27: *Circuits and gates:* both the circuits and gates of a city, and computer chips, made (like sand and glass) of silicon

31: *Raw-head* and *Bloody-Bones* were names of nursery bogeymen.

32ff: "Observation of the red shift in the spectra of distant stars revealed that the universe is expanding." ("Red shift": the spectrum shift of a celestial body towards longer wavelengths due to its receding from the viewer.) "If the total material in the universe exceeds a critical mass, gravity will eventually halt its expansion and the universe will implode for another big bang. Should the universe ever start to contract, this would be evident in a blue shift." (Joyce) Joyce comments in correspondence: "Reminds me of (& was prompted by) a description by Jean Danielou I read umpteen years ago of Origen's theory of multiple creation of the worlds through emanation from the Godhead, and their repeated resumption by that source."

36: The line puns on terms drawn from theatre: *gods:* those occupying a theatre's gallery; *explode:* to drive someone from the stage by clapping and hooting; *turn:* an act.

37: *Red giant:* a large, cool star; *white dwarf:* a faint, dead star

40: *Venus . . . Mars:* both the planets and the Greek gods (who were lovers in classical lore)

Cry Help: "This is worked from the Irish of Aogán O'Rathaille (c. 1675–1729)." (Joyce)
Dedication: for Brian Coffey, see p. 284

5   Spun by the rip my mainstay snapped
           arse breached with shit bile eats my gut
           to see our ground our shelter our wildness our civilized precincts
           hocked for a pittance by wasters

           Our rivers their frets and divisions stand still
10   black marshes and palace the Bride and the Boyne
           lake sound run red and the ominous seas
           since that jack took the tricks from our king

           Keen rain
           on the road unsettles me
15   no sound comes near but the roar
           of that unstoppable falls

           Proud master of salient and hollow of royal demesnes
           his stomach is lost with his lands
           now the hawk who holds fast those rents and accounts
20   knows no man as kin

           Come down too far from original heights
           temporal races fret rockface
           where raging headsprings supplement
           the river that drops through the settlements

25   I stop and Death rides up to me
           and the dragons are quenched in their courses
           and I'm bound to follow my leader down
           where His white ledger covers all the deal

                                                                        1995

5: *rip*: riptide—a disturbance of the water
   mainstay: the main rope supporting a ship's mast
9: *frets and divisions*: agitations and discords; but also the frets of a stringed instrument and the divisions
   (rapid melodic passages) played on them
10: *The Bride and the Boyne* are Irish rivers.
11: *lake sound*: Joyce puns on the less obvious meanings of the words: "lake" is the color crimson or scar-
   let, "sound" an inlet or channel. "O'Rahilly has Lough Derg [a lake in County Donegal] going red, which
   I take to be a pun, so: Lough Derg = lake sound (Irish *dearg* = red)" (Joyce, in correspondence)
12: *jack*: both the playing card and simply "a man"
17: *salient*: a projecting part of a fortification
   demesnes: domains
22: *races*: both "streams" and "ethnicities"
28: *ledger*: besides the obvious sense, this is also the word for a horizontal gravestone.
   deal: business deal; deal table; dealing of cards; and a type of wood used to make coffins

Tohu-bohu

FOR CLARE AND TOM

I

First things first. One time a friend of mine came in for a few empty
crates from a Mazda import agency. With a couple of rolls of felt he
transformed his poky yard into a well-appointed loft where he kept
fantails first and pouters, then tumblers, and finally some serious
5   racing birds. At that juncture the fancy breeds had to go because
their freaks disturbed the steady fliers. But he never banded his soft
birds for racing, or bothered with the mandatory clock, just released
them when he rose and let them settle back at evening to roost
reassuringly secure. In the end though he got thoroughly sick of
10   their ceaseless moaning, so he kicked out the lot of them, refitted
the wire grilles with glass, sanded, sealed, and papered down the
primitive walls, screeded the floor, and later on moved in himself,
the family, and all their traps. For a good week after in these novel
quarters he picked over an odd volume of Pliny's *Natural History,*
15   shaken intermittently by the indignant refugees beating like stormy
rain against the panes, and on the flat felt roof. This is a true story.

Title: cf. Genesis 1: "In the beginning God created the heaven and the earth. And the earth was without
form, and void [Hebrew *tohu-bohu,* 'chaos']."

1ff: The narrative of this section contains beneath it the lineaments of a creation myth. *Mazda* puns on
Ahura Mazda, the creation-god of Zoroastrian religion; in Zoroastrianism he is responsible for all that is
good in the universe, while Ahriman is responsible for all evil. This conception of a division in the cre-
ation was passed on to Manichaeism and Gnostic Christianity, for whom the material world itself was
evil; these schools of thought are considered heretical within orthodox Christianity. The expulsion of the
birds parallels the expulsion of the angels—Joyce notes: "as in 'The Turlough', Origen's cosmology is rel-
evant, with the expelled angels cascading as successive realms of emanation, in a succession of increas-
ingly imperfect worlds, until they finally reach the pits and are withdrawn again to the god-head's per-
fection" (again, the teachings of the Greek theologian Origen [185–254] are considered heretical). The
good week of line 13 echoes the week of creation.

1: *came in for:* was given

3: *poky:* small

4: *Fantails, pouters* and *tumblers* are all breeds of pigeon.

12: *screeded:* leveled

13: *traps:* belongings

14: The *Natural History* of *Pliny* the Elder (23/4–79) is a wide-ranging though often inaccurate miscellany
of scientific information.

II

> . . . *do not look upon me on the dung-heap*
>   *nor go and leave me cast out*
>   *and you will find me in the kingdoms.*
> *And do not look upon me when I am cast out among those who*
>   *are disgraced and in the least places,*
>   *nor laugh at me.*
> *And do not cast me out among those who are slain in violence.*
> *But I, I am compassionate and I am cruel.*
>   THUNDER PERFECT MIND

When the shattering
key turns clockwise
the golden tumblers fall

20   through courts
where suits
are duly packed and paid

the ward turns
from the crooked talon
25   lofty strut and pinion

down their powers
and dominations
to the striking jack

III

And now these carriers
30   wheel painfully aloft
ringed round with tokens

protocols addresses
codes conventions empty forms
and the streams freeze in their shadow

35   remorselessly they brood
on every post
spill milk

Epigraph: "Thunder Perfect Mind is one of the volumes comprising the Gnostic library found under the
   sands at Nag Hammadi." (Joyce)
19: A *tumbler* can be a pigeon; an acrobat; or (in a lock) the piece that holds the bolt in place until the key
   is turned.
23: *Wards* are the ridges inside a lock which prevent a key without matching notches from being inserted;
   the sense of "ward of court" is also present.
24: *talon:* punning on a term from card-play, signifying those cards not yet distributed to the players.
26: *Powers* and *dominations* are two of the ranks of angels in the traditional ninefold Christian hierarchy
   of angels.
28: *jack:* both the court card and the mechanical figure of a man that strikes the bell of a church clock
III: "The final section incorporates a number of technical terms used in computer networking." (Joyce)
29: *carriers:* refers simultaneously to carrier signals (in telecommunications), angels ("angel" literally
   means "messenger") and carrier pigeons.
37: Both male and female pigeons produce "pigeon milk," fed by regurgitation to their young.

and thick saltpetre
as they flap
40   from the twisted pair

to coax
all the news
comes down

so tell me
45   how would you put down
a lingering infestation

of goddamned angels?
set snares of blood
raise ghosts

50   and memories
for decoys
bait deadfalls

with true sleep?
or keep by the fire
55   a niptic cat

to stalk high winds
and pounce
on fallen stars?

they just don't get
60   the message yet!
suggestions please

so I can get
forever shut
of their close breath

65   fat with clay
stone floods
the midnight crashing

of their verminous wings

1995

38: Guano (bird droppings) is a source of *saltpetre*.
40: *twisted pair*: a name for the twined variety of ordinary phone cable
41: *coax*: "a standard abbreviation for coaxial cable. It was also the sound made by Aristophanes' frogs [in
  The Frogs]. . . . As the verb, to coax, it also indicates here the suasive intent of ostensibly objective news
  programmes, and their context of commercials" (Joyce, in correspondence).
52: A *deadfall* is a trap which drops a heavy weight.
55: "A niptic cat would share the watchful qualities exemplified by the Niptic Fathers of the Philokalia, a
  collection of texts written during the fourth to fifteenth centuries by spiritual masters of the Orthodox
  Christian tradition." (Joyce)

DENISE RILEY (b. 1948)

R ILEY WAS BORN IN CARLISLE AND EDUCATED AT CAMBRIDGE. SHE HAS WORKED AS AN editor in London and lectured at Goldsmiths' College; she currently teaches at the University of East Anglia. Her volumes of poetry include *Marxism for Infants* (1977), *Dry Air* (1985), *Stair Spirit* (1992), *Mop Mop Georgette* (1993) and *Selected Poems* (2000). She is the editor of *Poets on Writing: Britain 1970–1991* (1992) and the author of three books of prose: *War in the Nursery* (1983), *'Am I That Name': Feminism and the Category of 'Women' in History* (1988), and *The Words of Selves: Identification, Solidarity, Irony* (2000).

In *'Am I That Name'*, Riley writes: "That 'women' is indeterminate and impossible is no cause for lament. It is what makes feminism; which has hardly been an indiscriminate embrace anyway of the fragilities and peculiarities of the category."[1] Challenging identities "inside a designation"—to quote from "Affections must not"—Riley's poems largely resist the autobiographical narratives of much recent feminist poetry and foreground the self and the lyric "I" as constructed in language. The dance of pronouns in her poetry is willfully disorienting, "dis-locating our mis-placed trust," as Nigel Wheale writes, the "I" sometimes becoming "the object of the sentence rather than the subject."[2] Similar concerns with the permeable boundaries of identity—gendered identities and also national identities—help explain Riley's periodic inclusion of lines from popular music ("*Lure, 1963*") or Chuvash and Gaelic poetry ("Knowing in the Real World" and "Wherever You Are, Be Somewhere Else"). These poems, Riley remarks in an interview, raise the question of "where [the poet] *can* speak from—how smoothly coherent a speech you can truthfully present." She acknowledges that the lyricism of ballads and pop music "makes her envious" and wonders "does 'modernity' condemn us to a lack of affect?" One might read her poems as partly an effort to work through just that question. Speaking of her interest in the abstract painting of Gillian Ayres and "the painting references" in her poem "Red Shout," Riley notes that "there's an idea of containment and deliberate depression of affect being stepped aside from in this poem by an overspill, and of bleeding over the edges. So that the 'really human sign / as light and shocking as an annunciation' is credited to the power of rapid color to spill off its own margins and break the separate illness or intensity of focus of the isolated painter."[3] Painterly values meeting the dis-locations of self and, in Wheale's words, "the mordancy of what we see," combine to make for what one might call abstract lyric; here "lyric" has more to do with musicality than self-expression.

---

[1] *'Am I That Name': Feminism and the Category of 'Women' in History*, London, 1988, p. 113.
[2] "Colours—Ethics—Lyric, Voice: Review of Recent Poetry by Denise Riley," *Parataxis: modernism and modern writing*, vol. 4, 1993, p. 72.
[3] Romana Huk, "Denise Riley in Conversation," *P. N. Review*, vol. 21, no. 5, pp. 17–22.

Affections must not

This is an old fiction of reliability

is a weather presence, is a righteousness
is arms in cotton

this is what stands up in kitchens
5   is a true storm shelter
& is taken straight out of colonial history, master and slave

arms that I will not love folded nor admire for their 'strength'
linens that I will not love folded but will see flop open
tables that will rise heavily in the new wind & lift away, bearing their pre-
      cious burdens

10   of mothers who never were, nor white nor black
mothers who were always a set of equipment and a fragile balance
mothers who looked over a gulf through the cloud of an act & at times
      speechlessly saw it

inside a designation there are people permanently startled to bear it, the
      not-me against sociology
inside the kitchens there is realising of tightropes
15   Milk, if I do not continue to love you as deeply and truly as you want and
      need
that is us in the mythical streets again

support, support

the houses are murmuring with many small pockets of emotion
on which spongy grounds adults' lives are being erected and paid for daily
20   while their feet and their children's feet are tangled around like those of
      fen larks
in the fine steely wires which run to and fro between love and economics

affections must not support the rent

I. neglect. the house

                                    1978

Lure, 1963

Navy near-black cut in with lemon, fruity bright lime green.
I roam around around around around acidic yellows, globe
oranges burning, slashed cream, huge scarlet flowing
anemones, barbaric pink singing, radiant weeping When

Title: *Lure:* title of a painting by the British abstract painter Gillian Ayres. "The poem . . . quotes or
rephrases song lyrics: 'The Great Pretender' written by Buck Ram, recorded by The Platters, 'The Wan-
derer' written by Ernest Maresca, sung by Dion ['I roam around around around around'], 'It's In His Kiss'
by Rudy Clark, sung by Betty Everett, and the title of 'When Will I Be Loved' written by Phil Everly,
recorded by the Everly Brothers." (Riley's note)

5 will I be loved? Flood, drag to papery long brushes
   of deep violet, that's where it is, indigo, oh no, it's in
   his kiss. Lime brilliance. Obsessive song. Ink tongues.
   Black cascades trail and spatter darkly orange pools
   toward washed lakes, whose welling rose and milk
10 beribboned pillars melt and sag, I'm just a crimson
   kid that you won't date. Pear glow boys. Clean red.
   Fluent grey green, pine, broad stinging blue rough
   strips to make this floating space a burning place of
   whitest shores, a wave out on the ocean could never
15 move that way, flower, swell, don't ever make her blue.
   Oh yes I'm the great pretender. Red lays a stripe of darkest
   green on dark. My need is such I pretend too much, I'm
   wearing. And you're not listening to a word I say.

1992

When it's time to go

When an aggressively uncontrolled schadenfreude
reads a personal threat in everywhere
and so animatedly takes this as 'the political'
that the very kitchen colander shells out a neat
5 wehrmacht helmet of brown rice
   das schmeckt nach mehr!
   or when an inverse brand of professional unhappiness
   taps on its wristwatch 'as a realist I . . .'—then

set this boy free

10 No this isn't me, it's just my motor running

O great classic cadences of English poetry
We blush to hear thee lie
Above thy deep and dreamless.

1992

Pastoral

Gents in a landscape hang above their lands.
Their long keen shadows trace peninsulas on fields.
Englishness, Welshness, flow blankly out around them.
Hawks in good jackets lean into the wind, shriek 'lonely I:

When it's time to go: 1: *schadenfreude:* pleasure in someone else's misfortune
5: *wehrmacht:* the name used for the German Army from 1921 to 1945.
6: "it tastes of more!" (German)
9: cf. "Sleep," by John James (see p. 643), from his book *Dreaming Flesh:* "I beg you to free this boy."
12–13: cf. the carol "O Little Town of Bethlehem": "O little town of Bethlehem, / How still we see thee lie!
 / Above thy deep and dreamless sleep / The silent stars go by."

5   This sight is mine, but I can't think I am.
Those pale blue floods of watered silk have flounced indoors, I hear
their flick of vicious fans. I'll land and stow my feathered legs
and walk to find a sweet interior of beer'—These men are right:
it's hard to own perceptions setting out and in, but
10   settling with a shudder into a hired car as if into a coat
or bed, Rose Riley in the back, our lives in the hand of my calm
crossing the bealach past implausible farms and up and up the
breathless track of couldn't reverse now if I had to, I've not
had enough of this yet. Look out for those in our red car
15   so that it may be well; the road thread spins
out of the car's smooth mouth, a dream of ease slips back—

I don't know why it isn't any harder than this
I don't know why this light is evident
I fell into sleep, and that was a pure place
20   *I woke, it is so easy that I can only smile—*

A homely accident will do for that: so within days
I've one eye left that pulls to join the darkness
in which its brother sits; one eye's unharmed
yet I can't steer by that, my brain
25   would drag the shutters down, now that the dark
has got the balance. I, snowman, cinder for eye
bandaged white upon red, an icon of d.v.
must tap my blindfold way around
this mother and child, child and mother
30   silver hoop that I live in: who
will step in to help me. Inside the eye
taped closely shut, repeating suns
are fringed with cloud and race away
into each other, and as they hotly go
35   from brown to reddish-violet to ochre
they snake, like sunspot photographs
or lights which stream out from eclipsed moons;
they'll not keep still but whoosh and whoosh
in a poor video I can't switch off. The iris
40   is frayed insect wings; what if the
pupil's black should slop and run across its
sheeny brown and green, what if that black
spill out of its neat rigorous circle—
I haven't got a body, till it hurts—
45   eyes can mend fast: into the place of all of us
my sight returns and with it mastery
to track again the feather-trousered flights.

1992

6: *watered silk*: a lustrous silk with a wavy pattern
12: *bealach*: a narrow mountain pass
27: *d.v.*: "deo volente" (Latin): "God willing"

Wherever you are, be somewhere else

A body shot through, perforated, a tin sheet
beaten out then peppered with thin holes,
silvery, leaf-curled at their edges; light flies

5   right through this tracery, voices leap, slip side-
long, all faces split to angled facets: whichever
piece is glimpsed, that bit is what I am, held

in a look until dropped like an egg on the floor
let slop, crashed to slide and run, yolk yellow
for the live, the dead who worked through me.

10   Out of their lined shell the young snakes broke
past skin fronds stretched over sunless colour or
lit at a slant, or saturated grey—a fringe flapping

round nothing, frayed on a gape of glass, perspex
seen through, seen past, no name, just scrappy
15   filaments lifting and lifting over in the wind.

Draw the night right up over my eyes so that I
don't see and then I'm gone; push the soft hem
of the night into my mouth so that I stay quiet

when an old breeze buffets my face to muffle
20   me in terror of being left, or is that a far worse
terror of not being left. No. Inching flat out

over a glacier overhanging blackness I see no
edge but will tip where its glassy cold may stop
short and hard ice crash to dark air. What do

25   the worms sing, rearing up at the threshhold?
Floating a plain globe goes, the sky closes.
But I did see by it a soul trot on ahead of me.

I can try on these gothic riffs, they do make
a black twitchy cloak to both ham up and so
30   perversely dignify my usual fear of ends.

To stare at nothing, just to get it right, get
nothing right, with some faint idea of this
as a proper way to spend a life. No, what

I really mean to say instead is, come back
35   won't you, just all of you come back, and give
me one more go at doing it all again but doing it

The title "is based on the Nintendo Games Boy slogan; the italicised phrases in the poem are adapted from
the old Chuvash, from the play *The Peach Blossom Fan* by K'ung Shang-jen, and from the ballads 'Fair
Annie of Lochryan' and 'Sweet Willie and Fair Annie' in Alexander Gardner's *The Ballad Minstrelsy of
Scotland*, 1893" (Riley)

far better this time round—the work, the love stuff—
so I go to the wordprocessor longing for line cables
to loop out of the machine straight to my head

40   and back, as I do want to be only transmission—
in sleep alone I get articulate to mouth the part of
anyone and reel off others' characters until the focus

of a day through one-eyed self sets in again: go into it.
I must. *The flower breaks open to its bell of sound*
45   *that rings out through the woods.* I eat my knuckles

hearing that. I've only earned a modern, what, a flatness.
Or no, I can earn nothing, but maybe
some right to stop now and to say to you, Tell me.

—That plea for mutuality's not true. It's more ordinary that
50   flying light should flap me away into a stream of specks
a million surfaces without a tongue and I never have wanted

'a voice' anyway, nor got it. Alright. *No silver coin has been*
nailed to your house's forehead you dog-skin among the fox fur
where did you get that rosewater to make your skin so white?

55   *I did get that rosewater before I came to the light* grass
shakes in a wind running wild over tassels of barley
the sails were of the light green silk sewn of both gold

and white money take down take down the sails of silk set up
the sails of skin and something dark and blurred upon the ground
60   where something else patrols it, cool, nervous, calling out

Stop now. Hold it there. Balance. Be beautiful. Try.
—And I can't do this. I can't talk like any of this.
You hear me not do it.

                                                        1993

Knowing in the real world

A yellow glow slips from the brick houses.
Some steely clouds swell up over them.

One afternoon hour burns away until a rust-
coloured light sinks in towards evening

5   or any time at all when I fall straight through
myself to thud as onto the streaked floor of

a swimming pool drained out for winter, no
greeny depths but lined in blackened leaves.

Knowing in the real world: This poem like the last draws on Gardner's *Ballad Minstrelsy of Scotland* for
italicized passages.

Then the cold comes to tighten the air. In my room
10   I hear cars and the snow flying around the street.

I'm not outside anything: I'm not inside it either.
There's no democracy in beauty, I'm following

human looks. Though people spin away, don't
be thrown by their puzzling lives, later the lives

15   secrete their meaning. *The red sun's on the rain.*
Where do I put myself, if public life's destroyed.

Only to manage something blindingly sweet. I'm
too old now to want to be careful. Then I wasn't.

What you see is what you could have easily. You
20   could. Or take me home. Another kind of thought,

liquid behind speech, bleeds away from it altogether.
I washed my son in the morning milk.

Sliced into the shine of now, a hand on a blade.
A wound, taproot in its day, its red blossom in light.

25   The wind sheets slap the sea into ruffled wheatfields.
Angel, fish, paradise, rain of cherries.

                                                                1993

BARRY MACSWEENEY (1948–2000)

MACSWEENEY WAS BORN IN NEWCASTLE UPON TYNE AND EDUCATED AT RUTHERFORD Grammar School. He attended Harlow Technical College in Essex from 1966 to 1967 and then returned to Newcastle, where he worked as a reporter and editor for the *South Shields Gazette*. The precocious MacSweeney was already reading widely in the work of Arthur Rimbaud, Charles Baudelaire, and other nineteenth-century French poets by the time Basil Bunting introduced him to the work of the Objectivists and other modernist poets; J. H. Prynne encouraged his interest in English Romantic poetry. In the poems included here from *Hellhound Memos* (1993), the epigraph and some of the poems' language are taken from Robert Johnson, but the fourth section addresses Shelley, linking the English poet with the American blues musician in a composite "outsider" figure. Rock musicians such as Jim Morrison and poets such as Anne Sexton and Sylvia Plath enter into other MacSweeney poems, the latter especially in the second half of *The Book of Demons* (1997), which includes poems about MacSweeney's alcohol addiction and his treatment for it. Clive Bush writes that "It is no less than the destruction of the poet as a measure of value that MacSweeney takes as his theme and he takes it, too, from the bourgeoisie who like to see their artists wounded, crippled, dying, or in some way at least fatally produced by a culture they have, less-than-secretly, little desire to change."[1] The world of MacSweeney's poetry, he argues, is one in which "prospects for the young and poor are daunting" in a landscape overwhelmed by the "fetishised technological paraphernalia of late industrial capitalism."[2] Given equally to self-deprecating, comic moments and apocalyptic rage, to bile and nostalgia, MacSweeney's poems can occasionally suggest the influence of Bunting in their rhythms and prosodies if not in their popular idioms and theatrical personae.

The Boy from the Green Cabaret (1968) was MacSweeney's first substantial collection. It was followed by *Our Mutual Scarlet Boulevard* (1971), *Brother Wolf* (1971), and *Odes 1971–1978* (1978). *Black Torch* (1978) takes as its subject northern working-class culture and political dissent in mining communities from the Industrial Revolution through the late 1970s. *Ranter* (1985) meditates upon the seventeenth-century Levellers and other historical figures in a tradition of dissent. Other books include *Pearl* (1995), a sequence of often tender and celebratory poems in which a mute Northumbrian girl MacSweeney taught to read and write sometimes appears in a role akin to that of the traditional muse as well as in other guises, occasionally being imagined as the speaker of the poem.

---

[1] Introduction to *Worlds of New Measure: An Anthology of Five Contemporary British Poets,* ed. Clive Bush, London, 1997, p. 12.
[2] Ibid., p. 14.

from Hellhound Memos

FOR TERRY KELLY AND NICHOLAS JOHNSON

I got to keep movin'
I got to keep movin'
blues falling down like hail
U m m m m m m m m m m m m
blues falling down like hail
blues falling down like hail
And the days keep on worrying me
there's a hell hound on my trail
hell hound on my trail
hell hound on my trail
ROBERT JOHNSON

Sunk in my darkness at daylight.
Rain on lamb's oily wool
my anointment.
Sunk in my darkness in my cracked
5   braindrain.
Daydawn lies here spastic as anything.
Knockings, roarings, sounds arrive
from one more planet you have not been to.

Not one child leaps up to say bravo!

10   Sunk in my darkness, weeping in trimmed maythorn
by petrol stations. They want my discount, my
coupon crystal goblet.
My phlegm, your phlegm.

Weak-kneed sunk in my blueness, my sun
15   your sun. My fuck-up, your fuck-up.
My rain, your rain.

All aboard and welcome.

                 * * *

Sunk at my crossroads, hellhounds baying
broken from chains, lips, jaws
slavering with death notice, rape
on my left and right, filthy money, yellow Jerusalem.

Epigraph: Robert *Johnson* (1911–1938), the great Delta blues musician. The haunted, passionate quality of his music is evident in such recordings as "Hellhound on My Trail," "Me and the Devil Blues," and "Crossroads Blues." His short life ended when he was poisoned by a jealous husband.

12: *coupon crystal goblet:* a sales promotion from the early 1990s, in which petrol stations gave coupons with each fill-up; with the coupons customers collected sets of crystal drinking glasses.

4: *yellow:* the color of rapeseed (canola) in flower. EEC agricultural policy subsidizes farmers to grow canola. Substantial acreages were planted in the 1980s with this cash crop, which was unpopular because (1) it caused and aggravated hayfever and other allergies; (2) it spread into the hedgerows and the wild and stifled less hardy plants, thus upsetting habitats and the food chain; (3) it angered conservationists and nature-lovers.

5   I'd walk in there, turn the tables, rinse
the crowd with phlegm, make their shoes walk.
Swag wings at the con machines, blister
fingers of the three lemon fools. Sing mad,
merle mad, trill a bone, door stance finally
10   with contre-jour, say what next ammonite, how
is oxygenation, where's your Elvis lipcurl now?

* * *

Me the multiplex moron, multigenerational
multiplicity, many-fingered man with a violet
shell suit, stolen BMW and a rack of E. I'm here!

I used to be nowhere, now I'm all over the place.
5   I've had the garlic and thyme, the purging flax, blood and bone.
I've been to bed with the black pudding. Keep it.

I'm the only jackpot chancer on the job, estate joy-rider
extraordinaire. Bored in the listless
summer, when the boys in blue are in Marbella on the piss

10   I waft in or rev as is my nature, contrary to
council or ecclesiastical denial, and open up these
stolen microwaves. I turn them on and breathe.

I don't care what the damage is. Or the waste.
I enjoy the flames. I can scorch a line, a beautiful
15   blue and true line through the hull of your lives

and must say I like it better so. I adjust my visor
accordingly. Cut, cut, cut. It's my dark, dark memo,
almost a badge. I groove in the magenta heat. I lean

into it. I don't erect headstones, Hosanna those
20   sky-blue heavens in the fairy tales. I deliver.
Into a permanent darkness for the rest of your days.

I come down like slate-grey rain. That's all. No God available.

* * *

9: *merle:* blackbird (dialect)
10: *contre-jour:* back-lighting (in photography)
   ammonite: a type of fossilized shell, shaped like a spiral

3: *shell suit:* leisure suit in artificial fabric, modeled on the track suit: a working-class fashion of the '80s
  E: the drug Ecstasy
6: *black pudding:* a type of sausage made from blood and suet
7: *chancer:* risk-taker
  estate: housing estate (low-income housing)
9: *boys in blue:* policemen
  Marbella: a crowded holiday resort on the Costa del Sol in southern Spain, popular with young working people
  on the piss: drinking

FOR PBS ONE DAY EARLY

The very low odour tough acrylic formula
of B&Q Safe Paint with satin gloss finish
is venal. Civilisation too good a word for it.
Percy, why won't anyone leave us alone? Pass
5   The 10-litre can of Professional Obliterating Paint,
please. Pass the zinc-plated wing nuts, the spur
budget gold effect bracket and inspiration shelf.
Not to mention the Zamba Wall Shelving with Tool Rack.
Hardbeam I am for both of us against the intrusions.
10   Bysshe, tush, fash not, two hundred is nothing.
Wait until two thousand, then we'll justly explode!
The very floodlit light of heaven has already been
sold, as you predicted. Nothing to attract you
but the chard and sprouting broccoli. The rest is trash.
15   Babble, babble, babble. Slick, stink, stink.
Happy birthday, wake up, let's drown together!

* * *

Your tentship, your azureness, your cornflower
blue, flung over me, your right as rain, your
Bob's your uncle, please court my swelled heart.
Please spill me the dew from cusloppe's rim.
5   So much of life is weeping and stained
like broken spies, tables damp with distress,
the tea cold.
To frank a legend you say in Bodoni Bold: I
have boiled the earlies and now I can stand tall
10   in my yellow rape Jerusalem. Never believe it.
Prisoners in stripes, it was always so, nurses in white,
a marvel anyone lived.
Major minor not doing one thing about it.
And where, under this heaven, is my Mary?

* * *

Sky so very vast and blue. Puny we.
Lonnens ribbed against it.
Hellhound, thee with vast purchase, off, off!
my siren, my knocker, my foghorn, my bell.

Title: *PBS:* the poet Percy Bysshe Shelley (1792–1822), who drowned while sailing in the Bay of Spezia.
2: *B&Q:* name of a chain of do-it-yourself stores
9: *Hardbeam:* concrete lintel
10: *tush, fash not:* "hey look, don't worry" (dialect)
12: cf. Shelley's *Queen Mab* 5.177ff: "All things are sold: the very light of heaven / Is venal; earth's unsparing gifts of love / . . . Are bought and sold as in a public mart / Of undisguising selfishness. . . ."
14: Shelley was a vegetarian.

4: *cusloppe:* cowslip (an archaic spelling)
6: *spies:* spy apples
8: To *frank* is to stamp a letter with a mark indicating that postage has been paid; the sense here is perhaps "give currency to."
  Bodoni Bold: a style of typeface
9: *earlies:* early potatoes

2: *Lonnens:* lanes, roads (medieval English)

5   Off my loose nails, my gate furniture, my slide
       action latch, my epoxy-coated wire hasp, my B&Q
       gate bolt, my free delivered catalogue.

       So on a much-ignored and cloudy peak
       in south Cambridge between the passing traffic
10   Several great men will undo their XL vests
       And flex their special hinges.
       One will not. He is alert in black corduroy.

       Cut the chicken into large pieces.
       Bring the milk to boil in a heavy pan.
15   If you have a heat diffuser
       use it.
       Puree the remaining flesh.
       Chill until needed.

       Sense the stars and the dark water.

                                                      1993

15: *heat diffuser:* a wire object placed beneath a pot on the stove to spread the heat more efficiently

BILL GRIFFITHS (b. 1948)

GRIFFITHS WAS BORN IN KINGSBURY, MIDDLESEX AND EDUCATED AT LOCAL SCHOOLS and University College, London. As an associate of Eric Mottram and others he helped to develop the Poetry Society's National Poetry Centre in the 1970s before joining eleven other members of the Society's General Council in resigning when, as Mottram writes, "the Arts Council moved in to quash this action, by threatening to withdraw funds unless its own unelected representatives were placed on the committee of management and certain members of the organization sacked."[1] During the early 1970s, Griffiths was also briefly part of the biker culture in London, then lived in Germany before returning to Britain to live in Harrow, London. After his houseboat burned down he was homeless for two years before moving north, eventually to Seaham in County Durham, where he now resides again after having spent 1997–1999 cataloging the Mottram archive in London. During the 1980s, he studied Old English at King's College, London, earning a Ph.D. in 1986. His many publications include essays on local government in the Northeast and other prose reflecting his loyalty to the poor and dispossessed and his skepticism about current political and legal systems. Griffiths's books of poetry include *Cycles* (1974–1975), *Materia Boethiana* (1984), *The Book of the Boat* (1987), *A Tract Against the Giants* (1984), *On Ploiinus* (1990), *Bikers* (1990), *Darwin's Dialogues* (1991), *Rousseau & the Wicked* (1996), *Nomad Sense* (1998), and *Mr. Tapscott* (1999). He has also been active in small press publishing, with his own Pirate Press (later Amra Imprint).

As some of the details above suggest, Griffiths's life and activities challenge many received ideas of the poet's identity. He is a non-violent anarchist who is also a classically trained pianist and a scholar-translator of Old English, Celtic, and Germanic languages and cultures. Similarly, his poetry, which is rife with lexical and syntactical play and rhythms sometimes informed by his study of Anglo-Saxon, is impossible to categorize; the poet-critic Andrew Duncan has described it as "antiquarian, colloquial, and avant-garde, all at the same time."[2] At times a sardonic wit abuts archival display, as when in "A Guide to the Giants of England, A Tract Against the Giants" the poet's citations of Geoffrey of Monmouth and the Vulgate Bible on "giants" as they "come to Christian mention / and shape" is followed by the statement that "there were / pagans, then, / awf'ly puzzled," the colloquial contraction seeming to comment on the scholarly apparatus as much as the conflict of Christian and pagan cultures.[3] The

---

1 "The British Poetry Revival," *New British Poetries: The Scope of the Possible*, ed. Robert Hampson and Peter Barry, Manchester, 1993, pp. 19–20.
2 "Sorcery, bestiary and bone orchard," *Angel Exhaust*, vol 12, p. 119.
3 *A Tract Against the Giants: Poems and Texts*, Toronto, 1984, p. 13.

erudite archivist thus is also sometimes deadpan comic and gentle mimic of idioms; elsewhere, as in the following lines from *Rousseau & the Wicked,* Griffiths's anger is palpable: "The rich are a form of pollution."[4] Clive Bush writes of "the combination of mysticism and practical anarchism that characterizes Griffiths' work" and of the poet's interest in folklore as owing something to Romantic and Victorian models while actively resisting "sentimentalizing nostalgia." He argues that "perhaps Griffiths' greatest ability is to combine the severest of ethical judgments" with "a sense of open intellectual, social and historical curiosity."[5] In "Reekie" Griffiths's wit and learning are both evident, though a poem that ends by apostrophizing a candy-bar probably privileges the former.

---

[4] *Rousseau & the Wicked,* London, 1996, p. 29.
[5] *Out of Dissent: Five Contempoary British Poets,* London, 1997, pp. 211–303.

Reekie

As an art form I have always supported the cigarette. It is more
sociable than a pension, more reliable than health, a reward, a sig-
nal, the only compensation as antique as potato, tomato,
coffee, chocolate. Now they are disappearing, our cigarettes, in
5   favour of a moral concern for a world safe at last for the motoring
classes.

for only
the bus the bus
the omnibus
10   green is green, green, green,
dieselly clean

(If ever you are invited to compete under a set of rules, do check
first who made them; it can be important. Getting the balance
right.)

15   there are advantages:
the clean, sweet sweep of the nasal passages,
a labyrinthinity of
the lung overt to air,
the added sensitivity when you resort to other
20   drugs. Is a
eye-opener.

The great glory of the summer salmon sky I can now
and participate in the scent of the sex of roses
roll

Title: Reekie: smoky
10: "Green buses in Sunderland advertise their benefit to their environment" (Griffiths, in correspon-
dence)

25   the dawn psychophase
      before
      the tufted particulates of the
      gross sea-lorries that
      serve the leg-wide superstores
30   out of tankers Mexican
      with cinnabar and chocolate and cigars.

      The butter-farmers
      soon better
      outcrop the arty oil finers
35   or lose.
      Dead beets,
      dead liquor,
      else.

      When—
40   My Lord Sugar
      was hoyed from the high altar;
      the Caramels run for their lives.
      'Down with Rum!' shout the pale-skins,
      warned by their doctors that superficial racial convergence would only pro-
          voke skin-cancer.
45   Teeth, skin, lungs, stomachs—
      Let them pay for their own treatment!
      The rum 'n' chocolates will be priced from office.—
      Shamed and shorn and kept shut.

      Ancient alliances rent.
50   A little point import
      bit dimensional re depth
      of the place of pineapples.
      What angles / imbalances
      you admired in trinkets and godligold
55   fancy world Baroque
      it does you glimpse Rococo
      good

      The no-god
      that has said
60   'no reeking',
      that coffee-killer,
      pervert ex-kango did it,
      rankles.

      Behold! O Brink of Venture,
65   Other Titles.
      We are just as good, us,
      we are just as good, as. . . .

_____

27: *particulates*: air pollution
28: *sea-lorries*: freight trucks carrying goods from overseas
41: *hoyed*: thrown
62: *kango*: prison guard

It is not an empire—this offertorium
it is not a trade—a ocean religion.
70 No Romeo
concepting of Juliet over-back and
No India
dreaming of its Empress Kali, and
the fair 'change of fume—
75 just no one
had the reverence and knowledge of
as me of

The feathered leaf
a or-ish filigree
80 twink 'n' brown
stalk seg-quick with
ripe pattern
as bird-phoenix burns
and unrolls

85 I of the nose-deity
legumi-humiline
swaying, or helitropic zinc-sense
health of fashion.
Trade myself for
90 I ama rider in a pale skull.

unused I rise
pleased
I press
with tudor grace—
95 our Lord is man of grass
(I 'ceive his form as smoke)
in stook 'n' cloud makes
abundant bright
face.

100 This is me.
This is my cigarette. A soul. See.
It sees thee.

Ultimately for bells,
("only thing I dislike is bells")
105 rises and sinks, as tolls
times / wakes / slockens to sleep.

68: *offertorium*: a section of the mass service
73: *Kali*: Indian goddess of destruction
79: *or*: gold
81: *seg*: short for "segment"
85–90: "I would paraphrase: I of the nose deity, i.e., I formerly a smoker, could now drink beer, or sun-bathe or take healthy zinc tablets" (Griffiths, in correspondence). The Latin name of the hop plant is *Humulus lupulus.*
97: *stook*: a bundle of grainsheaves
106: *slockens*: northern dialect for "dampens down, wets, slakes"

How
we live the life of weeds
tangled teams

110   The moon-crow
dully glass bead eyes
notices
and knows
and notices
115   and knows.

look up my nose
behold the clear signs, good doctrine
in the delicate haywire
whirl
120   the fret the strap
straw-tickle linking
irrumpt
fracture-fold
sugar is salt is snow
125   I don't know

As the nicotine receded,
Ah! ah!
Lurked mistle-curvy retina
memorials
130   surge
first sleeping fore,
then to the wake—
I do
I do believe
135   and the new time-layer head
has its constants of aggression, love and war and work and sex
to hold to
to vow to.

I am not I
140   but Legacy.
A List
A Schedule
A Manifest

progress
145   as a process (or standard puppet)
an acclimatisation.

I am the temperate zone.
I have so much rainfall.
I tolerate a modicum of sun.

150   Now normal
all people
feelers 'n' 'tennae spread
and apart, interprompt
testing little crag-eggs of

155   each is.
         Shoulda wear jeans.

         Quality they said does not count
         but how black your breath

         Farewell,
160   so farewell,
         you tubes, you tarnishers;
         up here the baby-blue bum-clear nothing.
         Vanish ye what ye will.

         Where only orders damage your health.
165   Questions urge stress.
         And rhyme is the major cause of tinnitus.

         Then go on.
         What else?
         What else shall I give up?
170   Give up and gain?
         (But what is trezur un*less*
         ye're penni*less*?)

         Non nobis domine
         the perks, and tithes, preferments, and boxing of the box,
175   mogo-vendors
         of herbal collars,
                 collects

         O Twix!

                                                1998

166: *tinnitus:* a ringing in the ears

173: *Non nobis domine:* from Psalm 115: "Not unto us, Lord, not unto us, but unto thy name give glory, for thy mercy, and for thy truth's sake." Griffiths notes that it is from "a latin public school type song."

175: *mogo-vendors:* Mogadon is a trade name for nitrazepam, a sleeping pill.

177: *collects:* brief prayers said in church services

178: *Twix:* a brand of candybar

BRIAN CATLING (b. 1948)

B ORN IN LONDON, CATLING IS A SCULPTOR AND PERFORMANCE ARTIST AS WELL AS A poet. After many years teaching in London at Brighton Polytechnic and the Royal College of Art, he now lives in Oxford, where he is Head of Sculpture at the Ruskin School of Drawing and Fine Art and fellow of Linacre College, Oxford. He is also a guest lecturer at the Chelsea School of Art, the Royal Academy Schools, and Veslandets Kunstakademi in Bergen. He has performed throughout Europe and the Far East and been the subject of television films in Britain, Norway, and Japan. His work has been exhibited in galleries in London, Oxford, and Paris. His publications include *Necropathia* (1971), *The First Electron Heresy* (1972), *Vorticegarden* (1974), *The Tulpa Index* (1983), *Boschlog* (1987), *The Stumbling Block its Index* (1990), *Soundings, a Tractate of Absence* (1991), *Future Exiles: Three London Poets* (1992), which also has poems by Allen Fisher and Bill Griffiths, and *The Blindings* (1995).

In an interview with Ian Hunt, Catling says "I don't believe in sculpture. I don't believe in 'writing'. . . . As if there's anything called sculpture that can't be trespassed or diluted. . . ."[1] In challenging the shape and the separateness of various artforms, Catling is well within the tradition of an historical avant-garde. The poet and novelist Iain Sinclair once compared his commitment to "total invention" to that of the Vorticists Jacob Epstein, Wyndham Lewis, and Henri Gaudier-Brzeska; more recently Sinclair has spoken of Catling's "shamanism of intent" and the "impersonal passion" and "selfless intervention" evident in "coded constructions synthesized from the chaos of the streets—to which, after exhibition, they will be returned."[2] This last phrase refers especially to Catling's installations, which, as Catling says in his interview with Hunt, are "only here for one moment."[3] Their ephemerality makes them akin to performance, explicitly rejecting the cult of ownership, inheritance, and monumentality the visual arts are still burdened with.

Catling's remarks about his writing suggest an eclectic set of influences, though he has singled out the poems of Samuel Beckett as an important early influence. Others have noted a neo-Gothic sensibility shaping and shaped by the poems. *The Stumbling Block its Index* attempts "to write a sculpture," describing or "indexing" a non-existent work. Simon Jarvis argues that "the owner of *The Stumbling Block its Index* has not merely bought a non-existent sculpture, but one whose non-existence is multiple; which variously trips up the many objects attempting to stand in for it.

---

[1] *Parataxis: modernism and modern writing*, vol. 4 (1993), p. 47.
[2] *Conductors of Chaos: A Poetry Anthology*, p. xx.
[3] *Parataxis*, vol. 4, p. 49.

Like the god of negative theology, it is best known by what it is not."[4] Thus the paragraphs of the "index" posit the "stumbling block" variously as book, as "rock in the desert," "pillow to the dispossessed," and "night thing, that sits on the heart." Images of waste, decay, and expulsion dominate, as does a tone that might best be glossed by Sinclair's reference to Catling as the "Virgil" of "the dark ages between the death of Punk and the forced abdication of Margaret Thatcher."[5]

---

[4] "'The Cost of the Stumbling Block,'" *Parataxis*, vol. 4, p. 40.
[5] *Conductors of Chaos*, p. xx.

The Stumbling Block its Index

FOR THOSE WHO WALK THE STONY ROAD AND FOR THOSE WHO CANNOT
WALK WITH THEM

The Stumbling Block is a graphite font. This black plinth was once a brush or similar terminal that was the lips of an intense electrical arc. Industries proud and violent need spoke through it to turn the wheel or smelt
5 and cast the constructed challenge. Now abandoned it finds benediction in seclusion. It has softened its mouth to hold water, so that small animals and disjointed humans may drink or sign themselves in their passage.

The Stumbling Block has been used like an entrance
10 step to sharpen knives on. Its fossil bristle of tight stone forcing the heavy blades down to a hiss along one edge. These are knives of gleaming hubris, long intentions honed for malice. They are magnetized and have been placed to construct a lectern. Each blade holding the
15 next to form the platform. It may hold this index at its centre, hovering, placed outside in the aorta of streets. The removal of any of the blades from the assembled cluster will spill their fish bodies to the ground. The paper will drink any of the stains of their usage.

20 **The Stumbling Block** is an ark of extinction. A bouillon hive of the murdered past, frozen dry to a mass. Something has warmed its corner, the Oxoed grit bleeds a vein of contagion, virulent in its passion to embrace and swim in human tides.

25 **The Stumbling Block** is unfound to the stained and unclear eye. But its nest, its negative hollow, can be discovered in the mounds of waste and detritus that choke the streets. Its possible wedge, sphere or beam form is there; a vacant socket, easily trampled, destroyed
30 or cleared away. It is watching. Its obstinate grace squinting across the demonstrations of power.

1: *font*: a receptacle for holy water; but also, in printing, a set of type
12: *hubris*: overweening pride
22: *Oxo* is a brand of bouillon cube.

It is the light in the eye of the needle grown solid with anger, a fat sugar that clogs the passage to any kind of paradise.

35   **The Stumbling Block** is a bell that sounds a deeper voice than the throat of men. Their image and cry shrinks the world.

The communication of global gossip becomes a barbed wind of trivial penning; television enclosures of wired

40   indifference, the reduction of memory removes the open field and causes blurred shivers to be understood as the same thing. The bell hums as acceleration eradicates silence, the foundation for stillness is removed. The speed of language clones its own restless

45   manic hunger. The portable telephone, miniature televisions, satellites and their collection dishes are the cutlery for this gluttony.

The inedible thinness they devour is obvious. To feed this addiction soapy fictions are boiled from the skin

50   and bone of poverty. Tribes, villages, jungles and the very air itself can be wasted or burnt to secure a dry armpit in puppeted dramas of nightmare lives. Condensation is sweating inside the bell; a human modest sound that is unwelcome. It drips from the rim

55   in whispers and pools beneath its limited protection.

    The Stumbling Block is a shape shifter, a spirit bench that dwells in the cuffs of the expanding city. Over its worn layers of woven scars many forms have been stretched, clamped and tasted, licked and cut; reshaped.

60   Anointed by subtraction, they are put back on the blinking streets, patted and set loose. In the deep pocketed burrows of the bench, termite-size clones dream white directions to colour the tiredness of their somnambulistic donors.

65   **The Stumbling Block** is a barrel organ dragged to the site of a crime. Its tin cup catching rain as it judders on the pounding box. The moon is caught between its throat and the water, and in the black gleam of its varnished vibration. It spills dance into the causeways,

70   sucking revellers along the spindle of its cranked tune. They will spin and curl their lumpen massed centrifuge around the bellowing thing. The laughter is momentary but has soaked away the blood, only the scuffs of shoes and the scratched cobbles sing on.

75   **The Stumbling Block** is not a coffer, disguised by a wig of artifice. It cannot offer erudition or substitute lame emotions with its materiality. There is some recognition between it and other objects that attempt to trough or

---

55: *protection:* Bells have from antiquity been used to frighten away evil spirits.
71: *lumpen:* degraded; ugly

80 synthesize a human essence, but it is always a shallow
exchange.
The block expands in its sturdy isolation, it will not be
groomed for curation; the matted waxen direction
cannot be combed. Standing for a moment, when the
doors have shut in the bright lit gallery, alongside the
85 accepted and the pampered all polished to a single
purpose, snipped and fluttering their slit, coin eye cut in
their heads. The block stands with no such incision, no
access to its core. It will not simper for admiration or
love, it will not beg blind and inert for ownership. It has
90 no hollow to be filled by promise or paper. Its currency
is elsewhere. It offers itself in totality, without a price; an
obstinate gift to the imagination, a curve from the
seclusion of possession.

The Stumbling Block is an atlas swallowing its tongue,
95 falling into itself folding to a knot. The ultimate
substance of the knot is unknown, the previous
components fractured from their named concepts. The
wires of latitude are split from their soldered jointings;
snapped antennae waving in the stuttering wind,
100 shredded, gulping inward, tearing the skin lampshade of
Europe. Blue paper seas welling over the boundaries.
Wide daubs from the oceanic puddles discolour the
distinctions of territory and race, all accent is bleached,
all islands are merged. Mud and ink, paper and water
105 are scoured into another projection.

The Stumbling Block dreams from its possible paper
heart of the forest of its origins. Long wood holding a
canopy of shadows, undisturbed by men or other large
predatory beasts. That is the way it is remembered, the
110 days turned by the spokes of sunlight rotating in the
leaves. This timeless nostalgia rents a mite of bitterness
which is slowed and coloured by the quiet of the reverie.
Small movements are running through the trees, tiny
objects begin to drop from the high branches, they spin
115 and turn slowly in some hesitation against the gravity.
Coins, the sun giving a bruised glitter to their copper
edges. These are the coins of the poor, they have been
overcounted, turned and fingered ceaselessly in the hope
that they might be more. In pockets and brains their
120 uncertainties are lodged. The alloys heated and stained
by fear give up their task. The falling discs transmute in
the slowing air, being all substance until an organic
weight is reached, just before they land in the rich soft
ground. Here they will seed, husking away their
125 miserable dormant past, drinking life and fluidity,
swelling, a primal eye beginning to sense the light.

82: *curation:* display in a museum; but also "curing" (as leather)
98: *wires of latitude:* Globes were made by pasting paper over a wire skeleton.
100: The Nazis made *lampshades* from the skins of murdered Jews.

The **Stumbling Block** is a clock run on parable, whose telling ticks the escapement, and chews the time by in even linked bites.

130 The lead weights are classically inscribed with the word *mercy*; these inching metal lungs that ride past each other in the wooden dusk case, were originally made to aid the quick death of a thin simple man. Without them tied to his legs the wrench would have been slow,

135 strangling rather than snapping his life.

He was sentenced for the malice of burning fields. That luminous smoulder is grafted to the hands, so they may move ponderously through the dark.

The **Stumbling Block** was once a rock in a desert,

140 before it was cut and reshuffled in its aim at the city. It was then a marking stone for a tribe of wild dogs. They darkened its arid temperature, writing a grip into one of the perimeters of their elliptical spoors. The rock was an ornate scented gem in the collar of their nomadicy.

145 Generation after generation they layered their time without ever reaching its kernel.

These aboriginal creatures had avoided men, even though they were marked into legend by them. The early hunters praised their cunning and celebrated the

150 social organization of their pack, seeing kinship in their yellow eyes. The latter men shot them for scavengers, seeing only cruelty in the invasion of their fenced ignorance. Recent man is embarrassed by them, embarrassed by their own knowledge, unable to place

155 themselves in the taxonomy of a zoo. Arrows, traps, guns and poisons were known. Great distances would be plotted to circumnavigate these fears, while holding the loadstones as their foci. Disappearance of individuals was common. The survivors breeding around the void

160 to balance the velocity of their continuance.

Return of a lost one was unknown. So that the arrival of a lone beast at the rock, scenting the distance of its clan and furiously trying to clean itself in the stained sand, had never been seen. During its absence it had become

165 infected. The animal had been maimed, part of its finely tuned senses had been injured, blurred by a human that it was forced to live with, a man, a stranger in a distant city cage. They had circled each other, smelling, sleeping and marking each other's curves. A circus performed to

170 mythologize a lens for the man. The dog now spun deliriously about the stone, digging and scratching at its mute surface, trying to contact its history and meaning.

128: *escapement*: the device that controls the transfer of energy from a clock's power source to its counting mechanism
142: *grip*: a small ditch for carrying off water (or, as here, urine)
143: *spoors*: tracks
155: *taxonomy*: scientific classification of plants and animals
158: *loadstones*: magnets

Like glass its contagion screened the animal's core from
the recorded intimacies of its identity. It would attempt
175   to set itself in pursuit of its brethren, but would only
return shivering and exhausted in the crystal cold of
night, curling its rictus of sleep around the stone. For
months it stayed, growing thin and matted on poor
food, its ribs wheezed, its muzzle bald and blooded from
180   the manic rubbing against the rock to release a scent. It
would smell the bane in its urine staining a new and
alien line in the stone. The demented creature dug deep
into the sides, under its weight exposing its base,
loosening the roots. By the time the pack returned the
185   stone was free-standing and had tilted to a different
angle. They sensed their brother's disease before they
saw him. With teeth bared and hackles bristling like fins
they approached the changeling. The unpoisoned dog
part of him greeted the family as they tore him to pieces.
190   The blood slippery and fast oozing under the now
rejected stone.
Inside the dense mineral chemistry another compass
was breeding, its lightless magnetism accumulating
towards the cities. The ghosts of its timeless past
195   steaming from its surface.
The pack sang a terrible vapour before they left, a shrill
distance of voice. A song no coyote had ever sung
before.

The Stumbling Block is a book, either wedged to open
200   the wrong door or so massively closed that it takes at
least two to open it. It is gathered, this supine
architecture of information; a chained cathedral library
fastened against usage. A solid yolk of arrogance gloats
the cover and bindings with locks and closed
205   contrivances. Only the agreed scholar is given the
combination and candle, to lean into its interior. The
block has grown to grudge these limp intrusions,
preferring invention or accident as its chosen visitors.
Shadows can pick its lock, displaced images or sounds;
210   their filed teeth engaging with its heart.
To list these picks would weaken, break or distort their
touch, they are occulted tools only to be chewed over
after their clandestine use. The key is carried under the
tongue not in it, so that care is taken in its concealment.
215   It is possible to choke on its opening. One key might be
said thus: Our great-grandfathers carried rotting fish in

177: *rictus:* a set position (literally, a gaping jaw)
188: *changeling:* Fairies were said to steal babies, replacing them with fairy children (changelings); here
the word also suggests "shapeshifter" or "werewolf."
202: In earlier centuries the books in church libraries were *chained* to their shelves.
212: *occulted:* hidden
216: Decaying fish will glow phosphorescently in the dark. Catling comments on this passage in an inter-
view: "When people were mining in areas of great gas, and they couldn't take a flame in, they took bas-
kets of rotting fish. . . . As an analogy for knowledge, picking the lock to darkness, that seemed aston-
ishing to me." ("Spread Table, Spread Meat, Drink, and Bread: An interview with Brian Catling,"
Parataxis 4 [Summer 1993]: 42–57; p. 50)

baskets to the centre of the earth. Miles under the scalp
of grass, fuel was scraped and dug, ferried up to the air
above to be burnt for heat. In this compressed blindness
220   gases would swim against the lungs, smudging breath
with toxins. No flame could be opened to their hunger.
Decay became the only wick to prop the straining eyes.
The fluorescence of the sea collapsing into the ash of the
dark.
225   It is possible to feel the keys forming, the impression
stolen for a moment, pushed into the soap or wax at the
back of the mind.

The Stumbling Block is imitating a known thing; it or
rather they hang on a polite wall midway between the
230   museum floor and its mezzanine gallery. The muffled
carpet climbs the polished stairs that balances the wall in
its palm. The two rectangular wooden panels hang
there; a diptych of dark symmetry. Smoked varnish
holds the image in place, a pictorial aspic that seals the
235   time. The finely raised lines and delicate mapping that
are now fused to the wood are veins and nerves. The
boards were once table tops, on them the mass of
human   bodies   was   cut   away.   A   brutality   of
craftsmanship pruning the focus down to these thin
240   causeways of energy and sense. When the task was
completed and the fluids washed away, they dried,
waiting for the varnish to seal their secret portraits
closed. The block holds the memory and taste of this,
and is attempting to reformulate their future, using
245   them like wafers or baffles to sandwich another raw
sensual purpose.

The Stumbling Block has made itself of carbon paper,
sucking the increasingly obsolescent material from
offices at the centre of the city. It is compressed to
250   become a pivot; diamond-hard. The compacted density
smoulders in the deep night blue of its waxy, slippery
layers. The tiny scar letters are thick and noisy at its
centre, their planktonic clusters bite and disengage
continually, refocusing the chattering fusion. This mute
255   lexical friction gives the heat that powers the flexibility
of the shifting mass.
It can be heard only in the quiet times; its static, a
translucent muscle pulling between infinites.
In this manifestation the block is almost organic, a
260   writhing tank of cellular activity, straining between two
poles:
The expansion of its darkness, winged by the buzzing
particles, wants to unfold into the voracious speed of the

226: *Soap or wax* are used to surreptitiously copy keys.
233: *diptych:* a painting on two panels connected by a hinge
245: *baffles:* "sensual purpose" perhaps suggests the baffle of a loudspeaker, which increases the power of
   sound from the front by blocking out vibrations from the back.

stars; an explosive gleaming tracery to re-map the
265   heavens, to disappear through power into silence.

The other quietness it seeks is the hush of decay, the
implosion of language to the standstill of dust. A
shuddering instant halt that fractures the codex and
converts the block to tablets so that the twitching bodies
270   of words are confirmed to fossils the moment before
they grind themselves to luminous powder, which will
be lost into the scuffed crust of earth.

The Stumbling Block with some resentment shows
itself as a television set, the kind that lolls on street
275   corners or in flea markets, apparently broken. It will hiss
and fur the endless flutter of information, translating it
to a more meaningful blur.

The Stumbling Block suggests itself to become the
conjuror's table. A simple cloth of hope spread across its
280   complex bulk. The articulator stands on one side, the
customers on the other. They gape at the purity of the
perspective into which their meagre belongings will
disappear. Elemental forms are placed on the surface;
geomantic cones, hastily painted wooden house forms,
285   spheres of glass, rosy with dunce futures; and cardboard
discs that look like treasure. These small toys of
expectation are moved and turned so that the audience
may see that they contain nothing. They are the solid
trustworthy signatures of the operator's good
290   intentions. He even rolls up the sleeves of his tunic and
removes the gold Rolex from his arm so that no tricks
can be seen there. With eager tension and open eyes
they stack their coins with his and wait in sure
knowledge of their just rewards.
295   In time they dwindle, until the conjuror is alone, he
folds the cloth around the money and the instruments
of amazement, tying its neck carefully before leaving.
The block is powerless in this and can offer no succour
to those who shuffle away. Nor can it respond to the
300   pride of the conjuror. It has been feeding, and is slightly
foxed by the quantity of the vinegar grume of
disappointment that it has absorbed.

The Stumbling Block is being hunted. Extravagant
books of soap, perfumed with fear, have been placed in
305   the sunken zones. Dew will rub their musk to bathe the
causeways with heart-rending lures. Lanterns of ice are
offered to the early morning, light is stroked through

268: *codex:* a manuscript volume of ancient texts
284: Geomancy is a type of divination involving the reading of lines or figures.
291: *Rolex:* a brand of watch
301: *foxed:* (of a book's pages) discolored with reddish-brown spots
    grume: viscous fluid

their steaming chancels. These constructed spectres are
almost strong enough to catch and drain the
310   omnipotent cryptic grace of the block.

The Stumbling Block has become a pillow to the
dispossessed. It can be moulded to the need of its
companion, kneaded and pummelled so as not to lose
its hunched purchase on the slippery pavement. They
315   will warble and breathe into it, it becomes their mother
as their alcoholic dribble writes a sad and caustic text in
its interior. This wet laser chisel entwines their lineage
with fine scrollwork into the intricate memory of the
city. These are the inhabitants of the boundary, our
320   necessary shadows that are being cast further from the
warmth of their twins. The block gives itself completely
to these and will fierce itself against the bright sneers
and plastic credit blades that shave their humanity.
Without word or agreement, without plan or direction
325   they have begun to sleep a line. In the gutters and
elbows of curbs, in the approved architectural
contrivances they have threaded themselves in a
necklace cleated to ring a living, dreaming wall; a
perimeter fence. Their expulsion has constructed a cage
330   that concentrates the greed in its own bitter well.

The Stumbling Block is a night thing, that sits on the
heart. It will sip from the ribs of guilt, to breathe
luminous heat into flat shabby lungs elsewhere.

1990

308: The *chancel* is the section of the church behind the altar-rails, containing the altar and reserved for
   the clergymen and choir.
314: *purchase:* grip
318: *scrollwork:* carved decorations in the shape of a partly-unrolled scroll

ALAN HALSEY (b. 1949)

HALSEY WAS BORN IN CROYDON AND EDUCATED AT THE UNIVERSITY OF LONDON, where he took a degree in philosophy. Between 1979 and 1996, he ran The Poetry Bookshop in Hay-on-Wye. His books include *Auto Dada Café* (1987), *Five Years Out* (1989), *Reasonable Distance* (1992), *The Text of Shelley's Death* (1995), *A Robin Hood Book* (1996), and *Wittgenstein's Devil: Selected Writing 1978–98* (2000). He collaborated with David Annwn, Kelvin Corcoran, and Gavin Selerie in the book *Danse Macabre* (1997) and with Karen MacCormack in *Fit to Print* (1998). Halsey is also a painter, collagist, and book-illustrator, in this last capacity contributing drawings to Corcoran's *The Next Wave* (1990) and Selerie's *Azimuth* (1984). Since 1994, he has been the publisher of West House Books. He lives in Sheffield.

Tim Woods writes of the way, in Halsey's poetry, "words seem to fall over each other in their hurry to *work*," and of Halsey's fascination with the "metamorphosis of the word."[1] Phonic resonances and resemblances can seem to drive his poems, as in the opening of "Self-Portrait in a '90s Bestiary," or these lines from "Answering a New Year Letter, 1989": "While I'm for / getting by you're forgetting / truth derives from prepositions. . . ." The spirit suggested by such technique is partly ludic, but Halsey's playfulness rarely sacrifices the discursive power of the sentence. His poetry is charged by ethical and political concerns such as those suggested in lines from "For Reasonable Distance": "if that's the 21st century / coming in to land / or into money as / of now it will be trial / by ideal in an ordeal / world in which second- / hand minute particulars / discount the hours."[2] It should be noted that across his career thus far Halsey's poetic modes have been quite diverse, ranging from post-concrete alphabet poems to the mixture of prose and poetry in his *A Robin Hood Book,* which Gavin Selerie praises for its attentiveness to "the layers of accretion by which a legend develops" and its contrasting of "those who use the law as an instrument of their own profit" in contemporary Britain with "'a different order of value,' a longer reach of connexions between reach and supply."[3] In its occasional use of archaisms and myth, Halsey's poetry can suggest the influence of David Jones, but his search in his poems for a "passable order" in society and culture shares little with the Spenglerism and alienated conservatism of the older poet's work. Halsey seems most worried about linguistic and cultural systems when they approach the condition of stasis.

---

[1] "'Liquid Letters': Alan Halsey's *Five Year's Out*," *Fragmente*, vol. 3, 1991, p. 66.
[2] *Reasonable Distance*, Cambridge, 1992, p. 11.
[3] "Tracks Across the Wordland: The Work of Alan Halsey 1977–1996," *Pages* 397–420, 1996, p. 415.

Answering a New Year Letter, 1989

Clan destiny rules OK.
By naming no names
the way we're told every day
begins to seem to seem
5   like a great China being
broken up or down, a big pile-up
on the City of God bypass.
It's not the truth but the labels
which are liable to shift,
10   signed but not sealed or else
sealed but not delivered,
that's ventriloquism's debt
to lip-service. While I'm for
getting by you're forgetting
15   truth derives from prepositions
down here where we're always
up to something somebody
won't stand for but a totem
would, and for more
20   than tabulation prohibits.
At one below par
reason's parabled white,
parboiled, parcelled, pardoned
et seq.—all to explain
25   the apparent high levels
of deregulatory coincidence
as so-and-so is said to have said
in a context less familiar,
which is surely the point
30   of least contact, by the day.

                                        1992

Self-Portrait in a '90s Bestiary

Eternity's entirety's excuse
becoming chaos. Fitting odes
to the wrong occasions see me
marginalien in dream remin-

5: *great China being*: punning on "Great Chain of Being," a conception of the ordering of the universe that had a strong influence on Western thought down to the eighteenth century: in it, the universe contains an infinity of forms, which can be hierarchically ordered from the least of existences to the greatest (God himself). Halsey is linking this idea to the hierarchical cosmology of Taoism—the opening of this sentence draws on the *Tao Te Ching*'s first chapter: "The way [*tao*] that can be told is not the constant way; the name that can be named is not the constant name."

7: The great Christian theologian St Augustine (354–430) wrote *The City of God*, in which he distinguishes between the heavenly city of the elect and the earthly city of the damned.

18–20: cf. Freud's book *Totem and Taboo*

24: *et seq.*: "et sequentia" (Latin): "and the following"

Title: Medieval *bestiaries* were "natural histories of animals treated so that the peculiarities of animals shall convey a wholesome moral" (to quote *OED*'s 1871 citation).

5   aissance caught in categorical
     imperatives climbing up snakes
     and falling down letters off
     the edge of the map of monday
     when caveats for breakfast
10   make a workingman's day
     into a lifetime's achievement.
     Dirges, pal—watch how my
     opposite number in companion
     studies eats his tail then
15   my hat—*lapse grid*. If
     I am prepared to believe
     that the time-scale has been
     wiped as a personal matter
     from the public record then
20   does that explain the sepia tints
     developing at once in this shiny
     what we used to call saloon bar?
     A passable order never quite
     settles on the things men buy
25   and predecease, remarks the fellow
     with two heads and half a mind to
     the barflies and the world-
     weary oyster. Debt stifles
     debate. One makes millions but
30   many of the many only surface
     while the tigress burns in infinite
     redress shamefaced. The next moment
     is Bigfoot's last chance to prove
     fate favours him beneath the fin-
35   de-siècle moon before it sets
     out its terms and sets too.

                                                                 1992

An Essay on Translation

I.M. PETER HOY

How are the things by Hay-on-Wye
and what will you do when you are Death?
The painter has drawn a Parisian scene
characterized by decadence and various suggestions.
5   There is no end to appearance.

5–6: In the philosophy of Immanuel Kant *categorical imperatives* are universally binding moral laws.
9: *caveats:* warnings (from the Latin *caveat:* "let him beware")
34–35: *fin-/de-siécle:* end of the century

Title: *Translation:* three senses are operative: a translation of a text; relocation; an ascension from earth
   into heaven. Peter Hoy was a French scholar and a lecturer at Merton College, Oxford; he is best known
   as a bibliographer who edited and translated many modern French poets.
1: *Hay-on-Wye:* a Welsh border-town famed for its unusually large number of secondhand bookstores.
   Halsey ran the Poetry Bookshop in Hay-on-Wye from 1979 to 1996.

There is no end to likeness and fashion.
The things by Hay-on-Wye
show a scene muddle-mouthed and another
dry patch of rock 'n' roll melancholia.
10   There is a novice in the land
of the Dead who was a friend of mine.

Who is nervous as he was. Some
gather to the light, some
whistle and hum, some dowse,
15   some fall into a drowsy melancholia.
Some die after death. An old dream
of me gives the impression I need
certain books. The painter
has drawn a black river.

20   How are the things by the river?
Standing somewhat aside from the gathering there
is a novice I still call a friend of mine.
There is no end to likeness and appearance.

1996

19: *black river:* In Greek legend, the souls of the dead were ferried to the underworld over the river Styx
by the boatsman Charon.

GRACE NICHOLS (b. 1950)

N ICHOLS WAS BORN IN A SMALL VILLAGE ON THE GUYANA COAST. AFTER HIGH SCHOOL in Georgetown, she worked as a primary school teacher, a clerk at a telephone company, and a freelance reporter and journalist. She received a diploma in Communications from the University of Guyana. Nichols has written of her early interest in Guyanese and Amerindian folktale and stated that "It was only after coming to England in 1977 that poetry began to play a bigger and bigger part of my life. I started to read more of the work of other Caribbean and Black American poets. Having been surrounded by a lot of English poetry as a child I found that Caribbean poetry helped to put me in touch with the different rhythms, orality and atmosphere of our own culture."[1] The author of several collections of stories and poems for children, she has also published a novel, *Whole of the Morning Sky* (1986), and books of poems including *I is a long memoried woman* (1983), *The Fat Black Woman's Poems* (1984), *Lazy Thoughts of a Lazy Woman* (1989), and *Sunris* (1996). Her poems and performances have made her one of the most popular poets in England. She lives in Sussex and works as a freelance writer.

Nichols's poetry, especially in earlier volumes, employs the parallelisms and rhymes of popular poetry and song; the language of folktale as well as biblical idioms also inform the work. C. I. Innes has written that her poetry "challenges not only Western and Caribbean male traditions, but also a developing tradition of black women's writing, often a feature of the anthologies, that focuses on their suffering and portrays black women chiefly as victims of a white male patriarchy."[2] Nichols's poems about the "fat black woman" transform a stereotypical and derogatory image into a figure of strength; "IT'S BETTER TO DIE IN THE FLESH OF HOPE / THAN TO LIVE IN THE SLIMNESS OF DESPAIR" she writes in one poem. In "Skanking Englishman Between Trains" a young Englishman for whom a Caribbean patois and lifestyle is fashionable is gently mocked. "Long-Man" tells of an excursion with her family and friends to see the ley figure in Sussex thought to be of Saxon origin, but the mystery and "primitive pull / Of the pagan dimension" meets a more familiar and intimate world when we overhear the poet singing to her five-year-old a song borrowed from *The Wizard of Oz*. If the "fat black woman" would "place [her] X against a bowl of custard," defiantly affirming all that is used against her, Nichols's more autobiographical poems such as "Long-Man" celebrate domesticity and compassion.

---

[1] "Home Truths," in *Hinterland: Caribbean Poetry from the West Indies and Britain*, ed. E. A. Markham, Newcastle upon Tyne, 1989, p. 297.
[2] "Accent and Identity: Women Poets of Many Parts," in *Contemporary British Poetry: Essays in Theory and Criticism*, ed. James Acheson and Romana Huk, Albany, 1996, p. 329.

The Fat Black Woman Remembers

The fat black woman
remembers her Mama
and them days of playing
the Jovial Jemima

5   tossing pancakes
to heaven
in smokes of happy hearty
            murderous blue laughter

Starching and cleaning
10   O yes scolding and wheedling
pressing little white heads
against her big-aproned breasts
seeing down to the smallest fed
feeding her own children on Satanic bread

15   But this fat black woman ain't no Jemima
            Sure thing Honey/Yeah

                                  1984

The Fat Black Woman Versus Politics

The fat black woman
could see through politicians
like snake sees through rat
she knows the oil
5   that ease the tongue
she knows the soup-mouth tact
she knows the game
the lame race for fame
she knows the slippery hammer
10   wearing down upon the brain

In dreams she's seen them
stalking the corridors of power
faces behind a ballot-box cover
the fat black woman won't be their lover

15   But if you were to ask her
What's your greatest political ambition?
she'll be sure to answer

       To feed powercrazy politicians a manifesto of lard
       To place my X against a bowl of custard

                                  1984

Skanking Englishman Between Trains

Met him at Birmingham Station
small yellow hair Englishman
hi fi stereo swinging in one hand
walking in rhythm to reggae sound/Man

5   he was alive
he was full-o-jive
said he had a lovely
Jamaican wife

Said he couldn't remember
10   the taste of English food
I like mih drops
me johnny cakes
me peas and rice
me soup/Man

15   he was alive
he was full-o-jive
said he had a lovely
Jamaican wife

Said, showing me her photo
20   whenever we have a little quarrel
you know/to sweeten her up
I surprise her with a nice mango/Man

he was alive
he was full-o-jive
25   said he had a lovely Jamaican wife

1984

Title: *Skanking:* The word is glossed by line 4.
11: *drops:* a Jamaican cake made from coconut
12: *johnny cakes:* pancakes

Long-Man

(For Barbara Cole who first introduced us to the Long-Man
For Jan and Tim who came along
And to *The Druid Way* by Philip Carr-Gomm)

On open downland we're as open as he—
Me and Jan, Tim and John,
Kalera and Ayesha,
And the cracked-sun
5   Has once again withdrawn.
Leaving us to windy shawls
And pewtery greys
To newly mowed down
Fecund-earth which the rains
10   Had furrowed into clay.

Plod-Plod
Through the caking-blood
Of England's sod,
Our good shoes growing
15   Sulkier by the minute,
As is my five-year-old,
Whose hand a sixth sense
Tells me to hold,
Despite her intermittent tugging
20   On this our hill-god pilgrimage.

And even when she manages
To break free, I'm after her,
A wiser Demeter—
Swiftfooted and heavy
25   With apprehension.
Sensing the weald-spirits
In a primitive pull
Of the pagan dimension.

'We're off to see
30   The Long-Man, the wonderful
Long-Man of Wilmington,'
I sing, humouring her over
The timeless witchery
Of the landscape.

Title: "Reclining on the hills of the Southdown (halfway between Lewes and Eastbourne) is the mysterious figure of the Long-Man of Wilmington. Like the Cerne Giant in Dorset, he is carved out on the chalky hillside, reaching a height of 231 feet. . . . The Long-Man, or Green Man, of Wilmington continues to mystify generations of visitors and there is still much speculation as to whether he was carved out by the monks from the Wilmington Priory in the Middle Ages. Whether he is Saxon, Celtic or even Roman in origin, he remains naked, featureless and enigmatic. The silent figure of the Long-Man with his two staves invites us to solve the mystery." (Nichols' note)
23: *Demeter*: Greek goddess of agriculture; her daughter Persephone was snatched away by the underworld god Hades while picking flowers.
26: The *Weald* is a raised forested area in southeast England; on its rim are the chalk hillsides of the North and South Downs.

35 Meanwhile, as always, he's there,
Looming out of the green coombe
Of Windover's womb.

In our heart-searching
And soul-yearning
40 We come to stand before him,
But soon our luminous eyes
Are nailing him with a
Crucifixion of questions—
Who and Why and How he came to be.
45 Male, Female, or ancient
Presage of a new androgyny?

With the sun back out
Surely he is benevolent
Corn-God and Shepherd
50 Of the good harvest?

Sun-in and he's
The Phantom-Symbol
Of all our foreboding.
The Gatekeeper-Reaper
55 Who would reap us in.
The faceless frozen traveller.
Moongazer.
Green Man-Mirror,
Tricking our eyeballs on—
60 The cunning chameleon.

But going back over
The wet green swelling
The presumptuous Goddess in me
Looks back and catches him—
65 Off guard.
Poor wounded man,
The staves in his arms
No barrier to a woman like
She-who-would-break-them
70 And take him in her arms.

1996

36: *coombe:* valley on the flank of a hill

MEDBH McGUCKIAN (b. 1950)

DISCUSSING A PASSAGE FROM THE RUSSIAN POET OSIP MANDELSTAM BESIDE Mc-Guckian's poetry, Clair Wills argues that "Poetic speech is not linear but characterized by swift indirect motions; one image grows out of another, creating a crystallographic structure rather than one of preconceived form." This "swift convertibility of images" is the first thing the reader notices in many of McGuckian's poems, which are propelled from one metaphor or simile to another until the ostensible subject of the poem threatens to disappear altogether. As Wills notes, such elusive strategies do not seek to demonstrate McGuckian's ingenuity but rather to stress "the inappropriateness of 'naming' or fixing the poetic object."[1] In the early poem "Slips," McGuckian writes "My childhood is preserved as a nation's history, / My favorite fairytales the shells / Leased by the hermit crab"—as if the tactics of the hermit crab in making its home in a discarded shell are also those of the poet trying to make sense of her own felt experience under the weight of received accounts of nation and, or *as,* woman. The poem ends in an image identifying the power of metaphor and figure with singularity and an eroticized body: "I see my grandmother's death as a piece of ice, / My mother's slimness restored to her, / My own key slotted in your door—/ Tricks you might guess from this unfastened button, / A pen mislaid, a word misread, / My hair coming down in the middle of a conversation."

McGuckian was born into a Catholic family in Belfast and educated at a Dominican convent and Queen's University, Belfast, where she came to know the Northern Irish poets Seamus Heaney, Michael Longley, Paul Muldoon, and Ciaran Carson. She has taught at St. Patrick's Boys' College in East Belfast and been writer-in-residence at Queen's University, Belfast and the University of California, Berkeley. Her books include *Portrait of Joanna* (1980), *The Flower Master* (1982), *Venus and the Rain* (1984), *On Ballycastle Beach* (1988), *Marconi's Cottage* (1991), *Captain Lavender* (1994), and *Shelmalier* (1998). She lives in Belfast.

---

[1] *Improprieties: Politics and Sexuality in Northern Irish Poetry,* Oxford, 1993, p. 174.

Tulips

Touching the tulips was a shyness
I had had for a long time—such
Defensive mechanisms to frustrate the rain
That shakes into the sherry-glass

5   Of the daffodil, though scarcely
       Love's young dream; such present-mindedness
       To double-lock in tiers as whistle-tight,
       Or catch up on sleep with cantilevered
       Palms cupping elbows. It's their independence
10   Tempts them to this grocery of soul.

       Except, like all governesses, easily
       Carried away, in sunny
       Absences of mirrors they exalt themselves
       To ballets of revenge, a kind
15   Of twinness, an olympic way of earning,
       And are sacrificed to plot, their faces
       Lifted many times to the artistry of light—
       Its lovelessness a deeper sort
       Of illness than the womanliness
20   Of tulips with their bee-dark hearts.

                                                               1980

The Seed-Picture

       This is my portrait of Joanna—since the split
       The children come to me like a dumb-waiter,
       And I wonder where to put them, beautiful seeds
       With no immediate application . . . the clairvoyance
5   Of seed-work has opened up
       New spectrums of activity, beyond a second home.
       The seeds dictate their own vocabulary,
       Their dusty colours capture
       More than we can plan,
10   The mould on walls, or jumbled garages,
       Dead flower heads where insects shack . . .
       I only guide them not by guesswork
       In their necessary numbers,
       And attach them by the spine to a perfect bedding,
15   Woody orange pips, and tear-drop apple,
       The banana of the caraway, wrinkled pepper-corns,
       The pocked peach, or waterlily honesty,
       The seamed cherry stone so hard to break.

       Was it such self-indulgence to enclose her
20   In the border of a grandmother's sampler,
       Bonding all the seeds in one continuous skin,
       The sky resolved to a cloud the length of a man?
       To use tan linseed for the trees, spiky
       Sunflower for leaves, bright lentils
25   For the window, patna stars

The Seed-Picture: 17: *honesty:* a flowering plant whose semitransparent disc-like seedpods are used in
   dried flower arrangements; McGuckian likens them to waterlily-pads.
25: *patna stars:* i.e., star anise

For the floral blouse? Her hair
Is made of hook-shaped marigold, gold
Of pleasure for her lips, like raspberry grain.
The eyelids oatmeal, the irises
30   Of Dutch blue maw, black rape
For the pupils, millet
For the vicious beige circles underneath.
The single pearl barley
That sleeps around her dullness
35   Till it catches light, makes women
Feel their age, and sigh for liberation.

                                                                    1980

Slips

The studied poverty of a moon roof,
The earthenware of dairies cooled by apple trees,
The apple tree that makes the whitest wash . . .

But I forget names, remembering them wrongly
5   Where they touch upon another name,
A town in France like a woman's Christian name.

My childhood is preserved as a nation's history,
My favourite fairy tales the shells
Leased by the hermit crab.

10   I see my grandmother's death as a piece of ice,
My mother's slimness restored to her,
My own key slotted in your door—

Tricks you might guess from this unfastened button,
A pen mislaid, a word misread,
15   My hair coming down in the middle of a conversation.

                                                                    1982

Aviary

Well may you question the degree of falsehood
In my round-the-house men's clothes, when I seem
Cloaked for a journey, after just relearning to walk,
Or turning a swarthy aspect like a cache-
5   Enfant against all men. Some patterns have

27–28: *Gold of pleasure* is a grain, also known as "false flax" or "German sesame."
30: *maw:* mallow
    rape: rapeseed

Aviary: 4–5: *cache-enfant:* "a suppose, a Victorian kind of front-bustle to hide a pregnancy in dress"
  (McGuckian, in correspondence)

A very long repeat, and this includes a rose
Which has much in common with the rose
In your drawing, where you somehow put the garden
To rights. You call me aspen, tree of the woman's
10   Tongue, but if my longer and longer sentences
Prove me wholly female, I'd be persimmon,
And good kindling, to us both.
Remember
The overexcitement of mirrors, with their archways
15   Lending depth, until my compact selvedge
Frisks into a picot-edged valance, some
Swiss-fronted little shop? All this is as it
Should be, the disguise until those clear red
Bands of summerwood accommodate next
20   Winter's tardy ghost, your difficult daughter.

I can hear already in my chambered pith
The hammers of pianos, their fastigiate notes
Arranging a fine sight-screen for my nectary,
My trustful mop. And if you feel uncertain
25   Whether pendent foliage mitigates the damage
Done by snow, yet any wild bird would envy you
This aviary, whenever you free all the birds in me.

1984

The War Ending

In the still world
Between the covers of a book,
Silk glides through your name
Like a bee sleeping in a flower
5   Or a seal that turns its head to look
At a boy rowing a boat.

The fluttering motion of your hands
Down your body presses into my thoughts
As an enormous broken wave,
10   A rainbow or a painting being torn
Within me. I remove the hand
And order it to leave.

Your passion for light
Is so exactly placed,
15   I read them as eyes, mouth, nostrils,
Disappearing back into their mystery

15: *selvedge:* the edge of a piece of fabric, finished so as to prevent raveling
16: *picot-edged:* edged with ornamental loops
   valance: a drapery hung along the edge of a bed, altar, canopy, table, etc.
22: *fastigiate:* tapered upwards like a cone (said of trees)
23: *nectary:* the gland of a plant that secretes nectar

Like the war that has gone
Into us ending;

There you have my head,
20   A meeting of Irish eyes
With something English:
And now,
Today,
It bursts.

1991

The Albert Chain

Like an accomplished terrorist, the fruit hangs
from the end of a dead stem, under a tree
riddled with holes like a sieve. Breath smelling
of cinnamon retires into its dream to die there.
5   Fresh air blows in, morning breaks, then the mists
close in; a rivulet of burning air
pumps up the cinders from their roots,
but will not straighten in two radiant months
the twisted forest. Warm as a stable,
10   close to the surface of my mind,
the wild cat lies in the suppleness of life,
half-stripped of its skin, and in the square
beyond, a squirrel stoned to death
has come to rest on a lime tree.

15   I am going back into war, like a house
I knew when I was young: I am inside,
a thin sunshine, a night within a night,
getting used to the chalk and clay and bats
swarming in the roof. Like a dead man
20   attached to the soil which covers him,
I have fallen where no judgment can touch me,
its discoloured rubble has swallowed me up.
For ever and ever, I go back into myself:
I was born in little pieces, like specks of dust,
25   only an eye that looks in all directions can see me.
I am learning my country all over again,
how every inch of soil has been paid for
by the life of a man, the funerals of the poor.

Title: McGuckian's father's second name was *Albert,* a very British name; thus for him it was a kind of
"chain." *Albert chains* are popular gold-linked necklaces with a horizontal bar instead of a cross; prison-
ers would save up to buy one for their girlfriend. In a letter McGuckian notes of the image of the chain:
"The whole 1st stanza circles around that theme, something at the end of something else—the imperial
legacy of North Ireland. We are still bound to Victorian England which no longer exists except here."
14: *lime:* linden; though perhaps alluding to the caustic substance lime, in which the bodies of the exe-
cuted were placed in order that they might be the more quickly expunged.

I met someone I believed to be on the side
30 of the butchers, who said with tears, 'This
is too much.' I saw you nailed to a dry rock,
drawing after you under the earth the blue fringe
of the sea, and you cried out 'Don't move!'
as if you were already damned. You are muzzled
35 and muted, like a cannon improvised from an iron
pipe. You write to me generally at nightfall,
careful of your hands, bruised against bars:
already, in the prime of life, you belong
to the history of my country, incapable
40 in this summer of treason, of deliberate treason,
charming death away with the rhythm of your arm.

As if one part of you were coming to the rescue
of the other, across the highest part of the sky,
in your memory of the straight road flying past,
45 I uncovered your feet as a small refuge,
damp as winter kisses in the street,
or frost-voluptuous cider over
a fire of cuttings from the vine.
Whoever goes near you is isolated
50 by a double row of candles. I could escape
from any other prison but my own
unjust pursuit of justice
that turns one sort of poetry into another.

1994

50: *double row of candles:* i.e., at a wake

TONY LOPEZ (b. 1950)

LOPEZ WAS RAISED IN BRIXTON, SOUTH LONDON; HIS FATHER WAS A WORLD WAR II Hispanic refugee from North Africa, his mother a native of London. He published five crime and science-fiction novels with the New English Library between 1973 and 1976, before attending the University of Essex and then completing work for his Ph.D. at Gonville & Caius College, Cambridge, where he studied with J. H. Prynne. "Brought Forward" is one complete section of *False Memory* (1996), a modular sequence of 110 quatorzains. As elsewhere throughout the sequence, this poem employs jargon and phrases taken from marketing, biochemical, military, poetic, medical, financial, and similarly "specialized" discourses, welding these in an apparent syntactic continuity that heightens the reader's sense of their dizzying proliferation. The memory of Elizabethan sonnet sequences and their bucolic "Arcadia" meets the language of advertising in a kind of retro-pastoral, offering a grimly comic view of recent British history that is especially attuned to the impact of Thatcherite policies. The dominant mood of the sequence can be glimpsed, perhaps, in the book's first line—"And I don't see how we can win." If this suggests a conversational beginning *in medias res* the reader soon finds the "I" introduced here moved to other positions amid the poem's flattened and conjoined discourses. Andrew Crozier writes that, "In any of these stanzas language emits the toxic glow of an intertextuality for which a functioning media awareness is its sufficient context. . . . From the start this writing anticipates the post-modern as a future condition of the person."[1] Lopez's other books of poetry include *Snapshots* (1976), *Change* (1978), *The English Disease* (1978), *A Handbook of British Birds* (1982), *Abstract & Delicious* (1983), *A Theory of Surplus Labour* (1990), *Stress Management* (1994), and *Negative Equity* (1995). He is also the author of numerous critical essays and *The Poetry of W. S. Graham* (1989), which received a Blundell award from the Society of Authors. He teaches at the University of Plymouth, where he is Reader in Poetry.

---

[1] Review of *False Memory*, *The Poetry Project Newsletter*, New York, Summer 1998.

Brought Forward

This is not the time to write as if you believe
In a time of writing. Most authors view cell death
As a landmark or end point for experiments
With other goals in distantly related fields.

5   So I would have it, letting the grass grow over
       As we wade ashore in a costume re-enactment
       Of the grand colonial adventure. We call it
       "First landfall in Provincetown," after the event
       Unsettled by a cautious trading statement.
10   Posing as messengers of an unknown nature
       With all our cameras running: a repeat, a sequel,
       Filming some years after *Apocalypse Now.*
       The comparison between Prozac and Ecstasy
       May well be misleading and irresponsible.

15   Most molecular data points towards
       A lack of interest among teenage voters
       In Ms Windsor and her relatives. Hindsight
       Is a wonderful thing, the diet industry
       A capitalist dream. They cut open the woman
20   And took out her living foetus. The killer said
       That she wanted a baby of her own
       Designed for the next millennium. Nice chrome.
       Two-year contracts become one-year rolling
       Contracts when they expire. They follow
25   A programme towards their own death, reversible
       By specific experimental manoeuvres.
       Necrosis often affects whole sheets of cells
       Their ghostly outlines remain long after the event.

       Paparazzi on shopping trolleys peer over
30   Brick walls hoping to get one good shot
       Before she departs for Argentina. They are
       Unaware of immune surveillance systems.
       It's day 107 of the Maxwell trial—
       Rivals compare the free asset ratio
35   And pile into the stock. In long-term culture
       Or immunological killing
       Many forms of death may well exist
       Causing immediate semantic problems
       In key metabolic pathways. How like you this?
40   Power flotation will overshadow futures

8: The Pilgrims landed in 1620 at the harbor of what was to become the town of *Provincetown*, in Cape Cod, Massachusetts.

12: *Apocalypse Now* (1979, dir. Francis Ford Coppola) is a film about the Vietnam war based on Joseph Conrad's *Heart of Darkness*.

17: *Ms Windsor*: i.e., the Queen; the Royal Family is the House of Windsor.

27: *necrosis*: death of tissue

33: *Maxwell trial*: The financial difficulties of Robert Maxwell (1922–1991), newspaper and media tycoon, led him to appropriate money from his employees' pension funds. After his mysterious death, an apparent suicide (he disappeared from his yacht in the Atlantic, and his naked body was found in the water days later), his two sons were put on trial for their involvement in his shady financial dealings.

34: *free asset ratio*: "These are assets that are able to be realised in the short term (as opposed to the paper value of a company), an important indicator for the viability of a predatory takeover bid." (Lopez, in correspondence)

39: Cf. "They Flee From Me" by Sir Thomas Wyatt (c.1503–1542): "she me caught in her arms long and small, / Therewithal sweetly did me kiss / And softly said, 'Dear heart, how like you this?'"

40: *flotation*: a pun on the literal sense: to "float" is to issue stocks to finance a new company.

Taking down the taper for family credit
As a consequence of uncontrolled survival.

Who pays taxes? Cords of viable tumour cells
And strangled profits for the main operators
45   Interspersed with zones of neurosis
Growing nicely thank you under the Beta field.
"This may involve some unforeseen social costs"
He said, in a kindly voice, keeping busy
With secateurs in the arboretum,
50   "Some lose water and condense, others swell and lyse."
98 acres to house 5700
Procurement officials, a new railway station,
MOD budget up. They all have to eat lunch.
Think of the local building spend, orbital roads,
55   D-I-Y-sales: let's dry-line and re-concrete
The cellar. Let's put down a patio.

In olden days we could have had her beheaded
And cultured *seriatim* indefinitely
For the top-end of the catering trade:
60   Watch out Aberdeen Angus, wild salmon,
Investors wanting capital guarantee.
Managers of personal equity plans
Ended the week with a bounce. Gold collar workers
Appear to be sensitive to stagging
65   And demand for securities is bound to rise.
Every decile in the poorest 50%
Does somewhat better, though we have no idea
How such a mechanism is evoked or what
Metaphoric signals trigger the call
70   By neighbouring cells for programmed suicide.

Acrimonious Funk, the alleged author of this
Catastrophe, was watching a very sad
Documentary about the fate of *Britannia*.

46: *Beta field:* an oil field in the North Sea
49: *secateurs:* pruning shears
    arboretum: botanical tree-garden
50: *lyse:* disintegrate (said of cells)
52: *Procurement officials:* military officials in charge of procuring equipment and supplies
53: *MOD:* Ministry of Defense
54: *spend:* expenditure
    orbital roads: roads encircling the new development
55: *D-I-Y:* do-it-yourself—i.e., "home improvement"
    To *dry-line* is to apply a waterproof membrane between layers of a wall or floor, to stop dampness seeping through. The poem's do-it-yourself references allude to the murderers Fred and Rosemary West, whose cellar and garden when excavated in 1994 turned out to contain the bodies of women and children.
58: *seriatim:* one after the next
60: *Aberdeen Angus:* a premium breed of beef cattle
64: *stagging:* the practice of making multiple applications for a new company's shares when they come onto the market, thus securing more shares than needed for long-term investment; the surplus may then be sold quickly for large profit.
66: *decile:* in statistics, the tenth part of a sampled population; thus there are five deciles in the lower 50%.
73: *Britannia:* the Royal Yacht *Britannia;* the cost of refitting it was a controversial issue in 1995.

By that time we must have been at the party
75 Picking up regional specialities
From marquees sited at the enclave's edge
Which is when I began to smell freedom.
Women in head scarves pushing wheelbarrows
But all the men and teenage boys switched
80 To a January clear-out. Sub-couture touches
In the ethnic collection, a mix of synthetics
With a grubby *Virgin Atlantic* sweatshirt
Right out of the gym. For the cover we chose
A rusty railway track leading into a wood.

85 You may define a people by what they believe
And how they dance. For half in love with easeful death
They come to look at our experiments
To salvage from this debris. We walk the fields
Away from pretty homes and camp fires over
90 To the lonely place of our enactment.
Call it "remembering industry," call it
Anything you like. I seemed wise before the event
Because I had sole access to the statement.
These ceremonies are obsolete, like nature,
95 Like individual expression. The sequel
To life in our century begins about now.
Prospects are good for traders in ecstasy
Though predictions, I've heard, are irresponsible.

Not a family shot in the Christmas message
100 No queen of hearts. Burnt bodies in the woods
Laid out in star formation: peripheral
Target stimuli. A disused church, swords and flags,
Designed to be seen from the air. Workers for peace
Who cease upon the midnight with no pain
105 Finally robbed the morphine. Our heroine
Appears in a royal advert teaching orphans
To pronounce the queen's English: Spongiform
Encephalopathy Advisory Committee.
Sir Francis Drake sacked the city before this date
110 And is jolly in purple tights. We translate from

80: *Sub-couture:* ready-made, off-the-rack clothing produced by fashion houses
82: *Virgin Atlantic:* an airline company; Princess Diana was once photographed wearing a Virgin Atlantic sweatshirt in a gym.
86: *half in love with easeful death:* quoted, like line 104 below, from Keats' "Ode to a Nightingale."
99: *Christmas message:* i.e., the Queen's traditional Christmas address
100: *Burnt bodies . . . :* alludes to the 1995 Solar Temple cult murders in France (originally thought to be mass suicide); 14 of the victims were found laid out in star formation.
107ff: Bovine spongiform encephalopathy (BSE) is a fatal disease of cattle involving the deterioration of the brain. The first case in Britain was identified in 1986; fears over transmission of the disease to cattle outside the British Isles, and of its possibly causing a similar condition in humans (Creutzfeldt-Jakob Disease) through the eating of beef from infected cattle, led the European Commission to place an export ban on British cattle and beef in 1996 (which has since been gradually lifted). The Advisory Committee was formed in 1990.
109: The English Admiral *Sir Francis Drake* under Queen Elizabeth I was responsible for disrupting Spain's overseas empire and was crucial to the defeat of the Spanish Armada in 1588. He assaulted the Spanish port of Vigo in 1585.

The original Greek into animation:
Not a family shot in the Christmas message.

Tuesday morning we worked out the press release
And consultancy agreement, privy to all
115 In the common room. A song that endures
On the dance floor with the deputy Master
And editor of criminal evidence.
Not a time to throw hats in the air. Mouth freezing
Small talk of our era. No news from the star chamber
120 But healthcare buildings coming onto the market
Should have a local effect. Last year's *Armani*
Turns over to a woman hanged in a wood
At Tuzla. Next move is to blast open an aid route
For those lorries full of sheep at Brightlingsea.
125 Hypo-allergenic stabilised retinol
Puts spice in the ex-bobbysoxers' ginger cake.

Shabby on tarmac, his one-time flatmate said to me
He was able to keep his off-road car because
All kinds of fluffy girlie things got in the way
130 Like threads unravelling in Petticoat Lane.
Freud knew "totem" as an Algonquian word
He turned into ready money. Nicotine patches.
He was good at getting ideas across: up to speed
On Muroroa. Think of Justus Liebig
135 Who in 1910 invented fluid beef cubes
When Virginia spoke of high expectations
In public life. A headless bronze *King and Queen*
Prepared in brine vinegar and olive oil
Wrapped in squares of aluminium foil
140 Making sure all trademarks are acknowledged.

1996

116: *Master:* of a (British) public school, or a college
119: The Court of the *Star Chamber* existed from the fifteenth century to 1641: its name was a byword for arbitrariness and oppression.
123: *Tuzla:* a town in Bosnia
124: *Brightlingsea:* a town on the coast of Essex, which was the site of demonstrations against live export of animals to Europe.
125: *retinol:* vitamin A_1 (used in skin-creams)
126: *bobbysoxers:* adolescent girls
130: *Petticoat Lane:* site in London of a street market for antiques and second-hand goods, including clothes
131: *Algonquian:* a collective word for the languages spoken by a large number of North American native tribes.
134: *Muroroa:* A Pacific atoll which the French have used since 1966 for the testing of nuclear weapons, despite international protests.
137: *King and Queen:* A sculpture by the British sculptor Henry Moore (1898–1986); it had been recently vandalized.

MAGGIE O'SULLIVAN (b. 1951)

O'SULLIVAN WAS BORN OUTSIDE LINCOLN TO IRISH CATHOLIC PARENTS WHO MET IN
England. She moved to London in 1971 and worked for BBC-TV between 1973
and 1988, latterly as a researcher and production assistant on arts documentary films.
A film about Joseph Beuys was her last project before leaving London for Hebden
Bridge in West Yorkshire. O'Sullivan is also a visual artist and small press publisher
and editor. She has performed internationally, taught writing courses in a variety of
community and educational settings, and held residencies at institutions including
SUNY-Buffalo. Her publications include *An Incomplete Natural History* (1984), *From
the Handbook of That & Furriery* (1986), *Unofficial Word* (1988), *Ellen's Lament* (1993),
Excla (with Bruce Andrews, 1993), *In the House of the Shaman* (1993), *Palace of Rep-
tiles* (forthcoming), and *Red Shifts* (2000). She is the editor of *out of everywhere: lin-
guistically innovative poetry by women in North America & the UK* (1996).

O'Sullivan's work forces recognition of points of intersection between bardic tra-
ditions and the defamiliarizing practices of an avant-garde. Kurt Schwitters, Bob Cob-
bing, Basil Bunting, and Jerome Rothenberg are among the twentieth-century writers
whose work informs her own; the title of her book *In the House of the Shaman* is bor-
rowed from a drawing by Joseph Beuys, another important influence. As Jenny Gough
has written, there is in Ireland, where some of O'Sullivan's ancestors lived in areas
that did not see electricity until 1962, a long history of "female keeners" challenging
"state and church authorities or the social authority of men and family."[1] O'Sullivan's
poems embrace the oral, aural, visual, and sculptural qualities of language and
include mangled and fractured words as well as dialect, slang, and archaisms abutting
noncewords and loanwords. Her work is, Andrew Duncan writes, "frequently or even
normally about plants and animals: drawing on unconscious fantasies about occupy-
ing a different body, which, because of their roots in the physical grounds of our expe-
rience, are common and direct, but which are also creative and in conflict with rea-
son." The poems are, he adds, "violently shaped by sensations too rapid to amount to
knowledge," and recall for him the "crazed energy that rock music used to have."[2]
Shamanistic traditions are borrowed from in the name of an anarchistic critique of
the limits of standard linguistic practices. Archaic words such as "garb," Gough notes,
may be defined ("a bundle, a method or custom or a sheaf of grain") but equally sug-
gest "words not on the page but haunting the poem" such as "garbage" and "garble."[3]
It is hard to imagine a poetic practice more invested in the polyvalent, physical prop-
erties of language, or one for which paraphrase is a more futile task.

---

[1] *Contemporary Women Poets,* Detroit, 1998, p. 273.
[2] Review of *In the House of the Shaman, Angel Exhaust,* vol. 12, 1995, p. 113.
[3] Gough, p. 274.

Starlings

Lived Daily
　　or Both

　　Daily
　　the Living
5　　　　structuring
　　　　　　Bone-Seed,

　　Pelage,
　　　Aqueous,

　　　　　YONDERLY—
10　　　　　　lazybed of need—
　　CLOUD-SANG
　　　Tipsy Bobbles, Dowdy
　　　wander.Halt upon

　　　grinned jeers, gin's note
15　　someone's in the leading
　　　　　of small & the pitch meander ears

　　tune me gold
　　Dulthie pods,

　　　　　Lipper
20　　　　"Ochre harled

　　　ELECTRIC

　　CONTORTIONS—

　　　　　　　　　　　　　　　　1993

Our annotations to these selections are not meant to be complete or definitive, but to suggest some of the many semantic possibilities of O'Sullivan's often original and neologistic language use. The notes make no effort to account for a full range of possibilities nor to identify what might be read as abstract sonic and semantic play.

7: *Pelage:* an animal's fur, wool, or other covering; also suggesting "pelagic" (said of animals living near the surface of the ocean)

12: *Bobbles:* (as a verb) bobs; fumbles; (as a noun) the movement of water in commotion; a woolly ball for trimming dresses, hats, etc.; also perhaps suggesting "bobbery" (a noisy row) or "bob up" (to appear suddenly)

14: *gin:* both the drink and a snare

15: *leading:* besides the general senses of "guiding," "controlling," or "beginning," some specialized usages are pertinent: in music, "leading" is the stepwise movement of a voice from one note of a chord to one in the next, outlining the harmonic movement; in typography, it denotes the spacing between lines of type.

19: *Lipper:* ripple (as both verb and noun)

20: *harled:* dragged; knotted; also suggesting "herl" (a fiber; the barb of a feather)

Garb

THE TRAP IS
BENTED
BAREWISE
DEARED

5   politically emphatically in parliament today
               melted lowlands
               major misses   tabloid ballast
               Breeze Mount & Delph House   leukemia clusters
               flimsies in from cheek lino channels
10   inimical factors
               anorexia pressed   Topt Tusser
               chime warnings   beams lifted

BLOOD & FAND:
FELL NOISE
15   AT:

               Corruptly Sized
               Gallopers Chidden
               Knock-at-a-Tooth
               Pistols, Rifles, Secondhand Riddles
20   The Sleeve Alloys Only Flies
               Collusion Among Wanted
               Astringent Nouns
               Air
               Charms of Spider—
25   (Stolen
               Dandelion)—

RINGED SPIKE BALDER VISIBLES
BODHRAN BONES
IDIOT SCRAP

30   headless   legless peepshow bleating
               swigment   libra   loada tombla

PALEO BEVELS
BICKER PYRRHIC
BIG IT FEET
35   & DID:

9: *flimsies:* thin pieces of paper, used in a typewriter with a carbon to produce copies; bank notes (slang); the word also suggests the adjective "flimsy."

11: *Tusser:* coarse brown silk; Thomas Tusser was a sixteenth-century author of versified advice on agriculture.

13: *FAND:* to attempt or proceed; "found" (Scots); fond; also suggesting "fanned." Fand was the wife of the Irish sea-god Manannan, whom the hero Cu Chullainn became entranced with.

14: *FELL:* terrible, fierce; the noun "fell" means the pelt of an animal or a moorland ridge; as a verb, "to knock down."

27: *BALDER:* a god in Norse myth; young and beautiful, he was loved by all the gods except the evil trickster Loki, who engineered his death.

28: *BODHRAN:* traditional Celtic hand-held drum

33: *PYRRHIC:* an ancient Greek war-dance; in verse, a Pyrrhic foot consists of two weak syllables; a Pyrrhic victory is one achieved at great cost.

Hag Ma Lung Ma Lung Ma
Extra Fugitive Diction
Bossed
Plasticiser Tattooing Thus-Spheres
40   Crow Clattering Strictly
Ill-
Treat
Carrion Terminal
Hinges Gobbed & Wail

45   VERMILION
BRONZES:
(EAR MY STUTTER
EAR MY

Lights-Er Bags-Er
50   Flayed
Grinnel Crash the Fibres B & C Goose
Conjurations Owlyering Owlyering

THORN BULLIONS
ROCKING
55   TRAPS & SNARE:

Stereo Delve
Gut Ox Sea A Arrow Sea
Delved
Lapped Torso

60   HORO GEARING—
GAINERS
FLAPPIT, LITH—
URNS TURNS
THE WIND ONCE FOR PEWTER
65   PEWTER
MOANS A FAIL FAIL
FUNNING BEAK:

hunger, third or shade all the dear
the hers the him-ship, what shilling dear vcbn
70   time was ship said

MATH-TONNER
NUMB-DIMENSIONAL

3 2 grand triple alone
thirstly these
75   hempen signatorial strings
Sky Rolled Over Braille

WREN HERDING:
SNAKE WANTS:

62: *FLAPPIT*: flapped (Scots)

Navigational Tin Grug Hanged Man's
80   Treated Buckled Tetanus Rock Sirens
Make

1993

Hill Figures

nailed Eagles   beryl   alter vasish
    Owls, Blood-bed
    Bird-gear   turbulent
    Ruled

5   it,

    Raven

       blue acquiescing tar
       thread
   the.air.it.will.be.tinned.
10   pull—
     feather against call—

Crow-Shade
plumb, true

     hemispheres
15   (dwell-juggling)

      has shells,
      fan
      to
      resist—

20   Skull—

     alarge, Oth
       Twisted

    merry-go

    superates,
25   congregates,

     rolled-a-run

     lettering

     Autistic low
     twindom

80: *Sirens:* warning alarms, but also the female monsters of Greek myth who lived on an island in the Straits of Messina; their song had the power to draw sailors to their doom. In Homer's *Odyssey,* Odysseus outwits them by making his sailors stop their ears with wax; he himself listens to them and survives by having himself lashed to the mast.

29: The constellation Gemini is named after the twins Castor and Pollux, of whom Castor was mortal, Pollux immortal. When Castor was killed, Pollux refused his own immortality as it would separate them, so Zeus permitted them to live together half the year in the underworld, half with the gods on Mount Olympus.

30   to live in the Sky
                     to live Underground

                Eagerly
        as little names of both, Cow, horned to begin
                Horned to grow new

35   skinning torso
                    tinning lengths

                    fin-

                    bred-

                          Brinks

40   Bladder-on-Stick

                     hand-in, hand-outa, hand—

                sacri
                DOSAGES
                invert
45   reversionary
                morrow.

        BIRTH—

                herding

        —stomach footnight—
50   BIG STOOD SKULL SONGS—
                Bull-Roarer, penalty—

        elved X, chema-
                     tensions
                chema-
55   nexions: poisons

                pins, xins,
                          flicted

            rid out of hell
                reflectorised

60   —clanked—

            fanged, crowey, clotted into: buckled poly-scream
        drip wounds
            Bade.

                                                    1993

51: A *bullroarer* is a toy made of a piece of wood tied to the end of a thong; when whirled round it makes
  a loud noise.

PAUL MULDOON (b. 1951)

M ULDOON PUBLISHED HIS FIRST BOOK, *NEW WEATHER*, IN 1973, AND HE WAS STILL in his twenties when his second book, *Mules* (1977), appeared, cementing his reputation as the most promising Northern Irish poet of the generation succeeding Seamus Heaney's. In a review of *Mules*, Heaney praised Muldoon's "delight in the trickery and lechery that words are capable of."[1] Muldoon has in turn been conscious of the inevitable comparisons with Heaney, working references to him—sometimes critical ones—into several poems. Edna Longley speaks of how Muldoon's poetry "questions its own authority along with origins, foundations, heritage, precedent, preceptor and pedigree," describing his work as "a profound form of psycho-social linguistics which, by investigating structures of language, reveals 'the mechanism of the trap.'"[2] Muldoon's poetry absorbs sources as various as Raymond Chandler and Amerindian mythology, moving quickly between high and popular culture and flattening the distinctions between history, fiction, and myth. His accounts of Northern Ireland's complex colonial status are sometimes, as in "Meeting the British," refracted through stories of the interaction of English, French, and Native Americans in United States history. Such themes inform Muldoon's longest work, "Madoc: A Mystery," which draws on the Welsh myth of Madoc, whose supposed discovery of America prior to Columbus was used to justify English colonial adventure in America and Ireland. The poem imagines Robert Southey and Samuel Taylor Coleridge founding their proposed (but never established) utopian community in the United States; individual sections use the names of famous philosophers, critics, and scientists for their titles, and the poem is in part idiosyncratic meditation on the history of philosophy. "Quoof" is a deconstructed sonnet, a favorite form of Muldoon's. Muldoon ironically rhymes "sword" with "word" and makes a related point about the politics of language by putting "English" and "language" in positions where they "should" rhyme. Other off-rhymes such as "beast" and "breast" and "city" and "yeti" are equally barbed as Muldoon remembers a family word for "hot water bottle" and suggests language's ability simultaneously to empower, sustain, and exclude. "Incantata," an elegy for the artist Mary Farl Powers, is unusual in his oeuvre for its unironic tone and linear development; it achieves its considerable power through an extraordinary proliferation of details and names, as if it meant to be a modern version of François Villon's *ubi sunt*. Muldoon's books include *Why Brownlee Left* (1980), *Quoof* (1983), *Meeting the British*

---

[1] "The Mixed Marriage: Paul Muldoon," *Preoccupations: Selected Prose 1969–1978*, London, 1980, p. 213.
[2] *The Living Stream: Literature & Revisionism in Ireland*, Newcastle upon Tyne, 1994, pp. 197–98.

(1987), *Madoc* (1990), *The Annals of Chile* (1994), *New Selected Poems 1968–94* (1996), and *Hay* (1998). He edited *The Faber Book of Contemporary Irish Poetry* (1986).

　　Muldoon was born to Catholic parents in County Armagh and educated at St. Patrick's College, Armagh, and Queen's University, Belfast. For many years, he worked as a radio and television producer for BBC Northern Ireland and has since been writer-in-residence at Cambridge, Columbia, and most recently Princeton University. In the mid-1980s, he took up residence in the United States. In 1999–2000 he was Oxford Professor of Poetry.

Quoof

How often have I carried our family word
for the hot water bottle
to a strange bed,
as my father would juggle a red-hot half-brick
5　　in an old sock
to his childhood settle.
I have taken it into so many lovely heads
or laid it between us like a sword.

An hotel room in New York City
10　　with a girl who spoke hardly any English,
my hand on her breast
like the smouldering one-off spoor of the yeti
or some other shy beast
that has yet to enter the language.

　　　　　　　　　　　　　　　　　　　　　　　　　　1983

Meeting the British

We met the British in the dead of winter.
The sky was lavender

and the snow lavender-blue.
I could hear, far below,

5　　the sound of two streams coming together
(both were frozen over)

6: *settle*: a settle-bed, usable both as a bench and as a bed

Meeting the British: The setting of the poem is toward the end of Pontiac's Rebellion (1763–1764), an inter-tribal attack on British forts masterminded by the Native chief Pontiac. Lt. General Jeffrey Amherst, the commander-in-chief of the British forces in North America, and Col. Henry Bouquet, a soldier of Swiss descent in the British Army, in 1763 discussed the possibility of exterminating the native population by giving them blankets contaminated with smallpox, though it is not clear whether these plans were carried out. The poem is presumably set (as the exchange of tobacco in line 12 indicates) as peace treaty processes were beginning between the British and the Indian tribes.

and, no less strange,
myself calling out in French

across that forest-
10   clearing. Neither General Jeffrey Amherst

nor Colonel Henry Bouquet
could stomach our willow-tobacco.

As for the unusual
scent when the Colonel shook out his hand-

15   kerchief: *C'est la lavande,*
une fleur mauve comme le ciel.

They gave us six fishhooks
and two blankets embroidered with smallpox.

                                    1987

Incantata

IN MEMORY OF MARY FARL POWERS

I thought of you tonight, *a leanbh*, lying there in your long barrow
colder and dumber than a fish by Francisco de Herrera,
as I X-Actoed from a spud the Inca
glyph for a mouth: thought of that first time I saw your pink
5   spotted torso, distant-near as a nautilus,
when you undid your portfolio, yes indeedy,
and held the print of what looked like a cankered potato
at arm's length—your arms being longer, it seemed, than Lugh's.

Even Lugh of the Long (sometimes the Silver) Arm
10   would have wanted some distance between himself and the army-worms
that so clouded the sky over St Cloud you'd have to seal

15–16: "It's lavender, a flower that's mauve like the sky." In the era before the germ theory of disease, it
was thought that strong scents could ward off disease.

Incantata: The poem borrows its stanzaic form from W.B. Yeats's "In Memory of Major Robert Gregory."
Its structure is palindromic: rhymes are shared by the first and last stanzas, second and second-last, etc.
Title: "Incantata" is the feminine form of the Italian for "enchanted" or "spellbound"; but Muldoon has
said in correspondence that he had in mind the words "Inca" and "cantata."
Dedication: The Minnesota-born artist *Mary Farl Powers* was Muldoon's companion in the early 1980s.
She died in 1992.
1: *a leanbh:* "my dear" (Gaelic)
   barrow: grave-mound
2: The Spanish painter *Francisco de Herrera* the Younger (1622–1685) is known for his still-lifes with fish.
Cf. Yeats's poem "All Things Can Tempt Me": "Colder and dumber and deafer than a fish."
4–5: *pink / spotted torso:* the title of one of Powers's works, a print showing a woman carving a hieroglyph
into a potato. See Muldoon's poem "Mary Farl Powers *Pink Spotted Torso*," in *Quoof* (also alluded to in
line 128).
8: *Lugh:* a Celtic deity, known as "Lugh of the Long Arm," who possessed mastery of all arts and crafts;
he was associated by Greek writers with the god Apollo.
10: The *army-worm* is a moth caterpillar that moves from field to field destroying grass, grain, and other
crops.
11: *St Cloud:* a city in Minnesota

the doors and windows and steel
yourself against their nightmarish *déjeuner sur l'herbe:*
try as you might to run a foil
15   across their tracks, it was to no avail;
the army-worms shinnied down the stove-pipe on an army-worm rope.

I can hardly believe that, when we met, my idea of 'R and R'
was to get smashed, almost every night, on sickly-sweet Demerara
rum and Coke: as well as leaving you a grass widow
20   (remember how Krapp looks up 'viduity'?),
after eight or ten or twelve of those dark rums
it might be eight or ten or twelve o'clock before I'd land
back home in Landseer Street, deaf and blind
to the fact that not only was I all at sea, but in the doldrums.

25   Again and again you'd hold forth on your own version of Thomism,
your own *Summa*
Theologiae that in everything there is an order,
that the things of the world sing out in a great oratorio:
it was Thomism, though, tempered by *La Nausée,*
30   by His Nibs Sam Bethicket,
and by that Dublin thing, that an artist must walk down Baggott
Street wearing a hair-shirt under the shirt of Nessus.

'*D'éirigh me ar maidin,*' I sang, '*a tharraingt chun aoinigh mhóir*':
our first night, you just had to let slip that your secret amour
35   for a friend of mine was such
that you'd ended up lying with him in a ditch
under a bit of whin, or gorse, or furze,
somewhere on the border of Leitrim, perhaps, or Roscommon:
'gamine,' I wanted to say, 'kimono';
40   even then it was clear I'd never be at the centre of your universe.

Nor should I have been, since you were there already, your own *Ding*
an sich, no less likely to take wing

13: *déjeuner sur l'herbe:* picnic on the grass (title of an Impressionist painting by Édouard Manet)
17: *R and R:* rest and recuperation (military slang)
19: *grass widow:* a married woman whose husband is absent
20: *Krapp:* protagonist of *Krapp's Last Tape,* a play by the Irish playwright Samuel Beckett (1906–1989)
    viduity: widowhood
25: *Thomism:* the doctrines of medieval theologian St. Thomas Aquinas (1224/25–1274), author of the
    Summa Theologiae.
29: *La Nausée:* i.e., by existentialism and its sense of the absurdity of the human condition; *Nausea* is a
    novel by the existentialist philosopher Jean-Paul Sartre (1905–1980).
31: *Baggott Street* is a Dublin street noted for its nightlife.
32: *hair-shirt:* a shirt, made of rough animal hair, worn by the devout for self-mortification
    shirt of Nessus: a shirt given to Hercules by his wife Deineira: she had falsely been told it would win
    back his love. But it was in fact poisoned: clinging to his flesh, it caused him terrible suffering; to end it,
    Hercules killed himself by immolating himself on a pyre.
33: "I got up in the morning to go to the big fair" (Gaelic)
37: *Whin, gorse* and *furze* are all names for the gorsebush.
38: *Leitrim* and *Roscommon* are two (very poor) counties in western Ireland; they share a border.
39: *gamine:* tomboy, coquette
41–42: *Ding / an sich:* thing-in-itself; in the philosophy of Kant the thing-in-itself is unknowable; we can
    only know "phenomena."

than the Christ you drew for a Christmas card as a pupa
in swaddling clothes: and how resolutely you would pooh pooh
45   the idea I shared with Vladimir and Estragon,
with whom I'd been having a couple of jars,
that this image of the Christ-child swaddled and laid in the manger
could be traced directly to those army-worm dragoons.

I thought of the night Vladimir was explaining to all and sundry
50   the difference between *geantrai* and *suantrai*
and you remarked on how you used to have a crush
on Burt Lancaster as Elmer Gantry, and Vladimir went to brush
the ash off his sleeve with a legerdemain
that meant only one thing—'Why does he put up with this crap?'—
55   and you weighed in with 'To live in a dustbin, eating scrap,
seemed to Nagg and Nell a most eminent domain.'

How little you were exercised by those tiresome literary intrigues,
how you urged me to have no more truck
than the Thane of Calder
60   with a fourth estate that professes itself to be *'égalitaire'*
but wants only blood on the sand: yet, irony of ironies,
you were the one who, in the end,
got yourself up as a *retiarius* and, armed with net and trident,
marched from Mount Street to the Merrion Square arena.

65   In the end, you were the one who went forth to beard the lion,
you who took the DART line
every day from Jane's flat in Dun Laoghaire, or Dalkey,
dreaming your dream that the subterranean Dodder and Tolka
might again be heard above the *hoi polloi*
70   for whom Irish 'art' means a High Cross at Carndonagh or Corofin
and *The Book of Kells:* not until the lion cried craven
would the poor Tolka and the poor Dodder again sing out for joy.

I saw you again tonight, in your jump-suit, thin as a rake,
your hand moving in such a deliberate arc
75   as you ground a lithographic stone

43: *pupa:* a cocooned insect; a chrysalis
45: *Vladimir and Estragon:* The names are those of the anti-heroes of Beckett's play *Waiting for Godot.*
50: *geantrai:* light music, leading to easy laughter; *suantrai:* lullaby
52: *Burt Lancaster* played a charlatan in the 1960 film *Elmer Gantry.*
56: *Nagg and Nell:* husband and wife, they live in dustbins in Beckett's play *Endgame*
59: *Thane of Calder:* punning on "Thane of Cawdor" (Macbeth) and "John Calder," Beckett's publisher.
  Beckett was famously chary of the media.
60: *fourth estate:* the press
    égalitaire: "egalitarian" (French)
63: *retiarius:* a Roman gladiator armed with a trident and a net to entangle his opponent
64: *Mount Street:* location of the Graphic Studio (see line 189)
    Merrion Square: a posh area of Dublin; the square itself surrounds a public park
66: *DART line:* train line (Dublin Area Rapid Transit)
68: *Dodder and Tolka:* Dublin rivers, both now mostly built over except in the suburbs
69: *hoi polloi:* the general populace
70: *Carndonagh or Corofin:* locations of medieval Irish stone crosses, famed for their intricate carving.
71: *The Book of Kells:* a medieval Irish bible whose illuminations make it one of the greatest works of
  works of medieval art
    cried craven: gave in

that your hand and the stone blurred to one
and your face blurred into the face of your mother, Betty Wahl,
who took your failing, ink-stained hand
in her failing, ink-stained hand
80   and together you ground down that stone by sheer force of will.

I remember your pooh poohing, as we sat there on the 'Enterprise',
my theory that if your name is Powers
you grow into it or, at least,
are less inclined to tremble before the likes of this bomb-blast
85   further up the track: I myself was shaking like a leaf
as we wondered whether the I.R.A. or the Red
Hand Commandos or even the Red
Brigades had brought us to a standstill worthy of Hamm and Clov.

Hamm and Clov; Nagg and Nell; Watt and Knott;
90   the fact is that we'd been at a standstill long before the night
things came to a head,
long before we'd sat for half the day in the sweltering heat
somewhere just south of Killnasaggart
and I let slip a name—her name—off my tongue
95   and you turned away (I see it now) the better to deliver the sting
in your own tail, to let slip your own little secret.

I thought of you again tonight, thin as a rake, as you bent
over the copper plate of 'Emblements',
its tidal wave of army-worms into which you all but disappeared:
100   I wanted to catch something of its spirit
and yours, to body out your disembodied *vox
clamantis in deserto,* to let this all-too-cumbersome device
of a potato-mouth in a potato-face
speak out, unencumbered, from its long, low, mould-filled box.

105   I wanted it to speak to what seems always true of the truly great,
that you had a winningly inaccurate
sense of your own worth, that you would second-guess
yourself too readily by far, that you would rally to any cause
before your own, mine even,
110   though you detected in me a tendency to put
on too much artificiality, both as man and poet,
which is why you called me 'Polyester' or 'Polyurethane'.

81: *Enterprise:* an express train running from Belfast to Connolly Station, Dublin, every morning and
   evening; formerly a favorite target for bomb threats.
86–87: *Red / Hand Commandos:* a Belfast-based Protestant paramilitary terrorist organization
87–88: *Red / Brigades:* an Italian left-wing terrorist organization
88: *Hamm and Clov:* the main characters in *Endgame.* At the play's end they are both motionless onstage
   as the curtain falls.
89: *Watt and Knott:* the protagonist and his employer in Beckett's novel *Watt.*
101–2: *vox / clamantis in deserto:* "The voice of one crying in the wilderness" (Matt. 3:3)

That last time in Dublin, I copied with a quill dipped in oak-gall
onto a sheet of vellum, or maybe a human caul,
115   a poem for *The Great Book of Ireland*: as I watched the low
swoop over the lawn today of a swallow
I thought of your animated talk of Camille Pissarro
and André Derain's *The Turning Road, L'Estaque*:
when I saw in that swallow's nest a face in a mud-pack
120   from that muddy road I was filled again with a profound sorrow.

You must have known already, as we moved from the 'Hurly Burly'
to McDaid's or Riley's,
that something was amiss: I think you even mentioned a homeopath
as you showed off the great new acid-bath
125   in the Graphic Studio, and again undid your portfolio
to lay out your latest works; I try to imagine the strain
you must have been under, pretending to be as right as rain
while hearing the bells of a church from some long-flooded valley.

From the Quabbin reservoir, maybe, where the banks and bakeries
130   of a dozen little submerged Pompeii reliquaries
still do a roaring trade: as clearly as I saw your death-mask
in that swallow's nest, you must have heard the music
rise from the muddy ground between
your breasts as a nocturne, maybe, by John Field;
135   to think that you thought yourself so invulnerable, so inviolate,
that a little cancer could be beaten.

You must have known, as we walked through the ankle-deep clabber
with Katherine and Jean and the long-winded Quintus Calaber,
that cancer had already made such a breach
140   that you would almost surely perish:
you must have thought, as we walked through the woods
along the edge of the Quabbin,
that rather than let some doctor cut you open
you'd rely on infusions of hardock, hemlock, all the idle weeds.

113: The galls of the Aleppo oak are a source of Aleppo tannin, used in ink manufacture.
114: *vellum*: fine parchment (at one time made from calf's skin)
    caul: a membrane enclosing the foetus inside the womb
115: *The Great Book of Ireland*: a modern vellum book in which contemporary Irish poets were invited to
    write a poem.
117: *Camille Pissarro* (1830–1903), French Impressionist painter
118: *André Derain* (1880–1954), French painter who was one of the leaders of the Fauvists.
121: *the 'Hurly Burly'*: the Burlington Hotel
122: *McDaid's or Riley's*: pubs; McDaid's has a long literary tradition.
129: *Quabbin reservoir*: in Massachusetts
130: *Pompeii*: an ancient city in Italy, destroyed in 79 by the eruption of the volcano Mount Vesuvius; the
    city, and some of its inhabitants, were preserved perfectly beneath volcanic debris and ash.
    reliquaries: containers or shrines for sacred relics
134: *John Field* (1782–1837), Irish pianist and composer, the inventor of the nocturne
137: *clabber*: mud
144: Cf. *King Lear* 4.4.4–6: "hardocks, hemlock, nettles, cuckoo-flowers, / Darnel, and all the idle weeds
    that grow / In our sustaining corn."

145   I thought again of how art may be made, as it was by André Derain,
        of nothing more than a turn
        in the road where a swallow dips into the mire
        or plucks a strand of bloody wool from a strand of barbed wire
        in the aftermath of Chickamauga or Culloden
150   and builds from pain, from misery, from a deep-seated hurt,
        a monument to the human heart
        that shines like a golden dome among roofs rain-glazed and leaden.

        I wanted the mouth in this potato-cut
        to be heard far beyond the leaden, rain-glazed roofs of Quito,
155   to be heard all the way from the southern hemisphere
        to Clontarf or Clondalkin, to wherever your sweet-severe
        spirit might still find a toe-hold
        in this world: it struck me then how you would be aghast
        at the thought of my thinking you were some kind of ghost
160   who might still roam the earth in search of an earthly delight.

        You'd be aghast at the idea of your spirit hanging over this vale
        of tears like a jump-suited jump-jet whose vapour-trail
        unravels a sky: for there's nothing, you'd say, nothing over
        and above the sky itself, nothing but cloud-cover
165   reflected in a thousand lakes; it seems that Minne-
        sota itself means 'sky-tinted water', that the sky is a great slab
        of granite or iron ore that might at any moment slip
        back into the worked-out sky-quarry, into the worked-out sky-mines.

        To use the word 'might' is to betray you once too often, to betray
170   your notion that nothing's random, nothing arbitrary:
        the gelignite weeps, the hands fly by on the alarm clock,
        the 'Enterprise' goes clackety-clack
        as they all must; even the car hijacked that morning in the Cross,
        that was preordained, its owner spread on the bonnet
175   before being gagged and bound or bound
        and gagged, that was fixed like the stars in the Southern Cross.

        The fact that you were determined to cut yourself off in your prime
        because it was *pre*-determined has my eyes abrim:
        I crouch with Belacqua

149: *Chickamauga,* Georgia, was in 1863 the location of one of the bloodiest battles of the American Civil
  War; *Culloden,* in Scotland, was in 1746 the site of the defeat of the Jacobite Rebellion.
154: *Quito:* capital of Ecuador
156: *Clontarf or Clondalkin:* suburbs respectively north and south of Dublin
171: *gelignite:* gelatin dynamite (which exudes a liquid)
173: *the Cross:* Crossmaglen, a village just over the border into the Republic of Ireland, often the site of
  Republican activity.
174: *bonnet:* hood
179: *Belacqua:* a character in Dante's *Purgatorio,* a soul too indolent to attempt to ascend the mountain
  of Purgatory to Heaven. Beckett gave the name to the protagonist of a collection of stories, *More Pricks
  than Kicks.*

180   and Lucky and Pozzo in the Acacacac-
        ademy of Anthropopopometry, trying to make sense of the *'quaquaqua'*
        of that potato-mouth; that mouth as prim
        and proper as it's full of self-opprobrium,
        with its *'quaquaqua'*, with its 'Quoiquoiquoiquoiquoiquoiquoiq'.

185   That's all that's left of the voice of Enrico Caruso
        from all that's left of an opera-house somewhere in Matto Grosso,
        all that's left of the hogweed and horehound and cuckoo-pint,
        of the eighteen soldiers dead at Warrenpoint,
        of the Black Church clique and the Graphic Studio claque,
190   of the many moons of glasses on a tray,
        of the brewery-carts drawn by moon-booted drays,
        of those jump-suits worn under your bottle-green worsted cloak.

        Of the great big dishes of chicken lo mein and beef chow mein,
        of what's mine is yours and what's yours mine,
195   of the oxlips and cowslips
        on the banks of the Liffey at Leixlip
        where the salmon breaks through the either/or neither/nor nether
        reaches despite the temple-veil
        of itself being rent and the penny left out overnight on the rail
200   is a sheet of copper when the mail-train has passed over.

        Of the bride carried over the threshold, hey, only to alight
        on the limestone slab of another threshold,
        of the swarm, the cast,
        the colt, the spew of bees hanging like a bottle of Lucozade
205   from a branch the groom must sever,
        of Emily Post's ruling, in *Etiquette,*
        on how best to deal with the butler being in cahoots
        with the cook when they're both in cahoots with the chauffeur.

180: *Lucky and Pozzo:* characters in Beckett's *Waiting for Godot;* Muldoon quotes Lucky's speech in Act One, a nonsensical outpouring full of stuttering and repetition. "Anthropometry": the measurement of man

184: *Quoiquoi . . . :* said by the stuttering HCE in James Joyce's *Finnegans Wake*

185: *Enrico Caruso* (1873–1921), the great operatic tenor.

186: *Matto Grosso* is a state of Brazil, a remote frontier region; there is indeed an opera-house there, built at the turn of the century and recently refurbished; its story is told in Werner Herzog's film *Fitzcarraldo* (1982).

188: *Warrenpoint:* This 1979 attack on British soldiers is alluded to again at line 238.

189: *Black Church clique . . . Graphic Studio claque:* two groups of printmakers in Dublin. The *Black Church* is a Protestant church in Dublin, positioned in the middle of a road.

198–99: *temple-veil / . . . being rent:* as was that of the Temple in Jerusalem upon Christ's death

203–4: Once a bee colony has become overpopulated, the queen bee lays eggs from which a new queen will be born; then she and a portion of the worker bees leave in a swarm to find a new homesite. This may occur several times in a season: "The swarm of bees is the first and greatest number, the cast is the next, the colt the next, and the spew the least of all" (William Ellis, 1750, qtd. in *OED*).

204: *Lucozade:* an orange-colored, sweet, glucose-based fizzy drink; originally for the ill and convalescent

206: *Emily Post* (1872–1960), author of the bestseller *Etiquette: The Blue Book of Social Usage*

Of that poplar-flanked stretch of road between Leiden
210   and The Hague, of the road between Rathmullen and Ramelton,
where we looked so long and hard
for some trace of Spinoza or Amelia Earhart,
both of them going down with their engines on fire:
of the stretch of road somewhere near Urney
215   where Orpheus was again overwhelmed by that urge to turn
back and lost not only Eurydice but his steel-strung lyre.

Of the sparrows and finches in their bell of suet,
of the bitter-sweet
bottle of Calvados we felt obliged to open
220   somewhere near Falaise, so as to toast our new-found *copains*,
of the priest of the parish
who came enquiring about our 'status', of the hedge-clippers
I somehow had to hand, of him running like the clappers
up Landseer Street, of my subsequent self-reproach.

225   Of the remnants of Airey Neave, of the remnants of Mountbatten,
of the famous *andouilles*, of the famous *boudins*
noirs et blancs, of the barrel-vault
of the Cathedral at Rouen, of the flashlight, fat and roll of felt
on each of their sledges, of the music
230   of Joseph Beuys's pack of huskies, of that baldy little bugger
mushing them all the way from Berncastel through Bacarrat
to Belfast, his head stuck with honey and gold-leaf like a mosque.

Of Benjamin Britten's *Lachrymae*, with its gut-wrenching viola,
of Vivaldi's *Four Seasons*, of Frankie Valli's,
235   of Braque's great painting *The Shower of Rain*,

209ff: *Leiden* and *The Hague* are in the Netherlands, *Rathmullen and Ramelton* in Ireland.

212: The Dutch-Jewish philosopher Baruch *Spinoza* (1632–1677) was excommunicated by his synagogue for his unorthodox ideas in 1656; he lived in The Hague at the end of his life. The aviator *Amelia Earhart* (1897–1937) was the first woman to cross the Atlantic in an airplane, flying from Newfoundland to Ireland; her plane disappeared in 1937 while she was flying over the Pacific.

215: *Orpheus*: the musician of Greek myth; Orpheus's music convinced Hades, king of the underworld, to permit him to retrieve his dead wife Eurydice, on condition that he not look behind as he led her back to the world; he disobeyed, and she was lost.

219: *Calvados*: apple brandy, made in Calvados, a part of northern France also containing *Falaise*

220: *copains*: "friends" (French)

225: *Airey Neave*, a member of the British Parliament, was killed in 1979 by a car bomb planted by the Irish National Liberation Army. Lord *Mountbatten* (1900–79) was killed by a bomb planted on his boat by the Provisional I.R.A.

226–27: *andouilles . . . boudins / noirs et blancs*: types of sausage

227: *barrel-vault*: semicylindrical vaulted ceiling

230: *Joseph Beuys* (1921–1986), the German sculptor and performance artist; *fat, felt, honey* and *gold leaf* are substances that appear frequently in his work.

233: *Lachrymae (Reflections on a Song of Dowland)* is a composition for viola and piano (later arranged for viola and strings) by the British composer *Benjamin Britten* (1913–1976); its title means "tears."

234: *Frankie Valli* and the *Four Seasons* were a 1960s doo-wop group.

235: Georges *Braque* (1882–1963), Cubist painter

of the fizzy, lemon or sherbet-green *Ranus ranus*
plonked down in Trinity like a little Naugahyde pouffe,
of eighteen soldiers dead in Oriel,
of the weakness for a little fol-de-rol-de-rolly
240   suggested by the gap between the front teeth of the Wife of Bath.

Of *A Sunday Afternoon on the Island of La Grande Jatte,* of Seurat's
piling of tesserae upon tesserae
to give us a monkey arching its back
and the smoke arching out from a smoke-stack,
245   of Sunday afternoons in the Botanic Gardens, going with the flow
of the burghers of Sandy Row and Donegal
Pass and Andersonstown and Rathcoole,
of the army Landrover flaunt-flouncing by with its heavy furbelow.

Of Marlborough Park, of Notting Hill, of the Fitzroy Avenue
250   immortalized by Van 'His real name's Ivan'
Morrison, 'and him the dead spit
of Padraic Fiacc', of John Hewitt, the famous expat,
in whose memory they offer every year six of their best milch cows,
of the Bard of Ballymacarrett,
255   of every ungodly poet in his or her godly garret,
of Medhbh and Michael and Frank and Ciaran and 'wee' John Qughes.

Of the Belfast school, so called, of the school of hard knocks,
of your fervent eschewal of stockings and socks
as you set out to hunt down your foes
260   as implacably as the *tóraidheacht* through the Fews
of Redmond O'Hanlon, of how that 'd' and that 'c' aspirate

236: *Ranus ranus:* i.e., a frog (of the family *Ranidae*); Muldoon is glancing back at his poem "The Frog" in *Quoof,* in which it is playfully suggested that all the frogs in Ireland came from a single pair in Trinity College pond.

237: *pouffe:* a small, low, round, stuffed seat or footrest

240: The *Wife of Bath* is a character in Chaucer's *Canterbury Tales;* being gap-toothed was supposedly a sign of lechery.

241: *A Sunday Afternoon . . . :* the masterpiece of Georges Seurat (1859–1891), creator of the "pointillist" style of painting

242: *tesserae:* cubes of a mosaic

248: *furbelow:* an ornamental pleated border on a gown or petticoat; a flounce

249ff: This stanza concerns Belfast places and artists. There is a passing reference to *Fitzroy Avenue* in the song "Madame George" by the Belfast-born singer-songwriter Van Morrison.

252: *Padraic Fiacc* (b. 1924) and *John Hewitt* (1907–1987) are poets; Hewitt spent many years running an art gallery in Coventry.

256: Muldoon moves to Belfast poets of his own generation: Medbh McGuckian (see p. 784), Michael Longley, Frank Ormsby, Ciaran Carson and John Hughes. (Muldoon has wryly corrected the Gaelic orthography of McGuckian's name and indicated the aspirated "h" of the Belfast accent in his spelling of "Hughes.")

260: *tóraidheacht:* "pursuit" (Gaelic)
    the Fews: The Fews Forest in South Armagh, notorious for its brigands in the seventeenth and eighteenth centuries.

261: *Redmond O'Hanlon:* the subject of a popular folksong, a thief who steals from the rich to give to the poor; "Squire Johnston from the Fews" offers a reward of 400 pounds if he is caught and hanged, but no man will betray him and he successfully eludes the soldiers sent to hunt him.

in *tóraidheacht* make it sound like a last gasp in an oxygen-tent,
of your refusal to open a vent
but to breathe in spirit of salt, the mordant salt-spirit.

265   Of how mordantly hydrochloric acid must have scored and scarred,
of the claim that boiled skirrets
can cure the spitting of blood, of that dank
flat somewhere off Morehampton Road, of the unbelievable stink
of valerian or feverfew simmering over a low heat,
270   of your sitting there, pale and gaunt,
with that great prescriber of boiled skirrets, Dr John Arbuthnot,
your face in a bowl of feverfew, a towel over your head.

Of the great roll of paper like a bolt of cloth
running out again and again like a road at the edge of a cliff,
275   of how you called a Red Admiral a Red
Admirable, of how you were never in the red
on either the first or the last
of the month, of your habit of loosing the drawstring of your purse
and finding one scrunched-up, obstreperous
280   note and smoothing it out and holding it up, pristine and pellucid.

Of how you spent your whole life with your back to the wall,
of your generosity when all the while
you yourself lived from hand
to mouth, of Joseph Beuys's pack of hounds
285   crying out from their felt and fat 'Atone, atone, atone',
of Watt remembering the *'Krak! Krek! Krik!'*
of those three frogs' karaoke
like the still, sad, *basso continuo* of the great quotidian.

Of a ground bass of sadness, yes, but also a sennet of hautboys
290   as the fat and felt hounds of Beuys O'Beuys
bayed at the moon over a caravan
in Dunmore East, I'm pretty sure it was, or Dungarvan:
of my guest appearance in your self-portrait not as a hidalgo

---

264: *spirit of salt:* an early name for hydrochloric acid, which is used in the etching process
266: *skirrets:* water parsnips
268: *Morehampton Road:* in Dublin
271: *Dr John Arbuthnot* (1667–1735) was a noted friend of Alexander Pope and Jonathan Swift.
275: *Red Admiral:* a type of butterfly
285: Muldoon puns on "ochone," a Gaelic cry of lamentation.
286: At one point in Beckett's *Watt* the different cycles of three frogs' croaking are diagrammed down the page.
288: *basso continuo:* thorough-bass, a system of musical accompaniment used in the seventeenth and eighteenth centuries, in which a bass melody and skeletal harmonies are given, requiring some improvisation on the part of the performer to realize them. Cf. "the still, sad music of humanity" (Wordsworth, "Lines Composed a Few Miles Above Tintern Abbey," 91).
289: *ground bass:* a bass accompaniment consisting of a short phrase continually repeated.
       sennet: a musical flourish
       hautboys: oboes
290: *Beuys O'Beuys:* punning on the Irish expression "boys o boys."
291: *caravan:* trailer
293: *hidalgo:* Spanish nobleman; it is traditionally believed that many Irish have Spanish blood in their past.

from a long line
295   of hidalgos but a hound-dog, *a leanbh,*
a dog that skulks in the background, a dog that skulks and stalks.

Of that self-portrait, of the self-portraits by Rembrandt van Rijn,
of all that's revelation, all that's rune,
of all that's composed, all composed of odds and ends,
300   of that daft urge to make amends
when it's far too late, too late even to make sense of the clutter
of false trails and reversed horseshoe tracks
and the aniseed we took it in turn to drag
across each other's scents, when only a fish is dumber and colder.

305   Of your avoidance of canned goods, in the main,
on account of the exceeeeeeeeeeeeeeeedingly high risk of ptomaine,
of corned beef in particular being full of crap,
of your delight, so, in eating a banana as ceremoniously as Krapp
but flinging the skin over your shoulder like a thrush
310   flinging off a shell from which it's only just managed to disinter
a snail, like a stone-faced, twelfth-century
FitzKrapp eating his banana by the mellow, yellow light of a rush.

Of the 'Yes, let's go' spoken by Monsieur Tarragon,
of the early-ripening jardonelle, the tumorous jardon, the jargon
315   of jays, the jars
of tomato relish and the jars
of Victoria plums, absolutely *de rigueur* for a passable plum baba,
of the drawers full of balls of twine and butcher's string,
of Dire Straits playing 'The Sultans of Swing',
320   of the horse's hock suddenly erupting in those boils and buboes.

Of the Greek figurine of a pig, of the pig on a terracotta frieze,
of the sow dropping dead from some mysterious virus,
of your predilection for gammon
served with a sauce of coriander or cumin,
325   of the slippery elm, of the hornbeam or witch-, or even wych-,
hazel that's good for stopping a haemor-

303: The smell of *aniseed* will confuse a dog following the scent of a trail.
306: *ptomaine:* food poisoning
308: *Krapp* eats a *banana* at the opening of Beckett's play.
312: FitzKrapp: "Fitz" (Old French for "son of") was a prefix used in names among the medieval Anglo-
   Norman aristocracy.
   rush: a rushlight, a weak candle
313: *Yes, let's go* are the last words of *Waiting for Godot,* spoken by Estragon (whose name means "tarragon"
   in French).
314: *jardonelle:* for "jargonelle," a pear
   jardon: a tumor on the leg of a horse
320: *buboes:* swellings
323: *gammon:* ham
325: *slippery elm:* an extract from the bark of the slippery (red) elm used for traditional remedies. *Witch
   hazel* (or wych hazel) is a shrub said to have medicinal properties; the name is also used for the *horn-
   beam,* a type of birch.

rhage in mid-flow, of the merest of mere
hints of elderberry curing everything from sciatica to a stitch.

Of the decree *condemnator*, the decree *absolvitor*, the decree *nisi*,
330   of *Aosdána*, of *an chraobh cnuais*,
of the field of buckwheat
taken over by garget, inkberry, scoke—all names for pokeweed—
of *Mother Courage*, of *Arturo Ui*,
of those Sunday mornings spent picking at sesame
335   noodles and all sorts and conditions of dim sum,
of tea and ham sandwiches in the Nesbitt Arms hotel in Ardara.

Of the day your father came to call, of your leaving your sick-room
in what can only have been a state of delirium,
of how you simply wouldn't relent
340   from your vision of a blind
watch-maker, of your fatal belief that fate
governs everything from the honey-rust of your father's terrier's
eyebrows to the horse that rusts and rears
in the furrow, of the furrows from which we can no more deviate

345   than they can from themselves, no more than the map of Europe
can be redrawn, than that Hermes might make a harp from his *harpe*,
than that we must live in a vale
of tears on the banks of the Lagan or the Foyle,
than that what we have is a done deal,
350   than that the Irish Hermes,
Lugh, might have leafed through his vast herbarium
for the leaf that had it within it, Mary, to anoint and anneal,

than that Lugh of the Long Arm might have found in the midst of *lus
na leac* or *lus na treatha* or *Frannc-lus*,
355   in the midst of eyebright, or speedwell, or tansy, an antidote,

---

329: The *decree condemnator* and *decree absolvitor* are terms in Scottish law, the former expressing condemnation, the latter a decree in favor of the defender. The *decree nisi* is a divorce decree.

330: The Irish Arts Council established the *Aosdána* in 1983, an organization of artists limited to a maximum of 200 members; members are eligible for an annuity to permit them to concentrate on their work.
    an chraobh cnuais: "nut-laden bough" (Gaelic)

333: *Mother Courage and her Children* and *The Resistable Rise of Arturo Ui* are plays by Bertolt Brecht (1898–1956).

340ff: Fate is proverbially *blind;* the *watch-maker* is God (Muldoon alludes to William Paley's 1802 formulation of the theological "argument from design": just as the existence of a watch implies the existence of a watchmaker, so the existence of the world implies the existence of the God who created it).

343: *rusts:* is restive

346: *Hermes:* Greek messenger god and god of music and the arts (identified with the Roman god Mercury); his staff, the caduceus, is now the symbol of medicine. He was identified in Julius Caesar's *The Gallic War* with the Celtic god Lugh (see note to line 9).
    harpe: "knife" (Gaelic)

348: *Lagan:* a river southwest of Belfast
    Foyle: a river on which Derry (in Northern Ireland) is situated

351: *herbarium:* collection of dried plants

353–4: The Gaelic terms are translated in line 355.

355: *Eyebright, speedwell* and *tansy* are medicinal herbs.

than that this *Incantata*
might have you look up from your plate of copper or zinc
on which you've etched the row upon row
of army-worms, than that you might reach out, arrah,
360   and take in your ink-stained hands my own hands stained with ink.

1994

359: *arrah:* "An expletive expressing emotion or excitement, common in Anglo-Irish speech" (*OED*).

FRANK KUPPNER (b. 1951)

K UPPNER WAS BORN IN GLASGOW TO A SCOTTISH MOTHER AND A POLISH FATHER WHO came to Britain with the Polish army in 1945. He studied at the University of Glasgow and later qualified as an electronics engineer, a trade that he has never practiced. He has worked as a reviewer, typist, and visiting poet at the University of Edinburgh, though as he says in his 1989 self-interview in the magazine *Verse*, "the chief colours in my background have been the various calm greys of the DHHS" (Department of Health and Human Services).[1] His books of poetry include *A Bad Day for the Sung Dynasty* (1984), *The Intelligent Observation of Naked Women* (1987), and *Ridiculous! Absurd! Disgusting!* (1989). Other publications include the novels *A Very Quiet House* (1989), *Something Very Like Murder* (1994), *Everything Is Strange* (1997), and the prose book *A Concussed History of Scotland* (1990).

Kuppner favors long poems that are often unabashedly prosaic. *Ridiculous! Absurd! Disgusting!* takes its title from Arthur Rimbaud's characterization of his poetry long after he had abandoned writing it; the first of Kuppner's book's three sections is prose, the second a long poem in quatrains, the third a mixture of prose and several verse forms. Kuppner's ability to incorporate a wide range of reading from a variety of scientific and cultural fields might suggest comparisons with his fellow Scotsman Hugh MacDiarmid, as might his eclectic references to cultures and places remote from Scotland. *A Bad Day for the Sung Dynasty*, for instance, consists of 511 quatrains written after Kuppner read Oswald Siren's *Chinese Painting: Leading Masters and Principles*, with the quatrains borrowing some of their idiom, the book's blurb tells us, from "the common usage of translators of Chinese poetry." Ultimately, however, the ludic spirit of Kuppner's writing seems remote from the didacticism of MacDiarmid's later work; the poet-critic Robert Crawford writes that "Juxtaposition of the comic, the supposedly Immensely Significant, with the apparently trivial but essentially human details of mundanity is the hallmark of Kuppner's writing."[2] In his self-interview, Kuppner names Rimbaud and particularly the proto-surrealist Lautréamont as the "presiding spirits" in *Ridiculous! Absurd! Disgusting!* Philosophically, he adds, "I am a critical rationalist and, maybe, for myself, pointing inwards, I am some sort of Zen Buddhist."[3] "Eclipsing Binaries" makes good on its title by establishing and then undermining binary systems, allowing the reader the illusion of choice in the construction of the poem's phrases and sentences, while shifting the terms of relationship between the two options proffered.

---

[1] *Verse*, vol. 6, no. 2, June 1989, p. 50.
[2] *Identifying Poets: Self and Territory in Twentieth-Century Poetry*, Edinburgh, 1993, p. 122.
[3] *Verse*, p. 46.

Eclipsing Binaries

1. The Net

1.

I do not mind these <u>minutes</u> of silence
         moments
For, had <u>they</u> been noisy, they would also have ended
      we
And the tree <u>ignoring us</u> outside the window
        unnoticed
Would still be <u>ignoring us</u> <u>outside the window</u>
       signalling   somewhere inside

2.

5   Who lives, for instance, through <u>that wall there?</u>
               this wall here?
Is it not interesting that you <u>do not know?</u>
          can answer this?
Who is it who is in this room with <u>me?</u>
         you?
<u>Surely that ought to be at least a simpler question?</u>
Who is that raving lunatic on the television?

3.

<u>What is this net that holds us in place so insecurely?</u>
We are not fishes, are we? Were we ever?

10   <u>Might it not prove possible to slip through it entirely?</u>
I believe the fishes in general once did something like that.

Perhaps this <u>room</u> is still in <u>the water</u> anyway.
       arm   this room

<u>Why is it we are not drowning</u> in this invisible sea?
What is it we have sighted

4.

These <u>houses</u> which I can see out of your window trouble me
      cars
Obviously what <u>happens</u> inside them has to be called 'life'
       moves
15   But you are not inside any of those <u>houses</u>
              gardens
For you are here. <u>You are here, aren't you?</u>
      Oh my God, she is here

2. Doors

1.

A single <u>cloud</u>   <u>clinging to</u> a peak
      climber   balanced on

I throw a <u>large</u> flat <u>stone</u> into a <u>small flat</u> pool
       small   stone   vast
Is some <u>climber</u> looking at me from any of <u>those</u> mountains?
       animal   these

20   Is someone <u>looking at</u> you near that <u>quiet</u> suburban lane?
          touching   noisy

2.

This <u>large building</u> reminds me of your frown
     endless cloud
I suppose many people have <u>walked</u> through it
                hurried
I suppose some have <u>lingered longer</u>   than they should have done
          opened more doors
I <u>suppose</u> I <u>suppose</u> I <u>suppose</u> I <u>suppose</u> I <u>suppose</u>
  suppose inspect   reflect   remember   smile

3.

25   Apparently a great man once <u>killed himself</u> in that house
                    was attacked
Well, here is an even greater <u>man</u> standing at the entrance
                   fool
Wondering whether the <u>rain</u> which is not quite <u>falling</u> here
                 time   halting
<u>Is</u>   doing so nearby in the street where she was born
Is not

4.

So, this is the garden where you played as a young girl, is it?
What nonsense is this? This is just an ordinary garden.

30   I was already alive then, <u>throughout all of those moments</u>
                    apparently
<u>Breathing in</u> the air in the wrong places, as usual
Exhaling
<u>A not impossible distance away</u>
Who is this standing beside me now?

3. CLOUDS

1.

<u>What a window for</u> a single tree <u>to grow outside!</u>
If I were to be   this is the one I would wish to be.
<u>I could be jealous of that tree, if</u> I   <u>really tried</u>
Absurd   know
35   <u>You'd think it would relax</u>   at least <u>when she was elsewhere</u>
She ought to have been back   fifteen minutes ago

<u>But no: still it waves with its ridiculous enthusiasm</u>
That woman down there is also not her.

2.

I <u>suspect it cannot be healthy to be so envious of furniture</u>
   believe the weather forecast promised rain for this afternoon
I must try to <u>master</u> these <u>utterly reasonable</u> emotions
       prolong   woefully immature
Let me, for instance, look <u>out of the window, at the clouds</u>
                 at the clouds inside this room
40   Not a good idea! Let me <u>look back again</u>
            wait for the rain.

3.

<u>I would like to write your name upon the clouds</u>
Oh, colossal dictionary of never-used words!
Using a <u>fountain-pen</u> rather than an <u>artery</u>
      sneeze   word-processor
So that, when next <u>we walk up that street there</u>
          perhaps in the golden air of autumn
One upward glance would not go <u>unrewarded</u>
            unrecorded

4.

45   So many <u>flowers</u>   in the garden down there <u>this morning</u>
         clouds not   in mourning
If I knew their names <u>would</u> it make me happier?
           could
If they knew my <u>name</u>   could it make me unhappier?
       intentions
<u>Do you know how carefully your name was chosen?</u>
For why might we not spend an entire life in the grip of a name chosen at
   random, or in despair, or in moment of effortless flippancy?

4. Dust

1.

<u>But it will all have to end some time,</u> my darling, will it not?
But this newest sunlight will also fade,
50   However it has not yet ended <u>at this moment,</u> has it?
                 nor at this
<u>Not quite.</u> <u>Still not quite.</u> <u>And still not quite.</u>
Has it?   Has it?   Has it?
Why do we think we are <u>motionless?</u>
          going somewhere?

2.

<u>Steam is no doubt rising from the few remaining jungles</u>
I'm surprised it hasn't switched off yet?

<u>In the lungs of great rivers,</u> on this planet at least
Come, come; we are waiting

55   <u>In much much greater volume than it does from this new kettle</u>
It's boiling. Why doesn't the damn thing switch off?

Which, after a while, switches off with a sudden click.
Tea or coffee?

3.

We are the shadows cast in this room by <u>what?</u>
                                         whom?
And where is time when <u>they</u> are not moving?
                        eyes
<u>What would be here if we were not?</u>
Do you think anyone has ever died in this room?

60   <u>What is it all supposed to be disproving?</u>
I'll put the light on and dispel the gloom.

4.

Some dust on an outside <u>edge</u>   of a <u>cupboard door</u>
                          corner   spiral galaxy
Where else <u>in the universe</u>   would it prefer to be?
            but on my finger
At this present moment she is perhaps <u>moving towards me</u>
                                      saying something nonchalant
<u>How easy it is to forget</u> the utter stupidity of stars
How unimportant is

                                                          1989

GERALDINE MONK (b. 1952)

MONK WAS BORN IN BLACKBURN, LANCASHIRE AND LIVES TODAY IN SHEFFIELD. SHE earned a degree in English Studies at Sheffield Hallam University in 1988. She has been a creative writing tutor for Open College of the Arts and St. Luke's Hospice, Sheffield, and has held positions as visiting lecturer or poet at Chesterfield College of the Arts and SUNY-Buffalo. Much of her work has been outside the standard venues of poetry publishing, bringing her into contact with parallel experimentation in the art and music worlds, and she is well known as a performer of her poems. "Interregnum: The Performance" was part of The National Review of Live Art in 1993 and was performed at the ICA in London. "Hidden Cities," in which Monk and four others led bus tours around the major cities to present narratives alternative to British heritage narratives offered for the consumption of tourists, was commissioned for the Ruskin School of Fine Art and Drawing at Oxford University in 1995. In 1997, she was awarded a British Arts Council Bursary to tour England performing her texts with a saxophonist and cellist. Her selected poems were published as *The Sway of Precious Demons* (1992). *Interregnum* (1993) is a sequence of poems about the hanging, in 1612, of women from the Pendle area of East Lancashire who were accused of being witches; it mixes historical and other materials in a language occasionally borrowed from Gerard Manley Hopkins and George Fox. The CD *Hexentexts*, which includes recordings of poems from *Interregnum*, appeared in 1995.

Monk's poems owe something to traditions of visual poetry, allowing for effects such as the visual symmetry of "I"s in "Where?" Our desire to read this visual symmetry as emphasizing an isolated, sufficient, and balanced "I" at the literal center of the poem is immediately challenged when the poem's syntax suddenly shifts direction and slips from awe to confusion, deflating the discourse of the Romantic sublime. Brashly punning, predominantly lyric in tone, Monk's poems often attempt, as Linda Kinnahan writes, to disentangle "masculinist assumptions from a tradition of poetic authority."[1] They draw on the idioms of ballads and pop lyrics, while also evincing a Hopkins-like delight in forcing words into hyphenated combinations. "La Quinta del Sordo" was written in response to a series of etchings by Francisco Goya titled "Los Proverbios" (The Proverbs) or, alternatively, "Los Disparates" (The Follies), the grotesque and satirical "cold meat torsos" of Goya's work allowing for meditation on desire.

---

[1] "Experimental Poetics and the Lyric in British Women's Poetry: Geraldine Monk, Wendy Mulford, and Denise Riley," *Contemporary Literature*, vol. 37, n. 4, p. 644.

La Quinta del Sordo

Did they begin with
a sharp and a parched rasp
                    a hissling furnace
a gang of heckling menace

5   Did they come sooner or
sooner still
                    filtering through
goose kicking or belly snaking
with lobster arms and side stepping shadows

10   And they became yours all yours
sweet and sticky leeches of twilight
begging always and all ways with
slanted faces

15   a nerve instance —— threadbare
                    cold meat torsos

They needed you
They kneaded you —— exclusively

these draped men and dripping soldiers
these poor and animal antics
20   performing and consuming

How tight grew your creatures of myth
How tight grew the monkey wrench

                    * * *

                    I.

                    lunar masque

an equine head rears   a womans face bleeds white

prehensile lips   before ruin

bloodsucking and hooked in   two black trenches

5   rapacious horse play   crush down on cheekbones

crested and swollen   charcoal on chalk

with frenzy   choking black ivy
                            stricken
                            seaquake
10   of

Title: "The Country-house of the Deaf Man" (Spanish). This was the residence of the artist Francisco
Goya (1746–1828), who became deaf in his 40s (though the house was so named after a previous owner,
also deaf). Goya painted the walls of the Quinta with what are collectively known as the "black paint-
ings," dark and sinister images that include *Saturn Devouring his Children* and *The Witches' Sabbath*;
Monk has spoken of this poem's indebtedness to the brooding and enigmatic series of etchings from this
period of Goya's life that is known as the *Disparates* (Follies) or *Los Proverbios* (The Proverbs).

                              iron limbs
                             overwrought
                               straddle
                               airquake
15   and beyond
                            the aftermath
                             unblinking
                          the eye of a squid
                               devours
20   their future shadows
                         stretched and melted wax
                               frozen
                           partners in fatigue
                               seething
25   webbed and fossilized exhaustion

                                  2.

      We are gathered here today
      because peacocks are pretty birds
      and perfect monsters of iridescence
      Moreover the world has stumbled and tumbled viciously
5   off its floating circles and finally concussed under
      timid speech
      we shall begin to wail (sostenuto) with ill will and abundance
      Yes we have alighted here today keen and clever
      on the fallen margins of space and
10   unchangeable germ-plasms
      knowing why colours crack with moods and moving lips
      and telling no secrets of the bagged and sonic chieftains
      So all is safely gathered thin and perishing
      on its devious route to death
15   but we will not follow such wandering disasters
      we are too smug and swinging
      happy from this bough and bony thing

                                  3.

         You will go where I go where I and you go twinning
           this siamese disease forming bunches of limbs
                      fused in trepidation

         You remain me and I and you with these taunting
5   ligatures of skin binding mutual
                        assailants

                      Inextricable

                        we are
                  compulsory chaperons

Section 2: 7: sostenuto: sustained (said of a musical note)

10
a nexus of stretching
nerve
drained currents and
overheated desires

squabbling before
15
this obese gutter pressing crowd
this strata galvanized and quickened to animosity
to a baby old chick head revving up squawks to lasso
our hideous display

And here more hooks more eyes and this
20
fleshless wet bandaging of loneliness with black marrow gape

Come now
Let us beckon
Let us reckon hard
with this block vengeance

4·

Here we go sound around the one in the middle who we
shall riddle   the bulbous head pearing away we're
laughing at you   clenched fists may pray and black
out night to fight the   heardings AMPLIFICATIONS
5
go sound around and jutters through shutters and B
rained stained cellars   now you are the queen who'll
never be seen you're one on your own so far   from
home a pig in a choke/spoke more kindly of/a spoke in
the eye/s ticks bent will flick and pick up the pieces
10
of shadows we form for your   ultimate   annoyance
so turn a blind/fine/d eye look find/ers are keep/ers
and we are yours but it's only some fun so don't run
for a while just tow the line and you'll be   perhaps
and maybe wet with sweet dew if the morning ever or
15
never

5·

sabres topple HUNCH THAT knocks on fever
low BELLOWING shroud
hitting that largest MUSCLE shunting bloodrowned
crumpling at THE slightest shade
5
UNKNOWN
THE
HEART
breaking fierce A   wishing bone
THICKENING PEWTER
10
HUSK A
DRUM
sound BRITTLE WEAPON gargles
DILATING

```
                              AND
15                      CRISS A CROSS
                             NAILS
                              SH
         IMSHI             OUT         IMSHI
                           IMSHI
```

1980

Where?

```
      Went to mountains
                      everyone
                              on a tidal washy waving
                              crest of
5                             High up there!
                                    ROMANTICISM
                              and
                                    SUBLIME
                              headshakings of
10                                  I
                                    and
                                    I
                              don't know what
                              or not happened next
15                                  except
                              we roly-polied back
                              down again to
                                    DROWN
                              in a tidal washy wave
20                            of celluloid soap.
                                          (All of a sud.)
```

1990

18: *IMSHI:* "Go away!" (military slang)

10: *I and I* is Rastafarian idiom for "we."

LINTON KWESI JOHNSON (b. 1952)

JOHNSON WAS BORN IN CHAPLETON, JAMAICA AND AT AGE ELEVEN MOVED WITH HIS
family to Brixton in London. He was educated at Tulse Hill Comprehensive School
and Goldsmiths College of the University of London, where he studied sociology.
After graduation, he joined the Black Panthers and, as he has remarked in an inter-
view with Mervyn Morris, began writing poetry: "the Black Panthers had a black lit-
erature library and for me it was a new thing, you know, I didn't know there was such
a thing as black literature, I mean I thought books were only written by Europeans—
and I came across this book and began reading it, by W. E. B. Dubois, called *The Souls
of Black Folk.*"[1] Johnson helped organize a poetry workshop within the Black Panther
movement and started the group Rasta Love, in which poets performed with musi-
cians. In the mid-1970s, he joined the Race Today Collective, publishers of the jour-
nal *Race Today*, which the cultural historian Paul Gilroy has described as playing a
"central" role in building "links between black political organizations in different parts
of Britain as well as between British blacks and radical struggles elsewhere in the
world."[2] Johnson's first poems appeared in the magazine, and Race Today Publica-
tions brought out his first book, *Voices of the Living and the Dead* (1975). His second
book, *Dread Beat and Blood,* appeared the following year. His first LP, with the same
title, was released by Virgin Records, where Johnson had been working as a copy-
writer. A series of books including *Inglan is a Bitch* (1980) and his selected poems,
Tings and Times (1991), has followed, together with LPs and CDs released by Island
records and later by Johnson's own label. Johnson is an enormously popular performer
and has toured throughout Europe, reading poems with a backing band. His music
has helped him reach audiences much larger than those most poets enjoy; his com-
mitment to poetry is evident in his devotion of parts of each performance to the unac-
companied reading of his poems.

Johnson notes in his interview with Morris that he "coined the phrase 'dub
poetry'" in 1974 "as a way of talking about the deejays, the reggae deejays, because at
that time I tried to see them, and tried to argue that what they were doing was really
poetry, and that it had a lot in common with traditional African poetry in so far as it
was spontaneous, improvisatory and had a musical base." He speaks also of how
quickly "dub poetry" came to be used as an umbrella term to describe what poet-
peformers were doing. The term can be misleading, he notes, because it implies that
the poetry is added to the music, whereas the opposite is the case. Performance of the

---

1 "Interview with Linton Kwesi Johnson," in *Hinterland: Caribbean Poetry from the West Indies and
Britain*, Newcastle upon Tyne, 1989, p. 251.
2 *'There Ain't no Black in the Union Jack': The Cultural Politics of Race and Nation*, Chicago, 1987, p. 119.

826

written text allows interpretation, but Johnson's poems, while reflecting the influence of reggae rhythms and demotic oral traditions, are not improvised or spontaneous; they are recited rather than sung: "[my work] functions as poetry to be recited to poetry-listening audiences, something separate from the sound system tradition. Where the overlap comes is that we, all of us, have been inspired, and have been impressed, by the deejays."[3]

---

[3] "Interview," p. 256.

Mi Revalueshanary Fren

mi revalueshanary fren is nat di same agen
yu know fram wen?
fram di masses shatta silence—
staat fi grumble
5   fram pawty paramoncy tek a tumble
fram Hungary to Poelan to Romania
fram di cozy cyaasle dem staat fi crumble
wen wi buck-up wananada in a reaznin
mi fren always en up pan di same ting
10   dis is di sang im love fi sing:

Kaydar
e ad to go
Zhivkov
e ad to go
15   Husak
e ad to go
Honnicka
e ad to go
Chowcheskhu
20   e ad to go
jus like apartied
will av to go

awhile agoh mi fren an mi woz taakin
soh mi seh to im:

25   wat a way di eart a run nowadays, man
it gettin aadah by di day
fi know whey yu stan
cauz wen yu tink yu deh pan salid dry lan
wen yu teck a stack yu fine yu ina quick-san
30   yu noh notice ow di lanscape a shiff

7: *staat fi:* started to
9: *pan:* upon
11ff: The stanza names European Communist leaders who fell from power in 1988–1989: János *Kádár,* leader of Hungary; Todor *Zhivkov,* president of Bulgaria; Gustav *Husák,* president of Czechoslovakia; Erich *Honecker,* leader of East Germany; and Nicholae *Ceauşescu,* president of Romania; 1989 also saw the election of F.W. de Klerk as president of South Africa, who was to preside over the eventual dismantling of that country's apartheid system.
26: *aadah:* harder

is like valcanoe andah it an notn cyaan stap it
cauz tings jusa bubble an a bwoil doun below
strata sepahrate an refole
an wen yu tink yu reach di mountain tap
35   is a bran-new platow yu goh buck-up

mi revalueshanary fren shake im ed an im sigh
dis woz im reply:

Kaydar
e ad to go
40   Zhivkov
e ad to go
Husak
e ad to go
Honnicka
45   e ad to go
Chowcheskhu
e ad to go
jus like apartied
will av to go

50   well mi nevah did satisfy wid wat mi fren mek reply
an fi get a deepa meanin in di reaznin
mi seh to im:

well awrite
soh Garby gi di people dem glashnas
55   an it poze di Stallinist dem plenty prablem
soh Garby leggo peristrika pan dem
canfoundin bureacratic strategems
but wi haffi face up to di cole facks
im also open up pandora's bax
60   yes, people powa jus a showa evry howa
an everybady claim dem demacratic
but some a wolf an some a sheep
an dat is prablematic
noh tings like dat yu woulda call dialectic?

65   mi revalueshanary fren pauz awhile an im smile
den im look mi in mi eye an reply:

Kaydar
e ad to go
Zhivkov
70   e ad to go
Husak
e ad to go
Honnicka
e ad to go

54–56: Mikhail *Gorbachev* as the head of the Communist party in the USSR from 1985–1991 presided over the liberalization of the USSR and its eventual collapse; his watchwords were *glasnost* ("openness") and *perestroika* ("restructuring").

75   Chowcheskhu
e ad to go
jus like apartied
will av to go

well mi couldn elabarate
80   plus it woz gettin kinda late
soh in spite a mi lack af andahstandin
bout di meanin a di changes
in di east fi di wes, nonediless
an alldow mi av mi rezahvaeshans
85   bout di cansiquenses an implicaeshans
espehshally fi black libahraeshan
to bring di reaznin to a canclueshan
ah ad woz to agree wid mi fren
hopein dat wen wi meet up wance agen
90   wi coulda av a more fulla canvahsaeshan

soh mi seh to im, yu know wat?
im seh wat? mi seh:

Kaydar
e ad to go
95   Zhivkov
e ad to go
Husak
e ad to go
Honnicka
100   e ad to go
Chowcheskhu
e ad to go
jus like apartied
soon gaan

1991

MAURICE SCULLY (b. 1952)

SCULLY WAS BORN IN DUBLIN AND EDUCATED AT TRINITY COLLEGE, DUBLIN, WHERE she earned a degree in English and Irish. He has lived in Eire, Greece, Italy, and Lesotho. In the late 1970s, he attended St. Patrick's Teacher Training College for his teaching diploma. From 1981 to 1984, he edited the magazine *The Beau* and curated the Winding Stair reading series, a twice-monthly event featuring poets, painters, architects, musicians, and actors. Upon returning from Italy in 1986, he organized the Coelacanth Press festival, which took place over two months and brought poets including Peter Riley, Tom Raworth, Geraldine Monk, and Lee Harwood to Dublin. He taught in Lesotho between 1988 and 1990 and then returned to Dublin, where he now lives and works, teaching English as a foreign language and courses in literature and literacy at Dublin City University. Scully's books include *Five Freedoms of Movement* (1987) and a series of pamphlets and books that form part of a 300-page poem entitled *Livelihood: The Basic Colours* (1994), *Prelude* (1997), *Interlude* (1997), *Postlude* (1997), and *Steps* (1998).

Scully's work, particularly his long poem *Livelihood,* is difficult to excerpt, because of its emphasis on a poetics of process rather than the discrete poem. Given to versions of modernist *condensare,* the poetry is quick in its perceptual and syntactic leaps, incorporating everything from quotations from Plato to phrases from Sotho hymns. Many passages entitled "sonnet" might be thought of as "sonic-nets" and exist side by side with oblique echoes of literature in the Irish language. Writing of the music of Scully's poetry in *The Basic Colours,* James Keery notes a "lightness of touch": *The Basic Colours* uses and modifies found texts taken from the children's writer Enid Blyton, among other sources.[1] "Fire," one of several sequences from *Steps* with that title, concludes the volume; the book's dedication to the Swiss painter Paul Klee offers one window on Scully's aesthetic. It was Klee who, in his "Creative Credo" (1920), rejected the distinction between temporal and spatial art, arguing that "space, too, is a temporal concept," adding to this modernist proposition another: "Art does not reproduce the visible; rather, it makes visible."[2] A brief excerpt from *A Dictionary of Modern Painting* (1956) concerning Klee's non-figurative drawings might help the reader contemplate Scully's debt to him: "[Klee] creates his own world by twisting lines that sometimes recall honeycombs. Here and there he can be seen attempting a hieroglyphic, an indication of synthesized power, signs which are never static. . . . These drawings have a rhythm based on associations, contrasts, balancings and interruptions. In them are found what might be called directional arrows. . . . Houses hud-

---

[1] *P. N. Review,* vol. 22, no. 3, 1996, p. 50.
[2] *Theories of Modern Art: A Source Book by Artists and Critics,* ed. Herschel B. Chipp, Berkeley, 1968, pp. 182–86.

dled together in a village, vegetation springing upwards, the wake of fish in the water, flames dancing, the rise and fall of waves, the formation of crystals, roads and encounters, comings and goings—Klee gives form to everything which perpetually puzzles mankind, and he succeeds in suggesting its perpetual activity. By his blue foregrounds and grey backgrounds he gives space and vibrancy to his coloured planes."[3] Movement, color, mystery, and throughout a posture of receptiveness, a "Waiting Posture"—these are key to Scully's poetry.

---

[3] *A Dictionary of Modern Painting,* ed. Carlton Lake and Robert Mallard, New York, 1956, p. 140.

from Steps

Fire

A

suddenness of what snow does
to a doorstep when you
wake to it in the morning
early before almost anyone

5   (& why the verb *to be*
in so many languages
at such an angle should be
so irregular so often)

a slate gone there
10   emphatic & there too
yes the wind blew this way
not that when

(is a mystery to me.
where were you when they
15   named the name of money
in your name anyway?)

the snow fell graphic many
ways across you (curls joinctures
loops stops) to make the black & white
20   unmelting music of what is

•

B

being coiled into a deft, modified past
not in money-work but secret
difficulties darkness pleated
dovetailing deeper dark down to

25   an all-dimensional ground blackness
        being coiled into a deft, modified past
        hollowing, carving, cutting (I went out.
        I met nobody/I came back. Faced it.)
        the greedkeep, health, sanity, calmness where
30   the roots are, coiled, magnified,
        crystal spindles at the branch-heads,
        spasm of light

                    a wind that
                    turns a leaf on
35   the ground or
                    ientate
                    yourself.

                    —

                    grey black
                    stone ochre.
40   grey black
                    ochre clay.

                             •

        some monumental crap about gathering honey
        in the tympanum of a bank's facade
        small waterplanet tubby patriots
45   the minim of "known" history vertical siphon, pip.
        dogfish upriver, another world
        light through glass touching the light
        curtain reflected on the tabletop surface
        upside-down repelled
50   returns—
        pax! paxpax! pax!
        goes the fighting in the street
        being coiled into a deft, modified past.

                    —

                    grey black
55   ochre stone
                    grey black
                    ochre clay

                             •

43: *tympanum*: the recessed surface of a pediment (a triangular feature that in Classical-style architecture
    crowns the entrances of buildings): it is often decorated with relief sculptures and engraved mottos. The
    tympanum here belongs to the Allied Irish Banks building near Trinity College, Dublin: "usual tableau
    re INDUSTRY . . . sickles, ropes, anchors, a literate maid centre-stage consulting vasty tome, peasants,
    labourers & a beehive" (Scully, in correspondence).
45: *minim*: in music, a half-note; or, more generally, a little thing
51: *pax!*: Latin for "peace"

C

a triangle of sun
light on the
60   wall of a
shed.

           blue sky. join the
           dots. child-wit.
           the blue plane.
65   the blue
           plane
draws the eye
along then
down to
70   chim

           neys & rooftops. here
           we are. slightly
           closer to the
           heart of
75   creation (but still
not close enough)
at the base of
an old tree
(minute

80   grains of white quartz
           imprint of the nail
           in the mud/webb-
           ing between
           3 toes
85   & mare's tail sprung from the ooze
a spider web, ready) a small
bird buried. even that.
the tune complifact
scraptured.

90   five seagulls in V-form-
           ation & a quick
           sparrow too
           makin a
           mane.

95   it's wonderful to wake up sometimes
                to the feeling of time in the morning
                early, crisp, moving for a moment in
                the first day always, the clasp & bars
                of the metal gate in the hedge outside
100   (say) by the pathway where—can do on
                contact—the garden—you are—a glass

72ff: The epitaph of the Swiss artist Paul Klee (1879–1940), drawn from his diary, reads: "I cannot be
understood in purely earthly terms. For I can live as happily with the dead as with the unborn. Some-
what closer to the heart of all creation than is usual. But still far from being close enough."
85: *mare's tail:* a type of marsh plant
93–94: *makin a / mane:* lamenting; quoted from the Scottish ballad "The Twa Corbies" ("The Two
Ravens"): "As I was walking all alane, / I heard twa corbies making a mane." The ravens discuss eating
the body of a dead knight in the ditch nearby.

of cool water on the sunlit sill—in-
tricate tickle on the face—bright berry—
the air puckered where the silkseed
105   drifts *that*

held to the Waiting Posture, *that* music an instant
fit to stave only an order in a sea of which/&
orders. when a token's taken & returned
fluent—"beautiful ideas for prov-
110   iding truth"—a *legal-decision-*
trial-peace pouch in waiting
(pat)

                    clé deas
                         you could ex-
115   plain
                                   Peru
                    release the Trees
                         Animals
                                        Engines
120   joining the
                         Geometric Dance
                    on the shed wall
                                        of an evening
                    vertical to the *why* in yr pockets
125   (otherwise empty you go about with
                    proud & prim nonetheless)
                    mirrors gaps branch-formations
                    the very sight in the head—
                                   hills
130   stone outcrops—
                    staving off all aggressive parasites
                    & ear to the beat of breathing
                    returned renewed & singing
                                   why
135   /whirring pipsqueak/can't-thinking
                    why can't thinking
                         fit thinking fit
                         this   apt
                         black   black
140   *grey   red*
                         black   red
                         grey   grey
                              black

                                        •

                                                            1998

107: *stave:* both "stave off" and the "staff" on which music is notated
110ff: The frontispiece and backpiece of *Steps* depict a clay pouch, "from which the Sumerian logograph
    ◊ is derived, meaning, or thought to mean, *legal, decision, trial* or *peace.*" (Scully)
113: *clé deas:* "(say roughly 'clay, das'); Irish = 'left, right'—but also punningly: 'a good painting by Paul
    Klee'." (Scully, in correspondence)

JOHN WILKINSON (b. 1953)

W ILKINSON WAS BORN IN LONDON AND MOVED IN INFANCY TO CORNWALL, GROWING up there and in Devon. He was educated at a series of boarding schools and at Jesus College, Cambridge, where he took a double first in English. A fellowship at Harvard followed, allowing him to study the poetry of John Wieners. Wilkinson then moved to Birmingham and trained as a psychiatric nurse. In Birmingham he managed a psychiatric rehabilitation service for a Housing Association in the West Midlands. He has since held a position at the University of Wales devoted to training and service development for mental health agencies and is now commissioner and head of mental health for the East London and The City Health Authority, living in Cambridge and North London. The poems from Wilkinson's earliest small-press pamphlets are collected in *Oort's Cloud: Earlier Poems* (1999). Other books include *Clinical Notes* (1980), *Proud Flesh* (1986), *Flung Clear: Poems in Six Books* (1994), and *Sarn Helen* (1997).

Wilkinson is part of a second or third generation of Cambridge-educated poets whose work has led critics to posit the continuing existence of a "Cambridge School" consisting of poets influenced by the poetry of J. H. Prynne and his contemporaries. In an interview Wilkinson has said that it was the "range of rhetorical resources rather than . . . a body of knowledge" he discovered in Prynne's work that enabled a move beyond early poems "concerned with the becoming of the sentient subject" to a "more rhetorically various writing." Elsewhere in the interview, he remarks that "much of my life has been an attack on my well-spokenness. Both as a writer but also in terms of my employment, socially . . ."[1] It is tempting to relate such motives to the rebarbative surface of Wilkinson's poems, which, as Drew Milne writes, "seek to incorporate alien frames of reference as though they could be made into the expressive shapes of consciousness rather than left as so much dead matter of capitalism. . . . The triumphal dance of mind over matter, however, invariably dissolves into new negativities." Dense nets of internal allusions and echoes, Wilkinson's poems resist glossing; they establish multiple strands of argument and metaphor while setting contradictory definitions in motion. *Sarn Helen,* like many of Wilkinson's books, is a sequence of poems, here beginning *in medias res* with a poem with a slash for its title and "bayonetted" as its first word. Noting that its long lines suggest epic hexameter, Milne draws an analogy between reading the poem's "flights of fancy and . . . baroque sublime of figurative alienations . . . which speak of damaged lifeworlds" and the art of surfing the Net. Offered as a homage to Lynette Roberts, its title referring to a Roman road in Wales, the sequence is also, Milne argues, a kind of "nature poetry," albeit a nature poetry

---

1 "The John Wilkinson Interview," *Angel Exhaust,* vol. 8, 1992, pp. 76–90.

that "appears not simply to describe an external world but to cross refer residues of memory with a wariness towards the sentiments of collective false memory syndromes."[2] It is a poetry in which what might yet be—some perception that would adequately mirror the "soilage" of external worlds—is condemned "to bounce on the glimmerous pool" of public images and discourses, in which "elusive" and "skittering" perception is accompanied by colloquial admonition: "You've got some lip." Recognition of the objects and products of supposed needs as too often "guano, / hotly pursued" offers *Sarn Helen* its dominant tone of restless, accelerated disgust. Near the end of the last poem in the sequence, the reader encounters the lines "Flimsy / as I am I burrow in the fallopian waste of my making," as if this poetry in which it is not clear that any "calibration" will "serve to fold / edgeless radiant, erasive, your saved up fervencies" will nevertheless emerge as the poet's *habitus*.[3]

---

[2] "Flex & go," *Jacket*, accessed on the World Wide Web on [18 Feb. 2000]:
  http://www.jacket.zip.com.au/jacket03/milne-review.html
[3] *Sarn Helen*, p. 31.

from Sarn Helen

HOMAGE TO LYNETTE ROBERTS, AND FOR FRIENDS IN SWANSEA

> *Since the light of the star which was daguerrotyped took*
> *twenty years to traverse the space separating it from the earth,*
> *the ray which was fixed on the plate had consequently left the*
> *celestial sphere a long time before Daguerre had discovered the*
> *process by which we have just gained control of this light . . .*
>
> *I myself find in it monotony, that inexhaustible source of*
> *everything that makes a deep impression.*
> DELACROIX'S JOURNALS

"bayonetted"

/

bayonetted. If any will hear the truth must cling best
avoid blow dragonflies, cling on by nail-feasance
over a cataract which scours a giant curtain wall,
or was it short-of-time shrunk the unseeming aimless
5   river to a bank's sediment? Common seals luxuriate,

In reading these poems, it is important not to consider the verbal definitions put forward here as exclusive. Wilkinson's poems are dense nets of internal allusions and echoes, keeping several strands of metaphor and argument in currency simultaneously. Individual words may be exploited for more than one of these strands or contexts, sometimes bringing into play contradictory dictionary definitions. It can help to read the poems quickly a few times in order to gain a sense of the different strands before trying to make sense of a particular phrase. The extreme forward impetus of rhythm in the poems with longer lines is effective in carrying the reader across the knottiness of the syntax and the sometimes obscure words and phrases he uses.

Title: *Sarn Helen:* a Roman road in Wales, still in existence
Dedication: *Lynette Roberts,* the Welsh poet: see p. 348
Epigraph: *Eugéne Delacroix* (1798–1863), the French painter of the Romantic era
2: *feasance:* the execution of a duty or obligation (only now current in the word "malfeasance")
3: *curtain wall:* castle wall

transmitters pinned behind their perked-up ears,
breezes buffet from all directions Body-build them
into a race of top achievers, filing across hillsides
mewl within their gathering blades, a scopophilia
10   shrink-wraps the forest in its retailer's proud image
Preserving it while it speeds, dragnetting seagulls,
seagulls, choughs, a tinkers' brood they desolate
with far cries. Filaments shall creep though bated
shear the nucleus, threads by which I still revolve
15   shook where a deadeye holds the swarm by scent,
from bracken rising augural, on white stuff lightsome.
Bindings dishevelled dry & tighten on their windlass
mummify, screwing a bridge's tension dip & straight,
machines tramping open cropped ground beneath
20   go incognito in a high-wire infant parsing T-cells
Nose squashed on a greyprint, how will molten tar
fuse the cracks the drought shall visit? Canefrogs
jump the continent, leaf through springy signatures
closer than a razor-blade's width. Co-dependency
25   was our sick tract, gluey exudate we thought to pill,
thought in lieu of reagent so a pancake could solidify
honeycombed poor silicate, quivering to adjust
hand-to-hand remedial lets the day-out skaters pass
They throng the pentangle straw-fringed, slip-slide
30   through turnstiles like windows read seasons' entry.
Stronger the differences yet more shall they even out,
locally stabilised against their brushed & rolled-on
variety of roots affiliations. Affording scope for
trapped bubbles closing above the issue decompress
35   on the running crack we learnt to compère, calling
after names we program to overfly. Love of Mike
streams from a capsule still might generate Mike
Who. Repack his space with sex toys & a calculator.
Being obdurate ground a chain of buckets empties.
40   A scraping machine drew its blade on protuberances.
The vacuum sipped slowly like the seamed vessel
girds itself & counts on Count on a decent return,

9: *scopophilia:* voyeurism

15: *deadeye:* a round wood block pierced with three holes, through which a lanyard rope is threaded, which is used for extending a ship's shroud (a set of ropes attached to the mast to relieve it of sideways strain).

20: *T-cells:* cells responsible for the body's immune reactions

22: *Canefrogs:* Cane toads, native to South America, were introduced into Australia in 1935 to control sugarcane beetles; they have since themselves become pests, spreading over much of Australia. The toads exude poison through glands in their skin, and can also shoot it at attackers.

23: In bookmaking, sheets from the press are folded into *signatures;* in older books these were left uncut, so that a reader needed to slit open the pages of the book.

26: *reagent:* a substance employed in chemical reactions (e.g., for testing for another substance, as in litmus paper)
    pancake: glancing at "pancake makeup"

27: *silicate:* a salt formed by silicic acid; its structure indeed resembles a honeycomb. The passage perhaps also glances at the technological use of silicon in computer chips.

29: *pentangle:* the five-pointed diagram of a star, thought when inscribed on the ground to protect against the supernatural; it was used in conjuring to contain evil spirits.

34: A rapid reduction in air-pressure—as when a deepsea diver surfaces too quickly—leads to *decompression* sickness, as dissolved nitrogen is released from the body's tissues and forms *bubbles* in the joints.

35: *crack:* "split," but also "banter"

farting, a Wizard of Oz gale restocks what billows
caulked but incapable of self-evidence. As it imbibes
45   of the downdraught, belching short, distressed bouts,
send-storm shall abate & the crowsnest jiggle high-
vaunts to see behind lifts the nose of a coming storm,
compassed too by the arena. Drop its grey bundle
like on a scaffold television sours & is less buoyant.
50   But it seems their ionized stuff might over-rehearse
its early state of mobility, a platoon of engineering
squaddies drilled in straight lines for a lemming wave
spot & fox & it is their Passchendaele implodes in
reinforced trenches. The plasma sheath like a condom,
55   they start to expel communicative a flock of gulls
outperforms his spec, he will be a founding premise
this week of what he shortsees. Rewind the meter
dangles its supplement inside a white & careful box.
We took the ladle to the punchbowl frosted in a clear
60   tame stream. Around my arm the air was strapped.

"snap crackle & pop"

snap crackle & pop. Deliver us from passers-by of
accents & their affines. The fault was never outlandish
straws bubble with cuckoo-spit or the oak-apple
priority who may not draw on reserves But spiralled
5   like a run-time virus, flattening their strobe corn.
Their fields were laid waste before armies roll over,
prod then keyhole scanned the bales of rag, OCR
in passing, fleers of the covenant risen out of rushes,
proved as with psoriasis not cracks Come on down
10   Observe the halogen hob Take note of the library
of patristics, one volume open, scaredly consulted
flutters page to page will spot-buy a reduced yield

52: *squaddies:* soldiers, recruits
53: *fox:* (of a book's pages) become discolored with reddish-brown spots
    Passchendaele was a notorious battle of World War I, an attempt to break through German trench lines
that gained only five miles of ground at a cost of 250,000 casualties.
54: *plasma sheath:* a thin layer of space charge covering a surface in an ionized gas—e.g., a spacecraft or
airplane in the earth's ionosphere
56: A machine or computer *outperforms* its *spec* by exceeding its nominal capacity or capability.

1: Cf. the Lord's Prayer: "Deliver us from evil" (Matt. 6:13)
2: *affines:* kin
3: *cuckoo-spit:* a froth stuck to plants' stems or leaves that conceals insect larvae
    oak-apple: a growth on oak leaves produced by the gall-wasp
7: *keyhole scanned:* alluding to keyhole (high-precision) surgery
    OCR: optical character-recognition software, which translates the image of a text into characters
8: *fleers:* mocks; sneers
10: *halogen hob:* a high-tech stove burner that uses halogen tubes
11: *patristics:* writings by and on the Church Fathers; heredity

hinges down before listless scythes Whereat released
salivation smites those pillars that its pumping-house
15   water flooding the land floats poppies & pools wax.
With fire the granaries crackle then the aid convoys
load at a distant airport apples suffer anaesthesia,
sky-high transport brings to huts cornmeal, juices air,
forges like the house-martins season after season
20   pluck at their tatty binding but no cortisone sullies
read the figures off. The intervention bracket drum-
heads the first crop to ripen live on air, I hear you
sold down a connection those armourers high-fiving
on arrival make secure. A reconstruction package
25   quilts from logged bracken, bed for kine & impatient
floors trade the roots yet unlifted. Much like a gas
chamber meets television. The hydrothermal vents
suck the susceptive ocean & shall ordain its future
Child whose double straw froths through her glass,
30   drinking loose blowback with a fixed price collides.
Gangling the concrete across their bones had dowsed
pools by sticky hilt. The revenants mull things over
raggedy hole in the small end of the constant egg,
spewing to what lengths blue-silver arrows curve
35   E-mailed out from Imperial Rome, the flow of goods
sweeps up thought parochial once, was touched
cosmopolitan, a yak breeder, chewer of qat gyrate,
circling & self-righting under strict trial conditions.
Lighter & smaller yet they attract both touch & answer,
40   made to suck air dry will trash its palaeographic
loving solicitude, arrowheads of some elite forward
conning a headwind as the key its lock, as a coney
burrows thread as system. Bewildered they cut straw,
turn the stowaways, so commute the day's round
45   like a clepsydra who nod, a beam engine, schedules
for their life-pangs an inventory of variants I bridge
Spot-welding to a phantasm had wrinkled the flue-
columned smoke, blurred together seams immasked
that turbid to each other the air with nothing to it
50   stood on the paths which hitching over the orbital
parade vacancy. Their dumb fluffball is a material
mattering; its culture borne in the crop won't dissect
in carbohydrates, protein, vegetable hydrolisers:

20: *cortisone:* a steroid hormone, often used to treat inflammation
25: *kine:* cattle
27: *Hydrothermal vents* are the product of submarine volcanic activity or the movement of continental
  plates; they support unique deep-sea ecosystems.
28: *susceptive:* receptive; susceptible
32: *revenants:* people returned from exile; ghosts
37: *qat:* the leaf of a Middle-Eastern bush, mildly narcotic when chewed
40: *palaeographic:* pertaining to the study of ancient writings and inscriptions
41: *forward:* front edge; player in the front line of a soccer or rugby team
42: *conning:* scanning
    coney: rabbit
45: *clepsydra:* a water-clock
50: *orbital:* i.e., orbital road
52: *crop:* both a farm crop, and a bird's crop (a pouch forming an extension of its gullet, where food is pre-
  pared for digestion)

if votives of black hair & the joined-up alphabet
55   tirade the dog's nap, a pen-top & coin unmagnetic
jump to disengage any lead. Confounded in the face
conscripts you always—this too is ridiculous but so
I bore & cupped a blank face for an access code
beneath ladders & slides, the spider's web of ropes
60   strums what invisibly crosses through its counterbond.

"You've got some lip"

/

You've got some lip. A legionary
levels with the
sewer-rat, I might yet crack
the whip of a keyhole tracery,

5   this intracranial warm with soot,
writing a traceless
mirror out of
soilage, catapulting a skiff

to bounce on the glimmerous
10   delusory pool: what are the depths
believed in
you would sink towards,

impetus lost? You cross-remember
flitwork where the arch
15   breath dislodges
chunks of an old ceremonial

Scurrying like woodlice
carrying boats upon your backs,
feeling along the voussoirs
20   What a wheel was

So these may hang & grope
smudged on a lip,
deceived by a friendly camber
to be elusive, skittering

25   round their shelves,
sliding in clefts thick with guano

54: *votives*: priests
55: *nap*: the fur's surface

19: *voussoirs*: the stones of an arch
23: A *camber* is a slight curvature in the surface of a road; a *friendly camber* in a turn helps the car follow
   it.

hotly pursued, breathless. Savages,
prolapse your sights

30   on a penetralium slap in the middle,
your lenses having below-side
scratches cannot join
as diligent cross-hairs,

your resonant shout
won't crack the deep in a flitch
35   of dominion—no,
hang loose, something for all of us

swags in the monotone had fallen
calming the headwaters.
Slurp their
40   stinking rodent bolt-holes.

1997

28: A body part is *prolapsed* when it has slipped out of place or downwards from its correct location.
29: *penetralium:* inner part of a building, especially the inner shrine of a temple
34: *flitch:* a dense slice

JO SHAPCOTT (b. 1953)

ONE OF THE POEMS IN SHAPCOTT'S SECOND COLLECTION, *PHRASE BOOK* (1992), TELLS of its speaker's sudden transformation into a goat; the poem treats themes such as loneliness and desire and "the press of bodies" in crowds.[1] Such a procedure is fairly typical of her work, in which identity, gender, and the body are viewed from perspectives allowing for distance and, sometimes, gentle comedy. As Ian Gregson writes of an earlier book, what seems "distinctively Shapcott's own is a mingling of surreal fantasy with a kind of naturalism—an emphasis on sometimes gross physicality, on the body and its functions, or its implication in animality."[2] "Phrase Book" gives us the voice of a robotic "Englishwoman," her self-righteous national pride all that remains of an identity composed of contradictory and simplistic media-speak, her body a "Human Remains Pouch," her desire largely unavailable to her except as memory blurring into programed visions of Stealth bomber pilots. The "Mad Cow" poems offer us another view of "postmodern" identity as ecstatic, fluid, and open: the mad cow loves "the staggers" and "the wonderful holes in my brain," adding that "most brains are too / compressed. You need this spongy / generosity to let the others in." "The Mad Cow in Love" finds the mad cow dreaming of life as an angel, the poem drawing us past its absurd premise into its wistful meditation until a metaphor in the mad cow's intimate address to the lover transforms carnality or "animality" into necessity: "I want you earthly, / including all the global terrors and harms / which might come when we fall backwards / into the world of horn and hoof."

Shapcott was born in London and educated at Trinity College, Dublin, St. Hilda's College, Oxford, and Harvard. She has worked in the Education Office of the South Bank Centre and for the Arts Council. Her first book was *Electroplating the Baby* (1988), which contained among other poems a sequence about two famous literary couples—Robert Lowell and Elizabeth Hardwick, Robert Browning and Elizabeth Barrett Browning—that meditates upon sexual difference and creativity. Her most recent book, *My Life Asleep*, appeared in 1998. With Matthew Sweeney she is co-editor of the anthology *Emergency Kit: Poems for Strange Times* (1996).

---

[1] "Goat," *Phrase Book*, Oxford, 1992, p. 11.
[2] *Contemporary Poetry and Postmodernism*, New York, 1996, p. 245.

Phrase Book

I'm standing here inside my skin,
which will do for a Human Remains Pouch
for the moment. Look down there (up here).
Quickly. Slowly. This is my own front room

5   where I'm lost in the action, live from a war,
on screen. I am an Englishwoman, I don't understand you.
What's the matter? You are right. You are wrong.
Things are going well (badly). Am I disturbing you?

TV is showing bliss as taught to pilots:
10   Blend, Low silhouette, Irregular shape, Small,
Secluded. (Please write it down. Please speak slowly.)
Bliss is how it was in this very room

when I raised my body to his mouth,
when he even balanced me in the air,
15   or at least I thought so and yes the pilots say
yes they have caught it through the Side-Looking

Airborne Radar, and through the J-Stars.
I am expecting a gentleman (a young gentleman,
two gentlemen, some gentlemen). Please send him
20   (them) up at once. This is really beautiful.

Yes they have seen us, the pilots, in the Kill Box
on their screens, and played the routine for
getting us Stealthed, that is, Cleansed, to you and me,
Taken Out. They know how to move into a single room

25   like that, to send in with Pinpoint Accuracy, a hundred Harms.
I have two cases and a cardboard box. There is another
bag there. I cannot open my case—look out,
the lock is broken. Have I done enough?

Bliss, the pilots say, is for evasion
30   and escape. What's love in all this debris?
Just one person pounding another into dust,
into dust. I do not know the word for it yet.

Where is the British Consulate? Please explain.
What does it mean? What must I do? Where
35   can I find? What have I done? I have done
nothing. Let me pass please. I am an Englishwoman.

1992

The poem draws on both the language of phrasebooks and U.S. military jargon given currency during the
  Gulf War.
9: The acronym *BLISS* is taught to pilots to help them remember how to avoid radar.
17: *J-Stars:* Joint Surveillance and Target Attack Radar System
23: *Stealthed:* i.e., attacked by a stealth bomber plane
25: *Harms:* Homing Anti-Radar Missiles

The Mad Cow in Love

I want to be an angel and really think
I'm getting there with this mind of mine,
shrinking every day towards the cleanness,
the size of a baby animal's brain.
5   Trouble is, I want you to be an angel too
—and want that more if anything. It's one
of those demands I can't raise just like that,
evenings, when we're reading our different newspapers
you scanning your pages and me mine for an item
10   to start speech, make mouths smile, knees touch—something
in all that murder and mayhem to launch love.
You tell me you're looking for news of the self.
Do you want to be an angel? I know
the answer already and it's rough medicine.
15   But think of all the kinds there are, as many
as the different degrees of reaching
for the good. You might get away without
searching for the soul at all in those places,
today at least, you'd rather not get to know.
20   And angels do a variety of jobs:
the post of perpetual adoration might suit,
or divine messenger but I fancy for you
the government of the stars and all the elements.
I know you well enough to choose, after all this time
25   as foreign correspondent on the track of who you are,
looking for leads: your last screw, the food
you threw away, your strategic approaches
for living through the next hour. I don't mean it,
though, any of it. I want you earthly,
30   including all the global terrors and harms
which might come when we fall backwards
into the world of horn and hoof.

1992

Mad Cow Dance

I like to dance. Bang. I love to dance. Push.

It makes me savage and brilliant. Stomp. To
my own rhythm, rhythm. I lead or I don't

have a partner. No market for partners,
5   just this wide floor for the dance.
I think I was born here. Swoop. I don't care.

The Mad Cow In Love: Title: "Mad cow disease" is the popular name for bovine spongiform encephalopathy (BSE), a fatal disease of cattle involving the deterioration of the brain; the name comes from the erratic behaviour of the affected animals, which become nervous and aggressive and gradually lose muscular control. An epidemic of the disease occurred in British cattle in the late 1980s, and became an issue of international importance when it was discovered that the disease could be passed to humans, and that infected material had been entering the food chain over a substantial period of time.

Even if I'd been born in the back of a car

the chassis and each blessed spring
would have jumped as I leapt out

10   of my mum. Up. Down to the ocean, perhaps
the beach? Hah. Stone steps and stone walls,
the pebbled strand, try to stall my special

high-kicks for the sea. But fireflies

know I'm here, raving with light,
15   they swirl down my spine. Swish. My tail

goes bam, thwack against the backs
of my legs. Pleasure, local pleasure.
Listen, sitting-down reader, I reckon

faces would be red if you knew what

20   was next. The little fibres
of my muscles give me such a charge.

Bread and butter. Release. Ceasefire
between my legs and my brain. Sweet oil
flows down to my little hooves. I like

25   to turn and call to my friends in

northern towns: kick out, kick back, fruity,
for a second. We can meet among characters

who don't dance, and hoof it till dawn, gas
on and on even when we're moving the most.
30   Four legs increase splits into splats,

just watch me

become
pure product, pure

use,
35   pure perfume,
jasmine and fucked.

1992

MONIZA ALVI (b. 1954)

Alvi was born in Lehore, Pakistan and has lived in England since she was several months old. She was educated at the University of York, Whitelands College, and the London University Institute of Education, and now works as a teacher in London. Her books are *Peacock Luggage* (with Peter Daniels, 1992), *The Country at My Shoulder* (1993), and *A Bowl of Warm Air* (1996). She was one of the poets selected as part of the promotional events introducing a "New Generation" of British poets in 1996.

In the second half of *The Country at My Shoulder*, Alvi includes poems meditating on her relationship to her country of birth, which exists for her there partly as fantasy, as a country she can "prise" off a map, and also partly as an identity produced for her by others, by "Presents from my Aunts in Pakistan." Mostly Pakistan is simply remote, even unwanted: "I could never be as lovely / as those clothes—/ I longed for denim and corduroy."[1] In another poem, "India is manageable—smaller than / my hand, the Mahandi River / thinner than my lifetime."[2] Identity as written on the body assumes more threatening possibilities in "The Sari," which imagines the poet as "Inside my mother" looking out through a "glass porthole" only to see everyone from her family to local politicians peering in at her; they insist that "*Your body is your country.*"[3] Still another poem represents the poet's origins as a stone "like the one that tries / to fill the mango. / Inside it is the essence / of another continent." While the poet fears the removal of this stone, she also knows it would be better to "race away with it!"[4] Identity as it is shaped by the conflict between the discourse of others and one's own desires is mulled over in a conversational tone and manner owing something to Edward Thomas and Stevie Smith, the poems' simple if often idiosyncratic images also suggesting Jacques Prèvert: these are three poets Alvi names as influences in her note for *Contemporary Poets*.[5] *A Bowl of Warm Air,* which includes the three poems reprinted here, was written following Alvi's return visit to Pakistan. Here the difficulty of connecting with her origins and the incursion of the real often make for disappointment while, via simile, the poems incorporate details of life in Pakistan and India—as in "Grand Hotel," for instance, in which "Mock princes hover at table, / poorly paid, return / to shacks and open drains." A new consciousness of imperial history is suggested by "Fighter Planes," which begins with an image of green parrots

---

[1] "Presents from my Aunts in Pakistan," *The Country at My Shoulder,* Oxford, 1993, p. 30.
[2] "Map of India," p. 37.
[3] "The Sari," p. 36.
[4] "Domain," p. 42.
[5] *Contemporary Poets,* 6th edition, ed. Thomas Riggs, New York, 1996, p. 19.

nesting in fighter planes as the speaker admits that she had once "thought I could fly / and peck at little / bits of the world." "And If " reflects a new syntactic complexity in keeping with a view of identity as layered, its elusive core finally "unbearable," its shape no less subject to definition "by someone else" in Pakistan than in England.

And If

If you could choose a country
to belong to—
perhaps you had one
snatched away,
5   once offered to you
like a legend
in a basket covered with a cloth—

and if the sun were a simple flare,
the streets beating out
10   the streets, and your breath
lost on the road
with the Yadavs, herding cattle,
then you could rest, absorb
it all in the cool of the hills,

15   but still you might peel back one face
to retrieve another
and another, down to the face that is
unbearable, so clear
so complex, hinting at nations,
20   castes and sub-castes
and you would touch it once—

and if this Eastern track were
a gusty English lane
where rain makes mirrors
25   in the holes,
a rat lies lifeless, sodden
as an old floorcloth,
you'd be untouchable—as one

defined by someone else—
30   one who cleans the toilets,
burns the dead.

1996

The Wedding

I expected a quiet wedding
high above a lost city
a marriage to balance on my head

like a forest of sticks, a pot of water.
5   The ceremony tasted of nothing
had little colour—guests arrived

stealthy as sandalwood smugglers.
When they opened their suitcases
England spilled out.

10   They scratched at my veil
like beggars on a car window.
I insisted my dowry was simple—

a smile, a shadow, a whisper,
my house an incredible structure
15   of stiffened rags and bamboo.

We travelled along roads with English
names, my bridegroom and I.
Our eyes changed colour

like traffic-lights, so they said.
20   The time was not ripe
for us to view each other.

We stared straight ahead as if
we could see through mountains
breathe life into new cities.

25   I wanted to marry a country
take up a river for a veil
sing in the Jinnah Gardens

hold up my dream, tricky
as a snake-charmer's snake.
30   Our thoughts half-submerged

like buffaloes under dark water
we turned and faced each other
with turbulence

and imprints like maps on our hands.

1996

27: *Jinnah Gardens*: a popular park in Karachi

Grand Hotel

This is how life began—
with a Grand Hotel propelled
into the middle of India,

breathing fire and ice,
5   sucking in the world
and hurling it away.

All the living organisms roll
on the bed with stomach pains.
The bathroom almost gleams.

10   The carpet smells
of something old and fried,
though incense burns.

Mock princes hover at tables,
poorly paid, return
15   to shacks and open drains,

serve the invaders, oddly white
and semi-clad, armed with
sticks and cameras and maps.

1996

CAROL ANN DUFFY (b. 1955)

Duffy is best known for her dramatic monologues imagining the voices of character types rarely heard in poetry. "Psychopath" allows us to overhear the sick reasoning of a rapist and murderer; "Standing Female Nude" gives voice to a cynical "river-whore" posing for an artist. These poems and others try to represent the speech idioms and motives of degenerate or marginal figures while establishing an implied perspective from which their motivations and values can be scrutinized. As is the case with most dramatic monologues, Duffy's characters speak more than they know they speak, but not so much about themselves—it is not character per se that seems to be Duffy's first interest—as about a larger society's values, its language and images. The prostitute in "Standing Female Nude" allows Duffy to explore the ways women have often been represented by men in art: the artist "possesses me as he dips the brush / repeatedly into the paint." In "Psychopath," as Ian Gregson writes, the reader is propelled beyond the speaker's evil or sickness toward a "poetic voice speaking alongside the psychopathic one."[1] T. S. Eliot's *The Waste Land* resonates in "dull canal," for instance, and "My breath wipes me from the looking-glass" suggests a knowledge of the limits of representation no psychopath could frame so neatly.

Duffy was born in Glasgow and moved as a child to Staffordshire. She was educated at St. Joseph's Convent, Stafford Girl's High School, and the University of Liverpool, where she read philosophy. Her books of poetry are *Standing Female Nude* (1985), *Selling Manhattan* (1987), *The Other Country* (1990), *Mean Time* (1993), *The World's Wife* (1999), in which poems such as "Queen Kong" offer critical revisions of myth and popular culture, and *The Pamphlet* (1999). Duffy has been a visiting fellow at North Riding College, writer-in-residence at Southern Arts, Thamesdown, and editor of *Ambit* magazine. She lives in London and works as a freelance writer.

---

[1] *Contemporary Poetry and Postmodernism*, New York, 1996, p. 97.

Standing Female Nude

Six hours like this for a few francs.
Belly nipple arse in the window light,
he drains the colour from me. Further to the right,
Madame. And do try to be still.
5   I shall be represented analytically and hung

in great museums. The bourgeoisie will coo
at such an image of a river-whore. They call it Art.

Maybe. He is concerned with volume, space.
I with the next meal. You're getting thin,
10 Madame, this is not good. My breasts hang
slightly low, the studio is cold. In the tea-leaves
I can see the Queen of England gazing
on my shape. Magnificent, she murmurs
moving on. It makes me laugh. His name

15 is Georges. They tell me he's a genius.
There are times he does not concentrate
and stiffens for my warmth. Men think of their mothers.
He possesses me on canvas as he dips the brush
repeatedly into the paint. Little man,
20 you've not the money for the arts I sell.
Both poor, we make our living how we can.

I ask him Why do you do this? Because
I have to. There's no choice. Don't talk.
My smile confuses him. These artists
25 take themselves too seriously. At night I fill myself
with wine and dance around the bars. When it's finished
he shows me proudly, lights a cigarette. I say
Twelve francs and get my shawl. It does not look like me.

1985

And How Are We Today?

The little people in the radio are picking on me
again. It is sunny, but they are going to make it
rain. I do not like their voices, they have voices
like cold tea with skin on. I go O O O.

5 The flowers are plastic. There is all dust
on the petals. I go Ugh. Real flowers die,
but at least they are a comfort to us all.
I know them by name, listen. Rose. Tulip. Lily.

I live inside someone else's head. He hears me
10 with his stethoscope, so it is no use
sneaking home at five o'clock to his nice house
because I am in his ear going Breathe Breathe.

I might take my eye out and swallow it
to bring some attention to myself. Winston did.
15 His name was in the paper. For the time being
I make noises to annoy them and then I go BASTARDS.

1987

Psychopath

I run my metal comb through the D.A. and pose
my reflection between dummies in the window at Burton's.
Lamp light. Jimmy Dean. All over town, ducking and diving,
my shoes scud sparks against the night. She is in the canal.
5 Let me make myself crystal. With a good-looking girl crackling
in four petticoats, you feel like a king. She rode past me
on a wooden horse, laughing, and the air sang *Johnny,*
Remember Me. I turned the world faster, flash.

I don't talk much. I swing up beside them and do it
10 with my eyes. Brando. She was clean. I could smell her.
I thought, Here we go, old son. The fairground spun round us
and she blushed like candyfloss. You can woo them
with goldfish and coconuts, whispers in the Tunnel of Love.
When I zip up the leather, I'm in a new skin, I touch it
15 and love myself, sighing Some little lady's going to get lucky
tonight. My breath wipes me from the looking-glass.

We move from place to place. We leave on the last morning
with the scent of local girls on our fingers. They wear
our lovebites on their necks. I know what women want,
20 a handrail to Venus. She said *Please* and *Thank you*
to the toffee-apple, teddy-bear. I thought I was on, no error.
She squealed on the dodgems, clinging to my leather sleeve.
I took a swig of whisky from the flask and frenched it
down her throat. *No,* she said, *Don't,* like they always do.

25 Dirty Alice flicked my dick out when I was twelve.
She jeered. I nicked a quid and took her to the spinney.
I remember the wasps, the sun blazing as I pulled
her knickers down. I touched her and I went hard,
but she grabbed my hand and used that, moaning . . .
30 She told me her name on the towpath, holding the fish
in a small sack of water. We walked away from the lights.
She'd come too far with me now. She looked back, once.

A town like this would kill me. A gypsy read my palm.
She saw fame. I could be anything with my looks,
35 my luck, my brains. I bought a guitar and blew a smoke ring
at the moon. Elvis nothing. *I'm not that type,* she said.
Too late. I eased her down by the dull canal
and talked sexy. Useless. She stared at the goldfish, silent.
I grabbed the plastic bag. She cried as it gasped and wriggled
40 on the grass and here we are. A dog craps by a lamp post.

1: *D.A.*: short for "duck's arse," a 1950s haircut style "in which the hair at the back of the head is shaped
  like a duck's tail" (*OED*).
2: *Burton's*: a high street man's outfitters, providing low-budget sharp tailoring
5: *crystal*: i.e., crystal clear
7–8: *Johnny, Remember Me*: a 1961 hit single by John Leyton
26: *spinney*: a clump of small trees; copse

Mama, straight up, I hope you rot in hell. The old man
sloped off, sharpish. I saw her through the kitchen window.
The sky slammed down on my school cap, chicken licken.
Lady, Sweetheart, Princess I say now, but I never stay.
45   My sandwiches were near her thigh, then the Rent Man
lit her cigarette and I ran, ran . . . She is in the canal.
These streets are quiet, as if the town has held its breath
to watch the Wheel go round above the dreary homes.

No, don't. Imagine. One thump did it, then I was on her,
50   giving her everything I had. Jack the Lad, Ladies' Man.
Easier to say Yes. Easier to stay a child, wide-eyed
at the top of the helter-skelter. You get one chance in this life
and if you screw it you're done for, uncle, no mistake.
She lost a tooth. I picked her up, dead slim, and slid her in.
55   A girl like that should have a paid-up solitaire and high hopes,
but she asked for it. A right-well knackered outragement.

My reflection sucks a sour Woodbine and buys me a drink. Here's
looking at you. Deep down I'm talented. She found out. Don't mess
with me, angel, I'm no nutter. Over in the corner a dead ringer
60   for Ruth Ellis smears a farewell kiss on the lip of a gin-and-lime.
The barman calls Time. Bang in the centre of my skull,
there's a strange coolness. I could almost fly. Tomorrow
will find me elsewhere, with a loss of memory. Drink up son,
the world's your fucking oyster. Awopbopaloobop alopbimbam.

                                          1987

Translating the English, 1989

'. . . *and much of the poetry, alas, is lost in translation* . . .'

Welcome to my country! We have here Edwina Currie
and The Sun newspaper. Much excitement.
Also the weather has been most improving
even in February. Daffodils. (Wordsworth. Up North.) If you like
5   Shakespeare or even Opera we have too the Black Market.
For two hundred quids we are talking Les Miserables,
nods being as good as winks. Don't eat the eggs.
Wheel-clamp. Dogs. Vagrants. A tour of our wonderful

45: *Rent Man:* the man who came to collect the rent in the daytime, and thus, like the milkman, the
    stereotypical casual lover.
50: *Jack the Lad:* a cocky young man
52: *helter-skelter:* a funfair slide
55: *solitaire:* a single-diamond engagement ring
57: *Woodbine:* a brand of cigarette
60: *Ruth Ellis* in 1955 became the last woman to be hanged in Britain, for the murder of a faithless lover.
64: *Awopbopaloobop* . . . : a (slightly altered) quote from the Little Richard song "Tutti Frutti"

1: *Edwina Currie:* Minister of Food in Thatcher's government; a salmonella outbreak occurred during her
    term of office, hence "Don't eat the eggs" (line 7).
2: *The Sun:* a London newspaper owned by Rupert Murdoch, notable for its sensationalist journalism,
    right-wing political slant, and its nude "page three girls."
5: *Black Market:* i.e., for ticket scalpers

capital city is not to be missed. The Fergie,
10 The Princess Di and the football hooligan, truly you will
like it here, Squire. Also we can be talking crack, smack
and Carling Black Label if we are so inclined. Don't
drink the H_2O. All very proud we now have
a green Prime Minister. What colour yours? Binbags.
15 You will be knowing of Charles Dickens and Terry Wogan
and Scotland. All this can be arranged for cash no questions.
Ireland not on. Fish and chips and the Official Secrets Act
second to none. Here we go. We are liking
a smashing good time like estate agents and Neighbours,
20 also Brookside for we are allowed four Channels.
How many you have? Last night of Proms. Andrew
Lloyd-Webber. Jeffrey Archer. Plenty culture you will be agreeing.
Also history and buildings. The Houses of Lords. Docklands.
Many thrills and high interest rates for own good. Muggers.
25 Much lead in petrol. Filth. Rule Britannia and child abuse.
Electronic tagging, Boss, ten pints and plenty rape. Queen Mum.
Channel Tunnel. You get here fast no problem to my country
my country my country welcome welcome welcome.

1990

Poet for Our Times

I write the headlines for a Daily Paper.
It's just a knack one's born with all-right-Squire.
You do not have to be an educator,
just bang the words down like they're screaming *Fire!*
5 CECIL-KEAYS ROW SHOCK TELLS EYETIE WAITER.
ENGLAND FAN CALLS WHINGEING FROG A LIAR.

Cheers. Thing is, you've got to grab attention
with just one phrase as punters rush on by.
I've made mistakes too numerous to mention,
10 so now we print the buggers inches high.

12: *Carling Black Label:* a (downmarket) brand of lager
14: *a green Prime Minister:* Thatcher was of course nothing of the sort.
    Binbags: garbage bags
15: *Terry Wogan:* a popular Irish radio and TV talk-show host and middle of the road disc jockey
17: The British government invoked the *Official Secrets Act* (permitting the censorship of sensitive information) with great frequency, often in very trivial cases.
18: *Here we go:* a football (soccer) chant
19: *Neighbours:* a popular, long-running Australian teenage TV soap
20: *Brookside:* a soap opera on Channel Four
21: *Proms:* The BBC Henry Wood Promenade Concerts, based (though not exclusively held) in The Royal Albert Hall. The Last Night is televised, and ends with a round of nationalist songs such as "Land of Hope and Glory."
22: *Jeffrey Archer:* Lord Archer, popular novelist and politician
23: *Docklands:* refers to the massive speculative investment in London's Docklands, a flagship "enterprise zone" of Thatcher's government.
27: The excavation of the *Channel Tunnel,* an undersea rail connection linking Britain and France, began in 1987 and was completed in 1991.

5: The headline refers to the scandal resulting from an affair between Conservative minister Cecil Parkinson and his secretary Sarah Keays.

TOP MP PANTIE ROMP INCREASES TENSION.
RENT BOY: ROCK STAR PAID ME WELL TO LIE.

                I like to think that I'm a sort of poet
                for our times. My shout. Know what I mean?
15   I've got a special talent and I show it
                in punchy haikus featuring the Queen.
                DIPLOMAT IN BED WITH SERBO-CROAT.
                EASTENDERS' BONKING SHOCK IS WELL-OBSCENE.

                Of course, these days, there's not the sense of panic
20   you got a few years back. What with the box
                et cet. I wish I'd been around when the Titanic
                sank. To headline that, mate, would've been the tops.
                SEE PAGE 3 TODAY GENTS THEY'RE GIGANTIC.
                KINNOCK-BASHER MAGGIE PULLS OUT STOPS.

25   And, yes, I have a dream—make that a scotch, ta—
                that kids will know my headlines off by heart.
                IMMIGRANTS FLOOD IN CLAIMS HEATHROW WATCHER.
                GREEN PARTY WOMAN IS A NIGHTCLUB TART.
                The poem of the decade . . . *Stuff'em! Gotcha!*
30   The instant tits and bottom line of art.

                                                  1990

14: *My shout:* i.e., "Is my shout familiar?": my round (of drinks)
23: See note to line 2 of the preceding poem.
24: Neil *Kinnock* was leader of the Labour Party from 1983 to 1992; Margaret Thatcher was the Conservative Prime Minister from 1979 to 1990.
27: *Green Party:* British political party based upon ecological and community issues
29: *Stuff'em! Gotcha!:* famous headlines from *The Sun* newspaper during the 1982 Falklands War—the second celebrated the sinking of the Argentinian cruiser *General Belgrano*

CRIS CHEEK (b. 1955)

CHEEK WAS BORN IN ENFIELD, NORTHEAST LONDON, AND EDUCATED IN HIGHGATE, though after seeing Jimi Hendrix at the Albert Hall in 1967 he largely gave up on that official education to pursue what it neglected, reading widely in works by Shelley, Nerval, Baudelaire, Whitman, and others. Following an Arvon poetry course given by Eric Mottram and Jeff Nuttall in 1975, he was invited to workshops at the Poetry Society and there met Bob Cobbing, Allen Fisher, and Lawrence Upton. Alongside Cobbing, he was printshop manager at the Poetry Society and ran an open workshop that at its peak produced forty books a month; the do-it-yourself aesthetic among the London avant-garde and contemporary punk culture helped shape cheek's attitude to publishing and book production. He founded Bluff Books in 1976 and the journal *Rawz* soon after, publishing Fluxus artists, language poets, and concrete poets. Work with his, Upton's, and Clive Fencott's multi-vocal performance group *jgjgjgjg . . . (as long as you can say it that's our name)* led to an interest in performance that has found him working across and between artforms. In the United States in the late seventies, he came into contact with Marshall Reese, Kirby Malone, and other members of CoAccident; back in London in the early 1980s, he collaborated with Carlyle Reedy and then with new dance artists such as Kirstie Simpson and Michael C¹arke. Ongoing investigations of the borders between writing, voice, song, and music are evident in the variety of cheek's activities in years since; he has been the dancer-in-residence for the London borough of Tower Hamlets, co-director of the Voice Over Festival, reviewer for *The Times,* and with Sianed Jones and Philip Jeck part of the music group Slant; he has performed throughout Britain and in San Francisco and Amsterdam, worked in video, webcasting, installation art on the web, and arts development and curating. His radio program "The Music of Madagascar," made following a second trip to Africa, won a Sony Gold Award in 1995. He is bassist and clarinetist in the music group Garam Masala and editor and publisher of Sound & Language books and CDs. Together with appearances in most of the anthologies promoting a British avant-garde, his poetry has been published in books including *a present* (1980), *mud* (1984), *'stranger'* (1996), *f o g s* (2001), and *the canning town chronicle* (2001). The CD *skin upon skin,* containing versions of *'stranger'* and other texts performed to music, appeared in 1996; *Songs from Navigation,* a CD and book produced with Sianed Jones, appeared in 1998. He lives in Lowestoft and lectures in Performance Writing at Dartington College of Art.

The title of cheek's first collection of poems, *a present,* indicates his interest in writerly values inflected by performance; the book constructs a *possible* present, engaging everyday life with production values that emphasize meaning as emergent and provisional. As cheek's preface indicates, many of the poems began "in cars at traffic lights, improvised onto tape" and were later transcribed; the poems test the boundaries of the semantic and the extra-semantic, of what counts as affectively and cognitively significant, and what is before or beyond the word in gesture or noise. *'stranger,'* here in its third version, was written following cheek's stay in Madagascar and exhibits some of the conventions developed in his other poems, such as an eccentric capitalization that Ken Edwards has described as "recalling past spells of English literature."[1] Madagascar and the history of the empire are in the background as the poem explores the "poisons" as well as the attractions of false collectivities and sentimental identifications; the poem's narrator is both "creep" and agent of discovery, pursuing an existence beyond a "controlled form of loathing" and all that alienates him from the familiar, while remaining aware that the pursuit of discovery meets in the foreign a resistance that makes him "stranger."

---

[1] "Drizzle (on Trafalgar Road Old Kent Road): A Response to cris cheek's 'attributes ATTRIBUTES,'" *Pages: resources for the linguistically innovative poetries,* 1995, p. 333.

'stranger'

FOR TOM RAWORTH

I look up at the sky and I say I say to mysssssself, Every Day "What am I,
Doing with thisssssss creep?" and the answerrushes "Like," If water's
Running I'll Never hear it, "money, Creep!"
admit one shriek Comes   Close

5
Between pirating Skins of Distance
Vast, Imaginable Breath
Has perishable Homing with Fat
Time a syrup of irritant
Swing full stop

10
To a continuum arriving. 'Cut'
From a feeding frenzy. Horizon staggers up in beauty.

Silhouetting figures, Form the remnants of a Patchwork, sail
To animate a mutant Life or surf a fraying seam.
That six-toed shade which torches paraffin with sentiment to Strike
15
Note-hard, for tiny Far off ditch of land

Clutching, with pony fingers to a sweating plane.
For fears of truth exhausted clouds The Bones of Wishful
Social paths. Washed out to sea. A rendering,
Of roots up in the air with spray
20
To paint mistaken Identity.

Come fee dot dash hot. Is house a discarded Fruit?
A tendered verge? Where Welcome is
Unwelcome hit as tenant hearing tenant cry.

Dedication: *Tom Raworth:* see p. 613
1: cheek alludes to the phrase "I say, I say, I say," used as part of a vaudeville comedian's patter in leading up to a joke.
16: *pony:* slang for a £50 note

And meaning tilts from comprehension to aggression
25   As If, to emphasise or frame
            Variegated diversions of interpretation.

Forgetting—fleece—as in unguarded Crack activity
            The lot of it. A body politic
       Of bubbles, waking fast out of flattening dreams.

30   To Fish for cans bartering fantasies.
            Bland votes with printed faces
        Ashen, through oncoming headlights.
Reflecting nightgown's, blooming in her driver's eyes.
        A game of dash, concerning death. An edge
35   Littered profusely, with bleached shells
        And small bones, moulded into 'fetishes'?

            Inarticulate and ill at ease Fires
In the valley Twisted "up against the wall" cliches.
       Gun, holding an urge to piss home all
40   Advantage, Prized as turns of phrase.

            An overwhelming profusion, splintering
                 Sticks between tending
                 Rude metaphor for teeth
                 Through an open Rusting

45   Sum. Communications, far
                 From frequently so thin
                 Or frequency, so genuine.

        Frets, accompanying swallows of speech
            Girders, platt quaking dialect
50   Bridge; phantom outings of pitched location.

   Fireflies in this human, brain Preceeded by a quiet insistence
   Closeted by a contrivance Whose story remains a Story:
                 In others' words.

   A figure of security encrypting shadows with the volumes turned down low.
55   At one in the morning—a man and a woman almost motionless in bed,
        Flat on their backs and side by side, Listening—demurely
   To crackling Christian hymns wrung from a poorly tuned old radio.

            "Hey, stranger—I dreamed that you were"

Here, where it is always almost a perpetual daybreak, of misunderstandings that lie in
60   Between objects half seen, half truths Crawling, fumbling brass corruption.
            Partly lit doubts of humane incomprehension.
                 A prehensile compassion.

49: *platt:* "low" (German): the context might suggest "Plattdeutsch" (Low German)

Part dark for same That reason being word a piece of paper, off the Hook
Of hope, a Mass of tributary
65   Voices, drifting up out of these evening trees as smoke into a darkening
Sky, expands and travels.

'aturation . . . exile . . . from conventional obligatio'
Advising a nothing auto, choking waters "Rush!"—blue
Canvas with moorings, wind. Woke
70   Locked into a churning sweat. Crying
Hard, because I hadn't come
Home.

*

To paste among streaked over Clatter
Dreaming close friends were cobbles. Made a monster Together;
75   With a plastic bag, a ball of string partly unravelled
Fishing nets, willow charcoal and powdered tar,
Rooting sacks, dried human Faeces and dirty straw.

Drove along glittering—lines With overlapping—
leaves—Only footprints. And hid there.
80   Called 'there' home. On a bed of soft
Barks stripped from uprooted trees.
Pulped our excess and drank

Soup bled red with silt
Blown from dessicated lips.

85   A mistaken identity
leaving the discarded husk
of this burnt out planet
for trash.

Grooves gradually, drawing a hind
90   With a blunt pin. flooding, unsighted
Resonance defining buildings.
Gathering single claps into hooves from Thunder: spirits
Entire each other.

Mugged out of semblance. Muttering—waking with rain
95   Playing drums on upturned empty
Tins and pans

How people who live in the green slime
speak with those poorple who mine the brown sludge.

In the road outside the Hotel Baobab
100   Flashing tight white skirts under palms Pronounced sexual assetts
Assessed by headlights, winking bumpurrrr t-to bBumper
Ssssssspooled up to junctions for breakfast with pain "Baby"
's trying hard to shoot but film keeps jumping in Her frame.

And on an old hum
105   Teeming with cows
A blood puddle yoked to a sty

The Earth—burying
A small boy beating a squealing
Pig with a red hot stick

110   "and" . . at one at surround time, bird lures
Flit across corn, of ripening
Chrome
Smudging movements, to irrigate fracture.

Where the scent of a barrel of Orchids
115   Mixes with that of the shit from the ox
A poetry slick. To weave into opening mouth
Sticky rivers of future slang glo.m along roads of splice o

*

Dust layered onto dust hoods plumeing waters thickly onto grounds of shower.
Banana leaves breathe dripping evening spare.

120   A song, walking an island of schemes with a tornado of cares.
Tunes becoming mock slaughter to cheap Slough
Party more house out of mind than of body to castle, sleep
Welled into glands
Fading pathways of poppy flowers perfumed with rent.

125   Where gardens and streetwalks and gateways and
Commons respectfully sample.

A conversational
metered in prices
and weights transported
130   to an elegant, bread out of work,
whose fingers trading licks for cash
are caught—

listening to the waves of hunger.

And tongue an other language to get
135   throat and breath and lungs and heart
around one another, Switch
Language to hold, another
language to touch, smell Foil
A wake concerted kick
140   possess for shudder.

In need of nouriture an imam chants a bore-hole into resistance.
Creates a butterfry of consciousness.

Wide spread opium sesame wing Heads into reach of fan, ends
Mashed with a sickening crud, wheat appears to be a flag
145   Worn, as a false badge of knowledge

141: *nouriture*: both "nourishment" and "nurture, upbringing"
   imam: the prayer leader of a mosque

To sanction the dispersal of sense, in blobs
bobbing from blood to bloom, the operation
commemorative, Desert T-shirt wet Storm
bearing the plundering sanction
150   'We are the Thunder—WE ARE the
Lightning'.

*

Woke, to a
Low-toned Rub.
Hill that straighten itself trough, thought
155   finally clot. Being hauled.

An ornamental ox
through phosphorescence en
tranced

cloning a vacuous
160   'One' on behalf of any
expediency conversing confidently
within false categories
breathing rum, chiming the bull
by its horns resolved to tonic
165   as visitor and visited The Uninvited.

A shaved world, trapped
in a graveyard island of ancestors
giving far more than mere matters of fact.
Boiling with variant means between
170   competitive ideals of Paradise.

Worse than nothing.

Clop trick go densely patterned fan.
Of dice rolled into gin.
A subtle, culturally specific,
175   demarcation of public and private
a tendered verge meandered on.

"Stranger, that's far enough."
Nudging from spatial comforts
into a whipped back stooping to plant cure—vanishes.

*

180   Like, looking at the memory of a copy
blowing threaded paper clouds above a page. Washing drops onto stones.
Flash whisper of skin against slap
become potent more urgent, e-mergent bare
moanlight whose groaning forms luminous dunes.

148: Operation *Desert Storm* was the official name of the U.S. military action in the 1991 Gulf War.
150ff: The quoted phrase, notes cheek, "was a U.S. Gulf War T-shirt slogan for real."
164: *resolved to tonic:* (of a dissonant musical note) moved stepwise to the home note of the key of a piece of music

185 Revving an engine to steal attention.
Flirting cool furniture with blithe lids Closed.
A tidy splash on a mirror. A fear
Of belonging, an avoidance, of Cleaving to Incompletion

or an echo
190 of an echo of
a speech into stains.

Tone deaf stick lashings who
spoke, along school railings
Paramount noise.

*

195 She is paid off in a soup of sticky welcomes
through a lens of clap. As training
the nourishment of ineptitude
whittled from the fruits of millions of years
dive bombs into the Open sea
200 Pointing a camera at the perforating

skies
of difficult
lives.

*

A dubious return to flow
205 once might have been plundered
a stolen bedrock, creaking
with ecognomic, splashes drunk
through spoken door.

A hole emerging from a hole
210 turns money to distance
fuck-fuck for a bloodied gill on turtle stump.
Constructed literally as foul
Airs, gazing out of you
China
215 Kerala
Virginia
Venezuela
Rwanda
Georgia
220 Moravia
Banalia
Serbia
Macedonia
Cumbria
225 Ethiopia

215: *Kerala*: the most densely populated and religiously diverse state of India
224: *Cumbria*: a county in the north of England

                    Australia
                                    Guatemala
                    Libertalia
                    Sardinia
230   Banalia
                                    Nigeria
                    Korea
                             Somalia
                    Burma

235   Madagascar

                    Madagasssss   ss scar

        Hollowed and cast onto waters
          a walking stone, framed
            loops of refugee light
240   beached by inappropriate technology

                    As a drip
                 giving structure
                    to time

          varnished a meal coming out
245   through means of auction to obscurity.
          Points of rest, off balance points
            of movement, of disturbance
              or a shop by any name.

                        *

        Blatant backwaters of narrative sing, come
250   Come Undone in the shower and shake dry land.

              Sprinkle onto tight skins
                a release into puree
                  threw fantasy—

        To strike a society as fashion after liberty.
255   Pursued by frantic news wars shaped
                from travellers' mires
            and eagerly struggled to unravel
              the tangling delicacies, of influence.

        Pots in the kiln hang in that honeyed moment.
260   Reproducing airs to function taming
                dry falls into kiss well—
            cooked a sugar hook to catch on keep.

        Books leaving ribs textualized for a monument.
          Tins imprinted 'For Worldwide Passport'

228: *Libertalia:* a "legendary utopia," an "idealistic pirate colony founded by Captain Mission and Thomas
Trew in northern Madagascar near to Diego Suarez one hundred years before the French Revolution,
although coining similar baseline principles" (cheek).

265   "Stop that Clocking!"
                                Iron rooves flame humid air.

                         Transient openings onto truth and beauty.

                                Fat moments
                            That tremor weight from a muscle.
270   Where the garden and gardener are more alike
                                   to each other.

           Saline presents from belicose wrecks foundered on tortured coral
                       Wired up to both the positive and negative
                       Terminals. "Well, so everything is possible.
275   Now who's brought the cash?"

        Programming solely to engender. Where 'Killer Machine' is graffitied
        Onto buckled root of tree Spitting comes to grips with practice
           As a church releases its prurient mob with a sickening Gas.

                    OreThorough the sot wood seeps "I dug it ma. I dug it
280   Out ma. Ma". When a stranger is no longer a Stranger
                          taking hems out on a date to anger
                    Celibate Rifles, who bring collections from The Poor
               Assumptions lumped in dead heads under mouldy coats
                       forgotten with a swerve. Without a tray

285   the toy stood on the turning Wreck
                                 of climax and closure.

                            To distract from a diversionary tictac
                              or there isn't time for letters
                                 and you can't afford
290   to phone—country roads

                                 —going Home.

                         To belong is it, a social bereavement?
                         Can slap one heal the lions of sly?

                             Now—is poetry then
295   a process of arresting?
                                or of moving?

                        Aligning beyond the palms the blood
                            in a wasteland of solidarity
                            Plucked out of politeness
300   a controlled form of loathing.

285: Cf. "Casabianca," a popular poem by Felicia Hemans (1793–1835): "The boy stood on the burning deck / Whence all but he had fled; / The flame that lit the battle's wreck / Shone round him o'er the dead."

A cadence out of business is revisited

at Will, inverted where the heart is

there the sentimental hurt is—

there, the relative clutches.
305   Sponsoring these varnishing
threads a cloven tooth, to be pulled
wide, to chase my head
into a font of poisons
out beyond range—articulating
310   "I Believe"
with mouths tide open.

Then steeling time
to re-true
telling

315   canes that bend the clouds
with poise raiding convenience
clinging to the proliferations
of material recondition

through labor transitions
320   embodied by step gore retro-glow
lame view, to be leashed on
bleeched figurehead. Danger

paging a candidate
cast (lost) in surplus flesh
325   kicked, blent from austerity
into a slur of neglect
re-registered.

"hafahafa"[1]

---

[1] Literally meaning "strange" as given in *Les Guides de Poche de Madagasikara* (Societé Madprint, Anta-narivo, 1973). I quote from its Foreword, entitled "Here's a Friend": "So here you are in Madagascar, country of hospitality and where great value is placed on every effort to bring people together."

1993–1994 / 1996

ROBERT SHEPPARD (b. 1955)

IN THE AFTERWORD TO *FLOATING CAPITAL* (1991), AN ANTHOLOGY OF POETRY FROM London that Sheppard co-edited with Adrian Clarke, the reader finds a description of "strategies in the texts we have selected": "the virtual disappearance of citation, testimony, and varieties of 'unacknowledged legislation' in favour of a warier engagement with . . . materials, a politics of the sign."[1] Such strategies link the poetry in the anthology with post-structuralist critique and understand the politics of poetry as involving not just an ostensible subject matter, statement, or theme but the normative conventions of poetic discourse. The poet is thus charged with the task of constructing new models for discourse, and in Sheppard's case this often means rejecting a more traditional lyric speaker functioning as self-sufficient agent of perception. While much of the innovative poetry of the century has participated in the desire to construct new models for signifying that refuse to allow the reader to settle into the illusion that the poem is a transparent reflection of reality, in recent times the concerns outlined by Sheppard and Clarke are most often associated with Language Poetry in North America and the writing parallel to it in Britain, sometimes called "linguistically innovative poetry." Sheppard has been at the forefront of this movement, together with writers such as Clarke, Ken Edwards, Maggie O'Sullivan, and Ulli Freer, and while he has acknowledged his interest in the poetry of American Language Poets such as Barrett Watten, Lyn Hejinian, and Ron Silliman he has also insisted that the British contexts of his poetry as well as his debt to older British poets such as Allen Fisher and Lee Harwood be recognized. The sentence in "Internal Exile 1" about "Holding language in suspicion" and the colon allowing "reader" and "worker" to be juxtaposed indicate some of the rationales for Sheppard's poetic practice. "Internal Exile 1," like much of Sheppard's poetry, also can be read as critical of the sexual violence implicit in specific modes of representation. More recently Sheppard has extended this critique in *Empty Diaries* (1999), which deals with the history of the twentieth century through a series of female narrators who are at the same time conscious of their creation by a male writer. Most of Sheppard's poetry to date is part of a larger, ongoing project titled *Twentieth Century Blues*; "Internal Exile 1" and "The Materialization of Soap 1947," for instance, are part of *The Flashlight Sonata* (*Twentieth Century Blues* 6).

---

[1] Adrian Clarke and Robert Sheppard, "Afterword," *Floating Capital*, Elmwood, CT, 1991, p. 121.

Sheppard was educated at the University of East Anglia, where he earned a Ph.D. for a dissertation on contemporary British poetry and the work of Roy Fisher and Lee Harwood. His books include *The Flashlight Sonata* (1993) and a collection of his essays and reviews, *Far Language* (1999). He has edited two journals important to British innovative poetry, *Rock Drill* and *Pages*. He teaches at Edge Hill College and lives in Liverpool.

The Materialization of Soap 1947

Suspicion in the capital: the ecstasy
Of austerity rationing the uniforms.
It must be like air, natural and free,
But there's a shortage of nature in this
5   Land of torrents and the surrounding seas.
What is happening? He used to *prefer* words!
Feed me a well-trimmed cut of news.
We couldn't find any wheels, but we're happy,
A well-dressed pair: even on the wireless
10   You've got to keep up appearances,
Now we yearn for the parks and the azure skies
Of the tottering economies. . . . Pearl
Opened her palm over the sink to reveal
A fresh bar of soap. She smelt it; her favourite
15   Scent. She turned the hissing tap, and
The slippery unthought-of object lathered
Her chapped Cinderella hands. All she needed
Was her hero silk-parachuting into
Her perversely dissatisfied embrace. I
20   Prefer to talk to the dead, well-fed
On scraps that cannot be sold.
They died from Manchuria to Manchester.
I did not want to report this but I did.
The news is that another man has been held.
25   That much is reliable. Beyond that,
The monochrome world flickers
At the emotive edge of our fake memories:
Two frying morsels on the gas stove.

1993

Rationing and shortages continued in Britain for some time past the end of World War II.
18: *silk-parachuting:* "Surplus silk parachutes from the war were sometimes made into women's (under)
   clothes." (Sheppard, in correspondence)

Internal Exile 1

Out from germ-warm subterranean wind into
Business having just been, or about to be.
Hyphens, dashes, asterisks, strokes:
The silver number has been screwed. Red
5   Flag; blue light. One moment the man stands
With his arms tied behind his back; the next he falls
Head first from our chronicle. Pictures have pictures.
You are the real hero. The image—
That was like walking into somebody else's poem.
10   A public zipper porched shadow action. Heroes
Standing under cardboard captions. Masculinity sells
History: four guards on this side, four
On the other, changing according to
House demands. All the victims' outfits were
15   Manufactured by the Enemy. It was a fantastic
Feeling, going up stage and turning around for all
The judges. Her writing is content. Watches sold
Doubt as her underhand life expressed the
Heresies. Her clothes burn, turning stories,
20   Can add fur sovereign meaning
To line-sewn memory dust. Don't open the door; shut
Your eyes. To slam these columns you took this out.
The shimmering architectural fantasy
Of a slum, purpose built. Entry to that soft-furnished
25   Dream, riots hanging like petrol vapour
Over the black plastic rubbish bags,
Electric train-flashes crossing the page, from one of the
Languages which blows across Europe like ill-wind.
Bombs implode as a warning underscoring
30   The essential sentence. He says my
Mind is always somewhere else when I
Kiss her. This sentence is a variation. She's
Out on the porch, testing the day, transforming
Not only her, but the text, from which she
35   Could never be exiled. As soon as I write "the world",
It doesn't invert. Poverty less plentiful
But obscured by wealth and well-being.
The systems began to fail, in domestic adjustment.
The Chinese trains were nicer than the Russian ones.
40   This sentence is a variation of the next. The flow
Freed from compulsion. Trying to gauge it
All; the woman is not at her mirror. (Skip
A few pages; I will too.) Black girl in a tight leather
Skirt jumps into a waiting passenger-seat:
45   Pink folds of flesh for his mental
Speculum. I froze and sweated, wanted to burn
The insignia—but who would deck

Title: *Internal Exile* was the term used in the former USSR for exiling a citizen to Siberia.
46: *Speculum:* (1) a surgeon's instrument for dilating bodily orifices for inspection or operation; (2) a mir-
  ror

Themselves in the cloth pages
Of a tattered history? Pretend that some of
50 The sentences have been removed
Though your meaning heaps. Women desire a war;
Virus men built appearance. Wouldn't you prefer it
As a straight-out? The bike boys zooming in on each
Other's rolling captions? What was once
55 Familiar is now merely strange. Moving clouds behind
The birds rewind their film of homecoming. Swoop
Loop wires in light. A magpie flicker in dirty
Scruff eye. This has to be learned,
Holding language in suspicion. Posturing
60 About disaster, style demeans. A cold sore
On a child's mouth predicates a market
Full of bargains. What could she begin to say? How
Will she survive the questioning? Perhaps
It is only the uncurtained window-pane that
65 Throws the room back at us? Reader:
Worker. Walkman overspill rhythmed by the engine-
Driver's wiper-lashes. Another realism. She
Remarked the dome of her clichéd perception—
An image for later snuffmovie simulations: murder
70 Leads door to door. The crystal eye set in the wall.
They did not even notice that the effigies were of them.
Replace the object. She makes the unknown turn—
Feels at one moment a gobbet of raw meat in a
Porno film. She goes to the window to cry.

                                                                                1988, 1993

54: *rolling captions:* film credits
59: cf. Jean-Francois Lyotard, "Note on the Critical Function of the Work of Art," in *Driftworks* (New York,
   1984): "A poet is a man in a position to hold language . . . under suspicion."

DAVID DABYDEEN (b. 1955)

DABYDEEN WAS BORN IN GUYANA, THE DESCENDANT OF INDIANS WHO CAME TO THE Caribbean in the nineteenth century to work on British sugar plantations. As he has written, "In the 1960s the Americans invaded our country with money and guns," and his family chose to emigrate to England.[1] He read English at Cambridge and London University, completing his doctorate in 1982. He is director of the Centre for Research into Asian Migrations at the University of Warwick and author of critical studies including *Hogarth's Blacks: Images of Blacks in Eighteenth-Century English Art* (1985; 1987), *Hogarth, Walpole and Commercial Britain* (1988), and, with Paul Edwards, *Black Writers in Britain* (1991). He has also edited several books including *The Black Presence in English Literature* (1983) and published two novels.

In "On Not Being Milton: Nigger Talk in England Today" (1990), Dabydeen writes of the experience of black writers in England as follows: "Either you drop the epithet 'black' and think of yourself as a 'writer' (a few of us foolishly embrace this position, desirous of the status of 'writing' and knowing that 'black' is blighted)—that is, you cease dwelling on the nigger/tribal/nationalistic theme, you cease *folking* up the literature, and you become 'universal'—or else you perish in the backwater of small presses."[2] His first book of poetry, *Slave Song* (1984), contains poems written in a creolized English about the sadomasochistic dimensions of colonial experience and the cane-cutting culture of Guyana. The title poem of his second volume, *Coolie Odyssey* (1988), mixes fragments of "nation-language" with so-called standard English. The long poem "Turner," published in 1994 in the volume of that title, largely avoids creole, opting instead to explore in standard English the desire to invent new languages, histories, and "signs" as one of the legacies of the African diaspora. It was written as a response to J. M. W. Turner's painting "Slavers Throwing Overboard the Dead and Dying" (1840). In his preface, Dabydeen explains that

> My poem focuses on the submerged head of the African in the foreground of Turner's painting. It has been drowned in Turner's (and other artists') sea for centuries. When it awakens it can only partially recall the sources of its life, so it invents a body, a biography, and peoples an imagined landscape. Most of the names of birds, animals and fruit are made up. Ultimately, however, the African rejects the fabrication of an idyllic past. His real desire is to begin anew in the sea but he is too trapped by grievous memory to escape history. Although the sea has transformed him—bleached him of colour and compli-

---

[1] *Poetry Review*, vol. 84, no. 1, 1994, p. 25.
[2] *The State of the Language*, ed. Christopher Ricks and Leonard Michaels, Berkeley, 1990, p. 12.

cated his sense of gender—he still recognises himself as 'nigger.' The desire for transfiguration or newness or creative amnesia is frustrated. The agent of self-recognition is a stillborn child tossed overboard from a future ship. The child floats towards him. He wants to give it life, to mother it, but the child—his unconscious and his origin—cannot bear the future and its inventions, drowned as it is in memory of ancient cruelty. Neither can escape Turner's representation of them as exotic and sublime victims. Neither can describe themselves anew but are indelibly stained by Turner's language and imagery.[3]

Thus the poem, in which both the captain of the slave ship and the stillborn child are named "Turner," concerns the violent ruptures—the uprooting from origins and erasure of historical memory—that are among the legacies of slavery and the African diaspora. It raises the possibility that an existence "barren of ancestral memory" would be one "endowed richly with such emptiness / From which to dream, surmise, invent, immortalise" but ultimately confronts a reality in which "each must learn to live / Beadless in a foreign land; or perish." The word that would be "redemptive" cannot elude the woundedness that constitutes "the ground of memory."

---

[3] *Turner,* London, 1994, p. ix.

Coolie Odyssey

FOR MA, D. 1985

Now that peasantry is in vogue,
Poetry bubbles from peat bogs,
People strain for the old folk's fatal gobs
Coughed up in grates North or North East
5 'Tween bouts o' living dialect,
It should be time to hymn your own wreck,
Your house the source of ancient song:
Dry coconut shells cackling in the fireside
Smoking up our children's eyes and lungs,
10 Plantains spitting oil from a clay pot,
Thick sugary black tea gulped down.

The calves hustle to suck,
Bawling on their rope but are beaten back
Until the cow is milked.
15 Frantic children call to be fed.
Roopram the Idiot goes to graze his father's goats backdam
Dreaming that the twig he chews so viciously in his mouth
Is not a twig.

In a winter of England's scorn
20 We huddle together memories, hoard them from
The opulence of our masters.

You were always back home, forever
As canefield and whiplash, unchanging

16: The Dutch drained Guyana's swamplands in the eighteenth century with a series of canals, creating *backdams* to prevent further flooding from the outlying rivers and their tributaries.

As the tombstones in the old Dutch plot
25   Which the boys used for wickets playing ball.

Over here Harilall who regularly dodged his duties at the marketstall
To spin bowl for us in the style of Ramadhin
And afterwards took his beatings from you heroically
In the style of England losing
30   Is now known as the local Paki
Doing slow trade in his Balham cornershop.
Is it because his heart is not in business
But in the tumble of wickets long ago
To the roar of wayward boys?
35   Or is it because he spends too much time
Being chirpy with his customers, greeting
The tight-wrapped pensioners stalking the snow
With tropical smile, jolly small chat, credit?
They like Harilall, these muted claws of Empire,
40   They feel privileged by his grinning service,
They hear steelband in his voice
And the freeness of the sea.
The sun beams from his teeth.

Heaped up beside you Old Dabydeen
45   Who on Albion Estate clean dawn
Washed obsessively by the canal bank,
Spread flowers on the snake-infested water,
Fed the gods the food that Chandra cooked,
Bathed his tongue of the creole
50   Babbled by low-caste infected coolies.
His Hindi chants terrorised the watertoads
Flopping to the protection of bush.
He called upon Lord Krishna to preserve
The virginity of his daughters
55   From the Negroes,
Prayed that the white man would honour
The end-of-season bonus to Poonai
The canecutter, his strong, only son:
Chandra's womb being cursed by deities
60   Like the blasted land
Unconquerable jungle or weed
That dragged the might of years from a man.
Chandra like a deaf-mute moved about the house
To his command,
65   A fearful bride barely come-of-age
Year upon year swelling with female child.
Guilt clenched her mouth
Smothered the cry of bursting apart:
Wrapped hurriedly in a bundle of midwife's cloth
70   The burden was removed to her mother's safekeeping.

27: The West Indian cricket-player Sonny *Ramadhin* (b. 1929) was famed for his brilliant spin bowling.
30: *Paki:* offensive slang—short for "Pakistani"
31: *Balham:* a district of London; there is a large ethnic population in the area.
44: Dabydeen's mother is buried beside *Old Dabydeen,* her father.
53: *Krishna:* one of the major Hindu deities

He stamped and cursed and beat until he turned old
With the labour of chopping tree, minding cow, building fence
And the expense of his daughters' dowries.
Dreaming of India
75   He drank rum
Till he dropped dead
And was buried to the singing of Scottish Presbyterian hymns
And a hell-fire sermon from a pop-eyed bawling catechist,
By Poonai, lately baptised, like half the village.

80   Ever so old,
Dabydeen's wife,
Hobbling her way to fowl-pen,
Cussing low, chewing her cud, and lapsed in dream,
Sprinkling rice from her shrivelled hand.
85   Ever so old and bountiful,
Past where Dabydeen lazed in his mudgrave,
Idle as usual in the sun,
Who would dip his hand in a bowl of dhall and rice—
Nasty man, squelching and swallowing like a low-caste sow—
90   The bitch dead now!

The first boat chugged to the muddy port
Of King George's Town. Coolies come to rest
In El Dorado,
Their faces and best saris black with soot.
95   The men smelt of saltwater mixed with rum.
The odyssey was plank between river and land,
Mere yards but months of plotting
In the packed bowel of a white man's boat
The years of promise, years of expanse.

100   At first the gleam of the green land and the white folk and the Negroes,
The earth streaked with colour like a toucan's beak,
Kiskidees flame across a fortunate sky,
Canefields ripening in the sun
Wait to be gathered in armfuls of gold.

105   I have come back late and missed the funeral.
You will understand the connections were difficult.
Three airplanes boarded and many changes
Of machines and landscapes like reincarnations
To bring me to this library of graves,

79: In nineteenth-century Guyana, the Presbyterians had the job of converting the Indians (the Catholics, Methodists, etc., being preoccupied with the Africans); to this day the majority of Christian Guyanese Indians are Scottish Presbyterian.

88: *dhall:* a curry made from lentils, beans, or peas

91: Guyana was colonized by the Dutch beginning in the sixteenth century; their sugarcane plantations made use of black slaves from West Africa. Guyana changed hands several times during wars between the French and British between 1780 and 1815, with the British emerging victorious. The slave trade was abolished in 1807 and their full emancipation was gained in 1838; as a result planters began importing labor, most notably from India. Dabydeen is here imagining the first arrival of these laborers ("coolies") at the British port of Georgetown (so named after George III).

93: *El Dorado:* the legendary city of fabulous wealth

102: The *kiskidee* is a type of flycatcher with bright yellow plumage.

110 This small clearing of scrubland.
   There are no headstones, epitaphs, dates.
   The ancestors curl and dry to scrolls of parchment.
   They lie like texts
   Waiting to be written by the children
115 For whom they hacked and ploughed and saved
   To send to faraway schools.
   Is foolishness fill your head.
   Me dead.
   Dog-bone and dry-well
120 *Got no story to tell.*
   Just how me born stupid is so me gone.
   Still we persist before the grave
   Seeking fables.
   We plunder for the maps of El Dorado
125 To make bountiful our minds in an England
   Starved of gold.

   Albion village sleeps, hacked
   Out between bush and spiteful lip of river.
   Folk that know bone
130 Fatten themselves on dreams
   For the survival of days.
   Mosquitoes sing at a nipple of blood.
   A green-eyed moon watches
   The rheumatic agony of houses crutched up on stilts
135 Pecked about by huge beaks of wind,
   That bear the scars of ancient storms.
   Crappeau clear their throats in hideous serenade,
   Candleflies burst into suicidal flame.
   In a green night with promise of rain
140 You die.

   We mark your memory in songs
   Fleshed in the emptiness of folk,
   Poems that scrape bowl and bone
   In English basements far from home,
145 Or confess the lust of beasts
   In rare conceits
   To congregations of the educated
   Sipping wine, attentive between courses—
   See the applause fluttering from their white hands
150 Like so many messy table napkins.

               1988

137: *Crappean:* i.e., "crapauds" (French): toads

from Turner

I

Stillborn from all the signs. First a woman sobs
Above the creak of timbers and the cleaving
Of the sea, sobs from the depths of true
Hurt and grief, as you will never hear
5   But from woman giving birth, belly
Blown and flapping loose and torn like sails,
Rough sailors' hands jerking and tugging
At ropes of veins, to no avail. Blood vessels
Burst asunder, all below-deck are drowned.
10   Afterwards, stillness, but for the murmuring
Of women. The ship, anchored in compassion
And for profit's sake (what well-bred captain
Can resist the call of his helpless
Concubine, or the prospect of a natural
15   Increase in cargo?), sets sail again,
The part-born, sometimes with its mother,
Tossed overboard. Such was my bounty
Delivered so unexpectedly that at first
I could not believe this miracle of fate,
20   This longed-for gift of motherhood.
What was deemed mere food for sharks will become
My fable. I named it Turner
As I have given fresh names to birds and fish
And humankind, all things living but unknown,
25   Dimly recalled, or dead.

II

It plopped into the water and soon swelled
Like a brumplak seed that bursts buckshot
From its pod, falling into the pond
In the backdam of my mother's house, and fattening,
30   Where small boys like I was hold sticks to the water
For fish; branches stripped and shaped from the impala
Tree, no other, for we know—only the gods
Can tell how—that they bend so supple,
Almost a circle without snapping, yet strong
35   Enough to pull in a baby alligator.
Maybe by instinct, maybe the wisdom
Of our village elders passed down forever
(Until Turner came) which we suck in from birth
Like wood-smoke in my mother's kitchen,
40   Coconut shells stoking up a fire,
And I squat with my two sisters, small we are,
I don't know exactly how much in age—
Though since Turner's days I have learnt to count,
Weigh, measure, abstract, rationalise—

Dabydeen's note is quoted in the biographical headnote above.
4: *backdam*: see note to line 16 of "Coolie Odyssey," above.

45   But we are small enough nearly to pass
        Upright under the belly of the cow
        Whilst our father pulls the teats and wheezes
        Milk into a pakreet shell, swoosh, swoosh
        Swoosh, the sound still haunts, survives the roar
50   And crash and endless wash and lap
        Of waves, and we stoop under the belly
        Of the cow and I can see I am just
        Taller than its haunches, and when my sisters
        Kneel their heads reach its knees. We play
55   Games as our father milks, crawling under
        The belly like warriors, then springing up
        At the other side to hurl spears at enemies
        Hiding behind the chaltee tree in the cow-pen,
        From which we pick twigs each morning, chew the ends,
60   Brush our teeth clean. The cow moves its head
        To one side, watches us with covetous eyes
        As if it wants to play, but my father
        Will forbid it, for even when the milking is done,
        He will not let us jump on the cow's back,
65   Nor decorate its heels with the blue and yellow
        Bark of hemlik, nor put a chaktee straw
        Into its nostrils until it sneezes
        And snorts with laughter, but will lead it
        Straight to pasture, and send us off to school,
70   To Manu, the magician, who will teach
        Us how to squeeze, drain, blend, boil the juices
        Of herbs for medicines, or bandage the sprained
        Foot of a chicken. So the cow stands still,
        But looks at us with a harlot's eye and winks,
75   And we can see the mischief in its face
        Which our father can't because he's so far
        Behind, concentrating on his fingers as if
        Worshipping the gods, and it flicks its tail,
        Beating off flies, but really to join in,
80   To lash and surprise us as we wait in ambush
        Under its belly for the English
        To come from another village, who will plunder
        The crops, burn the huts, stampede the goats,
        Drag girls away by ropes.

XVIII

[487]   'Nigger,' it cries, naming me from some hoard
        Of superior knowledge, its tongue a viper's nest
        Guarding a lore buried by priests, philosophers,
490   Fugitives, which I will still ransack
        For pearls and coral beads to drape around
        Its body, covering the sores that the sea

45: *Manu:* in Indian myth, Manu is a figure similar to the Hebrew Noah, the sole human survivor of a great flood and thus the ancestor of modern humankind. Dabydeen in a 1994 interview with Kwame Dawes says that the name was chosen by accident from his memory, and that he was only made aware of its significance after the poem's publication.
487: *it:* the stillborn child

Bubbles on its skin, its strangulated neck
Issuing like an eel from its chest. 'Nigger,'
495   It cries, sensing its own deformity.
I look into its eyes to see my own coves,
My skin pitted and gathered like waves of sand.
I have become the sea's craft and will so shape
This creature's bone and cell and word beyond
500   Memory of obscene human form, but instead
It made me heed its distress at being
Human and alive, its anger at my
Coaxing it awake. For ever, it seemed,
Curled at my breast it drifted between death
505   And another mood, the waves slapping its face
Like my mother's hands summoning me back
To myself, at the edge of the pond. I stare
Into its face as into a daedal
Seed which Manu would hold up to the sky
510   For portents of flood, famine, or the crop
Of new births to supplement our tribe,
But even Manu could not prophesy
The shapes of death revolving in its eyes:
Bullwhips that play upon the backs of slaves
515   Hauling pillars of stone to a spot divined
By sorcerers whose throw of dice from whimsical
Hands appoints thousands to their deaths, arranges
Human bones like hieroglyphs to tell a prurient
Future age the ancient formulae of Empire.
520   A solitary vulture dips into one's fresh breast
As into an ink-well, wipes its beak upon
Another's parchment skin, writing its own
Version of events, whilst Pharaoh sleeps in cloths
Scented in the flow of female sacrifice.
525   Until a slave arose from the dead,
Cracking the seal of his mouth, waking
The buried with forbidden words. 'Revolt,'
He thundered, 'emancipation, blood', darkening
The sky with his lust, irrigating
530   Their stomachs, blooming courage in their skulls.
An army of sticks and sharpened flints flocked
Across the sands like ragged cacti, ripping
Down tents, encampments, cities, massacring
The men, scavenging the bellies of their wives
535   For scraps of joy. Wherever they settled
They made new deserts and new slaves. 'Revolt,'
He whispered, lifting aloft the Pharaoh's
Crown from a head chopped clean at the neck, hollowed
Into a drinking gourd. They cheered even as
540   They sipped at each other's throats in nostalgia
For death, except a child who slipped and limped
Away from the lap of men who loved him
Too much, broke him each night in frustration
Of their lives. Children appeared everywhere,

508: *daedal*: intricate

545   Strewn like dung at the root of palms
       As if to fertilise and succour them
       Against the desert, to memorialise
       In the spur of leaves the veins
       Once flowing with maternity. Everywhere,
550   Children trailing behind caravans heading
       North to the auction tents of Arabia,
       Sucking the air for any nipple of moisture.

XX

[578]   Shall I call to it even as the dead
         Survive catastrophe to speak in one
580   Redemptive and prophetic voice, even
         As a jackal breathing into bone
         Rouses familiar song? Shall I suckle
         It on tales of resurrected folk,
         Invent a sister, and another, as Manu would,
585   Pursing his lips so all the wrinkles
         On his face gathered like spokes around the hub
         Of his mouth and he would stare backwards
         Through his eye sockets into himself whilst
         We waited at his feet in dread of the word
590   That would spin suddenly from his throat,
         Cartwheel towards us, making us want
         To scatter, but we remained rooted
         At his feet in stunned obedience
         To his booming voice and his quivering
595   Fat manitou's body pouring forth sweat
         Enough to water all the animals
         Herded in the savannah? The first word
         Shot from his mouth, he stretched out his lizard's
         Tongue after it, retrieved it instantly
600   On the curled tip, closed his mouth, chewed. When he
         Grinded the word into bits he began his tale,
         One grain at a time fed to our lips
         Endlessly, the sack of his mouth bulging
         With wheat, until we grew sluggish and tame
605   With overeating, and fell asleep, his life-
         Long tale to be continued in dreams.
         Each morning, the milking of the cow done,
         Our father deposited us in Manu's hut
         For instruction. He resumed from the previous
610   Day, his hands still agile as he declaimed,
         His eyes frantically bright as if he was cursed
         To stay awake until his story ended. Only
         Then would the gods send him sleep, so peaceful
         And dark a sleep: the serpent's whisper, the lover's
615   Melody, the prisoner wailing the hours
         To his execution, the startled laughter
         Of the reprieved, no such sounds of triumph or loss
         Which he mimicked in his tale would awaken him.

595: *manitou*: i.e., "manatee": a water-cow

Now restlessly he sleeps, his duty unfulfilled,
620 His hands still gripped to the ghost of the sword
Turner insinuated into his belly,
Withdrew, sheathed, his mouth still open as if
Wanting to continue his tale. Only flies
Perform his obsequies, gathering on his tongue
625 To hum eulogies to our magician,
Our childhood, our promise, our broken
Word.

XXIV

720 Turner crammed our boys' mouths too with riches,
His tongue spurting strange potions upon ours
Which left us dazed, which made us forget
The very sound of our speech. Each night
Aboard ship he gave selflessly the nipple
725 Of his tongue until we learnt to say profitably
In his own language, *we desire you, we love*
You, we forgive you. He whispered eloquently
Into our ears even as we wriggled beneath him,
Breathless with pain, wanting to remove his hook
730 Implanted in our flesh. The more we struggled
Ungratefully, the more steadfast his resolve
To teach us words. He fished us patiently,
Obsessively, until our stubbornness gave way
To an exhaustion more complete than Manu's
735 Sleep after the sword bore into him
And we repeated in a trance the words
That shuddered from him: *blessed, angelic,*
Sublime; words that seemed to flow endlessly
From him, filling our mouths and bellies
740 Endlessly.

XXV

'Nigger,' it cries, loosening from the hook
Of my desire, drifting away from
My body of lies. I wanted to teach it
A redemptive song, fashion new descriptions
745 Of things, new colours fountaining out of form.
I wanted to begin anew in the sea
But the child would not bear the future
Nor its inventions, and my face was rooted
In the ground of memory, a ground stampeded
750 By herds of foreign men who swallow all its fruit
And leave a trail of dung for flies
To colonise; a tongueless earth, bereft
Of song except for the idiot witter
Of wind through a dead wood. 'Nigger'
755 It cries, naming itself, naming the gods,
The earth and its globe of stars. It dips

753: *witter*: chatter

Below the surface, frantically it tries to die,
To leave me beadless, nothing and a slave
To nothingness, to the white enfolding
760   Wings of Turner brooding over my body,
Stopping my mouth, drowning me in the yolk
Of myself. There is no mother, family,
Savannah fattening with cows, community
Of faithful men; no elders to foretell
765   The conspiracy of stars; magicians to douse
Our burning temples; no moon, no seed,
No priests to appease the malice of the gods
By gifts of precious speech—rhetoric antique
And lofty, beyond the grasp and cunning
770   Of the heathen and conquistador—
Chants, shrieks, invocations uttered on the first
Day spontaneously, from the most obscure
Part of the self when the first of our tribe
Awoke, and was lonely, and hazarded
775   Foliage of thorns, earth that still smouldered,
The piercing freshness of air in his lungs
In search of another image of himself.
No savannah, moon, gods, magicians
To heal or curse, harvests, ceremonies,
780   No men to plough, corn to fatten their herds,
No stars, no land, no words, no community,
No mother.

1994

RANDOLPH HEALY (b. 1956)

HEALY HAS WRITTEN THAT HIS FIRST BOOK, *25 POEMS* (1983), WAS PUBLISHED AT A moment when, for Irish poets writing in English, "Evoking an unmistakably Irish location [was] a primary aim, checkpoints being erected at every entrance to the tradition into which one could not pass without a certified 'sense of place.' "[1] His poems, rife with anagrams and acrostics and demonstrating familiarity not only with collage and other avant-garde techniques but also knowledge of the discourses and methods of logic, mathematics, neuroscience, and biology, have little to do with that tradition. This does not make his poems any less relevant to contemporary Irish life. The first poem in *25 Poems*, "Colonies of Belief," begins in laconic mimicry of logic's language of classification, only to proceed as if inevitably to discussion of the "logic" of colonization and its fate. Of his interest in "investigating the expressive potential of logic," Healy has written as follows: "It is possible to misrepresent the historical context of logic as a search for truth. A wholehearted attempt to uncover the picture of the world. However, in our century, such a search has been so hopelessly compromised as to have become something far more interesting. The instrument of orthodoxy, the scaffolding of the world, had begun to collapse under internal pressures. Freed from its former dogmatism it was now available to poetry."[2] While the discursive mode of Healy's early poems bears a faint resemblance to some of the poetry of Wallace Stevens, Healy's poem "Spirals Dance" indicates that he "prefer[s] bottomless chaos" to Stevensian order because of the former's "endlessly creative" potential.[3]

Arbor Vitae, the first part of which is included here, touches upon the possible referents of its title—the tree of life in Eden, the site in the cerebellum, a diagram in the Kabbalah, and a Persian carpet design—but its primary concern is the history of the deaf and signing in Ireland. While the creative potential of chaos interests Healy, his poems also express his concern for the people who have been abused or dispossessed by cultural and political systems erected in the name of logic or order. The anagrams for "chaos," which become a recurrent motif in "Arbor Vitae," might be read as a gesture of solidarity with deaf communities, whose world and language are other to but not less than the world and language of the hearing; the degree to which the resourcefulness and vitality of the deaf have not always been recognized by institutions purporting to educate them informs the narrative text of the poem. Noting that Healy is critical of "those systems which *forget the world* and use axiomatic theories to impose

---

[1] "Uncertain Questions," *boundary 2*, vol. 26, no. 1, 1999, p. 133
[2] Ibid., pp. 133–34.
[3] *Rana Rana!*, Bray, 1997, p. 26.

their will," David Annwn finds that Healy's poetry often presents a "cautious optimism" based upon the belief that "such systems will surely *die out*."[4]

Healy was born in Irvine, Scotland and moved to Dublin as a child. After leaving school at 14, he worked as a salesman, hoffmann presser, telex-typist, and security man before returning to Ballymun Community School and Trinity College, Dublin, where he studied mathematical sciences. He is the editor of Wild Honey Press, a publisher of exploratory Irish poetry, with authors such as Maurice Scully, Billy Mills, and Trevor Joyce on its list. Along with appearing in most of the journals and anthologies devoted to post-modern British and Irish poetry, Healy's poems have been published in a series of chapbooks: *Rana Rana!* (1997), *Flame* (1997), *Arbor Vitae* (1997), and *Scales* (1998). He lives outside Dublin in Bray, where he is a math and science teacher.

---

[4] "Vital Spirals Dancing: The Poetry of Randolph Healy," *Angel Exhaust*, vol. 17, 1999, p. 120.

Colonies of Belief

Not everything is flat, like a board.
You have the regular roundness of a ball.
And not everything so regular either.
The geometric dance of atoms in
5   molecules becomes, closer, a blur
of energy or, further, sandy rubble.
So not everything, it appears, is the same.
Some things are different. And not everything
is different in different ways.
10   Things form classes. And a class is a point
of interest from a particular
point of view. And some things have a point
of view which is formed from a small area
around the thing itself. And some things have
15   *consciousness* which lets them change their point
of view. Unless they choose not to.
But they can't choose always, and the few times
that they can may get them carried away
imagining they can always choose,
20   which is power. Power to think the small
area around them from which springs
their point of interest forming their point
of view is the pre-eminent area
of the globe. And that the occupiers
25   of this first patch on the planet should be
very powerful things and, in turn, band together
to become a very powerful Thing.
And in their ardour to spread the good news
of their prestige destroy the
30   consciousness of things which occupy
areas around their area by removing
their already limited faculty of choice.
That is by making possible only
one particular point of view.
35   Their own. But their unity is time-

dependent and eventually they
fall apart and stop being a very
powerful thing, sometimes becoming powerless
under the power of another or other points of view.

40 Sometimes when area unity breaks down,
individual integrity, which splits
events into right and wrong, becomes
of interest. To do the wrong thing for the
right reason or the right thing for the wrong
45 reason or the wrong thing for the wrong reason
is wrong. To do the right thing for the right
reason is right. If things cannot always
choose and therefore at those times behave
at random then wrongness should prevail
50 three to one unless things are under some
overpower. But rightness is a rule
holding the above relations with
wrongness, to select events and form two
classes, being stated by some thing.
55 And if that thing states the rule and states that
the rule is right then call it that thing's *belief.*
And if that thing behaves according to
its belief then it is *sincere, honest,*
and even *noble.* And noble things become a source
60 of rightness to themselves, every action
partaking of the becalming waters.

Sometimes conscious things forget the world.
They see everything from a point of view;
stay indoors discussing themselves;
65 allow no checks on their comfort; perform
irreversible experiments on
the area around them; calculate
theorems in axiomatic systems and
call it truth, forgetting that precision
70 is only gained at a very low level
of meaning, where there is little foresight
and less control; they swagger, dominate,
dabble, destroy, dream, exploit and die out.

1983

from Arbor Vitae

I

But there were some good ideas knocking around,
then, before the first word was spoken.
History.

Two Dominican Sisters, Srs. Mary Magdalen O'Farrell
5   and Mary Vincent Martin returned from France
with a sign dictionary and a number of teaching texts, 1846.
Fr. John Burke, Vincentian priest,
Englished these resources, in addition making signs
"softer and more feminine" for the girls
10   and "bolder and more masculine" for the boys.

Acosh, sacho, ohacs.

I get up early in the morning.
I wash my face and my hands.
I put my clothes on.

15   Casoh, hasoc.

St. Mary's School for Deaf Girls,
St. Joseph's School for Deaf Boys,
both residential, only hundreds of yards apart,
yet the lack of opportunity for contact between them
20   led to separate "men's signs" and "women's signs".
The difference between these became so great
that a belief arose among the girls
that another system had been brought from America for the boys.

"We were going out one day and for some reason I ran back into the house to get something out of the attic. Having been burgled four times I had installed a burglar alarm and stretching out on the ladder to open the trapdoor I accidentally set it off. The internal siren, called a sound bomb, instantly liquified my entire world and I fell to the floor. Everyone was screaming except Florence who was six months old at the time. No reaction at all in fact. This was our first indication that she might be deaf. We contacted a deaf woman, Wendy Murray, who over a period of two years taught our family to sign. Only later did we find out that sign language is prohibited in the deaf schools, parents being instructed not to as much as point at things in front of their child. This suppression of their natural language is based on the belief that a deaf child allowed to sign will never learn to speak. Steven Pinker, in *The Language Instinct,* describes the results of this policy, Oralism, as 'dismal'." (Healy's note). The full text of Healy's poem and his notes on it may be found at <*http://indigo.ie/~tjac/Poets/Randolph_Healy/Arbor_Vitae/arbor_vitae.htm*>.
Title: "tree of life" (Latin); Healy glosses: "the tree of life in the garden of Eden—a region in the cerebellum—an internet taxonomy project—a Persian carpet design—a diagram in the kabbalah—an actual tree."
12–14: "Deaf education offers a grim parallel to what Pearse called 'the murder machine', the systematic attempt of the English to obliterate the Irish language. The motif 'I get up early in the morning' translates an Irish language pseudo-narrative of the sixties which used to be taught in all the various tenses to schoolchildren. Deaf children are not taught the Irish language. Intensive voice training from the age of three hardly leaves time for the three R's. Politically, this was how deaf adults were excluded from teaching as one needed a qualification in Irish in order to enter University." (Healy)

Hosca, casho, scoha.

25   Hosac.

Start with radial strands, then go
alternately anticlockwise up and clockwise down
for four circumspins
then anticlockwise all the way to the centre
30   and home, sixty thousand individual movements later.
Ocsha, sacoh.
If moved before the end
will continue the web where it left off
however useless either result.

35   Günz, Mindel, Riss, Würm.

1946. Signing was no longer permitted
in the Girls' School (1956 in the Boys')
as oral methods became policy.

Why learn a sign when they might learn a word
40   *question mark.*

At the same time, the City of London was subsisting
on time lapse movies of William's Bon Chretiens
(seed to fruit in sixteen seconds)
lying hour upon hour in a poky flat
45   waiting for just the right time
being horribly aged by the wrong.

Write down the six combinations which begin with "CH".
Then swap the "H" with the third, fourth and fifth letter,
in turn, completing those twenty four which begin with "C".

50   Central doctrines:
That true language is lingual;
that one form of expression excludes another;
that failure is due to lack of effort.

Socha, hacos, ahsoc.

55   Out of the corners of our eyes we could see
a group pulling a plug of ice
hundreds of feet long out of the ground
trying to find out if the weather would hold.

Releasers of behaviour.

60   Transpose the "C" with each of the other four letters in turn
for the full list of one hundred and twenty.

35: *Günz . . . :* names of four ice ages
42: *William's Bon Chretien* is a variety of pear.
44: *poky:* cramped

Today,
fifty years later,
those still without language at the age of ten
65   are classified as being multiply handicapped
and transferred to a signing unit.
Ask *them* what it's like to have no native language.

Use your voice.

I will get up early in the morning.
70   I will wash my face and my hands.
I will put my clothes on.

Yes is open, two handed,
contact of horizontal and vertical.
No is a small, solitary, upright bird, closing.

75   Sohac, hasco, shoca.

In the omniscient landscape
every event was plotted as a point
all the lines between them exposed
every action every thought knitted into one cloth.

80   Back at the party, not even bothering to check the price,
we aimed lower, attempting to construe
what it was that underpinned each gesture,
assuming expression was an imperative,
even its evasion a loop in the autograph.

85   Shaco, cohas, ohasc.

Remove seat cushion,
embrace, grasping loops with hands, float.

Since love is a gift,
you cannot always choose what you get.
90   And, since no purchase is required,
no responsibility is accepted for any disappointment.

At that height, as if time had slowed,
I could feel my eardrum
vibrating like a puddle in the rain,
95   and a sickening feeling as I realised
that my car was not insured
for any loss or damage directly or indirectly
due to
        sahco, hsoca, oshac.

100   How much of us have they translated?
One or two pages of fragments.
        Good. But what progress?
They think much of it is nonsense and the rest a sealed book.

100: *How much of us* . . . : See note to line 127 below.

Excellent.

105 Acsho, scaho.

Deep signing is never used in front of hearing people.

I washed my face and my hands.

Total Communication,
the simultaneous use of speech and sign,
110 although in practice one atrophies
at the expense of the other.

Home is an array of data arising out of
membranes, pressure, chemo- and light sensors
and, even more so, out of post-sensual processing.
115 But I am a fragment of a shadow
cast by the coherence of energies
necessary to co-ordinate a colony of six trillion cells.

How do they even walk?
if not by a recursive sequence of points of collapse

120 I wish I had put my clothes on.

Oscah.

The unemployment rate among deaf people is 91%
Almost half of deaf school leavers have failed
to attain a reading age of nine years (1970's).

125 A sealed book.

O

Do or don't judge a city by its size, for
Example, this street, at one stage not even cobbled, hails
Originally from the sea, suggesting a
130 Xerox of some blue-green algae or perhaps
Yggdrassil apparently expanding as it
Reaches back into history, but
Intertwining, fusing, flexing against,

127: "No matter how good your hearing is there are things which you will not hear. In the stanza begin-
ning 'Do or don't judge a city by its size,' the vertical acrostic spells deoxyribonucleic acid. This will of
course be silent in any reading, particularly the way in which the syntax runs across line endings. (The
content extemporises on some remarks made by Wittgenstein where he compares language to a city.
Hearing educators have a history of refusing to recognise signing as a language possessing a grammar of
its own.) Deafness has a strongly genetic character. Apart from the obvious matter of heredity, deaf chil-
dren of deaf parents learn their natural language naturally, do not have to experience the oddity of being
taught their native language, and so can acquire language before the latency period has passed. Deaf
children of hearing parents are rarely so lucky. Here DNA is intended to represent something that
extends beyond an individual life while also suggesting uniqueness, one's personal secret. (Not all of
one's genes are manifested in one's own physical makeup.) The earlier stanza 'How much of us have they
translated?' refers to the human genome project, an attempt to completely decipher this furtive lan-
guage." (Healy)
131: *Yggdrasil*: the Tree of the World in Norse myth

Bumping into the funnelled walls
135   Overhanging the diminishing labour pool.
No one could have foreseen how
Unbridled the maze of little squares
Courtyards and streets would become.
Later additions are generally believed to
140   Enhance its fundamental character.
In any case, its persistence from ancient times,
Changed of course, but still very much alive,
And in constant use, attracting newcomers everyday,
Can be seen as a Swiss Army Knife of History,
145   Incorporating buzz words from every epoch,
Dated or still current.

Isn't it about time
you unfractured your accent
with ideas it was intended to pronounce?

150   I felt a forest under my skin.

Sahoc, ocahs, csoah.

Use your voice.

Chaos.

                                                     1997

151: "A recurrent motif is provided by the anagrams of the word chaos. This is partly a musical device,
partly to represent the disarray of the institutions, despite their obsession with order. Instructions are
given for working out all 120 anagrams, mirroring the way those in institutions are constantly told what
to do." (Healy)

JEAN "BINTA" BREEZE (b. 1957)

BREEZE EMERGED FROM THE WORLD OF JAMAICAN DUB POETRY IN THE EARLY 1980S AND today is among the best-known performance poets in the Caribbean, Britain, and Europe. Extending a long tradition of popular poetry in the Caribbean, which includes the work of calypso poet Louise Bennett, praised by Breeze for having "given the people's poetry back to them," dub poetry partly grew out of the practice of DJs who would improvise lyrics to read over recordings of reggae rhythms. Breeze, who has noted that dub poetry was mostly a male world when she began, brings a feminist perspective to dub poetry's traditional themes as they involve criticism of a modern, post-colonial urban life and occasional nostalgia for a simpler, rural life. "Cherry Tree Garden," with its quiet insistence on the importance of cultivating gardens with cherry trees "still in reach of children," is more typical of her work than the more declamatory "Riddym Ravings (The Mad Woman's Poem)." The latter poem has been described by Breeze as the work that helped her to see that her political concerns must emerge from her experience as a woman rather than her reading in C. L. R. James or Marx. Both "Cherry Tree Garden" and "Riddym Ravings" show that Breeze's poetry is not limited to standard dub poetry rhythms; she explains that "there is not enough experimentation with the form and it is becoming as constraining in its rhythms as the iambic pentameter."[1]

Breeze grew up in rural north-east Jamaica. She worked as a teacher before entering the Jamaican School of Drama, where she added the African name "Binta," which means "close to the heart." Her books include *Answers* (1983), *Riddym Ravings and Other Poems* (1988), *Spring Cleaning* (1992), and *On the Edge of an Island* (1997). Her career in performance began in Montego Bay in 1981; she first performed in England in 1985. She has been a contributing editor at *Critical Quarterly*, which under the general editorship of Colin MacCabe did much to secure academic attention for Black British writing and non-standard British poetry. Her recordings include *Word Soun' 'Ave Power, Reggae Power* (1985). She wrote the screenplay for the film *Hallelujah Anyhow* (1990). Breeze now divides her time between London and the Caribbean.

---

[1] "Can a Dub Poet Be a Woman?" *The Routledge Reader in Caribbean Literature,* ed. Alison Donnell and Sarah Lawson Welsh, London, 1996, pp. 498–500.

Riddym Ravings
(The Mad Woman's Poem)

de fus time dem kar me go a Bellevue
was fit di dactar an de landlord operate
an tek de radio outa mi head
troo dem seize de bed
5   weh did a gi mi cancer
an mek mi talk to nobady
ah di same night wen dem trow mi out fi no pay de rent
mi haffi sleep outa door wid de Channel One riddym box
an de D.J. fly up eena mi head
10   mi hear im a play seh

Eh, Eh,
no feel no way
town is a place dat ah really kean stay
dem kudda—ribbit mi han
15   *eh—ribbit mi toe*
mi waan go a country go look mango

fah wen hungry mek King St. pavement
bubble an dally in front a mi yeye
an mi foot start wanda falla fly
20   to de garbage pan eena de chinaman backlat
dem nearly chap aff mi han eena de butcha shap
fi de piece a ratten poke
ah de same time de mawga gal in front a mi
drap de laas piece a ripe banana
25   an mi—ben dung—pick i up—an nyam i
a dat time dem grab mi an kar mi back a Bellevue
dis time de dactar an de lanlord operate
an tek de radio plug outa mi head
den sen mi out, seh mi alright
30   but—as ah ketch back outa street
ah push een back de plug
an ah hear mi D.J. still a play, seh

1: *kar me go a Bellevue*: took me to the psychiatric hospital (*Bellevue* is a mental hospital in Kingston, Jamaica)
2: *fit*: for
4: *troo*: through (because)
5: *weh*: which
13: *kean*: can't
17ff: "When I'm hungry it makes King St. pavement bubble and move back and forth in front of my eyes, and my foot starts to wander, following flies . . ."
22: *poke*: pork
23: *mawga*: thin
25: *ben dung*: bend down
    nyam i: eat it
30: *as ah ketch back outa street*: once I was back on the street

     Eh, Eh,
     no feel no way
35   *town is a place dat ah really kean stay*
     dem kudda—ribbit mi han
     eh—ribbit mi toe
     mi waan go a country go look mango

     Ha Haah . . . Haa

40   wen mi fus come a town
     mi use to tell everybady 'mawnin'
     but as de likkle rosiness gawn outa mi face
     nobady nah ansa mi
     silence tun rags roun mi bady
45   in de mids a all de dead people dem
     a bawl bout de caast of livin
     an a ongle one ting tap mi fram go stark raving mad
     a wen mi siddung eena Parade
     a tear up newspaper fi talk to
50   sometime dem roll up
     an tun eena one a Uncle But sweet saaf
     yellow heart breadfruit
     wid piece a roas saalfish side a i
     an if likkle rain jus fall
55   mi get cocanat rundung fi eat i wid
     same place side a weh de country bus dem pull out
     an sometime mi a try board de bus
     an de canductor bwoy a halla out seh
     'dutty gal, kum affa de bus'
60   ah troo im no hear de riddym eena mi head
     same as de tape weh de bus driva a play, seh

     Eh, Eh,
     no feel no way
     town is a place dat ah really kean stay
65   *dem kudda—ribbit mi han*
     eh—ribbit mi toe
     mi waan go a country go look mango
     so country bus, ah beg yuh
     tek mi home
70   *to de place, where I belang*

     an di dutty bway jus run mi aff

     Well, dis mawnin, mi start out pon Spanish Town Road,
     fah mi deh go walk go home a country
     fah my granny use to tell mi how she walk fram wes

46: *bawl*: cry, complain
47: "and only one thing stopped me from going stark raving mad"
48: *Parade*: a street in Kingston
51: *sweet saaf*: sweetsop, a fruit also called "sweet apple."
55: *rundung*: juice
56: "beside this place the buses to the country pulled out" ("dem" after a noun denotes a plural).
72: *Spanish Town Road*: the route from Kingston to Spanish Town

75   come a town
        come sell food
        an mi waan ketch home befo dem put de price pon i'
        but mi kean go home dutty?
        fah mi parents dem did sen mi out clean
80   Ah!
        see wan stanpipe deh!
        so mi strip aff all de crocus bag dem
        an scrub unda mi armpit
        fah mi hear de two mawga gal dem laas nite
85   a laugh an seh
        who kudda breed smaddy like me?
        a troo dem no know seh a pure nice man
        weh drive car an have gun
        visit my piazza all dem four o'clock a mawnin
90   no de likkle dutty bwoy dem weh mi see dem a go home
        wid
        but as mi feel de clear water pon mi bady
        no grab dem grab mi
        an is back eena Bellevue dem kar mi
95   seh mi mad an a bade naked a street
        well dis time de dactar an de lanlord operate
        an dem tek de whole radio fram outa mi head
        but wen dem tink seh mi unda chloroform
        dem put i dung careless
100   an wen dem gawn
        mi tek de radio
        an mi push i up eena mi belly
        fi keep de baby company
        fah even if mi nuh mek i
105   me waan my baby know dis yah riddym yah
        fram before she bawn
        hear de D.J. a play, seh

        Eh, Eh,
        no feel no way
110   *town is a place dat ah really kean stay*
        dem kudda—ribbit mi han
        eh—ribbit mi toe
        mi waan go a country go look mango

        an same time
115   de dactar an de lanlord

77: *ketch:* go
81: *stanpipe:* standpipe (a public tap run off the mains)
82: *crocus bag:* a cloth bag used for carrying shopping, etc.
86: *smaddy:* somebody
87ff: "because they don't know that a very nice man who drives a car and has a gun visits my house every
     morning at four o'clock, unlike the dirty little boys I see them go home with."

trigger de electric shack
an mi hear de D.J. vice bawl out, seh

Murther
Pull up Missa Operator!

1988

Cherry Tree Garden

used to be
a cherry tree
in the garden
       wasn't no

5   well arranged
blossom bedded
softly shaded
        garden
no stones held

10   in soft moss
no garden chairs
or tinkling ice
in lime green glasses

no umbrellas

15   no winter's sleep

this square
wrenched
from swamps
dumped and hoed

20   crotons clutched
stubbornly
       and the mango knew
to earn its place
it had to produce more than

25   the usual crop
of juicy saints
       the sensible hibiscus
rooting from mere sticks
patrolled the border

30   was a cherry tree
in this garden

119: *Pull up:* i.e., referring back to the bus earlier in the poem

20: The *croton*, or variegated laurel, is a type of shrub or tree.

26: *saints:* The St. Julien mango is one of the most popular varieties.

catching the red
in the eyes of passing children

easily climbed
de-wormed
thriving

till

one night of ruthless
storm
pulled out its stump

what now
can we grow here
that's still in reach
of children

1992

BENJAMIN ZEPHANIAH (b. 1958)

IN THE LATE 1980S, ZEPHANIAH WAS SHORTLISTED FOR A FELLOWSHIP AT TRINITY College, Cambridge. Britain's tabloid media, including *The Sun,* took the opportunity to note that in his youth Zephaniah had been sent to an approved ("reform") school and done time in prison on burglary charges. The poet's opinion of *The Sun* is clear in the poem of that title included here. Bob Mole, introducing Zephaniah's *City Psalms* (1992), quotes from the *Oxford History of English Literature*'s entry on the fifteenth-century Scots poet Robert Henryson: "his observation is exact and detailed . . . he delights in homely phrases and in alliterative jingles drawing strength and colour from these popular elements . . . he knows the traditions and can extol them or laugh at them as the mood takes him."[1] For Mole, Zephaniah's poetry belongs in a tradition with "the tribal bards of Africa, the Gawain poet in Cheshire, Dunbar and Henryson in Scotland," but such sweeping genealogies seem to have more to do with the pursuit of academic sanction than the immediate origins of the poetry. Zephaniah's popularity, like Linton Kwesi Johnson's, has much to do with his forging links to other artforms, such as reggae music, with expanding the media poetry can use and testing the boundaries between spoken word and song. Behind both poets is the tradition of DJ toasters; Zephaniah himself worked briefly as a DJ in Handsworth.

Born in Birmingham, Zephaniah grew up in Jamaica and Handsworth. He has been writer-in-residence for the city of Liverpool and the Africa Arts Collective and active in promoting poetry in schools, youth clubs, prisons, and teacher training centers. His published plays and radio plays include *Hurricane Dub* (1988) and *Job Rocking* (1989). His records include *Dub Ranting* and *Us an Dem.* He has collaborated on other recordings with musicians such as Sinead O'Connor and appeared in films, TV programs, and on radio. His books also include *Pen Rhythm* (1981), *The Dread Affair* (1985), and *Propa Propaganda* (1996). He lives in London's East End.

---

[1] *City Psalms,* p. 9.

Money

(rant)

    Money mek a Rich man feel like a Big man
    It mek a Poor man feel like a Hooligan
    A One Parent family feels like some ruffians
    An dose who hav it don't seem to care a damn,
5   Money meks yu friend become yu enemy
    Yu start see tings very superficially
    Yu life is lived very artificially
    Unlike dose who live in Poverty.
    Money inflates yu ego
10   But money brings yu down
    Money causes problems anywea money is found,
    Food is what we need, food is necessary,
    Mek me grow my food
    An dem can eat dem money.

15   Money meks a singer singaloada crap
    Money keeps horses running round de track
    Money meks Marriages
    Money meks Divorce
    Money meks a Student tink about de course,
20   Money meks commercials
    Commercials mek money
    If yu don't hav money yu just watch more TV,
    Money can save us
    Still we feel doomed,
25   Plenty money burns ina Nuclear Mushroom.
    Money can't mek yu happy
    Money can't help yu when yu die,
    It seems dat dose who hav it continually live a lie.
    Children a dying
30   Spies a spying
    Refugees a fleeing
    Politicians a lying,
    So deals are done
    An webs are spun
35   Loans keep de Third World on de run,
    An de Bredda feels betta dan dis Bredda next door
    Cause dis Bredda's got money, but de Bredda's got more
    An de Bredda tinks dis Bredda's not a Bredda cause he's poor
    So dis Bredda kills de odder
40   Dat is Economic War.

    New world Economic War
    A bigga economic war means
    It may not be de East an de West anymore
    Now its de North an de South
45   Third World fall out
    Coffee an Oil is what its about
    It's Economic War
    Poor people hav de scar

Shots fired from de Stock Market floor,
50 So we work fe a living, how we try
An we try,
Wid so little time fe chilling
Like we living a lie.

Money meks a dream become reality
55 Money meks real life like a fantasy
Money has a habit of going to de head
I have some fe a rainy day underneath me bed,
Money problems mek it hard fe relax
Money meks it difficult fe get down to de facts
60 Money meks yu worship vanity an lies
Money is a drug wid legal eyes
Economists cum
Economists go
Yu try controlling yu cash flow
65 Food costs loads
House prices soar
An de Rich people try to dress like de Poor,
Nobody really understands de interest rate
When dere is interest den its all too late,
70 We cherish education
But how much do we pay?
Yu can't buy Race Relations or afford a holiday
Money can't mek you happy, yu happiness is paper thin
When yu are lonely yu will invite yu poor friends in.

75 Now dem sey is money culture time
Is dis culture yours, cause it is not mine
Money culture who?
Money culture what?
Money culture thrives where luv is not,
80 Dem can buy an sell till dem gu to Hell
Dem can tax de wisher at de wishing well,
Now Frankenstein cum fe privatise
Empire fools, get penny wise.
Every government will tek what dem can get
85 Every government is quick to feget
Every government can mek money by killing
Every government luvs money, no kidding,
But money is paper an paper will burn
So tink about trees as yu earn,
90 It could do good but it does more bad
Money is fake   and
You've been had.

Some study how fe manage it
Some study how fe spend it
95 Some people jus cannot comprehend it
Some study how fe move it from one country to another
Some study how fe study it an dem study fe ever,
Some people never see it yet dem work hard
Other never see it because dem carry cards,
100 Some people will grab it without nu thanks

An den mek it pile up in High Street banks.
Parents are hoping,
Some are not coping,
Some are jus managing,
105   Books need balancing,
Property is theft,
Nu money means death,
Yu pay fe yu rent den nothing left,
Some will pick a pocket
110   Some are paid fe stop it
Dose who are paid fe stop it are happy
Cause dey got it,
Some gu out an fight fe it
Some claim dem hav de right to it
115   People like me Granparents live long but never sight it.
Money made me gu out an rob
Den it made me gu looking fe a job,
Money made de Nurse an de Doctor immigrate
Money buys friends yu luv to hate,
120   Money made Slavery seem alright
Money brought de Bible an de Bible shone de light,
Victory to de penniless at grass roots sources
Who hav fe deal wid Market Forces,
Dat paper giant called Market Forces.

                                                        1992

The SUN

I believe the Blacks are bad
The Left is loony
God is Mad
This government's the best we've had
5   So I read The SUN.

I believe Britain is great
And other countries imitate
I am friendly with The State,
Daily, I read The SUN.

10   I am not too keen on foreign ones
But I don't mind some foreign bombs
Jungle bunnies play tom-toms,
But, I read The SUN.

Man, I don't like Russian spies
15   But we don't have none
I love lies,
I really do love Princess Di
I bet she reads The SUN.

Title: *The Sun* is a British tabloid newspaper notable for its right-wing political slant and topless "page three girls." The occasion for this poem is discussed in the headnote above.

Black people rob
20 Women should cook
And every poet is a crook,
I am told—so I don't need to look,
It's easy in The SUN.

Every hippie carries nits
25 And every Englishman love tits
I love Page Three and other bits,
I stare into The SUN.

I like playing bingo games
And witch-hunting to shame a name
30 But aren't newspapers all the same?
So why not read The SUN.

Don't give me truth, just give me gossip
And skeletons from people's closets,
I wanna be normal
35 And millions buy it,
I am blinded by The SUN.

1992

JACKIE KAY (b. 1961)

Born in Edinburgh to a Nigerian father and a Scottish mother, Kay was adopted by a white Glaswegian couple and grew up in Glasgow. She read English at the University of Stirling. She has been writer-in-residence at Hammersmith, London, and now works as a freelance writer in London. Besides her two principal collections of poetry, *The Adoption Papers* (1991) and *Other Lovers* (1993), she has published verse for children—*Two's Company* (1992) and *Three Has Gone* (1994)—and a biography of the blues singer Bessie Smith. *Twice Through the Heart,* a multimedia poem-documentary about a sixty-three-year-old woman sentenced to life for killing her physically and emotionally abusive husband, was shown in the BBC 2 *Words on Film* series in 1992. Kay has published plays including *Twilight Shift* (1994) and a novel, *Trumpet* (1998). Like her compatriot Liz Lochhead, an acknowledged influence, Kay is a popular performer of her poems.

In her poem "In My Country," Kay describes the experience of being watched by another woman "as if I were a superstition." Asked "Where do you come from?" the poem's speaker replies "'Here. These parts.'"[1] The assumptions about personal and national identity faced by a black woman in Scotland are the subject of many of Kay's poems. As C. L. Innes writes, the title sequence of *The Adoption Papers,* originally a radio play, "focuses on questions of personal identity within a society that sees African characteristics as abnormal; within that society, the adoptive parents provide an ideal of acceptance in which biological/racial inheritance is acknowledged but makes no difference to loving personal relationships or to the individual's place within the family or community. At the same time, these poems challenge what in Britain are commonly assumed connections between racial and cultural inheritance."[2] The core of the sequence treats autobiographical material, interweaving the voices of Kay as a child and her adoptive and birth mothers. Other poems in *The Adoption Papers* take up figures marginalized or "othered" by society, sometimes adopting their personas—men dying of AIDS, transvestites, lesbian lovers. The five-part sequence "Severe Gale 8" describes the lives of the poor in Margaret Thatcher's Britain, mixing documentary detail, protest, and fairy-tale fantasy: "The wind was revolutionary; / ducks and gulls and Canadian geese / levitated to catch flying pieces of bread."[3] While Glaswegian idioms and speech rhythms shape some of the voices in "Black Bottom," Kay's formal range extends to the rhymed couplets and quatrains

---

[1] 'In My Country,' *Other Lovers,* p. 14.
[2] "Accent and Identity: Women Poets of Many Parts," *Contemporary British Poetry: Essays in Theory and Criticism,* ed. James Acheson and Romana Huk, Albany, 1996, p. 337.
[3] "Severe Gale 8," *The Adoption Papers,* p. 6.

employed in *Twice Through the Heart* and the blues stanzas of her poems about Bessie Smith.

from The Adoption Papers

Chapter 7: Black Bottom

Maybe that's why I don't like
all this talk about her being black,
I brought her up as my own
as I would any other child
5   colour matters to the nutters;
but she says my daughter says
it matters to her

I suppose there would have been things
I couldn't understand with any child,
10   we knew she was coloured.
They told us they had no babies at first
and I chanced it didn't matter what colour it was
and they said *oh well are you sure*
in that case we have a baby for you—
15   to think she wasn't even thought of as a baby,
my baby, my baby

I chase his *Sambo Sambo* all the way from the school gate.
A fistful of anorak—What did you call me? Say that again.
Sam-bo. He plays the word like a bouncing ball
20   but his eyes move fast as ping pong.
I shove him up against the wall,
say that again you wee shite. *Sambo, sambo,* he's crying now

I knee him in the balls. What was that?
My fist is steel; I punch and punch his gut.
25   Sorry I didn't hear you? His tears drip like wax.
Nothing he heaves *I didn't say nothing.*
I let him go. He is a rat running. He turns
and shouts *Dirty Darkie* I chase him again.
Blonde hairs in my hand. Excuse me!
30   This teacher from primary 7 stops us.
Names? I'll report you to the headmaster tomorrow.
But Miss. Save it for Mr Thompson she says

My teacher's face cracks into a thin smile
Her long nails scratch the note well well

The Adoption Papers is the story of a black girl adopted by a white Scottish couple; her birth mother is a white Scotswoman, her father a Nigerian. Three voices tell the story—the daughter's is set in regular typeface, her adoptive mother's lines in sanserif, and her birth mother's in boldface.
Title: *Black Bottom:* a popular jazz dance of the 1920s

35   I see you were fighting yesterday, again.
        In a few years time you'll be a juvenile delinquent.
        Do you know what that is? Look it up in the dictionary.
        She spells each letter with slow pleasure.
        Read it out to the class.
40   Thug. Vandal. Hooligan. Speak up. Have you lost your tongue?

        To be honest I hardly ever think about it
        except if something happens, you know
        daft talk about darkies. Racialism.
        Mothers ringing my bell with their kids
45   crying *you tell. You tell. You tell.*
        —*No.* You tell your little girl to stop calling
        my little girl names and I'll tell my little girl
        to stop giving your little girl a doing.

        We're practising for the school show
50   I'm trying to do the Cha Cha and the Black Bottom
        but I can't get the steps right
        my right foot's left and my left foot's right
        my teacher shouts from the bottom
        of the class Come on, show

55   us what you can do I thought
        you people had it in your blood.
        My skin is hot as burning coal
        like that time she said Darkies are like coal
        in front of the whole class—my blood
60   what does she mean? I thought

        she'd stopped all that after the last time
        my dad talked to her on parents' night
        the other kids are all right till she starts;
        my feet step out of time, my heart starts
65   to miss beats like when I can't sleep at night—
        What Is In My Blood? The bell rings, it is time.

        Sometimes it is hard to know what to say
        that will comfort. Us two in the armchair;
        me holding her breath, 'they're ignorant
70   let's have some tea and cake, forget them'.

        Maybe it's really Bette Davis I want
        to be the good twin or even better the bad
        one or a nanny who drowns a baby in a bath.
        I'm not sure maybe I'd prefer Katharine
75   Hepburn tossing my red hair, having a hot
        temper. I says to my teacher Can't I be

71ff: The film stars here from Hollywood's golden years were noted for their glamor and strong personal-
    ities.

        Elizabeth Taylor, drunk and fat and she
        just laughed, not much chance of that.
        I went for an audition for *The Prime*
80   *of Miss Jean Brodie.* I didn't get a part
        even though I've been acting longer
        than Beverley Innes. So I have. Honest.

        Olubayo was the colour of peat
        when we walked out heads turned
85   **like horses, folk stood like trees**
        their eyes fixed on us—it made me
        burn, that hot glare; my hand
        would sweat down to his bone.
        Finally, alone, we'd melt
90   **nothing, nothing would matter**

        He never saw her. I looked for him in her;
        for a second it was as if he was there
        in that glass cot looking back through her.

        On my bedroom wall is a big poster
95   of Angela Davis who is in prison
        right now for nothing at all
        except she wouldn't put up with stuff.
        My mum says she is *only* 26
        which seems really old to me
100   but my mum says it is young
        just imagine, she says, being on
        America's Ten Most Wanted People's List at 26!
        I can't.
        Angela Davis is the only female person
105   I've seen (except for a nurse on TV)
        who looks like me. She had big hair like mine
        that grows out instead of down.
        My mum says it's called an *Afro.*
        If I could be as brave as her when I get older
110   I'll be OK.
        Last night I kissed her goodnight again
        and wondered if she could feel the kisses
        in prison all the way from Scotland.
        Her skin is the same too you know.
115   I can see my skin is that colour
        but most of the time I forget,
        so sometimes when I look in the mirror
        I give myself a bit of a shock
        and say to myself *Do you really look like this?*
120   as if I'm somebody else. I wonder if she does that.

79: *The Prime of Miss Jean Brodie* is a 1961 novel by the Scottish writer Muriel Spark; it gained especial
    popularity in its stage and film versions.
95: *Angela Davis* (b. 1944), black U.S. political activist; suspected of complicity in a 1970 courtroom shoot-
    ing in California which left four people dead, she became one of the FBI's most wanted criminals. After
    her arrest in New York, she was returned to California to stand trial, and was acquitted.

I don't believe she killed anybody.
It is all a load of phoney lies.
My dad says it's a set up.
I asked him if she'll get the electric chair
125   like them Roseberries he was telling me about.
No he says the world is on her side.
Well how come she's in there then I thinks.
I worry she's going to get the chair.
I worry she's worrying about the chair.
130   My dad says she'll be putting on a brave face.
He brought me a badge home which I wore
to school. It says FREE ANGELA DAVIS.
And all my pals says 'Who's she?'

                                                                    1991

125: Julius and Ethel Rosenberg were executed in 1953 (despite a worldwide campaign for clemency) for
selling U.S. nuclear weapons secrets to the USSR.

W. N. HERBERT (b. 1961)

\\ A NSWERMACHINE," THE FINAL POEM IN HERBERT'S *CABARET MCGONAGALL* (1996),
begins "Eh amna here tae tak yir caa: / Eh'm mebbe aff at thi fitbaa, / Eh mebbe
amna here at aa."[1] Thus an answering machine declares the speaker not at home or
off at a football match, the joke involving the machine's potentially total erasure of the
human. The previous poem in the same book, "Theory and Function of Invisibility,"
has as its first line "I want to be Colombo with no murders to solve."[2] Poems in Stan-
dard English sit next to those in Dundonian idiom: Herbert moves easily back and
forth between the two, much as he mixes cultural allusions. He is as likely to allude
to American TV shows as to the "thistledoon [that] blows over this land." Herbert
remarks on the utopian dimensions of his mixed practice in an author's note in *Angel
Exhaust* 9: "I write with a forked tongue, in that I use both English and Scots dialects.
In each of these I lie in a slightly different way. In Scots I pretend that my basic
dialect—Dundonian—hasn't been atrophied by cultural disdain and neglect, and still
has access to the broad vocabulary of the Scots dictionary. This creates the language
of a quasi-fictional country, not altogether different from the present status of 'Scot-
land.' In English I tell a slightly different lie; I pretend that poetry hasn't been
demoted to a position outside the main media, and can address the issues and topics
of those media."[3] In "The Postcards of Scotland," Herbert's language is for the most
part closer to Standard English than Dundonian dialect, but the poem relates to the
second "lie" mentioned above, scrutinizing the purportedly "authentic" Scotland pro-
duced by heritage and tourist industries. To an extent Herbert's eclectic concerns are
representative of the group of Scottish poets calling themselves Informationists. Her-
bert's and Richard Price's co-edited anthology of prose and poetry, *Contraflow on the
Super Highway* (1994), did much to promote the label and included work by Robert
Crawford, David Kinloch, Peter McCarey, Alan Riach, and the editors. According to
Price, the Informationist poets share an interest in "little-known information, social
history, and all kinds of 'underprivileged' facts. . . . In presenting information these
poets also scrutinise that very process, sometimes they parody it, often they extend it:
they meddle with 'enlightenment' itself."[4]

---

[1] *Cabaret McGonagall*, Newcastle upon Tyne, 1996, p. 128.
[2] Ibid., p. 126.
[3] *Angel Exhaust*, vol. 9, 1993, p. 65.
[4] "Approaching the Informationists," *Contraflow on the Super Highway*, ed. W. N. Herbert and Richard
Price, London, 1994, p. i.

William Herbert was born in Dundee and educated at Oxford University, where he earned a Ph.D. He has worked as a teacher and now is writer-in-residence in Dumfries and Galloway. With Richard Price, he edited a journal of Scottish poetry and culture, *Gairfish*. His other books include *Sharawaggi* (with Robert Crawford, 1990), *Dundee Doldrums* (1991), *Anither Music* (1991), *The Testament of the Reverend Thomas Dick* (1993), *Forked Tongue* (1994), and *The Laurelude* (1998). His critical study of Hugh MacDiarmid, *To Circumjack MacDiarmid*, appeared in 1992.

The Anxiety of Information

What is the tribe among whom women conceive
at the age of five
and die at the age of eight?
What is the tribe whose smell
5   puts crocodiles to flight?
Is it true that the ibis can be regarded as
the inventor of the enema?
Which is the bird that goes bald
in the turnip season?
10   What connection exists between
the lobes of the liver of the mouse
and the phases of the moon?

What is the name of the King of Epirus whose
big toe cured diseases
15   of the spleen?
The name of the woman of ancient Rome
who never spat?
The name of the historian who paid 21,000f
for a plate of speaking birds' tongues?
20   Of the poet whose mistress received
the attentions of an elephant?

Is it true that female quails
are so lascivious
that it is enough for them to hear the voice
25   of the male
in order to conceive?
That a serpent barked
when the Tarquins were expelled?
That Aristomenes of Messenia,
30   who killed 300 Spartans,
had a heart made of hair?

1996

6: *ibis*: a storklike wading bird
13: *Epirus*: coastal region of northwestern Greece and southern Albania
28: The Roman monarchy was abolished in 509 BC with the expulsion of Lucius *Tarquinus* Superbus, seventh king of Rome, and his family.
29: *Messenia* was enslaved by Sparta in the 8th century BC; in circa 650 BC the Messenians revolted under the leadership of *Aristomenes*.

The Postcards of Scotland

My country is being delivered repeatedly
onto the 'WELCOME' mat of my mind
with the light patter of postcards falling
like flattened raindrops; postcards from
5   its every moniply, its each extremity:
the drunk dog's profile of Fife,
the dangling penis of Kintyre,
the appendix of the Mull of Galloway,
the uvula of Ulva and the sputum and
10   spat-out dentures of the Western Isles,
the whale's maw of the Moray Firth
and the steam-snort cockade
of the Orkneys.
                       Every village sends me
15   its image like a sweetheart's *Vergissmeinnicht*,
to be carried in the wallet on
a dangerous journey,
for I am voyaging so far within
all thoughts of 'home',
20   it is as though I were stationary, and
it is they who fly away in every direction;
Scotland exploding like a hand-grenade until
its clachans catch up with the stars,
its cities collide with galaxies, scattering
25   the contents of their galleries, unspooling
their cinemas, bargain-basketing
their shopping precincts.

Only their postcards survive,
like the familiarity of light
30   still travelling from extinguished stars.

But what postcards can endure transmission
across such addressless gulfs, insertion
in such a black hole as
the letterbox of my discrimination?

35   Certainly the tartan-fringed idylls
of small dogs and pretty girls
hypnotised by the contents of a flapping kilt
despite the rubicund obesity of its owner
and the fact he wears his gingery beard
40   *sans* moustache:
                     nothing shall destroy
these; not even the incendiary glance
of the Angel of Death,

5: *moniply:* one of the chambers of the stomach of a ruminant (e.g., a cow, which has four)
15: *Vergissmeinnicht:* "forget-me-not" (German), the conclusion of a love letter
23: *clachans:* villages

for which reason Auld Clootie sends him them
45   weekly, along with their sib,
the fishermen catching Nessie,
because Auld Nick kens weel this degradation
of Thor's mythic encounter with
the Midgard Serpent
50   is a pain in the angelic butt.

But these I throw aside negligently
in the search for my true home.

Not the misty-lensed monstrosities
of quality pap-merchants, with
55   their dug-up zombie shots, their same old
purpling panoramas of hills and lochs
giving the glad eye in weathers that never were.
Nor the shampooing of sheep and the oiling
of Highland cattles' horns; nor
60   the photographic humping of Belties
and the image-maker's posing hand
fist-fucking the cute black bun. Nor
the fascinating 'Doors of Many Post Offices' shot,
presenting such a quaint contrast
65   to the work of Bernd und Hilla Becher
with series of urban water towers,
or the disused mines' pit-heads of Sanquhar,
and the lowland belt across of Fife.
Nor the orange and viridian 'Closes of Glasgow' series,
70   each tile personally signed
by Rennie Mackintosh, miraculously free
of asbestosis-tinged alcoholics' vomit.

Give me the postcards of municipal Scotland;
each caravan park lovingly identified
75   by a zen-succinct description printed
on a white border along the postcard's base:
each children's playpark accurately defined
down to the lack of smiles on the weans' faces;
each council flowerbed pointlessly recorded.
80   Here are the proud wastes of our city centres

44: *Auld Clootie:* like "Auld Nick," a nickname for the Devil
45: *sib:* kin
46: *Nessie:* the Loch Ness monster
47: *kens weel:* knows well
48: *Thor:* the Norse thunder-god, who tried but failed to defeat Jörmungand, the serpent of the world (or
   Midgard, Middle Earth)
60: *Belties:* Belted Galloway, a Scottish breed of cattle
65: The photographers *Bernd* and *Hilla Becher* are known for their images of industrial subject matter.
69: *Closes:* entryways to tenements (often decorated with colored tiles)
71: Charles *Rennie Mackintosh* (1868–1928), Glasgow-born Art Nouveau architect and designer
72: *asbestosis:* "A reference to bad industrial practice in Glasgow (and elsewhere)—people stripping out
   dangerous insulation without adequate protection, dying years later of asbestosis" (Herbert, in corre-
   spondence).
74: *caravan park:* trailer park
78: *weans':* children's

accurately seen for the first time,
begotten from the copulation
of councillors with cement-mixers,
the tight wads of backhanders jammed
85   up their quivering rectums.

Here is the genuine face of eternity,
where 'swimming pool' means
a kidney-shaped pond eighteen inches deep,
the colour of chopped jobbies
90   full of pale bodies and pink flotation aids;
where 'beach' is a silver fingernail,
clipped and spinning from the camera like
a boomerang covered in lice.
Observe the two old men leaning towards
95   the water, out of focus; they
are transfixed by a monster more fecund
than any Nessie: that brown weasel shape
is a wet spaniel bitch,
you have only to scratch
100   the postcard to release the perfume
of soggy dog. Observe
that child on the sliver of toe-cheese
called the 'beach' at Portpatrick:
she has one foot in a plastic bucket
105   forever. Paradise smells
of tarry seaweed, it tastes of sand
in lettuce and tomato sandwiches.
I couldn't think of never dying
anywhere else.

110   Here is my only home,
my Heaven; observe
these photographs of Mercat crosses
and town centres packed with Anglias,
the ghosts of Hillman Minxes.
115   Surely those figures eating fried egg rolls
behind the glass of Italian cafes
are the philosophers of the Enlightenment.
Surely that is Susan Ferrier gossiping
outside the crappy dress shop
120   with Margaret Oliphant. Surely

84: *backhanders:* bribes
89: *jobbies:* excrement
112: *Mercat crosses:* old, usually medieval town crosses, public monuments found in market (*mercat*)
    places.
113ff: Ford *Anglias* and *Hillman Minxes* are two archetypal 1960s car models, still to be found in such post-
    cards.
117: The late eighteenth century in Scotland is known as the Scottish *Enlightenment:* its luminaries
    included such writers as the philosopher David Hume, the economic theoretician Adam Smith, and the
    poet Robert Burns.
118ff: *Susan Ferrier* (1782–1854) and *Margaret Oliphant* (1828–97), Scottish novelists

Robert Burns is buying a haggis supper
from that chipper in Annan,
William Dunbar is stotting from
The Cement-Mixer's Arms.

125   Only in these images do I recognise
the beautiful nincompoop face
of my nation: the sullen brows
of the stultified young farmer
speeding out of shot;
130   the *Sweetheart Stout* expression
of the girl with a knife in her handbag.
Only in these postcards
can I ever be at rest.

                                                          1996

122: *chipper:* fish and chip shop
123: *William Dunbar* (?1465–?1530), Scots poet from a period (during the rule of James IV) often consid-
ered the "Golden Age" of Scottish poetry.
     stotting: walking drunkenly
130: *Sweetheart Stout:* "A brand of sweetish stout supposedly to be drunk by girlfriends—this is a descen-
dant of medicinal drinking. The label features a fresh-faced fifties lass in a red jumper you would say
might be the Scots equivalent of Lana Turner." (Herbert, in correspondence)

CAROLINE BERGVALL (b. 1962)

BERGVALL, OF FRANCO-NORWEGIAN NATIONALITY, WAS BORN IN HAMBURG, GERMANY and brought up in Geneva, Oslo, New York City, Paris, and Strasbourg. She was educated at the Université de la Sorbonne Nouvelle, Paris, and the University of Warwick, and now resides in London. She directs the program in Performance Writing at Dartington College of the Arts. As an emergent practice, performance writing seeks to destabilize oppositions between the ephemerality of performance and the fixity of print, often exploring trans-generic writing in hybrid media and sites. The American writer Steve Benson's description of his work as "site-specific engagements of circumstances proper to the social and physical properties of the event setting" describes one key element of performance writing; Bergvall's reference in her interview in *Binary Myths* (1998) to varieties of modern poetry alert to "the manipulation of non-verbal signs such as the space of the page . . . [and] typography" identifies another element relevant to the writers associated with performance writing.[1] Bergvall's publications include several that began as text-based performances and installations, including *Strange Passage* (1993) and *Éclat* (1996). The latter of these was first a guided tour of a domestic space, then later a live reading, before being rewritten for its book version. At each stage, collaboration—with visual artists, curators, and eventually the publisher cris cheek—was involved. Bergvall has also collaborated with the poet John Cayley. Her work has appeared in anthologies of exploratory writing such as *Out of Everywhere: linguistically innovative poetry by women in North America & the UK* (1996) and *Conductors of Chaos* (1996). She has translated the French-Canadian poet Nicole Brossard's *Typhon Dru* (1997).

"Les jets de la Poupee" is a section of a longer work entitled *GOAN ATOM*. A work in the tradition of the eclectic and crossbreeding wordplay of James Joyce, its most immediate precursors are the anagrammatic writing of Unica Zürn and the dolls and color photography of the Surrealist artist Hans Bellmer's *Les Jeux de la Poupée* ("Games of the Doll"). In Bellmer's "revolutionary approach to the female figure and photography," Herbert Lust writes, "the human body is a fearful package, or wounded sentence, with many parts that can be added to, subtracted from, multiplied, divided, shifted and rearranged like an anagram."[2] Sixty years after Bellmer's dolls, contemporary feminist theorists continue to show considerable interest in cyborgs, in a "prosthetic" body and the discursive construction of the body. Bergvall joins visual artists such as Cindy Sherman and Louise Bourgeois and writers such as Kathy Acker and Monique Wittig in taking up what she describes in her interview as "this post-

---

[1] *Binary Myths: Conversations with Contemporary Poets*, ed. Andy Brown, Exeter, 1998, p. 55.
[2] "For Women Are Endless Forms: Hans Bellmer's Dark Art," *Sulfur*, vol. 26, 1990, p. 36.

Beauvoir constructivism and body liberalism" as it reflects a "pressing obsession with transformation, metamorphosis as a field through which . . . conventions become problematised and gender games can be played out."[3] The poem's "Dolly," however, equally suggests a "constructivism" of another, more exactly technological sense: the cloning of the sheep "Dolly" in Scotland. Thus the poem might be said to be situated exactly at the center of questions destined to be crucial in the twenty-first century and involving sexuality, technology, agency, ethics, and identity.

---

[3]*Binary Myths*, p. 52.

Les jets de la Poupee

I

        Dolly
        sgot a wides lit
        down the lily
        sgot avide slot
5   donne a lolly
        to a head
        less cindy to slot in
        to lic
        kher shackle
10   good dottersum
        presses titbutt
        on for the puppe's
        panorama

        Nic
15   e roun
        ded olly

        Pops
        er
        body partson
20   to the flo
        ring the morning
        it's never matt
        ers what goes back
        on w

Title: "The jets [or spurts] of the Doll" (French). The title alludes to *Les Jeux de la Poupée* (*The Games of the Doll*, 1949), a collection of handtinted prints by the German artist Hans Bellmer (1902–1975); his work, influenced by the surrealists, is characterized by its erotic focus on the (often juvenile) female body. The dolls in his prints have been dissected and put back together, in contorted poses, with added or missing body parts. Bergvall notes (in correspondence) that the unnerving articulations of *Les Jeux de la Poupée* and the subtitle of his earlier *Poupée: Variations sur le montage d'une mineure articulée* (*Doll: Variations on the montage of an articulated minor*, 1934) "provided me with the syntactical basis for my own piece."

1: *Dolly:* In February 1997 a group of scientists in Edinburgh performed the first successful clone of an adult animal—a sheep, dubbed "Dolly."

4: *avide:* voracious (French)

5: *donne:* give (French)

7: *cindy:* alludes to the American photographer Cindy Sherman (b. 1954), whose *Untitled* series is referred to below (line 164).

12: *puppe:* doll; puppet (German).

25   here dolly
goodolly
in a
ny shape or form
wit one fine toast
30   erin the belly
wit no head
wit nos
ticky hairs
round the folly
35   and nof ingers at the tips
(or more)

In short
ALL OF
DOLLY'S
40   A FUNC

indy
likes hang
in
from the trees with
45   herl egs up in the air
while herl
egs dow
non the ground
li
50   kemy dolly's knees t
hey full of joins
they're full of joi
n

s

55   pleine didely
Suc
ha!
clever holly
polie penny
60   sits on the cha
irk daisy stickin gout
and a big bal looms in the
cranny
with ak not for the
65   hair sometimes blond
sum tied black again
st st
the wallpaper
or across
70   thes heets

Has got up elvis?
In a big way in

54–55: *s//pleine didely:* "splendidly," but punning on *pleine:* full; pregnant (French)

sclamation mark
fact e's got
75   2
and a central boule
shorts white ocks
end black shoes
for girls when e goe
80   e goe sout in the woods
in the dark
in a large coating
Watch baby hind! the tree
contracts a bunny ride
85   on sweaty bice
ickles
uch hairy crop

Still
a dirty doldo's
90   one fatpig
fruitcake
in the bowl of my pill
ow, naughty bumps
yternally croks
95   my rip
the stickout grappe
of your naval ma d'olliv ery bad
storms today
very bad

2

100   Enter HEADSTURGEONS
followed by
Enter MERCHANTS
followed by
Enter FISHMONGRELS
105   colon speech marks

Trouble in the Hous?

illy all tied up

Nothing random
about the errings
110   of this
fanny face once remove
able envelope
just stamp
or aply
115   anywhere
(twice culled more lovéd)
and who

76: *boule:* ball, bowl (French); "avoir une boule dans l'estomac" ("to have a ball in one's stomach") is colloquial French for "to feel stuffed" (after a meal).
96: *grappe:* cluster of grapes (French)

's the pretty mi-
in the double battery with bum
120   (who will eat the hen bouillon
Caroline will! Caroline will!)
-stake me for real

Enter WITNESS
(sucking on Lolly)
125   warf warf laffing
Sudnly arrosed
exclaims NO
workable pussy
ever su
130   posed to discharge at will
all over the factory
sclamation mark

AH YES
but sheeped
135   like a dolly
part out part ed
partout prenante
every little which way
right through the mid-
140   come 'n
gain a bit
come a kiss
(is made of this)
: it's a girl!
145   come a kiss
: and it's not
In fact it was
inconvenient
come again a bit,
150   *freddy*
(Nov. 18, 1819)

WITNESS a hole is some
fair ground to lims as these
(babybaby)
155   Easy not to know which is when
and wear is which
baby don't you cry
suck a collateral
screwed into one sprawled live
160   sized granpa
with a liver no blood pud
no rganic drill

137: *partout prenante:* "everywhere agreeing (or fascinating)" (French); punning on "parti pris," point of view, prejudice.
149–50: A quotation from the diary of Anne Lister of Halifax (1791–1840). Her diary was written in code; when it was eventually cracked it turned out to contain accounts of her lesbian affairs. As a result her descendants attempted to suppress it, and extracts were only published at last in the 1980s. The phrase here was a term of sexual endearment she used with one of her lovers.

do up e's mule
(Untitled #250)

165   Came pleated
out of box
capsized at the kenee
loose all the parts
R
170   olled out of the can
thrown up in the air
rolled towards the light
rolls into the light
Blt o by
175   bolt
hammered out
Every single P
art is a crown
to Ana and to Tom
180   falls back slowly
down to the ground
first held
then cut loose
and into the door

185   (It must be humbly AD
Mary by the lake
had a good
idea that is
"by some law
190   in my temperature"
quote MITTELD does not
consist
in cric-crac
crrr crr
195   ee
a ting out of void
but out of the ka
bone of dissectin grooms
unquote
200   Meaning
if we be wet in church
my sweet inventory
hol da
headup inflate
205   my lily pousse
my bridal suite

164: Cindy Sherman's photograph *Untitled, #250* (1992) is from a series of sexually explicit mannequin photos drawing on the work of Bellmer. It shows a figure reclining on a mass of hair, with an old man's head, a woman's swollen belly, and a legless pelvis; from the lips of its vagina emerges a string of what look like brown sausages, turds, or penises.
186ff: "Mary" is Mary Shelley, and lines 191–99 rework a passage from her 1831 introduction to *Franken-stein:* "Invention, it must be humbly admitted, does not consist in creating out of void, but out of chaos." *MITTELD* puns on the German "mittel," middle.
205: *pousse:* sprout, shoot (French)

every mouth is ador
every little blood
draws
210 out another
casing
(this mouse
has a big ear
spqueaks
215 Who ma
demi so?)
clusters
of body conc)

3

Entrate SLOB
220 w/ corporeal entourage
teeth hanging by the crowns.
Boof boof speaks
des trous des airs
des enfilades
225 half-wriggle
half-hook
and half-spit
at the limits of
perusal
230 Des compressions
des arrois
rejects of form
oratorical bypass colon
Mankind, that's me

235 MERCHANTS (Obviously not
comma
as good as begot in the lab

(Bah Bet her then
to combinations
240 where there was plenty
there's plenty more

Entre [clac] et [clac] CHORUS
A SCHOOL OF TEETH
upscaled
245 (head for a croupe
and a croupe for an eye)
loudly
speechmarks

223–24: *des trous:* holes (French); *des airs:* cf. the phrase "to put on airs"; *enfilade* is French slang for sexual penetration.
230: "constrictions" (French)
231: "desarroi" means "distress"; "arrois" means "in full attire / apparel"
242: "Between [clac] and [clac]" ("clac" being imitative of the sound of clacking teeth)
245: *croupe:* ass, arse (French slang)

Nothing can compare
250 sclamation mark
to the icdil of body—clac past
humanolo- clac
crowded physiques that mumble—clac
"lubrication" and mount one another's
255 rising melan—clac cholia

MERCHANTS
Is the ternal urgical
animated turn
tables
260 (sclaim) patent a son
for a boxo orgns

SPOOL OFF TEETH
Icdil of summerclac
and se living is ing
265 Lazy pick-nooks in
se fat gween of
feelds and postues
Doldi se Head wis wasline
Ffish are fwying
270 and se fig yours
a vewy good look in

MERCHANTS to
TVNTERVIEWER
colon speech marks
275 We're not acturally
against skin
(worn long in season)

Fuck skin
DOLLY ADOR
280 Fuck skin fresh can
can raise one leg say Mma, raise
the other say
Ppa
Some dram of kind
285 sclamating mark
Dolly says Kss
my fr
og
ock
290 Rub the genie tales
Some dream off kin
Some want a better make
another and-and
and and and and

251: *icdil*: puns on "idyll" and "un hic," French for "a snag"
263ff: cf. Gershwin's "Summertime": "Summertime an' the livin' is easy, / fish are jumpin' an' the cotton is
  high."

295   "finely structured mesh"
        "suitable scaffolds"
        seed a kleenex today
        to marrow the world
        much like
300   "growing an arm and hand"
        mol assumule eculargesse
        bandaged on not born slurpy
        quote Somday Independent
        22 Febr 1998
305   "The hurdle is nerve tissue"

                 2000

305: Bergvall quotes in this stanza from an article in the *Independent on Sunday* on the possibility of growing human flesh and limbs for reconstructive use. It concludes that nerve tissue would present the most obstacles to manufacture.

DREW MILNE (b. 1964)

Mᴵᴸɴᴇ ᴡᴀs ʙᴏʀɴ ɪɴ Eᴅɪɴʙᴜʀɢʜ ᴀɴᴅ ᴇᴅᴜᴄᴀᴛᴇᴅ ᴀᴛ Cᴀᴍʙʀɪᴅɢᴇ Uɴɪᴠᴇʀsɪᴛʏ. Hᴇ has been writer-in-residence at the Tate Gallery (1995) and a lecturer in the School of English and American Studies at the University of Sussex; he currently teaches at Trinity Hall College, Cambridge. From 1991 to 1996, he edited *Parataxis: modernism and modern writing*, publishing poetry, essays, and polemics. With *Angel Exhaust*, *fragmente*, and several other lively journals of the period, *Parataxis* was committed to a revaluation of post-1945 British poetry, but it also sustained an interest in pre-1945 modernists, publishing essays and reviews on imagism, Joyce, Pound, Lewis, Loy, H. D., Stein, and others. Milne's books of poetry include *Sheet Mettle* (1994), *Songbook* (1996), *Bench Marks* (1998), and *familiars* (1999). *How Peace Came* (1994) uses large, bold-faced typography resembling that of Wyndham Lewis's journal *Blast* (1914) and takes its title from a poster announcing the end of the general strike in 1926; the text was first designed for an installation. Milne has also co-edited, with Terry Eagleton, *A Marxist Reader* (1996) and published essays on Renaissance drama, Jacques Derrida, Herbert Marcuse, and Samuel Beckett.

The epigraph from Ian Hamilton Finlay accompanying Milne's "A Garden of Tears" helps to locate something essential to that poem and to much of Milne's work: "Certain gardens are described as retreats when they are really attacks." Perhaps the "garden" here might be thought of as the sonnet. In an author's note in *Angel Exhaust* 9, Milne outlines aspects of a poetics reflecting the influence of Theodor Adorno: "If poetry is the non-instrumental play of language, perhaps the instruments on which such play is made are the torn flesh and proud wounds of a divided body we call communication. The false hope is a singular voice rising above inarticulate cries to catch suffering in its spell. Voices rather than voice, then, and as writing."[1] "A Garden of Tears" is, in its form, a sonnet sequence, and as with most sonnet sequences "the state" of love is one of its concerns; the sequence also borrows some of its idiom and syntax from historical examples of the genre. But from the opening line of the sequence—"It's a long way from love to the state we're in"—it is clear that these are sonnets in which a more traditional idiom is disrupted or contaminated by political realities. "State" suggests the political state as much as the lovers' condition. The sequence is full of puns and substitutions such as this transformation of a line from the Psalms (one earlier reworked in Eliot's *The Waste Land*): "where we sat down, smiled, and remembered Sion, / or was it cyanide. . . ." While it makes sense to recognize Milne's use of poetry as a critical instrument, it should be added that criticism

---

[1] *Angel Exhaust*, vol. 9, 1993, p. 66.

in Milne's poems cannot be reduced to a set of paraphrasable propositions about "issues"—such as, in the present poem, nuclear weapons, conflict in the Middle East, or the Gulf War. For the critic James Keery, "A Garden of Tears" is notable for a "Concision and poignancy almost Empsonian, reminiscent of Empson's 'Aubade' in its simultaneous alienation and evocation of love, its finical syntax and rhythm and its zooming out from love to war."[2]

---

2 *P.N. Review*, vol. 22, no. 3, 1996, p. 50.

A Garden of Tears

Certain gardens are described as retreats when they are really attacks.
IAN HAMILTON FINLAY

I.

It's a long way from love to the state we're in
here where fish are just at sea, and to know is
a law of the land, or any old wonder
as nature calls—*chuchotement*—what the dickens
5   can such in hope springs diurnal add up to,
or float to, so languid through these crossed channels
where spirit is without duty and knows love
for the state bliss might be when words do wither:
go then, the way of steam ships and dictators,
10   go then softly, quick to the ends of this life,
ineffably melding where these be pardons
and there such sacrifice is all our hatred,
stored in sand for when stones can be heard to cry
that we fear no more the heat of the trident.

II.

Out that long dolour look you gave me to wean
this eldritch sadness stills the warm felt of breath
across whose cheek, and in tears, the curfew dries
as hope is salted round the lips in Gaza
5   stripped only so slowly to earth's hearing bone
that the face fires harsh amber from stone glances
which, once lit, extinguish this float glass plainsong,
or is it just pain in mosaic and jaw:
no, not that wish about the jowl, it is pain,
10   even the wall is weeping, seeping such rage
that breathing baffles, hung as a cluster of
camphire in the lost vineyards of Engedi,
where unmeasured song is suspended in brine
and barges drift, slightly stale, to the dead sea.

Epigraph: Ian Hamilton Finlay: see p. 466.
I: 4: *chuchotement*: whispering; rustling
II: 11–12: "My beloved is unto me as a cluster of camphire in the vineyards of En-gedi" (Song of Sol. 1:14).
  En-gedi is an oasis on the Dead Sea.
14: *the dead sea*: a salt lake on the border between Israel and Jordan

III.

Better you to me than I were to myself
but what water we were I'm against it still,
the turn on love is patience and thousand lies
while sleepless still loves we cannot sleep still with
5   are breathless but still lives we cannot breathe with,
til doubt gives in fear and throws the first light stone
against names we never made, and loving break,
our breast plate of sighs in armour of accord:
call it operation bouffe, a taking leave
10   in lost of means, burnt islands and grimaces,
that's one end or two, a rash passion of notes
whose calm call shall remain nameless, but is law,
where wills are alive with the sound of water,
water of our eyes falling, felt and all told.

IV.

The more is the pity, as to two touching,
any rainbow appears a bridge over war,
even if we do not live, nor even near,
but shuffle such as the colours of money
5   in the gross nets wading though this vale of tears
where an increase in size of relative debts
makes it *practically* unimaginable
that we can rely on natural forces
to stabilise our interest rates, back on track
10   where Zeus fuels the milky way of defence costs:
there is one other option, to allow growth
to grow and increase the critical value
of the deficit as a fraction of this
to what is, or what is still and always more.

V.

Well like as maybe, the quite gentle gripe
is like as new lost, place lost in window days
where never knowingly is ever the less,
still under sold over that tread of pages
5   whose count me in is the harvest epaulette
and sheaves of ornamental treason; our feed
of dutiful mésalliance thinks ring on rung
as our past tense in special offers does fade,
or passes the tell by date with new freedom
10   to rot spontaneously: you know the rot
I mean, I take it, and savour the flavour
of its passing, into the spirit of mould
where you would love, but let the reason be love,
and just as sure as the turning of the earth.

III: 9: *operation bouffe:* cf. "opera bouffe," comic opera

VI.

Come in the valley of the shadow of breath
where we are this kiss in impossible grief,
that never savoured wrench as now and never
when happen is, the thinking over descant
5   to once upon each other, folded in sums,
parts in inconstant disarray of ice
as this scream is, an only shade of dismay
that pulls each faceless tooth along to wisdom:
these are our lines upon each blowing birth bruise
10   dashed to lungs, as skin curls in such heavy fruit,
its lisp already for that day when one dies,
simply leaves, or forgets the flares of always,
left flickering stunned in early fear of now
when each feared for kiss is still a greater death.

VII.

What not curls unknown against the lip split,
spilt quite apart from what cannot wash, and does,
as perils timid flung in held afflatus
where reason grows its only slow friend in pain
5   and clasps of breath fail, fall then run asunder,
spun through in what parts to remain familiar
or is the part where lightning is nothing new,
is wrung to a crush of what will not wonder:
no, and no wonder you prefer the thunder
10   where the piano of dull skies falls through stairs
showering air over the broken meadows
which numberless sums of all our breaking parts
even the parting past does not wish for
or cannot hold still in a pity of ears.

VIII.

Count in tears through wine how it unwinding downs
out so much as a by your leaving now gone
while pleasures stretch out, bitten into the lost
something, as less of that empty slidden we
5   who were never this, never this in ease or
in that some kind of forgiveness for the rest,
as would remnants gather to back one's own sill
lying still among dreams there is no wish for
on such melisma drifting scars where there is,
10   after all, nothing natural about it:
no, not along that light flesh of which we dream
where tight skies are shocking to the blood of tears,
he among hers, she among his and never
but the saw in it, just this each in each saw.

IX.

It's a long way still where love our gulf is war,
here where arks are royal, ripe and for sinking,
our bonds are broke, such tearing kisses, and soil
makes shifts of our futures, a water of dust
5   whose ashen felt rubble bursts banks on the Clyde,
where we sat down, smiled, and remembered Sion,
or was it cyanide fixed in Prussian blue
of a mind broke in fear that death becomes me,
becomes we who were what falls out together,
10   as perishing tears tear up the sodding earth:
for as long as the sun takes to set its gloss
the labours of our loss are still glistening,
and where the going is over, gone over,
there we go, slightly pale, to the ends of love.

1994

IX: 5: *Clyde:* a river in Scotland that flows through Glasgow, and which used to be the location of its once very important shipbuilding industry.
6: cf. Psalm 137:1: "By the rivers of Babylon, there we sat down; yea, we wept, when we remembered Zion."
7: *Prussian blue:* a deep blue pigment, made from ferrocyanides treated with ferric salt

CATHERINE WALSH (b. 1964)

W ALSH WAS BORN IN DUBLIN AND GREW UP THERE AND IN RURAL WEXFORD. SHE
left school at 17 and worked in a variety of jobs, eventually leaving Ireland to
teach English in Barcelona. After a period in Spain and the south of England, she
returned to Ireland, living in Dublin and, since 1999, in County Limerick. With Billy
Mills, she edits hardPressed Poetry and its magazine, *The Journal*. Her books include
Short Stories (1989), *Pitch* (1994), and *idir eatortha and making tents* (1996), the Irish
in this last title translating as "in between."

Walsh's understanding of poetry as process might be glossed by the following lines
from "idir eatortha":"contending with space we box it, label it, extend / language fenc-
ing effect to move, ourselves, we extend / bridges of words. . . ."[1] Here Walsh seems
to posit the need for a language capable of defining the world—boxing and labeling—
only to say that poetry has more to do with moving toward the real than with grasp-
ing it in final definition. Syntax as well as proposition indicate a fluid relationship
between the namer and the thing named: both are changed by poetry's tentative prob-
ing of the world, skepticism competing with recognition or acknowledgement.
Ireland's history as a colonized place informs Walsh's rejection of an English pastoral
tradition, her sense of being "half the way" or "in between," traversing rather than
owning the land. Her poetry maps interior as well as geographical spaces, caught
between the "matter / of fact" and writing's struggle with "time / of the mind": "We
express how things used to be and can never express how things are or what's hap-
pening," Walsh remarks in an interview. In the same interview she expresses her dis-
may at the confining nature of a parochial Irish poetry in which the poet "must cele-
brate above all else [her] sense of Irishness and [her] sense of being part of an ongoing
linear tradition of Irish writers."[2] While they share something of the speed of intel-
lection of Tom Raworth's poetry and the condensed descriptive exactitude and quiet
reflection of Lorine Niedecker's, Walsh's poems are largely unprecedented in Ire-
land; Brian Coffey is perhaps the most significant influence among recent Irish poets.
Nevertheless, as Maurice Scully has argued, "In a most untraditional way [Walsh]
exploits, among other things, strands traditional to Irish poetry for centuries: the oral,
the complexly patterned and the lore of place." Here is a poetry, he adds, about "the
edge between voice, voices, and written down text," and in reading it we follow its
movement from "reading, to listening, to (over)hearing, to hearing (too much too lit-
tle), to watching, to doing, to thinking, to speaking, to omitting to speak, to singing."[3]

---

[1] *idir eatortha and making tents,* London, 1996, p. 39.
[2] *Prospect into Breath: Interviews with North and South Writers,* ed. Peterjon Skelt, Twickenham and
Wakefield, 1991, pp. 181–88.
[3] "Space," *Angel Exhaust* 17, 1999, p. 2.

from Pitch

Part Three

<pre>
          matter
      of fact
              poetical
                  fabulous

5   time

      of the mind

              making
      over instants

              (   )
10   stasis

      absorption
      (in terms of saturation   )
      farts in a bath

                      *

          realize
15   this is not memory
      conditions
      the state of the subject at
      the moment
      in question   being

20   making pictures
      to walk into wide
      edging   on

      the village to the bridge the terminus to the
      Rialto the bird to the shop the road to
25   the house this is the same place over
</pre>

23ff: The setting here is Dolphin's Barn, an area in Dublin a few miles southwest of the city center. The *village* is Rialto Village, location of a cinema also called the Rialto; the *grassed canal* is a former section of the Grand Canal, now a park; nearby is the small street *Portmahon* Drive. The *Big House* is Golden-bridge, a children's home.

the hill hospital bridge grassed canal topping
drowned children weeds the Big House in place
of kitchen gardens sloped terraces
6 houses to Portmahon

*

30   that's gone don't   dual again how to reach
through such preoccupation not to
even discreetly manipulate a shame
denying substance your form happy? now
there's a few of the clichés the gaunt'ling
35   effect startled mannerisms neither more nor
less differently

*

           having not forgotten
           smell colour
           of eye
40   hair tone
           flesh
           having not forgotten
           there should be
           some where eye
45   hair colour of
           voice smell
           having not forgotten
           some where tone
           of eyebrow lash
50   there should be
           colour it should
           be clear some
           where forgotten
           there white shirts
55   opening flap
           having
           not forgotten
           standing where
           some be
60   left

           that's all
           it rhymes with

*

road hedge ditch
twisting narrowly
65   to lane

level run in hill
here a rutted

             pothole climbed to
             the well

70   knotted roots sparse
             footholds smooth clay

             over the ditch
             stone flat pebbles
             cold water
75   running the
             rushes ragged

             primroses

             past spring groves beech chestnut bog-oak
             fairy ráth wild fruit clumping
80   hassocks of long bog grass

             this to the left some perspective
             beyond the river fast shallows
             waterfowl call occasional
             machine voice in song
85   carrying

                         *

             large long green barred gate
             small wooden pen gate
             small silver garden gate   (sunset?)
             small white wooden garden gate

90   (bower of wisteria)

             the bayleaf

             sweet william alyssum phlox
             flagstone crab apples   (on to the summer house)
             walk the other way
95   avoiding the bees
             small green iron garden gate

                         *

             I can't do any more than this
             certainly those insects
             appear on no other church accessories
100   of that period I have seen provenance
             this skin bone painted light the
             colours of your mornings how can

78: *bog-oak:* ancient oak preserved in a peat-bog, changed to a black color
79: *ráth:* hill-fort
80: *hassocks:* tufts
92: *sweet william alyssum phlox:* garden flowers

what I name anything *do* anything
while I all in out and for continue
105   knowing it slowly (so time) heavy with
denial of loss

*

the young in inverted commas gaping fuddled be spectacled "the old"
not the futile ancients caricatures of portent
the way it was she walked up the road so
110   slowly each long step long to prevent the need
for any one extra step her body shape
inverted capital L maintaining
momentum without pitching
straight on the head
115   with support of a shopping trolley
walking slacks flapping cuffs
homemade crooked pale greyblue
about 1976 conservative size
flares grey hair lovely blowing
120   out all full light that
clear skin sun on wrists
knuckled thick

years of
acceptilation
125   body weight

*

this does not give precedent

previous
dated

before or when
130   was
earlier

stratification
of experience
no narrative
135   easy in the mind

where are we   out there
on there   in side of what
knows?

which some ancestors deemed
140   themselves capable of remembering

124: *acceptilation*: the forgiveness of a debt

of which descendents selected for re-engendering
Declan says "are oo fished?"

*

not the voice below
stairs ringing
145   televised   the street
Italian   cars trucks full
house tired asleep but
for me   still

*

wet roof clear brown beyond
150   buffeted flowers till light changed
shade tone more than grey effectively
impeding adumbration moving
lines space (racing point to point)
how many in or out does it take
155   each an anchorage in view of the
wind (the sea) marathon
railway line sea side of a lonely
night walking dark rocks shift water
breaks

*

160   half the way
                                 home
                             on one
                           way streets

                                                  1994

HELEN MACDONALD (b. 1970)

MACDONALD WAS BORN IN SURREY AND EDUCATED AT CAMBRIDGE UNIVERSITY. FROM 1996 to 1999, she worked for the National Avian Research Center, Abu Dhabi, breeding falcons and assisting with the management of an international research program on the saker falcon. She is the editor of the British Falconers Club Newsletter and is currently completing graduate work at Darwin College, Cambridge, writing on the history of raptor conservation in the United States and the United Kingdom. Her publications include *Simple Objects* (1993), a section of the *Etruscan Reader 1* (1996) entitled "Safety Catch," and *Shaler's Fish* (2000).

The radiant particular, the "whatness" or *quidditas* of the "thing" prized by much modernist poetry has often set it at odds with "taxonomy" or classification, which seems to have little to do with our sensory experience of the world. Macdonald's poems acknowledge this desire for what one poem calls "demonstrations of thisness" overtly and also implicitly in their torqued, sprung syntax.[1] It is as if there were something equally descriptive of her poems' syntax in the lines from "Poem" about "a hawk / rousing one's mind from safety and tameable illness / to beautiful comprehension in the form of a hunch"; the hawk is seen "knocking at wind / or poise as it flows up along the face, an edge / clipped with rock and lifting, a movement // as if one were about to launch into speech of faith / at least a hoped conviction, spite of coincidence." The trust that naming engenders and requires, our struggle with ineffable experience in muddled words, the otherness of the natural world as it competes with the history of symbolic systems limiting or deflecting our engagement with it—"Bright the what, reins wherever you go"—these are among Macdonald's concerns.[2] "Poem" is an elegy for Bill Girden, a writer from New Mexico unknown to or "never met" by the poet, whose words nevertheless are valued here for their acceptance of the hawk as truly other and wild. When later in the poem Macdonald writes that "My pen crumples into a swan, it is singing / inauthenticate myth," the ambiguity of her sentence is such that it is not clear whether the pen *wounds* or *becomes* the swan. Might the pen "sing" a swan stripped of anthropomorphizing myth? Macdonald's poems seem fraught with just such questions as they blur figure and ground, subject and object, seeking a language—as another poem has it—that might "settle the account" while also "feeling weak and human somewhere."[3]

---

[1] "Phosphorous," *Etruscan Reader 1*, p. 21.
[2] "Poem," *Etruscan Reader 1*, p. 22.
[3] "Hitman.doc," *Etruscan Reader 1*, p. 27.

Taxonomy

Wren. Full song. No subsong. Call of alarm, spreketh & ought
damage the eyes with its form, small body, tail pricked up & beak like a
    hair

trailed through briars & at a distance scored with lime-scent in the nose
like scrapings from a goldsmiths' cuttle, rock alum and fair butter well-
    temped

5   which script goes is unrecognised by this one, is pulled by the ear
in anger the line at fault is under and inwardly drear as a bridge in winter

reared up inotherwise to seal the eyes through darkness, the bridge speaks
it does not speak, the starlings speak that steal the speech of men, *uc antea*

a spark that meets the idea of itself, apparently fearless.
10   Ah cruelty. & I had not stopped to think upon it

& I had not extended it into the world for love for naught.

                                        1997

Blackbird/Jackdaw/*Turdus/corvus/merula/monedula*

So. A spire pulled forward by gravity of anger into limes
brief ripple of disc-shaped serrated leaves & lineage

dropped into a ladle at dusk as swifts spit softly
overhead in lines from physics and buttons

5   slate, where it falls and falls. Battalions of heroes eh.
That is what we schemed to hear. Walls of them, with bad

luck on their side. What a curious pose you are holding
spare hopes for certainty she does, the heroes touch leaves

to their foreheads as they walk it is May, May damp May
10   on gravel.

                                         1997

Title: *Taxonomy:* the scientific classification of plants and animals
1: *subsong:* "a subdued, quiet birdsong . . . often heard deep in bushes. Victorians supposed it was young
  birds practising for the spring" (Macdonald, in correspondence)
   spreketh: speaks (a seventeenth-century spelling)
3: *lime-scent:* i.e. of the flowers of a lime (linden) tree
4: *goldsmiths' cuttle:* a cuttlefish bone, used to burnish gold
   temped: churned, mixed. The cures for diseases of hawks given in Edmund Bert's *Treatise of Hawks and
  Hawking* (1619) often include rock alum and butter.
7: *seal:* the eyes of recently trapped hawks were temporarily "seeled" (sewn up) in one stage of the train-
  ing process.
8: *uc antea:* the phrase is untraced; "antea" is Latin for "formerly."

Title: MacDonald's title intermingles the scientific names of the Old World blackbird (*Turdus merula*) and
  jackdaw (*Corvus monedula*).
1: *limes:* linden trees

Section VIII

Any idea is sufficient for the purpose you understand
this offensive on bright lines as bringing distinction

to militant bliss . . . all counter to what I deserve.
Can you tell what it is? Is it subservient to a wish

5   for deliberation, for a fine incision to split the junction
boxed so the lights go pop in a deal of amphoteric

glitter? Or dual clinker to fill the peace process
with incidental crimes; this is where gazes fit

and splinter rhymes from kit and kin and strip
10   the rest as if shopping. It is becoming clear.

Now, except at particular times, I do not think
it affects at all . . .

. . . huge indiscretions laying down an evening
for premeditated warmth and rescue . . .

15   running on though some lines were cut
simply to preserve the shadow of the impassive

& well, it's something to feed on
breaking crockery and trefoil for clover, so

engaging a manner that snaps
20   not that its extraordinary emotions have any

connection with positive pain.

1997

6: *amphoteric:* reacting with both acids and bases—acting as an acid in the presence of a base, and as a
base in the presence of an acid
7: *clinker:* a mistake, awkwardness
18: *trefoil:* a type of plant, resembling a four-leaf clover, and sometimes mistaken for the same

Poem

FOR BILL GIRDEN

Death, about which we are all thinking, death, I believe
is the only solution to this problem of how to be able to fly
PAUL NASH, *AERIAL FLOWERS*, 1945

To state the discovery of a country
& be in a time without rage, keeping wings
near yourself, as barred as buried in the day, crossly.
Some present results; a tree, a quail, a rock, a hawk
5   rousing one's mind from safety and tameable illness
to beautiful comprehension in the form of a hunch
as patience directs

the finishing line is a trail of feathers to brush.
You might resist the pall of earthly wings
10   wicker thrumming with sand and hysteria
no longer a word, no use, knocking at wind
or poise as it flows up along the face, an edge
clipped with rock and lifting, a movement

as if one were about to launch into speech of faith
15   at least a hoped conviction, spite of coincidence.
"This is hardly a flaw; it simply is" you say, then drop
like a lark in abeyance of song to mitigate sward.
My pen crumples into a swan, it is singing
inauthenticate myth, and not of future splendour.

20   I am glad. Some evidence a hymn without light. Fracas.
History. The building of a condominium.
It was true I had never met.
There was a strike on the glass; it was a bird.
I have never been to the desert.

1997

"The poem responds to an article by Bill Girden I read in the falconry anthology *A Bond with the Wild*. He died young, shortly after its publication. The article—which is particularly beautiful—describes a hawking expedition in the New Mexico desert, Girden flying his trained Cooper's Hawk in the dawn light." (Macdonald, in correspondence)

Epigraph: *Paul Nash* (1889–1946), British artist. "In his late essay, *Aerial Flowers*, Nash described his life-long ambition as 'just that of poor Icarus—to be able to launch into the air of my own volition and to sustain my flight like a bird'. His grave respiratory illness meant that despite being appointed official artist to the Air Ministry in WWII, he was unable to fly in aeroplanes." (Macdonald)

16: "The quotation . . . is Girden musing on his sudden realisation that his hawk is merely using him as a convenient hunting perch: that a shared, intense bond with this wild creature is illusory: the hawk exists in a different life-world entirely, and Girden has a epiphany in the New Mexico desert regarding the world and how we exist within it." (Macdonald)

Index of Authors

INDEX OF TITLES